LEADING CASES IN
CONSTITUTIONAL LAW

A COMPACT CASEBOOK FOR
A SHORT COURSE

2021 Edition

Jesse H. Choper
Earl Warren Professor of Public Law Emeritus,
University of California, Berkeley

Michael C. Dorf
Robert S. Stevens Professor of Law,
Cornell Law School

Richard H. Fallon, Jr.
Story Professor of Law,
Harvard Law School

Frederick Schauer
David and Mary Harrison Distinguished Professor of Law,
University of Virginia

AMERICAN CASEBOOK SERIES®

WEST
ACADEMIC
PUBLISHING

American Casebook Series is a trademark registered in the U.S. Patent and Trademark Office.

© West, a Thomson business, 2007, 2008
© 2009–2012 Thomson Reuters
© 2013 LEG, Inc. d/b/a West Academic Publishing
© 2014–2020 LEG, Inc. d/b/a West Academic
© 2021 LEG, Inc. d/b/a West Academic
      444 Cedar Street, Suite 700
      St. Paul, MN 55101
      1-877-888-1330

West, West Academic Publishing, and West Academic are trademarks of West Publishing Corporation, used under license.

Printed in the United States of America

ISBN: 978-1-64708-864-4

PREFACE

Published annually, this book—Leading Cases in Constitutional Law—typically includes all the significant opinions handed down during the Supreme Court's most recent Term, as well as previous Terms. The authors of this compact volume also produce a nearly 1800-page constitutional law casebook, but we have repeatedly heard some colleagues express the need for a shorter, less expensive, more bare-bones book for a basic course in constitutional law. This book fills the gap that our colleagues identified. By judicious editing of the most important decisions of the Supreme Court and careful summarizing of less significant cases, we have encompassed the "essentials" for a constitutional law course in this paperback volume.

This book's organization is very similar to that of our much larger and more traditional one, which includes an abundance of Notes and Comments. That larger book should serve as a resource for those who use this volume. Like the latest edition of the larger book, the selection of cases and organization of this book reflects fresh evaluations of the relevant materials. New cases have replaced old ones where appropriate, and additions have been balanced by judicious cuts.

Cases and statutory citations, as well as footnotes of the Court, have sometimes been omitted without specification; other omissions are indicated by asterisks or by brackets. The Court's footnotes are so identified. All other footnotes are ours.

JESSE H. CHOPER
MICHAEL C. DORF
RICHARD H. FALLON, JR.
FREDERICK SCHAUER

July 2021

TABLE OF CONTENTS

TABLE OF CASES

The principal cases are in bold type.

———

LEADING CASES IN
CONSTITUTIONAL LAW

A COMPACT CASEBOOK FOR
A SHORT COURSE

2021 Edition

CHAPTER 1

NATURE AND SCOPE OF JUDICIAL REVIEW

■ ■ ■

1. ORIGINS, EARLY CHALLENGES, AND CONTINUING CONTROVERSY

"Whoever hath an absolute authority to interpret any written or spoken laws, it is he who is truly the lawgiver, to all intents and purposes, and not the person who first spoke or wrote them."

—Bishop Hoadly's Sermon, preached
before the King, 1717.

MARBURY V. MADISON
5 U.S. (1 Cranch) 137, 2 L.Ed. 60 (1803).

[The framers of the Constitution expected the federal government to function without political parties, but by the end of President George Washington's second term, the country divided into Federalists and Democratic-Republicans (sometimes simply called Republicans, although not related to the modern Republican Party, which originated in the 1850s). In the election of 1800, the Republican candidate (and sitting Vice President) Thomas Jefferson defeated the Federalist candidate (and sitting President) John Adams. Jefferson was to take office in March 1801, but in January Adams nominated John Marshall, then Secretary of State, as fourth Chief Justice of the United States. Marshall assumed his judicial office in February but continued to serve as Secretary of State until the end of the Adams administration. During February, the lame-duck Federalist Congress passed (1) the Circuit Court Act, which, among other things, doubled the number of federal judges and (2) the Organic Act, which authorized appointment of 42 justices-of-the-peace in the District of Columbia. Senate confirmation of Adams' "midnight" appointees, virtually all Federalists, was completed one day before Jefferson's inauguration. Their commissions were signed by Adams and sealed by Acting Secretary of State Marshall, but due to time pressure, several for the justices-of-the-peace (including William Marbury) remained undelivered when Jefferson assumed the presidency the next day. Jefferson instructed the new Secretary of State, James Madison, to withhold delivery.

[Late in 1801, Marbury and several others sought a writ of mandamus (a kind of judicial order) in the Supreme Court to compel Madison to deliver the

1

commissions. The Court ordered Madison "to show cause why a mandamus should not issue" and the case was set for argument in the 1802 Term.

[While the case was pending, the new Republican Congress—incensed at Adams's efforts to entrench a Federalist judiciary and at the "Federalist" Court's order against a Republican cabinet officer—moved to repeal the Circuit Court Act. Federalist congressmen argued that repeal would violate Art. III's assurance of judicial tenure "during good behavior" and of the Constitution's plan for separation of powers assuring the independence of the Judiciary. It "was in this debate that for the first time since the initiation of the new Government under the Constitution there occurred a serious challenge of the power of the Judiciary to pass upon the constitutionality of Acts of Congress. Hitherto, [it had been the Republicans] who had sustained this power as a desirable curb on Congressional aggression and encroachment on the rights of the States, and they had been loud in their complaints at the failure of the Court to hold the Alien and Sedition laws unconstitutional. Now, however, in 1802, in order to counteract the Federalist argument that the Repeal Bill was unconstitutional and would be so held by the Court, [Republicans] advanced the proposition that the Court did not possess the power."[1]

[The Repeal Law passed early in 1802. To forestall its constitutional challenge in the Supreme Court until the political power of the new administration had been strengthened, Congress also eliminated the 1802 Supreme Court Term. Thus, the Court did not meet between December, 1801 and February, 1803. Although Marbury's case was not a challenge to the repeal of the Circuit Court Act, it was widely understood as carrying potential implications for the issues of judicial independence posed by that repeal.]

[On] 24th February, the following opinion of the court was delivered by CHIEF JUSTICE MARSHALL: * * *

No cause has been shown, and the present motion is for a mandamus. The peculiar delicacy of this case, the novelty of some of its circumstances, and the real difficulty attending the points which occur in it require a complete exposition of the principles on which the opinion to be given by the court is founded. * * *

1st. Has the applicant a right to the commission he demands? * * *

Mr. Marbury, [since] his commission was signed by the President and sealed by the Secretary of State, was appointed; and as the law creating the office gave the officer a right to hold for five years, independent of the executive, the appointment was not revocable, but vested in the officer legal rights, which are protected by the laws of his country.

To withhold his commission, therefore, is an act deemed by the court not warranted by law, but violative of a vested legal right. * * *

---

[1]   1 Charles Warren, *The Supreme Court in United States History* 215 (1922).

2dly. If he has a right, and that right has been violated, do the laws of his country afford him a remedy?

The very essence of civil liberty certainly consists in the right of every individual to claim the protection of the laws, whenever he receives an injury. One of the first duties of government is to afford that protection.

[The] government of the United States has been emphatically termed a government of laws, and not of men. It will certainly cease to deserve this high appellation, if the laws furnish no remedy for the violation of a vested legal right.

[W]here the heads of departments are the political or confidential agents of the executive, merely to execute the will of the president, or rather to act in cases in which the executive possesses a constitutional or legal discretion, nothing can be more perfectly clear than that their acts are only politically examinable. But where a specific duty is assigned by law, and individual rights depend upon the performance of that duty, it seems equally clear that the individual who considers himself injured, has a right to resort to the laws of his country for a remedy. * * *

It remains to be inquired whether,

3dly. He is entitled to the remedy for which he applies? This depends on,

1st. The nature of the writ applied for; and,

2dly. The power of this court.

1st. The nature of the writ. * * *

This writ, if awarded, would be directed to an officer of government, and its mandate to him would be, to use the words of Blackstone, "to do a particular thing therein specified, which appertains to his office and duty, and which the court has previously determined, or at least supposes, to be consonant to right and justice." Or, in the words of Lord Mansfield, the applicant, in this case, has a right to execute an office of public concern, and is kept out of possession of that right.

These circumstances certainly concur in this case.

Still, to render the mandamus a proper remedy, the officer to whom it is to be directed, must be one to whom, on legal principles, such writ may be directed; and the person applying for it must be without any other specific and legal remedy.

1st. With respect to the officer to whom it would be directed. The intimate political relation subsisting between the President of the United States and the heads of departments, necessarily renders any legal investigation of the acts of one of those high officers peculiarly irksome, as well as delicate; and excites some hesitation with respect to the propriety of entering into such investigation. Impressions are often received without much reflection or examination, and it is not wonderful that in such a case as this the assertion, by an individual, of his legal claims in a court of justice, to which claims it is the duty of that court to attend, should at first view be considered by some, as an attempt to intrude into the cabinet, and to intermeddle with the prerogatives of the executive.

It is scarcely necessary for the court to disclaim all pretensions to such a jurisdiction. An extravagance, so absurd and excessive, could not have been entertained for a moment. The province of the court is, solely, to decide on the rights of individuals, not to inquire how the executive, or executive officers, perform duties in which they have a discretion. Questions in their nature political, or which are, by the constitution and laws, submitted to the executive, can never be made in this court.

But [what] is there in the exalted station of the officer, which shall bar a citizen from asserting, in a court of justice, his legal rights, or shall forbid a court to listen to the claim, or to issue a mandamus, directing the performance of a duty, not depending on executive discretion, but on particular acts of congress, and the general principles of law?

[This], then, is a plain case for a mandamus, either to deliver the commission, or a copy of it from the record; and it only remains to be inquired,

Whether it can issue from this court.

The act to establish the judicial courts of the United States authorizes the supreme court "to issue writs of mandamus, in cases warranted by the principles and usages of law, to any courts appointed, or persons holding office, under the authority of the United States."[2]

The secretary of state, being a person holding an office under the authority of the United States, is precisely within the letter of the description; and if this court is not authorized to issue a writ of mandamus to such an officer, it must be because the law is unconstitutional, and therefore absolutely incapable of conferring the authority, and assigning the duties which its words purport to confer and assign.

[In] the distribution of [the judicial power of the United States] it is declared that "the supreme court shall have original jurisdiction in all cases affecting ambassadors, other public ministers and consuls, and those in which a state shall be a party. In all other cases, the supreme court shall have appellate jurisdiction."

It has been insisted, at the bar, that as the original grant of jurisdiction, to the supreme and inferior courts, is general, and the clause, assigning original jurisdiction to the supreme court, contains no negative or restrictive words, the

---

[2]　　§ 13 of the Judiciary Act of 1789 provided "[t]hat the Supreme Court shall have exclusive jurisdiction of all controversies of a civil nature, where a state is a party, except between a state and its citizens; and except also between a state and citizens of other states, or aliens, in which latter case it shall have original but not exclusive jurisdiction. And shall have exclusively all such jurisdiction of suits or proceedings against ambassadors or other public ministers, or their domestics, or domestic servants, as a court of law can have or exercise consistently with the law of nations; and original, but not exclusive jurisdiction of all suits brought by ambassadors or other public ministers, or in which a consul, or vice consul, shall be a party. And the trial of issues of fact in the Supreme Court in all actions at law against citizens of the United States shall be by jury. The Supreme Court shall also have appellate jurisdiction from the circuit courts and courts of the several states, in the cases hereinafter specially provided for; and shall have power to issue writs of prohibition to the district courts, when proceeding as courts of admiralty and maritime jurisdiction, and writs of mandamus, in cases warranted by the principles and usages of law, to any courts appointed, or persons holding office, under the authority of the United States."

power remains to the legislature, to assign original jurisdiction to that court in other cases than those specified in the article which has been recited; provided those cases belong to the judicial power of the United States.

If it had been intended to leave it in the discretion of the legislature to apportion the judicial power between the supreme and inferior courts according to the will of that body, it would certainly have been useless to have proceeded further than to have defined the judicial power, and the tribunals in which it should be vested. The subsequent part of the section is mere surplusage, is entirely without meaning, if such is to be the construction. If congress remains at liberty to give this court appellate jurisdiction, where the constitution has declared their jurisdiction shall be original; and original jurisdiction where the constitution has declared it shall be appellate; the distribution of jurisdiction, made in the constitution, is form without substance.

Affirmative words are often, in their operation, negative of other objects than those affirmed; and in this case, a negative or exclusive sense must be given to them, or they have no operation at all.

It cannot be presumed that any clause in the constitution is intended to be without effect; and, therefore, such a construction is inadmissible, unless the words require it.

[The] authority, therefore, given to the Supreme Court, by the Act establishing the judicial courts of the United States, to issue writs of mandamus to public officers, appears not to be warranted by the Constitution; and it becomes necessary to inquire whether a jurisdiction so conferred can be exercised.

The question whether an Act repugnant to the Constitution can become the law of the land, is a question deeply interesting to the United States; but, happily, not of an intricacy proportioned to its interest. It seems only necessary to recognize certain principles, supposed to have been long and well established, to decide it.

That the people have an original right to establish, for their future government, such principles as, in their opinion, shall most conduce to their own happiness, is the basis on which the whole American fabric has been erected. The exercise of this original right is a very great exertion; nor can it nor ought it to be frequently repeated. The principles, therefore, so established, are deemed fundamental. And as the authority from which they proceed is supreme, and can seldom act, they are designed to be permanent.

This original and supreme will organizes the government, and assigns to different departments their respective powers. It may either stop here, or establish certain limits not to be transcended by those departments.

The government of the United States is of the latter description. The powers of the legislature are defined and limited; and that those limits may not be mistaken, or forgotten, the constitution is written. To what purpose are powers limited, and to what purpose is that limitation committed to writing, if these limits may, at any time, be passed by those intended to be restrained? The distinction between a government with limited and unlimited powers is abolished, if those limits do not confine the persons on whom they are imposed, and if acts prohibited and acts allowed, are of equal obligation. It is a proposition too plain to be contested, that the constitution controls any legislative act repugnant to it; or, that the legislature may alter the constitution by an ordinary act.

Between these alternatives there is no middle ground. The constitution is either a superior paramount law, unchangeable by ordinary means, or it is on a level with ordinary legislative acts, and, like other acts, is alterable when the legislature shall please to alter it.

If the former part of the alternative be true, then a legislative act contrary to the constitution is not law: if the latter part be true, then written constitutions are absurd attempts, on the part of the people, to limit a power in its own nature illimitable.

Certainly all those who have framed written constitutions contemplate them as forming the fundamental and paramount law of the nation, and consequently, the theory of every such government must be, that an act of the legislature, repugnant to the constitution, is void.

This theory is essentially attached to a written constitution, and is, consequently, to be considered, by this court, as one of the fundamental principles of our society. It is not therefore to be lost sight of in the further consideration of this subject.

If an act of the legislature, repugnant to the Constitution, is void, does it, notwithstanding its invalidity, bind the courts, and oblige them to give it effect? Or, in other words, though it be not law, does it constitute a rule as operative as if it was a law? This would be to overthrow in fact what was established in theory; and would seem, at first view, an absurdity too gross to be insisted on. It shall, however, receive a more attentive consideration.

It is emphatically the province and duty of the judicial department to say what the law is. Those who apply the rule to particular cases, must of necessity expound and interpret that rule. If two laws conflict with each other, the courts must decide on the operation of each.

So if a law be in opposition to the constitution; if both the law and the constitution apply to a particular case, so that the court must either decide that case conformably to the law, disregarding the constitution; or conformably to the constitution, disregarding the law; the court must determine which of these conflicting rules governs the case. This is of the very essence of judicial duty.

If, then, the courts are to regard the constitution, and the constitution is superior to any ordinary act of the legislature, the constitution, and not such ordinary act, must govern the case to which they both apply.

Those then who controvert the principle that the constitution is to be considered in court, as a paramount law, are reduced to the necessity of maintaining that courts must close their eyes on the constitution, and see only the law.

This doctrine would subvert the very foundation of all written constitutions. It would declare that an Act which, according to the principles and theory of our government, is entirely void, is yet, in practice, completely obligatory. It would declare that if the legislature shall do what is expressly forbidden, such Act, notwithstanding the express prohibition, is in reality effectual. It would be giving to the legislature a practical and real omnipotence, with the same breath which professes to restrict their powers within narrow limits. It is prescribing limits, and declaring that those limits may be passed at pleasure.

That it thus reduces to nothing what we have deemed the greatest improvement on political institutions, a written constitution, would of itself be sufficient, in America, where written constitutions have been viewed with so much reverence, for rejecting the construction. But the peculiar expressions of the Constitution of the United States furnish additional arguments in favor of its rejection.

The judicial power of the United States is extended to all cases arising under the Constitution.

Could it be the intention of those who gave this power, to say that in using it the Constitution should not be looked into? That a case arising under the Constitution should be decided without examining the instrument under which it arises?

This is too extravagant to be maintained.

In some cases, then, the Constitution must be looked into by the judges. And if they can open it at all, what part of it are they forbidden to read or to obey?

There are many other parts of the Constitution which serve to illustrate this subject.

It is declared that "no tax or duty shall be laid on articles exported from any State." Suppose a duty on the export of cotton, of tobacco, or of flour; and a suit instituted to recover it. Ought judgment to be rendered in such a case? Ought the judges to close their eyes on the Constitution, and only see the law?

The Constitution declares "that no bill of attainder or ex post facto law shall be passed."

If, however, such a bill should be passed, and a person should be prosecuted under it, must the court condemn to death those victims whom the Constitution endeavors to preserve?

"No person," says the Constitution, "shall be convicted of treason unless on the testimony of two witnesses to the same overt act, or on confession in open court."

Here the language of the Constitution is addressed especially to the courts. It prescribes, directly for them, a rule of evidence not to be departed from. If the legislature should change that rule, and declare one witness, or a confession out of court, sufficient for conviction, must the constitutional principle yield to the legislative act?

From these, and many other selections which might be made, it is apparent, that the framers of the constitution contemplated that instrument as a rule for the government of courts, as well as of the legislature.

Why otherwise does it direct the judges to take an oath to support it? This oath certainly applies in an especial manner, to their conduct in their official character. How immoral to impose it on them, if they were to be used as the instruments, and the knowing instruments, for violating what they swear to support!

The oath of office, too, imposed by the legislature, is completely demonstrative of the legislative opinion on this subject. It is in these words: "I do solemnly swear that I will administer justice without respect to persons, and do equal right to the poor and to the rich; and that I will faithfully and impartially discharge all the duties incumbent on me as _____, according to the best of my abilities and understanding agreeably to the constitution and laws of the United States."

Why does a judge swear to discharge his duties agreeably to the constitution of the United States, if that constitution forms no rule for his government? If it is closed upon him, and cannot be inspected by him?

If such be the real state of things, this is worse than solemn mockery. To prescribe, or to take this oath, becomes equally a crime.

It is also not entirely unworthy of observation, that in declaring what shall be the supreme law of the land, the constitution itself is first mentioned; and not the laws of the United States generally, but those only which shall be made in pursuance of the constitution, have that rank.

Thus, the particular phraseology of the Constitution of the United States confirms and strengthens the principle, supposed to be essential to all written constitutions, that a law repugnant to the constitution is void; and that courts, as well as other departments, are bound by that instrument.

The rule must be discharged.[3]

———

"We are under a Constitution, but the Constitution is what the judges say it is."

—Charles Evans Hughes, Speech, 1907.

---

[3]   Six days later, the Supreme Court refused to consider whether the Circuit Court Act Repeal Law was constitutional, thus tacitly upholding it. *Stuart v. Laird*, 5 U.S. (1 Cranch) 299 (1803). After *Marbury*, the Court did not hold another act of Congress unconstitutional until *Dred Scott v. Sandford*, (1857), Ch. 9, Sec. 2, I.

COMMENTARY ON MARBURY

Further Historical Context

Marbury is most frequently cited as the case establishing the Supreme Court's power of judicial review, but the assumption that courts would decline to enforce unconstitutional laws appears to have been relatively widespread and uncontroversial in the early Republic.

Charles Warren, 1 *The Supreme Court in United States History* 232, 242–43 (1922): "Contemporary writings make it very clear that the republicans attacked the [*Marbury*] decision, not so much because it sustained the power of the court to determine the validity of congressional legislation, as because it enounced the doctrine that the court might issue mandamus to a cabinet official who was acting by direction of the president. In other words, Jefferson's antagonism to Marshall and the court at that time was due more to his resentment at the alleged invasion of his executive prerogative than to any so-called 'judicial usurpation' of the field of congressional authority. [It] seems plain [that Marshall might] have construed the language of the section of the judiciary act [to escape the necessity] to pass upon its constitutionality. Marshall naturally felt that in view of the recent attacks on judicial power it was important to have the great principle firmly established, and undoubtedly he welcomed the opportunity of fixing the precedent in a case in which his action would necessitate a decision in favor of his political opponents."

Text of the Constitution

Is the doctrine of "judicial review," which gives the Court power to declare an act of a coordinate branch of the government unconstitutional, compelled because a contrary rule "would subvert the very foundation of all written constitutions"?

William W. Van Alstyne, *A Critical Guide to Marbury v. Madison*, 1969 Duke L.J. 1: "[E]ven in Marshall's time (and to a great extent today), a number of nations maintained written constitutions and yet gave national legislative acts the full force of positive law without providing any constitutional check to guarantee the compatibility of those acts with their constitutions [e.g.,] France, Switzerland, and Belgium (and to some extent Great Britain where magna carta and other written instruments are roughly described as the constitution but where acts of parliament are not reviewable)."

The Oath

Does the "judges' oath" provision (Art. VI, cl. 3) furnish the necessary textual support for the doctrine of judicial review?

JUSTICE GIBSON, dissenting in *Eakin v. Raub*, 12 Serg. & Rawle 330 (Pa. 1825): "The oath to support the Constitution is not peculiar to the judges, but is taken indiscriminately by every officer of the government, and is designed rather as a test of the political principles of the man, than to bind the officer in the discharge of his duty: otherwise, it were difficult to determine, what operation it is to have in the case of a recorder of deeds, for instance, who, in execution of his office, has nothing to do with the Constitution. But granting it to relate to the official conduct of the judge, as well as every other officer, and not to his political principles, still, it must be understood in reference to supporting the Constitution, only as far as that may be involved in his official duty; and consequently, if his official duty does not comprehend an inquiry into the authority of the legislature, neither does his oath.

"[But] do not the judges do a positive act in violation of the Constitution, when they give effect to an unconstitutional law? Not if the law has been passed according to the forms established in the Constitution. The fallacy of the question is, in supposing that the judiciary adopts the acts of the legislature as its own; whereas, the enactment of a law and the interpretation of it are not concurrent acts, and as the judiciary is not required to concur in the enactment, neither is it in the breach of the constitution which may be the consequence of the enactment; the fault is imputable to the legislature, and on it the responsibility exclusively rests."

––––––

The Court as "Final" Arbiter

Thomas Jefferson, writing in 1804, 8 *The Writings of Thomas Jefferson* 310 (1897): "The judges, believing the [sedition law] constitutional, had a right to pass a sentence of fine and imprisonment; because that power was placed in their hands by the constitution. But the executive, believing the law to be unconstitutional, was bound to remit the execution of it; because that power has been confided to him by the constitution. The instrument meant that its co-ordinate branches should be checks on each other. But the opinion which gives to the judges the right to decide what laws are constitutional, and what not, not only for themselves in their own sphere of action, but for the legislative and executive also in their spheres, would make the judiciary a despotic branch."

––––––

Andrew Jackson, veto message in 1832 on Act to Recharter Bank of United States (the constitutionality of which had earlier been upheld by the Court), 2 *Messages and Papers of the Presidents* 576, 581–82 (James S. Richardson ed., 1900): "It is as much the duty of the house of representatives, of the senate, and of the president to decide upon the constitutionality of any bill or resolution which may be presented to them for passage or approval as it is of the supreme judges when it may be brought before them for judicial decision. The opinion of the judges has no more authority over congress than the opinion of congress has over the judges, and on that point the president is independent of both. The authority of the supreme court must not, therefore, be permitted to control the congress or the executive when acting in their legislative capacities, but to have only such influence as the force of their reasoning may deserve."

————

Abraham Lincoln, inaugural address in 1861, 2 Richardson, supra, at 5, 9–10: "I do not forget the position assumed by some that constitutional questions are to be decided by the Supreme Court, nor do I deny that such decisions must be binding in any case upon the parties to a suit as to the object of that suit, while they are also entitled to very high respect and consideration in all parallel cases by all other departments of the government. And while it is obviously possible that such decision may be erroneous in any given case, still the evil effect following it, being limited to that particular case, with the chance that it may be overruled and never become a precedent for other cases, can better be borne than could the evils of a different practice. At the same time, the candid citizen must confess that if the policy of the government upon vital questions affecting the whole people is to be irrevocably fixed by decisions of the Supreme Court, the instant they are made in ordinary litigation between parties in personal actions the people will have ceased to be their own rulers, having to that extent practically resigned their government into the hands of that eminent tribunal. Nor is there in this view any assault upon the court or the judges. It is a duty from which they may not shrink to decide cases properly brought before them, and it is no fault of theirs if others seek to turn their decisions to political purposes."

————

COOPER v. AARON, 358 U.S. 1 (1958) (also in Ch. 9, Sec. 2, III) arose several years after the landmark ruling in *Brown v. Board of Education* (1954) (Ch. 9, Sec. 2, II) that segregation of public school children on the basis of race violated the Fourteenth Amendment. A plan approved by the lower federal courts to desegregate Little Rock public schools was blocked by the Governor of Arkansas and other state officials. In the face of a federal court injunction, the Governor backed off, and National Guard soldiers, who had been called out to keep the public schools desegregated, were withdrawn. For a short time, black students were able to attend previously all-white public schools under the protection of federally-commanded troops. However, in early 1958, citing deep tension and concern about violence, the school board sought, and a federal court granted, a long postponement of the desegregation plan. The Court of Appeals reversed, and the Supreme Court affirmed—in an opinion delivered not by any one justice, as is ordinarily the case, but signed by all nine. Arkansas contended that because it was not a party to the litigation that culminated in the *Brown* ruling, it was not bound by that decision. This claim stirred the Supreme Court to make a broad and forceful statement about its supremacy in constitutional matters—as Laurence H. Tribe, *American Constitutional Law* 255 (3d ed. 2000) (hereinafter Tribe, 3d ed.) described it, "a statement uniquely punctuated by the Justices' individual signatures of the opinion." The Court wrote:

"Article VI of the Constitution makes the Constitution the 'supreme law of the land.' In 1803, Chief Justice Marshall, speaking for a unanimous Court, referring to the Constitution as 'the fundamental and paramount law of the nation,' declared [in] *Marbury* [the] basic principle that the federal judiciary is supreme in the exposition of the law of the Constitution, and that principle has ever since been respected by this Court and the Country as a permanent and indispensable feature of our constitutional system. It follows that the interpretation of the Fourteenth Amendment enunciated by this Court in the *Brown* case is the supreme law of the land. [Every] state legislator and executive and judicial officer is solemnly committed by oath taken pursuant to art. VI, cl. 3 'to support this Constitution.' * * * No state legislature or executive or judicial officer can war against the Constitution without violating his undertaking to support it. Chief Justice Marshall spoke for a unanimous court in saying that: 'If the legislatures of the several states may, at will, annul the judgments of the courts of the United States, and destroy the rights acquired under those judgments, the constitution itself becomes a solemn mockery * * * .' *United States v. Peters*, 5 Cranch 115. A Governor who asserts a power to nullify a federal court order is similarly restrained."

MARTIN v. HUNTER'S LESSEE
14 U.S. (1 Wheat.) 304, 4 L.Ed. 97 (1816).

[Lord Fairfax, a Virginia citizen, willed his Virginia land known as the Northern Neck of Virginia to his nephew, Martin, a British subject resident in England. In 1789, Virginia, acting pursuant to state laws confiscating lands owned by British subjects, granted land in the Northern Neck to Hunter. The latter brought an action of ejectment against Martin. The Virginia district court ruled for Martin, whose claim was fortified by the anti-confiscation clauses of the treaties of 1783 and 1794 with Great Britain. But the Virginia Court of Appeals reversed, holding that (1) the state's title to the Northern Neck had been perfected before any treaty and (2) in any event, a 1796 Act of Compromise between the Fairfax claimants and the state claimants, formally adopted by the Virginia legislature, had settled the matter against Martin.

[Acting for the purchasers of the Fairfax estate, John Marshall, then a member of the Virginia legislature, had negotiated the compromise. Since he and his brother had organized a syndicate which purchased 160,000 acres of Northern Neck from Martin in 1793, Marshall had a great interest in the case's outcome.

[In *Fairfax's Devisee v. Hunter's Lessee*, 11 U.S. (7 Cranch) 603 (1813), the Supreme Court (Marshall, C.J., not participating) reversed the Virginia Court of Appeals, ruling that Virginia had not perfected title to the Northern Neck prior to the grant to Hunter and that therefore the Treaty of 1794 confirmed the title remaining in Martin. Neither Story, J.'s majority opinion nor Johnson, J.'s dissent mentioned the Act of Compromise.

[The case was remanded to the Virginia Court of Appeals with instructions to enter judgment for appellant, but that court refused to obey the Supreme Court's mandate. All four judges then sitting maintained that insofar as it extended the appellate jurisdiction of the Supreme Court to "this court," § 25 of the Judiciary Act was unconstitutional. Judge Roane—Marshall's arch political enemy—and Judge Fleming (the two judges sitting when the court had decided the case against Martin on the merits) contended further that even if the Judiciary Act were valid the case had not properly been before the Supreme Court because the Virginia decision turned not upon a treaty, but on a matter of state law, the Act of Compromise.

[The case again came to the Supreme Court, Marshall again not sitting.[4]]

STORY, J., delivered the opinion of the court. * * *

The third article of the constitution is that which must principally attract our attention. [A]ppellate jurisdiction is given by the constitution to the supreme court, in all cases [within "the judicial power of the United States"] where it has not original jurisdiction; subject, however, to such exceptions and regulations as congress may prescribe. [W]hat is there to restrain its exercise over state tribunals, in the enumerated cases? [If] the judicial power extends to the case, it will be in vain to search in the letter of the constitution for any qualification as to the tribunal where it depends. It [is] plain, that the framers of the constitution did contemplate that cases within the judicial cognisance of the United States, not only might, but would, arise in the state courts, in the exercise of their ordinary jurisdiction [pointing to the supremacy clause]. Suppose, an indictment for a crime, in a state court, and the defendant should allege in his defence, that the crime was created by an ex post facto act of the state, must not the state court [have] a right to pronounce on the validity and sufficiency of the defence? [It] was foreseen, that in the exercise of their ordinary jurisdiction, state courts would incidentally take cognisance of cases arising under the constitution, the laws and treaties of the United States. Yet, to all these cases, the judicial power, by the very terms of the constitution, is to extend. It cannot extend, by original jurisdiction, if that was already rightfully and exclusively attached in the state courts, which (as has been already shown) may occur; it must, therefore, extend by appellate jurisdiction, or not at all. It would seem to follow, that the appellate power of the United States must, in such cases, extend to state tribunals.

[It] has been argued that such an appellate jurisdiction over state courts is inconsistent with the genius of our governments, and the spirit of the constitution. That the latter was never designed to act upon state sovereignties, but only upon the people, and that if the power exists it will materially impair the sovereignty of the states, and the independence of their courts. [But the Constitution] is crowded with provisions which restrain or annul the sovereignty of the states, in some of

---

4   For further exploration of the historical background, see 4 Albert J. Beveridge, *The Life of John Marshall* 144–61 (1919); 2 William W. Crosskey, *Politics and the Constitution* 785–817 (1953); 1 Charles Warren, *The Supreme Court in United States History* 442–53 (1922).

the highest branches of their prerogatives. The tenth section of the first article contains a long list of disabilities and prohibitions imposed upon the states. [The] language of the constitution is also imperative upon the states, as to the performance of many duties. It is imperative upon the state legislatures, to make laws prescribing the time, places and manner of holding elections for senators and representatives, and for electors of president and vice-president. And in these, as well as some other cases, congress have a right to revise, amend or supersede the laws which may be passed by state legislatures. When, therefore, the states are stripped of some of the highest attributes of sovereignty, and the same are given to the United States; when the legislatures of the states are, in some respects, under the control of congress, and in every case are, under the constitution, bound by the paramount authority of the United States; it is certainly difficult to support the argument, that the appellate power over the decisions of state courts is contrary to the genius of our institutions. The courts of the United States can, without question, revise the proceedings of the executive and legislative authorities of the states, and if they are found to be contrary to the constitution, may declare them to be of no legal validity. Surely, the exercise of the same right over judicial tribunals is not a higher or more dangerous act of sovereign power.

Nor can such a right be deemed to impair the independence of state judges. It is assuming the very ground in controversy, to assert that they possess an absolute independence of the United States. In respect to the powers granted to the United States, they are not independent; they are expressly bound to obedience, by the letter of the constitution.

[The] argument urged from the possibility of the abuse of the revising power, is equally unsatisfactory. [From] the very nature of things, the absolute right of decision, in the last resort, must rest somewhere—wherever it may be vested, it is susceptible of abuse. [A]dmitting that the judges of the state courts are, and always will be, of as much learning, integrity and wisdom, as those of the courts of the United States (which we very cheerfully admit), it does not aid the argument. It is manifest, that the constitution has proceeded upon a theory of its own, and given or withheld powers according to the judgment of the American people, by whom it was adopted. We can only construe its powers, and cannot inquire into the policy or principles which induced the grant of them. The constitution has presumed (whether rightly or wrongly, we do not inquire), that state attachments, state prejudices, state jealousies, and state interests, might sometimes obstruct, or control, or be supposed to obstruct or control, the regular administration of justice.

[This] is not all. A motive of another kind, perfectly compatible with the most sincere respect for state tribunals, might induce the grant of appellate power over their decisions. That motive is the importance, and even necessity of *uniformity* of decisions throughout the whole United States, upon all subjects within the purview of the constitution. Judges of equal learning and integrity, in different states, might differently interpret the statute, or a treaty of the United States, or even the constitution itself: if there were no revising authority to control these jarring and discordant judgments, and harmonize them into uniformity, the laws, the treaties and the constitution of the United States would be different, in different states, and might, perhaps, never have precisely the same construction, obligation or efficiency, in any two states. The public mischiefs that would attend such a state of things would be truly deplorable.

[On] the whole, the court are of opinion, that the appellate power of the United States does extend to cases pending in the state courts; and that the 25th section of the judiciary act, which authorizes the exercise of this jurisdiction in the specified cases, by a writ of error, is supported by the letter and spirit of the constitution. [It] is an historical fact, that this exposition of the constitution, extending its appellate power to state courts, was, previous to its adoption, uniformly and publicly avowed by its friends, and admitted by its enemies, as the basis of their respective reasonings, both in and out of the state conventions. It is an historical fact, that at the time when the judiciary act was submitted to the deliberations of the first congress, composed, as it was not only of men of great learning and ability, but of men who acted a principal part in framing, supporting or opposing that constitution, the same exposition was explicitly declared and admitted by the friends and by the opponents of that system. It is an historical fact, that the supreme court of the United States have, from time to time, sustained this appellate jurisdiction, in a great variety of cases, brought from the tribunals of many of the most important states in the Union, and that no state tribunal has ever breathed a judicial doubt on the subject or declined to obey the mandate of the supreme court, until the present occasion.

[The Court next rejected the contention that the case was not properly before it because the Virginia decision turned on the Act of Compromise.]

We have not thought it incumbent on us to give any opinion upon the question, whether this court have authority to issue a writ of mandamus to the court of appeals, to enforce the former judgments, as we did not think it necessarily involved in the decision of this cause.

It is the opinion of the whole court, that the judgment of the court of appeals of Virginia, rendered on the mandate in this cause, be reversed, and the judgment of the district court [be] affirmed.

JOHNSON, J. It will be observed, in this case, that the court disavows all intention to decide on the right to issue compulsory process to the state courts; thus leaving us, in my opinion, where the constitution and laws place us—supreme over persons and cases, so far as our judicial powers extend, but not asserting any compulsory control over the state tribunals. In this view, I acquiesce in their opinion, but not altogether in the reasoning or opinion of my brother who delivered it. * * *

NOTE

Uniformity. Consider Oliver Wendell Holmes, Jr., *Law and the Court, in Collected Legal Papers* 291, 295–96 (1920): "I do not think the United States would come to an end if we lost our power to declare an Act of Congress void. I do think the Union would be imperiled if we could not make that declaration as to the laws of the several states."

2. POLITICAL QUESTIONS

Does the principle of judicial review comprehend the Court's acting as "final arbiter" on *all* constitutional questions presented by a case properly within its jurisdiction? Or are some constitutional issues inappropriate for judicial resolution and thus nonjusticiable "political questions"? The Supreme Court has answered the former question in the negative and the latter in the affirmative, but its decisions have left a good deal of uncertainty and debate about when the political question doctrine does, and should, apply.

The Court gave a once-canonical formulation of its criteria for identifying political questions in BAKER v. CARR, 369 U.S. 186, 217 (1962): "Prominent on the surface of any case held to involve a political question is found a textually demonstrable constitutional commitment of the issue to a coordinate political department; or a lack of judicially discoverable and manageable standards for resolving it; or the impossibility of deciding without an initial policy determination of a kind clearly for nonjudicial discretion; or the impossibility of a court's undertaking independent resolution without expressing lack of the respect due coordinate branches of government; or an unusual need for unquestioning adherence to a political decision already made; or the potentiality of embarrassment from multifarious pronouncements by various departments on one question. Unless one of these formulations is inextricable from the case at bar, there should be no dismissal for non-justiciability on the ground of a political question's presence." In *Baker*, the Court, per BRENNAN, J., held that a suit challenging Tennessee's legislative apportionment scheme, under which some districts had vastly larger populations than others, presented a justiciable question under the Equal Protection Clause: "Judicial standards under the Equal Protection Clause are well developed[. This] case does, in one sense, involve the allocation of political power within a State, and the appellants might conceivably have added a claim under the Guaranty Clause. [Although *Colegrove v. Green*, 328 U.S. 549 (1946), had held a challenge to legislative redistricting nonjusticiable under the Guarantee Clause,[5] it does not follow that appellants may not be heard on the equal protection claim which in fact they tender."

FRANKFURTER, J., joined by Harlan, J., dissented: "The present case [is], in effect, a Guarantee Clause claim masquerading under a different label. But it cannot make the case more fit for judicial action that appellants invoke the Fourteenth Amendment rather than Art. IV, § 4, where, in fact, the gist of their complaint is the same." According to Frankfurter, J., involvement in legislative redistricting controversies would plunge the judiciary into a "political thicket."

---

5   The Court had also found Guarantee Clause cases to be nonjusticiable in *Pac. States Tel. & Tel. Co. v. Oregon*, 223 U.S. 118 (1912), and *Luther v. Borden*, 48 U.S. (7 How.) 1 (1849).

The Court again found the *Baker* criteria unsatisfied in POWELL v. McCORMACK, 395 U.S. 486 (1969), which arose when the House of Representatives refused to let flamboyant Harlem Congressman Adam Clayton Powell take his seat as a member of the 90th Congress. Although Powell met the age, citizenship, and residence requirements that Art. I, § 2, cl. 2 establishes for congressional service, the House voted to exclude him under Art. I, § 5, cl. 1 ("Each House shall be the Judge of the * * * Qualifications of its own Members"). The House based its decision on the report of a Select Committee "that Powell had asserted an unwarranted privilege and immunity from the processes of the courts of New York; that he had wrongfully diverted House funds for the use of others and himself; and that he had made false reports on expenditures of foreign currency to the Committee on House Administration." Powell sought, inter alia, a declaratory judgment that his exclusion was unconstitutional and that his salary should be paid by the Sergeant-at-Arms. The lower courts dismissed the complaint in light of Congress' textual prerogative to judge the "Qualifications of its own Members," but the Court, per WARREN, C.J., reversed:

"In order to determine whether there has been a textual commitment to a co-ordinate department of the Government, we must interpret the Constitution. [Our] examination of the relevant historical materials [including pre-Constitutional Convention precedents of the English Parliament and American colonial assemblies; the debates at the Constitutional Convention and state conventions; and early, as well as more recent, congressional precedents] leads us to the conclusion [that] the Constitution leaves the House without authority to *exclude* any person, duly elected by his constituents, who meets all of the requirements for membership expressly prescribed in" Art. I, § 2.

"Had the intent of the Framers emerged from these materials with less clarity, we would nevertheless have been compelled to resolve any ambiguity in favor of a narrow construction of the scope of Congress' power to exclude members-elect. A fundamental principle of our representative democracy is, in Hamilton's words, 'that the people should choose whom they please to govern them.' As Madison pointed out at the Convention, this principle is undermined as much by limiting whom the people can select as by limiting the franchise itself. * * * Unquestionably, Congress has an interest in preserving its institutional integrity, but in most cases that interest can be sufficiently safeguarded by the exercise of its power to punish its members for disorderly behavior and, in extreme cases, to expel a member with the concurrence of two-thirds." The Court expressed no view on what limitations may exist on Congress's power to "expel or otherwise punish" a member, under Art. I, § 5, cl. 2, once the member has been seated.

"Respondents' alternate contention is that the case presents a political question because judicial resolution of petitioners' claim would produce a 'potentially embarrassing confrontation between coordinate branches' of the Federal Government. But [our interpretation of Art. I, § 5] falls within the traditional role accorded courts to interpret the law, and does not involve a 'lack of the respect due [a] coordinate [branch] of government,' nor does it involve an 'initial policy determination of a kind clearly for nonjudicial discretion.' *Baker*. Our system of government requires that federal courts on occasion interpret the Constitution in a manner at variance with the construction given the document by another branch. The alleged conflict that such an adjudication may cause cannot justify the courts' avoiding their constitutional responsibility.

"Nor are any of the other formulations of a political question 'inextricable from the case at bar.' *Baker*. Petitioners seek a determination [for] which clearly there are 'judicially ... manageable standards.' Finally, a judicial resolution of petitioners' claim will not result in 'multifarious pronouncements by various departments on one question.' For, as we noted in *Baker*, it is the responsibility of this Court to act as the ultimate interpreter of the Constitution."

Cases subsequent to *Powell* left many unanswered questions, but no doubt that the Court regards some cases as presenting nonjusticiable questions. The next case so affirmed.

NIXON V. UNITED STATES
506 U.S. 224, 113 S.Ct. 732, 122 L.Ed.2d 1 (1993).

CHIEF JUSTICE REHNQUIST delivered the opinion of the Court.

Petitioner Walter L. Nixon, Jr., [a] former Chief Judge of the United States District Court for the Southern District of Mississippi, was convicted by a jury of two counts of making false statements before a federal grand jury and sentenced to prison. [On] May 10, 1989, the House of Representatives adopted three articles of impeachment for high crimes and misdemeanors. The first two articles charged Nixon with giving false testimony before the grand jury and the third article charged him with bringing disrepute on the Federal Judiciary.

After the House presented the articles to the Senate, the Senate voted to invoke its own Impeachment Rule XI, under which the presiding officer appoints a committee of Senators to "receive evidence and take testimony." The Senate committee held four days of hearings, during which 10 witnesses, including Nixon, testified. Pursuant to Rule XI, the committee presented the full Senate with a complete transcript of the proceeding and a report stating the uncontested facts and summarizing the evidence on the contested facts. Nixon and the House impeachment managers submitted extensive final briefs to the full Senate and delivered arguments from the Senate floor during the three hours set aside for oral argument in front of that body. Nixon himself gave a personal appeal, and several Senators posed questions directly to both parties. The Senate voted by more than the constitutionally required two-thirds majority to convict Nixon on the first two articles. The presiding officer then entered judgment removing Nixon from his office as United States District Judge.

Nixon thereafter commenced the present suit, arguing that Senate Rule XI violates the constitutional grant of authority to the Senate to "try" all impeachments because it prohibits the whole Senate from taking part in the evidentiary hearings. [The] District Court held that his claim was nonjusticiable and the Court of Appeals for the District of Columbia Circuit agreed.

A controversy is nonjusticiable—i.e., involves a political question—where there is "a textually demonstrable constitutional commitment of the issue to a coordinate political department; or a lack of judicially discoverable and manageable standards for resolving it." *Baker*, 369 U.S. at 217. [The] lack of judicially manageable standards may strengthen the conclusion that there is a textually demonstrable commitment to a coordinate branch.

In this case, we must examine Art. I, § 3, cl. 6, to determine the scope of authority conferred upon the Senate by the Framers regarding impeachment. It provides: "The Senate shall have the sole Power to try all Impeachments. When sitting for that Purpose, they shall be on Oath or Affirmation. When the President of the United States is tried, the Chief Justice shall preside: And no Person shall be convicted without the Concurrence of two thirds of the Members present." * * *

Petitioner argues that the word "try" in the first sentence imposes by implication an additional requirement on the Senate in that the proceedings must be in the nature of a judicial trial. From there petitioner goes on to argue that this limitation precludes the Senate from delegating to a select committee the task of hearing the testimony of witnesses * * * .

There are several difficulties with this position which lead us ultimately to reject it. The word "try," both in 1787 and later, has considerably broader meanings than those to which petitioner would limit it. [Thus], we cannot say that the Framers used the word "try" as an implied limitation on the method by which the Senate might proceed in trying impeachments. * * *

The conclusion that the use of the word "try" in the first sentence of the Impeachment Trial Clause lacks sufficient precision to afford any judicially manageable standard of review of the Senate's actions is fortified by the existence of the three very specific requirements that the Constitution does impose on the Senate when trying impeachments: the members must be under oath, a two-thirds vote is required to convict, and the Chief Justice presides when the President is tried. These limitations are quite precise, and their nature suggests that the Framers did not intend to impose additional limitations on the form of the Senate proceedings by the use of the word "try" in the first sentence.

Petitioner devotes only two pages in his brief to negating the significance of the word "sole" in the first sentence of Clause 6. [We] think that the word "sole" is of considerable significance. Indeed, the word "sole" appears only one other time in the Constitution—with respect to the House of Representatives' "*sole* Power of Impeachment." Art. I, § 2, cl. 5 (emphasis added). The common sense meaning of the word "sole" is that the Senate alone shall have authority to determine whether an individual should be acquitted or convicted. The dictionary definition bears this out. "Sole" is defined as "having no companion," "solitary," "being the only one," and "functioning . . . independently and without assistance or interference." If the courts may review the actions of the Senate in order to determine whether that body "tried" an impeached official, it is difficult to see how the Senate would be "functioning . . . independently and without assistance or interference."

Nixon [argues] that even if significance be attributed to the word "sole" in the first sentence of the clause, the authority granted is to the Senate, and this means that "the Senate—not the courts, not a lay jury, not a Senate Committee—shall try impeachments." Brief for Petitioner 42. It would be possible to read the first sentence of the Clause this way, but it is not a natural reading. Petitioner's interpretation would bring into judicial purview not merely the sort of claim made by petitioner, but other similar claims based on the conclusion that the word "Senate" has imposed by implication limitations on procedures which the Senate might adopt. Such limitations would be inconsistent with the construction of the Clause as a whole, which, as we have noted, sets out three express limitations in separate sentences.

The history and contemporary understanding of the impeachment provisions support our reading of the constitutional language. The parties do not offer evidence of a single word in the history of the Constitutional Convention or in contemporary commentary that even alludes to the possibility of judicial review in the context of the impeachment powers. [The] Framers labored over the question of where the impeachment power should lie. Significantly, in at least two considered scenarios the power was placed with the Federal Judiciary. [See] *The Federalist* No. 65. The Supreme Court was not the proper body because the Framers "doubted whether [it] would possess the degree of credit and authority" to carry out its judgment if it conflicted with the accusation brought by the Legislature—the people's representative. In addition, the Framers believed the Court was too small in number: "The awful discretion, which a court of impeachments must necessarily have, to doom to honor or to infamy the most confidential and the most distinguished characters of the community, forbids the commitment of the trust to a small number of persons." Id.

There are two additional reasons why the Judiciary, and the Supreme Court in particular, were not chosen to have any role in impeachments. First, the Framers recognized that most likely there would be two sets of proceedings for individuals who commit impeachable offenses—the impeachment trial and a separate criminal trial. In fact, the Constitution explicitly provides for two separate proceedings. See Art. I, § 3, cl. 7. The Framers deliberately separated the two forums to avoid raising the specter of bias and to ensure independent judgments. [Certainly] judicial review of the Senate's "trial" would introduce the same risk of bias as would participation in the trial itself.

Second, judicial review would be inconsistent with the Framers' insistence that our system be one of checks and balances. In our constitutional system, impeachment was designed to be the *only* check on the Judicial Branch by the Legislature. * * * Judicial involvement in impeachment proceedings, even if only for purposes of judicial review, is counterintuitive because it would eviscerate the "important constitutional check" placed on the Judiciary by the Framers. * * *

In addition to the textual commitment argument, we are persuaded that the lack of finality and the difficulty of fashioning relief counsel against justiciability. See *Baker*. We agree with the Court of Appeals that opening the door of judicial review to the procedures used by the Senate in trying impeachments would "expose the political life of the country to months, or perhaps years, of chaos." This lack of finality would manifest itself most dramatically if the President were impeached. The legitimacy of any successor, and hence his effectiveness, would be impaired severely, not merely while the judicial process was running its course, but during any retrial that a differently constituted Senate might conduct if its first judgment of conviction were invalidated. Equally uncertain is the question of what relief a court may give other than simply setting aside the judgment of conviction. Could it order the reinstatement of a convicted federal judge, or order Congress to create an additional judgeship if the seat had been filled in the interim?

Petitioner finally contends that a holding of nonjusticiability cannot be reconciled with our opinion in *Powell v. McCormack*. The relevant issue in *Powell* was whether courts could review the House of Representatives' conclusion that Powell was "unqualified" to sit as a Member because he had been accused of misappropriating public funds and abusing the process of the New York courts. We stated that the question of justiciability turned on whether the Constitution committed authority to the House to judge its members' qualifications, and if so, the extent of that commitment. Article I, § 5 provides that "Each House shall be the Judge of the Elections, Returns and Qualifications of its own Members." In turn, Art. I, § 2 specifies three requirements for membership in the House: The candidate must be at least 25 years of age, a citizen of the United States for no less than seven years, and an inhabitant of the State he is chosen to represent. We held that, in light of the three requirements specified in the Constitution, the word "qualifications"—of which the House was to be the Judge—was of a precise, limited nature. [The] decision as to whether a member satisfied these qualifications was placed with the House, but the decision as to what these qualifications consisted of was not.

In the case before us, there is no separate provision of the Constitution which could be defeated by allowing the Senate final authority to determine the meaning of the word "try" in the Impeachment Trial Clause. * * *

Affirmed.

JUSTICE STEVENS, concurring.

[Respect] for a coordinate Branch of the Government forecloses any assumption that improbable hypotheticals like those mentioned by Justice White and Justice Souter will ever occur. * * *

JUSTICE WHITE, with whom JUSTICE BLACKMUN joins, concurring in the judgment.

[The] Court is of the view that the Constitution forbids us even to consider [petitioner's constitutional] contention. I find no such prohibition and would therefore reach the merits of the claim. I concur in the judgment because the Senate fulfilled its constitutional obligation to "try" petitioner.

It should be said at the outset that, as a practical matter, it will likely make little difference whether the Court's or my view controls this case. This is so because the Senate has very wide discretion in specifying impeachment trial procedures and because it is extremely unlikely that the Senate would abuse its discretion and insist on a procedure that could not be deemed a trial by reasonable judges. [But] since the meaning of a constitutional provision is at issue, my disagreement with the Court should be stated.

[T]he issue in the political question doctrine is not whether the Constitutional text commits exclusive responsibility for a particular governmental function to one of the political branches. There are numerous instances of this sort of textual commitment, e.g., Art. I, § 8 [enumerating congressional powers], and it is not thought that disputes implicating these provisions are nonjusticiable. Rather, the issue is whether the Constitution has given one of the political branches final responsibility for interpreting the scope and nature of such a power.

[T]here are few, if any, explicit and unequivocal instances in the Constitution of this sort of textual commitment. [That] the word "sole" is found only in the House and Senate Impeachment Clauses demonstrates [only] that its purpose is to emphasize the distinct role of each in the impeachment process. As the majority notes, the Framers, following English practice, were very much concerned to separate the prosecutorial from the adjudicative aspects of impeachment. Giving each House "sole" power with respect to its role in impeachments effected this division of labor. While the majority is thus right to interpret the term "sole" to indicate that the Senate ought to " 'function independently and without assistance or interference,' " it wrongly identifies the judiciary, rather than the House, as the source of potential interference with which the Framers were concerned when they employed the term "sole."

Even if the Impeachment Trial Clause is read without regard to its companion clause, the Court's willingness to abandon its obligation to review the constitutionality of legislative acts merely on the strength of the word "sole" is perplexing. Consider, by comparison, the treatment of Art. I, § 1, which grants "All legislative powers" to the House and Senate. As used in that context "all" is nearly synonymous with "sole"—both connote entire and exclusive authority. Yet the Court has never thought it would unduly interfere with the operation of the Legislative Branch to entertain difficult and important questions as to the extent of the legislative power. * * *

[The] majority finds this case different from *Powell* only on the grounds that, whereas the qualifications of Art. I, § 2 are readily susceptible to judicial interpretation, the term "try" does not provide an "identifiable textual limit on the authority which is committed to the Senate." [Yet the] term "try" is hardly so elusive as the majority would have it. Were the Senate, for example, to adopt the practice of automatically entering a judgment of conviction whenever articles of impeachment were delivered from the House, it is quite clear that the Senate will have failed to "try" impeachments. Indeed in this respect, "try" presents no greater, and perhaps fewer, interpretive difficulties than some other constitutional standards that have been found amenable to familiar techniques of judicial construction, including, for example, "Commerce . . . among the several States," Art. I, § 8, cl. 3, and "due process of law." Amdt. 5.[3] * * *

JUSTICE SOUTER, concurring in the judgment.

[As] we cautioned in *Baker*, "the 'political question' label" tends "to obscure the need for case-by-case inquiry." The need for such close examination is nevertheless clear from our precedents, which demonstrate that the functional nature of the political question doctrine requires analysis of "the precise facts and posture of the particular case," and precludes "resolution by any semantic cataloguing."

[Whatever] considerations feature most prominently in a particular case, the political question doctrine is "essentially a function of the separation of powers," ibid., existing to restrain courts "from inappropriate interference in the business of the other branches of [the Federal] Government," and deriving in large part from prudential concerns about the respect we owe the political departments. Not all interference is inappropriate or disrespectful, however, and application of the doctrine ultimately turns, as Learned Hand put it, on "how importunately the occasion demands an answer." Learned Hand, *The Bill of Rights* 15 (1958).

This occasion does not demand an answer. The Impeachment Trial Clause [contemplates] that the Senate may determine, within broad boundaries, such subsidiary issues as the procedures for receipt and consideration of evidence necessary to satisfy its duty to "try" impeachments. Other significant considerations confirm a conclusion that this case presents a nonjusticiable political question: the "unusual need for unquestioning adherence to a political decision already made," as well as "the potentiality of embarrassment from multifarious pronouncements by various departments on one question." * * *

One can, nevertheless, envision different and unusual circumstances that might justify a more searching review of impeachment proceedings. If the Senate were to act in a manner seriously threatening the integrity of its results, convicting, say, upon a coin-toss, or upon a summary determination that an officer of the United States was simply "a bad guy," judicial interference might well be

---

[3]   [Ct's Note] The majority's in terrorem argument against justiciability—that judicial review of impeachments might cause national disruption and that the courts would be unable to fashion effective relief—merits only brief attention. In the typical instance, court review of impeachments would no more render the political system dysfunctional than has this litigation. Moreover, the same capacity for disruption was noted and rejected as a basis for not hearing *Powell*. The relief granted for unconstitutional impeachment trials would presumably be similar to the relief granted to other unfairly tried public employee-litigants. Finally, as applied to the special case of the President, the majority's argument merely points out that, were the Senate to convict the President without any kind of a trial, a constitutional crisis might well result. It hardly follows that the Court ought to refrain from upholding the Constitution in all impeachment cases. Nor does it follow that, in cases of Presidential impeachment, the Justices ought to abandon their constitutional responsibilities because the Senate has precipitated a crisis.

appropriate. In such circumstances, the Senate's action might be so far beyond the scope of its constitutional authority, and the consequent impact on the Republic so great, as to merit a judicial response despite the prudential concerns that would ordinarily counsel silence. "The political question doctrine, a tool for maintenance of governmental order, will not be so applied as to promote only disorder." *Baker.*

————

ZIVOTOFSKY v. CLINTON, 566 U.S. 189 (2012), per ROBERTS, C.J., rejected political question objections and held that the federal courts could determine the constitutionality of a statute requiring the State Department to list "Israel" as the place of birth on the passports of Americans born in Jerusalem who requested that listing. The State Department refused to comply with the law on the ground that, by purporting to recognize Jerusalem's status as part of Israel, it unconstitutionally interfered with the president's foreign affairs powers. It further argued that a suit seeking to compel compliance with the statute presented a political question. Without reference to additional factors considered in previous political question cases, the Court found that (1) there was no "textually demonstrable constitutional commitment of the issue" of the constitutionality of a federal statute to any branch other than the judiciary, and (2) "the textual, structural, and historical evidence put forward by the parties" revealed no lack of "judicially discoverable and manageable standards."

SOTOMAYOR, J., joined in relevant part by Breyer, J., concurred, emphasizing that in "rare case[s]" the Court should find questions nonjusticiable based principally on prudential considerations, but that this was not such a case. Alito, J., also concurred separately. BREYER, J., dissented, relying on a conjunction of "prudential considerations" that included the potential foreign policy ramifications of having U.S. passports denominate Jerusalem as part of Israel when Jerusalem's status is a subject of international contention.

RUCHO V. COMMON CAUSE
588 U.S. ___, 139 S.Ct. 2484, 204 L.Ed.2d 931 (2019).

CHIEF JUSTICE ROBERTS delivered the opinion of the Court.

Voters and other plaintiffs in North Carolina and Maryland challenged their States' congressional districting maps as unconstitutional partisan gerrymanders. The North Carolina plaintiffs complained that the State's districting plan discriminated against Democrats; the Maryland plaintiffs complained that their State's plan discriminated against Republicans. The plaintiffs alleged that the gerrymandering violated the First Amendment, the Equal Protection Clause of the Fourteenth Amendment, the Elections Clause, and Article I, § 2, of the Constitution.

[All agree that the partisan gerrymanders at issue in the two cases were deliberate and at least initially highly effective. In *Rucho*, the North Carolina case] one of the two Republicans chairing the redistricting committee [explained] that the map was drawn with the aim of electing ten Republicans and three Democrats because he did "not believe it [would be] possible to draw a map with 11 Republicans and 2 Democrats." One Democratic state senator objected that entrenching the 10–3 advantage for Republicans was not "fair, reasonable, [or] balanced" because, as recently as 2012, "Democratic congressional candidates had received more votes on a statewide basis than Republican candidates." [In] November 2016, North Carolina conducted congressional elections using the 2016 Plan [at issue in the litigation], and Republican candidates won 10 of the 13 congressional districts.

[The] second case before us is *Lamone v. Benisek.* In 2011, the Maryland Legislature—dominated by Democrats—undertook to redraw the lines of that State's eight congressional districts. The Governor at the time, Democrat Martin O'Malley, [appointed] a redistricting committee to help redraw the map. [The] Governor later testified that his aim was to "use the redistricting process to change the overall composition of Maryland's congressional delegation to 7 Democrats and 1 Republican by flipping" one district. [The] 2011 Plan accomplished that by moving roughly 360,000 voters out of the Sixth District and moving 350,000 new voters in. Overall, the Plan reduced the number of registered Republicans in the Sixth District by about 66,000 and increased the number of registered Democrats by about 24,000. The map was adopted by a party-line vote. It was used in the 2012 election and succeeded in flipping the Sixth District. A Democrat has held the seat ever since.

[In] these cases we are asked to decide an important question of constitutional law. "But before we do so, we must find that the question is presented in a 'case' or 'controversy' that is, in James Madison's words, 'of a Judiciary Nature.'" *DaimlerChrysler Corp. v. Cuno*, 547 U.S. 332, 342 (2006) (quoting 2 Records of the Federal Convention of 1787, p. 430 (M. Farrand ed. 1966)). [The] question here is whether there is an "appropriate role for the Federal Judiciary" in remedying the problem of partisan gerrymandering—whether such claims are claims of *legal* right, resolvable according to *legal* principles, or political questions that must find their resolution elsewhere.

Partisan gerrymandering is nothing new. Nor is frustration with it. [The] Framers addressed the election of Representatives to Congress in the Elections Clause. Art. I, § 4, cl. 1. That provision assigns to state legislatures the power to prescribe the "Times, Places and Manner of holding Elections" for Members of Congress, while giving Congress the power to "make or alter" any such regulations. [The Court here cited historical examples of congressional regulation before recognizing that only a requirement that states use single-member districts remains in place today.]

[Appellants] suggest that, through the Elections Clause, the Framers set aside electoral issues such as the one before us as questions that only Congress can resolve. We do not agree. In two areas—one-person, one-vote and racial gerrymandering—our cases have held that there is a role for the courts with respect to at least some issues that could arise from a State's drawing of congressional districts. See *Wesberry v. Sanders*, 376 U.S. 1 (1964); *Shaw v. Reno*, 509 U.S. 630 (1993).

But the history is not irrelevant. The Framers were aware of electoral districting problems and considered what to do about them. [At] no point was there a suggestion that the federal courts had a role to play. Nor was there any indication that the Framers had ever heard of courts doing such a thing.

[Partisan] gerrymandering claims have proved far more difficult to adjudicate [than one-person, one-vote cases and cases involving racial discrimination]. The basic reason is that, while it is illegal for a jurisdiction to depart from the one-person, one-vote rule, or to engage in racial discrimination in districting, "a jurisdiction may engage in constitutional political gerrymandering." *Hunt v. Cromartie*, 526 U.S. 541, 551 (1999) (citing *Bush v. Vera*, 517 U.S. 952, 968 (1996)).

To hold that legislators cannot take partisan interests into account when drawing district lines would essentially countermand the Framers' decision to entrust districting to political entities. The "central problem" is not determining whether a jurisdiction has engaged in partisan gerrymandering. It is "determining when political gerrymandering has gone too far." *Vieth* [*v. Jubelirer*, 541 U.S. 267, 296 (2004) (plurality opinion). The Court here recounted its prior confrontations will challenges to political gerrymandering. In *Davis v. Bandemer*, 478 U.S. 109 (1986), a majority thought the case was justiciable but splintered over the proper standard to apply. Four Justices (White, Brennan, Marshall, and Blackmun, JJ.) would have required proof of "intentional discrimination against an identifiable political group and an actual discriminatory effect on that group." Two Justices (Powell and Stevens, JJ.) would have focused on "whether the boundaries of the voting districts have been distorted deliberately and arbitrarily to achieve illegitimate ends." But O'Connor, J., joined by Burger, C.J., and Rehnquist, J., would have held that partisan gerrymandering claims pose political questions because the Equal Protection Clause simply "does not supply judicially manageable standards for resolving" them.

[Eighteen years later, in *Vieth*, Justice Scalia's plurality opinion also would have held challenges to gerrymanders nonjusticiable due to an absence of judicially manageable standards.] Kennedy, J., concurring in the judgment, noted "the lack of comprehensive and neutral principles for drawing electoral boundaries [and] the absence of rules to limit and confine judicial intervention." He nonetheless left open the possibility that "in another case a standard might emerge." Four Justices dissented.

[The] question [in appraising political gerrymandering claims] is one of degree: How to "provid[e] a standard for deciding how much partisan dominance is too much." *League of United Latin American Citizens v. Perry*, 548 U.S. 399, 420 (2006) (opinion of Kennedy, J.). And it is vital in such circumstances that the Court act only in accord with especially clear standards: "With uncertain limits, intervening courts—even when proceeding with best intentions—would risk assuming political, not legal, responsibility for a process that often produces ill will and distrust." *Vieth*, 541 U.S., at 307 (opinion of Kennedy, J.).

[Partisan] gerrymandering claims invariably sound in a desire for proportional representation. * * * "Our cases, however, clearly foreclose any claim that the Constitution requires proportional representation." [Unable] to claim that the Constitution requires proportional representation outright, plaintiffs inevitably ask the courts to make their own political judgment about how much representation particular political parties *deserve*—based on the votes of their supporters—and to rearrange the challenged districts to achieve that end. But federal courts are not equipped to apportion political power as a matter of fairness, nor is there any basis for concluding that they were authorized to do so.

[The] initial difficulty in settling on a "clear, manageable and politically neutral" test for fairness is that it is not even clear what fairness looks like in this context. [Fairness] may mean a greater number of competitive districts. [On] the other hand, perhaps the ultimate objective of a "fairer" share of seats in the congressional delegation is most readily achieved by yielding to the gravitational pull of proportionality and engaging in cracking and packing, to ensure each party its "appropriate" share of "safe" seats. [Or] perhaps fairness should be measured by adherence to "traditional" districting criteria, such as maintaining political subdivisions, keeping communities of interest together, and protecting incumbents.

[Deciding] among just these different visions of fairness (you can imagine many others) poses basic questions that are political, not legal. There are no legal standards discernible in the Constitution for making such judgments, let alone limited and precise standards that are clear, manageable, and politically neutral.

[Even] assuming the court knew which version of fairness to be looking for, there are no discernible and manageable standards for deciding whether there has been a violation. [Appellees] contend that if we can adjudicate one-person, one-vote claims, we can also assess partisan gerrymandering claims. [But] "vote dilution" in the one-person, one-vote cases refers to the idea that each vote must carry equal weight. [That] requirement does not extend to political parties. It does not mean that each party must be influential in proportion to its number of supporters.

Appellees and the dissent propose a number of "tests" for evaluating partisan gerrymandering claims, but none meets the need for a limited and precise standard that is judicially discernible and manageable. And none provides a solid grounding for judges to take the extraordinary step of reallocating power and influence between political parties.

[The District Court in the North Carolina case used a test that involved a "predominant" legislative purpose coupled with a demand for] a showing "that the dilution of the votes of supporters of a disfavored party in a particular district [is] likely to persist in subsequent elections such that an elected representative from the favored party in the district will not feel a need to be responsive to constituents who support the disfavored party."

[The] District Court's "predominant intent" prong is borrowed from the racial gerrymandering context. [If] district lines were drawn for the purpose of separating racial groups, then they are subject to strict scrutiny because "race-based decisionmaking is inherently suspect." But determining that lines were drawn on the basis of partisanship does not indicate that the districting was improper. A permissible intent—securing partisan advantage—does not become constitutionally impermissible, like racial discrimination, when that permissible intent "predominates."

The District Court tried to limit the reach of its test by requiring plaintiffs to show, in addition to predominant partisan intent, that vote dilution "is likely to persist" to such a degree that the elected representative will feel free to ignore the concerns of the supporters of the minority party. But "[t]o allow district courts to strike down apportionment plans on the basis of their prognostications as to the outcome of future elections . . . invites 'findings' on matters as to which neither judges nor anyone else can have any confidence." *Bandemer*, 478 U.S., at 160 (opinion of O'Connor, J.).

[The] District Courts also found partisan gerrymandering claims justiciable under the First Amendment, coalescing around a basic three-part test: proof of intent to burden individuals based on their voting history or party affiliation; an actual burden on political speech or associational rights; and a causal link between the invidious intent and actual burden. [To] begin, there are no restrictions on speech, association, or any other First Amendment activities in the districting plans at issue. [The] plaintiffs' argument is that partisanship in districting should be regarded as simple discrimination against supporters of the opposing party on the basis of political viewpoint. [It] provides no standard for determining when partisan activity goes too far.

As for actual burden, the slight anecdotal evidence found sufficient by the District Courts in these cases shows that this too is not a serious standard for separating constitutional from unconstitutional partisan gerrymandering. [How] much of a decline in voter engagement is enough to constitute a First Amendment burden? How many door knocks must go unanswered? How many petitions unsigned? How many calls for volunteers unheeded

The dissent proposes using a State's own districting criteria as a neutral baseline from which to measure how extreme a partisan gerrymander is. The dissent would have us line up all the possible maps drawn using those criteria according to the partisan distribution they would produce. Distance from the "median" map would indicate whether a particular districting plan harms supporters of one party to an unconstitutional extent.

As an initial matter, it does not make sense to use criteria that will vary from State to State and year to year as the baseline for determining whether a gerrymander violates the Federal Constitution. The degree of partisan advantage that the Constitution tolerates should not turn on criteria offered by the gerrymanderers themselves.

[Even] if we were to accept the dissent's proposed baseline, it would return us to "the original unanswerable question (How much political motivation and effect is too much?)." *Vieth*, 541 U.S., at 296–297 (plurality opinion). Would twenty percent away from the median map be okay? Forty percent? Sixty percent? Why or why not?

[The] dissent argues that there are other instances in law where matters of degree are left to the courts. True enough. But those instances typically involve constitutional or statutory provisions or common law confining and guiding the exercise of judicial discretion. [Here], on the other hand, the Constitution provides no basis whatever to guide the exercise of judicial discretion. [The] only provision in the Constitution that specifically addresses the matter assigns it to the political branches. See Art. I, § 4, cl. 1. [The Court next dismissed arguments based on the Elections Clause and Article I, § 2.]

Excessive partisanship in districting leads to results that reasonably seem unjust. But the fact that such gerrymandering is "incompatible with democratic principles," does not mean that the solution lies with the federal judiciary. [Federal] judges have no license to reallocate political power between the two major political parties, with no plausible grant of authority in the Constitution, and no legal standards to limit and direct their decisions.

[Our] conclusion does not condone excessive partisan gerrymandering. Nor does our conclusion condemn complaints about districting to echo into a void. The States, for example, are actively addressing the issue on a number of fronts. [The Court here described state legislation, state ballot initiatives, and state constitutional amendments to limit partisan gerrymandering.]

[As] noted, the Framers gave Congress the power to do something about partisan gerrymandering in the Elections Clause. [The Court here described several bills introduced in Congress.] We express no view on any of these pending proposals. We simply note that the avenue for reform established by the Framers, and used by Congress in the past, remains open. * * *

JUSTICE KAGAN, with whom JUSTICES GINSBURG, BREYER, and SOTOMAYOR join, dissenting.

For the first time ever, this Court refuses to remedy a constitutional violation because it thinks the task beyond judicial capabilities. [The] partisan gerrymanders in these cases deprived citizens of the most fundamental of their constitutional rights: the rights to participate equally in the political process, to join with others to advance political beliefs, and to choose their political representatives. [If] left unchecked, gerrymanders like the ones here may irreparably damage our system of government. And checking them is *not* beyond the courts. The majority's abdication comes just when courts across the country, including those below, have coalesced around manageable judicial standards to resolve partisan gerrymandering claims.

[The] majority concedes (really, how could it not?) that gerrymandering is "incompatible with democratic principles." [That] recognition would seem to demand a response. The majority offers two ideas * * *. One is that the political process can deal with the problem—a proposition so dubious on its face that I feel secure in delaying my answer for some time. The other is that political gerrymanders have always been with us. To its credit, the majority does not frame that point as an originalist constitutional argument. After all (as the majority rightly notes), racial and residential gerrymanders were also once with us, but the Court has done something about that fact. The majority's idea instead seems to be that if we have lived with partisan gerrymanders so long, we will survive.

That complacency has no cause. [While] bygone mapmakers may have drafted three or four alternative districting plans, today's mapmakers can generate thousands of possibilities at the touch of a key—and then choose the one giving their party maximum advantage (usually while still meeting traditional districting requirements). The effect is to make gerrymanders far more effective and durable than before, insulating politicians against all but the most titanic shifts in the political tides.

[Partisan] gerrymandering of the kind before us not only subverts democracy (as if that weren't bad enough). It violates individuals' constitutional rights as well. [That] practice implicates the Fourteenth Amendment's Equal Protection Clause. [And] partisan gerrymandering implicates the First Amendment too. That Amendment gives its greatest protection to political beliefs, speech, and association. Yet partisan gerrymanders subject certain voters to "disfavored treatment"—again, counting their votes for less—precisely because of "their voting history [and] their expression of political views." *Vieth*, 541 U.S., at 314 (opinion of Kennedy, J.).

[The] majority never disagrees; it appears to accept the "principle that each person must have an equal say in the election of representatives." And indeed, without this settled and shared understanding that cases like these inflict constitutional injury, the question of whether there are judicially manageable standards for resolving them would never come up.

So the only way to understand the majority's opinion is as follows: In the face of grievous harm to democratic governance and flagrant infringements on individuals' rights—in the face of escalating partisan manipulation whose compatibility with this Nation's values and law no one defends—the majority declines to provide any remedy. [I'll] give the majority this one—and important— thing: It identifies some dangers everyone should want to avoid. Judges should not be apportioning political power based on their own vision of electoral fairness, whether proportional representation or any other. And judges should not be striking down maps left, right, and center, on the view that every smidgen of politics is a smidgen too much. Respect for state legislative processes—and restraint in the exercise of judicial authority—counsels intervention in only egregious cases.

But in throwing up its hands, the majority misses something under its nose: What it says can't be done *has* been done. Over the past several years, federal courts across the country—including, but not exclusively, in the decisions below—have largely converged on a standard for adjudicating partisan gerrymandering claims (striking down both Democratic and Republican districting plans in the process).

[Start] with the standard the lower courts used. [B]oth courts (like others around the country) used basically the same three-part test to decide whether the plaintiffs had made out a vote dilution claim. As many legal standards do, that test has three parts: (1) intent; (2) effects; and (3) causation. First, the plaintiffs challenging a districting plan must prove that state officials' "predominant purpose" in drawing a district's lines was to "entrench [their party] in power" by diluting the votes of citizens favoring its rival. [Justice Kagan here cited *Common Cause v. Rucho*, 318 F. Supp. 3d 777, 805–806 (M.D.N.C. 2018).] Second, the plaintiffs must establish that the lines drawn in fact have the intended effect by "substantially" diluting their votes. [Justice Kagan here cited *Benisek v. Lamone*, 348 F. Supp. 3d 493, 498 (Md. 2018).] And third, if the plaintiffs make those showings, the State must come up with a legitimate, non-partisan justification to save its map. If you are a lawyer, you know that this test looks utterly ordinary. It is the sort of thing courts work with every day.

[The] majority's response to the District Courts' purpose analysis is discomfiting. The majority does not contest the lower courts' findings; how could it? Instead, the majority says that state officials' intent to entrench their party in power is perfectly "permissible," even when it is the predominant factor in drawing district lines. But that is wrong. [W]hen political actors have a specific and predominant intent to entrench themselves in power by manipulating district lines, that goes too far.

[On] to the second step of the analysis, where the plaintiffs must prove that the districting plan substantially dilutes their votes. [Consider] the sort of evidence used in North Carolina first. There, the plaintiffs demonstrated the districting plan's effects mostly by relying on what might be called the "extreme outlier approach." [The] approach—which also has recently been used in Michigan and Ohio litigation—begins by using advanced computing technology to randomly generate a large collection of districting plans that incorporate the State's physical and political geography and meet its declared districting criteria, *except for* partisan gain. [The] further out on the tail, the more extreme the partisan distortion and the more significant the vote dilution.

Using that approach, the North Carolina plaintiffs offered a boatload of alternative districting plans—all showing that the State's map was an out-out-out-outlier. One expert produced 3,000 maps, adhering in the way described above to the districting criteria that the North Carolina redistricting committee had used, other than partisan advantage. To calculate the partisan outcome of those maps, the expert also used the same election data (a composite of seven elections) that [a

North Carolina expert] had employed when devising the North Carolina plan in the first instance. [Every] single one of the 3,000 maps would have produced at least one more Democratic House Member than the State's actual map, and 77% would have elected three or four more. [Based] on those and other findings, the District Court determined that the North Carolina plan substantially dilutes the plaintiffs' votes.

Because the Maryland gerrymander involved just one district, the evidence in that case was far simpler—but no less powerful for that. [In] the old Sixth [District], 47% of registered voters were Republicans and only 36% Democrats. But in the new Sixth, 44% of registered voters were Democrats and only 33% Republicans. That reversal of the district's partisan composition translated into four consecutive Democratic victories, including in a wave election year for Republicans (2014). In what was once a party stronghold, Republicans now have little or no chance to elect their preferred candidate. The District Court thus found that the gerrymandered Maryland map substantially dilutes Republicans' votes.

[By] substantially diluting the votes of citizens favoring their rivals, the politicians of one party had succeeded in entrenching themselves in office. They had beat democracy.

The majority's broadest claim, as I've noted, is that this is a price we must pay because judicial oversight of partisan gerrymandering cannot be "politically neutral" or "manageable." [Consider] neutrality first. Contrary to the majority's suggestion, the District Courts did not have to—and in fact did not—choose among competing visions of electoral fairness. That is because they did not try to compare the State's actual map to an "ideally fair" one (whether based on proportional representation or some other criterion). Instead, they looked at the difference between what the State did and what the State would have done if politicians hadn't been intent on partisan gain. Or put differently, the comparator (or baseline or touchstone) is the result not of a judge's philosophizing but of the State's own characteristics and judgments.

[The] majority's sole response misses the point. According to the majority, "it does not make sense to use" a State's own (non-partisan) districting criteria as the baseline from which to measure partisan gerrymandering because those criteria "will vary from State to State and year to year." But that is a virtue, not a vice—a feature, not a bug.

[The] majority's "how much is too much" critique fares no better than its neutrality argument. How about the following for a first-cut answer: This much is too much. By any measure, a map that produces a greater partisan skew than any of 3,000 randomly generated maps (all with the State's political geography and districting criteria built in) reflects "too much" partisanship. Think about what I just said: The absolute worst of 3,001 possible maps. The *only one* that could produce a 10–3 partisan split even as Republicans got a bare majority of the statewide vote. And again: How much is too much? This much is too much: A map that without any evident non-partisan districting reason (to the contrary) shifted the composition of a district from 47% Republicans and 36% Democrats to 33% Republicans and 42% Democrats. A map that in 2011 was responsible for the largest partisan swing of a congressional district in the country.

And if the majority thought that approach too case-specific, it could have used the lower courts' general standard—focusing on "predominant" purpose and "substantial" effects—without fear of indeterminacy. I do not take even the majority to claim that courts are incapable of investigating whether legislators mainly intended to seek partisan advantage.

[Nor] is there any reason to doubt, as the majority does, the competence of courts to determine whether a district map "substantially" dilutes the votes of a rival party's supporters from the everything-but-partisanship baseline described above. [As] this Court recently noted, "the law is full of instances" where a judge's decision rests on "estimating rightly ... some matter of degree"—including the "substantial[ity]" of risk or harm.

[This] Court has long understood that it has a special responsibility to remedy violations of constitutional rights resulting from politicians' districting decisions. [The] need for judicial review is at its most urgent in cases like these. "For here, politicians' incentives conflict with voters' interests, leaving citizens without any political remedy for their constitutional harms." [*Gill v. Whitford*, 138 S.Ct. 1916, 1941 (2018),] (Kagan, J., concurring). Those harms arise because politicians want to stay in office. No one can look to them for effective relief.

[Here Kagan, J., argued that Congress and state political processes were unlikely to provide an effective remedy After noting that the majority had also recognized state courts as a possible source of relief—since the political question doctrine does not apply to them—she asked:] But what do those courts know that this Court does not? If they can develop and apply neutral and manageable standards to identify unconstitutional gerrymanders, why couldn't we?

[The] practices challenged in these cases imperil our system of government. Part of the Court's role in that system is to defend its foundations. None is more important than free and fair elections. With respect but deep sadness, I dissent.

3. DISCRETIONARY REVIEW

The most important current provisions governing the Court's appellate jurisdiction are 28 U.S.C.A. §§ 1254 (federal courts of appeals) and 1257 (state courts), both of which provide for review of lower court decisions only by "writ of certiorari"—a discretionary writ that permits the Court to decide for itself which cases most deserve its attention.[6]

---

[6]   Until 1988, Sections 1254 and 1257 both provided for appeal as of right in some cases, although they gave the Court discretion with respect to others. The Supreme Court's original jurisdiction, which typically comprises at most a handful of cases each year (mainly concerning "controversies between two or more states"), is presently governed by 28 U.S.C.A. § 1251.

In the exercise of its certiorari jurisdiction, the Court, in the words of Vinson, C.J., Address to the American Bar Association: The Work of the Federal Courts, *in* 69 S.Ct. v, vi (1949), is not "primarily concerned with the correction of errors in lower court decisions": "In almost all cases within the Court's appellate jurisdiction, the petitioner has already received one appellate review. [If] we took every case in which an interesting legal question is raised, or our prima facie impression is that the decision below is erroneous, we could not fulfill the Constitutional and statutory responsibilities placed upon the Court. To remain effective, the Supreme Court must continue to decide only those cases which present questions whose resolution will have immediate importance far beyond the particular facts and parties involved."

United States Supreme Court Rules

Rule 10. Considerations Governing Review on Writ of Certiorari

1. A review on writ of certiorari is not a matter of right, but of judicial discretion. A petition for a writ of certiorari will be granted only when there are special and important reasons therefor. The following, while neither controlling nor fully measuring the Court's discretion, indicate the character of reasons that will be considered: (a) When a United States court of appeals has rendered a decision in conflict with the decision of another United States court of appeals on the same matter; or has decided a federal question in a way in conflict with a state court of last resort; or has so far departed from the accepted and usual course of judicial proceedings, or sanctioned such a departure by a lower court, as to call for an exercise of this Court's power of supervision. (b) When a state court of last resort has decided a federal question in a way that conflicts with the decision of another state court of last resort or of a United States court of appeals. (c) When a state court or a United States court of appeals has decided an important question of federal law which has not been, but should be, settled by this Court, or has decided a federal question in a way that conflicts with applicable decisions of this Court. * * *

MARYLAND V. BALTIMORE RADIO SHOW, INC.
338 U.S. 912, 70 S.Ct. 252, 94 L.Ed. 562 (1950).

Opinion of JUSTICE FRANKFURTER respecting the denial of the petition for writ of certiorari. * * *

A variety of considerations underlie denials of the writ, and as to the same petition different reasons may lead different Justices to the same result. This is especially true of petitions for review on writ of certiorari to a State court. Narrowly technical reasons may lead to denials. [For detail, see Sec. 5 infra.] A decision may satisfy all these technical requirements and yet may commend itself for review to fewer than four members of the Court. Pertinent considerations of judicial policy here come into play. A case may raise an important question but the record may be cloudy. It may be desirable to have different aspects of an issue further illumined by the lower courts. Wise adjudication has its own time for ripening.

Since there are these conflicting and, to the uninformed, even confusing reasons for denying petitions for certiorari, it has been suggested from time to time that the Court indicate its reasons for denial. Practical considerations preclude. [The] time that would be required is prohibitive, apart from the fact as already indicated that different reasons not infrequently move different members of the Court. [It] becomes relevant here to note that failure to record a dissent from a denial of a petition for writ of certiorari in nowise implies that only the member of the Court who notes his dissent thought the petition should be granted. * * *

CHAPTER 2

NATIONAL LEGISLATIVE POWER

■ ■ ■

1. SOURCES AND NATURE

Introduction

By 1787, the minimal power of the national government under the Articles of Confederation—including its inability to directly raise armies, collect taxes, regulate foreign commerce, enforce domestic laws, and require the states to conform to the Peace Treaty with Great Britain[1]—produced what many considered to be a political crisis. Among the major defects in the Articles that led to the Constitutional Convention was the lack of authority to eliminate trade barriers erected by the individual states that treated other states like foreign nations and threatened to result in interstate commercial warfare.

The framers set out to construct a new central government that would have sufficient authority to address national problems but whose powers would be limited to those designated in the Constitution. The framers recognized the conflict between generalized grants of federal power (which might threaten the liberty of the people) and an overly specific listing of powers (which might leave the new government as ineffective as its predecessor). At one point, the Convention tentatively approved Virginia's proposal that the national legislature should have power "to legislate in all cases for the general interests of the Union, and also in those to which the States are separately incompetent." But the Committee on Detail's final report chose instead to enumerate a series of powers—mainly in Art. I, § 8—and to add at the end the power to "make all laws that shall be necessary and proper for carrying into execution the foregoing powers, and all other powers vested, by this Constitution."

Although the Necessary and Proper Clause was adopted by the Convention with little discussion, it was hardly understood uniformly. In 1791, shortly after the Constitution's ratification, before signing a bill chartering a national bank, President Washington sought opinions on its constitutionality. Secretary of the Treasury Alexander Hamilton argued that the Necessary and Proper Clause had to be interpreted broadly, and that the bank legislation was clearly constitutional. To him, laws "necessary" to carry out Congress' powers meant laws "needful,

---

[1]   See *The Federalist* No. 15 (Alexander Hamilton).

requisite, incidental, useful" to such powers. Limiting Congress' authority to strict necessity would unreasonably curtail the government's ability to act.

Secretary of State Thomas Jefferson argued that the bank would be flatly unconstitutional, strictly reading the Necessary and Proper Clause: a national bank was in no sense *essential* to carry out the duties of the federal government. If the clause were read so broadly as to make the bank "necessary," then Congress would effectively be authorized to enact any legislation that would be "convenient" in carrying out its goals, thus rendering the Convention's careful enumeration irrelevant.

Background of McCulloch v. Maryland. The first Bank of the United States engaged in a private banking business, but also acted as a depository for United States funds wherever it established branches. The preamble of the Act incorporating the Bank stated that its establishment "will be very conducive to the successful conducting of the national finances; will tend to give facility to the obtaining of loans, for the use of the government, in sudden emergencies; and will be productive of considerable advantages to trade and industry in general." The second Bank was incorporated over strenuous political opposition, and made itself extremely unpopular, particularly in the West and South, when it over-expanded credits and later drastically curtailed them, contributing to the failure of many state-incorporated banks. As a result, a number of states sought to exclude the Bank, either by state constitutional prohibitions against operating within the state any bank not chartered by the state, or by imposing heavy discriminatory taxes on such banks. The tax in *McCulloch* was one of the milder taxes.

McCULLOCH V. MARYLAND

17 U.S. (4 Wheat.) 316, 4 L.Ed. 579 (1819).

CHIEF JUSTICE MARSHALL delivered the opinion of the Court.

[Maryland taxed any bank operating in the state without state authority two percent of the face value of all banknotes issued unless it paid a $15,000 tax. The Maryland Court of Appeals upheld judgment for the statutory penalty against the cashier of the Baltimore branch of the Bank of United States for issuing bank notes without payment of the tax. The Supreme Court reversed.]

The first question [is], has Congress power to incorporate a bank? * * *

This government is acknowledged by all to be one of enumerated powers. [Among] the enumerated powers, we do not find that of establishing a bank or creating a corporation. But there is no phrase in the instrument which, like the Articles of Confederation [Article II: "Each state retains [every] power [not] expressly delegated."] excludes incidental or implied powers; and which requires that everything granted shall be expressly and minutely described. Even the tenth amendment, which was framed for the purpose of quieting the excessive jealousies which had been excited, omits the word "expressly," and declares only that the powers "not delegated to the United States, nor prohibited to the states, are reserved to the states or to the people"; thus leaving the question, whether the particular power which may become the subject of contest has been delegated to the one government, or prohibited to the other, to depend on a fair construction of the whole instrument. The men who drew and adopted this amendment had experienced the embarrassments resulting from the insertion of this word ["expressly"] in the Articles of Confederation, and probably omitted it to avoid those embarrassments. A constitution, to contain an accurate detail of all the subdivisions of which its great powers will admit, and of all the means by which they may be carried into execution, would partake of the prolixity of a legal code, and could scarcely be embraced by the human mind. It would probably never be understood by the public. Its nature, therefore, requires, that only its great outlines should be marked, its important objects designated, and the minor ingredients which composed those objects be deduced from the nature of the objects themselves. [In] considering this question, then, we must never forget, that it is *a constitution* we are expounding.

Although, among the enumerated powers of government, we do not find the word "bank," or "incorporation," we find the great powers to lay and collect taxes; to borrow money; to regulate commerce; to declare and conduct a war; and to raise and support armies and navies. The sword and the purse, all the external relations, and no inconsiderable portion of the industry of the nation, are intrusted to its government. It can never be pretended that these vast powers draw after them others of inferior importance, merely because they are inferior. [But] it may, with great reason be contended that a government, intrusted with such ample powers, on the due execution of which the happiness and prosperity of the nation so vitally depends, must also be intrusted with ample means for their execution. The power being given, it is the interest of the nation to facilitate its execution. It can never be their interest, and cannot be presumed to have been their intention, to clog and embarrass its execution by withholding the most appropriate means. [The] exigencies of the nation may require, that the treasure raised in the North should be transported to the South, that raised in the East conveyed to the West, or that this order should be reversed. Is that construction of the Constitution to be preferred which would render these operations difficult, hazardous, and expensive? Can we adopt that construction (unless the words imperiously require it) which would impute to the framers of that instrument, when granting these powers for the public good, the intention of impeding their exercise by withholding a choice of means? * * *

The creation of a corporation, it is said, appertains to sovereignty. This is admitted. But to what portion of sovereignty does it appertain? [In] America, the powers of sovereignty are divided between the government of the Union, and those of the states. They are each sovereign, with respect to the objects committed to it, and neither sovereign with respect to the objects committed to the other. [We] cannot well comprehend the process of reasoning which maintains, that a power appertaining to sovereignty cannot be connected with that vast portion of it which is granted to the general government, so far as it is calculated to subserve the legitimate objects of that government. The power of creating a corporation, though appertaining to sovereignty, is not, like the power of making war, or levying taxes, or of regulating commerce, a great substantive and independent power, which cannot be implied as incidental to other powers, or used as a means of executing them. It is never the end for which other powers are exercised, but a means by which other objects are accomplished. * * *

But the Constitution of the United States has not left the right of Congress to employ the necessary means, for the execution of the powers conferred on the government, to general reasoning. To its enumeration of powers is added that of [the Necessary and Proper Clause].

The counsel for the state of Maryland have urged [that] this clause, though in terms a grant of power, is not so in effect; but is really restrictive of the general right, which might otherwise be implied, of selecting means for executing the enumerated powers. [T]he argument on which most reliance is placed, is drawn from the peculiar language of this clause. Congress is not empowered by it to make all laws, which may have relation to the powers conferred on the government, but such only as may be *"necessary and proper"* for carrying them into execution. The word *"necessary"* is considered as controlling the whole sentence, and as limiting the right to pass laws for the execution of the granted powers, to such as are indispensable, and without which the power would be nugatory. That it excludes the choice of means, and leaves to Congress in each case, that only which is most direct and simple.

Is it true, that this is the sense in which the word "necessary" is always used? [If] reference be had to its use, in the common affairs of the world, or in approved authors, we find that it frequently imports no more than that one thing is convenient, or useful, or essential to another. To employ the means necessary to an end, is generally understood as employing any means calculated to produce the end, and not as being confined to those single means, without which the end would be entirely unattainable. [A] thing may be necessary, very necessary, absolutely or indispensably necessary. To no mind would the same idea be conveyed, by these several phrases. This comment on the word is well illustrated [by] the tenth section of the first article of the Constitution. It is, we think, impossible to compare the sentence which prohibits a state from laying "imposts, or duties on imports or exports, except what may be *absolutely* necessary for executing its inspection laws," with that which authorizes Congress "to make all laws which shall be necessary and proper for carrying into execution" the powers of the general government, without feeling a conviction that the convention understood itself to change materially the meaning of the word "necessary" by prefixing the word "absolutely." This word, then like others, is used in various senses; and in its construction, the subject, the context, the intention of the person using them, are all to be taken into view.

Let this be done in the case under consideration. The subject is the execution of those great powers on which the welfare of a nation essentially depends. It must have been the intention of those who gave these powers, to insure, as far as human prudence could insure, their beneficial execution. [This] provision is made in a constitution intended to endure for ages to come, and, consequently, to be adapted to the various crises of human affairs. To have prescribed the means by which government should, in all future time, execute its powers, would have been to change, entirely, the character of the instrument, and give it the properties of a legal code. It would have been an unwise attempt to provide, by immutable rules, for exigencies which, if foreseen at all must have been seen dimly, and which can be best provided for as they occur. To have declared that the best means shall not be used, but those alone without which the power given would be nugatory, would have been to deprive the legislature of the capacity to avail itself of experience, to exercise its reason, and to accommodate its legislation to circumstances. If we apply this principle of construction to any of the powers of the government, we shall find it so pernicious in its operation that we shall be compelled to discard [it.]

But the argument which most conclusively demonstrates the error of the construction contended for by the counsel for the state of Maryland, is founded on the intention of the convention, as manifested in the whole clause: * * *

1st. The clause is placed among the powers of Congress, not among the limitations on those powers.

2nd. Its terms purport to enlarge, not to diminish the powers vested in the government. It purports to be an additional power, not a restriction on those already granted. [If] no other motive for its insertion can be suggested, a sufficient one is found in the desire to remove all doubts respecting the right to legislate on that vast mass of incidental powers which must be involved in the Constitution, if that instrument be not a splendid bauble.

We admit, as all must admit, that the powers of the government are limited, and that its limits are not to be transcended. But we think the sound construction of the Constitution must allow to the national legislature that discretion, with respect to the means by which the powers it confers are to be carried into [execution]. Let the end be legitimate, let it be within the scope of the Constitution, and all means which are appropriate, which are plainly adapted to that end, which are not prohibited, but consist with the letter and spirit of the Constitution, are constitutional.

[If] a corporation may be employed indiscriminately with other means to carry into execution the powers of the government, no particular reason can be assigned for excluding the use of a bank, if required for its fiscal operations. [That] it is a convenient, a useful, and essential instrument in the prosecution of its fiscal operations, is not now a subject of controversy.

[But] were its necessity less apparent, none can deny its being an appropriate measure; and if it is, the degree of its necessity, as has been very justly observed, is to be discussed in another place. [S]hould Congress, under the pretext of executing its powers, pass laws for the accomplishment of objects not entrusted to the government; it would become the painful duty of this tribunal, should a case requiring such a decision come before it, to say that such an act was not the law of the land. But where the law is not prohibited, and is really calculated to effect any of the objects entrusted to the government, to undertake here to inquire into the degree of its necessity, would be to pass the line which circumscribes the judicial department, and to tread on legislative ground. * * *

[The Court invalidated Maryland's tax on the United States Bank, invoking the Supremacy Clause (Art. VI, cl. 2). This ruling and its progeny are considered in Sec. 5 infra.]

————

The most extensive recent consideration of the scope of implied powers, UNITED STATES v. COMSTOCK, 560 U.S. 126 (2010), per BREYER, J., used a multi-factor test to uphold "a federal civil-commitment statute [that] authorizes the Department of Justice to detain a mentally ill, sexually dangerous federal prisoner beyond the date the prisoner would otherwise be released. 18 U.S.C. § 4248. [The government] must first 'make all reasonable efforts to cause' the State where that person was tried, or the State where he is domiciled, to 'assume responsibility for his custody, care and treatment.'

"[I]n determining whether the Necessary and Proper Clause grants Congress the legislative authority to enact a particular federal statute, we look to see whether the statute constitutes a means that is rationally related to the implementation of a constitutionally enumerated power. Congress routinely exercises its authority to enact criminal laws in furtherance of, for example, its enumerated powers to regulate interstate and foreign commerce, to enforce civil rights, to spend funds for the general welfare, [and] so forth. [The federal government] has long been involved in the delivery of mental health care to federal prisoners, and has long provided for their civil commitment [including] insane criminals [who are sexually dangerous] upon the expiration of their terms of confinement.

"[Section] 4248 is 'reasonably adapted,' *United States v. Darby*, [Sec. 2, II, B infra], to Congress' power to act as a responsible federal custodian (a power that rests, in turn, upon federal criminal statutes that legitimately seek to implement constitutionally enumerated authority,) [and] Congress could have reasonably concluded [that] § 4248 satisfies 'review for means-end rationality,' i.e., that it satisfies the Constitution's insistence that a federal statute represent a rational means for implementing a constitutional grant of legislative authority.

["Nor] does this statute invade state sovereignty or otherwise improperly limit the scope of 'powers that remain with the States.' To the contrary, it requires *accommodation* of state interests. [The dissent's argument] that Congress' authority can be no more than one step removed from a specifically enumerated power [is] irreconcilable with our precedents. [A]s Chief Justice Marshall recognized in *McCulloch*, [from] the power to "to establish post offices and post roads" [has] been inferred the power and duty of *carrying* the mail along the post road, from one post office to another. And, from this *implied* power, has *again* been inferred the right to *punish* those who steal letters from the post office, or rob the mail.' " KENNEDY, J., and ALITO, J., concurred in the judgment.

THOMAS, J., joined by Scalia, J., dissented: Under *McCulloch*, "unless the end itself is 'legitimate,' the fit between means and end is irrelevant. "[The] Necessary and Proper Clause does not provide Congress with authority to enact any law simply because it furthers *other laws* Congress has enacted in the exercise of its incidental [authority]. Federal laws that criminalize conduct that interferes with enumerated powers, establish prisons for those who engage in that conduct, and set rules for the care and treatment of prisoners awaiting trial or serving a criminal sentence satisfy this test. [Civil] detention under § 4248, on the other hand, lacks any such connection to an enumerated power.

2. THE NATIONAL COMMERCE POWER

I. DEVELOPMENT OF BASIC CONCEPTS

GIBBONS V. OGDEN
22 U.S. (9 Wheat.) 1, 6 L.Ed. 23 (1824).

CHIEF JUSTICE MARSHALL delivered the opinion of the Court.

[A New York statute granted Livingston and Fulton the exclusive right to navigate steamboats in state waters; they assigned to Ogden the right to navigate between New York City and New Jersey. Ogden secured an injunction in the state courts against Gibbons, who was navigating two steamboats licensed under an act of Congress between New York and New Jersey.]

The appellant contends that this decree is erroneous, because the laws which purport to give the exclusive privilege it sustains, are repugnant [to] that clause in the constitution which authorizes Congress to [regulate] "commerce with foreign nations, and among the several states, and with the Indian tribes."

The subject to be regulated is commerce [and to] ascertain the extent of the power, it becomes necessary to settle the meaning of the word. The counsel for the appellee would limit it to traffic, to buying and selling, or the interchange of commodities, and do not admit that it comprehends navigation. This would restrict a general term, applicable to many objects, to one of its significations. Commerce, undoubtedly, is traffic, but it is something more: it is intercourse. It describes the commercial intercourse between nations, and parts of nations in all its branches, and is regulated by prescribing rules for carrying on that intercourse. [All] America understands, and has uniformly understood the word "commerce" to comprehend navigation, [and it] must have been so understood, when the Constitution was framed. The power over commerce, including navigation, was one of the primary objects for which the people of America adopted their government, and must have been contemplated in forming [it].

To what commerce does this power extend? [It] has, we believe, been universally admitted that these words comprehend every species of commercial intercourse between the United States and foreign nations. [If] this be the admitted meaning of the word, in its application to foreign nations, it must carry the same meaning throughout the sentences, and remain a unit, unless there be some plain intelligible cause which alters it.

The subject to which the power is next applied is to commerce "among the several States." The word "among" means intermingled with. [Commerce] among the states cannot stop at the external boundary-line of each state, but may be introduced into the interior. * * *

Comprehensive as the word "among" is, it may very properly be restricted to that commerce which concerns more states than one. [The] enumeration of the particular classes of commerce to which the power was to be extended [presupposes] something not enumerated; and that something, if we regard the language or the subject of the sentence, must be the exclusively internal commerce of a state. The genius and character of the whole government seem to be, that its action is to be applied to all the external concerns of the nation, and to those internal concerns which affect the states generally; but not to those which are completely within a particular state, which do not affect other states, and with which it is not necessary to interfere for the purpose of executing some of the general powers of the government. The completely internal commerce of a state, then, may be considered as reserved for the state itself.

But, in regulating commerce[,] the power of Congress does not stop at the jurisdictional lines of the several states. [What] is commerce "among" them; and how is it to be conducted? Can a trading expedition between two adjoining states commence and terminate outside of each? And if the trading intercourse be between two states remote from each other, must it not commence in one, terminate in the other, and probably pass through a third? Commerce among the states must, of necessity, be commerce with the states. [The] power of Congress, then, whatever it may be, must be exercised within the territorial jurisdiction of the several states.

[What] is this power? It is the power to regulate; that is, to prescribe the rule by which commerce is to be governed. This power, like all others vested in Congress, is complete in itself, may be exercised to its utmost extent, and acknowledges no limitations other than are prescribed in the Constitution. These are expressed in plain terms, and do not affect the questions which arise in this case. [If] as has always been understood, the sovereignty of Congress, though limited to specified objects, is plenary as to those objects, the power over commerce with foreign nations, and among the several States, is vested in Congress as absolutely as it would be in a single government, having in its constitution the same restrictions on the exercise of the power as are found in the constitution of the United States. [The] wisdom and the discretion of Congress, their identity with the people, and the influence which their constituents possess at elections, are, in this, as in many other instances, as that, for example, of declaring war, the sole restraints on which they have relied, to secure them from its abuse. They are the restraints on which the people must often rely solely, in all representative governments. * * *

[Ch. 4, Sec. 1 considers Marshall, C.J.'s discussion of Gibbons' claim that Congress' power to regulate commerce was exclusive, so that the New York law would be invalid even absent congressional action. The Court left that issue unresolved when it ruled that Ogden's claim of a steamboat monopoly under New York's law must yield to the federal law under which Gibbons held a license.]

The boats of the appellant were, we are told, employed in the transportation of passengers, and this is no part of that commerce which Congress may regulate. [But no] clear distinction is perceived between the power to regulate vessels employed in transporting men for hire, and property for hire. The subject is transferred to Congress, and no exception to the grant can be admitted which is not proved by the words or the nature of the thing. * * *[2]

NOTE

The Court's Commerce Clause concepts were first developed largely in cases challenging state regulatory laws and taxes as regulations of "commerce," which were claimed to be exclusively within the power of Congress. For a century, Congress left most business regulation to the states and made little use of its power to regulate commerce until the Interstate Commerce Act in 1887 and the Sherman Act in 1890.

Foundations for Extending the Reach of Congressional Power

CHAMPION V. AMES [THE LOTTERY CASE]
188 U.S. 321, 23 S.Ct. 321, 47 L.Ed. 492 (1903).

JUSTICE HARLAN delivered the opinion of the Court.

[The Federal Lottery Act, prohibiting interstate carriage of lottery tickets, was applied to shipping a box of tickets from Texas to California. Are] we prepared to say that [a] *prohibition* of the carriage of such articles from state to state is not a fit or appropriate mode for the *regulation* of that particular kind of commerce?

[If] a state, when considering legislation for the suppression of lotteries within its own limits, may properly take into view the evils, that inhere in the raising of money, in that mode, why may not Congress, invested with the power to regulate commerce among the several states, provide that such commerce shall not be polluted by the carrying of lottery tickets from one state to another? [I]t must not be forgotten that the power of Congress to regulate commerce among the states is

---

[2]   Johnson, J., concurred on the ground that the power of Congress to regulate commerce was exclusive.

plenary, is complete in itself, and is subject to no limitations except such as may be found in the Constitution. [What] clause can be cited which, in any degree, countenances the suggestion that one may, of right, carry or cause to be carried from one state to another that which will harm the public morals? * * *

Congress [does] not assume to interfere with traffic or commerce in lottery tickets carried on exclusively within the limits of any state, but has in view only commerce of that kind among the several [states]. Congress, for the purpose of guarding the people of the United States against the "widespread pestilence of lotteries" and to protect the commerce which concerns all the states, may [supplement] the action of those states—perhaps all of them—[for] the protection of the public morals. [It] said, in effect, that it would not permit the declared policy of the states [to] be overthrown or disregarded by the agency of interstate commerce. We should hesitate long before adjudging that an evil of such appalling character, carried on through interstate commerce, cannot be met and crushed by the only power competent to that end. * * *

It is said, however, [that] principle leads necessarily to the conclusion that Congress may arbitrarily exclude from commerce among the states any article, commodity, or thing, of whatever kind or nature, or however useful or valuable, which it may choose, no matter with what motive. [It] will be time enough to consider the constitutionality of such legislation when we must do so. [T]he possible abuse of a power is not an argument against its existence. * * *

CHIEF JUSTICE FULLER, with whom concur JUSTICE BREWER, JUSTICE SHIRAS, and JUSTICE PECKHAM, dissenting.

[The] power to suppress lotteries [belongs] to the states and not to Congress. To hold that Congress has general police power would be to hold that it may accomplish objects not intrusted to the general government, and to defeat the operation of the 10th Amendment.

[If] a lottery ticket is not an article of commerce, how can it become so [when] transported by an express company? [This] would be to say that everything is an article of commerce the moment it is taken to be transported from place to place, and of interstate commerce if from state to state. [The] necessary consequence is to take from the states all jurisdiction over the subject so far as interstate communication is concerned. It is a long step in the direction of wiping out all traces of state lines, and the creation of a centralized government. * * *

HOUSTON, EAST & WEST TEXAS RY. V. UNITED STATES [SHREVEPORT CASE]
234 U.S. 342, 34 S.Ct. 833, 58 L.Ed. 1341 (1914).

JUSTICE HUGHES delivered the opinion of the Court.

[The Interstate Commerce Commission fixed interstate railroad rates westward from Shreveport, La., to Texas markets. The ICC also ordered the affected railroads to raise their rates for intrastate shipments to the same Texas markets. The federally prescribed rates superseded rates that had been prescribed by the Texas Railroad Commission; the latter were lower for intrastate than for interstate traffic.[3]

[Where the power of Congress to regulate commerce] exists, it dominates. Interstate trade was not left to be destroyed or impeded by the rivalries of local government. The purpose was to make impossible the recurrence of the evils which had overwhelmed the Confederation, and to provide the necessary basis of national unity by insuring "uniformity of regulation against conflicting and discriminating state legislation." [Congress's] authority, extending to these interstate carriers as instruments of interstate commerce, necessarily embraces the right to control their operations in all matters having such a close and substantial relation to interstate traffic that the control is essential or appropriate to the security of that traffic, to the efficiency of the interstate service, and to the maintenance of conditions under which interstate commerce may be conducted upon fair terms and without molestation or hindrance.

[Congress may] prevent the common instrumentalities of interstate and intrastate commercial intercourse from being used in their intrastate operations to the injury of interstate commerce. This is not to say that Congress possesses the authority to regulate the internal commerce of a state, as such, but that it does possess the power to foster and protect interstate commerce, and to take all measures necessary or appropriate to that end, although intrastate transactions of interstate carriers may thereby be controlled.

This principle is applicable here. [In] removing the injurious discriminations against interstate traffic arising from the relation of intrastate to interstate rates, Congress is not bound to reduce the latter below what it may deem to be a proper standard, fair to the carrier and to the public. Otherwise, it could prevent the injury to interstate commerce only by the sacrifice of its judgment as to interstate rates. * * *

JUSTICE LURTON and JUSTICE PITNEY dissent.

---

[3]   For example, "a rate of 60 cents carried first-class traffic [160 miles] from Dallas, while the same rate [carried] the same class of traffic only 55 miles into Texas from Shreveport. [The] rate on wagons from Dallas to Marshall, Texas, 147.7 miles, was 36.8 cents, and from Shreveport to Marshall, 42 miles, 56 [cents]."

II. REGULATION OF NATIONAL ECONOMIC PROBLEMS

A. Limitations on the Commerce Power Through 1936

HAMMER V. DAGENHART

247 U.S. 251, 38 S.Ct. 529, 62 L.Ed. 1101 (1918).

JUSTICE DAY delivered the opinion of the Court.

[Ruling that Congress exceeded its commerce power by prohibiting interstate transportation of products from factories that used child labor, the Court distinguished the *Lottery* line of cases:] In each of these instances the use of interstate transportation was necessary to the accomplishment of harmful results. * * *

This element is wanting in the present case. [The] act in its effect does not regulate transportation among the states, but aims to standardize the ages at which children may be employed in mining and manufacturing within the states. The goods shipped are of themselves harmless. [B]efore transportation begins, the labor of their production is over, and the mere fact that they were intended for interstate commerce transportation does not make their production subject to federal control. [T]he production of articles, intended for interstate commerce, is a matter of local regulation. [If] it were otherwise, all manufacture intended for interstate shipment would be brought under federal control to the practical exclusion of the authority of the states, a result certainly not contemplated by the framers of the Constitution * * * .

It is further contended that the authority of Congress may be exerted [because] of the effect of the circulation of such goods in other states where the evil of this class of labor has been recognized by local legislation, [but t]here is no power vested in Congress to require the states to exercise their police power so as to prevent possible unfair competition. Many causes may cooperate to give one state, by reason of local laws or conditions, an economic advantage over others. The commerce clause was not intended to give to Congress a general authority to equalize such conditions. In some of the states laws have been passed fixing minimum wages for women, in others the local law regulates the hours of labor of women in various employments. Business done in such states may be at an economic disadvantage when compared with states which have no such regulations; surely, this fact does not give Congress the power to deny transportation in interstate commerce to those who carry on business where the hours of labor and the rate of compensation for women have not been fixed by a standard in use in other states and approved by Congress. [The] grant of power to Congress over the subject of interstate commerce [was] not to give it authority to control the states in their exercise of the police power over local trade and manufacture. [To] sustain this statute [would] sanction an invasion by the federal power of the control of a matter purely local in its character * * * .

JUSTICE HOLMES, [joined by McKENNA, BRANDEIS, and CLARKE, JJ.,] dissenting.

* * * Regulation means the prohibition of something, and when interstate commerce is the matter to be regulated I cannot doubt that the regulation may prohibit any part of such commerce that Congress sees fit to forbid[, despite] its possible reaction upon the conduct of the States in a matter upon which [they] are free from direct control. I [should] have thought that the most conspicuous decisions of this Court had made it clear that the power to regulate commerce and other constitutional powers could not be cut down or qualified by the fact that it might interfere with the carrying out of the domestic policy of any State. [They] may regulate their internal affairs and their domestic commerce as they like. But when they seek to send their products across the State line they are no longer within their rights. If there were no Constitution and no Congress their power to cross the line would depend upon their neighbors. Under the Constitution such commerce belongs not to the States but to Congress to regulate. It may carry out its views of public policy whatever indirect effect they may have upon the activities of the States. Instead of being encountered by a prohibitive tariff at her boundaries the State encounters the public policy of the United States which it is for Congress to express. [The] national welfare as understood by Congress may require a different attitude within its sphere from that of some self-seeking State. * * *

Constitutional Struggle:
The New Deal vs. The Great Depression

The Great Depression of the 1930s gave rise to unprecedented unemployment, drastic cutbacks in production, 60% declines in farm and labor income, widespread business and bank failures, and devastating home and farm mortgage foreclosures, all reacting with each other in an extraordinary downward spiral. Congress sought to respond using the Commerce Clause.

Early in the litigation over New Deal legislation, SCHECHTER POULTRY CORP. v. UNITED STATES, 295 U.S. 495 (1935), per HUGHES, C.J., struck down a Code, adopted under the National Industrial Recovery Act, to regulate trade practices, wages, hours, and collective bargaining in the New York poultry wholesale slaughtering market, where 96% of the poultry came from other states. Schechter bought birds only on the local market and, after slaughtering them, sold their meat only to local retailers. The Court ruled that the regulation fell outside the commerce power because the regulated conduct had no "direct" effect upon interstate commerce, but said little to clarify this, possibly because the major basis for invalidity was that the Act unconstitutionally delegated legislative power to the Act's Administrator, see Ch. 3, Sec. 2, I.

One year later, CARTER v. CARTER COAL CO., 298 U.S. 238 (1936), per SUTHERLAND, J., expanded on *Schechter's* "direct effect" test, ruling that the Commerce Clause did not give Congress power to require Bituminous Coal Code members to observe the hours and wages agreed to by producers of two-thirds of the nation's bituminous coal volume and one-half of its employed bituminous mine workers: "[T]he effect of the labor provisions of the [act] primarily falls upon production and not upon commerce; [p]roduction is a purely local activity. * * *

"That the production of every commodity intended for interstate sale and transportation has some effect upon interstate commerce may [be] freely granted; and we are brought to the final and decisive inquiry, whether here that effect is direct [or] indirect. The distinction is not formal, but substantial in the highest degree, as we pointed out in *Schechter*. 'If the commerce clause were construed [to] reach all enterprises and transactions which could be said to have an indirect effect upon interstate commerce, the federal authority would embrace practically all the activities of the people, and the authority of the state over its domestic concerns would exist only by sufferance of the federal government.' * * *

"Whether the effect of a given activity or condition is direct or indirect is not always easy to determine. The word 'direct' implies that the activity or condition invoked or blamed shall operate proximately—not mediately, remotely, or collaterally—to produce the effect. It connotes the absence of an efficient intervening agency or condition. And the extent of the effect bears no logical relation to its character. The distinction between a direct and an indirect effect turns, not upon the magnitude of either the cause or the effect, but entirely upon the manner in which the effect has been brought about. [It] is quite true that rules of law are sometimes qualified by considerations of degree, as the government argues. But the matter of degree has no bearing upon the question here, since that question is not—What is the *extent* of the local activity or condition, or the *extent* of the effect produced upon interstate commerce? but—What is the *relation* between the activity or condition and the effect?

"[The] only perceptible difference between [*Schechter*] and this is that in the *Schechter Case* the federal power was asserted with respect to commodities which had come to rest after their interstate transportation; while here, the case deals with commodities at rest before interstate commerce has begun. That difference is without significance."

B. Expansion of Commerce Power After 1936

By the 1936 Presidential election, the Court had invalidated six federal laws designed to advance President Franklin D. Roosevelt's New Deal program for economic recovery. More New Deal statutes still awaited the Court's scrutiny. These included the National Labor Relations Act, the Social Security Act (providing for both old age pensions and unemployment compensation), and the Public Utility Holding Company Act. In addition, new legislation was needed to replace the minimum labor standards lost in *Schechter* and *Carter Coal*.

After his overwhelming victory in the 1936 elections, President Roosevelt sought congressional approval of what became known popularly as the "Court Packing" plan, which would have authorized appointment of as many as six new justices, one to sit in addition to each justice over seventy years of age. In the first major Commerce Clause decision after *Carter*, several months before Congress rejected the Court-Packing plan,[4] NLRB v. JONES & LAUGHLIN STEEL CORP., 301 U.S. 1 (1937), the Court, per HUGHES, C.J., upheld application of the National Labor Relations Act to the nation's fourth-largest steel producer, most of whose production was shipped and sold in interstate commerce. The NLRB found that J&L had engaged in unfair labor practices by discharging employees at one of its plants: J&L's "argument rests upon the proposition that manufacturing in itself is not commerce. [Although] activities may be intrastate in character when separately considered, if they have such a close and substantial relation to interstate commerce that their control is essential or appropriate to protect that commerce from burdens and obstructions, Congress cannot be denied the power to exercise that control. Undoubtedly the scope of this power must be considered in the light of our dual system of government and may not be extended so as to embrace effects upon interstate commerce so indirect and remote [as to] obliterate the distinction between what is national and what is local and create a completely centralized government. The question is necessarily one of degree.

"[T]he stoppage of [J&L's] operations by industrial strife would have a most serious effect upon interstate commerce. In view of respondent's far-flung activities, it is idle to say that the effect would be indirect or remote. It is obvious that it would be immediate and might be catastrophic. We are asked to shut our eyes to the plainest facts of our national life and to deal with the question of direct and indirect effects in an intellectual vacuum. Because there may be but indirect and remote effects upon interstate commerce in connection with a host of local enterprises throughout the country, it does not follow that other industrial activities do not have such a close and intimate relation to interstate commerce as to make the presence of industrial strife a matter of the most urgent national concern." McReynolds J., joined by Van Devanter, Sutherland and Butler, JJ., dissented.

UNITED STATES V. DARBY
312 U.S. 100, 61 S.Ct. 451, 85 L.Ed. 609 (1941).

JUSTICE STONE delivered the opinion of the Court. * * *

The Fair Labor Standards [Act's] purpose [is] to exclude from interstate commerce goods produced [under] conditions detrimental to the maintenance of the minimum standards of living necessary for health and general well-being; and to prevent the use of interstate commerce [as] the means of spreading and perpetuating such substandard labor conditions among the workers of the several [states].

---

[4]   Two weeks earlier, *West Coast Hotel Co. v. Parrish* (1937), Ch. 5, Sec. 3, held that a state minimum wage law did not violate the Fourteenth Amendment Due Process Clause, overruling several earlier decisions.

The indictment charges that appellee is engaged, in the state of Georgia, in the business of acquiring raw materials, which he manufactures into finished lumber with the intent when manufactured, to ship it in interstate commerce * * * .

The prohibition of shipment of the proscribed goods in interstate commerce. Section 15(a)(1) prohibits, and the indictment charges, the shipment in interstate commerce, of goods produced for interstate commerce by employees whose wages and hours of employment do not conform to the requirements of the Act. * * *

While manufacture is not of itself interstate commerce the shipment of manufactured goods interstate is such commerce and the prohibition of such shipment by Congress is indubitably a regulation of the commerce. The power to regulate [extends] not only to those regulations which aid, foster and protect the commerce, but embraces those which prohibit it. It is conceded that the power of Congress to prohibit transportation in interstate commerce includes noxious articles, stolen articles, [and] articles such as intoxicating liquor or convict made goods, traffic in which is forbidden or restricted by the laws of the state of destination.

But it is said that the present prohibition falls within the scope of none of these categories; that while the prohibition is nominally a regulation of the commerce its motive or purpose is regulation of wages and hours of persons engaged in manufacture, the control of which has been reserved to the states and upon which Georgia and some of the states of destination have placed no restriction. [But] Congress, following its own conception of public policy concerning the restrictions which may appropriately be imposed on interstate commerce, is free to exclude from the commerce articles whose use in the states for which they are destined it may conceive to be injurious to the public health, morals or welfare even though the state has not sought to regulate their use. * * *

The motive and purpose of the present regulation are plainly to make effective the Congressional conception of public policy that interstate commerce should not be made the instrument of competition in the distribution of goods produced under substandard labor conditions. [The] motive and purpose of a regulation of interstate commerce are matters for the legislative judgment upon the exercise of which the Constitution places no restriction and over, which the courts are given no control. [Whatever] their motive and purpose, regulations of commerce which do not infringe some constitutional prohibition are within the plenary power conferred on Congress by the Commerce Clause. [We] conclude that the prohibition of the shipment interstate of goods produced under the forbidden substandard labor conditions is within the constitutional authority of Congress.

[T]hese principles of constitutional interpretation have been so long and repeatedly recognized by this Court as applicable to the Commerce Clause, that there would be little occasion for repeating them now were it not for the decision of this Court twenty-two years ago in *Dagenhart* [by] a bare majority of the Court over the powerful and now classic dissent of Mr. Justice Holmes. [*Dagenhart*] has not been followed. The distinction on which the decision was rested that

Congressional power to prohibit interstate commerce is limited to articles which in themselves have some harmful or deleterious property—a distinction which was novel when made and unsupported by any provision of the Constitution—has long since been abandoned. The thesis of the opinion that the motive of the prohibition or its effect to control in some measure the use or production within the states of the article thus excluded from the commerce can operate to deprive the regulation of its constitutional authority has long since ceased to have force. [It] should be and now is overruled.

Validity of the wage and hour requirements. Section 15(a)(2) and §§ 6 and 7 require employers to conform to the wage and hour provisions with respect to all employees engaged in the production of goods for interstate commerce. [T]he validity of the prohibition turns on the question whether [their employment] in the production of goods for interstate commerce is so related to the commerce and so affects it as to be within the reach of the power of Congress to regulate it.

[The] power of Congress to regulate interstate commerce extends to the regulation [of] activities intrastate which have a substantial effect on the commerce or the exercise of the Congressional power over it. [H]aving by the present Act adopted the policy of excluding from interstate commerce all goods produced for the commerce which do not conform to the specified labor standards, [Congress] may choose the means reasonably adapted to the attainment of the permitted end, even though they involve control of intrastate activities. Such legislation has often been sustained with respect to powers, other than the commerce power granted to the national government, when the means chosen, although not themselves within the granted power, were nevertheless deemed appropriate aids to the accomplishment of some purpose within an admitted power of the national government. [A] familiar like exercise of power is the regulation of intrastate transactions which are so commingled with or related to interstate commerce that all must be regulated if the interstate commerce is to be effectively controlled. [Similarly], Congress may require inspection and preventive treatment of all cattle in a disease infected area in order to prevent shipment in interstate commerce of some of the cattle without the treatment. [And] we have recently held that Congress in the exercise of its power to require inspection and grading of tobacco shipped in interstate commerce may compel such inspection and grading [at] local auction rooms from which a substantial part but not all of the tobacco sold is shipped in interstate commerce. *Currin v. Wallace*, 306 U.S. 1 (1939). * * *

We think also that § 15(a)(2), now under consideration, is sustainable independently of § 15(a)(1), which prohibits shipment or transportation of the proscribed goods. [Congress], to attain its objective in the suppression of nationwide competition in interstate commerce by goods produced under substandard labor conditions, has made no distinction as to the volume or amount of shipments in the commerce or of production for commerce by any particular shipper or producer. * * *

So far as *Carter* is inconsistent with this conclusion, its doctrine is limited in principle by the decisions under the Sherman Act and the National Labor Relations Act, which we have cited and which we follow.

Our conclusion is unaffected by the Tenth Amendment [which] states but a truism that all is retained which has not been surrendered. There is nothing in the history of its adoption to suggest that it was more than declaratory of the relationship between the national and state governments as it had been established by the Constitution before the amendment or that its purpose was other than to allay fears that the new national government might seek to exercise powers not granted, and that the states might not be able to exercise fully their reserved powers.[5]

Reversed.

NOTE

Local activities affecting commerce. (a) WICKARD v. FILBURN, 317 U.S. 111 (1942), per JACKSON, J., upheld a penalty imposed under the Agricultural Adjustment Act of 1938 on Filburn for raising 239 bushels of wheat in excess of his marketing allotment. Filburn's practice was to plant a small acreage of wheat, to sell some, feed some to livestock, and use some for home-consumed flour and for seed: "[This] Act extends federal regulation to production not intended in any part for commerce but wholly for consumption on the farm. [Questions] of the power of Congress are not to be decided by reference to any formula which would give controlling force to nomenclature such as 'production' and 'indirect.' [Even] if appellee's activity be local and though it may not be regarded as commerce, it may still, whatever its nature, be reached by Congress if it exerts a substantial economic effect on interstate commerce. * * *

"The wheat industry has been a problem industry for some years. [D]ecline in the export trade has left a large surplus in production which in connection with an abnormally large supply of wheat and other grains in recent years caused congestion in a number of markets; tied up railroad cars; and caused elevators in some instances to turn away grains, and railroads to institute embargoes to prevent further congestion. * * *

"The effect of consumption of home-grown wheat on interstate commerce is due to the fact that it constitutes the most variable factor in the disappearance of the wheat crop. Consumption on the farm where grown appears to vary in an amount greater than 20 per cent of average production. [The] effect of the statute before us is to restrict the amount which may be produced for market and the extent as well to which one may forestall resort to the market by producing to meet his own needs. That appellee's own contribution to the demand for wheat may be trivial by itself is not enough to remove him from the scope of federal regulation

---

[5]   The Court also held that the minimum wage and maximum hours provisions did not violate the Due Process Clause of the Fifth Amendment, citing *West Coast Hotel Co. v. Parrish*, Ch. 5, Sec. 3.

where, as here, his contribution, taken together with that of many others similarly situated, is far from trivial.

"[One] of the primary purposes of the Act in question was to increase the market price of wheat and to that end to limit the volume thereof that could affect the market. It can hardly be denied that a factor of such volume and variability as home-consumed wheat would have a substantial influence on price and market conditions. [Such wheat] overhangs the market and if induced by rising prices tends to flow into the market and check price increases. But if we assume that it is never marketed, it supplies a need of the man who grew it which would otherwise be reflected by purchases in the open market. Home-grown wheat in this sense competes with wheat in commerce. The stimulation of commerce is a use of the regulatory function quite as definitely as prohibitions or restrictions thereon. This record leaves us in no doubt that Congress may properly have considered that wheat consumed on the farm where grown if wholly outside the scheme of regulation would have a substantial effect in defeating and obstructing its purpose to stimulate trade therein at increased prices."

(b) MARYLAND v. WIRTZ, 392 U.S. 183 (1968), per HARLAN, J., upheld expanded congressional coverage of the Fair Labor Standards Act to include hospitals, nursing homes, and educational institutions—elementary, secondary, and higher education—whether private or public.[6] This was justified on two grounds: (1) the competitive position of an interstate enterprise is affected by *all* its labor costs, not simply the costs of employees producing goods for commerce; and (2) schools and hospitals are major users of goods imported from other states, and work stoppages involving their employees would interrupt this flow of goods across state lines.

(c) PEREZ v. UNITED STATES, 402 U.S. 146 (1971), per DOUGLAS, J., upheld the federal Consumer Credit Protection Act's ban on "extortionate credit transactions, though purely intrastate, [because they] may in the judgment of Congress affect interstate commerce. [R]eports and hearings [supplied] Congress with the knowledge that the loan shark racket provides organized crime with its second most lucrative source of revenue, [coerces] its victims into the commission of crimes against property, and causes the takeover by racketeers of legitimate businesses. * * *

"Congress need [not] make particularized findings in order to legislate. [But petitioner claims] that all that is involved in loan sharking is a traditionally local activity. [It] appears, instead, that loan sharking in its national setting is one way organized interstate crime holds its guns to the heads of the poor and the rich alike and syphons funds from numerous localities to finance its national operations." The Court rejected the contention that the extortionate activities of Perez were not shown to have any effect on commerce: "Where the *class of activities* is regulated

---

6   For application of the Act to state government activities, see Sec. 5, II infra.

and that *class* is within the reach of federal power, the courts have no power 'to excise, as trivial, individual instances' of the class. *Wirtz*." Stewart, J., dissented.

III. PROTECTION OF OTHER INTERESTS THROUGH THE COMMERCE CLAUSE

HEART OF ATLANTA MOTEL, INC. V. UNITED STATES
379 U.S. 241, 85 S.Ct. 348, 13 L.Ed.2d 258 (1964).

JUSTICE CLARK delivered the opinion of the Court. * * *

[Heart of Atlanta, near interstate highways, with 75% of its guests from other states and 216 rooms, refused to rent to African Americans. The issue presented was] the constitutionality of the Civil Rights Act of 1964[7] as applied to these facts.

[The] Senate Commerce Committee made it quite clear that the fundamental object of Title II was to vindicate [pursuant to the Equal Protection Clause of the Fourteenth Amendment] "the deprivation of personal dignity that surely accompanies denials of equal access to public establishments." At the same time, however, it noted that such an objective has been and could be readily achieved "by congressional action based on the commerce power of the Constitution." Our study of the legislative record [has] brought us to the conclusion that Congress possessed ample power [under the Commerce Clause], and we have therefore not considered the other grounds relied upon. * * *

While the Act [carried] no congressional findings the [legislative record is] replete with evidence of the burdens that discrimination by race or color places upon interstate commerce. This testimony included the fact that our people have become increasingly mobile with millions of all races traveling from State to State; that Negroes in particular have been the subject of discrimination in transient accommodations, having to travel great distances to secure the same; that often they have been unable to obtain accommodations and have had to call upon friends to put them up overnight; and that these conditions had become so acute as to require the listing of available lodging for Negroes in a special guidebook. [These] exclusionary practices were found to be nationwide [and, in the words of the Under Secretary of Commerce,] there is "no question that this discrimination in the North still exists to a large degree" and in the West and Midwest as well. This testimony indicated a qualitative as well as quantitative effect on interstate travel by Negroes. [As] for the latter, there was evidence that this uncertainty stemming from racial discrimination had the effect of discouraging travel on the part of a

---

[7]   Sec. 201(a) provided: "All persons shall be entitled to the full and equal enjoyment of the goods, services, facilities, [and] accommodations of any place of public accommodation * * * without discrimination or segregation on the ground of race, color, religion, or national origin." Sec. 201(b) defined each of several types of establishments as "a place of public accommodation [if] its operations affect [interstate or foreign commerce], or if discrimination or segregation by it is supported by State action." Sec. 201(c) provided that "any inn, hotel, motel or other establishment which provides lodging to transient guests" is a place of public accommodation whose "operations * * * affect commerce," except when a live-in owner rents five or fewer rooms.

substantial portion of the Negro community. [T]he voluminous testimony presents overwhelming evidence that discrimination by hotels and motels impedes interstate travel.

[The] same interest in protecting interstate commerce [led Congress to] extend the exercise of its power to gambling, to criminal enterprises, to deceptive practices in the sale of products, to fraudulent security transactions, to misbranding of drugs, [to] discrimination against shippers, to the protection of small business from injurious price cutting, [and] to racial discrimination by owners and managers of terminal restaurants.

That Congress was legislating against moral wrongs in many of these areas [does] not detract from the overwhelming evidence of the disruptive effect that racial discrimination has had on commercial intercourse.

[T]he power of Congress to promote interstate commerce also includes the power to [regulate] local activities in both the States of origin and destination, which might have a substantial and harmful effect upon that commerce. [Thus,] Congress may—as it has—prohibit racial discrimination by motels serving travelers, however "local" their operations may appear. * * *

[The concurring opinion of Douglas, J., appears after *Katzenbach v. McClung*, infra. Goldberg, J., also concurred.]

———

KATZENBACH v. McCLUNG, 379 U.S. 294 (1964), per CLARK, J., upheld application of Sec. 201 to Ollie's Barbecue, a Birmingham restaurant eleven blocks from an interstate highway. It catered to a family and white-collar trade, offering only a take-out service for African Americans: "There is no claim that interstate travelers frequented the restaurant, receiving about $70,000 worth of food which has moved in commerce [out of a total of $150,000].

"[A] comparison of per capita spending by Negroes in restaurants, theaters, and like establishments indicated less spending, after discounting income differences, in areas where discrimination is widely practiced. This condition, which was especially aggravated in the South, was attributed in the testimony of the Under Secretary of Commerce to racial segregation. This diminutive spending [has,] regardless of the absence of direct evidence, a close connection to interstate commerce. The fewer customers a restaurant enjoys the less food it sells and consequently the less it buys. [In] addition, there were many references to discriminatory situations causing wide unrest and having a depressant effect on general business conditions in the respective communities.

"Moreover there was an impressive array of testimony that discrimination in restaurants [obviously] discourages travel and obstructs interstate commerce for one can hardly travel without eating. Likewise, it was said, that discrimination deterred professional, as well as skilled, people from moving into areas where such practices occurred and thereby caused industry to be reluctant to establish there.

"[Here, as *in Darby*], Congress has determined for itself that refusals of service to Negroes have imposed burdens both upon the interstate flow of food and upon the movement of products generally. [This] does not preclude further examination by this Court. But where we find that the legislators, in light of the facts and testimony before them, have a rational basis for finding a chosen regulatory scheme necessary to the protection of commerce, our investigation is at an end. [The] absence of direct evidence connecting discriminatory restaurant service with the flow of interstate food, a factor on which the appellees place much reliance, is not, given the evidence as to the effect of such practices on other aspects of commerce, a crucial matter."

DOUGLAS, J., concurred: "Though I join the Court's opinion, I am somewhat reluctant [to] rest solely on the Commerce Clause. My reluctance is not due to any conviction that Congress lacks power to regulate commerce in the interests of human rights. It is rather my belief that [there] is a right of people to be free of state action that discriminates against them because of race. [Hence] I would prefer to rest on the assertion of legislative power contained in § 5 of the Fourteenth Amendment."[8]

IV. NEW LIMITATIONS IN THE 21st CENTURY

UNITED STATES V. MORRISON
529 U.S. 598, 120 S.Ct. 1740, 146 L.Ed.2d 658 (2000).

CHIEF JUSTICE REHNQUIST delivered the opinion of the Court.

[Petitioner Brzonkala, alleging that respondent, a fellow college student, repeatedly raped her, sued him under 42 U.S.C. § 13981 (part of the Violence Against Women Act of 1994) which provides a federal civil remedy for victims of gender-motivated violence. The United States intervened to defend § 13981's constitutionality.]

As we discussed at length in *United States v. Lopez*, 514 U.S. 549 (1995), our interpretation of the Commerce Clause has changed as our Nation has developed. [I]n the years since *Jones & Laughlin*, Congress has had considerably greater latitude in regulating conduct and transactions under the Commerce Clause than our previous case law permitted.

Lopez emphasized, however, [that] Congress' regulatory authority is not without effective bounds. [In] *Jones & Laughlin*, the Court warned that the scope of the interstate commerce power "must be considered in the light of our dual system of government and may not be extended so as to embrace effects upon interstate commerce so indirect and remote that to embrace them, in view of our

---

[8]   Goldberg, J., joined the opinion of the Court but in a separate opinion stated his view that the Fourteenth Amendment also authorized enactment of the Civil Rights Act, stressing that its "primary purpose" was "vindication of human dignity."

complex society, would effectually obliterate the distinction between what is national and what is local and create a completely centralized government."

As we observed in *Lopez*, modern Commerce Clause jurisprudence has "identified three broad categories of activity that Congress may regulate under its commerce power." "First, Congress may regulate the use of the channels of interstate commerce" (citing *Heart of Atlanta*; *Darby*). "Second, Congress is empowered to regulate and protect the instrumentalities of interstate commerce, or persons or things in interstate commerce, even though the threat may come only from intrastate activities" (citing *Shreveport*). "Finally, Congress' commerce authority includes the power to regulate those activities having a substantial relation to interstate commerce, i.e., those activities that substantially affect interstate commerce" (citing *Jones & Laughlin*).

Petitioners [seek] to sustain § 13981 as a regulation of activity that substantially affects interstate commerce. Given § 13981's focus on gender-motivated violence wherever it occurs (rather than violence directed at the instrumentalities of interstate commerce, interstate markets, or things or persons in interstate commerce), we agree that this is the proper inquiry.

[In] *Lopez*, [per REHNQUIST, C.J.], we held that the Gun-Free School Zones Act of 1990, 18 U.S.C. § 922(q)(1)(A), which made it a federal crime to knowingly possess a firearm in a school zone, exceeded Congress' authority under the Commerce Clause. Several significant considerations contributed to our decision.

First, we observed that § 922(q) was "a criminal statute that by its terms has nothing to do with 'commerce' or any sort of economic enterprise, however broadly one might define those terms." [A] fair reading of *Lopez* shows that the noneconomic, criminal nature of the conduct at issue was central to our decision in that case. See, e.g., ("Even *Wickard*, which is perhaps the most far reaching example of Commerce Clause authority over intrastate activity, involved economic activity in a way that the possession of a gun in a school zone does not"), ("Admittedly, a determination whether an intrastate activity is commercial or noncommercial may in some cases result in legal uncertainty. But, so long as Congress' authority is limited to those powers enumerated in the Constitution, and so long as those enumerated powers are interpreted as having judicially enforceable outer limits, congressional legislation under the Commerce Clause always will engender 'legal uncertainty' "), ("The possession of a gun in a local school zone is in no sense an economic activity that might, through repetition elsewhere, substantially affect any sort of interstate commerce"); see also id. (Kennedy, J., concurring) (stating that *Lopez* did not alter our "practical conception of commercial regulation" and that Congress may "regulate in the commercial sphere on the assumption that we have a single market and a unified purpose to build a stable national economy"), ("Were the Federal Government to take over the regulation of entire areas of traditional state concern, areas having nothing to do with the regulation of commercial activities, the boundaries between the spheres of federal and state authority would blur"), ("[In] a sense any conduct in this interdependent world of ours has an ultimate commercial origin or consequence, but we have not yet said the commerce power may reach so far"). * * *

The second consideration that we found important [was] that the statute contained "no express jurisdictional element which might limit its reach to a discrete set of firearm possessions that additionally have an explicit connection with or effect on interstate commerce." * * *

Third, we noted that neither § 922(q) "nor its legislative history contains express congressional findings regarding the effects upon interstate commerce of gun possession in a school zone." While "Congress normally is not required to make formal findings as to the substantial burdens that an activity has on interstate commerce," (citing *McClung, Perez*), the existence of such findings may "enable us to evaluate the legislative judgment that the activity in question substantially affects interstate commerce, even though no such substantial effect [is] visible to the naked eye."

Finally, our decision in *Lopez* rested in part on the fact that the link between gun possession and a substantial effect on interstate commerce was attenuated. The United States argued that the possession of guns may lead to violent crime, and that violent crime "can be expected to affect the functioning of the national economy in two ways. First, the costs of violent crime are substantial, and, through the mechanism of insurance, those costs are spread throughout the population. Second, violent crime reduces the willingness of individuals to travel to areas within the country that are perceived to be unsafe." The Government also argued that the presence of guns at schools poses a threat to the educational process, which in turn threatens to produce a less efficient and productive workforce, which will negatively affect national productivity and thus interstate commerce.

We rejected these "costs of crime" and "national productivity" arguments because they would permit Congress to "regulate not only all violent crime, but all activities that might lead to violent crime, regardless of how tenuously they relate to interstate commerce." We noted that, under this but-for reasoning: "Congress could regulate any activity that it found was related to the economic productivity of individual citizens: family law (including marriage, divorce, and child custody), for example. Under these theories, [it] is difficult to perceive any limitation on federal power, even in areas such as criminal law enforcement or education where States historically have been sovereign. Thus, if we were to accept the Government's arguments, we are hard pressed to posit any activity by an individual that Congress is without power to regulate."

With these principles underlying our Commerce Clause jurisprudence as reference points, the proper resolution of the present cases is clear. Gender-motivated crimes of violence are not, in any sense of the phrase, economic activity. While we need not adopt a categorical rule against aggregating the effects of any noneconomic activity in order to decide these cases, thus far in our Nation's history our cases have upheld Commerce Clause regulation of intrastate activity only where that activity is economic in nature.

Like the Gun-Free School Zones Act at issue in *Lopez*, § 13981 contains no jurisdictional element establishing that the federal cause of action is in pursuance of Congress' power to regulate interstate commerce. Although *Lopez* makes clear that such a jurisdictional element would lend support to the argument that § 13981 is sufficiently tied to interstate commerce, Congress elected to cast § 13981's remedy over a wider, and more purely intrastate, body of violent crime.

In contrast with the lack of congressional findings that we faced in *Lopez*, § 13981 *is* supported by numerous findings regarding the serious impact that gender-motivated violence has on victims and their families. But [as] we stated in *Lopez*, "Simply because Congress may conclude that a particular activity substantially affects interstate commerce does not necessarily make it so." (quoting *Hodel* (Rehnquist, J., concurring in judgment)). Rather, " 'whether particular operations affect interstate commerce sufficiently to come under the constitutional power of Congress to regulate them is ultimately a judicial rather than a legislative question, and can be settled finally only by this Court.' " (quoting *Heart of Atlanta* (Black, J., concurring)).

In these cases, Congress [found] that gender-motivated violence affects interstate commerce "by deterring potential victims from traveling interstate, from engaging in employment in interstate business, and from transacting with business, and in places involved in interstate commerce; [by] diminishing national productivity, increasing medical and other costs, and decreasing the supply of and the demand for interstate products." Given these findings and petitioners' arguments, the concern that we expressed in *Lopez* that Congress might use the Commerce Clause to completely obliterate the Constitution's distinction between national and local authority seems well founded. The reasoning that petitioners advance seeks to follow the but-for causal chain from the initial occurrence of violent crime (the suppression of which has always been the prime object of the States' police power) to every attenuated effect upon interstate commerce. If accepted, petitioners' reasoning would allow Congress to regulate any crime as long as the nationwide, aggregated impact of that crime has substantial effects on employment, production, transit, or consumption. Indeed, if Congress may regulate gender-motivated violence, it would be able to regulate murder or any other type of violence since gender-motivated violence, as a subset of all violent crime, is certain to have lesser economic impacts than the larger class of which it is a part.[7]

[The] regulation and punishment of intrastate violence that is not directed at the instrumentalities, channels, or goods involved in interstate commerce has

---

[7]   **[Ct's Note]** Justice Souter's theory [in dissent is] remarkable because it undermines this central principle of our constitutional system. As we have repeatedly noted, the Framers crafted the federal system of government so that the people's rights would be secured by the division of power. [No] doubt the political branches have a role in interpreting and applying the Constitution, but ever since *Marbury* this Court has remained the ultimate expositor of the constitutional text. [Justice] Souter's suggestion [that] from *Gibbons* on, public opinion has been the only restraint on the congressional exercise of the commerce power is true only insofar as it contends that political accountability is and has been the only limit on Congress' exercise of the commerce power within that power's outer bounds. As the language surrounding that relied upon by Justice Souter makes clear, *Gibbons* did not remove from this Court the authority to define that boundary.

always been the province of the States. See, e.g., *Cohens v. Virginia* (1821) [Ch. 1, Sec. 1 supra] (Marshall, C. J.) (stating that Congress "has no general right to punish murder committed within any of the States," and that it is "clear [that] congress cannot punish felonies generally"). Indeed, we can think of no better example of the police power, which the Founders denied the National Government and reposed in the States, than the suppression of violent crime and vindication of its victims. * * *

[The issue of Congress' power to enact § 13981 under § 5 of the Fourteenth Amendment is discussed in Ch. 11, Sec. 2, II.]

JUSTICE THOMAS, concurring.

The majority opinion correctly applies our decision in *Lopez* and I join it in full. I write separately only to express my view that the very notion of a "substantial effects" test under the Commerce Clause is inconsistent with the original understanding of Congress' powers and with this Court's early Commerce Clause cases. [Thomas, J.'s concurring opinion in *Lopez* contended:

["At the time the original Constitution was ratified, 'commerce' consisted of selling, buying, and bartering, as well as transporting for these purposes [in] contradistinction to productive activities such as manufacturing and agriculture. Alexander Hamilton, for example, repeatedly treated commerce, agriculture, and manufacturing as three separate endeavors. * * *

["The Constitution [does] not support the proposition that Congress has authority over all activities that 'substantially affect' interstate commerce. [After] all, if Congress may regulate all matters that substantially affect commerce, there is no need for the Constitution to specify that Congress may enact bankruptcy laws, cl. 4, or coin money and fix the standard of weights and measures, cl. 5, or punish counterfeiters of United States coin and securities, cl. 6. Likewise, Congress would not need the separate authority to establish post offices and post roads, cl. 7, or to grant patents and copyrights, cl. 8, or to 'punish Piracies and Felonies committed on the high Seas,' cl. 10. It might not even need the power to raise and support an Army and Navy, cls. 12 and 13, for fewer people would engage in commercial shipping if they thought that a foreign power could expropriate their property with ease. [An] interpretation of cl. 3 that makes the rest of § 8 superfluous simply cannot be correct."]

[Until] this Court replaces its existing Commerce Clause jurisprudence with a standard more consistent with the original understanding, we will continue to see Congress appropriating state police powers under the guise of regulating commerce.

JUSTICE SOUTER, with whom JUSTICE STEVENS, JUSTICE GINSBURG, and JUSTICE BREYER join, dissenting. * * *

One obvious difference from *Lopez* is the mountain of data assembled by Congress, here showing the effects of violence against women on interstate commerce. Passage of the Act in 1994 was preceded by four years of hearings [and] includes reports on gender bias from task forces in 21 [States]. Congress received evidence for the following findings:

"Three out of four American women will be victims of violent crimes sometime during their life." "[A]s many as 50 percent of homeless women and children are fleeing domestic violence." "[B]attering 'is the single largest cause of injury to women in the United States.'" "An estimated 4 million American women are battered each year by their husbands or partners." * * * "Between 2,000 and 4,000 women die every year from [domestic] abuse." "[A]rrest rates may be as low as 1 for every 100 domestic assaults." "[E]stimates suggest that we spend $5 to $10 billion a year on health care, criminal justice, and other social costs of domestic violence."

The evidence as to rape was similarly extensive, supporting these conclusions: "[The incidence of] rape rose four times as fast as the total national crime rate over the past 10 years." "According to one study, close to half a million girls now in high school will be raped before they graduate." "[T]hree-quarters of women never go to the movies alone after dark because of the fear of rape and nearly 50 percent do not use public transit alone after dark for the same reason." "[Forty-one] percent of judges surveyed believed that juries give sexual assault victims less credibility than other crime victims." "Less than 1 percent of all [rape] victims have collected damages." " '[A]n individual who commits rape has only about 4 chances in 100 of being arrested, prosecuted, and found guilty of any offense.'" "Almost one-quarter of convicted rapists never go to prison and another quarter received sentences in local jails where the average sentence is 11 months." "[A]lmost 50 percent of rape victims lose their jobs or are forced to quit because of the crime's severity." * * *

Congress thereby explicitly stated the predicate for the exercise of its Commerce Clause power. [T]he sufficiency of the evidence before Congress to provide a rational basis for the finding cannot seriously be questioned.

[The] Act would have passed muster at any time between *Wickard* in 1942 and *Lopez* in 1995, a period in which the law enjoyed a stable understanding that congressional power under the Commerce Clause, complemented by the authority of the Necessary and Proper Clause, extended to all activity that, when aggregated, has a substantial effect on interstate commerce. [T]his understanding was secure even against the turmoil at the passage of the Civil Rights Act of 1964, in the aftermath of which the Court not only reaffirmed the cumulative effects and rational basis features of the substantial effects test, but declined to limit the commerce power through a formal distinction between legislation focused on "commerce" and statutes addressing "moral and social wrongs," *Heart of Atlanta*.

[I]t is clear that some congressional conclusions about obviously substantial, cumulative effects on commerce are being assigned lesser values than the once-stable doctrine would assign them. These devaluations are accomplished [by] supplanting rational basis scrutiny with a new criterion of review.

[From] the fact that Art. I, § 8, cl. 3 grants an authority limited to regulating commerce, [it] does not at all follow that an activity affecting commerce nonetheless falls outside the commerce power, depending on the specific character of the activity, or the authority of a State to regulate it along with Congress. [H]istory has shown that categorical exclusions have proven as unworkable in practice as they are unsupportable in theory.

[I]t would not be inconsistent with the text of the Commerce Clause itself to declare "noncommercial" primary activity beyond or presumptively beyond the scope of the commerce power. That variant of categorical approach is not, however, the sole textually permissible way of defining the scope of the Commerce Clause, and any such neat limitation would at least be suspect in the light of the [Necessary and Proper Clause]. Accordingly, for significant periods of our history, the Court has defined the commerce power as plenary, unsusceptible to categorical exclusions. [In] the half century following the modern activation of the commerce power with passage of the Interstate Commerce Act in 1887, this Court from time to time created categorical enclaves beyond congressional reach by declaring such activities as "mining," "production," "manufacturing," and union membership to be outside the definition of "commerce" and by limiting application of the effects test to "direct" rather than "indirect" commercial consequences.

Since adherence to these formalistically contrived confines of commerce power in large measure provoked the judicial crisis of 1937, one might reasonably have doubted that Members of this Court would ever again toy with [it]. And yet [today's] enquiry into commercial purpose, first intimated by the *Lopez* concurrence (opinion of Kennedy, J.), is cousin to the intent-based analysis employed in *Hammer*, but rejected for Commerce Clause purposes in *Heart of Atlanta* and *Darby*.

Why is the majority tempted to reject the lesson so painfully learned in 1937? An answer emerges from contrasting *Wickard* with one of the predecessor cases it superseded. It was obvious in *Wickard* that growing wheat for consumption right on the farm was not "commerce" in the common vocabulary.[13] [Just] a few years before *Wickard*, however, it had certainly been no less obvious that "mining" practices could substantially affect commerce, even though *Carter Coal* had held mining regulation beyond the national commerce power. [T]he Court in *Carter Coal* had a reason for trying to maintain its categorical, formalistic distinction. [It] was still trying to create a laissez-faire world out of the 20th-century economy, and formalistic commercial distinctions were thought to be useful instruments in achieving that object. * * *

The Court finds it relevant that the statute addresses conduct traditionally subject to state prohibition under domestic criminal law. [Again,] history seems to be recycling, for the theory of traditional state concern as grounding a limiting principle has [been repudiated in *Garcia v. San Antonio Met. Trans. Auth.* (1985)

---

13   **[Ct's Note]** [If] substantial effects on commerce are proper subjects of concern under the Commerce Clause, what difference should it make whether the causes of those effects are themselves commercial? The Court's answer is that it makes a difference to federalism, and the legitimacy of the Court's new judicially derived federalism is the crux of our disagreement.

[Sec. 5, IV infra]], which held that the concept of "traditional governmental function" [was] incoherent.[14] * * *

The objection to reviving traditional state spheres of action as a consideration in commerce analysis [is] compounded by a further defect[:] the majority's rejection of the Founders' considered judgment that politics, not judicial review, should mediate between state and national interests as the strength and legislative jurisdiction of the National Government inevitably increased through the expected growth of the national economy. [quoting Madison (in *Federalist* No. 46), James Wilson at the Convention, and Marshall, C.J., in *Gibbons*]. * * *

[Nationwide] economic integration is the norm, the national political power has been augmented by its vast revenues, and the power of the States has been drawn down by the Seventeenth Amendment, eliminating selection of senators by state legislature in favor of direct election. [Amendments] that alter the balance of power between the National and State Governments, like the Fourteenth, or that change the way the States are represented within the Federal Government, like the Seventeenth, are not rips in the fabric of the Framers' Constitution, inviting judicial repairs. The Seventeenth Amendment may indeed have lessened the enthusiasm of the Senate to represent the States as discrete sovereignties, but the Amendment did not convert the judiciary into an alternate shield against the commerce power.

The Court [finds] no significance whatever in the state support for the Act based upon the States' acknowledged failure to deal adequately with gender-based violence in state courts, and the belief of their own law enforcement agencies that national action is essential. The National Association of Attorneys General supported the Act unanimously, and [as] the 1993 Senate Report put it, "The Violence Against Women Act is intended to respond both to the underlying attitude that this violence is somehow less serious than other crime and to the resulting failure of our criminal justice system to address such violence. Its goals are both symbolic and practical." [It] is, then, not the least irony of these cases that the States will be forced to enjoy the new federalism whether they want it or not. * * *

JUSTICE BREYER, with whom JUSTICE STEVENS joins, and with whom JUSTICE SOUTER and JUSTICE GINSBURG join as to Part I-A, dissenting.

No one denies the importance of the Constitution's federalist principles. [The] question is how the judiciary can [best] impose some meaningful limit, but not too great a limit, upon the scope of the legislative authority that the Commerce Clause delegates to Congress.

---

[14]　**[Ct's Note]** The Constitution of 1787 did, in fact, forbid some exercises of the commerce power. Article I, § 9, cl. 6, barred Congress from giving preference to the ports of one State over those of another. More strikingly, the Framers protected the slave trade from federal interference, see Art. I, § 9, cl. 1. [These] reservations demonstrate the plenary nature of the federal power; the exceptions prove the rule. [T]o suppose that enumerated powers must have limits is sensible; to maintain that there exist judicially identifiable areas of state regulation immune to the plenary congressional commerce power even though falling within the limits defined by the substantial effects test is to deny our constitutional history.

A.   Consider the problems. The "economic/noneconomic" distinction is not easy to apply. Does the local street corner mugger engage in "economic" activity or "noneconomic" activity when he mugs for money? Would evidence that desire for economic domination underlies many brutal crimes against women save the present statute?

The line becomes yet harder to draw given the need for exceptions. The Court itself would permit Congress to aggregate, hence regulate, "noneconomic" activity taking place at economic establishments. See *Heart of Atlanta*. And it would permit Congress to regulate where that regulation is "an essential part of a larger regulation of economic activity, in which the regulatory scheme could be undercut unless the intrastate activity were regulated." *Lopez*. Given the former exception, can Congress simply rewrite the present law and limit its application to restaurants, hotels, perhaps universities, and other places of public accommodation? Given the latter exception, can Congress save the present law by including it, or much of it, in a broader "Safe Transport" or "Workplace Safety" act?

More important, why should we give critical constitutional importance to the economic, or noneconomic, nature of an interstate-commerce-affecting cause? If chemical emanations through indirect environmental change cause identical, severe commercial harm outside a State, why should it matter whether local factories or home fireplaces release them? * * *

Most important, the Court's complex rules seem unlikely to help secure the very object that they seek, namely, the protection of "areas of traditional state regulation" from federal intrusion. The Court's rules, even if broadly interpreted, are underinclusive. The local pickpocket is no less a traditional subject of state regulation than is the local gender-motivated assault. Regardless, the Court reaffirms, as it should, Congress' well-established and frequently exercised power to enact laws that satisfy a commerce-related jurisdictional prerequisite—for example, that some item relevant to the federally regulated activity has at some time crossed a state line.

And in a world where most everyday products or their component parts cross interstate boundaries, Congress will frequently find it possible to redraft a statute using language that ties the regulation to the interstate movement of some relevant object, thereby regulating local criminal activity or, for that matter, family affairs. See, e.g., Child Support Recovery Act of 1992. [How] much would be gained, for example, were Congress to reenact the present law in the form of "An Act Forbidding Violence Against Women Perpetrated at Public Accommodations or by Those Who Have Moved in, or through the Use of Items that Have Moved in, Interstate Commerce"? Complex Commerce Clause rules creating fine distinctions that achieve only random results do little to further the important federalist interests that called them into being. That is why modern (pre-*Lopez*) case law rejected them. * * *

Since judges cannot change the [world,] Congress, not the courts, must remain primarily responsible for striking the appropriate state/federal balance. Congress is institutionally motivated to do so. Its Members represent state and local district interests. They consider the views of state and local officials when they legislate, and they have even developed formal procedures to ensure that such consideration takes place. See, e.g., Unfunded Mandates Reform Act of 1995. Moreover, Congress often can better reflect state concerns for autonomy in the details of sophisticated statutory schemes than can the judiciary, which cannot easily gather the relevant facts and which must apply more general legal rules and categories.

* * * Congress focused the federal law upon documented deficiencies in state legal systems. And it tailored the law to prevent its use in certain areas of traditional state concern, such as divorce, alimony, or child custody. Consequently, the law before us seems to represent an instance, not of state/federal conflict, but of state/federal efforts to cooperate in order to help solve a mutually acknowledged national problem.

[I] continue to agree with Justice Souter that the Court's traditional "rational basis" approach is sufficient. But I recognize that the law in this area is unstable and that time and experience may demonstrate both the unworkability of the majority's rules and the superiority of Congress' own procedural approach—in which case the law may evolve towards a rule that, in certain difficult Commerce Clause cases, takes account of the thoroughness with which Congress has considered the federalism issue.[9] * * *

GONZALES V. RAICH

545 U.S. 1, 125 S.Ct. 2195, 162 L.Ed. 2d 1 (2005).

JUSTICE STEVENS delivered the opinion of the Court.

[The Controlled Substances Act, part of "a comprehensive regime to combat the international and interstate traffic in illicit drugs", "prohibited the local cultivation and use of marijuana" even when in compliance with state law authorizing its use for medical purposes.]

Wickard establishes that Congress can regulate purely intrastate activity that is not itself "commercial," in that it is not produced for sale [if] Congress had a rational basis for believing that, when viewed in the aggregate, leaving home-consumed wheat outside the regulatory scheme would have a substantial influence on price and market conditions. Here too, Congress had a rational basis for concluding that leaving home-consumed marijuana outside federal control would similarly affect price and market conditions [given] the likelihood that the high demand in the interstate market will draw such marijuana into that market [and given] the enforcement difficulties that attend distinguishing between marijuana cultivated locally and marijuana grown elsewhere, and concerns about diversion into illicit channels [which] would leave a gaping hole in the CSA.

---

[9]   The question of whether the national political process or judicial review is more desirable and effective in "safeguarding" federalism is considered further in Sec. 5, II infra.

[Respondents] nonetheless insist that the CSA cannot be constitutionally applied to their activities because Congress did not make a specific finding that the intrastate cultivation and possession of marijuana for medical purposes based on the recommendation of a physician would substantially affect the larger interstate marijuana market. [But] we have never required ["that legislation must contain detailed findings proving that each activity regulated within a comprehensive statute is essential to the statutory scheme"] absent a special concern such as the protection of free speech.

[I]n both *Lopez* and *Morrison*, the parties asserted that a particular statute or provision fell outside Congress' commerce power in its entirety. This distinction is pivotal for we have often reiterated that "[w]here the class of activities is regulated and that class is within the reach of federal power, the courts have no power 'to excise, as trivial, individual instances' of the class." *Perez.* [Unlike the conduct targeted in] *Lopez* and *Morrison*, the activities regulated by the CSA are quintessentially economic[—]production, distribution, and consumption of commodities for which there is an established, and lucrative, interstate market.

[I]f, as the principal dissent contends, the personal cultivation, possession, and use of marijuana for medicinal purposes is beyond the " 'outer limits' of Congress' Commerce Clause authority," (O'Connor, J., dissenting), it must also be true that such personal use of marijuana (or any other homegrown drug) for recreational purposes is also beyond those "outer limits," whether or not a State elects to authorize or even regulate such use. Justice Thomas' separate dissent suffers from the same sweeping implications. [One] need not have a degree in economics to understand why a nationwide exemption for the vast quantity of marijuana (or other drugs) locally cultivated for personal use (which presumably would include use by friends, neighbors, and family members) may have a substantial impact on the interstate market for this extraordinarily popular substance. The congressional judgment that an exemption for such a significant segment of the total market would undermine the orderly enforcement of the entire regulatory scheme is entitled to a strong presumption of validity. Indeed, that judgment is not only rational, but "visible to the naked eye," *Lopez*, under any commonsense appraisal of the probable consequences of such an open-ended exemption.

[The dissents' limiting] the activity to marijuana possession and cultivation "in accordance with state law" cannot serve to place respondents' activities beyond congressional reach. The Supremacy Clause unambiguously provides that if there is any conflict between federal and state law, federal law shall prevail. * * *[38] [The]

---

[38]   **[Ct's Note]** California's decision (made 34 years after the CSA was enacted) to impose "stric[t] controls" on the "cultivation and possession of marijuana for medical purposes," (Thomas, J., dissenting), cannot retroactively divest Congress of its authority under the Commerce Clause.

[Thomas, J.'s dissent responded: "The majority apparently believes that even if States prevented any medical marijuana from entering the illicit drug market, and thus even if there were no need for the CSA to govern medical marijuana users, we should uphold the CSA under the *Commerce* Clause and the *Necessary* and Proper Clause. [T]o invoke the Supremacy Clause, as the majority does, is to beg the question. The CSA displaces California's Compassionate Use notion that California law has surgically excised a discrete activity that is hermetically sealed off from the larger interstate marijuana market is a dubious proposition,[10] and, more importantly, one that Congress could have rationally rejected. * * *

JUSTICE SCALIA, concurring in the judgment [to describe a "more nuanced doctrinal foundation" and to respond to O'Connor, J.'s dissent].

[Although *Lopez* and *Morrison*] rejected the argument that Congress may regulate *noneconomic* activity based solely on the effect that it may have on interstate commerce through a remote chain of inferences, [under the Necessary and Proper Clause, Congress has] regulatory authority over intrastate activities that are not themselves part of interstate commerce [even when they] do not themselves substantially affect interstate commerce [if they are] "an essential part of a larger regulation of economic activity, in which the regulatory scheme could be undercut unless the intrastate activity were regulated." [*Lopez*.] Unlike the power to regulate activities that have a substantial effect on interstate commerce, the power to enact laws enabling effective regulation of interstate commerce can only be exercised in conjunction with congressional regulation of an interstate market. [Therefore, that] simple possession [of drugs] is a noneconomic activity is immaterial to whether it can be prohibited as a necessary part of a larger regulation. Rather, Congress's authority to enact all of these prohibitions of intrastate controlled-substance activities depends only upon whether they are appropriate means of achieving the legitimate end of eradicating [illegal] substances from interstate commerce. [T]hat the CSA regulates an area typically left to state regulation [is] not enough to render federal regulation an inappropriate means. * * *

JUSTICE O'CONNOR, with whom CHIEF JUSTICE REHNQUIST and JUSTICE THOMAS join, dissenting.

This case exemplifies the role of States as laboratories. The States' core police powers have always included authority to define criminal law and to protect the health, safety, and welfare of their citizens. [Today's] decision suggests that the federal regulation of local activity is immune to Commerce Clause challenge because Congress chose to act with an ambitious, all-encompassing statute, rather than piecemeal. [If so], then *Lopez* stands for nothing more than a drafting guide: Congress should have described the relevant crime as "transfer or possession of a firearm anywhere in the nation"—thus including commercial and noncommercial activity, and clearly encompassing some activity with assuredly substantial effect on interstate commerce. [This is] a signal to Congress to enact legislation that is more extensive and more intrusive into the domain of state power. If the Court

---

Act if the CSA is constitutional as applied to respondents' conduct, but that is the very question at issue."]

[10]   The Court refers here to O'Connor, J's argument "that California's Compassionate Use Act and similar state legislation may well isolate activities relating to medicinal marijuana from the illicit market," through controls such as the requirement of a "recommendation by a physician" and "an identification card system for qualified patients."

always defers to Congress as it does today, little may be left to the notion of enumerated powers. * * *

A number of objective markers are available to confine the scope of constitutional review here. Both federal and state legislation [recognize] that medical and nonmedical (i.e., recreational) uses of drugs are realistically distinct and can be segregated, and regulate them differently. [Moreover] it is relevant that this case involves the interplay of federal and state regulation in areas of criminal law and social policy, where "States lay claim by right of history and expertise." *Lopez* (Kennedy, J., concurring); see also *Morrison*. [To] ascertain whether Congress' encroachment is constitutionally justified in this case, then, I would focus here on the personal cultivation, possession, and use of marijuana for medicinal purposes.

[It] will not do to say that Congress may regulate noncommercial activity simply because it may have an effect on the demand for commercial goods, or because the noncommercial endeavor can, in some sense, substitute for commercial activity. Most commercial goods or services have some sort of privately producible analogue. Home care substitutes for daycare. Charades games substitute for movie tickets. Backyard or windowsill gardening substitutes for going to the supermarket. To draw the line wherever private activity affects the demand for market goods is to draw no line at all, and to declare everything economic. [As for *Wickard*, in] contrast to the CSA's limitless assertion of power, Congress provided an exemption within the AAA for small producers. [Thus] *Wickard* did not hold or imply that small-scale production of commodities is always economic, and automatically within Congress' reach.

[S]omething more than mere assertion is required when Congress purports to have power over local activity whose connection to an interstate market is not self-evident. Otherwise, the Necessary and Proper Clause will always be a back door for unconstitutional federal regulation. [And] here, in part because common sense suggests that medical marijuana users may be limited in number, [the] effect of those activities on interstate drug traffic is not self-evidently substantial.

In this regard, again, this case is readily distinguishable from *Wickard* [because] the parties had "stipulated a summary of the economics of the wheat industry" [which showed] that consumption of homegrown wheat was the most variable factor in the size of the national wheat crop, and that on-site consumption could have the effect of varying the amount of wheat sent to market by as much as 20 percent. [The] Court recognizes that "the record in the *Wickard* case itself established the causal connection between the production for local use and the national market" and argues that "we have before us findings by Congress *to the same effect*." The Court refers to a series of declarations in the introduction to the CSA saying that (1) local distribution and possession of controlled substances causes "swelling" in interstate traffic; (2) local production and distribution cannot be distinguished from interstate production and distribution; (3) federal control over intrastate incidents "is essential to effective control" over interstate drug trafficking. These bare declarations cannot be compared to the record before the Court in *Wickard*. [If] as the Court claims, today's decision does not break with precedent, how can it be that voluminous findings, documenting extensive hearings about the specific topic of violence against women, did not pass constitutional muster in *Morrison,* while the CSA's abstract, unsubstantiated, generalized findings about controlled substances do? * * *

JUSTICE THOMAS, dissenting.

[The] Government contends that banning ["a distinct and separable subclass (local growers and users of state-authorized, medical marijuana)"] is "necessary and proper for carrying into Execution" its regulation of interstate drug trafficking. However, in order to be "necessary," the intrastate ban [must] be an "obvious, simple, and direct relation" between the intrastate ban and the regulation of interstate commerce. *Sabri v. United States*, [Sec. 3, II infra] (Thomas, J., concurring in judgment).

[E]ven assuming Congress has "obvious" and "plain" reasons why regulating intrastate cultivation and possession is necessary to regulating the interstate drug trade, none of those reasons applies to medical marijuana. [E]ven assuming that States' controls allow some seepage of medical marijuana into the illicit drug market, [i]t is difficult to see how this vast market could be affected by diverted medical cannabis, let alone in a way that makes regulating intrastate medical marijuana obviously essential to controlling the interstate drug market. [I]t is implausible that this Court could set aside entire portions of the United States Code as outside Congress' power in *Lopez* and *Morrison,* but it cannot engage in the more restrained practice of invalidating particular applications of the CSA that are beyond Congress' power. This Court has regularly entertained as-applied challenges under constitutional provisions, including the Commerce Clause, see *McClung*; *Heart of Atlanta*; *Wickard*. There is no reason why, when Congress exceeds the scope of its commerce power, courts may not invalidate Congress' overreaching on a case-by-case basis.

[The] majority's rewriting of the Commerce Clause seems to be rooted in the belief that, unless the Commerce Clause covers the entire web of human activity, Congress will be left powerless to regulate the national economy effectively. The interconnectedness of economic activity is not a modern phenomenon unfamiliar to the Framers. *Lopez* (Thomas, J., concurring). Moreover, the Framers understood what the majority does not appear to fully appreciate: There is a danger to concentrating too much, as well as too little, power in the Federal Government. This Court [has] casually allowed the Federal Government to strip States of their ability to regulate *intra* state commerce—not to mention a host of local activities, like mere drug possession, that are not commercial. * * *11

---

11   In *Taylor v. United States*, 136 S.Ct. 2074 (2016), the Court, in an opinion by Alito, J., applied *Raich* to construe the jurisdictional element of a federal statute that was deemed to reach to the full extent of the Commerce power. "In order to obtain a conviction under the Hobbs Act for the robbery or attempted robbery of a drug dealer," the Court wrote, "the Government need not show that the drugs that a defendant stole or attempted to steal either traveled or were destined

NATIONAL FEDERATION OF INDEPENDENT
BUSINESS V. SEBELIUS

567 U.S. 519, 132 S.Ct. 2566, 183 L.Ed.2d 450 (2012).

CHIEF JUSTICE ROBERTS announced the judgment of the Court and delivered the opinion of the Court with respect to Parts I, II, and III-C, an opinion with respect to Part IV, in which JUSTICE BREYER and JUSTICE KAGAN join, and an opinion with respect to Parts III-A, III-B, and III-D. * * *

I. In 2010, Congress enacted the Patient Protection and Affordable Care Act [ACA], to increase the number of Americans covered by health insurance and decrease the cost of health care. [It does so mainly by prohibiting insurance companies from (a) denying coverage for preexisting conditions, and (b) charging unhealthy persons higher premiums than healthy ones.] [This] case concerns constitutional challenges to two key provisions[:] the individual mandate and the Medicaid expansion.[12]

The individual mandate requires most Americans to maintain "minimum essential" health insurance coverage [and] those who do not comply with the mandate must make a [payment] to the Federal Government [which] the Act describes as a "penalty," calculated as a percentage of household income, subject to a floor based on a specified dollar amount and a ceiling based on the average annual premium the individual would have to pay for qualifying private health insurance.[13] [The Eleventh Circuit held that the individual mandate exceeds Congress's power under the Commerce Clause. The Sixth and D.C. Circuits reached the opposite conclusion.]

[III. A.1.] Congress has never attempted to rely on the [commerce power] to compel individuals not engaged in commerce to purchase an unwanted product.[3] [The] power to *regulate* commerce presupposes the existence of commercial activity to be regulated. If the power to "regulate" something included the power to create it, many of the provisions in the Constitution would be superfluous. For example, [the] power to regulate the armed forces or the value of money. [As] expansive as our cases construing the scope of the commerce power have been, [they] uniformly describe the power as reaching "activity" [citing *Lopez, Perez, Jones & Laughlin*].

Wickard has long been regarded as "perhaps the most far reaching example of Commerce Clause authority over intrastate activity," but the Government's theory in this case would go much further. Under *Wickard* it is within Congress's

---

for transport across state lines." Thomas, J., dissented on the ground that the ruling "extends our already expansive, flawed commerce-power precedents."

 12 The Medicaid expansion is discussed in Sec. 3, I infra.

 13 Part II of the opinion held that the Anti-Injunction Act—which provides that "no suit for the purpose of restraining the assessment or collection of any tax shall be maintained in any court"—did not bar the suit, because the payment did not constitute a "tax" within the statute's meaning.

 3 **[Ct's Note]** The examples of other congressional mandates cited by Justice Ginsburg are not to the contrary. Each of those mandates—to report for jury duty, to register for the draft, to purchase firearms in anticipation of militia service, to exchange gold currency for paper currency, and to file a tax return—are based on constitutional provisions other than the Commerce Clause.

power to regulate the market for wheat by supporting its price. But price can be supported by increasing demand as well as by decreasing supply. The aggregated decisions of some consumers not to purchase wheat have a substantial effect on the price of wheat, just as decisions not to purchase health insurance have on the price of insurance. Congress can therefore command that those not buying wheat do so. [The] farmer in *Wickard* was at least actively engaged in the production of wheat, and the Government could regulate that activity because of its effect on commerce. The Government's theory here would effectively override that limitation, by establishing that individuals may be regulated under the Commerce Clause whenever enough of them are not doing something the Government would have them do.

[To] consider a different example in the health care market, many Americans do not eat a balanced diet, [a] larger percentage of the total population than those without health insurance. The failure of that group to have a healthy diet increases health care costs, to a greater extent than the failure of the uninsured to purchase insurance. [Under] the Government's theory, Congress could address the diet problem by ordering everyone to buy vegetables.

[To] an economist, perhaps, there is no difference between activity and inactivity; both have measurable economic effects on commerce. But the distinction between doing something and doing nothing would not have been lost on the Framers, who were "practical statesmen," not metaphysical philosophers, ["]dealing with the facts of political life as they understood them, putting into form the government they were creating, and prescribing in language clear and intelligible the powers that government was to take." *South Carolina v. United States*, 199 U.S. 437 (1905).

[The Government argues] that because sickness and injury are unpredictable but unavoidable, "the uninsured as a class are active in the market for health care, which they regularly seek and obtain." The individual mandate "merely regulates how individuals finance and pay for that active participation—requiring that they do so through insurance, rather than through attempted self-insurance with the back-stop of shifting costs to others." [But t]he phrase "active in the market" cannot obscure the fact that most of those regulated by the individual mandate are not currently engaged in any commercial activity involving health care. [The] proposition that Congress may dictate the conduct of an individual today because of prophesied future activity finds no support in our precedent. * * *

2.   The Government next contends that Congress has the power under the Necessary and Proper Clause to enact the individual mandate because it is an "integral part of a comprehensive scheme of economic regulation" [that requires insurance companies to provide coverage even to those with preexisting medical conditions—a requirement that would be financially unsustainable if currently healthy individuals were not required to purchase coverage.] Under this argument, it is not necessary to consider the effect that an individual's inactivity may have on

interstate commerce; it is enough that Congress regulated commercial activity in a way that requires the regulation of inactivity to be effective.

[Although] the [Necessary and Proper] Clause gives Congress authority to "legislate on that vast mass of incidental powers which must be involved in the constitution," it does not license the exercise of any "great substantive and independent power[s]" beyond those specifically enumerated. *McCulloch.* [W]e have been very deferential to Congress's determination that a regulation is "necessary." [But] we have also carried out our responsibility to declare unconstitutional those laws that undermine the structure of government established by the Constitution [on the ground that they] are not "proper [means] for carrying into Execution" Congress's enumerated powers.

[Each] of our prior cases upholding laws under that Clause involved exercises of authority derivative of, and in service to, a granted power. For example, we have upheld provisions permitting continued confinement of those already in federal custody when they could not be safely released, [*Comstock*]. The individual mandate, by contrast, vests Congress with the extraordinary ability to create the necessary predicate to the exercise of an enumerated power. This is in no way an authority that is "narrow in scope," *Comstock*, or "incidental" to the exercise of the commerce power, *McCulloch*. Rather, such a conception of the Necessary and Proper Clause would work a substantial expansion of federal authority. No longer would Congress be limited to regulating under the Commerce Clause those who by some preexisting activity bring themselves within the sphere of federal regulation. Instead, Congress could reach beyond the natural limit of its authority and draw within its regulatory scope those who otherwise would be outside of it. Even if the individual mandate is "necessary" to the Act's insurance reforms, such an expansion of federal power is not a "proper" means for making those reforms effective.

The Government relies primarily on our decision in *Raich*, [but that case] did not involve the exercise of any "great substantive and independent power," *McCulloch*, of the sort at issue here. Instead, it concerned only the constitutionality of "individual *applications* of a concededly valid statutory scheme." *Raich.* * * *[14]

[SCALIA, KENNEDY, THOMAS and ALITO, JJ., filed a long separate dissent, other parts of which are reproduced below, Sec. 3, I infra. Although they agreed with the conclusions of and made similar arguments to Roberts, C.J. regarding the Commerce and Necessary and Proper Clauses, they did not join any part of his opinion. With regard to the Commerce Clause issue, they took special pains to distinguish *Raich* as "no precedent for what Congress has done here. That case's prohibition of growing (cf. *Wickard*), and of possession (cf. innumerable federal statutes) did not represent the expansion of the federal power to direct into a broad new field. The mandating of economic activity does.

---

[14]   Roberts, C.J.'s opinion of the Court in Part III-C, upholding the individual mandate under the taxing power, is in Sec. 3 infra.

["Moreover, *Raich* is far different from the Individual Mandate in another respect[: the] growing and possession prohibitions were the only practicable way of enabling the prohibition of interstate traffic in marijuana to be effectively enforced. Intrastate marijuana could no more be distinguished from interstate marijuana than, for example, endangered-species trophies obtained before the species was federally protected can be distinguished from trophies obtained afterwards—which made it necessary and proper to prohibit the sale of all such trophies, see *Andrus v. Allard*, 444 U.S. 51 (1979).

["With the present statute, by contrast, there are many [ways]. For instance, those who did not purchase insurance could be subjected to a surcharge when they do enter the health insurance system. Or they could be denied a full income tax credit given to those who do purchase the insurance."]

JUSTICE GINSBURG, with whom JUSTICE SOTOMAYOR joins, and with whom JUSTICE BREYER and JUSTICE KAGAN join as to Parts I, II, III, and IV, concurring in part, concurring in the judgment in part, and dissenting in part.

* * * I [would hold] that the Commerce Clause authorizes Congress to enact the minimum coverage provision.

[I.] The large number of individuals without health insurance, Congress found, heavily burdens the national health-care market. [Unlike] markets for most products, however, the inability to pay for care does not mean that an uninsured individual will receive no care. Federal and state law, as well as professional obligations and embedded social norms, require hospitals and physicians to provide care when it is most needed, regardless of the patient's ability to pay. * * *

Health-care providers do not absorb these bad debts. Instead, they raise their prices, passing along the cost of uncompensated care to those who do pay reliably: the government and private insurance companies. In response, private insurers increase their premiums. [The] net result: Those with health insurance subsidize the medical care of those without it. As economists would describe what happens, the uninsured "free ride" on those who pay for health insurance. The size of this subsidy is considerable. Congress found that the cost-shifting just described "increases family [insurance] premiums by on average over $1,000 a year." [Moreover, since] those without insurance generally lack access to preventative care, they do not receive treatment for conditions—like hypertension and diabetes—that can be successfully and affordably treated if diagnosed early on. When sickness finally drives the uninsured to seek care, once treatable conditions have escalated into grave health problems, requiring more costly and extensive intervention. * * *

States cannot resolve the problem of the uninsured on their own. [A] universal health-care system, if adopted by an individual State, would be "bait to the needy and dependent elsewhere, encouraging them to migrate and seek a haven of repose." *Helvering v. Davis* [Sec. 3, II infra. To] cover the increased costs, a State would have to raise taxes, and private health-insurance companies would have to increase premiums [which] would, in turn, encourage businesses and healthy individuals to leave the State. [Facing] that risk, individual States are unlikely to take the initiative in addressing the problem of the uninsured, even though solving that problem is in all States' best interests. Congress' intervention was needed to overcome this collective action impasse.

Aware that a national solution was required, Congress could have taken over the health-insurance market by establishing a tax-and-spend federal program like Social Security. Such a program, commonly referred to as a single-payer system (where the sole payer is the Federal Government), would have left little, if any, room for private enterprise or the States. [Instead] the ACA [is] a solution that retains a robust role for private insurers and state governments. * * *

In the 1990s, several States—including New York, New Jersey, Washington, Kentucky, Maine, New Hampshire, and Vermont—enacted [ACA-type] laws without requiring universal acquisition of insurance coverage. The results were disastrous. "All seven states suffered from skyrocketing insurance premium costs, reductions in individuals with coverage, and reductions in insurance products and providers." * * * Massachusetts, Congress was told, cracked the adverse selection problem. By requiring most residents to obtain insurance, the Commonwealth ensured that insurers would not be left with only the sick as customers. * * *[2]

[II.] The Commerce Clause, it is widely acknowledged, "was the Framers' response to the central problem that gave rise to the Constitution itself." The Framers' solution[,] as they perceived it, granted Congress the authority to enact economic legislation "in all Cases for the general Interests of the Union, and also in those Cases to which the States are separately incompetent." 2 Records of the Federal Convention of 1787. * * *[15]

Consistent with the Framers' intent, we have repeatedly emphasized that Congress' authority under the Commerce Clause is dependent upon "practical" considerations, including "actual experience." *Jones & Laughlin*; see *Wickard*; *Lopez* (Kennedy, J., concurring). When appraising such legislation, we ask only (1) whether Congress had a "rational basis" for concluding that the regulated activity substantially affects interstate commerce, and (2) whether there is a "reasonable connection between the regulatory means selected and the asserted ends." [Numerous citations omitted. W]e presume the statute under review is constitutional and may strike it down only on a "plain showing" that Congress acted irrationally. *Morrison*.

[Beyond] dispute, Congress had a rational basis for concluding that the uninsured, as a class, substantially affect interstate commerce. Those without insurance consume billions of dollars of health-care products and services each year. Those goods are produced, sold, and delivered largely by national and

---

[2]   **[Ct's Note]** Despite its success, Massachusetts' medical-care providers still administer substantial amounts of uncompensated care, much of that to uninsured patients from out-of-state.

[15]   In their separate dissent (which was a concurrence on the Commerce Clause issue), Scalia, Kennedy, Thomas and Alito, JJ., responded that "Article I contains no whatever-it-takes-to-solve-a-national problem power."

regional companies who routinely transact business across state lines. The uninsured also cross state lines to receive care. [Their] inability to pay for a significant portion of that consumption drives up market prices, foists costs on other consumers, and reduces market efficiency and stability. [T]he decision to forgo insurance is hardly inconsequential or equivalent to "doing nothing." [Giving] individuals a strong incentive to [insure,] Congress had good reason to believe, would reduce the number of uninsured and, correspondingly, mitigate the adverse impact the uninsured have on the national health-care market.

[Even] assuming, for the moment, that Congress lacks authority under the Commerce Clause to "compel individuals not engaged in commerce to purchase an unwanted product," such a limitation would be inapplicable here. Everyone will, at some point, consume health-care products and services. [But,] the Chief Justice insists, the uninsured cannot be considered active in the market for health care, because "[t]he proximity and degree of connection between the [uninsured today] and [their] subsequent commercial activity is too lacking."

This argument has multiple flaws. First, more than 60% of those without insurance visit a hospital or doctor's office each year. Nearly 90% will within five [years.] Equally evident, Congress has no way of separating those uninsured individuals who will need emergency medical care today (surely their consumption of medical care is sufficiently imminent) from those who will not need medical services for years to come. [See] *Perez* ("[W]hen it is necessary in order to prevent an evil to make the law embrace more than the precise thing to be prevented it may do so.") [It] is Congress' role, not the Court's, to delineate the boundaries of the market the Legislature seeks to regulate.

[C]ontrary to The Chief Justice's contention, our precedent does [indeed] acknowledge Congress' authority, under the Commerce Clause, to direct the conduct of an individual today (the farmer in *Wickard*, stopped from growing excess wheat; the plaintiff in *Raich*, ordered to cease cultivating marijuana) because of a prophesied future transaction (the eventual sale of that wheat or marijuana in the interstate market). Congress' actions are even more rational in this case, where the future activity (the consumption of medical care) is certain to occur, the sole uncertainty being the time the activity will take place. [Thus, it is not] accurate to say that the minimum coverage provision "compel[s] individuals . . . to purchase an unwanted product." * * *

At bottom, The Chief Justice's and the joint dissenters' "view that an individual cannot be subject to Commerce Clause regulation absent voluntary, affirmative acts that enter him or her into, or affect, the interstate market expresses a concern for individual liberty that [is] more redolent of Due Process Clause arguments." Plaintiffs have abandoned any argument pinned to substantive due process, however, and now concede that the provisions here at issue do not offend the Due Process Clause.

Underlying the Chief Justice's view [is] a fear that the commerce power would otherwise know no limits. [But] the unique attributes of the health-care market render everyone active in that market and give rise to a significant free-riding problem that does not occur in other markets. * * *

Supplementing these legal restraints is a formidable check on congressional power: the democratic process. As the controversy surrounding the passage of the Affordable Care Act attests, purchase mandates are likely to engender political resistance. [Additionally, the Chief Justice] emphasizes the provision's novelty. [But as] our national economy grows and changes, we have recognized, Congress must adapt to the changing "economic and financial realities." * * *

[III.] Asserting that the Necessary and Proper Clause does not authorize the minimum coverage provision, the Chief Justice focuses on the word "proper." A mandate to purchase health insurance is not "proper" [because] it is less "narrow in scope" than other laws this Court has upheld under the Necessary and Proper Clause (citing *Comstock*). [But how] is a judge to decide [whether] Congress employed an "independent power," or merely a "derivative" one? Whether the power used is "substantive," or just "incidental"? The instruction The Chief Justice, in effect, provides lower courts: You will know it when you see it. * * *

3. THE NATIONAL TAXING AND SPENDING POWERS

Art. I, § 8, cl. 1, grants Congress power "to lay and collect taxes, duties, imposts and excises, to pay the debts and provide for the common defense and general welfare of the United States." Its language includes both power to tax and to spend. In general, neither the text of Section 8 nor any case law restricts the purposes for which Congress may spend money. This section primarily concerns the use of the taxing and spending powers to achieve regulatory ends.

The Court has long recognized that Congress may use its taxing power as both a "necessary and proper" way to enforce its regulatory powers, and as a way to raise revenue which may produce "incidental" regulatory effects. The issues raised by the latter use of the taxing power, and analogous use of the spending power, declined in importance as the expanded view of Congress' regulatory powers between 1936 and 1995 left few occasions for Congress to resort to taxing or spending for regulatory purposes. But the limitations imposed on the commerce power by *Lopez* and *Morrison* (as well as on Congress' ability to enforce the Civil War Amendments, see Ch. 11, Sec. 2) have given the national taxing and spending powers a potentially renewed importance.

I. REGULATION THROUGH TAXING

Between 1922 and 1935, the Court thwarted congressional efforts to bypass its narrow interpretation of the Commerce Clause by imposing burdensome taxes for deviation from a specified course of conduct beyond the congressional power to regulate.[16] Because Congress has had little occasion to resort to the taxing power for regulatory purposes after *Darby* and *Wickard* approved a greatly expanded commerce power, the Court has not found it necessary to review critically the distinction it drew in the *Child Labor Tax Case* (1922) between (a) taxes it condemned as a "penalty" for departure from a detailed and specified course of conduct and (b) those typical excise taxes it sustained on sales or businesses set at a burdensome amount designed to discourage the taxed activity.[17]

In NATIONAL FEDERATION OF INDEPENDENT BUSINESS v. SEBELIUS, Sec. 2, IV, ROBERTS, C.J.'s opinion for the Court (Part III-C) held that the "exaction the Affordable Care Act imposes on those without health insurance looks like a tax in many respects. The [individual mandate payment] is paid to the Treasury by 'taxpayer[s]' when they file their tax returns. It does not apply to individuals who do not pay federal income taxes because their household income is less than the threshold in the Internal Revenue Code. For taxpayers who do owe the payment, its amount is determined by such familiar factors as taxable income, number of dependents, and joint filing status. The requirement to pay is found in the Internal Revenue Code and enforced by the IRS, [which] must assess and collect it 'in the same manner as taxes.' This process yields the essential feature of any tax: it produces at least some revenue for the Government. *Kahriger.* Indeed, the payment is expected to raise about $4 billion per year by 2017.

"It is of course true that the Act describes the payment as a 'penalty,' not a 'tax.' But that label [does] not determine whether the payment may be viewed as an exercise of Congress's taxing power. [See] *Nelson v. Sears, Roebuck & Co.,* 312 U.S. 359 (1941) ("In passing on the constitutionality of a tax law, we are concerned only with its practical operation, not its definition or the precise form of descriptive words which may be applied to it"); *United States v. Sotelo,* 436 U.S. 268 (1978) ("That the funds due are referred to as a 'penalty' does not alter their essential character as taxes"). * * *[7]

"The same analysis here suggests that the [individual mandate] payment may for constitutional purposes be considered a tax, not a penalty: First, for most Americans the amount due will be far less than the price of insurance, and, by statute, it can never be more.[8] It may often be a reasonable financial decision to

---

16   *Bailey v. Drexel Furniture Co.* (Child Labor Tax Case), 259 U.S. 20 (1922) (struck down a ten percent net profit tax on manufacturers who employed children deviating from standards like those in *Dagenhart); Hill v. Wallace,* 259 U.S. 44 (1922) (struck down tax on futures contracts in grain unless made through a board of trade meeting federal requirements); *United States v. Constantine,* 296 U.S. 287 (1935) (struck down tax on liquor manufacturers and dealers operating in violation of state law). Since 1935, no federal tax with a regulatory effect has been invalidated.

17   *McCray v. United States,* 195 U.S. 27 (1904); *United States v. Doremus,* 249 U.S. 86 (1919).

7   [Ct's Note] *Sotelo,* in particular, would seem to refute the joint dissent's contention that we have "never" treated an exaction as a tax if it was denominated a penalty. * * *

8   [Ct's Note] In 2016, for example, individuals making $35,000 a year are expected to owe the IRS about $60 for any month in which they do not have health insurance. Someone with an annual income of $100,000 a year would likely owe about $200. The price of a qualifying insurance policy is projected to be around $400 per month.

make the payment rather than purchase insurance, unlike the 'prohibitory' financial punishment in the *Child Labor Tax Case*. Second, the individual mandate contains no scienter requirement. Third, the payment is collected solely by the IRS through the normal means of taxation—except that the Service is not allowed to use those means most suggestive of a punitive sanction, such as criminal prosecution. * * *

"None of this is to say that the payment is not intended to affect individual conduct. [I]t is plainly designed to expand health insurance coverage. But taxes that seek to influence conduct are nothing new. [Today,] federal and state taxes can compose more than half the retail price of cigarettes, not just to raise more money, but to encourage people to quit smoking. And we have upheld such obviously regulatory measures as taxes on selling marijuana and sawed-off shotguns. * * *

"Indeed, it is estimated that four million people each year will choose to pay the IRS rather than buy insurance. [That] suggests that Congress did not think it was creating four million outlaws. * * *[18]

"There may, however, be a more fundamental objection to a tax on those who lack health insurance. [The] Court today holds that our Constitution protects us from federal regulation under the Commerce Clause so long as we abstain from the regulated activity. [But] Congress's use of the Taxing Clause to encourage buying something is, by contrast, not new. Tax incentives already promote, for example, purchasing homes and professional educations. * * *

"Second, Congress's ability to use its taxing power to influence conduct is not without limits. [See *Child Labor Tax Case*. More] recently we have declined to closely examine the regulatory motive or effect of revenue-raising measures. See *Kahriger* (collecting cases). We have nonetheless maintained that 'there comes a time in the extension of the penalizing features of the so-called tax when it loses its character as such and becomes a mere penalty with the characteristics of regulation and punishment.' *Department of Revenue of Mont. v. Kurth Ranch*, 511 U.S., at 779 (1994).

"We have already explained that the [individual mandate] payment's practical characteristics pass muster as a tax under our narrowest interpretations of the taxing power. [W]e need not here decide the precise point at which an exaction becomes so punitive that the taxing power does not authorize it. * * *

"Third, although the breadth of Congress's power to tax is greater than its power to regulate commerce, the taxing power does not give Congress the same degree of control over individual behavior. [It] is limited to requiring an individual to pay money into the Federal Treasury, no more. If a tax is properly paid, the Government has no power to compel or punish individuals subject to it. We do not make light of the severe burden that taxation—especially taxation motivated by a

---

[18]   The Court also rejected the argument that the individual mandate violates the Direct Tax Clause, Art. 1, § 9, ch. 4.

regulatory purpose—can impose. But imposition of a tax nonetheless leaves an individual with a lawful choice to do or not do a certain act, so long as he is willing to pay a tax levied on that choice."

SCALIA, KENNEDY, THOMAS and ALITO JJ., dissented: The individual mandate "is either a penalty or else a tax. [But] we know of no case [in] which the imposition was, for constitutional purposes, both. [The] issue is not whether Congress had the *power* to frame the minimum-coverage provision as a tax, but whether it *did* so.

"[In] this case, there is simply no way, 'without doing violence to the fair meaning of the words used' to escape what Congress enacted: a mandate that individuals maintain minimum essential coverage, enforced by a penalty. [We] have never held that any exaction imposed for violation of the law is an exercise of Congress' taxing power—even when the statute calls it a tax, much less when (as here) the statute repeatedly *calls* it a penalty. * * *

"So the question is, quite simply, whether the exaction here is imposed for violation of the law. It unquestionably is. [T]hat Congress (in its own words) 'imposed . . . a penalty' for failure to buy insurance is alone sufficient to render that failure unlawful. [W]e have never—*never*—treated as a tax an exaction which faces up to the critical difference between a tax and a penalty, and explicitly denominates the exaction a 'penalty.' Eighteen [times], Congress called the exaction in § 5000A(b) a 'penalty.' [T]he nail in the coffin is that the mandate and penalty are located in Title I of the Act, its operative core, rather than where a tax would be found—in Title IX, containing the Act's 'Revenue Provisions.' "[19]

II. REGULATION THROUGH SPENDING

Several decisions in the 1930s dealt with congressional attempts to regulate by use of the spending power. United States v. Butler, 297 U.S. 1 (1936), rejected a law that paid farmers to reduce acreage. Steward Machine Co. v. Davis, 301 U.S. 548 (1937), upheld Congress's unemployment compensation program that gave employers a 90 percent credit on a federal tax imposed on them if they made payments to a state's unemployment compensation fund that met federal requirements. Helvering v. Davis, 301 U.S. 619 (1937), held that what is in the nation's "general welfare" is left to Congress. See also United States v. Gerlach Live Stock Co., 339 U.S. 725 (1950) (ruling that Congress's power to spend for the general welfare was "limited only by the requirement that it shall be exercised for the common benefit as distinguished from some mere local purpose").

---

[19] The Tax Cuts and Jobs Act of 2017 lowered the tax due to $0 for anyone who is otherwise subject to the individual mandate. A federal district court found that this change rendered the mandate unconstitutional and found further that the invalid mandate was not severable from the rest of the Affordable Care Act, which the court declared unconstitutional in its entirety. A federal appeals court agreed in substantial part, but the Supreme Court ordered the lawsuit dismissed on the ground that neither the individual nor state plaintiffs had Article III standing. *See California v. Texas*, 141 S.Ct. 2104 (2021).

SOUTH DAKOTA V. DOLE
483 U.S. 203, 107 S.Ct. 2793, 97 L.Ed.2d 171 (1987).

CHIEF JUSTICE REHNQUIST delivered the opinion of the Court.

[In] 1984 Congress enacted 23 U.S.C. § 158 [withholding 5%] of federal highway funds otherwise allocable from States "in which the purchase or public possession [of] any alcoholic beverage by a person who is less than twenty-one years of age is lawful." * * *

The spending power is of course not unlimited, *Pennhurst State School and Hospital v. Halderman*, 451 U.S. 1 (1981). [The] first of these limitations is derived from the language of the Constitution itself: the exercise of the spending power must be in pursuit of "the general welfare." In considering whether a particular expenditure is intended to serve general public purposes, courts should defer substantially to the judgment of Congress. *Helvering*.[2] Second, we have required that if Congress desires to condition the States' receipt of federal funds, it "must do so unambiguously, [enabling] the States to [be] cognizant of the consequences of their participation." *Pennhurst.* Third, our cases have suggested (without significant elaboration) that conditions on federal grants might be illegitimate if they are unrelated "to the federal interest in particular national projects or programs." *Massachusetts v. United States*, 435 U.S. 444 (1978) (plurality opinion). Finally, we have noted that other constitutional provisions may provide an independent bar to the conditional grant of federal funds.

South Dakota does not seriously claim that § 158 is inconsistent with any of the first three restrictions mentioned [above.] Indeed, the condition imposed by Congress is directly related to one of the main purposes for which highway funds are expended—safe interstate travel. [A] Presidential commission appointed to study alcohol-related accidents and fatalities on the Nation's highways concluded that the lack of uniformity in the States' drinking ages created "an incentive to drink and drive" because "young persons commut[e] to border States where the drinking age is lower." * * *

The remaining question about the validity of § 158—and the basic point of disagreement between the parties—is whether the Twenty-first Amendment constitutes an "independent constitutional bar." [Petitioner] asserts that "Congress may not use the spending power to regulate that which it is prohibited from regulating directly under the Twenty-first Amendment." But our cases [have] established that the constitutional limitations on Congress when exercising its spending power are less exacting than those on its authority to regulate directly.

[In] *Oklahoma v. Civil Service Comm'n*, 330 U.S. 127 (1947), the Court considered the validity of the Hatch Act insofar as it was applied to political activities of state officials whose employment was financed in whole or in part with

---

[2]   **[Ct's Note]** The level of deference to the congressional decision is such that the Court has questioned whether "general welfare" is a judicially enforceable restriction at all. See *Buckley v. Valeo*, 424 U.S. 1 (1976) (per curiam).

federal funds. The State contended that an order under this provision to withhold certain federal funds unless a state official was removed invaded its sovereignty in violation of the Tenth Amendment. [See Sec. 5 infra.] Though finding that "the United States is not concerned with, and has no power to regulate, local political activities as such of state officials," the Court nevertheless held that the Federal Government "does have power to fix the terms upon which its money allotments to states shall be disbursed." The Court found no violation of the State's sovereignty because the State could, and did, adopt "the 'simple expedient' of not yielding to what she urges is federal coercion. The offer of benefits to a state by the United States dependent upon cooperation by the state with federal plans, assumedly for the general welfare, is not unusual."

[T]he language in our earlier opinions stands for the unexceptionable proposition that the [spending] power may not be used to induce the States to engage in activities that would themselves be unconstitutional. Thus, [a] grant of federal funds conditioned on invidiously discriminatory state action or the infliction of cruel and unusual punishment would be an illegitimate exercise of the Congress' broad spending power. But no such claim can be or is made here. Were South Dakota to succumb to the blandishments offered by Congress and raise its drinking age to 21, [it] would not violate the constitutional rights of anyone.

Our decisions have recognized that in some circumstances the financial inducement offered by Congress might be so coercive as to pass the point at which "pressure turns into compulsion." *Steward.* Here, however, Congress has directed only that a State desiring to establish a minimum drinking age lower than 21 lose a relatively small percentage of certain federal highway funds. [A] conditional grant of federal money of this sort is [not] unconstitutional simply by reason of its success in achieving the congressional objective. [T]he enactment of [drinking age] laws remains the prerogative of the States not merely in theory but in fact. Even if Congress might lack the power to impose a national minimum drinking age directly, we conclude that encouragement to state action found in § 158 is a valid use of the spending power. * * *

JUSTICE O'CONNOR, dissenting.

[T]he Court's application of the requirement that the condition imposed be reasonably related to the purpose for which the funds are expended is cursory and unconvincing. [When] Congress appropriates money to build a highway, it is entitled to insist that the highway be a safe one. But it is not entitled to insist [that] the State impose or change regulations in other areas of the State's social and economic life because of an attenuated or tangential relationship to highway use or safety. Indeed, if the rule were otherwise, the Congress could effectively regulate almost any area of a State's social, political, or economic life on the theory that use of the interstate transportation system is somehow enhanced. If, for example, the United States were to condition highway moneys upon moving the state capital, I suppose it might argue that interstate transportation is facilitated by locating local governments in places easily accessible to interstate highways—or, conversely, that highways might become overburdened if they had to carry traffic to and from the state capital. In my mind, such a relationship is hardly more attenuated than the one which the Court finds supports § 158.

There is a clear place at which the Court can draw the line between permissible and impermissible conditions on federal grants. [It] turns on whether the requirement specifies in some way how the money should be spent, so that Congress' intent in making the grant will be effectuated. [A] requirement that is not such a specification is not a condition, but a regulation, which is valid only if it falls within one of Congress' delegated regulatory powers. [The] error in *Butler* was not the Court's conclusion that the Act was essentially regulatory, but rather its crabbed view of the extent of Congress' regulatory power under the Commerce Clause.

[If] the spending power is to be limited only by Congress' notion of the general welfare, the reality, given the vast financial resources of the Federal Government, is that the Spending Clause gives "power to the Congress to tear down the barriers, to invade the states' jurisdiction, and to become a parliament of the whole people, subject to no restrictions save such as are self-imposed." This, of course, as *Butler* held, was not the Framers' plan and it is not the meaning of the Spending Clause. Our later cases are consistent with the notion that, under the spending power, the Congress may only condition grants in ways that can fairly be said to be related to the expenditure of federal funds [discussing *Oklahoma v. CSC*. But] a condition that a State will raise its drinking age to 21 [has] nothing to do with how the funds Congress has appropriated are expended. Rather [it] is a regulation determining who shall be able to drink liquor. As such it is not justified by the spending power. * * *

———

SABRI v. UNITED STATES, 541 U.S. 600 (2004), per SOUTER, J., held that Congress had power to make it a crime to bribe state or local officials whose government agency received federal funds in excess of $10,000 in any year: "Congress has authority under the Spending Clause [to] see to it that taxpayer dollars appropriated under that power are in fact spent for the general welfare, and not frittered away in graft or on projects undermined when funds are siphoned off or corrupt public officers are derelict about demanding value for dollars. See generally *McCulloch* (establishing review for means-ends rationality under the Necessary and Proper Clause)."

THOMAS, J., concurring in the judgment, observed that "the Court appears to hold that the Necessary and Proper Clause authorizes the exercise of any power that is no more than a 'rational means' to effectuate one of Congress' enumerated powers. [The Court] does not explain how there could be any federal interest in 'prosecut[ing]' a bribe paid to a city's meat inspector in connection with a substantial transaction just because the city's parks department had received a federal grant of $10,000,' *United States v. Santopietro*, 166 F.3d 88 (2d Cir.1999). It would be difficult to describe the chain of inferences and assumptions in which the Court would have to indulge to connect such a bribe to a federal interest in any federal funds or programs as being 'plainly adapted' to their protection."

———

In NATIONAL FEDERATION OF INDEPENDENT BUSINESS v. SEBELIUS, Sec. 2, IV, supra, ROBERTS, C.J.'s opinion (Part IV), joined by Breyer and Kagan, JJ., addressed the ACA's "Medicaid expansion": "The States also contend that the Medicaid expansion exceeds Congress's authority under the Spending Clause. They claim that Congress is coercing the States to adopt the changes it wants by threatening to withhold all of a State's Medicaid grants, unless the State accepts the new expanded funding and complies with the conditions that come with it.

"[The] current Medicaid program requires States to cover only certain discrete categories of needy individuals—pregnant women, children, needy families, the blind, the elderly, and the disabled. [On] average States cover only those unemployed parents who make less than 37 percent of the federal poverty level, and only those employed parents who make less than 63 percent of the poverty line.

"The Medicaid provisions of the Affordable Care Act, in contrast, require States to expand their Medicaid programs by 2014 to cover all individuals under the age of 65 with incomes below 133 percent of the federal poverty line. The Act [also] provides that the Federal Government will pay 100 percent of the costs of covering these newly eligible individuals through 2016. In the following years, the federal payment level gradually decreases, to a minimum of 90 percent. In light of the expansion in coverage mandated by the Act, the Federal Government estimates that its Medicaid spending will increase by approximately $100 billion per year, nearly 40 percent above current levels.

"[O]ur cases have recognized [that] Congress may use its spending power to create incentives for States to act in accordance with federal policies. But when 'pressure turns into compulsion,' *Steward Machine*, the legislation [would] threaten the political accountability key to our federal system. '[W]here the Federal Government directs the States to regulate, it may be state officials who will bear the brunt of public disapproval, while the federal officials who devised the regulatory program may remain insulated from the electoral ramifications of their decision.' *New York v. United States.* [T]his danger is heightened when Congress acts under the Spending Clause, because Congress can use that power to implement federal policy it could not impose directly under its enumerated powers. * * *

"The States [argue] that the Medicaid expansion is far from the typical case [in] the way it has structured the funding: Instead of simply refusing to grant the new funds to States that will not accept the new conditions, Congress has also threatened to withhold those States' existing Medicaid funds. [In *Dole*,] we found that the inducement was not impermissibly coercive, because Congress was offering only 'relatively mild encouragement to the States.' We observed that 'all

South Dakota would lose if she adheres to her chosen course as to a suitable minimum drinking age is 5%' of her highway funds. In fact, the federal funds at stake constituted less than half of one percent of South Dakota's budget at the time. * * *

"In this case, the financial 'inducement' Congress has chosen is much more than 'relatively mild encouragement'—it is a gun to the head. [A] State that opts out of the Affordable Care Act's expansion in health care coverage thus stands to lose not merely 'a relatively small percentage' of its existing Medicaid funding, but *all* of it. Medicaid spending accounts for over 20 percent of the average State's total budget, with federal funds covering 50 to 83 percent of those costs.

"[T]he Government claims that the Medicaid expansion is properly viewed merely as a modification of the existing program because [the] original Medicaid provisions contain a clause expressly reserving '[t]he right to alter, amend, or repeal any provision' of that statute. So it does. But [a] State confronted with statutory language reserving the right to 'alter' or 'amend' [might] reasonably assume that Congress was entitled to make adjustments to the Medicaid program as it developed. [The] Medicaid expansion, however, accomplishes a shift in kind, not merely degree. [It] is no longer a program to care for the neediest among us, but rather an element of a comprehensive national plan to provide universal health insurance coverage.[14] * * *

"The Court in *Steward Machine* did not attempt to 'fix the outermost line' where persuasion gives way to coercion. [We] have no need to fix a line either.[20] It is enough for today that wherever that line may be, this statute is surely beyond it."[21]

GINSBURG, J., joined by Sotomayor, J., dissented: The Chief Justice *"for the first time ever*—finds an exercise of Congress' spending power unconstitutionally coercive.

---

[14]   **[Ct's Note]** Justice Ginsburg suggests that the States can have no objection to the Medicaid expansion, because "Congress could have repealed Medicaid [and,] [t]hereafter, could have enacted Medicaid II, a new program combining the pre-2010 coverage with the expanded coverage required by the ACA." But it would certainly not be that easy. Practical constraints would plainly inhibit, if not preclude, [putting] every feature of Medicaid on the table for political reconsideration. * * *

[20]   The joint opinion of Scalia, Kennedy, Thomas, and Alito, JJ., dissenting, concurred in the result of this Part of Roberts, C.J.'s opinion, adding that "whether federal spending legislation crosses the line from enticement to coercion is often difficult to determine, and courts should not conclude that legislation is unconstitutional on this ground unless the coercive nature of an offer is unmistakably clear. In this case, however, there can be no doubt."

[21]   Roberts, C.J., held that under the ACA's severability clause, Congress intended that, if the Medicaid expansion were found unconstitutional, it would be fully remedied by permitting the states that wished to do so to decline the federal funding for the expansion without having *all* federal funding for Medicaid withdrawn. Ginsburg, J., joined by Sotomayor, J., who dissented on the merits of the Medicaid expansion ruling (see below), agreed with Roberts, C.J.'s view that "the Medicaid Act's severability clause determines the appropriate remedy." The joint dissent of Scalia, Kennedy, Thomas, and Alito, JJ., would invalidate the expansion in full, and since they would find that both the individual mandate and the expansion are invalid, "all other provisions of the Act must fail as well."

"Medicaid, as amended by the ACA, however, is not two spending programs; it is a single [program]. Given past expansions, plus express statutory warning that Congress may change the requirements participating States must meet, there can be no tenable claim that the ACA fails for lack of [notice.] Congress is simply requiring States to do what States have long been required to do to receive Medicaid funding: comply with the conditions Congress prescribes for participation. [Even] if courts were inclined to second-guess Congress' conception of the character of its legislation, how would reviewing judges divine whether an Act of Congress, purporting to amend a law, is in reality not an amendment, but a new creation? At what point does an extension become so large that it 'transforms' the basic law? * * *

"Since 1965, Congress has amended the Medicaid program on more than 50 occasions, sometimes quite sizably. Most relevant here, between 1988 and 1990, Congress [added] millions to the Medicaid-eligible population. Between 1966 and 1990, annual federal Medicaid spending grew from \$631.6 million to \$42.6 billion; state spending rose to \$31 billion over the same period. * * *

"Compared to past alterations, the ACA is notable for the extent to which the Federal Government will pick up the tab. [The] Congressional Budget Office (CBO) projects that States will spend 0.8% more than they would have, absent the [ACA.] Whatever the increase in state obligations after the ACA, it will pale in comparison to the increase in federal funding.

"Finally, any fair appraisal of Medicaid would require acknowledgment of the considerable autonomy States enjoy under the [Act.] States, as first-line administrators, will continue to guide the distribution of substantial resources among their needy populations. [U]ndoubtedly the interests of federalism are better served when States retain a meaningful role in the implementation of a program of such importance.[17]

"The Chief Justice appears to find [a] requirement that, when spending legislation is first passed, or when States first enlist in the federal program, Congress must provide clear notice of conditions it might later impose. If I understand his point correctly, it was incumbent on Congress, in 1965, to warn the States clearly of the size and shape potential changes to Medicaid might take. And absent such notice, sizable changes could not be made mandatory. Our decisions do not support such a requirement.

"[In] *Bowen v. Public Agencies Opposed to Social Security Entrapment*, 477 U.S. 41 (1986), [Congress] changed Social Security from a program voluntary for the States [to cover their employees] to one from which they could not escape. [By] including in the Act 'a clause expressly reserving to it "[t]he right to alter, amend, or repeal any provision" of the Act,' we [unanimously] held, Congress put States on notice that the Act 'created no contractual rights.' As *Bowen* indicates, no State

---

[17]   **[Ct's Note]** The Chief Justice and the joint dissenters perceive in cooperative federalism a "threa[t]" to "political accountability." [But] Medicaid's status as a federally funded, state-administered program is hardly hidden from view.

could reasonably have read § 1304 [of the Medicaid Act] as reserving to Congress authority to make adjustments only if modestly sized. [In] short, given § 1304, this Court's construction of § 1304's language in *Bowen,* and the enlargement of Medicaid in the years since 1965, a State would be hard put to complain that it lacked fair notice when, in 2010, Congress altered Medicaid to embrace a larger portion of the Nation's poor.

"[When] future Spending Clause challenges arrive, as they likely will in the wake of today's decision, how will litigants and judges assess whether 'a State has a legitimate choice whether to accept the federal conditions in exchange for federal funds'? Are courts to measure the number of dollars the Federal Government might withhold for noncompliance? The portion of the State's budget at stake? And which State's—or States'—budget is determinative: the lead plaintiff, all challenging States (26 in this case, many with quite different fiscal situations), or some national median? Does it matter [that] the coercion state officials in fact fear is punishment at the ballot box for turning down a politically popular federal grant? [The] coercion inquiry, therefore, appears to involve political judgments that defy judicial calculation."

4.   FOREIGN AFFAIRS POWER

The preceding materials on the commerce, taxing, and spending powers should provide adequate background for consideration of issues relating to the many other congressional powers. This section, however, involves a significant, atypical congressional power.

I.   TREATIES AS A SOURCE OF LEGISLATIVE POWER

MISSOURI v. HOLLAND, 252 U.S. 416 (1920), per HOLMES, J., upheld a federal statute implementing a treaty with Canada that obligated both countries to seek legislation[22] protecting birds that traversed both countries, and were valued for food and as destroyers of insects harmful to vegetation: "[It] is not enough to refer to the Tenth Amendment [because] by Article 2, Section 2, the power to make treaties is delegated expressly, and by Article 6 treaties [are] declared the supreme law of the land.[23] If the treaty is valid there can be no dispute about the validity of the statute [as] a necessary and proper means to execute the powers of the Government.

"[It] is said [that] there are [constitutional limits] to the treaty-making power, and that one such limit is that what an act of Congress could not do unaided, in derogation of the powers reserved to the States, a treaty cannot do. [Acts] of

---

[22]   Thus, the treaty was not, by its terms, "self-executing" but rather required congressional implementation. See *Medellin v. Texas* (2008), Ch. 3, Sec. 1, I.

[23]   "[A] treaty is placed on the same footing [with] an act of legislation. [When] the two relate to the same subject, the courts will always endeavor to construe them so as to give effect to both, [but] if the two are inconsistent, the one last in date will control the other." *Whitney v. Robertson,* 124 U.S. 190 (1888).

Congress are the supreme law of the land only when made in pursuance of the Constitution, while treaties are declared to be so when made under the authority of the United States. It is open to question whether the authority of the United States means more than the formal acts prescribed to make the convention. We do not mean to imply that there are no qualifications to the treaty-making power; but they must be ascertained in a different way. It is obvious that there may be matters of the sharpest exigency for the national well being that an act of Congress could not deal with but that a treaty followed by such an act could, and it is not lightly to be assumed that, in matters requiring national action, 'a power which must belong to and somewhere reside in every civilized government' is not to be found. [W]hen we are dealing with words [in] the Constitution of the United States, we must realize that they have called into life a being the development of which could not have been foreseen completely by the most gifted of its begetters. It was enough for them to realize or to hope that they had created an organism; it has taken a century and has cost their successors much sweat and blood to prove that they created a nation. The case before us must be considered in the light of our whole experience and not merely in that of what was said a hundred years ago. The treaty in question does not contravene any prohibitory words to be found in the Constitution. The only question is whether it is forbidden by some invisible radiation from the general terms of the Tenth Amendment. We must consider what this country has become in deciding what that amendment has reserved. * * *

"Here a national interest of very nearly the first magnitude is involved. It can be protected only by national action in concert with that of another power. The subject matter is only transitorily within the State and has no permanent habitat therein. But for the treaty and the statute there soon might be no birds for any powers to deal with. We see nothing in the Constitution that compels the Government to sit by while a food supply is cut off and the protectors of our forests and our crops are destroyed. It is not sufficient to rely upon the States. The reliance is vain, and were it otherwise, the question is whether the United States is forbidden to act. We are of opinion that the treaty and statute must be upheld." Van Devanter and Pitney, JJ., dissented without opinion.

————

In BOND v. UNITED STATES, 572 U.S. 844 (2014), the Court, per ROBERTS, C.J., interpreted the Chemical Weapons Convention Implementation Act of 1998, which had been enacted by Congress to implement the international Convention on the Prohibition of the Development, Production, Stockpiling, and Use of Chemical Weapons and on Their Destruction, to be "consistent with the principles of federalism inherent in our constitutional structure," so as not to apply to an attempt by a vengeful wife to poison a woman with whom her husband had an affair, thus avoiding the constitutional question of the scope and continuing vitality of *Missouri v. Holland*. This was "a statute concerned with acts of war, assassination, and terrorism, [not] local criminal activity, which has traditionally been the responsibility of the States."

Three Justices concurred in the judgment and addressed the constitutional issue. SCALIA, J., joined by Thomas, J., and in part by Alito, J., found "clear beyond doubt" that the statute covered petitioner's conduct and was authorized by the treaty. But, he went on, "beginning in the last half of the last century, many treaties [touch] almost every aspect of domestic civil, political, and cultural life." Statutes implementing treaties must therefore rely upon "independent (though quite robust) Article I, § 8 powers." Accordingly, "[t]he Constitution's text and structure show that there is" nothing to *Holland*'s "*ipse dixit.*"

THOMAS, J., joined by Scalia, J., and in part by Alito, J., reasoned that "even if a treaty may reach some local matters," the "original understanding" of the Framers and "post-ratification theory and practice" showed that treaties "must [be] limited to international intercourse [rather than] purely domestic matters."

5.   APPLYING NATIONAL POWERS TO STATE GOVERNMENTS: INTERGOVERNMENTAL IMMUNITIES

I.   ORIGINS OF IMMUNITIES

Intergovernmental immunity as a constitutional limit on state and federal power started with McCULLOCH v. MARYLAND, Sec. 1 supra, which held invalid Maryland's taxes on the Bank of United States: "[The] great principle [that sustains the bank's] claim to be exempted from the power of the state to tax its operations [is] that the Constitution and the laws made in pursuance thereof are supreme. [From this, other] propositions are deduced as corollaries[:] 1st. That a power to create implies a power to preserve. 2d. That a power to destroy, if wielded by a different hand, is hostile to, and incompatible with, these powers to create and to preserve. 3d. That where this repugnancy exists, that authority which is supreme must control. [That] the power of taxing [the bank] by the states may be exercised so as to destroy it, is too obvious to be denied."

Since *McCulloch* the Court has never questioned absolute federal immunity from state taxation without the consent of Congress. But such immunity has been restricted to state taxes imposed on the United States itself, or an agency or instrumentality so closely connected to the Government that the two cannot realistically be viewed as separate entities, at least insofar as the activity being taxed is concerned. Meanwhile, invoking *McCulloch*, many cases afforded state officials a fairly broad immunity from federal taxes. But beginning in 1938, this line of cases was abandoned.

II.   STATE IMMUNITY FROM FEDERAL REGULATION

MARYLAND v. WIRTZ (1968), Sec. 2, II, B, per HARLAN, J., upheld application of the Fair Labor Standards Act to state schools and hospitals, stressing that "Congress has 'interfered with' these state functions only to the extent of providing that when the state employs people in performing such functions it is subject to the same restrictions as a wide range of other employers whose activities affect commerce. * * * " Douglas, J., joined by Stewart, J., dissented.

NATIONAL LEAGUE OF CITIES v. USERY, 426 U.S. 833 (1976), per REHNQUIST, J., overruled *Wirtz* on this issue: Federal regulation of the wages, hours, and overtime compensation for those whom states employ "to carry out their governmental functions" would increase costs and "substantially restructure" ways by which "state and local governments [discharge] their dual function of administering the public law and furnishing public services." It is not within Congress' commerce power "to directly displace the States' freedom to structure integral operations in areas of traditional governmental functions." Though "not untroubled by [possible] implications of the Court's opinion," BLACKMUN, J., joined it "with the understanding" that it "adopts a balancing approach, and does not outlaw federal power where the federal interest is demonstrably greater and [state compliance] would be essential." Brennan, J., joined by White, Marshall and Stevens, JJ., dissented.

During the next seven years, the *National League of Cities* principle was unsuccessfully urged upon the Court five times. The first two decisions were unanimous.[24] In the next two, Blackmun, J., joined the *National League of Cities* dissenters to rule 5–4 that the principle was not applicable.[25] The fifth follows:

GARCIA V. SAN ANTONIO METROPOLITAN TRANSIT AUTHORITY
469 U.S. 528, 105 S.Ct. 1005, 83 L.Ed.2d 1016 (1985).

JUSTICE BLACKMUN delivered the opinion of the Court.

[The Court upheld application of the Fair Labor Standards Act wage and hour provisions to a municipally-owned and operated mass transit system.]

The prerequisites for governmental immunity under *National League of Cities* were summarized by this Court in *Hodel*[:] First, it is said that the federal statute at issue must regulate "the 'States as States.' " Second, the statute must "address

---

[24]   *Hodel v. Virginia Surface Mining* (1981), note 4 after *Heart of Atlanta*, Sec. 2, III supra (upholding federal regulation of surface mining); *United Transp. Union v. Long Island R. R.*, 455 U.S. 678 (1982) (holding that operation of Long Island R.R. was not a "traditional government function").

[25]   *Federal Energy Regulatory Comm'n (FERC) v. Mississippi*, 456 U.S. 742 (1982) (upholding federal law requiring, inter alia, that state energy regulators "consider" adopting specified standards); *Equal Employment Opportunity Comm'n v. Wyoming*, 460 U.S. 226 (1983) (upholding federal ban on mandatory age retirement for state game wardens as not involving a "serious federal intrusion").

matters that are indisputably 'attribute[s] of state sovereignty.' " Third, state compliance with the federal obligation must "directly impair [the States'] ability 'to structure integral operations in areas of traditional governmental functions.' " Finally, the relation of state and federal interests must not be such that "the nature of the federal [interest] justifies state submission." The controversy in the present cases has focused on the [third] requirement. * * *

The distinction [between governmental and proprietary functions that] the Court discarded as unworkable in the field of tax immunity has proved no more fruitful in the field of regulatory immunity under the Commerce Clause. Neither do any of the alternative standards that might be employed to distinguish between protected and unprotected governmental functions appear manageable. We rejected the possibility of making immunity turn on a purely historical standard of "tradition" in *United Transp. Union v. Long Island R. R.*, 455 U.S. 678 (1982) [because] it prevents a court from accommodating changes in the historical functions of States [that] have resulted in a number of once-private functions like education being assumed by the States and their subdivisions. * * *

We believe, however, that there is a more fundamental problem at work [here]. The essence of our federal system is that within the realm of authority left open to them under the Constitution, the States must be equally free to engage in any activity that their citizens choose for the common weal. [Any] rule of state immunity that looks to the "traditional," "integral," or "necessary" nature of governmental functions inevitably invites an unelected federal judiciary to make decisions about which state policies it favors and which ones it dislikes. [If] there are to be limits on the Federal Government's power to interfere with state functions—as undoubtedly there are—we must look elsewhere to find them. * * *

We doubt that courts ultimately can identify principled constitutional limitations on the scope of Congress' Commerce Clause powers over the States merely by relying on a priori definitions of state sovereignty. In part, this is because of the elusiveness of objective criteria for "fundamental" elements of state sovereignty, a problem we have witnessed in the search for "traditional governmental functions." There is, however, a more fundamental reason: [the] States unquestionably do "retai[n] a significant measure of sovereign authority." [But the] fact that the States remain sovereign as to all powers not vested in Congress or denied them by the Constitution offers no guidance about where the frontier between state and federal power lies. In short, we have no license to employ freestanding conceptions of state sovereignty when measuring congressional authority under the Commerce Clause. [In] *The Federalist* No. 39 (J. Madison), [a] different measure of state sovereignty emerges. [T]he principal means chosen by the Framers to ensure the role of the States in the federal system lies in the structure of the Federal Government itself. It is no novelty to observe that the composition of the Federal Government was designed in large part to protect the States from overreaching by Congress.[11] [The] States were vested with indirect

---

11   **[Ct's Note]** See, e.g., Jesse H. Choper, *Judicial Review and the National Political Process* 175 (1980); Herbert Wechsler, *The Political Safeguards of Federalism: The Role of the*

influence over the House of Representatives and the Presidency by their control of electoral qualifications and their role in presidential elections. They were given more direct influence in the Senate, where each State received equal representation and each Senator was to be selected by the legislature of his State. The significance attached to the [former] is underscored by the prohibition of any constitutional amendment divesting a State of equal representation without the State's consent. Art. V.

The extent to which the structure of the Federal Government itself was relied on to insulate the interests of the States is evident in the views of the Framers. James Madison explained that the Federal Government "will partake sufficiently of the spirit [of the States], to be disinclined to invade the rights of the individual States, or the prerogatives of their governments." *The Federalist* No. 46. * * *

The effectiveness of the federal political process in preserving the States' interests is apparent even today. [T]he States have been able to direct a substantial proportion of federal revenues into their own treasuries in the form of general and program-specific grants in aid. [At] the same time [they] have been able to exempt themselves from a wide variety of obligations imposed by Congress under the Commerce Clause. For example, the Federal Power Act, the National Labor Relations Act, the Labor-Management Reporting and Disclosure Act, the Occupational Safety and Health Act, the Employee Retirement Insurance Security Act, and the Sherman Act all contain express or implied exemptions for States and their subdivisions. The fact that some federal statutes such as the FLSA extend general obligations to the States cannot obscure the extent to which the political position of the States in the federal system has served to minimize the burdens that the States bear under the Commerce Clause.

[A]gainst this background, we are convinced that [a]ny substantive restraint on the exercise of Commerce Clause powers must find its justification in the procedural nature of this basic limitation, and it [must] be tailored to compensate for possible failings in the national political process. [W]e perceive nothing in the overtime and minimum-wage requirements of the FLSA, as applied to SAMTA, that is destructive of state [sovereignty]. SAMTA faces nothing more than the same minimum-wage and overtime obligations that hundreds of thousands of other employers, public as well as private, have to meet.[26] [The] political process ensures that laws that unduly burden the States will not be promulgated. * * * *National League of Cities* is overruled. * * *

JUSTICE POWELL, with whom CHIEF JUSTICE BURGER, JUSTICE REHNQUIST, and JUSTICE O'CONNOR join, dissenting.

States in the Composition and Selection of the National Government, 54 Colum.L.Rev. 543 (1954); D. Bruce La Pierre, *The Political Safeguards of Federalism, Redux: Intergovernmental Immunity and the States as Agents of the Nation,* 60 Wash.U.L.Q. 779 (1982).

[26]   The Court noted that when the FLSA subjected state mass-transit systems to higher costs, the federal government simultaneously provided "substantial countervailing financial assistance."

[T]oday's decision effectively reduces the Tenth Amendment to meaningless rhetoric when Congress acts pursuant to the Commerce Clause. * * * *National League of Cities* [adopted] a familiar type of balancing test [which] explicitly weighed the seriousness of the problem addressed by the federal legislation [against] the effects of compliance on State sovereignty.[5] * * *

Members of Congress are elected from the various States, but once in office they are members of the federal government. Although the States participate in the Electoral College, this is hardly a reason to view the President as a representative of the States' interest against federal encroachment. We noted recently "the hydraulic pressure inherent within each of the separate Branches to exceed the outer limits of its [power]." *INS v. Chadha*, [Ch. 3, Sec. 2, II]. The Court offers no reason to think that this pressure will not operate when Congress seeks to invoke its powers under the Commerce Clause.[9]

[The] fact that Congress generally does not transgress constitutional limits on its power to reach State activities does not make judicial review any less necessary to rectify the cases in which it does do so. [J]udicial enforcement of the Tenth Amendment is essential to maintaining the federal system. [Indeed,] the Court's view of federalism appears to relegate the States to precisely the trivial role that opponents of the Constitution feared they would occupy.

[Under] the balancing test [the] state interest [in this case] is compelling. The financial impact on States and localities of displacing their control over wages, hours, overtime regulations, pensions, and labor relations with their employees could have serious, as well as unanticipated, effects on state and local planning, budgeting, and the levying of taxes. [I]ntracity mass transit system [is] a classic example of the type of service traditionally provided by local government. It [is] indistinguishable in principle from the traditional services of providing and maintaining streets, public lighting, traffic control, water, and sewerage systems. Services of this kind are precisely those "with which citizens are more 'familiarly and minutely conversant.'" The *Federalist*, No. 46. State and local officials [know] that their constituents and the press respond to the adequacy, fair distribution, and cost of these services. It is this kind of state and local control and accountability

---

[5]   **[Ct's Note]** In undertaking such balancing, we have considered [the] strength of the federal interest in the challenged legislation and the impact of exempting the States from its reach. Central to our inquiry into the federal interest is how closely the challenged action implicates the central concerns of the Commerce Clause, viz., the promotion of a national economy and free trade among the states. [On] the other hand, we have also assessed the injury done to the States if forced to comply with federal Commerce Clause enactments.

[9]   **[Ct's Note]** * * * Professor Wechsler, whose seminal article in 1954 proposed the view adopted by the Court today, [wrote]: "National action [has] always been regarded as exceptional in our polity, an intrusion to be justified by some necessity, the special rather than the ordinary case." Not only is the premise of this view clearly at odds with the proliferation of national legislation over the past 30 years, but "a variety of structural and political changes in this century have combined to make Congress particularly *insensitive* to state and local values." Advisory Comm'n on Intergovernmental Relations, *Regulatory Federalism: Policy, Process, Impact and Reform* 50 (1984). The adoption of the Seventeenth Amendment (providing for direct election of senators), the weakening of political parties on the local level, and the rise of national media, among other things, have made Congress increasingly less representative of State and local interests, and more likely to be responsive to the demands of various national constituencies.

that the Framers understood would insure the vitality and preservation of the federal system that the Constitution explicitly requires. * * *[27]

PRINTZ V. UNITED STATES

521 U.S. 898, 117 S.Ct. 2365, 138 L.Ed.2d 914 (1997).

JUSTICE SCALIA delivered the opinion of the Court.

[Under an interim provision of the] Brady Handgun Violence Prevention Act[, r]egulated firearms dealers are required to forward Brady Forms not to a federal officer or employee, but to the CLEOs ["chief law enforcement officers"], whose obligation [is] to make "reasonable efforts" within five days to determine whether the sales reflected in the forms are lawful. While the CLEOs are subjected to no federal requirement that they prevent the sales determined to be unlawful (it is perhaps assumed that their state-law duties will require prevention or apprehension), they are empowered to grant, in effect, waivers of the federally prescribed 5-day waiting period for handgun purchases by notifying the gun dealers that they have no reason to believe the transactions would be illegal.

The petitioners here object to being pressed into federal service * * * . Because there is no constitutional text speaking to this precise question, the answer to the CLEOs' challenge must be sought in historical understanding and practice, in the structure of the Constitution, and in the jurisprudence of this Court.

[The Court concluded that the relevant historical practice "tends to negate" Congress's power to impose federal responsibilities on state officers without the States' consent. E]nactments of the early Congresses [contain] no evidence of an assumption that the Federal Government may command the States' executive power in the absence of a particularized constitutional authorization, [such as the Extradition Clause of Art IV, Sec. 2.][28]

[We] turn next to consideration of the structure of the Constitution. [We] have set forth the historical record in more detail elsewhere, see *New York v. United States*, [505 U.S. 144 (1992), per O'Connor, J. (discussed below)], and need not repeat it here. It suffices to repeat the conclusion: "The Framers explicitly chose a Constitution that confers upon Congress the power to regulate individuals, not States." [This] separation of the two spheres is one of the Constitution's structural protections of liberty. [The] power of the Federal Government would be augmented immeasurably if it were able to impress into its service—and at no cost to itself—the police officers of the 50 States. [F]ederal control of state officers would [also] have an effect upon [the] separation and equilibration of powers between the three

---

[27]   While joining the separate Powell and O'Connor dissents, Rehnquist, J., withheld full acceptance of their "balancing" approaches and concluded: "[U]nder any one of these approaches the judgment in this case should be affirmed," as they all rely on "a principle that will, I am confident, in time again command the support of a majority of this Court."

[28]   The dissents argued: "Absent even a modicum of textual foundation for its judicially crafted constitutional rule, there should be a presumption that if the Framers had actually intended such a rule, at least one of them would have mentioned it."

branches of the Federal Government itself. The Constitution [says] the President "shall take Care that the Laws be faithfully executed," personally and through officers whom he appoints. [The] Brady Act effectively transfers this responsibility to thousands of CLEOs in the 50 States, who are left to implement the program without meaningful Presidential control. [T]he power of the President would be subject to reduction, if Congress could act as effectively without the President as with him, by simply requiring state officers to execute its laws.[12]

[Recent] opinions of ours have made clear that the Federal Government may not compel the States to implement, by legislation or executive action, federal regulatory programs. [*Hodel*] concluded that the Surface Mining Control and Reclamation Act of 1977 [merely] made compliance with federal standards a precondition to continued state regulation in an otherwise pre-empted field. In *Federal Energy Regulatory Comm'n (FERC) v. Mississippi*, 456 U.S. 742 (1982), we construed the most troubling provisions of the Public Utility Regulatory Policies Act of 1978 to contain only the "command" that state agencies "consider" federal standards.[29] * * *

When we were at last confronted squarely with a federal statute that unambiguously required the States to enact or administer a federal regulatory program, our decision should have come as no surprise. At issue in *New York* [were] the so-called "take title" provisions of the Low-Level Radioactive Waste Policy Amendments Act of 1985, which required States either to enact legislation providing for the disposal of radioactive waste generated within their borders, or to take title to, and possession of, the waste—effectively requiring the States either to legislate pursuant to Congress's directions, or to implement an administrative solution. We concluded that Congress could constitutionally require the states to do neither.* * *

The Government contends that *New York* is distinguishable on the following ground: unlike the "take title" provisions invalidated there, [the] Brady Act does not require state legislative or executive officials to make policy. [But is] it really true that there is no policymaking involved in deciding, for example, what "reasonable efforts" shall be expended to conduct a background check? It may well satisfy the Act for a CLEO to direct that (a) no background checks will be conducted that divert personnel time from pending felony investigations, and (b) no

---

[12] **[Ct's Note]** There is not, as the dissent believes, "tension" between the proposition that impressing state police officers into federal service will massively augment federal power, and the proposition that it will also sap the power of the Federal Presidency. It is quite possible to have a more powerful Federal Government that is, by reason of the destruction of its Executive unity, a less efficient one. The dissent is correct that control by the unitary Federal Executive is also sacrificed when States voluntarily administer federal programs, but the condition of voluntary state participation significantly reduces the ability of Congress to use this device as a means of reducing the power of the Presidency.

[29] *FERC*, per Blackmun, J., emphasized that because "Congress could have preempted the field of utility regulation, at least insofar as private rather than state activity is concerned, [the Act] should not be invalid simply because, out of deference to state authority, Congress adopted a less intrusive scheme and allowed the States to continue regulating in the area on the condition that they *consider* the suggested federal standards."

background check will be permitted to consume more than one-half hour of an officer's time. [Even assuming,] that the Brady Act leaves no "policymaking" discretion with the States, we fail to see how that improves rather than worsens the intrusion upon state sovereignty. Preservation of the States as independent and autonomous political entities is arguably less undermined by requiring them to make policy in certain fields than [by] "reduc[ing] [them] to puppets of a ventriloquist Congress." * * *

The Government purports to find support for its proffered distinction of *New York* [in] *Testa v. Katt*, 330 U.S. 386 (1947), [which] stands for the proposition that state courts cannot refuse to apply federal law—a conclusion mandated by the terms of the Supremacy Clause. [T]hat says nothing about whether state executive officers must administer federal law. * * *

The Government also maintains that requiring state officers to perform discrete, ministerial tasks specified by Congress does not violate the principle of *New York* because it does not diminish the accountability of state or federal officials.[30] [But by] forcing state governments to absorb the financial burden of implementing a federal regulatory program, Members of Congress can take credit for "solving" problems without having to ask their constituents to pay for the solutions with higher federal taxes. And even when the States are not forced to absorb the [costs,] they are still put in the position of taking the blame for its burdensomeness and for its defects. Under the present law, for example, it will be the CLEO [not] some federal official, who will be blamed for any error (even one in the designated federal database) that causes a purchaser to be mistakenly rejected.

[The] Brady Act, the dissent asserts, is different [from the directives at issue in] *New York* because the former is addressed to individuals—namely CLEOs— while the latter were directed to the State itself. [But while] the Brady Act is directed to "individuals," it is directed to them in their official capacities. * * *

Finally, the Government puts forward a cluster of arguments [under] the heading: "The Brady Act serves very important purposes, is most efficiently administered by CLEOs during the interim period, and places a minimal and only temporary burden upon state officers." [Assuming] the mentioned factors were true, they might be relevant if we were evaluating whether the incidental application to the States of a federal law of general applicability excessively interfered with the functioning of state governments. But where, as here, it is the whole object of the law to direct the functioning of the state executive, and hence

---

[30]   The *New York* Court reasoned that "where the Federal Government compels States to regulate, the accountability of both state and federal officials is diminished. If the citizens of New York, for example, do not consider that making provision for the disposal of radioactive waste is in their best interest, they may elect state officials who share their view. That view can always be preempted under the Supremacy Clause if is contrary to the national view, but in such a case it is the Federal Government that makes the decision in full view of the public, and it will be federal officials that suffer the consequences if the decision turns out to be detrimental or unpopular. But where the Federal Government directs the States to regulate, it may be state officials who will bear the brunt of public disapproval, while the federal officials who devised the regulatory program may remain insulated from the electoral ramifications of their decision."

to compromise the structural framework of dual sovereignty, such a "balancing" analysis is inappropriate.[17] * * *

JUSTICE O'CONNOR, concurring.

[T]he Court appropriately refrains from deciding [whether] purely ministerial reporting requirements imposed by Congress on state and local authorities pursuant to its Commerce Clause powers are similarly invalid. See, e.g., 42 U.S.C. § 5779(a) (requiring state and local law enforcement agencies to report cases of missing children to the Department of Justice).[31]

JUSTICE STEVENS, with whom JUSTICE SOUTER, JUSTICE GINSBURG, and JUSTICE BREYER join, dissenting. * * *

[S]ince the ultimate issue is one of power, we must consider its implications in times of national emergency. Matters such as the enlistment of air raid wardens, the administration of a military draft, the mass inoculation of children to forestall an epidemic, or perhaps the threat of an international terrorist, may require a national response before federal personnel can be made available to respond. If the Constitution empowers Congress and the President to make an appropriate response, is there anything in the Tenth Amendment [that] forbids the enlistment of state officers to make that response effective? * * *

Unlike the First Amendment, which prohibits the enactment of a category of laws that would otherwise be authorized by Article I, the Tenth Amendment [does] not purport to limit the scope or the effectiveness of the exercise of powers that are delegated to Congress.[32] Thus, the Amendment provides no support for a rule that immunizes local officials from obligations that might be imposed on ordinary citizens.[2] [The] majority expresses special concern that were its rule not adopted

---

[17]   **[Ct's Note]** The dissent observes that "Congress could require private persons, such as hospital executives or school administrators, to provide arms merchants with relevant information about a prospective purchaser's fitness to own a weapon," and that "the burden on police officers [imposed by the Brady Act] would be permissible if a similar burden were also imposed on private parties with access to relevant data." That is undoubtedly true, but [t]he Brady Act does not merely require CLEOs to report information in their private possession. It requires them to provide information that belongs to the State and is available to them only in their official capacity; and to conduct investigations in their official capacity, by examining databases and records that only state officials have access to. In other words, the suggestion that extension of this statute to private citizens would eliminate the constitutional problem posits the impossible.

[31]   The Court commented that "federal statutes [which] require only the provision of information to the Federal Government, do not involve the precise issue before us [here]." Thomas, J., who joined the Court's opinion, also concurred.

[32]   *New York*, however, explained that "the Tenth Amendment confirms that the power of the Federal Government is subject to limits that may, in a given instance, reserve power to the States. [It] thus directs us to determine [whether] an incident of state sovereignty is protected by a limitation on an Article I power."

[2]   **[Ct's Note]** Recognizing the force of the argument, the Court suggests that this reasoning is in error because—even if it is responsive to the submission that the Tenth Amendment roots the principle set forth by the majority today—it does not answer the possibility that the Court's holding can be rooted in a "principle of state sovereignty" mentioned nowhere in the constitutional text. As a ground for invalidating important federal legislation, this argument is remarkably weak. The majority's further claim that, while the Brady Act may be legislation "necessary" to Congress' execution of its undisputed Commerce Clause authority to regulate firearms sales, it is nevertheless not "proper" because it violates state sovereignty, is wholly

the Federal Government would be able to avail itself of the services of state government officials "at no cost to itself." But this [problem] of imposing so-called "unfunded mandates" on the States has been identified and meaningfully addressed by Congress in recent legislation.[18] * * *

Perversely, [by] limiting the ability of the Federal Government to enlist state officials in the implementation of its programs, the Court creates incentives for the National Government to aggrandize itself. In the name of State's rights, the majority would have the Federal Government create vast national bureaucracies to implement its policies.[33]

Finally, the majority provides an incomplete explanation of our decision in *Testa* [which] unanimously held that state courts of appropriate jurisdiction must occupy themselves adjudicating claims brought by private litigants under the federal Emergency Price Control Act of 1942, regardless of how otherwise crowded their dockets might be with state-law matters. That is a much greater imposition on state sovereignty than the Court's characterization of the [case]. Even if the Court were correct [that] it was the reference to judges in the Supremacy Clause [that] dictated the result in *Testa*, the Court's implied *expressio unius* argument that the Framers therefore did not intend to permit the enlistment of other state officials is implausible. [The] notion that the Framers would have had no reluctance to "press state judges into federal service" against their will but would have regarded the imposition of a similar—indeed, far lesser—burden on town constables as an intolerable affront to principles of state sovereignty can only be considered perverse. * * *

JUSTICE BREYER, with whom JUSTICE STEVENS joins, dissenting.

---

circular. [Our] ruling in *New York* that the Commerce Clause does not provide Congress the authority to require States to enact legislation—a power that affects States far closer to the core of their sovereign authority—does nothing to support the majority's unwarranted extension of that reasoning today.

[18]   [Ct's Note] The majority also makes the more general claim that requiring state officials to carry out federal policy causes states to "tak[e] the blame" for failed programs. The Court cites no empirical authority to support the proposition. [Unlike] state legislators, local government executive officials routinely take action in response to a variety of sources of authority: local ordinance, state law, and federal law. It doubtless may therefore require some sophistication to discern under which authority an executive official is acting. [But] the majority's rule neither creates nor alters this basic truth. The problem is of little real consequence in any event, because to the extent that a particular action proves politically unpopular, we may be confident that elected officials charged with implementing it will be quite clear to their constituents where the source of the misfortune lies. These cases demonstrate the point. Sheriffs Printz and Mack have made public statements, including their decisions to serve as plaintiffs in these actions, denouncing the Brady Act.

[33]   White, J., joined by Blackmun and Stevens, JJ., dissenting in *New York*, made a similar argument: "The ultimate irony of the decision today is that in its formalistically rigid obeisance to 'federalism,' the Court gives Congress fewer incentives to defer to the wishes of state officials in achieving local solutions to local problems. This legislation was a classic example of Congress acting as arbiter among the States in their attempts to accept responsibility for managing a problem of grave import. The States urged the National Legislature not to impose [a] solution to the country's low-level radioactive waste management problems. [By] invalidating the measure designed to ensure compliance for recalcitrant States, such as New York, the Court upsets the delicate compromise achieved among the States."

[T]he fact that there is not more precedent—that direct federal assignment of duties to state officers is not common—likely reflects, not a widely shared belief that any such assignment is incompatible with basic principles of federalism, but rather a widely shared practice of assigning such duties in other ways. See, e.g., *Dole* (spending power); *New York* (general statutory duty); *FERC* (pre-emption). Thus, there is neither need nor reason to find in the Constitution an absolute principle, the inflexibility of which poses a surprising and technical obstacle to the enactment of a law that Congress believed necessary to solve an important national problem.* * *[34]

———

RENO v. CONDON, 528 U.S. 141 (2000), per REHNQUIST, C.J., unanimously upheld Congress's power under the Commerce Clause to pass the Driver's Privacy Protection Act, which barred state motor vehicle departments from disclosing (or selling) personal information (such as name, address, telephone number, vehicle description, Social Security number, medical information, and photograph) required for a driver's license or car registration: "[T]he vehicle information [is] used by insurers, manufacturers, direct marketers, and others engaged in interstate commerce [and] by various public and private entities for matters related to interstate motoring. * * *

"We agree [that] the DPPA's provisions will require time and effort on the part of state employees ["to learn and apply its complex provisions"], but reject the State's argument that the DPPA violates the principles laid down in either *New York* or *Printz*. [Such] 'commandeering' [is] an inevitable consequence of regulating ["States acting purely as commercial sellers."] That a State wishing to engage in certain activity must take administrative and sometimes legislative action to comply with federal standards regulating that activity is a commonplace that presents no constitutional defect.

"[The] DPPA does not require the States in their sovereign capacity to regulate their own citizens. The DPPA regulates the States as the owners of databases. It does not require the South Carolina Legislature to enact any laws or regulations, and it does not require state officials to assist in the enforcement of federal statutes regulating private individuals. We accordingly conclude that the DPPA is consistent with the constitutional principles enunciated in *New York* and *Printz*."

Nor does the DPPA "regulate the States exclusively. [It] regulates [the] States as initial suppliers of the information in interstate commerce and private resellers or redisclosers of that information in commerce."

———

---

[34] Souter, J., dissented, noting that "I do not read any of *The Federalist* material as requiring the conclusion that Congress could require administrative support without an obligation to pay fair value for it."

A federal statute, the Professional and Amateur Sports Protection Act (PASPA), forbids states from "authoriz[ing]" sports gambling. In MURPHY v. NAT'L COLLEGIATE ATHLETIC ASS'N, 138 S.Ct. 1461 (2018), respondent and the U.S. government acknowledged that Congress may not "compel a State to enact legislation," but argued that PASPA merely forbade states with existing sports gambling prohibitions from enacting certain new laws that would partially repeal such prohibitions. The Court rejected the distinction between compulsion and prohibition. PASPA, ALITO, J., wrote for the Court, "unequivocally dictates what a state legislature may and may not do. [It] is as if federal officers were installed in state legislative chambers and were armed with the authority to stop legislators from voting on any offending proposals. A more direct affront to state sovereignty is not easy to imagine." The majority distinguished *Reno v. Condon* on the ground that PASPA, unlike the DPPA, regulated only the state, rather than applying "equally to state and private actors." THOMAS, J., BREYER, J., and GINSBURG, J., joined in whole by Sotomayor, J., and in part by Breyer, J., each filed separate opinions setting forth their respective views about the appropriate remedial consequences for other provisions of PASPA, which the majority deemed nonseverable from the invalid one.

CHAPTER 3

DISTRIBUTION OF FEDERAL POWERS: SEPARATION OF POWERS

■ ■ ■

This chapter addresses the distribution of powers *within* the federal government. Its principal concern is how the Constitution's text and structure, and the separation-of-powers and checks-and-balances concepts they embody, define the powers of Congress and the Executive. A related issue is the extent to which a power expressly granted to one branch must be exercised to avoid interference with the power of another branch. These matters are considered in this chapter's three sections: (1) presidential action affecting "congressional powers"; (2) congressional action affecting "presidential powers"; and (3) executive privilege and immunity.

1. PRESIDENTIAL ACTION AFFECTING "CONGRESSIONAL" POWERS

I. INTERNAL MATTERS: DOMESTIC LAWMAKING

YOUNGSTOWN SHEET & TUBE CO. V. SAWYER [THE STEEL SEIZURE CASE]
343 U.S. 579, 72 S.Ct. 863, 96 L.Ed. 1153 (1952).

JUSTICE BLACK delivered the opinion of the Court. * * *

We are asked to decide whether [President Truman] was acting within his constitutional power when he issued an order directing the Secretary of Commerce [Sawyer] to take possession of and operate most of the Nation's steel mills. The mill owners argue that the President's order amounts to lawmaking, a legislative function which the Constitution has expressly confided to the Congress and not to the President. The Government's position is that the order was made on findings of the President and that his action was necessary to avert a national catastrophe which would inevitably result from a stoppage of steel production [during the Korean War].

[When efforts to settle a labor dispute—including reference to the Federal Wage Stabilization Board—failed, the union called a nationwide strike to begin April 9, 1952. Finding that the strike would jeopardize national defense, a few hours before the strike deadline the President issued Executive Order 10340, directing the Secretary of Commerce to take possession of most of the country's steel mills and keep them operating. The President sent a message to Congress reporting his actions on the next day. On May 3, the Court granted direct review of a U.S. District Court order that enjoined the Secretary's possession of the steel mills, and set argument for May 12. On June 2, the Court upheld the injunction, ruling the seizure unconstitutional.]

The President's power, if any, to issue the order must stem either from an act of Congress or from the Constitution itself.

[T]he use of the seizure [to] prevent work stoppage was not only unauthorized by any congressional enactment; prior to this controversy, Congress had refused to adopt that method of settling labor disputes. When the [Labor Management Relations Act of 1947] was under [consideration], Congress rejected an amendment which would have authorized such governmental seizures in cases of emergency. [Instead], the plan sought to bring about settlements by use of the customary devices of mediation, conciliation, investigation by boards of inquiry, and public reports. In some instances temporary injunctions were authorized to provide cooling-off periods. All this failing, unions were left free to strike after a secret vote by employees.[1] * * *

It is clear that if the President had authority to issue the order he did, it must be found in some provision of the Constitution. [The] contention is that presidential power should be implied from the aggregate of his powers under the Constitution. Particular reliance is placed on provisions in Article II which say that "The executive Power shall be vested in a President"; that "he shall take Care that the Laws be faithfully executed"; and that he "shall be Commander in Chief of the Army and Navy of the United States." * * *

We cannot with faithfulness to our constitutional system hold that the Commander in Chief of the Armed Forces has the ultimate power as such to take possession of private property in order to keep labor disputes from stopping production. This is a job for the Nation's lawmakers, not for its military authorities. [In] the framework of our Constitution, the President's power to see that the laws are faithfully executed refutes the idea that he is to be a lawmaker. The Constitution limits his functions in the lawmaking process to the recommending of laws he thinks wise and the vetoing of laws he thinks bad. And the Constitution is neither silent nor equivocal about who shall make laws which the President is to execute. The first section of the first article says that "All legislative Powers herein granted shall be vested in a Congress of the United States." * * *

The President's order does not direct that a congressional policy be executed in a manner prescribed by Congress—it directs that a presidential policy be executed in a manner prescribed by the President. The preamble of the order itself, like that of many statutes, sets out reasons why the President believes certain

---

[1] Sections 206–210 of the Act provided that "[w]henever in the opinion of the President [a] threatened or actual strike [will], if permitted to occur or to continue, imperil the national health or safety," on the President's initiative, the strike could be enjoined while a board of inquiry studied the dispute, but that the strike could continue after 80 days if the employees reject the employer's last offer of settlement. The President was then obligated under the Act to report on the emergency to Congress.

policies should be adopted, proclaims these policies as rules of conduct to be followed, and again, like a statute, authorizes a government official to promulgate additional rules and regulations. [The] power of Congress to adopt such public policies as those proclaimed by the order is beyond question. It can authorize the taking of private property for public use. It can make laws regulating the relationships between employers and employees, prescribing rules designed to settle labor disputes, and fixing wages and working conditions in certain fields of our economy. The Constitution did not subject this lawmaking power of Congress to presidential or military supervision or control.

It is said that other Presidents without congressional authority have taken possession of private business enterprises in order to settle labor disputes. But even if this be true, Congress has not thereby lost its exclusive constitutional authority to make [laws].

Affirmed.

JUSTICE FRANKFURTER, concurring.

Although the considerations relevant to the legal enforcement of the principle of separation of powers seem to me more complicated and flexible than may appear from what Mr. Justice Black has written, I join his opinion because I thoroughly agree with the application of the principle to this case. * * *

[We] must [put] to one side consideration of what powers the President would have had if there had been no legislation whatever bearing on the authority asserted by the seizure, or if the seizure had been only for a short, explicitly temporary period, to be terminated automatically unless Congressional approval were given. These and other questions, like or unlike, are not now here. [It] cannot be contended that the President would have had power to issue this order had Congress explicitly negated such authority in formal legislation. [And Congress's decision reflected in the Labor Management Relations Act of 1947 should be given the same effect, since] Congress has expressed its will to withhold this power from the President as though it had said so in so many words. [It has] said to the President, "You may not seize. Please report to us and ask for seizure power if you think it is needed in a specific [situation]."

[The] content of the three authorities of government is not to be derived from an abstract analysis. The areas are partly interacting, not wholly disjointed. The Constitution is a framework for government. Therefore the way the framework has consistently operated fairly establishes that it has operated according to its true nature. Deeply embedded traditional ways of conducting government cannot supplant the Constitution or legislation, but they give meaning to the words of a text. [But the] list of executive assertions of the power of seizure in circumstances comparable to the present reduces to three in the six-month period from June to December of 1941. [T]hese three isolated instances do not add up [to] the kind of executive construction of the Constitution [necessary to justify the action here]. Nor do they come to us sanctioned by the long-continued acquiescence of Congress. * * *

JUSTICE JACKSON, concurring.

The actual art of governing under our Constitution does not and cannot conform to judicial definitions of the power of any of its branches based on isolated clauses or even single Articles torn from context. While the Constitution diffuses power the better to secure liberty, it also contemplates that practice will integrate the dispersed powers into a workable government. It enjoins upon its branches separateness but interdependence, autonomy but reciprocity. Presidential powers are not fixed but fluctuate, depending upon their disjunction or conjunction with those of Congress. We may well begin by a somewhat over-simplified grouping of practical situations in which a President may doubt, or others may challenge, his powers. * * *

1.   When the President acts pursuant to an express or implied authorization of Congress, his authority is at its maximum, for it includes all that he possesses in his own right plus all that Congress can delegate. * * *

2.   When the President acts in absence of either a congressional grant or denial of authority, he can only rely upon his own independent powers, but there is a zone of twilight in which he and Congress may have concurrent authority, or in which its distribution is uncertain. Therefore, congressional inertia, indifference or quiescence may sometimes, at least as a practical matter, enable, if not invite, measures on independent presidential responsibility. In this area, any actual test of power is likely to depend on the imperatives of events and contemporary imponderables rather than on abstract theories of law.

3.   When the President takes measures incompatible with the expressed or implied will of Congress, his power is at its lowest ebb, for then he can rely only upon his own constitutional powers minus any constitutional powers of Congress over the matter. Courts can sustain exclusive Presidential control in such a case only by disabling the Congress from acting upon the subject. Presidential claim to a power at once so conclusive and preclusive must be scrutinized with caution, for what is at stake is the equilibrium established by our constitutional system.

Into which of these classifications does this executive seizure of the steel industry fit? It is eliminated from the first by admission, for it is conceded that no congressional authorization exists for this seizure. [It] seems clearly eliminated from [the "second category,"] because Congress has not left seizure of private property an open field but has covered it by three statutory policies inconsistent with this seizure [e.g., fn. 1, none of which] were invoked. In choosing a different and inconsistent way of his own, the President cannot claim that it is necessitated or invited by failure of Congress to legislate upon the occasions, grounds and methods for seizure of industrial properties.

This leaves the current seizure to be justified only by the severe tests under the third grouping, [where] we can sustain the President only by holding that seizure of such strike-bound industries is within his domain and beyond control by Congress. [I] cannot accept the view that [Art. II, § 1, cl. 1, vesting "the executive power" in the President] is a grant in bulk of all conceivable executive power but regard it as an allocation to the presidential office of the generic powers thereafter stated.

The [Commander in Chief] appellation is sometimes advanced as support for any presidential action, internal or external, involving use of force, the idea being that it vests power to do anything, anywhere, that can be done with an army or navy. [But the] Constitution expressly places in Congress power "to raise and *support* Armies" and "to *provide* and *maintain* a Navy." (Emphasis supplied.) [Congress] alone controls the raising of revenues and their appropriation and may determine in what manner and by what means they shall be spent for military and naval procurement. I suppose no one would doubt that Congress can take over war supply as a Government enterprise. * * *

The third clause in which the Solicitor General finds seizure powers is that "he shall take Care that the Laws be faithfully executed." That authority must be matched against [the Due Process Clause of the Fifth Amendment]. One [clause] gives a governmental authority that reaches so far as there is law, the other gives a private right that authority shall go no farther. * * *

The Solicitor General lastly grounds support of the seizure upon nebulous, inherent powers never expressly granted but said to have accrued to the office from the customs and claims of preceding administrations. The plea is for a resulting power to deal with a crisis or an emergency according to the necessities of the case, the unarticulated assumption being that necessity knows no law. Loose and irresponsible use of adjectives colors all non-legal and much legal discussion of presidential powers. "Inherent" powers, "implied" powers, "incidental" powers, "plenary" powers, "war" powers and "emergency" powers are used, often interchangeably and without fixed or ascertainable meanings. * * *

In view of the ease, expedition and safety with which Congress can grant and has granted large emergency powers, certainly ample to embrace this crisis, I am quite unimpressed with the argument that we should affirm possession of them without statute. Such power either has no beginning or it has no end. If it exists, it need submit to no legal restraint. I am not alarmed that it would plunge us straightway into dictatorship, but it is at least a step in that wrong direction.

[The] Executive, except for recommendation and veto, has no legislative power. The executive action we have here originates in the individual will of the President and represents an exercise of authority without law. [With] all its defects, delays, and inconveniences, men have discovered no technique for long preserving free government except that the Executive be under the law, and that the law be made by parliamentary deliberations. * * *[2]

---

2   Burton, J., concurred in Black, J.'s opinion but also wrote a separate concurrence, similar in thrust to those of Frankfurter and Jackson, JJ., stressing that "the President's [order] invaded the jurisdiction of Congress," which "reserved to itself" the remedy of seizure. Douglas, J., concurred in Black, J.'s opinion, noting that "the branch of government that has the power to pay compensation for a seizure [Congress] is the only one able to authorize a seizure [under] the condemnation provision in the Fifth Amendment." Clark, J., concurred in the judgment because "Congress had prescribed methods to be followed by the President in meeting the emergency at

CHIEF JUSTICE VINSON, with whom JUSTICE REED and JUSTICE MINTON join, dissenting.

[The dissent emphasized the country's international commitments for economic and military aid to preserve the free world and congressional action directing the President to strengthen the armed forces. It called attention to the legislation directly related to supporting the Korean War. It quoted affidavits showing the enormous demand for steel in vital defense programs and attesting that a work stoppage would imperil the national defense.] Accordingly, if the President has any power under the Constitution to meet a critical situation in the absence of express statutory authorization, there is no basis whatever for criticizing the exercise of such power in this case.

[Our] Presidents have on many occasions exhibited the leadership contemplated by the Framers when they made the President Commander in Chief, and imposed upon him the trust to "take Care that the Laws be faithfully executed." With or without explicit statutory authorization, Presidents have [dealt] with national emergencies by acting promptly [to] enforce legislative programs, at least to save those programs until Congress could act. Congress and the courts have responded to such executive initiative with consistent approval. [Historic episodes from George Washington to Franklin D. Roosevelt were summarized in 17 pages. A brief excerpt follows:]

Some six months before Pearl Harbor, a dispute at a single aviation [plant] interrupted a segment of the production of military aircraft. [President] Roosevelt ordered the seizure of the plant "pursuant to the powers vested in [him as] Commander in Chief of the Army and Navy of the United States." The Attorney General (Jackson) vigorously proclaimed that the President had the moral duty to keep this Nation's defense effort a "going concern." [A]lso prior to Pearl Harbor, the President ordered the seizure of a ship-building company and an aircraft parts plant. Following the declaration of war, [five] additional industrial concerns were seized to avert interruption of needed production. During the same period, the President directed seizure of the Nation's coal mines to remove an obstruction to the effective prosecution of the war.

[This] is but a cursory summary of executive leadership. But it amply demonstrates that Presidents have taken prompt action to enforce the laws and protect the country whether or not Congress happened to provide in advance for the particular method of execution. [T]he fact that Congress and the courts have consistently recognized and given their support to such executive action indicates that such a power of seizure has been accepted throughout our history.

Flexibility as to mode of execution [of the laws] to meet critical situations is a matter of practical necessity. [The] broad executive power granted by Article II [cannot], it is said, be invoked to avert disaster. Instead, the President must confine himself to sending a message to Congress recommending action. Under this

---

hand, [but] in the absence of such action by Congress, the President's independent power to act depends upon the gravity of the situation confronting the nation."

messenger-boy concept of the Office, the President cannot even act to preserve legislative programs from destruction so that Congress will have something left to act upon.

[T]here [is no] question of unlimited executive power in this case. The President himself closed the door to any such claim when he sent his Message to Congress stating his purpose to abide by any action of Congress, whether approving or disapproving his seizure action [or] regulating the manner in which the mills were to be administered and returned to the owners. [J]udicial, legislative and executive precedents throughout our history demonstrate that in this case the President acted in full conformity with his duties under the Constitution. * * *

———

DAMES & MOORE v. REGAN, 453 U.S. 654 (1981), per REHNQUIST, J., unanimously upheld presidential executive orders to implement an executive agreement between Iran and the United States securing release of American hostages held in Iran for 15 months in 1979–81. The executive agreement called for termination of "all litigation between the government of each party and the nationals of the other" and for settlement of pending claims through binding arbitration before a tribunal established under the agreement. The executive orders (1) suspended all claims in American courts that were within the jurisdiction of the claims tribunal, (2) nullified all prejudgment attachments against Iran's assets in actions against Iran in American courts, and (3) ordered transfer to Iran of all its assets in U.S. banks, except for one billion dollars to cover awards against Iran by the claims tribunal.

Dames & Moore's prejudgment attachment of Iranian bank assets, to secure its large claim for services rendered to Iran, was vacated pursuant to the executive orders. The Court rejected Dames & Moore's challenge: "Because the President's action in nullifying the attachments [was] taken pursuant to specific congressional authorization [under the International Emergency Economic Powers Act (IEEPA)][3] it is 'supported by the strongest of presumptions and the widest latitude of judicial interpretation, and the burden of persuasion would rest heavily upon any who might attack it.' [Youngstown] (Jackson, J., concurring). [We] cannot say that petitioner has sustained that heavy burden. A contrary ruling would mean that the Federal Government as a whole lacked the power exercised by the President, and that we are not prepared to say."

By contrast, "neither the IEEPA nor the Hostage Act constitutes specific authorization of the President's action suspending claims. [But this is] not to say that these statutory provisions are entirely irrelevant to the question of the validity of the President's [action.] Congress cannot anticipate and legislate with regard to every possible action the President may find it necessary to take. [E]nactment of

---

[3] Section 1702(a)(1)(B) of IEEPA empowered the President to "compel," "nullify," or "prohibit" any "transfer" with respect to, or transactions involving, any property subject to the jurisdiction of the United States in which any foreign country has any interest.

legislation closely related to the question of the President's authority in a particular case which evinces legislative intent to accord the President broad discretion may be considered to 'invite' 'measures on independent presidential responsibility.' *Youngstown* (Jackson, J., concurring). At least this is so where there is no contrary indication of legislative intent and when, as here, there is a history of congressional acquiescence in conduct of the sort engaged in by the President. * * *

"Crucial to our decision today is the conclusion that Congress has implicitly approved the practice of claim settlement by executive agreement. This is best demonstrated by Congress' enactment of the International Claims Settlement Act of 1949. The Act had two purposes: (1) to allocate to United States nationals funds received in the course of an executive claims settlement with Yugoslavia, and (2) to provide a procedure whereby funds resulting from future settlements could be distributed. To achieve these ends Congress created the International Claims Commission, now the Foreign Claims Settlement Commission, [and] gave it jurisdiction to make final and binding decisions with respect to claims by United States nationals against settlement funds. By creating a procedure to implement future settlement agreements, Congress placed its stamp of approval on such agreements. Indeed, the legislative history of the Act observed that the United States was seeking settlements with countries other than Yugoslavia and [stated] that the bill contemplates settlements of a similar nature in the future.

"[As] Justice Frankfurter pointed out in *Youngstown*, 'a systematic, unbroken executive practice, long pursued to the knowledge of the Congress and never before questioned [may] be treated as a gloss on "Executive Power" vested in the President by § 1 of Art. II.' [Our] conclusion is buttressed by the fact that the means chosen by the President to settle the claims of American nationals provided an alternative forum, the Claims Tribunal, which is capable of providing meaningful relief. [Just] as importantly, [we are] clearly not confronted with a situation in which Congress has in some way resisted the exercise of Presidential authority. * * *

"We do not decide that the President possesses plenary power to settle claims, even as against foreign governmental entities. [But] where, as here, the settlement of claims has been determined to be a necessary incident to the resolution of a major foreign policy dispute between our country and another, and where, as here, we can conclude that Congress acquiesced in the President's action, we are not prepared to say that the President lacks the power to settle such claims."

———

MEDELLIN v. TEXAS, 552 U.S. 491 (2008), per ROBERTS, C.J., invalidated President George W. Bush's "Memorandum" that state courts must adhere to the International Court of Justice's decision that the Vienna Convention on Consular Relations required (1) that law enforcement authorities inform arrested foreign nationals of their right to notify their consulate of their detention, and if this was not done, (2) that the United States provide reconsideration of convictions without regard to state procedural default rules:[4] While the treaty "constitutes an *international* law obligation on the part of the United States," it is "not domestic law unless Congress has either enacted implementing statutes or the treaty itself conveys an intention that it be 'self-executing' and is ratified on these terms. [Because] none of [the] treaty sources creates binding federal law in the absence of implementing legislation, and because it is uncontested that no such legislation exists, we conclude that the [ICJ's decision] is not automatically binding domestic law."

As for the President's independent constitutional power under Art. II, "given the absence of congressional legislation, [the] non-self-executing treaties at issue here did not 'express[ly] or implied[ly]' vest the President with the unilateral authority to make them self-executing. Accordingly, the President's Memorandum does not fall within the first category of the *Youngstown* framework. [When] the President asserts the power to 'enforce' a non-self-executing treaty by unilaterally creating domestic law, he acts in conflict with the implicit understanding of the ratifying Senate [and] is therefore within Justice Jackson's third category, not the first or even the second."

Dames & Moore is "based on the view that 'a systematic, unbroken, executive practice, long pursued to the knowledge of the Congress and never before questioned,' can 'raise a presumption that the [action] had been [taken] in pursuance of its consent.' *Dames & Moore*. [The] President's Memorandum is not supported by a 'particularly longstanding practice' of congressional acquiescence. [Indeed,] the Government has not identified a single instance in which the President has attempted (or Congress has acquiesced in) a Presidential directive issued to state courts, much less one that reaches deep into the heart of the State's police powers and compels state courts to reopen final criminal judgments and set aside neutrally applicable state laws. [The] Executive's narrow and strictly limited authority to settle international claims disputes pursuant to an executive agreement cannot stretch so far as to support the current Presidential Memorandum."

BREYER, J., joined by Souter and Ginsburg, JJ. dissented, concluding that "a strong line of precedent, likely reflecting the views of the Founders, indicates that the treaty provisions [and the ICJ judgment] address themselves to the Judicial Branch and consequently are self-executing." STEVENS, J., concurred in the Court's judgment, although agreeing largely with Breyer, J., because "the text and history of the Supremacy Clause, as well as this Court's treaty-related cases, do not support a presumption against self-execution. I also endorse the proposition that the [treaty] is itself self-executing and judicially enforceable." But its unclear language leaves the manner of compliance "to the political, not the judicial department."

---

[4]   Petitioner, a Mexican national, was convicted of gang rape and murder and sentenced to death. Although he had been given the *Miranda* warnings prior to his confession, he was not informed of his Vienna Convention rights. The Texas courts refused to consider this claim because he had not raised it in timely fashion.

II. EXTERNAL MATTERS: FOREIGN AFFAIRS AND WAR

UNITED STATES V. CURTISS-WRIGHT EXPORT CORP.
299 U.S. 304, 57 S.Ct. 216, 81 L.Ed. 255 (1936).

JUSTICE SUTHERLAND delivered the opinion of the Court.

[A joint resolution of Congress authorized the President to prohibit the sale of arms to Bolivia and Paraguay, which were engaged in armed conflict, if the President found that such prohibition would "contribute to the reestablishment of peace between those countries." The President proclaimed an embargo, and Curtiss-Wright was indicted for violating its terms. The lower court found the joint resolution an unconstitutional delegation of legislative power.]

The powers of the federal government in respect of foreign or external affairs and those in respect of domestic or internal affairs [are] different, both in respect of their origin and their nature. The broad statement that the federal government can exercise no powers except those specifically enumerated in the Constitution, and such implied powers as are necessary and proper to carry into effect the enumerated powers, is categorically true only in respect of our internal affairs.

As a result of the separation from Great Britain by the colonies acting as a unit, the powers of external sovereignty passed from the Crown not to the colonies severally, but to the colonies in their collective and corporate capacity as the United States of America. [The] powers to declare and wage war, to conclude peace, to make treaties, to maintain diplomatic relations with other sovereignties, if they had never been mentioned in the Constitution, would have vested in the federal government as necessary concomitants of nationality.

[Another difference is that] participation in the exercise of power [over external affairs] is significantly limited. In this vast external realm, [the] President alone has the power to speak or listen as a representative of the nation. He *makes* treaties with the advice and consent of the Senate; but he alone negotiates [and] the Senate cannot intrude. [As] Marshall said [in] the House of Representatives, "The President is the sole organ of the nation in its external relations, and its sole representative with foreign nations."

It is important [that] we are here dealing not alone with an authority vested in the President by an exertion of legislative power, but with such an authority plus the very delicate, plenary and exclusive power of the President as the sole organ of the federal government in the field of international relations. [If] embarrassment—perhaps serious embarrassment—is to be avoided and success for our aims achieved, congressional legislation [must] often accord to the President a degree of discretion and freedom from statutory restriction which would not be admissible were domestic affairs alone involved. Moreover, he, not Congress, has the better opportunity of knowing the conditions which prevail in foreign countries, and especially is this true in time of war. He has his confidential sources of information. [Secrecy] in respect of information gathered by them may be highly necessary. [In] the light of the foregoing observations, it is evident that this court should not be in haste to apply a general rule which will have the effect of condemning legislation like that under review as constituting an unlawful delegation of legislative power. * * *

Reversed.[5]

ZIVOTOFSKY v. KERRY, 576 U.S. 1 (2015), per KENNEDY, J., held that an act of Congress [§ 214(d)], requiring the Secretary of State to allow citizens born in Jerusalem to list their place of birth as 'Israel' on passports, "directly contradicts [the] carefully calibrated and longstanding Executive branch policy of neutrality toward Jerusalem," thus interfering with the President's "exclusive power to grant formal recognition to a foreign sovereign," as shown by the "Constitution's text and structure, as well as precedent and history":

"It is a logical and proper inference" that the "Reception Clause, which directs that the President 'shall receive Ambassadors and other public Ministers,' Art. II, § 3, [should] be understood to acknowledge his power to recognize other nations." In addition, Art. II, § 2, cl. 2 provides that the President "shall nominate * * * Ambassadors as well as 'other public Ministers and Consuls.'" This includes "dispatch[ing] other diplomatic agents [and] engaging in direct diplomacy with foreign heads of state and their ministers." The power that "the President may unilaterally effect recognition—and the lack of any similar power vested in Congress—[as well] as "functional considerations, suggest [that] the Nation must have a single policy regarding which governments are legitimate in the eyes of the United States." Thus, "the President since the founding has exercised this unilateral power to recognize new states—and the Court has endorsed the practice," [thereby] illustrating that "the Court has long considered recognition to be the exclusive prerogative of the Executive [and] the sole organ of the federal government in the field of international relations. [To] be effective in negotiations over a formal recognition determination, it must be evident to his counterparts abroad that he speaks for the Nation on that precise question." Nor does *Curtiss-Wright* indicate that "the Executive is not free from the ordinary controls and checks of Congress merely because foreign affairs are at issue.

"[This] is not to say Congress may not express its disagreement with the President in myriad ways. For example, it may enact an embargo, decline to confirm an ambassador, or even declare war. But none of these acts would alter the President's recognition decision."[6]

THOMAS, J., concurred in the judgment in part and dissented in part. "Our Constitution vests the residual foreign affairs powers of the Federal Government—

---

[5]   McReynolds, J., dissented without opinion. Stone, J., did not participate.

[6]   Breyer, J., joined the Court's opinion but added "that this case presents a political question. See *Zivotofsky v. Clinton*," Ch. 1, Sec. 2.

i.e., those not specifically enumerated in the Constitution—in the President by way of Article II's Vesting Clause. [It] includes all powers originally understood as falling within the 'executive power' of the Federal Government. [The] President has long regulated passports under his residual foreign affairs power, [preceded "in England, by the King; in the colonies, by the Continental Congress; and in the United States, by President Washington and every President since,"] and this portion of § 214(d) does not fall within any of Congress' enumerated powers. By contrast, § 214(d) poses no such problem insofar as it regulates consular reports of birth abroad. [These] were ["historically associated with" and] were developed to effectuate the naturalization laws, [and fall] within Congress' enumerated powers under the Naturalization and Necessary and Proper Clauses."

SCALIA, J., joined by Roberts, C.J. and Alito, J., dissented: "One would think that if Congress may grant Zivotofsky a passport and a birth report [under its naturalization power], it may also require these papers to record his birthplace as 'Israel.' [W]hen faced with alternative ways to carry its powers into execution, Congress has the 'discretion' to choose the one it deems 'most beneficial to the people,' *McCulloch*, [and] thus has the right to decide that recording birthplaces as 'Israel' makes for better foreign policy. Or that regardless of international politics, a passport or birth report should respect its bearer's conscientious belief that Jerusalem belongs to Israel. * * *

"I agree that the Constitution *empowers* the President to extend recognition on behalf of the United States, but I find it a much harder question whether it makes that power exclusive. [In any event,] § 214(d) plainly does not concern recognition [which]is a formal legal act with effects under international law. [M]aking a notation in a passport or birth report does not encumber the Republic with any international obligations. * * *

"Even if the Constitution gives the President sole power to extend recognition, it does not give him sole power to make all decisions relating to foreign disputes over sovereignty. To the contrary, a fair reading of Article I's [power] to "regulate Commerce with foreign Nations," § 8, cl. 3, includes power to regulate imports from Gibraltar as British goods or as Spanish goods. [There] is no question that Congress may, if it wishes, pass laws that openly flout treaties made by the President. [Today's] holding puts the implied power to recognize territorial claims (which the Court infers from the power to recognize states, which it infers from the responsibility to receive ambassadors) on a higher footing than the express power to make treaties."

ROBERTS, C.J., joined by Alito, J., filed a separate dissent: "Never before has this Court accepted a President's direct defiance of an Act of Congress in the field of foreign affairs. We have instead stressed that the President's power reaches 'its lowest ebb' when he contravenes the express will of Congress [*Youngstown* (Jackson, J., concurring.) At] the founding, "there was no reason to view the reception clause as a source of discretionary authority for the president.

"[E]ven if the President does have exclusive recognition power, he still cannot prevail in this case, because the statute at issue *does not implicate recognition*. [N]either Congress nor the Executive Branch regards § 214(d) as a recognition determination. * * *

"If the President's so-called general foreign relations authority does not permit him to countermand a State's lawful action [*Medellin*], it surely does not authorize him to disregard an express statutory directive enacted by Congress, which—unlike the States—has extensive foreign relations powers of its own."

2. CONGRESSIONAL ACTION AFFECTING "PRESIDENTIAL" POWERS

I. DELEGATION OF RULEMAKING POWER

YAKUS v. UNITED STATES, 321 U.S. 414 (1944): The World War II emergency price control act authorized the president-appointed administrator to issue regulations establishing maximum prices and rents [w]hen in the administrator's judgment prices "have risen or threaten to rise in a manner inconsistent with the purposes of this act." The administrator was to "make adjustments for such relevant factors as he may determine and deem to be of general applicability." The Court, per STONE, C.J., upheld this delegation: "The Act [is] an exercise by Congress of its legislative power. In it Congress has stated the legislative objective, has prescribed the method of achieving that objective—maximum price fixing—and has laid down standards to guide the administrative determination of both the occasions for the exercise of the price-fixing power, and the particular prices to be established.

"The Act is unlike the National Industrial Recovery Act [in] *Schechter Poultry Corp.*, [Ch. 2, Sec. 2, II, A], which proclaimed in the broadest terms its purpose 'to rehabilitate industry and to conserve natural resources.' It prescribed no method of attaining that end save by the establishment of codes of fair competition, the nature of whose permissible provisions was left undefined. It provided no standards to which those codes were to conform.

"[The] Constitution [does] not require that Congress find for itself every fact upon which it desires to base legislative action. [The] essentials of the legislative function [are] preserved when Congress has specified the basic conditions of fact upon whose existence or occurrence, ascertained from relevant data by a designated administrative agency, it directs that its statutory command shall be effective. It is no objection that [this calls] for the exercise of judgment, and for the formulation of subsidiary administrative policy within the prescribed statutory framework." Only Roberts, J., dissented on the delegation issue.[7]

---

[7]   In only two cases, both involving New Deal legislation, has the Court invalidated congressional delegation of legislative power to a federal officer or agency. *Schechter*, supra; *Panama Refining Co. v. Ryan*, 293 U.S. 388 (1935). See also *Carter v. Carter Coal Co.*, Ch. 2, Sec.

———

WHITMAN v. AMERICAN TRUCKING ASSN'S, INC., 531 U.S. 457 (2001), per SCALIA, J. held that the Clean Air Act's delegation to the EPA to set air quality standards—"the attainment and maintenance of which [are] requisite to protect the public health" with "an adequate margin of safety"—stated an "intelligible principle." THOMAS, J., agreed, but was "not convinced that the intelligible principle doctrine serves to prevent all cessions of legislative power. [On a future day], I would be willing to address the question whether our delegation jurisprudence has strayed too far from our Founders' understanding of separation of powers."

———

The broad scope of Congress's power to delegate in the modern administrative state is further emphasized by UNITED STATES v. MEAD, 533 U.S. 218 (2001), which concerned a federal agency's interpretation of a statutory authorization when "Congress has not directly addressed the precise question at issue." The Court held that "if Congress has explicitly left a gap for the agency to fill," the agency's interpretations of its governing statute are valid "unless they are procedurally arbitrary, capricious, or manifestly contrary to the statute"; if the delegation is "implicit rather than explicit," the agency's interpretation is valid if "reasonable." If the authorization is neither explicit nor implicit, "considerable weight should be accorded to an executive department's construction of a statutory scheme it is entrusted to administer," with the outcome ultimately based on multiple factors. In addition to this judicial "deference" to the agency's interpretations, "an agency to which Congress has delegated policymaking responsibilities may, within the limits of that delegation, properly rely upon the incumbent administration's views of wise policy to inform its judgments. While agencies are not directly accountable to the people, the Chief Executive is [and may appropriately resolve] the competing interests which Congress itself either inadvertently did not resolve, or intentionally left to be resolved by the agency charged with the administration of the statute in light of everyday realities."

II. LEGISLATIVE AND LINE ITEM VETOES

INS v. CHADHA
462 U.S. 919, 103 S.Ct. 2764, 77 L.Ed.2d 317 (1983).

CHIEF JUSTICE BURGER delivered the opinion of the Court.

[The Immigration and Nationality Act authorized the Attorney General to suspend deportation of a deportable alien if he met specified conditions and would suffer "extreme hardship" if deported. It required a report to Congress on each suspension. Sec. 244(c)(2) provided that if, within a specified period thereafter,

---

2, II, A, invalidating a congressional delegation to a private industry association with a potentially adverse interest to the objects of the regulation.

either house of Congress "passes a resolution stating [that] it does not favor the suspension [the] Attorney General shall thereupon deport such alien." The Attorney General suspended the deportation of Chadha. Accepting a House Committee's conclusion that Chadha did not satisfy the hardship requirements, the House of Representatives passed a resolution that the "deportation should not be suspended." It was not submitted to the Senate, nor "presented to the President" under Art. I, § 7.]

Although not "hermetically" sealed from one another, the powers delegated to the three Branches are functionally identifiable. [Whether] actions taken by either House are, in law and fact, an exercise of legislative power depends not on their form but upon "whether they contain matter which is properly to be regarded as legislative in its character and effect."

[In] purporting to exercise power defined in Art. I, § 8, cl. 4, to "establish an uniform Rule of Naturalization," the House took action that had the purpose and effect of altering the legal rights, duties, and relations of persons, including the Attorney General, Executive Branch officials and Chadha, all outside the legislative branch. [The] one-House veto operated in [this case] to overrule the Attorney General and mandate Chadha's deportation; absent the House action, Chadha would remain in the United States. Congress has *acted* and its action has altered Chadha's status.

The legislative character of the one-House veto in [this case] is confirmed by the character of the congressional action it supplants. Neither the House of Representatives nor the Senate contends that, absent the veto provision in § 244(c)(2), either of them, or both of them acting together, could effectively require the Attorney General to deport an alien once the Attorney General, in the exercise of legislatively delegated authority,[16] had determined the alien should remain in the United States. Without the challenged provision in § 244(c)(2), this could have been achieved, if at all, only by legislation requiring deportation. * * *

The nature of the decision implemented by the one-House veto in [this case] further manifests its legislative character. After long experience with the clumsy, time-consuming private bill procedure, Congress made a deliberate choice to delegate to [the] Attorney General, the authority to allow deportable aliens to remain in this country in certain specified circumstances. [Disagreement] with the Attorney General's decision on Chadha's deportation—that is, Congress' decision to deport Chadha—no less than Congress' original choice to delegate to the

---

    16   [Ct's Note] Congress protests that affirming the Court of Appeals in [favor of Chadha] will sanction "lawmaking by the Attorney General." * * * Executive action under legislatively delegated authority that might resemble "legislative" action in some respects is not subject to the approval of both Houses of Congress and the President for the reason that the Constitution does not so require. That kind of Executive action is always subject to check by the terms of the legislation that authorized it; and if that authority is exceeded it is open to judicial review as well as the power of Congress to modify or revoke the authority entirely. A one-House veto is clearly legislative in both character and effect and is not so checked; the need for the check provided by Art. I, §§ 1, 7, is therefore clear. Congress' authority to delegate portions of its power to administrative agencies provides no support for the argument that Congress can constitutionally control administration of the laws by way of a Congressional veto.

Attorney General the authority to make that decision, involves determinations of policy that Congress can implement in only one way; bicameral passage followed by presentment to the President. Congress must abide by its delegation of authority until that delegation is legislatively altered or revoked.[19]

Finally, we see that when the Framers intended to authorize either House of Congress to act alone and outside of its prescribed bicameral legislative role, they narrowly and precisely defined the procedure for such action [in] only[: the House of Representatives' power to initiate impeachments, and the Senate's powers to try impeachments, to confirm presidential appointments, and to approve treaties.]

The bicameral requirement, the Presentment Clauses, the President's veto, and Congress' power to override a veto were intended to erect enduring checks on each Branch and to protect the people from the improvident exercise of power by mandating certain prescribed steps. [In] purely practical terms, it is obviously easier for action to be taken by one House without submission to the President; but it is crystal clear from the records of the Convention, contemporaneous writings and debates, that the Framers ranked other values higher than efficiency. [The] choices we discern as having been made in the Constitutional Convention [were] consciously made by men who had lived under a form of government that permitted arbitrary governmental acts to go unchecked. There is no support in the Constitution or decisions of this Court for the proposition that the cumbersomeness and delays often encountered in complying with explicit constitutional standards may be avoided, either by the Congress or by the President. * * *

JUSTICE POWELL concurring in the judgment.

[In] my view, the case [may] be decided on a narrower ground. When Congress finds that a particular person does not satisfy the statutory criteria for permanent residence in this country it has assumed a judicial function in violation of the principle of separation of powers. [The Framers'] concern that a legislature should not be able unilaterally to impose a substantial deprivation on one person was expressed not only in [the] general allocation of power, but also in more specific provisions, such as the Bill of Attainder Clause, Art. I, § 9, cl. 3[, both of which] reflect the Framers' concern that trial by a legislature lacks the safeguards necessary to prevent the abuse of power. * * *

JUSTICE WHITE dissenting. * * *

---

19   [Ct's Note] This does not mean that Congress is required to capitulate to "the accretion of policy control by forces outside its chambers." [Beyond] the obvious fact that Congress ultimately controls administrative agencies in the legislation that creates them, other means of control, such as durational limits on authorizations and formal reporting requirements, lie well within Congress' constitutional power. See also n.9, supra.

[Fn. 9 stated: "Without the one-House veto, § 244 resembles the 'report and wait' provision approved by the Court in *Sibbach v. Wilson & Co.*, 312 U.S. 1 (1941). [The statute in] *Sibbach* did *not* provide that Congress could unilaterally veto the Federal Rules. Rather, it gave Congress the opportunity to review the Rules before they became effective and to pass legislation barring their effectiveness if the Rules were found objectionable. This technique was used by Congress when it acted in 1973 to stay, and ultimately to revise, the proposed Rules of Evidence."]

The prominence of the legislative veto mechanism in our contemporary political system [has] become a central means by which Congress secures the accountability of executive and independent agencies. Without the legislative veto, Congress is faced with a Hobson's choice: either to refrain from delegating the necessary authority, leaving itself with a hopeless task of writing laws with the requisite specificity to cover endless special circumstances across the entire policy landscape, or in the alternative, to abdicate its lawmaking function to the Executive Branch and independent agencies. To choose the former leaves major national problems unresolved; to opt for the latter risks unaccountable policymaking by those not elected to fill that role. Accordingly, over the past five decades, the legislative veto has been placed in nearly 200 statutes[:] reorganization, budgets, foreign affairs, war powers, and regulation of trade, safety, energy, the environment, and the economy. [T]he increasing reliance of Congress upon the legislative veto suggests that the alternatives to which Congress must now turn are not entirely satisfactory.[10]

The history of the legislative veto also makes clear that it has not been a sword with which Congress has struck out to aggrandize itself at the expense of the other branches—the concerns of Madison and Hamilton. Rather, the veto has been a means of defense, a reservation of ultimate authority necessary if Congress is to fulfill its designated role under Art. I as the Nation's lawmaker. While the President has often objected to particular legislative vetoes, generally those left in the hands of congressional Committees, the Executive has more often agreed to legislative review as the price for a broad delegation of authority. * * *

[The] power to exercise a legislative veto is not the power to write new law without bicameral approval or Presidential consideration. The veto must be authorized by statute and may only negative what an Executive department or independent agency has proposed. On its face, the legislative veto no more allows one House of Congress to make law than does the Presidential veto confer such power upon the President. * * *

If Congress may delegate lawmaking power to independent and Executive agencies, it is most difficult to understand Art. I as prohibiting Congress from also reserving a check on legislative power for itself. Absent the veto, the agencies receiving delegations of legislative or quasi-legislative power may issue regulations having the force of law without bicameral approval and without the President's signature. It is thus not apparent why the reservation of a veto over the exercise of that legislative power must be subject to a more exacting test. In both cases, it is enough that the initial statutory authorizations comply with the Art. I requirements. * * *

The central concern of the presentation and bicameralism requirements of Art. I is that when a departure from the legal status quo is undertaken, it is done

---

10   [Ct's Note] While Congress could write certain statutes with greater specificity, it is unlikely that this is a realistic or even desirable substitute for the legislative veto. [Political volatility] and [t]he controversial nature of many issues would prevent Congress from reaching agreement on many major problems if specificity were required in their enactments.

with the approval of the President and both Houses of Congress—or, in the event of a Presidential veto, a two-thirds majority in both Houses. This interest is fully satisfied by the operation of § 244(c)(2). The President's approval is found in the Attorney General's action in recommending to Congress that the deportation order for a given alien be suspended. The House and the Senate indicate their approval of the Executive's action by not passing a resolution of disapproval within the statutory period. Thus, a change in the legal status quo—the deportability of the alien—is consummated only with the approval of each of the three relevant actors. The disagreement of any one of the three maintains the alien's pre-existing status. * * *

———

Two weeks after *Chadha*, PROCESS GAS CONSUMERS GROUP v. CONSUMER ENERGY COUNCIL OF AMERICA, 463 U.S. 1216 (1983), summarily affirmed decisions invalidating a one-house legislative veto of regulatory rulemaking by the Federal Energy Regulatory Commission and a two-house veto of such rulemaking by the Federal Trade Commission. Rehnquist, J., would have noted probable jurisdiction and set the cases for oral argument. Powell, J., took no part. WHITE, J., dissented: "Where the veto is placed as a check upon the actions of the independent regulatory agencies, the Art. I analysis relied upon in *Chadha* has a particularly hollow ring. [These] regulations have the force of law without the President's concurrence; nor can he veto. [To] invalidate the [legislative veto,] which allows Congress to maintain some control over the lawmaking process, merely guarantees that the independent agencies, once created, for all practical purposes are a fourth branch of the Government not subject to the direct control of either Congress or the Executive Branch."

CLINTON v. NEW YORK
524 U.S. 417, 118 S.Ct. 2091, 141 L.Ed.2d 393 (1998).

JUSTICE STEVENS delivered the opinion of the Court.

[The Line Item Veto Act gave the President the power to "cancel in whole" three types of provisions that have been enacted by Congress and signed into law: "(1) any dollar amount of discretionary budget authority; (2) any item of new direct spending; or (3) any limited tax benefit." The President exercised his "line item veto" to nullify the two provisions involved in this case: a section of the Balanced Budget Act of 1997 that waived the federal government's statutory authority to seek recoupment of as much as $2.6 billion in taxes that New York had levied against Medicare providers, and a section of the Taxpayers Relief Act of 1997, which authorized favorable tax treatment of certain parties selling food processing facilities to farmers' cooperatives.]

The Act requires the President [to] determine, with respect to each cancellation, that it will "(i) reduce the Federal budget deficit; (ii) not impair any essential Government functions; and (iii) not harm the national interest."

Moreover, he must transmit a special message to Congress notifying it of each cancellation within five calendar days.

[If] a "disapproval bill" pertaining to a special message is enacted into law, the cancellations set forth in that message become "null and void." The Act sets forth a detailed expedited procedure for the consideration of a "disapproval bill," but no such bill was passed for [the] cancellations involved in these cases. A majority vote of both Houses is sufficient to enact a disapproval bill. The Act does not grant the President the authority to cancel a disapproval bill, but he does, of course, retain his constitutional authority to veto such a bill.

[There] are important differences between the President's "return" of a bill pursuant to Article I, § 7, and the exercise of the President's cancellation authority pursuant to the Line Item Veto Act. The constitutional return takes place before the bill becomes law; the statutory cancellation occurs after the bill becomes law. The constitutional return is of the entire bill; the statutory cancellation is of only a part. Although the Constitution expressly authorizes the President to play a role in the process of enacting statutes, it is silent on the subject of unilateral Presidential action that either repeals or amends parts of duly enacted statutes.

There are powerful reasons for construing constitutional silence on this profoundly important issue as equivalent to an express prohibition. The procedures governing the enactment of statutes set forth [in] Article I were the product of the great debates and compromises that produced the Constitution itself. [Our] first President understood the text of the Presentment Clause as requiring that he either "approve all the parts of a Bill, or reject it in toto." What has emerged in these cases from the President's exercise of his statutory cancellation powers, however, are truncated versions of two bills that passed both Houses of Congress. They are not the product of the "finely wrought" procedure that the Framers designed.

[The] Government contends that the cancellations were [not repeals or vetoes in the constitutional sense, but] merely exercises of discretionary authority granted to the President by the Balanced Budget Act and the Taxpayer Relief Act read in light of the previously enacted Line Item Veto Act. [In] *Field v. Clark*, 143 U.S. 649 (1892), the Court upheld the constitutionality of the Tariff Act of 1890. That statute contained a "free list" of almost 300 specific articles that were exempted from import duties[, but] directed the President to suspend [the] exemption for sugar, molasses, coffee, tea, and hides "whenever, and so often" as he [determined] that any country producing and exporting those products imposed duties on the agricultural products of the United States that he deemed to be "reciprocally unequal and unreasonable."

[But there are] critical differences between the power to suspend the exemption from import duties and the power to cancel portions of a duly enacted statute. First, the exercise of the suspension power was contingent upon a condition that did not exist when the Tariff Act was passed: the imposition of "reciprocally unequal and unreasonable" import duties by other countries. In contrast, the exercise of the cancellation power within five days after the enactment of the Balanced Budget and Tax Reform Acts necessarily was based on the same conditions that Congress evaluated when it passed those statutes. Second, under the Tariff Act, when the President determined that the contingency had arisen, he had a duty to suspend; in contrast, [the Line Item Veto Act] did not qualify his discretion to cancel or not to cancel. * * *

Neither are we persuaded by the Government's contention that the President's authority to cancel new direct spending and tax benefit items is no greater than his traditional authority to decline to spend appropriated funds. [The] critical difference between this statute and all of its predecessors [is] that unlike any of them, this Act gives the President the unilateral power to change the text of duly enacted statutes.

[Because] we conclude that the Act's cancellation provisions violate Article I, § 7, [we] find it unnecessary to consider [whether] the Act [impermissibly delegates lawmaking authority to the President].

JUSTICE KENNEDY, concurring. * * *

Liberty is always at stake when one or more of the branches seek to transgress the separation of powers. Separation of powers was designed to implement a fundamental insight: concentration of power in the hands of a single branch is a threat to liberty. [If] a citizen who is taxed has the measure of the tax or the decision to spend determined by the Executive alone, without adequate control by the citizen's Representatives in Congress, liberty is threatened.

JUSTICE BREYER, with whom JUSTICE O'CONNOR and JUSTICE SCALIA join as to Part III, dissenting.* * *

Imagine that the canceled New York health care tax provision at issue here [said] *"that the President may prevent the just-mentioned provision from having legal force or effect if he determines x, y and z.* (Assume x, y and z to be the same determinations required by the Line Item Veto Act)." [One] could not say that a President who "prevents" the deeming language from "having legal force or effect" has either repealed or amended this particular hypothetical statute. Rather, the President has exercised the power it explicitly delegates to him. He has executed the law, not repealed it.

It could make no significant difference to this linguistic point were the italicized proviso to appear, not as part of [the statute's text] but, instead, at the bottom of the statute page, say referenced by an asterisk, with a statement that it applies to every spending provision in the act next to which a similar asterisk appears. And that being so, it could make no difference if that proviso appeared, instead, in a different, earlier-enacted law, along with legal language that makes it applicable to every future spending provision picked out according to a specified formula.

But, of course, this last-mentioned possibility is this very case. [T]hat the Act's procedures differ from the Constitution's exclusive procedures for enacting (or repealing) legislation is beside the point. The Act itself was enacted in accordance with these procedures, and its failure to require the President to satisfy those procedures does not make the Act unconstitutional. * * *

JUSTICE SCALIA, with whom JUSTICE O'CONNOR joins, and with whom JUSTICE BREYER joins as to Part III, concurring in part and dissenting in part. * * *

[Article I, § 7] of the Constitution obviously prevents the President from canceling a law that Congress has not authorized him to cancel. [But] that is not this case. [Article I, § 7] no more categorically prohibits the Executive reduction of congressional dispositions in the course of implementing statutes that authorize such reduction, than it categorically prohibits the Executive augmentation of congressional dispositions in the course of implementing statutes that authorize such augmentation—generally known as substantive rulemaking.

[Insofar] as the degree of political, "law-making" power conferred upon the Executive is concerned, there is not a dime's worth of difference between Congress's authorizing the President to cancel a spending item, and Congress's authorizing money to be spent on a particular item at the President's discretion. And the latter has been done since the Founding of the Nation. From 1789–1791, the First Congress made lump-sum appropriations for the entire Government—"sums not exceeding" specified amounts for broad purposes. From a very early date Congress also made permissive individual appropriations, leaving the decision whether to spend the money to the President's unfettered discretion. * * *

III. APPOINTMENT AND REMOVAL OF OFFICERS

Art. II, Sec. 2, cl.2 states the President's power to "appoint * * * Officers of the United States," but nowhere does the Constitution address the power to remove officers, an issue disputed in the First Congress concerning President Washington's authority to unilaterally remove the Secretary of the Department of Foreign Affairs. MYERS v. UNITED STATES, 272 U.S. 52 (1926), ruled that the President's authority included the power to remove executive officers of the United States, even when their appointment was subject to the advice and consent of the Senate. HUMPHREY'S EXECUTOR v. UNITED STATES, 295 U.S. 602 (1935), held that Congress could limit the grounds for removal of a Commissioner of the Federal Trade Commission. Distinguishing *Myers*, which involved a postmaster, the *Humphreys* Court said that the earlier case "not be accepted as controlling our decision here. A postmaster is an executive officer restricted to the performance of executive functions. [*Myers*] finds support in the theory that such an officer is merely one of the units in the executive department [and] the decision goes far enough to include all purely executive officers. It goes no farther."

———

BUCKLEY v. VALEO, 424 U.S. 1 (1976), per curiam, invalidated the Federal Election Campaign Act's provision for the Federal Election Commission (FEC) because it assigned appointment of two commissioners to the President pro tem of the Senate and two to the Speaker of the House of Representatives, leaving two for Presidential appointment: "[A]ny appointee exercising significant authority pursuant to the laws of the United States is an 'Officer of the United States,' and must, therefore, be appointed in the manner prescribed by [the Appointments Clause]. While the second part of the Clause authorizes Congress to vest the appointment of the officers described in that part in 'the Courts of Law, or in the Heads of Departments,' neither the Speaker of the House nor the President pro tempore of the Senate comes within this language.

"[The] position that because Congress has been given explicit and plenary authority to regulate a field of activity, it must therefore have the power to appoint those who are to administer the regulatory statute is both novel and contrary to the language of the Appointments Clause [which] controls the appointment of the members of a typical administrative agency even though its functions, as this Court recognized in *Humphrey's Executor*, may be 'predominantly quasi-judicial and quasi-legislative' rather than executive. The Court in that case carefully emphasized that although the members of such agencies were to be independent of the Executive in their day-to-day operations, the Executive was not excluded from selecting them. * * *

"All aspects of the Act are brought within the Commission's broad administrative powers: rulemaking, advisory opinions, and determinations of eligibility for funds and even for federal elective office itself. These functions [are] of kinds usually performed by independent regulatory agencies or by some department in the Executive Branch under the direction of an Act of Congress. [Yet] each of these functions also represents the performance of a significant governmental duty exercised pursuant to a public law. While the President may not insist that such functions be delegated to an appointee of his removable at will, *Humphrey's Executor,* none of them operates merely in aid of congressional authority to legislate or is sufficiently removed from the administration and enforcement of public law to allow it to be performed by the present Commission."

BOWSHER v. SYNAR, 478 U.S. 714 (1986): The Balanced Budget and Emergency Deficit Act of 1985 set maximum yearly permissible deficits with the goal of reducing the federal deficit to zero by 1991. If needed to keep the deficit within the maximum, the Act required across-the-board cuts, half in defense programs and half elsewhere. Sec. 251 set out the procedure: (1) For each year the directors of the Office of Management and Budget and of the Congressional Budget Office were to estimate the deficit and calculate, program by program, the cuts required to meet the goal, and to report their estimates and calculations to the Comptroller General. (2) After reviewing the directors' figures, the Comptroller was to report to the President on the estimates and required budget reductions. (3) The President was then to issue an order placing in effect reductions specified by the Comptroller, unless within a specified period Congress met the deficit goal in other ways. The Court, per BURGER, C.J., held this procedure unconstitutional:

"Congress cannot reserve for itself the power of removal of an officer charged with the execution of the laws except by impeachment. [To] permit an officer controlled by Congress to execute the laws would be, in essence, to permit a congressional veto. Congress could simply remove, or threaten to remove, an officer for executing the laws in any fashion found to be unsatisfactory to Congress. [*Chadha.*] With these principles in mind, we turn to consideration of whether the Comptroller General is controlled by Congress.

"[Although] the Comptroller General is nominated by the President from a list of three individuals recommended by the Speaker of the House of Representatives and the President pro tempore of the Senate, and confirmed by the Senate,[8] he is removable only at the initiative of Congress [not] only by impeachment but also by joint resolution of Congress 'at any [time'].[7] [T]he removal powers over the Comptroller General's office dictate that he will be subservient to Congress.

"[The] Comptroller General heads the General Accounting Office, 'an instrumentality of the United States Government independent of the executive departments,' which was created by Congress [in] 1921 [because] it believed that it 'needed an officer, responsible to it alone, to check upon the application of public funds in accordance with appropriations.' Harvey C. Mansfield, *The Comptroller General* 65 (1939).

"It is clear that Congress has consistently viewed the Comptroller General as an officer of the Legislative Branch. [T]he Comptrollers General have also viewed themselves as part of the Legislative Branch. [The] remaining question is whether the Comptroller General has been assigned [executive powers under the Act].

"[Under] § 251, the Comptroller General must exercise judgment concerning facts that affect the application of the Act. He must also interpret the provisions of the Act to determine precisely what budgetary calculations are required. Decisions of that kind are typically made by officers charged with executing a statute.

In deciding the remedy, the Court invalidated the procedure that gave "executive" authority to the Comptroller General, resorting to the Act's "fallback" provisions[9] that were to take effect "[i]n the event [*any*] of the reporting procedures described in section 251 are invalidated."[10]

WHITE, J., dissented: "Determining the level of spending by the Federal Government is [a] peculiarly legislative function, and one expressly committed to Congress by Art. I, § 9. [Delegating] the execution of this legislation—that is, the

---

8   The Comptroller General was limited to a single 15-year term.

7   **[Ct's Note]** Although the President could veto such a joint resolution, the veto could be overridden by a two-thirds vote of both Houses of Congress. Thus, the Comptroller General could be removed in the face of Presidential opposition. [We] therefore read the removal provision as authorizing removal by Congress alone.

9   Under the fallback provisions, Congress makes the ultimate budget decision by joint resolution, which is subject to Presidential veto unless overridden by two-thirds votes in both houses of Congress.

10   Stevens, J., joined by Marshall, J., concurred in the judgment but dissented from "labeling the function assigned to the Comptroller General as 'executive powers.'"

power to apply the Act's criteria and make the required calculations—to an officer independent of the President's will does not deprive the President of any power that he would otherwise have or that is essential to the performance of the duties of his office. Rather, the result of such a delegation, from the standpoint of the President, is no different from the result of more traditional forms of appropriation: under either system, the level of funds available to the Executive Branch to carry out its duties is not within the President's discretionary control.

" * * * Congress may remove the Comptroller only through a joint resolution, which by definition must be passed by both Houses and signed by the President. [In] other words, a removal of the Comptroller under the statute *satisfies the requirements of bicameralism and presentment laid down in Chadha.* "[Those] who have studied the office agree that the procedural and substantive limits on the power of Congress and the President to remove the Comptroller make dislodging him against his will practically impossible."[11]

MORRISON V. OLSON
487 U.S. 654, 108 S.Ct. 2597, 101 L.Ed.2d 569 (1988).

CHIEF JUSTICE REHNQUIST delivered the opinion of the Court.

[The Ethics in Government Act of 1978 called for appointment of an "independent counsel" to investigate, and, if appropriate, to prosecute certain high-ranking government officials[12] for violating almost any federal criminal law. Upon receipt of information that the Attorney General considers "sufficient grounds," the Attorney General conducts a preliminary investigation and then reports to a special division of the Court of Appeals for the District of Columbia Circuit whether there are "reasonable grounds to believe that further investigation or prosecution is warranted." If so, the Attorney General must request the Special Division to appoint, and provide it with sufficient information to enable it to appoint, "an appropriate independent counsel and define that independent counsel's prosecutorial jurisdiction."[13] The Act grants the independent counsel the "full power and independent authority" of the Department of Justice to investigate and prosecute. The department must suspend all its investigations and proceedings regarding any matter referred to independent counsel. The Special Division

---

[11]   Blackmun, J., separately dissenting, agreed with White, J., that it was "unrealistic" to claim that the removal power makes the Comptroller General "subservient to Congress." But to the extent removal power was found incompatible with the constitutional separation of powers, he would "cure" it by refusing to allow congressional removal "—if it ever is attempted—and not by striking down the central provisions of the Deficit Control Act."

[12]   These included the President, Vice-President, cabinet officers, high ranking officers in the Executive Office of the President and the Justice Department, and the like.

[13]   The Act created the Special Division of three Circuit Court Judges appointed by the Chief Justice of the United States for two-year terms. The Court upheld the Special Division's authority to appoint the independent counsel and specify her jurisdiction. It invoked the Appointments Clause reference to courts of law appointing "inferior officers," the congruity of "a court having the power to appoint prosecutorial officers" with a "court's normal functions," and the Act's ban on Special Division judges' participation in other matters relating to the independent counsel.

appointed Morrison to investigate a charge of perjury before the House Judiciary Committee by Olson, an Assistant Attorney General.]

[We turn to the question] whether the provision of the Act restricting the Attorney General's power to remove the independent counsel to only those instances in which he can show "good cause," taken by itself, impermissibly interferes with the President's exercise of his constitutionally appointed functions. [Unlike] both *Bowsher* and *Myers,* this case does not involve an attempt by Congress itself to gain a role in the removal of executive officials. [The] Act instead puts the removal power squarely in the hands of the Executive Branch. [There] is no requirement of congressional approval of the Attorney General's removal decision, though the decision is subject to judicial review. * * *

Appellees contend [that] when a "purely executive" official is involved, the governing precedent is *Myers,* not *Humphrey's Executor.* And, under *Myers,* the President must have absolute discretion to discharge "purely" executive officials at will. We undoubtedly did rely on the terms "quasi-legislative" and "quasi-judicial" to distinguish the officials involved in *Humphrey's Executor* and *Wiener* from those in *Myers,* but our present considered view is that the determination of whether the Constitution allows Congress to impose a "good cause"-type restriction on the President's power to remove an official cannot be made to turn on whether or not that official is classified as "purely executive." The analysis contained in our removal cases is designed not to define rigid categories of those officials who may or may not be removed at will by the President, but to ensure that Congress does not interfere with the President's exercise of the "executive power" [under] Article II. *Myers* was undoubtedly correct in its holding, and in its broader suggestion that there are some "purely executive" officials who must be removable by the President at will if he is to be able to accomplish his constitutional role.[29] [At] the other end of the spectrum from *Myers,* the characterization of the agencies in *Humphrey's Executor* and *Wiener* as "quasi-legislative" or "quasi-judicial" in large part reflected our judgment that it was not essential to the President's proper execution of his Article II powers that these agencies be headed up by individuals who were removable at will.[30] [There] is no real dispute that the functions performed by the independent counsel are "executive" in the sense that they are law enforcement functions that typically have been undertaken by officials within the Executive Branch. As we noted above, however, the independent counsel is an inferior officer under the Appointments Clause, with limited jurisdiction and tenure and lacking

---

[29]   [Ct's Note] The dissent says that the language of Article II vesting the executive power of the United States in the President requires that every officer of the United States exercising any part of that power must serve at the pleasure of the President and be removable by him at will. This rigid demarcation—a demarcation incapable of being altered by law in the slightest degree, and applicable to tens of thousands of holders of offices neither known nor foreseen by the Framers—depends upon an extrapolation from general constitutional language which we think is more than the text will bear. * * *

[30]   [Ct's Note] The terms also may be used to describe the circumstances in which Congress might be more inclined to find that a degree of independence from the Executive, such as that afforded by a "good cause" removal standard, is necessary to the proper functioning of the agency or official. It is not difficult to imagine situations in which Congress might desire that an official performing "quasi-judicial" functions, for example, would be free of executive or political control.

policymaking or significant administrative authority. Although the counsel exercises no small amount of discretion and judgment in deciding how to carry out his or her duties under the Act, we simply do not see how the President's need to control the exercise of that discretion is so central to the functioning of the Executive Branch as to require as a matter of constitutional law that the counsel be terminable at will by the President.

[Here], as with the provision of the Act conferring the appointment authority of the independent counsel on the special court, the congressional determination to limit the removal power of the Attorney General was essential, in the view of Congress, to establish the necessary independence of the office. We do not think that this limitation as it presently stands sufficiently deprives the President of control over the independent counsel to interfere impermissibly with his constitutional obligation to ensure the faithful execution of the laws.

The final question to be addressed is whether the Act, taken as a whole, violates the principle of separation of powers. [We] observe first that this case does not involve an attempt by Congress to increase its own powers at the expense of the Executive Branch. [Similarly], we do not think that the Act works any *judicial* usurpation of properly executive functions. [T]he Special Division has no power to appoint an independent counsel sua sponte; it may only do so upon the specific request of the Attorney General, and the courts are specifically prevented from reviewing the Attorney General's decision not to seek appointment.

Finally, we do not think that the Act "impermissibly undermine[s]" the powers of the Executive Branch. [It] is undeniable that the Act reduces the amount of control or supervision that the Attorney General and, through him, the President exercises over the investigation and prosecution of a certain class of alleged criminal activity. * * *

JUSTICE SCALIA, dissenting.

[It] effects a revolution in our constitutional jurisprudence for the Court, once it has determined that (1) purely executive functions are at issue here, and (2) those functions have been given to a person whose actions are not fully within the supervision and control of the President, nonetheless to proceed further to sit in judgment of whether "the President's need to control the exercise of [the independent counsel's] discretion is *so central* to the functioning of the Executive Branch" as to require complete control (emphasis added), whether the conferral of his powers upon someone else "*sufficiently* deprives the President of control over the independent counsel [and] whether "the Act give[s] the Executive Branch *sufficient* control over the independent counsel to ensure that the President is able to perform his constitutionally assigned duties" (emphasis added). It is not for us to determine [how] much of the purely executive powers of government must be within the full control of the President. The Constitution prescribes that they *all* are.

[Before] this statute was passed, the President, in taking action disagreeable to the Congress, or an executive officer giving advice to the President or testifying before Congress concerning one of those many matters on which the two branches are from time to time at odds, could be assured that his acts and motives would be adjudged—insofar as the decision whether to conduct a criminal investigation and to prosecute is concerned—in the Executive Branch, that is, in a forum attuned to the interests and the policies of the Presidency. That was one of the natural advantages the Constitution gave to the Presidency, just as it gave Members of Congress (and their staffs) the advantage of not being prosecutable for anything said or done in their legislative capacities. [It] deeply wounds the President, by substantially reducing the President's ability to protect himself and his staff. That is the whole object of the law, of course, and I cannot imagine why the Court believes it does not succeed.

[Worse] than what [the Court] has done, however, is the manner in which it has done it. A government of laws means a government of rules. Today's decision on the basic issue of fragmentation of executive power is ungoverned by rule, and hence ungoverned by law. It extends into the very heart of our most significant constitutional function the "totality of the circumstances" mode of analysis that this Court has in recent years become fond of. Taking all things into account, we conclude that the power taken away from the President here is not really *too* much. The next time executive power is assigned to someone other than the President we may conclude, taking all things into account, that it *is* too much. That opinion, like this one, will not be confined by any rule[;] it is ad hoc judgment. And it fails to explain why it is not true that—as the text of the Constitution seems to require, as the Founders seemed to expect, and as our past cases have uniformly assumed—all purely executive power must be under the control of the President. * * *14

MISTRETTA v. UNITED STATES, 488 U.S. 361 (1989), per BLACKMUN, J., upheld the Sentencing Reform Act of 1984, which created the U.S. Sentencing Commission, charged with devising guidelines for federal sentencing that would establish, within the limits of existing law, ranges of determinate sentences for categories of offenses and defendants according to specified factors, "among others." The Commission was established as an independent commission in the Judicial Branch, consisting of seven voting members appointed by the President, of whom three must be federal judges:

"[Jackson, J.'s *Youngstown* opinion] summarized the pragmatic, flexible view of differentiated governmental power to which we are heir. [As a general principle], 'executive or administrative duties of a nonjudicial nature may not be imposed on [Art. III judges].' *Morrison.* Nonetheless, we have recognized significant exceptions [as in] *Sibbach* [fn. 19 in *Chadha*, in which] we upheld a challenge to certain rules promulgated under the Rules Enabling Act of 1934, which conferred upon the Judiciary the power to promulgate federal rules of civil procedure." Thus, the constitutionality of conferring rulemaking authority on federal judges lay within

---

14   Kennedy, J., took no part.

the "twilight area" recognized by Jackson, J. In light of the judiciary's traditional role in sentencing, there was nothing "incongruous" about the judicial role on the Commission and no "vesting within the Judiciary [of] responsibilities that more appropriately belong to another Branch." Whatever "constitutional problems might arise if the powers of the Commission were vested in a court, the Commission is not a court, does not exercise judicial power, and is not controlled by or accountable to members of the Judicial Branch. The Commission [is] an independent agency in every relevant sense." Moreover, "placement of the Sentencing Commission in the Judicial Branch has not increased the Branch's authority. Prior to the passage of the Act, the Judicial Branch, as an aggregate, decided precisely the questions assigned to the Commission: what sentence is appropriate to what criminal conduct under what circumstances." Nor did this "extrajudicial assignment" undermine the integrity or independence of the Judicial Branch, nor "threaten, either in fact or in appearance, [its] impartiality."[15]

METROPOLITAN WASHINGTON AIRPORTS AUTH. v. CITIZENS FOR ABATEMENT OF AIRPORT NOISE, 501 U.S. 252 (1991), per STEVENS, J., invalidated a compact between the District of Columbia and Virginia, approved by Congress, leasing Reagan and Dulles airports from the federal government. The compact conditioned the lease on the vesting of veto power over the management of the airports in a Review Board consisting of nine members of Congress, selected from designated congressional committees but serving in their "individual" capacities. If the powers of the Review Board were "executive," congressional involvement in their exercise was impermissible under *Bowsher*. If the functions of the Review Board were instead classified as legislative, the arrangement ran afoul of principles laid down in *Chadha*: This statute is "a blueprint for extensive expansion of the legislative power beyond its constitutionally defined role. [Congress] could [use] similar expedients to enable its Members or its agents to retain control, outside the ordinary legislative process, of the activities of state grant recipients charged with executing virtually every aspect of national policy."[16]

FREE ENTERPRISE FUND v. PUBLIC COMPANY ACCOUNTING OVERSIGHT BOARD, 561 U.S. 477 (2010): Respondent (Board), which has "expansive powers" over the accounting industry, was created by the Sarbanes-Oxley Act of 2002 as

[15] Only Scalia, J., dissented. He would uphold "delegation of legislative authority" under "congressionally prescribed standards" only "in conjunction with the lawful exercise of executive or judicial power. [The] whole theory of *lawful* congressional 'delegation' is [that] a certain degree of discretion, and thus of lawmaking, *inheres* in most executive or judicial action, and it is up to Congress, by the relative specificity or generality of its statutory commands, to determine—up to a point—how small or how large that degree shall be. [But] the lawmaking function of the Sentencing Commission is completely divorced from any responsibility for execution of the law or adjudication of private rights under the law. [The] only governmental power the Commission possesses is the power to make law; and it is not the Congress."

[16] White, J., joined by Rehnquist, C.J., and Marshall, J., dissented.

part of a set of reforms in response to a "series of celebrated accounting debacles." Its five members are appointed by the SEC, which has oversight of the Board but cannot remove Board members except "for good cause." SEC Commissioners "cannot themselves be removed by the President except [for] inefficiency, neglect of duty, or malfeasance in office." The Court, per ROBERTS, C.J., held this to "contravene the Constitution's separation of powers" because it was "contrary to Article II's vesting of the executive power in the President":

"[In *Humphrey's Executor* and *Morrison*], "only one level of protected tenure separated the President from an officer exercising executive power. [The] Act before us [not] only protects Board members from removal except [under a "rigorous good-cause standard"], but withdraws from the President any decision on whether that good cause exists. That decision is vested instead in other tenured officers—the Commissioners—none of whom is subject to the President's direct control. [The] President therefore cannot hold the Commission fully accountable for the Board's conduct to the same extent that he may hold the Commission accountable for everything else that it does. * * *[4] [Moreover, neither] respondents nor the dissent explain why the Board's task, unlike so many others, requires *more* than one layer of insulation from the President. [The] parties have identified only a handful of isolated positions [in the government] in which inferior officers might be protected by two levels of good-cause tenure. [But none, such as "civil service tenure-protected employees in independent agencies or administrative law judges,"] are similarly situated to the Board."[17]

BREYER, J., joined by Stevens, Ginsburg and Sotomayor, JJ., dissented: Our governmental system involves "vast numbers of subjects, concerned with vast numbers of different problems [within] many different kinds of administrative structures, exercising different kinds of administrative authority. [Compared] to Congress and the President, the Judiciary possesses an inferior understanding of the realities of administration, and the manner in which power, including and most especially political power, operates in context."

The dissent emphasized that since "the Commission's control over the Board's investigatory and legal functions is virtually absolute [then], as a practical matter, the President's control over the Board should prove sufficient as well. [Moreover, the] Accounting Board members supervise, and are themselves, technical professional experts [and] the justification for insulating the 'technical experts' on the Board from fear of losing their jobs due to political influence is particularly

---

[4]   **[Ct's Note]** [Without] a second layer of protection, the Commission has no excuse for retaining an officer who is not faithfully executing the law. With the second layer in place, the Commission can shield its decision from Presidential review by finding that good cause is absent—a finding that, given the Commission's own protected tenure, the President cannot easily overturn. * * *

[17]   Without dissent, the Court also held that "the Board members have been validly appointed": The Commission, whose members are "Officers of the United States," "constitutes a 'Departmen[t]' for purposes of the Appointments Clause," "the Board members are inferior officers whose appointment Congress may permissibly vest in a 'Hea[d] of Departmen[t].' "

strong. [H]istorically, this regulatory subject matter—financial regulation—has been thought to exhibit a particular need for independence."

———————

NLRB v. CANNING, 573 U.S. 513 (2014), per BREYER, J., held that President Obama's "appointment of three of the Board's five members, during a 3-day 'pro-forma' recess of the Senate," was invalid under the Appointments Clause, which allows for recess appointments "so that the President can ensure the continued functioning of the Federal Government when the Senate is away": Under "the longstanding 'practice of the government' *McCulloch*, [the] phrase 'the recess' includes an intra-session recess of substantial length." * * *

"History also offers strong support. [Since 1929,] Congress has shortened its inter-session breaks as it has taken longer and more frequent intra-session breaks; Presidents have correspondingly [made] thousands of intra-session recess appointments. [We] think the Framers likely did intend the Clause to apply to a new circumstance that so clearly falls within its essential purposes, where doing so is consistent with the Clauses's language. [T]he most likely reason the Framers did not place a textual floor underneath the word 'recess' is that they did not foresee the *need* for one. [And] they might not have anticipated that intra-session recesses would become lengthier and more significant than inter-session [ones. As to] how long a recess must be in order to fall within the Clause, [we] conclude, in light of historical practice, that a recess of more than 3 days but less than 10 days is presumptively too short to fall within the Clause. We add the word 'presumptively' to leave open the possibility that some very unusual circumstance—a national catastrophe, for instance, that renders the Senate unavailable but calls for an urgent response—could demand the exercise of the recess-appointment power during a shorter break.

"[As to] the scope of the phrase 'vacancies *that may happen* during the recess of the Senate,' [all] agree that the phrase applies to vacancies that initially occur during a recess. But does it also 'apply to vacancies that initially occur before a recess and continue to exist during the recess? In our view the phrase applies to both kinds of vacancy [because its] purpose is to permit the President to obtain the assistance of subordinate officers when the Senate, due to its recess, cannot confirm [them.] Historical practice over the past 200 years strongly favors the broader interpretation [as] Presidents since Madison have made many recess appointments filling vacancies that initially occurred prior to a recess."

As for "calculation of the length of the Senate's 'recess,' [the] President made the recess appointments before us on January 4, 2012, in between the January 3 and the January 6 pro forma sessions. [W]e conclude that when the Senate declares that it is in session and possesses the capacity, under its own rules, to conduct business, it is in session for purposes of the Clause [and] Senate rules make clear that, once in session, the Senate can act even if it has earlier said that it would not."

Since the appointments in the case were during a recess of only three days, they were not within the President's authority.

SCALIA, J., joined by Roberts, C.J., and Thomas and Alito, JJ., concurred in the judgment but submitted a long, detailed disagreement, qualifying or contradicting the Court's rationale point by point. He emphasized "the folly of interpreting constitutional provisions designed to establish 'a structure of government that would protect liberty,' *Bowsher,* on the narrow-minded assumption that their only purpose is to make the government run as efficiently as possible."

As a matter of both "plain meaning [and] historical practice," (1) Recess is "the gap between sessions and [the] appointments at issue here are invalid because they undisputedly were made during the Senate's session;" and] (2) "vacancies" are those "that arise during the recess in which they are filled."

———

SEILA LAW LLC v. CONSUMER FINANCIAL PROTECTION BUREAU, 140 S.Ct. 2183 (2020), concerned a restriction on the President's power to remove the Director of the Consumer Financial Protection Bureau (CFPB) prior to the expiration of a five-year term. The Supreme Court, per ROBERTS, C.J., held the restriction unconstitutional:

"In the wake of the 2008 financial crisis, Congress [through the Dodd-Frank Act] established the [CFPB], an independent regulatory agency tasked with ensuring that consumer debt products are safe and transparent. In organizing the CFPB, Congress deviated from the structure of nearly every other independent administrative agency in our history. Instead of placing the agency under the leadership of a board with multiple members, Congress provided that the CFPB would be led by a single Director, who serves for a longer term than the President and cannot be removed by the President except for inefficiency, neglect, or malfeasance. The CFPB Director has no boss, peers, or voters to report to. Yet the Director wields vast rulemaking, enforcement, and adjudicatory authority over a significant portion of the U.S. economy. The question before us is whether this arrangement violates the Constitution's separation of powers.

"Our precedents have recognized only two exceptions to the President's unrestricted removal power. In *Humphrey's Executor* we held that Congress could create expert agencies led by a *group* of principal officers removable by the President only for good cause. And in *United States v. Perkins,* 116 U.S. 483 (1886) [which upheld tenure protections for a naval cadet-engineer], and *Morrison* we held that Congress could provide tenure protections to certain *inferior* officers with narrowly defined duties.

"We are now asked to extend these precedents to a new configuration: an independent agency that wields significant executive power and is run by a single individual who cannot be removed by the President unless certain statutory criteria are met. We decline to take that step. While we need not and do not revisit our prior decisions allowing certain limitations on the President's removal power, there are compelling reasons not to extend those precedents to the novel context of an independent agency led by a single Director. Such an agency lacks a foundation in historical practice and clashes with constitutional structure by concentrating power in a unilateral actor insulated from Presidential control."

The Court nonetheless denied relief to the petitioner, a California-based law firm that provided debt-related legal services to clients and that resisted a subpoena from the CFPB on the ground that, in light of the unconstitutional tenure protection for the Director, the agency had no lawful authority. In a portion of his lead opinion joined only by Alito and Kavanaugh, JJ., the Chief Justice rejected petitioner's plea: "The provisions of the Dodd-Frank Act bearing on the CFPB's structure and duties remain fully operative without the offending tenure restriction. Those provisions are capable of functioning independently, and there is nothing in the text or history of the Dodd-Frank Act that demonstrates Congress would have preferred *no* CFPB to a CFPB supervised by the President. Quite the opposite. [The] Dodd-Frank Act contains an express severability clause." Because the Justices who dissented on the merits concurred in the judgment with respect to severability, the petitioner was denied relief but the CFPB Director was rendered subject to removal at will by the President.

THOMAS, J., joined by Gorsuch, J., concurred in the merits: "*Humphrey's Executor* does not comport with the Constitution. [The] Constitution does not permit the creation of officers exercising 'quasi-legislative' and 'quasi-judicial powers' in 'quasi-legislative' and 'quasi-judicial agencies.' No such powers or agencies exist. Congress lacks the authority to delegate its legislative power, and it cannot authorize the use of judicial power by officers acting outside of the bounds of Article III. Nor can Congress create agencies that straddle multiple branches of Government. The Constitution sets out three branches of Government and provides each with a different form of power—legislative, executive, and judicial. [If] any remnant of *Humphrey's Executor* is still standing, it certainly is not enough to justify the numerous, unaccountable independent agencies that currently exercise vast executive power outside the bounds of our constitutional structure."

With respect to the remedy, THOMAS, J., joined by Gorsuch, J., dissented: "The Federal Judiciary does not have the power to excise, erase, alter, or otherwise strike down a statute. And the Court's reference to severability as a 'remedy' is inaccurate. Traditional remedies—like injunctions, declarations, or damages—operate with respect to specific parties, not on legal rules in the abstract [citations and internal quotation marks omitted]."

KAGAN, J., joined by Ginsburg, Breyer, and Sotomayor, JJ., concluded that "*if* the agency's removal provision is unconstitutional, it should be severed," but dissented on the merits: "The majority offers the civics class version of separation of powers—call it the Schoolhouse Rock definition of the phrase. [Yet,] as James Madison stated, the creation of distinct branches 'did not mean that these departments ought to have no partial agency in, or no controul over the acts of each other.' The Federalist No. 47. "[Congress's] choice to put a single director, rather than a multimember commission, at the CFPB's head violates no principle of separation of powers. [To] make sense on the majority's own terms, the distinction between singular and plural agency heads must rest on a theory about why the former more easily 'slip' from the President's grasp. But [the] opposite is more likely to be true: To the extent that such matters are measurable, individuals are easier than groups to supervise."

The Court relied on *Seila Law* in COLLINS v. YELLEN, 141 S.Ct. 1761 (2021), to invalidate the Federal Housing Finance Agency (FHFA), which is tasked by statute with supervising mortgage financing companies Fannie Mae and Freddie Mac. Congress placed the FHFA under a single Director removable by the President only "for cause." ALITO, J., spoke for the Court. Rejecting the contention that the FHFA's limited responsibilities relative to those of the CFPB distinguished *Seila Law*, he wrote that "the nature and breadth of an agency's authority is not dispositive in determining whether Congress may limit the President's power to remove its head. The President's removal power serves vital purposes even when the officer subject to removal is not the head of one of the largest and most powerful agencies."

3. EXECUTIVE PRIVILEGE AND IMMUNITY

UNITED STATES v. NIXON, 418 U.S. 683 (1974), grew out of the burglary of the Democratic national headquarters in the Watergate hotel during the 1972 presidential campaign, by employees of the president's re-election committee. After investigations by the press and a Senate committee revealed involvement by high officials in the Nixon administration, the President authorized appointment of a special prosecutor, who subpoenaed presidential tapes and documents based on an indictment, naming Nixon an unindicted "co-conspirator" and charging seven of his staff and political associates with obstructing justice and other Watergate-related offenses. The Court, per BURGER, C.J., rejected Nixon's claim of executive privilege against the subpoena: "The President's counsel [reads] the Constitution as providing an absolute privilege of confidentiality for all presidential communications. Many decisions of this Court, however, have unequivocally reaffirmed the holding of *Marbury v. Madison* that '[i]t is emphatically the province and duty of the judicial department to say what the law is.' [Notwithstanding] the deference each branch must accord the others, the 'judicial power of the United States' [can] no more be shared with the Executive Branch than the Chief Executive, for example, can share with the judiciary the veto power.

"[T]he President's counsel urges [the] valid need for protection of communications between high government officials and those who advise and assist them in the performance of their manifold duties; the importance of this confidentiality is too plain to require further discussion. Human experience teaches that those who expect public dissemination of their remarks may well temper candor with a concern for appearances and for their own interests to the detriment of the decisionmaking process. Whatever the nature of the privilege of confidentiality of presidential communications in the exercise of Art. II powers, the privilege can be said to derive from the supremacy of each branch within its own assigned area of constitutional duties. Certain powers and privileges flow from the nature of enumerated powers; the protection of the confidentiality of presidential communications has similar constitutional underpinnings. * * *

"However, neither the doctrine of separation of powers, nor the need for confidentiality of high level communications, without more, can sustain an absolute, unqualified presidential privilege of immunity from judicial process under all circumstances. [When] the privilege depends solely on the broad, undifferentiated claim of public interest in the confidentiality of such conversations, a confrontation with other values arises. Absent a claim of need to protect military, diplomatic, or sensitive national security secrets, we find it difficult to accept the argument that even the very important interest in confidentiality of presidential communications is significantly diminished by production of such material for in camera inspection with all the protection that a district court will be obliged to provide.

"The impediment that an absolute, unqualified privilege would place in the way of the primary constitutional duty of the Judicial Branch to do justice in criminal prosecutions would plainly conflict with the function of the courts under Art. III. In designing the structure of our Government [the] Framers [sought] to provide a comprehensive system, but the separate powers were not intended to operate with absolute independence.

"[The need for confidentiality justifies] a presumptive privilege for presidential communications. [But] this presumptive privilege must be considered in light of our historic commitment to the rule of law. [To] ensure that justice is done, it is imperative to the function of courts that compulsory process be available for the production of evidence needed either by the prosecution or by the defense. * * *

"In this case the President [does] not place his claim of privilege on the ground [of] military or diplomatic secrets[, where courts] have traditionally shown the utmost deference to presidential [responsibilities]. No case of the Court [has] extended this high degree of deference to a President's generalized interest in confidentiality. * * *

"The right to the production of all evidence at a criminal trial similarly has constitutional dimensions. The Sixth Amendment explicitly confers upon every defendant in a criminal trial the right 'to be confronted with the witnesses against him' and 'to have compulsory process for obtaining witnesses in his favor.' Moreover, the Fifth Amendment also guarantees that no person shall be deprived of liberty without due process of law. It is the manifest duty of the courts to vindicate those guarantees and to accomplish that it is essential that all relevant and admissible evidence be produced.

"In this case we must weigh the importance of the general privilege of confidentiality of presidential communications in performance of [the President's] responsibilities against the inroads of such a privilege on the fair administration of criminal justice.[19] The interest in preserving confidentiality is weighty indeed and entitled to great respect. However, we cannot conclude that advisers will be moved to temper the candor of their remarks by the infrequent occasions of disclosure because of the possibility that such conversations will be called for in the context of a criminal prosecution.

"On the other hand, [the] constitutional need for production of relevant evidence in a criminal proceeding is specific and central to the fair adjudication of a particular criminal case in the administration of justice. Without access to specific facts a criminal prosecution may be totally frustrated. [The] generalized assertion of privilege must yield to the demonstrated, specific need for evidence in a pending criminal trial."[18]

After his departure from office, President Nixon was sued by Fitzgerald, who claimed that Nixon and White House aides caused him to be fired from his federal job (for "whistle-blowing") in violation of his statutory and constitutional rights. NIXON v. FITZGERALD, 457 U.S. 731 (1982), per POWELL, J., affirmed summary dismissal of the action against Nixon: A President is entitled to *absolute immunity* from "damages liability predicated on his official acts."[27] This immunity is "a functionally mandated incident of the President's unique office, rooted in the constitutional tradition of the separation of powers and supported by our history. [As] is the case with prosecutors and judges—for whom absolute immunity now is established—a President must concern himself with matters likely to 'arouse the most intense feelings.' Yet [it] is in precisely such cases that there exists the greatest public interest in providing an official 'the maximum ability to deal fearlessly and impartially with' the duties of his office [where he] must make the most sensitive and far-reaching decisions entrusted to any official under our constitutional system. [In] view of the special nature of the President's constitutional office and functions, we think it appropriate to recognize absolute Presidential immunity from damages liability for acts within the 'outer perimeter' of his official responsibility. * * *

"A rule of absolute immunity for the President will not leave the Nation without sufficient protection against misconduct on the part of the chief executive. There remains the constitutional remedy of impeachment. In addition, there are formal and informal checks on Presidential action that do not apply with equal force to other executive officials. The President is subjected to constant scrutiny by the press. Vigilant oversight by Congress also may serve to deter Presidential

---

[19]   [Ct's Note] We are not here concerned with the balance between the President's generalized interest in confidentiality and the need for relevant evidence in civil litigation, nor with that between the confidentiality interest and congressional demands for information, nor with the President's interest in preserving state secrets.

[18]   Rehnquist, J., did not participate.

[27]   [Ct's Note] [Our] holding today need only be that the President is absolutely immune from civil damages liability for his official acts in the absence of explicit affirmative action by Congress.

abuses of office, as well as [a] desire to earn re-election, the need to maintain prestige as an element of Presidential influence, and a President's traditional concern for his historical stature."

WHITE, J., joined by Brennan, Marshall and Blackmun, JJ., dissented: "Attaching absolute immunity to the office of the President, rather than to particular activities that the President might perform, places the President above the law. [The] wholesale claim that the President is entitled to absolute immunity in all of his actions stands on no firmer ground than did the claim that all presidential communications are entitled to an absolute privilege *[Nixon I]*. Therefore, whatever may be true of the necessity of such a broad immunity in certain areas of executive responsibility,[30] the only question that must be answered here is whether the dismissal of employees falls within a constitutionally assigned executive function, the performance of which would be substantially impaired by the possibility of a private action for damages. I believe it does not."[19]

———

CLINTON v. JONES, 520 U.S. 681 (1997): An Arkansas state employee, filed a federal civil suit against President Clinton, seeking damages for " 'abhorrent' sexual advances that she vehemently rejected," allegedly made while he was governor of Arkansas. The Court, per STEVENS, J., rejected Clinton's effort to have the suit dismissed without prejudice, and the statute of limitations tolled, until expiration of his term: "Petitioner's strongest argument [relies] on separation of powers. [He] contends that this particular case—as well as the potential additional litigation that [it] may spawn—may impose an unacceptable burden on the President's time and energy, and thereby impair the effective performance of his office. [But this] predictive judgment finds little support in either history or the relatively narrow compass of the issues raised in this particular case. [In] the more than 200-year history of the Republic, only three sitting Presidents have been subjected to suits for their private actions. [It therefore] seems unlikely that a deluge of such litigation will ever engulf the Presidency. As for the case at hand, if properly managed by the District Court, it appears to us highly unlikely to occupy any substantial amount of petitioner's time.

"[We] have long held that when the President takes official action, the Court has the authority to determine whether he has acted within the law. [E.g., *Youngstown*. If] the Judiciary may severely burden the Executive Branch by reviewing the legality of the President's official conduct, and if it may direct appropriate process to the President himself [e.g., *Nixon I*], it must follow that the federal courts have power to determine the legality of his unofficial conduct [including that occurring before he became President.]

---

30   **[Ct's Note]** [A] clear example would be instances in which the President participates in prosecutorial decisions.

19   Blackmun, J., joined by Brennan and Marshall, JJ., also dissented.

"The District Court has broad discretion to stay proceedings as an incident to its power to control its own docket [and] potential burdens on the President [are] appropriate matters for the District Court to evaluate in its management of the case. The high respect that is owed to the Office of the Chief Executive [is] a matter that should inform the conduct of the entire proceeding, including the timing and scope of discovery." Nonetheless, "the proponent of a stay bears the burden of establishing its need." And so far there was "nothing in the record to enable a judge to assess the potential harm that may ensue from scheduling the trial promptly after discovery is concluded."

BREYER, J., concurred in the judgment only, noting that "once the President sets forth and explains a conflict between judicial proceeding and public duties, [the] Constitution permits a judge to schedule a trial in an ordinary civil damages action [only] within the constraints of a constitutional principle [that] forbids a federal judge in such a case to interfere with the President's discharge of his public duties." Breyer, J., was less "sanguine" than the majority that permitting suits against sitting Presidents would not lead to a proliferation of such actions. He would make clear that the Constitution does "not grant a single judge more than a very limited power to second guess a President's reasonable determination (announced in open court) of his scheduling needs."

TRUMP v. VANCE, 140 S.Ct. 2412 (2020), addressed, in a criminal context, a question the Court specifically left open in *Clinton*: whether a sitting President enjoys any kind of immunity in actions in *state* court. A state prosecutor in New York City initiated a wide-ranging investigation and on behalf of a grand jury issued a subpoena *duces tecum* to an accounting firm seeking financial records of President Trump and his businesses beginning six years before and continuing into his presidency. The President argued that he enjoys absolute immunity from state criminal processes while in office. All nine members of the Court rejected the absolute immunity claim.

ROBERTS, C.J., wrote for the Court: "In our judicial system, 'the public has a right to every man's evidence.' Since the earliest days of the Republic, 'every man' has included the President of the United States. Beginning with Jefferson and carrying on through Clinton, Presidents have uniformly testified or produced documents in criminal proceedings when called upon by federal courts. This case involves—so far as we and the parties can tell—the first *state* criminal subpoena directed to a President. The President contends that the subpoena is unenforceable."

Chief Justice Roberts began by describing the long history of federal courts compelling, and of Presidents complying with, subpoenas, with special focus on the treason trial of Aaron Burr, at which Chief Justice Marshall, riding circuit, presided. *See United States v. Burr*, 25 F.Cas. 30 (No. 14,692d) (CC Va. 1807). "Burr moved for a subpoena *duces tecum* directed at Jefferson. [The] prosecution opposed the request, arguing that a President could not be subjected to such a subpoena and that the [document Burr sought] might contain state secrets. [The] President, Marshall declared, does not 'stand exempt from the general provisions of the constitution.' [At] common law the 'single reservation' to the duty to testify in response to a subpoena was 'the case of the king,' whose 'dignity' was seen as 'incompatible' with appearing 'under the process of the court.' But, as Marshall explained, a king is born to power and can 'do no wrong.' The President, by contrast, is 'of the people' and subject to the law. According to Marshall, the sole argument for exempting the President from testimonial obligations was that his 'duties as chief magistrate demand his whole time for national objects.' But, in Marshall's assessment, those demands were 'not unremitting.' And should the President's duties preclude his attendance at a particular time and place, a court could work that out upon return of the subpoena. Marshall also rejected the prosecution's argument that the President was immune from a subpoena *duces tecum* because executive papers might contain state secrets. 'A subpoena duces tecum,' he said, 'may issue to any person to whom an ordinary subpoena may issue.' [In] the two centuries since the Burr trial, successive Presidents have accepted Marshall's ruling that the Chief Executive is subject to subpoena.

"[The President] argues that the Supremacy Clause gives a sitting President absolute immunity from state criminal subpoenas because compliance with those subpoenas would categorically impair a President's performance of his Article II functions. The Solicitor General, arguing on behalf of the United States, agrees with much of the President's reasonin g but does not commit to his bottom line. Instead, the Solicitor General urges us to resolve this case by holding that a state grand jury subpoena for a sitting President's personal records must, at the very least, 'satisfy a heightened standard of need . . . .'

"[The President concedes] that state grand juries are free to investigate a sitting President with an eye toward charging him after the completion of his term. [His] objection therefore must be limited to the *additional* distraction caused by the subpoena itself. But that argument runs up against the 200 years of precedent establishing that Presidents, and their official communications, are subject to judicial process even when the President is under investigation.

"[The] President next claims that the stigma of being subpoenaed will undermine his leadership at home and abroad. Notably, the Solicitor General does not endorse this argument, perhaps because we have twice denied absolute immunity claims by Presidents in cases involving allegations of serious misconduct [citing Presidents Nixon and Clinton].

"[Finally,] the President and the Solicitor General [argue] that, while federal prosecutors are accountable to and removable by the President, the 2,300 district attorneys in this country are responsive to local constituencies, local interests, and local prejudices. [While] we cannot ignore the possibility that state prosecutors may have political motivations, [state and federal law] protect against the predicted abuse. [Moreover, t]he Supremacy Clause prohibits state judges and prosecutors from interfering with a President's official duties. [Any] effort to manipulate a President's policy decisions or to retaliate against a President for official acts through issuance of a subpoena would thus be an unconstitutional attempt to influence a superior sovereign exempt from such obstacles. We generally assume that state courts and prosecutors will observe constitutional limitations. Failing that, federal law allows a President to challenge any allegedly unconstitutional influence in a federal forum, as the President has done here [citations and internal quotation marks omitted].

"[Thus,] we cannot conclude that absolute immunity is necessary or appropriate under Article II or the Supremacy Clause. Our dissenting colleagues agree. [On] that point the Court is unanimous."

The Court next considered "whether a state grand jury subpoena seeking a President's private papers must satisfy a heightened need standard." It rejected such a standard "for three reasons. First, such a heightened standard would extend protection designed for official documents to the President's private papers. [Second,] heightened protection against state subpoenas is [not] necessary for the Executive to fulfill his Article II functions. [If] the state subpoena is not issued to manipulate, the documents themselves are not protected, and the Executive is not impaired, then nothing in Article II or the Supremacy Clause supports holding state subpoenas to a higher standard than their federal counterparts. Finally, in the absence of a need to protect the Executive, the public interest in fair and effective law enforcement cuts in favor of comprehensive access to evidence."

Having rejected the President's and Solicitor General's categorical arguments, the Court allowed the possibility of "subpoena-specific constitutional challenges" and accordingly remanded to the lower courts.

KAVANAUGH, J., joined by Gorsuch, J., concurred in the judgment. Agreeing with the Court's rejection of absolute immunity, he would have applied the "demonstrated, specific need" standard of *Nixon*, which he distinguished from the "heightened need" standard proposed by the Solicitor General: "The *Nixon* standard ensures that a prosecutor's interest in subpoenaed information is sufficiently important to justify an intrusion on the Article II interests of the Presidency [and] reduces the risk of subjecting a President to unwarranted burdens, because it provides that a prosecutor may obtain a President's information only in certain defined circumstances. Although the Court adopted the *Nixon* standard in a different Article II context—there, involving the confidentiality of official, privileged information—[there] are also important Article II (and Supremacy Clause) interests at stake here."

THOMAS, J., also wrote separately in what he styled a dissent, although he agreed with the Court that the President lacks "absolute immunity from *issuance* of the subpoena. But he may be entitled to relief against its *enforcement*. [The] majority recognizes that the President can seek relief from enforcement, but it does not vacate and remand for the lower courts to address this question. I would do so and instruct them to apply the standard articulated by Chief Justice Marshall in

Burr: If the President is unable to comply because of his official duties, then he is entitled to injunctive and declaratory relief."

ALITO, J., also dissented, emphasizing that the President was effectively a target of the investigation. "In *McCulloch v. Maryland* [Ch. 2, Sec. 1], Maryland's sovereign taxing power had to yield, and in a similar way, a State's sovereign power to enforce its criminal laws must accommodate the indispensable role that the Constitution assigns to the Presidency. This must be the rule with respect to a state prosecution of a sitting President. Both the structure of the Government established by the Constitution and the Constitution's provisions on the impeachment and removal of a President make it clear that the prosecution of a sitting President is out of the question.

"If a sitting President were charged in New York County, would he be arrested and fingerprinted? He would presumably be required to appear for arraignment in criminal court, where the judge would set the conditions for his release. Could he be sent to Rikers Island or be required to post bail? Could the judge impose restrictions on his travel? If the President were scheduled to travel abroad— perhaps to attend a G-7 meeting—would he have to get judicial approval? [The] law applies equally to all persons, including a person who happens for a period of time to occupy the Presidency. But there is no question that the nature of the office demands in some instances that the application of laws be adjusted at least until the person's term in office ends.

"I agree with the Court that not all [subpoenas to the President] should be barred. There may be situations in which there is an urgent and critical need for the subpoenaed information. The situation in the Burr trial, where the documents at issue were sought by a criminal defendant to defend against a charge of treason, is a good example. But in a case like the one at hand, a subpoena should not be allowed unless a heightened standard is met."

———

TRUMP v. MAZARS USA, LLP, 140 S.Ct. 2019 (2020), was decided the same day as *Trump v. Vance*. ROBERTS, C.J., again wrote for the Court: "[T]hree committees of the U. S. House of Representatives issued four subpoenas seeking information about the finances of President Donald J. Trump, his children, and affiliated businesses. We have held that the House has authority under the Constitution to issue subpoenas to assist it in carrying out its legislative responsibilities. The House asserts that the financial information sought here— encompassing a decade's worth of transactions by the President and his family— will help guide legislative reform in areas ranging from money laundering and terrorism to foreign involvement in U. S. elections. The President contends that the House lacked a valid legislative aim and instead sought these records to harass him, expose personal matters, and conduct law enforcement activities beyond its authority.

"[The] President's information is sought not by prosecutors or private parties in connection with a particular judicial proceeding, but by committees of Congress that have set forth broad legislative objectives. Congress and the President—the two political branches established by the Constitution—have an ongoing relationship that the Framers intended to feature both rivalry and reciprocity. [Historically], disputes over congressional demands for presidential documents have not ended up in court. Instead, they have been hashed out [politically]." Chief Justice Roberts then described negotiations and compromises reached between Congress and Presidents Washington, Jefferson, Reagan, and Clinton.

"Quoting *Nixon*, the President asserts that the House must establish a 'demonstrated, specific need' for the financial information, just as the Watergate special prosecutor was required to do in order to obtain the tapes. And drawing on *Senate Select Committee on Presidential Campaign Activities v. Nixon*, 498 F.2d 725 (1974)—the D.C. Circuit case refusing to enforce the Senate subpoena for the tapes—the President and the Solicitor General argue that the House must show that the financial information is 'demonstrably critical' to its legislative purpose. We disagree that these demanding standards apply here. Unlike the cases before us, *Nixon* and *Senate Select Committee* involved Oval Office communications over which the President asserted executive privilege. That privilege safeguards the public interest in candid, confidential deliberations within the Executive Branch. [The] standards proposed by the President and the Solicitor General—if applied outside the context of privileged information—would risk seriously impeding Congress in carrying out its responsibilities. The President and the Solicitor General would apply the same exacting standards to *all* subpoenas for the President's information, without recognizing distinctions between privileged and nonprivileged information, between official and personal information, or between various legislative objectives. Such a categorical approach would represent a significant departure from the longstanding way of doing business between the branches, giving short shrift to Congress's important interests in conducting inquiries to obtain the information it needs to legislate effectively.

"[The] House meanwhile would have us ignore that these suits involve the President. Invoking our precedents concerning investigations that did not target the President's papers, the House urges us to uphold its subpoenas because they relate to a valid legislative purpose or concern a subject on which legislation could be had [citations and internal quotation marks omitted]. Far from accounting for separation of powers concerns, the House's approach aggravates them by leaving essentially no limits on the congressional power to subpoena the President's personal records. Any personal paper possessed by a President could potentially 'relate to' a conceivable subject of legislation, for Congress has broad legislative powers that touch a vast number of subjects. The President's financial records could relate to economic reform, medical records to health reform, school transcripts to education reform, and so on. Indeed, at argument, the House was unable to identify *any* type of information that lacks some relation to potential legislation.

"[Congressional] subpoenas for the President's personal information implicate weighty concerns regarding the separation of powers. Neither side, however, identifies an approach that accounts for these concerns. [A] balanced approach is necessary. [First,] courts should carefully assess whether the asserted legislative purpose warrants the significant step of involving the President and his papers. [Congress] may not rely on the President's information if other sources could reasonably provide Congress the information it needs in light of its particular legislative objective. [Second], to narrow the scope of possible conflict between the branches, courts should insist on a subpoena no broader than reasonably necessary to support Congress's legislative objective. [Third], courts should be attentive to the nature of the evidence offered by Congress to establish that a subpoena advances a valid legislative purpose. The more detailed and substantial the evidence of Congress's legislative purpose, the better. [Fourth], courts should be careful to assess the burdens imposed on the President by a subpoena. [Other] considerations may be pertinent as well; one case every two centuries does not afford enough experience for an exhaustive list." The Court remanded for application of the foregoing criteria.

THOMAS, J., dissented: "I would hold that Congress has no power to issue a legislative subpoena for private, nonofficial documents—whether they belong to the President or not. Congress may be able to obtain these documents as part of an investigation of the President, but to do so, it must proceed under the impeachment power."

ALITO, J., also dissented. Although he assumed *arguendo* that Congress may issue a subpoena to the President in the exercise of its legislative powers in some circumstances, he thought the Court's conditions were too permissive. He contended that "the House should provide a description of the type of legislation being considered, and while great specificity is not necessary, the description should be sufficient to permit a court to assess whether the particular records sought are of any special importance. The House should also spell out its constitutional authority to enact the type of legislation that it is contemplating, and it should justify the scope of the subpoenas in relation to the articulated legislative needs. In addition, it should explain why the subpoenaed information, as opposed to information available from other sources, is needed. Unless the House is required to make a showing along these lines, I would hold that enforcement of the subpoenas cannot be ordered."

CHAPTER 4

STATE POWER TO REGULATE

■ ■ ■

Introduction

As discussed in Ch. 2, the Commerce Clause is principally a grant of legislative power to Congress. From the beginning, however, it has been assumed that the grant of authority to Congress necessarily implies a withdrawal of at least some regulatory power from the states, even though the Commerce Clause does not expressly negate state power.[1] This chapter explores the impact of national legislative authority on the states' power to regulate. The focus is on the "dormant Commerce Clause," the term commonly used to refer to the Commerce Clause in cases in which Congress possesses regulatory power but has not exercised it. Since the early nineteenth century, the Supreme Court has invoked the dormant Commerce Clause to invalidate various types of state legislation affecting interstate commerce on the ground that such legislation is incompatible with national interests.

When Congress enacts valid legislation under the Commerce Clause (and thus asserts its power, rather than leaving it "dormant"), there is no doubt that Congress can preclude, displace, or "preempt" state law.

CROSBY v. NATIONAL FOREIGN TRADE COUNCIL, 530 U.S. 363, 372–73 (2000), summarized the relevant principles as follows: "A fundamental principle of the Constitution is that Congress has the power to preempt state law. Art. VI, cl. 2; *Gibbons v. Ogden* [Sec. 1 infra]. Even without an express provision for preemption, we have found that state law must yield to a congressional Act in at least two circumstances. When Congress intends federal law to 'occupy the field,' [all] state law in that area is preempted. And even if Congress has not occupied the field, state law is naturally preempted to the extent of any conflict with a federal statute. We will find preemption where it is impossible for a private party to comply with both state and federal law, and where 'under the circumstances of [a] particular case, [the challenged state law] stands as an obstacle to the accomplishment and execution of the full purposes and objectives of Congress.'" The basic concept of preemption is taken for granted, rather than studied, in the materials that follow.[2] Once the principle is accepted, preemption questions

---

[1]   Except for the special, express limits on tonnage duties and duties on imports and exports. Art. I, § 10.

[2]   For a more extensive introduction, see John F. Manning & Matthew C. Stephenson, *Legislation and Regulation* 284–303 (2d ed. 2013).

essentially involve the interpretation of federal statutes, not the Constitution, and are better addressed in a course on statutory interpretation.

Accepting that valid federal legislation will "preempt" any incompatible state law, this chapter considers issues that arise in contexts in which Congress has the power to legislate but has not done so.

1. STATE REGULATION WHEN CONGRESS'S POWER IS "DORMANT": HISTORY AND FUNDAMENTAL ISSUES

In GIBBONS v. OGDEN (1824), Ch. 2, Sec. 2, I supra, MARSHALL, C.J., in the course of upholding federal regulatory power over interstate navigation and recognizing its preemptive force when exercised, discussed but did not decide whether the grant of commerce power to Congress impliedly excluded all state regulation of interstate and foreign commerce: "In support of [the argument for concurrent or joint federal and state regulatory power] it is said, that [the states] possessed it as an inseparable attribute of sovereignty, before the formation of the constitution, and still retain it, except so far as they have surrendered it by that instrument; that this principle results from the nature of the government, and is secured by the tenth amendment; that an affirmative grant of power is not exclusive, unless in its own nature it be such that the continued exercise of it by the former possessor is inconsistent with the grant, and that this is not of that description.

"The appellant [contends, however], that full power to regulate a particular subject, implies the whole power, and leaves no residuum; that a grant of the whole is incompatible with the existence of a right in another to any part of it.

"[The] grant of the power to lay and collect taxes is, like the power to regulate commerce, made in general terms, [but it] is capable of residing in, and being exercised by, different authorities at the same time. [When], then, each government exercises the power of taxation, neither is exercising the power of the other. But, when a State proceeds to regulate commerce with foreign nations, or among the several States, it is exercising the very power that is granted to Congress, and is doing the very thing which Congress is authorized to do. There is no analogy, then, between the power of taxation and the power of regulating commerce.

"[The] inspection laws are said to be regulations of commerce, and are certainly recognized in the constitution, as being passed in the exercise of a power remaining with the States. That inspection laws may have a remote and considerable influence on commerce, will not be denied; but that a power to regulate commerce is the source from which the right to pass them is derived, cannot be admitted. The object of inspection laws, is to improve the quality of articles produced by the labor of a [country]. They act upon the subject before it becomes an article of foreign commerce, or of commerce among the States, and prepare it for that purpose. They form a portion of that immense mass of legislation, which embraces every thing within the territory of a State, not surrendered to the general government: all which can be most advantageously exercised by the States themselves. Inspection laws, quarantine laws, health laws of every description, as well as laws for regulating the internal commerce of a State, and those which respect turnpike roads, ferries, &c., are component parts of this mass.

"No direct general power over these objects is granted to Congress; and, consequently, they remain subject to State legislation. [It] is obvious, that the government of the Union, in the exercise of its express powers, that, for example, of regulating commerce with foreign nations and among the States, may use means that may also be employed by a State, in the exercise of its acknowledged powers; that, for example, of regulating commerce within the State. [If] a State, in passing laws on subjects acknowledged to be within its control, and with a view to those subjects, shall adopt a measure of the same character with one which Congress may adopt, it does not derive its authority from the particular power which has been granted, but from some other, which remains with the State, and may be executed by the same means. All experience shows, that the same measures, or measures scarcely distinguishable from each other, may flow from distinct powers; but this does not prove that the powers themselves are [identical. The] acknowledged power of a State to regulate its police, its domestic trade, and to govern its own citizens, may enable it to legislate on this subject to a considerable [extent].

"It has been contended by the counsel for the appellant, that, as the word to 'regulate' implies in its nature, full power over the thing to be regulated, it excludes, necessarily, the action of all others that would perform the same operation on the same thing. That regulation is designed for the entire result, applying to those parts which remain as they were, as well as to those which are altered. It produces a uniform whole, which is as much disturbed and deranged by changing what the regulating power designs to leave untouched, as that on which it has operated. There is great force in this argument, and the Court is not satisfied that it has been refuted."

––––––––

An early judicial response to the question of exclusive vs. concurrent power involved an appeal to the states' "police" power—a power not to regulate "commerce" but to protect citizens in ways that might sometimes affect commerce. Invocation of the idea of state police power permitted the Court to uphold state legislation that aimed to achieve permissible goals, even when the legislation had effects on interstate commerce.

WILLSON v. BLACK-BIRD CREEK MARSH CO., 27 U.S. (2 Pet.) 245 (1829), per MARSHALL, C.J., upheld a Delaware statute authorizing a dam that obstructed a small navigable stream, impeding the passage of a boat licensed by the federal navigation laws: "The act of assembly by which the plaintiffs were authorized to construct their dam, shows plainly that this is one of those many creeks, passing through a deep level marsh adjoining the Delaware [River], up which the tide flows for some distance. The value of the property on its banks must be enhanced by excluding the water from the marsh, and the health of the inhabitants probably improved. Measures calculated to produce these objects, provided they do not come into collision with the powers of the general government, are undoubtedly within those [police powers] which are reserved to the states. But the measure authorized by this act stops a navigable creek, and must be supposed to abridge the rights of those who have been accustomed to use it.

"[If] Congress had passed any act which bore upon the case; any act in execution of the power to regulate commerce, the object of which was to control state legislation over those small navigable creeks into which the tide flows, and which abound throughout the lower country of the middle and southern states; we should feel not much difficulty in saying that a state law coming in conflict with such act would be void. But Congress has passed no such act. The repugnancy of the law of Delaware to the constitution is placed entirely on its repugnancy to the power to regulate commerce with foreign nations and among the several states; a power which has not been so exercised as to affect the question.

"We do not think that the act empowering the [company] to place a dam across the creek, can, under all the circumstances of the case, be considered as repugnant to the power to regulate commerce in its dormant state, or as being in conflict with any law passed on the subject."

COOLEY V. BOARD OF WARDENS
53 U.S. (12 How.) 299, 13 L.Ed. 996 (1852).

JUSTICE CURTIS delivered the opinion of the Court.

[The Court upheld Pennsylvania's 1803 law that required ships using the Philadelphia port to hire a local pilot,[3] considered in the light of a 1789 act of Congress providing that harbors and ports of the United States shall "continue to be regulated in conformity with the existing laws of the States [or] with such laws as the States [may] hereafter enact."]

If the Constitution excluded the States from making any law regulating commerce, certainly Congress cannot regrant, or in any manner reconvey to the States that power. And yet this act of 1789 gives its sanction only to laws enacted by the [States]. Entertaining these views we are brought [to the] question, whether the grant of the commercial power to Congress, did *per se* deprive the States of all power to regulate [pilots].

[When] it is said that the nature of the power requires that it should be exercised exclusively by Congress, it must be intended to refer to the subjects of that power, and to say they are of such a nature as to require exclusive legislation

---

[3]   Ships not doing so were required to pay a fee for "the use of the society for the relief of distressed and decayed pilots" and their families.

by Congress. Now the power to regulate commerce, embraces a vast field, containing not only many, but exceedingly various subjects, quite unlike in their nature; some imperatively demanding a single uniform rule, operating equally on the commerce of the United States in every port; and some, like the subject now in question, as imperatively demanding that diversity, which alone can meet the local necessities of navigation.

Either absolutely to affirm, or deny that the nature of this power requires exclusive legislation by Congress, is to lose sight of the nature of the subjects of this power, and to assert concerning all of them, what is really applicable but to a part. Whatever subjects of this power are in their nature national, or admit only of one uniform system, or plan of regulation, may justly be said to be of such a nature as to require exclusive legislation by Congress. That this cannot be affirmed of laws for the regulation of pilots and pilotage is plain. The act of 1789 contains a clear and authoritative declaration by the first Congress, that the nature of this subject is such, that until Congress should find it necessary to exert its power, it should be left to the legislation of the States; that it is local and not national; that it is likely to be the best provided for, not by one system, or plan of regulations, but by as many as the legislative discretion of the several States should deem applicable to the local peculiarities of the ports within their limits.

[The] practice of the States, and of the national government, has been in conformity with this declaration, from the origin of the national government to this time; and the nature of the subject, when examined, is such as to leave no doubt of the superior fitness and propriety, not to say the absolute necessity, of different systems of regulation, drawn from local knowledge and experience, and conformed to local wants. How then can we say, that by the mere grant of power to regulate commerce, the States are deprived of all the power to legislate on this subject, because from the nature of the power the legislation of Congress must be exclusive? * * *4

2. BASIC DOCTRINAL PRINCIPLES AND THEIR APPLICATION

Although the Court, since *Cooley*, has regularly reviewed state legislation for possible conflict with the negative implications of the Commerce Clause, uncertainty and controversy have persisted concerning the standard against which legislation should be tested. Through the nineteenth and into the twentieth century, the *Cooley* distinction between subjects that did and did not require national uniformity was consistently applied to invalidate purposefully discriminatory regulations that favored local interests. However, other applications were less certain. After the turn of the twentieth century, the Court frequently distinguished between "direct" burdens on commerce, which were impermissible, and "indirect" burdens that could be sustained. But observers complained that these labels were conclusory and, what is more, that it had become

---

4   Daniel, J., concurred on other grounds. McLean and Wayne, JJ., dissented.

"difficult, if not impossible" to tell "whether these expressions merely constituted different methods of stating the *Cooley* doctrine, or whether the Court was applying different tests."

In *Di Santo v. Pennsylvania*, 273 U.S. 34, 44 (1927), Stone, J., dissenting, mounted a forceful attack on the direct-indirect "formula." In its place, he suggested a balancing test, under which the validity of a state regulation would depend upon whether "a consideration of all the facts and circumstances, such as the nature of the regulation, its function, the character of the business involved and the actual effect on the flow of commerce, leads to the conclusion that the regulation concerns interests peculiarly local and does not infringe the national interest in maintaining the freedom of commerce across state lines."[5]

Two decades later, the Court adopted a balancing approach in *Southern Pacific Co. v. Arizona*, 325 U.S. 761 (1945), involving a challenge to a state law prohibiting railroad trains of more than 14 passenger or 70 freight cars. In an opinion by Stone, C.J., the Court framed the judicial inquiry as turning on "the nature and extent of the burden which the state regulation of interstate trains, adopted as a safety measure, imposes on interstate commerce, and whether the relative weights of the state and national interests" justify the prohibition.

In the modern era that *Di Santo* and *Southern Pacific* inaugurated, judicial review under the dormant Commerce Clause has occurred within a sharply two-tiered framework. Under it, state regulations that *purposely* or *facially* discriminate against interstate commerce—such as restrictions on the sale of goods imported from other states—are invalid unless supported by an extraordinary justification.

WYOMING v. OKLAHOMA, 502 U.S. 437, 454–55 (1992), formulated this aspect of the doctrine as follows: "[The] 'negative' aspect of the Commerce Clause prohibits economic protectionism—that is, regulatory measures designed to benefit in-state economic interests by burdening out-of-state competitors. When a state statute clearly discriminates against interstate commerce, it will be struck down unless the discrimination is demonstrably justified by a valid factor unrelated to economic protectionism. Indeed, when the state statute amounts to simple economic protectionism, a 'virtually per se rule of invalidity' has applied."

By contrast, when state regulations only "incidentally" (rather than facially or purposefully) restrict the flow of interstate commerce—for example, by regulating containers in which an item of commerce can be marketed, regardless of where it was produced—the Court will balance the national and local interests at stake. The most frequently invoked formulation of the balancing formula was first articulated in PIKE v. BRUCE CHURCH, INC., 397 U.S. 137, 142 (1970): "Where [a state statute] regulates evenhandedly to effectuate a legitimate local public interest, and its effects on interstate commerce are only incidental, it will be upheld unless the burden imposed on such commerce is clearly excessive in relation

---

[5]   Holmes and Brandeis, JJ., joined Stone, J.'s dissent.

to the putative local benefits. If a legitimate local purpose is found, then the question becomes one of degree. And the extent of the burden that will be tolerated [will] depend on the nature of the local interest involved, and on whether it could be promoted as well with a lesser impact on interstate activities."

As you read the cases that follow, consider whether the Court's two-tiered analytical framework, including the balancing test articulated in *Pike*, (i) is constitutionally defensible and (ii) actually describes the Court's processes of decision.

I. STATUTES THAT DISCRIMINATE ON THEIR FACES AGAINST INTERSTATE COMMERCE

BALDWIN V. G.A.F. SEELIG, INC.
294 U.S. 511, 55 S.Ct. 497, 79 L.Ed. 1032 (1935).

JUSTICE CARDOZO delivered the opinion of the Court.

[New York regulated the minimum prices at which producers could sell milk to dealers. It also prohibited the sale in New York of milk bought outside the state at lower prices. The Court held the prohibitions invalid.]

New York has no power to project its legislation into Vermont by regulating the price to be paid in that state for milk acquired there. [It] is equally without power to prohibit the introduction within her territory of milk of wholesome quality acquired in Vermont, whether at high prices or [low]. Accepting those postulates, New York asserts her power to outlaw milk so introduced by prohibiting its sale thereafter if the price that has been paid for it to the farmers of Vermont is less than would be owing in like circumstances to farmers in New York. The importer in that view may keep his milk or drink it, but sell it he may not.

Such a power, if exerted, will set a barrier to traffic between one state and another as effective as if customs duties, equal to the price differential, had been laid upon the thing transported.

[Nice] distinctions [between] direct and indirect burdens [are] irrelevant when the avowed purpose of the obstruction, as well as its necessary tendency, is to suppress or mitigate the consequences of competition between the states. [If] New York, in order to promote the economic welfare of her farmers, may guard them against competition with the cheaper prices of Vermont, the door has been opened to rivalries and reprisals that were meant to be averted by subjecting commerce between the states to the power of the nation.

The argument is pressed upon us, however, that the end to be served by the Milk Control Act is something more than the economic welfare of the farmers. [The] end to be served is the maintenance of a regular and adequate supply of pure and wholesome milk; the supply being put in jeopardy when the farmers of the state are unable to earn a living income. [On] that assumption we are asked to say that intervention will be upheld as a valid exercise by the state of its internal police power, though there is an incidental obstruction to commerce between one state and another. [Let] such an exception be admitted, and all that a state will have to do in times of stress and strain is to say that its farmers and merchants and workmen must be protected against competition from without, lest they go upon the poor relief lists or perish altogether. To give entrance to that excuse would be to invite a speedy end of our national solidarity. The Constitution was framed under the dominion of a political philosophy less parochial in range. It was framed upon the theory that the peoples of the several states must sink or swim together, and that in the long run prosperity and salvation are in union and not division.

[Another argument] seeks to establish [that] farmers who are underpaid will be tempted to save the expense of sanitary precautions. [But] the evils springing from uncared for cattle must be remedied by measures of repression more direct and certain than the creation of a parity of prices between New York and other states. Appropriate certificates may be exacted from farmers in Vermont and elsewhere (*Mintz v. Baldwin*, 289 U.S. 346; *Reid v. Colorado*, 187 U.S. 137); milk may be excluded if necessary safeguards have been omitted; but commerce between the states is burdened unduly when one state regulates by indirection the prices to be paid to producers in another, in the faith that augmentation of prices will lift up the level of economic welfare, and that this will stimulate the observance of sanitary requirements in the preparation of the [product.] Whatever relation there may be between earnings and sanitation is too remote and indirect to justify obstructions to the normal flow of commerce in its movement between states.

[What] is ultimate is the principle that one state in its dealings with another may not place itself in a position of economic isolation. Formulas and catch-words are subordinate to this over-mastering requirement. Neither the power to tax nor the police power may be used by the state of destination with the aim and effect of establishing an economic barrier against competition with the products of another state or the labor of its residents. Restrictions so contrived are an unreasonable clog upon the mobility of commerce. They set up what is equivalent to a rampart of customs duties designed to neutralize advantages belonging to the place of origin. They are thus hostile in conception as well as burdensome in result. The form of the packages in such circumstances is immaterial, whether they are original or broken. The importer must be free from imposts framed for the very purpose of suppressing competition from without and leading inescapably to the suppression so intended. * * *

———

In DEAN MILK CO. v. MADISON, 340 U.S. 349 (1951), the Court addressed a Madison, Wisconsin, ordinance that prohibited the sale of milk not processed at approved pasteurization plants within five miles of Madison's central square. Writing for the Court, Clark, J., found that "reasonable and adequate alternatives are available. If Madison prefers to rely upon its own officials for inspection of distant milk sources, such inspection is readily open to it without hardship for it could charge the actual and reasonable cost of such inspection to the importing producers and processors. [Alternatively, Madison could exclude] milk not produced and pasteurized conformably to standards as high as those enforced by the receiving city." Quoting *Baldwin*, the Court therefore concluded that "the regulation must yield to the principle that 'one state in its dealings with another may not place itself in a position of economic isolation.'"

The Court added in a footnote: "It is immaterial that Wisconsin milk from outside the Madison area is subjected to the same proscription as that moving in interstate commerce."

Black, J., joined by Douglas and Minton, JJ., dissented. The dissent argued that "[n]either of the alternatives suggested by the Court would assure the people of Madison as pure a supply of milk as they receive under their own ordinance." Further, the dissent critiqued the "reasonable alternatives" approach: "[W]hile the "reasonable alternative" concept has been invoked to protect First Amendment rights, [it] has not heretofore been considered an appropriate weapon for striking down local health laws. [In] my view, to use this ground now elevates the right to traffic in commerce for profit above the power of the people to guard the purity of their daily diet of [milk]."

PHILADELPHIA V. NEW JERSEY
437 U.S. 617, 98 S.Ct. 2531, 57 L.Ed.2d 475 (1978).

JUSTICE STEWART delivered the opinion of the Court.

[Operators of New Jersey landfills, and out-of-state cities that had agreements with them for waste disposal, brought a Commerce Clause challenge against Ch. 363, N.J.Laws, 1973, which provided: "No person shall bring into this State any solid or liquid waste which originated or was collected outside [the] State." The New Jersey Supreme Court upheld the statute, ruling that it advanced vital health and environmental objectives with no economic discrimination against interstate commerce and that its substantial benefits outweighed its "slight" burden on interstate commerce. The Supreme Court reversed.]

[The] New Jersey Supreme Court questioned whether the interstate movement of [wastes] is "commerce" at all within the meaning of the Commerce Clause. [All] objects of interstate trade merit Commerce Clause protection; none is excluded by definition at the outset. [Just] as Congress has power to regulate the interstate movement of these wastes, States are not free from constitutional scrutiny when they restrict that movement.

[The] opinions of the Court through the years have reflected an alertness to the evils of "economic isolation" and protectionism, while at the same time recognizing that incidental burdens on interstate commerce may be unavoidable when a State legislates to safeguard the health and safety of its people. Thus, where simple economic protectionism is effected by state legislation, a virtually per se rule of invalidity has been erected. See, e.g., *Baldwin*. [But] where other legislative objectives are credibly advanced and there is no patent discrimination against interstate trade, the Court has adopted a much more flexible approach, the general contours of which were outlined in [*Pike*]. [The] crucial inquiry, therefore, must be directed to determining whether ch. 363 is basically a protectionist measure, or whether it can fairly be viewed as a law directed to legitimate local concerns, with effects upon interstate commerce that are only incidental.

The purpose of ch. 363 is set out in the [statute]: "The Legislature finds and determines that [the] volume of solid and liquid waste continues to rapidly increase, that the treatment and disposal of these wastes continues to pose an even greater threat to the quality of the environment of New Jersey, that the available and appropriate landfill sites within the State are being diminished, that the environment continues to be threatened by the treatment and disposal of waste which originated or was collected outside the State." [The] state court additionally found that New Jersey's existing landfill sites will be exhausted within a few years; that to go on using these sites or to develop new ones will take a heavy environmental [toll;] that new techniques to divert waste from landfills to other methods of disposal and resource recovery processes are under development, but that these changes will require time; and finally, that "the extension of the lifespan of existing landfills, resulting from the exclusion of out-of-state waste, may be of crucial importance in preventing further virgin wetlands or other undeveloped lands from being devoted to landfill purposes."

[The] dispute about ultimate legislative purpose need not be resolved, because [the] evil of protectionism can reside in legislative means as well as legislative ends. Thus, it does not matter whether the ultimate aim of ch. 363 is to reduce the waste disposal costs of New Jersey residents or to save remaining open lands from pollution, for we assume New Jersey has every right to protect its residents' pocketbooks as well as their environment. And it may be assumed as well that New Jersey may pursue those ends by slowing the flow of *all* waste into the State's remaining landfills, even though interstate commerce may incidentally be affected. But whatever New Jersey's ultimate purpose, it may not be accomplished by discriminating against articles of commerce coming from outside the State unless there is some reason, apart from their origin, to treat them differently. Both on its face and in its plain effect, ch. 363 violates this principle of nondiscrimination.

[Also] relevant here are the Court's decisions holding that a State may not accord its own inhabitants a preferred right of access over consumers in other States to natural resources located within its borders. [E.g.,] *West v. Kansas Natural Gas Co.*, 221 U.S. 229 (1911). [On] its face, [the New Jersey law] imposes on out-of-state commercial interests the full burden of conserving the State's remaining landfill space. It is true that in our previous cases the scarce natural resource was itself the article of commerce, whereas here the scarce resource and the article of commerce are distinct. But that difference is without consequence. In both instances, the State has overtly moved to slow or freeze the flow of commerce for protectionist reasons. It does not matter that the State has shut the article of commerce inside the State in one case and outside the State in the other. What is crucial is the attempt by one State to isolate itself from a problem common to many by erecting a barrier against the movement of interstate trade.

[It] is true that certain quarantine laws have not been considered forbidden protectionist measures, even though they were directed against out-of-state commerce. But those quarantine laws banned the importation of articles such as diseased livestock that required destruction as soon as possible because their very movement risked contagion and other evils. Those laws thus did not discriminate against interstate commerce as such, but simply prevented traffic in noxious articles, whatever their origin.

The New Jersey statute is not such a quarantine law. There has been no claim here that the very movement of waste into or through New Jersey endangers health, or that waste must be disposed of as soon and as close to its point of generation as possible. The harms caused by waste are said to arise after its disposal in landfill sites, and at that point, as New Jersey concedes, there is no basis to distinguish out-of-state waste from domestic waste. If one is inherently harmful, so is the other. Yet New Jersey has banned the former while leaving its landfill sites open to the latter. The New Jersey law blocks the importation of waste in an obvious effort to saddle those outside the State with the entire burden of slowing the flow of refuse into New Jersey's remaining landfill sites. That legislative effort is clearly impermissible under the Commerce Clause of the Constitution.

Today, cities in Pennsylvania and New York find it expedient or necessary to send their waste into New Jersey for disposal, and New Jersey claims the right to close its borders to such traffic. Tomorrow, cities in New Jersey may find it expedient or necessary to send their waste into Pennsylvania or New York for disposal, and those States might then claim the right to close their borders. The Commerce Clause will protect New Jersey in the future, just as it protects her neighbors now, from efforts by one State to isolate itself in the stream of interstate commerce from a problem shared by all.

JUSTICE REHNQUIST, with whom CHIEF JUSTICE BURGER joins, dissenting.

[New] Jersey should be free under our past precedents to prohibit the importation of solid waste because of the health and safety problems that such waste poses to its citizens. The fact that New Jersey continues to, and indeed must continue to, dispose of its own solid waste does not mean that New Jersey may not prohibit the importation of even more solid waste into the State.

[I] do not see why a State may ban the importation of items whose movement risks contagion, but cannot ban the importation of items which, although they may be transported into the State without undue hazard, will then simply pile up in an ever increasing danger to the public's health and safety. The Commerce Clause was not drawn with a view to having the validity of state laws turn on such pointless distinctions.

[T]hat New Jersey has left its landfill sites open for domestic waste does not, of course, mean that solid waste is not innately harmful. Nor does it mean that New Jersey prohibits importation of solid waste for reasons other than the health and safety of its population. New Jersey must out of sheer necessity treat and dispose of its solid waste in some fashion, just as it must treat New Jersey cattle suffering from hoof-and-mouth disease. It does not follow that New Jersey must, under the Commerce Clause, accept solid waste or diseased cattle from outside its borders and thereby exacerbate its problems. * * *

————

With *Philadelphia*, compare MAINE v. TAYLOR, 477 U.S. 131 (1986), per BLACKMUN, J., upheld a Maine law that prohibited importation into Maine of live baitfish that competed with Maine's native baitfish industry. The Court relied on two district court findings: (1) "Maine 'clearly has a legitimate and substantial purpose in prohibiting the importation of live bait fish' because 'substantive uncertainties' surrounded the effects that baitfish parasites would have on the State's unique population of wild fish, and the consequences of introducing non-native species were similarly unpredictable"; and (2) "less discriminatory means of protecting against these threats were currently unavailable" despite the "abstract possibility" of developing acceptable testing procedures in the future. The Court added:

"[A] State must make reasonable efforts to avoid restraining the free flow of commerce across its borders, but it is not required to develop new and unproven means of protection at an uncertain cost. Appellee, of course, is free to work on his own or in conjunction with other bait dealers to develop scientifically acceptable sampling and inspection procedures for golden shiners; if and when such procedures are developed, Maine no longer may be able to justify its import ban. The State need not join in those efforts, however, and it need not pretend they already have succeeded.

"[The] evidence in this case amply supports the District Court's findings that Maine's ban on the importation of live baitfish serves legitimate local purposes that could not adequately be served by available nondiscriminatory alternatives. This is not a case of arbitrary discrimination against interstate commerce; the record suggests that Maine has legitimate reasons, 'apart from their origin, to treat [out-of-state baitfish] differently,' *Philadelphia*."

STEVENS, J., dissented, contending that "uncertainty" and "[a]mbiguity about dangers and alternatives should actually defeat, rather than sustain, the discriminatory measure." His summary: "There is something fishy about this case."

————

SPORHASE v. NEBRASKA, 458 U.S. 941 (1982), per STEVENS, J., held invalid a Nebraska law requiring denial of a permit to withdraw and transport water for use in an adjoining state unless that state "grants reciprocal rights" to withdraw and transport its water for use in Nebraska. Rejecting an earlier precedent,[6] the Court ruled that ground water is an "article of commerce," requiring Commerce Clause analysis of state laws restricting its transfer to other states: "[Because] Colorado forbids the exportation of its ground water, the reciprocity provision operates as an explicit barrier to commerce between the two states. [Nebraska] therefore bears the initial burden of demonstrating a close fit between the reciprocity requirement and its asserted local purpose. [The] reciprocity requirement does not survive the 'strictest scrutiny' reserved for facially discriminatory legislation."

TENNESSEE WINE AND SPIRITS RETAILERS ASS'N v. TENNESSEE ALCOHOLIC BEVERAGE COMM'N, 139 S.Ct. 2449 (2019), invalidated a Tennessee statute that imposed a two-year duration-of-residency requirement for licenses to own and operate liquor stores. Writing for a 7–2 majority, ALITO, J., began by noting recent criticisms of dormant Commerce Clause doctrine, but he responded by citing original historical expectations that the Constitution would provide "protection against a broad swathe of state protectionist measures." Within the existing doctrinal framework, Tennessee's principal defense of its discriminatory residency test rested on § 2 of the Twenty-first Amendment, which provides that "[t]he transportation or importation into any State, Territory, or possession of the United States for delivery or use therein of intoxicating liquors, in violation of the laws thereof, is hereby prohibited." Despite some early judicial suggestions that § 2 gave the states plenary control over all matters involving alcohol, the Court had subsequently recognized that it must "scrutinize state alcohol laws for compliance with many constitutional provisions," including the First and Fourteenth Amendments. With respect to the dormant Commerce Clause, examination of relevant history "convince[s] us that the aim of § 2 was not to give states a free hand to restrict the importation of alcohol." GORSUCH, J., joined by THOMAS, J., dissented: "[T]hose who ratified the [Twenty-first] Amendment wanted the States to be able to regulate the sale of liquor free of judicial meddling under the dormant Commerce Clause."

II. CONGRESSIONAL AUTHORIZATION OF STATE REGULATION

Cooley v. Board of Wardens, Sec. 1, supra, assumed that "Congress cannot regrant" regulatory power to the states once the power of regulation has been given to Congress under the Commerce Clause. But *Cooley* was not the Court's last word.

PRUDENTIAL INS. CO. v. BENJAMIN, 328 U.S. 408 (1946), per RUTLEDGE, J., upheld Congress's power to authorize state taxes that discriminate against interstate commerce and thereby insulate such taxes from challenge under the dormant Commerce Clause:[7] "Prudential chiefly relies [on] cases which have

---

6   *Hudson County Water Co. v. McCarter*, 209 U.S. 349 (1908).

7   *Prudential* upheld a South Carolina statute that imposed a tax on gross insurance premiums from South Carolina businesses but exempted South Carolina insurance companies.

outlawed state taxes found to discriminate against interstate commerce. [Those cases] presented no question of the validity of such a tax where Congress had taken affirmative action consenting to it or purporting to give it validity.

"[In] all the variations of Commerce Clause theory it has never been the law that what the states may do in the regulation of commerce, Congress being silent, is the full measure of its power. Much less has this boundary been thought to confine what Congress and the states acting together may [accomplish].

"[The] cases most important for the decision in this cause [are] the ones involving situations where the silence of Congress or the dormancy of its power has been taken judicially, [as] forbidding state action, only to have Congress later disclaim the prohibition or undertake to nullify it. Not yet has this Court held such a disclaimer invalid or that state action supported by it could not stand. On the contrary, in each instance it has given effect to the congressional judgment contradicting its own previous one.

"[The McCarran Act] was a determination by Congress that state taxes, which in its silence might be held invalid as discriminatory, do not place on interstate insurance business a burden which it is unable generally to bear or should not bear in the competition with local business. Such taxes were not uncommon among the states, and the statute clearly included South Carolina's tax now in issue.

"That judgment was one of policy and reflected long and clear experience. For, notwithstanding the long incidence of the tax and its payment by Prudential without question prior to the *South-Eastern* decision, the record of Prudential's continuous success in South Carolina over decades refutes any idea that payment of the tax handicapped it in any way tending to exclude it from competition with local business or with domestic insurance companies.

"[This] broad authority [over commerce] Congress may exercise alone [or] in conjunction with coordinated action by the states, in which case limitations imposed for the preservation of their powers become inoperative and only those designed to forbid action altogether by any power or combination of powers in our governmental system remain effective. Here both Congress and South Carolina have acted, and in complete coordination, to sustain the tax. It is therefore reinforced by the exercise of all the power of government residing in our scheme. [Congress and the states] were not forbidden to cooperate or by doing so to achieve legislative consequences, particularly in the great fields of regulating commerce and taxation, which, to some extent at least, neither could accomplish in isolated exertion."

The Court ruled that Congress had authorized such taxes by the McCarran Act, which made insurance companies subject to state taxes and regulations after *United States v. South-Eastern Underwriters Ass'n*, 322 U.S. 533 (1944), had given rise to doubts about state power over interstate insurance business.

Although Congress can waive impediments to state discrimination under the Commerce Clause, Congress cannot waive individual rights to be free from discrimination under the Privileges and Immunities Clause of Art. IV, see Sec. 4 of this chapter, or the Equal Protection Clause of the Fourteenth Amendment, see Ch. 9. The leading equal protection case on state protectionism, METROPOLITAN LIFE INS. CO. v. WARD, 470 U.S. 869 (1985), per POWELL, J., struck down a discriminatory state tax on out-of-state insurance companies under the Equal Protection Clause, notwithstanding the statute's immunity from attack on dormant Commerce Clause grounds under the McCarran Act and *Prudential Ins. Co.*

Although *Metropolitan Life Ins.* makes clear that Congress cannot authorize equal protection violations, a leading commentator describes the case as an "aberration" in finding that state legislation discriminating against out-of-state businesses violates the Equal Protection Clause. Tribe 2d ed., at 526 n.34. Compare *Northeast Bancorp, Inc. v. Board of Governors*, 472 U.S. 159, 172–73 (1985) (holding that Congress had authorized Massachusetts and Connecticut laws imposing reciprocity requirements on out-of-state banks that seek to acquire in-state banks and that the laws were not violations of the Equal Protection Clause).

III. DISCRIMINATORY STATUTES THAT FAVOR GOVERNMENTAL RATHER THAN PRIVATE ENTITIES

UNITED TRASH HAULERS ASS'N V. ONEIDA-HERKIMER SOLID WASTE MANAGEMENT AUTH.
550 U.S. 330, 127 S.Ct. 1786, 167 L.Ed.2d 655 (2007).

CHIEF JUSTICE ROBERTS delivered the opinion of the Court, except as to Part II-D.[8]

[In the 1980s, Oneida and Herkimer Counties in New York faced a "solid waste crisis." The counties had uneasy relationships with local waste processors, who were infiltrated by organized crime elements that chronically fixed prices and drastically overcharged. Further, local landfills were operating without permits and violating state regulations, thereby causing environmental damage and costing the public tens of millions of dollars. In response, the State of New York created the Oneida-Herkimer Solid Waste Management Authority and authorized the Counties to impose "appropriate and reasonable limitations on competition." In 1989, the Counties enacted "flow control" ordinances requiring that all solid waste collected within the counties be delivered to the Authority for processing. A trade association of solid waste management companies sued, alleging that the flow control ordinance violated the dormant Commerce Clause by discriminating against interstate commerce.]

---

[8]   Souter, Ginsburg, and Breyer, JJ., joined in Part II-D.

"Flow control" ordinances require trash haulers to deliver solid waste to a particular waste processing facility. [As the Court pointed out in *C & A Carbone, Inc. v. Clarkstown*, 511 U.S. 383 (1994), "what makes garbage a profitable business is not its own worth but the fact that its possessor must pay to get rid of it. In other words, the article of commerce is not so much the solid waste itself, but rather the service of processing and disposing of it. In] this case, we face flow control ordinances quite similar to the one invalidated in *Carbone*[, which involved mandated delivery to a private processing facility with close links to the town]. The only salient difference is that the laws at issue here require haulers to bring waste to facilities owned and operated by a state-created public benefit corporation. We find this difference constitutionally significant. Disposing of trash has been a traditional government activity for years, and laws that favor the government in such areas [do not] discriminate against interstate commerce for purposes of the Commerce Clause.

[II-C.] The flow control ordinances in this case benefit a clearly public facility, while treating all private companies exactly the same. Because the question is now squarely presented on the facts of the case before us, we decide that such flow control ordinances do not discriminate against interstate commerce for purposes of the dormant Commerce Clause.

Compelling reasons justify treating these laws differently from laws favoring particular private businesses over their competitors. Conceptually, of course, any notion of discrimination assumes a comparison of substantially similar entities. But States and municipalities are not private businesses—far from it. Unlike private enterprise, government is vested with the responsibility of protecting the health, safety, and welfare of its citizens. These important responsibilities set state and local government apart from a typical private business.

[As] our local processing cases demonstrate, when a law favors in-state business over out-of-state competition, rigorous scrutiny is appropriate because the law is often the product of "simple economic protectionism." Laws favoring local government, by contrast, may be directed toward any number of legitimate goals unrelated to protectionism. Here the flow control ordinances enable the Counties to pursue particular policies with respect to the handling and treatment of waste generated in the Counties, while allocating the costs of those policies on citizens and businesses according to the volume of waste they generate.

[The] dormant Commerce Clause is not a roving license for federal courts to decide what activities are appropriate for state and local government to undertake, and what activities must be the province of private market competition. [It] is not the office of the Commerce Clause to control the decision of the voters on whether government or the private sector should provide waste management services. "The Commerce Clause significantly limits the ability of States and localities to regulate or otherwise burden the flow of interstate commerce, but it does not elevate free trade above all other values." *Maine v. Taylor*.

We should be particularly hesitant to interfere with the Counties' efforts under the guise of the Commerce Clause because [w]aste disposal is both typically and traditionally a local government function. [The policy] of the State of New York favors "displac[ing] competition with regulation or monopoly public control" in this area. We may or may not agree with that approach, but nothing in the Commerce Clause vests the responsibility for that policy judgment with the Federal Judiciary.

Finally, it bears mentioning that the most palpable harm imposed by the ordinances—more expensive trash removal—is likely to fall upon the very people who voted for the laws. Our dormant Commerce Clause cases often find discrimination when a State shifts the costs of regulation to other States. [Here,] the citizens and businesses of the Counties bear the costs of the ordinances. There is no reason to step in and hand local businesses a victory they could not obtain through the political process.

We hold that the Counties' flow control ordinances, which treat in-state private business interests exactly the same as out-of-state ones, do not discriminate against interstate commerce for purposes of the dormant Commerce Clause.

[II-D] [In a section joined only by Souter, Ginsburg, and Breyer, JJ., Chief Justice Roberts proceeded to analyze the Counties' flow-control ordinance under the *Pike* balancing test, quoted in the Introduction to this Section. The trial court] could not detect any disparate impact on out-of-state as opposed to in-state businesses. [Yet the ordinances deliver public benefits by increasing] recycling in at least two ways. [First,] they create enhanced incentives for recycling and proper disposal of other kinds of waste. [Second,] by requiring all waste to be deposited at Authority facilities, the Counties have markedly increased their ability to enforce recycling laws. If the haulers could take waste to any disposal site, achieving an equal level of enforcement would be much more costly, if not impossible. For these reasons, any arguable burden the ordinances impose on interstate commerce does not exceed their public benefits.

JUSTICE SCALIA, concurring in part.

I join Part I and Parts II-A through II-C of the Court's opinion. I write separately to reaffirm my view that the so-called "negative" Commerce Clause is an unjustified judicial invention, not to be expanded beyond its existing domain. The historical record provides no grounds for reading the Commerce Clause to be other than what it says—an authorization for Congress to regulate commerce. I have been willing to enforce on *stare decisis* grounds a "negative" self-executing Commerce Clause in two situations: (1) against a state law that facially discriminates against interstate commerce, and (2) against a state law that is indistinguishable from a type of law previously held unconstitutional by this Court. As today's opinion makes clear, the flow-control law at issue in this case meets neither condition.

[I] am unable to join Part II-D of the principal opinion, in which the plurality performs so-called "*Pike* balancing." Generally speaking, the balancing of various values is left to Congress—which is precisely what the Commerce Clause (the real Commerce Clause) envisions.

JUSTICE THOMAS, concurring in the judgment.

I concur in the judgment. Although I joined [*Carbone*], I no longer believe it was correctly decided. The negative Commerce Clause has no basis in the Constitution and has proved unworkable in practice. As the debate between the majority and dissent shows, application of the negative Commerce Clause turns solely on policy considerations, not on the Constitution. Because this Court has no policy role in regulating interstate commerce, I would discard the Court's negative Commerce Clause jurisprudence.

JUSTICE ALITO, with whom JUSTICE STEVENS and JUSTICE KENNEDY join, dissenting.

This case cannot be meaningfully distinguished from *Carbone.* As the Court itself acknowledges, "[t]he only salient difference" between the cases is that the ordinance invalidated in *Carbone* discriminated in favor of a privately owned facility, whereas the laws at issue here discriminate in favor of facilities owned and operated by a state-created public benefit corporation. The Court relies on the distinction between public and private ownership to uphold the flow-control laws, even though a straightforward application of *Carbone* would lead to the opposite result. The public-private distinction drawn by the Court is both illusory and without precedent.

[The] only real difference between the facility at issue in *Carbone* and its counterpart in this case is that title to the former had not yet formally passed to the municipality. The Court exalts form over substance in adopting a test that turns on this technical distinction[.]

[I] see no basis for the Court's assumption that discrimination in favor of an in-state facility owned by the government is likely to serve legitimate goals unrelated to protectionism. Discrimination in favor of an in-state government facility serves local economic interests, inuring to the benefit of local residents who are employed at the facility, local businesses that supply the facility with goods and services, and local workers employed by such businesses. It is therefore surprising to read in the opinion of the Court that state discrimination in favor of a state-owned business is not likely to be motivated by economic protectionism.

[Proper] analysis under the dormant Commerce Clause involves more than an inquiry into whether the challenged Act is in some sense directed toward [legitimate] goals unrelated to protectionism; equally important are the means by which those goals are realized. If the chosen means take the form of a statute that discriminates against interstate commerce—either on its face or in practical effect—then "the burden falls on [the enacting government] to demonstrate both that the statute 'serves a legitimate local purpose,' and that this purpose could not be served as well by available nondiscriminatory means." *Maine v. Taylor.*

[T]hese laws discriminate against interstate commerce (generally favoring local interests over nonlocal interests), but are defended on the ground that they serve legitimate goals unrelated to protectionism (e.g., health, safety, and protection of the environment). And while I do not question that the laws at issue in this case serve legitimate goals, the laws offend the dormant Commerce Clause because those goals could be attained effectively through nondiscriminatory means.

The Court next suggests that deference to legislation discriminating in favor of a municipal landfill is especially appropriate considering that [w]aste disposal is both typically and traditionally a local government function. I disagree on two grounds.

First, this Court has previously recognized that any standard "that turns on a judicial appraisal of whether a particular governmental function is 'integral' or 'traditional' " is "unsound in principle and unworkable in practice." *Garcia v. San Antonio Metropolitan Transit Authority*, Ch. 2, Sec. 5, IV supra. [Second,] most of the garbage in this country is still managed by the private sector. In that respect, the Court is simply mistaken in concluding that waste disposal is "typically" a local government function.

Equally unpersuasive is the Court's suggestion that the flow-control laws do not discriminate against interstate commerce because they treat in-state private business interests exactly the same as out-of-state ones. [T]his Court has long recognized that a burden imposed by a State upon interstate commerce is not to be sustained simply because the statute imposing it applies alike to the people of all the States, including the people of the State enacting such statute.

———

DEPARTMENT OF REV. v. DAVIS, 553 U.S. 328 (2008), per SOUTER, J., upheld a Kentucky income tax statute that exempted interest on bonds issued by Kentucky and its political subdivisions, but not on bonds issued by other states or their local governments: "Municipal bonds currently finance roughly two-thirds of capital expenditures by state and local governments [and] by the turn of the millennium, over '$1.5 trillion in municipal bonds were outstanding.' Differential tax schemes like Kentucky's have a long pedigree, too. [Today], 41 states have laws like the one before us.

"It follows a fortiori from *United Haulers* that Kentucky must prevail. In *United Haulers,* we explained that a government function is not susceptible to standard dormant Commerce Clause scrutiny owing to its likely motivation by legitimate objectives distinct from the simple economic protectionism the Clause abhors. [In] fact, this emphasis on the public character of the enterprise supported by the tax preference is just a step in addressing a fundamental element of dormant Commerce Clause jurisprudence, the principle that 'any notion of discrimination assumes a comparison of substantially similar entities.' [Viewed] through this lens, the Kentucky tax scheme parallels the ordinance upheld in *United Haulers:* it 'benefit[s] a clearly public [issuer, that is, Kentucky and its municipalities], while treating all private [issuers] exactly the same.' There is no forbidden discrimination because Kentucky, as a public entity, does not have to treat itself as being 'substantially similar' to the other bond issuers in the market."

Having found no forbidden discrimination, Souter, J., also concluded that the balancing test of *Pike v. Bruce Church, Inc.*, did not apply because "the current record and scholarly material convince us that the Judicial Branch is not institutionally suited to draw reliable conclusions of the kind that would be necessary." For example, the Court was not well situated to predict whether national capital markets would accommodate the bonds issued by smaller municipalities in the absence of tax benefits for in-state purchasers or whether "capital [would] to some degree simply dry up, eliminating a class of municipal improvements. [What] is most significant about these cost-benefit questions is not even the difficulty of answering them or the inevitable uncertainty of the predictions that might be made in trying to come up with answers, but the unsuitability of the judicial process and judicial forums for making whatever predictions and reaching whatever answers are possible at all."

Stevens, J., filed a concurring opinion. Roberts, C.J., and Scalia, J., also declined to join parts of the majority opinion. Thomas, J., concurred in the judgment only, on the ground that the Court's dormant Commerce Clause jurisprudence lacked constitutional foundations and should be abandoned altogether.

KENNEDY, J., joined by Alito, J., dissented: "The Court holds the Kentucky law is valid because bond issuance fulfills a public function [but] the premise is wrong. The law in question operates on those who hold the bonds and trade them, not those who issue them." Moreover, even if the case were about bond issuance rather than taxation, "the discrimination against interstate commerce would be too plain and prejudicial to be sustained. [A] state has no authority to use its taxing power to erect local barriers to out-of-state goods or commodities. Nothing in our cases even begins to suggest this rule is inapplicable simply because the State uses a discriminatory tax to favor its own enterprise."

Kennedy, J., thought that the Court's reliance on *United Haulers* was misplaced, for the ordinance upheld there "applied equally to interstate and in-state commerce. [Nondiscrimination], not just state involvement, was central to the rationale."

IV. STATUTES THAT DO NOT DISCRIMINATE ON THEIR FACES BUT NEVERTHELESS BURDEN INTERSTATE COMMERCE

As noted above, at least since the 1945 decision in *Southern Pacific Co. v. Arizona*, 325 U.S. 761, the Court has said that it will apply some form of balancing test to gauge the permissibility under the Commerce Clause of state legislation that does not discriminate on its face and has a legitimate local purpose but "incidentally" burdens interstate commerce. An example, suggested above in the Notes and Questions following *Baldwin v. Seelig*, would be a state law that forbade the in-state sale of milk produced by cattle that had been fed a hormone deemed dangerous to human health by the state legislature. If the statute were challenged by milk producers in other states, a balancing test would apply. If one asks why, it may be important that, in nearly all dormant Commerce Clause cases that do not involve a facial discrimination against interstate commerce, the challenged statute has had a "discriminatory effect": It has imposed greater burdens on out-of-state than on in-state interests or enterprises—as the imagined statute regulating the sale of milk from hormone-fed cattle would have if most or all dairy farmers in the state that imposed the rule did not feed their cows the allegedly suspect hormone but if many farmers in other states did.

In cases of this kind, a loosely connected family of "process-based" theories attempts to build on the insight of Stone, J.'s famous footnote four in *United States v. Carolene Products*, Ch. 5, Sec. 3 infra: although courts should generally not reweigh policy judgments made by legislatures, the presumption that legislatures should be trusted to make such judgments dissolves when affected interests are not fairly represented in a state's political process—making them analogous to members of "discrete and insular minorities." This concern with the fairness of the states' political processes also echoes through much of the case law. See Tribe 3d ed., at 1052, citing *Southern Pacific*: "Because regulation unduly burdening or discriminating against interstate or foreign commerce or out-of-state enterprise has been thought to result from the inherently limited constituency to which each state or local legislature is accountable, the [Court] has viewed with suspicion any state action which imposes special or distinct burdens on out-of-state interests unrepresented in the state's political process."

As you study the cases in this Part, consider whether the Court's balancing methodology is consistent and principled—or whether, as Scalia, J., has argued,[9] the Court should, and typically has, invalidated state legislation only when it believes that the legislature had an impermissibly protectionist purpose of aiding local economic actors at the expense of their out-of-state competitors.

———

BREARD v. ALEXANDRIA, 341 U.S. 622 (1951), per REED, J., upheld, over a Commerce Clause claim, an ordinance forbidding door-to-door soliciting of orders for the sale of merchandise other than food, as applied to Breard and his crew of sales persons seeking subscriptions to out-of-state magazines.[10] The Court viewed the ordinance as protecting an important social interest in residential privacy: "Unwanted knocks on the door by day or night are a nuisance, or worse, to peace and quiet. [As] the exigencies of trade are not ordinarily expected to have a higher rating constitutionally than the tranquillity of the fireside, responsible municipal

---

9   See *Bendix Autolite Corp. v. Midwesco Enterprises, Inc.* infra.
10   The Court also denied a freedom of the press claim.

officers have sought a way to curb the annoyances while preserving complete freedom for desirable visitors to the homes." No less restrictive alternative was available. "The idea of barring classified salesmen from homes by means of notices posted by individual householders was rejected early as less practical than an ordinance regulating solicitors."

Although acknowledging that "the local retail merchant [has] not been unmindful of the effective competition furnished by house-to-house selling" and recognizing "the importance to publishers of our many periodicals" of house-to-house solicitation, the Court found it constitutionally adequate that the "usual methods of seeking business are left open by the ordinance." "That such methods do not produce as much business as house-to-house canvassing is, constitutionally, [immaterial.] Taxation that threatens interstate commerce with prohibition or discrimination is bad, but regulation that leaves out-of-state sellers on the same basis as local sellers cannot be invalid for that reason."

The Court was "not willing even to appraise the suggestion, unsupported in the record, that [widespread use of comparable ordinances] springs predominantly from the selfish influence of local merchants. [When] there is a reasonable basis for legislation to protect the social, as distinguished from the economic, welfare of a community, it is not for this Court because of the Commerce Clause to deny the exercise locally of the sovereign power of Louisiana."

VINSON, C.J., joined by Douglas, J., dissented: "I think it plain that a 'blanket prohibition' upon appellant's solicitation discriminates against and unduly burdens interstate commerce in favoring local retail merchants. 'Whether or not it was so intended, those are its necessary effects.' The fact that this ordinance exempts solicitation by the essentially local purveyors of farm products [by exempting food vendors] shows that local economic interests are relieved of the burdensome effects of the ordinance."

———————

HUNT v. WASHINGTON STATE APPLE ADVERTISING COMM'N, 432 U.S. 333 (1977), per BURGER, C.J., ruled unanimously that North Carolina violated the Commerce Clause when it barred sale in the state of closed apple containers bearing any grade marks except those of the U.S. Department of Agriculture ("U.S.D.A.") or a "not graded" mark. The regulation was challenged on behalf of Washington apple growers, who routinely packed their apples in containers bearing Washington grades. On account of a 60-year-old state system of inspection, grading, and advertising for Washington apples, these grades were viewed in the trade as equivalent or superior to the U.S.D.A. grades.

In ruling against North Carolina, the Chief Justice held that, once a state regulation has been found to have a disproportionately adverse effect on interstate commerce, the burden shifts onto the state to justify its regulation. Though noting "some indications" of an "economic protection motive," the Court did not question the "declared purpose of protecting consumers from deception and fraud in the market place," in which apples bearing divergent grading standards from seven states competed with North Carolina apples. But the mere fact that "state legislation furthers matters of legitimate local concern, even in the health and consumer protection areas, does not end the inquiry. [Rather], when such state legislation comes into conflict with the Commerce Clause's overriding requirement of a national 'common market,' we are confronted with the task of effecting an accommodation of the competing national and local interests. *Pike.*

"[T]he challenged statute has the practical effect of not only burdening interstate sales of Washington apples, but also discriminating against them. This discrimination takes various forms. [The statute raised] the costs of doing business in the North Carolina market for Washington apple growers and dealers, while leaving those of their North Carolina counterparts unaffected.[11] [The] statute [stripped] away from the Washington apple industry the competitive and economic advantages it has earned for itself through its expensive inspection and grading system. [By] prohibiting Washington growers and dealers from marketing apples under their State's grades, the statute has a leveling effect which insidiously operates to the advantage of local apple producers."

The Court further reasoned that, "[w]hen discrimination against commerce of the type we have found is demonstrated, the burden falls on the state to justify it in terms of the local benefit flowing from the statute and the unavailability of nondiscriminatory alternatives adequate to preserve the local interests at stake. *Dean Milk*; *Baldwin.*" The state did not meet this burden. By permitting no grades at all, the statute "can hardly be thought to eliminate the problems of deception and confusion created by the multiplicity of different state grades." And a nondiscriminatory alternative was available by permitting state grades to be used on the same containers as USDA grades.

————

MINNESOTA v. CLOVER LEAF CREAMERY CO., 449 U.S. 456 (1981), considered a statute held to be even-handed on its face. The Court, per BRENNAN, J., upheld a state law that banned nonreturnable milk containers made of plastic but permitted other nonreturnable milk containers, largely cartons made of pulpwood. The legislature had found that use of nonreturnable plastic containers "presents a solid waste management problem for the state, promotes energy waste, and depletes natural resources" in violation of a legislative policy to encourage "the reduction of the amount and type of material entering the solid waste stream." The Court upheld the statute, even though most of the plastic containers originated out of state and most of the pulpwood containers originated in state:

"[Minnesota's statute] does not effect 'simple protectionism,' but 'regulates even-handedly' by prohibiting all milk retailers from selling their products in

---

[11] To sell apples in the North Carolina market, Washington growers had to obliterate Washington grades imprinted on their standard containers, repack all shipments to North Carolina, or pack and store specially marked containers of apples.

plastic, nonreturnable milk containers, without regard to whether the milk, the containers, or the sellers are from outside the State. [Since] the statute does not discriminate between interstate and intrastate commerce, the controlling question is whether the incidental burden imposed on interstate commerce [is] 'clearly excessive in relation to the putative local benefits.' *Pike.* We conclude that it is not. [Within] Minnesota, business will presumably shift from manufacturers of plastic nonreturnable containers to producers of paperboard cartons, refillable bottles, and plastic pouches, but there is no reason to suspect that the gainers will be Minnesota firms, or the losers out-of-state firms. Indeed, two of the three dairies, the sole milk retailer, and the sole milk container producer challenging the statute in this litigation are Minnesota firms.[17]

"Pulpwood producers are the only Minnesota industry likely to benefit significantly from the Act at the expense of out-of-state firms. Respondents point out that plastic resin, the raw material used for making plastic nonreturnable milk jugs, is produced entirely by non-Minnesota firms, while pulpwood, used for making paperboard, is a major Minnesota product. Nevertheless, it is clear that respondents exaggerate the degree of burden on out-of-state interests, both because plastics will continue to be used in the production of plastic pouches, plastic returnable bottles, and paperboard itself, and because out-of-state pulpwood producers will presumably absorb some of the business generated by the Act.

"Even granting that the out-of-state plastics industry is burdened relatively more heavily than the Minnesota pulpwood industry, we find that this burden is not 'clearly excessive' in light of the substantial state interest in promoting conservation of energy and other natural resources and easing solid waste disposal problems. [We] find these local benefits ample to support Minnesota's decision under the Commerce Clause. Moreover, we find that no approach with 'a lesser impact on interstate activities,' *Pike*, is [available].

"In *Exxon* [*Corp. v. Maryland*, 437 U.S. 117 (1978), we] stressed that the Commerce Clause 'protects the interstate market, not particular interstate firms, from prohibitive or burdensome regulations.' A nondiscriminatory regulation serving substantial state purposes is not invalid simply because it causes some business to shift from a predominantly out-of-state industry to a predominantly in-state industry. Only if the burden on interstate commerce clearly outweighs the State's legitimate purposes does such a regulation violate the Commerce Clause."[12]

BENDIX AUTOLITE CORP. v. MIDWESCO ENTERPRISES, INC., 486 U.S. 888 (1988), is noteworthy largely because of the argument presented in a much-noticed concurring opinion by Scalia, J. The Court, per KENNEDY, J., applied *Pike*

---

[17]   [Ct's Note] The existence of major in-state interests adversely affected by the Act is a powerful safeguard against legislative abuse.

[12]   Powell, J., and Stevens, J., each dissenting separately, would have referred the Commerce Clause issue back to the Minnesota Supreme Court.

balancing to invalidate an Ohio statute that tolled the statute of limitations when foreign corporations did not appoint an agent to accept process for the exercise of general judicial jurisdiction: "Where the burden of a state regulation falls on interstate commerce, restricting its flow in a manner not applicable to local business or trade, there may be either a discrimination that renders the regulation invalid without more, or cause to weigh and assess the State's putative interests against the interstate burden to determine if the burden imposed is a reasonable one. [We] find that the burden imposed on interstate commerce by the tolling statute exceeds any local interest that the state might advance.

"[The] Ohio statutory scheme [forces] a foreign corporation to choose between exposure to the general jurisdiction of Ohio courts or forfeiture of the limitations defense, remaining subject to suit in Ohio in perpetuity. Requiring a foreign corporation to appoint an agent for service in all cases and to defend itself with reference to all transactions, including those in which it did not have the minimum contacts necessary for supporting personal jurisdiction, is a significant [burden].

"The ability to execute service of process on foreign corporations and entities is an important factor to consider in assessing the local interest. [However,] Ohio cannot justify its statute as a means of protecting its residents from corporations who become liable for acts done within the State but later withdraw from the jurisdiction, for it is conceded by all parties that the Ohio long-arm statute would have permitted service on Midwesco throughout the period of limitations."

SCALIA, J., concurred in the judgment: "I cannot confidently assess whether the Court's evaluation and balancing of interests in this case is right or wrong. [He pointed out uncertainties regarding both the burden on a foreign corporation and the benefits to local interests.]

"Having [roughly] evaluated the interests on both sides, [the] Court then proceeds to judge which is more important. This process is ordinarily called 'balancing,' *Pike,* but the scale analogy is not really appropriate, since the interests on both sides are incommensurate. It is more like judging whether a particular line is longer than a particular rock is heavy. All I am really persuaded of by the Court's opinion is that the burdens the Court labels 'significant' are more determinative of its decision than the benefits it labels 'important.' Were it not for the brief implication that there is here a discrimination unjustified by *any* state interest, I suggest an opinion could as persuasively have been written coming out the opposite way. We sometimes make similar 'balancing' judgments in determining how far the needs of the State can intrude upon the liberties of the individual, but that is of the essence of the courts' function as the nonpolitical branch. Weighing the governmental interests of a State against the needs of interstate commerce is, by contrast, a task squarely within the responsibility of Congress, and 'ill suited to the judicial function.'

"I would therefore abandon the 'balancing' approach to these negative Commerce Clause cases, first explicitly adopted [in] *Pike,* and leave essentially legislative judgments to the Congress. Issues already decided I would leave untouched, but would adopt for the future an analysis more appropriate to our role and our abilities. [In] my view, a state statute is invalid under the Commerce Clause if, and only if, it accords discriminatory treatment to interstate commerce in a respect not required to achieve a lawful state purpose. When such a validating purpose exists, it is for Congress and not us to determine it is not significant enough to justify the burden on [commerce].

"Because the present statute discriminates against interstate commerce by applying a disadvantageous rule against nonresidents for no valid state purpose that requires such a rule, I concur in the judgment that the Ohio statute violates the Commerce Clause."

V.   SUBSIDIES AND LINKAGES

NEW ENERGY CO. OF IND. v. LIMBACH, 486 U.S. 269 (1988), per SCALIA, J., invalidated an Ohio statute that provided a tax credit to users of a gasoline substitute, ethanol, that was produced in Ohio or in a state that gave a reciprocal tax credit for Ohio-produced ethanol. The Court ruled unanimously that Ohio discriminated in violation of the Commerce Clause when it denied the tax credit for ethanol produced in Indiana, which granted a direct subsidy to Indiana ethanol producers, but furnished no reciprocal tax credit: "The Ohio provision at issue here explicitly deprives certain products of generally available beneficial tax treatment because they are made in certain other states, and thus on its face appears to violate the cardinal requirement of nondiscrimination.

"[It] has not escaped our notice that the appellant here, which is eligible to receive a cash subsidy under Indiana's program for in-state ethanol producers, is the potential beneficiary of a scheme no less discriminatory than the one that it attacks, and no less effective in conferring a commercial advantage over out-of-state competitors. To believe the Indiana scheme is valid, however, is not to believe that the Ohio scheme must be valid as well. The Commerce Clause does not prohibit all state action designed to give its residents an advantage in the marketplace, but only action of that description *in connection with the State's regulation of interstate commerce*. Direct subsidization of domestic industry does not ordinarily run afoul of that prohibition; discriminatory taxation of out-of-state manufacturers does."

WEST LYNN CREAMERY, INC. V. HEALY
512 U.S. 186, 114 S.Ct. 2205, 129 L.Ed.2d 157 (1994).

JUSTICE STEVENS delivered the opinion of the Court.

[Massachusetts taxed all sales of milk by wholesalers to Massachusetts retailers, regardless of whether the milk was produced in or out of state. The proceeds of the tax went to a fund used to make subsidy payments to Massachusetts milk producers.]

The paradigmatic example of a law discriminating against interstate commerce is the protective tariff or customs duty, which taxes goods imported from other states, but does not tax similar products produced in state. A tariff is an attractive measure because it simultaneously raises revenue and benefits local producers by burdening their out-of-state competitors. Nevertheless, it violates the principle of the unitary national market by handicapping out-of-state competitors, thus artificially encouraging in-state production even when the same goods could be produced at lower cost in other states.

[In] fact, tariffs against the products of other states are so patently unconstitutional that our cases reveal not a single attempt by any state to enact one. Instead, the cases are filled with state laws that aspire to reap some of the benefits of tariffs by other means.

[Massachusetts' combination of a facially nondiscriminatory tax with a subsidy to in-state farmers] is clearly unconstitutional. Its avowed purpose and its undisputed effect are to enable higher cost Massachusetts dairy farmers to compete with lower cost dairy farmers in other States. [The net result is to make] milk produced out of State more expensive. Although the tax also applies to milk produced in Massachusetts, its effect on Massachusetts producers is entirely (indeed more than) offset by the subsidy provided exclusively to Massachusetts dairy farmers. Like an ordinary tariff, the tax is thus effectively imposed only on out-of-state products.

[Respondent] argues that the payments to Massachusetts dairy farmers from the Dairy Equalization Fund are valid, because subsidies are constitutional exercises of state power, and that the order premium which provides money for the Fund is valid, because it is a nondiscriminatory tax. [Even] granting respondent's assertion that both components of the pricing order would be constitutional standing alone,[15] the pricing order nevertheless must fall. [R]espondent errs in assuming that the constitutionality of the pricing order follows logically from the constitutionality of its component parts. By conjoining a tax and a subsidy, Massachusetts has created a program more dangerous to interstate commerce than either part alone. Nondiscriminatory measures, like the evenhanded tax at issue here, are generally upheld, in spite of any adverse effects on interstate commerce, in part because "[t]he existence of major in-state interests adversely affected [is] a powerful safeguard against legislative abuse." However, when a nondiscriminatory tax is coupled with a subsidy to one of the groups hurt by the tax, a state's political processes can no longer be relied upon to prevent legislative abuse, because one of the in-state interests which would otherwise lobby against the tax has been mollified by the subsidy. So, in this case, one would ordinarily have expected at least three groups to lobby against the order premium, which, as a tax, raises the price (and hence lowers demand) for milk: dairy farmers, milk dealers, and consumers. But because the tax was coupled with a subsidy, one of the most

---

[15] **[Ct's Note]** We have never squarely confronted the constitutionality of subsidies, and we need not do so now. We have, however, noted that "[d]irect subsidization of domestic industry does not ordinarily run afoul" of the negative Commerce Clause. *New Energy.*

powerful of these groups, Massachusetts dairy farmers, instead of exerting their influence against the tax, were in fact its primary supporters.

[Respondent] also argues that "the operation of the [scheme] disproves any claim of protectionism," because "*only* in-state consumers feel the effect of any retail price increase [and] [t]he dealers themselves [have] a substantial in-state presence." This argument, if accepted, would undermine almost every discriminatory tax case. State taxes are ordinarily paid by in-state businesses and consumers, yet if they discriminate against out-of-state products, they are unconstitutional. [The] cost of a tariff is also borne primarily by local consumers, yet a tariff is the paradigmatic Commerce Clause violation.

SCALIA, J., joined by THOMAS, J., concurred in the judgment.

[The] Court notes that, in funding this subsidy, Massachusetts has taxed milk produced in other States, and thus "not only assists local farmers, but burdens interstate commerce." But the same could be said of almost all subsidies funded from general state revenues, which almost invariably include monies from use taxes on out-of-state products. And even where the funding does not come in any part from taxes on out-of-state goods, "merely assist[ing]" in-state businesses unquestionably neutralizes advantages possessed by out-of-state enterprises. Such subsidies, particularly where they are in the form of cash or (what comes to the same thing) tax forgiveness, are often admitted to have as their purpose—*indeed, are nationally advertised as having as their purpose*—making it more profitable to conduct business in-state than elsewhere, i.e., distorting normal market incentives.

[There] are at least four possible devices that would enable a State to produce the economic effect that Massachusetts has produced here: (1) a discriminatory tax upon the industry, imposing a higher liability on out-of-state members than on their in-state competitors; (2) a tax upon the industry that is nondiscriminatory in its assessment, but that has an "exemption" or "credit" for in-state members; (3) a nondiscriminatory tax upon the industry, the revenues from which are placed into a segregated fund, which fund is disbursed as "rebates" or "subsidies" to in-state members of the industry (the situation at issue in this case); and (4) with or without nondiscriminatory taxation of the industry, a subsidy for the in-state members of the industry, funded from the State's general revenues. It is long settled that the first of these methodologies is unconstitutional under the negative Commerce Clause. The second of them, "exemption" from or "credit" against a "neutral" tax, is no different in principle from the first, and has likewise been held invalid. The fourth methodology, application of a state subsidy from general revenues, is so far removed from what we have hitherto held to be unconstitutional, that prohibiting it must be regarded as an extension of our negative-Commerce-Clause jurisprudence and therefore, to me, unacceptable. See *Limbach*. Indeed, in my view our negative-Commerce-Clause cases have already approved the use of such subsidies. See *Hughes*.

[The] issue before us in the present case is whether the third of these methodologies must fall. Although the question is close, I conclude it would not be a principled point at which to disembark from the negative-Commerce-Clause train. The only difference between methodology (2) (discriminatory "exemption" from nondiscriminatory tax) and methodology (3) (discriminatory refund of nondiscriminatory tax) is that the money is taken and returned rather than simply left with the favored in-state taxpayer in the first place. The difference between (3) and (4), on the other hand, is the difference between assisting in-state industry through discriminatory taxation, and assisting in-state industry by other means.

I would therefore allow a State to subsidize its domestic industry so long as it does so from nondiscriminatory taxes that go into the State's general revenue fund. Perhaps, as some commentators contend, that line comports with an important economic reality: a State is less likely to maintain a subsidy when its citizens perceive that the money (in the general fund) is available for any number of competing, non-protectionist purposes. That is not, however, the basis for my position, for as the Chief Justice explains, "[a]nalysis of interest group participation in the political process may serve many useful purposes, but serving as a basis for interpreting the dormant Commerce Clause is not one of them." [I] draw the line where I do because it is a clear, rational line.

REHNQUIST, C.J., joined by BLACKMUN, J., dissenting.

The Court is less than just in its description of the reasons which lay behind the Massachusetts law which it strikes down. The law undoubtedly sought to aid struggling Massachusetts dairy farmers, beset by steady or declining prices and escalating costs. [Massachusetts] has dealt with this problem by providing a subsidy to aid its beleaguered dairy farmers. In case after case, we have approved the validity under the Commerce Clause of such enactments. ["Direct] subsidization of domestic industry does not ordinarily run afoul of [the dormant Commerce Clause]; discriminatory taxation of out-of-state manufacturers does." *Limbach*.

["Denial] of the right to experiment may be fraught with serious consequences to the Nation. It is one of the happy incidents of the federal system that a single courageous State may, if its citizens choose, serve as a laboratory; and try novel social and economic experiments without risk to the rest of the country." [*New State Ice Co. v. Liebmann*, 285 U.S. 262, 311 (1932) (Brandeis, J., dissenting). The] wisdom of a messianic insistence on a grim sink-or-swim policy of laissez-faire economics would be debatable had Congress chosen to enact it; but Congress has done nothing of the kind. It is the Court which has imposed the policy under the dormant Commerce Clause, a policy which bodes ill for the values of federalism which have long animated our constitutional jurisprudence.

3. THE STATE AS A MARKET PARTICIPANT

REEVES, INC. v. STAKE

447 U.S. 429, 100 S.Ct. 2271, 65 L.Ed.2d 244 (1980).

JUSTICE BLACKMUN delivered the opinion of the Court.

[Responding to a 1919 cement shortage, South Dakota built and operated a cement plant, which sold to both in-state and out-of-state buyers. The latter bought 40% of the plant's production in the mid-70s. When booming construction caused a cement shortage in 1978, the state "reaffirmed its policy of supplying all South Dakota customers" before offering cement to buyers from out of state. Reeves, an out-of-state buyer for 20 years, challenged South Dakota's preferential sales policy as a violation of the Commerce Clause.]

The issue in this case is whether, consistent with the Commerce Clause, the State of South Dakota, in a time of shortage, may confine the sale of cement that it produces solely to its residents. [The court of appeals upheld the law]. It concluded that the state had "simply acted in a proprietary capacity," as permitted by *Hughes v. Alexandria Scrap Corp.*, 426 U.S. 794 (1976).

Alexandria Scrap concerned a Maryland program designed to remove abandoned automobiles from the State's roadways and junkyards. To encourage recycling, a "bounty" was offered for every Maryland-title junk car converted into scrap. [The law] imposed more exacting documentation requirements on out-of-state than in-state processors. [*Alexandria Scrap*] did not involve "the kind of action with which the Commerce Clause is concerned." Unlike prior cases voiding state laws inhibiting interstate trade, "Maryland has not sought to prohibit the flow of [junk cars], or to regulate the conditions under which it may occur. Instead, it has entered into the market itself to bid up their price as a purchaser, in effect, of a potential article of interstate commerce," and has restricted "its trade to its own citizens or businesses within the State."

Having characterized Maryland as a market participant, rather than as a market regulator, the Court found no reason to "believe the Commerce Clause was intended to require independent justification for [the State's] action." The Court couched its holding in unmistakably broad terms. "Nothing in the purposes animating the Commerce Clause prohibits a State, in the absence of congressional action, from participating in the market and exercising the right to favor its own citizens over others."

The basic distinction drawn in *Alexandria Scrap* between States as market participants and States as market regulators makes good sense and sound law. As that case explains, the Commerce Clause responds principally to state taxes and regulatory measures impeding free private trade in the national marketplace. [There] is no indication of a constitutional plan to limit the ability of the States themselves to operate freely in the free market. See Laurence H. Tribe, *American Constitutional Law* 336 (1978) ("[T]he Commerce Clause was directed, as an historical matter, only at regulatory and taxing actions taken by states in their sovereign capacity."). The precedents comport with this distinction.[9]

Restraint in this area is also counseled by considerations of state sovereignty, the role of each State "as guardian and trustee for its people," and "the long recognized right of trader or manufacturer, engaged in an entirely private business, freely to exercise his own independent discretion as to parties with whom he will deal." *United States v. Colgate & Co.*, 250 U.S. 300, 307 (1919). Moreover, state proprietary activities may be, and often are, burdened with the same restrictions imposed on private market participants. Evenhandedness suggests that, when acting as proprietors, States should similarly share existing freedoms from federal constraints, including the inherent limits of the Commerce Clause. Finally, as this case illustrates, the competing considerations in cases involving state proprietary action often will be subtle, complex, politically charged, and difficult to assess under traditional Commerce Clause analysis. Given these factors, *Alexandria Scrap* wisely recognizes that, as a rule, the adjustment of interests in this context is a task better suited for Congress than this Court.

[We] find the label "protectionism" of little help in this context. The State's refusal to sell to buyers other than South Dakotans is "protectionist" only in the sense that it limits benefits generated by a state program to those who fund the state treasury and whom the State was created to serve. Petitioner's argument apparently also would characterize as "protectionist" rules restricting to state residents the enjoyment of state educational institutions, energy generated by a state-run plant, police and fire protection, and agricultural improvement and business development programs. Such policies, while perhaps "protectionist" in a loose sense, reflect the essential and patently unobjectionable purpose of state government—to serve the citizens of the State.

[Cement] is not a natural resource, like coal, timber, wild game, or minerals. Cf. *Hughes v. Oklahoma* (minnows); *Philadelphia v. New Jersey* (landfill sites). It is the end-product of a complex process whereby a costly physical plant and human labor act on raw materials. South Dakota has not sought to limit access to the State's limestone or other materials used to make cement. Nor has it restricted the ability of private firms or sister States to set up plants within its borders.

JUSTICE POWELL, with whom JUSTICE BRENNAN, JUSTICE WHITE, and JUSTICE STEVENS join, dissenting.

The application of the Commerce Clause to this case should turn on the nature of the governmental activity involved. [In] procuring goods and services for the operation of government, a State may act without regard to the private

---

[9]   [**Ct's Note**] *Alexandria Scrap* does not stand alone. In *American Yearbook Co. v. Askew*, 339 F.Supp. 719 (M.D.Fla.1972), a three-judge District Court upheld a Florida statute requiring the State to obtain needed printing services from in-state shops. It reasoned that "state proprietary functions" are exempt from Commerce Clause scrutiny. This Court affirmed summarily. 409 U.S. 904 (1972). Numerous courts have rebuffed Commerce Clause challenges directed at similar preferences that exist in "a substantial majority of the states." Note, 58 Iowa L.Rev. 576 (1973). [The opinion cites state court decisions from eight states.]

marketplace and remove itself from the reach of the Commerce Clause. See *American Yearbook Co.* [footnote 9 of the majority opinion, supra]. But when a State itself becomes a participant in the private market for other purposes, the Constitution forbids actions that would impede the flow of interstate commerce. These categories recognize no more than the "constitutional line between the State as Government and the State as trader." *New York v. United States,* [326 U.S. 572 (1946)].

The Court holds that South Dakota, like a private business, should not be governed by the Commerce Clause when it enters the private market. But precisely because South Dakota is a State, it cannot be presumed to behave like an enterprise "engaged in an entirely private business." A State frequently will respond to market conditions on the basis of political rather than economic concerns. To use the Court's terms, a State may attempt to act as a "market regulator" rather than a "market participant." In that situation, it is a pretense to equate the State with a private economic actor. State action burdening interstate trade is no less state action because it is accomplished by a public agency authorized to participate in the private market.

[Unlike] the market subsidies at issue in *Alexandria Scrap,* the marketing policy of the South Dakota Cement Commission has cut off interstate trade.[3] The State can raise such a bar when it enters the market to supply its own needs. In order to ensure an adequate supply of cement for public uses, the State can withhold from interstate commerce the cement needed for public projects.

The State, however, has no parallel justification for favoring private, in-state customers over out-of-state customers.[4] In response to political concerns that likely would be inconsequential to a private cement producer, South Dakota has shut off its cement sales to customers beyond its borders. That discrimination constitutes a direct barrier to trade "of the type forbidden by the Commerce Clause, and involved in previous cases." *Alexandria Scrap.* The effect on interstate trade is the same as if the state legislature had imposed the policy on private cement producers. The Commerce Clause prohibits this severe restraint on commerce.

———

SOUTH-CENTRAL TIMBER DEVELOPMENT, INC. v. WUNNICKE, 467 U.S. 82 (1984), held that the market participant concept did not free Alaska from Commerce Clause invalidation of the state's contractual requirement that

---

[3]   **[Ct's Note]** One distinction between a private and a governmental function is whether the activity is supported with general tax funds, as was the case for the reprocessing program in *Alexandria Scrap,* or whether it is financed by the revenues it generates. In this case, South Dakota's cement plant has supported itself for many years. There is thus no need to consider the question whether a state-subsidized business could confine its sales to local residents.

[4]   **[Ct's Note]** The consequences of South Dakota's "residents-first" policy were devastating to petitioner Reeves, Inc., a Wyoming firm. For 20 years, Reeves had purchased about 95% of its cement from the South Dakota plant. When the State imposed its preference for South Dakota residents in 1978, Reeves had to reduce its production by over 75%. As a result, its South Dakota competitors were in a vastly superior position to compete for work in the region.

purchasers of state-owned standing timber must generally saw it into "cants" less than nine inches wide before shipping it out of state. WHITE, J.'S plurality opinion, joined by Brennan, Blackmun, and Stevens, JJ., stressed that the requirement reached beyond the market transaction in which the state participated: "[The] market-participant doctrine permits a state to influence 'a discrete, identifiable class of economic activity in which [it] is a major participant.' Contrary to the state's contention, the doctrine is not carte blanche to impose any conditions that the state has the economic power to dictate, and does not validate any requirement merely because the state imposes it upon someone with whom it is in contractual privity.

"The limit of the market-participant doctrine must be that it allows a State to impose burdens on commerce within the market in which it is a participant, but allows it to go no further. The State may not impose conditions, whether by statute, regulation, or contract, that have a substantial regulatory effect outside of that particular market. Unless the 'market' is relatively narrowly defined, the doctrine has the potential of swallowing up the rule that States may not impose substantial burdens on interstate commerce even if they act with the permissible state purpose of fostering local industry.

"At the heart of the dispute in this case is a disagreement about the definition of the market. Alaska contends that it is participating in the processed timber market, although it acknowledges that it participates in no way in the actual processing. South-Central argues, on the other hand, that although the State may be a participant in the timber market, it is using its leverage in that market to exert a regulatory effect in the processing market, in which it is not a participant. We agree with the latter position.

"[We] reject the contention that a State's action as a market regulator may be upheld against Commerce Clause challenge on the ground that the State could achieve the same end as a market participant. We therefore find it unimportant for present purposes that the State could support its processing industry by selling only to Alaska processors, by vertical integration, or by direct subsidy."

Having found the Commerce Clause applicable, the opinion concluded that Alaska's log processing requirement fell within the *Pike* and *Philadelphia* "rule of virtual per se invalidity" because of its "protectionist nature."[13]

REHNQUIST, J., joined by O'Connor, J., dissented: "Alaska is merely paying the buyer of the timber indirectly, by means of a reduced price, to hire Alaska residents to process the timber. Under existing precedent, the State could accomplish that same result in any number of ways. [T]he State could choose to sell its timber only

---

[13]   Powell, J., joined by Burger, C.J., would have remanded the foregoing issues for consideration by the court of appeals. But they joined Part II of White, J.'s opinion, which considered the relevance of a longstanding federal policy forbidding shipment from Alaska of unprocessed timber from federal lands. This federal policy did not negate the implied invalidity, under the Commerce Clause, of a similar state policy for timber harvested from state lands: for "a state regulation to be removed from the reach of the dormant Commerce Clause, congressional intent must be unmistakably clear."

to those companies that maintain active primary-processing plants in Alaska. *Reeves.* Or the State could directly subsidize the primary-processing industry within the State. *Alexandria Scrap.* The State could even pay to have the logs processed and then enter the market only to sell processed logs. It seems to me unduly formalistic to conclude that the one path chosen by the State as best suited to promote its concerns is the path forbidden it by the Commerce Clause."

4. INTERSTATE PRIVILEGES AND IMMUNITIES CLAUSE

Art. IV, § 2, cl. 1 provides that "The Citizens of each State shall be entitled to all Privileges and Immunities of Citizens in the several States." In most cases, the relationship between the dormant Commerce Clause and the Privileges and Immunities Clause is "mutually reinforcing." *Hicklin v. Orbeck*, 437 U.S. 518, 531 (1978). As a result, many of the claims brought under the dormant Commerce Clause could equally well be brought under the Privileges and Immunities Clause and vice versa. Nonetheless, the overlap between the dormant Commerce and the Privileges and Immunities Clauses is not complete.

One clear and important difference is that corporations cannot sue under the Privileges and Immunities Clause because they are not "citizens." *Paul v. Virginia*, 75 U.S. 168 (1868). Claims on behalf of corporations must thus be brought under the dormant Commerce Clause if they are to be brought at all.

Other differences are more subtle. As you read the following materials on the Privileges and Immunities Clause, you should keep the following questions in mind. First, what exactly are the "Privileges and Immunities of Citizens" that Art. IV, § 2, cl. 1 protects? Only if a state regulation impairs a privilege or immunity of citizenship will it trigger an inquiry into whether it can nevertheless be justified under applicable standards. Second, is the applicable test for the permissibility of state infringements on the "Privileges and Immunities of Citizens" more or less stringent than the test for state violations of the Commerce Clause? Third, to what extent, if any, does the Privileges and Immunities Clause undermine the significance of "the market participant exception" to dormant Commerce Clause doctrine?

UNITED BUILDING & CONSTRUCTION TRADES COUNCIL V. MAYOR OF CAMDEN
465 U.S. 208, 104 S.Ct. 1020, 79 L.Ed.2d 249 (1984).

JUSTICE REHNQUIST delivered the opinion of the Court.

A municipal ordinance of the city of Camden, New Jersey, requires that at least 40% of the employees of contractors and subcontractors working on city construction projects be Camden residents. Appellant, the United Building and Construction Trades Council of Camden County and Vicinity (Council), challenges that ordinance as a violation of the Privileges and Immunities Clause, Art. IV, § 2, cl. 1, of the United States Constitution [and] as unconstitutional under the Commerce Clause.

Citing *Reeves* and *Alexandria Scrap*, the [New Jersey Supreme Court] held that the resident quota was not subject to challenge under the Commerce Clause because the State was acting as a market participant rather than as a market regulator. [Since] the Council filed its appeal, [this Court] decided *White*, which held that an executive order of the Mayor of Boston, requiring that at least 50% of all jobs on construction projects funded in whole or in part by city funds be filled with bona fide city residents, was immune from scrutiny under the Commerce Clause because Boston was acting as a market participant rather than as a market regulator. In light of the decision in *White*, appellant has abandoned its Commerce Clause challenge. [The] only question left [is] whether the [ordinance] violates the Privileges and Immunities Clause.

[The City argues] that the Clause only applies to laws passed by a *State*. [But the] fact that the ordinance [is] municipal [does] not somehow place it outside the scope of the Privileges and Immunities Clause. [What] would be unconstitutional if done directly by the State can no more readily be accomplished by a city deriving its authority from the State. [Nor can we accept] that the Privileges and Immunities Clause does not apply to an ordinance that discriminates solely on the basis of *municipal* residency. The Clause is phrased in terms of *state* citizenship and was designed "to place the citizens of each State upon the same footing with citizens of other States, as far as the advantages resulting from citizenship in those States are concerned." [But we] have never read the Clause so literally as to apply it only to distinctions based on state citizenship. [A] person who is not residing in a given State is ipso facto not residing in a city within that State. Thus, whether the exercise of a privilege is conditioned on state residency or on municipal residency he will just as surely be excluded.

[It] is true that New Jersey citizens not residing in Camden will be affected by the ordinance as well as out-of-state citizens. And it is true that the disadvantaged New Jersey residents have no claim under the Privileges and Immunities Clause. *Slaughter-House Cases*. But New Jersey residents at least have a chance to remedy at the polls any discrimination against them. Out-of-state citizens have no similar opportunity.

[Application] of the Privileges and Immunities Clause to a particular instance of discrimination against out-of-state residents entails a two-step inquiry. As an initial matter, the Court must decide whether the ordinance burdens one of those privileges and immunities protected by the Clause. *Baldwin v. Montana Fish and Game Comm'n.*, 436 U.S. 371 (1978).[14] Not all forms of discrimination against citizens of other States are constitutionally suspect: "Some distinctions between residents and nonresidents merely reflect the fact that this is a Nation composed

---

[14]   *Baldwin* upheld Montana's license fee for hunting elk—which was $225 for non-residents, compared with $30 for residents—on the ground that hunting for sport was not a protected "fundamental" right under the Privileges and Immunities Clause.

of individual States, and are permitted; other distinctions are prohibited because they hinder the formation, the purpose, or the development of a single Union of those States. Only with respect to those 'privileges' and 'immunities' bearing upon the vitality of the Nation as a single entity must the State treat all citizens, resident and nonresident, equally." Ibid.

As a threshold matter, then, we must determine whether an out-of-state resident's interest in employment on public works contracts in another State is sufficiently "fundamental" to the promotion of interstate harmony so as to "fall within the purview of the Privileges and Immunities Clause." Id.

Certainly, the pursuit of a common calling [(that is, a job)] is one of the most fundamental of those privileges protected by the Clause. Many, if not most, of our cases expounding the Privileges and Immunities Clause have dealt with this basic and essential activity. See, e.g., *Hicklin v. Orbeck*, 437 U.S. 518 (1978); *Toomer v. Witsell*, 334 U.S. 385 (1948). Public employment, however, is qualitatively different from employment in the private sector; it is a subspecies of the broader opportunity to pursue a common calling. We have held that there is no fundamental right to government employment for purposes of the Equal Protection Clause. *Massachusetts Bd. of Retirement v. Murgia*, [Ch. 9, Sec. 4, III infra]. Cf. *McCarthy v. Philadelphia Civil Service Comm'n*, 424 U.S. 645 (1976) (rejecting equal protection challenge to municipal residency requirement for municipal workers). And in *White*, we held that for purposes of the Commerce Clause everyone employed on a city public works project is, "in a substantial if informal sense, 'working for the city.'"

It can certainly be argued that for purposes of the Privileges and Immunities Clause everyone affected by the Camden ordinance is also "working for the city" and, therefore, has no grounds for complaint when the city favors its own residents. But we decline to transfer mechanically into this context an analysis fashioned to fit the Commerce Clause. Our decision in *White* turned on a distinction between the city acting as a market participant and the city acting as a market regulator. [But] the distinction between market participant and market regulator relied upon in *White* to dispose of the Commerce Clause challenge is not dispositive in this context. The two Clauses have different aims and set different standards for state conduct.

The Commerce Clause acts as an implied restraint upon state regulatory powers. Such powers must give way before the superior authority of Congress to legislate on (or leave unregulated) matters involving interstate commerce. When the State acts solely as a market participant, no conflict between state regulation and federal regulatory authority can arise. *White; Reeves; Alexandria Scrap*. The Privileges and Immunities Clause, on the other hand, imposes a direct restraint on state action in the interests of interstate harmony.

[In] *Hicklin,* we struck down as a violation of the Privileges and Immunities Clause an "Alaska Hire" statute containing a resident-hiring preference for all employment related to the development of the State's oil and gas resources. Alaska argued in that case that "because the oil and gas that are the subject of Alaska Hire are *owned* by the State, this ownership, of itself, is sufficient justification for the Act's discrimination against nonresidents, and takes the Act totally without the scope of the Privileges and Immunities Clause." We concluded, however, that the State's interest in controlling those things it claims to own is not absolute. "Rather than placing a statute completely beyond the Clause, the State's ownership of the property with which the statute is concerned is a factor—although often the crucial factor—to be considered in evaluating whether the statute's discrimination against noncitizens violates the Clause." Much the same analysis, we think, is appropriate to a city's efforts to bias private employment decisions in favor of its residents on construction projects funded with public moneys. The fact that Camden is expending its own funds or funds it administers in accordance with the terms of a grant is certainly a factor—perhaps the crucial factor—to be considered in evaluating whether the statute's discrimination violates the Privileges and Immunities Clause. But it does not remove the Camden ordinance completely from the purview of the Clause.

[The] conclusion that Camden's ordinance discriminates against a protected privilege does not, of course, end the inquiry. We have stressed in prior cases that "[l]ike many other constitutional provisions, the privileges and immunities clause is not an absolute." *Toomer.* It does not preclude discrimination against citizens of other States where there is a "substantial reason" for the difference in treatment. "[T]he inquiry in each case must be concerned with whether such reasons do exist and whether the degree of discrimination bears a close relation to them."

[Every] inquiry under the Privileges and Immunities Clause "must [be] conducted with due regard for the principle that the States should have considerable leeway in analyzing local evils and in prescribing appropriate cures." This caution is particularly appropriate when a government body is merely setting conditions on the expenditure of funds it controls. The Alaska Hire statute at issue in *Hicklin* swept within its strictures not only contractors and subcontractors dealing directly with the State's oil and gas; it also covered suppliers who provided goods and services to those contractors and subcontractors. We invalidated the Act as "an attempt to force virtually all businesses that benefit in some way from the economic ripple effect of Alaska's decision to develop its oil and gas resources to bias their employment practices in favor of the State's residents." No similar "ripple effect" appears to infect the Camden ordinance. It is limited in scope to employees working directly on city public works projects.

Nonetheless, we find it impossible to evaluate Camden's justification on the record as it now stands. No trial has ever been held in the case. No findings of fact have been made. [We], therefore, [remand for] proceedings not inconsistent with this opinion.

JUSTICE BLACKMUN, dissenting.

[The] Framers had every reason to believe that interstate discrimination based on municipal residence would be dealt with by the States themselves. [Nor] is this mechanism for relief merely a theoretical one; in the past decade several States, including California and Georgia, have repealed or forbidden protectionist ordinances like the one at issue here. [Because] I believe that the [Privileges and Immunities Clause] does not apply to discrimination based on municipal residence, I dissent.

———

McBURNEY v. YOUNG, 569 U.S. 221 (2013), per ALITO, J., unanimously rejected an argument that Virginia's Freedom of Information Act (FOIA) violated the Privileges and Immunities Clause by granting Virginia citizens, but not out-of-staters, access to all public records: "Petitioners allege that Virginia's citizens-only FOIA provision violates four different 'fundamental' privileges or immunities: the opportunity to pursue a common calling, the ability to own and transfer property, access to the Virginia courts, and access to public information. [Although the challenged provision] has the incidental effect of preventing citizens of other States from making a profit by trading on information contained in state records[, the] Court has struck laws down as violating the privilege of pursuing a common calling only when those laws were enacted for the protectionist purpose of burdening out-of-state citizens. [Here,] the distinction that the statute makes between citizens and noncitizens has a distinctly nonprotectionist aim. The state FOIA essentially represents a mechanism by which those who ultimately hold sovereign power (*i.e.*, the citizens of the Commonwealth) may obtain an accounting from the public officials to whom they delegate the exercise of that power.

"[If] a State prevented out-of-state citizens from accessing records—like title documents and mortgage records—that are necessary to the transfer of property, the State might well run afoul of the Privileges and Immunities Clause. Virginia, however, does not prevent citizens of other States from obtaining such documents. [Requiring] noncitizens to conduct a few minutes of Internet research in lieu of using a relatively cumbersome state FOIA process cannot be said to impose any significant burden on noncitizens' ability to own or transfer property in Virginia.

"[Although] the Privileges and Immunities Clause 'secures citizens of one State the right to resort to the courts of another, equally with the citizens of the latter State,' [the] Court has made clear that 'the constitutional requirement is satisfied if the non-resident is given access [upon] terms which in themselves are reasonable and adequate. [Virginia's] rules of civil procedure provide for both discovery and subpoenas duces tecum. There is no reason to think that those mechanisms are insufficient to provide noncitizens with any relevant, nonprivileged documents needed in litigation.

"Finally, we [cannot] agree that the Privileges and Immunities Clause covers [a] broad right [of access to public information]. No such right was recognized at common law. [Nor] is such a sweeping right 'basic to the maintenance or well-being of the Union.'

"[Petitioners' dormant Commerce Clause challenge also fails because] Virginia's FOIA law neither 'regulates' nor 'burdens' interstate commerce; rather, it merely provides a service to local citizens that would not otherwise be available at all."

CHAPTER 5

SUBSTANTIVE PROTECTION OF
ECONOMIC INTERESTS

■ ■ ■

Introduction

Most of the remaining chapters of this book concern constitutional limits on government power, independent of limits arising out of the horizontal and vertical distribution of powers among the branches and levels of government. Sometimes called "negative" limits or simply "rights," they are identical, or nearly so, whether applied to state or federal governments, but are based on different sources. Art. I, § 9 and the Bill of Rights (comprising the first nine amendments) give rise to the major limits on the federal government, while Art. I, § 10 and the Reconstruction Amendments (i.e., the Thirteenth, Fourteenth, and Fifteenth Amendments) give rise to most of the limits on state and local government. This chapter recounts the early development of constitutional rights and then focuses on rights protecting economic interests. Since the late 1930s, courts have protected economic rights less robustly than some other kinds of rights, but the Supreme Court's early treatment of economic rights frames its treatment of other rights, and in some contexts protection for economic rights remains substantial.

1. ORIGINS OF SUBSTANTIVE DUE PROCESS

A first-time reader of the Constitution might think that the Ninth Amendment and the Privileges or Immunities Clause of the Fourteenth Amendment serve as important textual grounds for rights that are not expressly enumerated in the text. However, for reasons that will be discussed at length below, historically the Due Process Clauses of the Fifth and Fourteenth Amendments have played a larger role. Yet the terms of those provisions refer only to "process" and thus appear to limit only the *procedures* by which government affects life, liberty, and property. How, then, can the Due Process Clauses be invoked to impose limits on the *substance* of governmental regulations and other activities? That these clauses embody *any* limits on the substance of legislation requires some initial explanation.

I.   EARLY EXPRESSIONS OF THE NOTION THAT GOVERNMENTAL AUTHORITY HAS IMPLIED LIMITS

An early expression of the view that there are implied or inherent limits on governmental power did not rely on the Due Process Clause of the Fifth Amendment or any other specific constitutional provision. In CALDER v. BULL, 3 U.S. (3 Dall.) 386 (1798), the Supreme Court rejected the claim of potential heirs that a Connecticut statute amounted to an ex post facto law (because the ex post facto clause only applies to criminal laws). Two Justices engaged in a notable exchange over whether it would ever be appropriate to strike down legislation without regard to explicit constitutional limitations.

CHASE, J., said yes: "I cannot subscribe to the omnipotence of a State Legislature, or that it is absolute and without control; although its authority should not be expressly restrained by the Constitution, or fundamental law of the State. The people of the United States erected their constitutions, or forms of government, to establish justice, to promote the general welfare, to secure the blessings of liberty, and to protect their persons and property from violence. The purposes for which men enter into society will determine the nature and terms of the social compact; and as they are the foundation of the legislative power, they will decide what are the proper objects of it. The nature and ends of legislative power will limit the exercise of it. This fundamental principle flows from the very nature of our free Republican governments, that no man should be compelled to do what the laws do not require; nor to refrain from acts which the laws permit. There are acts which the Federal, or State, Legislature cannot do, without exceeding their authority. There are certain vital principles in our free Republican governments, which will determine and overrule an apparent and flagrant abuse of legislative power; as to authorize manifest injustice by positive law; to take away that security for personal liberty, or private property, for the protection whereof the government was established. An ACT of the legislature (for I cannot call it a law), contrary to the great first principles of the social compact, cannot be considered a rightful exercise of legislative authority. [A] few instances will suffice to explain what I mean. A law that punished a citizen for an innocent action or, in other words, for an act, which, when done, was in violation of no existing law; a law that destroys, or impairs, the lawful private contracts of citizens; a law that makes a man a Judge in his own cause; or a law that takes property from A and gives it to B: It is against all reason and justice, for a people to intrust a Legislature with SUCH powers; and therefore, it cannot be presumed that they have done it. The genius, the nature, and the spirit, of our State Governments, amount to a prohibition of such acts of legislation; and the general principles of law and reason forbid them. [To] maintain that our Federal, or State Legislature possesses such powers, if they had not been expressly restrained, would, in my opinion, be a political heresy, altogether inadmissible in our free republican governments."

IREDELL, J., disagreed: "[If] a government, composed of Legislative, Executive and Judicial departments, were established, by a constitution which imposed no limits on the legislative power, the consequence would inevitably be, that whatever the legislative power chose to enact, would be lawfully enacted, and the judicial power could never interpose to pronounce it void. It is true, that some speculative jurists have held, that a legislative act against natural justice must, in itself, be void; but I cannot think that, under such a government any Court of Justice would possess a power to declare it so. [I]t has been the policy of all the American states, which have, individually, framed their state constitutions, since the revolution, and of the people of the United States, when they framed the Federal Constitution, to define with precision the objects of the legislative power, and to restrain its exercise within marked and settled boundaries. If any act of Congress, or of the Legislature of a state, violates those constitutional provisions, it is unquestionably void. [If], on the other hand, the Legislature of the Union, or the Legislature of any member of the Union, shall pass a law, within the general scope of their constitutional power, the Court cannot pronounce it to be void, merely because it is, in their judgment, contrary to the principles of natural justice. The ideas of natural justice are regulated by no fixed standard: the ablest and the purest men have differed upon the subject; and all that the Court could properly say, in such an event, would be that the Legislature (possessed of an equal right of opinion) had passed an act which, in the opinion of the judges, was inconsistent with the abstract principles of natural justice."

In BARRON v. MAYOR AND CITY COUNCIL OF BALTIMORE, 32 U.S. (7 Pet.) 243 (1833), in the course of rejecting appellant's argument that by ruining the use of his wharf the city had violated the Fifth Amendment guarantee that private property shall not be "taken for public use, without just compensation," the Court, per MARSHALL, C.J., held that the Bill of Rights applied only to the federal government: "[The] great revolution which established the constitution of the United States was not effected without immense opposition. Serious fears were extensively entertained that [the new national powers] might be exercised in a manner dangerous to liberty. In almost every convention by which the constitution was adopted, amendments to guard against the abuse of power were recommended. These amendments demanded security against the apprehended encroachments of the general government. [They] contain no expression indicating an intention to apply them to the state governments. This court cannot so apply them."

Concurring in the judgment in *Washington v. Glucksberg*, (1997) (Ch. 6, Sec. 3), which rejected the argument that there is a constitutional right to physician-assisted suicide, SOUTER, J., noted that the physicians who asserted this right "also invoke two centuries of American constitutional practice in recognizing unenumerated substantive limits on governmental action." "Although this practice has neither rested on any single textual basis nor expressed a consistent theory, [the] persistence of substantive due process in our cases points to the legitimacy of the modern justification for such judicial review.

"[Before] the ratification of the Fourteenth Amendment, substantive constitutional review resting on a theory of unenumerated rights occurred largely in the state courts applying state constitutions that commonly contained either due process clauses like that of the Fifth Amendment (and later the Fourteenth) or the textual antecedents of such clauses, repeating Magna Carta's guarantee of 'the law of the land.' On the basis of such clauses, or of general principles untethered to specific constitutional language, state courts evaluated the constitutionality of a wide range of statutes.

"Even in this early period, however, this Court anticipated the developments that would presage both the Civil War and the ratification of the Fourteenth Amendment, by making it clear on several occasions that it too had no doubt of the judiciary's power to strike down legislation that conflicted with important but unenumerated principles of American government. [In] FLETCHER v. PECK, 6 Cranch 87 (1810), [the Court] struck down an Act of the Georgia Legislature that purported to rescind a sale of public land ab initio and reclaim title for the State, and so deprive subsequent, good-faith purchasers of property conveyed by the original grantees. The Court rested the invalidation on alternative sources of authority: the specific prohibitions against bills of attainder, ex post facto laws, laws impairing contracts in Article 1, § 10, of the Constitution; and 'general principles which are common to our free institutions,' by which Chief Justice Marshall meant that a simple deprivation of property by the State could not be an authentically 'legislative' Act.

"*Fletcher* was not, though, the most telling early example of such review. For its most salient instance in the Court before the adoption of the Fourteenth Amendment was, of course, the case that the Amendment would in due course overturn, DRED SCOTT v. SANDFORD, 19 How. 393 (1857). Unlike *Fletcher*, *Dred Scott* was textually based on a due process clause (in the Fifth Amendment, applicable to the National Government), and it was in reliance on that Clause's protection of property that the Court invalidated the Missouri Compromise. This substantive protection of an owner's property in a slave taken to the territories was traced to the absence of any enumerated power to affect that property granted to the Congress by Article 1 of the Constitution, the implication being that the Government had no legitimate interest that could support the earlier congressional compromise. The ensuing judgment of history needs no recounting here."

II.   FOURTEENTH AMENDMENT

Historical background. The grounds asserted in the early cases for protecting economic (and other) interests from legislative power could not long prevail in the face of the growing acceptance of the federal and state constitutions as the only sources of judicially enforceable limitations on legislative power. Thus, proponents of constitutional limits on state and local government needed to look elsewhere. Yet apart from a few provisions enumerated in Article 1, § 10, before Reconstruction, the federal constitution provided little basis for challenging state or local laws. The Thirteenth Amendment forbidding slavery and involuntary servitude was ratified in 1865, but freeing the slaves did not produce the fruits of freedom due to "Black Codes" and other repressive measures adopted in the states of the former Confederacy. The plight of African Americans was reflected in the Civil Rights Act of 1866, which Congress passed over the veto of President Andrew Johnson. It recognized "all persons born in United States" as United States citizens, and gave to "such citizens, of every race or color, without regard to any previous condition of slavery [the] same right, in every State and Territory in the United States, to make and enforce contracts, to sue, be parties, and give evidence, to inherit, purchase, lease, sell, hold, and convey real and personal property, and to full and equal benefit of all laws and proceedings for the security of person and property, as is enjoyed by white citizens." To remove doubts about the Act's constitutionality, Congress also proposed what became the Fourteenth Amendment. In addition to setting forth privileges and immunities, due process, and equal protection provisions as limitations on the states, it authorized Congress to enact legislation to "enforce this article."

SLAUGHTER-HOUSE CASES
83 U.S. (16 Wall.) 36, 21 L. Ed. 394 (1873).

JUSTICE MILLER delivered the opinion of the Court.

[A Louisiana law granted a monopoly to operate slaughterhouses in the New Orleans area, regarding this an "appropriate," "stringent, and effectual" means to "remove from the more densely populated part of the city, the noxious slaughter-houses and large and offensive collections of animals." Excluded butchers claimed that the law violated their right "to exercise their trade" and invoked the 13th and 14th Amendments.]

This court is thus called upon for the first time to give construction to [these Amendments. The Civil War] being over, those who had succeeded in re-establishing the authority of the Federal government were not content to permit [the] great act of emancipation to rest on the actual results of the contest or the proclamation of the Executive, both of which might have been questioned in after times, and they determined to place this main and most valuable result in the Constitution of the restored Union as one of its fundamental articles. Hence the [13th Amendment]. To withdraw the mind from the contemplation of this grand yet simple declaration of the personal freedom of all the human race within the jurisdiction of this government [and] with a microscopic search endeavor to find in it a reference to servitudes, which may have been attached to property in certain localities, requires an effort, to say the least of it.

[The] process of restoring to their proper relations with the Federal government and with the other States those which had sided with the [rebellion] developed the fact that, notwithstanding the formal recognition by those States of the abolition of slavery, the condition of the slave race would, without further protection of the Federal government, be almost as bad as it was before. Among the first acts of legislation adopted by several of the States [were] laws which imposed upon the colored race onerous disabilities and burdens, and curtailed their rights [to] such an extent that their freedom was of little value. [These] circumstances [forced] upon the statesmen who had conducted the Federal government in safety through [the war], and who supposed that by [the 13th Amendment] they had secured the result of their labors, the conviction that something more was necessary in the way of constitutional protection to the unfortunate race who had suffered so much. They accordingly [proposed the 14th Amendment]. A few years' experience satisfied [those] who had been the authors of the other two amendments that [these] were inadequate for the protection of life, liberty, and property, without which freedom to the slave was no boon. [It] was urged that a race of men distinctively marked as was the negro, living in the midst of another and dominant race, could never be fully secured in their person and their property without the right of suffrage. Hence [the 15th Amendment].

[In] the light of this recapitulation of events, almost too recent to be called history, [and] on the most casual examination of the language of these amendments, no one can fail to be impressed with the one pervading purpose found in them all, [and] without which none of them would have been even suggested; we mean the freedom of the slave race [and] the protection of the newly-made freeman and citizen from the oppressions of those who had formerly exercised unlimited dominion over him. It is true that only the fifteenth amendment, in terms, mentions the negro, [but] it is just as true that each of the other articles was addressed to the grievances of that race, and designed to remedy them as the fifteenth. We do not say that no one else but the negro can share in this protection. [But] what we do say [is] that in any fair and just construction of any section or phrase of these amendments, it is necessary to look to the purpose which [was] the pervading spirit of them all, the evil which they were designed to remedy.

[The] first section of the [14th Amendment], to which our attention is more specially invited, opens with a definition of citizenship—not only citizenship of the United States, but citizenship of the States. * * * 'All persons born or naturalized in the United States, and subject to the jurisdiction thereof, are citizens of the United States and of the State wherein they reside.' [The section] overturns the *Dred Scott* decision by making *all persons* born within the United States [citizens] of the United States. [The] next observation is more important in view of the arguments of counsel in the present case. [T]he distinction between citizenship of the United States and citizenship of a State is clearly recognized and established. Not only may a man be a citizen of the United States without being a citizen of a State, but an important element is necessary to convert the former into the latter. He must reside within the State to make him a citizen of it, but it is only necessary that he should be born or naturalized in the United States to be a citizen of the Union.

[We] think [the distinction between citizenship of the United States and citizenship of a State] of great weight in this argument, because the next paragraph of this same section, which is the one mainly relied on by plaintiffs in error, speaks only of privileges and immunities of citizens of the United States, and does not speak of those of citizens of the several States. The argument, however, in favor of the plaintiffs rests wholly on the assumption that the citizenship is the same, and the privileges and immunities guaranteed by the clause are the same. The language is, 'No state shall make or enforce any law which shall abridge the privileges or immunities of citizens of *the United States.*' It is a little remarkable, if this clause was intended as a protection to the citizen of a State against the legislative power of his own State, that the word citizen of the State should be left out when it is so carefully used, and used in contradistinction to citizens of the United States, in the very sentence which precedes it. It is too clear for argument that the change in phraseology was adopted understandingly and with a purpose.

Of the privileges and immunities of the citizen of the United States, and of the privileges and immunities of the citizen of the State, and what they respectively are, we will presently consider; but we wish to state here that it is only the former which are placed by this clause under the protection of the federal Constitution, and that the latter, whatever they may be, are not intended to have any additional protection by this paragraph of the amendment.

The first occurrence of the words 'privileges and immunities' in our constitutional history, is to be found in [the] articles of the old Confederation. [Art. IV, § 2 of the Constitution states:] 'The citizens of each State shall be entitled to all the privileges and immunities of citizens of the several States.' [It] did not create those rights, which it called privileges and immunities of citizens of the States. It threw around them in that clause no security for the citizen of the State in which they were claimed or exercised. Nor did it profess to control the power of the State governments over the rights of its own citizens. Its sole purpose was to declare to the several States, that whatever those rights, as you grant or establish them to your own citizens, or as you limit or qualify [them], the same, neither more nor less, shall be the measure of the rights of citizens of other States within your jurisdiction.

[Up] to the adoption of the recent amendments, no claim or pretense was set up that those rights depended on the Federal government for their existence or protection, beyond the very few express limitations which the Federal Constitution imposed upon the States—such, for instance, as the prohibition against ex post facto laws, bills of attainder, and laws impairing the obligation of contracts. But with the exception of these and a few other restrictions, the entire domain of the privileges and immunities of citizens of the States [lay] within the constitutional and legislative power of the States, and without that of the Federal government. Was it the purpose of the fourteenth amendment, by the simple declaration that no State should make or enforce any law which shall abridge the privileges and immunities of *citizens of the United States,* to transfer the security and protection of all the civil rights [from] the States to the Federal government? And where it is declared that Congress shall have the power to enforce that article, was it intended to bring within the power of Congress the entire domain of civil rights heretofore belonging exclusively to the States?

[Such] a construction [would] constitute this court a perpetual censor upon all legislation of the States, on the civil rights of their own citizens, with authority to nullify such as it did not approve as consistent with those rights, as they existed at the time of the adoption of this amendment. [Such a construction] radically changes the whole theory of the relations of the State and Federal governments to each other and of both these governments to the people. [We] are convinced that no such results were intended by the Congress which proposed these amendments, nor by the legislatures of the States which ratified them.

[The] argument has not been much pressed in these cases that the defendant's charter deprives the plaintiffs of their property without due process of law, or that it denies to them the equal protection of the law. The first of these paragraphs has been in the Constitution since the adoption of the Fifth Amendment, as a restraint upon the Federal power. It is also to be found in some form of expression in the constitutions of nearly all the States, as a restraint upon the power of the States. [U]nder no construction of that provision that we have ever seen, or any that we deem admissible, can the restraint imposed [by] Louisiana upon the exercise of their trade by the butchers of New Orleans be held to be a deprivation of property within the meaning of that provision.

[In] the light of the history of these amendments, and the pervading purpose of them, [it] is not difficult to give a meaning to [the equal protection] clause. [Laws discriminating against] the newly emancipated negroes [were] the evil to be remedied by this clause, and by it such laws are forbidden. [We] doubt very much whether any action of a State not directed by way of discrimination against the negroes as a class, or on account of their race, will ever be held to come within the purview of this provision. It is so clearly a provision for that race and that emergency, that a strong case would be necessary for its application to any other. [Unquestionably the recent war] added largely to the number of those who believe in the necessity of a strong National government. But, however pervading this sentiment, and however it may have contributed to the adoption of the amendments we have been considering, we do not see in those amendments any purpose to destroy the main features of the general system.

JUSTICE FIELD, J., joined by CHIEF JUSTICE CHASE, JUSTICE SWAYNE, and JUSTICE BRADLEY, dissenting.

[The] question presented [is] whether the recent [amendments] protect the citizens of the United States against the deprivation of their common rights by State legislation. In my judgment, the fourteenth amendment does afford such [protection]. The amendment does not attempt to confer any new privileges or immunities upon citizens, or to enumerate or define those already existing. It assumes that there are such privileges and immunities which belong of right to citizens as such, and ordains that they shall not be abridged by State legislation.

If this inhibition [only] refers, as held by the [majority], [to] such privileges and immunities as were before its adoption specially designated in the Constitution or necessarily implied as belonging to citizens of the United States, it was a vain and idle enactment, which accomplished nothing, and most unnecessarily excited Congress and the people on its passage. With privileges and immunities thus designated or implied no State could ever have interfered by its laws, and no new constitutional provision was required to inhibit such interference. [But] if the amendment refers to the natural and inalienable rights which belong to all citizens, the inhibition has a profound significance and consequence.

[The] terms, privileges and immunities, are not new in the amendment; they were in the Constitution before the amendment was adopted. They are found in [Art. IV, § 2.] In *Corfield v. Coryell*, 6 F.Cas. 546 (No. 3,230) (C.C.E.D.Pa.1825), Mr. Justice Washington said he had "no hesitation in confining these expressions to those privileges and immunities which were, in their nature, fundamental; which belong of right to the citizens of all free governments." [This] appears to me to be a sound construction of the clause in question. [Clearly] among [these rights] must be placed the right to pursue a lawful employment in a lawful manner, without other restraint than such as equally affects all persons. In the discussions in Congress upon the passage of the Civil Rights Act repeated reference was made to this language of Mr. Justice Washington. It was cited by Senator Trumbull with the observation that it enumerated the very rights belonging to a citizen of the United States set forth in the first section of the act.

[The] privileges and immunities designated in [Art. IV, § 2] are, then, according to the decision cited, those which of right belong to the citizens of all free governments. [What] the clause in question did for the protection of the citizens of one State against hostile and discriminating legislation of other States, the fourteenth amendment does for the protection of every citizen of the United States against hostile and discriminating legislation against him in favor of others, whether they reside in the same or in different [States].

This equality of right, with exemption from all disparaging and partial enactments, in the lawful pursuits of life, throughout the whole country, is the distinguishing privilege of citizens of the United States. To them, everywhere, all pursuits, all professions, all avocations are open without other restrictions than such as are imposed equally upon all others of the same age, sex, and condition. The State may prescribe such regulations for every pursuit and calling of life as will promote the public health, secure the good order and advance the general prosperity of society, but when once prescribed, the pursuit or calling must be free to be followed by every citizen who is within the conditions designated, and will conform to the regulations. This is the fundamental idea upon which our institutions rest, and unless adhered to in the legislation of the country our government will be a republic only in name. The fourteenth amendment, in my judgment, makes it essential to the validity of the legislation of every State that this equality of right should be respected.

JUSTICE BRADLEY, dissenting.

[In] my judgment, it was the intention of the people of this country in adopting [the 14th] amendment to provide National security against violation by the States of the fundamental rights of the citizen. [A] law which prohibits a large class of citizens from adopting a lawful employment, or from following a lawful employment previously adopted, does deprive them of liberty as well as property, without due process of law. [Such] a law also deprives those citizens of the equal protection of the laws. [It] is futile to argue that none but persons of the African race are intended to be benefitted by this amendment. They may have been the primary cause of the amendment, but its language is general, embracing all citizens, and I think it was purposely so expressed. The mischief to be remedied was not merely slavery and its incidents and consequences; but that spirit of insubordination and disloyalty to the National government which had troubled the country for so many years in some of the States, and that intolerance of free speech and free discussion which often rendered life and property insecure, and led to much unequal legislation.

[But] great fears are expressed that this construction of the amendment will lead to enactments by Congress interfering with the internal affairs of the States. [In] my judgment no such practical inconveniences would arise. Very little, if any, legislation on the part of Congress would be required to carry the amendment into effect. Like the prohibition against passing a law impairing the obligation of a contract, it would execute itself. [Even] if the business of the National courts should be increased, Congress could easily supply the remedy by increasing their number and efficiency. The great question is: What is the true construction of the amendment? [The] argument from inconvenience ought not to have a very controlling influence in questions of this sort. The National will and National interest are of far greater importance.

———

In *McDonald v. City of Chicago*, Ch. 6, Sec. 6, the Privileges or Immunities Clause was offered as the basis for making the right to bear arms and, by implication, other provisions of the Bill of Rights, applicable to the states. Despite acknowledging a substantial body of scholarly literature arguing that *Slaughter-House* was wrongly decided, Justice Alito's opinion for the Court ultimately rested incorporation of that right and other rights on the Due Process Clause.

2. THE *LOCHNER* ERA

I. THE ROAD TO *LOCHNER*

Despite the *Slaughter-House* majority's suggestion that the Fourteenth Amendment was relevant only to cases involving the equal rights of formerly enslaved African Americans and their descendants, within a relatively short time the Court began to give the amendment a broader interpretation, especially in cases involving economic rights. The shift was presaged in *Munn v. Illinois*, 94 U.S. (4 Otto) 113 (1876). The Court, per WAITE, C.J., upheld a state law regulating the rates charged by grain elevators, pointing out that private property may be regulated when it is "affected with a public interest." However, the Court made a comment that was to be relied upon years later to justify judicial review of economic regulation: "Undoubtedly, in mere private contracts, relating to matters in which the public has no interest, what is reasonable must be ascertained judicially." Over a decade later, *Mugler v. Kansas*, 123 U.S. 623 (1887), upheld a state law prohibiting intoxicating beverages, but the Court, per HARLAN, J., made clear that not every statute said to be enacted for the promotion of "the public morals, the public health, or the public safety" would be sustained. If a law supposedly enacted pursuant to the police powers of the state "has no real or substantial relation to these objects, or is a palpable invasion of rights secured by the fundamental law, it is the duty of the courts to so adjudge."

ALLGEYER v. LOUISIANA, 165 U.S. 578 (1897), was the first reasoned Supreme Court decision actually to hold that the substance of economic legislation violated Fourteenth Amendment Due Process. A unanimous Court, per PECKHAM, J., struck down a Louisiana law prohibiting any act in the state that directly or indirectly facilitated a contract for marine insurance on state property with a company not licensed to do business in the state. Although the opinion hinted that Louisiana might have impermissibly extended the reach of its laws beyond its territorial limits, the ruling was ultimately based on individual liberty rather than horizontal federalism. According to the Court, the statute exceeded the police power of the state and deprived the defendants of their Fourteenth Amendment liberty to contract for insurance: "The 'liberty' mentioned in that amendment means, not only the right of the citizen to be free from the mere physical restraint of his person, but [also includes] the right of the citizen to be free in the enjoyment of all his faculties, to be free to use them in all lawful ways; to live and work where he will; [to] pursue any livelihood or avocation; and for that purpose to enter into all contracts which may be proper, necessary, and essential to his carrying out to a successful conclusion the purposes above mentioned."

LOCHNER v. NEW YORK
198 U.S. 45, 25 S.Ct. 539, 49 L.Ed. 937 (1905).

JUSTICE PECKHAM delivered the opinion of the Court.

[The Court held invalid a New York statute forbidding employment in a bakery for more than 60 hours per week or 10 hours per day.]

The statute necessarily interferes with the right of contract between the employer and employees. [The] general right to make a contract in relation to his business is part of the liberty of the individual protected by the 14th Amendment. [*Allgeyer*.] The right to purchase or to sell labor is part of the liberty protected by this amendment, unless there are circumstances which exclude the right. There are, however, certain powers, existing in the sovereignty of each state in the Union, somewhat vaguely termed police powers, the exact description and limitation of which have not been attempted by the courts. [This court has] upheld the exercise of the police powers of the states in many cases, [among them] *Holden v. Hardy*, 169 U.S. 366 (1898), [where it] was held that the kind of employment, mining, smelting, etc., and the character of the employees in such kinds of labor, were such as to make it reasonable and proper for the State to interfere to prevent the employees from being constrained by the rules laid down by the proprietors in regard to labor. [There] is nothing in *Holden v. Hardy* which covers the case now before us.

It must, of course, be conceded that there is a limit to the valid exercise of the police power by the state. [Otherwise] the 14th Amendment would have no efficacy and the legislatures of the states would have unbounded power. [In] every case that comes before this court, therefore, where legislation of this character is concerned, and where the protection of the Federal Constitution is sought, the question necessarily arises: Is this a fair, reasonable, and appropriate exercise of the police power of the state, or is it an unreasonable, unnecessary, and arbitrary interference with the right of the individual to his personal liberty, or to enter into those contracts in relation to labor which may seem to him appropriate or necessary for the support of himself and his family? Of course the liberty of contract relating to labor includes both parties to it. The one has as much right to purchase as the other to sell labor. This is not a question of substituting the judgment of the court for that of the legislature. If the act be within the power of the state it is valid, although the judgment of the court might be totally opposed to the enactment of such a law. But the question would still remain: Is it within the police power of the State? and that question must be answered by the court.

The question whether this act is valid as a labor law, pure and simple, may be dismissed in a few words. There is no reasonable ground for interfering with the liberty of person or the right of free contract, by determining the hours of labor, in the occupation of a baker. There is no contention that bakers as a class are not equal in intelligence and capacity to men in other trades or manual occupations, or that they are not able to assert their rights and care for themselves without the protecting arm of the state. [They] are in no sense wards of the state. Viewed in the light of a purely labor law, with no reference whatever to the question of health, we think that a law like the one before us involves neither the safety, the morals, nor the welfare, of the public, and that the interest of the public is not in the slightest degree affected by such an act. The law must be upheld, if at all, as a law pertaining to the health of the individual engaged in the occupation of a baker. It does not affect any other portion of the public than those who are engaged in that occupation. Clean and wholesome bread does not depend upon whether the baker works but ten hours per day or only sixty hours a week. [There] is, in our judgment, no reasonable foundation for holding this to be necessary or appropriate as a health law to safeguard the public health, or the health of the individuals who are following the trade of a baker.

[We] think that there can be no fair doubt that the trade of a baker, in and of itself, is not an unhealthy one to that degree which would authorize the legislature to interfere with the right to labor, and with the right of free contract on the part of the individual, either as employer or employee. [Some] occupations are more healthy than others, but we think there are none which might not come under the power of the legislature to supervise and control the hours of working therein, if the mere fact that the occupation is not absolutely and perfectly healthy is to confer that right upon the legislative department of the government. [It] is unfortunately true that labor, even in any department, may possibly carry with it the seeds of unhealthiness. But are we all, on that account, at the mercy of legislative majorities? A printer, a tinsmith, a locksmith, a carpenter, a cabinet maker, a dry goods clerk, a bank's, a lawyer's, or a physician's clerk, or a clerk in almost any kind of business, would all come under the power of the legislature, on this assumption. No trade, no occupation, no mode of earning one's living, could escape this all-pervading power, and the acts of the legislature in limiting the hours of labor in all employments would be valid, although such limitation might seriously cripple the ability of the laborer to support himself and his family.

[It] is also urged [that] it is to the interest of the state that its population should be strong and robust, and therefore any legislation which may be said to tend to make people healthy must be valid as health laws, enacted under the police power. If this be a valid argument and a justification for this kind of legislation, it follows that the protection of the Federal Constitution from undue interference with liberty of person and freedom of contract is visionary, wherever the law is sought to be justified as a valid exercise of the police power. Scarcely any law but might find shelter under such assumptions. [Not] only the hours of employees, but the hours of employers, could be regulated, and doctors, lawyers, scientists, all professional men, as well as athletes and artisans, could be forbidden to fatigue their brains and bodies by prolonged hours of exercise, lest the fighting strength of the state be impaired. We mention these extreme cases because the contention is extreme. We do not believe in the soundness of the views which uphold this law. [The] act is not, within any fair meaning of the term, a health law, but is an illegal interference with the rights of individuals, both employers and employees, to make contracts regarding labor upon such terms as they may think best, or which they may agree upon with the other parties to such contracts. Statutes of the nature of that under review, limiting the hours in which grown and intelligent men may labor to earn their living, are mere meddlesome interferences with the rights of the individual, and they are not saved from condemnation by the claim that they are passed in the exercise of the police power and upon the subject of the health of the individual whose rights are interfered with, unless there be some fair ground, reasonable in and of itself, to say that there is material danger to the public health, or to the health of the employees, if the hours of labor are not curtailed.

[This] interference on the part of the legislatures of the several states with the ordinary trades and occupations of the people seems to be on the increase. [It] is impossible for us to shut our eyes to the fact that many of the laws of this character, while passed under what is claimed to be the police power for the purpose of protecting the public health or welfare, are, in reality, passed from other motives. We are justified in saying so when, from the character of the law and the subject upon which it legislates, it is apparent that the public health or welfare bears but the most remote relation to the law. * * *

JUSTICE HARLAN (with whom JUSTICE WHITE and JUSTICE DAY concurred) dissenting: * * *

I take it to be firmly established that what is called the liberty of contract may, within certain limits, be subjected to regulations designed and calculated to promote the general welfare, or to guard the public health, the public morals, or the public safety. [It] is plain that this statute was enacted in order to protect the physical well-being of those who work in bakery and confectionery establishments. [The] statute must be taken as expressing the belief of the people of New York that, as a general rule, and in the case of the average man, labor in excess of sixty hours during a week in such establishments may endanger the health of those who thus labor. Whether or not this be wise legislation it is not the province of the court to inquire. Under our systems of government the courts are not concerned with the wisdom or policy of legislation. So that in determining the question of power to interfere with liberty or contract, the court may inquire whether the means devised by the state are germane to an end which may be lawfully accomplished and have a real or substantial relation to the protection of health, as involved in the daily work of the persons, male and female, engaged in bakery and confectionery establishments. But when this inquiry is entered upon I find it impossible, in view of common experience, to say that there is here no real or substantial relation between the means employed by the state and the end sought to be accomplished by its legislation. Nor can I say that the statute has no appropriate or direct connection with that protection to health which each state owes to her citizens or that it is not promotive of the health of the employees in question or that the regulation prescribed by the state is utterly unreasonable and extravagant or wholly arbitrary. Still less can I say that the statute is, beyond question, a plain, palpable invasion of rights secured by the fundamental law.

[The dissenting opinion cited statistics on the health problems of workers, pointing out that long hours, night hours, and difficult working conditions, such as excessive heat and exposure to flour dust, were injurious to the health of bakers, who] seldom live over their fiftieth year. [We] judicially know that the question of the number of hours during which a workman should continuously labor has been, for a long period, and is yet, a subject of serious consideration among civilized peoples, and by those having special knowledge of the laws of health. [We] also judicially know that the number of hours that should constitute a day's labor in particular occupations involving the physical strength and safety of workmen has been the subject of enactments by Congress and by nearly all of the states. Many, if not most, of those enactments fix eight hours as the proper basis of a day's labor.

I do not stop to consider whether any particular view of this economic question presents the sounder theory. [It] is enough for the determination of this case [that] the question is one about which there is room for debate and for an honest difference of opinion. There are many reasons of a weighty, substantial character, based upon the experience of mankind, in support of the theory that, all things considered, more than ten hours' steady work each day, from week to week, in a bakery or confectionery establishment, may endanger the health and shorten the lives of the workmen, thereby diminishing their physical and mental capacity to serve the State and to provide for those dependent upon them.

If such reasons exist that ought to be the end of this case, for the state is not amenable to the judiciary, in respect of its legislative enactments, unless such enactments are plainly, palpably, beyond all question, inconsistent with the Constitution of the United States. * * *

JUSTICE HOLMES dissenting: * * *

This case is decided upon an economic theory which a large part of the country does not entertain. If it were a question whether I agree with that theory, I should desire to study it further and long before making up my mind. But I do not conceive that to be my duty, because I strongly believe that my agreement or disagreement has nothing to do with the right of a majority to embody their opinions in law. It is settled by various decisions of this court that state constitutions and state laws may regulate life in many ways which we as legislators might think as injudicious, or if you like as tyrannical, as this, and which, equally with this, interfere with the liberty to contract. Sunday laws and usury laws are ancient examples. A more modern one is the prohibition of lotteries. The liberty of the citizen to do as he likes so long as he does not interfere with the liberty of others to do the same, which has been a shibboleth for some well-known writers, is interfered with by school laws, by the Post Office, by every state or municipal institution which takes his money for purposes thought desirable, whether he likes it or not. The 14th Amendment does not enact Mr. Herbert Spencer's *Social Statics*. [A] Constitution is not intended to embody a particular economic theory, whether of paternalism and the organic relation of the citizen to the state or of laissez faire. It is made for people of fundamentally differing views, and the accident of our finding certain opinions natural and familiar, or novel, and even shocking, ought not to conclude our judgment upon the question whether statutes embodying them conflict with the Constitution of the United States.

General propositions do not decide concrete cases. [But] I think that the proposition just stated, if it is accepted, will carry us far toward the end. [I] think that the word "liberty," in the 14th Amendment, is perverted when it is held to prevent the natural outcome of a dominant opinion, unless it can be said that a rational and fair man necessarily would admit that the statute proposed would infringe fundamental principles as they have been understood by the traditions of our people and our law. It does not need research to show that no such sweeping condemnation can be passed upon the statute before us. * * *

II. THREE DECADES OF CONTROL
OVER LEGISLATIVE POLICY

Although the *Lochner*-era Court professed that reasonable exercises of the police power would be upheld, regardless of the underlying policy, the received wisdom holds that the Court frequently substituted its judgment of the wisdom of economic regulation said to interfere with contract and property interests for that of Congress and state legislatures, doing so most freely in cases involving labor legislation, regulation of prices, and limitations on entry into business. With regularity Holmes, J., dissented from these rulings, joined later by Brandeis and Stone, JJ., and Hughes, C.J.

1.   *Hours of labor.* Notwithstanding the holding of *Lochner*, in 1908 the Court sustained regulation of work hours for women in MULLER v. OREGON, 208 U.S. 412 (1908), basing the decision on sex-based stereotypes. The Court, per BREWER, J., thought it plain that "woman's physical structure" put her at a disadvantage in the struggle for subsistence and that because "healthy mothers are essential to vigorous offspring, the physical well-being of woman becomes an object of public interest." The "inherent difference[s] between the two sexes," continued the Court, "justify special legislation restricting or qualifying the conditions under which [women] should be permitted to toil." The majority was influenced by a so-called "Brandeis brief," which furnished the Court with empirical evidence in support of regulation of hours of labor for women. Felix Frankfurter successfully followed the same technique as counsel in BUNTING v. OREGON, 243 U.S. 426 (1917), in which a 5–3 Court appeared to overrule *Lochner* (but not its philosophy) when it sustained a regulation of work hours for men in manufacturing establishments.

2.   *Anti-union discrimination.* The Court struck down both federal and state labor legislation forbidding discrimination by employers for union activity and prohibiting employers from requiring employees to sign "yellow dog" contracts, i.e., agreements not to remain or become union members.

ADAIR v. UNITED STATES, 208 U.S. 161 (1908) (5th Amendment); COPPAGE v. KANSAS, 236 U.S. 1 (1915) (14th Amendment). The opinion in *Adair* was written by HARLAN, J., one of the dissenters in *Lochner*. He deemed the "right of a person to sell his labor upon such terms as he deems proper [to be] the same as the right of the purchaser to prescribe the conditions." An employer and his employees "have equality of right, and any legislation that disturbs that equality is an arbitrary interference with the liberty of contract." PITNEY, J., speaking for the Court in *Coppage*, proclaimed that the Fourteenth Amendment protects "the right to make contracts" and an "interference with this liberty so serious as that now under consideration, and so disturbing of equality of right, must be deemed to be arbitrary, unless it be supportable as a reasonable exercise of the police power of the state." The Court was not impressed by the argument that "employees, as a rule, are not financially able to be as independent in making contracts for the sale of their labor as are employers in making a contract of purchase thereof." It is "from the nature of things impossible," responded the Court, "to uphold freedom of contract and the right of private property without at the same time recognizing as legitimate those inequalities of fortune that are the necessary result of the exercise of those rights." HOLMES, J., dissented: "[A] workman not unnaturally may believe that only by belonging to a union can he secure a contract that shall be fair to him. [If] that belief, whether right or wrong, may be held by a reasonable man, it seems to me that it may be enforced by law in order to establish the equality of position between the parties in which liberty of contract begins."

These restrictive decisions were distinguished away in *Texas & N.O.R. Co. v. Brotherhood of Ry. & S.S. Clerks*, 281 U.S. 548 (1930) and *NLRB v. Jones & Laughlin Steel Corp.*, 301 U.S. 1 (1937). They were finally expressly overruled in *Phelps Dodge Corp. v. NLRB*, 313 U.S. 177 (1941) and *Lincoln Fed. Labor Union v. Northwestern Iron & Met. Co.* (1949), Sec. 3 infra.

In EPIC SYSTEMS CORP. v. LEWIS, 138 S.Ct. 1612 (2018), the Court, per GORSUCH, J., held that the Federal Arbitration Act rendered enforceable employment contracts requiring arbitration and thus precluding employees from bringing a class action to enforce provisions of the federal Fair Labor Standards Act and related state law claims. Dissenting for herself and three colleagues, GINSBURG, J., recounted congressional efforts in the wake of *Coppage* to protect workers against yellow dog contracts, deeming the Court's decisions sustaining those efforts a "retreat from its *Lochner*-era contractual-'liberty' decisions." In response, the majority opined that "like most apocalyptic warnings, this one proves a false alarm. [Our] decision does nothing to override Congress's policy judgments."

3. ***Regulation of wages.*** Six years after it had upheld regulation of *hours* of labor in *Bunting*, the Court, per SUTHERLAND, J., ruled that a federal statute prescribing minimum *wages* for women in the District of Columbia violated due process.

ADKINS v. CHILDREN'S HOSPITAL, 261 U.S. 525 (1923): The Court emphasized that, although "freedom of contract" is subject to a great variety of restraints, it "is, nevertheless, the general rule and restraint the exception, and the exercise of legislative authority to abridge it can be justified only by the existence of exceptional circumstances." "[This] is not a law dealing with any business charged with a public interest or with public work," continued the Court, nor is it "for the protection of persons under legal disability or for the prevention of fraud. It is simply and exclusively a price-fixing law, confined to adult women, [who] are legally as capable of contracting for themselves as men." The Court noted that the Nineteenth Amendment had recently been adopted, thus reducing the civil inferiority of women almost to the "vanishing point." Therefore, "liberty of contract" could not be subjected to greater infringement in the case of women than of men.

HOLMES, J., dissenting, expressed his inability to "understand the principle on which the power to fix a minimum for the wages of women can be denied by those who admit the power to fix a maximum for their hours of work." As for the recent adoption of the Nineteenth Amendment, he wrote that it "will need more than [that] to convince me that there are no differences between men and women, or that legislation cannot take those differences into account."

4.   ***Regulation of prices.*** The Court also held that regulation of prices for commodities and services violated due process except for a limited class of businesses "affected with a public interest." *Nebbia v. New York* (1934) severely limited these rulings and they were expressly overruled in *Olsen v. Nebraska ex rel. Western Ref. & Bond Ass'n* (1941), both in Sec. 3 infra.

3. THE ABANDONMENT OF *LOCHNER*

NEBBIA V. NEW YORK
291 U.S. 502, 54 S.Ct. 505, 78 L.Ed. 940 (1934).

JUSTICE ROBERTS delivered the opinion of the Court.

[In 1933, after a year's legislative study of the state's dairy industry, New York enacted a law establishing a Milk Control Board with power to fix maximum and minimum retail prices. The Board fixed nine cents per quart as the price to be charged by a retail store. Nebbia, the proprietor of a grocery, was convicted of selling milk below the minimum price.]

[Under] our form of government the use of property and the making of contracts are normally matters of private and not of public concern. The general rule is that both shall be free of governmental interference. But neither property rights nor contract rights are absolute; for government cannot exist if the citizen may at will use his property to the detriment of his fellows, or exercise his freedom of contract to work them harm. Equally fundamental with the private right is that of the public to regulate it in the common interest. [T]he guaranty of due process [demands] only that the law shall not be unreasonable, arbitrary, or capricious, and that the means selected shall have a real and substantial relation to the object sought to be attained. [A] regulation valid for one sort of business, or in given circumstances, may be invalid for another sort, or for the same business under other circumstances, because the reasonableness of each regulation depends upon the relevant facts.

[The opinion then summarized many different kinds of business and property regulations and controls previously sustained against due process attacks.]

The legislative investigation of 1932 was persuasive of the fact [that] unrestricted competition aggravated existing evils and the normal law of supply and demand was insufficient to correct maladjustments detrimental to the community. The inquiry disclosed destructive and demoralizing competitive conditions and unfair trade practices which resulted in retail price cutting and reduced the income of the farmer below the cost of production. [The Legislature] believed conditions could be improved by preventing destructive price-cutting by stores which, due to the flood of surplus milk, were able to buy at much lower prices than the larger distributors and to sell without incurring the delivery costs of the latter. [In] the light of the facts the [Milk Control Board's] order appears not to be unreasonable or arbitrary, or without relation to the purpose to prevent ruthless competition from destroying the wholesale price structure on which the farmer depends for his livelihood, and the community for an assured supply of milk. But we are told that because the law essays to control prices it denies due process. Notwithstanding the admitted power to correct existing economic ills by appropriate regulation of business, [the] appellant urges that direct fixation of prices is a type of regulation absolutely forbidden. [The] argument runs that the public control of rates or prices is per se unreasonable and unconstitutional, save as applied to businesses affected with a public interest; that a business so affected is [one] such as is commonly called a public utility; or a business in its nature a monopoly. [But] if, as must be conceded, the industry is subject to regulation in the public interest, what constitutional principle bars the state from correcting existing maladjustments by legislation touching prices? We think there is no such principle. The due process clause makes no mention of sales or of prices any more than it speaks of business or contracts or buildings or other incidents of property. The thought seems nevertheless to have persisted that there is something peculiarly sacrosanct about the price one may charge for what he makes or sells, and that, however able to regulate other elements of manufacture or trade, with incidental effect upon price, the state is incapable of directly controlling the price itself. This view was negatived many years ago. *Munn v. Illinois.*

"[Affected] with a public interest" is the equivalent of "subject to the exercise of the police power" and it is plain that nothing more was intended by the expression. [It] is clear that there is no closed class or category of businesses affected with a public interest, and the function of courts in the application of the Fifth and Fourteenth Amendments is to determine in each case whether circumstances vindicate the challenged regulation as a reasonable exertion of governmental authority or condemn it as arbitrary or discriminatory. The phrase "affected with a public interest" can, in the nature of things, mean no more than that an industry, for adequate reason, is subject to control for the public good. [There] can be no doubt that upon proper occasion and by appropriate measures the state may regulate a business in any of its aspects, including the prices to be charged for the products or commodities it sells.

So far as the requirement of due process is concerned, [a] state is free to adopt whatever economic policy may reasonably be deemed to promote public welfare, and to enforce that policy by legislation adapted to its purpose. The courts are without authority either to declare such policy, or, when it is declared by the legislature, to override it. If the laws passed are seen to have a reasonable relation to a proper legislative purpose, and are neither arbitrary nor discriminatory, the requirements of due process are satisfied. [With] the wisdom of the policy adopted, with the adequacy or practicability of the law enacted to forward it, the courts are both incompetent and unauthorized to deal. * * *

JUSTICE MCREYNOLDS, joined by JUSTICE VAN DEVANTER, JUSTICE SUTHERLAND, and JUSTICE BUTLER, dissenting:

[P]lainly, I think, this Court must have regard to the wisdom of the enactment. At least, we must inquire concerning its purpose and decide whether the means proposed have reasonable relation to something within legislative power—whether the end is legitimate, and the means appropriate. [Here,] we find direct interference with guaranteed rights defended upon the ground that the purpose was to promote the public welfare by increasing milk prices at the farm. [The] court below [has] not attempted to indicate how higher charges at stores to impoverished customers when the output is excessive and sale prices by producers are unrestrained, can possibly increase receipts at the farm. [It] appears to me wholly unreasonable to expect this legislation to accomplish the proposed end— increase of prices at the farm. [Not] only does the statute interfere arbitrarily with the rights of the little grocer to conduct his business according to standards long accepted—complete destruction may follow; but it takes away the liberty of 12,000,000 consumers. [Grave] concern for embarrassed farmers is everywhere; but this should neither obscure the rights of others nor obstruct judicial appraisement of measures proposed for relief. The ultimate welfare of the producer, like that of every other class, requires dominance of the Constitution.

———

WEST COAST HOTEL CO. v. PARRISH, 300 U.S. 379 (1937), dealt the decisive blow. The decision overruled *Adkins v. Children's Hospital* and sustained a state minimum wage law for women. A 5–4 majority, per HUGHES, C.J., devoted substantial space to the reasons for regulation of women's wages: "What can be closer to the public interest than the health of women and their protection from unscrupulous and overreaching employers? [The] Legislature of the state was clearly entitled to consider [the] fact that [women] are in the class receiving the least pay, that their bargaining power is relatively weak, and that they are the ready victims of those who would take advantage of their necessitous circumstances. The Legislature was entitled to adopt measures to reduce the evils of the 'sweating system,' the exploiting of workers at wages so low as to be insufficient to meet the bare cost of living, thus making their very helplessness the occasion of a most injurious competition. [What] these workers lose in wages the taxpayers are called upon to pay. [We] may take judicial notice of the unparalleled demands for relief which arose during the recent period of depression. [The] community is not bound to provide, what is in effect a subsidy for unconscionable employers. [Even] if the wisdom of the policy be regarded as debatable and its effects uncertain, still the Legislature is entitled to its judgment."

As for the contention that the law violated "freedom of contract": "What is this freedom? The Constitution does not speak of freedom of contract. It [prohibits] the deprivation of liberty without due process of law [and in so doing] the Constitution does not recognize an absolute and uncontrollable liberty. [Liberty] under the Constitution [is] necessarily subject to the restraints of due process, and regulation which is reasonable in relation to its subject and is adopted in the interests of the community is due process. [We] think [*Adkins*] was a departure from the true application of the principles governing the regulation by the state of the relation of employer and employed." Sutherland, J., joined by Van Devanter, McReynolds, and Butler, JJ., dissented.

Footnote 4 of the *Carolene Products Case*

UNITED STATES v. CAROLENE PRODUCTS CO., 304 U.S. 144 (1938), upheld the constitutionality of a federal statute that prohibited the shipment in interstate commerce of "filled milk," defined as a compound of skimmed milk and a fat or oil other than milk fat. Appellee argued that the legislation violated both the commerce and due process clauses. The government countered that appellee's product posed a danger to the public. Writing for the Court, STONE, J., took the position that economic regulatory legislation, such as the statute at issue, was entitled to a presumption of constitutionality and should be upheld if supported by any rational basis. "Where the existence of a rational basis for legislation whose constitutionality is attacked depends upon facts beyond the sphere of judicial notice," continued Stone, "such facts may properly be made the subject of judicial inquiry, and the constitutionality of a statute predicated upon the existence of a particular state of facts may be challenged by showing to the court that those facts have ceased to exist. [But] by their very nature such inquiries, where the legislative judgment is drawn in question, must be restricted to the issue whether any state of facts either known or which could reasonably be assumed affords support for it." Under this approach, the challenged legislation easily passed constitutional muster. In the course of writing his opinion, Stone, J., dropped a footnote (fn. 4) that appears to have predicted many of the civil rights and civil liberties decisions of the ensuing decades. It reads as follows:

"There may be narrower scope for operation of the presumption of constitutionality when legislation appears on its face to be within a specific prohibition of the Constitution, such as those of the first ten Amendments, which are deemed equally specific when held to be embraced within the Fourteenth.

"It is unnecessary to consider now whether legislation which restricts those political processes which can ordinarily be expected to bring about repeal of undesirable legislation, is to be subjected to more exacting judicial scrutiny under the general prohibitions of the Fourteenth than are most other types of legislation [referring to cases dealing with restrictions on voting rights and freedom of expression and political association].

"Nor need we enquire whether similar considerations enter into the review of statutes directed at particular religious, or national, or racial minorities[:] whether prejudice against discrete and insular minorities may be a special condition, which tends seriously to curtail the operation of those political processes ordinarily to be relied upon to protect minorities, and which may call for a correspondingly more searching judicial inquiry."

The 1940s, 50s and 60s: A Far Cry from *Lochner*

West Coast Hotel was followed quickly by a number of cases upholding New Deal legislation as falling within congressional power to regulate interstate commerce. See, e.g., *NLRB v. Jones & Laughlin Steel Corp.*, 301 U.S. 1 (1937) (the National Labor Relations Act); *United States v. Darby*, 312 U.S. 100 (1941) (the Fair Labor Standards Act); *Wickard v. Filburn*, 317 U.S. 111 (1942) (the Agricultural Adjustment Act). A great deal of state economic legislation was also sustained against challenges asserting economic rights. Some representative cases follow:

OLSEN v. NEBRASKA, 313 U.S. 236 (1941), upheld a Nebraska statute fixing maximum fees for employment agencies. DOUGLAS, J.'s, unanimous opinion bluntly rejected the state court's reliance on *Ribnik v. McBride*, 277 U.S. 350 (1928), which had held a similar statute violative of due process: "[Respondents] insist that special circumstances must be shown to support the validity of such drastic legislation as price-fixing, [that] legislative limitation of maximum fees for employment agencies is certain to react unfavorably upon those members of the community for whom it is most difficult to obtain jobs, [and that] there are no conditions which the legislature might reasonably believe would redound to the public injury unless corrected by such legislation. [We] are not concerned, however, with the wisdom, need, or appropriateness of the legislation. Differences of opinion on that score suggest a choice which 'should be left where [it] was left by the Constitution—to the states and to Congress.' *Ribnik,* dissenting opinion. [In the] final analysis, the only constitutional prohibitions or restraints which respondents have suggested for the invalidation of this legislation are those notions of public policy embedded in earlier decisions of this Court but which, as Mr. Justice Holmes long ago admonished, should not be read into the Constitution."

In LINCOLN FEDERAL LABOR UNION v. NORTHWESTERN IRON & METAL CO., 335 U.S. 525 (1949), a unanimous Court, per BLACK, J., sustained a state law that barred a preference for union membership in employment decisions. The Court noted that at least since *Nebbia*, it had "steadily rejected the due process philosophy enunciated in the [*Lochner-Coppage*] line of cases" and returned closer to the earlier constitutional principle that states may legislate "against what are found to be injurious practices in their internal commercial and business affairs, so long as their laws do not run afoul of some specific federal constitutional prohibition [or] some valid federal law."

WILLIAMSON v. LEE OPTICAL OF OKLAHOMA, INC., 348 U.S. 483 (1955), where a unanimous Court, per DOUGLAS, J., upheld an Oklahoma law regulating opticians and optometrists, illustrates the great distance the Court had moved away from *Lochner* by the 1950s.

The law prohibited opticians from fitting or duplicating lenses without a prescription from an ophthalmologist or optometrist. "In practical effect, it means that no optician can fit old glasses into new frames or supply a lens, whether it be a new lens or one to duplicate a lost or broken lens, without a prescription." The lower court invalidated the law because an optician of ordinary skill could read a prescription from a broken lens fragment. The Supreme Court reversed despite its acknowledgment that the "law may exact a needless, wasteful requirement in many cases. But it is for the legislature, not the courts, to balance the advantages and disadvantages of [the] requirement. [The] legislature might have concluded that the frequency of occasions when a prescription is necessary was sufficient to justify this regulation of the fitting of eyeglasses. [Or] the legislature may have concluded that eye examinations were so critical [that] every change in frames and every duplication of a lens should be accompanied by a prescription from a medical expert. To be sure, the present law does not require a new examination of the eyes every time the frames are changed or the lenses duplicated. [But] the law need not be in every respect logically consistent with its aims to be constitutional. [The] day is gone when this Court uses the Due Process Clause [to] strike down state laws, regulatory of business and industrial conditions, because they may be unwise, improvident, or out of harmony with a particular school of thought."

A provision of the law that prohibited soliciting the sale of eyeglass frames was challenged on the ground that it regulated in a commercial area "only casually related to the visual care of the public." The Court responded: "[The] legislature might conclude that to regulate [lenses] effectively, it would have to regulate [eyeglass frames]. The advertiser of frames may be using his ads to bring in customers who will buy lenses."

Yet another provision of the law prohibited retail stores from renting space to optometrists. The Court rejected the challenge to this measure as well, viewing it as "an attempt to free the profession, to as great an extent as possible, from all taints of commercialism. It certainly might be easy for an optometrist with space in a retail store to be merely a front for the retail establishment. [We] cannot say that the regulation has no rational relation [to the setting of professional standards] and therefore is beyond constitutional bounds."

In FERGUSON v. SKRUPA, 372 U.S. 726 (1963), the Court, per BLACK, J., without a dissent, rejected a due process challenge to a state law barring all but lawyers from the business of debt adjusting. And it did so in the strongest terms: "Under the system of government created by our Constitution, it is up to legislatures, not courts, to decide on the wisdom and utility of legislation. [The] doctrine that prevailed in *Lochner, Coppage, Adkins*, [and] like cases [has] long since been discarded. We have returned to the original constitutional proposition that courts do not substitute their social and economic beliefs for the judgment of legislative bodies, who are elected to pass laws. [Whether] the legislature takes for its textbook Adam Smith, Herbert Spencer, Lord Keynes or some other is no concern of ours." HARLAN, J., concurred in the judgment on the ground that "[this] measure bears a rational relation to a constitutionally permissible objective."

PUNITIVE DAMAGE CONSTRAINTS

Do more recent decisions placing some limits on punitive damage awards constitute a partial return of robust judicial review of economic regulation under the rubric of substantive due process?

BMW OF NORTH AMERICA, INC. v. GORE, 517 U.S. 559 (1996), marked the first time that the Court found that a punitive damages award violated due process on the ground that it was "grossly excessive," considering such factors as the degree of reprehensibility of the defendant's conduct and the disparity between the harm suffered by the plaintiff and the punitive damage award. The defendant had been assessed $2 million in punitive damages for having knowingly failed to tell an automobile buyer that, at a cost of $600, it had repainted portions of his new $40,000 car, thereby lowering its potential resale value by about 10 percent. A 5–4 majority, per STEVENS, J., recognized that prior cases had "consistently rejected the notion that the constitutional line is marked by a simple mathematical formula, even one that compares actual *and potential* damages to the punitive award." The Court added: "When the ratio is a breathtaking 500 to 1, however, the award must surely 'raise a suspicious judicial eyebrow.' "

SCALIA, J., joined by Thomas, J., dissented: "[What] the Fourteenth Amendment's procedural guarantee assures is an opportunity to contest the reasonableness of a damages judgment in state court; but there is no federal guarantee a damages award actually *be* reasonable." In a separate dissent, GINSBURG, J., joined by REHNQUIST, C.J., maintained that "[the] Court is not well equipped for this mission. [It] has only a vague concept of substantive due process, a 'raised eyebrow' test, as its ultimate guide."

———

STATE FARM MUT. AUTO INS. CO. v. CAMPBELL, 538 U.S. 408 (2003), struck down another punitive damages award. The case involved a $145 million punitive damages award where full compensatory damages were only $1 million. A 6–3 majority, per KENNEDY, J., observed: "[Due process] prohibits the imposition of grossly excessive or arbitrary punishments on a tortfeasor. [We] decline again to impose a bright-line ratio which a punitive damages award cannot exceed. Our jurisprudence and the principles it has now established demonstrate, however, that, in practice, few awards exceeding a single-digit ratio between punitive and compensatory damages, to a significant degree, will satisfy due process." Scalia, Thomas, and Ginsburg, JJ., each filed separate dissents.

———

PHILIP MORRIS v. WILLIAMS, 549 U.S. 346 (2007), addressed a question about the purpose of punitive damages. A jury ordered the defendant tobacco company to pay $821,000 in compensatory damages to the widow of a smoker for negligence and deceit. A punitive damages award of $79.5 million followed the trial judge's refusal to instruct the jury "not to punish the defendant for the impact of its alleged misconduct on other persons, who may bring lawsuits of their own in which other juries can resolve their claims," after the plaintiff's attorney had urged jurors to "think about how many other Jesse Williams in the last 40 years in the State of Oregon there have been." The Oregon Supreme Court sustained the award, but a 5–4 majority, per BREYER, J., vacated that judgment and held that a punitive damages award based upon a jury's "desire to *punish* the defendant for harming persons who are not before the court" would violate the defendant's right to due process.

STEVENS, J., dissented: "[I] see no reason why an interest in punishing a wrongdoer 'for harming persons who are not before the court' should not be taken into consideration when assessing the appropriate sanction for reprehensible conduct." GINSBURG, J., joined by Scalia and Thomas, JJ., wrote a separate dissent, contending that the punitive damages award was not in fact aimed at punishing the defendant for harm to third parties but for the reprehensibility of the conduct. THOMAS, J., also dissented separately, reiterating his "view that 'the Constitution does not constrain the size of punitive damage awards.' "

———

BROWNING-FERRIS INDUSTRIES OF VERMONT v. KELCO DISPOSAL, INC., 492 U.S. 257 (1989), ruled out the Eighth Amendment's prohibition on "excessive fines" as an alternative basis for limiting punitive damages. The Court, per BLACKMUN, J., acknowledged that "[the] Eighth Amendment received little debate in the First Congress," and that "the Excessive Fines Clause received even less attention." Nonetheless, on the basis of the "undisputed purpose and history of the Amendment generally," the majority concluded that it does not apply in private civil litigation. In an opinion concurring in part and dissenting in part, O'CONNOR, J., joined by Stevens, J., relied on historical studies of the same period to reach the opposite conclusion.

4. OTHER LIMITS ON ECONOMIC LEGISLATION: THE PROHIBITION AGAINST "TAKING" "PRIVATE PROPERTY" WITHOUT JUST COMPENSATION

The Fifth Amendment limits the federal government's power of eminent domain: "nor shall private property be taken for a public use without just compensation." This specific provision of the Bill of Rights was one of the first to be deemed binding on the states via Fourteenth Amendment due process. See *Chicago, B. & Q. R. Co. v. Chicago*, 166 U.S. 226 (1897); *Missouri Pac. Ry. Co. v. Nebraska*, 164 U.S. 403 (1896). Perhaps because the "Takings Clause" is a specifically enumerated limit, the post-*West Coast Hotel* retreat from robust protection of economic liberty under the general rubric of substantive due process did not eliminate robust judicial scrutiny of takings. This section briefly considers some of the most puzzling questions that arise under the Takings Clause.

What Government Action Should Be Regarded as a "Taking," Requiring Just Compensation?

In *Pennsylvania Coal Co. v. Mahon*, 260 U.S. 393 (1922), the Court, per HOLMES, J., observed that "the general rule at least is that while property may be regulated to a certain extent, if regulation goes too far it will be recognized as a taking." Such a "rule" may strike many as at best an uninformative tautology. But is the "general rule" represented by the modern cases any more helpful?

The question presented in PENN CENTRAL TRANSP. CO. v. NEW YORK CITY, 438 U.S. 104 (1978), was whether a preservation commission's denial of approval for Penn Central to construct a 55-story office building on the roof of its property—Grand Central Terminal, which had been designated as a "landmark"—constituted a "taking." In holding that it did not, the Court, per BRENNAN, J., emphasized that the denial of approval to build the structure "does not interfere in any way" with the present and past uses of the Terminal. "More importantly, on this record, we must regard the [restriction] as permitting Penn Central not only to profit from the Terminal but also to obtain a 'reasonable return' on its investment."

The *Penn Central* Court recognized that "what constitutes a 'taking' [has] proved to be a problem of considerable difficulty. [T]his Court, quite simply, has been unable to develop any 'set formula' for determining when 'justice and fairness' require that economic injuries caused by public action be compensated by the government, rather than remain disproportionately concentrated on a few persons. [A] 'taking' may more readily be found," noted the Court, "when the interference with property can be characterized as a physical invasion by government [than] when interference arises from some public program adjusting the benefits and burdens of economic life to promote the common good."

A good illustration of the doctrinal significance of a "physical invasion" is *Loretto v. Teleprompter Manhattan CATV Corp.*, 458 U.S. 419 (1982), which held that a state law requiring landlords to allow television cable companies to install cable facilities in their apartment buildings amounted to a "taking," despite the fact that the facilities occupied at most only one and one-half cubic feet of the landlord's property.

The Court applied *Loretto* in HORNE v. DEP'T OF AGRICULTURE, 576 U.S. 350 (2015). Under the authority of a federal statute enacted during the Great Depression, the Secretary of Agriculture ordered raisin growers to set aside a portion of their crop for the federal government to dispose as it saw fit, with net proceeds from government sales, if any, distributed to growers. The petitioners refused to comply with orders requiring the sacrifice of 47 percent of their raisins in one year and 30 percent in another, arguing that the program was a taking. The Court, per ROBERTS, C.J., agreed. Finding "[n]othing in th[e] history [of the Takings Clause to] suggest[ ] that personal property was any less protected against physical appropriation than real property," he deemed this "physical appropriation of personal property" subject to the *per se* rule of *Loretto*. SOTOMAYOR, J., dissented on the ground that the *per se* rule of *Loretto* ought not to apply where the growers retained at least one "stick" in the bundle of property rights in their raisins, namely "the right to receive some money for the[ ] disposition" of the raisins reserved for the government.

The Court has also considered categorical treatment appropriate where the regulation denies *all* economically beneficial or productive use of land. A good illustration is LUCAS v. SOUTH CAROLINA COASTAL COUNCIL, 505 U.S. 1003 (1992), where the enactment of an anti-erosion law prevented the owner from erecting any permanent habitable structure on his land. The Court, per SCALIA, J., observed: "[R]egulations that leave the owner of land without economically beneficial or productive options for its use—typically, as here, by requiring land to be left substantially in its natural state—carry with them a heightened risk that private property is being pressed into some form of public service under the guise of mitigating serious public harm. [When] the owner of real property has been called upon to sacrifice *all* economically beneficial uses in the name of the common good, that is, to leave the property economically idle, he has suffered a taking."

———

In STOP THE BEACH RENOURISHMENT, INC. v. FLORIDA DEPT. OF ENVIRONMENTAL PROTECTION, 560 U.S. 702 (2010), all eight participating justices agreed that a Florida Supreme Court ruling did not constitute a "judicial taking," but four (SCALIA, J., joined by Roberts, C.J., and Thomas and Alito, JJ.) would have used the case to establish the proposition that a *judicial decision* can constitute an unlawful taking: "The Takings Clause bars *the State* from taking private property without paying for it, no matter which branch is the instrument of the taking. [If] a legislature *or a court* declares that what was once an established right of private property no longer exists, it has taken that property, no less than if the State had physically appropriated it or destroyed its value by regulation." The other four participating justices did not reach the question whether judicial actions can ever result in a taking.

How to Determine the "Denominator" in Calculating Whether a Regulatory Taking Has Occurred?

To determine whether a regulation deprives an owner of all economically beneficial use of his or her property, courts must compare what is restricted against the whole. What is the whole? In *Penn Central*, the property owner argued that the regulation restricted all of the "air rights" above Grand Central Terminal, but the Court rejected that framing, treating the relevant parcel as encompassing the underlying land and building as well. In MURR v. WISCONSIN, 137 S.Ct. 1933 (2017), state and local law implementing a federally-imposed conservation mandate restricted development on certain lots with less than an acre of developable land, while also restricting the sale of adjacent lots under common ownership by merging them into one parcel. Members of the Murr family acquired two adjacent lots at different times and wanted to sell one of them to pay for development on the other, but were forbidden from doing so. They argued that each lot was a separate parcel for takings purposes and that the restrictions on one of the lots left them with no economically beneficial use of that lot. The Court, per KENNEDY, J., disagreed with the Murrs' characterization of the relevant parcel. Invoking the principle that the Takings Clause protects property owners' "reasonable expectations," the Court held that "no single consideration can supply the exclusive test for determining the denominator. Instead, courts must consider a number of factors. These include the treatment of the land under state and local law; the physical characteristics of the land; and the prospective value of the regulated land." Evaluating these factors, the Court concluded that the state "merger provision" was "a legitimate exercise of government power," and thus the relevant parcel comprised both lots. The composite parcel retained substantial economically beneficial use, so there was no *per se* taking under *Lucas*; and the "coordinated federal, state, and local effort to preserve [a] river and surrounding land" resulted in "a reasonable land-use regulation," so there was also no taking "under the more general test of *Penn Central*."

ROBERTS, C.J., joined by THOMAS and ALITO, JJ., dissented from the Court's multi-factor test on the ground that it led to "double counting" of the state's interest by first factoring in the reasonableness of the regulation in determining the proper parcel and then considering the regulation's reasonableness in applying *Penn Central*. The Chief Justice would have relied on state law alone to define each plot. In response to the majority's argument that the merger provision was part of state law, the dissent complained that it was a special rule created by the Wisconsin courts for regulatory takings cases, rather than an "ordinary principle[ ] of Wisconsin property law."

THOMAS, J., also dissented for himself alone, suggesting that in a future case the Court should "take a fresh look at our regulatory takings jurisprudence, to see whether it can be grounded in the original public meaning of the Takings Clause of the Fifth Amendment or the Privileges or Immunities Clause of the Fourteenth Amendment."

What Constitutes "Property" for Purposes of the Takings Clause?

The Takings Clause applies where a *specific* interest in physical or intellectual property is involved. But no opinion of the Court has held that the Takings Clause applies when a *general obligation* to pay money to the government or to a third party is at issue. Extension of Takings Clause doctrine to such general obligations might threaten to revive *Lochner*-style review.

In EASTERN ENTERPRISES v. APFEL, 524 U.S. 498 (1998), the Court struck down a federal statute that imposed a monetary assessment on the prior owner of a coal mine that would have been used to fund benefits for now-retired miners who had once worked for the coal mine. However, there was no opinion of the Court. Speaking for four Justices, O'CONNOR, J., concluded that as the statute affected Eastern Enterprises, it violated the Takings Clause. Concurring in the judgment, but rejecting the plurality's Takings Clause analysis, KENNEDY, J., concluded that the statute "must be invalidated as contrary to essential due process principles" because it went "far outside the bounds of retroactivity permissible under our law." It is noteworthy that (a) the O'Connor plurality seemed to avoid reliance upon the Due Process Clause at least in part out of fear of resurrecting *Lochner*, but (b) Justice Kennedy, argued forcefully that the plurality's adoption of a "novel and expansive concept of a taking" did not avoid the "normative judgment" that would otherwise need to be made under the due process rubric. Likewise, STEVENS, J., dissenting, joined by Souter, Ginsburg and Breyer, JJ., concluded that whether the statute "is analyzed under the Takings Clause or the Due Process Clause" the company "has not carried its burden of overcoming the presumption of constitutionality accorded to an Act of Congress."

Thus, a four-Justice plurality had maintained that a general obligation could be the subject of a taking, but five Justices (in concurring and dissenting opinions) had disagreed.

KELO V. NEW LONDON

545 U.S. 469, 125 S.Ct. 2655, 162 L.Ed.2d 439 (2005).

JUSTICE STEVENS delivered the opinion of the Court.

[Decades of economic decline prompted state and local officials to target New London, Conn. (hereinafter City), and especially its Fort Trumbell area, for economic revitalization. The task was assigned chiefly to the New London Development Corp. (NLDC), a private entity. Shortly thereafter, the pharmaceutical company Pfizer announced that it would build a $300 million facility on a site immediately adjacent to Fort Trumbell. Local planners hoped that the new facility would catalyze the area's rejuvenation.

[The city council approved the NLDC plan and authorized the entity to purchase property or to acquire it by exercising eminent domain in the City's name. When petitioners in the case, nine persons who owned 15 properties in Fort Trumbell, refused to sell, the City initiated condemnation proceedings. The properties were not blighted or otherwise in poor condition. Rather, they were condemned only because they happened to be in the development area. Petitioner brought this action in state court, maintaining that the City's taking of their properties would violate the "public use" restriction in the Takings Clause. The state supreme court disagreed.]

[The] disposition of this [case] turns on the question whether the City's development plan serves a "public purpose." Without exception, our cases have defined that concept broadly, reflecting our longstanding policy of deference to legislative judgments in this field. [For] more than a century, our public use jurisprudence has wisely eschewed rigid formulas and intrusive scrutiny in favor of affording legislatures broad latitude in determining what public needs justify the use of the takings power.

Those who govern the City were not confronted with the need to remove blight in the Fort Trumbull area, but their determination that the area was sufficiently distressed to justify a program of economic rejuvenation is entitled to our deference. The City has carefully formulated an economic development plan that it believes will provide appreciable benefits to the community, including—but by no means limited to—new jobs and increased tax revenue. [Because] that plan unquestionably serves a public purpose, the takings challenged here satisfy the public use requirement of the Fifth Amendment.

[Petitioners] contend that using eminent domain for economic development impermissibly blurs the boundary between public and private takings. Again, our cases foreclose this objection. Quite simply, the government's pursuit of a public purpose will often benefit individual private parties.

[It] is further argued that without a bright-line rule nothing would stop a city from transferring citizen *A*'s property to citizen *B* for the sole reason that citizen *B* will put the property to a more productive use and thus pay more taxes. Such a one-to-one transfer of property, executed outside the confines of an integrated development plan, is not presented in this case. While such an unusual exercise of government power would certainly raise a suspicion that a private purpose was afoot, the hypothetical cases posited by petitioners can be confronted if and when they arise. They do not warrant the crafting of an artificial restriction on the concept of public use.

[We] emphasize that nothing in our opinion precludes any State from placing further restrictions on its exercise of the takings power. Indeed, many States already impose "public use" requirements that are stricter than the federal baseline. [This] Court's authority, however, extends only to determining whether the City's proposed condemnations are for a "public use" within the meaning of the Fifth Amendment to the Federal Constitution. Because over a century of our case law interpreting that provision dictates an affirmative answer to that question, we may not grant petitioners the relief that they seek. * * *

JUSTICE KENNEDY, concurring.

[A] court confronted with a plausible accusation of impermissible favoritism to private parties should treat the objection as a serious one and review the record to see if it has merit, though with the presumption that the government's actions were reasonable and intended to serve a public purpose. Here, the trial court [did so and] concluded [that] benefitting Pfizer was not "the primary motivation or effect of this development plan." [This] case, then, survives the meaningful rational-basis review that in my view is required under the Public Use Clause. [While] there may be categories of cases in which the transfers are so suspicious, or the procedures employed so prone to abuse, or the purported benefits are so trivial or implausible, that courts should presume an impermissible private purpose, no such circumstances are present in this case. * * *

JUSTICE O'CONNOR, with whom CHIEF JUSTICE REHNQUIST, JUSTICE SCALIA, and JUSTICE THOMAS join, dissenting.

[To] reason, as the Court does, that the incidental public benefits resulting from the subsequent ordinary use of private property render economic development takings "for public use" is to wash out any distinction between private and public use of property—and thereby effectively to delete the words "for public use" from the Takings Clause of the Fifth Amendment.

[Where] is the line between "public" and "private" property use? [Were] the political branches the sole arbiters of the public-private distinction, the Public Use Clause would amount to little more than hortatory fluff. An external, judicial check on how the public use requirement is interpreted, however limited, is necessary if this constraint on government power is to retain any meaning.

[This case] presents an issue of first impression: Are economic development takings constitutional? I would hold that they are not.

[The] Court protests that it does not sanction the bare transfer from A to B for B's benefit. It suggests two limitations on what can be taken after today's decision. First, it maintains a role for courts in ferreting out takings whose sole purpose is to bestow a benefit on the private transferee—without detailing how courts are to conduct that complicated inquiry. [The] trouble with economic development takings is that private benefit and incidental public benefit are, by definition, merged and mutually reinforcing. In this case, for example, any boon for Pfizer or the plan's developer is difficult to disaggregate from the promised public gains in taxes and jobs.

Even if there were a practical way to isolate the motives behind a given taking, the gesture toward a purpose test is theoretically flawed. If it is true that incidental public benefits from new private use are enough to ensure the "public purpose" in a taking, why should it matter, as far as the Fifth Amendment is concerned, what inspired the taking in the first place?

[A] second proposed limitation is implicit in the Court's opinion. The logic of today's decision is that eminent domain may only be used to upgrade—not downgrade—property. At best this makes the Public Use Clause redundant with the Due Process Clause, which already prohibits irrational government action. [In] any event, this constraint has no realistic import. For who among us can say she already makes the most productive or attractive possible use of her property? The specter of condemnation hangs over all property. Nothing is to prevent the State from replacing any Motel 6 with a Ritz-Carlton, any home with a shopping mall, or any farm with a factory.

[Any] property may now be taken for the benefit of another private party, but the fallout from this decision will not be random. The beneficiaries are likely to be those citizens with disproportionate influence and power in the political process, including large corporations and development firms. As for the victims, the government now has license to transfer property from those with fewer resources to those with more. The Founders cannot have intended this perverse result. * * *

JUSTICE THOMAS, dissenting.

[There] is no justification [for] affording almost insurmountable deference to legislative conclusions that a use serves a "public use." [W]e would not defer to a legislature's determination of the various circumstances that establish, for example, when a search of a home would be reasonable, or when a convicted double-murderer may be shackled during a sentencing proceeding without on-the-record findings, or when state law creates a property interest protected by the Due Process Clause. [I] would revisit our Public Use Clause cases and consider returning to the original meaning of the Public Use Clause: that the government may take property only if it actually uses or gives the public a legal right to use the property. * * *

LAWS "IMPAIRING THE OBLIGATION OF CONTRACTS"

Art. 1, § 10, prohibits the states from enacting any "Law impairing the Obligation of Contracts." (Unlike some provisions in § 10, no parallel provision of Art. 1, § 9, restricts the federal government.) Although Marshall Court case law construed the provision broadly, modern doctrine gives it a narrower scope.

In HOME BUILDING & LOAN ASS'N v. BLAISDELL, 290 U.S. 398 (1934)— decided the same year the *Nebbia* case struck the economic due process doctrine a heavy blow—the Court upheld what might be called a "debtor relief law" despite its retrospective impact. *Blaisdell* arose as follows: During the Great Depression, Minnesota enacted a Mortgage Moratorium Law—a law that was to remain in effect "only during the continuance of the emergency and in no event beyond May 1, 1935"—which gave the state courts the authority to extend the redemption period after real estate foreclosure sales provided the mortgagor paid a reasonable part of the rental value of the property. Thus mortgagees could not obtain possession of the real estate and convey title to new purchasers as they would have been able to do if a mortgage moratorium law had not been adopted.

A 5–4 majority, per HUGHES, C.J., upheld the challenged law. Recalling the origins of the clause, the Court first stated: "The widespread distress following the revolutionary period, and the plight of debtors, had called forth in the States an ignoble array of legislative schemes for the defeat of creditors and the invasion of contractual obligations. Legislative interferences had been so numerous and extreme that the confidence essential to prosperous trade had been undermined and the utter destruction of credit was threatened. [It] was necessary to interpose the restraining power of a central authority in order to secure the foundations even of 'private faith.' "

The Court nonetheless distinguished what it called "broad expressions" in earlier opinions and found that Minnesota's law "does not impair the integrity of the mortgage indebtedness. The obligation for interest remains. [Aside] from the extension of time, the other conditions of redemption are unaltered. [While] the mortgagee-purchaser is debarred from actual possession, he has, so far as rental value is concerned, the equivalent of possession during the extended period. [Not] only is the constitutional provision qualified by the measure of control which the state retains over remedial processes, but the state also continues to possess authority to safeguard the vital interests of its people. [Not] only are existing laws read into contracts in order to fix obligations as between the parties, but the reservation of existing attributes of sovereign power is also read into contracts as a postulate of the legal order. [The Constitution would not] permit the state to adopt as its policy the repudiation of debts or the destruction of contracts or the denial of means to enforce them. But it does not follow that conditions may not arise in which a temporary restraint of enforcement may be consistent with the spirit and purpose of the constitutional provision and thus found to be within the range of the reserved power of the state to protect the vital interests of the community."

UNITED STATES TRUST CO. v. NEW JERSEY, 431 U.S. 1 (1977), was a rare post-*Lochner*-era case finding a violation of the contract clause. To assure bondholders of the Port Authority of New York and New Jersey that the Authority would not in the future take over mass transit deficit operations beyond its financial reserves in 1962, the two states entered into a covenant limiting the numbers of such operations the Authority would absorb. In 1974, however, in order to subsidize more mass transportation, both states repealed the legislation implementing the covenant. A 4–3 majority, per Blackmun, J., agreed with the bondholders that the retroactive repeal of the covenant, which reduced the financial security of their bonds, violated the contract clause.

The following year the Court found another violation of the contract clause:

In ALLIED STRUCTURAL STEEL CO. v. SPANNAUS, 438 U.S. 234 (1978), petitioner had adopted a pension plan that vested pension rights only when an employee had worked to age 65, or 15 years to age 60 or 20 years to age 55. However, Minnesota then enacted a law requiring employers of 100 workers or more who had established employee pension plans and who then went out of business in the state to pay full pensions to all its Minnesota employees who had worked ten years or more. A 6–3 majority, per STEWART, J., held that the law could not survive challenge under the contract clause: The law had "change[d] the company's obligations in an area where the element of reliance was vital—the funding of a pension plan" and "impose[d] a completely unexpected liability in potentially disabling amounts." Moreover, the law did not "deal with a situation remotely approaching the broad and desperate emergency economic conditions of the early 1930s—conditions of which the Court in *Blaisdell* took official notice."

BRENNAN, J., wrote forceful dissenting opinions in both the *U.S. Trust* and *Allied Steel* cases. Noting that *U.S. Trust* was "the first case in some 40 years in which this Court has seen fit to invalidate purely economic and social legislation on the strength of the Contract Clause," he feared that the case might signal "a return to substantive constitutional review of States' policies and a new resolve to protect property owners whose interest or circumstances may happen to appeal to Members of this Court." Dissenting in *Allied Steel*, Brennan, J., maintained that the majority's "conversion of the Contract Clause into a limitation on the power of states to enact laws that impose duties additional to obligations assumed under private contracts must inevitably produce results difficult to square with any rational conception of a constitutional order." The "necessary consequence" of the majority's approach "is to vest judges with broad subjective discretion to protect property interests that happen to appeal to them."

Although the Court thus appeared to have revitalized the contract clause, it retreated sharply in two unanimous 1983 rulings: *Energy Reserves Group v. Kansas Power & Light Co.*, 459 U.S. 400 (upholding a Kansas law that imposed price controls on intrastate gas and prohibited natural gas producers from raising the purchase price despite provisions in contracts with consumers for raising the purchase price in the event of changes in the law); *Exxon Corp. v. Eagerton*, 462 U.S. 176 (upholding an Alabama law prohibiting oil producers from passing increases in a severance tax on to consumers despite pre-existing contracts requiring purchasers to reimburse producers for such taxes).

CHAPTER 6

PROTECTION OF INDIVIDUAL RIGHTS: DUE PROCESS, THE BILL OF RIGHTS, AND UNENUMERATED RIGHTS

■ ■ ■

1. APPLICABILITY OF THE BILL OF RIGHTS TO THE STATES; NATURE AND SCOPE OF FOURTEENTH AMENDMENT DUE PROCESS

I. INCORPORATION THEORIES

Barron v. Mayor and City Council of Baltimore, (Ch. 5, Sec. 1, I) held that the individual rights protected by the Bill of Rights impose limits on the federal government but not on state or local government. Did the adoption of the Fourteenth Amendment reverse *Barron*? For many years, the Supreme Court said that it did not. *Twining v. New Jersey*, 211 U.S. 78 (1908) and *Palko v. Connecticut*, 302 U.S. 319 (1937) rejected the view that the Fourteenth Amendment made all of the provisions of the Bill of Rights fully applicable to the states.[1] But the Court recognized that "it is possible that some of the personal rights safeguarded by the first eight Amendments against national action may also be safeguarded against state action, because a denial of them would be a denial of due process" (*Twining*) or because "the specific pledges of particular amendments have been found to be implicit in the concept of ordered liberty, and thus, through the Fourteenth Amendment, become valid as against the states" (*Palko*). And the Court in this period found among the procedural requirements of due process certain rules paralleling provisions of the first eight amendments. For example, *Powell v. Alabama*, 287 U.S. 45 (1932), held that defendants in a capital case were denied due process when a state refused them the aid of counsel. "The logically critical thing, however," explained Harlan, J., years later, "was not that the rights had been found in the Bill of Rights, but that they were deemed * * * fundamental."[2]

Under the "ordered liberty"/"fundamental fairness" test, which procedural safeguards included in the Bill of Rights were applicable to the states and which

---

[1]   *Palko,* which held that the Fourteenth Amendment did not encompass at least certain aspects of the double jeopardy prohibition of the Fifth Amendment, was overruled in *Benton v. Maryland*, 395 U.S. 784 (1969). The *Twining* view that the Fifth Amendment privilege against self-incrimination is not incorporated in the Fourteenth was rejected in *Malloy v. Hogan* (1964), discussed below.

[2]   *Duncan v. Louisiana* (1968) (dissent joined by Stewart, J.), discussed below.

were not? Consider CARDOZO, J., speaking for the *Palko* Court: "[There] emerges the perception of a rationalizing principle which gives to discrete instances a proper order and coherence. The right to trial by jury and the immunity from prosecution except as the result of an indictment [are] not of the very essence of a scheme of ordered liberty. To abolish them is not to violate a 'principle of justice so rooted in the traditions and conscience of our people as to be ranked as fundamental.' Few would be so narrow or provincial as to maintain that a fair and enlightened system of justice would be impossible without them. What is true of jury trials and indictments is true also, as the cases show, of the immunity from compulsory self-incrimination. This too might be lost, and justice still be done.

"[We] reach a different plane of social and moral values when we pass [to those provisions of the Bill of Rights] brought within the Fourteenth Amendment by a process of absorption. These in their origin were effective against the federal government alone. If the Fourteenth Amendment has absorbed them, the process of absorption has had its source in the belief that neither liberty nor justice would exist if they were sacrificed. This is true, for illustration, of freedom of thought and speech. Of that freedom one may say that it is the matrix, the indispensable condition, of nearly every other form of freedom. [Fundamental] too in the concept of due process, and so in that of liberty, is the thought that condemnation shall be rendered only after trial. The hearing, moreover, must be a real one, not a sham or pretense. [The] decision [in *Powell*] did not turn upon the fact that the benefit of counsel would have been guaranteed to the defendants by [the] Sixth Amendment if they had been prosecuted in a federal court [but on] the fact that in the particular situation laid before us [the aid] of counsel was essential to the substance of a hearing."

ADAMSON v. CALIFORNIA
332 U.S. 46, 67 S.Ct. 1672, 91 L.Ed. 1903 (1947).

JUSTICE REED delivered the opinion of the Court.

[Adamson was convicted of first-degree murder after a state court trial in which the rules of evidence allowed his failure] to explain or to deny evidence against him to be commented upon by court and by counsel and to be considered by court and jury. The defendant did not testify.

[We] shall assume [that application of the rule challenged here] would infringe defendant's privilege against self-incrimination under the Fifth Amendment if this were a trial in a court of the United States under a similar law. Such an assumption does not determine appellant's rights under the Fourteenth Amendment. It is settled law that the clause of the Fifth Amendment, protecting a person against being compelled to be a witness against himself, is not made effective by the Fourteenth Amendment as a protection against state action on the ground that freedom from testimonial compulsion is a right of national citizenship, or because it is a personal privilege or immunity secured by the Federal Constitution as one of the rights of man that are listed in the Bill of Rights.

[Defendant also] contends that if the privilege against self-incrimination is not a right protected by the privileges and immunities clause of the Fourteenth Amendment against state action, [it] inheres in the right to a fair trial. A right to a fair trial is a right admittedly protected by the due process clause of the Fourteenth Amendment. [The] due process clause of the Fourteenth Amendment, however, does not draw all the rights of the federal Bill of Rights under its protection. That contention was made and rejected in *Palko*. [Nothing] has been called to our attention that either the framers of the Fourteenth Amendment or the states that adopted intended its due process clause to draw within its scope the earlier amendments to the Constitution. * * *

JUSTICE FRANKFURTER, concurring.

[The Fourteenth] Amendment neither comprehends the specific provisions by which the founders deemed it appropriate to restrict the federal government nor is it confined to them. The Due Process Clause of the Fourteenth Amendment has an independent potency, precisely as does the Due Procee Clause of the Fifth Amendment in relation to the Federal Government.

[Those] reading the English language with the meaning which it ordinarily conveys, those conversant with the political and legal history of the concept of due process, those sensitive to the relations of the States to the central government as well as the relation of some of the provisions of the Bill of Rights to the process of justice, would hardly recognize the Fourteenth Amendment as a cover for the various explicit provisions of the first eight Amendments. Some of these are enduring reflections of experience with human nature, while some express the restricted views of Eighteenth-Century England regarding the best methods for the ascertainment of facts. The notion that the Fourteenth Amendment was a covert way of imposing upon the States all the rules which it seemed important to Eighteenth Century statesmen to write into the Federal Amendments, was rejected by judges who were themselves witnesses of the process by which the Fourteenth Amendment became part of the Constitution. * * *

Indeed, the suggestion that the Fourteenth Amendment incorporates the first eight Amendments as such is not unambiguously urged. [There] is suggested merely a selective incorporation of the first eight Amendments into the Fourteenth Amendment. Some are in and some are out, but we are left in the dark as to which are in and which are out. [If] the basis of selection is merely that those provisions of the first eight Amendments are incorporated which commend themselves to individual justices as indispensable to the dignity and happiness of a free man, we are thrown back to a merely subjective test. [In] the history of thought "natural law" has a much longer and much better founded meaning and justification than such subjective selection of the first eight Amendments for incorporation into the Fourteenth. * * *

JUSTICE BLACK, with whom JUSTICE DOUGLAS joins, dissenting.

[The provisions of the Bill of Rights] may be thought outdated abstractions by some. And it is true that they were designed to meet ancient evils. But they are the same kind of human evils that have emerged from century to century wherever excessive power is sought by the few at the expense of the many. In my judgment the people of no nation can lose their liberty so long as a Bill of Rights like ours survives and its basic purposes are conscientiously interpreted, enforced and respected so as to afford continuous protection against old, as well as new, devices and practices which might thwart those purposes. I fear to see the consequences of the Court's practice of substituting its own concepts of decency and fundamental justice for the language of the Bill of Rights as its point of departure in interpreting and enforcing that Bill of Rights. [I] would follow what I believe was the original purpose of the Fourteenth Amendment—to extend to all the people of the nation the complete protection of the Bill of Rights.

[T]o pass upon the constitutionality of statutes by looking to the particular standards enumerated in the Bill of Rights and other parts of the Constitution is one thing; to invalidate statutes because of application of "natural law" deemed to be above and undefined by the Constitution is another. In the one instance, courts proceeding within clearly marked constitutional boundaries seek to execute policies written into the Constitution; in the other they roam at will in the limitless area of their own beliefs as to reasonableness and actually select policies, a responsibility which the Constitution entrusts to the legislative representatives of the people. * * *

JUSTICE MURPHY, with whom JUSTICE RUTLEDGE joins, dissenting.

I agree that the specific guarantees of the Bill of Rights should be carried over intact into the first section of the Fourteenth Amendment. But I am not prepared to say that the latter is entirely and necessarily limited by the Bill of Rights. Occasions may arise where a proceeding falls so far short of conforming to fundamental standards of procedure as to warrant constitutional condemnation in terms of a lack of due process despite the absence of a specific provision of the Bill of Rights. * * *

———

Post-*Adamson* cases continued the process of selective incorporation, but both the pattern of results and the Court's language shifted. DUNCAN v. LOUISIANA, 391 U.S. 145 (1968), illustrates the change. It held the Sixth Amendment right to jury trial applicable to the states via the Fourteenth Amendment. WHITE, J., speaking for the *Duncan* majority, described the incorporation inquiry this way:

"Earlier the Court can be seen as having asked, when inquiring into whether some particular procedural safeguard was required of a State, if a civilized system could be imagined that would not accord the particular protection. [The] recent cases, on the other hand, have proceeded upon the valid assumption that state criminal processes are not imaginary and theoretical schemes but actual systems bearing virtually every characteristic of the common-law system that has been developing contemporaneously in England and in this country. The question thus is whether given this kind of system a particular procedure is fundamental—

whether, that is, a procedure is necessary to an Anglo-American regime of ordered liberty. [It] might be said that the limitation in question is not necessarily fundamental to fairness in every criminal system that might be imagined but is fundamental in the context of the criminal processes maintained by the American States."

HARLAN, J., joined by Stewart, J., dissented: "Even if I could agree that the question before us is whether Sixth Amendment jury trial is totally 'in' or totally 'out' [see Part II infra], I can find in the Court's opinion no real reasons for concluding that it should be 'in'. The basis for differentiating among clauses in the Bill of Rights cannot be that [only] some are old and much praised, or that only some have played an important role in the development of federal law. These things are true of all. The Court says that some clauses are more 'fundamental' than others, but [uses] this word in a sense that would have astonished Mr. Justice Cardozo and which, in addition, is of no help. The word does not mean 'analytically critical to procedural fairness' for no real analysis of the role of the jury in making procedures fair is even attempted. Instead, the word turns out to mean 'old,' 'much praised,' and 'found in the Bill of Rights.' The definition of 'fundamental' thus turns out to be circular."

———

Although the Court has remained unwilling to accept the total incorporationists' reading of the Fourteenth Amendment, in the 1960s it held that the Fourteenth Amendment incorporated nearly all of the provisions of the Bill of Rights. As WHITE, J., observed in *Duncan*: "In resolving conflicting claims concerning the meaning of this spacious [Fourteenth Amendment] language, the Court has looked increasingly to the Bill of Rights for guidance. [The Fourteenth Amendment] now protects the right to compensation for property taken by the State; the rights of speech, press, and religion covered by the First Amendment; the Fourth Amendment rights to be free from unreasonable searches and seizures and to have excluded from criminal trials any evidence illegally seized; the right guaranteed by the Fifth Amendment to be free of compelled self-incrimination; and the Sixth Amendment rights to counsel, to a speedy and public trial; to confrontation of opposing witnesses; and to compulsory process for obtaining witnesses."

Most of the incorporation cases that divided the Warren Court involved rights of suspects in criminal investigations and prosecutions.[3] Such rights can be understood as part of the "process" that is "due" to a person before he or she is deprived of life or liberty. However, the foregoing catalogue also includes non-procedural rights, such as speech, press, and religion. Can these rights be incorporated via the Fourteenth Amendment's Due Process Clause without

---

[3]   In the area of criminal procedure, the Court has come very close to incorporating all of the relevant Bill of Rights guarantees. But one exception remains on the books. *Hurtado v. California*, 110 U.S. 516 (1884), refused to apply to the states the Fifth Amendment requirement that prosecution be initiated by grand jury indictment.

reliance on the concept of *substantive* due process? Is it notable that the Court did not distinguish between procedural and substantive rights in this context?

II. IS THE BILL OF RIGHTS INCORPORATED "JOT-FOR-JOT"?

In the 1960s, the Court seemed to be incorporating not only the general concept of federal rights, but applying each incorporated provision to the states *to the exact same extent* it applied to the federal government. Thus, BRENNAN, J., observed for a majority in *Malloy v. Hogan*, 378 U.S. 1 (1964): "We have held that the guarantees of the First Amendment, the prohibition of unreasonable searches and seizures of the Fourth Amendment, and the right to counsel guaranteed by the Sixth Amendment, are all to be enforced against the States under the Fourteenth Amendment *according to the same standards that protect those personal rights against federal encroachment*. [The] Court thus has rejected the notion that the Fourteenth Amendment applies to the States only a 'watered-down, subjective version of the individual guarantees of the Bill of Rights.' " (Emphasis added.) As WHITE, J., wrote for the majority in *Duncan:* "Because we believe that trial by jury in criminal cases is fundamental to the American scheme of justice, we hold that the Fourteenth Amendment guarantees a right of jury trial in all criminal cases which—*were they to be tried in a federal court*—would come within the Sixth Amendment's guarantee." (Emphasis added.)

HARLAN, J., was the most persistent and powerful critic of the *Malloy-Duncan* approach to Fourteenth Amendment Due Process. "The consequence," he protested in his *Malloy* dissent, "is inevitably disregard of all relevant differences which may exist between state and federal criminal law and its enforcement. The ultimate result is compelled uniformity, which is inconsistent with the purpose of our federal system and which is achieved either by encroachment on the State's sovereign powers or by dilution in federal law enforcement of the specific protections found in the Bill of Rights."

III. A NEW WAVE OF INCORPORATION LITIGATION

McDonald v. Chicago (Sec. 6 infra) presented the question whether the Second Amendment right to keep and bear arms is incorporated as an individual right against state and local governments. In Part II.D of his majority opinion, ALITO, J., looked back on various cases dealing with the relationship between the Bill of Rights and Fourteenth Amendment Due Process: Although "the Court never has embraced Justice Black's 'total incorporation' theory, [it] eventually incorporated almost all of the provisions of the Bill of Rights." During the 1960s, the Court "abandoned three of [the] characteristics of the earlier period. The Court made it clear that the governing standard is not whether *any* 'civilized system [can] be imagined that would not accord the particular protection.' *Duncan*. Instead, the Court inquired whether a particular Bill of Rights guarantee is fundamental to *our* scheme of ordered liberty and system of justice.

"[The] Court also shed any reluctance to hold that rights guaranteed by the Bill of Rights met the requirements for protection under the Due Process Clause. [Only] a handful of the Bill of Rights protections remain unincorporated."

———

In TIMBS v. INDIANA, 139 S.Ct. 682 (2019), GINSBURG, J., wrote for the Court that "the historical and logical case for concluding that the Fourteenth Amendment incorporates the Excessive Fines Clause is overwhelming." The Court rejected the State's contention that the Fourteenth Amendment did not incorporate the Clause's application to civil *in rem* forfeitures that are at least partly punitive. The decision was unanimous in result, but THOMAS, J., concurred only in the judgment. Adhering to a view he expressed in *McDonald* (Sec. 6 infra), he would have relied on the Fourteenth Amendment's Privileges or Immunities Clause as the basis for incorporation. Concurring in the majority opinion, GORSUCH, J., "acknowledge[d]" that "[a]s an original matter . . . the appropriate vehicle for incorporation may well be the Fourteenth Amendment's Privileges or Immunities Clause, rather than, as this Court has long assumed, the Due Process Clause." However, he continued, "nothing in this case turns on that question, and, regardless of the precise vehicle, there can be no serious doubt that the Fourteenth Amendment requires the States to respect the freedom from excessive fines enshrined in the Eighth Amendment."

———

RAMOS v. LOUISIANA, 140 S.Ct. 1390 (2020), presented the question whether the Sixth Amendment requirement of a unanimous twelve-person jury in serious criminal cases is incorporated. GORSUCH, J., wrote for the Court: "In 48 States and federal court, a single juror's vote to acquit is enough to prevent a conviction. But not in Louisiana. Along with Oregon, Louisiana has long punished people based on 10-to-2 verdicts. [Wherever] we might look to determine what the term 'trial by an impartial jury trial' meant at the time of the Sixth Amendment's adoption—whether it's the common law, state practices in the founding era, or opinions and treatises written soon afterward—the answer is unmistakable. A jury must reach a unanimous verdict in order to convict.

"There can be no question either that the Sixth Amendment's unanimity requirement applies to state and federal criminal trials equally. This Court has long explained that the Sixth Amendment right to a jury trial is 'fundamental to the American scheme of justice' and incorporated against the States under the Fourteenth Amendment. This Court has long explained, too, that incorporated provisions of the Bill of Rights bear the same content when asserted against States as they do when asserted against the federal government. So if the Sixth Amendment's right to a jury trial requires a unanimous verdict to support a conviction in federal court, it requires no less in state court.

"How, despite these seemingly straightforward principles, have Louisiana's and Oregon's laws managed to hang on for so long? It turns out that the Sixth

Amendment's otherwise simple story took a strange turn. [In] *Apodaca* v. *Oregon,* 406 U.S. 404 (1972), [four] dissenting Justices would not have hesitated to strike down the States' laws, recognizing that the Sixth Amendment requires unanimity and that this guarantee is fully applicable against the States under the Fourteenth Amendment. But a four-Justice plurality [declared] that the real question [was] whether unanimity serves an important 'function' in 'contemporary society.' [Justice] Powell agreed that, as a matter of 'history and precedent, the Sixth Amendment requires a unanimous jury verdict to convict.' But, on the other hand, he argued that the Fourteenth Amendment does not render this guarantee against the federal government fully applicable against the States. In this way, Justice Powell doubled down on his belief in 'dual-track' incorporation—the idea that a single right can mean two different things depending on whether it is being invoked against the federal or a state government.

"[Even] if we accepted the premise that *Apodaca* established a precedent, no one on the Court today is prepared to say it was rightly decided, and *stare decisis* isn't supposed to be the art of methodically ignoring what everyone knows to be true. [Louisiana and Oregon] credibly claim that the number of nonunanimous felony convictions still on direct appeal are somewhere in the hundreds, and retrying or plea bargaining these cases will surely impose a cost. But new rules of criminal procedures usually do, often affecting significant numbers of pending cases across the whole country."

SOTOMAYOR and KAVANAUGH, JJ., each wrote a partial concurrence explaining their respective views of *stare decisis*. Thomas, J., concurred in the judgment, reiterating his view that the Fourteenth Amendment's Privileges or Immunities Clause provides the proper basis for incorporation. *See McDonald, infra,* Sec. 6.

ALITO, J., joined by Roberts, C.J., and Kagan, J., dissented on *stare decisis* grounds: The Court "imposes a potentially crushing burden on the courts and criminal justice systems of [Louisiana and Oregon]. Whatever one may think about the correctness of [*Apodaca*], it has elicited enormous and entirely reasonable reliance. And before this Court decided to intervene, the decision appeared to have little practical importance going forward. Louisiana has now abolished non-unanimous verdicts, and Oregon seemed on the verge of doing the same until the Court intervened."

IV. BODILY EXTRACTIONS

BLACK, J.'s argument for total incorporation leaned heavily on the idea that the specific provisions of the Bill of Rights provide much greater guidance to judges than the generalities of due process. Yet most language in the Bill of Rights is itself general, at least when specific problems arise under a particular phrase. In such cases, does dwelling on the language simply shift the focus of broad judicial inquiry from the extremely broad "due process" to such very broad terms as "freedom of speech," "establishment of religion," "unreasonable searches and seizures," "excessive bail," "cruel and unusual punishments," and "the assistance of counsel"?

In considering whether the right to counsel attaches at the time of arrest, preliminary hearing, arraignment, or not until the trial itself, or includes probation and parole revocation hearings, or applies to juvenile delinquency proceedings, deportation hearings, or civil commitments, or, where the defendant is indigent, includes the right to *assigned* counsel or an assigned psychiatrist at state expense, how helpful is the Sixth Amendment language entitling an accused to "the assistance of counsel for his defense"? Is the specificity or direction of this language significantly greater than that of the Due Process Clause standing alone? Put differently, do cases construing "enumerated" rights employ a different methodology from those involving "unenumerated" rights?

To turn to another cluster of problems—which form the basis for this part— in considering whether, and under what conditions, the police may direct the pumping of a person's stomach to uncover incriminating evidence, or the taking of a blood sample from him, without his consent, do the specific guarantees in the Bill of Rights against "unreasonable searches and seizures" and against compelling a person to be "a witness against himself" free the Court from the demands of appraising and judging involved in answering these questions by interpreting the Due Process Clause?

———

ROCHIN v. CALIFORNIA, 342 U.S. 165 (1952): "Having 'some information' that [Rochin] was selling narcotics, three deputy sheriffs [forced] open the door to [his] room" and found him "sitting partly dressed on the side of the bed, upon which his wife was lying. On a 'night stand' beside the bed the deputies spied two capsules. When asked 'Whose stuff is this?' Rochin seized the capsules and put them in his mouth. A struggle ensued, in the course of which the three officers 'jumped upon him' and [unsuccessfully] attempted to extract the capsules. [Rochin] was handcuffed and taken to a hospital. At the direction of one of the officers a doctor forced an emetic solution through a tube into Rochin's stomach against his will. This 'stomach pumping' produced vomiting. In the vomited matter were found two capsules which proved to contain morphine. [Rochin] was convicted [of possessing morphine] and sentenced to sixty days' imprisonment. The chief evidence against him was the two capsules."

The Court, per FRANKFURTER, J., concluded that the officers' conduct violated Fourteenth Amendment due process: "This is conduct that shocks the conscience. Illegally breaking into the privacy of the petitioner, the struggle to open his mouth and remove what was there, the forcible extraction of his stomach's contents—this course of proceeding by agents of government to obtain evidence is bound to offend even hardened sensibilities. They are methods too close to the rack and the screw to permit of constitutional differentiation. [Due] process of law, as a historic and generative principle, precludes defining, and thereby confining, [civilized] standards of conduct more precisely than to say that convictions cannot be brought about by methods that offend 'a sense of justice.' It would be a stultification of the responsibility which the course of constitutional history has cast upon this Court to hold that in order to convict a man the police cannot extract by force what is in his mind but can extract what is in his stomach. [E]ven though statements contained in them may be independently established as true[,] [c]oerced confessions offend the community's sense of fair play and decency. So here, to sanction the brutal conduct which naturally enough was condemned by the court whose judgment is before us, would be to afford brutality the cloak of law. Nothing would be more calculated to discredit law and thereby to brutalize the temper of a society."

BLACK, J., concurring, maintained that the Fifth Amendment's protection against compelled self-incrimination applied to the states and that "a person is compelled to be a witness against himself not only when he is compelled to testify, but also when as here, incriminating evidence is forcibly taken from him by a contrivance of modern science." In his view, "faithful adherence to the specific guarantees in the Bill of Rights insures a more permanent protection of individual liberty than that which can be afforded by the nebulous [Fourteenth Amendment due process] standards stated by the majority."

DOUGLAS, J., concurring, also would have rested the decision on the privilege against self-incrimination.

––––––––

BREITHAUPT v. ABRAM, 352 U.S. 432 (1957), set a high threshold for finding a *Rochin* violation. In *Breithaupt*, the police took a blood sample from an unconscious person who had been involved in a fatal automobile collision. A majority, per CLARK, J., affirmed a manslaughter conviction based on the blood sample (which showed intoxication). The Court distinguished the stomach-pumping in *Rochin* as "brutal" and "offensive." By contrast, in *Breithaupt* the Court emphasized that the sample was taken "under the protective eye of a physician" and that "the blood test procedure has become routine in our everyday life." The "interests of society in the scientific determination of intoxication, one of the great causes of the mortal hazards of the road," outweighed "so slight an intrusion" of a person's body.

WARREN, C.J., joined by Black and Douglas, JJ., dissenting, deemed *Rochin* controlling, and argued that police efforts to curb the narcotics traffic, involved in *Rochin,* "is surely a state interest of at least as great magnitude as the interest in highway law enforcement. [Only] personal reaction to the stomach pump and the blood test can distinguish the [two cases]."

DOUGLAS, J., joined by Black, J., dissented, maintaining that "if the decencies of a civilized state are the test, it is repulsive to me for the police to insert needles into an unconscious person in order to get the evidence necessary to convict him, whether they find the person unconscious, give him a pill which puts him to sleep, or use force to subdue him."

Nine years later, the Court upheld the taking by a physician, at police direction, of a blood sample from an injured person, over his objection.

———

SCHMERBER v. CALIFORNIA, 384 U.S. 757 (1966). In affirming the conviction for operating a vehicle while under the influence of intoxicating liquor, a 5–4 majority, per BRENNAN, J., ruled: (1) that the extraction of blood from petitioner under the aforementioned circumstances "did not offend" that "sense of justice" "of which we spoke in *Rochin*," thus reaffirming *Breithaupt*; (2) that the Fifth Amendment privilege against self-incrimination, now binding on the states, "protects an accused only from being compelled to testify against himself, or otherwise provide the State with evidence of a testimonial or communicative nature, and that the withdrawal of blood and use of the analysis in question [did] not involve compulsion to these ends"; and (3) that the Fourth Amendment protection against unreasonable searches and seizures, now binding on the states, was satisfied because: (a) "there was plainly probable cause" to arrest and charge petitioner and to suggest "the required relevance and likely success of a test of petitioner's blood for alcohol"; (b) the officer "might reasonably have believed that he was confronted with an emergency, in which the delay necessary to obtain a warrant, under the circumstances, threatened 'the destruction of evidence' "; and (c) "the test chosen to measure petitioner's blood-alcohol level was a reasonable one" that "was performed in a reasonable manner."

BLACK, J., joined by Douglas, J., dissenting, expressed incredulity at the majority's "conclusion that compelling a person to give his blood to help the State convict him is not equivalent to compelling him to be a witness against himself. [It] is a strange hierarchy of values that allows the State to extract a human being's blood to convict him of a crime because of the blood's content but proscribes compelled production of his lifeless papers."

———

WINSTON v. LEE, 470 U.S. 753 (1985), per BRENNAN, J., held that the surgical removal of a bullet from the body of an objecting suspect required more than ordinary probable cause to believe that the bullet would provide evidence of crime. "A compelled surgical intrusion into an individual's body for evidence," the Court explained in distinguishing *Schmerber*, "implicates expectations of privacy and security of such magnitude that the intrusion may be 'unreasonable' even if likely to produce evidence of a crime." The decision relied only on the Fourth Amendment (as incorporated) and did not directly address the question whether the intrusion could also be said to violate the Due Process Clause under the theory of *Rochin*.

2. REPRODUCTIVE FREEDOM

Introductory Note on the Right of "Privacy"

The cases in this section and the following three sections concern the so-called right of "privacy." They involve some of the most controversial constitutional issues of the post-*Lochner* era, especially abortion. These materials raise a variety of distinct questions that the Court and commentators sometimes treat as intersecting or overlapping: (1) does the Constitution authorize judges to recognize rights not expressly set forth in the text?; (2) if so, how should the content of those rights be discerned?; (3) applying the proper approach, what rights should be recognized?; and (4) under what circumstances may government infringe such rights?

None of the foregoing questions arises *only* in the context of the right to privacy. What then accounts for the unusually heated debate about the right of privacy in the current era? As you read the materials in this section, consider whether the issues of constitutional interpretation posed are especially difficult or whether, instead, the underlying substantive issues are especially divisive.

———

Two *Lochner*-era cases are often cited as antecedents of the modern right to privacy. In *Meyer v. Nebraska*, 262 U.S. 390 (1923), the Court reversed the conviction of a parochial teacher who taught an elementary student in German, in violation of a state law forbidding instruction in any language but English. *Pierce v. Society of Sisters*, 268 U.S. 510 (1925), invalidated a law that required parents to send their children to public school through the eighth grade, insofar as it forbade sending them to private school. Although *Meyer* and *Pierce* can be understood as protecting freedom of speech, they were decided long before the cases incorporating the Bill of Rights and relied in substantial part on principles of economic liberty. In addition, the Court in *Pierce* described both cases as protecting "the liberty of parents and guardians to direct the upbringing and education of children under their control."

———

BUCK v. BELL, 274 U.S. 200 (1927), per HOLMES, J., upheld a sterilization law applicable to "mental defectives" in state institutions: "Carrie Buck is a feeble-minded white woman who was committed to the State Colony [for Epileptics and Feeble Minded]. She is the daughter of a feeble-minded mother in the same institution, and the mother of an illegitimate feeble-minded child. [We] have seen more than once that the public welfare may call upon the best citizens for their lives. It would be strange if it could not call upon those who already sap the strength of the State for these lesser sacrifices, often not felt to be such by those concerned, in order to prevent our being swamped with incompetence. It is better for all the world if, instead of waiting to execute degenerate offspring for crime or to let them starve for their imbecility, society can prevent those who are manifestly unfit from continuing their kind. The principle that sustains compulsory vaccination is broad enough to cover cutting the Fallopian tubes. Three generations of imbeciles are enough."

———

SKINNER v. OKLAHOMA, 316 U.S. 535 (1942), per DOUGLAS, J., invalidated Oklahoma's Habitual Criminal Sterilization Act, which authorized the sterilization of persons previously convicted and imprisoned two or more times for crimes "amounting to felonies involving moral turpitude" and thereafter convicted of such a felony and sentenced to prison. (Petitioner was convicted of robbery with firearms after having previously been convicted for the same crime as well as for "stealing chickens.") The Act expressly exempted embezzlement, political offenses, and revenue act violations from the category of moral turpitude felonies. Thus, one convicted three times of larceny could be subjected to sterilization, but the embezzler could not—although "the nature of the two crimes is intrinsically the same" and they are otherwise punishable in the same manner. The Court found that the Oklahoma law "runs afoul of the equal protection clause" because—

"We are dealing here with legislation which involves one of the basic civil rights of man. Marriage and procreation are fundamental to the very existence and survival of the race. [In] evil or reckless hands [the power to sterilize] can cause races or types which are inimical to the dominant group to wither and disappear. There is no redemption for the individual whom the law touches. [He] is forever deprived of a basic liberty. We mention these matters [in] emphasis of our view that strict scrutiny of the classification which a State makes in a sterilization law is essential, lest unwittingly, or otherwise, invidious discriminations are made against groups or types of individuals in violation of the constitutional guaranty of just and equal laws."

The Court distinguished *Buck* this way: "[It] was pointed out [in that case] that 'so far as the operations enable those who otherwise must be kept confined to be returned to the world, and thus open the asylum to others, the equality aimed at will be more nearly reached.' Here there is no such saving feature."

STONE, C.J., concurring in the result in *Skinner*, thought that "the real question [is] not one of equal protection, but whether the wholesale condemnation of a class to such an invasion of personal liberty, without opportunity to any individual to show that his is not the type of case which would justify resort to it, satisfies the demands of due process. [A] law which condemns, without hearing, all the individuals of a class to so harsh a measure as the present because some or even many merit condemnation, is lacking in the first principles of due process."

JACKSON, J., concurred in both the majority and the separate opinion of Stone, C.J., arguing that equal protection and due process provided alternative grounds for the holding.

GRISWOLD V. CONNECTICUT

381 U.S. 479, 85 S.Ct. 1678, 14 L.Ed.2d 510 (1965).

JUSTICE DOUGLAS delivered the opinion of the Court.

Appellant Griswold is Executive Director of the Planned Parenthood League of Connecticut. Appellant Buxton [is] Medical Director for the League at its Center in New Haven—a center open [when] appellants were arrested. They gave information, instruction, and medical advice to *married persons* as to the means of preventing conception. [Fees] were usually charged, although some couples were serviced free.

[The constitutionality of two Connecticut statutes is involved.] [One] provides: "Any person who uses any drug, medicinal article or instrument for the purpose of preventing conception shall be fined not less than fifty dollars or imprisoned not less than sixty days nor more than one year or be both fined and imprisoned." [The other] provides: "Any person who assists, abets, counsels, causes, hires or commands another to commit any offense may be prosecuted and punished as if he were the principal offender." The appellants were found guilty as accessories and fined $100 each.

[We] are met with a wide range of questions that implicate the Due Process Clause. [Overtones] of some arguments suggest that *Lochner* should be our guide. But we decline that invitation. [We] do not sit as a super-legislature to determine the wisdom, need, and propriety of laws that touch economic problems, business affairs, or social conditions. This law, however, operates directly on an intimate relation of husband and wife and their physician's role in one aspect of that relation.

The association of people is not mentioned in the Constitution nor in the Bill of Rights. The right to educate a child in a school of the parents' choice—whether public or private or parochial—is also not mentioned. Nor is the right to study any particular subject or any foreign language. Yet the First Amendment has been construed to include certain of those rights. [See] *Pierce* [and] *Meyer*. [T]he State may not, consistently with the spirit of the First Amendment, contract the spectrum of available knowledge. The right of freedom of speech and press includes not only the right to utter or to print, but the right to distribute, the right to receive, the right to read and freedom of inquiry, freedom of thought, and freedom to teach—indeed the freedom of the entire university community. Without those peripheral rights the specific rights would be less secure. And so we reaffirm the principle [of] *Pierce* [and] *Meyer*.

In *NAACP v. Alabama* [Ch. 7, Sec. 9], we protected the "freedom to associate and privacy in one's associations," noting that freedom of association was a peripheral First Amendment right. [In] other words, the First Amendment has a penumbra where privacy is protected from governmental intrusion. In like context, we have protected forms of "association" that are not political in the customary sense but pertain to the social, legal, and economic benefit of the members. *NAACP v. Button*, 371 U.S. 415 (1963). [W]hile [association] is not expressly included in the First Amendment its existence is necessary in making the express guarantees fully meaningful.

The foregoing cases suggest that specific guarantees in the Bill of Rights have penumbras, formed by emanations from those guarantees that help give them life and substance. Various guarantees create zones of privacy. The right of association contained in the penumbra of the First Amendment is one, as we have seen. The Third Amendment in its prohibition against the quartering of soldiers "in any house" [is] another facet of that privacy. The Fourth Amendment [is another]. The Fifth Amendment in its Self-Incrimination Clause enables the citizen to create a zone of privacy which government may not force him to surrender to his detriment. The Ninth Amendment provides: "The enumeration in the Constitution, of certain rights, shall not be construed to deny or disparage others retained by the people." * * *

The present case, then, concerns a relationship lying within the zone of privacy created by several fundamental constitutional guarantees. And it concerns a law which, in forbidding the *use* of contraceptives rather than regulating their manufacture or sale, seeks to achieve its goals by means having a maximum destructive impact upon that relationship. Such a law cannot stand in light of the familiar principle [that] a "governmental purpose to control or prevent activities constitutionally subject to state regulation may not be achieved by means which sweep unnecessarily broadly and thereby invade the area of protected freedoms." *NAACP v. Alabama.* Would we allow the police to search the sacred precincts of marital bedrooms for telltale signs of the use of contraceptives? The very idea is repulsive to the notions of privacy surrounding the marriage relationship.

We deal with a right of privacy older than the Bill of Rights * * * . Marriage is a coming together for better or for worse, hopefully enduring, and intimate to the degree of being sacred. It is an association that promotes a way of life, not causes; a harmony in living, not political faiths; a bilateral loyalty, not commercial or social projects. Yet it is an association for as noble a purpose as any involved in our prior decisions.

Reversed.

JUSTICE GOLDBERG, whom CHIEF JUSTICE WARREN and JUSTICE BRENNAN join, concurring.

I [join the Court's opinion]. Although I have not accepted the view that "due process" as used in the Fourteenth Amendment includes all of the first eight Amendments, I do agree that the concept of liberty protects those personal rights that are fundamental, and is not confined to the specific terms of the Bill of Rights. My conclusion that [liberty] embraces the right of marital privacy though that right is not mentioned explicitly in the Constitution is supported both by numerous decisions [and] by the language and history of the Ninth Amendment [which] reveal that the Framers of the Constitution believed that there are additional fundamental rights, protected from governmental infringement. [The] Ninth Amendment shows a belief of the Constitution's authors that fundamental rights exist that are not expressly enumerated in the first eight amendments and an intent that the list of rights included there not be deemed exhaustive.

[Surely] the Government, absent a showing of a compelling subordinating state interest, could not decree that all husbands and wives must be sterilized after two children have been born to them. Yet by [the dissenters'] reasoning such an invasion of marital privacy would not be subject to constitutional challenge because, while it might be "silly," no provision of the Constitution specifically prevents the Government from curtailing the marital right to bear children and raise a family. * * *

JUSTICE HARLAN, concurring in the judgment.

I fully agree with the judgment [but cannot] join the Court's opinion [as] it seems to me to evince an approach [in which] the Due Process Clause of the Fourteenth Amendment does not touch this Connecticut statute unless the enactment is found to violate some right assured by the letter or penumbra of the Bill of Rights. [W]hat I find implicit in the Court's opinion is that the "incorporation" doctrine may be used to *restrict* the reach of Fourteenth Amendment Due Process. For me this is just as unacceptable constitutional doctrine as is the use of the "incorporation" approach to *impose* upon the States all the requirements of the Bill of Rights.

[The] proper constitutional inquiry in this case is whether this Connecticut statute infringes the Due Process Clause of the Fourteenth Amendment because the enactment violates basic values "implicit in the concept of ordered liberty." For reasons stated at length in my dissenting opinion in *Poe v. Ullman* [discussed below], I believe that it does. While the relevant inquiry may be aided by resort to one or more of the provisions of the Bill of Rights, it is not dependent on them or any of their radiations.

[While] I could not more heartily agree that judicial "self restraint" is an indispensable ingredient of sound constitutional adjudication, I do submit that the formula suggested [by the dissenters] for achieving it is more hollow than real. "Specific" provisions of the Constitution, no less than "due process," lend themselves as readily to "personal" interpretations by judges whose constitutional outlook is simply to keep the Constitution in supposed "tune with the times".

[Judicial self-restraint] will be achieved in this area, as in other[s], only by continual insistence upon respect for the teachings of history, solid recognition of the basic values that underlie our society, and wise appreciation of the great roles that the doctrines of federalism and separation of powers have played in establishing and preserving American freedoms. Adherence to these principles will not, of course, obviate all constitutional differences of opinion among judges, nor should it. Their continued recognition will, however, go farther toward keeping most judges from roaming at large in the constitutional field than will the interpolation into the Constitution of an artificial and largely illusory restriction on the content of the Due Process Clause.

[Dissenting from the jurisdictional ruling in POE v. ULLMAN, 367 U.S. 497 (1961), which failed to reach the merits of an earlier constitutional challenge to the Connecticut anti-birth control statute, Harlan, J., had maintained that the statute, "as construed to apply to these appellants, violates the Fourteenth Amendment" because "a statute making it a criminal offense for *married couples* to use contraceptives is an intolerable and unjustifiable invasion of privacy in the conduct of the most intimate concerns of an individual's personal life." Harlan, J., "would not suggest that adultery, homosexuality, fornication and incest are immune from criminal enquiry, however privately practiced," but "the intimacy of husband and wife is necessarily an essential and accepted feature of the institution of marriage, an institution which the State not only must allow, but which always and in every age it has fostered and protected. It is one thing when the State exerts its power either to forbid extra-marital sexuality altogether, or to say who may marry, but it is quite another when, having acknowledged a marriage and the intimacies inherent in it, it undertakes to regulate by means of the criminal law the details of that intimacy."

[Although the state had "argued the constitutional permissibility of the moral judgment underlying" the challenged statute, Harlan, J., could not find anything that "even remotely suggests a justification for the obnoxiously intrusive means it has chosen to effectuate that policy." He deemed "the utter novelty" of the statute "conclusive." "Although the Federal Government and many States have at one time or another [prohibited or regulated] the distribution of contraceptives, none [has] made the *use* of contraceptives a crime. Indeed, a diligent search has revealed that no nation, including several which quite evidently share Connecticut's moral policy, had seen fit to effectuate that policy by the means presented here."

[Because the constitutional challenges to the Connecticut statute "draw their basis from no explicit language of the Constitution, and have yet to find expression in any decision of this Court," Harlan, J., deemed it "desirable at the outset to state the framework of Constitutional principles in which I think the issue must be judged":

["Were due process merely a procedural safeguard it would fail to reach those situations where the deprivation of life, liberty or property was accomplished by legislation which by operating in the future could, given even the fairest possible procedure in application to individuals, nevertheless destroy the enjoyment of all three. [I]t is not the particular enumeration of rights in the first eight Amendments which spells out the reach of Fourteenth Amendment due process, but rather [those concepts embracing] rights 'which [are] *fundamental;* which belong [to] the citizens of all free governments.'

["[T]hrough the course of this Court's decisions [due process] has represented the balance which our Nation, built upon postulates of respect for the liberty of the individual, has struck between that liberty and the demands of organized society. [The] balance of which I speak is the balance struck by this country, having regard to what history teaches are the traditions from which it developed as well as the traditions from which it broke. That tradition is a living thing. A decision of this Court which radically departs from it could not long survive, while a decision which builds on what has survived is likely to be sound. No formula could serve as a substitute, in this area, for judgment and restraint.

["[The] full scope of the liberty guaranteed by the Due Process Clause cannot be found in or limited by the precise terms of the specific guarantees elsewhere provided in the Constitution. This 'liberty' is not a series of isolated points pricked out in terms of the taking of property; the freedom of speech, press, and religion; the right to keep and bear arms; the freedom from unreasonable searches and seizures; and so on. It is a rational continuum which, broadly speaking, includes a freedom from all substantial arbitrary impositions and purposeless restraints and which also recognizes, what a reasonable and sensitive judgment must, that certain interests require particularly careful scrutiny of the state needs asserted to justify their abridgment. Cf. *Skinner.*"]

JUSTICE WHITE, concurring in the judgment.

In my view this Connecticut law as applied to married couples deprives them of "liberty" without [the due process] guaranteed by the Fourteenth Amendment against arbitrary or capricious [denials]. Surely the right [to] be free of regulation of the intimacies of the marriage relationship, "come[s] to this Court with a momentum for respect lacking when appeal is made to liberties which derive merely from shifting economic arrangements." *Kovacs v. Cooper*, 336 U.S. 77 (1949) (opinion of Frankfurter, J.).

The Connecticut anti-contraceptive statute deals rather substantially with this relationship. [And] the clear effect of these statutes, as enforced, is to deny disadvantaged citizens of Connecticut, those without either adequate knowledge or resources to obtain private counseling, access to medical assistance and up-to-date information in respect to proper methods of birth control. In my view, a statute with these effects bears a substantial burden of justification when attacked under the Fourteenth Amendment.

[The] statute is said to serve the State's policy against all forms of promiscuous or illicit sexual relationships, be they premarital or extramarital, concededly a permissible and legitimate legislative goal. [But] I wholly fail to see how the ban on the use of contraceptives by married couples in any way reinforces the State's ban on illicit sexual relationships. [Perhaps] the theory is that the flat ban on use prevents married people from possessing contraceptives and without the ready availability of such devices for use in the marital relationship, there will be no or less temptation to use them in extramarital ones. This reasoning rests on the premise that married people will comply with the ban in regard to their marital relationship, notwithstanding total nonenforcement in this context and apparent nonenforcibility, but will not comply with criminal statutes prohibiting extramarital affairs and the anti-use statute in respect to illicit sexual relationships, a premise whose validity has not been demonstrated and whose intrinsic validity is not very evident. At most the broad ban is of marginal utility to the declared objective. A statute limiting its prohibition on use to persons engaging in the prohibited relationship would serve the end posited by Connecticut in the same way, and with the same effectiveness, or ineffectiveness, as the broad anti-use statute under attack in this case. I find nothing in this record justifying the sweeping scope of this statute. * * *

JUSTICE BLACK, with whom JUSTICE STEWART joins, dissenting.

[The] Court talks about a constitutional "right of privacy" as though there is some constitutional provision or provisions forbidding any law ever to be passed which might abridge the "privacy" of individuals. But there is not. There are, of course, guarantees in certain specific constitutional provisions [such as the Fourth Amendment] which are designed in part to protect privacy at certain times and places with respect to certain activities. [But] I think it belittles [the Fourth] Amendment to talk about it as though it protects nothing but "privacy." * * *

One of the most effective ways of diluting or expanding a constitutionally guaranteed right is to substitute for the crucial word or words of a constitutional guarantee another word or words, more or less flexible and more or less restricted in meaning. This fact is well illustrated by the use of the term "right of privacy" as a comprehensive substitute for the Fourth Amendment's guarantee against "unreasonable searches and seizures." * * * I like my privacy as well as the next one, but I am nevertheless compelled to admit that government has a right to invade it unless prohibited by some specific constitutional provision.

[This] brings me to the arguments made by [the concurring justices]. I discuss the due process and Ninth Amendment arguments together because on analysis they turn out to be the same thing—merely using different words to claim for this Court and the federal judiciary power to invalidate any legislative act [that] it considers to be arbitrary, capricious, unreasonable, or oppressive, or this Court's belief that a particular state law under scrutiny has no "rational or justifying" purpose, or is offensive to a "sense of fairness and justice." If these formulas based on "natural justice" [are] to prevail, they require judges to determine what is or is not constitutional on the basis of their own appraisal of what laws are unwise or unnecessary. [I] do not believe that we are granted power by the Due Process Clause or any [other] provisions [to do so].

Of the cases on which my [Brothers] rely so heavily, undoubtedly the reasoning of two of them supports their result here—[*Meyer* and *Pierce*]. *Meyer* [relying on *Lochner,*] held unconstitutional, as an "arbitrary" and unreasonable interference with the right of a teacher to carry on his occupation and of parents to hire him, a state law forbidding the teaching of modern foreign languages to young children in the schools.[7] [*Pierce,* per McReynolds, J.] said that a state law requiring that all children attend public schools interfered unconstitutionally with the property rights of private school corporations because it was an "arbitrary, unreasonable, and unlawful interference" which threatened "destruction of their business and property." Without expressing an opinion as to whether either of those cases reached a correct result in light of our later decisions applying the First Amendment to the States through the Fourteenth, I merely point out that the reasoning stated in *Meyer* and *Pierce* was the same natural law due process philosophy which many later opinions repudiated, and which I cannot accept.

---

7   [Ct's Note] In *Meyer,* in the very same sentence quoted in part by my Brethren in which he asserted that the Due Process Clause gave an abstract and inviolable right "to marry, establish a home and bring up children," Justice McReynolds asserted also that the Due Process Clause prevented States from interfering with "the right of the individual to contract."

[My] Brother Goldberg [says] that the Ninth Amendment as well as the Due Process Clause can be used by this Court as authority to strike down all state legislation which this Court thinks violates "fundamental principles of liberty and justice," or is contrary to the "traditions and collective conscience of our people." [One] would certainly have to look far beyond the language of the Ninth Amendment to find that the Framers vested in this Court any such awesome veto powers over lawmaking. [The Ninth] Amendment was passed [to] limit the Federal Government to the powers granted expressly or by necessary implication. [This] fact is perhaps responsible for the peculiar phenomenon that for a period of a century and a half no serious suggestion was ever made that [that] Amendment, enacted to protect state powers against federal invasion, could be used as a weapon of federal power to prevent state legislatures from passing laws they consider appropriate to govern local affairs. * * *

JUSTICE STEWART, whom JUSTICE BLACK joins, dissenting.

[T]his is an uncommonly silly law. As a practical matter, the law is obviously unenforceable, except in the oblique context of the present case. As a philosophical matter, I believe the use of contraceptives in the relationship of marriage should be left to personal and private [choice]. As a matter of social policy, I think professional counsel about methods of birth control should be available to all, so that each individual's choice can be meaningfully made. But we are not [asked] whether we think this law is unwise, or even asinine. We are asked to hold that it violates the United States Constitution. And that I cannot do.

In the course of its opinion the Court refers to no less than six Amendments [but] does not say which of these Amendments, if any, it thinks is infringed by this Connecticut law. [As] to the First, Third, Fourth, and Fifth Amendments, I can find nothing in any of them to invalidate this Connecticut law, even assuming that all those amendments are fully applicable against the States. [The] Ninth Amendment, like its companion the Tenth [was adopted] simply to make clear that the adoption of the Bill of Rights did not alter the plan that the *Federal* Government was to be a government of express and limited powers, and that all rights and powers not delegated to it were retained by the people and the individual States. Until today no member of this Court has ever suggested that the Ninth Amendment meant anything [else].

––––––

Griswold invalidated a ban on the *use* of contraceptives by *married* couples. EISENSTADT v. BAIRD, 405 U.S. 438 (1972), overturned a conviction for violating a Massachusetts law making it a felony to *distribute* contraceptive materials, *except* in the case of registered physicians and pharmacists furnishing the materials to *married* persons. The Court, per BRENNAN, J., concluded that, because the statute was riddled with exceptions making contraceptives freely available and because, if protection of health were the rationale, the statute would be both discriminatory and overbroad, "the goals of deterring premarital sex and regulating the distribution of potentially harmful articles cannot reasonably be regarded as legislative aims." "[V]iewed as a prohibition on contraception per se" the statute "violates the rights of single persons under the Equal Protection Clause." For, "whatever the rights of the individual to access to contraceptives may be, the rights must be the same for the unmarried and the married alike.

"If under *Griswold* the distribution of contraceptives to married persons cannot be prohibited, a ban on distribution to unmarried persons would be equally impermissible. It is true that in *Griswold* the right of privacy in question inhered in the marital relationship. Yet the marital couple is not an independent entity with a mind and heart of its own, but an association of two individuals each with a separate intellectual and emotional makeup. If the right of privacy means anything, it is the right of the *individual,* married or single, to be free from unwarranted governmental intrusion into matters so fundamentally affecting a person as the decision whether to bear or beget a child. On the other hand, if *Griswold* is no bar to a prohibition on the distribution of contraceptives, the State could not, consistently with the Equal Protection Clause, outlaw distribution to unmarried but not to married persons. In each case the evil, as perceived by the State, would be identical, and the underinclusion would be invidious."[4]

BURGER, C.J., dissented, "see[ing] nothing in the Fourteenth Amendment or any other part of the Constitution that even vaguely suggests that these medicinal forms of contraceptives must be available in the open market. [By] relying on *Griswold* in the present context, the Court has passed beyond the penumbras of the specific guarantees into the uncircumscribed area of personal predilections."

ROE V. WADE

410 U.S. 113, 93 S.Ct. 705, 35 L.Ed.2d 147 (1973).

JUSTICE BLACKMUN delivered the opinion of the Court.

[Jane] Roe alleged that she was unmarried and pregnant [and] that she was unable to get a "legal" abortion in Texas because her life did not appear to be threatened by the continuation of her pregnancy. [R]estrictive criminal abortion laws [like Texas's] in effect in a majority of States [today] derive from statutory changes effected, for the most part, in the latter half of the 19th century, [but] at common law, at the time of the adoption of our Constitution, and throughout the major portion of the 19th century, [a] woman enjoyed a substantially broader right to terminate a pregnancy than she does in most States today. [Three] reasons have been advanced to explain historically the enactment of criminal abortion laws in the 19th century and to justify their continued existence.

It has been argued occasionally that these laws were the product of a Victorian social concern to discourage illicit sexual conduct. Texas, however, does not

---

4   Douglas, J., who joined the Court's opinion, also concurred on free speech grounds. White, J., joined by Blackmun, J., concurred in the judgment on the ground that the record did not establish either that the particular contraceptive at issue was dangerous or that the defendant was unmarried. Powell and Rehnquist, JJ., did not participate.

advance this justification [and] it appears that no court or commentator has taken the argument seriously.

[A] second reason is [that when] most criminal abortion laws were first enacted, the procedure was a hazardous one for the woman. [But modern] medical data indicat[e] that abortion in early pregnancy, that is, prior to the end of first trimester, although not without its risk, is now relatively safe.

[The] third reason is the State's interest—some phrase it in terms of duty—in protecting prenatal life. Some of the argument for this justification rests on the theory that a new human life is present from the moment of conception. [Only] when the life of the pregnant mother herself is at stake, balanced against the life she carries within her, should the interest of the embryo or fetus not prevail. [In] assessing the State's interest, recognition may be given to the less rigid claim that as long as at least *potential* life is involved, the State may assert interests beyond the protection of the pregnant woman alone. [It] is with these interests, and the weight to be attached to them, that this case is concerned.

The Constitution does not explicitly mention any right of privacy. [But] the Court has recognized that a right of personal privacy, or a guarantee of certain areas or zones of privacy, does exist under the Constitution. In varying contexts the Court or individual Justices have, indeed, found at least the roots of that right in the First Amendment; in the Fourth and Fifth Amendments; in the penumbras of the Bill of Rights, *Griswold;* in the Ninth Amendment, id. (Goldberg, J., concurring); or in the concept of liberty guaranteed by the first section of the Fourteenth Amendment, see *Meyer.* These decisions make it clear that only personal rights that can be deemed "fundamental" or "implicit in the concept of ordered liberty," are included in this guarantee of personal privacy. They also make it clear that the right has some extension to activities relating to marriage; procreation; contraception; family relationships; and child rearing and education.

This right of privacy, whether it be founded in the Fourteenth Amendment's concept of personal liberty [as] we feel it is, [or] in the [Ninth Amendment], is broad enough to encompass a woman's decision whether or not to terminate her pregnancy. The detriment that the State would impose upon the pregnant woman by denying this choice altogether is apparent. Specific and direct harm medically diagnosable even in early pregnancy may be [involved]. Psychological harm may be imminent. Mental and physical health may be taxed by child care. There is also the distress, for all concerned, associated with the unwanted child, and there is the problem of bringing a child into a family already unable, psychologically and otherwise, to care for it. In other cases, as in this one, the additional difficulties and continuing stigma of unwed motherhood may be involved. All these are factors the woman and her responsible physician necessarily will consider in consultation.

[Where] certain "fundamental rights" are involved, the Court has held that regulation limiting these rights may be justified only by a "compelling state interest," and that legislative enactments must be narrowly drawn to express only the legitimate state interests at stake.

[Appellee argues] that the fetus is a "person" within the language and meaning of the Fourteenth Amendment. [If so,] appellant's case, of course, collapses, for the fetus' right to life would then be guaranteed specifically by the Amendment.

[The] Constitution does not define "person" in so many words. [The Court then listed each provision in which the word appears.] But in nearly all these instances, the use of the word is such that it has application only postnatally. None indicates, with any assurance, that it has any possible pre-natal application. All this, together with our observation that throughout the major portion of the 19th century prevailing legal abortion practices were far freer [than] today, persuades us that the word "person," as used in the Fourteenth Amendment, does not include the unborn. [Thus,] we pass on to other considerations.

The pregnant woman cannot be isolated in her privacy. She carries an embryo and, later, a fetus. [The] situation therefore is inherently different from marital intimacy, or bedroom possession of obscene material, or marriage, or procreation, or education, with which *Eisenstadt, Griswold,* [and other cases were] concerned.

[Texas] urges that, apart from the Fourteenth Amendment, life begins at conception and is present throughout pregnancy, and that, therefore, the State has a compelling interest in protecting that life from and after conception. We need not resolve the difficult question of when life begins. When those trained [in] medicine, philosophy, and theology are unable to arrive at any consensus, the judiciary, at this point in the development of man's knowledge, is not in a position to speculate as to the answer.

[W]e do not agree that, by adopting one theory of life, Texas may override the rights of the pregnant woman that are at stake. We repeat, however, that the State does have an important and legitimate interest in preserving and protecting the health of the pregnant woman [and] that it has still *another* important and legitimate interest in protecting the potentiality of human life. These interests are separate and distinct. Each grows in substantiality as the woman approaches term and, at a point during pregnancy, each becomes "compelling."

With respect to [the] interest in the health of the mother, the "compelling" point, in the light of present medical knowledge, is at approximately the end of the first trimester. This is so because of the now-established medical fact that until the end of the first trimester mortality in abortion may be less than mortality in normal childbirth. [Hence,] for the period of pregnancy prior to this "compelling" point, the attending physician, in consultation with his patient, is free to determine, without regulation by the State, that in his medical judgment the patient's pregnancy should be terminated. If that decision is reached, the judgment may be effectuated by an abortion free of interference by the State.

With respect to [the] interest in potential life, the "compelling" point is at viability [which "is usually placed at about seven months (28 weeks) but may occur earlier, even at 24 weeks."] This is so because the fetus then presumably has the capability of meaningful life outside the mother's womb. State regulation protective of fetal life after viability thus has both logical and biological justifications. If the State is interested in protecting fetal life after viability, it may go as far as to proscribe abortion during that period except when it is necessary to preserve the life or health of the mother. Measured against these standards, [the Texas statute] sweeps too broadly [and] therefore, cannot survive the constitutional attack made upon it here.

* * *

JUSTICE STEWART, concurring.

In 1963, this Court, in *Ferguson v. Skrupa* [Ch. 5, Sec. 3], purported to sound the death knell for the doctrine of substantive due process, [but] [b]arely two years later, in *Griswold,* the Court held a Connecticut birth control law unconstitutional. [T]he *Griswold* decision can be rationally understood only as a holding that the Connecticut statute substantively invaded the "liberty" that is protected by the Due Process Clause of the Fourteenth Amendment. As so understood, *Griswold* stands as one in a long line of pre-*Skrupa* cases decided under the doctrine of substantive due process, and I now accept it as such.

* * *

JUSTICE DOUGLAS, concurring [in *Doe* as well as in *Roe*].

While I join the opinion of the Court, I add a few words.

[The] Ninth Amendment obviously does not create federally enforceable rights. [But] a catalogue of [the rights "retained by the people"] includes customary, traditional, and time-honored rights, amenities, privileges, and immunities that come within the sweep of "the Blessings of Liberty" mentioned in the preamble to the Constitution. Many of them, in my view, come within the meaning of the term "liberty" as used in the Fourteenth Amendment. * * *

JUSTICE WHITE, with whom JUSTICE REHNQUIST joins, dissenting.

[The claim] before us is that for [various] reasons, or for no reason at all, and without asserting or claiming any threat to life or health, any woman is entitled to an abortion at her request if she is able to find a medical advisor willing to [perform it]. The Court for the most part sustains this position [and] simply fashions and announces a new constitutional right [and], with scarcely any reason or authority for its action, invests that right with sufficient substance to override most existing state abortion statutes. The upshot is that the people and the legislatures of the 50 States are constitutionally disentitled to weigh the relative importance of the continued existence and development of the fetus, on the one hand, against a spectrum of possible impacts on the mother, on the other hand. As an exercise of raw judicial power, the Court perhaps has authority [but] in my view its judgment is an improvident and extravagant exercise of the power of judicial review * * * .

JUSTICE REHNQUIST, dissenting. * * *

I have difficulty in concluding [that] the right of "privacy" is involved in this case. [Texas] bars the performance of a medical abortion by a licensed physician on a plaintiff such as Roe. A transaction resulting in an operation such as this is not "private" in the ordinary usage of that word. Nor is the "privacy" that the Court finds here even a distant relative of the freedom from searches and seizures protected by the Fourth Amendment.

[Constitutional] liberty is not guaranteed absolutely against deprivation, only against deprivation without due process of law. The test traditionally applied in the area of social and economic legislation is whether or not a law such as that challenged has a rational relation to a valid state objective. [If] the Texas statute were to prohibit an abortion even where the mother's life is in jeopardy, I have little doubt that such a statute would lack a rational relation to a valid state objective under the test stated in *Williamson v. Lee Optical Co.* [Ch. 5, Sec. 3]. But the Court's sweeping invalidation of any restrictions on abortion during the first trimester is impossible to justify under that standard, and the conscious weighing of competing factors that the Court's opinion apparently substitutes for the established test is far more appropriate to a legislative judgment than to a judicial one.

[While] the Court's opinion quotes from the dissent of Mr. Justice Holmes in *Lochner*, the result it reaches is more closely attuned to the majority opinion of Mr. Justice Peckham in that case. [The] decision here to break pregnancy into three distinct terms and to outline the permissible restrictions the State may impose in each one, for example, partakes more of judicial legislation than it does of a determination of the intent of the drafters of the Fourteenth Amendment.

[By] the time of the adoption of the Fourteenth Amendment in 1868, there were at least 36 laws enacted by state or territorial legislatures limiting abortion. While many States have amended or updated their laws, 21 of the laws on the books in 1868 remain in effect today. [There] apparently was no question concerning the validity of [the Texas] provision or of any of the other state statutes when the Fourteenth Amendment was adopted. The only conclusion possible from this history is that the drafters did not intend to have the Fourteenth Amendment withdraw from the States the power to legislate with respect to this matter. * * *

DOE v. BOLTON, 410 U.S. 179 (1973), the companion case to *Roe v. Wade*, per BLACKMUN, J., invalidated several provisions of a Georgia abortion law. The Court first rejected the claim that a provision permitting a physician to perform an abortion "based upon his best clinical judgment that an abortion is necessary" was unconstitutionally vague. However, despite the fact that the Georgia statute was patterned after the American Law Institute's Model Penal Code (1962), which had served as the model for recent legislation in about one-fourth of the states, the Court invalidated substantial portions of the statute. Struck down were requirements: (1) that the abortion be performed in an accredited hospital; (2) that the procedure be approved by a hospital staff abortion committee; and (3) that the performing physician's judgment be confirmed by independent examinations of the patient by two other physicians. "[T]he woman's right to receive medical care in accordance with her licensed physician's best judgment and the physician's right to administer it are substantially limited by this statutorily imposed overview."

Abortion Funding

1.   MAHER v. ROE, 432 U.S. 464 (1977), per POWELL, J., sustained Connecticut's use of Medicaid funds to reimburse women for the costs of childbirth and "medically necessary" first trimester abortions (defined to include "psychiatric necessity"), but not for the costs of elective or nontherapeutic first trimester abortions.

On "the central question"—"whether the regulation 'impinges upon a fundamental right explicitly or implicitly protected by the Constitution' "—the Court held that *Roe* did not establish "an unqualified 'constitutional right to an abortion,' " but only a "right protect[ing] the woman from unduly burdensome interference with her freedom to decide whether to terminate her pregnancy. It implies no limitation on the authority of a State to make a value judgment favoring childbirth over abortion, and to implement that judgment by the allocation of public funds. [The] indigency that may make it difficult—and in some cases, perhaps, impossible—for some women to have abortions is neither created nor in any way affected by the [regulation.]"

BRENNAN, J., joined by Marshall and Blackmun, JJ., dissented, accusing the majority of "a distressing insensitivity to the plight of impoverished pregnant women." The "disparity in funding [clearly] operates to coerce indigent pregnant women to bear children they would not otherwise choose to have, and just as clearly, this coercion can only operate upon the poor, who are uniquely the victims of this form of financial pressure."

2.   *The Hyde Amendment.* Title XIX of the Social Security Act established the Medicaid program to provide federal financial assistance to states choosing to reimburse certain costs of medical treatment for needy persons. Since 1976, various versions of the so-called Hyde Amendment have limited federal funding of abortions under the Medicaid program to those necessary to save the life of the mother and certain other exceptional circumstances.

HARRIS v. McRAE, 448 U.S. 297 (1980), per STEWART, J., found no constitutional violation: "The present case does differ factually from *Maher* insofar as that case involved a failure to fund nontherapeutic abortions, whereas the Hyde Amendment withholds funding of certain medically necessary abortions. [But] regardless of [how] the freedom of a woman to choose to terminate her pregnancy for health reasons [is characterized], it simply does not follow that [this freedom] carries with it a constitutional entitlement to the financial resources to avail herself of the full range of protected choices. [T]he Hyde Amendment leaves an indigent woman with at least the same range of choice in deciding whether to obtain a medically necessary abortion as she would have had if Congress had chosen to subsidize no health care costs at all.

"[Acceptance of appellees' argument] would mark a drastic change in our understanding of the Constitution. It cannot be that because government may not prohibit the use of contraceptives, *Griswold,* or prevent parents from sending their child to a private school, *Pierce,* government, therefore, has an affirmative constitutional obligation to assure that all persons have the financial resources to obtain contraceptives or send their children to private [schools.]"

Four justices dissented—Brennan, Marshall and Blackmun, JJ. (the three *Maher* dissenters), and Stevens, J. who had joined the opinion of the Court in *Maher.* STEVENS, J., maintained that the instant case presented "[a] fundamentally different question" from the one decided in *Maher:* "[This case involves] the pool of benefits that Congress created by enacting [Title XIX]. Individuals who satisfy two neutral criteria—financial need and medical need—are entitled to equal access to that pool. The question is whether certain persons who satisfy those criteria may be denied access to benefits solely because they must exercise the constitutional right to have an abortion in order to obtain the medical care they need. Our prior cases plainly dictate the answer."

The other three dissenters wrote separately, each voicing agreement with Stevens, J.'s analysis. BRENNAN, J., joined by Marshall and Blackmun, JJ., maintained: "[W]hat the Court fails to appreciate is that it is not simply the woman's indigency that interferes with her freedom of choice, but the combination of her own poverty and the Government's unequal subsidization of abortion and childbirth."

The Court extended *Maher* and *McRae* in *Rust v. Sullivan,* 500 U.S. 173 (1991), upholding federal regulations prohibiting private physicians receiving federal funds for "family planning services" from providing abortion information to a woman client except when a pregnancy places her life in peril. (The free speech aspects of this case are discussed at Ch. 7, Sec. 7, I.)

The Patient Protection and Affordable Care Act extended the Hyde Amendment to the federal subsidies for which individuals purchasing health insurance on "exchanges" may be eligible. Although the Act itself does not forbid insurance plans offered on the exchanges from covering abortion, it does proportionately reduce subsidies for such plans and requires the segregation of funds. In addition, the Act authorizes states to "prohibit abortion coverage in [all] qualified health plans" offered on state exchanges. 42 U.S.C. § 18023.

The Court Reaffirms "the Essential Holding of *Roe*"

PLANNED PARENTHOOD OF SOUTHEASTERN PENNSYLVANIA V. CASEY

505 U.S. 833, 112 S.Ct. 2791, 120 L.Ed.2d 674 (1992).

JUSTICE O'CONNOR, JUSTICE KENNEDY, and JUSTICE SOUTER announced the judgment of the Court and delivered the opinion of the Court with respect to Parts

I, II, III, V-A, V-C, and VI, an opinion with respect to Part V-E, in which JUSTICE STEVENS joins, and an opinion with respect to Parts IV, V-B, and V-D.

I.   Liberty finds no refuge in a jurisprudence of doubt. Yet 19 years after our holding that the Constitution protects a woman's right to terminate her pregnancy in its early stages, *Roe v. Wade,* that definition of liberty is still questioned. Joining the respondents as amicus curiae, the United States, as it has done in five other cases in the last decade, again asks us to overrule *Roe.*

[*Roe's*] essential holding, the holding we reaffirm, has three parts. First is a recognition of the right of the woman to choose to have an abortion before viability and to obtain it without undue interference from the State. Before viability, the State's interests are not strong enough to support a prohibition of abortion or the imposition of a substantial obstacle to the woman's effective right to elect the procedure. Second is a confirmation of the State's power to restrict abortions after fetal viability, if the law contains exceptions for pregnancies which endanger a woman's life or health. And third is the principle that the State has legitimate interests from the outset of the pregnancy in protecting the health of the woman and the life of the fetus that may become a child. These principles do not contradict one another; and we adhere to each. * * *

III.   [When] this Court reexamines a prior holding, [we] may ask whether the rule has proven to be intolerable simply in defying practical workability; whether the rule is subject to a kind of reliance that would lend a special hardship to the consequences of overruling and add inequity to the cost of repudiation; whether related principles of law have so far developed as to have left the old rule no more than a remnant of abandoned doctrine; or whether facts have so changed or come to be seen so differently, as to have robbed the old rule of significant application or justification. [Although] *Roe* has engendered opposition, it has in no sense proven "unworkable," representing as it does a simple limitation beyond which a state law is unenforceable.

[To] eliminate the issue of reliance [would] be simply to refuse to face the fact that for two decades of economic and social developments, people have organized intimate relationships and made choices that define their views of themselves and their places in society, in reliance on the availability of abortion in the event that contraception should fail. The ability of women to participate equally in the economic and social life of the Nation has been facilitated by their ability to control their reproductive lives.

[Even] on the assumption that the central holding of *Roe* was in error, that error would go only to the strength of the state interest in fetal protection, not to the recognition afforded by the Constitution to the woman's liberty. The latter aspect of the decision fits comfortably within the framework of the Court's prior decisions including *Skinner, Griswold,* [and] *Eisenstadt,* the holdings of which are "not a series of isolated points," but mark a "rational continuum." *Poe v. Ullman* (Harlan, J., dissenting).

[The] sustained and widespread debate *Roe* has provoked calls for some comparison between that case and others of comparable dimension that have responded to national controversies and taken on the impress of the controversies addressed. Only two such decisional lines from the past century present themselves for examination, and in each instance the result reached by the Court accorded with the principles we apply today.

The first example is that line of cases identified with *Lochner v. New York* [Ch. 5, Sec. 2, I] (1905) [and] *Adkins v. Children's Hospital* [Ch. 5, Sec. 2, II] (1923). [Fourteen] years later, *West Coast Hotel Co. v. Parrish* [Ch. 5, Sec. 3] (1937) signaled the demise of *Lochner* by overruling *Adkins*. In the meantime, the Depression had come and, with it, the lesson that seemed unmistakable to most people by 1937, that the interpretation of contractual freedom protected in *Adkins* rested on fundamentally false factual assumptions about the capacity of a relatively unregulated market to satisfy minimal levels of human welfare. [The] facts upon which the earlier case had premised a constitutional resolution of social controversy had proven to be untrue, and history's demonstration of their untruth not only justified but required the new choice of constitutional principle that *West Coast Hotel* announced.

[The] second comparison that 20th century history invites is with the cases employing the separate-but-equal rule for applying the Fourteenth Amendment's equal protection guarantee. They began with *Plessy v. Ferguson* [Ch. 9, Sec. 2, II], holding that legislatively mandated racial segregation in public transportation works no denial of equal protection. [But this rule was] repudiated in *Brown v. Board of Education* [Ch. 9, Sec. 2, II].

[The *Brown* Court observed] that whatever may have been the understanding in *Plessy*'s time of the power of segregation to stigmatize those who were segregated with a "badge of inferiority," it was clear by 1954 that legally sanctioned segregation had just such an effect, to the point that racially separate public educational facilities were deemed inherently unequal. Society's understanding of the facts upon which a constitutional ruling was sought in 1954 was thus fundamentally different from the basis claimed for the decision in 1896. While we think *Plessy* was wrong the day it was decided, we must also recognize that the *Plessy* Court's explanation for its decision was so clearly at odds with the facts apparent to the Court in 1954 that the decision to reexamine *Plessy* was on this ground alone not only justified but required.

[Because] neither the factual underpinnings of *Roe*'s central holding nor our understanding of it has changed [the] Court could not pretend to be reexamining the prior law with any justification beyond a present doctrinal disposition to come out differently from the Court of 1973. To overrule prior law for no other reason than that would run counter to the view repeated in our cases, that a decision to overrule should rest on some special reason over and above the belief that a prior case was wrongly decided.

[Overruling] *Roe*'s central holding would not only reach an unjustifiable result under principles of stare decisis, but would seriously weaken the Court's capacity to exercise the judicial power and to function as the Supreme Court of a Nation dedicated to the rule of law. [The] Court's power lies [in] its legitimacy, a product of substance and perception that shows itself in the people's acceptance of the Judiciary as fit to determine what the Nation's law means and to declare what it demands.

[Where,] in the performance of its judicial duties, the Court decides a case in such a way as to resolve the sort of intensely divisive controversy reflected in *Roe* and those rare, comparable cases, its decision has a dimension that the resolution of the normal case does not carry. [To] overrule under fire in the absence of the most compelling reason to reexamine a watershed decision would subvert the Court's legitimacy beyond any serious question.

IV.   [We] conclude that the basic decision in *Roe* was based on a constitutional analysis which we cannot now repudiate. The woman's liberty is not so unlimited, however, that from the outset the State cannot show its concern for the life of the unborn, and at a later point in fetal development the State's interest in life has sufficient force so that the right of the woman to terminate the pregnancy can be restricted. [We] conclude the line should be drawn at viability, so that before that time the woman has a right to choose to terminate her pregnancy. We adhere to this principle for two reasons. First [is] the doctrine of stare decisis. [We] have twice reaffirmed [*Roe*] in the face of great opposition. [The] second reason is that the concept of viability, as we noted in *Roe,* is the time at which there is a realistic possibility of maintaining and nourishing a life outside the womb, so that the independent existence of the second life can in reason and all fairness be the object of state protection that now overrides the rights of the woman. [The] viability line also has, as a practical matter, an element of fairness. In some broad sense it might be said that a woman who fails to act before viability has consented to the State's intervention on behalf of the developing child. [The] woman's right to terminate her pregnancy before viability is the most central principle of *Roe*.

[On] the other side of the equation is the interest of the State in the protection of potential life. [We] do not need to say whether each of us, had we been Members of the Court when the valuation of the State interest came before it as an original matter, would have concluded, as the *Roe* Court did, that its weight is insufficient to justify a ban on abortions prior to viability even when it is subject to certain exceptions. The matter is not before us in the first instance, and coming as it does after nearly 20 years of litigation in *Roe*'s wake we are satisfied that the immediate question is not the soundness of *Roe*'s resolution of the issue, but the precedential force that must be accorded to its holding. And we have concluded that the essential holding of *Roe* should be reaffirmed.

Yet it must be remembered that *Roe* speaks with clarity in establishing not only the woman's liberty but also the State's "important and legitimate interest in potential life." That portion [of] *Roe* has been given too little acknowledgement and implementation by the Court in its subsequent cases. [We] reject the trimester framework, which we do not consider to be part of the essential holding of *Roe.* Measures aimed at ensuring that a woman's choice contemplates the consequences for the fetus do not necessarily interfere with the right recognized in *Roe,* although those measures have been found to be inconsistent with the rigid trimester framework announced in that case.

[In] our view, the undue burden standard is the appropriate means of reconciling the State's interest with the woman's constitutionally protected liberty. [A] finding of an undue burden is a shorthand for the conclusion that a state regulation has the purpose or effect of placing a substantial obstacle in the path of a woman seeking an abortion of a nonviable fetus. A statute with this purpose is invalid because the means chosen by the State to further the interest in potential life must be calculated to inform the woman's free choice, not hinder it.

[What] is at stake is the woman's right to make the ultimate decision, not a right to be insulated from all others in doing so. Regulations which do no more than create a structural mechanism by which the State, or the parent or guardian of a minor, may express profound respect for the life of the unborn are permitted, if they are not a substantial obstacle to the woman's exercise of the right to choose. [Unless] it has that effect on her right of choice, a state measure designed to persuade her to choose childbirth over abortion will be upheld if reasonably related to that goal. Regulations designed to foster the health of a woman seeking an abortion are valid if they do not constitute an undue burden.

[We] give this summary:

(a) To protect the central right recognized by *Roe* while at the same time accommodating the State's profound interest in potential life, we will employ the undue burden analysis as explained in this opinion. An undue burden exists, and therefore a provision of law is invalid, if its purpose or effect is to place a substantial obstacle in the path of a woman seeking an abortion before the fetus attains viability.

(b) We reject the rigid trimester framework of *Roe.* To promote the State's profound interest in potential life, throughout pregnancy the State may take measures to ensure that the woman's choice is informed, and measures designed to advance this interest will not be invalidated as long as their purpose is to persuade the woman to choose childbirth over abortion. These measures must not be an undue burden on the right.

(c) As with any medical procedure, the State may enact regulations to further the health or safety of a woman seeking an abortion. Unnecessary health regulations that have the purpose or effect of presenting a substantial obstacle to a woman seeking an abortion impose an undue burden on the right.

(d) Our adoption of the undue burden analysis does not disturb the central holding of *Roe,* and we reaffirm that holding. [A] State may not prohibit any woman from making the ultimate decision to terminate her pregnancy before viability.

(e)   We also reaffirm *Roe*'s holding that "subsequent to viability, the State in promoting its interest in the potentiality of human life may, if it chooses, regulate, and even proscribe, abortion except where it is necessary, in appropriate medical judgment, for the preservation of the life or health of the mother."

These principles control our assessment of the Pennsylvania statute, and we now turn to the issue of the validity of its challenged provisions.

V.   [The lead opinion applied the undue burden test to five provisions of the Pennsylvania Abortion Control Act of 1982 as amended in 1988 and 1989. In addition to the analysis included below, the joint opinion upheld the law's definition of a medical emergency and its reporting requirements.]

B.   [Except] in a medical emergency, the statute requires that at least 24 hours before performing an abortion a physician inform the woman of the nature of the procedure, the health risks of the abortion and of childbirth, and the "probable gestational age of the unborn child." The physician or a qualified nonphysician must inform the woman of the availability of printed materials published by the State describing the fetus and providing information about medical assistance for childbirth, information about child support from the father, and a list of agencies which provide adoption and other services as alternatives to abortion.

[The] idea that important decisions will be more informed and deliberate if they follow some period of reflection does not strike us as unreasonable, particularly where the statute directs that important information become part of the background of the decision.

[The] findings of fact [indicate] that for those women who have the fewest financial resources, those who must travel long distances, and those who have difficulty explaining their whereabouts to husbands, employers, or others, the 24-hour waiting period will be "particularly burdensome." These findings are troubling in some respects, but they do not demonstrate that the waiting period constitutes an undue burden. [Under] the undue burden standard a State is permitted to enact persuasive measures which favor childbirth over abortion, even if those measures do not further a health interest. And while the waiting period does limit a physician's discretion, that is not, standing alone, a reason to invalidate it. In light of the construction given the statute's definition of medical emergency by the Court of Appeals, and the District Court's findings, we cannot say that the waiting period imposes a real health risk.

[C.]   Section 3209 of Pennsylvania's abortion law provides, except in cases of medical emergency, that no physician shall perform an abortion on a married woman without receiving a signed statement from the woman that she has notified her spouse that she is about to undergo an abortion. The woman has the option of providing an alternative signed statement certifying that her husband is not the man who impregnated her; that her husband could not be located; that the pregnancy is the result of spousal sexual assault which she has reported; or that the woman believes that notifying her husband will cause him or someone else to inflict bodily injury upon her. A physician who performs an abortion on a married woman without receiving the appropriate signed statement will have his or her license revoked, and is liable to the husband for damages.

[Various studies of domestic violence] and the District Court's findings reinforce what common sense would suggest. In well-functioning marriages, spouses discuss important intimate decisions such as whether to bear a child. But there are millions of women in this country who are the victims of regular physical and psychological abuse at the hands of their husbands. Should these women become pregnant, they may have very good reasons for not wishing to inform their husbands of their decision to obtain an abortion.

[The] spousal notification requirement is thus likely to prevent a significant number of women from obtaining an abortion. It does not merely make abortions a little more difficult or expensive to obtain; for many women, it will impose a substantial obstacle. We must not blind ourselves to the fact that the significant number of women who fear for their safety and the safety of their children are likely to be deterred from procuring an abortion as surely as if the Commonwealth had outlawed abortion in all cases.

[Section] 3209's real target is narrower even than the class of women seeking abortions identified by the State: it is married women seeking abortions who do not wish to notify their husbands of their intentions and who do not qualify for one of the statutory exceptions to the notice requirement. The unfortunate yet persisting conditions we document above will mean that in a large fraction of the cases in which § 3209 is relevant, it will operate as a substantial obstacle to a woman's choice to undergo an abortion. It is an undue burden, and therefore invalid.

This conclusion is in no way inconsistent with our decisions upholding parental notification or consent requirements. Those enactments, and our judgment that they are constitutional, are based on the quite reasonable assumption that minors will benefit from consultation with their parents and that children will often not realize that their parents have their best interests at heart. We cannot adopt a parallel assumption about adult women. [Section] 3209 embodies a view of marriage consonant with the common-law status of married women but repugnant to our present understanding of marriage and of the nature of the rights secured by the Constitution. Women do not lose their constitutionally protected liberty when they marry.

D. [Except] in a medical emergency, an unemancipated young woman under 18 may not obtain an abortion unless she and one of her parents (or guardian) provides informed consent. [If] neither a parent nor a guardian provides consent, a court may authorize the performance of an abortion upon a determination that the young woman is mature and capable of giving informed consent and has in fact given her informed consent, or that an abortion would be in her best interests. [Our] cases establish, and we reaffirm today, that a State may require a minor seeking an abortion to obtain the consent of a parent or guardian, provided that there is an adequate judicial bypass procedure.

[VI.] Our Constitution is a covenant running from the first generation of Americans to us and then to future generations. It is a coherent succession. Each generation must learn anew that the Constitution's written terms embody ideas and aspirations that must survive more ages than one. We accept our responsibility not to retreat from interpreting the full meaning of the covenant in light of all of our precedents. We invoke it once again to define the freedom guaranteed by the Constitution's own promise, the promise of liberty. * * *

JUSTICE STEVENS, concurring in part and dissenting in part. * * *

[I] accept what is implicit in the Court's analysis, namely, a reaffirmation of *Roe*'s explanation of *why* the State's obligation to protect the life or health of the mother must take precedence over any duty to the unborn. The Court in *Roe* carefully considered, and rejected, the State's argument "that the fetus is a 'person' within the language and meaning of the Fourteenth Amendment."

[The] State may promote its preferences by funding childbirth, by creating and maintaining alternatives to abortion, and by espousing the virtues of family; but it must respect the individual's freedom to make such judgments. [Justice Stevens deemed unconstitutional the 24-hour waiting period and those sections requiring a woman to be provided with a wide "range of materials clearly designed to persuade her to choose not to undergo the abortion." But he did not find constitutionally objectionable those sections requiring the physician to inform a woman of the nature and risks of the abortion procedure and the medical risks of carrying to term for these "are neutral requirements comparable to those imposed in other medical procedures."]

JUSTICE BLACKMUN, concurring in part, concurring in the judgment in part, and dissenting in part.

[The] Constitution and decisions of this Court require [us] to subject all non-de-minimis abortion regulations to strict scrutiny. Under this standard, the Pennsylvania statute's provisions requiring content-based counseling, a 24-hour delay, informed parental consent, and reporting of abortion-related information must be invalidated. [R]estrictive abortion laws force women to endure physical invasions far more substantial than those this Court has held to violate the constitutional principle of bodily integrity in other contexts. See, e.g., *Winston*; *Rochin* [Sec. 1, IV supra]. [Because] motherhood has a dramatic impact on a woman's educational prospects, employment opportunities, and self-determination, restrictive abortion laws deprive her of basic control over her life.

[A] State's restrictions on a woman's right to terminate her pregnancy also implicate constitutional guarantees of gender equality. [By] restricting the right to terminate pregnancies, the State conscripts women's bodies into its service, forcing women to continue their pregnancies, suffer the pains of childbirth, and in most instances, provide years of maternal care. The State does not compensate women for their services; instead, it assumes that they owe this duty as a matter of course. This assumption—that women can simply be forced to accept the "natural" status and incidents of motherhood—appears to rest upon a conception of women's role that has triggered the protection of the Equal Protection Clause. The joint opinion recognizes that these assumptions about women's place in society "are no longer consistent with our understanding of the family, the individual, or the Constitution."

CHIEF JUSTICE REHNQUIST, with whom JUSTICE WHITE, JUSTICE SCALIA, and JUSTICE THOMAS join, concurring in the judgment in part and dissenting in part.

The joint opinion, following its newly minted variation on stare decisis, retains the outer shell of *Roe* but beats a wholesale retreat from the substance of that case. We believe that *Roe* was wrongly decided, and that it can and should be overruled consistently with our traditional approach to stare decisis in constitutional cases. We would adopt the approach of the plurality in *Webster* and uphold the challenged provisions of the Pennsylvania statute in their entirety.

[Unlike] marriage, procreation and contraception, abortion "involves the purposeful termination of potential life." The abortion decision must therefore "be recognized as sui generis, different in kind from the others that the Court has protected under the rubric of personal or family privacy and autonomy." One cannot ignore the fact that a woman is not isolated in her pregnancy, and that the decision to abort necessarily involves the destruction of a fetus.

[Nor] do the historical traditions of the American people support the view that the right to terminate one's pregnancy is "fundamental." The common law which we inherited from England made abortion after "quickening" an offense. At the time of the adoption of the Fourteenth Amendment, statutory prohibitions or restrictions on abortion were commonplace; in 1868, at least 28 of the then-37 States and 8 Territories had statutes banning or limiting abortion. By the turn of the century virtually every State had a law prohibiting or restricting abortion on its books. By the middle of the present century, a liberalization trend had set in. But 21 of the restrictive abortion laws in effect in 1868 were still in effect in 1973 when *Roe* was decided, and an overwhelming majority of the States prohibited abortion unless necessary to preserve the life or health of the mother. On this record, it can scarcely be said that any deeply rooted tradition of relatively unrestricted abortion in our history supported the classification of the right to abortion as "fundamental" under the Due Process Clause of the Fourteenth Amendment.

[Having] failed to put forth any evidence to prove any true reliance [on *Roe*], the joint opinion's argument is based solely on generalized assertions about the national psyche, on a belief that the people of this country have grown accustomed to the *Roe* decision over the last 19 years and have "ordered their thinking and living around" it. As an initial matter, one might inquire how the joint opinion can view the "central holding" of *Roe* as so deeply rooted in our constitutional culture, when it so casually uproots and disposes of that same decision's trimester framework. Furthermore, at various points in the past, the same could have been said about this Court's erroneous decisions that the Constitution allowed "separate but equal" treatment of minorities or that "liberty" under the Due Process Clause protected "freedom of contract." [The] simple fact that a generation or more had grown used to these major decisions did not prevent the Court from correcting its errors in those cases, nor should it prevent us from correctly interpreting the Constitution here.

[The] sum of the joint opinion's labors in the name of stare decisis and "legitimacy" is this: *Roe* stands as a sort of judicial Potemkin Village, which may be pointed out to passers-by as a monument to the importance of adhering to precedent. But behind the facade, an entirely new method of analysis, without any roots in constitutional law, is imported to decide the constitutionality of state laws regulating abortion. Neither stare decisis nor "legitimacy" are truly served by such an effort.

[The Chief Justice then discussed each of the challenged provisions and concluded that each should be upheld.]

JUSTICE SCALIA, with whom CHIEF JUSTICE REHNQUIST, JUSTICE WHITE, and JUSTICE THOMAS join, concurring in the judgment in part and dissenting in part.

[The] issue in [these cases] [is] not whether the power of a woman to abort her unborn child is a "liberty" in the absolute sense; or even whether it is a liberty of great importance to many women. Of course it is both. The issue is whether it is a liberty protected by the Constitution of the United States. I am sure it is not. I reach that conclusion not because of anything so exalted as my views concerning the "concept of existence, of meaning, of the universe, and of the mystery of human life." Rather, I reach it for the same reason I reach the conclusion that bigamy is not constitutionally protected—because of two simple facts: (1) the Constitution says absolutely nothing about it, and (2) the longstanding traditions of American society have permitted it to be legally proscribed.

[To] the extent I can discern *any* meaningful content in the "undue burden" standard as applied in the joint opinion, it appears to be that a State may not regulate abortion in such a way as to reduce significantly its incidence. The joint opinion repeatedly emphasizes that an important factor in the "undue burden" analysis is whether the regulation "prevent[s] a significant number of women from obtaining an abortion," whether a "significant number of women [are] likely to be deterred from procuring an abortion," and whether the regulation often "deters" women from seeking abortions. We are not told, however, what forms of "deterrence" are impermissible or what degree of success in deterrence is too much to be tolerated.

[I] cannot agree with, indeed I am appalled by, the Court's suggestion that the decision whether to stand by an erroneous constitutional decision must be strongly influenced—*against* overruling, no less—by the substantial and continuing public opposition the decision has generated. [In] my history-book, the Court was covered with dishonor and deprived of legitimacy by *Dred Scott v. Sandford* [Ch. 9, Sec. 2, I], an erroneous (and widely opposed) opinion that it did not abandon, rather than by *West Coast Hotel,* which produced the famous "switch in time" from the Court's erroneous (and widely opposed) constitutional opposition to the social measures of the New Deal. (Both *Dred Scott* and one line of the cases resisting the New Deal rested upon the concept of "substantive due process" that the Court praises and employs today.)

[By] continuing the imposition of a rigid national rule instead of allowing for regional differences, the Court merely prolongs and intensifies the anguish. We should get out of this area, where we have no right to be, and where we do neither ourselves nor the country any good by remaining.

Purported Health Regulations

WHOLE WOMAN'S HEALTH V. HELLERSTEDT
___ U.S. ___, 136 S.Ct. 2292, 195 L.Ed.2d 665 (2016).

JUSTICE BREYER delivered the opinion of the Court.

In *Planned Parenthood v. Casey,* a plurality of the Court concluded that there "exists" an "undue burden" on a woman's right to decide to have an abortion, and consequently a provision of law is constitutionally invalid, if the *"purpose or effect"* of the provision *"is to place a substantial obstacle* in the path of a woman seeking an abortion before the fetus attains viability." (Emphasis added.) The plurality added that "[u]nnecessary health regulations that have the purpose or effect of presenting a substantial obstacle to a woman seeking an abortion impose an undue burden on the right."

We must here decide whether two provisions of Texas' House Bill 2 violate the Federal Constitution as interpreted in *Casey*. The first provision, which we shall call the *"admitting-privileges requirement,"* says that "[a] physician performing or inducing an abortion . . . must, on the date the abortion is performed or induced, have active admitting privileges at a hospital that . . . is located not further than 30 miles from the location at which the abortion is performed or induced."

[The] second provision, which we shall call the *"surgical-center requirement,"* says that "the minimum standards for an abortion facility must be equivalent to the minimum standards adopted under [the Texas Health and Safety Code section] for ambulatory surgical centers."

We conclude that neither of these provisions offers medical benefits sufficient to justify the burdens upon access that each imposes. Each places a substantial obstacle in the path of women seeking a previability abortion, each constitutes an undue burden on abortion access and each violates the [Fourteenth Amendment].

I. [B.] The District Court [received] stipulations from the parties and depositions from the parties' experts. The court conducted a 4-day bench trial. It heard, among other testimony, the opinions from expert witnesses for both sides. On the basis of the stipulations, depositions, and testimony, that court [concluded, *inter alia*, that: after the admitting-privileges requirement went into effect, the number of licensed abortion facilities operating in Texas was reduced from more than 40 to just over half as many; if the surgical center provision were to go into effect, the number of abortion facilities would be reduced to as few as seven or eight; these abortion facilities would exist only in the state's major metropolitan areas;] the suggestion that "that these seven or eight providers could meet the demand of the entire state stretches credulity"[; these reductions would greatly increase travel distances for many women in the state;] "[t]he great weight of evidence demonstrates that, before the act's passage, abortion in Texas was extremely safe with particularly low rates of serious complications and virtually no deaths occurring on account of the procedure"[; "a]bortion, as regulated by the State before the enactment of House Bill 2, has been shown to be much safer, in terms of minor and serious complications, than many common medical procedures not subject to such intense regulation and scrutiny"[; and t]he "cost of coming into compliance" with the surgical-center requirement "for existing clinics is significant," "undisputedly approach[ing] 1 million dollars," and "most likely exceed[ing] 1.5 million dollars," with "[s]ome . . . clinics" unable to "comply due to physical size limitations of their sites." [Based on these findings, the district court enjoined both provisions of the Texas law, but that ruling was reversed by a panel of the U.S. Court of Appeals for the Fifth Circuit.] * * *

III. *Undue Burden—Legal Standard*

[The] Court of Appeals wrote that a state law is "constitutional if: (1) it does not have the purpose or effect of placing a substantial obstacle in the path of a woman seeking an abortion of a nonviable fetus; and (2) it is reasonably related to (or designed to further) a legitimate state interest." The Court of Appeals went on to hold that "the district court erred by substituting its own judgment for that of the legislature" when it conducted its "undue burden inquiry," in part because "medical uncertainty underlying a statute is for resolution by legislatures, not the courts." (citing *Gonzales v. Carhart*, 550 U.S. 124 (2007) [(upholding federal Partial Birth Abortion Ban Act)]).

The Court of Appeals' articulation of the relevant standard is incorrect. The first part of the Court of Appeals' test may be read to imply that a district court should not consider the existence or nonexistence of medical benefits when considering whether a regulation of abortion constitutes an undue burden. The rule announced in *Casey,* however, requires that courts consider the burdens a law imposes on abortion access together with the benefits those laws confer. And the second part of the test is wrong to equate the judicial review applicable to the regulation of a constitutionally protected personal liberty with the less strict review applicable where, for example, economic legislation is at issue. See *Williamson v. Lee Optical of Okla., Inc.,* [Ch. 5, Sec. 3]. The Court of Appeals' approach simply does not match the standard that this Court laid out in *Casey,* which asks courts to consider whether any burden imposed on abortion access is "undue."

The statement that legislatures, and not courts, must resolve questions of medical uncertainty is also inconsistent with this Court's case law. Instead, the Court, when determining the constitutionality of laws regulating abortion procedures, has placed considerable weight upon evidence and argument presented in judicial proceedings. In *Casey,* for example, we relied heavily on the District Court's factual findings and the research-based submissions of *amici* in declaring a portion of the law at issue unconstitutional. [And], in *Gonzales* the Court, while pointing out that we must review legislative "factfinding under a deferential standard," added that we must not "place dispositive weight" on those "findings." *Gonzales* went on to point out that the "*Court retains an independent constitutional duty to review factual findings where constitutional rights are at stake.*" (Emphasis added). Although there we upheld a statute regulating abortion, we did not do so solely on the basis of legislative findings explicitly set forth in the statute, noting that "evidence presented in the District Courts contradicts" some of the legislative findings. In these circumstances, we said, "[u]ncritical deference to Congress' factual findings . . . is inappropriate."

Unlike in *Gonzales,* the relevant statute here does not set forth any legislative findings. Rather, one is left to infer that the legislature sought to further a constitutionally acceptable objective (namely, protecting women's health). For a district court to give significant weight to evidence in the judicial record in these circumstances is consistent with this Court's case law. [The] District Court [did] not simply substitute its own judgment for that of the legislature. It considered the evidence in the record—including expert evidence, presented in stipulations, depositions, and testimony. It then weighed the asserted benefits against the burdens. We hold that, in so doing, the District Court applied the correct legal standard.

IV. *Undue Burden—Admitting-Privileges Requirement*

[Before] the enactment of H.B. 2, doctors who provided abortions were required to "have admitting privileges *or* have a working arrangement with a physician(s) who has admitting privileges at a local hospital in order to ensure the necessary back up for medical complications." The new law changed this requirement by requiring that a "physician performing or inducing an abortion . . . must, on the date the abortion is performed or induced, have active admitting privileges at a hospital that . . . is located not further than 30 miles from the location at which the abortion is performed or induced." [The] purpose of the admitting-privileges requirement is to help ensure that women have easy access to a hospital should complications arise during an abortion procedure. But the District Court found that it brought about no such health-related benefit. The court found that "[t]he great weight of evidence demonstrates that, before the act's passage, abortion in Texas was extremely safe with particularly low rates of serious complications and virtually no deaths occurring on account of the procedure." Thus, there was no significant health-related problem that the new law helped to cure.

[When] directly asked at oral argument whether Texas knew of a single instance in which the new requirement would have helped even one woman obtain better treatment, Texas admitted that there was no evidence in the record of such a case. This answer is consistent with the findings of the other Federal District

Courts that have considered the health benefits of other States' similar admitting-privileges laws.

[An *amicus*] brief describes the undisputed general fact that "hospitals often condition admitting privileges on reaching a certain number of admissions per year." Returning to the District Court record, we note that, in direct testimony, the president of Nova Health Systems, implicitly relying on this general fact, pointed out that it would be difficult for doctors regularly performing abortions at the El Paso clinic to obtain admitting privileges at nearby hospitals because "[d]uring the past 10 years, over 17,000 abortion procedures were performed at the El Paso clinic [and n]ot a single one of those patients had to be transferred to a hospital for emergency treatment, much less admitted to the hospital." In a word, doctors would be unable to maintain admitting privileges or obtain those privileges for the future, because the fact that abortions are so safe meant that providers were unlikely to have any patients to admit.

[The] record contains sufficient evidence that the admitting-privileges requirement led to the closure of half of Texas' clinics, or thereabouts. Those closures meant fewer doctors, longer waiting times, and increased crowding. Record evidence also supports the finding that after the admitting-privileges provision went into effect, the "number of women of reproductive age living in a county . . . more than 150 miles from a provider increased from approximately 86,000 to 400,000 . . . and the number of women living in a county more than 200 miles from a provider from approximately 10,000 to 290,000." We recognize that increased driving distances do not always constitute an "undue burden." See *Casey* (joint opinion). But here, those increases are but one additional burden, which, when taken together with others that the closings brought about, and when viewed in light of the virtual absence of any health benefit, lead us to conclude that the record adequately supports the District Court's "undue burden" conclusion.

The dissent [argues that some] clinics may have closed for other reasons [but] petitioners satisfied their burden to present evidence of causation by presenting direct testimony as well as plausible inferences to be drawn from the timing of the clinic closures. The District Court credited that evidence and concluded from it that H.B. 2 in fact led to the clinic closures. The dissent's speculation that perhaps other evidence, not presented at trial or credited by the District Court, might have shown that some clinics closed for unrelated reasons does not provide sufficient ground to disturb the District Court's factual finding on that issue.

In the same breath, the dissent suggests that one benefit of H.B. 2's requirements would be that they might "force unsafe facilities to shut down." [But d]etermined wrongdoers, already ignoring existing statutes and safety measures, are unlikely to be convinced to adopt safe practices by a new overlay of regulations. [Pre-existing] Texas law already contained numerous detailed regulations covering abortion facilities, including a requirement that facilities be inspected at least annually.

[V.] *Undue Burden—Surgical-Center Requirement*

[Prior] to enactment of the [surgical-center] requirement, Texas law required abortion facilities to meet a host of health and safety requirements. Under those pre-existing laws, facilities were subject to annual reporting and recordkeeping requirements; a quality assurance program; personnel policies and staffing requirements, physical and environmental requirements; infection control standards; disclosure requirements; patient-rights standards; and medical- and clinical-services standards, including anesthesia standards. These requirements are policed by random and announced inspections, at least annually, as well as administrative penalties, injunctions, civil penalties, and criminal penalties for certain violations[.]

[There] is considerable evidence in the record supporting the District Court's findings indicating that the statutory provision requiring all abortion facilities to meet all surgical-center standards does not benefit patients and is not necessary. [The] record makes clear that the surgical-center requirement provides no benefit when complications arise in the context of an abortion produced through medication. That is because, in such a case, complications would almost always arise only after the patient has left the facility. The record also contains evidence indicating that abortions taking place in an abortion facility are safe—indeed, safer than numerous procedures that take place outside hospitals and to which Texas does not apply its surgical-center requirements, [such as childbirth, colonoscopy, and liposuction]. And Texas partly or wholly grandfathers (or waives in whole or in part the surgical-center requirement for) about two-thirds of the facilities to which the surgical-center standards apply. But it neither grandfathers nor provides waivers for any of the facilities that perform abortions. [The] record evidence thus supports the ultimate legal conclusion that the surgical-center requirement is not necessary.

[At] the same time, the record provides adequate evidentiary support for the District Court's conclusion that the surgical-center requirement places a substantial obstacle in the path of women seeking an abortion. [In addition], common sense suggests that, more often than not, a physical facility that satisfies a certain physical demand will not be able to meet five times that demand without expanding or otherwise incurring significant costs. [And] the fact that so many facilities were forced to close by the admitting-privileges requirement means that hiring more physicians would not be quite as simple as the dissent suggests. Courts are free to base their findings on commonsense inferences drawn from the evidence. And that is what the District Court did here.

[More] fundamentally, in the face of no threat to women's health, Texas seeks to force women to travel long distances to get abortions in crammed-to-capacity superfacilities. Patients seeking these services are less likely to get the kind of individualized attention, serious conversation, and emotional support that doctors at less taxed facilities may have offered. Healthcare facilities and medical professionals are not fungible commodities. Surgical centers attempting to accommodate sudden, vastly increased demand, may find that quality of care declines. Another commonsense inference that the District Court made is that these effects would be harmful to, not supportive of, women's health. [We] agree with the District Court that the surgical-center requirement, like the admitting-privileges requirement, provides few, if any, health benefits for women, poses a substantial obstacle to women seeking abortions, and constitutes an "undue burden" on their constitutional right to do so. * * *

JUSTICE GINSBURG, concurring.

[When] a State severely limits access to safe and legal procedures, women in desperate circumstances may resort to unlicensed rogue practitioners, *faute de mieux,* at great risk to their health and safety.

JUSTICE THOMAS, dissenting.

[Whatever] scrutiny the majority applies to Texas' law, it bears little resemblance to the undue-burden test the Court articulated in *Casey* and its successors. Instead, the majority eviscerates important features of that test to return to a regime like the one that *Casey* repudiated. I remain fundamentally opposed to the Court's abortion jurisprudence. Even taking *Casey* as the baseline, however, the majority radically rewrites the undue-burden test in three ways. First, today's decision requires courts to "consider the burdens a law imposes on abortion access together with the benefits those laws confer." Second, today's opinion tells the courts that, when the law's justifications are medically uncertain, they need not defer to the legislature, and must instead assess medical justifications for abortion restrictions by scrutinizing the record themselves. Finally, even if a law imposes no "substantial obstacle" to women's access to abortions, the law now must have more than a "reasonabl[e] relat[ion] to . . . a legitimate state interest." These precepts are nowhere to be found in *Casey* or its successors, and transform the undue-burden test to something much more akin to strict scrutiny.

[The] majority's furtive reconfiguration of the standard of scrutiny applicable to abortion restrictions also points to a deeper problem. The undue-burden standard is just one variant of the Court's tiers-of-scrutiny approach to constitutional adjudication. And the label the Court affixes to its level of scrutiny in assessing whether the government can restrict a given right—be it "rational basis," intermediate, strict, or something else—is increasingly a meaningless formalism. As the Court applies whatever standard it likes to any given case, nothing but empty words separates our constitutional decisions from judicial fiat.

Though the tiers of scrutiny have become a ubiquitous feature of constitutional law, they are of recent vintage. Only in the 1960s did the Court begin in earnest to speak of "strict scrutiny" versus reviewing legislation for mere rationality, and to develop the contours of these tests. See Richard H. Fallon, *Strict Judicial Scrutiny*, 54 UCLA L.Rev. 1267 (2007). In short order, the Court adopted strict scrutiny as the standard for reviewing everything from race-based classifications under the Equal Protection Clause to restrictions on constitutionally protected speech. Then the tiers of scrutiny proliferated into ever more gradations. *Casey*'s undue-burden test added yet another right-specific test on the spectrum between rational-basis and strict-scrutiny review.

[If] our recent cases illustrate anything, it is how easily the Court tinkers with levels of scrutiny to achieve its desired result. [It] is now easier for the government to restrict judicial candidates' campaign speech than for the Government to define marriage—even though the former is subject to strict scrutiny and the latter was supposedly subject to some form of rational-basis review. [These] labels now mean little. [The] Court should abandon the pretense that anything other than policy preferences underlies its balancing of constitutional rights and interests in any given case.

[The] Court has simultaneously transformed judicially created rights like the right to abortion into preferred constitutional rights, while disfavoring many of the rights actually enumerated in the Constitution. But our Constitution renounces the notion that some constitutional rights are more equal than others. A plaintiff either possesses the constitutional right he is asserting, or not—and if not, the judiciary has no business creating ad hoc exceptions so that others can assert rights that seem especially important to vindicate. A law either infringes a constitutional right, or not; there is no room for the judiciary to invent tolerable degrees of encroachment. Unless the Court abides by one set of rules to adjudicate constitutional rights, it will continue reducing constitutional law to policy-driven value judgments until the last shreds of its legitimacy disappear.

Today's decision will prompt some to claim victory, just as it will stiffen opponents' will to object. But the entire Nation has lost something essential. [I] respectfully dissent.

JUSTICE ALITO, with whom CHIEF JUSTICE ROBERTS and JUSTICE THOMAS join, dissenting.[5]

[Under] our cases, petitioners must show that the admitting privileges and [ambulatory surgical center ("ASC")] requirements impose an "undue burden" on women seeking abortions. And in order to obtain the sweeping relief they seek— facial invalidation of those provisions—they must show, at a minimum, that these provisions have an unconstitutional impact on at least a "large fraction" of Texas women of reproductive age. Such a situation could result if the clinics able to comply with the new requirements either lacked the requisite overall capacity or were located too far away to serve a "large fraction" of the women in question.

Petitioners did not make that showing. Instead of offering direct evidence, they relied on two crude inferences. First, they pointed to the number of abortion clinics that closed after the enactment of H.B. 2, and asked that it be inferred that

---

[5]   Most of the dissent argued that the plaintiffs' claims were barred by claim preclusion because they had previously brought an unsuccessful pre-enforcement facial challenge to the admitting privileges requirement. It also argued that facial invalidation was an improper remedy because of the Texas law's broad severability clause. The discussion of claim preclusion and severability have been omitted from both the majority and this dissent.

all these closures resulted from the two challenged provisions. They made little effort to show why particular clinics closed. Second, they pointed to the number of abortions performed annually at ASCs before H.B. 2 took effect and, because this figure is well below the total number of abortions performed each year in the State, they asked that it be inferred that ASC-compliant clinics could not meet the demands of women in the State. Petitioners failed to provide any evidence of the actual capacity of the facilities that would be available to perform abortions in compliance with the new law—even though they provided this type of evidence in their first case to the District Court at trial and then to this Court in their application for interim injunctive relief.

I do not dispute the fact that H.B. 2 caused the closure of some clinics. Indeed, it seems clear that H.B. 2 was intended to force unsafe facilities to shut down. [While] there can be no doubt that H.B. 2 caused some clinics to cease operation, the absence of proof regarding the reasons for particular closures is a problem because some clinics have or may have closed for at least four reasons other than the two H.B. 2 requirements at issue here. These are:

1.   *H.B. 2's restriction on medication abortion.* In their first case, petitioners challenged the provision of H.B. 2 that regulates medication abortion, but that part of the statute was upheld by the Fifth Circuit and not relitigated in this case. The record in this case indicates that in the first six months after this restriction took effect, the number of medication abortions dropped by 6,957 (compared to the same period the previous year).

2.   *Withdrawal of Texas family planning funds.* In 2011, Texas passed a law preventing family planning grants to providers that perform abortions and their affiliates. In the first case, petitioners' expert admitted that some clinics closed "as a result of the defunding," and [this] withdrawal appears specifically to have caused multiple clinic closures in West Texas.

3.   *The nationwide decline in abortion demand.* Petitioners' expert testimony relies on a study from the Guttmacher Institute which concludes that "the national abortion rate has resumed its decline, and *no evidence was found that the overall drop in abortion incidence was related to the decrease in providers or to restrictions implemented between 2008 and 2011.*"

4.   *Physician retirement (or other localized factors).* Like everyone else, most physicians eventually retire, and the retirement of a physician who performs abortions can cause the closing of a clinic or a reduction in the number of abortions that a clinic can perform. When this happens, the closure of the clinic or the reduction in capacity cannot be attributed to H.B. 2 unless it is shown that the retirement was caused by the admitting privileges or surgical center requirements as opposed to age or some other factor.

[Neither] petitioners nor the District Court properly addressed these complexities in assessing causation—and for no good reason. [Because] there was ample reason to believe that some closures were caused by these other factors, the District Court's failure to ascertain the reasons for clinic closures means that, on the record before us, there is no way to tell which closures actually count. Petitioners—who, as plaintiffs, bore the burden of proof—cannot simply point to temporal correlation and call it causation.

[Applying] what the Court terms "common sense," the Court infers that the ASCs that performed abortions at the time of H.B. 2's enactment lacked the capacity to perform all the abortions sought by women in Texas. [The] Court's inference has obvious limitations. First, it is not unassailable "common sense" to hold that current utilization equals capacity. [Faced] with increased demand, ASCs could potentially increase the number of abortions performed without prohibitively expensive changes. Among other things, they might hire more physicians who perform abortions, utilize their facilities more intensively or efficiently, or shift the mix of services provided. Second, what matters for present purposes is not the capacity of just those ASCs that performed abortions prior to the enactment of H.B. 2 but the capacity of those that would be available to perform abortions after the statute took effect. And since the enactment of H.B. 2, the number of ASCs performing abortions has increased by 50%—from six in 2012 to nine today.

[The] Court asserts that, after the admitting privileges requirement took effect, clinics "were not able to accommodate increased demand," but petitioners' own evidence suggested that the requirement had *no* effect on capacity. On this point, like the question of the reason for clinic closures, petitioners did not discharge their burden, and the District Court did not engage in the type of analysis that should have been conducted before enjoining an important state law.

[I] do not dismiss the situation of those women who would no longer live within 150 miles of a clinic as a result of H.B. 2. But under current doctrine such localized problems can be addressed by narrow as-applied challenges. * * *

———————

In JUNE MEDICAL SERVICES L. L. C. v. RUSSO, 140 S.Ct. 2103 (2020). BREYER, J., again delivered the judgment, although here, unlike in *Whole Woman's Health*, he spoke only for a plurality consisting of himself and Ginsburg, Sotomayor, and Kagan, JJ. The Court considered "the constitutionality of a Louisiana statute, Act 620, that is almost word-for-word identical to Texas' admitting-privileges law. As in *Whole Woman's Health*, the District Court found that the statute offers no significant health benefit. It found that conditions on admitting privileges common to hospitals throughout the State have made and will continue to make it impossible for abortion providers to obtain conforming privileges for reasons that have nothing to do with the State's asserted interests in promoting women's health and safety. And it found that this inability places a substantial obstacle in the path of women seeking an abortion. As in *Whole Woman's Health*, the substantial obstacle the Act imposes, and the absence of any health-related benefit, led the District Court to conclude that the law imposes an undue burden and is therefore unconstitutional." Because the appeals court nonetheless found distinctions between the Louisiana and Texas laws in their application, it upheld Act 620. The Court reversed, invalidating it as indistinguishable from the Texas law.

Crediting the district court's factual findings as not clearly erroneous, the plurality observed that Act 620 "would leave Louisiana with just one clinic with one provider to serve the 10,000 women annually who seek abortions in the State. Working full time in New Orleans, [that one doctor, identified in the record as] Doe 5 would be able to absorb no more than about 30% of the annual demand for abortions in Louisiana. And because Doe 5 does not perform abortions beyond 18 weeks, women between 18 weeks and the state legal limit of 20 weeks would have little or no way to exercise their constitutional right to an abortion.

"Those women not altogether prevented from obtaining an abortion would face other burdens. As in *Whole Woman's Health*, the reduction in abortion providers caused by Act 620 would inevitably mean 'longer waiting times, and increased crowding.' The District Court heard testimony that delays in obtaining an abortion increase the risk that a woman will experience complications from the procedure and may make it impossible for her to choose a noninvasive medication abortion.

"Even if they obtain an appointment at a clinic, women who might previously have gone to a clinic in Baton Rouge or Shreveport would face increased driving distances. New Orleans is nearly a five hour drive from Shreveport; it is over an hour from Baton Rouge; and Baton Rouge is more than four hours from Shreveport. The impact of those increases would be magnified by Louisiana's requirement that every woman undergo an ultrasound and receive mandatory counseling at least 24 hours before an abortion. A Shreveport resident seeking an abortion who might previously have obtained care at one of that city's local clinics would either have to spend nearly 20 hours driving back and forth to Doe 5's clinic twice, or else find overnight lodging in New Orleans. As the District Court stated, both experts and laypersons testified that the burdens of this increased travel would fall disproportionately on poor women, who are least able to absorb them.

"[The] District Court found that the admitting-privileges requirement serves no 'relevant credentialing function.' [H]ospitals can, and do, deny admitting privileges for reasons unrelated to a doctor's ability safely to perform abortions. And Act 620's requirement that physicians obtain privileges at a hospital within 30 miles of the place where they perform abortions further constrains providers for reasons that bear no relationship to competence. [Further,] the District Court found that the admitting-privileges requirement 'does not conform to prevailing medical standards and will not improve the safety of abortion in Louisiana.' As in *Whole Woman's Health*, the [State] introduced no evidence 'showing that patients have better outcomes when their physicians have admitting privileges' or 'of any instance in which an admitting privileges requirement would have helped even one woman obtain better treatment.'

"[This] case is similar to, nearly identical with, *Whole Woman's Health*. And the law must consequently reach a similar conclusion. Act 620 is unconstitutional."

ROBERTS, C.J., concurred in the judgment: "I joined the dissent in *Whole Woman's Health* and continue to believe that the case was wrongly decided. The question today however is not whether *Whole Woman's Health* was right or wrong, but whether to adhere to it in deciding the present case. [The] legal doctrine of *stare decisis* requires us, absent special circumstances, to treat like cases alike. The Louisiana law imposes a burden on access to abortion just as severe as that imposed by the Texas law, for the same reasons. Therefore Louisiana's law cannot stand under our precedents.

"[The parties] agree that the undue burden standard announced in *Casey* provides the appropriate framework to analyze Louisiana's law. Neither party has asked us to reassess the constitutional validity of that standard. [Under] *Casey*, the State may not impose an undue burden on the woman's ability to obtain an abortion.

"[The] plurality repeats today that the undue burden standard requires courts 'to weigh the law's asserted benefits against the burdens it imposes on abortion access.' " [Nothing] about *Casey* suggested that a weighing of costs and benefits of an abortion regulation was a job for the courts. [The] upshot of *Casey* is clear: The several restrictions that did not impose a substantial obstacle were constitutional, while the restriction that did impose a substantial obstacle was unconstitutional. To be sure, the Court at times discussed the benefits of the regulations, including when it distinguished spousal notification from parental consent. But in the context of *Casey*'s governing standard, these benefits were not placed on a scale opposite the law's burdens. Rather, *Casey* discussed benefits in considering the threshold requirement that the State have a 'legitimate purpose' and that the law be 'reasonably related to that goal.' So long as that showing is made, the only question for a court is whether a law has the 'effect of placing a substantial obstacle in the path of a woman seeking an abortion of a nonviable fetus.' *Casey* repeats that 'substantial obstacle' standard nearly verbatim no less than 15 times.

"[Nonetheless, w]e should respect the statement in *Whole Woman's Health* that it was applying the undue burden standard of *Casey*. [Here] the plurality expressly acknowledges that we are not considering how to analyze an abortion regulation that does not present a substantial obstacle. [In] this case, *Casey*'s requirement of finding a substantial obstacle before invalidating an abortion regulation is therefore a sufficient basis for the decision, as it was in *Whole Woman's Health*. In neither case, nor in *Casey* itself, was there call for consideration of a regulation's benefits, and nothing in *Casey* commands such consideration. Under principles of *stare decisis*, I agree with the plurality that the determination in *Whole Woman's Health* that Texas's law imposed a substantial obstacle requires the same determination about Louisiana's law. Under those same principles, I would adhere to the holding of *Casey*, requiring a substantial obstacle before striking down an abortion regulation."

THOMAS, J., dissented chiefly on the ground that the plaintiffs should be denied third-party standing.

ALITO, J, joined in full by Gorsuch, J., and in different parts by Thomas and Kavanaugh, JJ., dissented. In portions of his dissent in which all the dissenters concurred, he agreed with the Chief Justice that *Casey* "rules out the balancing test adopted in *Whole Woman's Health*. *Whole Woman's Health* simply misinterpreted *Casey* [and] should be overruled insofar as it changed the *Casey* test. Unless *Casey* is reexamined—and Louisiana has not asked us to do that—the test it adopted should remain the governing standard.

"[In] any event, contrary to the view taken by the plurality and (seemingly) by the Chief Justice, there is ample evidence in the record showing that admitting privileges help to protect the health of women by ensuring that physicians who perform abortions meet a higher standard of competence than is shown by the mere possession of a license to practice. In deciding whether to grant admitting privileges, hospitals typically undertake a rigorous investigative process to ensure that a doctor is responsible and competent and has the training and experience needed to perform the procedures for which the privileges are sought. [Both] the plurality and the Chief Justice err in concluding that the admitting-privileges requirement serves no valid purpose.

"They also err in their assessment of Act 620's likely effect on access to abortion. [Because] the Louisiana law was not allowed to go into effect for any appreciable time, it was necessary for the District Court to predict what its effects would be. Attempting to do that, the court apparently concluded that none of the doctors who currently perform abortions in the State would be replaced if the admitting privileges requirement forced them to leave abortion practice. [The] finding was based on a fundamentally flawed test. In attempting to ascertain how many of the doctors who perform abortions in the State would have to leave abortion practice for lack of admitting privileges, the District Court received evidence in a variety of forms—some live testimony, but also deposition transcripts, declarations, and even letters from counsel—about the doctors' unsuccessful efforts to obtain privileges. The District Court considered whether these doctors had proceeded in 'good faith'; it found that they all met that standard; and it therefore concluded that the law would leave the State with very few abortion providers. [However, w]hen the District Court made its assessment of the doctors' 'good faith,' enforcement of Act 620 had been preliminarily enjoined, and the doctors surely knew that enforcement would be permanently barred if the lawsuit was successful. Thus, the doctors had everything to lose and nothing to gain by obtaining privileges."

GORSUCH, J. dissented on multiple grounds, including an objection that in crediting the district court's findings, the Court slighted the state legislature.

KAVANAUGH, J., also briefly dissented separately, expressing agreement with the conclusion of Alito, J., "that the Court should remand the case for a new trial and additional factfinding under the appropriate legal standards."

———

In DOBBS v. JACKSON WOMEN'S HEALTH, *cert. granted*, 2021 WL 1951792 (2021), the Supreme Court will consider the constitutionality of a Mississippi statute barring most abortions after 15 weeks of pregnancy. Although the petition presented three questions, the Court granted review on only one: "Whether all pre-viability prohibitions on elective abortions are unconstitutional."

3. RIGHT TO DIE

WASHINGTON V. GLUCKSBERG
521 U.S. 702, 117 S.Ct. 2258, 138 L.Ed.2d 772 (1997).

CHIEF JUSTICE REHNQUIST delivered the opinion of the Court.

The question presented in this case is whether Washington's prohibition against "caus[ing]" or "aid[ing]" a suicide offends the Fourteenth Amendment to the United States Constitution. We hold that it does not.

[Respondents, four physicians who declared they would assist terminally ill, suffering patients in ending their lives if not for Washington's assisted-suicide ban, and Compassion in Dying, a nonprofit organization that counseled people considering physician-assisted suicide, sought a declaration that Washington's statute is, on its face, unconstitutional. They were originally joined by three gravely ill plaintiffs, who died before the case reached the Supreme Court. The respondents asserted "the existence of a liberty interest protected by the Fourteenth Amendment which extends to a personal choice by a mentally competent, terminally ill adult to commit physician-assisted suicide." They relied primarily on *Casey* and *Cruzan v. Director, Missouri Dep't of Health*, 497 U.S. 261 (1990). Following a severe automobile accident, Nancy Beth Cruzan was in a persistent vegetative state for many years and had virtually no chance of regaining her cognitive faculties. She was being kept alive by means of a feeding and hydration tube inserted into her stomach. When Nancy's parents sought to discontinue the tubal feeding but were rebuffed by officials of the state hospital where Nancy was a patient, they turned to the courts. The state supreme court ruled that, in the absence of a living will, they had to show clear and convincing evidence of Nancy's wish to be free of life support and that they had failed to do so. The U.S. Supreme Court affirmed 5–4, per Rehnquist, C.J., but assumed for purposes of the case that a *competent* person would have "a constitutionally protected right to refuse lifesaving hydration and nutrition."]

We begin, as we do in all due process cases, by examining our Nation's history, legal traditions, and practices. In almost every State—indeed, in almost every western democracy—it is a crime to assist a suicide. The States' assisted-suicide bans are not innovations. Rather, they are longstanding expressions of the States' commitment to the protection and preservation of all human life. [Indeed], opposition to and condemnation of suicide—and, therefore, of assisting suicide— are consistent and enduring themes of our philosophical, legal, and cultural heritages. More specifically, for over 700 years, the Anglo-American common-law tradition has punished or otherwise disapproved of both suicide and assisting suicide.

[For] the most part, the early American colonies adopted the common-law approach. [Over] time, however, [the] colonies abolished [the] harsh common-law penalties [such as forfeiture of the suicide's property. However,] the movement away from the common law's harsh sanctions did not represent an acceptance of suicide, [but instead] reflected the growing consensus that it was unfair to punish the suicide's family for his wrongdoing.

[That] suicide remained a grievous, though nonfelonious, wrong is confirmed by the fact that colonial and early state legislatures and courts did not retreat from prohibiting assisting suicide. [And] the prohibitions against assisted suicide never contained exceptions for those who were near death. [In] this century, the [American Law Institute's] Model Penal Code also prohibited "aiding" suicide, prompting many States to enact or revise their assisted-suicide bans. The code's drafters observed that "the interests in the sanctity of life that are represented by the criminal homicide laws are threatened by one who expresses a willingness to participate in taking the life of another, even though the act may be accomplished with the consent, or at the request, of the suicide victim."

Though deeply rooted, the States' assisted-suicide bans have in recent years been reexamined and, generally, reaffirmed. Because of advances in medicine and technology, Americans today are increasingly likely to die in institutions, from chronic illnesses. Public concern and democratic action are therefore sharply focused on how best to protect dignity and independence at the end of life, with the result that there have been many significant changes in state laws and in the attitudes these laws reflect. Many States, for example, now permit "living wills," surrogate health-care decisionmaking, and the withdrawal or refusal of life-sustaining medical treatment. At the same time, however, voters and legislators continue for the most part to reaffirm their States' prohibitions on assisting suicide.

The Washington statute at issue in this case was enacted in 1975 as part of a revision of that State's criminal code. Four years later, Washington passed its Natural Death Act, which specifically stated that the "withholding or withdrawal of life-sustaining treatment [shall] not, for any purpose, constitute a suicide" and that "[n]othing in this chapter shall be construed to condone, authorize, or approve mercy killing * * * ." In 1991, Washington voters rejected a ballot initiative which, had it passed, would have permitted a form of physician-assisted suicide. Washington then added a provision to the Natural Death Act expressly excluding physician-assisted suicide.

California voters rejected an assisted-suicide initiative similar to Washington's in 1993. On the other hand, in 1994, voters in Oregon enacted, also through ballot initiative, that State's "Death With Dignity Act," which legalized physician-assisted suicide for competent, terminally ill adults. Since the Oregon vote, many proposals to legalize assisted-suicide have been and continue to be introduced in the States' legislatures, but none has been enacted.

[Thus], the States are currently engaged in serious, thoughtful examinations of physician-assisted suicide and other similar issues. For example, New York State's Task Force on Life and the Law—an ongoing, blue-ribbon commission composed of doctors, ethicists, lawyers, religious leaders, and interested laymen—was convened in 1984 and commissioned with "a broad mandate to recommend public policy on issues raised by medical advances." [After] studying physician-assisted suicide, however, the Task Force unanimously concluded that "[l]egalizing assisted suicide and euthanasia would pose profound risks to many individuals who are ill and vulnerable. [T]he potential dangers of this dramatic change in public policy would outweigh any benefit that might be achieved."

[The] Due Process Clause guarantees more than fair process, and the "liberty" it protects includes more than the absence of physical restraint. [The] Clause also provides heightened protection against government interference with certain fundamental rights and liberty interests. [We] have also assumed, and strongly suggested, that the Due Process Clause protects the traditional right to refuse unwanted lifesaving medical treatment. *Cruzan.*

But we "ha[ve] always been reluctant to expand the concept of substantive due process because guideposts for responsible decisionmaking in this unchartered area are scarce and open-ended." By extending constitutional protection to an asserted right or liberty interest, we, to a great extent, place the matter outside the arena of public debate and legislative action. We must therefore "exercise the utmost care whenever we are asked to break new ground in this field," lest the liberty protected by the Due Process Clause be subtly transformed into the policy preferences of the Members of this Court.

Our established method of substantive-due-process analysis has two primary features: First, we have regularly observed that the Due Process Clause specially protects those fundamental rights and liberties which are, objectively, "deeply rooted in this Nation's history and tradition." [Second], we have required in substantive-due-process cases a "careful description" of the asserted fundamental liberty interest.

[We] have a tradition of carefully formulating the interest at stake in substantive-due-process cases. For example, although *Cruzan* is often described as a "right to die" case, we were, in fact, more precise: We assumed that the Constitution granted competent persons a "constitutionally protected right to refuse lifesaving hydration and nutrition." The Washington statute at issue in this case prohibits "aid[ing] another person to attempt suicide" and, thus, the question before us is whether the "liberty" specially protected by the Due Process Clause includes a right to commit suicide which itself includes a right to assistance in doing so.

[We] are confronted with a consistent and almost universal tradition that has long rejected the asserted right, and continues explicitly to reject it today, even for terminally ill, mentally competent adults. To hold for respondents, we would have to reverse centuries of legal doctrine and practice, and strike down the considered policy choice of almost every State.

[Respondents] contend that in *Cruzan* we "acknowledged that competent, dying persons have the right to direct the removal of life-sustaining medical treatment and thus hasten death" and that "the constitutional principle behind recognizing the patient's liberty to direct the withdrawal of artificial life support applies at least as strongly to the choice to hasten impending death by consuming lethal medication." [The] right assumed in *Cruzan,* however, was not simply deduced from abstract concepts of personal autonomy. Given the common-law rule that forced medication was a battery, and the long legal tradition protecting the decision to refuse unwanted medical treatment, our assumption was entirely consistent with this Nation's history and constitutional traditions. The decision to commit suicide with the assistance of another may be just as personal and profound as the decision to refuse unwanted medical treatment, but it has never enjoyed similar legal protection. Indeed, the two acts are widely and reasonably regarded as quite distinct. In *Cruzan* itself, we recognized that most States outlawed assisted suicide—and even more do today—and we certainly gave no intimation that the right to refuse unwanted medical treatment could be somehow transmuted into a right to assistance in committing suicide.

Respondents also rely on *Casey.* [The] Court of Appeals, like the District Court, found *Casey* " 'highly instructive' " and " 'almost prescriptive' " for determining " 'what liberty interest may inhere in a terminally ill person's choice to commit suicide.' " [Similarly], respondents emphasize the statement in *Casey* that: "At the heart of liberty is the right to define one's own concept of existence, of meaning, of the universe, and of the mystery of human life. Beliefs about these matters could not define the attributes of personhood were they formed under compulsion of the State."

By choosing this language, the Court's opinion in *Casey* described, in a general way and in light of our prior cases, those personal activities and decisions that this Court has identified as so deeply rooted in our history and traditions, or so fundamental to our concept of constitutionally ordered liberty, that they are protected by the Fourteenth Amendment. [That] many of the rights and liberties protected by the Due Process Clause sound in personal autonomy does not warrant the sweeping conclusion that any and all important, intimate, and personal decisions are so protected, and *Casey* did not suggest otherwise.

The history of the law's treatment of assisted suicide in this country has been and continues to be one of the rejection of nearly all efforts to permit it. That being the case, our decisions lead us to conclude that the asserted "right" to assistance in committing suicide is not a fundamental liberty interest protected by the Due Process Clause. The Constitution also requires, however, that Washington's assisted-suicide ban be rationally related to legitimate government interests. This requirement is unquestionably met here. As the court below recognized, Washington's assisted-suicide ban implicates a number of state interests.

First, Washington has an "unqualified interest in the preservation of human life." *Cruzan.* The State's prohibition on assisted suicide, like all homicide laws, both reflects and advances its commitment to this interest.

[The] Court of Appeals also recognized Washington's interest in protecting life, but held that the "weight" of this interest depends on the "medical condition and the wishes of the person whose life is at stake." Washington, however, has rejected this sliding-scale approach and, through its assisted-suicide ban, insists that all persons' lives, from beginning to end, regardless of physical or mental condition, are under the full protection of the law. [As] we have previously affirmed, the States "may properly decline to make judgments about the 'quality' of life that a particular individual may enjoy," *Cruzan.* This remains true, as *Cruzan* makes clear, even for those who are near death.

Relatedly, all admit that suicide is a serious public-health problem, especially among persons in otherwise vulnerable groups. [Those] who attempt suicide—terminally ill or not—often suffer from depression or other mental disorders. [Research] indicates, however, that many people who request physician-assisted suicide withdraw that request if their depression and pain are treated. The New York Task Force, however, expressed its concern that, because depression is difficult to diagnose, physicians and medical professionals often fail to respond adequately to seriously ill patients' needs. Thus, legal physician-assisted suicide could make it more difficult for the State to protect depressed or mentally ill persons, or those who are suffering from untreated pain, from suicidal impulses.

The State also has an interest in protecting the integrity and ethics of the medical profession. [The] American Medical Association, like many other medical and physicians' groups, has concluded that "[p]hysician-assisted suicide is fundamentally incompatible with the physician's role as healer." [And] physician-assisted suicide could, it is argued, undermine the trust that is essential to the doctor-patient relationship by blurring the time-honored line between healing and harming.

Next, the State has an interest in protecting vulnerable groups—including the poor, the elderly, and disabled persons—from abuse, neglect, and mistakes. The Court of Appeals dismissed [this] concern, [but we] have recognized [the] real risk of subtle coercion and undue influence in end-of-life situations. *Cruzan.* [If] physician-assisted suicide were permitted, many might resort to it to spare their families the substantial financial burden of end-of-life health-care costs. The State's interest here goes beyond protecting the vulnerable from coercion; it extends to protecting disabled and terminally ill people from prejudice, negative and inaccurate stereotypes, and [societal indifference].

[Finally,] the State may fear that permitting assisted suicide will start it down the path to voluntary and perhaps even involuntary euthanasia. [The] Court of Appeal's decision, and its expansive reasoning, provide ample support for the State's concerns. [This] concern is further supported by evidence about the practice of euthanasia in the Netherlands. The Dutch government's own [1990 study] suggests that, despite the existence of various reporting procedures, euthanasia in the Netherlands has not been limited to competent, terminally ill adults who are enduring physical suffering, and that regulation of the practice may not have prevented abuses in cases involving vulnerable persons, including severely disabled neonates and elderly persons suffering from dementia. [Washington], like most other States, reasonably ensures against this risk by banning, rather than regulating, assisting suicide.

We need not weigh exactingly the relative strengths of these various interests. They are unquestionably important and legitimate, and Washington's ban on assisted suicide is at least reasonably related to their promotion and protection. We therefore hold that [the challenged Washington statute] does not violate the Fourteenth Amendment, either on its face or "as applied to competent, terminally ill adults who wish to hasten their deaths by obtaining medication prescribed by their doctors."[24]

[Throughout] the Nation, Americans are engaged in an earnest and profound debate about the morality, legality, and practicality of physician-assisted suicide. Our holding permits this debate to continue, as it should in a democratic society.
* * *

JUSTICE O'CONNOR, concurring.[*]

[The] Court frames the issue [as] whether the Due Process Clause of the Constitution protects a "right to commit suicide which itself includes a right to assistance in doing so," and concludes that our Nation's history, legal traditions, and practices do not support the existence of such a right. I join the Court's opinions because I agree that there is no generalized right to "commit suicide." But respondents urge us to address the narrower question whether a mentally competent person who is experiencing great suffering has a constitutionally cognizable interest in controlling the circumstances of his or her imminent death. I see no need to reach that question in the context of the facial challenges to the New York and Washington laws at issue here. [The] parties and *amici* agree that in these States a patient who is suffering from a terminal illness and who is experiencing great pain has no legal barriers to obtaining medication, from qualified physicians, to alleviate that suffering, even to the point of causing unconsciousness and hastening death. In this light, even assuming that we would recognize such an interest, I agree that the State's interests in protecting those

---

[24]   [Ct's Note] [We] reject the Court of Appeals' specific holding that the statute is unconstitutional "as applied" to a particular class. Justice Stevens agrees with this holding, but would not "foreclose the possibility that an individual plaintiff seeking to hasten her death, or a doctor whose assistance was sought, could prevail in a more particularized challenge." Our opinion does not absolutely foreclose such a claim. However, given our holding that the Due Process Clause of the Fourteenth Amendment does not provide heightened protection to the asserted liberty interest in ending one's life with a physician's assistance, such a claim would have to be quite different from the ones advanced by respondents here.

[*]   [Ct's Note] Justice Ginsburg concurs in the Court's judgments substantially for the reasons stated in this opinion. Justice Breyer joins this opinion except insofar as it joins the opinions of the Court. [O'Connor, J.'s opinion also constitutes her concurring opinion in the companion case of *Vacco v. Quill*.]

who are not truly competent or facing imminent death, or those whose decisions to hasten death would not truly be voluntary, are sufficiently weighty to justify a prohibition against physician-assisted suicide.

Every one of us at some point may be affected by our own or a family member's terminal illness. There is no reason to think the democratic process will not strike the proper balance between the interests of terminally ill, mentally competent individuals who would seek to end their suffering and the State's interests in protecting those who might seek to end life mistakenly or under pressure.

[In] sum, there is no need to address the question whether suffering patients have a constitutionally cognizable interest in obtaining relief from the suffering that they may experience in the last days of their lives. There is no dispute that dying patients in Washington and New York can obtain palliative care, even when doing so would hasten their deaths. The difficulty in defining terminal illness and the risk that a dying patient's request for assistance in ending his or her life might not be truly voluntary justifies the prohibitions on assisted suicide we uphold here.

JUSTICE STEVENS, concurring in the judgments.[6]

[Today,] the Court decides that Washington's statute prohibiting assisted suicide is not invalid "on its face," that is to say, in all or most cases in which it might be applied. That holding, however, does not foreclose the possibility that some applications of the statute might well be invalid.

[The *Cruzan*] Court assumed that the interest in liberty protected by the Fourteenth Amendment encompassed the right of a terminally ill patient to direct the withdrawal of life-sustaining treatment. [That] assumption [was] supported by the common-law tradition protecting the individual's general right to refuse unwanted medical treatment. [However,] [g]iven the irreversible nature of her illness and the progressive character of her suffering, Nancy Cruzan's interest in refusing medical care was incidental to her more basic interest in controlling the manner and timing of her death. [The] source of Nancy Cruzan's right to refuse treatment was not just a common-law rule. Rather, this right is an aspect of a far broader and more basic concept of freedom that is even older than the common law. This freedom embraces, not merely a person's right to refuse a particular kind of unwanted treatment, but also her interest in dignity, and in determining the character of the memories that will survive long after her death.

[Thus,] the common-law right to protection from battery, which included the right to reject medical treatment in most circumstances, did not mark "the outer limits of the substantive sphere of liberty" that supported the Cruzan family's decision to hasten Nancy's death. *Casey*. [Whatever] the outer limits of the concept may be, it definitely includes protection for matters "central to personal dignity and autonomy." *Casey*.

[The] *Cruzan* case demonstrated that some state intrusions on the right to decide how death will be encountered are also intolerable. The now-deceased

---

[6]   This opinion also constitutes Stevens, J.'s concurring opinion in *Vacco v. Quill*, infra.

plaintiffs in this action may in fact have had a liberty interest even stronger than Nancy Cruzan's because, not only were they terminally ill, they were suffering constant and severe pain. Avoiding intolerable pain and the indignity of living one's final days incapacitated and in agony is certainly "[a]t the heart of [the] liberty [to] define one's own concept of existence, of meaning, of the universe, and of the mystery of human life."

[Although] there is no absolute right to physician-assisted suicide, *Cruzan* makes it clear that some individuals who no longer have the option of deciding whether to live or to die because they are already on the threshold of death have a constitutionally protected interest that may outweigh the State's interest in preserving life at all costs. The liberty interest at stake in a case like this differs from, and is stronger than, both the common-law right to refuse medical treatment and the unbridled interest in deciding whether to live or die. It is an interest in deciding how, rather than whether, a critical threshold shall be crossed.

The state interests supporting a general rule banning the practice of physician-assisted suicide do not have the same force in all [cases]. Properly viewed, [the interest in preserving human life] is not a collective interest that should always outweigh the interests of a person who because of pain, incapacity, or sedation finds her life intolerable, but rather, an aspect of individual freedom.

[Allowing] the individual, rather than the State, to make judgments " 'about the 'quality' of life that a particular individual may enjoy' " does not mean that the lives of terminally-ill, disabled people have less value than the lives of those who are healthy. Rather, it gives proper recognition to the individual's interest in choosing a final chapter that accords with her life story, rather than one that demeans her values and poisons memories of her.

[The] State's legitimate interest in preventing abuse does not apply to an individual who is not victimized by abuse, who is not suffering from depression, and who makes a rational and voluntary decision to seek assistance in dying. [Encouraging] the development and ensuring the availability of adequate pain treatment is of utmost importance; palliative care, however, cannot alleviate all pain and suffering. [An] individual adequately informed of the care alternatives thus might make a rational choice for assisted suicide. For such an individual, the State's interest in preventing potential abuse and mistake is only minimally implicated.

[Unlike] the Court of Appeals, I would not say as a categorical matter that [the] state interests are invalid as to the entire class of terminally ill, mentally competent patients. I do not, however, foreclose the possibility that an individual plaintiff seeking to hasten her death, or a doctor whose assistance was sought, could prevail in a more particularized challenge.

JUSTICE SOUTER, concurring in the judgment.

[The question presented] is whether [state law] sets up one of those "arbitrary impositions" or "purposeless restraints" at odds with the Due Process Clause of the

Fourteenth Amendment. *Poe v. Ullman* (Harlan, J., dissenting). I conclude that [it does not], but I write separately to give my reasons for analyzing the substantive due process claims as I do, and for rejecting this one.

[The] persistence of substantive due process in our cases points to the legitimacy of the modern justification for such judicial review found in Justice Harlan's dissent in *Poe*,[4] [while] the acknowledged failures of some of these cases point with caution to the difficulty raised by the present claim.

[The *Poe* dissent] is a reminder that the business of [substantive due process] review is not the identification of extratextual absolutes but scrutiny of a legislative resolution (perhaps unconscious) of clashing principles, each quite possibly worthy in and of itself, but each to be weighed within the history of our values as a people. It is a comparison of the relative strengths of opposing claims that informs the judicial task, not a deduction from some first premise. Thus informed, judicial review still has no warrant to substitute one reasonable resolution of the contending positions for another, but authority to supplant the balance already struck between the contenders only when it falls outside the realm of the reasonable.

[Constitutional] recognition of the right to bodily integrity underlies the assumed right, good against the State, to require physicians to terminate artificial life support, *Cruzan,* [and] the affirmative right to obtain medical intervention to cause abortion, see *Casey.* It is, indeed, in the abortion cases that the most telling recognitions of the importance of bodily integrity and the concomitant tradition of medical assistance have occurred. [The] analogies between the abortion cases and this one are several. Even though the State has a legitimate interest in discouraging abortion, the Court recognized a woman's right to a physician's counsel and care. Like the decision to commit suicide, the decision to abort potential life can be made irresponsibly and under the influence of others, and yet the Court has held in the abortion cases that physicians are fit assistants. Without physician assistance in abortion, the woman's right would have too often amounted to nothing more than a right to self-mutilation, and without a physician to assist in the suicide of the dying, the patient's right will often be confined to crude methods of causing death, most shocking and painful to the decedent's survivors.

[The] State claims interests in protecting patients from mistakenly and involuntarily deciding to end their lives, and in guarding against both voluntary and involuntary euthanasia. [The] argument is that a progression would occur, obscuring the line between the ill and the dying, and between the responsible and the unduly influenced, until ultimately doctors and perhaps others would abuse a limited freedom to aid suicides. [Respondents] propose an answer to all this, the answer of state regulation with teeth. Legislation proposed in several States, for example, would authorize physician-assisted suicide but require two qualified

---

4   **[Ct's Note]** The status of the Harlan dissent in *Poe v. Ullman* is shown by the Court's adoption of its result in *Griswold* and by the Court's acknowledgment of its status and adoption of its reasoning in *Casey.* * * *

physicians to confirm the patient's diagnosis, prognosis, and competence; and would mandate that the patient make repeated requests witnessed by at least two others over a specified timespan; and would impose reporting requirements and criminal penalties for various acts of coercion.

But at least at this moment there are reasons for caution in predicting the effectiveness of the teeth proposed. Respondents' proposals, as it turns out, sound much like the guidelines now in place in the Netherlands, the only place where experience with physician-assisted suicide and euthanasia has yielded empirical evidence about how such regulations might affect actual practice. [There] is, however, a substantial dispute today about what the Dutch experience shows. Some commentators marshall evidence that the Dutch guidelines have in practice failed to protect patients from involuntary euthanasia and have been violated with impunity. This evidence is contested. The day may come when we can say with some assurance which side is right, but for now it is the substantiality of the factual disagreement, and the alternatives for resolving it, that matter. They are, for me, dispositive of the due process claim at this time.

[It] is assumed in this case, and must be, that a State's interest in protecting those unable to make responsible decisions and those who make no decisions at all entitles the State to bar aid to any but a knowing and responsible person intending suicide, and to prohibit euthanasia. How, and how far, a State should act in that interest are judgments for the State, but the legitimacy of its action to deny a physician the option to aid any but the knowing and responsible is beyond question.

[While] I do not decide for all time that respondents' claim should not be recognized, I acknowledge the legislative institutional competence as the better one to deal with that claim at this time.

JUSTICE GINSBURG, concurring in the judgments.

I concur in the Court's judgments in these cases substantially for the reasons stated by Justice O'Connor in her concurring opinion.

JUSTICE BREYER, concurring in the judgments.

I believe that Justice O'Connor's views, which I share, have greater legal significance than the Court's opinion suggests. I join her separate opinion, except insofar as it joins the majority. And I concur in the judgments. I shall briefly explain how I differ from the Court.

I agree with the Court in *Vacco v. Quill,* [infra] that the articulated state interests justify the distinction drawn between physician assisted suicide and withdrawal of life-support. I also agree [that] the critical question in both of the cases before us is whether "the 'liberty' specially protected by the Due Process Clause includes a right" of the sort that the respondents assert. I do not agree, however, with the Court's formulation of that claimed "liberty" interest. The Court describes it as a "right to commit suicide with another's assistance." But I would not reject the respondents' claim without considering a different formulation, for which our legal tradition may provide greater support. That formulation would use words roughly like a "right to die with dignity." But irrespective of the exact words used, at its core would lie personal control over the manner of death, professional medical assistance, and the avoidance of unnecessary and severe physical suffering—combined.

[I] do not believe, however, that this Court need or now should decide whether [a right to die with dignity] is "fundamental." That is because, in my view, the avoidance of severe physical pain (connected with death) would have to comprise an essential part of any successful claim and because, as Justice O'Connor points out, the laws before us do not *force* a dying person to undergo that kind of pain.

[Were] the legal circumstances different—for example, were state law to prevent the provision of palliative care, including the administration of drugs as needed to avoid pain at the end of life—then the law's impact upon serious and otherwise unavoidable physical pain (accompanying death) would be more directly at issue. And as Justice O'Connor suggests, the Court might have to revisit its conclusions in these cases.

———————

In a companion case to *Glucksberg*, VACCO v. QUILL, 521 U.S. 793 (1997), the Court rejected the argument that because New York permits competent persons to refuse lifesaving medical treatment, and the refusal of such treatment is "essentially the same thing" as physician-assisted suicide, the state's assisted suicide ban violates the Equal Protection Clause. REHNQUIST, C.J., again wrote for the Court: "[The] Equal Protection Clause [embodies] a general rule that States must treat like cases alike but may treat unlike cases accordingly. If a legislative classification or distinction 'neither burdens a fundamental right nor targets a suspect class, we will uphold [it] so long as it bears a rational relation to some legitimate end.' *Romer v. Evans* [Ch. 9, Sec. 4, I]. [On] their faces, neither New York's ban on assisting suicide nor its statutes permitting patients to refuse medical treatment treat anyone differently from anyone else or draw any distinctions between persons. *Everyone,* regardless of physical condition, is entitled, if competent, to refuse unwanted lifesaving medical treatment; *no one* is permitted to assist a suicide.

"[The] Court of Appeals, however, concluded that some terminally ill people— those who are on life-support systems—are treated differently from those who are not, in that the former may 'hasten death' by ending treatment, but the latter may not 'hasten death' through physician-assisted suicide. This conclusion depends on the submission that ending or refusing lifesaving medical treatment 'is nothing more nor less than assisted suicide.' Unlike the Court of Appeals, we think the distinction between assisting suicide and withdrawing life-sustaining treatment, a distinction widely recognized and endorsed in the medical profession and in our legal traditions, is both important and logical; it is certainly rational.

"The distinction comports with fundamental legal principles of causation and intent. First, when a patient refuses life-sustaining medical treatment, he dies from an underlying fatal disease or pathology; but if a patient ingests lethal medication prescribed by a physician, he is killed by that medication. [Furthermore,] a physician who withdraws, or honors a patient's refusal to begin, life-sustaining medical treatment purposefully intends, or may so intend, only to respect his patient's wishes and 'to cease doing useless and futile or degrading things to the patient when [the patient] no longer stands to benefit from them.' The same is true when a doctor provides aggressive palliative care; in some cases, painkilling drugs may hasten a patient's death, but the physician's purpose and intent is, or may be, only to ease his patient's pain. A doctor who assists a suicide, however, 'must, necessarily and indubitably, intend primarily that the patient be made dead.' Similarly, a patient who commits suicide with a doctor's aid necessarily has the specific intent to end his or her own life, while a patient who refuses or discontinues treatment might not. [The] law has long used actors' intent or purpose to distinguish between two acts that may have the same result. [Put] differently, the law distinguishes actions taken 'because of' a given end from actions taken 'in spite of' their unintended but foreseen consequences.

"[We] disagree with respondents' claim that the distinction between refusing lifesaving medical treatment and assisted suicide is 'arbitrary' and 'irrational.'[11] [By] permitting everyone to refuse unwanted medical treatment while prohibiting anyone from assisting a suicide, New York law follows a longstanding and rational distinction. New York's reasons for recognizing and acting on this distinction— including prohibiting intentional killing and preserving life; preventing suicide; maintaining physicians' role as their patients' healers; protecting vulnerable people from indifference, prejudice, and psychological and financial pressure to end their lives; and avoiding a possible slide towards euthanasia—are discussed in greater detail in our opinion in *Glucksberg*. These valid and important public interests easily satisfy the constitutional requirement that a legislative classification bear a rational relation to some legitimate end."

STEVENS, J., concurring in the judgment, "agree[d] that the distinction between permitting death to ensue from an underlying fatal disease and causing it to occur by the administration of medication or other means provides a constitutionally sufficient basis for the State's classification." However, unlike the Court, he was "not persuaded that in all cases there will in fact be a significant difference between the intent of the physicians, the patients or the families in the two situations."[7]

---

[11]   [Ct's Note] Respondents also argue that the State irrationally distinguishes between physician-assisted suicide and "terminal sedation," a process respondents characterize as "induc[ing] barbiturate coma and then starv[ing] the person to death." Petitioners insist, however, that " '[a]lthough proponents of physician-assisted suicide and euthanasia contend that terminal sedation is covert physician-assisted suicide or euthanasia, the concept of sedating pharmacotherapy is based on informed consent and the principle of double effect.' " Just as a State may prohibit assisting suicide while permitting patients to refuse unwanted lifesaving treatment, it may permit palliative care related to that refusal, which may have the foreseen but unintended "double effect" of hastening the patient's death.

[7]   Souter, J., who concurred in the judgment, observed that the reasons which led him to conclude that the challenged statute in *Glucksberg* was "not arbitrary under the due process

4. SEXUAL LIBERTY

BOWERS V. HARDWICK
478 U.S. 186, 106 S.Ct. 2841, 92 L.Ed.2d 140 (1986).

JUSTICE WHITE delivered the opinion of the Court.

In August 1982, respondent [was] charged with violating the Georgia statute criminalizing sodomy[1] by committing that act with another adult male in the bedroom of respondent's home. After a preliminary hearing, the District Attorney decided not to present the matter to the grand jury unless further evidence developed.

Respondent then brought suit in the Federal District Court, challenging the constitutionality of the statute insofar as it criminalized consensual sodomy. [The] District Court [dismissed the suit] for failure to state a claim. [The] Court of Appeals for the Eleventh Circuit reversed, holding] that the Georgia statute violated respondent's fundamental rights because his homosexual activity is a private and intimate association that is beyond the reach of state regulation by reason of the Ninth Amendment and the Due Process Clause. [We reverse.]

This case does not require a judgment on whether laws against sodomy between consenting adults in general, or between homosexuals in particular, are wise or desirable. [T]he issue presented is whether the Federal Constitution confers a fundamental right upon homosexuals to engage in sodomy and hence invalidates the laws of the many States that still make such conduct illegal and have done so for a very long time. The case also calls for some judgment about the limits of the Court's role in carrying out its constitutional mandate.

[Striving] to assure itself and the public that announcing rights not readily identifiable in the Constitution's text involves much more than the imposition of the Justices' own choice of values on the States and the Federal Government, the Court has sought to identify the nature of the rights qualifying for heightened judicial protection. In *Palko* it was said that this category includes those fundamental liberties that are "implicit in the concept of ordered liberty," such that "neither liberty nor justice would exist if [they] were sacrificed." A different description of fundamental liberties appeared in *Moore v. East Cleveland* (opinion of Powell, J.) [Sec. 5, I infra], where they are characterized as those liberties that are "deeply rooted in this Nation's history and tradition."

---

standard also support the distinction between assistance to suicide, which is banned, and practices such as termination of artificial life support and death-hastening pain medication, which are permitted."

1　　**[Ct's Note]** Ga.Code Ann. § 16–6–2 (1984) provides, in pertinent part, as follows:

"(a) A person commits the offense of sodomy when he performs or submits to any sexual act involving the sex organs of one person and the mouth or anus of [another].

"(b) A person convicted of the offense of sodomy shall be punished by imprisonment for not less than one nor more than 20 [years]."

It is obvious to us that neither of these formulations would extend a fundamental right to homosexuals to engage in acts of consensual sodomy. Proscriptions against that conduct have ancient roots. Sodomy was a criminal offense at common law and was forbidden by the laws of the original thirteen States when they ratified the Bill of Rights. In 1868, when the Fourteenth Amendment was ratified, all but 5 of the 37 States in the Union had criminal sodomy laws. In fact, until 1961, all 50 States outlawed sodomy, and today, 24 States and the District of Columbia continue to provide criminal penalties for sodomy performed in private and between consenting adults. Against this background, to claim that a right to engage in such conduct is "deeply rooted in this Nation's history and tradition" or "implicit in the concept of ordered liberty" is, at best, facetious.

Nor are we inclined to take a more expansive view of our authority to discover new fundamental rights imbedded in the Due Process Clause. The Court is most vulnerable and comes nearest to illegitimacy when it deals with judge-made constitutional law having little or no cognizable roots in the language or design of the Constitution. [There] should be, therefore, great resistance to expand the substantive reach of [the due process clauses], particularly if it requires redefining the category of rights deemed to be fundamental. Otherwise, the Judiciary necessarily takes to itself further authority to govern the country without express constitutional authority.

[Respondent], however, asserts that the result should be different where the homosexual conduct occurs in the privacy of the home. [Yet] otherwise illegal conduct is not always immunized whenever it occurs in the home. Victimless crimes, such as the possession and use of illegal drugs, do not escape the law where they are committed at home. [And] if respondent's submission is limited to the voluntary sexual conduct between consenting adults, it would be difficult, except by fiat, to limit the claimed right to homosexual conduct while leaving exposed to prosecution adultery, incest, and other sexual crimes even though they are committed in the home. We are unwilling to start down that road.

Even if the conduct at issue here is not a fundamental right, respondent asserts that there must be a rational basis for the law and that there is none in this case other than the presumed belief of a majority of the electorate in Georgia that homosexual sodomy is immoral and unacceptable. [The] law, however, is constantly based on notions of morality, and if all laws representing essentially moral choices are to be invalidated under the Due Process Clause, the courts will be very busy indeed. [Reversed.]

CHIEF JUSTICE BURGER, concurring.

[To] hold that the act of homosexual sodomy is somehow protected as a fundamental right would be to cast aside millennia of moral teaching. * * *

JUSTICE POWELL, concurring.

[I] agree with the Court that there is no fundamental right [such] as that claimed by respondent. [This] is not to suggest, however, that respondent may not be protected by the Eighth Amendment. [The] Georgia statute at issue in this case authorizes a court to imprison a person for up to 20 years for a single private, consensual act of sodomy. In my view, a prison sentence for such conduct—certainly a sentence of long duration—would create a serious Eighth Amendment issue. [In] this case, however, respondent has not been tried, much less convicted and sentenced. * * *

JUSTICE BLACKMUN, with whom JUSTICE BRENNAN, JUSTICE MARSHALL, and JUSTICE STEVENS join, dissenting.

[We] must analyze respondent's claim in the light of the values that underlie the constitutional right to privacy. If that right means anything, it means that, before Georgia can prosecute its citizens for making choices about the most intimate aspects of their lives, it must do more than assert that the choice they have made is an " 'abominable crime not fit to be named among Christians.' "

[The] Court's almost obsessive focus on homosexual activity is particularly hard to justify in light of the broad language Georgia has used. Unlike the Court, the Georgia Legislature has not proceeded on the assumption that homosexuals are so different from other citizens that their lives may be controlled in a way that would not be tolerated if it limited the choices of those other citizens. Rather, Georgia has provided that "[a] person commits the offense of sodomy when he performs or submits to any sexual act involving the sex organs of one person and the mouth or anus of another." The sex or status of the persons who engage in the act is irrelevant as a matter of state law.

[Only] the most willful blindness could obscure the fact that sexual intimacy is "a sensitive, key relationship of human existence, central to family life, community welfare, and the development of human personality." The fact that individuals define themselves in a significant way through their intimate sexual relationships with others suggests, in a Nation as diverse as ours, that there may be many "right" ways of conducting those relationships, and that much of the richness of a relationship will come from the freedom an individual has to *choose* the form and nature of these intensely personal bonds.

[The] assertion that "traditional Judeo-Christian values proscribe" the conduct involved cannot provide an adequate justification for [the law]. That certain, but by no means all, religious groups condemn the behavior at issue gives the State no license to impose their judgments on the entire citizenry. The legitimacy of secular legislation depends instead on whether the State can advance some justification for its law beyond its conformity to religious doctrine.

[I] can only hope that [the] Court soon will reconsider its analysis and conclude that depriving individuals of the right to choose for themselves how to conduct their intimate relationships poses a far greater threat to the values most deeply rooted in our Nation's history than tolerance of nonconformity could ever do. * * *

JUSTICE STEVENS, with whom JUSTICE BRENNAN and JUSTICE MARSHALL join, dissenting.

Like the statute that is challenged in this case, the rationale of the Court's opinion applies equally to the prohibited conduct regardless of whether the parties who engage in it are married or unmarried, or are of the same or different sexes. Sodomy was condemned as an odious and sinful type of behavior during the formative period of the common law. That condemnation was equally damning for heterosexual and homosexual sodomy. Moreover, it provided no special exemption for married couples. The license to cohabit and to produce legitimate offspring simply did not include any permission to engage in sexual conduct that was considered a "crime against nature."

[The] Court has posited as a justification for the Georgia statute "the presumed belief of a majority of the electorate in Georgia that homosexual sodomy is immoral and unacceptable." But the Georgia electorate has expressed no such belief—instead, its representatives enacted a law that presumably reflects the belief that *all sodomy* is immoral and unacceptable. Unless the Court is prepared to conclude that such a law is constitutional, it may not rely on the work product of the Georgia Legislature to support its holding. For the Georgia statute does not single out homosexuals as a separate class meriting special disfavored treatment. [Moreover, the] record of nonenforcement, in this case and in the last several decades, belies the Attorney General's representations about the importance of the State's selective application of its generally applicable law. * * *

LAWRENCE V. TEXAS

539 U.S. 558, 123 S.Ct. 2472, 156 L.Ed.2d 508 (2003).

JUSTICE KENNEDY delivered the opinion of the Court.

Liberty protects the person from unwarranted government intrusions into a dwelling or other private places. In our tradition the State is not omnipresent in the home. And there are other spheres of our lives and existence, outside the home, where the State should not be a dominant presence. Freedom extends beyond spatial bounds. Liberty presumes an autonomy of self that includes freedom of thought, belief, expression, and certain intimate conduct. The instant case involves liberty of the person both in its spatial and in its more transcendent dimensions. The question before the Court is the validity of a Texas statute making it a crime for two persons of the same sex to engage in certain intimate sexual conduct.

Houston [police officers] were dispatched to a private residence in response to a reported weapons disturbance. They entered an apartment [where] Lawrence resided. The right of the police to enter does not seem to have been questioned. The officers observed Lawrence and another man, Tyron Garner, engaging in a sexual act. The two petitioners were arrested, held in custody overnight, and charged and convicted before a Justice of the Peace.

The complaints described their crime as "deviate sexual intercourse, namely anal sex, with a member of the same sex (man)." The applicable state [law] provides: "A person commits an offense if he engages in deviate sexual intercourse with another individual of the same sex." The statute defines "[d]eviate sexual intercourse" as follows:

"(A) any contact between any part of the genitals of one person and the mouth or anus of another person; or

"(B) the penetration of the genitals or the anus of another person with an object."

[Petitioners were convicted. The Texas Court of Appeals rejected their constitutional arguments, considering *Bowers v. Hardwick* controlling. The Supreme Court granted certiorari to consider whether petitioners' convictions violated the Equal Protection or Due Process Clauses and whether *Hardwick* should be overruled.]

We conclude the case should be resolved by determining whether the petitioners were free as adults to engage in the private conduct in the exercise of their liberty under the Due Process Clause of the Fourteenth Amendment to the Constitution. For this inquiry we deem it necessary to reconsider the Court's holding in *Bowers*. [The Court then discussed *Griswold*, *Eisenstadt*, *Roe*, and *Carey*.] *Roe* recognized the right of a woman to make certain fundamental decisions affecting her destiny and confirmed once more that the protection of liberty under the Due Process Clause has a substantive dimension of fundamental significance in defining the rights of the person.

[The] facts in *Bowers* had some similarities to the instant case. [One] difference between the two cases is that the Georgia statute prohibited the conduct whether or not the participants were of the same sex, while the Texas statute, as we have seen, applies only to participants of the same sex.

[The] Court began its substantive discussion in *Bowers* as follows: "The issue presented is whether the Federal Constitution confers a fundamental right upon homosexuals to engage in sodomy and hence invalidates the laws of the many States that still make such conduct illegal and have done so for a very long time." That statement, we now conclude, discloses the Court's own failure to appreciate the extent of the liberty at stake. To say that the issue in *Bowers* was simply the right to engage in certain sexual conduct demeans the claim the individual put forward, just as it would demean a married couple were it to be said marriage is simply about the right to have sexual intercourse. The laws involved in *Bowers* and here are, to be sure, statutes that purport to do no more than prohibit a particular sexual act. Their penalties and purposes, though, have more far-reaching consequences, touching upon the most private human conduct, sexual behavior, and in the most private of places, the home. The statutes do seek to control a personal relationship that, whether or not entitled to formal recognition in the law, is within the liberty of persons to choose without being punished as criminals.

This, as a general rule, should counsel against attempts by the State, or a court, to define the meaning of the relationship or to set its boundaries absent injury to a person or abuse of an institution the law protects. It suffices for us to acknowledge that adults may choose to enter upon this relationship in the confines of their homes and their own private lives and still retain their dignity as free persons. When sexuality finds overt expression in intimate conduct with another person, the conduct can be but one element in a personal bond that is more enduring. The liberty protected by the Constitution allows homosexual persons the right to make this choice.

Having misapprehended the claim of liberty there presented to it, and thus stating the claim to be whether there is a fundamental right to engage in consensual sodomy, the *Bowers* Court said: "Proscriptions against that conduct have ancient roots." In academic writings, and in many of the scholarly amicus briefs filed to assist the Court in this case, there are fundamental criticisms of the historical premises relied upon by the majority and concurring opinions in *Bowers*. We need not enter this debate in the attempt to reach a definitive historical judgment, but the following considerations counsel against adopting the definitive conclusions upon which *Bowers* placed such reliance.

At the outset it should be noted that there is no longstanding history in this country of laws directed at homosexual conduct as a distinct matter. [The] absence of legal prohibitions focusing on homosexual conduct may be explained in part by noting that according to some scholars the concept of the homosexual as a distinct category of person did not emerge until the late 19th century. [Thus] early American sodomy laws were not directed at homosexuals as such but instead sought to prohibit nonprocreative sexual activity more generally. This does not suggest approval of homosexual conduct. It does tend to show that this particular form of conduct was not thought of as a separate category from like conduct between heterosexual persons.

Laws prohibiting sodomy do not seem to have been enforced against consenting adults acting in private. [Instead] of targeting relations between consenting adults in private, 19th-century sodomy prosecutions typically involved relations between men and minor girls or minor boys, relations between adults involving force, relations between adults implicating disparity in status, or relations between men and animals.

[The infrequency of prosecutions in consensual cases] makes it difficult to say that society approved of a rigorous and systematic punishment of the consensual acts committed in private and by adults. The longstanding criminal prohibition of homosexual sodomy upon which the *Bowers* decision placed such reliance is as consistent with a general condemnation of nonprocreative sex as it is with an established tradition of prosecuting acts because of their homosexual character.

[Far] from possessing "ancient roots," *Bowers,* American laws targeting same-sex couples did not develop until the last third of the 20th century. The reported decisions concerning the prosecution of consensual, homosexual sodomy between adults for the years 1880–1995 are not always clear in the details, but a significant number involved conduct in a public place. It was not until the 1970s that any State singled out same-sex relations for criminal prosecution, and only nine States have done so. [Over] the course of the last decades, States with same-sex prohibitions have moved toward abolishing them.

In summary, the historical grounds relied upon in *Bowers* are more complex than the majority opinion and the concurring opinion by Chief Justice Burger indicate. Their historical premises are not without doubt and, at the very least, are overstated.

It must be acknowledged, of course, that the Court in *Bowers* was making the broader point that for centuries there have been powerful voices to condemn homosexual conduct as immoral. [This does] not answer the question before us, however. The issue is whether the majority may use the power of the State to enforce these views on the whole society through operation of the criminal law. "Our obligation is to define the liberty of all, not to mandate our own moral code." *Casey.*

[Our] laws and traditions in the past half century [show] an emerging awareness that liberty gives substantial protection to adult persons in deciding how to conduct their private lives in matters pertaining to sex. "[H]istory and tradition are the starting point but not in all cases the ending point of the substantive due process inquiry." *Sacramento v. Lewis*, 523 U.S. 833 (1998) (Kennedy, J., concurring). This emerging recognition should have been apparent when *Bowers* was decided. In 1955 the American Law Institute promulgated the Model Penal Code and made clear that it did not recommend or provide for "criminal penalties for consensual sexual relations conducted in private." [In] 1961 Illinois changed its laws to conform to the Model Penal Code. Other States soon followed.

In *Bowers* the Court referred to the fact that before 1961 all 50 States had outlawed sodomy, and that at the time of the Court's decision 24 States and the District of Columbia had sodomy laws. Justice Powell pointed out that these prohibitions often were being ignored, however. Georgia, for instance, had not sought to enforce its law for decades.

[The] sweeping references by Chief Justice Burger to the history of Western civilization and to Judeo-Christian moral and ethical standards did not take account of other authorities pointing in an opposite direction. A committee advising the British Parliament recommended in 1957 repeal of laws punishing homosexual conduct. Parliament enacted the substance of those recommendations 10 years later. Of even more importance, almost five years before *Bowers* was decided the European Court of Human Rights considered a case with parallels to *Bowers* and to today's case. [The] court held that the laws proscribing [consensual homosexual conduct] were invalid under the European Convention on Human Rights. *Dudgeon v. United Kingdom*, 45 Eur.Ct.H.R. (1981).

[In] our own constitutional system the deficiencies in *Bowers* became even more apparent in the years following its announcement. The 25 States with laws prohibiting the relevant conduct referenced in the *Bowers* decision are reduced now to 13, of which 4 enforce their laws only against homosexual conduct. In those States where sodomy is still proscribed, whether for same-sex or heterosexual conduct, there is a pattern of nonenforcement with respect to consenting adults acting in private. The State of Texas admitted in 1994 that as of that date it had not prosecuted anyone under those circumstances. Two principal cases decided after *Bowers* cast its holding into even more doubt [discussing *Casey* and *Romer v. Evans*, Ch. 9, Sec. 4, I].

[As] an alternative argument in this case, counsel for the petitioners and some amici contend that *Romer* provides the basis for declaring the Texas statute invalid under the Equal Protection Clause. That is a tenable argument, but we conclude the instant case requires us to address whether *Bowers* itself has continuing validity. Were we to hold the statute invalid under the Equal Protection Clause some might question whether a prohibition would be valid if drawn differently, say, to prohibit the conduct both between same-sex and different-sex participants.

Equality of treatment and the due process right to demand respect for conduct protected by the substantive guarantee of liberty are linked in important respects, and a decision on the latter point advances both interests. If protected conduct is made criminal and the law which does so remains unexamined for its substantive validity, its stigma might remain even if it were not enforceable as drawn for equal protection reasons. When homosexual conduct is made criminal by the law of the State, that declaration in and of itself is an invitation to subject homosexual persons to discrimination both in the public and in the private spheres. The central holding of *Bowers* has been brought in question by this case, and it should be addressed. Its continuance as precedent demeans the lives of homosexual persons.

The stigma this criminal statute imposes, moreover, is not trivial. The offense, to be sure, is but [a] minor offense in the Texas legal system. Still, it remains a criminal offense with all that imports for the dignity of the persons charged. The petitioners will bear on their record the history of their criminal convictions. Just this Term we rejected various challenges to state laws requiring the registration of sex offenders. We are advised that if Texas convicted an adult for private, consensual homosexual conduct under the statute here in question the convicted person would come within the registration laws of a least four States were he or she to be subject to their jurisdiction. This underscores the consequential nature of the punishment and the state-sponsored condemnation attendant to the criminal prohibition. Furthermore, the Texas criminal conviction carries with it the other collateral consequences always following a conviction, such as notations on job application forms, to mention but one example.

The foundations of *Bowers* have sustained serious erosion from our recent decisions in *Casey* and *Romer*. When our precedent has been thus weakened, criticism from other sources is of greater significance. In the United States criticism of *Bowers* has been substantial and continuing, disapproving of its reasoning in all respects, not just as to its historical assumptions. The courts of five different States have declined to follow it in interpreting provisions in their own state constitutions parallel to the Due Process Clause of the Fourteenth Amendment.

To the extent *Bowers* relied on values we share with a wider civilization, it should be noted that the reasoning and holding in *Bowers* have been rejected elsewhere. The European Court of Human Rights has followed not *Bowers* but its own decision in *Dudgeon.* Other nations, too, have taken action consistent with an affirmation of the protected right of homosexual adults to engage in intimate, consensual conduct. The right the petitioners seek in this case has been accepted as an integral part of human freedom in many other countries. There has been no showing that in this country the governmental interest in circumscribing personal choice is somehow more legitimate or urgent.

[In] *Casey* we noted that when a court is asked to overrule a precedent recognizing a constitutional liberty interest, individual or societal reliance on the existence of that liberty cautions with particular strength against reversing course. [The] holding in *Bowers,* however, has not induced detrimental reliance comparable to some instances where recognized individual rights are involved. Indeed, there has been no individual or societal reliance on *Bowers* of the sort that could counsel against overturning its holding once there are compelling reasons to do so. *Bowers* itself causes uncertainty, for the precedents before and after its issuance contradict its central holding.

[Justice] Stevens' [dissenting] analysis, in our view, should have been controlling in *Bowers* and should control here. *Bowers* was not correct when it was decided, and it is not correct today. It ought not to remain binding precedent. *Bowers v. Hardwick* should be and now is overruled.

The present case does not involve minors. It does not involve persons who might be injured or coerced or who are situated in relationships where consent might not easily be refused. It does not involve public conduct or prostitution. It does not involve whether the government must give formal recognition to any relationship that homosexual persons seek to enter. The case does involve two adults who, with full and mutual consent from each other, engaged in sexual practices common to a homosexual lifestyle. The petitioners are entitled to respect for their private lives. The State cannot demean their existence or control their destiny by making their private sexual conduct a crime. Their right to liberty under the Due Process Clause gives them the full right to engage in their conduct without intervention of the government. "It is a promise of the Constitution that there is a realm of personal liberty which the government may not enter." *Casey.* The Texas statute furthers no legitimate state interest which can justify its intrusion into the personal and private life of the individual.

Had those who drew and ratified the Due Process Clauses of the Fifth Amendment or the Fourteenth Amendment known the components of liberty in its manifold possibilities, they might have been more specific. They did not presume to have this insight. They knew times can blind us to certain truths and later generations can see that laws once thought necessary and proper in fact serve only to oppress. As the Constitution endures, persons in every generation can invoke its principles in their own search for greater freedom. * * *

JUSTICE O'CONNOR, concurring in the judgment.

[O'Connor, J., did not join the Court in overruling *Bowers*, but agreed that the Texas statute was unconstitutional, relying on the Equal Protection Clause. See Ch. 9, Sec. 4, I, infra.] That this law as applied to private, consensual conduct is unconstitutional under the Equal Protection Clause does not mean that other laws distinguishing between heterosexuals and homosexuals would similarly fail under rational basis review. Texas cannot assert any legitimate state interest here, such as national security or preserving the traditional institution of marriage. * * *

JUSTICE SCALIA, with whom CHIEF JUSTICE REHNQUIST and JUSTICE THOMAS join, dissenting.

[N]owhere does the Court's opinion declare that homosexual sodomy is a "fundamental right" under the Due Process Clause; nor does it subject the Texas law to the standard of review that would be appropriate (strict scrutiny) if homosexual sodomy *were* a "fundamental right." Thus, while overruling the *outcome* of *Bowers,* the Court leaves strangely untouched its central legal conclusion: "[R]espondent would have us announce [a] fundamental right to engage in homosexual sodomy. This we are quite unwilling to do." Instead the Court simply describes petitioners' conduct as "an exercise of their liberty"—which it undoubtedly is—and proceeds to apply an unheard-of form of rational-basis review that will have far-reaching implications beyond this case.

[I] do not myself believe in rigid adherence to stare decisis in constitutional cases; but I do believe that we should be consistent rather than manipulative in invoking the doctrine. Today's opinions in support of reversal do not bother to distinguish—or indeed, even bother to mention—the paean to stare decisis coauthored by three Members of today's majority in *Casey.* There, when stare decisis meant preservation of judicially invented abortion rights, the widespread criticism of *Roe* was strong reason to *reaffirm* [it]. Today, however, the widespread opposition to *Bowers,* a decision resolving an issue as "intensely divisive" as the issue in *Roe,* is offered as a reason in favor of *overruling* it. Gone, too, is any "enquiry" (of the sort conducted in *Casey*) into whether the decision sought to be overruled has "proven 'unworkable.' "

Today's approach to stare decisis invites us to overrule an erroneously decided precedent (including an "intensely divisive" decision) *if:* (1) its foundations have been "eroded" by subsequent decisions; (2) it has been subject to "substantial and continuing" criticism; and (3) it has not induced "individual or societal reliance" that counsels against overturning. The problem is that *Roe* itself—which today's majority surely has no disposition to overrule—satisfies these conditions to at least the same degree as *Bowers.*

(1) A preliminary digressive observation with regard to the first factor: The Court's claim that *Casey* "casts some doubt" upon the holding in *Bowers* (or any other case, for that matter) does not withstand analysis. As far as its holding is concerned, *Casey* provided a *less* expansive right to abortion than did *Roe, which was already on the books when Bowers was decided.* And if the Court is referring not to the holding of *Casey,* but to the dictum of its famed sweet-mystery-of-life passage (" 'At the heart of liberty is the right to define one's own concept of existence, of meaning, of the universe, and of the mystery of human life' "): That "casts some doubt" upon either the totality of our jurisprudence or else (presumably the right answer) nothing at all. I have never heard of a law that attempted to restrict one's "right to define" certain concepts; and if the passage calls into question the government's power to regulate *actions based on* one's self-defined "concept of existence, etc.," it is the passage that ate the rule of law.

I do not quarrel with the Court's claim that *Romer* "eroded" the "foundations" of *Bowers'* rational-basis holding. But *Roe* and *Casey* have been equally "eroded" by *Glucksberg,* which held that *only* fundamental rights which are " 'deeply rooted in this Nation's history and tradition' " qualify for anything other than rational basis scrutiny under the doctrine of "substantive due process." *Roe* and *Casey,* of course, subjected the restriction of abortion to heightened scrutiny without even attempting to establish that the freedom to abort *was* rooted in this Nation's tradition.

(2) *Bowers,* the Court says, has been subject to "substantial and continuing [criticism], disapproving of its reasoning in all respects, not just as to its historical assumptions." Exactly what those nonhistorical criticisms are, and whether the Court even agrees with them, are left unsaid. [Of] course, *Roe* too (and by extension *Casey*) had been (and still is) subject to unrelenting criticism, including criticism from the two commentators cited by the Court today.

(3) That leaves, to distinguish the rock-solid, unamendable disposition of *Roe* from the readily overrulable *Bowers,* only the third factor. "[T]here has been," the Court says, "no individual or societal reliance on *Bowers* of the sort that could counsel against overturning its [holding]." It seems to me that the "societal reliance" on the principles confirmed in *Bowers* and discarded today has been overwhelming. Countless judicial decisions and legislative enactments have relied on the ancient proposition that a governing majority's belief that certain sexual behavior is "immoral and unacceptable" constitutes a rational basis for regulation. [L]aws against bigamy, same-sex marriage, adult incest, prostitution, masturbation, adultery, fornication, bestiality, and obscenity are likewise sustainable only in light of *Bowers'* validation of laws based on moral choices. Every single one of these laws is called into question by today's decision. [The] impossibility of distinguishing homosexuality from other traditional "morals" offenses is precisely why *Bowers* rejected the rational-basis challenge. "The law," it said, "is constantly based on notions of morality, and if all laws representing essentially moral choices are to be invalidated under the Due Process Clause, the courts will be very busy indeed."

What a massive disruption of the current social order, therefore, the overruling of *Bowers* entails. Not so the overruling of *Roe,* which would simply have restored the regime that existed for centuries before 1973, in which the permissibility of and restrictions upon, abortion were determined legislatively State-by-State. [To] tell the truth, it does not surprise me, and should surprise no one, that the Court has chosen today to revise the standards of stare decisis set forth in *Casey.* It has thereby exposed *Casey's* extraordinary deference to precedent for the result-oriented expedient that it is.

Having decided that it need not adhere to stare decisis, the Court still must establish that *Bowers* was wrongly decided and that the Texas statute, as applied to petitioners, is unconstitutional. [The Texas law at issue] undoubtedly imposes constraints on liberty. So do laws prohibiting prostitution, recreational use of heroin, and, for that matter, working more than 60 hours per week in a bakery. But there is no right to "liberty" under the Due Process Clause, though today's opinion repeatedly makes that claim. [The] Fourteenth Amendment *expressly allows* States to deprive their citizens of "liberty," *so long as "due process of law" is provided.*

[Our] opinions applying the doctrine known as "substantive due process" hold that the Due Process Clause prohibits States from infringing *fundamental* liberty interests, unless the infringement is narrowly tailored to serve a compelling state interest. *Glucksberg.* We have held repeatedly, in cases the Court today does not overrule, that *only* fundamental rights qualify for this so-called "heightened scrutiny" protection—that is, rights which are " 'deeply rooted in this Nation's history and tradition.' " [All] other liberty interests may be abridged or abrogated pursuant to a validly enacted state law if that law is rationally related to a legitimate state interest.

Bowers held [that] a right to engage in homosexual sodomy was not "deeply rooted in this Nation's history and tradition." The Court today does not overrule this holding. Not once does it describe homosexual sodomy as a "fundamental right" or a "fundamental liberty interest," nor does it subject the Texas statute to strict scrutiny. Instead, [the] Court concludes that the application of Texas's statute to petitioners' conduct fails the rational-basis test, and overrules *Bowers'* holding to the contrary[:] "The Texas statute furthers no legitimate state interest which can justify its intrusion into the personal and private life of the individual."

[The] Court's description of "the state of the law" at the time of *Bowers* only confirms that *Bowers* was right. [*Griswold*] *expressly disclaimed* any reliance on the doctrine of "substantive due process," and grounded the so-called "right to privacy" in penumbras of constitutional provisions *other than* the Due Process Clause. *Eisenstadt,* likewise had nothing to do with "substantive due process"; it invalidated a Massachusetts law prohibiting the distribution of contraceptives to unmarried persons solely on the basis of the Equal Protection Clause.

[*Roe*] recognized that the right to abort an unborn child was a "fundamental right" protected by the Due Process Clause. The *Roe* Court, however, made no attempt to establish that this right was " 'deeply rooted in this Nation's history and tradition' "; instead, it based its conclusion that "the Fourteenth Amendment's concept of personal liberty [is] broad enough to encompass a woman's decision whether or not to terminate her pregnancy" on its own normative judgment that antiabortion laws were undesirable. We have since rejected *Roe*'s holding that regulations of abortion must be narrowly tailored to serve a compelling state interest, see *Casey*, (joint opinion of O'Connor, Kennedy, and Souter, JJ.); (Rehnquist, C.J., concurring in judgment in part and dissenting in part)—and thus, by logical implication, *Roe*'s holding that the right to abort an unborn child is a "fundamental right."

[After] discussing the history of antisodomy laws, the Court proclaims that, "it should be noted that there is no longstanding history in this country of laws directed at homosexual conduct as a distinct matter." This observation in no way casts into doubt the "definitive [historical] conclusion" on which *Bowers* relied: that our Nation has a longstanding history of laws prohibiting *sodomy in general*—regardless of whether it was performed by same-sex or opposite-sex couples.

[It] is (as *Bowers* recognized) entirely irrelevant whether the laws in our long national tradition criminalizing homosexual sodomy were "directed at homosexual conduct as a distinct matter." Whether homosexual sodomy was prohibited by a law targeted at same-sex sexual relations or by a more general law prohibiting both homosexual and heterosexual sodomy, the only relevant point is that it *was* criminalized—which suffices to establish that homosexual sodomy is not a right "deeply rooted in our Nation's history and tradition." The Court today agrees that homosexual sodomy was criminalized and thus does not dispute the facts on which Bowers *actually* relied.

Next the Court makes the claim, again unsupported by any citations, that "[l]aws prohibiting sodomy do not seem to have been enforced against consenting adults acting in private." The key qualifier here is "acting in private"—since the Court admits that sodomy laws *were* enforced against consenting adults (although the Court contends that prosecutions were "infrequent."). I do not know what "acting in private" means; surely consensual sodomy, like heterosexual intercourse, is rarely performed on stage. If all the Court means by "acting in private" is "on private premises, with the doors closed and windows covered," it is entirely unsurprising that evidence of enforcement would be hard to come by. [Surely] that lack of evidence would not sustain the proposition that consensual sodomy on private premises with the doors closed and windows covered was regarded as a "fundamental right," even though all other consensual sodomy was criminalized. [*Bowers*'] conclusion that homosexual sodomy is not a fundamental right "deeply rooted in this Nation's history and tradition" is utterly unassailable.

Realizing that fact, the Court instead says: "[W]e think that our laws and traditions in the past half century are of most relevance here. These references show *an emerging awareness* that liberty gives substantial protection to adult persons in deciding how to conduct their private lives *in matters pertaining to sex*."

(Emphasis added). [The] statement is factually false. States continue to prosecute all sorts of crimes by adults "in matters pertaining to sex": prostitution, adult incest, adultery, obscenity, and child pornography. Sodomy laws, too, have been enforced "in the past half century," in which there have been 134 reported cases involving prosecutions for consensual, adult, homosexual sodomy.

[In] any event, an "emerging awareness" is by definition not "deeply rooted in this Nation's history and tradition[s]," as we have said "fundamental right" status requires. Constitutional entitlements do not spring into existence because some States choose to lessen or eliminate criminal sanctions on certain behavior. Much less do they spring into existence, as the Court seems to believe, because *foreign nations* decriminalize conduct. The *Bowers* majority opinion *never* relied on "values we share with a wider civilization," but rather rejected the claimed right to sodomy on the ground that such a right was not " 'deeply rooted in *this Nation's* history and tradition' " (emphasis added).

[I] turn now to the ground on which the Court squarely rests its holding: the contention that there is no rational basis for the law here under attack. This proposition is so out of accord with our jurisprudence—indeed, with the jurisprudence of *any* society we know—that it requires little discussion.

The Texas statute undeniably seeks to further the belief of its citizens that certain forms of sexual behavior are "immoral and unacceptable," *Bowers*—the same interest furthered by criminal laws against fornication, bigamy, adultery, adult incest, bestiality, and obscenity. *Bowers* held that this *was* a legitimate state interest. The Court today reaches the opposite conclusion. [It] embraces instead Justice Stevens' declaration in his *Bowers* dissent, that "the fact that the governing majority in a State has traditionally viewed a particular practice as immoral is not a sufficient reason for upholding a law prohibiting the practice." This effectively decrees the end of all morals legislation. If, as the Court asserts, the promotion of majoritarian sexual morality is not even a *legitimate* state interest, none of the above-mentioned laws can survive rational-basis review.

[Today's] opinion is the product of a Court, which is the product of a law-profession culture, that has largely signed on to the so-called homosexual agenda, by which I mean the agenda promoted by some homosexual activists directed at eliminating the moral opprobrium that has traditionally attached to homosexual conduct. [The] Association of [American] Law Schools (to which any reputable law school *must* seek to belong) excludes from membership any school that refuses to ban from its job-interview facilities a law firm (no matter how small) that does not wish to hire as a prospective partner a person who openly engages in homosexual conduct.

One of the most revealing statements in today's opinion is the Court's grim warning that the criminalization of homosexual conduct is "an invitation to subject homosexual persons to discrimination both in the public and in the private spheres." It is clear from this that the Court has taken sides in the culture war, departing from its role of assuring, as neutral observer, that the democratic rules of engagement are observed. Many Americans do not want persons who openly engage in homosexual conduct as partners in their business, as scoutmasters for their children, as teachers in their children's schools, or as boarders in their home. They view this as protecting themselves and their families from a lifestyle that they believe to be immoral and destructive. The Court views it as "discrimination" which it is the function of our judgments to deter. So imbued is the Court with the law profession's anti-anti-homosexual culture, that it is seemingly unaware that the attitudes of that culture are not obviously "mainstream"; that in most States what the Court calls "discrimination" against those who engage in homosexual acts is perfectly legal; that proposals to ban such "discrimination" under Title VII have repeatedly been rejected by Congress; that in some cases such "discrimination" is *mandated* by federal statute, see 10 U.S.C. § 654(b)(1) (mandating discharge from the armed forces of any service member who engages in or intends to engage in homosexual acts); and that in some cases such "discrimination" is a constitutional right, see *Boy Scouts of America v. Dale*, [Ch. 7, Sec. 9, II]. Let me be clear that I have nothing against homosexuals, or any other group, promoting their agenda through normal democratic means. Social perceptions of sexual and other morality change over time, and every group has the right to persuade its fellow citizens that its view of such matters is the best. [But] persuading one's fellow citizens is one thing, and imposing one's views in absence of democratic majority will is something else. I would no more *require* a State to criminalize homosexual acts—or, for that matter, display *any* moral disapprobation of them—than I would *forbid* it to do so. What Texas has chosen to do is well within the range of traditional democratic action, and its hand should not be stayed through the invention of a brand-new "constitutional right" by a Court that is impatient of democratic change.

[One] of the benefits of leaving regulation of this matter to the people rather than to the courts is that the people, unlike judges, need not carry things to their logical conclusion. The people may feel that their disapprobation of homosexual conduct is strong enough to disallow homosexual marriage, but not strong enough to criminalize private homosexual acts—and may legislate accordingly. The Court today pretends that it possesses a similar freedom of action, so that that we need not fear judicial imposition of homosexual marriage, as has recently occurred in Canada (in a decision that the Canadian Government has chosen not to appeal). At the end of its opinion—after having laid waste the foundations of our rational-basis jurisprudence—the Court says that the present case "does not involve whether the government must give formal recognition to any relationship that homosexual persons seek to enter." Do not believe it. More illuminating than this bald, unreasoned disclaimer is the progression of thought displayed by an earlier passage in the Court's opinion, which notes the constitutional protections afforded to "personal decisions relating to *marriage,* procreation, contraception, family relationships, child rearing, and education," and then declares that "[p]ersons in a homosexual relationship may seek autonomy for these purposes, just as heterosexual persons do" (emphasis added). Today's opinion dismantles the structure of constitutional law that has permitted a distinction to be made between heterosexual and homosexual unions, insofar as formal recognition in marriage is concerned. If moral disapproval of homosexual conduct is "no legitimate state interest" for purposes of proscribing that conduct; and if, as the Court coos (casting aside all pretense of neutrality), "[w]hen sexuality finds overt expression in intimate conduct with another person, the conduct can be but one element in a personal bond that is more enduring"; what justification could there possibly be for denying the benefits of marriage to homosexual couples exercising "[t]he liberty protected by the Constitution"? Surely not the encouragement of procreation, since the sterile and the elderly are allowed to marry. This case "does not involve" the issue of homosexual marriage only if one entertains the belief that principle and logic have nothing to do with the decisions of this Court. Many will hope that, as the Court comfortingly assures us, this is so. * * *

JUSTICE THOMAS, dissenting.

I join Justice Scalia's dissenting opinion. I write separately to note that the law before the Court today "is ... uncommonly silly." *Griswold* (Stewart, J., dissenting). If I were a member of the Texas Legislature, I would vote to repeal it. Punishing someone for expressing his sexual preference through noncommercial consensual conduct with another adult does not appear to be a worthy way to expend valuable law enforcement resources.

Notwithstanding this, I recognize that as a Member of this Court I am not empowered to help petitioners and others similarly situated. My duty, rather, is to "decide cases 'agreeably to the Constitution and laws of the United States.' " And, just like Justice Stewart, I "can find [neither in the Bill of Rights nor any other part of the Constitution a] general right of privacy" or as the Court terms it today, the "liberty of the person both in its spatial and more transcendent dimensions."

5. FAMILY LIFE AND MARRIAGE

As illustrated by cases like *Griswold* and *Roe*, modern substantive due process doctrine concerns questions about whether to become a parent. But as cases like *Meyer* and *Pierce* illustrate, the Supreme Court has long protected decisions about *how* to form families as well.

I. FAMILY COMPOSITION AND LIVING QUARTERS

Relying on earlier decisions sustaining local zoning regulations, BELLE TERRE v. BORAAS, 416 U.S. 1 (1974), per DOUGLAS, J., upheld a village ordinance restricting land use to one-family dwellings (defining "family" to mean not more than two unrelated persons living together as a single housekeeping unit, and expressly excluding from the term lodging, boarding, fraternity or multiple-dwelling houses). Appellees, who had leased their houses to six unrelated college students, challenged the ordinance, inter alia, on the ground that it "trenches on the newcomers' rights of privacy." The Court disagreed: "We deal with economic and social legislation where legislatures have historically drawn lines which we respect [if the law] bears 'a rational relationship to a (permissible) state objective.'

[Boarding] houses, fraternity houses, and the like present urban problems. [The] police power is not confined to elimination of filth, stench, and unhealthy places."

MARSHALL, J., dissented: The law burdened "fundamental rights of association and privacy," and thus required extraordinary justification, not a mere showing that the ordinance "bears a rational relationship to the accomplishment of legitimate governmental objectives." He viewed "the right to 'establish a home' " as an "essential part" of Fourteenth Amendment liberty and maintained that "the choice of household companions"—which "involves deeply personal considerations as to the kind and quality of intimate relationships within the home"—"surely falls within the ambit of the right to privacy protected by the Constitution." The state's purposes "could be as effectively achieved by means of an ordinance that did not discriminate on the basis of constitutionally protected choices of lifestyle."

———

Distinguishing *Belle Terre* as involving an ordinance "affect[ing] only *unrelated* individuals," MOORE v. EAST CLEVELAND, 431 U.S. 494 (1977), invalidated a housing ordinance that limited occupancy to single families, but defined "family" so as to forbid appellant from having her two grandsons live with her. (It did not permit living arrangements if, as in this case, the grandchildren were cousins rather than brothers.) POWELL, J., announcing the Court's judgment and joined by Brennan, Marshall, and Blackmun, JJ., struck down the ordinance on substantive due process grounds:

"[O]n its face [the ordinance] selects certain categories of relatives who may live together and declares that others may not. [When] a city undertakes such intrusive regulation of the family [the] usual judicial deference to the legislature is inappropriate. 'This Court has long recognized that freedom of personal choice in matters of marriage and family life is one of the liberties protected by [due process].' [When] the government intrudes on choices concerning family living arrangements, this Court must examine carefully the importance of the governmental interests advanced and the extent to which they are served by the challenged regulation. [T]hus examined, this ordinance cannot survive." Although the city's goals—preventing overcrowding, minimizing congestion and avoiding financial strain on its school system—were "legitimate," the ordinance served them "marginally, at best."

"[T]he history of the *Lochner* [era] counsels caution and restraint [but] it does [not] require what the city urges here: cutting off any protection of family rights at the first convenient, if arbitrary boundary—the boundary of the nuclear family. [Appropriate] limits on substantive due process come not from drawing arbitrary lines but rather from careful 'respect for the teachings of history [and] solid recognition of the basic values that underlie our society.' *Griswold* (Harlan, J., concurring). Our decisions establish that the Constitution protects the sanctity of the family precisely because the institution of the family is deeply rooted in this Nation's history and tradition. [Ours] is by no means a tradition limited to respect for [the] nuclear family. The tradition of uncles, aunts, cousins, and especially grandparents sharing a household along with parents and children has roots equally venerable and equally deserving of constitutional recognition. [*Pierce*] struck down an Oregon law requiring all children to attend the State's public schools, holding that the Constitution 'excludes any general power of the State to standardize its children by forcing them to accept instruction from public teachers only.' By the same token the Constitution prevents East Cleveland from standardizing its children and its adults by forcing all to live in certain narrowly defined family patterns.[8]

STEWART, J., joined by Rehnquist, J., dissented, rejecting the argument that "the importance of the 'extended family' in American society" renders appellant's "decision to share her residence with her grandsons, [like] the decisions involved in bearing and raising children, [an] aspect of 'family life' also entitled to substantive [constitutional] protection. [To] equate this interest with the fundamental decisions to marry and to bear and raise children is to extend the limited substantive contours of the Due Process Clause beyond recognition."

WHITE, J., also dissented, writing: "I cannot believe that the interest in residing with more than one set of grandchildren is one that calls for any kind of heightened protection under the Due Process Clause." He maintained that Powell, J.'s application of heightened scrutiny "suggests a far too expansive charter for this Court. [What] the deeply rooted traditions of the country are is arguable; which of them deserve the protection of the Due Process Clause is even more debatable."

II. MARRIAGE

In LOVING v. VIRGINIA, 388 U.S. 1 (1967) (also at Ch. 9, Sec. 2, II), the Court held, per WARREN, C.J., that a state statutory scheme designed to prevent marriages between persons of different races not only violated the Equal Protection Clause, but deprived the Lovings of liberty without due process. The Court recalled that in *Skinner*, it had described marriage as "one of the 'basic civil rights of man.' " It "surely" is a deprivation of liberty without due process, declared the Court, "[t]o deny this fundamental freedom on so unsupportable a basis as the racial classifications embodied in these statutes." Because racial discrimination played so large a role in the *Loving* case, its due process ruling was largely overlooked.

————

ZABLOCKI v. REDHAIL, 434 U.S. 374 (1978), invalidated a Wisconsin law forbidding marriage by any resident with minor children not in his custody whom he is under court order to support, unless he proves compliance with the support obligation and that the children "are not then and are not likely thereafter to

---

[8]   Brennan, J., joined by Marshall, J., concurred, characterizing the ordinance as "senseless," "arbitrary" and "eccentric" and as reflecting "cultural myopia" and "a depressing insensitivity toward the economic and emotional needs of a very large part of our society." He called the "extended family" "virtually a means of survival" for many poor and minority families. "[The] 'nuclear family' is the pattern so often found in much of white suburbia," but "the Constitution cannot [tolerate] the imposition by government upon the rest of us of white suburbia's preference in patterns of family living." Stevens, J., concurred in the result.

become public charges." Appellee and the woman he desired to marry were expecting a child, but he was denied a marriage license because he had not satisfied his support obligations to his illegitimate child who had been a public charge since birth. In striking down the marriage prohibition under the "fundamental rights" branch of equal protection doctrine (Ch. 9, Sec. 5) the Court, per MARSHALL, J., observed:

"Since our past decisions make clear that the right to marry is of fundamental importance, and since the classification at issue here significantly interferes with the exercise of that right, we believe that 'critical examination' of the state interests advanced in support of the classification is required. [Cases] subsequent to *Griswold* and *Loving* have routinely categorized the decision to marry as among the personal decisions protected by the right of privacy. [It] is not surprising that the decision to marry has been placed on the same level of importance as decisions relating to procreation, childbirth, child rearing, and family relationships [for] it would make little sense to recognize a right of privacy with respect to other matters of family life and not with respect to the decision to enter the relationship that is the foundation of the family in our society. [If] appellee's right to procreate means anything at all, it must imply some right to enter the only relationship in which the [state] allows sexual relations legally to take place.

"By reaffirming the fundamental character of the right to marry, we do not mean to suggest that every state regulation which relates in any way to the incidents of or prerequisites for marriage must be subjected to rigorous scrutiny. [The] statutory classification at issue here, however, clearly does interfere directly and substantially with the right to marry. [Some] of those in the affected class, like appellee, will never be able to obtain the necessary court order, because they either lack the financial means to meet their support obligations or cannot prove that their children will not become public charges. These persons are absolutely prevented from getting married. Many others, able in theory to satisfy the statute's requirements, will be sufficiently burdened by having to do so that they will in effect be coerced into forgoing their right to marry. And even those who can be persuaded to meet the statute's requirements suffer a serious intrusion into their freedom of choice in an area in which we have held such freedom to be fundamental.

"When a statutory classification significantly interferes with the exercise of a fundamental right, it cannot be upheld unless it is supported by sufficiently important state interests and is closely tailored to effectuate only those interests. [The] State already has numerous other means for exacting compliance with support obligations, means that are at least as effective as the instant statute's and yet do not impinge upon the right to marry."

STEWART, J., who concurred in the judgment, rejected the view that the Wisconsin statute violated equal protection. As he saw it, "the problem in this case is not one of discriminatory classifications, but of unwarranted encroachment upon a constitutionally protected freedom." He deemed the statute unconstitutional "because it exceeds the bounds of permissible state regulation of marriage." He continued:

"I do not agree [that] there is a 'right to marry' in the constitutional sense. [Surely], for example, a State may legitimately say that no one can marry his or her sibling, that no one can marry who is not at least 14 years old, that no one can marry without first passing an examination for venereal disease, or that no one can marry who has a living husband or wife. But, just as surely, in regulating the intimate human relationship of marriage, there is a limit beyond which a State may not constitutionally go.

"[The] State's legitimate concern with the financial soundness of prospective marriages must stop short of telling people they may not marry because they are too poor or because they might persist in their financial irresponsibility. [A] legislative judgment so alien to our traditions and so offensive to our shared notions of fairness offends the Due Process Clause. [Equal] protection doctrine has become the Court's chief instrument for invalidating state laws. Yet, in a case like this one, the doctrine is no more than substantive due process by another name. [The] message of the Court's opinion is that Wisconsin may not use its control over marriage to achieve the objectives of the state statute. Such restrictions on basic governmental power are at the heart of substantive due process. The Court is understandably reluctant to rely on substantive due process. But to embrace the essence of that doctrine under the guise of equal protection serves no purpose but obfuscation."

POWELL, J., concurred in the judgment, but wrote separately "because the majority's rationale sweeps too broadly in an area which traditionally has been subject to pervasive state regulation [which] has included bans on incest, bigamy, and homosexuality, as well as various preconditions to marriage, such as blood tests. Likewise, a showing of fault on the part of one of the partners traditionally has been a prerequisite to the dissolution of an unsuccessful union. A 'compelling state purpose' inquiry would cast doubt on the network of restrictions that the States have fashioned to govern marriage and divorce.

"[But the] Wisconsin measure in this case does not pass muster under either due process or equal protection standards. [As for the state's 'collection device' justification, the] vice inheres [in] the failure to make provision for those without the means to comply with child-support obligations. [As for the state interest in preserving] the ability of marriage applicants to support their prior issue by preventing them from incurring new obligations, [the law is] so grossly underinclusive with respect to this objective, given the many ways that additional financial obligations may be incurred by the applicant quite apart from a contemplated marriage, that the classification 'does not bear a fair and substantial relation to the object of the legislation.' "

STEVENS, J., concurred: "Under this statute, a person's economic status may determine his eligibility to enter into a lawful marriage. A noncustodial parent whose children are 'public charges' may not marry even if he has met his court-ordered obligations. Thus, within the class of parents who have fulfilled their court-ordered obligations, the rich may marry and the poor may not. This type of statutory discrimination is, I believe, totally unprecedented, as well as inconsistent with our tradition of administering justice equally to the rich and to the poor."[9]

In TURNER v. SAFLEY, 482 U.S. 78 (1987), a unanimous Court, per O'CONNOR, J., ruled that the right to marry, deemed to be "a fundamental right" in *Loving* and *Zablocki*, remained so in the prison setting. Thus, it struck down a prison regulation that permitted inmates to marry only when the prison superintendent gave approval for "compelling reasons," which, in practice meant only "pregnancy or birth of a child." After recognizing that "the right to marry is subject to substantial restrictions as a result of incarceration," the Court went on: "Many important attributes of marriage remain, however, after taking into account the limitations imposed by prison life. First, inmate marriages, like others, are expressions of emotional support and public commitment. [In] addition, many religions recognize marriage as having spiritual significance. Third, most inmates eventually will be released [and] therefore most inmate marriages are formed in the expectation that they ultimately will be fully consummated. Finally, marital status often is a pre-condition to the receipt of government benefits, [property] rights, [and] other, less tangible, benefits (e.g., legitimation of children born out of wedlock). [Taken together], these remaining elements are sufficient to form a constitutionally protected marital relationship in the prison context."

In UNITED STATES v. WINDSOR, 570 U.S. 744 (2013), the Court, per KENNEDY, J., invalidated Section 3 of the Defense of Marriage Act, (DOMA) which, for federal purposes defined marriage as a union of a man and a woman even if state law recognized same-sex marriage. The decision rested on equal protection grounds, supplemented by federalism concerns: given the historical deference the federal government had accorded "to state-law policy decisions with respect to domestic relations," Congress's departure from that pattern was seen as evidence of the impermissible purpose of imposing "a stigma upon all who enter into same-sex marriages made lawful by the unquestioned authority of the States." The Court did not decide whether there is a constitutional right to state recognition of same-sex marriage, either as a matter of substantive due process or equal protection, but SCALIA, J., joined by Thomas, J., predicted in dissent that such recognition was "inevitable" in light of the majority's rationale.

---

[9]   Rehnquist, J., the sole dissenter, "view[ed] this legislative judgment in the light of the traditional presumption of validity." He concluded that the law, "despite its imperfections, is sufficiently rational to satisfy the demands of the Fourteenth Amendment."

OBERGEFELL V. HODGES

576 U.S. 644, 135 S.Ct. 2584, 192 L.Ed.2d 609 (2015).

JUSTICE KENNEDY delivered the opinion of the Court.

The Constitution promises liberty to all within its reach, a liberty that includes certain specific rights that allow persons, within a lawful realm, to define and express their identity. The petitioners in these cases seek to find that liberty by marrying someone of the same sex and having their marriages deemed lawful on the same terms and conditions as marriages between persons of the opposite sex.

I.   [The] petitioners are 14 same-sex couples and two men whose same-sex partners are deceased. The respondents are state officials responsible for enforcing the laws in question. The petitioners claim the respondents violate the Fourteenth Amendment by denying them the right to marry or to have their marriages, lawfully performed in another State, given full recognition.

II.   A. [From] their beginning to their most recent page, the annals of human history reveal the transcendent importance of marriage. The lifelong union of a man and a woman always has promised nobility and dignity to all persons, without regard to their station in life. Marriage is sacred to those who live by their religions and offers unique fulfillment to those who find meaning in the secular realm. Its dynamic allows two people to find a life that could not be found alone, for a marriage becomes greater than just the two persons. Rising from the most basic human needs, marriage is essential to our most profound hopes and aspirations.

[The] respondents say [it] would demean a timeless institution if the concept and lawful status of marriage were extended to two persons of the same sex. [Yet f]ar from seeking to devalue marriage, the petitioners seek it for themselves because of their respect—and need—for its privileges and responsibilities. And their immutable nature dictates that same-sex marriage is their only real path to this profound commitment.

B.   [Marriage]—even as confined to opposite-sex relations—has evolved over time. For example, marriage was once viewed as an arrangement by the couple's parents based on political, religious, and financial concerns; but by the time of the Nation's founding it was understood to be a voluntary contract between a man and a woman. As the role and status of women changed, the institution further evolved. Under the centuries-old doctrine of coverture, a married man and woman were treated by the State as a single, male-dominated legal entity. As women gained legal, political, and property rights, and as society began to understand that women have their own equal dignity, the law of coverture was abandoned. These and other developments in the institution of marriage over the past centuries were not mere superficial changes. Rather, they worked deep transformations in its structure, affecting aspects of marriage long viewed by many as essential.

[This] Court first gave detailed consideration to the legal status of homosexuals in *Bowers v. Hardwick.* There it upheld the constitutionality of a

Georgia law deemed to criminalize certain homosexual acts. Ten years later, in *Romer* [Ch. 9, Sec. 4, I], the Court invalidated an amendment to Colorado's Constitution that sought to foreclose any branch or political subdivision of the State from protecting persons against discrimination based on sexual orientation. Then, in 2003, the Court overruled *Bowers,* holding that laws making same-sex intimacy a crime "demea[n] the lives of homosexual persons." *Lawrence.* Two Terms ago, in *Windsor* this Court invalidated [the Defense of Marriage Act] to the extent it barred the Federal Government from treating same-sex marriages as valid even when they were lawful in the State where they were licensed. DOMA, the Court held, impermissibly disparaged those same-sex couples "who wanted to affirm their commitment to one another before their children, their family, their friends, and their community."

III. [The] right to marry is fundamental under the Due Process Clause. [It] cannot be denied that this Court's cases describing the right to marry presumed a relationship involving opposite-sex partners. The Court, like many institutions, has made assumptions defined by the world and time of which it is a part. Still, [i]n defining the right to marry [our] cases have identified essential attributes of that right based in history, tradition, and other constitutional liberties inherent in this intimate bond. And in assessing whether the force and rationale of its cases apply to same-sex couples, the Court must respect the basic reasons why the right to marry has been long protected. This analysis compels the conclusion that same-sex couples may exercise the right to marry. The four principles and traditions to be discussed demonstrate that the reasons marriage is fundamental under the Constitution apply with equal force to same-sex couples.

A first premise of the Court's relevant precedents is that the right to personal choice regarding marriage is inherent in the concept of individual autonomy. This abiding connection between marriage and liberty is why *Loving* invalidated interracial marriage bans under the Due Process Clause. [The] nature of marriage is that, through its enduring bond, two persons together can find other freedoms, such as expression, intimacy, and spirituality. This is true for all persons, whatever their sexual orientation.

[A] second principle in this Court's jurisprudence is that the right to marry is fundamental because it supports a two-person union unlike any other in its importance to the committed individuals. [Marriage] responds to the universal fear that a lonely person might call out only to find no one there. It offers the hope of companionship and understanding and assurance that while both still live there will be someone to care for the other. As this Court held in *Lawrence,* same-sex couples have the same right as opposite-sex couples to enjoy intimate association. *Lawrence* invalidated laws that made same-sex intimacy a criminal act. [But] while *Lawrence* confirmed a dimension of freedom that allows individuals to engage in intimate association without criminal liability, it does not follow that freedom stops there. Outlaw to outcast may be a step forward, but it does not achieve the full promise of liberty.

A third basis for protecting the right to marry is that it safeguards children and families and thus draws meaning from related rights of childrearing, procreation, and education. See *Pierce*; *Meyer*. [Under] the laws of the several States, some of marriage's protections for children and families are material. But marriage also confers more profound benefits. By giving recognition and legal structure to their parents' relationship, marriage allows children "to understand the integrity and closeness of their own family and its concord with other families in their community and in their daily lives." *Windsor*. Marriage also affords the permanency and stability important to children's best interests. As all parties agree, many same-sex couples provide loving and nurturing homes to their children, whether biological or adopted. And hundreds of thousands of children are presently being raised by such couples. Most States have allowed gays and lesbians to adopt, either as individuals or as couples, and many adopted and foster children have same-sex parents. This provides powerful confirmation from the law itself that gays and lesbians can create loving, supportive families. [The] marriage laws at issue here thus harm and humiliate the children of same-sex couples.

That is not to say the right to marry is less meaningful for those who do not or cannot have children. An ability, desire, or promise to procreate is not and has not been a prerequisite for a valid marriage in any State. In light of precedent protecting the right of a married couple not to procreate, it cannot be said the Court or the States have conditioned the right to marry on the capacity or commitment to procreate. The constitutional marriage right has many aspects, of which childbearing is only one.

Fourth and finally, this Court's cases and the Nation's traditions make clear that marriage is a keystone of our social order. [While] the States are in general free to vary the benefits they confer on all married couples, they have throughout our history made marriage the basis for an expanding list of governmental rights, benefits, and responsibilities, [including]: taxation; inheritance and property rights; rules of intestate succession; spousal privilege in the law of evidence; hospital access; medical decisionmaking authority; adoption rights; the rights and benefits of survivors; birth and death certificates; professional ethics rules; campaign finance restrictions; workers' compensation benefits; health insurance; and child custody, support, and visitation rules. [The] States have contributed to the fundamental character of the marriage right by placing that institution at the center of so many facets of the legal and social order.

There is no difference between same- and opposite-sex couples with respect to this principle. Yet by virtue of their exclusion from that institution, same-sex couples are denied the constellation of benefits that the States have linked to marriage. This harm results in more than just material burdens. Same-sex couples are consigned to an instability many opposite-sex couples would deem intolerable in their own lives. As the State itself makes marriage all the more precious by the significance it attaches to it, exclusion from that status has the effect of teaching that gays and lesbians are unequal in important respects. It demeans gays and lesbians for the State to lock them out of a central institution of the Nation's society. [Laws] excluding same-sex couples from the marriage right impose stigma and injury of the kind prohibited by our basic charter.

[Respondents invoke] *Glucksberg*, which called for a " 'careful description' " of fundamental rights. [*Glucksberg*] did insist that liberty under the Due Process Clause must be defined in a most circumscribed manner, with central reference to specific historical practices. Yet while that approach may have been appropriate for the asserted right there involved (physician-assisted suicide), it is inconsistent with the approach this Court has used in discussing other fundamental rights, including marriage and intimacy. *Loving* did not ask about a "right to interracial marriage"; *Turner* did not ask about a "right of inmates to marry"; and *Zablocki* did not ask about a "right of fathers with unpaid child support duties to marry." [If] rights were defined by who exercised them in the past, then received practices could serve as their own continued justification and new groups could not invoke rights once denied.

[Many] who deem same-sex marriage to be wrong reach that conclusion based on decent and honorable religious or philosophical premises, and neither they nor their beliefs are disparaged here. But when that sincere, personal opposition becomes enacted law and public policy, the necessary consequence is to put the imprimatur of the State itself on an exclusion that soon demeans or stigmatizes those whose own liberty is then denied.

[The] right of same-sex couples to marry that is part of the liberty promised by the Fourteenth Amendment is derived, too, from that Amendment's guarantee of the equal protection of the laws. The Due Process Clause and the Equal Protection Clause are connected in a profound way, though they set forth independent principles. Rights implicit in liberty and rights secured by equal protection may rest on different precepts and are not always co-extensive, yet in some instances each may be instructive as to the meaning and reach of the other. In any particular case one Clause may be thought to capture the essence of the right in a more accurate and comprehensive way, even as the two Clauses may converge in the identification and definition of the right. This interrelation of the two principles furthers our understanding of what freedom is and must become.

[In] interpreting the Equal Protection Clause, the Court has recognized that new insights and societal understandings can reveal unjustified inequality within our most fundamental institutions that once passed unnoticed and unchallenged. To take but one period, this occurred with respect to marriage in the 1970s and 1980s. Notwithstanding the gradual erosion of the doctrine of coverture, invidious sex-based classifications in marriage remained common through the mid-20th century. These classifications denied the equal dignity of men and women. One State's law, for example, provided in 1971 that "the husband is the head of the family and the wife is subject to him; her legal civil existence is merged in the husband, except so far as the law recognizes her separately, either for her own protection, or for her benefit." Ga.Code Ann. § 53–501 (1935). Responding to a new awareness, the Court invoked equal protection principles to invalidate laws imposing sex-based inequality on marriage. [Numerous citations omitted.] Like *Loving* and *Zablocki,* these precedents show the Equal Protection Clause can help to identify and correct inequalities in the institution of marriage, vindicating precepts of liberty and equality under the Constitution.

[This] dynamic also applies to same-sex marriage. It is now clear that the challenged laws burden the liberty of same-sex couples, and it must be further acknowledged that they abridge central precepts of equality. Here the marriage laws enforced by the respondents are in essence unequal: same-sex couples are denied all the benefits afforded to opposite-sex couples and are barred from exercising a fundamental right. Especially against a long history of disapproval of their relationships, this denial to same-sex couples of the right to marry works a grave and continuing harm.

[The] Court now holds that same-sex couples may exercise the fundamental right to marry. No longer may this liberty be denied to them. [T]he State laws challenged by Petitioners in these cases are now held invalid to the extent they exclude same-sex couples from civil marriage on the same terms and conditions as opposite-sex couples.

IV. [The] respondents warn there has been insufficient democratic discourse before deciding an issue so basic as the definition of marriage. [Yet] there has been far more deliberation than this argument acknowledges. There have been referenda, legislative debates, and grassroots campaigns, as well as countless studies, papers, books, and other popular and scholarly writings. There has been extensive litigation in state and federal courts. [An Appendix listed lower court cases.] Judicial opinions addressing the issue have been informed by the contentions of parties and counsel, which, in turn, reflect the more general, societal discussion of same-sex marriage and its meaning that has occurred over the past decades. [Ma]ny of the central institutions in American life—state and local governments, the military, large and small businesses, labor unions, religious organizations, law enforcement, civic groups, professional organizations, and universities—have devoted substantial attention to the question. This has led to an enhanced understanding of the issue—an understanding reflected in the arguments now presented for resolution as a matter of constitutional law.

The dynamic of our constitutional system is that individuals need not await legislative action before asserting a fundamental right. The Nation's courts are open to injured individuals who come to them to vindicate their own direct, personal stake in our basic charter. [It] is of no moment whether advocates of same-sex marriage now enjoy or lack momentum in the democratic process.

[The] respondents also argue allowing same-sex couples to wed will harm marriage as an institution by leading to fewer opposite-sex marriages. This may occur, the respondents contend, because licensing same-sex marriage severs the connection between natural procreation and marriage. That argument, however, rests on a counterintuitive view of opposite-sex couple's decisionmaking processes regarding marriage and parenthood. Decisions about whether to marry and raise children are based on many personal, romantic, and practical considerations; and it is unrealistic to conclude that an opposite-sex couple would choose not to marry simply because same-sex couples may do so.

[Finally], it must be emphasized that religions, and those who adhere to religious doctrines, may continue to advocate with utmost, sincere conviction that, by divine precepts, same-sex marriage should not be condoned. The First Amendment ensures that religious organizations and persons are given proper protection as they seek to teach the principles that are so fulfilling and so central to their lives and faiths, and to their own deep aspirations to continue the family structure they have long revered. The same is true of those who oppose same-sex marriage for other reasons. In turn, those who believe allowing same-sex marriage is proper or indeed essential, whether as a matter of religious conviction or secular belief, may engage those who disagree with their view in an open and searching debate. The Constitution, however, does not permit the State to bar same-sex couples from marriage on the same terms as accorded to couples of the opposite sex.

V. These cases also present the question whether the Constitution requires States to recognize same-sex marriages validly performed out of State. As made clear by the case of Obergefell and Arthur, and by that of DeKoe and Kostura, the recognition bans inflict substantial and continuing harm on same-sex couples. [The] Court, in this decision, holds same-sex couples may exercise the fundamental right to marry in all States. It follows that the Court also must hold—and it now does hold—that there is no lawful basis for a State to refuse to recognize a lawful same-sex marriage performed in another State on the ground of its same-sex character.

* * *

No union is more profound than marriage, for it embodies the highest ideals of love, fidelity, devotion, sacrifice, and family. In forming a marital union, two people become something greater than once they were. As some of the petitioners in these cases demonstrate, marriage embodies a love that may endure even past death. It would misunderstand these men and women to say they disrespect the idea of marriage. Their plea is that they do respect it, respect it so deeply that they seek to find its fulfillment for themselves. Their hope is not to be condemned to live in loneliness, excluded from one of civilization's oldest institutions. They ask for equal dignity in the eyes of the law. The Constitution grants them that right.

CHIEF JUSTICE ROBERTS, with whom JUSTICE SCALIA and JUSTICE THOMAS join, dissenting.

[Although] the policy arguments for extending marriage to same-sex couples may be compelling, the legal arguments for requiring such an extension are not. The fundamental right to marry does not include a right to make a State change its definition of marriage. And a State's decision to maintain the meaning of marriage that has persisted in every culture throughout human history can hardly be called irrational. In short, our Constitution does not enact any one theory of marriage. The people of a State are free to expand marriage to include same-sex couples, or to retain the historic definition.

Today, however, the Court takes the extraordinary step of ordering every State to license and recognize same-sex marriage. Many people will rejoice at this decision, and I begrudge none their celebration. But for those who believe in a government of laws, not of men, the majority's approach is deeply disheartening. Supporters of same-sex marriage have achieved considerable success persuading their fellow citizens—through the democratic process—to adopt their view. That ends today. Five lawyers have closed the debate and enacted their own vision of marriage as a matter of constitutional law. Stealing this issue from the people will for many cast a cloud over same-sex marriage, making a dramatic social change that much more difficult to accept.

[The] Court invalidates the marriage laws of more than half the States and orders the transformation of a social institution that has formed the basis of human society for millennia, for the Kalahari Bushmen and the Han Chinese, the Carthaginians and the Aztecs. Just who do we think we are?

It can be tempting for judges to confuse our own preferences with the requirements of the law. But as this Court has been reminded throughout our history, the Constitution "is made for people of fundamentally differing views." *Lochner v. New York* [Ch. 5, Sec. 2, I] (1905) (Holmes, J., dissenting). [The] majority today neglects that restrained conception of the judicial role. It seizes for itself a question the Constitution leaves to the people, at a time when the people are engaged in a vibrant debate on that question.

I.   [Petitioners] and their *amici* base their arguments on the "right to marry" and the imperative of "marriage equality." There is no serious dispute that, under our precedents, the Constitution protects a right to marry and requires States to apply their marriage laws equally. The real question in these cases is what constitutes "marriage," or—more precisely—*who decides* what constitutes "marriage"? The majority largely ignores these questions, relegating ages of human experience with marriage to a paragraph or two.

A.   [The] universal definition of marriage as the union of a man and a woman is no historical coincidence. Marriage did not come about as a result of a political movement, discovery, disease, war, religious doctrine, or any other moving force of world history—and certainly not as a result of a prehistoric decision to exclude gays and lesbians. It arose in the nature of things to meet a vital need: ensuring that children are conceived by a mother and father committed to raising them in the stable conditions of a lifelong relationship.

The premises supporting this concept of marriage are so fundamental that they rarely require articulation. The human race must procreate to survive. Procreation occurs through sexual relations between a man and a woman. When sexual relations result in the conception of a child, that child's prospects are generally better if the mother and father stay together rather than going their separate ways. Therefore, for the good of children and society, sexual relations that can lead to procreation should occur only between a man and a woman committed to a lasting bond. Society has recognized that bond as marriage. And by bestowing a respected status and material benefits on married couples, society encourages men and women to conduct sexual relations within marriage rather than without.

[This] singular understanding of marriage has prevailed in the United States throughout our history. [Early] Americans drew heavily on legal scholars like William Blackstone, who regarded marriage between "husband and wife" as one of the "great relations in private life," and philosophers like John Locke, who described marriage as "a voluntary compact between man and woman" centered on "its chief end, procreation" and the "nourishment and support" of children.

[As] the majority notes, some aspects of marriage have changed over time. Arranged marriages have largely given way to pairings based on romantic love. States have replaced coverture, the doctrine by which a married man and woman became a single legal entity, with laws that respect each participant's separate status. Racial restrictions on marriage, which "arose as an incident to slavery" to promote "White Supremacy," were repealed by many States and ultimately struck down by this Court. *Skinner*. [But] these developments [did not] work any transformation in the core structure of marriage as the union between a man and a woman. If you had asked a person on the street how marriage was defined, no one would ever have said, "Marriage is the union of a man and a woman, where the woman is subject to coverture." The majority may be right that the "history of marriage is one of both continuity and change," but the core meaning of marriage has endured.

II.   [The] majority purports to identify four "principles and traditions" in this Court's due process precedents that support a fundamental right for same-sex couples to marry. In reality, however, the majority's approach has no basis in principle or tradition, except for the unprincipled tradition of judicial policymaking that characterized discredited decisions such as *Lochner*.

A.   [To] avoid repeating *Lochner*'s error of converting personal preferences into constitutional mandates, our modern substantive due process cases have stressed the need for "judicial self-restraint." *Collins v. Harker Heights*, 503 U.S. 115 (1992). Our precedents have required that implied fundamental rights be "objectively, deeply rooted in this Nation's history and tradition," and "implicit in the concept of ordered liberty, such that neither liberty nor justice would exist if they were sacrificed." *Glucksberg*. Although the Court articulated the importance of history and tradition to the fundamental rights inquiry most precisely in *Glucksberg*, many other cases both before and after have adopted the same approach.

Proper reliance on history and tradition of course requires looking beyond the individual law being challenged, so that every restriction on liberty does not supply its own constitutional justification. The Court is right about that. But given the few "guideposts for responsible decisionmaking in this unchartered area," *Collins*, "an approach grounded in history imposes limits on the judiciary that are more meaningful than any based on [an] abstract formula." *Moore.*

B.   The majority acknowledges none of this doctrinal background, and it is easy to see why: Its aggressive application of substantive due process breaks sharply with decades of precedent and returns the Court to the unprincipled approach of *Lochner*.

1.   [Prior] cases do not hold, of course, that anyone who wants to get married has a constitutional right to do so. They instead require a State to justify barriers to marriage as that institution has always been understood. In *Loving,* the Court held that racial restrictions on the right to marry lacked a compelling justification. In *Zablocki,* restrictions based on child support debts did not suffice. In *Turner,* restrictions based on status as a prisoner were deemed impermissible.

None of the laws at issue in those cases purported to change the core definition of marriage as the union of a man and a woman. The laws challenged in *Zablocki* and *Turner* did not define marriage as "the union of a man and a woman, *where neither party owes child support or is in prison.*" Nor did the interracial marriage ban at issue in *Loving* define marriage as "the union of a man and a woman *of the same race.*" Removing racial barriers to marriage therefore did not change what a marriage was any more than integrating schools changed what a school was. As the majority admits, the institution of "marriage" discussed in every one of these cases "presumed a relationship involving opposite-sex partners." In short, the "right to marry" cases stand for the important but limited proposition that particular restrictions on access to marriage *as traditionally defined* violate due process. These precedents say nothing at all about a right to make a State change its definition of marriage, which is the right petitioners actually seek here.

2.   [Neither] *Lawrence* nor any other precedent in the privacy line of cases supports the right that petitioners assert here. Unlike criminal laws banning contraceptives and sodomy, the marriage laws at issue here involve no government intrusion. They create no crime and impose no punishment. Same-sex couples remain free to live together, to engage in intimate conduct, and to raise their families as they see fit. No one is "condemned to live in loneliness" by the laws challenged in these cases—no one. At the same time, [the] privacy cases provide no support for the majority's position, because petitioners do not seek privacy. Quite the opposite, they seek public recognition of their relationships, along with corresponding government benefits.

3.   [One] immediate question invited by the majority's position is whether States may retain the definition of marriage as a union of two people. Although the majority randomly inserts the adjective "two" in various places, it offers no reason at all why the two-person element of the core definition of marriage may be preserved while the man-woman element may not. Indeed, from the standpoint of history and tradition, a leap from opposite-sex marriage to same-sex marriage is much greater than one from a two-person union to plural unions, which have deep roots in some cultures around the world. If the majority is willing to take the big

leap, it is hard to see how it can say no to the shorter one. It is striking how much of the majority's reasoning would apply with equal force to the claim of a fundamental right to plural marriage. [I] do not mean to equate marriage between same-sex couples with plural marriages in all respects. There may well be relevant differences that compel different legal analysis. But if there are, petitioners have not pointed to any.

III. In addition to their due process argument, petitioners contend that the Equal Protection Clause requires their States to license and recognize same-sex marriages. [Yet] the majority fails to provide even a single sentence explaining how the Equal Protection Clause supplies independent weight for its position. [In] any event, the marriage laws at issue here do not violate the Equal Protection Clause, because distinguishing between opposite-sex and same-sex couples is rationally related to the States' "legitimate state interest" in "preserving the traditional institution of marriage." *Lawrence* (O'Connor, J., concurring in judgment).

[The] equal protection analysis might be different, in my view, if we were confronted with a more focused challenge to the denial of certain tangible benefits. Of course, those more selective claims will not arise now that the Court has taken the drastic step of requiring every State to license and recognize marriages between same-sex couples.

IV. Nowhere is the majority's extravagant conception of judicial supremacy more evident than in its description—and dismissal—of the public debate regarding same-sex marriage. Yes, the majority concedes, on one side are thousands of years of human history in every society known to have populated the planet. But on the other side, there has been "extensive litigation," "many thoughtful District Court decisions," "countless studies, papers, books, and other popular and scholarly writings," and "more than 100" *amicus* briefs in these cases alone. What would be the point of allowing the democratic process to go on? It is high time for the Court to decide the meaning of marriage, based on five lawyers' "better informed understanding" of "a liberty that remains urgent in our own era." The answer is surely there in one of those *amicus* briefs or studies.

[By] deciding this question under the Constitution, the Court removes it from the realm of democratic decision. There will be consequences to shutting down the political process on an issue of such profound public significance. Closing debate tends to close minds. People denied a voice are less likely to accept the ruling of a court on an issue that does not seem to be the sort of thing courts usually decide. [H]owever heartened the proponents of same-sex marriage might be on this day, it is worth acknowledging what they have lost, and lost forever: the opportunity to win the true acceptance that comes from persuading their fellow citizens of the justice of their cause. And they lose this just when the winds of change were freshening at their backs.

[Respect] for sincere religious conviction has led voters and legislators in every State that has adopted same-sex marriage democratically to include accommodations for religious practice. The majority's decision imposing same-sex marriage cannot, of course, create any such accommodations. The majority graciously suggests that religious believers may continue to "advocate" and "teach" their views of marriage. The First Amendment guarantees, however, the freedom to "*exercise*" religion. Ominously, that is not a word the majority uses.

* * *

[If] you are among the many Americans—of whatever sexual orientation—who favor expanding same-sex marriage, by all means celebrate today's decision. Celebrate the achievement of a desired goal. Celebrate the opportunity for a new expression of commitment to a partner. Celebrate the availability of new benefits. But do not celebrate the Constitution. It had nothing to do with it.

JUSTICE SCALIA, with whom JUSTICE THOMAS joins, dissenting.

[When] the Fourteenth Amendment was ratified in 1868, every State limited marriage to one man and one woman, and no one doubted the constitutionality of doing so. That resolves these cases. When it comes to determining the meaning of a vague constitutional provision—such as "due process of law" or "equal protection of the laws"—it is unquestionable that the People who ratified that provision did not understand it to prohibit a practice that remained both universal and uncontroversial in the years after ratification. We have no basis for striking down a practice that is not expressly prohibited by the Fourteenth Amendment's text, and that bears the endorsement of a long tradition of open, widespread, and unchallenged use dating back to the Amendment's ratification. Since there is no doubt whatever that the People never decided to prohibit the limitation of marriage to opposite-sex couples, the public debate over same-sex marriage must be allowed to continue.

[Hubris] is sometimes defined as o'erweening pride; and pride, we know, goeth before a fall. The Judiciary is the "least dangerous" of the federal branches because it has "neither Force nor Will, but merely judgment; and must ultimately depend upon the aid of the executive arm" and the States, "even for the efficacy of its judgments."[26] With each decision of ours that takes from the People a question properly left to them—with each decision that is unabashedly based not on law, but on the "reasoned judgment" of a bare majority of this Court—we move one step closer to being reminded of our impotence.

JUSTICE THOMAS, with whom JUSTICE SCALIA joins, dissenting.

[In] the American legal tradition, liberty has long been understood as individual freedom *from* governmental action, not as a right *to* a particular governmental entitlement. [The] founding-era idea of civil liberty as natural liberty constrained by human law necessarily involved only those freedoms that existed *outside of* government.

[Petitioners] cannot claim [that] the States have restricted their ability to go about their daily lives as they would be able to absent governmental restrictions.

---

[26]   [Ct's Note] *The Federalist* No. 78 (A. Hamilton).

Petitioners do not ask this Court to order the States to stop restricting their ability to enter same-sex relationships, to engage in intimate behavior, to make vows to their partners in public ceremonies, to engage in religious wedding ceremonies, to hold themselves out as married, or to raise children. The States have imposed no such restrictions. Nor have the States prevented petitioners from approximating a number of incidents of marriage through private legal means, such as wills, trusts, and powers of attorney.

Instead, the States have refused to grant them governmental entitlements. Petitioners claim that as a matter of "liberty," they are entitled to access privileges and benefits that exist solely *because of* the government. [But] receiving governmental recognition and benefits has nothing to do with any understanding of "liberty" that the Framers would have recognized.

JUSTICE ALITO, with whom JUSTICE SCALIA and JUSTICE THOMAS join, dissenting.

[Today], more than 40% of all children in this country are born to unmarried women. This development undoubtedly is both a cause and a result of changes in our society's understanding of marriage. While, for many, the attributes of marriage in 21st-century America have changed, those States that do not want to recognize same-sex marriage have not yet given up on the traditional understanding. They worry that by officially abandoning the older understanding, they may contribute to marriage's further decay. It is far beyond the outer reaches of this Court's authority to say that a State may not adhere to the understanding of marriage that has long prevailed, not just in this country and others with similar cultural roots, but also in a great variety of countries and cultures all around the globe.

[Today's decision] will be used to vilify Americans who are unwilling to assent to the new orthodoxy. In the course of its opinion, the majority compares traditional marriage laws to laws that denied equal treatment for African-Americans and women. The implications of this analogy will be exploited by those who are determined to stamp out every vestige of dissent. Perhaps recognizing how its reasoning may be used, the majority attempts, toward the end of its opinion, to reassure those who oppose same-sex marriage that their rights of conscience will be protected. We will soon see whether this proves to be true. I assume that those who cling to old beliefs will be able to whisper their thoughts in the recesses of their homes, but if they repeat those views in public, they will risk being labeled as bigots and treated as such by governments, employers, and schools.

6. THE RIGHT TO KEEP AND BEAR ARMS

DISTRICT OF COLUMBIA V. HELLER

554 U.S. 570, 128 S.Ct. 2783, 171 L.Ed.2d 637 (2008).

JUSTICE SCALIA delivered the opinion of the Court.

[The] District of Columbia generally prohibits the possession of handguns. It is a crime to carry an unregistered firearm, and the registration of handguns is prohibited. Wholly apart from that prohibition, no person may carry a handgun without a license, but the chief of police may issue licenses for 1-year periods. District of Columbia law also requires residents to keep their lawfully owned firearms, such as registered long guns, "unloaded and disassembled or bound by a trigger lock or similar device" unless they are located in a place of business or are being used for lawful recreational activities.

Respondent Dick Heller is a D.C. special police officer authorized to carry a handgun while on duty. [He] applied for a registration certificate for a handgun that he wished to keep at home, but the District refused. He [sued,] seeking, on Second Amendment grounds, to enjoin the city from enforcing the bar on the registration of handguns, the licensing requirement insofar as it prohibits the carrying of a firearm in the home without a license, and the trigger-lock requirement insofar as it prohibits the use of "functional firearms within the home."

[The] Second Amendment provides: "A well regulated Militia, being necessary to the security of a free State, the right of the people to keep and bear Arms, shall not be infringed." In interpreting this text, we are guided by the principle that "[t]he Constitution was written to be understood by the voters; its words and phrases were used in their normal and ordinary as distinguished from technical meaning."

[The] two sides in this case have set out very different interpretations of the Amendment. Petitioners and today's dissenting Justices believe that it protects only the right to possess and carry a firearm in connection with militia service. Respondent argues that it protects an individual right to possess a firearm unconnected with service in a militia, and to use that arm for traditionally lawful purposes, such as self-defense within the home.

The Second Amendment is naturally divided into two parts: its prefatory clause and its operative clause. The former does not limit the latter grammatically, but rather announces a purpose. [Although] this structure of the Second Amendment is unique in our Constitution, other legal documents of the founding era, particularly individual-rights provisions of state constitutions, commonly included a prefatory statement of purpose.

[Putting] all of [the Second Amendment's] textual elements together, we find that they guarantee the individual right to possess and carry weapons in case of confrontation. This meaning is strongly confirmed by the historical background of the Second Amendment. We look to this because it has always been widely understood that the Second Amendment, like the First and Fourth Amendments, codified a *pre-existing* right. The very text of the Second Amendment implicitly recognizes the pre-existence of the right and declares only that it "shall not be infringed."

[By] the time of the founding, the right to have arms had become fundamental for English subjects. Blackstone, whose works, we have said, "constituted the preeminent authority on English law for the founding generation," cited the arms provision of the Bill of Rights as one of the fundamental rights of Englishmen. His description of it cannot possibly be thought to tie it to militia or military service. It was, he said, "the natural right of resistance and self-preservation," and "the right of having and using arms for self-preservation and defence[.]" Other contemporary authorities concurred.

[There] seems to us no doubt, on the basis of both text and history, that the Second Amendment conferred an individual right to keep and bear arms. Of course the right was not unlimited, just as the First Amendment's right of free speech was not. Thus, we do not read the Second Amendment to protect the right of citizens to carry arms for *any sort* of confrontation, just as we do not read the First Amendment to protect the right of citizens to speak for *any purpose*.

[Does] the preface fit with an operative clause that creates an individual right to keep and bear arms? It fits perfectly, once one knows the history that the founding generation knew and that we have described above. That history showed that the way tyrants had eliminated a militia consisting of all the able-bodied men was not by banning the militia but simply by taking away the people's arms, enabling a select militia or standing army to suppress political opponents. This is what had occurred in England that prompted codification of the right to have arms in the English Bill of Rights.

The debate with respect to the right to keep and bear arms, as with other guarantees in the Bill of Rights, was not over whether it was desirable (all agreed that it was) but over whether it needed to be codified in the Constitution. During the 1788 ratification debates, the fear that the federal government would disarm the people in order to impose rule through a standing army or select militia was pervasive in Antifederalist rhetoric. [It] was understood across the political spectrum that the right helped to secure the ideal of a citizen militia, which might be necessary to oppose an oppressive military force if the constitutional order broke down. It is therefore entirely sensible that the Second Amendment's prefatory clause announces the purpose for which the right was codified: to prevent elimination of the militia. The prefatory clause does not suggest that preserving the militia was the only reason Americans valued the ancient right; most undoubtedly thought it even more important for self-defense and hunting. But the threat that the new Federal Government would destroy the citizens' militia by taking away their arms was the reason that right—unlike some other English rights—was codified in a written Constitution.

[Justice] Stevens places overwhelming reliance upon this Court's decision in *United States v. Miller*, 307 U.S. 174 (1939). [According to Justice Stevens, *Miller* holds that] the Second Amendment "protects the right to keep and bear arms for certain military purposes, but [it] does not curtail the legislature's power to regulate the nonmilitary use and ownership of weapons."

[But] *Miller* did not hold that and cannot possibly be read to have held that. [It] upheld against a Second Amendment challenge two men's federal convictions for transporting an unregistered short-barreled shotgun [in] violation of the National Firearms Act. It is entirely clear that the Court's basis for saying that the Second Amendment did not apply was [that] the *type of weapon at issue* was not eligible for Second Amendment protection. [We] read *Miller* to say only that the Second Amendment does not protect those weapons not typically possessed by law-abiding citizens for lawful purposes, such as short-barreled shotguns. That accords with the historical understanding of the scope of the right.

In the aftermath of the Civil War, there was an outpouring of discussion of the Second Amendment in Congress and in public discourse, as people debated whether and how to secure constitutional rights for newly free slaves. Since those discussions took place 75 years after the ratification of the Second Amendment, they do not provide as much insight into its original meaning as earlier sources. Yet those born and educated in the early 19th century faced a widespread effort to limit arms ownership by a large number of citizens; their understanding of the origins and continuing significance of the Amendment is instructive.

Blacks were routinely disarmed by Southern States after the Civil War. Those who opposed these injustices frequently stated that they infringed blacks' constitutional rights to keep and bear arms. Needless to say, the claim was not that blacks were being prohibited from carrying arms in an organized state militia. [It] was plainly the understanding in the post-Civil War Congress that the Second Amendment protected an individual right to use arms for self-defense.

[Like] most rights, the right secured by the Second Amendment is not unlimited. [For] example, the majority of the 19th-century courts to consider the question held that prohibitions on carrying concealed weapons were lawful under the Second Amendment or state analogues. Although we do not undertake an exhaustive historical analysis today of the full scope of the Second Amendment, nothing in our opinion should be taken to cast doubt on longstanding prohibitions on the possession of firearms by felons and the mentally ill, or laws forbidding the carrying of firearms in sensitive places such as schools and government buildings, or laws imposing conditions and qualifications on the commercial sale of arms.[26]

We also recognize another important limitation on the right to keep and carry arms. *Miller* said [that] the sorts of weapons protected were those "in common use

---

[26] **[Ct's Note]** We identify these presumptively lawful regulatory measures only as examples; our list does not purport to be exhaustive.

at the time." We think that limitation is fairly supported by the historical tradition of prohibiting the carrying of "dangerous and unusual weapons."

[It] may be objected that if weapons that are most useful in military service— M-16 rifles and the like—may be banned, then the Second Amendment right is completely detached from the prefatory clause. But as we have said, the conception of the militia at the time of the Second Amendment's ratification was the body of all citizens capable of military service, who would bring the sorts of lawful weapons that they possessed at home to militia duty. It may well be true today that a militia, to be as effective as militias in the 18th century, would require sophisticated arms that are highly unusual in society at large. Indeed, it may be true that no amount of small arms could be useful against modern-day bombers and tanks. But the fact that modern developments have limited the degree of fit between the prefatory clause and the protected right cannot change our interpretation of the right.

We turn finally to the law at issue here. [The] inherent right of self-defense has been central to the Second Amendment right. The handgun ban amounts to a prohibition of an entire class of "arms" that is overwhelmingly chosen by American society for that lawful purpose. The prohibition extends, moreover, to the home, where the need for defense of self, family, and property is most acute. Under any of the standards of scrutiny that we have applied to enumerated constitutional rights,[27] banning from the home "the most preferred firearm in the nation to 'keep' and use for protection of one's home and family" would fail constitutional muster.

[It] is no answer to say, as petitioners do, that it is permissible to ban the possession of handguns so long as the possession of other firearms (i.e., long guns) is allowed. It is enough to note [that] the American people have considered the handgun to be the quintessential self-defense weapon. There are many reasons that a citizen may prefer a handgun for home defense: It is easier to store in a location that is readily accessible in an emergency; it cannot easily be redirected or wrestled away by an attacker; it is easier to use for those without the upper-body strength to lift and aim a long gun; it can be pointed at a burglar with one hand while the other hand dials the police. Whatever the reason, handguns are the most popular weapon chosen by Americans for self-defense in the home, and a complete prohibition of their use is invalid.

We must also address the District's requirement (as applied to respondent's handgun) that firearms in the home be rendered and kept inoperable at all times. This makes it impossible for citizens to use them for the core lawful purpose of self-defense and is hence unconstitutional.

[Justice Breyer] criticizes us for declining to establish a level of scrutiny for evaluating Second Amendment restrictions. He proposes, explicitly at least, none of the traditionally expressed levels (strict scrutiny, intermediate scrutiny, rational

---

[27]   [Ct's Note] Justice Breyer correctly notes that this law, like almost all laws, would pass rational-basis scrutiny. But [if] all that was required to overcome the right to keep and bear arms was a rational basis, the Second Amendment would be redundant with the separate constitutional prohibitions on irrational laws, and would have no effect.

basis), but rather a judge-empowering "interest-balancing inquiry" that "asks whether the statute burdens a protected interest in a way or to an extent that is out of proportion to the statute's salutary effects upon other important governmental interests." [Justice] Breyer arrives at his interest-balanced answer: because handgun violence is a problem, because the law is limited to an urban area, and because there were somewhat similar restrictions in the founding period (a false proposition that we have already discussed), the interest-balancing inquiry results in the constitutionality of the handgun ban. QED.

We know of no other enumerated constitutional right whose core protection has been subjected to a freestanding "interest-balancing" approach. The very enumeration of the right takes out of the hands of government—even the Third Branch of Government—the power to decide on a case-by-case basis whether the right is *really worth* insisting upon. A constitutional guarantee subject to future judges' assessments of its usefulness is no constitutional guarantee at all. [We] would not apply an "interest-balancing" approach to the prohibition of a peaceful neo-Nazi march through Skokie. See [*Collin v. Smith*, Ch. 7, Sec. 2, I]. The First Amendment contains the freedom-of-speech guarantee that the people ratified, which included exceptions for obscenity, libel, and disclosure of state secrets, but not for the expression of extremely unpopular and wrong-headed views. The Second Amendment is no different. Like the First, it is the very *product* of an interest-balancing by the people—which Justice Breyer would now conduct for them anew.

[We] are aware of the problem of handgun violence in this country, and we take seriously the concerns raised by [many] who believe that prohibition of handgun ownership is a solution. The Constitution leaves the District of Columbia a variety of tools for combating that problem, including some measures regulating handguns. But the enshrinement of constitutional rights necessarily takes certain policy choices off the table. These include the absolute prohibition of handguns held and used for self-defense in the home. Undoubtedly some think that the Second Amendment is outmoded in a society where our standing army is the pride of our Nation, where well-trained police forces provide personal security, and where gun violence is a serious problem. That is perhaps debatable, but what is not debatable is that it is not the role of this Court to pronounce the Second Amendment extinct.

JUSTICE STEVENS, with whom JUSTICE SOUTER, JUSTICE GINSBURG, and JUSTICE BREYER join, dissenting.

The question presented by this case is not whether the Second Amendment protects a "collective right" or an "individual right." Surely it protects a right that can be enforced by individuals. But a conclusion that the Second Amendment protects an individual right does not tell us anything about the scope of that right.

Guns are used to hunt, for self-defense, to commit crimes, for sporting activities, and to perform military duties. The Second Amendment plainly does not protect the right to use a gun to rob a bank; it is equally clear that it *does* encompass the right to use weapons for certain military purposes. Whether it also protects the right to possess and use guns for nonmilitary purposes like hunting and personal self-defense is the question presented by this case. The text of the Amendment, its history, and our decision in *United States* v. *Miller*, provide a clear answer to that question.

The Second Amendment was adopted to protect the right of the people of each of the several States to maintain a well-regulated militia. It was a response to concerns raised during the ratification of the Constitution that the power of Congress to disarm the state militias and create a national standing army posed an intolerable threat to the sovereignty of the several States. Neither the text of the Amendment nor the arguments advanced by its proponents evidenced the slightest interest in limiting any legislature's authority to regulate private civilian uses of firearms. Specifically, there is no indication that the Framers of the Amendment intended to enshrine the common-law right of self-defense in the Constitution. [The] view of the Amendment we took in *Miller*—that it protects the right to keep and bear arms for certain military purposes, but that it does not curtail the Legislature's power to regulate the nonmilitary use and ownership of weapons—is both the most natural reading of the Amendment's text and the interpretation most faithful to the history of its adoption.

[The] Court concludes its opinion by declaring that it is not the proper role of this Court to change the meaning of rights "enshrine[d]" in the Constitution. But the right the Court announces was not "enshrined" in the Second Amendment by the Framers; it is the product of today's law-changing decision. * * *

JUSTICE BREYER, with whom JUSTICE STEVENS, JUSTICE SOUTER, and JUSTICE GINSBURG join, dissenting.

[The] majority's conclusion is wrong for two independent reasons. The first reason is that set forth by Justice Stevens—namely, that the Second Amendment protects militia-related, not self-defense-related, interests. These two interests are sometimes intertwined. To assure 18th-century citizens that they could keep arms for militia purposes would necessarily have allowed them to keep arms that they could have used for self-defense as well. But self-defense alone, detached from any militia-related objective, is not the Amendment's concern.

The second independent reason is that the protection the Amendment provides is not absolute. [The] District's law is consistent with the Second Amendment even if that Amendment is interpreted as protecting a wholly separate interest in individual self-defense. That is so because the District's regulation, which focuses upon the presence of handguns in high-crime urban areas, represents a permissible legislative response to a serious, indeed life-threatening, problem.

[T]he law is tailored to the urban crime problem in that it is local in scope and thus affects only a geographic area both limited in size and entirely urban; the law concerns handguns, which are specially linked to urban gun deaths and injuries, and which are the overwhelmingly favorite weapon of armed criminals; and at the same time, the law imposes a burden upon gun owners that seems proportionately no greater than restrictions in existence at the time the Second Amendment was adopted. In these circumstances, the District's law falls within the zone that the Second Amendment leaves open to regulation by legislatures.

[Respondent] proposes that the Court adopt a "strict scrutiny" test, which would require reviewing with care each gun law to determine whether it is "narrowly tailored to achieve a compelling governmental interest." But the majority implicitly, and appropriately, rejects that suggestion by broadly approving a set of laws—prohibitions on concealed weapons, forfeiture by criminals of the Second Amendment right, prohibitions on firearms in certain locales, and governmental regulation of commercial firearm sales—whose constitutionality under a strict scrutiny standard would be far from clear.

[I] would simply adopt [an] interest-balancing inquiry explicitly. The fact that important interests lie on both sides of the constitutional equation suggests that review of gun-control regulation is not a context in which a court should effectively presume either constitutionality (as in rational-basis review) or unconstitutionality (as in strict scrutiny). Rather, "where a law significantly implicates competing constitutionally protected interests in complex ways," the Court generally asks whether the statute burdens a protected interest in a way or to an extent that is out of proportion to the statute's salutary effects upon other important governmental interests. Any answer would take account both of the statute's effects upon the competing interests and the existence of any clearly superior less restrictive alternative. Contrary to the majority's unsupported suggestion that this sort of "proportionality" approach is unprecedented, the Court has applied it in various constitutional contexts, including election-law cases, speech cases, and due process cases.

[A]ny self-defense interest at the time of the Framing could not have focused exclusively upon urban-crime related dangers. Two hundred years ago, most Americans, many living on the frontier, would likely have thought of self-defense primarily in terms of outbreaks of fighting with Indian tribes, rebellions, [marauders], and crime-related dangers to travelers on the roads, on footpaths, or along waterways.

[Nor,] for that matter, am I aware of any evidence that *handguns* in particular were central to the Framers' conception of the Second Amendment. The lists of militia-related weapons in the late 18th-century state statutes appear primarily to refer to other sorts of weapons, muskets in particular.

[A] contrary view, as embodied in today's decision, will have unfortunate consequences. The decision will encourage legal challenges to gun regulation throughout the Nation. Because it says little about the standards used to evaluate regulatory decisions, it will leave the Nation without clear standards for resolving those challenges. And litigation over the course of many years, or the mere specter of such litigation, threatens to leave cities without effective protection against gun violence and accidents during that time.

[I] can understand how reasonable individuals can disagree about the merits of strict gun control as a crime-control measure, even in a totally urbanized area.

But I cannot understand how one can take from the elected branches of government the right to decide whether to insist upon a handgun-free urban populace in a city now facing a serious crime problem and which, in the future, could well face environmental or other emergencies that threaten the breakdown of law and order.

[The] majority says that that Amendment protects those weapons "typically possessed by law-abiding citizens for lawful purposes." This definition conveniently excludes machineguns, but permits handguns, which the majority describes as "the most popular weapon chosen by Americans for self-defense in the home." But what sense does this approach make? [On] the majority's reasoning, if tomorrow someone invents a particularly useful, highly dangerous self-defense weapon, Congress and the States had better ban it immediately, for once it becomes popular Congress will no longer possess the constitutional authority to do so. In essence, the majority determines what regulations are permissible by looking to see what existing regulations permit. There is no basis for believing that the Framers intended such circular reasoning.

[I] conclude that the District's measure is a proportionate, not a disproportionate, response to the compelling concerns that led the District to adopt it. * * *

McDONALD V. CITY OF CHICAGO

561 U.S. 742, 130 S.Ct. 3020, 177 L.Ed.2d 894 (2010).

JUSTICE ALITO announced the judgment of the Court and delivered the opinion of the Court with respect to Parts I, II-A, II-B, II-D, III-A, and III-B, in which THE CHIEF JUSTICE, JUSTICE SCALIA, JUSTICE KENNEDY, and JUSTICE THOMAS, join, and an opinion with respect to Parts II-C, IV, and V, in which THE CHIEF JUSTICE, JUSTICE SCALIA and JUSTICE KENNEDY, join.

Two years ago, in *Heller*, we held that the Second Amendment protects the right to keep and bear arms for the purpose of self-defense, and we struck down a District of Columbia law that banned the possession of handguns in the home. The city of Chicago (City) and the village of Oak Park, a Chicago suburb, have laws that are similar to the District of Columbia's, but Chicago and Oak Park argue that their laws are constitutional because the Second Amendment has no application to the States. We have previously held that most of the provisions of the Bill of Rights apply with full force to both the Federal Government and the States. Applying the standard that is well established in our case law, we hold that the Second Amendment right is fully applicable to the States.

[II-B.] Today, many legal scholars dispute the correctness of the narrow *Slaughter-House* interpretation.

[II-C.] For many decades, the question of the rights protected by the Fourteenth Amendment against state infringement has been analyzed under the Due Process Clause of that Amendment and not under the Privileges or Immunities Clause. We therefore decline to disturb the *Slaughter-House* holding.

[II-D. Nearly all provisions of the Bill of Rights have been "incorporated" in a way that provides the same level of protection against the states as they provide against the federal government. See p. 420 supra. The relevant inquiry is] whether a particular Bill of Rights guarantee is fundamental to *our* scheme of ordered liberty and system of justice.

[III.] With this framework in mind, we now turn directly to the question whether the Second Amendment right to keep and bear arms is incorporated in the concept of due process. In answering that question [we] must decide whether the right to keep and bear arms is fundamental to *our* scheme of ordered liberty, *Duncan* [or] whether this right is "deeply rooted in this Nation's history and tradition." *Washington v. Glucksberg* [p. 484 supra].

A.   Our decision in *Heller* points unmistakably to the answer. Self-defense is a basic right, recognized by many legal systems from ancient times to the present day, and in *Heller*, we held that individual self defense is "the *central component*" of the Second Amendment right [and] "deeply rooted" in the Nation's history and tradition.

[B.] [After] the Civil War, many of the over 180,000 African Americans who served in the Union Army returned to the States of the old Confederacy, where systematic efforts were made to disarm them and other blacks. [Union] Army commanders took steps to secure the rights of all citizens to keep and bear arms, but the 39th Congress concluded that legislative action was necessary. Its efforts to safeguard the right to keep and bear arms demonstrate that the right was still recognized to be fundamental.

[The] Civil Rights Act of 1866, which was considered at the same time as the Freedmen's Bureau Act, [sought] to protect the right of all citizens to keep and bear arms. [The] unavoidable conclusion is that the Civil Rights Act, like the Freedmen's Bureau Act, aimed to protect "the constitutional right to bear arms" and not simply to prohibit discrimination. [Congress], however, ultimately deemed these legislative remedies insufficient. Southern resistance, Presidential vetoes, and this Court's pre-Civil-War precedent persuaded Congress that a constitutional amendment was necessary to provide full protection for the rights of blacks. Today, it is generally accepted that the Fourteenth Amendment was understood to provide a constitutional basis for protecting the rights set out in the Civil Rights Act of 1866.

[Despite] all this evidence, municipal respondents contend that Congress, in the years immediately following the Civil War, merely sought to outlaw "discriminatory measures taken against freedmen, which it addressed by adopting a non-discrimination principle" and that even an outright ban on the possession of firearms was regarded as acceptable, "so long as it was not done in a discriminatory manner." [This] argument is implausible.

[IV.] [Municipal] respondents, in effect, ask us to treat the right recognized in *Heller* as a second-class right, subject to an entirely different body of rules than the other Bill of Rights guarantees that we have held to be incorporated into the Due Process Clause.

Municipal respondents' main argument is nothing less than a plea to disregard 50 years of incorporation precedent and return (presumably for this case only) to a bygone era. [According] to municipal respondents, if it is possible to imagine *any* civilized legal system that does not recognize a particular right, then the Due Process Clause does not make that right binding on the States. Therefore, [because many countries] either ban or severely limit handgun ownership, it must follow that no right to possess such weapons is protected by the Fourteenth Amendment.

This line of argument is, of course, inconsistent with the long-established standard we apply in incorporation cases. And the present-day implications of [this] argument are stunning. For example, many of the rights that our Bill of Rights provides for persons accused of criminal offenses are virtually unique to this country. If *our* understanding of the right to a jury trial, the right against self-incrimination, and the right to counsel were necessary attributes of *any* civilized country, it would follow that the United States is the only civilized Nation in the world.

[Municipal] respondents maintain that the Second Amendment differs from all of the other provisions of the Bill of Rights because it concerns the right to possess a deadly implement and thus has implications for public safety. [But this] is not the only constitutional right that has controversial public safety implications. All of the constitutional provisions that impose restrictions on law enforcement and on the prosecution of crimes fall into the same category.

JUSTICE THOMAS, concurring in part and concurring in the judgment.

I agree with the Court that the Fourteenth Amendment makes the right to keep and bear arms set forth in the Second Amendment "fully applicable to the States." I write separately because I believe there is a more straightforward path to this conclusion, one that is more faithful to the Fourteenth Amendment's text and history.

[I] cannot agree that the [Second Amendment] is enforceable against the States through a clause that speaks only to "process." Instead, the right to keep and bear arms is a privilege of American citizenship that applies to the States through the Fourteenth Amendment's Privileges or Immunities Clause.

[The] notion that a constitutional provision that guarantees only "process" before a person is deprived of life, liberty or property could define the substance of [unenumerated] rights strains credulity for even the most casual user of words. Moreover, this fiction is a particularly dangerous one. The one theme that links the Court's substantive due process precedents together is their lack of a guiding principle to distinguish "fundamental" rights that warrant protection from nonfundamental rights that do not. Today's decision illustrates the point. Replaying a debate that has endured from the inception of the Court's substantive due process jurisprudence, the dissent lauds the "flexibility" in this Court's substantive due process doctrine, while the plurality makes yet another effort to impose principled restraints on its exercise. But neither side argues that the meaning they attribute to the Due Process Clause was consistent with public understanding at the time of its ratification.

[After a long discussion of the meaning of the terms "privileges" and "immunities," the Congressional debates on the Fourteenth Amendment, what the ratifying public understood the Privileges or Immunities Clause to mean, and the civil rights legislation adopted by the 39th Congress in 1866, Thomas, J., concluded that] the record makes plain that the Framers of the Privileges or Immunities Clause and the ratifying-era public understood—just as the Framers of the Second Amendment did—that the right to keep and bear arms was essential to the preservation of liberty. The record makes equally plain that they deemed this right necessary to include in the minimum baseline of federal rights that the Privileges or Immunities Clause established in the wake of the War over slavery. [I] agree with the Court that the Second Amendment is fully applicable to the States. I do so because the right to keep and bear arms is guaranteed by the Fourteenth Amendment as a privilege of American citizenship.

JUSTICE BREYER, with whom JUSTICE GINSBURG and JUSTICE SOTOMAYOR join, dissenting.

[We] are aware of no argument that gun-control regulations target or are passed with the purpose of targeting "discrete and insular minorities." *Carolene Products* [Ch. 5, Sec. 3]. Nor will incorporation help to assure equal respect for individuals. Unlike the First Amendment's rights of free speech, free press, assembly, and petition, the private self-defense right does not comprise a necessary part of the democratic process that the Constitution seeks to establish. Unlike the First Amendment's religious protections, the Fourth Amendment's protection against unreasonable searches and seizures, the Fifth and Sixth Amendments' insistence upon fair criminal procedure, and the Eighth Amendment's protection against cruel and unusual punishments, the private self-defense right does not significantly seek to protect individuals who might otherwise suffer unfair or inhumane treatment at the hands of a majority.

[D]etermining the constitutionality of a particular state gun law requires finding answers to complex empirically based questions of a kind that legislatures are better able than courts to make. [Does] the presence of a child in the house matter? Does the presence of a convicted felon in the house matter? [When] do registration requirements become severe to the point that they amount to an unconstitutional ban? [The] difficulty of finding answers to these questions is exceeded only by the importance of doing so. Firearms cause well over 60,000 deaths and injuries in the United States each year. Those who live in urban areas, police officers, women, and children, all may be particularly at risk. And gun regulation may save their lives. Some experts have calculated, for example, that

Chicago's handgun ban has saved several hundred lives, perhaps close to 1,000, since it was enacted in 1983.

[At] the same time, the opponents of regulation cast doubt on these studies. And who is right? [Suppose] studies find more accidents and suicides where there is a handgun in the home than where there is a long gun in the home or no gun at all. To what extent do such studies justify a ban? What if opponents of the ban put forth counter studies? In answering such questions judges cannot simply refer to judicial homilies, such as Blackstone's 18th-century perception that a man's home is his castle. Nor can the plurality so simply reject, by mere assertion, the fact that "incorporation will require judges to assess the costs and benefits of firearms restrictions."

[N]othing in 18th-, 19th-, 20th-, or 21st-century history shows a consensus that the right to private armed defense, as described in *Heller*, is "deeply rooted in this Nation's history or tradition" or is otherwise "fundamental." Indeed, incorporating the right recognized in *Heller* may change the law in many of the 50 States. Read in the majority's favor, the historical evidence is at most ambiguous. And, in the absence of any other support for its conclusion, ambiguous history cannot show that the Fourteenth Amendment incorporates a private right of self-defense against the States.

JUSTICE STEVENS, dissenting.

[I] agree with the plurality that there are weighty arguments supporting petitioners' [Due Process contention]. But these arguments are less compelling than the plurality suggests; they are much less compelling when applied outside the home; and their validity does not depend on the Court's holding in *Heller*. For that holding sheds no light on the meaning of the Due Process Clause. [Our] decisions construing that Clause to render various procedural guarantees in the Bill of Rights enforceable against the States likewise tell us little about the meaning of the word "liberty" in the Clause or about the scope of its protection of nonprocedural rights. This is a substantive due process case.

[A] key constraint on substantive due process analysis is respect for the democratic process. If a particular liberty interest is already being given careful consideration in, and subjected to ongoing calibration by, the States, judicial enforcement may not be appropriate. When the Court declined to establish a general right to physician-assisted suicide, for example, it did so in part because "the States [were] currently engaged in serious, thoughtful examinations of physician-assisted suicide and other similar issues," rendering judicial intervention both less necessary and potentially more disruptive. *Glucksberg*. Conversely, we have long appreciated that more "searching" judicial review may be justified when the rights of "discrete and insular minorities"—groups that may face systematic barriers in the political system—are at stake. *Carolene Products Co.*

[Recognizing] a new liberty right is a momentous step. It takes that right, to a considerable extent, "outside the arena of public debate and legislative action."

Glucksberg. Sometimes that momentous step must be taken; some fundamental aspects of personhood, dignity, and the like do not vary from State to State, and demand a baseline of protection. But sensitivity to the interaction between the intrinsic aspects of liberty and the practical realities of contemporary society provides an important tool for guiding judicial discretion. This sensitivity is an aspect of a deeper principle: the need to approach our work with humility and caution.

[While] I agree with the Court that our substantive due process cases offer a principled basis for holding that petitioners have a constitutional right to possess a usable firearm in the home, I am ultimately persuaded that a better reading of our case law supports the city of Chicago. I would not foreclose the possibility that a particular plaintiff—say, an elderly widow who lives in a dangerous neighborhood and does not have the strength to operate a long gun—may have a cognizable liberty interest in possessing a handgun. But I cannot accept petitioners' broader submission. A number of factors, taken together, lead me to this conclusion.

First, firearms have a fundamentally ambivalent relationship to liberty. Just as they can help homeowners defend their families and property from intruders, they can help thugs and insurrectionists murder innocent victims. [Amici] calculate that approximately one million Americans have been wounded or killed by gunfire in the last decade.

[T]he right to possess a firearm of one's choosing is different in kind from the liberty interests we have recognized under the Due Process Clause. [I] do not doubt for a moment that many Americans feel deeply passionate about firearms [but] it does not appear to be the case that the ability to own a handgun, or any particular type of firearm, is critical to leading a life of autonomy, dignity, or political equality. [The] liberty interest asserted by petitioners is also dissimilar from those we have recognized in its capacity to undermine the security of others. [The] handgun is itself a tool for crime; the handgun's bullets *are* the violence.

[Although] it may be true that Americans' interest in firearm possession and state-law recognition of that interest are 'deeply rooted' in some important senses, it is equally true that the States have a long and unbroken history of regulating firearms. The idea that States may place substantial restrictions on the right to keep and bear arms short of complete disarmament is, in fact, far more entrenched than the notion that the Federal Constitution protects any such right.

Across the Nation, States and localities vary significantly in the patterns and problems of gun violence they face, as well as in the traditions and cultures of lawful gun use they claim. The city of Chicago, for example, faces a pressing challenge in combating criminal street gangs. Most rural areas do not. The city of Chicago has a high population density, which increases the potential for a gunman to inflict mass terror and casualties. Most rural areas do not. [Given] that relevant background conditions diverge so much across jurisdictions, the Court ought to pay particular heed to state and local legislatures' "right to experiment." *New State Ice Co. v. Liebmann*, 285 U.S. 262 (1932). (Brandeis, J., dissenting.)

[The] strength of a liberty claim must be assessed in connection with its status in the democratic process. [Neither] petitioners nor those most zealously committed to their views represent a group or a claim that is liable to receive unfair treatment at the hands of the majority. On the contrary, petitioners' views are supported by powerful participants in the legislative process.

[Justice] Scalia's method invites not only bad history, but also bad constitutional law. [In] evaluating a claimed liberty interest (or any constitutional claim for that matter), it makes perfect sense to give history significant weight. [But] it makes little sense to give history dispositive weight in every case. And it makes *especially* little sense to answer questions like whether the right to bear arms is "fundamental" by focusing only on the past, given that both the practical significance and the public understandings of such a right often change as society changes.

[The] concern runs still deeper. Not only can historical views be less than completely clear or informative, but they can also be wrong. [It] is not the role of federal judges to be amateur historians. And it is not fidelity to the Constitution to ignore its use of deliberately capacious language, in an effort to transform foundational legal commitments into narrow rules of decision. [The] net result of Justice Scalia's supposedly objective analysis is to vest federal judges—ultimately a majority of the judges on this Court—with unprecedented lawmaking powers in an area in which they have no special qualifications, and in which the give-and-take of the political process has functioned effectively for decades. * * *

JUSTICE SCALIA, concurring.[10]

I join the Court's opinion. Despite my misgivings about Substantive Due Process as an original matter, I have acquiesced in the Court's incorporation of certain guarantees in the Bill of Rights "because it is both long established and narrowly limited." This case does not require me to reconsider that view, since straightforward application of settled doctrine suffices to decide it. I write separately only to respond to some aspects of Justice Stevens' dissent.

[Exactly] what is covered [under the view of Stevens, J.] is not clear. But whatever else is in, he *knows* that the right to keep and bear arms is out, despite its being as "deeply rooted in this Nation's history and tradition" as a right can be, see *Heller*.

Justice Stevens also argues that requiring courts to show "respect for the democratic process" should serve as a constraint. That is true, but [he] would have them show respect in an extraordinary manner. In his view, if a right "is already being given careful consideration in, and subjected to ongoing calibration by, the States, judicial enforcement may not be appropriate." In other words, a right, such

---

[10]   This concurrence has been relocated to follow the dissent of Stevens, J., to which it responds.

as the right to keep and bear arms, that has long been recognized but on which the States are considering restrictions, apparently deserves *less* protection, while a privilege the political branches (instruments of the democratic process) have withheld entirely and continue to withhold, deserves *more*. That topsy-turvy approach conveniently accomplishes the objective of ensuring that the rights this Court held protected in *Casey*, *Lawrence*, and other such cases fit the theory—but at the cost of insulting rather than respecting the democratic process.

[Justice Stevens makes] the odd assertion that "firearms have a fundamentally ambivalent relationship to liberty," since sometimes they are used to cause (or sometimes accidentally produce) injury to others. [The] criterion, [is] inherently manipulable. Surely Justice Stevens does not mean that the Clause covers only rights that have *zero* harmful effect on *anyone*. Otherwise even the First Amendment is out.

[Justice] Stevens next suggests that the Second Amendment right is not fundamental because it is "different in kind" from other rights we have recognized. [Even] though he does "not doubt for a moment that many Americans * * * see [firearms] as critical to their way of life as well as to their security," he pronounces that owning a handgun is not "critical to leading a life of autonomy, dignity, or political equality." Who says? Deciding what is essential to an enlightened, liberty-filled life is an inherently political, moral judgment—the antithesis of an objective approach that reaches conclusions by applying neutral rules to verifiable evidence.

[Justice] Stevens' final reason for rejecting incorporation of the Second Amendment reveals, more clearly than any of the others, the game that is afoot. Assuming that there is a "plausible constitutional basis" for holding that the right to keep and bear arms is incorporated, he asserts that we ought not to do so *for prudential reasons*. Even if we had the authority to withhold rights that are within the Constitution's command (and we assuredly do not), two of the reasons Justice Stevens gives for abstention show just how much power he would hand to judges. The States' "right to experiment" with solutions to the problem of gun violence, he says, is at its apex here because "the best solution is far from clear." That is true of most serious social problems—whether, for example, "the best solution" for rampant crime is to admit confessions unless they are affirmatively shown to have been coerced, but see *Miranda v. Arizona*, 384 U.S. 436 (1966), or to permit jurors to impose the death penalty without a requirement that they be free to consider "any relevant mitigating factor."

[The] question to be decided is not whether the historically focused method is a *perfect means* of restraining aristocratic judicial Constitution-writing; but whether it is the *best means available* in an imperfect world. Or indeed, even more narrowly than that: whether it is demonstrably much better than what Justice Stevens proposes. I think it beyond all serious dispute that it is much less subjective, and intrudes much less upon the democratic process. [In] the most controversial matters brought before this Court—for example, the constitutionality of prohibiting abortion, assisted suicide, or homosexual sodomy, or the constitutionality of the death penalty—*any* historical methodology, under *any* plausible standard of proof, would lead to the same conclusion. Moreover, the methodological differences that divide historians, and the varying interpretive assumptions they bring to their work, are nothing compared to the differences among the American people (though perhaps not among graduates of prestigious law schools) with regard to the moral judgments Justice Stevens would have courts pronounce. * * *

CHAPTER 7

FREEDOM OF EXPRESSION
AND ASSOCIATION

■ ■ ■

1. THE SCOPE AND STRENGTH OF
THE FIRST AMENDMENT

The First Amendment provides that "Congress shall make no law * * * abridging the freedom of speech, or of the press." Some have stressed that no law means NO LAW. For example, Black, J., dissenting in *Konigsberg v. State Bar*, 366 U.S. 36 (1961) argued that the "First Amendment's unequivocal command [shows] that the men who drafted our Bill of Rights did all the 'balancing' that was to be done in this field."

Yet laws forbidding or regulating speech are commonplace. Laws against perjury, blackmail, and fraud prohibit speech. So does much of the law of contracts. And most of antitrust law, securities law, and the regulatory activity of the Federal Trade Commission and the Food and Drug Administration is focused on speech regulation as well. Black, J., himself conceded that speech pursued as an integral part of criminal conduct was beyond First Amendment protection. Indeed, no one contends that citizens are free to say anything, anywhere, at any time. As Holmes, J., famously observed, citizens are not free to yell "fire" falsely in a theater.

But the spectre of a man crying fire falsely in the theater plagues First Amendment theory, largely because the phrase is of scant assistance in formulating principles to separate the protected from the unprotected. Too much of our lives involves "speech" in the literal sense to expect that the First Amendment can even be relevant to such a vast proportion of human existence. And speech interacts with too many other values in too many complicated ways to expect that a single formula will prove productive.

These broad questions recur in numerous specific contexts. Are advocates of illegal conduct, child pornographers, advertisers of cigarettes and alcohol, and publishers of libel relevantly similar to the person in the theater, or are they instead engaged in freedom of speech? And what about publications that invade the privacy of citizens or officials? Or citizens who wish to speak on government property? And which property? Is there a right of access to the print or broadcast media, such that government might force private owners to grant access for speakers? Does the First Amendment offer protection for the wealthy, for powerful corporations, and for media conglomerates against government attempts to assure greater equality in the intellectual marketplace? Can government demand information about private political associations or reporters' confidential sources? Does the First Amendment require government to produce information it might otherwise withhold? And the list goes on.

The Court has tended to approach questions such as these without much attention to the language or history of the First Amendment and with no commitment to any general theory. Rather, it has sought to develop principles in more case-specific and topic-specific contexts and has produced a complex and conflicting body of constitutional precedent. Many of the principles were first developed in a line of cases involving the advocacy of illegal action, and these cases are commonly understood to mark the beginning of the modern First Amendment.

I.   ADVOCACY OF ILLEGAL ACTION

A.   Emerging Principles

SCHENCK V. UNITED STATES
249 U.S. 47, 39 S.Ct. 247, 63 L.Ed. 470 (1919).

JUSTICE HOLMES delivered the opinion of the Court.

This [indictment charges] a conspiracy to violate the Espionage Act of June 15, 1917 by causing and attempting to cause insubordination in the military and naval forces of the United States, and to obstruct the recruiting and enlistment service of the United States, when the United States was at war with the German Empire, to-wit, that the defendants wilfully conspired to have printed and circulated to men who had been called and accepted for military service a document set forth and alleged to be calculated to cause such insubordination and obstruction. [The] defendants were found guilty on all the counts. They set up the First Amendment to the Constitution forbidding Congress to make any law abridging the freedom of speech, or of the press.

[The] document in question upon its first printed side recited the first section of the Thirteenth Amendment, said that the idea embodied in it was violated by the Conscription Act and that a conscript is little better than a convict. In impassioned language it intimated that conscription was despotism in its worst form and a monstrous wrong against humanity in the interest of Wall Street's chosen few. It said "Do not submit to intimidation," but in form at least confined itself to peaceful measures such as a petition for the repeal of the act. The other and later printed side of the sheet was headed "Assert Your Rights." It stated reasons for alleging that any one violated the Constitution when he refused to recognize "your right to assert your opposition to the draft," and went on "If you do not assert and support your rights, you are helping to deny or disparage rights which it is the solemn duty of all citizens and residents of the United States to retain." It described the arguments on the other side as coming from cunning politicians and a mercenary capitalist press, and even silent consent to the conscription law as helping to support an infamous conspiracy. It denied the power to send our citizens away to foreign shores to shoot up the people of other lands, and added that words could not express the condemnation such cold-blooded ruthlessness deserves, winding up "You must do your share to maintain, support and uphold the rights of the people of this country." Of course the documents would not have been sent unless it had been intended to have some effect, and we do not see what effect it could be expected to have upon persons subject to the draft except to influence them to obstruct the carrying of it out. The defendants do not deny that the jury might find against them on this point. * * *

But it is said, suppose that that was the tendency of this circular, it is protected by the First Amendment to the Constitution. [It] well may be that the prohibition of laws abridging the freedom of speech is not confined to previous restraints, although to prevent them may have been the main purpose, as intimated in Patterson v. Colorado, 205 U.S. 454 [1907]. We admit that in many places and in ordinary times the defendants in saying all that was said in the circular would have been within their constitutional rights. But the character of every act depends upon the circumstances in which it is done. The most stringent protection of free speech would not protect a man in falsely shouting fire in a theatre and causing a panic. It does not even protect a man from an injunction against uttering words that may have all the effect of force. The question in every case is whether the words used are used in such circumstances and are of such a nature as to create a clear and present danger that they will bring about the substantive evils that Congress has a right to prevent. It is a question of proximity and degree. When a nation is at war many things that might be said in time of peace are such a hindrance to its effort that their utterance will not be endured so long as men fight and that no Court could regard them as protected by any constitutional right. It seems to be admitted that if an actual obstruction of the recruiting service were proved, liability for words that produced that effect might be enforced. The statute punishes conspiracies to obstruct [conscription] as well as actual obstruction. If the act, (speaking, or circulating a paper,) its tendency and the intent with which it is done are the same, we perceive no ground for saying that success alone warrants making the act a crime. * * *

Judgments affirmed.[1]

---

[1]   See also *Frohwerk v. United States*, 249 U.S. 204 (1919), where a unanimous Court, per Holmes, J., sustained a conviction for conspiracy to obstruct recruiting, in violation of the Espionage Act, by means of newspaper articles praising the spirit and strength of the German nation, criticizing the decision to send American troops to France, maintaining that the government was giving false and hypocritical reasons for its course of action, and implying that "the guilt of those who voted the unnatural sacrifice" is greater than the wrong of those who seek to escape by resistance: "[*Schenck* decided] that a person may be convicted of a conspiracy to obstruct recruiting by words of persuasion. [S]o far as the language of the articles goes there is not much to choose between expressions to be found in them and those before us in *Schenck*." "[The] First Amendment while prohibiting legislation against free speech cannot have been [intended] to give immunity for every possible use of language. [Neither] Hamilton nor Madison, nor any other competent person then or later, ever supposed that to make criminal the counselling of murder [would] be an unconstitutional interference with free speech."

DEBS v. UNITED STATES, 249 U.S. 211 (1919): Defendant was convicted of violating the Espionage Act for obstructing and attempting to obstruct the recruiting service and for causing and attempting to cause insubordination and disloyalty in the armed services. He was given a ten-year prison sentence on each count, to run concurrently. His criminal conduct consisted of giving the anti-war speech described in the opinion at the state convention of the Socialist Party of Ohio, held at a park in Canton, Ohio, on a June 16, 1918 Sunday afternoon before a general audience of 1,200 persons. At the time of the speech, defendant was a national political figure. In affirming, HOLMES, J., observed for a unanimous Court:

"The main theme of the speech was socialism, its growth, and a prophecy of its ultimate success. With that we have nothing to do, but if a part or the manifest intent of the more general utterances was to encourage those present to obstruct the recruiting service and if in passages such encouragement was directly given, the immunity of the general theme may not be enough to protect the speech. [Defendant had come to the park directly from a nearby jail, where he had visited three socialists imprisoned for obstructing the recruiting service. He expressed sympathy and admiration for these persons and others convicted of similar offenses, and then] said that the master class has always declared the war and the subject class has always fought the battles—that the subject class has had nothing to gain and all to lose, including their lives; [and that] 'You have your lives to lose; you certainly ought to have the right to declare war if you consider a war necessary.' [He next said of a woman serving a ten-year sentence for obstructing the recruiting service] that she had said no more than the speaker had said that afternoon; that if she was guilty so was [he].

"There followed personal experiences and illustrations of the growth of socialism, a glorification of minorities, and a prophecy of the success of [socialism], with the interjection that 'you need to know that you are fit for something better than slavery and cannon fodder.' [Defendant's] final exhortation [was] 'Don't worry about the charge of treason to your masters; but be concerned about the treason that involves yourselves.' The defendant addressed the jury himself, and while contending that his speech did not warrant the charges said 'I have been accused of obstructing the war. I admit it. Gentlemen, I abhor war. I would oppose the war if I stood alone.' The statement was not necessary to warrant the jury in finding that one purpose of the speech, whether incidental or not does not matter, was to oppose not only war in general but this war, and that the opposition was so expressed that its natural and intended effect would be to obstruct recruiting. If that was intended and if, in all the circumstances, that would be its probable effect, it would not be protected by reason of its being part of a general program and expressions of a general and conscientious belief.

"[Defendant's constitutional objections] based upon the First Amendment [were] disposed of in *Schenck*. [T]he admission in evidence of the record of the conviction [of various persons he mentioned in his speech was proper] to show what he was talking about, to explain the true import of his expression of sympathy and to throw light on the intent of the address. [Properly admitted, too, was an 'Antiwar Proclamation and Program' adopted the previous year, coupled with testimony that shortly before his speech defendant had stated that he approved it]. Its first recommendation was, 'continuous, active, and public opposition to the war, through demonstrations, mass petitions, and all other means within our power.' Evidence that the defendant accepted this view and this declaration of his duties at the time that he made his speech is evidence that if in that speech he used words tending to obstruct the recruiting service he meant that they should have that effect. [T]he jury were most carefully instructed that they could not find the defendant guilty for advocacy of any of his opinions unless the words used had as their natural tendency and reasonably probable effect to obstruct the recruiting service [and] unless the defendant had the specific intent to do so in his mind."

* * *

MASSES PUBLISHING CO. v. PATTEN, 244 Fed. 535 (S.D.N.Y.1917): The Postmaster of New York advised plaintiff that an issue of his monthly revolutionary journal, *The Masses,* would be denied the mails under the Espionage Act since it tended to encourage the enemies of the United States and to hamper the government in its conduct of the war. The Postmaster subsequently specified as objectionable several cartoons entitled, e.g., "Conscription," "Making the World Safe for Capitalism"; several articles admiring the "sacrifice" of conscientious objectors and a poem praising two persons imprisoned for conspiracy to resist the draft. Plaintiff sought a preliminary injunction against the postmaster from excluding its magazine from the mails. LEARNED HAND, D.J., granted relief:

"[The postmaster maintains] that to arouse discontent and disaffection among the people with the prosecution of the war and with the draft tends to promote a mutinous and insubordinate temper among the troops. This [is] true; men who become satisfied that they are engaged in an enterprise dictated by the unconscionable selfishness of the rich, and effectuated by a tyrannous disregard for the will of those who must suffer and die, will be more prone to insubordination than those who have faith in the cause and acquiesce in the means. Yet to interpret the word 'cause' [in the statutory language forbidding one to 'willfully cause' insubordination in the armed forces] so broadly would [necessarily involve] the suppression of all hostile criticism, and of all opinion except what encouraged and supported the existing policies, or which fell within the range of temperate argument. * * * Assuming that the power to repress such opinion may rest in Congress in the throes of a struggle for the very existence of the state, its exercise is so contrary to the use and wont of our people that only the clearest expression of such a power justifies the conclusion that it was intended.

"The defendant's position, therefore, in so far as it involves the suppression of the free utterance of abuse and criticism of the existing law, or of the policies of the war, is not, in my judgment, supported by the language of the statute. Yet there has always been a recognized limit to such expressions. [One] may not counsel or advise others to violate the law as it stands. Words are not only the keys of persuasion, but the triggers of action, and those which have no purport but to counsel the violation of law cannot by any latitude of interpretation be a part of that public opinion which is the final source of government in a democratic state. [If] one stops short of urging upon others that it is their duty or their interest to resist the law, it seems to me one should not be held to have attempted to cause its violation. If that be not the test, I can see no escape from the conclusion that under this section every political agitation which can be shown to be apt to create a seditious temper is illegal. I am confident that by such language Congress had no such revolutionary purpose in view.

"It seems to me, however, quite plain that none of the language and none of the cartoons in this paper can be thought directly to counsel or advise insubordination or mutiny, without a violation of their meaning quite beyond any tolerable understanding. I come, therefore to the [provision of the Act forbidding] any one from willfully obstructing [recruiting or enlistment]. I am not prepared to assent to the plaintiff's position that this only refers to acts other than words, nor that the act thus defined must be shown to have been successful. One may obstruct without preventing, and the mere obstruction is an injury to the service; for it throws impediments in its way. Here again, however, since the question is of the expression of opinion, I construe the sentence, so far as it restrains public utterance, [as] limited to the direct advocacy of resistance to the recruiting and enlistment service. If so, the inquiry is narrowed to the question whether any of the challenged matter may be said to advocate resistance to the draft, taking the meaning of the words with the utmost latitude which they can bear.

"[It] is plain enough that the [magazine] has the fullest sympathy for [those who resist the draft or obstruct recruiting], that it admires their courage, and that it presumptively approves their conduct. [Moreover,] these passages, it must be remembered, occur in a magazine which attacks with the utmost violence the draft and the war. That such comments have a tendency to arouse emulation in others is clear enough, but that they counsel others to follow these examples is not so plain. Literally at least they do not, and while, as I have said, the words are to be taken, not literally, but according to their full import, the literal meaning is the starting point for interpretation. One may admire and approve the course of a hero without feeling any duty to follow him. There is not the least implied intimation in these words that others are under a duty to follow. The most that can be said is that, if others do follow, they will get the same admiration and the same approval. * * *

"When the question is of a statute constituting a crime, it seems to me that there should be more definite evidence of the act. The question before me is quite the same as what would arise upon a motion to dismiss an indictment at the close of the proof: Could any reasonable man say, not that the indirect result of the language might be to arouse a seditious disposition, for that would not be enough, but that the language directly advocated resistance to the draft? I cannot think that upon such language any verdict would stand."[2]

JUSTICE HOLMES—DISSENTING IN
ABRAMS V. UNITED STATES
250 U.S. 616, 624, 40 S.Ct. 17, 20, 63 L.Ed. 1173, 1178 (1919).

[In the summer of 1918, the United States sent a small body of marines to Siberia. The defendants opposed the "capitalist" invasion of Russia, and characterized it as an attempt to crush the Russian Revolution. Shortly thereafter, they printed two leaflets and distributed several thousand copies in New York City. Many of the copies were thrown from a window where one defendant was employed; others were passed around at radical meetings. Both leaflets supported Russia against the United States; one called upon workers to unite in a general strike. There was no evidence that workers responded to the call.

[The Court upheld the defendants' convictions for conspiring to violate two provisions of the 1918 amendments to the Espionage Act. One count prohibited language intended to "incite, provoke and encourage resistance to the United States"; the other punished those who urged curtailment of war production. As the Court interpreted the statute, an intent to interfere with efforts against a *declared* war was a necessary element of both offenses. Since the United States had not declared war upon Russia, "the main task of the government was to establish an [*intention*] *to interfere with the war with Germany.*" The Court found intent on the principle that "Men must be held to have intended, and to be accountable for, the effects which their acts were likely to produce. Even if their primary purpose and intent was to aid the cause of the Russian Revolution, the plan of action which they adopted necessarily involved, before it could be realized, defeat of the war program of the United States * * * ."

[HOLMES, J., dissented, joined in his opinion by BRANDEIS, J.]

[I] am aware of course that the word "intent" as vaguely used in ordinary legal discussion means no more than knowledge at the time of the act that the consequences said to be intended will ensue. [But,] when words are used exactly, a deed is not done with intent to produce a consequence unless that consequence is the aim of the deed. It may be obvious, and obvious to the actor, that the consequence will follow, and he may be liable for it even if he regrets it, but he does not do the act with intent to produce it unless the aim to produce it is the proximate motive of the specific act although there may be some deeper motive behind.

---

[2]   In reversing, 246 Fed. 24 (1917), the Second Circuit observed: "If the natural and probable effect of what is said is to encourage resistance to a law, and the words are used in an endeavor to persuade to resistance, it is immaterial that the duty to resist is not mentioned, or the interest of the person addressed in resistance is not suggested. That one may willfully obstruct the enlistment service, without advising in direct language against enlistments, and without stating that to refrain from enlistment is a duty or in one's interest, seems to us too plain for controversy."

It seems to me that this statute must be taken to use its words in a strict and accurate sense. They would be absurd in any other. A patriot might think that we were wasting money on aeroplanes, or making more cannon of a certain kind than we needed, and might advocate curtailment with success, yet even if it turned out that the curtailment hindered and was thought by other minds to have been obviously likely to hinder the United States in the prosecution of the war, no one would hold such conduct a crime. * * *

I never have seen any reason to doubt that the questions of law that alone were before this Court in the cases of *Schenck, Frohwerk* and *Debs* were rightly decided. I do not doubt for a moment that by the same reasoning that would justify punishing persuasion to murder, the United States constitutionally may punish speech that produces or is intended to produce a clear and imminent danger that it will bring about forthwith certain substantive evils that the United States constitutionally may seek to prevent. The power undoubtedly is greater in time of war than in time of peace because war opens dangers that do not exist at other times.

But as against dangers peculiar to war, as against others, the principle of the right to free speech is always the same. It is only the present danger of immediate evil or an intent to bring it about that warrants Congress in setting a limit to the expression of opinion where private rights are not concerned. Congress certainly cannot forbid all effort to change the mind of the country. Now nobody can suppose that the surreptitious publishing of a silly leaflet by an unknown man, without more, would present any immediate danger that its opinions would hinder the success of the government arms or have any appreciable tendency to do so. Publishing those opinions for the very purpose of obstructing, however, might indicate a greater danger and at any rate would have the quality of an attempt. * * *

I do not see how anyone can find the intent required by the statute in any of the defendants' words. The leaflet advocating a general strike is the only one that affords even a foundation for the charge, and [its only object] is to help Russia and stop American intervention there against the popular government—not to impede the United States in the war that it was carrying on. * * *

In this case sentences of twenty years imprisonment have been imposed for the publishing of two leaflets that I believe the defendants had as much right to publish as the Government has to publish the Constitution of the United States now vainly invoked by them. [E]ven if what I think the necessary intent were shown; the most nominal punishment seems to me all that possibly could be inflicted, unless the defendants are to be made to suffer not for what the indictment alleges but for the creed that they avow—[which,] although made the subject of examination at the trial, no one has a right even to consider in dealing with the charges before the Court.

Persecution for the expression of opinions seems to me perfectly logical. If you have no doubt of your premises or your power and want a certain result with all your heart you naturally express your wishes in law and sweep away all opposition. To allow opposition by speech seems to indicate that you think the speech impotent, as when a man says that he has squared the circle, or that you do not care whole-heartedly for the result, or that you doubt either your power or your premises. But when men have realized that time has upset many fighting faiths, they may come to believe even more than they believe the very foundations of their own conduct that the ultimate good desired is better reached by free trade in ideas—that the best test of truth is the power of the thought to get itself accepted in the competition of the market, and that truth is the only ground upon which their wishes safely can be carried out. That at any rate is the theory of our Constitution. It is an experiment, as all life is an experiment. Every year if not every day we have to wager our salvation upon some prophecy based upon imperfect knowledge. While that experiment is part of our system I think that we should be eternally vigilant against attempts to check the expression of opinions that we loathe and believe to be fraught with death, unless they so imminently threaten immediate interference with the lawful and pressing purposes of the law that an immediate check is required to save the country. [Only] the emergency that makes it immediately dangerous to leave the correction of evil counsels to time warrants making any exception to the sweeping command, "Congress shall make no law * * * abridging the freedom of speech." Of course I am speaking only of expressions of opinion and exhortations, which were all that were uttered [here].

The "Marketplace of Ideas"

Is the competition of the market—the marketplace of ideas, as it is now put—as the "best test of truth" an empirical and not a philosophical claim? Consider Frederick Schauer, *Facts and the First Amendment*, 57 UCLA L.Rev. 897 (2010): "Once we fathom the full scope of factors other than the truth of a proposition that might determine which propositions individuals or groups will accept and which they will reject—the charisma, authority, or persuasiveness of the speaker; the consistency between the proposition and the prior beliefs of the hearer; the consistency between the proposition and what the hearer believes that other hearers believe; the frequency with which the proposition is uttered; the extent to which the proposition is communicated with photographs and other visual or aural embellishments; the extent to which the proposition will make the reader or listener feel good or happy for content-independent reasons; and almost countless others—we can see that placing faith in the superiority of truth over all of these other attributes of a proposition in explaining acceptance and rejection requires a substantial degree of faith in pervasive human rationality and an almost willful disregard of the masses of scientific and marketing research to the contrary."

Contrast Holmes, J.'s statement of the "marketplace of ideas" argument with John Milton's statement in *Areopagitica* (1644): "And though all the winds of doctrine were let loose to play upon the earth, so Truth be in the field, we do injuriously by licensing and prohibiting to misdoubt her strength. Let her and

Falsehood grapple; who ever knew Truth put to the worse, in a free and open encounter?" Holmes, J., claims that the competition of the market is the best test of truth; Milton maintains that truth will emerge in a free and open encounter. How would one verify either hypothesis? Might Holmes be referring only to political or policy truth, where it is plausible that truth is *defined* by the marketplace of ideas rather than being located by it?

In UNITED STATES v. ALVAREZ (2012), Sec. 4, VI, infra, a local office holder falsely claimed at a public meeting to have been awarded the Congressional Medal of Honor. A federal statute—the Stolen Valor Act—made that representation a crime, but the Court, per Kennedy, J., held that the statute violated the First Amendment. Is the marketplace of ideas the best way of determining whether Mr. Alvarez had been awarded the medal? The best way of determining whether the claims of astrology are true? Global warming? The number of casualties in a natural disaster? More broadly, what is the role of the marketplace of ideas in determining factual and scientific truth?

B. State Sedition Laws

A second group of cases in the initial development of First Amendment doctrine involved state "sedition laws" of two types: criminal anarchy laws, typified by the New York statute in *Gitlow,* infra, and criminal syndicalism laws similar to the California statute in *Whitney,* infra. Most states enacted anarchy and syndicalism statutes between 1917 and 1921, in response to World War I and the fear of Bolshevism that developed in its wake, but the first modern sedition law was passed by New York in 1902, soon after the assassination of President McKinley and at a time of substantial labor union activism. The law, which prohibited not only actual or attempted assassinations or conspiracies to assassinate, but advocacy of anarchy as well, lay idle for nearly twenty years, until the *Gitlow* prosecution.

GITLOW v. NEW YORK, 268 U.S. 652 (1925): Defendant was a member of the Left Wing Section of the Socialist Party and a member of its National Council, which adopted a "Left Wing Manifesto," condemning the dominant "moderate Socialism" for its recognition of the necessity of the democratic parliamentary state; advocating the necessity of accomplishing the "Communist Revolution" by a militant and "revolutionary Socialism" based on "the class struggle"; and urging the development of mass political strikes for the destruction of the parliamentary state. Defendant arranged for printing and distributing, through the mails and otherwise, 16,000 copies of the Manifesto in the Left Wing's official organ, The Revolutionary Age. There was no evidence of any effect from the publication and circulation of the Manifesto.

In sustaining a conviction under the New York "criminal anarchy" statutes, prohibiting the "advocacy, advising or teaching the duty, necessity or propriety of overthrowing or overturning organized government by force or violence" and the publication or distribution of such matter, the majority, per SANFORD, J., stated that for present purposes we may and do assume[3] that First Amendment freedoms of expression "are among the fundamental personal rights and 'liberties' protected by the due process clause of the Fourteenth Amendment from impairment by the States," but ruled:

"By enacting the present statute the State has determined, through its legislative body, that utterances advocating the overthrow of organized government by force, violence and unlawful means, are so inimical to the general welfare and involve such danger of substantive evil that they may be penalized in the exercise of its police power. That determination must be given great weight. Every presumption is to be indulged in favor of the validity of the statute. And the case is to be considered 'in the light of the principle that the State is primarily the judge of regulations required in the interest of public safety and welfare'; and that its police 'statutes may only be declared unconstitutional where they are arbitrary or unreasonable attempts to exercise authority vested in the State in the public interest.' That utterances inciting to the overthrow of organized government by unlawful means, present a sufficient danger of substantive evil to bring their punishment within the range of legislative discretion, is clear. Such utterances, by their very nature, involve danger to the public peace and to the security of the State. They threaten breaches of the peace and ultimate revolution. And the immediate danger is none the less real and substantial, because the effect of a given utterance cannot be accurately foreseen. The State cannot reasonably be required to measure the danger from every such utterance in the nice balance of a jeweler's scale. A single revolutionary spark may kindle a fire that, smoldering for a time, may burst into a sweeping and destructive conflagration. It cannot be said that the State is acting arbitrarily or unreasonably when in the exercise of its judgment as to the measures necessary to protect the public peace and safety, it seeks to extinguish the spark without waiting until it has enkindled the flame or blazed into the conflagration. It cannot reasonably be required to defer the adoption of measures for its own peace and safety until the revolutionary utterances lead to actual disturbances of the public peace or imminent and immediate danger of its own destruction; but it may, in the exercise of its judgment, suppress the threatened danger in its incipiency.

"[It] is clear that the question in [this case] is entirely different from that involved in those cases where the statute merely prohibits certain acts involving the danger of substantive evil, without any reference to language itself, and it is sought to apply its provisions to language used by the defendant for the purpose of bringing about the prohibited results. There, if it be contended that the statute cannot be applied to the language used by the defendant because of its protection by the freedom of speech or press, it must necessarily be found, as an original question, without any previous determination by the legislative body, whether the specific language used involved such likelihood of bringing about the substantive evil as to deprive it of the constitutional protection. In such cases it has been held

---

[3]   *Gitlow* is generally cited for the proposition that the First Amendment applies to state restrictions.

that the general provisions of the statute may be constitutionally applied to the specific utterance of the defendant if its natural tendency and probable effect was to bring about the substantive evil which the legislative body might prevent. *Schenck; Debs.* And the general statement in the *Schenck* case that the 'question in every case is whether the words are used in such circumstances and are of such a nature as to create a clear and present danger that they will bring about the substantive evils,' [was] manifestly intended, as shown by the context, to apply only in cases of this class, and has no application to those like the present, where the legislative body itself has previously determined the danger of substantive evil arising from utterances of a specified character."

HOLMES, J., joined by Brandeis, J., dissented: "The general principle of free speech, it seems to me, must be taken to be included in the Fourteenth Amendment, in view of the scope that has been given to the word 'liberty' as there used, although perhaps it may be accepted with a somewhat larger latitude of interpretation than is allowed to Congress by the sweeping language that governs or ought to govern the laws of the United States. If I am right then I think that the criterion sanctioned by the full Court in *Schenck* applies. [It] is true that in my opinion this criterion was departed from in *Abrams,* but the convictions that I expressed in that case are too deep for it to be possible for me as yet to believe that it [has] settled the law. If what I think the correct test is applied it is manifest that there was no present danger of an attempt to overthrow the government by force on the part of the admittedly small minority who shared the defendant's views. It is said that this manifesto was more than a theory, that it was an incitement. Every idea is an incitement. It offers itself for belief and if believed it is acted on unless some other belief outweighs it or some failure of energy stifles the movement at its birth. The only difference between the expression of an opinion and an incitement in the narrower sense is the speaker's enthusiasm for the result. Eloquence may set fire to reason. But whatever may be thought of the redundant discourse before us it had no chance of starting a present conflagration. If in the long run the beliefs expressed in proletarian dictatorship are destined to be accepted by the dominant forces of the community, the only meaning of free speech is that they should be given their chance and have their way.

"If the publication of this document had been laid as an attempt to induce an uprising against government at once and not at some indefinite time in the future it would have presented a different question. The object would have been one with which the law might deal, subject to the doubt whether there was any danger that the publication could produce any result, or in other words, whether it was not futile and too remote from possible consequences. But the indictment alleges the publication and nothing more."

WHITNEY V. CALIFORNIA

274 U.S. 357, 47 S.Ct. 641, 71 L.Ed. 1095 (1927).

JUSTICE SANFORD delivered the opinion of the Court.

[Charlotte Anita Whitney was convicted of violating the 1919 Criminal Syndicalism Act of California whose pertinent provisions were]:

"Section 1. The term 'criminal syndicalism' as used in this act is hereby defined as any doctrine or precept advocating, teaching or aiding and abetting the commission of crime, sabotage (which word is hereby defined as meaning willful and malicious physical damage or injury to physical property), or unlawful acts of force and violence or unlawful methods of terrorism as a means of accomplishing a change in industrial ownership or control, or effecting any political change.

"Sec. 2. Any person who: * * * 4. Organizes or assists in organizing, or is or knowingly becomes a member of, any organization, society, group or assemblage of persons organized or assembled to advocate, teach or aid and abet criminal syndicalism; * * * Is guilty of a felony and punishable by imprisonment."

The first count of the information, on which the conviction was had, charged that on or about November 28, 1919, in Alameda County, the defendant, in violation of the Criminal Syndicalism Act, "did then and there unlawfully, willfully, wrongfully, deliberately and feloniously organize and assist in organizing, and was, is, and knowingly became a member of [a group] organized and assembled to advocate, teach, aid and abet criminal syndicalism." * * *

1. While it is not denied that the evidence warranted the jury in finding that the defendant became a member of and assisted in organizing the Communist Labor Party of California, and that this was organized to advocate, teach, aid or abet criminal syndicalism as defined by the Act, it is urged that the Act, as here construed and applied, deprived the defendant of her liberty without due process of law. [Defendant's] argument is, in effect, that the character of the state organization could not be forecast when she attended the convention; that she had no purpose of helping to create an instrument of terrorism and violence; that she "took part in formulating and presenting to the convention a resolution which, if adopted, would have committed the new organization to a legitimate policy of political reform by the use of the ballot"; that it was not until after the majority of the convention turned out to be "contrary minded, and other less temperate policies prevailed" that the convention could have taken on the character of criminal syndicalism; and that as this was done over her protest, her mere presence in the convention, however violent the opinions expressed therein, could not thereby become a crime. This contention [is in effect] an effort to review the weight of the evidence for the purpose of showing that the defendant did not join and assist in organizing the Communist Labor Party of California with a knowledge of its unlawful character and purpose. This question, which is foreclosed by the verdict of the jury, [is] one of fact merely which is not open to review in this Court, involving as it does no constitutional question whatever. * * *

[That a state] may punish those who abuse [freedom of speech] by utterances inimical to the public welfare, tending to incite to crime, disturb the public peace, or endanger the foundations of organized government and threaten its overthrow by unlawful means, is not open to question. [*Gitlow*].

The essence of the offense denounced by the Act is the combining with others in an association for the accomplishment of the desired ends through the advocacy and use of criminal and unlawful methods. It partakes of the nature of a criminal conspiracy. That such united and joint action involves even greater danger to the public peace and security than the isolated utterances and acts of individuals is clear. We cannot hold that, as here applied, the Act is an unreasonable or arbitrary exercise of the police power of the State, unwarrantably infringing any right of free speech, assembly or association, or that those persons are protected from punishment by the due process clause who abuse such rights by joining and furthering an organization thus menacing the peace and welfare of the State. * * *

Affirmed.

JUSTICE BRANDEIS (concurring.) * * *

The felony which the statute created is a crime very unlike the old felony of conspiracy or the old misdemeanor of unlawful assembly. The mere act of assisting in forming a society for teaching syndicalism, of becoming a member of it, or assembling with others for that purpose is given the dynamic quality of crime. There is guilt although the society may not contemplate immediate promulgation of the doctrine. Thus the accused is to be punished, not for attempt, incitement or conspiracy, but for a step in preparation, which, if it threatens the public order at all, does so only remotely. The novelty in the prohibition introduced is that the statute aims, not at the practice of criminal syndicalism, nor even directly at the preaching of it, but at association with those who propose to preach it.

Despite arguments to the contrary which had seemed to me persuasive, it is settled that the due process clause of the Fourteenth Amendment applies to matters of substantive law as well as to matters of procedure. Thus all fundamental rights comprised within the term liberty are protected by the federal Constitution from invasion by the states. The right of free speech, the right to teach and the right of assembly are, of course, fundamental rights. These may not be denied or abridged. But, although the rights of free speech and assembly are fundamental, they are not in their nature absolute. Their exercise is subject to restriction, if the particular restriction proposed is required in order to protect the state from destruction or from serious injury, political, economic or moral. That the necessity which is essential to a valid restriction does not exist unless speech would produce, or is intended to produce, a clear and imminent danger of some substantive evil which the state constitutionally may seek to prevent has been settled. See *Schenck*.

[The] Legislature must obviously decide, in the first instance, whether a danger exists which calls for a particular protective measure. But where a statute is valid only in case certain conditions exist, the enactment of the statute cannot alone establish the facts which are essential to its validity. Prohibitory legislation has repeatedly been held invalid, because unnecessary, where the denial of liberty involved was that of engaging in a particular business. The powers of the courts to strike down an offending law are no less when the interests involved are not property rights, but the fundamental personal rights of free speech and assembly.

This Court has not yet fixed the standard by which to determine when a danger shall be deemed clear; how remote the danger may be and yet be deemed present; and what degree of evil shall be deemed sufficiently substantial to justify resort to abridgment of free speech and assembly as the means of protection. To reach sound conclusions on these matters, we must bear in mind why a state is, ordinarily, denied the power to prohibit dissemination of social, economic and political doctrine which a vast majority of its citizens believes to be false and fraught with evil consequence.

Those who won our independence believed that the final end of the state was to make men free to develop their faculties, and that in its government the deliberative forces should prevail over the arbitrary. They valued liberty both as an end and as a means. They believed liberty to be the secret of happiness and courage to be the secret of liberty. They believed that freedom to think as you will and to speak as you think are means indispensable to the discovery and spread of political truth; that without free speech and assembly discussion would be futile; that with them, discussion affords ordinarily adequate protection against the dissemination of noxious doctrine; that the greatest menace to freedom is an inert people; that public discussion is a political duty; and that this should be a fundamental principle of the American government. They recognized the risks to which all human institutions are subject. But they knew that order cannot be secured merely through fear of punishment for its infraction; that it is hazardous to discourage thought, hope and imagination; that fear breeds repression; that repression breeds hate; that hate menaces stable government; that the path of safety lies in the opportunity to discuss freely supposed grievances and proposed remedies; and that the fitting remedy for evil counsels is good ones. Believing in the power of reason as applied through public discussion, they eschewed silence coerced by law—the argument of force in its worst form. Recognizing the occasional tyrannies of governing majorities, they amended the Constitution so that free speech and assembly should be guaranteed.

Fear of serious injury cannot alone justify suppression of free speech and assembly. Men feared witches and burnt women. It is the function of speech to free men from the bondage of irrational fears. To justify suppression of free speech there must be reasonable ground to fear that serious evil will result if free speech is practiced. There must be reasonable ground to believe that the danger apprehended is imminent. There must be reasonable ground to believe that the evil to be prevented is a serious one. Every denunciation of existing law tends in some measure to increase the probability that there will be violation of it. Condonation of a breach enhances the probability. Expressions of approval add to the probability. Propagation of the criminal state of mind by teaching syndicalism increases it. Advocacy of lawbreaking heightens it still further. But even advocacy of violation, however reprehensible morally, is not a justification for denying free speech where the advocacy falls short of incitement and there is nothing to indicate that the advocacy would be immediately acted on. The wide difference between advocacy and incitement, between preparation and attempt, between assembling and conspiracy, must be borne in mind. In order to support a finding of clear and present danger it must be shown either that immediate serious violence was to be expected or was advocated, or that the past conduct furnished reason to believe that such advocacy was then contemplated.

Those who won our independence by revolution were not cowards. They did not fear political change. They did not exalt order at the cost of liberty. To courageous, self-reliant men, with confidence in the power of free and fearless reasoning applied through the processes of popular government, no danger flowing from speech can be deemed clear and present, unless the incidence of the evil apprehended is so imminent that it may befall before there is opportunity for full discussion. If there be time to expose through discussion the falsehood and fallacies, to avert the evil by the processes of education, the remedy to be applied is more speech, not enforced silence. Only an emergency can justify repression. Such must be the rule if authority is to be reconciled with freedom. Such, in my opinion, is the command of the Constitution. It is therefore always open to Americans to challenge a law abridging free speech and assembly by showing that there was no emergency justifying it.

Moreover, even imminent danger cannot justify resort to prohibition of these functions essential to effective democracy, unless the evil apprehended is relatively serious. Prohibition of free speech and assembly is a measure so stringent that it would be inappropriate as the means for averting a relatively trivial harm to society. A police measure may be unconstitutional merely because the remedy, although effective as means of protection, is unduly harsh or oppressive. Thus, a state might, in the exercise of its police power, make any trespass upon the land of another a crime, regardless of the results or of the intent or purpose of the trespasser. It might, also, punish an attempt, a conspiracy, or an incitement to commit the trespass. But it is hardly conceivable that this court would hold constitutional a statute which punished as a felony the mere voluntary assembly with a society formed to teach that pedestrians had the moral right to cross uninclosed, unposted, waste lands and to advocate their doing so, even if there was imminent danger that advocacy would lead to a trespass. The fact that speech is likely to result in some violence or in destruction of property is not enough to justify its suppression. There must be the probability of serious injury to the State. Among free men, the deterrents ordinarily to be applied to prevent crime are education and punishment for violations of the law, not abridgement of the rights of free speech and assembly.

* * * Whenever the fundamental rights of free speech and assembly are alleged to have been invaded, it must remain open to a defendant to present the issue whether there actually did exist at the time a clear danger, whether the danger, if any, was imminent, and whether the evil apprehended was one so

substantial as to justify the stringent restriction interposed by the Legislature. The legislative declaration, like the fact that the statute was passed and was sustained by the highest court of the State, creates merely a rebuttable presumption that these conditions have been satisfied.

Whether in 1919, when Miss Whitney did the things complained of, there was in California such clear and present danger of serious evil, might have been made the important issue in the case. She might have required that the issue be determined either by the court or the jury. She claimed below that the statute as applied to her violated the federal Constitution; but she did not claim that it was void because there was no clear and present danger of serious evil, nor did she request that the existence of these conditions of a valid measure thus restricting the rights of free speech and assembly be passed upon by the court or a jury. On the other hand, there was evidence on which the court or jury might have found that such danger existed. I am unable to assent to the suggestion in the opinion of the court that assembling with a political party, formed to advocate the desirability of a proletarian revolution by mass action at some date necessarily far in the future, is not a right within the protection of the Fourteenth Amendment. In the present case, however, there was other testimony which tended to establish the existence of a conspiracy, on the part of members of the International Workers of the World, to commit present serious crimes, and likewise to show that such a conspiracy would be furthered by the activity of the society of which Miss Whitney was a member. Under these circumstances the judgment of the State court cannot be disturbed. * * *

JUSTICE HOLMES joins in this opinion.

C. Communism and Illegal Advocacy

Kent Greenawalt, *Speech and Crime*, 1980 Am.B.Found.Res.J. 645, describes the pattern for much of the period between *Whitney* and *Dennis* infra: "[T]he clear and present danger formula emerged as the applicable standard not only for the kinds of issues with respect to which it originated but also for a wide variety of other First Amendment problems. If the Court was not always very clear about the relevance of that formula to those different problems, its use of the test, and its employment of ancillary doctrines, did evince a growing disposition to protect expression." By 1951, however, anti-communist sentiment was a powerful theme in American politics. The Soviet Union had detonated a nuclear weapon; communists had firm control of the Chinese mainland; the Korean War had reached a stalemate; Alger Hiss had been convicted of perjury in congressional testimony concerning alleged spying activities for the Soviet Union while a State Department official; and Senator Joseph McCarthy of Wisconsin had created a national sensation by accusations that many "card carrying Communists" held important State Department jobs.

DENNIS V. UNITED STATES

341 U.S. 494, 71 S.Ct. 857, 95 L.Ed. 1137 (1951).

CHIEF JUSTICE VINSON announced the judgment of the Court and an opinion in which JUSTICE REED, JUSTICE BURTON and JUSTICE MINTON join.

Petitioners were indicted in July, 1948, for violation of the conspiracy provisions of the Smith Act during the period of April, 1945, to July, 1948. * * * A verdict of guilty as to all the petitioners was [affirmed by the Second Circuit]. We granted certiorari, limited to the following two questions: (1) Whether either § 2 or § 3 of the Smith Act, inherently or as construed and applied in the instant case, violates the First Amendment and other provisions of the Bill of Rights; (2) whether either § 2 or § 3 of the Act, inherently or as construed and applied in the instant case, violates the First and Fifth Amendments, because of indefiniteness.

Sections 2 and 3 of the Smith Act provide as follows:

"Sec. 2.

"(a) It shall be unlawful for any person—

"(1) to knowingly or willfully advocate, abet, advise, or teach the duty, necessity, desirability, or propriety of overthrowing or destroying any government in the United States by force or violence, or by the assassination of any officer of any such government; * * *

"Sec. 3. It shall be unlawful for any person to attempt to commit, or to conspire to commit, any of the acts prohibited by the provisions [of] this title."

The indictment charged the petitioners with wilfully and knowingly conspiring (1) to organize as the Communist Party of the United States of America a society, group and assembly of persons who teach and advocate the overthrow and destruction of the Government of the United States by force and violence, and (2) knowingly and wilfully to advocate and teach the duty and necessity of overthrowing and destroying the Government of the United States by force and violence. The indictment further alleged that § 2 of the Smith Act proscribes these acts and that any conspiracy to take such action is a violation of § 3 of the Act.

The trial of the case extended over nine months, six of which were devoted to the taking of evidence, resulting in a record of 16,000 pages. Our limited grant of the writ of certiorari has removed from our consideration any question as to the sufficiency of the evidence to support the jury's determination that petitioners are guilty of the offense charged. Whether on this record petitioners did in fact advocate the overthrow of the Government by force and violence is not before us, and we must base any discussion of this point upon the conclusions stated in the opinion of the Court of Appeals, which treated the issue in great detail [and] held that the record supports the following broad conclusions: [that] the Communist Party is a highly disciplined organization, adept at infiltration into strategic positions, use of aliases, and double-meaning language; that the Party is rigidly controlled; that Communists, unlike other political parties, tolerate no dissension from the policy laid down by the guiding [forces]; that the literature of the Party and the statements and activities of its leaders, petitioners here, advocate, and the general goal of the Party was, during the period in question, to achieve a successful overthrow of the existing order by force and violence. * * *

The obvious purpose of the statute is to protect existing Government, not from change by peaceable, lawful and constitutional means, but from change by violence, revolution and terrorism. That it is within the *power* of the Congress to protect the Government of the United States from armed rebellion is a proposition which requires little discussion. Whatever theoretical merit there may be to the argument that there is a "right" to rebellion against dictatorial governments is without force where the existing structure of the government provides for peaceful and orderly change. We reject any principle of governmental helplessness in the face of preparation for revolution, which principle, carried to its logical conclusion, must lead to anarchy. No one could conceive that it is not within the power of Congress to prohibit acts intended to overthrow the Government by force and violence. The question with which we are concerned here is not whether Congress has such *power,* but whether the *means* which it has employed conflict with the First and Fifth Amendments to the Constitution.

One of the bases for the contention that the means which Congress has employed are invalid takes the form of an attack on the face of the statute on the grounds that by its terms it prohibits academic discussion of the merits of Marxism-Leninism, that it stifles ideas and is contrary to all concepts of a free speech and a free press. [This] is a federal statute which we must interpret as well as judge. Herein lies the fallacy of reliance upon the manner in which this Court has treated judgments of state courts. Where the statute as construed by the state court transgressed the First Amendment, we could not but invalidate the judgments of conviction.

The very language of the Smith Act negates the interpretation which petitioners would have us impose on that Act. It is directed at advocacy, not discussion. Thus, the trial judge properly charged the jury that they could not convict if they found that petitioners did "no more than pursue peaceful studies and discussions or teaching and advocacy in the realm of ideas." * * * Congress did not intend to eradicate the free discussion of political theories, to destroy the traditional rights of Americans to discuss and evaluate ideas without fear of governmental sanction. * * *

But although the statute is not directed at the hypothetical cases which petitioners have conjured, its application in this case has resulted in convictions for the teaching and advocacy of the overthrow of the Government by force and violence, which, even though coupled with the intent to accomplish that overthrow, contains an element of speech. For this reason, we must pay special heed to the demands of the First Amendment marking out the boundaries of speech.

[T]he basis of the First Amendment is the hypothesis that speech can rebut speech, propaganda will answer propaganda, free debate of ideas will result in the wisest governmental policies. [An] analysis of the leading cases in this Court which have involved direct limitations on speech, however, will demonstrate that both the majority of the Court and the dissenters in particular cases have recognized that this is not an unlimited, unqualified right, but that the societal value of speech must, on occasion, be subordinated to other values and considerations. * * *

Although no case subsequent to *Whitney* and *Gitlow* has expressly overruled the majority opinions in those cases, there is little doubt that subsequent opinions have inclined toward the Holmes-Brandeis rationale. * * *

In this case we are squarely presented with the application of the "clear and present danger" test, and must decide what that phrase imports. We first note that many of the cases in which this Court has reversed convictions by use of this or similar tests have been based on the fact that the interest which the State was attempting to protect was itself too insubstantial to warrant restriction of speech. * * * Overthrow of the Government by force and violence is certainly a substantial enough interest for the Government to limit speech. Indeed, this is the ultimate value of any society, for if a society cannot protect its very structure from armed internal attack, it must follow that no subordinate value can be protected. If, then, this interest may be protected, the literal problem which is presented is what has been meant by the use of the phrase "clear and present danger" of the utterances bringing about the evil within the power of Congress to punish.

Obviously, the words cannot mean that before the Government may act, it must wait until the putsch is about to be executed, the plans have been laid and the signal is awaited. If Government is aware that a group aiming at its overthrow is attempting to indoctrinate its members and to commit them to a course whereby they will strike when the leaders feel the circumstances permit, action by the Government is required. The argument that there is no need for Government to concern itself, for Government is strong, it possesses ample powers to put down a rebellion, it may defeat the revolution with ease needs no answer. For that is not the question. Certainly an attempt to overthrow the Government by force, even though doomed from the outset because of inadequate numbers or power of the revolutionists, is a sufficient evil for Congress to prevent. The damage which such attempts create both physically and politically to a nation makes it impossible to measure the validity in terms of the probability of success, or the immediacy of a successful attempt. In the instant case the trial judge charged the jury that they could not convict unless they found that petitioners intended to overthrow the Government "as speedily as circumstances would permit." This does not mean, and could not properly mean, that they would not strike until there was certainty of success. What was meant was that the revolutionists would strike when they thought the time was ripe. We must therefore reject the contention that success or probability of success is the criterion.

The situation with which Justices Holmes and Brandeis were concerned in *Gitlow* was a comparatively isolated event, bearing little relation in their minds to any substantial threat to the safety of the community. [They] were not confronted with any situation comparable to the instant one—the development of an apparatus designed and dedicated to the overthrow of the Government, in the context of world crisis after crisis.

Chief Judge Learned Hand, writing for the majority below, interpreted the phrase as follows: "In each case [courts] must ask whether the gravity of the 'evil,' discounted by its improbability, justifies such invasion of free speech as is necessary to avoid the danger." We adopt this statement of the rule. As articulated by Chief Judge Hand, it is as succinct and inclusive as any other we might devise at this time. * * *

Likewise, we are in accord with the court below, which affirmed the trial court's finding that the requisite danger existed. The mere fact that from the period 1945 to 1948 petitioners' activities did not result in an attempt to overthrow the Government by force and violence is of course no answer to the fact that there was a group that was ready to make the attempt. The formation by petitioners of such a highly organized conspiracy, with rigidly disciplined members subject to call when the leaders, these petitioners, felt that the time had come for action, coupled with the inflammable nature of world conditions, similar uprisings in other countries, and the touch-and-go nature of our relations with countries with whom petitioners were in the very least ideologically attuned, convince us that their convictions were justified on this score. And this analysis disposes of the contention that a conspiracy to advocate, as distinguished from the advocacy itself, cannot be constitutionally restrained, because it comprises only the preparation. It is the existence of the conspiracy which creates the danger. * * *

Although we have concluded that the finding that there was a sufficient danger to warrant the application of the statute was justified on the merits, there remains the problem of whether the trial judge's treatment of the issue was correct. He charged the jury, in relevant part, as follows: "In further construction and interpretation of the statute I charge you that it is not the abstract doctrine of overthrowing or destroying organized government by unlawful means which is denounced by this law, but the teaching and advocacy of action for the accomplishment of that purpose, by language reasonably and ordinarily calculated to incite persons to such action. Accordingly, you cannot find the defendants or any of them guilty of the crime charged unless you are satisfied beyond a reasonable doubt that they conspired to organize a society, group and assembly of persons who teach and advocate the overthrow or destruction of the Government of the United States by force and violence and to advocate and teach the duty and necessity of overthrowing or destroying the Government of the United States by force and violence, with the intent that such teaching and advocacy be of a rule or principle of action and by language reasonably and ordinarily calculated to incite persons to such action, all with the intent to cause the overthrow or destruction of the Government of the United States by force and violence as speedily as circumstances would permit. * * *

"If you are satisfied that the evidence establishes beyond a reasonable doubt that the defendants, or any of them, are guilty of a violation of the statute, as I have interpreted it to you, I find as matter of law that there is sufficient danger of a substantive evil that the Congress has a right to prevent to justify the application of the statute under the First Amendment of the Constitution. This is matter of law about which you have no concern. * * * "

It is thus clear that he reserved the question of the existence of the danger for his own determination, and the question becomes whether the issue is of such a nature that it should have been submitted to the jury.

[When] facts are found that establish the violation of a statute, the protection against conviction afforded by the First Amendment is a matter of law. The doctrine that there must be a clear and present danger of a substantive evil that Congress has a right to prevent is a judicial rule to be applied as a matter of law by the courts. The guilt is established by proof of facts. Whether the First Amendment protects the activity which constitutes the violation of the statute must depend upon a judicial determination of the scope of the First Amendment applied to the circumstances of the case.

[In] *Schenck* this Court itself examined the record to find whether the requisite danger appeared, and the issue was not submitted to a jury. And in every later case in which the Court has measured the validity of a statute by the "clear and present danger" test, that determination has been by the court, the question of the danger not being submitted to the jury. * * * Petitioners intended to overthrow the Government of the United States as speedily as the circumstances would permit. Their conspiracy to organize the Communist Party and to teach and advocate the overthrow of the Government of the United States by force and violence created a "clear and present danger" of an attempt to overthrow the Government by force and violence. They were properly and constitutionally convicted * * * .

Affirmed.

JUSTICE CLARK took no part in the consideration or decision of this case.

JUSTICE FRANKFURTER, concurring in affirmance of the judgment.

[The] demands of free speech in a democratic society as well as the interest in national security are better served by candid and informed weighing of the competing interests, within the confines of the judicial process, than by announcing dogmas too inflexible for the non-Euclidian problems to be solved.

But how are competing interests to be assessed? Since they are not subject to quantitative ascertainment, the issue necessarily resolves itself into asking, who is to make the adjustment?—who is to balance the relevant factors and ascertain which interest is in the circumstances to prevail? Full responsibility for the choice cannot be given to the courts. Courts are not representative bodies. They are not designed to be a good reflex of a democratic society. Their judgment is best informed, and therefore most dependable, within narrow limits. Their essential quality is detachment, founded on independence. History teaches that the independence of the judiciary is jeopardized when courts become embroiled in the passions of the day and assume primary responsibility in choosing between competing political, economic and social pressures.

Primary responsibility for adjusting the interests which compete in the situation before us of necessity belongs to the Congress. [We] are to set aside the judgment of those whose duty it is to legislate only if there is no reasonable basis for [it]. Free-speech cases are not an exception to the principle that we are not legislators, that direct policy-making is not our province. How best to reconcile competing interests is the business of legislatures, and the balance they strike is a judgment not to be displaced by ours, but to be respected unless outside the pale of fair judgment. [A] survey of the relevant decisions indicates that the results which we have reached are on the whole those that would ensue from careful weighing of conflicting interests. The complex issues presented by regulation of speech in public places by picketing, and by legislation prohibiting advocacy of crime have been resolved by scrutiny of many factors besides the imminence and gravity of the evil threatened. The matter has been well summarized by a reflective student of the Court's work. "The truth is that the clear-and-present-danger test is an oversimplified judgment unless it takes account also of a number of other factors: the relative seriousness of the danger in comparison with the value of the occasion for speech or political activity; the availability of more moderate controls than those which the state has imposed; and perhaps the specific intent with which the speech or activity is launched. No matter how rapidly we utter the phrase 'clear and present danger,' or how closely we hyphenate the words, they are not a substitute for the weighing of values. They tend to convey a delusion of certitude when what is most certain is the complexity of the strands in the web of freedoms which the judge must disentangle." Paul Freund, *On Understanding the Supreme Court* 27–28 [1949]. * * *

To make validity of legislation depend on judicial reading of events still in the womb of time—a forecast, that is, of the outcome of forces at best appreciated only with knowledge of the topmost secrets of nations—is to charge the judiciary with duties beyond its equipment. * * *

Even when moving strictly within the limits of constitutional adjudication, judges are concerned with issues that may be said to involve vital finalities. The too easy transition from disapproval of what is undesirable to condemnation as unconstitutional, has led some of the wisest judges to question the wisdom of our scheme in lodging such authority in courts. But it is relevant to remind that in sustaining the power of Congress in a case like this nothing irrevocable is done. The democratic process at all events is not impaired or restricted. Power and responsibility remain with the people and immediately with their representation. All the Court says is that Congress was not forbidden by the Constitution to pass this enactment and that a prosecution under it may be brought against a conspiracy such as the one before us. * * *

JUSTICE JACKSON, concurring.

[E]ither by accident or design, the Communist stratagem outwits the antianarchist pattern of statute aimed against "overthrow by force and violence" if qualified by the doctrine that only "clear and present danger" of accomplishing that result will sustain the prosecution.

The "clear and present danger" test was an innovation by Mr. Justice Holmes in the *Schenck* case, reiterated and refined by him and Mr. Justice Brandeis in later cases, all arising before the era of World War II revealed the subtlety and efficacy of modernized revolutionary techniques used by totalitarian parties. In those cases, they were faced with convictions under so-called criminal syndicalism statutes aimed at anarchists but which, loosely construed, had been applied to punish socialism, pacifism, and left-wing ideologies, the charges often resting on farfetched inferences which, if true, would establish only technical or trivial violations. They proposed "clear and present danger" as a test for the sufficiency of evidence in particular cases.

I would save it, unmodified, for application as a "rule of reason" in the kind of case for which it was devised. When the issue is criminality of a hotheaded speech on a street corner, or circulation of a few incendiary pamphlets, or parading by some zealots behind a red flag, or refusal of a handful of school children to salute our flag, it is not beyond the capacity of the judicial process to gather, comprehend, and weigh the necessary materials for decision whether it is a clear and present danger of substantive evil or a harmless letting off of steam. It is not a prophecy, for the danger in such cases has matured by the time of trial or it was never present. The test applies and has meaning where a conviction is sought to be based on a speech or writing which does not directly or explicitly advocate a crime but to which such tendency is sought to be attributed by construction or by implication from external circumstances. The formula in such cases favors freedoms that are vital to our society, and, even if sometimes applied too generously, the consequences cannot be grave. But its recent expansion has extended, in particular to Communists, unprecedented immunities. Unless we are to hold our Government captive in a judge-made verbal trap, we must approach the problem of a well-organized, nation-wide conspiracy, such as I have described, as realistically as our predecessors faced the trivialities that were being prosecuted until they were checked with a rule of reason.

I think reason is lacking for applying that test to this case.

If we must decide that this Act and its application are constitutional only if we are convinced that petitioner's conduct creates a "clear and present danger" of violent overthrow, we must appraise imponderables, including international and national phenomena which baffle the best informed foreign offices and our most experienced politicians. We would have to foresee and predict the effectiveness of Communist propaganda, opportunities for infiltration, whether, and when, a time will come that they consider propitious for action, and whether and how fast our existing government will deteriorate. And we would have to speculate as to whether an approaching Communist coup would not be anticipated by a nationalistic fascist movement. No doctrine can be sound whose application requires us to make a prophecy of that sort in the guise of a legal decision. The judicial process simply is not adequate to a trial of such far-flung issues. The answers given would reflect our own political predilections and nothing more.

The authors of the clear and present danger test never applied it to a case like this, nor would I. If applied as it is proposed here, it means that the Communist plotting is protected during its period of incubation; its preliminary stages of organization and preparation are immune from the law; the Government can move only after imminent action is manifest, when it would, of course, be too late.

The highest degree of constitutional protection is due to the individual acting without conspiracy. But even an individual cannot claim that the Constitution protects him in advocating or teaching overthrow of government by force or violence. I should suppose no one would doubt that Congress has power to make such attempted overthrow a crime. But the contention is that one has the constitutional right to work up a public desire and will to do what it is a crime to attempt. I think direct incitement by speech or writing can be made a crime, and I think there can be a conviction without also proving that the odds favored its success by 99 to 1, or some other extremely high ratio. * * *

What really is under review here is a conviction of conspiracy, after a trial for conspiracy, on an indictment charging conspiracy, brought under a statute outlawing conspiracy. With due respect to my colleagues, they seem to me to discuss anything under the sun except the law of conspiracy. * * *

The Constitution does not make conspiracy a civil right. [Although] I consider criminal conspiracy a dragnet device capable of perversion into an instrument of injustice in the hands of a partisan or complacent judiciary, it has an established place in our system of law, and no reason appears for applying it only to concerted action claimed to disturb interstate commerce and withholding it from those claimed to undermine our whole Government. * * *

I do not suggest that Congress could punish conspiracy to advocate something, the doing of which it may not punish. Advocacy or exposition of the doctrine of communal property ownership, or any political philosophy unassociated with advocacy of its imposition by force or seizure of government by unlawful means could not be reached through conspiracy prosecution. But it is not forbidden to put down force or violence, it is not forbidden to punish its teaching or advocacy, and the end being punishable, there is no doubt of the power to punish conspiracy for the purpose. * * *

JUSTICE BLACK, dissenting. * * *

So long as this Court exercises the power of judicial review of legislation, I cannot agree that the First Amendment permits us to sustain laws suppressing freedom of speech and press on the basis of Congress' or our own notions of mere "reasonableness." Such a doctrine waters down the First Amendment so that it amounts to little more than an admonition to Congress. The Amendment as so construed is not likely to protect any but those "safe" or orthodox views which rarely need its protection. I must also express my objection to the holding because, as Mr. Justice Douglas' dissent shows, it sanctions the determination of a crucial issue of fact by the judge rather than by the jury. * * *

Public opinion being what it now is, few will protest the conviction of these Communist petitioners. There is hope, however, that in calmer times, when present pressures, passions and fears subside, this or some later Court will restore the First Amendment liberties to the high preferred place where they belong in a free society.

JUSTICE DOUGLAS, dissenting.

If this were a case where those who claimed protection under the First Amendment were teaching the techniques of sabotage, the assassination of the President, the filching of documents from public files, the planting of bombs, the art of street warfare, and the like, I would have no doubts. The freedom to speak is not absolute; the teaching of methods of terror and other seditious conduct should be beyond the pale along with obscenity and immorality. This case was argued as if those were the facts. The argument imported much seditious conduct into the record. That is easy and it has popular appeal, for the activities of Communists in plotting and scheming against the free world are common knowledge. But the fact is that no such evidence was introduced at the trial. There is a statute which makes a seditious conspiracy unlawful. Petitioners, however, were not charged with a "conspiracy to overthrow" the Government. They were charged with a conspiracy to form a party and groups and assemblies of people who teach and advocate the overthrow of our Government by force or violence and with a conspiracy to advocate and teach its overthrow by force and violence. It may well be that indoctrination in the techniques of terror to destroy the Government would be indictable under either statute. But the teaching which is condemned here is of a different character.

So far as the present record is concerned, what petitioners did was to organize people to teach and themselves teach the Marxist-Leninist doctrine contained chiefly in four books: *Foundations of Leninism* by Stalin (1924); *The Communist Manifesto* by Marx and Engels (1848); *State and Revolution* by Lenin (1917); *History of the Communist Party of the Soviet Union* (B.) (1939).

Those books are to Soviet Communism what *Mein Kampf* was to Nazism. If they are understood, the ugliness of Communism is revealed, its deceit and cunning are exposed, the nature of its activities becomes apparent, and the chances of its success less likely. That is not, of course, the reason why petitioners chose these books for their classrooms. They are fervent Communists to whom these volumes are gospel. They preached the creed with the hope that some day it would be acted upon.

The opinion of the Court does not outlaw these texts nor condemn them to the fire, as the Communists do literature offensive to their creed. But if the books themselves are not outlawed, if they can lawfully remain on library shelves, by what reasoning does their use in a classroom become a crime? It would not be a crime under the Act to introduce these books to a class, though that would be teaching what the creed of violent overthrow of the Government is. The Act, as construed, requires the element of intent—that those who teach the creed believe in it. The crime then depends not on what is taught but on who the teacher is. That is to make freedom of speech turn not on *what is said,* but on the *intent* with which it is said. Once we start down that road we enter territory dangerous to the liberties of every citizen. * * *

The vice of treating speech as the equivalent of overt acts of a treasonable or seditious character is emphasized by a concurring opinion, which by invoking the law of conspiracy makes speech do service for deeds which are dangerous to society. [N]ever until today has anyone seriously thought that the ancient law of conspiracy could constitutionally be used to turn speech into seditious conduct. Yet that is precisely what is suggested. I repeat that we deal here with speech alone, not with speech *plus* acts of sabotage or unlawful conduct. Not a single seditious act is charged in the indictment. To make a lawful speech unlawful because two men conceive it is to raise the law of conspiracy to appalling proportions. * * *

There comes a time when even speech loses its constitutional immunity. Speech innocuous one year may at another time fan such destructive flames that it must be halted in the interests of the safety of the Republic. That is the meaning of the clear and present danger test. When conditions are so critical that there will be no time to avoid the evil that the speech threatens, it is time to call a halt. Otherwise, free speech which is the strength of the Nation will be the cause of its destruction.

Yet free speech is the rule, not the exception. The restraint to be constitutional must be based on more than fear, on more than passionate opposition against the speech, on more than a revolted dislike for its contents. There must be some immediate injury to society that is likely if speech is allowed. * * *

I had assumed that the question of the clear and present danger, being so critical an issue in the case, would be a matter for submission to the jury. [The] Court, I think, errs when it treats the question as one of law.

Yet, whether the question is one for the Court or the jury, there should be evidence of record on the issue. This record, however, contains no evidence whatsoever showing that the acts charged viz., the teaching of the Soviet theory of revolution with the hope that it will be realized, have created any clear and present danger to the Nation. The Court, however, rules to the contrary. [The majority] might as well say that the speech of petitioners is outlawed because Soviet Russia and her Red Army are a threat to world peace.

The nature of Communism as a force on the world scene would, of course, be relevant to the issue of clear and present danger of petitioners' advocacy within the United States. But the primary consideration is the strength and tactical position of petitioners and their converts in this country. On that there is no evidence in the record. If we are to take judicial notice of the threat of Communists within the nation, it should not be difficult to conclude that *as a political party* they are of little consequence. Communists in this country have never made a respectable or serious showing in any election. I would doubt that there is a village, let alone a city or county or state, which the Communists could carry. Communism in the world scene is no bogeyman; but Communism as a political faction or party in this country plainly is. Communism has been so thoroughly exposed in this country that it has been crippled as a political force. Free speech has destroyed it as an effective political party. It is inconceivable that those who went up and down this country preaching the doctrine of revolution which petitioners espouse would have any success. In days of trouble and confusion, when bread lines were long, when the unemployed walked the streets, when people were starving, the advocates of a short-cut by revolution might have a chance to gain adherents. But today there are no such conditions. The country is not in despair; the people know Soviet Communism; the doctrine of Soviet revolution is exposed in all of its ugliness and the American people want none of it.

[Unless] and until extreme and necessitous circumstances are shown our aim should be to keep speech unfettered and to allow the processes of law to be invoked only when the provocateurs among us move from speech to action. * * *

––––––––

Dennis distinguished. In 1954, Senator Joseph McCarthy was censured by the United States Senate for acting contrary to its ethics and impairing its dignity. In 1957, when the convictions of 14 "second string" communist leaders reached the Supreme Court in YATES v. UNITED STATES, 354 U.S. 298 (1957), McCarthy had died, as had McCarthyism. Strong anti-communist sentiment persisted, but the political atmosphere in *Yates'* 1957 was profoundly different from that of *Dennis* 1951. HARLAN, J., distinguishing *Dennis,* construed the Smith Act narrowly: "[The] essence of the *Dennis* holding was that indoctrination of a group in preparation for future violent action, as well as exhortation to immediate action, by advocacy found to be directed to 'action for the accomplishment' of forcible overthrow, to violence as 'a rule or principle of action,' and employing 'language of incitement,' is not constitutionally protected when the group is of sufficient size and cohesiveness, is sufficiently oriented towards action, and other circumstances are such as reasonably to justify apprehension that action will occur. This is quite a different thing from the view of the District Court here that mere doctrinal justification of forcible overthrow, if engaged in with the intent to accomplish overthrow, is punishable per se under the Smith Act. [T]he trial court's statement that the proscribed advocacy must include the 'urging,' 'necessity,' and 'duty' of forcible overthrow, and not merely its 'desirability' and 'propriety,' may not be regarded as a sufficient substitute for charging that the Smith Act reaches only advocacy of action for the overthrow of government by force and violence. The essential distinction is that those to whom the advocacy is addressed must be urged to *do* something, now or in the future, rather than merely to *believe* in something."

Applying this standard, Harlan J., acquitted 5 defendants and remanded to the lower court for proceedings against the remaining defendants.

After *Yates*, the government sought to prosecute Communists for being members of an organization advocating the overthrow of the government by force and violence. The Court in *Scales v. United States*, 367 U.S. 203 (1961), and *Noto v. United States*, 367 U.S. 290 (1961), interpreted the membership clause to require that the organization engage in advocacy of the sort described in *Yates* and that the members be active and aware of the organization's advocacy and its specific intent to bring about speedy violent overthrow.

Seven years after *Scales* and *Noto*, Dr. Benjamin Spock, Rev. William Sloan Coffin, and others were convicted of conspiring to counsel and abet Selective Service registrants to refuse to have their draft cards in their possession and to disobey other duties under the Selective Service Act of 1967. Spock signed a document entitled "A Call to Resist Illegitimate Authority," which "had 'a double aspect: in part it was a denunciation of governmental policy [in Vietnam] and, in part, it involved a public call to resist the duties imposed by the [Selective Service] Act.' UNITED STATES v. SPOCK, 416 F.2d 165 (1st Cir.1969), per ALDRICH, J., ruled that Spock should have been acquitted: The primary basis for the court's conclusion was that the trial court had impermissibly (in a criminal case) given the jury special questions, rather than simply requiring a general verdict. But the court also addressed the First Amendment issues: "[Spock] was one of the drafters of the Call, but this does not evidence the necessary intent to adhere to its illegal aspects. [H]is speech was limited to condemnation of the war and the draft, and lacked any words or content of counselling. The jury could not find proscribed advocacy from the mere fact [that] he hoped the frequent stating of his views might give young men 'courage to take active steps in draft resistance.' This is a natural consequence of vigorous speech. Similarly, Spock's actions lacked the clear character necessary to imply specific intent under the First Amendment standard. [H]e was at [a] demonstration, [but took] no part in its planning. [His statements at this demonstration did not extend] beyond the general anti-war, anti-draft remarks he had made before. His attendance is as consistent with a desire to repeat this speech as it is to aid a violation of the law. The dissent would fault us for drawing such distinctions, but it forgets [that] expressing one's views in broad areas is not foreclosed by knowledge of the consequences, and the important lesson of *Noto, Scales* and *Yates* that one may belong to a group, knowing of its illegal aspects, and still not be found to adhere thereto."

D. A Modern "Restatement"

BRANDENBURG V. OHIO

395 U.S. 444, 89 S.Ct. 1827, 23 L.Ed.2d 430 (1969).

PER CURIAM.

The appellant, a leader of a Ku Klux Klan group, was convicted under [a 1919] Ohio Criminal Syndicalism statute of "advocat[ing] the duty, necessity, or propriety of crime, sabotage, violence, or unlawful methods of terrorism as a means of accomplishing industrial or political reform" and of "voluntarily assembl[ing] with any society, group or assemblage of persons formed to teach or advocate the doctrines of criminal syndicalism." He was fined $1,000 and sentenced to one to 10 years' imprisonment. * * *

The record shows that a man, identified at trial as the appellant, telephoned an announcer-reporter on the staff of a Cincinnati television station and invited him to come to a Ku Klux Klan "rally" to be held at a farm in Hamilton County. With the cooperation of the organizers, the reporter and a cameraman attended the meeting and filmed the events. Portions of the films were later broadcast on the local station and on a national network.

The prosecution's case rested on the films and on testimony identifying the appellant as the person who communicated with the reporter and who spoke at the rally. The State also introduced into evidence several articles appearing in the film, including a pistol, a rifle, a shotgun, ammunition, a Bible, and a red hood worn by the speaker in the films.

One film showed 12 hooded figures, some of whom carried firearms. They were gathered around a large wooden cross, which they burned. No one was present other than the participants and the newsmen who made the film. Most of the words uttered during the scene were incomprehensible when the film was projected, but scattered phrases could be understood that were derogatory of Negroes and, in one instance, of Jews. Another scene on the same film showed the appellant, in Klan regalia, making a speech. The speech, in full, was as follows:

"This is an organizers' meeting. We have had quite a few members here today which are—we have hundreds, hundreds of members throughout the State of Ohio. I can quote from a newspaper clipping from the Columbus Ohio Dispatch, five weeks ago Sunday morning. The Klan has more members in the State of Ohio than does any other organization. We're not a revengent organization, but if our President, our Congress, our Supreme Court, continues to suppress the white, Caucasian race, it's possible that there might have to be some revengence taken.

"We are marching on Congress July the Fourth, four hundred thousand strong. From there we are dividing into two groups, one group to march on St. Augustine, Florida, the other group to march into Mississippi. Thank you."

The second film showed six hooded figures one of whom, later identified as the appellant, repeated a speech very similar to that recorded on the first film. The reference to the possibility of "revengence" was omitted, and one sentence was added: "Personally, I believe the nigger should be returned to Africa, the Jew returned to Israel." Though some of the figures in the films carried weapons, the speaker did not.

[*Whitney*] sustained the constitutionality of California's Criminal Syndicalism Act, the text of which is quite similar to that of the laws of Ohio. The Court upheld the statute on the ground that, without more, "advocating" violent means to effect political and economic change involves such danger to the security of the State that the State may outlaw it. But *Whitney* has been thoroughly discredited by later decisions [such as *Dennis* which] have fashioned the principle that the constitutional guarantees of free speech and free press do not permit a State to forbid or proscribe advocacy of the use of force or of law violation except where such advocacy is directed to inciting or producing imminent lawless action and is likely to incite or produce such action. As we said in *Noto*, "the mere abstract teaching [of] the moral propriety or even moral necessity for a resort to force and violence, is not the same as preparing a group for violent action and steeling it to such action." See also *Bond v. Floyd*. A statute which fails to draw this distinction impermissibly intrudes upon the freedoms guaranteed by the First and Fourteenth Amendments. It sweeps within its condemnation speech which our Constitution has immunized from governmental control. Cf. *Yates* * * * .

Measured by this test, Ohio's Criminal Syndicalism Act cannot be sustained. The Act punishes persons who "advocate or teach the duty, necessity, or propriety" of violence "as a means of accomplishing industrial or political reform"; or who publish or circulate or display any book or paper containing such advocacy; or who "justify" the commission of violent acts "with intent to exemplify, spread or advocate the propriety of the doctrines of criminal syndicalism"; or [who] "voluntarily assemble" with a group formed "to teach or advocate the doctrines of criminal syndicalism." Neither the indictment nor the trial judge's instructions to the jury in any way refined the statute's bald definition of the crime in terms of mere advocacy not distinguished from incitement to imminent lawless action.

Accordingly, we are here confronted with a statute which, by its own words and as applied, purports to punish mere advocacy and to forbid, on pain of criminal punishment, assembly with others merely to advocate the described type of action. Such a statute falls within the condemnation of the First and Fourteenth Amendments. The contrary teaching of *Whitney* cannot be supported, and that decision is therefore overruled.

Reversed.

JUSTICE BLACK, concurring.

I agree with the views expressed by Mr. Justice Douglas in his concurring opinion in this case that the "clear and present danger" doctrine should have no place in the interpretation of the First Amendment. I join the Court's opinion, which, as I understand it, simply cites *Dennis*, but does not indicate any agreement on the Court's part with the "clear and present danger" doctrine on which *Dennis* purported to rely.

JUSTICE DOUGLAS, concurring.

While I join the opinion of the Court, I desire to enter a caveat.

[Whether] the war power—the greatest leveler of them all—is adequate to sustain [the "clear and present danger"] doctrine is debatable. The dissents in *Abrams* [and other cases] show how easily "clear and present danger" is manipulated to crush what Brandeis called "the fundamental right of free men to strive for better conditions through new legislation and new institutions" by argument and discourse even in time of war. Though I doubt if the "clear and present danger" test is congenial to the First Amendment in time of a declared war, I am certain it is not reconcilable with the First Amendment in days of peace. * * *

Mr. Justice Holmes, though never formally abandoning the "clear and present danger" test, moved closer to the First Amendment ideal when he said in dissent in *Gitlow* [quoting the passage beginning, "Every idea is an incitement."] We have never been faithful to the philosophy of that dissent.

"[In *Dennis,* we distorted] the 'clear and present danger' test beyond recognition. [I] see no place in the regime of the First Amendment for any 'clear and present danger' test whether strict and tight as some would make it or free-wheeling as the Court in *Dennis* rephrased it.

NOTES AND QUESTIONS

1. Why did the Court say that pre-*Brandenburg* decisions "have fashioned the principle" that advocacy may not be prohibited "except [where] directed to inciting or producing *imminent* lawless action *and* * * * *likely* to incite or produce such action"? Didn't *Dennis*, *Yates* and *Scales* deny that the unlawful action advocated need be "imminent" or that the advocacy must be "likely" to produce the forbidden action?

2. Does *Brandenburg* adopt the *Masses* incitement test as a major part of the required showing? Does the idea of incitement require explicit words, as suggested in Hand's *Masses* opinion, or explicit intent to produce the advocated effect, or both? If one wants to argue that *Brandenburg* adopted *Masses*, is there anything to be made of the phrase "directed to" in the *Brandenburg* test? Is "directed to" a reference to speaker intent or to the conventional meaning of the speaker's words? Alternatively, did *Yates* adopt the *Masses* test? If so, does its favorable citation in *Brandenburg* constitute an adoption of the *Masses* test?

3. The *Brandenburg* "inciting or producing imminent lawless action" standard was the basis for reversal of a disorderly conduct conviction in HESS v. INDIANA, 414 U.S. 105 (1973) (per curiam). After antiwar demonstrators on the Indiana University campus had blocked a public street, police moved them to the curbs on either side. As an officer passed him, appellant stated loudly, "We'll take

the fucking street later [or again]," which led to his disorderly conduct conviction. His statement, observed the Court, "was not addressed to any person or group in particular" and "his tone, although loud, was no louder than that of the other people in the area. [At] best, [the] statement could be taken as counsel for present moderation; at worst, it amounted to nothing more than advocacy of illegal action at some indefinite future time." This was insufficient, under *Brandenburg,* to punish appellant's words, as the State had, on the ground that they had a "tendency to produce violence." It could not be said that appellant "was advocating, in the normal sense, any action" and there was "no evidence" that "his words were intended to produce, and likely to produce, *imminent* disorder."

REHNQUIST, J., joined by Burger, C.J., and Blackmun, J., dissented: "The simple explanation for the result in this case is that the majority has interpreted the evidence differently from the courts below." The dissenters quarreled with the Court's conclusion that appellant's advocacy "was not directed towards inciting imminent action. [T]here are surely possible constructions of the statement which would encompass more or less immediate and continuing action against the police. They should not be rejected out of hand because of an unexplained preference for other acceptable alternatives."

4.   Does *Brandenburg* apply to advocacy of trivial crimes, whether political or not? To advocacy of trespass across a lawn? Of littering? See Brandeis in Whitney, referring to "substantial" and "serious" evils.

5.   Does *Brandenburg* apply to solicitation of crime in non-public or non-ideological contexts? For analysis of the issues raised by the shift in context from public to private or in subject matter from ideological to non-ideological, see Kent Greenawalt, *Speech, Crime and the Uses of Language* (1989).

6.   Should *Brandenburg* be construed to protect threats? Nuremberg Files, an anti-abortion Web site included the names, addresses, photographs, and license plate numbers of those who provided abortions or were prominent pro-choice advocates together with their family members. Protected? On the First Amendment and threats, see *Virginia v. Black* (2003), Sec. 1, I, D infra. Does *Brandenburg* apply unmodified to the provision of crime-facilitating factual information? To tort actions against those whose words may have been a causal contributor to a crime?[4]

7.   Congress prohibits the providing of material support or resources to any organization designated by the Secretary of State to be a foreign terrorist organization. Plaintiffs sought to provide support to either of two such

---

[4]   On the application of *Brandenburg* to the provision of information likely to facilitate crime, a prominent example arose from the publication by Paladin Press of a book entitled *Hit Man: A Technical Manual for Independent Contractors.* James Perry relied on the book's instructions to kill three people. *Rice v. Paladin Enterprises*, 128 F.3d 233 (4th Cir. 1997). Consider also *Herceg v. Hustler Magazine, Inc.*, 814 F.2d 1017 (5th Cir. 1987) (refusing, on the authority of *Brandenburg,* to find tort liability where juvenile died while attempting an act of autoerotic asphyxiation described in magazine); *Olivia N. v. National Broadcasting Co.*, 178 Cal.Rptr. 888 (Cal.Ct.App. 1981) (disallowing tort liability against television broadcaster for broadcasting a description of a sexual assault subsequently copied by juveniles in committing such an assault).

organizations: the Kurdistan Workers Party ("PKK") and the Liberation Tigers of Tamil Eelam ("LTTE"). Specifically, they wished to provide support in order to train members of the PKK to use law to peacefully resolve disputes; to teach PKK how to petition representative bodies such as the United Nations for relief; and/or to engage in political advocacy on behalf of Kurds who live in Turkey or on behalf of the LTTE. HOLDER v. HUMANITARIAN LAW PROJECT, 561 U.S. 1 (2010), per ROBERTS, C.J., held that the congressional prohibition could constitutionally be applied to training and expert advice for peaceful speech activities even if the provision of such support was not intended to assist in the unlawful activities of the organization. Roberts, C.J., emphasized that the statute does not cover independent advocacy on behalf of such organizations or even membership in such organizations. Rather, it covers support including training, expert advice, or speech under the direction of or in coordination with an organization designated as terrorist in character.

Roberts, C.J., did not deny that the support was a form of presumptively protected speech, but deferred to the findings of the Congressional and Executive Branches that the organizations were "so tainted by their criminal conduct that any contribution to such an organization facilitates that conduct." He argued that support frees up other resources, helps to legitimize such organizations, and strains U.S. relationships with its allies. The skills taught could be used in manipulative ways and might gain further monetary gains for such organizations. Roberts, C.J., concluded that the prohibitions were necessary to further an urgent objective of the highest order.

BREYER, J., joined by Ginsburg and Sotomayor, JJ., dissenting, argued that the decision interfered with centrally important peaceful speech activities. He argued that peaceful advocacy should ordinarily be protected whether or not it was coordinated with a designated terrorist organization.

II. REPUTATION AND PRIVACY

In an important article, Harry Kalven coined the phrase "two level theory," *The Metaphysics of the Law of Obscenity*, 1960 Sup.Ct.Rev. 1. As he described it, *Beauharnais,* infra, and other cases employed a First Amendment methodology that classified speech at two levels. Some speech—libel, obscenity, "fighting words"—was thought to be so bereft of social utility as to be beneath First Amendment protection. At the second level, speech of constitutional value was thought to be protected unless it presented a clear and present danger of a substantive evil. In some respects Kalven was plainly correct. No one seriously claims that the First Amendment is applicable to ordinary contract law, which imposes liability based on spoken or written words, or to most of the law of wills, which does much the same thing, or to the law of blackmail, perjury, and much else. Indeed, albeit with less unanimity, the First Amendment is not understood even to be relevant to most of the regulatory activities of the Securities and Exchange Commission, the Federal Trade Commission, and the Food and Drug Administration, each of which is largely in the business of regulating the use of words. And if one corporate executive uses words to propose to an executive of a competitor company that they charge the same prices, and if the second executive uses words to agree to the arrangement, they will both be in plain violation of the price-fixing dimensions of the Sherman Antitrust Act, with nary an objection from the First Amendment.

In other areas, however, Kalven's two-level account appears to be weakening, as the following materials on libel and privacy indicate. The purpose is not to offer a detailed examination of libel and privacy law, but to use the initial exclusion of defamation from First Amendment coverage, and the subsequent erosion of that exclusion, to explore First Amendment methods and values that go beyond defamation and privacy.

A. Group Libel

BEAUHARNAIS v. ILLINOIS, 343 U.S. 250 (1952), per FRANKFURTER, J., sustained a statute prohibiting exhibition in any public place of any publication portraying "depravity, criminality, unchastity, or lack of virtue of a class of citizens, of any race, color, creed or religion [which exposes such citizens] to contempt, derision or obloquy or which is productive of breach of the peace or riots." The Court affirmed a conviction for distributing of a leaflet which petitioned the Mayor and City Council of Chicago "to halt the further encroachment, harassment and invasion of white people, their property, neighborhoods and persons by the Negro"; called for "one million self respecting white people in Chicago to unite"; and warned that if "the need to prevent the white race from becoming mongrelized by the Negro will not unite us, then the [aggressions], rapes, robberies, knives, guns, and marijuana of the Negro, surely will.":

"Today every American jurisdiction [punishes] libels directed at individuals. '[There] are certain well-defined and narrowly limited classes of speech, the prevention and punishment of which have never been thought to raise any constitutional problem. These include the lewd and obscene, the profane, the libelous, and the insulting or "fighting" words—those which by their very utterance inflict injury or tend to incite to an immediate breach of the peace. It has been well observed that such utterances are no essential part of any exposition of ideas, and are of such slight social value as a step to truth that any benefit that may be derived from them is clearly outweighed by the social interest in order and morality. "Resort to epithets or personal abuse is not in any proper sense communication of information or opinion safeguarded by the Constitution, and its punishment as a criminal act would raise no question under that instrument." *Cantwell v. Connecticut*, [Ch. 8, Sec. 2].' Such were the views of a unanimous Court in *Chaplinsky v. New Hampshire*, Sec. 1, IV, A infra.

"No one will gainsay that it is libelous falsely to charge another with being a rapist, robber, carrier of knives and guns, and user of marijuana. The [question is whether the fourteenth amendment] prevents a State from punishing such libels— as criminal libel has been defined, limited and constitutionally recognized time out of mind—directed at designated collectivities and flagrantly disseminated. [I]f an utterance directed at an individual may be the object of criminal sanctions, we cannot deny to a State power to punish the same utterance directed at a defined group, unless we can say that this is a wilful and purposeless restriction unrelated to the peace and well-being of the State.

"Illinois did not have to look beyond her own borders to await the tragic experience of the last three decades to conclude that wilful purveyors of falsehood concerning racial and religious groups promote strife and tend powerfully to obstruct the manifold adjustments required for free, orderly life in a metropolitan, polyglot community. From the murder of the abolitionist Lovejoy in 1837 to the Cicero riots of 1951, Illinois has been the scene of exacerbated tension between races, often flaring into violence and destruction. In many of these outbreaks, utterances of the character here in question, so the Illinois legislature could conclude, played a significant [part].

"In the face of this history and its frequent obligato of extreme racial and religious propaganda, we would deny experience to say that the Illinois legislature was without reason in seeking ways to curb false or malicious defamation of racial and religious groups, made in public places and by means calculated to have a powerful emotional impact on those to whom it was presented.

"[It would] be arrant dogmatism, quite outside the scope of our authority[, for] us to deny that the Illinois Legislature may warrantably believe that a man's job and his educational opportunities and the dignity accorded him may depend as much on the reputation of the racial and religious group to which he willynilly belongs, as on his own merits. This being so, we are precluded from saying that speech concededly punishable when immediately directed at individuals cannot be outlawed if directed at groups with whose position and esteem in society the affiliated individual may be inextricably involved. * * *

"As to the defense of truth, Illinois in common with many States requires a showing not only that the utterance state the facts, but also that the publication be made 'with good motives and for justifiable ends'. Both elements are necessary if the defense is to prevail. [The] teaching of a century and a half of criminal libel prosecutions in this country would go by the board if we were to hold that Illinois was not within her rights in making this combined requirement. Assuming that defendant's offer of proof directed to a part of the defense was adequate, it did not satisfy the entire requirement which Illinois could exact."

The Court ruled that the trial court properly declined to require the jury to find a "clear and present danger": "Libelous utterances not being within the area of constitutionally protected speech, it is unnecessary, either for us or for the State courts, to consider the issues behind the phrase 'clear and present danger.' Certainly no one would contend that obscene speech, for example, may be punished only upon a showing of such circumstances. Libel, as we have seen, is in the same class."

BLACK, J., joined by Douglas, J., dissented: "[The Court] acts on the bland assumption that the First Amendment is wholly irrelevant. [Today's] case degrades

First Amendment freedoms to the 'rational basis' level. [We] are cautioned that state legislatures must be left free to 'experiment' and to make legislative judgments. [State] experimentation in curbing freedom of expression is startling and frightening doctrine in a country dedicated to self-government by its people.

"[As] 'constitutionally recognized,' [criminal libel] has provided for punishment of false, malicious, scurrilous charges against individuals, not against huge groups. This limited scope of the law of criminal libel is of no small importance. It has confined state punishment of speech and expression to the narrowest of areas involving nothing more than private feuds. Every expansion of the law of criminal libel so as to punish discussion of matters of public concern means a corresponding invasion of the area dedicated to free expression by the First Amendment.

"[If] there be minority groups who hail this holding as their victory, they might consider the possible relevancy of this ancient remark: 'Another such victory and I am undone.'"

REED, J., joined by Douglas, J., dissenting, argued that the statute was unconstitutionally vague: "These words—'virtue,' 'derision,' and 'obloquy'—have neither general nor special meanings well enough known to apprise those within their reach as to limitations on speech. Philosophers and poets, thinkers of high and low degree from every age and race have sought to expound the meaning of virtue. [Are] the tests of the Puritan or the Cavalier to be applied, those of the city or the farm, the Christian or non-Christian, the old or the young?"

DOUGLAS, J., dissented: "Hitler and his Nazis showed how evil a conspiracy could be which was aimed at destroying a race by exposing it to contempt, derision, and obloquy. I would be willing to concede that such conduct directed at a race or group in this country could be made an indictable offense. For such a project would be more than the exercise of free speech. [It] would be free speech plus.

"I would also be willing to concede that even without the element of conspiracy there might be times and occasions when the legislative or executive branch might call a halt to inflammatory talk, such as the shouting of 'fire' in a school or a theatre.

"My view is that if in any case other public interests are to override the plain command of the First Amendment, the peril of speech must be clear and present, leaving no room for argument, raising no doubts as to the necessity of curbing speech in order to prevent disaster."

JACKSON, J., dissenting, argued that the Fourteenth Amendment does not incorporate the first, as such, but permits the states more latitude than the Congress. He concluded, however, that due process required the trier of fact to evaluate the evidence as to the truth and good faith of the speaker and the clarity and presence of the danger. He was unwilling to assume danger from the tendency of the words and felt that the trial court had precluded the defendant's efforts to show truth and good motives.

B. Public Officials and Seditious Libel

NEW YORK TIMES CO. V. SULLIVAN
376 U.S. 254, 84 S.Ct. 710, 11 L.Ed.2d 686 (1964).

JUSTICE BRENNAN delivered the opinion of the Court.

[Sullivan, the Montgomery, Ala. police commissioner, sued the New York Times and four black Alabama clergymen for alleged libelous statements in a paid, full-page fund-raising advertisement signed by a "Committee to defend Martin Luther King and the struggle for freedom in the South." The advertisement stated that "truckloads of police armed with shotguns and tear-gas ringed Alabama State College Campus" in Montgomery, and that "the Southern violators [have] bombed [Dr. King's] home, assaulted his person [and] arrested him seven times." In several respects the statements were untrue. Several witnesses testified that they understood the statements to refer to Sullivan because he supervised Montgomery police. Sullivan proved he did not participate in the events described. He offered no proof of pecuniary loss.[3] Pursuant to Alabama law, the trial court submitted the libel issue to the jury, giving general and punitive damages instructions. It returned a $500,000 verdict for Sullivan against all of the defendants.] We hold that the rule of law applied by the Alabama courts is constitutionally deficient for failure to provide the safeguards for freedom of speech and of the press that are required by the First and Fourteenth Amendments in a libel action brought by a public official against critics of his official conduct. We further hold that under the proper safeguards the evidence presented in this case is constitutionally insufficient to support the judgment for respondent.

I.   [The] publication here [communicated] information, expressed opinion, recited grievances, protested claimed abuses, and sought financial support on behalf of a movement whose existence and objectives are matters of the highest public interest and concern. That the Times was paid for publishing the advertisement is as immaterial in this connection as is the fact that newspapers and books are sold. [*Smith v. California*, Sec. 1, III, B infra.] Any other conclusion would discourage newspapers from carrying "editorial advertisements" of this type, and so might shut off an important outlet for the promulgation of information and ideas by persons who do not themselves have access to publishing facilities.

II.   Under Alabama law [once] "libel per se" has been established, the defendant has no defense as to stated facts unless he can persuade the jury that they were true in all their particulars. [His] privilege of "fair comment" for expressions of opinion depends on the truth of the facts upon which the comment is based. [Unless] he can discharge the burden of proving truth, general damages are presumed, and may be awarded without proof of pecuniary injury.

---

[3]   **[Ct's Note]** Approximately 394 copies of the edition [containing] the advertisement were circulated in Alabama. Of these, about 35 copies were distributed in Montgomery County. The total circulation of the Times for that day was approximately 650,000 copies.

[Respondent] relies heavily, as did the Alabama courts, on statements of this Court to the effect that the Constitution does not protect libelous publications. Those statements do not foreclose our inquiry here. None of the cases sustained the use of libel laws to impose sanctions upon expression critical of the official conduct of public officials. [L]ibel can claim no talismanic immunity from constitutional limitations. It must be measured by standards that satisfy the First Amendment.

The First Amendment, said Judge Learned Hand, "presupposes that right conclusions are more likely to be gathered out of a multitude of tongues, than through any kind of authoritative selection. To many this is, and always will be, folly; but we have staked upon it our all." [Thus] we consider this case against the background of a profound national commitment to the principle that debate on public issues should be uninhibited, robust, and wide-open, and that it may well include vehement, caustic, and sometimes unpleasantly sharp attacks on government and public officials. The present advertisement, as an expression of grievance and protest on one of the major public issues of our time, would seem clearly to qualify for the constitutional protection. The question is whether it forfeits that protection by the falsity of some of its factual statements and by its alleged defamation of respondent.

Authoritative interpretations of the First Amendment guarantees have consistently refused to recognize an exception for any test of truth—whether administered by judges, juries, or administrative officials—and especially not one that puts the burden of proving truth on the speaker. [E]rroneous statement is inevitable in free debate, and [it] must be protected if the freedoms of expression are to have the "breathing space" that they "need [to] survive."

[Injury] to official reputation affords no more warrant for repressing speech that would otherwise be free than does factual error. Where judicial officers are involved, this Court has held that concern for the dignity and reputation of the courts does not justify the punishment as criminal contempt of criticism of the judge or his decision. This is true even though the utterance contains "half-truths" and "misinformation." Such repression can be justified, if at all, only by a clear and present danger of the obstruction of justice. If judges are to be treated as "men of fortitude, able to thrive in a hardy climate," surely the same must be true of other government officials, such as elected city commissioners. Criticism of their official conduct does not lose its constitutional protection merely because it is effective criticism and hence diminishes their official reputations.

If neither factual error nor defamatory content suffices to remove the constitutional shield from criticism of official conduct, the combination of the two elements is no less inadequate. This is the lesson to be drawn from the great controversy over the Sedition Act of 1798, 1 Stat. 596, which first crystallized a national awareness of the central meaning of the First Amendment. [Although] the Sedition Act was never tested in this Court, the attack upon its validity has carried the day in the court of history. Fines levied in its prosecution were repaid by Act of Congress on the ground that it was unconstitutional. * * * Jefferson, as President, pardoned those who had been convicted and sentenced under the Act and remitted their fines. [Its] invalidity [has] also been assumed by Justices of this Court. [These] views reflect a broad consensus that the Act, because of the restraint it imposed upon criticism of government and public officials, was inconsistent with the First Amendment. * * *

What a State may not constitutionally bring about by means of a criminal statute is likewise beyond the reach of its civil law of libel. The fear of damage awards under a rule such as that invoked by the Alabama courts here may be markedly more inhibiting than the fear of prosecution under a criminal statute. [The] judgment awarded in this case—without the need for any proof of actual pecuniary loss—was one thousand times greater than the maximum fine provided by the Alabama criminal [libel law], and one hundred times greater than that provided by the Sedition Act. And since there is no double-jeopardy limitation applicable to civil lawsuits, this is not the only judgment that may be awarded against petitioners for the same publication.[18] Whether or not a newspaper can survive a succession of such judgments, the pall of fear and timidity imposed upon those who would give voice to public criticism is an atmosphere in which the First Amendment freedoms cannot [survive].

The state rule of law is not saved by its allowance of the defense of truth. A defense for erroneous statements honestly made is no less essential here than was the requirement of proof of guilty knowledge which, in *Smith v. California,* we held indispensable to a valid conviction of a bookseller for possessing obscene writings for [sale].

A rule compelling the critic of official conduct to guarantee the truth of all his factual assertions—and to do so on pain of libel judgments virtually unlimited in amount—leads to a comparable "self-censorship." Allowance of the defense of truth, with the burden of proving it on the defendant, does not mean that only false speech will be deterred.[19] [Under] such a rule, would-be critics of official conduct may be deterred from voicing their criticism, even though it is believed to be true and even though it is in fact true, because of doubt whether it can be proved in court or fear of the expense of having to do so. They tend to make only statements which "steer far wider of the unlawful zone." The rule thus dampens the vigor and limits the variety of public [debate].

The constitutional guarantees require, we think, a federal rule that prohibits a public official from recovering damages for a defamatory falsehood relating to his official conduct unless he proves that the statement was made with "actual

---

18   [Ct's Note] The Times states that four other libel suits based on the advertisement have been filed against it by [others]; that another $500,000 verdict has been awarded in [one]; and that the damages sought in the other three total $2,000,000.

19   [Ct's Note] Even a false statement may be deemed to make a valuable contribution to the public debate, since it brings about "the clearer perception and livelier impression of truth, produced by its collision with error." Mill, *On Liberty* 15 (1955).

malice"—that is, with knowledge that it was false or with reckless disregard of whether it was false or [not].[5]

Such a privilege for criticism of official conduct is appropriately analogous to the protection accorded a public official when *he* is sued for libel by a private citizen. In *Barr v. Matteo*, 360 U.S. 564 (1959), this Court held the utterance of a federal official to be absolutely privileged if made "within the outer perimeter" of his duties. The States accord the same immunity to statements of their highest officers, although some differentiate their lesser officials and qualify the privilege they enjoy. But all hold that all officials are protected unless actual malice can be proved. The reason for the official privilege is said to be that the threat of damage suits would otherwise "inhibit the fearless, vigorous, and effective administration of policies of government" and "dampen the ardor of all but the most resolute, or the most irresponsible, in the unflinching discharge of their duties." *Barr.* Analogous considerations support the privilege for the citizen-critic of government. It is as much his duty to criticize as it is the official's duty to administer. [It] would give public servants an unjustified preference over the public they serve, if critics of official conduct did not have a fair equivalent of the immunity granted to the officials themselves. We conclude that such a privilege is required by the First and Fourteenth Amendments.

III.   [W]e consider that the proof presented to show actual malice lacks the convincing clarity[6] which the constitutional standard demands, and hence that it would not constitutionally sustain the judgment for respondent under the proper rule of law. [T]here is evidence that the Times published the advertisement without checking its accuracy against the news stories in the Times' own files. The mere presence of the stories in the files does [not] establish that the Times "knew" the advertisement was false, since the state of mind required for actual malice would have to be brought home to the persons in the Times' organization having responsibility for the publication of the advertisement. With respect to the failure of those persons to make the check, the record shows that they relied upon their knowledge of the good reputation of many [whose] names were listed as sponsors of the advertisement, and upon the letter from A. Philip Randolph, known to them as a responsible individual, certifying that the use of the names was authorized. There was testimony that the persons handling the advertisement saw nothing in it that would render it unacceptable under the Times' policy of rejecting advertisements containing "attacks of a personal character"; their failure to reject it on this ground was not unreasonable. We think the evidence against the Times supports at most a finding of negligence in failing to discover the misstatements,

---

[5]   "Reckless disregard" is often misunderstood. *St. Amant v. Thompson,* 390 U.S. 727 (1968) emphasized that reckless disregard is publishing while "in fact entertain[ing] serious doubts about the truth of the publication," and *Garrison v. Louisiana,* 379 U.S. 64 (1964) held the standard to require a "high degree of awareness of probable falsity." Under both *St. Amant* and *Garrison,* "reckless disregard" requires a degree of knowledge beyond common law recklessness.

[6]   See *Bose Corp. v. Consumers Union,* 466 U.S. 485 (1984), holding that appellate courts "must exercise independent judgment and determine whether the record establishes actual malice with convincing clarity." On the requirement of independent appellate review in First Amendment cases generally, see also *Jacobellis v. Ohio,* 378 U.S. 188 (1964).

and is constitutionally insufficient to show the recklessness that is required for a finding of actual malice.

[T]he evidence was constitutionally defective in another respect: it was incapable of supporting the jury's finding that the allegedly libelous statements were made "of and concerning" respondent. [On this point, the Supreme Court of Alabama] based its ruling on the proposition that: "[The] average person knows that municipal agents, such as police and firemen, and others, are under the control and direction of the city governing body, and more particularly under the direction and control of a single commissioner. In measuring the performance or deficiencies of such groups, praise or criticism is usually attached to the official in complete control of the body."

This proposition has disquieting implications for criticism of governmental conduct. [It would transmute] criticism of government, however impersonal it may seem on its face, into personal criticism, and hence potential libel, of the officials of whom the government is composed. [Raising] as it does the possibility that a good-faith critic of government will be penalized for his criticism, the proposition relied on by the Alabama courts strikes at the very center of the constitutionally protected area of free expression. We hold that such a proposition may not constitutionally be utilized to establish that an otherwise impersonal attack on governmental operations was a libel of an official responsible for those operations. Since it was relied on exclusively here, and there was no other evidence to connect the statements with respondent, the evidence was constitutionally insufficient to support a finding that the statements referred to respondent. * * *

JUSTICE BLACK, with whom JUSTICE DOUGLAS joins (concurring).

* * * "Malice," even as defined by the Court, is an elusive, abstract concept, hard to prove and hard to disprove. The requirement that malice be proved provides at best an evanescent protection for the right critically to discuss public affairs and certainly does not measure up to the sturdy safeguard embodied in the First Amendment. Unlike the Court, therefore, I vote to reverse exclusively on the ground that the Times and the individual defendants had an absolute, unconditional constitutional right to publish in the Times advertisement their criticisms of the Montgomery agencies and [officials].

The half-million-dollar verdict [gives] dramatic proof [that] state libel laws threaten the very existence of an American press virile enough to publish unpopular views on public affairs and bold enough to criticize the conduct of public officials. [B]riefs before us show that in Alabama there are now pending eleven libel suits by local and state officials against the Times seeking $5,600,000, and five such suits against the Columbia Broadcasting System seeking $1,700,000. Moreover, this technique for harassing and punishing a free press—now that it has been shown to be possible—is by no means limited to cases with racial overtones; it can be used in other fields where public feelings may make local as well as out-of-state newspapers easy prey for libel verdict seekers.

In my opinion the Federal Constitution has dealt with this deadly danger to the press in the only way possible without leaving the press open to destruction— by granting the press an absolute immunity for criticism of the way public officials do their public duty.

[This] Nation, I suspect, can live in peace without libel suits based on public discussions of public affairs and public officials. But I doubt that a country can live in freedom where its people can be made to suffer physically or financially for criticizing their government, its actions, or its officials. * * *[7]

The First Amendment and democracy. Professor Harry Kalven observed that the *New York Times* decision was moving toward "the theory of free speech that Alexander Meiklejohn has been offering us for some fifteen years now." Harry Kalven, *The New York Times Case: A Note on "The Central Meaning of the First Amendment,"* 1964 Sup.Ct.Rev. 191. Indeed Kalven reported Alexander Meiklejohn's view that the case was " 'an occasion for dancing in the streets.' " Meiklejohn argued that "[The] principle of the freedom of speech springs from the necessities of the program of self-government. [It] is a deduction from the basic American agreement that public issues shall be decided by universal suffrage. [When] a question of policy is 'before the house,' free men choose to meet it not with their eyes shut, but with their eyes open. To be afraid of ideas, any idea, is to be unfit for self-government. [The] guarantee given by the First Amendment is not, then, assured to all speaking. It is assured only to speech which bears, directly or indirectly, upon issues with which voters have to deal—only, therefore, to the consideration of matters of public interest. Private speech, or private interest in speech [has] no claim whatever to the protection of the First Amendment." Alexander Meiklejohn, *Free Speech and Its Relation to Self-Government* (1948).

Public figures. In CURTIS PUB. CO. v. BUTTS and ASSOCIATED PRESS v. WALKER, 388 U.S. 130 (1967), the Court extended the *New York Times* principle to non-governmental "public officials." HARLAN, J., contended that because public figures were not subject to the restraints of the political process, any criticism of them was not akin to seditious libel and was, therefore, a step removed from the central meaning of the First Amendment. Nonetheless, he argued that public figure actions should not be left entirely to the vagaries of state defamation law and would have required that public figures show "highly unreasonable conduct constituting an extreme departure from the standards of investigation and reporting ordinarily adhered to by responsible publishers" as a prerequisite to recovery. In response, WARREN, C.J., argued that the inapplicability of the restraints of the political process to public figures underscored the importance for

---

[7]   Goldberg, J., joined by Douglas, J., concurring, asserted that for "the citizen and [the] press an absolute unconditional privilege to criticize official conduct," but maintained that the imposition of liability for "[p]urely private defamation" did not abridge the First Amendment because it had "little to do with the political ends of a self-governing society." And see *Dun & Bradstreet, Inc. v. Greenmoss Builders, Inc.,* 472 U.S. 749 (1985).

uninhibited debate about their activities since "public opinion may be the only instrument by which society can attempt to influence their conduct." He observed that increasingly "the distinctions between governmental and private sectors are blurred," that public figures, like public officials, "often play an influential role in ordering society," and as a class have a ready access to the mass media "both to influence policy and to counter criticism of their views and activities." He concluded that the *New York Times* rule should be extended to public figures. Four other justices in *Butts* and *Walker* were willing to go at least as far as Warren, C.J., and subsequent cases have settled on the position that public figures must meet the *New York Times* requirements in order to recover in a defamation action.

C. Private Individuals and Public Figures

GERTZ V. ROBERT WELCH, INC.
418 U.S. 323, 94 S.Ct. 2997, 41 L.Ed.2d 789 (1974).

JUSTICE POWELL delivered the opinion of the Court.

[Respondent published *American Opinion,* a monthly outlet for the John Birch Society. It published an article falsely stating that Gertz, a lawyer, was the "architect" in a "communist frameup" of a policeman convicted of murdering a youth whose family Gertz represented in resultant civil proceedings, and that Gertz had a "criminal record" and had been an officer in a named "Communist-fronter" organization that advocated violent seizure of our government. In Gertz' libel action there was evidence that *Opinion*'s managing editor did not know the statements were false and had relied on the reputation of the article's author and prior experience with the accuracy of his articles. After a $50,000 verdict for Gertz, the trial court entered judgment n.o.v., concluding that the *New York Times* rule applied to any discussion of a "public issue." The court of appeals affirmed, ruling that the publisher did not have the requisite "awareness of probable falsity." The Court held that *New York Times* did not apply to defamation of private individuals, but remanded for a new trial "because the jury was allowed to impose liability without fault [and] to presume damages without proof of injury."]

II.   The principal issue in this case is whether a newspaper or broadcaster that publishes defamatory falsehoods about an individual who is neither a public official nor a public figure may claim a constitutional privilege against liability for the injury inflicted by those statements. * * *

In his opinion for the plurality in *Rosenbloom,* Mr. Justice Brennan took the *Times* privilege one step further [than *Butts* and *Walker*]. He concluded that its protection should extend to defamatory falsehoods relating to private persons if the statements concerned matters of general or public interest. He abjured the suggested distinction between public officials and public figures on the one hand and private individuals on the other. He focused instead on society's interest in learning about certain issues: "If a matter is a subject of public or general interest, it cannot suddenly become less so merely because a private individual is involved or because in some sense the individual did not choose to become involved." Thus, under the plurality opinion, a private citizen involuntarily associated with a matter of general interest has no recourse for injury to his reputation unless he can satisfy the demanding requirements of the *Times* [test].

III. [Under] the First Amendment there is no such thing as a false idea. However pernicious an opinion may seem, we depend for its correction not on the conscience of the judges and juries but on the competition of other ideas. But there is no constitutional value in false statements of fact. Neither the intentional lie nor the careless error materially advances society's interest in "uninhibited, robust, and wide-open" debate on public issues. * * *

Although the erroneous statement of fact is not worthy of constitutional protection, it is nevertheless inevitable in free debate. [P]unishment of error runs the risk of inducing a cautious and restrictive exercise of the constitutionally guaranteed freedoms of speech and press. [The] First Amendment requires that we protect some falsehood in order to protect speech that matters.

The need to avoid self-censorship by the news media is, however, not the only societal value at issue. [The] legitimate state interest underlying the law of libel is the compensation of individuals for the harm inflicted on them by defamatory falsehoods. We would not lightly require the State to abandon this purpose, for, as Mr. Justice Stewart has reminded us, the individual's right to the protection of his own good name "reflects no more than our basic concept of the essential dignity and worth of every human being—a concept at the root of any decent system of ordered liberty. * * * " *Rosenblatt.*

Some tension necessarily exists between the need for a vigorous and uninhibited press and the legitimate interest in redressing wrongful injury. [In] our continuing effort to define the proper accommodation between these competing concerns, we have been especially anxious to assure to the freedoms of speech and press that "breathing space" essential to their fruitful exercise. To that end this Court has extended a measure of strategic protection to defamatory falsehood.

The *New York Times* standard defines the level of constitutional protection appropriate to the context of defamation of [public figures and those who hold governmental office]. Plainly many deserving plaintiffs, including some intentionally subjected to injury, will be unable to surmount the barrier of the *New York Times* test. [For] the reasons stated below, we conclude that the state interest in compensating injury to the reputation of private individuals requires that a different rule should obtain with respect to them.

[W]e have no difficulty in distinguishing among defamation plaintiffs. The first remedy of any victim of defamation is self-help—using available opportunities to contradict the lie or correct the error and thereby to minimize its adverse impact on reputation. Public officials and public figures usually enjoy significantly greater access to the channels of effective communication and hence have a more realistic opportunity to counteract false statements than private individuals normally enjoy.[9] Private individuals are therefore more vulnerable to injury, and the state interest in protecting them is correspondingly greater.

More important than the likelihood that private individuals will lack effective opportunities for rebuttal, there is a compelling normative consideration underlying the distinction between public and private defamation plaintiffs. An individual who decides to seek governmental office must accept certain necessary consequences of that involvement in public affairs. He runs the risk of closer public scrutiny than might otherwise be the case. [Those] classed as public figures stand in a similar [position.]

Even if the foregoing generalities do not obtain in every instance, the communications media are entitled to act on the assumption that public officials and public figures have voluntarily exposed themselves to increased risk of injury from defamatory falsehoods concerning them. No such assumption is justified with respect to a private individual. He has not accepted public office nor assumed an "influential role in ordering society." *Butts.* He has relinquished no part of his interest in the protection of his own good name, and consequently he has a more compelling call on the courts for redress of injury inflicted by defamatory falsehood. Thus, private individuals are not only more vulnerable to injury than public officials and public figures; they are also more deserving of recovery.

For these reasons we conclude that the States should retain substantial latitude in their efforts to enforce a legal remedy for defamatory falsehood injurious to the reputation of a private individual. The extension of the *Times* test proposed by the *Rosenbloom* [*v. Metromedia*, 403 U.S. 29 (1971)][8] plurality would abridge this legitimate state interest to a degree that we find unacceptable. And it would occasion the additional difficulty of forcing state and federal judges to decide on an ad hoc basis which publications address issues of "general or public interest" and which do not—to determine, in the words of Mr. Justice Marshall, "what information is relevant to self-government." *Rosenbloom.* We doubt the wisdom of committing this task to the conscience of judges. [The] "public or general interest" test for determining the applicability of the *Times* standard to private defamation actions inadequately serves both of the competing values at stake. On the one hand, a private individual whose reputation is injured by defamatory falsehood that does concern an issue of public or general interest has no recourse unless he can meet the rigorous requirements of *Times.* This is true despite the factors that distinguish the state interest in compensating private individuals from the analogous interest involved in the context of public persons. On the other hand, a publisher or broadcaster of a defamatory error which a court deems unrelated to an issue of public or general interest may be held liable in damages even if it took

---

[9]   **[Ct's Note]** Of course, an opportunity for rebuttal seldom suffices to undo harm of defamatory falsehood. Indeed, the law of defamation is rooted in our experience that the truth rarely catches up with a lie. But the fact that the self-help remedy of rebuttal, standing alone, is inadequate to its task does not mean that it is irrelevant to our inquiry.

[8]   The *Rosenbloom* plurality would have extended the *New York Times* rule to statements of general or public interest, without regard to the public or official status of the plaintiff.

every reasonable precaution to ensure the accuracy of its assertions. And liability may far exceed compensation for any actual injury to the plaintiff, for the jury may be permitted to presume damages without proof of loss and even to award punitive damages.

We hold that, so long as they do not impose liability without fault, the States may define for themselves the appropriate standard of liability for a publisher or broadcaster of defamatory falsehood injurious to a private individual. This approach provides a more equitable boundary between the competing concerns involved here. It recognizes the strength of the legitimate state interest in compensating private individuals for wrongful injury to reputation, yet shields the press and broadcast media from the rigors of strict liability for defamation. At least this conclusion obtains where, as here, the substance of the defamatory statement "makes substantial danger to reputation apparent." *Butts*. This phrase places in perspective the conclusion we announce today. Our inquiry would involve considerations somewhat different from those discussed above if a State purported to condition civil liability on a factual misstatement whose content did not warn a reasonably prudent editor or broadcaster of its defamatory potential. Cf. *Time, Inc. v. Hill* [Part D infra]. Such a case is not now before us, and we intimate no view as to its proper resolution.

IV. [T]he strong and legitimate state interest in compensating private individuals for injury to reputation [extends] no further than compensation for actual injury. For the reasons stated below, we hold that the States may not permit recovery of presumed or punitive damages, at least when liability is not based on a showing of knowledge of falsity or reckless disregard for the truth.

The common law of defamation is an oddity of tort [law]. Juries may award substantial sums as compensation for supposed damage to reputation without any proof that such harm actually occurred. [This] unnecessarily compounds the potential of any system of liability for defamatory falsehood to inhibit the vigorous exercise of First Amendment freedoms [and] invites juries to punish unpopular opinion rather than to compensate individuals for injury sustained by the publication of a false fact. More to the point, the States have no substantial interest in securing for plaintiffs such as this petitioner gratuitous awards of money damages far in excess of any actual injury.

We would not, of course, invalidate state law simply because we doubt its wisdom, but here we are attempting to reconcile state law with a competing interest grounded in the constitutional command of the First Amendment. It is therefore appropriate to require that state remedies for defamatory falsehood reach no farther than is necessary to protect the legitimate interest involved. It is necessary to restrict defamation plaintiffs who do not prove knowledge of falsity or reckless disregard for the truth to compensation for actual injury. We need not define "actual injury," as trial courts have wide experience in framing appropriate jury instructions in tort action. Suffice it to say that actual injury is not limited to out-of-pocket loss. Indeed, the more customary types of actual harm inflicted by defamatory falsehood include impairment of reputation and standing in the community, personal humiliation, and mental anguish and suffering. Of course, juries must be limited by appropriate instructions, and all awards must be supported by competent evidence concerning the injury, although there need be no evidence which assigns an actual dollar value to the injury.

We also find no justification for allowing awards of punitive damages against publishers and broadcasters held liable under state-defined standards of liability for defamation. In most jurisdictions jury discretion over the amounts awarded is limited only by the gentle rule that they not be excessive. Consequently, juries assess punitive damages in wholly unpredictable amounts bearing no necessary relation to the actual harm caused. And they remain free to use their discretion selectively to punish expressions of unpopular views. [J]ury discretion to award punitive damages unnecessarily exacerbates the danger of media self-censorship; [punitive] damages are wholly irrelevant to the state interest that justifies a negligence standard for private defamation actions. They are not compensation for injury. Instead, they are private fines levied by civil juries to punish reprehensible conduct and to deter its future occurrence. In short, the private defamation plaintiff who establishes liability under a less demanding standard than that stated by *Times* may recover only such damages as are sufficient to compensate him for actual injury.

V.   Notwithstanding our refusal to extend the *New York Times* privilege to defamation of private individuals, respondent contends that we should affirm the judgment below on the ground that petitioner is [a] public figure. [That] designation may rest on either of two alternative bases. In some instances an individual may achieve such pervasive fame or notoriety that he becomes a public figure for all purposes and in all contexts. More commonly, an individual voluntarily injects himself or is drawn into a particular public controversy and thereby becomes a public figure for a limited range of issues. In either case such persons assume special prominence in the resolution of public questions.

Petitioner has long been active in community and professional affairs. He has served as an officer of local civic groups and of various professional organizations, and he has published several books and articles on legal subjects. Although petitioner was consequently well known in some circles, he had achieved no general fame or notoriety in the community. None of the prospective jurors called at the trial had ever heard of petitioner prior to this litigation, and respondent offered no proof that this response was atypical of the local population. We would not lightly assume that a citizen's participation in community and professional affairs rendered him a public figure for all purposes. Absent clear evidence of general fame or notoriety in the community, and pervasive involvement in the affairs of society, an individual should not be deemed a public personality for all aspects of his life. It is preferable to reduce the public-figure question to a more meaningful context by looking to the nature and extent of an individual's participation in the particular controversy giving rise to the defamation.

In this context it is plain that petitioner was not a public figure. He played a minimal role at the coroner's inquest, and his participation related solely to his representation of a private client. He took no part in the criminal prosecution of Officer Nuccio. Moreover, he never discussed either the criminal or civil litigation with the press and was never quoted as having done so. He plainly did not thrust himself into the vortex of this public issue, nor did he engage the public's attention in an attempt to influence its outcome. We are persuaded that the trial court did not err in refusing to characterize petitioner as a public figure for the purpose of this litigation.

We therefore conclude that the *New York Times* standard is inapplicable to this case and that the trial court erred in entering judgment for respondent. Because the jury was allowed to impose liability without fault and was permitted to presume damages without proof of injury, a new trial is necessary.

JUSTICE BRENNAN, dissenting.

[While the Court's] arguments are forcefully and eloquently presented, I cannot accept them for the reasons I stated in *Rosenbloom:* "The *New York Times* standard was applied to libel of a public official or public figure to give effect to the Amendment's function to encourage ventilation of public issues, not because the public official has any less interest in protecting his reputation than an individual in private life. [In] the vast majority of libels involving public officials or public figures, the ability to respond through the media will depend on the same complex factor on which the ability of a private individual depends: the unpredictable event of the media's continuing interest in the story. Thus the unproved, and highly improbable, generalization that an as yet [not fully defined] class of 'public figures' involved in matters of public concern will be better able to respond through the media than private individuals also involved in such matters seems too insubstantial a reed on which to rest a constitutional distinction."

[Adoption], by many States, of a reasonable care standard in cases where private individuals are involved in matters of public interest—the probable result of today's decision—[will] lead to self-censorship since publishers will be required carefully to weigh a myriad of uncertain factors before publication. The reasonable care standard is "elusive," it saddles the press with "the intolerable burden of guessing how a jury might assess the reasonableness of steps taken by it to verify the accuracy of every reference to a name, picture or portrait." Under a reasonable care regime, publishers and broadcasters will have to make pre-publication judgments about juror assessment of such diverse considerations as the size, operating procedures, and financial condition of the news gathering system, as well as the relative costs and benefits of instituting less frequent and more costly reporting at a higher level of accuracy. [And] most hazardous, the flexibility which inheres in the reasonable care standard will create the danger that a jury will convert it into "an instrument for the suppression of those 'vehement, caustic, and sometimes unpleasantly sharp attacks,' [which] must be protected if the guarantees of the First and Fourteenth Amendments are to prevail." *Monitor Patriot Co.*

[A] jury's latitude to impose liability for want of due care poses a far greater threat of suppressing unpopular views than does a possible recovery of presumed or punitive damages. Moreover, the Court's broad-ranging examples of "actual injury" [allow] a jury bent on punishing expression of unpopular views a formidable weapon for doing so. [E]ven a limitation of recovery to "actual injury"—however much it reduces the size or frequency of recoveries—will not provide the necessary elbow room for First Amendment expression. "[The] very possibility of having to engage in litigation, an expensive and protracted process, is threat enough to cause discussion and debate to 'steer far wider of the unlawful zone' thereby keeping protected discussion from public cognizance. * * * " *Rosenbloom.*

[I] reject the argument that my *Rosenbloom* view improperly commits to judges the task of determining what is and what is not an issue of "general or public interest." [Performance] of this task [will] not always be easy. But surely the courts, the ultimate arbiters of all disputes concerning clashes of constitutional values, would only be performing one of their traditional functions in undertaking this duty. [The] public interest is necessarily broad; any residual self-censorship that may result from the uncertain contours of the "general or public interest" concept should be of far less concern to publishers and broadcasters than that occasioned by state laws imposing liability for negligent falsehood. * * *

JUSTICE WHITE, dissenting.

[T]he Court, in a few printed pages, has federalized major aspects of libel law by declaring unconstitutional in important respects the prevailing defamation law in all or most of the 50 States. * * *

I.   [These] radical changes in the law and severe invasions of the prerogatives of the States [should] at least be shown to be required by the First Amendment or necessitated by our present circumstances. Neither has been [demonstrated.]

The central meaning of *New York Times,* and for me the First Amendment as it relates to libel laws, is that seditious libel—criticism of government and public officials—falls beyond the police power of the State. In a democratic society such as ours, the citizen has the privilege of criticizing his government and its officials. But neither *New York Times* nor its progeny suggest that the First Amendment intended in all circumstances to deprive the private citizen of his historic recourse to redress published falsehoods damaging to reputation or that, contrary to history and precedent, the amendment should now be so interpreted. Simply put, the First Amendment did not confer a "license to defame the citizen." Douglas, *The Right of the People* 38 (1958).

[T]he law has heretofore put the risk of falsehood on the publisher where the victim is a private citizen and no grounds of special privilege are invoked. The Court would now shift this risk to the victim, even though he has done nothing to invite the calumny, is wholly innocent of fault, and is helpless to avoid his injury. I doubt that jurisprudential resistance to liability without fault is sufficient ground for employing the First Amendment to revolutionize the law of libel, and in my view, that body of legal rules poses no realistic threat to the press and its service to the public. The press today is vigorous and robust. To me, it is quite incredible to suggest that threats of libel suits from private citizens are causing the press to refrain from publishing the truth. I know of no hard facts to support that proposition, and the Court furnishes none.

[I]f the Court's principal concern is to protect the communications industry from large libel judgments, it would appear that its new requirements with respect to general and punitive damages would be ample protection. Why it also feels compelled to escalate the threshold standard of liability I cannot fathom, particularly when this will eliminate in many instances the plaintiff's possibility of securing a judicial determination that the damaging publication was indeed false, whether or not he is entitled to recover money damages. [I] find it unacceptable to distribute the risk in this manner and force the wholly innocent victim to bear the injury; for, as between the two, the defamer is the only culpable party. It is he who circulated a falsehood that he was not required to publish. * * *

TIME, INC. v. FIRESTONE, 424 U.S. 448 (1976), per REHNQUIST, J., held that persons who have not assumed a role of especial prominence in the affairs of society are not public figures unless they have " 'thrust themselves to the forefront of particular public controversies in order to influence the resolution of the issues involved.' " A divorce proceeding involving one of America's wealthiest industrial families and containing testimony concerning the extramarital sexual activities of the parties thus did not involve a "public controversy," "even though the marital difficulties of extremely wealthy individuals may be of interest to some portion of the reading public." Nor did the filing of a divorce suit, or the holding of press conferences.

D. Emotional Distress

HUSTLER MAGAZINE v. FALWELL, 485 U.S. 46 (1988), per REHNQUIST, C.J., held that public figures and public officials offended by a mass media parody could not recover for the tort of intentional infliction of emotional distress without a showing of *New York Times* malice. Parodying a series of liquor advertisements in which celebrities speak about their "first time," the editors of *Hustler* chose plaintiff Jerry Falwell (a nationally famous minister, host of a nationally syndicated television show, and founder of the Moral Majority political organization) "as the featured celebrity and drafted an alleged 'interview' with him in which he states that his 'first time' was during a drunken incestuous rendezvous with his mother in an outhouse. The *Hustler* parody portrays [Falwell] and his mother 'as drunk and immoral,' and suggests that [Falwell] is a hypocrite who preaches only when he is drunk. In small print at the bottom of the page, the ad contains the disclaimer, 'ad parody—not to be taken seriously.' The magazine's table of contents also lists the ad as 'Fiction; Ad and Personality Parody.' * * *

"We must decide whether a public figure may recover damages for emotional harm caused by the publication of an ad parody offensive to him, and doubtless gross and repugnant in the eyes of most. [Falwell] would have us find that a State's interest in protecting public figures from emotional distress is sufficient to deny First Amendment protection to speech that is patently offensive and is intended to inflict emotional injury, even when that speech could not reasonably have been interpreted as stating actual facts about the public figure involved. * * *

"Generally speaking the law does not regard the intent to inflict emotional distress as one which should receive much solicitude, and it is quite understandable that most if not all jurisdictions have chosen to make it civilly culpable where the conduct in question is sufficiently 'outrageous.' But in the world of debate about public affairs, many things done with motives that are less than admirable are protected by the First Amendment. '[Debate] on public issues will not be uninhibited if the speaker must run the risk that it will be proved in court that he spoke out of hatred; even if he did speak out of hatred, utterances honestly believed contribute to the free interchange of ideas and the ascertainment of truth.' *Garrison.* Thus while such a bad motive may be deemed controlling for purposes of tort liability in other areas of the law, we think the First Amendment prohibits such a result in the area of public debate about public figures.

"Were we to hold otherwise, there can be little doubt that political cartoonists and satirists would be subjected to damage awards without any showing that their work falsely defamed its subject. * * *

"There is no doubt that the caricature of [Falwell] and his mother published in Hustler is at best a distant cousin of [traditional] political cartoons [and] a rather poor relation at that. If it were possible by laying down a principled standard to separate the one from the other, public discourse would probably suffer little or no harm. But we doubt that there is any such standard, and we are quite sure that the pejorative description 'outrageous' does not supply one. 'Outrageousness' in the area of political and social discourse has an inherent subjectiveness about it which would allow a jury to impose liability on the basis of the jurors' tastes or views, or perhaps on the basis of their dislike of a particular expression.

"We conclude that public figures and public officials may not recover for the tort of intentional infliction of emotional distress by reason of publications such as the one here at issue without showing in addition that the publication contains a false statement of fact which was made with 'actual malice,' i.e., with knowledge that the statement was false or with reckless disregard as to whether or not it was true."

———

The father of a deceased Marine brought an action for intentional infliction of emotional distress, intrusion upon seclusion, and civil conspiracy against a fundamentalist church and its members for demonstrating near the Marine's funeral with signs, detailed in the Court's opinion below, including "Thank God for Dead Soldiers."

SNYDER v. PHELPS, 562 U.S. 443 (2011), per ROBERTS, C.J., held that the speech was protected and immune from tort liability: "A jury held members of the Westboro Baptist Church liable for millions of dollars in damages for picketing near a soldier's funeral service. The picket signs reflected the church's view that the United States is overly tolerant of sin and that God kills American soldiers as punishment. The question presented is whether the First Amendment shields the church members from tort liability for their speech in this case. [The] church had notified the authorities in advance of its intent to picket at the time of the funeral, and the picketers complied with police instructions in staging their demonstration. The picketing took place within a 10- by 25-foot plot of public land adjacent to a public street, behind a temporary fence. That plot was approximately 1,000 feet from the church where the funeral was held. Several buildings separated the picket site from the church. The Westboro picketers displayed their signs for about 30 minutes before the funeral began and sang hymns and recited Bible verses. None of the picketers entered church property or went to the cemetery. They did not yell or use profanity, and there was no violence associated with the picketing. The funeral procession passed within 200 to 300 feet of the picket site. Although Snyder testified that he could see the tops of the picket signs as he drove to the funeral, he did not see what was written on the signs until later that night, while watching a news broadcast covering the event. A few weeks after the funeral, one of the picketers posted a message on Westboro's Web site discussing the picketing and containing religiously oriented denunciations of the Snyders, interspersed among lengthy Bible quotations. Snyder discovered the posting, referred to by the parties as the 'epic,' during an Internet search for his son's name. The epic is not properly before us and does not factor in our analysis. * * *

"A trial was held on the remaining claims. At trial, Snyder described the severity of his emotional injuries. He testified that he is unable to separate the thought of his dead son from his thoughts of Westboro's picketing, and that he often becomes tearful, angry, and physically ill when he thinks about it. Expert witnesses testified that Snyder's emotional anguish had resulted in severe depression and had exacerbated pre-existing health conditions.

"To succeed on a claim for intentional infliction of emotional distress in Maryland, a plaintiff must demonstrate that the defendant intentionally or recklessly engaged in extreme and outrageous conduct that caused the plaintiff to suffer severe emotional distress. The Free Speech Clause of the First Amendment [can] serve as a defense in state tort suits, including suits for intentional infliction of emotional distress.

"Whether the First Amendment prohibits holding Westboro liable for its speech in this case turns largely on whether that speech is of public or private concern, as determined by all the circumstances of the case. '[S]peech on matters of public concern [is] at the heart of the First Amendment's protection.' * * *

" '[N]ot all speech is of equal First Amendment importance,' however, and where matters of purely private significance are at issue, First Amendment protections are often less rigorous. That is because restricting speech on purely private matters does not implicate the same constitutional concerns as limiting speech on matters of public interest: '[T]here is no threat to the free and robust debate of public issues; there is no potential interference with a meaningful dialogue of ideas'; and the 'threat of liability' does not pose the risk of 'a reaction of self-censorship' on matters of public import.

"Speech deals with matters of public concern when it can 'be fairly considered as relating to any matter of political, social, or other concern to the community,' or when it 'is a subject of legitimate news interest; that is, a subject of general interest and of value and concern to the public,' The arguably 'inappropriate or controversial character of a statement is irrelevant to the question whether it deals with a matter of public concern.' * * *

"Deciding whether speech is of public or private concern requires us to examine the 'content, form, and context' of that speech, 'as revealed by the whole record.' [In] considering content, form, and context, no factor is dispositive, and it is necessary to evaluate all the circumstances of the speech, including what was said, where it was said, and how it was said.

"The 'content' of Westboro's signs plainly relates to broad issues of interest to society at large, rather than matters of 'purely private concern.' The placards read 'God Hates the USA/Thank God for 9/11,' 'America is Doomed,' 'Don't Pray for the USA,' 'Thank God for IEDs,' 'Fag Troops,' 'Semper Fi Fags,' 'God Hates Fags,' 'Maryland Taliban,' 'Fags Doom Nations,' 'Not Blessed Just Cursed,' 'Thank God for Dead Soldiers,' 'Pope in Hell,' 'Priests Rape Boys,' 'You're Going to Hell,' and 'God Hates You.' While these messages may fall short of refined social or political commentary, the issues they highlight—the political and moral conduct of the United States and its citizens, the fate of our Nation, homosexuality in the military, and scandals involving the Catholic clergy—are matters of public import. The signs certainly convey Westboro's position on those issues, in a manner designed [to] reach as broad a public audience as possible. And even if a few of the signs-such as 'You're Going to Hell' and 'God Hates You'—were viewed as containing messages related to Matthew Snyder or the Snyders specifically, that would not change the fact that the overall thrust and dominant theme of Westboro's demonstration spoke to broader public issues.

"Apart from the content of Westboro's signs, Snyder contends that the 'context' of the speech—its connection with his son's funeral—makes the speech a matter of private rather than public concern. The fact that Westboro spoke in connection with a funeral, however, cannot by itself transform the nature of Westboro's speech. Westboro's signs, displayed on public land next to a public street, reflect the fact that the church finds much to condemn in modern society. Its speech is 'fairly characterized as constituting speech on a matter of public concern,' and the funeral setting does not alter that conclusion. * * *

"Snyder goes on to argue that Westboro's speech should be afforded less than full First Amendment protection 'not only because of the words' but also because the church members exploited the funeral 'as a platform to bring their message to a broader audience.' * * * Westboro's choice to convey its views in conjunction with Matthew Snyder's funeral made the expression of those views particularly hurtful to many, especially to Matthew's father. The record makes clear that the applicable legal term—'emotional distress'—fails to capture fully the anguish Westboro's choice added to Mr. Snyder's already incalculable grief. But Westboro conducted its picketing peacefully on matters of public concern at a public place adjacent to a public street. * * *

"Westboro's choice of where and when to conduct its picketing is not beyond the Government's regulatory reach—it is 'subject to reasonable time, place, or manner restrictions' that are consistent with the standards announced in this Court's precedents. Maryland now has a law imposing restrictions on funeral picketing. To the extent these laws are content neutral, they raise very different questions from the tort verdict at issue in this case. Maryland's law, however, was not in effect at the time of the events at issue here, so we have no occasion to consider how it might apply to facts such as those before us, or whether it or other similar regulations are constitutional.

"The record confirms that any distress occasioned by Westboro's picketing turned on the content and viewpoint of the message conveyed, rather than any interference with the funeral itself. A group of parishioners standing at the very spot where Westboro stood, holding signs that said 'God Bless America' and 'God Loves You,' would not have been subjected to liability. It was what Westboro said that exposed it to tort damages. * * *

"Given that Westboro's speech was at a public place on a matter of public concern, that speech is entitled to 'special protection' under the First Amendment. Such speech cannot be restricted simply because it is upsetting or arouses contempt. * * *

"The jury here was instructed that it could hold Westboro liable for intentional infliction of emotional distress based on a finding that Westboro's picketing was 'outrageous.' Outrageousness, 'however, is a highly malleable standard with' an inherent subjectiveness about it which would allow a jury to impose liability on the basis of the jurors 'tastes or views, or perhaps on the basis of their dislike of a particular expression.' [What] Westboro said, [and] how and where it chose to say it, is entitled to 'special protection' under the First Amendment, and that protection cannot be overcome by a jury finding that the picketing was outrageous.

"For all these reasons, the jury verdict imposing tort liability on Westboro for intentional infliction of emotional distress must be set aside."

BREYER, J., concurred: "I agree with the Court and join its opinion. That opinion restricts its analysis here to the matter raised in the petition for certiorari, namely, Westboro's picketing activity. The opinion does not examine in depth the effect of television broadcasting. Nor does it say anything about Internet postings. The Court holds that the First Amendment protects the picketing that occurred here, primarily because the picketing addressed matters of 'public concern.' * * *

"Westboro's means of communicating its views consisted of picketing in a place where picketing was lawful and in compliance with all police directions. The picketing could not be seen or heard from the funeral ceremony itself. And Snyder testified that he saw no more than the tops of the picketers' signs as he drove to the funeral. To uphold the application of state law in these circumstances would punish Westboro for seeking to communicate its views on matters of public concern without proportionately advancing the State's interest in protecting its citizens against severe emotional harm. Consequently, the First Amendment protects Westboro. As I read the Court's opinion, it holds no more."

ALITO, J., dissented: "Our profound national commitment to free and open debate is not a license for the vicious verbal assault that occurred in this case. Petitioner Albert Snyder is not a public figure. He is simply a parent whose son, Marine Lance Corporal Matthew Snyder, was killed in Iraq. Mr. Snyder wanted what is surely the right of any parent who experiences such an incalculable loss: to bury his son in peace. But respondents, members of the Westboro Baptist Church, deprived him of that elementary right. They first issued a press release and thus turned Matthew's funeral into a tumultuous media event. They then appeared at the church, approached as closely as they could without trespassing, and launched a malevolent verbal attack on Matthew and his family at a time of acute emotional vulnerability. As a result, Albert Snyder suffered severe and lasting emotional injury. The Court [holds] that the First Amendment protected respondents' right to brutalize Mr. Snyder. I cannot agree.

"Respondents and other members of their church have strong opinions on certain moral, religious, and political issues, and the First Amendment ensures that they have almost limitless opportunities to express their views. They may write and distribute books, articles, and other texts; they may create and disseminate video and audio recordings; they may circulate petitions; they may speak to individuals and groups in public forums and in any private venue that wishes to accommodate them; they may picket peacefully in countless locations; they may appear on television and speak on the radio; they may post messages on the Internet and send out e-mails. And they may express their views in terms that are 'uninhibited,' 'vehement,' and 'caustic.'

"It does not follow, however, that they may intentionally inflict severe emotional injury on private persons at a time of intense emotional sensitivity by launching vicious verbal attacks that make no contribution to public debate. To protect against such injury, 'most if not all jurisdictions' permit recovery in tort for the intentional infliction of emotional distress (or IIED). * * *

"Although the elements of the IIED tort are difficult to meet, respondents long ago abandoned any effort to show that those tough standards were not satisfied here. On appeal, they chose not to contest the sufficiency of the evidence. They did not dispute that Mr. Snyder suffered 'wounds that are truly severe and incapable of healing themselves. 'Nor did they dispute that their speech was 'so outrageous in character, and so extreme in degree, as to go beyond all possible bounds of decency, and to be regarded as atrocious, and utterly intolerable in a civilized community.' Instead, they maintained that the First Amendment gave them a license to engage in such conduct. * * *

"On the morning of Matthew Snyder's funeral, respondents could have chosen to stage their protest at countless locations. They could have picketed the United States Capitol, the White House, the Supreme Court, the Pentagon, or any of the more than 5,600 military recruiting stations in this country. They could have returned to the Maryland State House or the United States Naval Academy, where they had been the day before. They could have selected any public road where pedestrians are allowed. (There are more than 4,000,000 miles of public roads in the United States.) They could have staged their protest in a public park. (There are more than 20,000 public parks in this country) They could have chosen any Catholic church where no funeral was taking place. (There are nearly 19,000 Catholic churches in the United States.) But of course, a small group picketing at any of these locations would have probably gone unnoticed.

"The Westboro Baptist Church, however, has devised a strategy that remedies this problem. As the Court notes, church members have protested at nearly 600 military funerals. They have also picketed the funerals of police officers, firefighters, and the victims of natural disasters, accidents, and shocking crimes. And in advance of these protests, they issue press releases to ensure that their protests will attract public attention. This strategy works because it is expected that respondents' verbal assaults will wound the family and friends of the deceased and because the media is irresistibly drawn to the sight of persons who are visibly in grief. The more outrageous the funeral protest, the more publicity the Westboro Baptist Church is able to obtain. * * *

"[T]he Court finds that 'the overall thrust and dominant theme of [their] demonstration spoke to' broad public issues. [T]his portrayal is quite inaccurate; respondents' attack on Matthew was of central importance. But in any event, I fail to see why actionable speech should be immunized simply because it is interspersed with speech that is protected. The First Amendment allows recovery for defamatory statements that are interspersed with nondefamatory statements on matters of public concern, and there is no good reason why respondents' attack on Matthew Snyder and his family should be treated differently. * * *

"[T]he Court finds it significant that respondents' protest occurred on a public street, but this fact alone should not be enough to preclude IIED liability. To be sure, statements made on a public street may be less likely to satisfy the elements of the IIED tort than statements made on private property, but there is no reason why a public street in close proximity to the scene of a funeral should be regarded as a free-fire zone in which otherwise actionable verbal attacks are shielded from liability. If the First Amendment permits the States to protect their residents from the harm inflicted by such attacks—and the Court does not hold otherwise—then the location of the tort should not be dispositive. A physical assault may occur without trespassing; it is no defense that the perpetrator had 'the right to be where [he was].' And the same should be true with respect to unprotected speech. [D]efamatory statements are [not] immunized when they occur in a public place, and there is no good reason to treat a verbal assault based on the conduct or character of a private figure like Matthew Snyder any differently.

"One final comment about the opinion of the Court is in order. The Court suggests that the wounds inflicted by vicious verbal assaults at funerals will be prevented or at least mitigated in the future by new laws that restrict picketing within a specified distance of a funeral. It is apparent, however, that the enactment of these laws is no substitute for the protection provided by the established IIED tort; according to the Court, the verbal attacks that severely wounded petitioner in this case complied with the new Maryland law regulating funeral picketing. And there is absolutely nothing to suggest that Congress and the state legislatures, in enacting these laws, intended them to displace the protection provided by the well-established IIED tort.

"The real significance of these new laws is not that they obviate the need for IIED protection. Rather, their enactment dramatically illustrates the fundamental point that funerals are unique events at which special protection against emotional assaults is in [order.] Allowing family members to have a few hours of peace without harassment does not undermine public debate. I would [hold] that, in this setting, the First Amendment permits a private figure to recover for the intentional infliction of emotional distress caused by speech on a matter of private concern."

False news. Should injury to a particular person be a prerequisite to state regulation of plainly and factually false publications? Consider *Keeton v. Hustler Magazine, Inc.*, 465 U.S. 770 (1984): "False statements of fact harm both the subject of the falsehood *and* the readers of the statement. New Hampshire may rightly employ its libel laws to discourage the deception of its citizens." Could New Hampshire make it a criminal offense to publish false statements with knowledge of their falsity without any requirement of injury to a particular person? See *United States v. Alvarez*, Sec. 4, VI, F infra. Could a state impose sanctions for intentionally false statements made in the course of a political campaign? Cf. *Brown v. Hartlage*, 456 U.S. 45 (1982), suggesting that *Times v. Sullivan* is applicable in such situations.

E. Disclosure of Private Facts

FLORIDA STAR V. B.J.F.

491 U.S. 524, 109 S.Ct. 2603, 105 L.Ed.2d 443 (1989).

JUSTICE MARSHALL delivered the opinion of the Court.

Florida Stat. § 794.03 (1987) makes it unlawful to "print, publish, or broadcast [in] any instrument of mass communication" the name of the victim of a sexual offense. Pursuant to this statute, appellant The Florida Star was found civilly liable for publishing the name of a rape victim which it had obtained from a publicly released police report. [B.J.F.] testified that she had suffered emotional distress from the publication of her name. She stated that she had heard about the article from fellow workers and acquaintances; that her mother had received several threatening phone calls from a man who stated that he would rape B.J.F. again; and that these events had forced B.J.F. to change her phone number and residence, to seek police protection, and to obtain mental health counseling. [The jury] awarded B.J.F. $75,000 in compensatory damages and $25,000 in punitive damages. * * *

[We do not] accept appellant's invitation to hold broadly that truthful publication may never be punished consistent with the First Amendment. Our cases have carefully eschewed reaching this ultimate question, mindful that the future may bring scenarios which prudence counsels our not resolving anticipatorily. See, e.g., *Near v. Minnesota,* [Sec. 4, I, B] (hypothesizing "publication of the sailing dates of transports or the number and location of troops"); see also *Garrison v. Louisiana* (endorsing absolute defense of truth "where discussion of public affairs is concerned," but leaving unsettled the constitutional implications of truthfulness "in the discrete area of purely private libels"). Indeed, in [*Cox Broadcasting v. Cohn,* 420 U.S. 469 (1975)], we pointedly refused to answer even the less sweeping question "whether truthful publications may ever be subjected to civil or criminal liability" for invading "an area of privacy" defined by the State. [We] continue to believe that the sensitivity and significance of the interests presented in clashes between First Amendment and privacy rights counsel relying on limited principles that sweep no more broadly than the appropriate context of the instant case.

In our view, this case is appropriately analyzed with reference to [the] limited First Amendment principle [we] articulated in *Smith v. Daily Mail Pub. Co.,* 443 U.S. 97 (1979): "[I]f a newspaper lawfully obtains truthful information about a matter of public significance then state officials may not constitutionally punish publication of the information, absent a need to further a state interest of the highest order." * * *

Applied to the instant case, the *Daily Mail* principle clearly commands reversal. The first inquiry is whether the newspaper "lawfully obtain[ed] truthful information about a matter of public significance." It is undisputed that the news article describing the assault on B.J.F. was accurate. In addition, appellant lawfully obtained B.J.F.'s name. Appellee's argument to the contrary is based on the fact that under Florida law, police reports which reveal the identity of the victim of a sexual offense are not among the matters of "public record" which the public, by law, is entitled to inspect. But the fact that state officials are not required to disclose such reports does not make it unlawful for a newspaper to receive them when furnished by the government. Nor does the fact that the Department apparently failed to fulfill its obligation under § 794.03 not to "cause or allow to [be] published" the name of a sexual offense victim make the newspaper's ensuing receipt of this information unlawful. Even assuming the Constitution permitted a State to proscribe *receipt* of information, Florida has not taken this step. It is, clear, furthermore, that the news article concerned "a matter of public significance[.]" That is, the article generally, as opposed to the specific identity contained within it, involved a matter of paramount public import: the commission, and investigation, of a violent crime which had been reported to authorities.

The second inquiry is whether imposing liability on appellant [serves] "a need to further a state interest of the highest order." Appellee argues that a rule punishing publication furthers three closely related interests: the privacy of victims of sexual offenses; the physical safety of such victims, who may be targeted for retaliation if their names become known to their assailants; and the goal of encouraging victims of such crimes to report these offenses without fear of exposure.

At a time in which we are daily reminded of the tragic reality of rape, it is undeniable that these are highly significant interests. [We] do not rule out the possibility that, in a proper case, imposing civil sanctions for publication of the name of a rape victim might be so overwhelmingly necessary to advance these interests as to satisfy the *Daily Mail* standard. For three independent reasons, however, imposing liability for publication under the circumstances of this case is too precipitous a means of advancing these interests to convince us that there is a "need" [for] Florida to take this extreme step.

First is the manner in which appellant obtained the identifying information in question. [B.J.F.'s] identity would never have come to light were it not for the erroneous, if inadvertent, inclusion by the Department of her full name in an incident report made available in a press room open to the public. [Where] as here, the government has failed to police itself in disseminating information, it is clear [that] the imposition of damages against the press for its subsequent publication can hardly be said to be a narrowly tailored means of safeguarding anonymity.

That appellant gained access to the information in question through a government news release makes it especially likely that, if liability were to be imposed, self-censorship would result. Reliance on a news release is a paradigmatically "routine newspaper reporting techniqu[e]." The government's issuance of such a release, without qualification, can only convey to recipients that the government considered dissemination lawful, and indeed expected the recipients to disseminate the information further. Had appellant merely reproduced the news release prepared and released by the Department, imposing civil damages would surely violate the First Amendment. The fact that appellant converted the police report into a news story by adding the linguistic connecting tissue necessary to transform the report's facts into full sentences cannot change this result.

A second problem with Florida's imposition of liability for publication is the broad sweep of the negligence per se standard applied under the civil cause of action implied from § 794.03. Unlike claims based on the common law tort of invasion of privacy, civil actions based on § 794.03 require no case-by-case findings that the disclosure of a fact about a person's private life was one that a reasonable person would find highly offensive. On the contrary, under the per se theory of negligence adopted by the courts below, liability follows automatically from publication. This is so regardless of whether the identity of the victim is already known throughout the community; whether the victim has voluntarily called public attention to the offense; or whether the identity of the victim has otherwise become a reasonable subject of public concern—because, perhaps, questions have arisen whether the victim fabricated an assault by a particular person. Nor is there a scienter requirement of any kind under § 794.03, engendering the perverse result that truthful publications challenged pursuant to this cause of action are less protected by the First Amendment than even the least protected defamatory falsehoods: those involving purely private figures, where liability is evaluated under a standard, usually applied by a jury, of ordinary negligence. See *Gertz.* * * *

Third, and finally, the facial underinclusiveness of § 794.03 raises serious doubts about whether Florida is, in fact, serving, with this statute, the significant interests which appellee invokes in support of affirmance. Section 794.03 prohibits the publication of identifying information only if this information appears in an "instrument of mass communication," a term the statute does not define. Section 794.03 does not prohibit the spread by other means of the identities of victims of sexual offenses. An individual who maliciously spreads word of the identity of a rape victim is thus not covered, despite the fact that the communication of such information to persons who live near, or work with, the victim may have consequences equally devastating as the exposure of her name to large numbers of strangers.

When a State attempts the extraordinary measure of punishing truthful publication in the name of privacy, it must demonstrate its commitment to advancing this interest by applying its prohibition evenhandedly, to the small-time disseminator as well as the media giant. Where important First Amendment interests are at stake, the mass scope of disclosure is not an acceptable surrogate for injury. Without more careful and inclusive precautions against alternative forms of dissemination, we cannot conclude that Florida's selective ban on publication by the mass media satisfactorily accomplishes its stated purpose.

Our holding today is limited. We do not hold that truthful publication is automatically constitutionally protected, or that there is no zone of personal privacy within which the State may protect the individual from intrusion by the press, or even that a State may never punish publication of the name of a victim of a sexual offense. We hold only that where a newspaper publishes truthful information which it has lawfully obtained, punishment may [be] imposed, if at all, only when narrowly tailored to a state interest of the highest order, and that no such interest is satisfactorily served by imposing liability to appellant under the facts of this case. * * *

JUSTICE SCALIA, concurring in part and concurring in the judgment.

I think it sufficient to decide this case to rely upon the third ground set forth in the Court's opinion: that a law cannot be regarded as protecting an interest "of the highest order" and thus as justifying a restriction upon truthful speech, when it leaves appreciable damage to that supposedly vital interest unprohibited. In the present case, I would anticipate that the rape victim's discomfort at the dissemination of news of her misfortune among friends and acquaintances would be at least as great as her discomfort at its publication by the media to people to whom she is only a name. Yet the law in question does not prohibit the former in either oral or written form. Nor is it at all clear [that] Florida's general privacy law would prohibit such gossip. Nor, finally, is it credible that the interest meant to be served by the statute is the protection of the victim against a rapist still at large— an interest that arguably would extend only to mass publication. There would be little reason to limit a statute with that objective to rape alone; or to extend it to all rapes, whether or not the felon has been apprehended and confined. In any case, the instructions here did not require the jury to find that the rapist was at large.

This law has every appearance of a prohibition that society is prepared to impose upon the press but not upon itself. Such a prohibition does not protect an interest "of the highest order." For that reason, I agree that the judgment of the court below must be reversed.

JUSTICE WHITE, with whom THE CHIEF JUSTICE and JUSTICE O'CONNOR join, dissenting.

"Short of homicide, [rape] is the 'ultimate violation of self.' " *Coker v. Georgia*, [433 U.S. 584 (1977)] (opinion of White, J.). For B.J.F., however, the violation she suffered at a rapist's knife-point marked only the beginning of her ordeal. [Yet] today, the Court holds that a jury award of $75,000 to compensate B.J.F. for the harm she suffered due to the Star's negligence is at odds with the First Amendment. I do not accept this result.

[T]he three "independent reasons" the Court cites for reversing the judgment for B.J.F. [do not] support its result. The first of these reasons [is] the fact "appellant gained access to [B.J.F.'s name] through a government news release." [But the] "release" of information provided by the government was not, as the Court says, "without qualification." As the Star's own reporter conceded at trial, the crime incident report that inadvertently included B.J.F.'s name was posted in a room that contained signs making it clear that the names of rape victims were not matters of public record, and were not to be published. The Star's reporter indicated that she understood that she "[was not] allowed to take down that information" (i.e., B.J.F.'s name) and that she "[was] not supposed to take the information from the police department." Thus, by her own admission the posting of the incident report did not convey to the Star's reporter the idea that "the government considered dissemination lawful"; the Court's suggestion to the contrary is inapt. * * *

Unfortunately, as this case illustrates, mistakes happen: even when States take measures to "avoid" disclosure, sometimes rape victim's names are found out. As I see it, it is not too much to ask the press, in instances such as this, to respect simple standards of decency and refrain from publishing a victim's name, address, and/or phone number.

Second, the Court complains [that] a newspaper might be found liable under the Florida courts' negligence per se theory without regard to a newspaper's scienter or degree of fault. The short answer to this complaint is that whatever merit the Court's argument might have, it is wholly inapposite here, where the jury found that appellant acted with "reckless indifference towards the rights of others," a standard far higher than the *Gertz* standard the Court urges as a constitutional minimum today.

But even taking the Court's concerns in the abstract, they miss the mark. [The] Court says that negligence per se permits a plaintiff to hold a defendant liable without a showing that the disclosure was "of a fact about a person's private life [that] a reasonable person would find highly offensive." But the point here is that the legislature—reflecting popular sentiment—has determined that disclosure of the fact that a person was raped is categorically a revelation that reasonable people find offensive. And as for the Court's suggestion that the Florida courts' theory permits liability without regard for whether the victim's identity is already known, or whether she herself has made it known—these are facts that would surely enter into the calculation of damages in such a case. In any event, none of these mitigating factors was present [here].

Third, the Court faults the Florida criminal statute for being underinclusive. [But] our cases which have struck down laws that limit or burden the press due to their underinclusiveness have involved situations where a legislature has singled out one segment of the news media or press for adverse treatment. Here, the Florida law evenhandedly covers all "instrument[s] of mass communication" no matter their form, media, content, nature or purpose. It excludes neighborhood gossips because presumably the Florida Legislature has determined that neighborhood gossips do not pose the danger and intrusion to rape victims that "instrument[s] of mass communication" do. [Florida] wanted to prevent the widespread distribution of rape victim's names, and therefore enacted a statute tailored almost as precisely as possible to achieving that end. * * *

At issue in this case is whether there is any information about people, which—though true—may not be published in the press. [The] Court accepts appellant's invitation to obliterate one of the most note-worthy legal inventions of the 20th-Century: the tort of the publication of private facts. Even if the Court's opinion does not say as much today, such obliteration will follow inevitably from the Court's conclusion here. [Today,] we hit the bottom of the slippery slope.

I would find a place to draw the line higher on the hillside: a spot high enough to protect B.J.F.'s desire for privacy and peace-of-mind in the wake of a horrible personal tragedy. There is no public interest in publishing the names, addresses, and phone numbers of persons who are the victims of crime—and no public interest in immunizing the press from liability in the rare cases where a State's efforts to protect a victim's privacy have failed. Consequently, I respectfully dissent.

————

During the course of a cell phone conversation, the president of a local teacher's union, Kane, told his chief labor negotiator, Bartnicki: "If they're not gonna move for three percent, we're gonna have to go to their, their homes * * * To blow off their front porches, we'll have to do some work on some of those guys. (PAUSES). Really, uh, really and truthfully because this is, you know, this is bad news." The conversation was illegally intercepted by an unknown person and was sent to the head of a local taxpayer's organization, Yocum, who in turn, shared it with school board members and a local broadcaster, Vopper. Vopper played the tape on his radio show. Bartnicki and Kane brought an action against Yocum and Vopper invoking state and federal laws prohibiting the disclosure of material known to be unlawfully intercepted.

BARTNICKI v. VOPPER, 532 U.S. 514 (2001), per STEVENS, J., held the statutes unconstitutional as applied to circumstances in which the defendants played no role in the illegal acquisition of the material, their access to the conversation was obtained lawfully, and the conversation was about a public issue: "We agree with petitioners that 18 U.S.C. § 2511(1)(c), as well as its Pennsylvania analog, is in fact a content-neutral law of general applicability. [In] this case, the basic purpose of the statute at issue is to 'protec[t] the privacy of wire[, electronic,] and oral communication. The statute does not distinguish based on the content of the intercepted conversations, nor is it justified by reference to the content of those conversations. Rather, the communications at issue are singled out by virtue of the fact that they were illegally intercepted—by virtue of the source, rather than the subject matter.

"On the other hand, the naked prohibition against disclosures is fairly characterized as a regulation of pure speech. Unlike the prohibition against the 'use' of the contents of an illegal interception in § 2511(1)(d), subsection (c) is not a regulation of conduct. It is true that the delivery of a tape recording might be regarded as conduct, but given that the purpose of such a delivery is to provide the recipient with the text of recorded statements, it is like the delivery of a handbill or a pamphlet, and as such, it is the kind of 'speech' that the First Amendment protects.

"[As] a general matter, 'state action to punish the publication of truthful information seldom can satisfy constitutional standards.' *Daily Mail.* [The] Government identifies two interests served by the statute—first, the interest in removing an incentive for parties to intercept private conversations, and second, the interest in minimizing the harm to persons whose conversations have been illegally intercepted. We assume that those interests adequately justify the prohibition in § 2511(1)(d) against the interceptor's own use of information that he or she acquired by violating § 2511(1)(a), but it by no means follows that punishing disclosures of lawfully obtained information of public interest by one not involved in the initial illegality is an acceptable means of serving those ends.

"The normal method of deterring unlawful conduct is to impose an appropriate punishment on the person who engages in it. If the sanctions that presently attach to a violation of § 2511(1)(a) do not provide sufficient deterrence, perhaps those sanctions should be made more severe. But it would be quite remarkable to hold that speech by a law-abiding possessor of information can be suppressed in order to deter conduct by a non-law-abiding third party.

"[With] only a handful of exceptions, the violations of § 2511(1)(a) that have been described in litigated cases have been motivated by either financial gain or domestic disputes. In virtually all of those cases, the identity of the person or persons intercepting the communication has been known. Moreover, petitioners cite no evidence that Congress viewed the prohibition against disclosures as a response to the difficulty of identifying persons making improper use of scanners and other surveillance devices and accordingly of deterring such conduct, and there is no empirical evidence to support the assumption that the prohibition against disclosures reduces the number of illegal interceptions.

"Although this case demonstrates that there may be an occasional situation in which an anonymous scanner will risk criminal prosecution by passing on information without any expectation of financial reward or public praise, surely this is the exceptional case. Moreover, there is no basis for assuming that imposing sanctions upon respondents will deter the unidentified scanner from continuing to engage in surreptitious interceptions. Unusual cases fall far short of a showing that there is a 'need of the highest order' for a rule supplementing the traditional means of deterring antisocial conduct. The justification for any such novel burden on expression must be 'far stronger than mere speculation about serious harms.' Accordingly, the Government's first suggested justification for applying § 2511(1)(c) to an otherwise innocent disclosure of public information is plainly insufficient.[19]

---

[19]   **[Ct's Note]** Our holding, of course, does not apply to punishing parties for obtaining the relevant information unlawfully. "It would be frivolous to assert—and no one does in these cases—that the First Amendment, in the interest of securing news or otherwise, confers a license on either the reporter or his news sources to violate valid criminal laws. Although stealing documents or private wiretapping could provide newsworthy information, neither reporter nor source is immune from conviction for such conduct, whatever the impact on the flow of news."

"The Government's second argument, however, is considerably stronger. Privacy of communication is an important interest, [and] the fear of public disclosure of private conversations might well have a chilling effect on private speech. [Accordingly], it seems to us that there are important interests to be considered on both sides of the constitutional calculus. In considering that balance, we acknowledge that some intrusions on privacy are more offensive than others, and that the disclosure of the contents of a private conversation can be an even greater intrusion on privacy than the interception itself. As a result, there is a valid independent justification for prohibiting such disclosures by persons who lawfully obtained access to the contents of an illegally intercepted message, even if that prohibition does not play a significant role in preventing such interceptions from occurring in the first place.

"We need not decide whether that interest is strong enough to justify the application of § 2511(c) to disclosures of trade secrets or domestic gossip or other information of purely private concern. In other words, the outcome of the case does not turn on whether § 2511(1)(c) may be enforced with respect to most violations of the statute without offending the First Amendment. The enforcement of that provision in this case, however, implicates the core purposes of the First Amendment because it imposes sanctions on the publication of truthful information of public concern.

"In this case, privacy concerns give way when balanced against the interest in publishing matters of public importance. [The] months of negotiations over the proper level of compensation for teachers at the Wyoming Valley West High School were unquestionably a matter of public concern, and respondents were clearly engaged in debate about that concern. That debate may be more mundane than the Communist rhetoric that inspired Justice Brandeis' classic opinion in *Whitney v. California*, but it is no less worthy of constitutional protection."

BREYER, J., joined by O'Connor, J., concurred: "[As] a general matter, despite the statutes' direct restrictions on speech, the Federal Constitution must tolerate laws of this kind because of the importance of these privacy and speech-related objectives. [Nonetheless], looked at more specifically, the statutes, as applied in these circumstances, do not reasonably reconcile the competing constitutional objectives. Rather, they disproportionately interfere with media freedom. For one thing, the broadcasters here engaged in no unlawful activity other than the ultimate publication of the information another had previously obtained. [For] another thing, the speakers had little or no legitimate interest in maintaining the privacy of the particular conversation. That conversation involved a suggestion about 'blow[ing] off . . . front porches' and 'do[ing] some work on some of these guys,' thereby raising a significant concern for the safety of others. Where publication of private information constitutes a wrongful act, the law recognizes a privilege allowing the reporting of threats to public safety. [Even] where the danger may have passed by the time of publication, that fact cannot legitimize the speaker's earlier privacy expectation. Nor should editors, who must make a publication decision quickly, have to determine present or continued danger before publishing this kind of threat.

"Further, the speakers themselves, the president of a teacher's union and the union's chief negotiator, were 'limited public figures,' for they voluntarily engaged in a public controversy. They thereby subjected themselves to somewhat greater public scrutiny and had a lesser interest in privacy than an individual engaged in purely private affairs. [This] is not to say that the Constitution requires anyone, including public figures, to give up entirely the right to private communication, i.e., communication free from telephone taps or interceptions. But the subject matter of the conversation at issue here is far removed from that in situations where the media publicizes truly private matters.

"Thus, in finding a constitutional privilege to publish unlawfully intercepted conversations of the kind here at issue, the Court does not create a 'public interest' exception that swallows up the statutes' privacy-protecting general rule. Rather, it finds constitutional protection for publication of intercepted information of a special kind. Here, the speakers' legitimate privacy expectations are unusually low, and the public interest in defeating those expectations is unusually high."

REHNQUIST, C.J., joined by Scalia and Thomas, JJ., dissented: "Technology now permits millions of important and confidential conversations to occur through a vast system of electronic networks. These advances, however, raise significant privacy concerns. We are placed in the uncomfortable position of not knowing who might have access to our personal and business e-mails, our medical and financial records, or our cordless and cellular telephone conversations. In an attempt to prevent some of the most egregious violations of privacy, the United States, the District of Columbia, and 40 States have enacted laws prohibiting the intentional interception and knowing disclosure of electronic communications. The Court holds that all of these statutes violate the First Amendment insofar as the illegally intercepted conversation touches upon a matter of 'public concern,' an amorphous concept that the Court does not even attempt to define. [The] Court's decision diminishes [the] purposes of the First Amendment: chilling the speech of the millions of Americans who rely upon electronic technology to communicate each day. * * *

"The Court correctly observes that these are 'content-neutral law[s] of general applicability' which serve recognized interests of the 'highest order': 'the interest in individual privacy [and] in fostering private speech.' It nonetheless subjects these laws to the strict scrutiny normally reserved for governmental attempts to censor different viewpoints or ideas. There is scant support, either in precedent or in reason, for the Court's tacit application of strict scrutiny.

"[I]t is obvious that the *Daily Mail* cases upon which the Court relies do not address the question presented here. Our decisions themselves made this clear: 'The *Daily Mail* principle does not settle the issue whether, in cases where information has been acquired unlawfully by a newspaper or by a source, the government may ever punish not only the unlawful acquisition, but the ensuing publication as well.' *Florida Star*. [Undaunted], the Court places an inordinate amount of weight upon the fact that the receipt of an illegally intercepted communication has not been criminalized. But this hardly renders those who knowingly receive and disclose such communications 'law-abiding,' and it certainly does not bring them under the *Daily Mail* principle. The transmission of the intercepted communication from the eavesdropper to the third party is itself illegal; and where, as here, the third party then knowingly discloses that communication, another illegal act has been committed. The third party in this situation cannot be likened to the reporters in the *Daily Mail* cases, who lawfully obtained their information through consensual interviews or public documents. * * *

"The 'dry up the market' theory, which posits that it is possible to deter an illegal act that is difficult to police by preventing the wrongdoer from enjoying the fruits of the crime, is neither novel nor implausible. It is a time-tested theory that undergirds numerous laws, such as the prohibition of the knowing possession of stolen goods. [Reliance] upon the 'dry up the market' theory is both logical and eminently reasonable, and our precedents make plain that it is 'far stronger than mere speculation.'

"These statutes also protect the important interests of deterring clandestine invasions of privacy and preventing the involuntary broadcast of private communications. [These] statutes undeniably protect this venerable right of privacy. [The] Court concludes that the private conversation between Gloria Bartnicki and Anthony Kane is somehow a 'debate * * * worthy of constitutional protection.' Perhaps the Court is correct that '[i]f the statements about the labor negotiations had been made in a public arena—during a bargaining session, for example—they would have been newsworthy.' The point, however, is that Bartnicki and Kane had no intention of contributing to a public 'debate' at all, and it is perverse to hold that another's unlawful interception and knowing disclosure of their conversation is speech 'worthy of constitutional protection.' * * *

"The Constitution should not protect the involuntary broadcast of personal conversations. Even where the communications involve public figures or concern public matters, the conversations are nonetheless private and worthy of protection. Although public persons may have forgone the right to live their lives screened from public scrutiny in some areas, it does not and should not follow that they also have abandoned their right to have a private conversation without fear of it being intentionally intercepted and knowingly disclosed."

———

The 1976 Copyright Act provided copyright protection until 50 years after an author's death. The Copyright Term Extension Act of 1998 ("CTEA") extended the term to 70 years for new and existing copyrights.

ELDRED v. ASHCROFT, 537 U.S. 186 (2003), per GINSBURG, J., upheld the Act against a claim that the extended copyright protection to already existing intellectual property was unconstitutional: "Petitioners [argue] that the CTEA is a content-neutral regulation of speech that fails heightened judicial review under the First Amendment. We reject petitioners' plea for imposition of uncommonly strict scrutiny on a copyright scheme that incorporates its own speech-protective purposes and safeguards. The Copyright Clause and First Amendment were adopted close in time. This proximity indicates that, in the Framers' view, copyright's limited monopolies are compatible with free speech principles. Indeed, copyright's purpose is to *promote* the creation and publication of free expression. * * *

"In addition to spurring the creation and publication of new expression, copyright law contains built-in First Amendment accommodations. First, it distinguishes between ideas and expression and makes only the latter eligible for copyright protection. [Due] to this distinction, every idea, theory, and fact in a copyrighted work becomes instantly available for public exploitation at the moment of publication.

"Second, the 'fair use' defense allows the public to use not only facts and ideas contained in a copyrighted work, but also expression itself in certain circumstances. [The] fair use defense affords considerable 'latitude for scholarship and comment,' and even for parody. The CTEA itself supplements these traditional First Amendment safeguards. First, it allows libraries, archives, and similar institutions to 'reproduce' and 'distribute, display, or perform in facsimile or digital form' copies of certain published works 'during the last 20 years of any term of copyright [for] purposes of preservation, scholarship, or research' if the work is not already being exploited commercially and further copies are unavailable at a reasonable price. Second, Title II of the CTEA, known as the Fairness in Music Licensing Act of 1998, exempts small businesses, restaurants, and like entities from having to pay performance royalties on music played from licensed radio, television, and similar facilities. * * *

"The First Amendment securely protects the freedom to make—or decline to make—one's own speech; it bears less heavily when speakers assert the right to make other people's speeches. To the extent such assertions raise First Amendment concerns, copyright's built-in free speech safeguards are generally adequate to address them. [W]hen, as in this case, Congress has not altered the traditional contours of copyright protection, further First Amendment scrutiny is unnecessary."

BREYER, J., dissented: "The Copyright Clause and the First Amendment seek related objectives—the creation and dissemination of information. When working in tandem, these provisions mutually reinforce each other, the first serving as an 'engine of free expression,' the second assuring that government throws up no obstacle to its dissemination. At the same time, a particular statute that exceeds proper Copyright Clause bounds may set Clause and Amendment at cross-purposes, thereby depriving the public of the speech-related benefits that the Founders, through both, have promised. [The] majority [invokes] the 'fair use' exception, and it notes that copyright law itself is restricted to protection of a work's expression, not its substantive content. Neither the exception nor the restriction, however, would necessarily help those who wish to obtain from electronic databases material that is not there—say, teachers wishing their students to see albums of Depression Era photographs, to read the recorded words of those who actually lived under slavery, or to contrast, say, Gary Cooper's heroic portrayal of Sergeant York with filmed reality from the battlefield of Verdun. Such harm, and more, will occur despite the 1998 Act's exemptions and despite the other 'First Amendment safeguards' in which the majority places its trust. The statute falls outside the scope of legislative power that the Copyright Clause, read in light of the First Amendment, grants to Congress."

IV. OBSCENITY

A. The Search for a Rationale

Roth v. United States, 354 U.S. 476 (1957) held that obscenity was "not within the area of constitutionally protected speech or press" because, drawing from *Chaplinsky,* infra, such utterances were *"no essential part of any exposition of ideas, and are of such slight social value as a step to truth that any benefit that may be derived from them is clearly outweighed by the social interest in order and morality."* [Emphasis in original]. The Court determined that sexually explicit material was not necessarily obscene. Instead the determination of obscenity was "whether to the average person, applying contemporary community standards, the dominant theme of the material taken as a whole appeals to prurient interest." Such material, according to the Court, was "utterly without redeeming social importance."

Despite *Roth's* view that obscene speech had no First Amendment value, *Stanley v. Georgia,* 394 U.S. 557 (1969) concluded that the First Amendment protected the possession of obscene material in the home. The Court argued that the right "to receive information and ideas, regardless of their social worth, is fundamental to our free society," distinguishing the public distribution of obscene materials on the ground that there was a greater danger that such material might fall into the hands of children or "intrude on the sensibilities or privacy of the general public."

Many commentators believed that *Roth* and *Stanley* left the law in an unstable position. *Roth* had announced that obscenity was without constitutional value but offered no workable definition; *Stanley* seemed to some to suggest that public showings of obscene material might be constitutional if children were excluded and if individuals were not exposed to the material without informed consent. *Paris Adult Theatre,* infra, attempted to provide a rationale for the regulation of obscenity that would prevent the showing of obscene material in public theaters; *Miller,* infra, sought to crystallize the definition of obscenity.

PARIS ADULT THEATRE I v. SLATON

413 U.S. 49, 93 S.Ct. 2628, 37 L.Ed.2d 446 (1973).

CHIEF JUSTICE BURGER delivered the opinion of the Court.

[The entrance to Paris Adult Theatres I & II was conventional and displayed no pictures. Signs read: "Adult Theatre—You must be 21 and able to prove it. If viewing the nude body offends you, Please Do Not Enter." The District Attorney, nonetheless, had brought an action to enjoin the showing of two films that the Georgia Supreme Court described as "hard core pornography" leaving "little to the imagination." The Georgia Supreme Court assumed that the adult theaters in question barred minors and gave a full warning to the general public of the nature of the films involved, but held that the showing of the films was not constitutionally protected.]

[We] categorically disapprove the theory [that] obscene, pornographic films acquire constitutional immunity from state regulation simply because they are exhibited for consenting adults only. [Although we have] recognized the high importance of the state interest in regulating the exposure of obscene materials to juveniles and unconsenting adults, this Court has never declared these to be the only legitimate state interests permitting regulation of obscene material.

[W]e hold that there are legitimate state interests at stake in stemming the tide of commercialized obscenity, even assuming it is feasible to enforce effective safeguards against exposure to juveniles and to the passerby. [These] include the interest of the public in the quality of life and the total community environment, the tone of commerce in the great city centers, and, possibly, the public safety itself. The Hill-Link Minority Report of the Commission on Obscenity and Pornography indicates that there is at least an arguable correlation between obscene material and crime. Quite apart from sex crimes, however, there remains one problem of large proportions aptly described by Professor Bickel: "It concerns the tone of the society, the mode, or to use terms that have perhaps greater currency, the style and quality of life, now and in the future. A man may be entitled to read an obscene book in his room, or expose himself indecently there. [We] should protect his privacy. But if he demands a right to obtain the books and pictures he wants in the market, and to foregather in public places—discreet, if you will, but accessible to all—with others who share his tastes, *then to grant him his right is to affect the world about the rest of us, and to impinge on other privacies.* Even supposing that each of us can, if he wishes, effectively avert the eye and stop the ear (which, in truth, we cannot), what is commonly read and seen and heard and done intrudes upon us all, want it or not." 22 *The Public Interest* 25 (Winter, 1971). [T]here is a "right of the Nation and of the States to maintain a decent [society]," *Jacobellis* (Warren, C.J., dissenting).

But, it is argued, there is no scientific data which conclusively demonstrates that exposure to obscene materials adversely affects men and women or their society. It is urged [that], absent such a demonstration, any kind of state regulation is "impermissible." We reject this argument. It is not for us to resolve empirical uncertainties underlying state legislation, save in the exceptional case where that legislation plainly impinges upon rights protected by the Constitution itself. [Although] there is no conclusive proof of a connection between antisocial behavior and obscene material, the legislature of Georgia could quite reasonably determine that such a connection does or might exist. In deciding *Roth,* this Court implicitly accepted that a legislature could legitimately act on such a conclusion to protect *"the social interest in order and morality."*

From the beginning of civilized societies, legislators and judges have acted on various unprovable assumptions. Such assumptions underlie much lawful state regulation of commercial and business affairs. The same is true of the federal securities, antitrust laws and a host of other federal regulations. [Likewise], when legislatures and administrators act to protect the physical environment from pollution and to preserve our resources of forests, streams and parks, they must act on such imponderables as the impact of a new highway near or through an existing park or wilderness area. [The] fact that a congressional directive reflects unprovable assumptions about what is good for the people, including imponderable aesthetic assumptions, is not a sufficient reason to find that statute unconstitutional.

If we accept the unprovable assumption that a complete education requires certain books, and the well nigh universal belief that good books, plays, and art lift the spirit, improve the mind, enrich the human personality and develop character, can we then say that a state legislature may not act on the corollary assumption that commerce in obscene books, or public exhibitions focused on obscene conduct, have a tendency to exert a corrupting and debasing impact leading to antisocial behavior? [The] sum of experience, including that of the past two decades, affords an ample basis for legislatures to conclude that a sensitive, key relationship of human existence, central to family life, community welfare, and the development of human personality, can be debased and distorted by crass commercial exploitation of sex. Nothing in the Constitution prohibits a State from reaching such a conclusion and acting on it legislatively simply because there is no conclusive evidence or empirical data.

[Nothing] in this Court's decisions intimates that there is any "fundamental" privacy right "implicit in the concept of ordered liberty" to watch obscene movies in places of public accommodation. [W]e have declined to equate the privacy of the home relied on in *Stanley* with a "zone" of "privacy" that follows a distributor or a consumer of obscene materials wherever he goes.[9]

[W]e reject the claim that Georgia is here attempting to control the minds or thoughts of those who patronize theatres. Preventing unlimited display or distribution of obscene material, which by definition lacks any serious literary,

---

[9]   The Court has limited *Stanley* to its facts, holding that Stanley did not apply to the possession of child pornography even in the home, *Osborne v. Ohio,* 495 U.S. 103 (1990), and that *Stanley* did not protect the mailing of obscene material to consenting adults, *United States v. Reidel,* 402 U.S. 351 (1971), or transporting or importing obscene materials for private use, *United States v. Orito,* 413 U.S. 139 (1973); *United States v. 12 200-Ft. Reels,* 413 U.S. 123 (1973).

artistic, political, or scientific value as communication, is distinct from a control of reason and the intellect.

[Finally], petitioners argue that conduct which directly involves "consenting adults" only has, for that sole reason, a special claim to constitutional protection. Our Constitution establishes a broad range of conditions on the exercise of power by the States, but for us to say that our Constitution incorporates the proposition that conduct involving consenting adults only is always beyond state regulation,[14] is a step we are unable to take.[15] [The] issue in this context goes beyond whether someone, or even the majority, considers the conduct depicted as "wrong" or "sinful." The States have the power to make a morally neutral judgment that public exhibition of obscene material, or commerce in such material, has a tendency to injure the community as a whole, to endanger the public safety, or to jeopardize, in Mr. Chief Justice Warren's words, the States' "right [to] maintain a decent society." *Jacobellis* (dissenting). * * *

JUSTICE BRENNAN, with whom JUSTICE STEWART and JUSTICE MARSHALL join, dissenting.

[I] am convinced that the approach initiated 15 years ago in *Roth* and culminating in the Court's decision today, cannot bring stability to this area of the law without jeopardizing fundamental First Amendment values, and I have concluded that the time has come to make a significant departure from that [approach].

[The] decision of the Georgia Supreme Court rested squarely on its conclusion that the State could constitutionally suppress these films even if they were displayed only to persons over the age of 21 who were aware of the nature of their contents and who had consented to viewing them. [I] am convinced of the invalidity of that conclusion [and] would therefore vacate the [judgment]. I have no occasion to consider the extent of State power to regulate the distribution of sexually oriented materials to juveniles or to unconsenting [adults]. [*Stanley*] reflected our emerging view that the state interests in protecting children and in protecting unconsenting adults may stand on a different footing from the other asserted state interests. It may well be, as one commentator has argued, that "exposure to [erotic material] is for some persons an intense emotional experience. A communication of this nature, imposed upon a person contrary to his wishes, has all the characteristics of a physical assault. [And it] constitutes an invasion of his [privacy]." [But] whatever the strength of the state interests in protecting juveniles and unconsenting adults from exposure to sexually oriented materials, those interests cannot be asserted in defense of the holding of the Georgia Supreme Court, [which] assumed for the purposes of its decision that the films in issue were

---

14   [Ct's Note] Cf. John Stuart Mill, *On Liberty* 13 (1955).

15   [Ct's Note] The state statute books are replete with constitutionally unchallenged laws against prostitution, suicide, voluntary self-mutilation, brutalizing "bare fist" prize fights, and duels, although these crimes may only directly involve "consenting adults." Statutes making bigamy a crime surely cut into an individual's freedom to associate, but few today seriously claim such statutes violate the First Amendment or any other constitutional provision.

exhibited only to persons over the age of 21 who viewed them willingly and with prior knowledge of the nature of their contents. [The] justification for the suppression must be found, therefore, in some independent interest in regulating the reading and viewing habits of consenting [adults].

In *Stanley* we pointed out that "[t]here appears to be little empirical basis for" the assertion that "exposure to obscene materials may lead to deviant sexual behavior or crimes of sexual violence." In any event, we added that "if the State is only concerned about printed or filmed materials inducing antisocial conduct, we believe that in the context of private consumption of ideas and information we should adhere to the view that '[a]mong free men, the deterrents ordinarily to be applied to prevent crime are education and punishment for violations of the [law].' "

Moreover, in *Stanley* we rejected as "wholly inconsistent with the philosophy of the First Amendment," the notion that there is a legitimate state concern in the "control [of] the moral content of a person's thoughts." [The] traditional description of state police power does embrace the regulation of morals as well as the health, safety, and general welfare of the citizenry. [But] the State's interest in regulating morality by suppressing obscenity, while often asserted, remains essentially unfocused and ill-defined. And, since the attempt to curtail unprotected speech necessarily spills over into the area of protected speech, the effort to serve this speculative interest through the suppression of obscene material must tread heavily on rights protected by the First Amendment. * * *

In short, while I cannot say that the interests of the State—apart from the question of juveniles and unconsenting adults—are trivial or nonexistent, I am compelled to conclude that these interests cannot justify the substantial damage to constitutional rights and to this Nation's judicial machinery that inevitably results from state efforts to bar the distribution even of unprotected material to consenting adults.

JUSTICE DOUGLAS, dissenting. * * *

"Obscenity" at most is the expression of offensive ideas. There are regimes in the world where ideas "offensive" to the majority (or at least to those who control the majority) are suppressed. There life proceeds at a monotonous pace. Most of us would find that world offensive. One of the most offensive experiences in my life was a visit to a nation where bookstalls were filled only with books on mathematics and [religion.]

I am sure I would find offensive most of the books and movies charged with being obscene. But in a life that has not been short, I have yet to be trapped into seeing or reading something that would offend me. I never read or see the materials coming to the Court under charges of "obscenity," because I have thought the First Amendment made it unconstitutional for me to act as a censor. * * *

———

KINGSLEY INT'L PICTURES CORP. v. REGENTS, 360 U.S. 684 (1959), per STEWART, J., underlined the distinction between obscenity and non-obscene "portrayal of sex" in art and literature. *Kingsley* held invalid New York's denial of a license to exhibit the film *Lady Chatterley's Lover* pursuant to a statute requiring such denial when a film "portrays acts of sexual immorality [as] desirable, acceptable or proper patterns of behavior": "[What] New York has done, [is] to prevent the exhibition of a motion picture because that picture advocates an idea— that adultery under certain circumstances may be proper behavior. Yet the First Amendment's basic guarantee is of freedom to advocate ideas. The State, quite simply, has thus struck at the very heart of constitutionally protected liberty."

B. A Revised Standard

MILLER V. CALIFORNIA
413 U.S. 15, 93 S.Ct. 2607, 37 L.Ed.2d 419 (1973).

CHIEF JUSTICE BURGER delivered the opinion of the Court. [The Court remanded, "for proceedings not inconsistent" with the opinion's obscenity standard, Miller's conviction under California's obscenity law for mass mailing of unsolicited pictorial advertising brochures depicting men and women in a variety of group sexual activities.]

This is one of a group of "obscenity-pornography" cases being reviewed by the Court in a re-examination of standards enunciated in earlier cases involving what Mr. Justice Harlan called "the intractable obscenity problem." [I]n this context [we] are called on to define the standards which must be used to identify obscene material that a State may [regulate].

[Nine years after *Roth*], in *Memoirs v. Massachusetts*, 383 U.S. 413 (1966), the Court veered sharply away from the Roth concept and, with only three Justices in the plurality opinion, articulated a new test of obscenity. The plurality held that under the *Roth* definition "as elaborated in subsequent cases, three elements must coalesce: it must be established that (a) the dominant theme of the material taken as a whole appeals to a prurient interest in sex; (b) the material is patently offensive because it affronts contemporary community standards relating to the description or representation of sexual matters; and (c) the material is utterly without redeeming social value." [While] *Roth* presumed "obscenity" to be "utterly without redeeming social importance," *Memoirs* required that to prove obscenity it must be affirmatively established that the material is "*utterly* without redeeming social value."

Thus, even as they repeated the words of *Roth,* the *Memoirs* plurality produced a drastically altered test that called on the prosecution to prove a negative, i.e., that the material was "*utterly* without redeeming social value"—a burden virtually impossible to discharge under our criminal standards of proof. [Apart] from the initial formulation in *Roth,* no majority of the Court has at any given time been able to agree on a standard to determine what constitutes obscene, pornographic material subject to regulation under the States' police power. This is not remarkable, for in the area of freedom of speech and press the courts must always remain sensitive to any infringement on genuinely serious literary, artistic, political, or scientific expression. * * *

II.   This much has been categorically settled by the Court, that obscene material is unprotected by the First Amendment. [We] acknowledge, however, the inherent dangers of undertaking to regulate any form of expression. State statutes designed to regulate obscene materials must be carefully limited. As a result, we now confine the permissible scope of such regulation to works which depict or describe sexual conduct. That conduct must be specifically defined by the applicable state law, as written or authoritatively construed. A state offense must also be limited to works which, taken as a whole, appeal to the prurient interest in sex, which portray sexual conduct in a patently offensive way, and which, taken as a whole, do not have serious literary, artistic, political, or scientific value.

The basic guidelines for the trier of fact must be: (a) whether "the average person, applying contemporary community standards" would find that the work, taken as a whole, appeals to the prurient interest, (b) whether the work depicts or describes, in a patently offensive way, sexual conduct specifically defined by the applicable state law, and (c) whether the work, taken as a whole, lacks serious literary, artistic, political, or scientific value. We do not adopt as a constitutional standard the "*utterly* without redeeming social value" test of *Memoirs;* that concept has never commanded the adherence of more than three Justices at one time. If a state law that regulates obscene material is thus limited, as written or construed, the First Amendment values applicable to the States [are] adequately protected by the ultimate power of appellate courts to conduct an independent review of constitutional claims when necessary.

We emphasize that it is not our function to propose regulatory schemes for the States. [It] is possible, however, to give a few plain examples of what a state statute could define for regulation under the second part (b) of the standard announced in this opinion, supra:

(a)   Patently offensive representations or descriptions of ultimate sexual acts, normal or perverted, actual or simulated.

(b)   Patently offensive representations or descriptions of masturbation, excretory functions, and lewd exhibition of the genitals.[10]

Sex and nudity may not be exploited without limit by films or pictures exhibited or sold in places of public accommodation any more than live sex and

---

10   *Jenkins v. Georgia*, 418 U.S. 153 (1974), unanimously held the film *Carnal Knowledge* not obscene because it did not ' "depict or describe patently offensive 'hard core' sexual conduct" ' as required by *Miller:* "[While there] are scenes in which sexual conduct including 'ultimate sexual acts' is to be understood to be taking place, the camera does not focus on the bodies of the actors at such times. There is no exhibition whatever of the actors' genitals, lewd or otherwise, during these scenes. There are occasional scenes of nudity, but nudity alone is not enough to make material legally obscene under the *Miller* standards."

nudity can be exhibited or sold without limit in such public places.[8] At a minimum, prurient, patently offensive depiction or description of sexual conduct must have serious literary, artistic, political, or scientific value to merit First Amendment protection. For example, medical books for the education of physicians and related personnel necessarily use graphic illustrations and descriptions of human anatomy. In resolving the inevitably sensitive questions of fact and law, we must continue to rely on the jury system, accompanied by the safeguards that judges, rules of evidence, presumption of innocence and other protective features [provide].

Mr. Justice Brennan [has] abandoned his former positions and now maintains that no formulation of this Court, the Congress, or the States can adequately distinguish obscene material unprotected by the First Amendment from protected expression, *Paris Adult Theatre* (Brennan, J., dissenting). Paradoxically, Justice Brennan indicates that suppression of unprotected obscene material is permissible to avoid exposure to unconsenting adults, as in this case, and to juveniles, although he gives no indication of how the division between protected and nonprotected materials may be drawn with greater precision for these purposes than for regulation of commercial exposure to consenting adults only. Nor does he indicate where in the Constitution he finds the authority to distinguish between a willing "adult" one month past the state law age of majority and a willing "juvenile" one month younger.

Under the holdings announced today, no one will be subject to prosecution for the sale or exposure of obscene materials unless these materials depict or describe patently offensive "hard core" sexual conduct specifically defined by the regulating state law, as written or construed. We are satisfied that these specific prerequisites will provide fair notice to a dealer in such materials that his public and commercial activities may bring prosecution. If the inability to define regulated materials with ultimate, god-like precision altogether removes the power of the States or the Congress to regulate, then "hard core" pornography may be exposed without limit to the juvenile, the passerby, and the consenting adult alike, as indeed, Mr. Justice Douglas contends.

[N]o amount of "fatigue" should lead us to adopt a convenient "institutional" rationale—an absolutist, "anything goes" view of the First Amendment—because it will lighten our burdens. [Nor] should we remedy "tension between state and federal courts" by arbitrarily depriving the States of a power reserved to them under the Constitution, a power which they have enjoyed and exercised continuously from before the adoption of the First Amendment to this day. "Our duty admits of no 'substitute for facing up to the tough individual problems of constitutional judgment involved in every obscenity case.'" *Jacobellis* (opinion of Brennan, J.).

---

8   [Ct's Note] Although we are not presented here with the problem of regulating lewd public conduct itself, the States have greater power to regulate nonverbal, physical conduct than to suppress depictions or descriptions of the same behavior. * * *

III. Under a national Constitution, fundamental First Amendment limitations on the powers of the States do not vary from community to community, but this does not mean that there are, or should or can be, fixed, uniform national standards of precisely what appeals to the "prurient interest" or is "patently offensive." These are essentially questions of fact, and our nation is simply too big and too diverse for this Court to reasonably expect that such standards could be articulated for all 50 States in a single formulation, even assuming the prerequisite consensus exists. When triers of fact are asked to decide whether "the average person, applying contemporary community standards" would consider certain materials "prurient," it would be unrealistic to require that the answer be based on some abstract formulation. The adversary system, with lay jurors as the usual ultimate fact finders in criminal prosecutions, has historically permitted triers-of-fact to draw on the standards of their community, guided always by limiting instructions on the law. To require a State to structure obscenity proceedings around evidence of a *national* "community standard" would be an exercise in [futility].

We conclude that neither the State's alleged failure to offer evidence of "national standards," nor the trial court's charge that the jury consider state community standards, were constitutional errors. Nothing in the First Amendment requires that a jury must consider hypothetical and unascertainable "national standards" when attempting to determine whether certain materials are obscene as a matter of [fact].

It is neither realistic nor constitutionally sound to read the First Amendment as requiring that the people of Maine or Mississippi accept public depiction of conduct found tolerable in Las Vegas, or New York City. People in different States vary in their tastes and attitudes, and this diversity is not to be strangled by the absolutism of imposed uniformity. As the Court made clear in *Mishkin,* the primary concern with requiring a jury to apply the standard of "the average person, applying contemporary community standards" is to be certain that, so far as material is not aimed at a deviant group, it will be judged by its impact on an average person, rather than a particularly susceptible or sensitive person—or indeed a totally insensitive one. [We] hold the requirement that the jury evaluate the materials with reference to "contemporary standards of the State of California" serves this protective purpose and is constitutionally adequate.

[In] sum we (a) reaffirm the *Roth* holding that obscene material is not protected by the First Amendment, (b) hold that such material can be regulated by the States, subject to the specific safeguards enunciated above, without a showing that the material is "*utterly* without redeeming social value," and (c) hold that obscenity is to be determined by applying "contemporary community standards," not "national standards." * * *

JUSTICE DOUGLAS, dissenting. * * *

My contention is that until a civil proceeding has placed a tract beyond the pale, no criminal prosecution should be sustained. For no more vivid illustration of vague and uncertain laws could be designed than those we have fashioned. [If] a specific book [or] motion picture has in a civil proceeding been condemned as obscene and review of that finding has been completed, and thereafter a person publishes [or] displays that particular book or film, then a vague law has been made specific. There would remain the underlying question whether the First Amendment allows an implied exception in the case of obscenity. I do not think it does and my views on the issue have been stated over and again. But at least a criminal prosecution brought at that juncture would not violate the time-honored void-for-vagueness test.

JUSTICE BRENNAN, with whom JUSTICE STEWART and JUSTICE MARSHALL join, dissenting.

In my dissent in *Paris Adult Theatre,* decided this date, I noted that I had no occasion to consider the extent of state power to regulate the distribution of sexually oriented material to juveniles or the offensive exposure of such material to unconsenting adults. [I] need not now decide whether a statute might be drawn to impose, within the requirements of the First Amendment, criminal penalties for the precise conduct at issue here. For it is clear [the] statute under which the prosecution was brought is unconstitutionally overbroad, and therefore invalid on its face. * * *

[In his *Paris* dissent, Brennan, J., joined by Stewart and Marshall, JJ., argued that the state interests in regulating obscenity were not strong enough to justify the degree of vagueness. He criticized not only the Court's standard in *Miller,* but also a range of alternatives:]

II.   [The] essence of our problem [is] that we have been unable to provide "sensitive tools" to separate obscenity from other sexually oriented but constitutionally protected speech, so that efforts to suppress the former do not spill over into the suppression of the latter. * * *

III.   Our experience with the *Roth* approach has certainly taught us that the outright suppression of obscenity cannot be reconciled with the fundamental principles of the First and Fourteenth Amendments. For we have failed to formulate a standard that sharply distinguishes protected from unprotected speech, and out of necessity, we have resorted to the *Redrup* approach, which resolves cases as between the parties, but offers only the most obscure guidance to legislation, adjudication by other courts, and primary conduct. [T]he vagueness problem would be largely of our own creation if it stemmed primarily from our failure to reach a consensus on any one standard. But after 15 years of experimentation and debate I am reluctantly forced to the conclusion that none of the available formulas, including the one announced today, can reduce the vagueness to a tolerable level while [striking] an acceptable balance between the protections of the First and Fourteenth Amendments, on the one hand, and on the other the asserted state interest in regulating the dissemination of certain sexually oriented materials. Any effort to draw a constitutionally acceptable boundary on state power must resort to such indefinite concepts as "prurient interest," "patent offensiveness," "serious literary value," and the like. The meaning of these concepts necessarily varies with the experience, outlook, and even idiosyncrasies of the person defining them. Although we have assumed that obscenity does exist and that we "know it when [we] see it," *Jacobellis* (Stewart, J., concurring), we are manifestly unable to describe it in advance except by reference to concepts so elusive that they fail to distinguish clearly between protected and unprotected speech.

[Added to the inherent vagueness of standards] is the further complication that the obscenity of any particular item may depend upon nuances of presentation and the context of its dissemination. See *Ginzburg*. [N]o one definition, no matter how precisely or narrowly drawn, can possibly suffice for all situations, or carve out fully suppressible expression from all media without also creating a substantial risk of encroachment upon the guarantees of the Due Process Clause and the First Amendment. [The] resulting level of uncertainty is utterly intolerable, not alone because it makes "[b]ookselling [a] hazardous profession," *Ginsberg* (Fortas, J., dissenting), but as well because it invites arbitrary and erratic enforcement of the law. [We] have indicated that "stricter standards of permissible statutory vagueness may be applied to a statute having a potentially inhibiting effect on speech; a man may the less be required to act at his peril here, because the free dissemination of ideas may be the loser." * * *

The problems of fair notice and chilling protected speech are very grave standing alone. But [a] vague statute in this area creates a third [set] of problems. These [concern] the institutional stress that inevitably results where the line separating protected from unprotected speech is excessively vague. [Almost] every obscenity case presents a constitutional question of exceptional difficulty. [As] a result of our failure to define standards with predictable application to any given piece of material, there is no probability of regularity in obscenity decisions by state and lower federal courts. [O]ne cannot say with certainty that material is obscene until at least five members of this Court, applying inevitably obscure standards, have pronounced it [so].

[The] severe problems arising from the lack of fair notice, from the chill on protected expression, and from the stress imposed on the state and federal judicial machinery persuade me that a significant change in direction is urgently required. I turn, therefore, to the alternatives. * * *

IV. 1. The approach requiring the smallest deviation from our present course would be to draw a new line between protected and unprotected speech, still permitting the States to suppress all material on the unprotected side of the line. In my view, clarity cannot be obtained pursuant to this approach except by drawing a line that resolves all doubts in favor of state power and against the guarantees of the First Amendment. We could hold, for example, that any depiction or description of human sexual organs, irrespective of the manner or purpose of the portrayal, is outside the protection of the First Amendment and therefore open to suppression by the States. That formula would, no doubt, offer much fairer notice

[and] give rise to a substantial probability of regularity in most judicial determinations under the standard. But such a standard would be appallingly overbroad, permitting the suppression of a vast range of literary, scientific, and artistic masterpieces. Neither the First Amendment nor any free community could possibly tolerate such a standard.

2.   [T]he Court today recognizes that a prohibition against any depiction or description of human sexual organs could not be reconciled with the guarantees of the First Amendment. But the Court [adopts] a restatement of the *Roth-Memoirs* definition of obscenity [that] permits suppression if the government can prove that the materials lack "*serious* literary, artistic, political or scientific value." [In] *Roth* we held that certain expression is obscene, and thus outside the protection of the First Amendment, precisely *because* it lacks even the slightest redeeming social value. [The] Court's approach necessarily assumes that some works will be deemed obscene—even though they clearly have *some* social value—because the State was able to prove that the value, measured by some unspecified standard, was not sufficiently "serious" to warrant constitutional protection. That result [is] nothing less than a rejection of the fundamental First Amendment premises and rationale of the *Roth* opinion and an invitation to widespread suppression of sexually oriented speech. Before today, the protections of the First Amendment have never been thought limited to expressions of *serious* literary or political value.

[T]he Court's approach [can] have no ameliorative impact on the cluster of problems that grow out of the vagueness of our current standards. Indeed, even the Court makes no argument that the reformulation will provide fairer notice to booksellers, theatre owners, and the reading and viewing public. Nor does the Court contend that the approach will provide clearer guidance to law enforcement officials or reduce the chill on protected expression. * * *

Of course, the Court's restated *Roth* test does limit the definition of obscenity to depictions of physical conduct and explicit sexual acts. And that limitation may seem, at first glance, a welcome and clarifying addition to the *Roth-Memoirs* formula. But just as the agreement in *Roth* on an abstract definition of obscenity gave little hint of the extreme difficulty that was to follow in attempting to apply that definition to specific material, the mere formulation of a "physical conduct" test is no assurance that it can be applied with any greater facility. [The] Court surely demonstrates little sensitivity to our own institutional problems, much less the other vagueness-related difficulties, in establishing a system that requires us to consider whether a description of human genitals is sufficiently "lewd" to deprive it of constitutional protection; whether a sexual act is "ultimate"; whether the conduct depicted in materials before us fits within one of the categories of conduct whose depiction the state or federal governments have attempted to suppress; and a host of equally pointless inquiries. * * *

If the application of the "physical conduct" test to pictorial material is fraught with difficulty, its application to textual material carries the potential for extraordinary abuse. Surely we have passed the point where the mere written description of sexual conduct is deprived of First Amendment protection. Yet the test offers no guidance to us, or anyone else, in determining which written descriptions of sexual conduct are protected, and which are not.

Ultimately, the reformulation must fail because it still leaves in this Court the responsibility of determining in each case whether the materials are protected by the First Amendment. * * *

3.   I have also considered the possibility of reducing our own role, and the role of appellate courts generally, in determining whether particular matter is obscene. Thus, [we] might adopt the position that where a lower federal or state court has conscientiously applied the constitutional standard, its finding of obscenity will be no more vulnerable to reversal by this Court than any finding of fact. [E]ven if the Constitution would permit us to refrain from judging for ourselves the alleged obscenity of particular materials, that approach would solve at best only a small part of our problem. For while it would mitigate the institutional stress, [it] would neither offer nor produce any cure for the other vices of vagueness. Far from providing a clearer guide to permissible primary conduct, the approach would inevitably lead to even greater uncertainty and the consequent due process problems of fair notice. And the approach would expose much protected, sexually oriented expression to the vagaries of jury determinations. Plainly, the institutional gain would be more than offset by the unprecedented infringement of First Amendment rights.

4.   Finally, I have considered the view, urged so forcefully since 1957 by our Brothers Black and Douglas, that the First Amendment bars the suppression of any sexually oriented expression. That position would effect a sharp reduction, although perhaps not a total elimination, of the uncertainty that surrounds our current approach. Nevertheless, I am convinced that it would achieve that desirable goal only by stripping the States of power to an extent that cannot be justified by the commands of the Constitution, at least so long as there is available an alternative approach that strikes a better balance between the guarantee of free expression and the States' legitimate interests.

* * * I would hold, therefore, that at least in the absence of distribution to juveniles or obtrusive exposure to unconsenting adults, the First and Fourteenth Amendments prohibit the state and federal governments from attempting wholly to suppress sexually oriented materials on the basis of their allegedly "obscene" contents. Nothing in this approach precludes those governments from taking action to serve what may be strong and legitimate interests through regulation of the manner of distribution of sexually oriented material.

VI.   * * * I do not pretend to have found a complete and infallible [answer]. Difficult questions must still be faced, notably in the areas of distribution to juveniles and offensive exposure to unconsenting adults. Whatever the extent of state power to regulate in those areas, it should be clear that the view I espouse today would introduce a large measure of clarity to this troubled area, would reduce the institutional pressure on this Court and the rest of the State and Federal judiciary, and would guarantee fuller freedom of expression while leaving room for the protection of legitimate governmental interests. * * *

C. Vagueness and Overbreadth: An Overview

The doctrines of "vagueness" and "overbreadth" referred to in Brennan, J.'s dissents are deeply embedded in First Amendment jurisprudence. At first glance, the doctrines appear discrete. A statute that prohibits the use of the words "kill" and "President" in the same sentence may not be vague, but it is certainly overbroad even though some sentences using those words may be unprotected. Conversely, a vague statute may not be overbroad; it may not pertain to First Amendment freedoms at all, or it may clearly be intended to exclude all protected speech from its prohibition but use vague language to accomplish that purpose.

Ordinarily, however, the problems of "vagueness" and "overbreadth" are closely related. An Airport Commissioners resolution banning all "First Amendment activities" in the Los Angeles International Airport was declared overbroad in *Board of Airport Commissioners v. Jews for Jesus*, 482 U.S. 569 (1987). Literally read the statute would have prevented anyone from talking or reading in the airport. But if the language literally covers a variety of constitutionally protected activities, it *cannot be read literally*. If the statute cannot be read according to its terms, however, problems of vagueness will often emerge. To be sure, statutes may be interpreted in ways that will avoid vagueness or overbreadth difficulties. It is established doctrine, for example, that an attack based either upon vagueness or overbreadth will be unsuccessful in federal court if the statute in question is "readily subject to a narrowing construction by the state courts." *Young v. American Mini Theatres, Inc.*, 427 U.S. 50 (1976). Moreover, "[f]or the purpose of determining whether a state statute is too vague and indefinite to constitute valid legislation [the Court takes] 'the statute as though it read precisely as the highest court of the State has interpreted it.' " *Wainwright v. Stone*, 414 U.S. 21 (1973). Under this policy, a litigant can be prosecuted successfully for violating a statute that by its terms appears vague or overbroad but is interpreted by the state court in the same prosecution to mean something clearer or narrower than its literal language would dictate. The harshness of this doctrine is mitigated somewhat by the fact that "unexpected" or "unforeseeable" judicial constructions in such contexts violate due process.

Somewhat more complicated is the issue of when general attacks on a statute are permitted. Plainly litigants may argue that statutes are vague as to their own conduct or that their own speech is protected. In other words, litigants are always free to argue that a statute is invalid "as applied" to their own conduct. The dispute concerns when litigants can attack a statute without reference to their own conduct, an attack sometimes called "on its face."

A separate question is: when should such attacks result in partial or total invalidation of a statute? The terminology has become as confused as the issues. The Court has frequently referred to facial attacks on statutes in a way that embraces attempts at either partial or total invalidation. In some opinions, however, it uses the term "facial attack" or "on its face" to refer only to arguments seeking total invalidation of a statute.

Terminology aside, one of the recurrent questions has been the extent to which litigants may argue that a statute is unconstitutionally overbroad even though their own conduct would not otherwise be constitutionally protected. This is often characterized as a standing issue. Ordinarily litigants do not have standing to raise the rights of others. But it has been argued that litigants should have standing to challenge overbroad statutes even if their own conduct would be otherwise unprotected in order to prevent a chilling effect on freedom of speech. Alternatively, it has been argued that no standing problem is genuinely presented because "[u]nder 'conventional' standing principles, a litigant has always had the right to be judged in accordance with a constitutionally valid rule of law." Henry Monaghan, *Overbreadth*, 1981 S.Ct.Rev. 1. On this view, if a statute is unconstitutionally overbroad, it is not a valid rule of law, and any defendant prosecuted under the statute has standing to make that claim. However the issue may be characterized, White, J., contended for many years that a litigant whose own conduct is unprotected should not prevail on an overbreadth challenge without a showing that the statute's overbreadth is "real and substantial." After much litigation, White, J., finally prevailed. The "substantial" overbreadth doctrine now burdens all litigants who argue that a statute should be declared overbroad when their own conduct would otherwise be unprotected.

Less clear are the circumstances in which a litigant whose conduct *is* protected can go beyond a claim that the statute is unconstitutional "as applied" because litigants are always free to argue that their own conduct is protected. Moreover, the Court has stated that "[t]here is no reason to limit challenges to case-by-case 'as applied' challenges when the statute [in] all its applications falls short of constitutional demands." *Secretary of State of Maryland v. Joseph H. Munson Co.*, 467 U.S. 947 (1984). How far beyond this the Court will go is unclear. In *Brockett v. Spokane Arcades, Inc.*, 472 U.S. 491 (1985), it referred to the "normal rule that partial, rather than facial invalidation" of statutes is to be preferred and observed that: "[A]n individual whose own speech or expressive conduct may validly be prohibited or sanctioned is permitted to challenge a statute on its face because it also threatens others not before the court—those who desire to engage in legally protected expression but who may refrain from doing so rather than risk prosecution or undertake to have the law declared partially invalid. If the overbreadth is 'substantial,' the law may not be enforced against anyone, including the party before the court, until it is narrowed to reach only unprotected activity, whether by legislative action or by judicial construction or partial invalidation.

"It is otherwise where the parties challenging the statute are those who desire to engage in protected speech that the overbroad statute purports to punish, or who seek to publish both protected and unprotected material. There is then no want of a proper party to challenge the statute, no concern that an attack on the statute will be unduly delayed or protected speech discouraged. The statute may forthwith be declared invalid to the extent that it reaches too far, but otherwise left intact."

Brockett takes the view that it must give standing to the otherwise unprotected to raise an overbreadth challenge, in order to secure the rights of those whose speech should be protected. But it sees no purpose in giving standing to the protected in order to secure rights for those whose speech should not be protected. This position is not without its ironies. In some circumstances, a litigant whose speech is unprotected will be in a better position than one whose speech is protected, at least if the litigant's goal is completely to stop enforcement of a statute.

Finally, what of cases when it is uncertain whether the litigant's speech is protected? Should courts consider as applied attacks before proceeding to overbreadth attacks? *Board of Trustees v. Fox,* 492 U.S. 462 (1989), declared it "not the usual judicial practice" and "generally undesirable" to proceed to an overbreadth challenge without first determining whether the statute would be valid as applied, but the Court has not specified the considerations relevant to separating the "usual" judicial practice from the unusual.

The issues with respect to vagueness challenges are similar. White, J., maintained that vagueness challenges should be confined to "as applied" attacks unless a statute were vague in all of its applications. Accordingly, if a statute clearly proscribed the conduct of a particular defendant, to allow that defendant to challenge a statute for vagueness would in his view have been "to confound vagueness and overbreadth." *Kolender v. Lawson,* 461 U.S. 352 (1983) (White, J., dissenting). In response, the Court stated that a facial attack upon a statute need not depend upon a showing of vagueness in all of a statute's applications: "[W]e permit a facial challenge if a law reaches 'a substantial amount of constitutionally protected conduct,'" Moreover, the Court has previously allowed litigants to raise the vagueness issue "even though there is no uncertainty about the impact of the ordinances on their own rights." *Young.* But see, e.g., *Broadrick v. Oklahoma,* 413 U.S. 601 (1973), in which White, J., writing for the Court, suggested that standing to raise the vagueness argument should not be permitted in this situation.

Less clear are the circumstances in which litigants whose conduct is *not* clearly covered by a statute can go beyond an "as applied" attack. One approach would be to apply the same rule to all litigants, e.g., allowing total invalidation of statutes upon a showing of a "substantial" vagueness. In *Kolender,* the Court made no determination whether the statute involved was vague as to the defendant's own conduct; arguably, the opinion implied that it made no difference. Another approach would analogize to the approach suggested in *Brockett* for overbreadth challenges. Thus, a court might refrain from total invalidation of a statute and confine itself to striking the vague part insofar as the vague part seems to cover protected speech, leaving the balance of the statute intact. *Kolender* itself recites that the Court has "traditionally regarded vagueness and overbreadth as logically related and similar doctrines," but the Court's attitudes toward vagueness remain unclear.

V. "FIGHTING WORDS," OFFENSIVE WORDS AND HOSTILE AUDIENCES

A. Fighting Words

CHAPLINSKY v. NEW HAMPSHIRE, 315 U.S. 568 (1942): In the course of proselytizing on the streets, appellant, a Jehovah's Witness, denounced organized religion. Despite the city marshal's warning to "go slow" because his listeners were upset with his attacks on religion, appellant continued and a disturbance occurred. At this point, a police officer led appellant toward the police station, without arresting him. While en route, appellant again encountered the city marshal who had previously admonished him. Appellant then said to the marshal (he claimed, but the marshal denied, in response to the marshal's cursing him): "You are a God damned racketeer" and "a damned Fascist and the whole government of Rochester are Fascists or agents of Fascists." He was convicted of violating a state statute forbidding anyone to address "any offensive, derisive or annoying word to any other person who is lawfully in any [public place] [or] call[ing] him by any offensive or derisive name." The Court, per MURPHY, J., upheld the conviction:

"There are certain well-defined and narrowly limited classes of speech, the prevention and punishment of which have never been thought to raise any Constitutional problem. These include the lewd and obscene, the profane, the libelous, and the insulting or 'fighting' words—those which by their very utterance inflict injury or tend to incite an immediate breach of the peace. [S]uch utterances are no essential part of any exposition of ideas, and are of such slight social value as a step to truth that any benefit that may be derived from them is clearly outweighed by the social interest in order and morality. * * *

"On the authority of its earlier decisions, the state court declared that the statute's purpose was to preserve the public peace, no words being 'forbidden except such as have a direct tendency to cause acts of violence by the person to whom, individually, the remark is addressed'. It was further said: 'The word "offensive" is not to be defined in terms of what a particular addressee thinks. [The] test is what men of common intelligence would understand would be words likely to cause an average addressee to fight. [The] English language has a number of words and expressions which by general consent are "fighting words" when said without a disarming smile. [Such] words, as ordinary men know, are likely to cause a fight. So are threatening, profane or obscene revilings. Derisive and annoying words can be taken as coming within the purview of the statute as heretofore interpreted only when they have this characteristic of plainly tending to excite the addressee to a breach of the peace. [The] statute, as construed, does no more than prohibit the face-to-face words plainly likely to cause a breach of the peace by the addressee, words whose speaking constitute a breach of the peace by the speaker—including "classical fighting words", words in current use less "classical" but equally likely to cause violence, and other disorderly words, including profanity, obscenity and threats.'

"[A] statute punishing verbal acts, carefully drawn so as not unduly to impair liberty of expression, is not too vague for a criminal law. * * * "Nor can we say that the application of the statute to the facts disclosed by the record substantially or unreasonably impinges upon the privilege of free speech. Argument is unnecessary to demonstrate that the appellations 'damn racketeer' and 'damn Fascist' are epithets likely to provoke the average person to retaliation, and thereby cause a breach of the peace.

"The refusal of the state court to admit evidence of provocation and evidence bearing on the truth or falsity of the utterances is open to no Constitutional objection. Whether the facts sought to be proved by such evidence constitute a defense to the charge or may be shown in mitigation are questions for the state court to determine. Our function is fulfilled by a determination that the challenged statute, on its face and as applied, does not contravene the Fourteenth Amendment."

B. Hostile Audiences

TERMINIELLO v. CHICAGO, 337 U.S. 1 (1949): Petitioner "vigorously, if not viciously" criticized various political and racial groups and condemned "a surging, howling mob" gathered in protest outside the auditorium in which he spoke. He called his adversaries "slimy scum," "snakes," "bedbugs," and the like. Those inside the hall could hear those on the outside yell, "Fascists, Hitlers!" The crowd outside tried to tear the clothes off those who entered. About 28 windows were broken; stink bombs were thrown. But in charging the jury, the trial court defined "breach of the peace" to include speech which "stirs the public to anger, *invites dispute,* [or] brings about a condition of unrest (emphasis added)." A 5–4 majority, per DOUGLAS, J., struck down the breach of peace ordinance as thus construed: "[A] function of free speech under our system of government is to invite dispute. It may indeed best serve its high purpose when it induces a condition of unrest, creates dissatisfaction with conditions as they are, or even stirs people to anger. [That] is why freedom of speech, though not absolute, *Chaplinsky,* is nevertheless protected against censorship or punishment, unless shown likely to produce a clear and present danger of a serious substantive evil that rises far above public inconvenience, annoyance, or unrest."

———

FEINER v. NEW YORK, 340 U.S. 315 (1951): Petitioner made a speech on a street corner in a predominantly black residential section of Syracuse, N.Y. A crowd of 75 to 80 persons, black and white, gathered around him, and several pedestrians had to go into the highway in order to pass by. A few minutes after he started, two police officers arrived and observed the rest of the meeting. In the course of his speech, publicizing a meeting of the Young Progressives of America to be held that evening in a local hotel and protesting the revocation of a permit to hold the meeting in a public school auditorium, petitioner referred to the President as a "bum," to the American Legion as "a Nazi Gestapo," and to the Mayor of

Syracuse as a "champagne-sipping bum" who "does not speak for the Negro people." He also indicated in an excited manner: "The Negroes don't have equal rights; they should rise up in arms and fight for them."

These statements "stirred up a little excitement." One man indicated that if the police did not get that "S * * * O * * * B* * * " off the stand, he would do so himself. There was not yet a disturbance, but according to police testimony "angry muttering and pushing." In the words of the arresting officer, he "stepped in to prevent it from resulting in a fight." After disregarding two requests to stop speaking, petitioner was arrested and convicted for disorderly conduct. The Court, per VINSON, C.J., affirmed: "The language of *Cantwell* is appropriate here. '[Nobody would] suggest that the principle of freedom of speech sanctions incitement to riot or that religious liberty connotes the privilege to exhort others to physical attack upon those belonging to another sect. When clear and present danger of riot, disorder, interference with traffic upon the public street or other immediate threat to public safety, peace, or order, appears, the power of the State to prevent or punish is obvious.'

"[It] is one thing to say that the police cannot be used as an instrument for the suppression of unpopular views, and another to say that, when as here the speaker passes the bounds of argument or persuasion and undertakes incitement to riot, they are powerless to prevent a breach of the peace. Nor in this case can we condemn the considered judgment of three New York courts approving the means which the police, faced with a crisis, used in the exercise of their power and duty to preserve peace and order."

BLACK, J., dissented: "The Court's opinion apparently rests on this reasoning: The policeman, under the circumstances detailed, could reasonably conclude that serious fighting or even riot was imminent; therefore he could stop petitioner's speech to prevent a breach of peace; accordingly, it was 'disorderly conduct' for petitioner to continue speaking in disobedience of the officer's request. As to the existence of a dangerous situation on the street corner, it seems far-fetched to suggest that the 'facts' show any imminent threat of riot or uncontrollable disorder. It is neither unusual nor unexpected that some people at public street meetings mutter, mill about, push, shove, or disagree, even violently, with the speaker. Indeed, it is rare where controversial topics are discussed that an outdoor crowd does not do some or all of these things. Nor does one isolated threat to assault the speaker forebode disorder. Especially should the danger be discounted where, as here, the person threatening was a man whose wife and two small children accompanied him and who, so far as the record shows, was never close enough to petitioner to carry out the threat.

"Moreover, assuming that the 'facts' did indicate a critical situation, I reject the implication of the Court's opinion that the police had no obligation to protect petitioner's constitutional right to talk. The police of course have power to prevent breaches of the peace. But if, in the name of preserving order, they ever can interfere with a lawful public speaker, they first must make all reasonable efforts to protect him. * * *

"Finally, I cannot agree with the Court's statement that petitioner's disregard of the policeman's unexplained request amounted to such 'deliberate defiance' as would justify an arrest or conviction for disorderly conduct. On the contrary, I think that the policeman's action was a 'deliberate defiance' of ordinary official duty as well as of the constitutional right of free speech. Here petitioner was 'asked' then 'told' then 'commanded' to stop speaking, but a man making a lawful address is certainly not required to be silent merely because an officer directs it."

DOUGLAS, J., joined by Minton, J., dissented: "A speaker may not, of course, incite a riot any more than he may incite a breach of the peace by the use of 'fighting words'. But this record shows no such extremes. It shows an unsympathetic audience and the threat of one man to haul the speaker from the stage. It is against that kind of threat that speakers need police protection. If they do not receive it and instead the police throw their weight on the side of those who would break up the meetings, the police become the new censors of speech."

———

Edwards v. South Carolina, 372 U.S. 229 (1963), reversed a breach of the peace conviction of civil rights demonstrators who refused to disperse within 15 minutes of a police command. The Court maintained that the 200 to 300 onlookers did not threaten violence and that police protection was ample. It described the situation as a "far cry from [*Feiner*]." In addition to *Edwards*, see also *Gregory v. City of Chicago*, 394 U.S. 111 (1969), and *Cox v. Louisiana*, 379 U.S. 536 (1965), both of which, like *Edwards*, involved civil rights demonstrators confronted by actually or potentially hostile audiences. In both cases the Court followed *Edwards* and refused to allow a potentially hostile audience and potential violence to justify restrictions on the speakers.

In many confrontations between speakers and hostile audiences, the costs of additional police protection, sometimes effective and sometimes not, have run to hundreds of thousands or millions of dollars. If those costs may not constitutionally be imposed on the original speakers (see *Forsyth County v. Nationalist Movement*, 505 U.S. 123 (1992)), and may not for the same reasons be imposed on those who lawfully demonstrate against lawful speakers, may they be imposed on those who unlawfully interfere with speakers? If not, either as a matter of constitutional law or practical reality, do speakers have the ability to impose substantial costs on governments with whom they disagree?

C. Offensive Words

COHEN V. CALIFORNIA

403 U.S. 15, 91 S.Ct. 1780, 29 L.Ed.2d 284 (1971).

JUSTICE HARLAN delivered the opinion of the Court.

[Defendant was convicted of violating that part of a general California disturbing-the-peace statute which prohibits "maliciously and willfully disturb[ing] the peace or quiet of any neighborhood or person" by "offensive conduct." He had worn a jacket bearing the plainly visible words "Fuck the Draft" in a Los Angeles courthouse corridor, where women and children were present. He testified that he did so as a means of informing the public of the depth of his feelings against the Vietnam War and the draft. He did not engage in, nor threaten, any violence, nor was anyone who saw him violently aroused. Nor was there any evidence that he uttered any sound prior to his arrest. In affirming, the California Court of Appeal construed "offensive conduct" to mean "behavior which has a tendency to provoke *others* to acts of violence or to in turn disturb the peace" and held that the state had proved this element because it was "reasonably foreseeable" that defendant's conduct "might cause others to rise up to commit a violent act against [him] or attempt to forceably remove his jacket."]

In order to lay hands on the precise issue which this case involves, it is useful first to canvass various matters which this record does *not* present.

The conviction quite clearly rests upon the asserted offensiveness of the *words* Cohen used to convey his message to the public. The only "conduct" which the State sought to punish is the fact of communication. Thus, we deal here with a conviction resting solely upon "speech," not upon any separately identifiable conduct which allegedly was intended by Cohen to be perceived by others as expressive of particular views but which, on its face, does not necessarily convey any message and hence arguably could be regulated without effectively repressing Cohen's ability to express himself. Further, the State certainly lacks power to punish Cohen for the underlying content of the message the inscription conveyed. At least so long as there is no showing of an intent to incite disobedience to or disruption of the draft, Cohen could not, consistently with the First and Fourteenth Amendments, be punished for asserting the evident position on the inutility or immorality of the draft his jacket reflected.

Appellant's conviction, then, rests squarely upon his exercise [of] "freedom of speech" [and] can be justified, if at all, only as a valid regulation of the manner in which he exercised that freedom, not as a permissible prohibition on the substantive message it conveys. This does not end the inquiry, of course, for the First and Fourteenth Amendments have never been thought to give absolute protection to every individual to speak whenever or wherever he pleases, or to use any form of address in any circumstances that he chooses. In this vein, too, however, we think it important to note that several issues typically associated with such problems are not presented here.

In the first place, Cohen was tried under a statute applicable throughout the entire State. Any attempt to support this conviction on the ground that the statute seeks to preserve an appropriately decorous atmosphere in the courthouse where Cohen was arrested must fail in the absence of any language in the statute that would have put appellant on notice that certain kinds of otherwise permissible speech or conduct would nevertheless, under California law, not be tolerated in certain places. No fair reading of the phrase "offensive conduct" can be said sufficiently to inform the ordinary person that distinctions between certain locations are thereby created.

In the second place, [this] case cannot be said to fall within those relatively few categories of instances where prior decisions have established the power of government to deal more comprehensively with certain forms of individual expression simply upon a showing that such a form was employed. This is not, for example, an obscenity case. Whatever else may be necessary to give rise to the States' broader power to prohibit obscene expression, such expression must be, in some significant way, erotic. It cannot plausibly be maintained that this vulgar allusion to the Selective Service System would conjure up such psychic stimulation in anyone likely to be confronted with Cohen's crudely defaced jacket.

This Court has also held that the States are free to ban the simple use, without a demonstration of additional justifying circumstances, of so-called "fighting words," those personally abusive epithets which, when addressed to the ordinary citizen, are, as a matter of common knowledge, inherently likely to provoke violent reaction. While the four-letter word displayed by Cohen in relation to the draft is not uncommonly employed in a personally provocative fashion, in this instance it was clearly not "directed to the person of the hearer." No individual actually or likely to be present could reasonably have regarded the words on appellant's jacket as a direct personal insult. Nor do we have here an instance of the exercise of the State's police power to prevent a speaker from intentionally provoking a given group to hostile reaction. There is [no] showing that anyone who saw Cohen [violently] aroused or that appellant intended such a result.

[T]he mere presumed presence of unwitting listeners or viewers does not serve automatically to justify curtailing all speech capable of giving offense. While this Court has recognized that government may properly act in many situations to prohibit intrusion into the privacy of the home of unwelcome views and ideas which cannot be totally banned from the public dialogue, we have at the same time consistently stressed that "we are often 'captives' outside the sanctuary of the home and subject to objectionable speech." The ability of government, consonant with the Constitution, to shut off discourse solely to protect others from hearing it is, in other words, dependent upon a showing that substantial privacy interests are being invaded in an essentially intolerable manner. Any broader view of this authority would effectively empower a majority to silence dissidents simply as a matter of personal predilections.

[Given] the subtlety and complexity of the factors involved if Cohen's "speech" was otherwise entitled to constitutional protection, we do not think the fact that some unwilling "listeners" in a public building may have been briefly exposed to it can serve to justify this breach of the peace conviction where, as here, there was no evidence that persons powerless to avoid appellant's conduct did in fact object to it, and where [unlike another portion of the same statute barring the use of "vulgar, profane or indecent language within [the] hearing of women or children, in a loud and boisterous manner"], the [challenged statutory provision] evinces no concern [with] the special plight of the captive auditor, but, instead, indiscriminately sweeps within its prohibitions all "offensive conduct" that disturbs "any neighborhood or person."

Against this background, the issue flushed by this case stands out in bold relief. It is whether California can excise, as "offensive conduct," one particular scurrilous epithet from the public discourse, either upon the theory of the court below that its use is inherently likely to cause violent reaction or upon a more general assertion that the States, acting as guardians of public morality, may properly remove this offensive word from the public vocabulary.

The rationale of the California court is plainly untenable. At most it reflects an "undifferentiated fear or apprehension of disturbance [which] is not enough to overcome the right to freedom of expression." *Tinker* [Sec. 7, II infra]. We have been shown no evidence that substantial numbers of citizens are standing ready to strike out physically at whoever may assault their sensibilities with execrations like that uttered by Cohen. There may be some persons about with such lawless and violent proclivities, but that is an insufficient base upon which to erect, consistently with constitutional values, a governmental power to force persons who wish to ventilate their dissident views into avoiding particular forms of expression. The argument amounts to little more than the self-defeating proposition that to avoid physical censorship of one who has not sought to provoke such a response by a hypothetical coterie of the violent and lawless, the States may more appropriately effectuate that censorship themselves.

Admittedly, it is not so obvious that the [First Amendment disables] the States from punishing public utterance of this unseemly expletive in order to maintain what they regard as a suitable level of discourse within the body politic. We think, however, that examination and reflection will reveal the shortcomings of a contrary viewpoint.

[The] constitutional right of free expression is powerful medicine in a society as diverse and populous as ours. It is designed and intended to remove governmental restraints from the arena of public discussion, putting the decision as to what views shall be voiced largely into the hands of each of us, in the hope that use of such freedom will ultimately produce a more capable citizenry and more perfect polity and in the belief that no other approach would comport with the premise of individual dignity and choice upon which our political system rests.

To many, the immediate consequence of this freedom may often appear to be only verbal tumult, discord, and even offensive utterance. These are, however, within established limits, in truth necessary side effects of the broader enduring values which the process of open debate permits us to achieve. That the air may at times seem filled with verbal cacophony is, in this sense not a sign of weakness but of strength. We cannot lose sight of the fact that, in what otherwise might seem a trifling and annoying instance of individual distasteful abuse of a privilege, these fundamental societal values are truly implicated. * * *

Against this perception of the constitutional policies involved, [more] particularized considerations that peculiarly call for reversal of this conviction. First, the principle contended for by the State seems inherently boundless. How is one to distinguish this from any other offensive word? Surely the State has no right to cleanse public debate to the point where it is grammatically palatable to the most squeamish among us. Yet no readily ascertainable general principle exists for stopping short of that result were we to affirm the judgment below. For, while the particular four-letter word being litigated here is perhaps more distasteful than most others of its genre, it is nevertheless often true that one man's vulgarity is another's lyric. Indeed, we think it is largely because governmental officials cannot make principled distinctions in this area that the Constitution leaves matters of taste and style so largely to the individual.

Additionally, we cannot overlook the fact, because it is well illustrated by the episode involved here, that much linguistic expression serves a dual communicative function: it conveys not only ideas capable of relatively precise, detached explication, but otherwise inexpressible emotions as well. In fact, words are often chosen as much for their emotive as their cognitive force. We cannot sanction the view that the Constitution, while solicitous of the cognitive content of individual speech, has little or no regard for that emotive function which, practically speaking, may often be the more important element of the overall message sought to be communicated. * * *

Finally, and in the same vein, we cannot indulge the facile assumption that one can forbid particular words without also running a substantial risk of suppressing ideas in the process. Indeed, governments might soon seize upon the censorship of particular words as a convenient guise for banning the expression of unpopular views. We have been able [to] discern little social benefit that might result from running the risk of opening the door to such grave results.

It is, in sum, our judgment that, absent a more particularized and compelling reason for its actions, the State may not, consistently with the First and Fourteenth Amendments, make the simple public display here involved of this single four-letter expletive a criminal offense. * * *

[BLACKMUN, J., joined by Burger, C.J., and Black, J., dissented for two reasons: (1) "Cohen's absurd and immature antic [was] mainly conduct and little speech" and the case falls "well within the sphere of *Chaplinsky*"; (2) although it declined to review the state court of appeals' decision in *Cohen,* the California Supreme Court subsequently narrowly construed the breach-of-the-peace statute in another case and *Cohen* should be remanded to the California Court of Appeal in the light of this subsequent construction. White, J., concurred with the dissent on the latter ground.]

A series of cases in the early 1970s reversed convictions involving abusive language. *Gooding v. Wilson*, 405 U.S. 518 (1972), invalidated a Georgia ordinance primarily because it had been previously applied to "utterances where there was no likelihood that the person addressed would make an immediate violent response." *Lewis v. New Orleans*, 415 U.S. 130 (1974), ruled that vulgar or offensive speech was protected under the First Amendment. Because the statute punished "opprobrious language," it was deemed by the Court to embrace words that do not " 'by their very utterance inflict injury or tend to invite an immediate breach of the peace.' "

Although *Gooding* seemed to require a danger of immediate violence, *Lewis* recited that infliction of injury was sufficient. Dissenting in both cases, BURGER, C.J., and Blackmun and Rehnquist, JJ., complained that the majority invoked vagueness and overbreadth analysis "indiscriminately without regard to the nature of the speech in question, the possible effect the statute or ordinance has upon such speech, the importance of the speech in relation to the exposition of ideas, or the purported or asserted community interest in preventing that speech." The dissenters focused upon the facts of the cases (e.g., Gooding to a police officer: "White son of a bitch, I'll kill you," "You son of a bitch, I'll choke you to death," and "You son of a bitch, if you ever put your hands on me again, I'll cut you to pieces."). They complained that the majority had relegated the facts to "footnote status, conveniently distant and in less disturbing focus."

VI. COMMERCIAL SPEECH

VIRGINIA STATE BOARD OF PHARMACY V. VIRGINIA CITIZENS CONSUMER COUNCIL
425 U.S. 748, 96 S.Ct. 1817, 48 L.Ed.2d 346 (1976).

JUSTICE BLACKMUN delivered the opinion of the Court.

[The Court held invalid a Virginia statute that made advertising the prices of prescription drugs "unprofessional conduct," subjecting pharmacists to license suspension or revocation. Prescription drug prices strikingly varied within the same locality, in Virginia and nationally, sometimes by several hundred percent. Such drugs were dispensed exclusively by licensed pharmacists but 95% were prepared by manufacturers, not compounded by the pharmacists.]

[Appellants] contend that the advertisement of prescription drug prices is outside the protection of the First Amendment because it is "commercial speech." There can be no question that in past decisions the Court has given some indication that commercial speech is unprotected.

Last Term, in *Bigelow v. Virginia*, 421 U.S. 809 (1975), the notion of unprotected "commercial speech" all but passed from the scene. We reversed a conviction for violation of a Virginia statute that made the circulation of any publication to encourage or promote the processing of an abortion in Virginia a misdemeanor. [The] advertisement in question, in addition to announcing that abortions were legal in New York, offered the services of a referral agency in that State. [We] concluded that "the Virginia courts erred in their assumptions that advertising, as such, was entitled to no First Amendment protection," and we observed that the "relationship of speech to the marketplace of products or of services does not make it valueless in the marketplace of ideas."

Some fragment of hope for the continuing validity of a "commercial speech" exception arguably might have persisted because of the subject matter of the advertisement in *Bigelow*. We noted that in announcing the availability of legal abortions in New York, the advertisement "did more than simply propose a commercial transaction. It contained factual material of clear 'public interest.'" And, of course, the advertisement related to activity with which, at least in some respects, the State could not interfere. * * *

Here, [the] question whether there is a First Amendment exception for "commercial speech" is squarely before us. Our pharmacist does not wish to editorialize on any subject, cultural, philosophical, or political. He does not wish to report any particularly newsworthy fact, or to make generalized observations even about commercial matters. The "idea" he wishes to communicate is simply this: "I will sell you the X prescription drug at the Y price." Our question, then, is whether this communication is wholly outside the protection of the First Amendment.

V.   [Speech] does not lose its First Amendment protection because money is spent to project it, as in a paid advertisement. [*New*] *York Times Co. v. Sullivan.* Speech likewise is protected even though it is carried in a form that is "sold" for profit. [Our] question is whether speech which does "no more than propose a commercial transaction," is so removed from any "exposition of ideas," and from "truth, science, morality, and arts in general, in its diffusion of liberal sentiments on the administration of Government", *Roth,* that it lacks all protection. Our answer is that it is not.

Focusing first on the individual parties to the transaction that is proposed in the commercial advertisement, we may assume that the advertiser's interest is a purely economic one. That hardly disqualifies him for protection under the First Amendment. * * *

As to the particular consumer's interest in the free flow of commercial information, that interest may be [far keener] than his interest in the day's most urgent political debate. Appellees' case in this respect is a convincing one. Those whom the suppression of prescription drug price information hits the hardest are the poor, the sick, and particularly the aged. A disproportionate amount of their income tends to be spent on prescription drugs; yet they are the least able to learn, by shopping from pharmacist to pharmacist, where their scarce dollars are best spent. When drug prices vary as strikingly as they do, information as to who is charging what [could] mean the alleviation of physical pain or the enjoyment of basic necessities.

Generalizing, society also may have a strong interest in the free flow of commercial information. [Obviously,] not all commercial messages contain the same or even [great] public interest element. There are few to which such an element, however, could not be added. Our pharmacist, for example, could cast himself as a commentator on store-to-store disparities in drug prices, giving his own and those of a competitor as proof. We see little point in requiring him to do so, and little difference if he does not.

Moreover, [another] consideration suggests that no line between publicly "interesting" or "important" commercial advertising and the opposite kind could ever be drawn. Advertising, however tasteless and excessive it sometimes may seem, is nonetheless dissemination of information as to who is producing and selling what product, for what reason, and at what price. So long as we preserve a predominantly free enterprise economy, the allocation of our resources in large measure will be made through numerous private economic decisions. It is a matter of public interest that those decisions, in the aggregate, be intelligent and well informed. To this end, the free flow of commercial information is indispensable. And if it is indispensable to the proper allocation of resources in a free enterprise system, it is also indispensable to the formation of intelligent opinions as to how that system ought to be regulated or altered. [Even] if the First Amendment were thought to be primarily an instrument to enlighten public decision making in a democracy, we could not say that the free flow of information does not serve that goal.

Arrayed against these substantial individual and societal interests are a number of justifications for the advertising ban. These have to do principally with maintaining a high degree of professionalism on the part of licensed pharmacists. [Price] advertising, it is argued, will place in jeopardy the pharmacist's expertise and, with it, the customer's health. It is claimed that the aggressive price competition that will result from unlimited advertising will make it impossible for the pharmacist to supply professional services in the compounding, handling, and dispensing of prescription drugs. Such services are time-consuming and expensive; if competitors who economize by eliminating them are permitted to advertise their resulting lower prices, the more painstaking and conscientious pharmacist will be forced either to follow suit or to go out of business. [It] is further claimed that advertising will lead people to shop for their prescription drugs among the various pharmacists who offer the lowest prices, and the loss of stable pharmacist-customer relationships will make individual [attention] impossible. Finally, it is argued that damage will be done to the professional image of the pharmacist. This image, that of a skilled and specialized craftsman, attracts talent to the profession and reinforces the better habits of those who are in [it].

The strength of these proffered justifications is greatly undermined by the fact that high professional standards, to a substantial extent, are guaranteed by the close regulation to which pharmacists [are] subject.

The challenge now made, however, is based on the First Amendment. This casts the Board's justifications in a different light, for on close inspection it is seen that the State's protectiveness of its citizens rests in large measure on the advantages of their being kept in ignorance. The advertising ban does not directly affect professional standards one way or the other. It affects them only through the reactions it is assumed people will have to the free flow of drug price information. There is no claim that the advertising ban in any way prevents the cutting of corners by the pharmacist who is so inclined. That pharmacist is likely to cut corners in any event. The only effect the advertising ban has on him is to insulate him from price competition and to open the way for him to make a substantial, and perhaps even excessive, profit in addition to providing an inferior service. The more painstaking pharmacist is also protected but, again, it is a protection based in large part on public ignorance.

It appears to be feared that if the pharmacist who wishes to provide low cost, and assertedly low quality, services is permitted to advertise, he will be taken up on his offer by too many unwitting customers. They will choose the low-cost, low-quality service and drive the "professional" pharmacist out of business. [They] will go from one pharmacist to another, following the discount, and destroy the pharmacist-customer relationship. They will lose respect for the profession because it advertises. All this is not in their best interests, and all this can be avoided if they are not permitted to know who is charging what.

[A]n alternative to this highly paternalistic approach [is] to assume that this information is not in itself harmful, that people will perceive their own best interests if only they are well enough informed, and that the best means to that end is to open the channels of communication rather than to close them. If they are truly open, nothing prevents the "professional" pharmacist from marketing his own assertedly superior product, and contrasting it with that of the low-cost, high-volume prescription drug retailer. But the choice among these alternative approaches is not ours to make or the Virginia General Assembly's. It is precisely this kind of choice, between the dangers of suppressing information, and the dangers of its misuse if it is freely available, that the First Amendment makes for [us].

VI. In concluding that commercial speech, like other varieties, is protected, we of course do not hold that it can never be regulated in any way. Some forms of commercial speech regulation are surely permissible. We mention a few. [There] is no claim, for example, that the prohibition on prescription drug price advertising is a mere time, place, and manner restriction. We have often approved restrictions of that kind provided that they are justified without reference to the content of the regulated speech, that they serve a significant governmental interest, and that in so doing they leave open ample alternative channels for communication of the information. Whatever may be the proper bounds of time, place, and manner restrictions on commercial speech, they are plainly exceeded by this Virginia statute, which singles out speech of a particular content and seeks to prevent its dissemination completely.

Nor is there any claim that prescription drug price advertisements are forbidden because they are false or misleading in any way. Untruthful speech, commercial or otherwise, has never been protected for its own sake. *Gertz.* Obviously much commercial speech is not provably false, or even wholly false, but only deceptive or misleading. We foresee no obstacle to a State's dealing effectively with this problem.[24] The First Amendment, as we construe it today, does not prohibit the State from insuring that the stream of commercial information flows cleanly as well as freely.

Also, there is no claim that the transactions proposed in the forbidden advertisements are themselves illegal in any way. Finally, the special problems of the electronic broadcast media are likewise not in this case.

What is at issue is whether a State may completely suppress the dissemination of concededly truthful information about entirely lawful activity, fearful of that information's effect upon its disseminators and its recipients. [We] conclude that the answer to this one is in the [negative].

JUSTICE STEWART, concurring.

[I] write separately to explain why I think today's decision does not preclude [governmental regulation of false or deceptive advertising]. The Court has on several occasions addressed the problems posed by false statements of fact in libel cases. [Factual] errors are inevitable in free debate, and the imposition of liability for [such errors] can "dampe[n] the vigor and limi[t] the variety of public debate" by inducing "self-censorship." [In] contrast to the press, which must often attempt to assemble the true facts from sketchy and sometimes conflicting sources under the pressure of publication deadlines, the commercial advertiser generally knows the product or service he seeks to sell and is in a position to verify the accuracy of his factual representations before he disseminates them. The advertiser's access to

---

[24]   **[Ct's Note]** [C]ommon sense differences between speech that does "no more than propose a commercial transaction," *Pittsburgh Press* and other varieties [suggest] that a different degree of protection is necessary to insure that the flow of truthful and legitimate commercial information is unimpaired. The truth of commercial speech, for example, may be more easily verifiable by its disseminator than, let us say, news reporting or political commentary, in that ordinarily the advertiser seeks to disseminate information about a specific product or service that he himself provides and presumably knows more about than anyone else. Also, commercial speech may be more durable than other kinds. Since advertising is the sine qua non of commercial profits, there is little likelihood of its being chilled by proper regulation and foregone entirely.

Attributes such as these, the greater objectivity and hardiness of commercial speech, may make it less necessary to tolerate inaccurate statements for fear of silencing the speaker. They may also make it appropriate to require that a commercial message appear in such a form, or include such additional information, warnings and disclaimers, as are necessary to prevent its being deceptive. They may also make inapplicable the prohibition on prior restraints. * * *

the truth about his product and its price substantially eliminates any danger that governmental regulation of false or misleading price or product advertising will chill accurate and nondeceptive commercial [expression].

Since the factual claims contained in commercial price or product advertisements relate to tangible goods or services, they may be tested empirically and corrected to reflect the truth without in any manner jeopardizing the free dissemination of thought. Indeed, the elimination of false and deceptive claims serves to promote the one facet of commercial price and product advertising that warrants First Amendment protection—its contribution to the flow of accurate and reliable information relevant to public and private decision making.

JUSTICE REHNQUIST, dissenting.

[Under] the Court's opinion the way will be open not only for dissemination of price information but for active promotion of prescription drugs, liquor, cigarettes and other products the use of which it has previously been thought desirable to discourage. Now, however, such promotion is protected by the First Amendment so long as it is not misleading or does not promote an illegal product or [enterprise].

The Court speaks of the consumer's interest in the free flow of commercial information. [This] should presumptively be the concern of the Virginia Legislature, which sits to balance [this] and other claims in the process of making laws such as the one here under attack. The Court speaks of the importance in a "predominantly free enterprise economy" of intelligent and well-informed decisions as to allocation of resources. While there is again much to be said for the Court's observation as a matter of desirable public policy, there is certainly nothing in the United States Constitution which requires the Virginia Legislature to hew to the teachings of Adam Smith in its legislative decisions regulating the pharmacy profession. E.g., *Nebbia v. New York; Olsen v. Nebraska* [Ch. 5, Sec. 3].

[There] are undoubted difficulties with an effort to draw a bright line between "commercial speech" on the one hand and "protected speech" on the other, and the Court does better to face up to these difficulties than to attempt to hide them under labels. In this case, however, the Court has unfortunately substituted for the wavering line previously thought to exist between commercial speech and protected speech a no more satisfactory line of its own—that between "truthful" commercial speech, on the one hand, and that which is "false and misleading" on the other. The difficulty with this line is not that it wavers, but on the contrary that it is simply too Procrustean to take into account the congeries of factors which I believe could, quite consistently with the [First Amendment] properly influence a legislative decision with respect to commercial advertising.

[S]uch a line simply makes no allowance whatever for what appears to have been a considered legislative judgment in most States that while prescription drugs are a necessary and vital part of medical care and treatment, there are sufficient dangers attending their widespread use that they simply may not be promoted in the same manner as hair creams, deodorants, and toothpaste. The very real dangers that general advertising for such drugs might create in terms of encouraging, even though not sanctioning, illicit use of them by individuals for whom they have not been prescribed, or by generating patient pressure upon physicians to prescribe them are simply not dealt with in the Court's [opinion].

OHRALIK v. OHIO STATE BAR ASS'N, 436 U.S. 447 (1978), upheld the indefinite suspension of an attorney for violating the anti-solicitation provisions of the Ohio Code of Professional Responsibility. Those provisions generally do not allow lawyers to recommend themselves to anyone who has not sought "their advice regarding employment of a lawyer."

"In-person solicitation by a lawyer of remunerative employment is a business transaction in which speech is an essential but subordinate component. While this does not remove the speech from the protection of the First Amendment, as was held in *Bates* [*v. State Bar,* 433 U.S. 350 (1977), protecting attorney advertising] and *Virginia Pharmacy,* it lowers the level of appropriate judicial scrutiny. [A] lawyer's procurement of remunerative employment is a subject only marginally affected with First Amendment concerns. It falls within the State's proper sphere of economic and professional regulation. While entitled to some constitutional protection, appellant's conduct is subject to regulation in furtherance of important state [interests].

In CENTRAL HUDSON GAS & ELEC. CORP. v. PUBLIC SERV. COMM'N, 447 U.S. 557 (1980), the Court, per POWELL, J., characterized the prior commercial speech cases as embracing a special test:

"In commercial speech cases, then, a four-part analysis has developed. At the outset, we must determine whether the expression is protected by the First Amendment. For commercial speech to come within that provision, it at least must concern lawful activity and not be misleading. Next, we ask whether the asserted governmental interest is substantial. If both inquiries yield positive answers, we must determine whether the regulation directly advances the governmental interest asserted, and whether it is not more extensive than is necessary to serve that interest."

LORILLARD TOBACCO CO. v. REILLY
533 U.S. 525, 121 S.Ct. 2404, 150 L.Ed.2d 532 (2001).

JUSTICE O'CONNOR delivered the opinion of the Court.

In January 1999, the Attorney General of Massachusetts promulgated comprehensive regulations governing the advertising and sale of cigarettes, smokeless tobacco, and cigars. Petitioners, a group of cigarette, smokeless tobacco, and cigar manufacturers and retailers, filed suit in Federal District Court claiming that the regulations violate federal law and the United States Constitution.

I.   [The Court observed that the purpose of the restrictions was "to eliminate deception and unfairness in the way cigarettes and smokeless tobacco products are marketed, sold and distributed in Massachusetts in order to address the incidence of cigarette smoking and smokeless tobacco use by children under legal age [and] to prevent access to such products by underage consumers. The similar purpose of the cigar regulations is 'to eliminate [the] false perception that cigars are a safe alternative to cigarettes [and] to prevent access to such products by underage consumers.' " Among other things the restrictions prohibited outdoor advertising, "including advertising in enclosed stadiums and advertising from within a retail establishment that is directed toward or visible from the outside of the establishment, in any location that is within a 1,000 foot radius of any public playground, playground area in a public park, elementary school or secondary school."].

II.   [The Court concluded that the Federal Cigarette Labeling and Advertising Act of 1965 as amended, prevented states and localities from regulating the location of cigarette advertising.]

III. By its terms, the FCLAA's pre-emption provision only applies to cigarettes. Accordingly, we must evaluate the smokeless tobacco and cigar petitioners' First Amendment challenges to the State's outdoor and point-of-sale advertising regulations. The cigarette petitioners did not raise a pre-emption challenge to the sales practices regulations. Thus, we must analyze the cigarette as well as the smokeless tobacco and cigar petitioners' claim that certain sales practices regulations for tobacco products violate the First Amendment.

A.   [Petitioners] urge us to reject the *Central Hudson* analysis and apply strict scrutiny. [But] we see "no need to break new ground. *Central Hudson*, as applied in our more recent commercial speech cases, provides an adequate basis for decision.

Only the last two steps of *Central Hudson*'s four-part analysis are at issue here. The Attorney General has assumed for purposes of summary judgment that petitioners' speech is entitled to First Amendment protection. With respect to the second step, none of the petitioners contests the importance of the State's interest in preventing the use of tobacco products by minors.

The third step of *Central Hudson* [requires] that "the speech restriction directly and materially advanc[e] the asserted governmental interest. 'This burden is not satisfied by mere speculation or conjecture; rather, a governmental body seeking to sustain a restriction on commercial speech must demonstrate that the harms it recites are real and that its restriction will in fact alleviate them to a material degree.' " We do not, however, require that "empirical data [come] accompanied by a surfeit of background information. [W]e have permitted litigants to justify speech restrictions by reference to studies and anecdotes pertaining to different locales altogether, or even, in a case applying strict scrutiny, to justify restrictions based solely on history, consensus, and 'simple common sense.' "

The last step of the *Central Hudson* analysis "complements" the third step, "asking whether the speech restriction is not more extensive than necessary to serve the interests that support it." We have made it clear that "the least restrictive means" is not the standard; instead, the case law requires a reasonable " 'fit between the legislature's ends and the means chosen to accomplish those ends, [a] means narrowly tailored to achieve the desired objective.' " * * *

B.   [1.] The smokeless tobacco and cigar petitioners [maintain] that although the Attorney General may have identified a problem with underage cigarette smoking, he has not identified an equally severe problem with respect to underage use of smokeless tobacco or cigars. The smokeless tobacco petitioner emphasizes the "lack of parity" between cigarettes and smokeless tobacco. The cigar petitioners catalogue a list of differences between cigars and other tobacco products, including the characteristics of the products and marketing strategies. The petitioners finally contend that the Attorney General cannot prove that advertising has a causal link to tobacco use such that limiting advertising will materially alleviate any problem of underage use of their products.

In previous cases, we have acknowledged the theory that product advertising stimulates demand for products, while suppressed advertising may have the opposite effect. *United States v. Edge Broadcasting Co.*, 509 U.S. 418 (1993). The Attorney General cites numerous studies to support this theory in the case of tobacco products[, providing] ample documentation of the problem with underage use of smokeless tobacco and cigars. In addition, we disagree with petitioners' claim that there is no evidence that preventing targeted campaigns and limiting youth exposure to advertising will decrease underage use of smokeless tobacco and cigars. On this record and in the posture of summary judgment, we are unable to conclude that the Attorney General's decision to regulate advertising of smokeless tobacco and cigars in an effort to combat the use of tobacco products by minors was based on mere "speculation [and] conjecture."

2.   Whatever the strength of the Attorney General's evidence to justify the outdoor advertising regulations, however, we conclude that the regulations do not satisfy the fourth step of the *Central Hudson* analysis. [The] outdoor advertising regulations prohibit any smokeless tobacco or cigar advertising within 1,000 feet of schools or playgrounds. In the District Court, petitioners maintained that this prohibition would prevent advertising in 87% to 91% of Boston, Worcester, and Springfield. The 87% to 91% figure appears to include not only the effect of the regulations, but also the limitations imposed by other generally applicable zoning restrictions. The Attorney General disputed petitioners' figures but "concede[d] that the reach of the regulations is substantial." * * *

In some geographical areas, these regulations would constitute nearly a complete ban on the communication of truthful information about smokeless tobacco and cigars to adult consumers. The breadth and scope of the regulations, and the process by which the Attorney General adopted the regulations, do not demonstrate a careful calculation of the speech interests involved. * * *

The Attorney General apparently selected the 1,000-foot distance based on the FDA's decision to impose an identical 1,000-foot restriction when it attempted to regulate cigarette and smokeless tobacco advertising. But [the] degree to which speech is suppressed—or alternative avenues for speech remain available—under a particular regulatory scheme tends to be case specific [for] although a State or locality may have common interests and concerns about underage smoking and the effects of tobacco advertisements, the impact of a restriction on speech will undoubtedly vary from place to place. The FDA's regulations would have had widely disparate effects nationwide. Even in Massachusetts, the effect of the Attorney General's speech regulations will vary based on whether a locale is rural, suburban, or urban. The uniformly broad sweep of the geographical limitation demonstrates a lack of tailoring. * * *

The State's interest in preventing underage tobacco use is substantial, and even compelling, but it is no less true that the sale and use of tobacco products by adults is a legal activity. We must consider that tobacco retailers and manufacturers have an interest in conveying truthful information about their products to adults, and adults have a corresponding interest in receiving truthful information about tobacco products. [In] some instances, Massachusetts' outdoor advertising regulations would impose particularly onerous burdens on speech. For example, we disagree with the Court of Appeals' conclusion that because cigar manufacturers and retailers conduct a limited amount of advertising in comparison to other tobacco products, "the relative lack of cigar advertising also means that the burden imposed on cigar advertisers is correspondingly small." If some retailers have relatively small advertising budgets, and use few avenues of communication, then the Attorney General's outdoor advertising regulations potentially place a greater, not lesser, burden on those retailers' speech. * * *

JUSTICE KENNEDY, with whom JUSTICE SCALIA joins, concurring in part and concurring in the judgment.

The obvious overbreadth of the outdoor advertising restrictions suffices to invalidate them under the fourth part of the test in *Central Hudson*. [My] continuing concerns that the test gives insufficient protection to truthful, nonmisleading commercial speech require me to refrain from expressing agreement with the Court's application of the third part of *Central Hudson*.

JUSTICE THOMAS, concurring in part and concurring in the judgment

I join the opinion of the Court (with the exception of Part III-B-1). * * *

I have observed previously that there is no "philosophical or historical basis for asserting that 'commercial' speech is of 'lower value' than 'noncommercial' speech." Indeed, I doubt whether it is even possible to draw a coherent distinction between commercial and noncommercial speech.

It should be clear that if these regulations targeted anything other than advertising for commercial products—if, for example, they were directed at billboards promoting political candidates—all would agree that the restrictions should be subjected to strict scrutiny. In my view, an asserted government interest in keeping people ignorant by suppressing expression "is per se illegitimate and can no more justify regulation of 'commercial' speech than it can justify regulation of 'noncommercial' speech." That is essentially the interest asserted here. * * *

JUSTICE SOUTER, concurring in part and dissenting in part.

I join Parts I, II-C, II-D, III-A, III-B-1, III-C, and III-D of the Court's opinion. I join Part I of the opinion of Justice Stevens concurring in the judgment in part and dissenting in part. I respectfully dissent from Part III-B-2 of the opinion of the Court, and like Justice Stevens would remand for trial on the constitutionality of the 1,000-foot limit.

JUSTICE STEVENS, with whom JUSTICE GINSBURG and JUSTICE BREYER join, and with whom JUSTICE SOUTER joins as to Part I, concurring in part, concurring in the judgment in part, and dissenting in part. * * *

I.   [Stevens, J., argued that the Federal Cigarette Labeling and Advertising Act of 1965 did not preclude state and local regulation of the location of cigarette advertising.]

II.   *The 1,000-Foot Rule.* I am in complete accord with the Court's analysis of the importance of the interests served by the advertising restrictions. As the Court lucidly explains, few interests are more "compelling," than ensuring that minors do not become addicted to a dangerous drug before they are able to make a mature and informed decision as to the health risks associated with that substance. [Nevertheless,] noble ends do not save a speech-restricting statute whose means are poorly tailored. Such statutes may be invalid for two different reasons. First, the means chosen may be insufficiently related to the ends they purportedly serve. Alternatively, the statute may be so broadly drawn that, while effectively achieving its ends, it unduly restricts communications that are unrelated to its policy aims.

To my mind, the 1,000-foot rule does not present a tailoring problem of the first type. For reasons cogently explained in our prior opinions and in the opinion of the Court, we may fairly assume that advertising stimulates consumption and, therefore, that regulations limiting advertising will facilitate efforts to stem consumption. Furthermore, if the government's intention is to limit consumption by a particular segment of the community—in this case, minors—it is appropriate, indeed necessary, to tailor advertising restrictions to the areas where that segment of the community congregates—in this case, the area surrounding schools and playgrounds.

However, I share the majority's concern as to whether the 1,000-foot rule unduly restricts the ability of cigarette manufacturers to convey lawful information to adult consumers. This, of course, is a question of line-drawing. [E]fforts to protect children from exposure to harmful material will undoubtedly have some spillover effect on the free speech rights of adults. [Though] many factors plausibly enter the equation when calculating whether a child-directed location restriction goes too far in regulating adult speech, one crucial question is whether the regulatory scheme leaves available sufficient "alternative avenues of communication." Because I do not think the record contains sufficient information to enable us to answer that question, I would vacate the award of summary judgment upholding the 1,000-foot rule and remand for trial on that issue. * * *

––––––––

In EXPRESSIONS HAIR DESIGN v. SCHNEIDERMAN, 137 S.Ct. 1144 (2017), the Court considered a New York statute that prohibited merchants from imposing a surcharge for the use of credit cards when the imposition of the surcharge was necessarily committed by use of speech. Reversing the Second Circuit and remanding for reconsideration in light of the applicable First Amendment standards, the Court, per Roberts, C.J., said that "while we agree with the Court of Appeals that § 518 regulates a relationship between a sticker price and the price charged to credit card users, we cannot accept its conclusion that § 518 is nothing more than a mine-run price regulation. In regulating the communication of prices rather than prices themselves, § 518 regulates speech." BREYER, J., concurred in the judgment. "I agree with the Court that New York's statute regulates speech. But that is because virtually all government regulation affects speech. Human relations take place through speech. And human relations include community activities of all kinds—commercial and otherwise. When the government seeks to regulate those activities, it is often wiser not to try to distinguish between 'speech' and 'conduct.' Instead, we can [simply] ask whether, or how, a challenged statute, rule, or regulation affects an interest that the First Amendment protects.

2. THE PROBLEM OF CONTENT REGULATION

CHICAGO POLICE DEPT. v. MOSLEY, 408 U.S. 92 (1972), invalidated an ordinance banning all picketing within 150 feet of a school building while the school is in session and one half-hour before and afterwards, except "the peaceful picketing of any school involved in a labor dispute." The suit was brought by a federal postal employee who, for seven months prior to enactment of the ordinance, had frequently picketed a high school in Chicago. "During school hours and usually by himself, Mosley would walk the public sidewalk adjoining the school, carrying a sign that read: 'Jones High School practices black discrimination. Jones High School has a black quota.' His lonely crusade was always peaceful, orderly, and [quiet]." The Court, per MARSHALL, J., viewed the ordinance as drawing "an impermissible distinction between labor picketing and other peaceful picketing": "The central problem with Chicago's ordinance is that it describes permissible picketing in terms of its subject matter. Peaceful picketing on the subject of a school's labor-management dispute is permitted, but all other peaceful picketing is prohibited. The operative distinction is the message on a picket sign. But, above all else, the First Amendment means that government has no power to restrict expression because of its message, its ideas, its subject matter, or its content.

"[U]nder the Equal Protection Clause, not to mention the First Amendment itself,[11] government may not grant the use of a forum to people whose views it finds acceptable, but deny use to those wishing to express less favored or more controversial views. And it may not select which issues are worth discussing or debating in public facilities. There is an 'equality of status in the field of ideas,' and government must afford all points of view an equal opportunity to be heard. Once a forum is opened up to assembly or speaking by some groups, government may not prohibit others from assembling or speaking on the basis of what they intend to say. Selective exclusions from a public forum may not be based on content alone, and may not be justified by reference to content alone.

R.A.V. v. St. Paul
505 U.S. 377, 112 S.Ct. 2538, 120 L.Ed.2d 305 (1992).

JUSTICE SCALIA delivered the opinion of the Court.

In the predawn hours of June 21, 1990, petitioner and several other teenagers allegedly assembled a crudely-made cross by taping together broken chair legs. They then allegedly burned the cross inside the fenced yard of a black family that lived across the street from the house where petitioner was staying. Although this conduct could have been punished under any of a number of laws, one of the two provisions under which respondent city of St. Paul chose to charge petitioner (then a juvenile) was the St. Paul Bias-Motivated Crime Ordinance, which provides: "Whoever places on public or private property a symbol, object, appellation, characterization or graffiti, including, but not limited to, a burning cross or Nazi swastika, which one knows or has reasonable grounds to know arouses anger, alarm or resentment in others on the basis of race, color, creed, religion or gender commits disorderly conduct and shall be guilty of a misdemeanor." * * *

I.   [W]e accept the Minnesota Supreme Court's authoritative statement that the ordinance reaches only those expressions that constitute "fighting words" within the meaning of Chaplinsky. [W]e nonetheless conclude that the ordinance is facially unconstitutional in that it prohibits otherwise permitted speech solely on the basis of the subjects the speech addresses.

[From] 1791 to the present, our society, like other free but civilized societies, has permitted restrictions upon the content of speech in a few limited areas, which are "of such slight social value as a step to truth that any benefit that may be derived from them is clearly outweighed by the social interest in order and morality." *Chaplinsky.* * * *

We have sometimes said that these categories of expression are "not within the area of constitutionally protected speech," *Roth; Beauharnais; Chaplinsky.* [But] such statements must be taken in context, however, and are no more literally

---

    [11]   *Consolidated Edison Co. v. Public Service Comm'n*, 447 U.S. 530 (1980), abandoned equal protection and cited *Mosley* as a First Amendment case: "The First Amendment's hostility to content-based regulation extends not only to restrictions on particular viewpoints, but also to prohibition of public discussion of an entire topic."

true than is the occasionally repeated shorthand characterizing obscenity "as not being speech at all." What they mean is that these areas of speech can, consistently with the First Amendment, be regulated *because of their constitutionally proscribable content* (obscenity, defamation, etc.)—not that they are categories of speech entirely invisible to the Constitution, so that they may be made the vehicles for content discrimination unrelated to their distinctively proscribable content. Thus, the government may proscribe libel; but it may not make the further content discrimination of proscribing *only* libel critical of the government.

Our cases surely do not establish the proposition that the First Amendment imposes no obstacle whatsoever to regulation of particular instances of such proscribable expression, so that the government "may regulate [them] freely," (White, J., concurring in judgment). That would mean that a city council could enact an ordinance prohibiting only those legally obscene works that contain criticism of the city government or, indeed, that do not include endorsement of the city government. Such a simplistic, all-or-nothing-at-all approach to First Amendment protection is at odds with common sense and with our jurisprudence as well. It is not true that "fighting words" have at most a "de minimis" expressive content or that their content is *in all respects* "worthless and undeserving of constitutional protection"; sometimes they are quite expressive indeed. We have not said that they constitute "*no* part of the expression of ideas," but only that they constitute "no *essential* part of any exposition of ideas."

The proposition that a particular instance of speech can be proscribable on the basis of one feature (e.g., obscenity) but not on the basis of another (e.g., opposition to the city government) is commonplace, and has found application in many contexts. We have long held, for example, that nonverbal expressive activity can be banned because of the action it entails, but not because of the ideas it expresses— so that burning a flag in violation of an ordinance against outdoor fires could be punishable, whereas burning a flag in violation of an ordinance against dishonoring the flag is not. Similarly, we have upheld reasonable "time, place, or manner" restrictions, but only if they are "justified without reference to the content of the regulated speech." And just as the power to proscribe particular speech on the basis of a noncontent element (e.g., noise) does not entail the power to proscribe the same speech on the basis of a content element; so also, the power to proscribe it on the basis of *one* content element (e.g., obscenity) does not entail the power to proscribe it on the basis of *other* content elements.

In other words, the exclusion of "fighting words" from the scope of the First Amendment simply means that, for purposes of that Amendment, the unprotected features of the words are, despite their verbal character, essentially a "non-speech" element of communication. Fighting words are thus analogous to a noisy sound truck: Each [is,] a "mode of speech,"; both can be used to convey an idea; but neither has, in and of itself, a claim upon the First Amendment. As with the sound truck, however, so also with fighting words: The government may not regulate use based on hostility—or favoritism—towards the underlying message expressed.

[The] prohibition against content discrimination that we assert the First Amendment requires is not absolute. It applies differently in the context of proscribable speech than in the area of fully protected speech. [When] the basis for the content discrimination consists entirely of the very reason the entire class of speech at issue is proscribable, no significant danger of idea or viewpoint discrimination exists. Such a reason, having been adjudged neutral enough to support exclusion of the entire class of speech from First Amendment protection, is also neutral enough to form the basis of distinction within the class. To illustrate: A State might choose to prohibit only that obscenity which is the most patently offensive *in its prurience*—i.e., that which involves the most lascivious displays of sexual activity. But it may not prohibit, for example, only that obscenity which includes offensive *political* messages. And the Federal Government can criminalize only those threats of violence that are directed against the President, see 18 U.S.C. § 871—since the reasons why threats of violence are outside the First Amendment (protecting individuals from the fear of violence, from the disruption that fear engenders, and from the possibility that the threatened violence will occur) have special force when applied to the person of the President. But the Federal Government may not criminalize only those threats against the President that mention his policy on aid to inner cities. And to take a final example (one mentioned by Justice Stevens), a State may choose to regulate price advertising in one industry but not in others, because the risk of fraud (one of the characteristics of commercial speech that justifies depriving it of full First Amendment protection) is in its view greater there. But a State may not prohibit only that commercial advertising that depicts men in a demeaning fashion.

Another valid basis for according differential treatment to even a content-defined subclass of proscribable speech is that the subclass happens to be associated with particular "secondary effects" of the speech, so that the regulation is *"justified* without reference to the content of [the] speech," *Renton, infra.* A State could, for example, permit all obscene live performances except those involving minors. Moreover, since words can in some circumstances violate laws directed not against speech but against conduct (a law against treason, for example, is violated by telling the enemy the nation's defense secrets), a particular content-based subcategory of a proscribable class of speech can be swept up incidentally within the reach of a statute directed at conduct rather than speech. Thus, for example, sexually derogatory "fighting words," among other words, may produce a violation of Title VII's general prohibition against sexual discrimination in employment practices. Where the government does not target conduct on the basis of its expressive content, acts are not shielded from regulation merely because they express a discriminatory idea or philosophy.

These bases for distinction refute the proposition that the selectivity of the restriction is "even arguably 'conditioned upon the sovereign's agreement with what a speaker may intend to say.' " There may be other such bases as well. Indeed, to validate such selectivity (where totally proscribable speech is at issue) it may not even be necessary to identify any particular "neutral" basis, so long as the nature of the content discrimination is such that there is no realistic possibility that official suppression of ideas is afoot. (We cannot think of any First Amendment interest that would stand in the way of a State's prohibiting only those obscene motion pictures with blue-eyed actresses.) Save for that limitation, the regulation of "fighting words," like the regulation of noisy speech, may address some offensive instances and leave other, equally offensive, instances alone.

II.   [Although] the phrase in the ordinance, "arouses anger, alarm or resentment in others," has been limited by the Minnesota Supreme Court's construction to reach only those symbols or displays that amount to "fighting words," the remaining, unmodified terms make clear that the ordinance applies only to "fighting words" that insult, or provoke violence, "on the basis of race, color, creed, religion or gender." Displays containing abusive invective, no matter how vicious or severe, are permissible unless they are addressed to one of the specified disfavored topics. Those who wish to use "fighting words" in connection with other ideas—to express hostility, for example, on the basis of political affiliation, union membership, or homosexuality—are not covered. The First Amendment does [permit] special prohibitions [on] disfavored subjects.

In its practical operation, moreover, the ordinance goes even beyond mere content discrimination, to actual viewpoint discrimination. Displays containing some words—odious racial epithets, for example—would be prohibited to proponents of all views. But "fighting words" that do not themselves invoke race, color, creed, religion, or gender—aspersions upon a person's mother, for example— would seemingly be usable ad libitum in the placards of those arguing *in favor* of racial, color, etc. tolerance and equality, but could not be used by that speaker's opponents. One could hold up a sign saying, for example, that all "anti-Catholic bigots" are misbegotten; but not that all "papists" are, for that would insult and provoke violence "on the basis of religion." St. Paul has no such authority to license one side of a debate to fight freestyle, while requiring the other to follow Marquis of Queensbury Rules.

[T]he reason why fighting words are categorically excluded from the protection of the First Amendment is not that their content communicates any particular idea, but that their content embodies a particularly intolerable (and socially unnecessary) *mode* of expressing *whatever* idea the speaker wishes to convey. St. Paul has not singled out an especially offensive mode of expression—it has not, for example, selected for prohibition only those fighting words that communicate ideas in a threatening (as opposed to a merely obnoxious) manner. Rather, it has proscribed fighting words of whatever manner that communicate messages of racial, gender, or religious intolerance.

[St. Paul] argues that the ordinance [is] aimed only at the "secondary effects" of the speech, see *Renton.* According to St. Paul, the ordinance is intended, "not to impact on [sic] the right of free expression of the accused," but rather to "protect against the victimization of a person or persons who are particularly vulnerable because of their membership in a group that historically has been discriminated against." Even assuming that an ordinance that completely proscribes, rather than merely regulates, a specified category of speech can ever be considered to be directed only to the secondary effects of such speech, it is clear that the St. Paul ordinance is not directed to secondary effects within the meaning of *Renton*. As we said in *Boos* "[l]isteners' reactions to speech are not the type of 'secondary effects' we referred to in *Renton*." * * *[7]

Finally, St. Paul [asserts] that the ordinance helps to ensure the basic human rights of members of groups that have historically been subjected to discrimination, including the right of such group members to live in peace where they wish. We do not doubt that these interests are compelling, and that the ordinance can be said to promote them. But the "danger of censorship" presented by a facially content-based statute requires that that weapon be employed only where it is "*necessary* to serve the asserted [compelling] interest". The existence of adequate content-neutral alternatives thus "undercut[s] significantly" any defense of such a statute, casting considerable doubt on the government's protestations that "the asserted justification is in fact an accurate description of the purpose and effect of the law." [An] ordinance not limited to the favored topics, for example, would have precisely the same beneficial effect. In fact the only interest distinctively served by the content limitation is that of displaying the city council's special hostility towards the particular biases thus singled out. That is precisely what the First Amendment forbids.

[Let] there be no mistake about our belief that burning a cross in someone's front yard is reprehensible. But St. Paul has sufficient means at its disposal to prevent such behavior without adding the First Amendment to the fire. * * *

JUSTICE WHITE, with whom JUSTICE BLACKMUN and JUSTICE O'CONNOR join, and with whom JUSTICE STEVENS joins except as to Part I(A), concurring in the judgment. * * *

I.A. [T]he majority holds that the First Amendment protects those narrow categories of expression long held to be undeserving of First Amendment protection—at least to the extent that lawmakers may not regulate some fighting words more strictly than others because of their content. [Should] the government want to criminalize certain fighting words, the Court now requires it to criminalize all fighting words.

To borrow a phrase, "Such a simplistic, all-or-nothing-at-all approach to First Amendment protection is at odds with common sense and with our jurisprudence as well." It is inconsistent to hold that the government may proscribe an entire

---

[7]   **[Ct's Note]** St. Paul has not argued in this case that the ordinance merely regulates that subclass of fighting words which is most likely to provoke a violent response. But even if one assumes (as appears unlikely) that the categories selected may be so described, that would not justify selective regulation under a "secondary effects" theory. The only reason why such expressive conduct would be especially correlated with violence is that it conveys a particularly odious message; because the "chain of causation" thus *necessarily* "run[s] through the persuasive effect of the expressive component" of the conduct, it is clear that the St. Paul ordinance regulates on the basis of the "primary" effect of the speech—i.e., its persuasive (or repellent) force.

category of speech because the content of that speech is evil, but that the government may not treat a subset of that category differently without violating the First Amendment; the content of the subset is by definition worthless and undeserving of constitutional protection.

The majority's observation that fighting words are "quite expressive indeed," is no answer. Fighting words are not a means of exchanging views, rallying supporters, or registering a protest; they are directed against individuals to provoke violence or to inflict injury. Therefore, a ban on all fighting words or on a subset of the fighting words category would restrict only the social evil of hate speech, without creating the danger of driving viewpoints from the marketplace.

Therefore, the Court's insistence on inventing its brand of First Amendment underinclusiveness puzzles me. [T]he Court's new "underbreadth" creation [invites] the continuation of expressive conduct that in this case is evil and worthless in First Amendment terms until the city of St. Paul cures the underbreadth by adding to its ordinance a catch-all phrase such as "and all other fighting words that may constitutionally be subject to this ordinance."

II.   * * * I would decide the case on overbreadth grounds. * * *

In construing the St. Paul ordinance, [I understand the Minnesota Supreme Court] to have ruled that St. Paul may constitutionally prohibit expression that "by its very utterance" causes "anger, alarm or resentment." Our fighting words cases have made clear, however, that [t]he mere fact that expressive activity causes hurt feelings, offense, or resentment does not render the expression unprotected. [The] ordinance is therefore fatally overbroad and invalid on its face.

JUSTICE BLACKMUN, concurring in the judgment.

[B]y deciding that a State cannot regulate speech that causes great harm unless it also regulates speech that does not (setting law and logic on their heads), the Court seems to abandon the categorical approach, and inevitably to relax the level of scrutiny applicable to content-based laws. [The] simple reality is that the Court will never provide child pornography or cigarette advertising the level of protection customarily granted political speech. If we are forbidden from categorizing, as the Court has done here, we shall reduce protection across the board. * * *

[There] is the possibility that this case will not significantly alter First Amendment jurisprudence, but, instead, will be regarded as an aberration—a case where the Court manipulated doctrine to strike down an ordinance whose premise it opposed, namely, that racial threats and verbal assaults are of greater harm than other fighting words. I fear that the Court has been distracted from its proper mission by the temptation to decide the issue over "politically correct speech" and "cultural diversity," neither of which is presented here. If this is the meaning of today's opinion, it is perhaps even more regrettable.

I see no First Amendment values that are compromised by a law that prohibits hoodlums from driving minorities out of their homes by burning crosses on their lawns, but I see great harm in preventing the people of Saint Paul from specifically punishing the race-based fighting words that so prejudice their community. * * *

JUSTICE STEVENS, with whom JUSTICE WHITE and JUSTICE BLACKMUN join as to Part I, concurring in the judgment. * * *

I.   [Our] First Amendment decisions have created a rough hierarchy in the constitutional protection of speech. Core political speech occupies the highest, most protected position; commercial speech and nonobscene, sexually explicit speech are regarded as a sort of second-class expression; obscenity and fighting words receive the least protection of all. Assuming that the Court is correct that this last class of speech is not wholly "unprotected," it certainly does not follow that fighting words and obscenity receive the *same* sort of protection afforded core political speech. Yet in ruling that proscribable speech cannot be regulated based on subject matter, the Court does just that. Perversely, this gives fighting words *greater* protection than is afforded commercial speech. If Congress can prohibit false advertising directed at airline passengers without also prohibiting false advertising directed at bus passengers and if a city can prohibit political advertisements in its buses while allowing other advertisements, it is ironic to hold that a city cannot regulate fighting words based on "race, color, creed, religion or gender" while leaving unregulated fighting words based on "union membership or homosexuality." * * * Perhaps because the Court recognizes these perversities, it quickly offers some ad hoc limitations on its newly extended prohibition on content-based regulations.

[T]he Court recognizes that a State may regulate advertising in one industry but not another because "the risk of fraud (one of the characteristics that justifies depriving [commercial speech] of full First Amendment protection)" in the regulated industry is "greater" than in other industries. "[O]ne of the characteristics that justifies" the constitutional status of fighting words is that such words "by their very utterance inflict injury or tend to incite an immediate breach of the peace." *Chaplinsky.* Certainly a legislature that may determine that the risk of fraud is greater in the legal trade than in the medical trade may determine that the risk of injury or breach of peace created by race-based threats is greater than that created by other threats. * * *

III.   [Unlike] the Court, I do not believe that all content-based regulations are equally infirm and presumptively invalid; unlike Justice White, I do not believe that fighting words are wholly unprotected by the First Amendment. To the contrary, I believe our decisions establish a more complex and subtle analysis, one that considers the content and context of the regulated speech, and the nature and scope of the restriction on speech. * * * Whatever the allure of absolute doctrines, it is just too simple to declare expression "protected" or "unprotected" or to proclaim a regulation "content-based" or "content-neutral."

[The] St. Paul ordinance regulates speech not on the basis of its subject matter or the viewpoint expressed, but rather on the basis of the *harm* the speech causes. * * * Contrary to the Court's suggestion, the ordinance regulates only a subcategory of expression that causes *injuries based on* "race, color, creed, religion or gender," not a subcategory that involves *discussions* that concern those characteristics. * * *

WISCONSIN v. MITCHELL, 508 U.S. 476 (1993), per REHNQUIST, C.J., found no First Amendment violation when Wisconsin permitted a sentence for aggravated battery to be enhanced on the ground that the white victim had been selected because of his race. The Court observed that, unlike *R.A.V.*, the Wisconsin statute was aimed at conduct, not speech, that a chilling effect on speech was unlikely, that the focus on motive was no different from that employed in anti-discrimination statutes, and that bias-inspired conduct is more likely "to provoke retaliatory crimes, inflict distinct emotional harms on their victims, and incite community unrest."

In 1952, Virginia declared it a felony publicly to burn a cross with the intent of intimidating any person or group of persons. In 1968, Virginia added a provision that any such burning shall be prima facie evidence of an intent to intimidate. Barry Black led a Ku Klux Klan rally in which a cross was burned after a series of speeches marked by racial hostility, including one speaker saying that he "would love to take a .30/.30 and just random[ly] shoot the blacks." Forty to fifty cars passed the site during the rally, and eight to ten houses were located in its vicinity. The trial court used a Virginia Model Instruction that "the burning of a cross by itself is sufficient evidence from which you may infer the required intent."

Richard Elliot and Jonathan O'Mara attempted to burn a cross at the residence of an African-American. O'Mara pled guilty of attempted burning, reserving the right to challenge the statute; Elliot was convicted in a trial in which the jury was instructed that the Commonwealth had to show the intent to burn the cross and the intent to intimidate. The trial court did not instruct on the meaning of the prima facie provision of the statute, nor did it give the Model Instruction.

The Virginia Supreme Court declared the statute unconstitutional in light of *R.A.V.* and overturned the convictions of the three defendants.

VIRGINIA v. BLACK, 538 U.S. 343 (2003), per O'CONNOR, J., upheld the cross burning with intent to intimidate provision, struck down the prima facie evidence provision as interpreted by the jury instruction in the Black case, and, thereby, affirmed the dismissal of Black's prosecution while vacating and remanding for further proceedings with respect to Elliot and O'Mara: "[T]he First Amendment [permits] a State to ban a 'true threat.' Intimidation in the constitutionally proscribable sense of the word is a type of true threat. [The] First Amendment permits Virginia to outlaw cross burnings done with the intent to intimidate because burning a cross is a particularly virulent form of intimidation. Instead of prohibiting all intimidating messages, Virginia may choose to regulate this subset of intimidating messages in light of cross burning's long and pernicious history as a signal of impending violence. Thus, just as a State may regulate only that obscenity which is the most obscene due to its prurient content, so too may a State choose to prohibit only those forms of intimidation that are most likely to inspire fear of bodily harm. A ban on cross burning carried out with the intent to intimidate is fully consistent with our holding in *R.A.V.* and is proscribable under the First Amendment."

In a section of the opinion joined by Rehnquist, C.J., Stevens and Breyer, JJ., O'Connor, J., addressed the prima facie evidence provision: "The Supreme Court of Virginia has not ruled on the meaning of the prima facie evidence provision. It has, however, stated that 'the act of burning a cross alone, with no evidence of intent to intimidate, will nonetheless suffice for arrest and prosecution and will insulate the Commonwealth from a motion to strike the evidence at the end of its case-in-chief.' The jury in the case of Richard Elliott did not receive any instruction on the prima facie evidence provision, and the provision was not an issue in the case of Jonathan O'Mara because he pleaded guilty. The court in Barry Black's case, however, instructed the jury that the provision means: 'The burning of a cross, by itself, is sufficient evidence from which you may infer the required intent.'

"The prima facie evidence provision, as interpreted by the jury instruction, renders the statute unconstitutional. Because this jury instruction is the Model Jury Instruction, and because the Supreme Court of Virginia had the opportunity to expressly disavow the jury instruction, the jury instruction's construction of the prima facie provision 'is a ruling on a question of state law that is as binding on us as though the precise words had been written into' the statute. [As] construed by the jury instruction, the prima facie provision strips away the very reason why a State may ban cross burning with the intent to intimidate. The prima facie evidence provision permits a jury to convict in every cross-burning case in which defendants exercise their constitutional right not to put on a defense. And even where a defendant like Black presents a defense, the prima facie evidence provision makes it more likely that the jury will find an intent to intimidate regardless of the particular facts of the case. The provision permits the Commonwealth to arrest, prosecute, and convict a person based solely on the fact of cross burning itself.

"The act of burning a cross may mean that a person is engaging in constitutionally proscribable intimidation. But that same act may mean only that the person is engaged in core political speech. The prima facie evidence provision in this statute blurs the line between these two meanings of a burning cross. As interpreted by the jury instruction, the provision chills constitutionally protected political speech because of the possibility that a State will prosecute—and potentially convict—somebody engaging only in lawful political speech at the core of what the First Amendment is designed to protect. * * *

"For these reasons, the prima facie evidence provision, as interpreted through the jury instruction and as applied in Barry Black's case, is unconstitutional on its face. We recognize that the Supreme Court of Virginia has not authoritatively interpreted the meaning of the prima facie evidence provision. Unlike Justice

Scalia, we refuse to speculate on whether *any* interpretation of the prima facie evidence provision would satisfy the First Amendment. Rather, all we hold is that because of the interpretation of the prima facie evidence provision given by the jury instruction, the provision makes the statute facially invalid at this point."

SCALIA, J., joined by Thomas, J., concurring and dissenting, agreed that the cross burning/intimidation portion of the statute was constitutional, but he denied that the prima facie evidence aspect of the statute was unconstitutional on its face. In a portion of his opinion not joined by Thomas, J., Scalia J., nonetheless concurred with the plurality's view that that the jury instruction was invalid: "I believe the prima-facie-evidence provision in Virginia's cross-burning statute is constitutionally unproblematic. Nevertheless, because the Virginia Supreme Court has not yet offered an authoritative construction of [that provision], I concur in the Court's decision to vacate and remand the judgment with respect to respondents Elliott and O'Mara. I also agree that respondent Black's conviction cannot stand. As noted above, the jury in Black's case was instructed that '[t]he burning of a cross, *by itself,* is sufficient evidence from which you may infer the required intent.' Where this instruction has been given, it is impossible to determine whether the jury has rendered its verdict (as it must) in light of the entire body of facts before it—*including* evidence that might rebut the presumption that the cross burning was done with an intent to intimidate—or, instead, has chosen to ignore such rebuttal evidence and focused exclusively on the fact that the defendant burned a cross. Still, I cannot go along with the Court's decision to affirm the judgment with respect to Black. In that judgment, the Virginia Supreme Court, having erroneously concluded that § 18.2–423 is overbroad, not only vacated Black's conviction, but dismissed the indictment against him as well. Because I believe the constitutional defect in Black's conviction is rooted in a jury instruction and not in the statute itself, I would not dismiss the indictment and would permit the Commonwealth to retry Black if it wishes to do so."

SOUTER, J., joined by Kennedy and Ginsburg, JJ., concurring in part and dissenting in part, argued that both the cross burning/intimidation section and the prima facie evidence section were unconstitutional: "I agree with the majority that the Virginia statute makes a content-based distinction within the category of punishable intimidating or threatening expression, the very type of distinction we considered in *R.A.V.* I disagree that any exception should save Virginia's law from unconstitutionality under the holding in *R.A.V.* or any acceptable variation of it. [Because] of the burning cross's extraordinary force as a method of intimidation, the *R.A.V.* exception most likely to cover the statute is the first of the three mentioned there, which the *R.A.V.* opinion called an exception for content discrimination on a basis that 'consists entirely of the very reason the entire class of speech at issue is proscribable.' This is the exception the majority speaks of here as covering statutes prohibiting 'particularly virulent' proscribable expression. [*RAV*] explained that when the subcategory is confined to the most obviously proscribable instances, 'no significant danger of idea or viewpoint discrimination exists,' and the explanation was rounded out with some illustrative examples. None of them, however, resembles the case before us. * * *

"As I see the likely significance of the evidence provision, its primary effect is to skew jury deliberations toward conviction in cases where the evidence of intent to intimidate is relatively weak and arguably consistent with a solely ideological reason for burning. To understand how the provision may work, recall that the symbolic act of burning a cross, without more, is consistent with both intent to intimidate and intent to make an ideological statement free of any aim to threaten. One can tell the intimidating instance from the wholly ideological one only by reference to some further circumstance. In the real world, of course, and in real-world prosecutions, there will always be further circumstances, and the factfinder will always learn something more than the isolated fact of cross burning. Sometimes those circumstances will show an intent to intimidate, but sometimes they will be at least equivocal, as in cases where a white supremacist group burns a cross at an initiation ceremony or political rally visible to the public. In such a case, if the factfinder Black's case is aware of the prima facie evidence provision, as the jury was in respondent, the provision will have the practical effect of tilting the jury's thinking in favor of the prosecution. [The] provision will thus tend to draw nonthreatening ideological expression within the ambit of the prohibition of intimidating expression. * * *

"To the extent the prima facie evidence provision skews prosecutions, then, it skews the statute toward suppressing ideas. Thus, the appropriate way to consider the statute's prima facie evidence term, in my view, is not as if it were an overbroad statutory definition amenable to severance or a narrowing construction. The question here is not the permissible scope of an arguably overbroad statute, but the claim of a clearly content-based statute to an exception from the general prohibition of content-based proscriptions, an exception that is not warranted if the statute's terms show that suppression of ideas may be afoot. Accordingly, the way to look at the prima facie evidence provision is to consider it for any indication of what is afoot. And if we look at the provision for this purpose, it has a very obvious significance as a mechanism for bringing within the statute's prohibition some expression that is doubtfully threatening though certainly distasteful."

THOMAS, J., dissenting, maintained that the statute was constitutional: "Although I agree with the majority's conclusion that it is constitutionally permissible to 'ban . . . cross burning carried out with intent to intimidate,' I believe that the majority errs in imputing an expressive component to the activity in question. In my view, whatever expressive value cross burning has, the legislature simply wrote it out by banning only intimidating conduct undertaken by a particular means. A conclusion that the statute prohibiting cross burning with intent to intimidate sweeps beyond a prohibition on certain conduct into the zone of expression overlooks not only the words of the statute but also reality.

" 'The world's oldest, most persistent terrorist organization is not European or even Middle Eastern in origin. Fifty years before the Irish Republican Army was organized, a century before Al Fatah declared its holy war on Israel, the Ku Klux Klan was actively harassing, torturing and murdering in the United States. Today [its] members remain fanatically committed to a course of violent opposition to social progress and racial equality in the United States.' M. Newton & J. Newton, *The Ku Klux Klan: An Encyclopedia* vii (1991). * * *

"As the Solicitor General points out, the association between acts of intimidating cross burning and violence is well documented in recent American history. [Virginia's] experience has been no exception. [In] February 1952, in light of [a] series of cross burnings and attendant reports that the Klan, 'long considered dead in Virginia, is being revitalized in Richmond,' Governor Battle announced that 'Virginia might well consider passing legislation to restrict the activities of the Ku Klux Klan.' [As] newspapers reported at the time, the bill was 'to ban the burning of crosses and other similar evidences of *terrorism.*' * * *

"Strengthening [my] conclusion, that the legislature sought to criminalize terrorizing *conduct* is the fact that at the time the statute was enacted, racial segregation was not only the prevailing practice, but also the law in Virginia. And, just two years after the enactment of this statute, Virginia's General Assembly embarked on a campaign of 'massive resistance' in response to *Brown v. Board of Education*. It strains credulity to suggest that a state legislature that adopted a litany of segregationist laws self-contradictorily intended to squelch the segregationist message. Even for segregationists, violent and terroristic conduct, the Siamese twin of cross burning, was intolerable. The ban on cross burning with intent to intimidate demonstrates that even segregationists understood the difference between intimidating and terroristic conduct and racist expression. It is simply beyond belief that, in passing the statute now under review, the Virginia legislature was concerned with anything but penalizing conduct it must have viewed as particularly vicious.

"Accordingly, this statute prohibits only conduct, not expression. And, just as one cannot burn down someone's house to make a political point and then seek refuge in the First Amendment, those who hate cannot terrorize and intimidate to make their point. In light of my conclusion that the statute here addresses only conduct, there is no need to analyze it under any of our First Amendment tests.

"[Even] assuming that the statute implicates the First Amendment, in my view, the fact that the statute permits a jury to draw an inference of intent to intimidate from the cross burning itself presents no constitutional problems. [The] inference is rebuttable and, as the jury instructions given in this case demonstrate, Virginia law still requires the jury to find the existence of each element, including intent to intimidate, beyond a reasonable doubt."

————

Under 15 U.S.C. § 1052(a), the Patent and Trademark Office (PTO) may deny registration to any trademark that may "disparage . . . or bring . . . into contemp[t] or disrepute" any "persons, living or dead." Relying on this provision, the PTO denied trademark registration to a dance-rock band who wished to register the band's name—"The Slants." The band, whose members are Asian-Americans, used the name in an attempt to deprive the term of its traditional derogatory meaning as disparaging of those of Asian descent. In MATAL v. TAM, 137 S.Ct. 1744 (2017), the Supreme Court unanimously held that § 1052's "disparagement clause" represented unconstitutional viewpoint discrimination. Announcing the judgment of the Court, ALITO, J. delivered an opinion that was unanimous in interpreting the disparagement clause's reference to "persons" as including the disparagement of racial or ethnic groups. And the opinion also represented the view of a unanimous Court in rejecting the argument that trademark registration was a form of government speech, thus making even viewpoint discrimination constitutionally permissible. (see infra, Sec. 7, and especially *Walker v. Texas Division, Sons of Confederate Veterans, Inc.*, Sec. 7, II, and *Pleasant Grove City v. Summum*, Sec. 7, II). "[I]t is far-fetched to suggest that the content of a registered mark is government speech. [I]f trademarks represent government speech, what does the Government have in mind when it advises Americans to 'make believe' (Sony), 'Think different' (Apple), 'Just do it' (Nike), or 'Have it your way' (Burger King)? [None] of our government speech cases even remotely supports the idea that registered trademarks are government speech."

Having concluded that trademarks are not government speech, Alito, now speaking only for himself, Roberts, CJ, and Thomas and Breyer, JJ, also concluded that trademark registration was neither the kind of government subsidy that might also be awarded on content- and viewpoint-based grounds (see *Rust v. Sullivan*, infra, Sec. 7, II), nor the type of government program (see *Davenport v. Washington Educ. Ass'n*, infra, Sec. 9, I) that may, again, be based on content or viewpoint. As a result of the inapplicability of none of these justifications for content- or viewpoint-discrimination, Alito found it unnecessary to address the question whether trademarks were commercial speech, because, he said, "the disparagement clause cannot withstand even *Central Hudson* (supra, Sec. 3, II) review. [No] matter how the [government's] point is phrased, its unmistakable thrust is this: The Government has an interest in preventing speech expressing ideas that offend. And, as we have explained, that idea strikes at the heart of the First Amendment. Speech that demeans on the basis of race, ethnicity, gender, religion, age, disability, or any other similar ground is hateful; but the proudest boast of our free speech jurisprudence is that we protect the freedom to express the 'thought that we hate.' *United States v. Schwimmer*, 279 U.S. 644 (1929) (Holmes, J., dissenting). [We] hold that the disparagement clause violates the [First] Amendment."

KENNEDY, J., writing for himself and Ginsburg, Sotomayor, and Kagan, JJ., agreed that "§ 1052(a) constitutes viewpoint discrimination—a form of speech suppression so potent that it must be subject to rigorous constitutional scrutiny. The Government's action and the statute on which it is based cannot survive this scrutiny. [The] test for viewpoint discrimination is whether—within the relevant subject category—the government has singled out a subset of messages for disfavor based on the views expressed. [Here] the law [reflects] the Government's disapproval of a subset of messages it finds offensive. This is the essence of viewpoint discrimination." Concluding that the "narrow" government speech and government program "exceptions" were inapplicable, and that even characterization of the speech as "commercial" "does not serve as a blanket exemption from the First Amendment's requirement of viewpoint neutrality," Kennedy concluded by joining the Court's opinion in part and concurring in the judgment.

––––––

Two Terms after *Matal v. Tam*, the Court revisited the issue in IANCU v. BRUNETTI, 139 S.Ct. 2294 (2019), holding that the Lanham Act's prohibition on registration for "immoral or scandalous" trademarks constituted impermissible viewpoint-based discrimination. At issue was an attempted registration of the trademark FUCT by the clothing manufacturer that used these four letters, allegedly pronounced as four separate letters, as the brand for its clothing line. Relying substantially on *Matal*, the Court, with KAGAN, J., writing the majority opinion, rejected the argument that this standard was a viewpoint-neutral restriction on the manner in which a point of view could be expressed but was not itself a viewpoint-based standard. The Court also rejected the government's arguments that the statutory criteria were not facially invalid but only that there had been errors in application by trademark examiners in applying the criteria, as well as the argument that the statute could be subject to a saving narrowing construction.

Concurring, JUSTICE ALITO noted that a statute precluding registration of "vulgar terms" could be valid, but that "[v]iewpoint discrimination is poison to a free society. But in many countries with constitutions or legal traditions that claim to protect freedom of speech, serious viewpoint discrimination is now tolerated, and such discrimination has become increasingly prevalent in this country. At a time when free speech is under attack, it is especially important for this Court to remain firm on the principle that the First Amendment does not tolerate viewpoint discrimination."

ROBERTS, C.J., BREYER, J., and SOTOMAYOR, J., each wrote opinions concurring in part and dissenting in part. All three agreed with the majority that the "immoral" component was impermissibly viewpoint-based, but that that it could be excised by the Court leaving the "scandalous" element in place, an element that for all three was sufficiently close a restriction on only the lewd or the profane that it could be understood as not being viewpoint-based. JUSTICE BREYER's opinion also objected the Court's continuing reliance on rigid First Amendment categories, believing that the Court should focus on the "more basic proportionality question" whether the harm to the First Amendment's interests was disproportionate to the government's regulatory objectives.

I. "HATE SPEECH" AND THE *SKOKIE* CONTROVERSY

COLLIN v. SMITH, 578 F.2d 1197 (7th Cir.), cert. denied, 439 U.S. 916 (1978), per PELL, J., struck down a Village of Skokie "Racial Slur" Ordinance, making it a misdemeanor to disseminate any material (defined to include "public display of markings and clothing of symbolic significance") promoting and inciting racial or religious hatred. The Village sought to apply this ordinance to the display of swastikas and military uniforms by the NSPA, a "Nazi organization" that planned to demonstrate for some 20–30 minutes in front of the Skokie Village Hall.

"Although there was some evidence that some individuals "might have difficulty restraining their reactions to the Nazi demonstration," the Village "does not rely on a fear of responsive violence to justify the ordinance, and does not even suggest that there will be any physical violence if the march is held. This confession takes the case out of the scope of *Brandenburg* and *Feiner*. [It] also eliminates any argument based on the fighting words doctrine of *Chaplinsky*, [which] applied only to words with a direct tendency to cause violence by the persons to whom, individually, the words were addressed."

The court rejected the argument that the Nazi march, with its display of swastikas and uniforms, "will create a substantive evil that it has a right to prohibit: the infliction of psychic trauma on resident holocaust survivors [some 5,000] and other Jewish residents. [The] problem with engrafting an exception on the First Amendment for such situations is that they are indistinguishable in principle from speech that 'invite[s] dispute [or] induces a condition of unrest [or] even stirs people to anger,' *Terminiello*. Yet these are among the 'high purposes' of the First Amendment. [Where,] as here, a crime is made of a silent march, attended only by symbols and not by extrinsic conduct offensive in itself, we think the words of *Street v. New York*, 394 U.S. 576 (1969), are very much on point: '[A]ny shock effect [must] be attributed to the content of the ideas expressed. [P]ublic expression of ideas may not be prohibited merely because the ideas are themselves offensive to some of their hearers.' "

Nor was the court impressed with the argument that the proposed march was "not speech, [but] rather an invasion, intensely menacing no matter how peacefully conducted" (most of Skokie's residents are Jewish): "There *need be* no captive audience, as Village residents may, if they wish, simply avoid the Village Hall for thirty minutes on a Sunday afternoon, which no doubt would be their normal course of conduct on a day when the Village Hall was not open in the regular course of business. Absent such intrusion or captivity, there is no justifiable substantial privacy interest to save [the ordinance], when it attempts, by fiat, to declare the entire Village, at all times, a privacy zone that may be sanitized from the offensiveness of Nazi ideology and symbols."

UNITED STATES V. O'BRIEN
391 U.S. 367, 88 S.Ct. 1673, 20 L.Ed.2d 672 (1968).

CHIEF JUSTICE WARREN delivered the opinion of the Court.

On the morning of March 31, 1966, David Paul O'Brien and three companions burned their Selective Service registration certificates on the steps of the South Boston Courthouse. A sizable crowd, including several [FBI agents] witnessed the event. Immediately after the burning, members of the crowd began attacking O'Brien [and he was ushered to safety by an FBI agent.] O'Brien stated to FBI agents that he had burned his registration certificate because of his beliefs, knowing that he was violating federal law.

[For this act, O'Brien was convicted in federal court.] He [told] the jury that he burned the certificate publicly to influence others to adopt his antiwar beliefs, as he put it, "so that other people would reevaluate their positions with Selective Service, with the armed forces, and reevaluate their place in the culture of today, to hopefully consider my position."

The indictment upon which he was tried charged that he "wilfully and knowingly did mutilate, destroy, and change by burning [his] Registration Certificate; in violation of [§ 462(b)(3) of the Universal Military Training and Service Act of 1948], amended by Congress in 1965 (adding the words italicized below), so that at the time O'Brien burned his certificate an offense was committed by any person, "who forges, alters, *knowingly destroys, knowingly mutilates,* or in any manner changes any such certificate * * *." (Italics supplied.)

[On appeal, the] First Circuit held the 1965 Amendment unconstitutional as a law abridging freedom of speech. At the time the Amendment was enacted, a regulation of the Selective Service System required registrants to keep their registration certificates in their "personal possession at all times." Wilful violations of regulations promulgated pursuant to the Universal Military Training and Service Act were made criminal by statute. The Court of Appeals, therefore, was of the opinion that conduct punishable under the 1965 Amendment was already punishable under the nonpossession regulation, and consequently that the Amendment served no valid purpose; further, that in light of the prior regulation, the Amendment must have been "directed at public as distinguished from private destruction." On this basis, the Court concluded that the 1965 Amendment ran afoul of the First Amendment by singling out persons engaged in protests for special treatment. * * *

When a male reaches the age of 18, he is required by the Universal Military Training and Service Act to register with a local draft board. He is assigned a Selective Service number, and within five days he is issued a registration certificate. Subsequently, and based on a questionnaire completed by the registrant, he is assigned a classification denoting his eligibility for induction, and "[a]s soon as practicable" thereafter he is issued a Notice of Classification. * * *

Both the registration and classification certificates bear notices that the registrant must notify his local board in writing of every change in address, physical condition, and occupational, marital, family, dependency, and military status, and of any other fact which might change his classification. Both also contain a notice that the registrant's Selective Service number should appear on all communications to his local board.

[The 1965] Amendment does not distinguish between public and private destruction, and it does not punish only destruction engaged in for the purpose of expressing views. A law prohibiting destruction of Selective Service certificates no more abridges free speech on its face than a motor vehicle law prohibiting the destruction of drivers' licenses, or a tax law prohibiting the destruction of books and records.

O'Brien nonetheless argues [first] that the 1965 Amendment is unconstitutional [as] applied to him because his act of burning his registration certificate was protected "symbolic speech" within the First Amendment. [He claims that] the First Amendment guarantees include all modes of "communication of ideas by conduct," and that his conduct is within this definition because he did it in "demonstration against the war and against the draft."

We cannot accept the view that an apparently limitless variety of conduct can be labeled "speech" whenever the person engaging in the conduct intends thereby to express an idea. However, even on the assumption that the alleged communicative element in O'Brien's conduct is sufficient to bring into play the First Amendment, it does not necessarily follow that the destruction of a registration certificate is constitutionally protected activity. This Court has held that when "speech" and "nonspeech" elements are combined in the same course of conduct, a sufficiently important governmental interest in regulating the nonspeech element can justify incidental limitations on First Amendment freedoms. To characterize the quality of the governmental interest which must appear, the Court has employed a variety of descriptive terms: compelling; substantial; subordinating; paramount; cogent; strong. [W]e think it clear that a government regulation is sufficiently justified if it is within the constitutional power of the government; if it furthers an important or substantial governmental interest; if the governmental interest is unrelated to the suppression of free expression; and if the incidental restriction on alleged First Amendment freedom is no greater than is essential to the furtherance of that interest. We find that the 1965 Amendment meets all of these requirements, and consequently that O'Brien can be constitutionally convicted for violating it. [Pursuant to its power to classify and conscript manpower for military service], Congress may establish a system of registration for individuals liable for training and service, and may require such individuals within reason to cooperate in the registration system. The issuance of certificates indicating the registration and eligibility classification of individuals is a legitimate and substantial administrative aid in the functioning of this system. And legislation to insure the continuing availability of issued certificates serves a legitimate and substantial purpose in the system's administration.

[O'Brien] essentially adopts the position that [Selective Service] certificates are so many pieces of paper designed to notify registrants of their registration or classification, to be retained or tossed in the wastebasket according to the convenience or taste of the registrant. Once the registrant has received notification, according to this view, there is no reason for him to retain the certificates. [However, the registration and classification certificates serve] purposes in addition to initial notification. Many of these purposes would be defeated by the certificates' destruction or mutilation. Among these are [simplifying verification of the registration and classification of suspected delinquents, evidence of availability for induction in the event of emergency, ease of communication between registrants and local boards, continually reminding registrants of the need to notify local boards of changes in status].

The many functions performed by Selective Service certificates establish [that] Congress has a legitimate and substantial interest in preventing their wanton and unrestrained destruction and assuring their continuing availability by punishing people who knowingly and wilfully destroy or mutilate them. And we are unpersuaded that the pre-existence of the nonpossession regulations in any way negates this interest.

In the absence of a question as to multiple punishment, it has never been suggested that there is anything improper in Congress providing alternative statutory avenues of prosecution to assure the effective protection of one and the same interest. Here, the pre-existing avenue of prosecution was not even statutory. Regulations may be modified or revoked from time to time by administrative discretion. Certainly, the Congress may change or supplement a regulation.

[The] gravamen of the offense defined by the statute is the deliberate rendering of certificates unavailable for the various purposes which they may serve. Whether registrants keep their certificates in their personal possession at all times, as required by the regulations, is of no particular concern under the 1965 Amendment, as long as they do not mutilate or destroy the certificates so as to render them unavailable. [The 1965 amendment] is concerned with abuses involving *any* issued Selective Service certificates, not only with the registrant's own certificates. The knowing destruction or mutilation of someone else's certificates would therefore violate the statute but not the nonpossession regulations.

We think it apparent that the continuing availability to each registrant of his Selective Service certificates substantially furthers the smooth and proper functioning of the system that Congress has established to raise armies. * * *

It is equally clear that the 1965 Amendment specifically protects this substantial governmental interest. We perceive no alternative means that would more precisely and narrowly assure the continuing availability of issued Selective Service certificates than a law which prohibits their wilful mutilation or destruction. The 1965 Amendment prohibits such conduct and does nothing more. [The] governmental interest and the scope of the 1965 Amendment are limited to preventing a harm to the smooth and efficient functioning of the Selective Service System. When O'Brien deliberately rendered unavailable his registration certificate, he wilfully frustrated this governmental interest. For this noncommunicative impact of his conduct, and for nothing else, he was convicted.* * *

O'Brien finally argues that the 1965 Amendment is unconstitutional as enacted because what he calls the "purpose" of Congress was "to suppress freedom of speech." We reject this argument because under settled principles the purpose of Congress, as O'Brien uses that term, is not a basis for declaring this legislation unconstitutional.

It is a familiar principle of constitutional law that this Court will not strike down an otherwise constitutional statute on the basis of an alleged illicit legislative motive.

[I]f we were to examine legislative purpose in the instant case, we would be obliged to consider not only [the statements of the three members of Congress who addressed themselves to the amendment, all viewing draft-card burning as a brazen display of unpatriotism] but also the more authoritative reports of the Senate and House Armed Services Committees. [B]oth reports make clear a concern with the "defiant" destruction of so-called "draft cards" and with "open" encouragement to others to destroy their cards, [but they] also indicate that this concern stemmed from an apprehension that unrestrained destruction of cards would disrupt the smooth functioning of the Selective Service System. * * *

Reversed.

JUSTICE HARLAN concurring. * * *

I wish to make explicit my understanding that [the Court's analysis] does not foreclose consideration of First Amendment claims in those rare instances when an "incidental" restriction upon expression, imposed by a regulation which furthers an "important or substantial" governmental interest and satisfies the Court's other criteria, in practice has the effect of entirely preventing a "speaker" from reaching a significant audience with whom he could not otherwise lawfully communicate. This is not such a case, since O'Brien manifestly could have conveyed his message in many ways other than by burning his draft card.

JUSTICE DOUGLAS, dissenting.

[Douglas, J., thought that "the underlying and basic problem in this case" was the constitutionality of a draft "in the absence of a declaration of war" and that the case should be put down for reargument on this question. The following Term, concurring in *Brandenburg*, he criticized *O'Brien* on the merits. After recalling that the Court had rejected O'Brien's First Amendment argument on the ground that "legislation to insure the continuing availability of issued certificates serves a legitimate and substantial purpose in the [selective service] system's administration," he commented: "But O'Brien was not prosecuted for not having his draft card available when asked for by a federal agent. He was indicted, tried, and convicted for burning the card. And this Court's affirmance [was not] consistent with the First Amendment." He observed, [in] *Brandenburg:* ["Action is often a method of expression and within the protection of the First Amendment. Suppose one tears up his own copy of the Constitution in eloquent protest to a decision of this Court. May he be indicted? Suppose one rips his own Bible to shreds to celebrate his departure from one 'faith' and his embrace of atheism. May he be indicted? * * *]

Evidence of motive. The *O'Brien* majority declines to consider evidence of actual congressional motivation, preferring an official statement of purpose or a potentially permissible motive. Does the Court's squeamishness about looking at the actual motivations of the members of Congress survive *Wallace v. Jaffree* and *Edwards v. Aguillard*, Ch. 8, Sec. 1, III? The question whether allegedly illicit governmental motive can invalidate an otherwise permissible governmental action remains actively contested but with little resolution. In *Masterpiece Cakeshop, Ltd. v. Colorado Civil Rights Commission*, 138 S.Ct. 1719 (2018), Ch. 8, Sec. 2, the Court upheld the claim of a baker who argued that applying the Colorado anti-discrimination statute against him because of his refusal, on grounds of religious belief, to create a wedding cake for a same-sex marriage was a restriction on his religious belief. In agreeing with the baker, however, the majority avoided deciding when someone such as the baker is entitled to a constitutionally-mandated exemption on free exercise grounds from a law of general application enacted and applied without reference to religion. Instead, the majority's decision was based almost exclusively on evidence from the Civil Rights Commission's hearings, evidence suggesting active hostility by some of the commissioners to the content and sincerity of the baker's religious beliefs. In so holding, the Court relied heavily on *Church of the Lukumi Babalu Aye, Inc. v. Hialeah* (1993), Ch. 8, Sec. 2, further reinforcing the view that illicit motive is especially relevant in free exercise cases. But in *Trump v. Hawaii*, Ch. 8, infra, the Court refused to treat the President's anti-Muslim statements as grounds for invalidating an otherwise constitutionally permissible immigration restriction, leaving open a range questions about when official motivation is or is not relevant. If what *O'Brien* and *Trump v. Hawaii* have in common is a reluctance to look at statements of motivation by a coordinate branch of the federal government, then *O'Brien*'s statements about congressional motivation may apply with less force to state legislation, as the cases described above may suggest. But if a willingness to look at evidence of actual motivation is a special function of freedom of religion concerns, a plausible inference from *Church of the Lukumi Babalu Aye, Wallace v. Jaffree, Edwards v. Aguillard*, and other cases, then the extent to which such evidence will be important in free speech cases remains uncertain.

TEXAS V. JOHNSON

491 U.S. 397, 109 S.Ct. 2533, 105 L.Ed.2d 342 (1989).

JUSTICE BRENNAN delivered the opinion of the Court.

[Gregory] Lee Johnson was convicted of desecrating a flag in violation of Texas law.[1]

I.   While the Republican National Convention was taking place in Dallas in 1984, respondent Johnson participated in a political demonstration dubbed the "Republican War Chest Tour." [The] demonstration ended in front of Dallas City Hall, where Johnson unfurled the American flag, doused it with kerosene, and set it on fire. While the flag burned, the protestors chanted, "America, the red, white, and blue, we spit on you." [No] one was physically injured or threatened with injury, though several witnesses testified that they had been seriously offended by the flag-burning. * * *

II.   Johnson was convicted of flag desecration for burning the flag rather than for uttering insulting words. [We] must first determine whether Johnson's burning of the flag constituted expressive conduct, permitting him to invoke the First Amendment in challenging his conviction. If his conduct was expressive, we next decide whether the State's regulation is related to the suppression of free expression. *O'Brien.* If the State's regulation is not related to expression, then the less stringent standard we announced in *O'Brien* for regulations of noncommunicative conduct controls. If it is, then we are outside of *O'Brien*'s test, and we must ask whether this interest justifies Johnson's conviction under a more demanding standard. A third possibility is that the State's asserted interest is simply not implicated on these facts, and in that event the interest drops out of the picture. * * *

In deciding whether particular conduct possesses sufficient communicative elements to bring the First Amendment into play, we have asked whether "[a]n intent to convey a particularized message was present, and [whether] the likelihood was great that the message would be understood by those who viewed it." [In] *Spence v. Washington*, 418 U.S. 405 (1974), for example, we emphasized that Spence's taping of a peace sign to his flag was "roughly simultaneous with and concededly triggered by the Cambodian incursion and the Kent State tragedy." The State of Washington had conceded [that] Spence's conduct was a form of

---

[1]   **[Ct's Note]** Tex.Penal Code Ann. § 42.09 (1989) provides in full: "§ 42.09. Desecration of Venerated Object

"(a) A person commits an offense if he intentionally or knowingly desecrates:

"(1) a public monument;

"(2) a place of worship or burial; or

"(3) a state or national flag.

"(b) For purposes of this section, 'desecrate' means deface, damage, or otherwise physically mistreat in a way that the actor knows will seriously offend one or more persons likely to observe or discover his action.

"(c) An offense under this section is a Class A misdemeanor."

communication, and we stated that "the State's concession is inevitable on this record."

III. In order to decide whether *O'Brien*'s test [applies] we must decide whether Texas has asserted an interest in support of Johnson's conviction that is unrelated to the suppression of expression.

A.   Texas claims that its interest in preventing breaches of the peace justifies Johnson's conviction for flag desecration. However, no disturbance of the peace actually occurred or threatened to occur because of Johnson's burning of the flag. [The] only evidence offered by the State at trial to show the reaction to Johnson's actions was the testimony of several persons who had been seriously offended by the flag-burning.

The State's position, therefore, amounts to a claim that an audience that takes serious offense at particular expression is necessarily likely to disturb the peace and that the expression may be prohibited on this basis. [W]e have not permitted the Government to assume that every expression of a provocative idea will incite a riot, but have instead required careful consideration of the actual circumstances surrounding such expression, asking whether the expression "is directed to inciting or producing imminent lawless action and is likely to incite or produce such action." *Brandenburg*. To accept Texas' arguments that it need only demonstrate "the potential for a breach of the peace," and that every flag-burning necessarily possesses that potential, would be to eviscerate our holding in *Brandenburg*. This we decline to do.

Nor does Johnson's expressive conduct fall within that small class of "fighting words" that are "likely to provoke the average person to retaliation, and thereby cause a breach of the peace." *Chaplinsky*. No reasonable onlooker would have regarded Johnson's generalized expression of dissatisfaction with the policies of the Federal Government as a direct personal insult or an invitation to exchange fisticuffs.

We thus conclude that the State's interest in maintaining order is not implicated on these facts. * * *

B.   The State also asserts an interest in preserving the flag as a symbol of nationhood and national unity. [The] State, apparently, is concerned that such conduct will lead people to believe either that the flag does not stand for nationhood and national unity, but instead reflects other, less positive concepts, or that the concepts reflected in the flag do not in fact exist, that is, we do not enjoy unity as a Nation. These concerns blossom only when a person's treatment of the flag communicates some message, and thus are related "to the suppression of free expression" within the meaning of *O'Brien*. We are thus outside of *O'Brien*'s test altogether.

IV.   It remains to consider whether the State's interest in preserving the flag as a symbol of nationhood and national unity justifies Johnson's conviction. [If Johnson] had burned the flag as a means of disposing of it because it was dirty or torn, he would not have been convicted of flag desecration under this Texas law: federal law designates burning as the preferred means of disposing of a flag "when it is in such condition that it is no longer a fitting emblem for display," 36 U.S.C. § 176(k), and Texas has no quarrel with this means of disposal. The Texas law is thus not aimed at protecting the physical integrity of the flag in all circumstances, but is designed instead to protect it only against impairments that would cause serious offense to others.

Whether Johnson's treatment of the flag violated Texas law thus depended on the likely communicative impact of his expressive conduct. Our decision in *Boos v. Barry*, 485 U.S. 312 (1988), tells us that this restriction on Johnson's expression is content-based. In *Boos*, we considered the constitutionality of a law prohibiting "the display of any sign within 50 feet of a foreign embassy if that sign tends to bring that foreign government into 'public odium' or 'public disrepute.' " Rejecting the argument that the law was content-neutral because it was justified by "our international law obligation to shield diplomats from speech that offends their dignity," we held that "[t]he emotive impact of speech on its audience is not a 'secondary effect' " unrelated to the content of the expression itself.

According to the principles announced in *Boos*, Johnson's political expression was restricted because of the content of the message he conveyed. We must therefore subject the State's asserted interest in preserving the special symbolic character of the flag to "the most exacting scrutiny." *Boos.* * * *

If there is a bedrock principle underlying the First Amendment, it is that the Government may not prohibit the expression of an idea simply because society finds the idea itself offensive or disagreeable. [We] have not recognized an exception to this principle even where our flag has been involved. [We] never before have held that the Government may ensure that a symbol be used to express only one view of that symbol or its referents. Indeed, in *Schacht v. United States*, 398 U.S. 58 (1970), we invalidated a federal statute permitting an actor portraying a member of one of our armed forces to " 'wear the uniform of that armed force if the portrayal does not tend to discredit that armed force.' " This proviso, we held, "which leaves Americans free to praise the war in Vietnam but can send persons like Schacht to prison for opposing it, cannot survive in a country which has the First Amendment."

We perceive no basis on which to hold that the principle underlying our decision in *Schacht* does not apply to this case. To conclude that the Government may permit designated symbols to be used to communicate only a limited set of messages would be to enter territory having no discernible or defensible boundaries. Could the Government, on this theory, prohibit the burning of state flags? Of copies of the Presidential seal? Of the Constitution? In evaluating these choices under the First Amendment, how would we decide which symbols were sufficiently special to warrant this unique status? To do so, we would be forced to consult our own political preferences, and impose them on the citizenry, in the very way that the First Amendment forbids us to do.

There is, moreover, no indication—either in the text of the Constitution or in our cases interpreting it—that a separate judicial category exists for the American flag alone. Indeed, we would not be surprised to learn that the persons who framed our Constitution and wrote the Amendment that we now construe were not known for their reverence for the Union Jack. The First Amendment does not guarantee that other concepts virtually sacred to our Nation as a whole—such as the principle that discrimination on the basis of race is odious and destructive—will go unquestioned in the marketplace of ideas. See *Brandenburg*. We decline, therefore, to create for the flag an exception to the joust of principles protected by the First Amendment.

It is not the State's ends, but its means, to which we object. It cannot be gainsaid that there is a special place reserved for the flag in this Nation, and thus we do not doubt that the Government has a legitimate interest in making efforts to "preserv[e] the national flag as an unalloyed symbol of our country." We reject the suggestion, urged at oral argument by counsel for Johnson, that the Government lacks "any state interest whatsoever" in regulating the manner in which the flag may be displayed. Congress has, for example, enacted precatory regulations describing the proper treatment of the flag, see 36 U.S.C. §§ 173–177, and we cast no doubt on the legitimacy of its interest in making such recommendations. To say that the Government has an interest in encouraging proper treatment of the flag, however, is not to say that it may criminally punish a person for burning a flag as a means of political protest. "National unity as an end which officials may foster by persuasion and example is not in question. The problem is whether under our Constitution compulsion as here employed is a permissible means for its achievement."

[W]e submit that nobody can suppose that this one gesture of an unknown man will change our Nation's attitude towards its flag. See *Abrams* (Holmes, J., dissenting). Indeed, Texas' argument that the burning of an American flag " 'is an act having a high likelihood to cause a breach of the peace,' " and its statute's implicit assumption that physical mistreatment of the flag will lead to "serious offense," tend to confirm that the flag's special role is not in danger; if it were, no one would riot or take offense because a flag had been burned.

We are tempted to say, in fact, that the flag's deservedly cherished place in our community will be strengthened, not weakened, by our holding today. Our decision is a reaffirmation of the principles of freedom and inclusiveness that the flag best reflects, and of the conviction that our toleration of criticism such as Johnson's is a sign and source of our strength. Indeed, one of the proudest images of our flag, the one immortalized in our own national anthem, is of the bombardment it survived at Fort McHenry. It is the Nation's resilience, not its rigidity, that Texas sees reflected in the flag—and it is that resilience that we reassert today.

The way to preserve the flag's special role is not to punish those who feel differently about these matters. It is to persuade them that they are wrong. [We] can imagine no more appropriate response to burning a flag than waving one's own, no better way to counter a flag-burner's message than by saluting the flag that burns, no surer means of preserving the dignity even of the flag that burned than by—as one witness here did—according its remains a respectful burial. * * *

JUSTICE KENNEDY, concurring. * * *

Our colleagues in dissent advance powerful arguments why respondent may be convicted for his expression, reminding us that among those who will be dismayed by our holding will be some who have had the singular honor of carrying the flag in battle. And I agree that the flag holds a lonely place of honor in an age when absolutes are distrusted and simple truths are burdened by unneeded apologetics.

With all respect to those views, I do not believe the Constitution gives us the right to rule as the dissenting members of the Court urge, however painful this judgment is to announce. Though symbols often are what we ourselves make of them, the flag is constant in expressing beliefs Americans share, beliefs in law and peace and that freedom which sustains the human spirit. The case here today forces recognition of the costs to which those beliefs commit us. It is poignant but fundamental that the flag protects those who hold it in contempt.

For all the record shows, this respondent was not a philosopher and perhaps did not even possess the ability to comprehend how repellent his statements must be to the Republic itself. But whether or not he could appreciate the enormity of the offense he gave, the fact remains that his acts were speech, in both the technical and the fundamental meaning of the Constitution. So I agree with the Court that he must go free.

CHIEF JUSTICE REHNQUIST, with whom JUSTICE WHITE and JUSTICE O'CONNOR join, dissenting.

In holding this Texas statute unconstitutional, the Court ignores Justice Holmes' familiar aphorism that "a page of history is worth a volume of logic." *New York Trust Co. v. Eisner*, 256 U.S. 345 (1921). * * *

The American flag [throughout] more than 200 years of our history, has come to be the visible symbol embodying our Nation. It does not represent the views of any particular political party, and it does not represent any particular political philosophy. The flag is not simply another "idea" or "point of view" competing for recognition in the marketplace of ideas. Millions and millions of Americans regard it with an almost mystical reverence regardless of what sort of social, political, or philosophical beliefs they may have. I cannot agree that the First Amendment invalidates the Act of Congress, and the laws of 48 of the 50 States, which make criminal the public burning of the flag.

More than 80 years ago in *Halter v. Nebraska* [205 U.S. 34 (1907)], this Court upheld the constitutionality of a Nebraska statute that forbade the use of representations of the American flag for advertising purposes upon articles of merchandise. The Court there said: "For that flag every true American has not simply an appreciation but a deep affection. * * * Hence, it has often occurred that insults to a flag have been the cause of war, and indignities put upon it, in the presence of those who revere it, have often been resented and sometimes punished on the spot."

Only two Terms ago, in *San Francisco Arts & Athletics, Inc. v. United States Olympic Committee*, [483 U.S. 522 (1987)], the Court held that Congress could grant exclusive use of the word "Olympic" to the United States Olympic Committee. The Court thought that this "restrictio[n] on expressive speech properly [was] characterized as incidental to the primary congressional purpose of encouraging and rewarding the USOC's activities." As the Court stated, "when a word [or symbol] acquires value 'as the result of organization and the expenditure of labor, skill, and money' by an entity, that entity constitutionally may obtain a limited property right in the word [or symbol]." Surely Congress or the States may recognize a similar interest in the flag.

[T]he public burning of the American flag by Johnson was no essential part of any exposition of ideas, and at the same time it had a tendency to incite a breach of the peace. Johnson was free to make any verbal denunciation of the flag that he wished; indeed, he was free to burn the flag in private. He could publicly burn other symbols of the Government or effigies of political leaders. He did lead a march through the streets of Dallas, and conducted a rally in front of the Dallas City Hall. He engaged in a "die-in" to protest nuclear weapons. He shouted out various slogans during the march, including: "Reagan, Mondale which will it be? Either one means World War III"; "Ronald Reagan, killer of the hour, Perfect example of U.S. power"; and "red, white and blue, we spit on you, you stand for plunder, you will go under." For none of these acts was he arrested or prosecuted. [As] with "fighting words," so with flag burning, for purposes of the First Amendment: It is "no essential part of any exposition of ideas, and [is] of such slight social value as a step to truth that any benefit that may be derived from [it] is clearly outweighed" by the public interest in avoiding a probable breach of the peace. * * *

The result of the Texas statute is obviously to deny one in Johnson's frame of mind one of many means of "symbolic speech." Far from being a case of "one picture being worth a thousand words," flag burning is the equivalent of an inarticulate grunt or roar that, it seems fair to say, is most likely to be indulged in not to express any particular idea, but to antagonize others. [The] Texas statute [left Johnson] with a full panoply of other symbols and every conceivable form of verbal expression to express his deep disapproval of national policy. Thus, in no way can it be said that Texas is punishing him because his hearers—or any other group of people—were profoundly opposed to the message that he sought to convey. Such opposition is no proper basis for restricting speech or expression under the First Amendment. It was Johnson's use of this particular symbol, and not the idea that he sought to convey by it or by his many other expressions, for which he was punished. * * *

The Court concludes its opinion with a regrettably patronizing civics lecture, presumably addressed to the Members of both Houses of Congress, the members of the 48 state legislatures that enacted prohibitions against flag burning, and the troops fighting under that flag in Vietnam who objected to its being burned: "The way to preserve the flag's special role is not to punish those who feel differently about these matters. It is to persuade them that they are wrong." The Court's role as the final expositor of the Constitution is well established, but its role as a platonic guardian admonishing those responsible to public opinion as if they were truant school children has no similar place in our system of government. * * *

Uncritical extension of constitutional protection to the burning of the flag risks the frustration of the very purpose for which organized governments are instituted. The Court decides that the American flag is just another symbol, about which not only must opinions pro and con be tolerated, but for which the most minimal public respect may not be enjoined. The government may conscript men into the Armed Forces where they must fight and perhaps die for the flag, but the government may not prohibit the public burning of the banner under which they fight. I would uphold the Texas statute as applied in this case.

JUSTICE STEVENS, dissenting. * * *

Even if flag burning could be considered just another species of symbolic speech under the logical application of the rules that the Court has developed in its interpretation of the First Amendment in other contexts, this case has an intangible dimension that makes those rules inapplicable.

A country's flag is a symbol of more than "nationhood and national unity." [T]he American flag [is] more than a proud symbol of the courage, the determination, and the gifts of nature that transformed 13 fledgling Colonies into a world power. It is a symbol of freedom, of equal opportunity, of religious tolerance, and of goodwill for other peoples who share our aspirations. The symbol carries its message to dissidents both at home and abroad who may have no interest at all in our national unity or survival.

The value of the flag as a symbol cannot be measured. Even so, I have no doubt that the interest in preserving that value for the future is both significant and legitimate. Conceivably that value will be enhanced by the Court's conclusion that our national commitment to free expression is so strong that even the United States as ultimate guarantor of that freedom is without power to prohibit the desecration of its unique symbol. But I am unpersuaded. The creation of a federal right to post bulletin boards and graffiti on the Washington Monument might enlarge the market for free expression, but at a cost I would not pay. Similarly, in my considered judgment, sanctioning the public desecration of the flag will tarnish its value—both for those who cherish the ideas for which it waves and for those who desire to don the robes of martyrdom by burning it. That tarnish is not justified by the trivial burden on free expression occasioned by requiring that an available, alternative mode of expression—including uttering words critical of the flag be employed.

It is appropriate to emphasize certain propositions that are not implicated by this case. [The] statute does not compel any conduct or any profession of respect for any idea or any symbol. [Nor] does the statute violate "the government's paramount obligation of neutrality in its regulation of protected communication." The content of respondent's message has no relevance whatsoever to the case. The concept of "desecration" does not turn on the substance of the message the actor intends to convey, but rather on whether those who view the act will take serious offense. Accordingly, one intending to convey a message of respect for the flag by burning it in a public square might nonetheless be guilty of desecration if he knows that others—perhaps simply because they misperceive the intended message—will be seriously offended. Indeed, even if the actor knows that all possible witnesses will understand that he intends to send a message of respect, he might still be guilty of desecration if he also knows that this understanding does not lessen the offense taken by some of those witnesses. The case has nothing to do with "disagreeable ideas." It involves disagreeable conduct that, in my opinion, diminishes the value of an important national asset.

[Had respondent] chosen to spray paint—or perhaps convey with a motion picture projector—his message of dissatisfaction on the facade of the Lincoln Memorial, there would be no question about the power of the Government to prohibit his means of expression. The prohibition would be supported by the legitimate interest in preserving the quality of an important national asset. Though the asset at stake in this case is intangible, given its unique value, the same interest supports a prohibition on the desecration of the American flag.

The ideas of liberty and equality have been an irresistible force in motivating leaders like Patrick Henry, Susan B. Anthony, and Abraham Lincoln, schoolteachers like Nathan Hale and Booker T. Washington, the Philippine Scouts who fought at Bataan, and the soldiers who scaled the bluff at Omaha Beach. If those ideas are worth fighting for—and our history demonstrates that they are—it cannot be true that the flag that uniquely symbolizes their power is not itself worthy of protection from unnecessary desecration.

In response to *Johnson,* Congress passed, by an overwhelming majority, the Flag Protection Act of 1989, which attached criminal penalties to the knowing mutilation, defacement, burning, maintaining on the floor or ground, or trampling upon any flag of the United States.

UNITED STATES v. EICHMAN, 496 U.S. 310 (1990), per BRENNAN, J., invalidated the statute: "Although the Flag Protection Act contains no explicit content-based limitation on the scope of prohibited conduct, it is nevertheless clear that the Government's asserted *interest* is 'related "to the suppression of free expression" and concerned with the content of such expression. The Government's interest in protecting the 'physical integrity' of a privately owned flag rests upon a perceived need to preserve the flag's status as a symbol of our Nation and certain national ideals. But the mere destruction or disfigurement of a particular physical manifestation of the symbol, without more, does not diminish or otherwise affect the symbol itself in any way. For example, the secret destruction of a flag in one's own basement would not threaten the flag's recognized meaning. Rather, the Government's desire to preserve the flag as a symbol for certain national ideals is implicated 'only when a person's treatment of the flag communicates [a] message' to others that is inconsistent with those ideals."

STEVENS, J., joined by Rehnquist, C.J., White and O'Connor, JJ., dissenting, argued that the government's "legitimate interest in protecting the symbolic value of the American flag" outweighed the free speech interest. In describing the flag's symbolic value he stated that the flag "inspires and motivates the average citizen to make personal sacrifices in order to achieve societal goals of overriding importance; at all times, it serves as a reminder of the paramount importance of pursuing the ideals that characterize our society. * * * [T]he communicative value of a well-placed bomb in the Capital does not entitle it to the protection of the First Amendment. Burning a flag is not, of course, equivalent to burning a public building. Assuming that the protester is burning his own flag, it causes no physical harm to other persons or to their property. The impact is purely symbolic, and it is apparent that some thoughtful persons believe that impact far from depreciating the value of the symbol, will actually enhance its meaning. I most respectfully disagree."

———————

Community for Creative Non-Violence (CCNV) sought to conduct a wintertime demonstration near the White House in Lafayette Park and the Mall to dramatize the plight of the homeless. The National Park Service authorized the erection of two symbolic tent cities for purposes of the demonstration, but denied CCNV's request that demonstrators be permitted to sleep in the tents. National Park Service regulations permit camping (the "use of park land for living accommodation purposes such as sleeping activities") in National Parks only in campgrounds designated for that purpose.

CLARK v. COMMUNITY FOR CREATIVE NON-VIOLENCE, 468 U.S. 288 (1984), per WHITE, J., rejected CCNV's claim that the regulations could not be constitutionally applied against its demonstration: "We need not differ with the view of the Court of Appeals that overnight sleeping in connection with the demonstration is expressive conduct protected to some extent by the First Amendment.[5] We assume for present purposes, but do not decide, that such is the case, cf. *O'Brien,* but this assumption only begins the inquiry. Expression, whether oral or written or symbolized by conduct, is subject to reasonable time, place, or manner restrictions. We have often noted that restrictions of this kind are valid

———————

[5]   [Ct's Note] We reject the suggestion of the plurality below, however, that the burden on the demonstrators is limited to "the advancement of a plausible contention" that their conduct is expressive. Although it is common to place the burden upon the Government to justify impingements on First Amendment interests, it is the obligation of the person desiring to engage in assertedly expressive conduct to demonstrate that the First Amendment even applies. To hold otherwise would be to create a rule that all conduct is presumptively expressive.

provided that they are justified without reference to the content of the regulated speech, that they are narrowly tailored to serve a significant governmental interest, and that they leave open ample alternative channels for communication of the information.

"It is also true that a message may be delivered by conduct that is intended to be communicative and that, in context, would reasonably be understood by the viewer to be communicative. Symbolic expression of this kind may be forbidden or regulated if the conduct itself may constitutionally be regulated, if the regulation is narrowly drawn to further a substantial governmental interest, and if the interest is unrelated to the suppression of free speech. *O'Brien.*

"[That] sleeping, like the symbolic tents themselves, may be expressive and part of the message delivered by the demonstration does not make the ban any less a limitation on the manner of demonstrating, for reasonable time, place, or manner regulations normally have the purpose and direct effect of limiting expression but are nevertheless valid. Neither does the fact that sleeping, arguendo, may be expressive conduct, rather than oral or written expression, render the sleeping prohibition any less a time, place, or manner regulation. To the contrary, the Park Service neither attempts to ban sleeping generally nor to ban it everywhere in the parks. It has established areas for camping and forbids it elsewhere, including Lafayette Park and the Mall. Considered as such, we have very little trouble concluding that the Park Service may prohibit overnight sleeping in the parks involved here.

"The requirement that the regulation be content-neutral is clearly satisfied. The courts below accepted that view, and it is not disputed here that the prohibition on camping, and on sleeping specifically, is content-neutral and is not being applied because of disagreement with the message presented. Neither was the regulation faulted, nor could it be, on the ground that without overnight sleeping the plight of the homeless could not be communicated in other ways. The regulation otherwise left the demonstration intact, with its symbolic city, signs, and the presence of those who were willing to take their turns in a day-and-night vigil. Respondents do not suggest that there was, or is, any barrier to delivering to the media, or to the public by other means, the intended message concerning the plight of the homeless.

"It is also apparent to us that the regulation narrowly focuses on the Government's substantial interest in maintaining the parks in the heart of our Capital in an attractive and intact condition, readily available to the millions of people who wish to see and enjoy them by their presence. To permit camping—using these areas as living accommodations—would be totally inimical to these purposes, as would be readily understood by those who have frequented the National Parks across the country and observed the unfortunate consequences of the activities of those who refuse to confine their camping to designated areas.

"It is urged by [CCNV] that if the symbolic city of tents was to be permitted and if the demonstrators did not intend to cook, dig, or engage in aspects of camping other than sleeping, the incremental benefit to the parks could not justify the ban on sleeping, which was here an expressive activity said to enhance the message concerning the plight of the poor and homeless. We cannot agree. In the first place, we seriously doubt that the First Amendment requires the Park Service to permit a demonstration in Lafayette Park and the Mall involving a 24-hour vigil and the erection of tents to accommodate 150 people. Furthermore, although we have assumed for present purposes that the sleeping banned in this case would have an expressive element, it is evident that its major value to this demonstration would be facilitative. Without a permit to sleep, it would be difficult to get the poor and homeless to participate or to be present at all.

"Beyond this, however, it is evident from our cases that the validity of this regulation need not be judged solely by reference to the demonstration at hand. Absent the prohibition on sleeping, there would be other groups who would demand permission to deliver an asserted message by camping in Lafayette Park. Some of them would surely have as credible a claim in this regard as does CCNV, and the denial of permits to still others would present difficult problems for the Park Service. With the prohibition, however, as is evident in the case before us, at least some around-the-clock demonstrations lasting for days on end will not materialize, others will be limited in size and duration, and the purposes of the regulation will thus be materially served. Perhaps these purposes would be more effectively and not so clumsily achieved by preventing tents and 24-hour vigils entirely in the core areas. But the Park Service's decision to permit nonsleeping demonstrations does not, in our view, impugn the camping prohibition as a valuable, but perhaps imperfect, protection to the parks. If the Government has a legitimate interest in ensuring that the National Parks are adequately protected, which we think it has, and if the parks would be more exposed to harm without the sleeping prohibition than with it, the ban is safe from invalidation under the First Amendment as a reasonable regulation of the manner in which a demonstration may be carried out. * * *

"[The] foregoing analysis demonstrates that the Park Service regulation is sustainable under the four-factor standard of *O'Brien,* for validating a regulation of expressive conduct, which, in the last analysis is little, if any, different from the standard applied to time, place, or manner restrictions. No one contends that aside from its impact on speech a rule against camping or overnight sleeping in public parks is beyond the constitutional power of the Government to enforce. And for the reasons we have discussed above, there is a substantial Government interest in conserving park property, an interest that is plainly served by, and requires for its implementation, measures such as the proscription of sleeping that are designed to limit the wear and tear on park properties. That interest is unrelated to suppression of expression.

"We are unmoved by the Court of Appeals' view that the challenged regulation is unnecessary, and hence invalid, because there are less speech-restrictive alternatives that could have satisfied the Government interest in preserving park lands. [The] Court of Appeals' suggestions that the Park Service minimize the possible injury by reducing the size, duration, or frequency of demonstrations would still curtail the total allowable expression in which demonstrators could engage, whether by sleeping or otherwise, and these suggestions represent no more than a disagreement with the Park Service over how much protection the core parks require or how an acceptable level of preservation is to be attained. We do not believe, however, that either *United States v. O'Brien* or the time, place, or manner decisions assign to the judiciary the authority to replace the Park Service as the manager of the Nation's parks or endow the judiciary with the competence to judge how much protection of park lands is wise and how that level of conservation is to be [attained.]"

BURGER, C.J., joined the Court's opinion: "[CCNV's] attempt at camping in the park is a form of 'picketing'; it is conduct, not speech. [It] trivializes the First Amendment to seek to use it as a shield in the manner asserted here."

MARSHALL, J., joined by Brennan, J., dissented: "The majority assumes, without deciding, that the respondents' conduct is entitled to constitutional protection. The problem with this assumption is that the Court thereby avoids examining closely the reality of respondents' planned expression. The majority's approach denatures respondents' asserted right and thus makes all too easy identification of a Government interest sufficient to warrant its abridgment.

"[Missing] from the majority's description is any inkling that Lafayette Park and the Mall have served as the sites for some of the most rousing political demonstrations in the Nation's history. [The] primary purpose for making *sleep* an integral part of the demonstration was 'to re-enact the central reality of homelessness' and to impress upon public consciousness, in as dramatic a way as possible, that homelessness is a widespread problem, often ignored, that confronts its victims with life-threatening deprivations. As one of the homeless men seeking to demonstrate explained: 'Sleeping in Lafayette Park or on the Mall, for me, is to show people that conditions are so poor for the homeless and poor in this city that we would actually sleep *outside* in the winter to get the point across.' * * * Here respondents clearly intended to protest the reality of homelessness by sleeping outdoors in the winter in the near vicinity of the magisterial residence of the President of the United States. In addition to accentuating the political character of their protest by their choice of location and mode of communication, respondents also intended to underline the meaning of their protest by giving their demonstration satirical names. Respondents planned to name the demonstration on the Mall 'Congressional Village,' and the demonstration in Lafayette Park, 'Reaganville II.' * * *

"Although sleep in the context of this case is symbolic speech protected by the First Amendment, it is nonetheless subject to reasonable time, place, and manner restrictions. I agree with the standard enunciated by the majority. I conclude, however, that the regulations at issue in this case, as applied to respondents, fail to satisfy this [standard].

"[T]here are no substantial Government interests advanced by the Government's regulations as applied to respondents. All that the Court's decision advances are the prerogatives of a bureaucracy that over the years has shown an implacable hostility toward citizens' exercise of First Amendment [rights].

"The disposition of this case impels me to make two additional observations. First, in this case, as in some others involving time, place, and manner restrictions, the Court has dramatically lowered its scrutiny of governmental regulations once it has determined that such regulations are content-neutral. The result has been the creation of a two-tiered approach to First Amendment cases: while regulations that turn on the content of the expression are subjected to a strict form of judicial review, regulations that are aimed at matters other than expression receive only a minimal level of scrutiny. [The] Court has seemingly overlooked the fact that content-neutral restrictions are also capable of unnecessarily restricting protected expressive activity. [The] Court [has] transformed the ban against content distinctions from a floor that offers all persons at least equal liberty under the First Amendment into a ceiling that restricts persons to the protection of First Amendment equality—but nothing more.[14] The consistent imposition of silence upon all may fulfill the dictates of an evenhanded content-neutrality. But it offends our 'profound national commitment to the principle that debate on public issues should be uninhibited, robust, and wide-open'. *New York Times v. Sullivan.*

"Second, the disposition of this case reveals a mistaken assumption regarding the motives and behavior of Government officials who create and administer content-neutral regulations. The Court's salutary skepticism of governmental decisionmaking in First Amendment matters suddenly dissipates once it determines that a restriction is not content-based. The Court evidently assumes that the balance struck by officials is deserving of deference so long as it does not appear to be tainted by content discrimination. What the Court fails to recognize is that public officials have strong incentives to overregulate even in the absence of an intent to censor particular views. This incentive stems from the fact that of the two groups whose interests officials must accommodate—on the one hand, the interests of the general public and, on the other, the interests of those who seek to use a particular forum for First Amendment activity—the political power of the former is likely to be far greater than that of the latter."

————

New York Public Health law authorizes the forced closure of a building for one year if it has been used for the purpose of "lewdness, assignation or prostitution." A civil complaint alleged that prostitution solicitation and sexual activities by patrons were occurring at an adult bookstore within observation of the proprietor.

---

[14]   **[Ct's Note]** Furthermore, [a] content-neutral regulation that restricts an inexpensive mode of communication will fall most heavily upon relatively poor speakers and to points of view that such speakers typically espouse. This sort of latent inequality is very much in evidence in this case, for respondents lack the financial means necessary to buy access to more conventional modes of persuasion. * * *

Accordingly, the complaint called for the closure of the building for one year. There was no claim that any books in the store were obscene. The New York Court of Appeals held that the closure remedy violated the First Amendment because it was broader than necessary to achieve the restriction against illicit sexual activities. It reasoned that an injunction against the alleged sexual conduct could further the state interest without infringing on First Amendment values.

ARCARA v. CLOUD BOOKS, INC., 478 U.S. 697 (1986), per BURGER, C.J., reversed, holding that the closure remedy did not require any First Amendment scrutiny: "This Court has applied First Amendment scrutiny to a statute regulating conduct which has the incidental effect of burdening the expression of a particular political opinion. *O'Brien.* * * *

"We have also applied First Amendment scrutiny to some statutes which, although directed at activity with no expressive component, impose a disproportionate burden upon those engaged in protected First Amendment activities. In *Minneapolis Star & Tribune v. Minnesota Commissioner of Revenue,* 460 U.S. 575 (1983), we struck down a tax imposed on the sale of large quantities of newsprint and ink because the tax had the effect of singling out newspapers to shoulder its burden. [Even] while striking down the tax in *Minneapolis Star,* we emphasized: 'Clearly, the First Amendment does not prohibit all regulation of the press. It is beyond dispute that the States and the Federal Government can subject newspapers to generally applicable economic regulations without creating constitutional problems.'

"The New York Court of Appeals held that the *O'Brien* test for permissible governmental regulation was applicable to this case because the closure order sought by petitioner would also impose an incidental burden upon respondents' bookselling activities. [But] unlike the symbolic draft card burning in *O'Brien,* the sexual activity carried on in this case manifests absolutely no element of protected expression. In *Paris Adult Theatre,* we underscored the fallacy of seeking to use the First Amendment as a cloak for obviously unlawful public sexual conduct by the diaphanous device of attributing protected expressive attributes to that conduct. First Amendment values may not be invoked by merely linking the words 'sex' and 'books.'

"Nor does the distinction drawn by the New York Public Health Law inevitably single out bookstores or others engaged in First Amendment protected activities for the imposition of its burden, as did the tax struck down in *Minneapolis Star.* [If] the city imposed closure penalties for demonstrated Fire Code violations or health hazards from inadequate sewage treatment, the First Amendment would not aid the owner of premises who had knowingly allowed such violations to persist. * * *

"It is true that the closure order in this case would require respondents to move their bookselling business to another location. Yet we have not traditionally subjected every criminal and civil sanction imposed through legal process to 'least restrictive means' scrutiny simply because each particular remedy will have some effect on the First Amendment activities of those subject to sanction."

O'CONNOR, J., joined by Stevens, J., concurred: "I agree that the Court of Appeals erred in applying a First Amendment standard of review where, as here, the government is regulating neither speech nor an incidental, non-expressive effect of speech. Any other conclusion would lead to the absurd result that any government action that had some conceivable speech-inhibiting consequences, such as the arrest of a newscaster for a traffic violation, would require analysis under the First Amendment."

BLACKMUN, J., joined by Brennan and Marshall, JJ., dissented: "Until today, this Court has never suggested that a State may suppress speech as much as it likes, without justification, so long as it does so through generally applicable regulations that have 'nothing to do with any expressive conduct.' * * *

"At some point, of course, the impact of state regulation on First Amendment rights become so attenuated that it is easily outweighed by the state interest. But when a State directly and substantially impairs First Amendment activities, such as by shutting down a bookstore, I believe that the State must show, at a minimum, that it has chosen the least restrictive means of pursuing its legitimate objectives. The closure of a bookstore can no more be compared to a traffic arrest of a reporter than the closure of a church could be compared to the traffic arrest of its clergyman.

"A State has a legitimate interest in forbidding sexual acts committed in public, including a bookstore. An obvious method of eliminating such acts is to arrest the patron committing them. But the statute in issue does not provide for that. Instead, it imposes absolute liability on the bookstore simply because the activity occurs on the premises. And the penalty—a mandatory 1-year closure—imposes an unnecessary burden on speech. Of course 'linking the words "sex" and "books" is not enough to extend First Amendment protection to illegal sexual activity, but neither should it suffice to remove First Amendment protection from books situated near the site of such activity. The State's purpose in stopping public lewdness cannot justify such a substantial infringement of First Amendment rights. * * *

"Petitioner has not demonstrated that a less restrictive remedy would be inadequate to abate the nuisance. The Court improperly attempts to shift to the bookseller the responsibility for finding an alternative site. But surely the Court would not uphold a city ordinance banning all public debate on the theory that the residents could move somewhere else."

Generally applicable laws. A newspaper published the name of a confidential source who it believed had misled it for political reasons. The source sued for breach of contract and prevailed in the Minnesota Supreme Court.

COHEN v. COWLES MEDIA CO., 501 U.S. 663 (1991), per White, J., affirmed, dismissing the First Amendment claim with the observation that "generally applicable laws do not offend the First Amendment simply because their enforcement against the press has incidental effects on its ability to gather and report the news."

REED V. GILBERT
576 U.S. 155, 135 S.Ct. 2218, 192 L.Ed.2d 236 (2015).

JUSTICE THOMAS delivered the opinion of the Court.

The town of Gilbert, Arizona (or Town), has adopted a comprehensive code governing the manner in which people may display outdoor signs. The Sign Code identifies various categories of signs based on the type of information they convey, then subjects each category to different restrictions. One of the categories is "Temporary Directional Signs Relating to a Qualifying Event," loosely defined as signs directing the public to a meeting of a nonprofit group. The Code imposes more stringent restrictions on these signs than it does on signs conveying other messages. We hold that these provisions are content-based regulations of speech that cannot survive strict scrutiny.

I.A. The Sign Code prohibits the display of outdoor signs anywhere within the Town without a permit, but it then exempts 23 categories of signs from that requirement. These exemptions include everything from bazaar signs to flying banners. Three categories of exempt signs are particularly relevant here.

The first is "Ideological Sign[s]." This category includes any "sign communicating a message or ideas for noncommercial purposes that is not a Construction Sign, Directional Sign, Temporary Directional Sign Relating to a Qualifying Event, Political Sign, Garage Sale Sign, or a sign owned or required by a governmental agency." Of the three categories discussed here, the Code treats ideological signs most favorably, allowing them to be up to 20 square feet in area and to be placed in all "zoning districts" without time limits.

The second category is "Political Sign[s]." This includes any "temporary sign designed to influence the outcome of an election called by a public body." The Code treats these signs less favorably than ideological signs. The Code allows the placement of political signs up to 16 square feet on residential property and up to 32 square feet on nonresidential property, undeveloped municipal property, and "rights-of-way." These signs may be displayed up to 60 days before a primary election and up to 15 days following a general election.

The third category is "Temporary Directional Signs Relating to a Qualifying Event." This includes any "Temporary Sign intended to direct pedestrians, motorists, and other passersby to a 'qualifying event.'" A "qualifying event" is defined as any "assembly, gathering, activity, or meeting sponsored, arranged, or promoted by a religious, charitable, community service, educational, or other similar non-profit organization." The Code treats temporary directional signs even less favorably than political signs. Temporary directional signs may be no larger than six square feet. They may be placed on private property or on a public right-of-way, but no more than four signs may be placed on a single property at any time. And, they may be displayed no more than 12 hours before the "qualifying event" and no more than 1 hour afterward.

B.   Petitioners Good News Community Church and its pastor [wish] to advertise the time and location of their Sunday church services. The Church is a small, cash-strapped entity that owns no building, so it holds its services at elementary schools or other locations in or near the Town. In order to inform the public about its services, which are held in a variety of different locations, the Church began placing 15 to 20 temporary signs around the Town, frequently in the public right-of-way abutting the street. The signs typically displayed the Church's name, along with the time and location of the upcoming service. Church members would post the signs early in the day on Saturday and then remove them around midday on Sunday. The display of these signs requires little money and manpower, and thus has proved to be an economical and effective way for the Church to let the community know where its services are being held each week.

This practice caught the attention of the Town's Sign Code compliance manager, who twice cited the Church for violating the Code. The first citation noted that the Church exceeded the time limits for displaying its temporary directional signs. The second citation referred to the same problem, along with the Church's failure to include the date of the event on the signs. [Pastor] Reed contacted the Sign Code Compliance Department in an attempt to reach an accommodation. His efforts proved unsuccessful. Shortly thereafter, petitioners filed a complaint in the United States District Court for the District of Arizona, arguing that the Sign Code abridged their freedom of speech. [The] District Court denied the petitioners' motion for a preliminary injunction. The Court of Appeals for the Ninth Circuit affirmed, holding that the Sign Code's provision regulating temporary directional signs did not regulate speech on the basis of content. [It] then remanded for the District Court to determine in the first instance whether the Sign Code's distinctions among temporary directional signs, political signs, and ideological signs nevertheless constituted a content-based regulation of speech. On remand, the District Court granted summary judgment in favor of the Town. The Court of Appeals again affirmed, holding that the Code's sign categories were content neutral. We granted certiorari, and now reverse.

II.A.   Under [the Free Speech Clause], a government, including a municipal government vested with state authority, "has no power to restrict expression because of its message, its ideas, its subject matter, or its content." [Mosley] Content-based laws—those that target speech based on its communicative content—are presumptively unconstitutional and may be justified only if the government proves that they are narrowly tailored to serve compelling state interests. [R.A.V.]

Government regulation of speech is content based if a law applies to particular speech because of the topic discussed or the idea or message expressed. This commonsense meaning of the phrase "content based" requires a court to consider whether a regulation of speech "on its face" draws distinctions based on the message a speaker conveys. Some facial distinctions based on a message are obvious, defining regulated speech by particular subject matter, and others are more subtle, defining regulated speech by its function or purpose. Both are distinctions drawn based on the message a speaker conveys, and, therefore, are subject to strict scrutiny.

Our precedents have also recognized a separate and additional category of laws that, though facially content neutral, will be considered content-based regulations of speech: laws that cannot be " 'justified without reference to the content of the regulated speech,' " or that were adopted by the government "because of disagreement with the message [the speech] conveys." Those laws, like those that are content based on their face, must also satisfy strict scrutiny.

B.   The Town's Sign Code is content based on its face. It defines "Temporary Directional Signs" on the basis of whether a sign conveys the message of directing the public to church or some other "qualifying event." It defines "Political Signs" on the basis of whether a sign's message is "designed to influence the outcome of an election." And it defines "Ideological Signs" on the basis of whether a sign "communicat[es] a message or ideas" that do not fit within the Code's other categories. It then subjects each of these categories to different restrictions.

The restrictions in the Sign Code that apply to any given sign thus depend entirely on the communicative content of the sign. If a sign informs its reader of the time and place a book club will discuss John Locke's Two Treatises of Government, that sign will be treated differently from a sign expressing the view that one should vote for one of Locke's followers in an upcoming election, and both signs will be treated differently from a sign expressing an ideological view rooted in Locke's theory of government. More to the point, the Church's signs inviting people to attend its worship services are treated differently from signs conveying other types of ideas. On its face, the Sign Code is a content-based regulation of speech. We thus have no need to consider the government's justifications or purposes for enacting the Code to determine whether it is subject to strict scrutiny.

C.   In reaching the contrary conclusion, the Court of Appeals offered several theories to explain why the Town's Sign Code should be deemed content neutral. None is persuasive.

1.   The Court of Appeals first determined that the Sign Code was content neutral because the Town "did not adopt its regulation of speech [based on] disagree[ment] with the message conveyed," and its justifications for regulating temporary directional signs were "unrelated to the content of the sign." In its brief to this Court, the United States similarly contends that a sign regulation is content neutral—even if it expressly draws distinctions based on the sign's communicative content—if those distinctions can be " 'justified without reference to the content of

the regulated speech.' But this analysis skips the crucial first step in the content-neutrality analysis: determining whether the law is content neutral on its face. A law that is content based on its face is subject to strict scrutiny regardless of the government's benign motive, content-neutral justification, or lack of "animus toward the ideas contained" in the regulated speech. We have thus made clear that " '[i]llicit legislative intent is not the sine qua non of a violation of the First Amendment,' " and a party opposing the government "need adduce 'no evidence of an improper censorial motive.' " Although "a content-based purpose may be sufficient in certain circumstances to show that a regulation is content based, it is not necessary. In other words, an innocuous justification cannot transform a facially content-based law into one that is content neutral.

That is why we have repeatedly considered whether a law is content neutral on its face *before* turning to the law's justification or purpose. Because strict scrutiny applies either when a law is content based on its face or when the purpose and justification for the law are content based, a court must evaluate each question before it concludes that the law is content neutral and thus subject to a lower level of scrutiny. [Innocent] motives do not eliminate the danger of censorship presented by a facially content-based statute, as future government officials may one day wield such statutes to suppress disfavored speech. That is why the First Amendment expressly targets the operation of the laws—*i.e.,* the "abridg[ement] of speech"—rather than merely the motives of those who enacted them. [One] could easily imagine a Sign Code compliance manager who disliked the Church's substantive teachings deploying the Sign Code to make it more difficult for the Church to inform the public of the location of its services. Accordingly, we have repeatedly "rejected the argument that 'discriminatory . . . treatment is suspect under the First Amendment only when the legislature intends to suppress certain ideas.' " We do so again today.

2. The Court of Appeals next reasoned that the Sign Code was content neutral because it "does not mention any idea or viewpoint, let alone single one out for differential treatment." It reasoned that, for the purpose of the Code provisions, "[i]t makes no difference which candidate is supported, who sponsors the event, or what ideological perspective is asserted." The Town seizes on this reasoning, insisting that "content based" is a term of art that "should be applied flexibly" with the goal of protecting "viewpoints and ideas from government censorship or favoritism." In the Town's view, a sign regulation that "does not censor or favor particular viewpoints or ideas" cannot be content based. The Sign Code allegedly passes this test because its treatment of temporary directional signs does not raise any concerns that the government is "endorsing or suppressing 'ideas or viewpoints,' " and the provisions for political signs and ideological signs "are neutral as to particular ideas or viewpoints" within those categories.

This analysis conflates two distinct but related limitations that the First Amendment places on government regulation of speech. Government discrimination among viewpoints—or the regulation of speech based on "the specific motivating ideology or the opinion or perspective of the speaker"—is a "more blatant" and "egregious form of content discrimination." But it is well established that "[t]he First Amendment's hostility to content-based regulation extends not only to restrictions on particular viewpoints, but also to prohibition of public discussion of an entire topic."

Thus, a speech regulation targeted at specific subject matter is content based even if it does not discriminate among viewpoints within that subject matter. For example, a law banning the use of sound trucks for political speech—and only political speech—would be a content-based regulation, even if it imposed no limits on the political viewpoints that could be expressed. The Town's Sign Code likewise singles out specific subject matter for differential treatment, even if it does not target viewpoints within that subject matter. Ideological messages are given more favorable treatment than messages concerning a political candidate, which are themselves given more favorable treatment than messages announcing an assembly of like-minded individuals. That is a paradigmatic example of content-based discrimination.

3.   Finally, the Court of Appeals characterized the Sign Code's distinctions as turning on " 'the content-neutral elements of who is speaking through the sign and whether and when an event is occurring.' " That analysis is mistaken on both factual and legal grounds.

To start, the Sign Code's distinctions are not speaker based. The restrictions for political, ideological, and temporary event signs apply equally no matter who sponsors them. If a local business, for example, sought to put up signs advertising the Church's meetings, those signs would be subject to the same limitations as such signs placed by the Church. And if Reed had decided to display signs in support of a particular candidate, he could have made those signs far larger—and kept them up for far longer—than signs inviting people to attend his church services. If the Code's distinctions were truly speaker based, both types of signs would receive the same treatment.

In any case, the fact that a distinction is speaker based does not, as the Court of Appeals seemed to believe, automatically render the distinction content neutral. Because "[s]peech restrictions based on the identity of the speaker are all too often simply a means to control content," [Citizens United, infra] we have insisted that "laws favoring some speakers over others demand strict scrutiny when the legislature's speaker preference reflects a content preference." Thus, a law limiting the content of newspapers, but only newspapers, could not evade strict scrutiny simply because it could be characterized as speaker based. Likewise, a content-based law that restricted the political speech of all corporations would not become content neutral just because it singled out corporations as a class of speakers. Characterizing a distinction as speaker based is only the beginning—not the end—of the inquiry.

[As] with speaker-based laws, the fact that a distinction is event based does not render it content neutral. The Court of Appeals cited no precedent from this Court supporting its novel theory of an exception from the content-neutrality requirement for event-based laws. As we have explained, a speech regulation is content based if the law applies to particular speech because of the topic discussed or the idea or message expressed. A regulation that targets a sign because it conveys an idea about a specific event is no less content based than a regulation that targets a sign because it conveys some other idea. Here, the Code singles out signs bearing a particular message: the time and location of a specific event. This type of ordinance may seem like a perfectly rational way to regulate signs, but a clear and firm rule governing content neutrality is an essential means of protecting the freedom of speech, even if laws that might seem "entirely reasonable" will sometimes be "struck down because of their content-based nature."

III. Because the Town's Sign Code imposes content-based restrictions on speech, those provisions can stand only if they survive strict scrutiny. [Thus,] it is the Town's burden to demonstrate that the Code's differentiation between temporary directional signs and other types of signs, such as political signs and ideological signs, furthers a compelling governmental interest and is narrowly tailored to that end.

The Town cannot do so. It has offered only two governmental interests in support of the distinctions the Sign Code draws: preserving the Town's aesthetic appeal and traffic safety. Assuming for the sake of argument that those are compelling governmental interests, the Code's distinctions fail as hopelessly underinclusive.

Starting with the preservation of aesthetics, temporary directional signs are "no greater an eyesore," than ideological or political ones. Yet the Code allows unlimited proliferation of larger ideological signs while strictly limiting the number, size, and duration of smaller directional ones. The Town cannot claim that placing strict limits on temporary directional signs is necessary to beautify the Town while at the same time allowing unlimited numbers of other types of signs that create the same problem.

The Town similarly has not shown that limiting temporary directional signs is necessary to eliminate threats to traffic safety, but that limiting other types of signs is not. The Town has offered no reason to believe that directional signs pose a greater threat to safety than do ideological or political signs. If anything, a sharply worded ideological sign seems more likely to distract a driver than a sign directing the public to a nearby church meeting.

In light of this underinclusiveness, the Town has not met its burden to prove that its Sign Code is narrowly tailored to further a compelling government interest. Because a " 'law cannot be regarded as protecting an interest of the highest order, and thus as justifying a restriction on truthful speech, when it leaves appreciable damage to that supposedly vital interest unprohibited,' " the Sign Code fails strict scrutiny.

IV. Our decision today will not prevent governments from enacting effective sign laws. The Town asserts that an " 'absolutist' " content-neutrality rule would render "virtually all distinctions in sign laws . . . subject to strict scrutiny," but that is not the case. Not "all distinctions" are subject to strict scrutiny, only *content-based* ones are. Laws that are *content neutral* are instead subject to lesser scrutiny.

The Town has ample content-neutral options available to resolve problems with safety and aesthetics. For example, its current Code regulates many aspects of signs that have nothing to do with a sign's message: size, building materials, lighting, moving parts, and portability. And on public property, the Town may go a long way toward entirely forbidding the posting of signs, so long as it does so in an evenhanded, content-neutral manner. * * * We acknowledge that a city might reasonably view the general regulation of signs as necessary because signs "take up space and may obstruct views, distract motorists, displace alternative uses for land, and pose other problems that legitimately call for regulation. At the same time, the presence of certain signs may be essential, both for vehicles and pedestrians, to guide traffic or to identify hazards and ensure safety. A sign ordinance narrowly tailored to the challenges of protecting the safety of pedestrians, drivers, and passengers—such as warning signs marking hazards on private property, signs directing traffic, or street numbers associated with private houses—well might survive strict scrutiny. The signs at issue in this case, including political and ideological signs and signs for events, are far removed from those purposes. As discussed above, they are facially content based and are neither justified by traditional safety concerns nor narrowly tailored.

We reverse the judgment of the Court of Appeals and remand the case for proceedings consistent with this opinion.

JUSTICE ALITO, with whom JUSTICE KENNEDY and JUSTICE SOTOMAYOR join, concurring.

I join the opinion of the Court but add a few words of further explanation.

As the Court holds, what we have termed "content-based" laws must satisfy strict scrutiny. Content-based laws merit this protection because they present, albeit sometimes in a subtler form, the same dangers as laws that regulate speech based on viewpoint. Limiting speech based on its "topic" or "subject" favors those who do not want to disturb the status quo. Such regulations may interfere with democratic self-government and the search for truth. * * *

JUSTICE BREYER, concurring in the judgment.

I join JUSTICE KAGAN's separate opinion.

[Content] discrimination, while helping courts to identify unconstitutional suppression of expression, cannot and should not *always* trigger strict scrutiny. To say that it is not an automatic "strict scrutiny" trigger is not to argue against that concept's use. I readily concede, for example, that content discrimination, as a conceptual tool, can sometimes reveal weaknesses in the government's rationale for a rule that limits speech. If, for example, a city looks to litter prevention as the rationale for a prohibition against placing newsracks dispensing free advertisements on public property, why does it exempt other newsracks causing similar litter? I also concede that, whenever government disfavors one kind of speech, it places that speech at a disadvantage, potentially interfering with the free marketplace of ideas and with an individual's ability to express thoughts and ideas that can help that individual determine the kind of society in which he wishes to live, help shape that society, and help define his place within it.

Nonetheless, in these latter instances to use the presence of content discrimination automatically to trigger strict scrutiny and thereby call into play a strong presumption against constitutionality goes too far. That is because virtually all government activities involve speech, many of which involve the regulation of speech. Regulatory programs almost always require content discrimination. And to hold that such content discrimination triggers strict scrutiny is to write a recipe for judicial management of ordinary government regulatory activity.

Consider a few examples of speech regulated by government that inevitably involve content discrimination, but where a strong presumption against constitutionality has no place. Consider governmental regulation of securities, (e.g., requirements for content that must be included in a registration statement); of energy conservation labeling-practices (requirements for content that must be included on labels of certain consumer electronics); of prescription drugs, (requiring a prescription drug label to bear the symbol "Rx only"); of doctor-patient confidentiality, (requiring confidentiality of certain medical records, but allowing a physician to disclose that the patient has HIV to the patient's spouse or sexual partner); of income tax statements, (requiring taxpayers to furnish information about foreign gifts received if the aggregate amount exceeds $10,000); of commercial airplane briefings, (requiring pilots to ensure that each passenger has been briefed on flight procedures, such as seatbelt fastening); of signs at petting zoos, e.g., N.Y. Gen. Bus. Law Ann. § 399–ff(3) (West Cum. Supp. 2015) (requiring petting zoos to post a sign at every exit " 'strongly recommend[ing] that persons wash their hands upon exiting the petting zoo area' "); and so on.

[I] recognize that the Court could escape the problem by watering down the force of the presumption against constitutionality that "strict scrutiny" normally carries with it. But, in my view, doing so will weaken the First Amendment's protection in instances where "strict scrutiny" should apply in full force.

The better approach is to generally treat content discrimination as a strong reason weighing against the constitutionality of a rule where a traditional public forum, or where viewpoint discrimination, is threatened, but elsewhere treat it as a rule of thumb, finding it a helpful, but not determinative legal tool, in an appropriate case, to determine the strength of a justification. I would use content discrimination as a supplement to a more basic analysis, which, tracking most of our First Amendment cases, asks whether the regulation at issue works harm to First Amendment interests that is disproportionate in light of the relevant regulatory objectives. Answering this question requires examining the seriousness of the harm to speech, the importance of the countervailing objectives, the extent to which the law will achieve those objectives, and whether there are other, less restrictive ways of doing so. Admittedly, this approach does not have the simplicity of a mechanical use of categories. But it does permit the government to regulate speech in numerous instances where the voters have authorized the government to regulate and where courts should hesitate to substitute judicial judgment for that of administrators. * * *

JUSTICE KAGAN, with whom JUSTICE GINSBURG and JUSTICE BREYER join, concurring in the judgment.

Countless cities and towns across America have adopted ordinances regulating the posting of signs, while exempting certain categories of signs based on their subject matter. For example, some municipalities generally prohibit illuminated signs in residential neighborhoods, but lift that ban for signs that identify the address of a home or the name of its owner or occupant. In other municipalities, safety signs such as "Blind Pedestrian Crossing" and "Hidden Driveway" can be posted without a permit, even as other permanent signs require one. Elsewhere, historic site markers—for example, "George Washington Slept Here"—are also exempt from general regulations. And similarly, the federal Highway Beautification Act limits signs along interstate highways unless, for instance, they direct travelers to "scenic and historical attractions" or advertise free coffee.

Given the Court's analysis, many sign ordinances of that kind are now in jeopardy. [And] although the majority holds out hope that some sign laws with subject-matter exemptions "might survive" that stringent review, the likelihood is that most will be struck down. After all, it is the "rare case[ ] in which a speech restriction withstands strict scrutiny." [Williams-Yulee, infra]. To clear that high bar, the government must show that a content-based distinction "is necessary to serve a compelling state interest and is narrowly drawn to achieve that end." So on the majority's view, courts would have to determine that a town has a compelling interest in informing passersby where George Washington slept. And likewise, courts would have to find that a town has no other way to prevent hidden-driveway mishaps than by specially treating hidden-driveway signs. (Well-placed speed bumps? Lower speed limits? Or how about just a ban on hidden driveways?) The consequence—unless courts water down strict scrutiny to something unrecognizable—is that our communities will find themselves in an unenviable bind: They will have to either repeal the exemptions that allow for helpful signs on streets and sidewalks, or else lift their sign restrictions altogether and resign themselves to the resulting clutter.

Although the majority insists that applying strict scrutiny to all such ordinances is "essential" to protecting First Amendment freedoms, I find it challenging to understand why that is so. This Court's decisions articulate two important and related reasons for subjecting content-based speech regulations to the most exacting standard of review. The first is "to preserve an uninhibited marketplace of ideas in which truth will ultimately prevail." The second is to ensure that the government has not regulated speech "based on hostility—or favoritism—towards the underlying message expressed." Yet the subject-matter exemptions included in many sign ordinances do not implicate those concerns. Allowing residents, say, to install a light bulb over "name and address" signs but no others does not distort the marketplace of ideas. Nor does that different treatment give rise to an inference of impermissible government motive.

We apply strict scrutiny to facially content-based regulations of speech, in keeping with the rationales just described, when there is any "realistic possibility that official suppression of ideas is afoot." That is always the case when the regulation facially differentiates on the basis of viewpoint. It is also the case (except in non-public or limited public forums) when a law restricts "discussion of an entire topic" in public debate. We have stated that "[i]f the marketplace of ideas is to remain free and open, governments must not be allowed to choose 'which issues are worth discussing or debating.' " And we have recognized that such subject-matter restrictions, even though viewpoint-neutral on their face, may "suggest[ ] an attempt to give one side of a debatable public question an advantage in expressing its views to the people." Subject-matter regulation, in other words, may have the intent or effect of favoring some ideas over others. When that is realistically possible—when the restriction "raises the specter that the Government may effectively drive certain ideas or viewpoints from the marketplace"—we insist that the law pass the most demanding constitutional scrutiny. But when that is not realistically possible, we may do well to relax our guard so that "entirely reasonable" laws imperiled by strict scrutiny can survive. This point is by no means new. Our concern with content-based regulation arises from the fear that the government will skew the public's debate of ideas—so when "that risk is inconsequential, . . . strict scrutiny is unwarranted." To do its intended work, of course, the category of content-based regulation triggering strict scrutiny must sweep more broadly than the actual harm; that category exists to create a buffer zone guaranteeing that the government cannot favor or disfavor certain viewpoints. But that buffer zone need not extend forever. We can administer our content-regulation doctrine with a dose of common sense, so as to leave standing laws that in no way implicate its intended function.

And indeed we have done just that: Our cases have been far less rigid than the majority admits in applying strict scrutiny to facially content-based laws— including in cases just like this one. [In *Ladue v. Gilleo*, 512 U.S. 43 (1994)], the Court assumed *arguendo* that a sign ordinance's exceptions for address signs, safety signs, and for-sale signs in residential areas did not trigger strict scrutiny. We did not need to, and so did not, decide the level-of-scrutiny question because the law's breadth made it unconstitutional under any standard.

The majority could easily have taken *Ladue*'s tack here. The Town of Gilbert's defense of its sign ordinance—most notably, the law's distinctions between directional signs and others—does not pass strict scrutiny, or intermediate scrutiny, or even the laugh test. The Town, for example, provides no reason at all for prohibiting more than four directional signs on a property while placing no limits on the number of other types of signs. Similarly, the Town offers no coherent justification for restricting the size of directional signs to 6 square feet while allowing other signs to reach 20 square feet. The best the Town could come up with at oral argument was that directional signs "need to be smaller because they need to guide travelers along a route." Why exactly a smaller sign better helps travelers get to where they are going is left a mystery. The absence of any sensible basis for these and other distinctions dooms the Town's ordinance under even the intermediate scrutiny that the Court typically applies to "time, place, or manner" speech regulations. Accordingly, there is no need to decide in this case whether strict scrutiny applies to every sign ordinance in every town across this country containing a subject-matter exemption.

I suspect this Court and others will regret the majority's insistence today on answering that question in the affirmative. As the years go by, courts will discover that thousands of towns have such ordinances, many of them "entirely reasonable." And as the challenges to them mount, courts will have to invalidate one after the other. (This Court may soon find itself a veritable Supreme Board of Sign Review.) And courts will strike down those democratically enacted local laws even though no one—certainly not the majority—has ever explained why the vindication of First Amendment values requires that result. Because I see no reason why such an easy case calls for us to cast a constitutional pall on reasonable regulations quite unlike the law before us, I concur only in the judgment.

3. GOVERNMENT PROPERTY AND THE PUBLIC FORUM

The question of when persons can speak on public property has come to be known as public forum doctrine. But "[t]he public forum saga began, and very nearly ended," Geoffrey Stone, *Fora Americana: Speech in Public Places*, 1974 Sup.Ct.Rev. 233, with an effort by Holmes, J., then on the Supreme Judicial Court of Massachusetts, "to solve a difficult First Amendment problem by simplistic resort to a common-law concept," Vincent Blasi, *Prior Restraints on Demonstrations*, 68 Mich.L.Rev. 1482 (1970). For holding religious meetings on the Boston Common, a preacher was convicted under an ordinance prohibiting "any public address" upon publicly-owned property without a permit from the mayor. In upholding the permit ordinance Holmes, J., observed: "For the legislature absolutely or conditionally to forbid public speaking in a highway or public park is no more an infringement of rights of a member of the public than for the owner of a private house to forbid it in the house." *Commonwealth v. Davis*, 39 N.E. 113 (Mass 1895). On appeal, a unanimous Supreme Court adopted the Holmes position, 167 U.S. 43 (1897): "[T]he right to absolutely exclude all right to use [public property], necessarily includes the authority to determine under what circumstances such use may be availed of, as the greater power contains the lesser."

This view survived until HAGUE v. C.I.O., 307 U.S. 496 (1939), which rejected Jersey City's claim that its ordinance requiring a permit for an open air meeting was justified by the "plenary power" rationale of *Davis*. In rejecting the *Davis* dictum, ROBERTS, J., in a plurality opinion, uttered a famous "counter dictum," which has played a central role in the evolution of public forum theory: "Wherever the title of streets and parks may rest, they have immemorially been held in trust for the use of the public and, time out of mind, have been used for purposes of assembly, communicating thoughts between citizens, and discussing public questions. Such use of the streets and public places has, from ancient times, been a part of the privileges, immunities, rights, and liberties of citizens. [This privilege of a citizen] is not absolute, but relative, and must be exercised in subordination to the general comfort and convenience, and in consonance with peace and good order; but it must not, in the guise of regulation, be abridged or denied." Eight months later, the *Hague* dictum was given impressive content by Roberts, J., for the Court, in *Schneider* infra.

I. FOUNDATION CASES

A. Mandatory Access

SCHNEIDER v. IRVINGTON, 308 U.S. 147 (1939), per ROBERTS, J., invalidated several ordinances prohibiting leafleting on public streets or other public places: "Municipal authorities, as trustees for the public, have the duty to keep their communities' streets open and available for movement of people and property, the primary purpose to which the streets are dedicated. So long as legislation to this end does not abridge the constitutional liberty of one rightfully upon the street to impart information through speech or the distribution of literature, it may lawfully regulate the conduct of those using the streets. For example, a person could not exercise this liberty by taking his stand in the middle of a crowded street, contrary to traffic regulations, and maintain his position to the stoppage of all traffic; a group of distributors could not insist upon a constitutional right to form a cordon across the street and to allow no pedestrian to pass who did not accept a tendered leaflet; nor does the guarantee of freedom of speech or of the press deprive a municipality of power to enact regulations against throwing literature broadcast in the streets. Prohibition of such conduct would not abridge the constitutional liberty since such activity bears no necessary relationship to the freedom to speak, write, print or distribute information or opinion. * * *

"In *Lovell v. Griffin*, 303 U.S. 444 (1938), this court held void an ordinance which forbade the distribution by hand or otherwise of literature of any kind without written permission from the city manager. [Similarly] in *Hague v. C.I.O.*, an ordinance was held void on its face because it provided for previous administrative censorship of the exercise of the right of speech and assembly in appropriate public places." The [ordinances] under review do not purport to license distribution but all of them absolutely prohibit it in the streets and, one of them, in other public places as well.

"The motive of the legislation under attack in Numbers 13, 18 and 29 is held by the courts below to be the prevention of littering of the streets and, although the alleged offenders were not charged with themselves scattering paper in the streets, their convictions were sustained upon the theory that distribution by them encouraged or resulted in such littering. We are of opinion that the purpose to keep the streets clean and of good appearance is insufficient to justify an ordinance which prohibits a person rightfully on a public street from handing literature to one willing to receive it. Any burden imposed upon the city authorities in cleaning and caring for the streets as an indirect consequence of such distribution results from the constitutional protection of the freedom of speech and press. This constitutional protection does not deprive a city of all power to prevent street littering. There are obvious methods of preventing littering. Amongst these is the punishment of those who actually throw papers on the streets.

"It is suggested that [the] ordinances are valid because their operation is limited to streets and alleys and leaves persons free to distribute printed matter in other public places. But, as we have said, the streets are natural and proper places for the dissemination of information and opinion; and one is not to have the exercise of his liberty of expression in appropriate places abridged on the plea that it may be exercised in some other place."

MCREYNOLDS, J., "is of opinion that the judgment in each case should be affirmed."

NOTES AND QUESTIONS

1.   COX v. NEW HAMPSHIRE, 312 U.S. 569 (1941), per HUGHES, C.J., upheld convictions of sixty-eight Jehovah's Witnesses for parading without a permit. They had marched in four or five groups (with perhaps twenty others) along the sidewalk in single file carrying signs and handing out leaflets: "[T]he state court considered and defined the duty of the licensing authority and the rights of the appellants to a license for their parade, with regard only to consideration of time, place and manner so as to conserve the public convenience."

2.   *Cox* said there was nothing "contrary to the Constitution" in the exaction of a fee " 'incident to the administration of the [licensing] Act and to the maintenance of public order in the matter licensed.' " In *Forsyth County v. The Nationalist Movement*, 505 U.S. 123 (1992), however, the Court held that speech cannot be financially burdened by imposing security expenses on speakers likely to be confronted by hostile audiences.

3.   *Reasonable time, place, and manner regulations.* (a) As *Cox* reveals, a right of access to a public forum does not guarantee immunity from reasonable time, place, and manner regulations. In HEFFRON v. INTERNATIONAL SOC. FOR KRISHNA CONSCIOUSNESS, 452 U.S. 640 (1981), for example, the Court, per WHITE, J., upheld a state fair rule prohibiting the distribution of printed material or the solicitation of funds except from a duly licensed booth on the fairgrounds. The Court noted that consideration of a forum's special attributes is relevant to the determination of reasonableness, and the test of reasonableness is whether the restrictions "are justified without reference to the content of the regulated speech, that they serve a significant governmental

interest, and that in doing so they leave open ample alternative channels for communication of the information."

WARD v. ROCK AGAINST RACISM, 491 U.S. 781 (1989), per KENNEDY, J., observes that "[E]ven in a public forum the government may impose reasonable restrictions on the time, place, or manner of protected speech, provided the restrictions 'are justified without reference to the content of the regulated speech, that they are narrowly tailored to serve a significant governmental interest, and that they leave open ample alternative channels for communication of the information.' " The case reasserts that the *O'Brien* test is little different from the time, place, and manner test, and then states: "[A] regulation of the time, place, or manner of protected speech must be narrowly tailored to serve the government's legitimate content-neutral interests but [it] need not be the least-restrictive or least-intrusive means of doing so. Rather, the requirement of narrow tailoring is satisfied 'so long as [the] regulation promotes a substantial government interest that would be achieved less effectively absent the regulation.' To be sure, this standard does not mean that a time, place, or manner regulation may burden substantially more speech than is necessary to further the government's legitimate interests. Government may not regulate expression in such a manner that a substantial portion of the burden on speech does not serve to advance its goals."

INTERNATIONAL SOCIETY FOR KRISHNA CONSCIOUSNESS, INC. v. LEE

505 U.S. 672, 112 S.Ct. 2701, 120 L.Ed.2d 541 (1992).

CHIEF JUSTICE REHNQUIST delivered the opinion of the Court.

* * * Petitioner International Society for Krishna Consciousness, Inc. (ISKCON) is a not-for-profit religious corporation whose members perform a ritual known as sankirtan. The ritual consists of " 'going into public places, disseminating religious literature and soliciting funds to support the religion.' " The primary purpose of this ritual is raising funds for the movement.

Respondent [was] the police superintendent of the Port Authority of New York and New Jersey and was charged with enforcing the regulation at issue. The Port Authority owns and operates three major airports in the greater New York City area [which] collectively form one of the world's busiest metropolitan airport complexes. By decade's end they are expected to serve at least 110 million passengers annually. * * *

The Port Authority has adopted a regulation forbidding within the terminals the repetitive solicitation of money or distribution of literature [but permitting] solicitation and distribution on the sidewalks outside the terminal buildings. The regulation effectively prohibits petitioner from performing sankirtan in the terminals. * * *

It is uncontested that the solicitation at issue in this case is a form of speech protected under the First Amendment. But it is also well settled that the government need not permit all forms of speech on property that it owns and controls. Where the government is acting as a proprietor, managing its internal operations, rather than acting as lawmaker with the power to regulate or license, its action will not be subjected to the heightened review to which its actions as a lawmaker may be subject. * * *

[Our] cases reflect, either implicitly or explicitly, a "forum-based" approach for assessing restrictions that the government seeks to place on the use of its property. Under this approach, regulation of speech on government property that has traditionally been available for public expression is subject to the highest scrutiny. Such regulations survive only if they are narrowly drawn to achieve a compelling state interest. *Perry.* The second category of public property is the designated public forum, whether of a limited or unlimited character—property that the state has opened for expressive activity by part or all of the public. Id.[12] Regulation of such property is subject to the same limitations as that governing a traditional public forum. Finally, there is all remaining public property. Limitations on expressive activity conducted on this last category of property must survive only a much more limited review. The challenged regulation need only be reasonable, as long as the regulation is not an effort to suppress the speaker's activity due to disagreement with the speaker's view.

[Our] precedents foreclose the conclusion that airport terminals are public fora. Reflecting the general growth of the air travel industry, airport terminals have only recently achieved their contemporary size and character. [Moreover,] even within the rather short history of air transport, it is only "[i]n recent years [that] it has become a common practice for various religious and non-profit organizations to use commercial airports as a forum for the distribution of literature, the solicitation of funds, the proselytizing of new members, and other similar activities." 45 Fed.Reg. 35314 (1980). Thus, the tradition of airport activity does not demonstrate that airports have historically been made available for speech activity. Nor can we say that these particular terminals, or airport terminals generally, have been intentionally opened by their operators to such activity; the frequent and continuing litigation evidencing the operators' objections belies any such claim. * * *

Petitioner attempts to circumvent the history and practice governing airport activity by pointing our attention to the variety of speech activity that it claims historically occurred at various "transportation nodes" such as rail stations, bus stations, wharves, and Ellis Island. Even if we were inclined to accept petitioner's historical account[,] we think that such evidence is of little import for two reasons. First, much of the evidence is irrelevant to *public* fora analysis, because sites such as bus and rail terminals traditionally have had *private* ownership. The development of privately owned parks that ban speech activity would not change the public fora status of publicly held parks. But the reverse is also true. The

---

[12]   In interpreting this approach, *Perry Educ. Ass'n v. Perry Local Educators' Ass'n*, 460 U.S. 37 (1983), stated in its footnote 7 that: "a public forum may be created for a limited purpose such as use by certain groups or for discussion of certain subjects.?

practices of privately held transportation centers do not bear on the government's regulatory authority over a publicly owned airport.

Second, the relevant unit for our inquiry is an airport, not "transportation nodes" generally. When new methods of transportation develop, new methods for accommodating that transportation are also likely to be needed. And with each new step, it therefore will be a new inquiry whether the transportation necessities are compatible with various kinds of expressive activity. [The] "security magnet," for example, is an airport commonplace that lacks a counterpart in bus terminals and train stations. And public access to air terminals is also not infrequently restricted—just last year the Federal Aviation Administration required airports for a 4-month period to limit access to areas normally publicly accessible. To blithely equate airports with other transportation centers, therefore, would be a mistake. [T]he record demonstrates that Port Authority management considers the purpose of the terminals to be the facilitation of passenger air travel, not the promotion of expression. Even if we look beyond the intent of the Port Authority to the manner in which the terminals have been operated, the terminals have never been dedicated (except under the threat of court order) to expression in the form sought to be exercised [here]. Thus, we think that neither by tradition nor purpose can the terminals be described as satisfying the standards we have previously set out for identifying a public forum.

The restrictions here challenged, therefore, need only satisfy a requirement of reasonableness. * * *

We have on many prior occasions noted the disruptive effect that solicitation may have on business. "Solicitation requires action by those who would respond: The individual solicited must decide whether or not to contribute (which itself might involve reading the solicitor's literature or hearing his pitch), and then, having decided to do so, reach for a wallet, search it for money, write a check, or produce a credit card." *United States v. Kokinda*, 497 U.S. 720 (1990). Passengers who wish to avoid the solicitor may have to alter their path, slowing both themselves and those around them. The result is that the normal flow of traffic is impeded. This is especially so in an airport, where "air travelers, who are often weighted down by cumbersome baggage [may] be hurrying to catch a plane or to arrange ground transportation." Delays may be particularly costly in this setting, as a flight missed by only a few minutes can result in hours worth of subsequent inconvenience.

In addition, face to face solicitation presents risks of duress that are an appropriate target of regulation. The skillful, and unprincipled, solicitor can target the most vulnerable, including those accompanying children or those suffering physical impairment and who cannot easily avoid the solicitation. The unsavory solicitor can also commit fraud through concealment of his affiliation or through deliberate efforts to shortchange those who agree to purchase. Compounding this problem is the fact that, in an airport, the targets of such activity frequently are on tight schedules. This in turn makes such visitors unlikely to stop and formally complain to airport authorities. As a result, the airport faces considerable difficulty in achieving its legitimate interest in monitoring solicitation activity to assure that travelers are not interfered with unduly.

[T]he sidewalk areas outside the terminals [are] frequented by an overwhelming percentage of airport users. [W]e think it would be odd to conclude that the Port Authority's terminal regulation is unreasonable despite the Port Authority having otherwise assured access to an area universally traveled. * * *

Moreover, "[if] petitioner is given access, so too must other groups. "Obviously, there would be a much larger threat to the State's interest in crowd control if all other religious, nonreligious, and noncommercial organizations could likewise move freely." As a result, we conclude that the solicitation ban is reasonable. * * *

JUSTICE O'CONNOR, concurring in 91–155 [on the solicitation issue] and concurring in the judgment in 91–339 [on the distribution of literature issue]. * * *

I concur in the Court's opinion in No. 91–155 and agree that publicly owned airports are not public fora. [This], however, does not mean that the government can restrict speech in whatever way it likes. * * *

"The reasonableness of the Government's restriction [on speech in a nonpublic forum] must be assessed in light of the purpose of the forum and all the surrounding circumstances." *Cornelius.* " '[C]onsideration of a forum's special attributes is relevant to the constitutionality of a regulation since the significance of the governmental interest must be assessed in light of the characteristic nature and function of the particular forum involved.' " *Kokinda.* In this case, the "special attributes" and "surrounding circumstances" of the airports operated by the Port Authority are determinative. Not only has the Port Authority chosen *not* to limit access to the airports under its control, it has created a huge complex open to travelers and nontravelers alike. The airports house restaurants, cafeterias, snack bars, coffee shops, cocktail lounges, post offices, banks, telegraph offices, clothing shops, drug stores, food stores, nurseries, barber shops, currency exchanges, art exhibits, commercial advertising displays, bookstores, newsstands, dental offices and private clubs. The International Arrivals Building at JFK Airport even has two branches of Bloomingdale's.

We have said that a restriction on speech in a nonpublic forum is "reasonable" when it is "consistent with the [government's] legitimate interest in 'preserv[ing] the property [for] the use to which it is lawfully dedicated.' " *Perry.* [The] reasonableness inquiry, therefore, is not whether the restrictions on speech are "consistent [with] preserving the property" for air travel, but whether they are reasonably related to maintaining the multipurpose environment that the Port Authority has deliberately created.

Applying that standard, I agree with the Court in No. 91–155 that the ban on solicitation is reasonable. [In] my view, however, the regulation banning leafletting [cannot] be upheld as reasonable on this record. I therefore concur in the judgment in No. 91–339 striking down that prohibition. [W]e have expressly noted that leafletting does not entail the same kinds of problems presented by face-to-face solicitation. Specifically, "[o]ne need not ponder the contents of a leaflet or pamphlet in order mechanically to take it out of someone's [hand]. 'The distribution of literature does not require that the recipient stop in order to receive the message the speaker wishes to convey; instead the recipient is free to read the message at a later time.'" With the possible exception of avoiding litter, it is difficult to point to any problems intrinsic to the act of leafletting that would make it naturally incompatible with a large, multipurpose forum such as those at issue here. * * *

Of course, it is still open for the Port Authority to promulgate regulations of the time, place, and manner of leafletting which are "content-neutral, narrowly tailored to serve a significant government interest, and leave open ample alternative channels of communication." For example, during the many years that this litigation has been in progress, the Port Authority has not banned sankirtan completely from JFK International Airport, but has restricted it to a relatively uncongested part of the airport terminals, the same part that houses the airport chapel. In my view, that regulation meets the standards we have applied * * * .

JUSTICE KENNEDY, with whom JUSTICE BLACKMUN, JUSTICE STEVENS, and JUSTICE SOUTER join as to Part I, concurring in the judgment.

I.   [The Court] leaves the government with almost unlimited authority to restrict speech on its property by doing nothing more than articulating a non-speech-related purpose for the area, and it leaves almost no scope for the development of new public forums absent the rare approval of the government. The Court's error [in] analysis is a classification of the property that turns on the government's own definition or decision, unconstrained by an independent duty to respect the speech its citizens can voice there. The Court acknowledges as much, by reintroducing today into our First Amendment law a strict doctrinal line between the proprietary and regulatory functions of government which I thought had been abandoned long ago.

[Public] places are of necessity the locus for discussion of public issues, as well as protest against arbitrary government action. At the heart of our jurisprudence lies the principle that in a free nation citizens must have the right to gather and speak with other persons in public places. The recognition that certain government-owned property is a public forum provides open notice to citizens that their freedoms may be exercised there without fear of a censorial government, adding tangible reinforcement to the idea that we are a free people. * * *

The Court's analysis rests on an inaccurate view of history. The notion that traditional public forums are property which have public discourse as their principal purpose is a most doubtful fiction. The types of property that we have recognized as the quintessential public forums are streets, parks, and sidewalks. It would seem apparent that the principal purpose of streets and sidewalks, like airports, is to facilitate transportation, not public discourse. [Similarly,] the purpose for the creation of public parks may be as much for beauty and open space as for discourse. Thus under the Court's analysis, even the quintessential public forums would appear to lack the necessary elements of what the Court defines as a public forum. * * *

One of the places left in our mobile society that is suitable for discourse is a metropolitan airport [because] in these days an airport is one of the few government-owned spaces where many persons have extensive contact with other members of the public. Given that private spaces of similar character are not subject to the dictates of the First Amendment, it is critical that we preserve these areas for protected speech. [If] the objective, physical characteristics of the property at issue and the actual public access and uses which have been permitted by the government indicate that expressive activity would be appropriate and compatible with those uses, the property is a public forum. [The] possibility of some theoretical inconsistency between expressive activities and the property's uses should not bar a finding of a public forum, if those inconsistencies can be avoided through simple and permitted regulations.

The second category of the Court's jurisprudence, the so-called designated forum, provides little, if any, additional protection for speech. [I] do not quarrel with the fact that speech must often be restricted on property of this kind to retain the purpose for which it has been designated. And I recognize that when property has been designated for a particular expressive use, the government may choose to eliminate that designation. But this increases the need to protect speech in other places, where discourse may occur free of such restrictions. In some sense the government always retains authority to close a public forum, by selling the property, changing its physical character, or changing its principal use. Otherwise the State would be prohibited from closing a park, or eliminating a street or sidewalk, which no one has understood the public forum doctrine to require. The difference is that when property is a protected public forum the State may not by fiat assert broad control over speech or expressive activities; it must alter the objective physical character or uses of the property, and bear the attendant costs, to change the property's forum status.

Under this analysis, it is evident that the public spaces of the Port Authority's airports are public forums. First, the District Court made detailed findings [that] show that the public spaces in the airports are broad, public thoroughfares full of people and lined with stores and other commercial activities. An airport corridor is of course not a street, but that is not the proper inquiry. The question is one of physical similarities, sufficient to suggest that the airport corridor should be a public forum for the same reasons that streets and sidewalks have been treated as public forums by the people who use them.

Second, the airport areas involved here are open to the public without restriction. Plaintiffs do not seek access to the secured areas of the airports, nor do I suggest that these areas would be public forums. And while most people who come to the Port Authority's airports do so for a reason related to air travel, [this] does not distinguish an airport from streets or sidewalks, which most people use for travel. * * *

Third, and perhaps most important, it is apparent from the record, and from the recent history of airports, that when adequate time, place, and manner regulations are in place, expressive activity is quite compatible with the uses of major airports. The Port Authority [argues] that the problem of congestion in its airports' corridors makes expressive activity inconsistent with the airports' primary purpose, which is to facilitate air travel. The First Amendment is often inconvenient. But that is besides the point. Inconvenience does not absolve the government of its obligation to tolerate speech. * * *

[A] grant of plenary power allows the government to tilt the dialogue heard by the public, to exclude many, more marginal voices. [We] have long recognized that the right to distribute flyers and literature lies at the heart of the liberties guaranteed by the Speech and Press Clauses of the First Amendment. The Port Authority's rule, which prohibits almost all such activity, is among the most restrictive possible of those liberties. The regulation is in fact so broad and restrictive of speech, Justice O'Connor finds it void even under the standards applicable to government regulations in nonpublic forums. I have no difficulty deciding the regulation cannot survive the far more stringent rules applicable to regulations in public forums. The regulation is not drawn in narrow terms and it does not leave open ample alternative channels for communication. * * *

JUSTICE SOUTER, with whom JUSTICE BLACKMUN and JUSTICE STEVENS join, concurring in the judgment in No. 91–339 [on the distribution of literature issue] and dissenting in No. 91–155 [on the solicitation issue].

[I] do not think the Port Authority's solicitation ban leaves open the "ample" channels of communication required of a valid content-neutral time, place and manner restriction. A distribution of preaddressed envelopes is unlikely to be much of an alternative. The practical reality of the regulation, which this Court can never ignore, is that it shuts off a uniquely powerful avenue of communication for organizations like the International Society for Krishna Consciousness, and may, in effect, completely prohibit unpopular and poorly funded groups from receiving funds in response to protected solicitation. * * *

LEE V. INTERNATIONAL SOCIETY FOR KRISHNA CONSCIOUSNESS, INC.
505 U.S. 830, 112 S.Ct. 2709, 120 L.Ed.2d 669 (1992).

PER CURIAM.

For the reasons expressed in the opinions of Justice O'Connor, Justice Kennedy, and Justice Souter in *ISKCON v. Lee,* the judgment of the Court of Appeals holding that the ban on distribution of literature in the Port Authority airport terminals is invalid under the First Amendment is affirmed.

CHIEF JUSTICE REHNQUIST, with whom JUSTICE WHITE, JUSTICE SCALIA and JUSTICE THOMAS join, dissenting.

Leafletting [must] be evaluated against a backdrop of the substantial congestion problem facing the Port Authority and with an eye to the cumulative impact that will result if all groups are permitted terminal access. Viewed in this light, I conclude that the distribution ban, no less than the solicitation ban, is reasonable.

[The] weary, harried, or hurried traveler may have no less desire and need to avoid the delays generated by having literature foisted upon him than he does to avoid delays from a financial solicitation. And while a busy passenger perhaps may succeed in fending off a leafletter with minimal disruption to himself by agreeing simply to take the proffered material, this does not completely ameliorate the dangers of congestion flowing from such leafletting. Others may choose not simply to accept the material but also to stop and engage the leafletter in debate, obstructing those who follow. Moreover, those who accept material may often simply drop it on the floor once out of the leafletter's range, creating an eyesore, a safety hazard, and additional cleanup work for airport staff. * * *

LEHMAN v. SHAKER HEIGHTS, 418 U.S. 298 (1974), held that a public transit system could sell commercial advertising space for cards on its vehicles while refusing to sell space for "political" or "public issue" advertising. BLACKMUN, J., joined by Burger, C.J., and White and Rehnquist, JJ., ruled that the card space is not a public forum and found the city's decision reasonable because it minimized "chances of abuse, the appearance of favoritism, and the risk of imposing upon a captive audience." DOUGLAS, J., concurring, maintained that political messages and commercial messages were both offensive and intrusive to captive audiences, noted that the commercial advertising policy was not before the Court, and voted to deny a right to spread a political message to a captive audience. BRENNAN, J., joined by Stewart, Marshall, and Powell, JJ., dissenting, observed that the "city's solicitous regard for 'captive riders' [has] a hollow ring in the present case where [it] has opened its rapid transit system as a forum for communication."

BURSON v. FREEMAN, 504 U.S. 191 (1992), upheld the statute. BLACKMUN, J., joined by Rehnquist, C.J., and White and Kennedy, JJ., argued that the 100 foot zone was a public forum, that the regulation was based on the content of the speech, that the state was required to show that its statute was necessary to achieve a compelling state interest and narrowly drawn to achieve that end, and determined that this was the "rare case" in which strict scrutiny against content regulation could be satisfied: "There is [ample evidence] that political candidates have used campaign workers to commit voter intimidation or electoral fraud. In contrast, there is simply no evidence that political candidates have used other forms of solicitation or exit polling to commit such electoral abuses. [The] First Amendment does not require states to regulate for problems that do not exist. * * *

"Here, the State, as recognized administrator of elections, has asserted that the exercise of free speech rights conflicts with another fundamental right, the right to cast a ballot in an election free from the taint of intimidation and fraud. A long history, a substantial consensus, and simple common sense shows that some restricted zone around polling places is necessary to protect that fundamental right. Given the conflict between those two rights, we hold that requiring solicitors to stand 100 feet from the entrances to polling places does not constitute an unconstitutional compromise."

SCALIA, J., agreed with Blackmun, J., that the regulation was justified, but maintained that the area around a polling place is not a public forum: "If the category of 'traditional public forum' is to be a tool of analysis rather than a conclusory label, it must remain faithful to its name and derive its content from *tradition*. Because restrictions on speech around polling places are as venerable a part of the American tradition as the secret ballot, [Tennessee's statute] does not restrict speech in a traditional public forum. [I] believe that the [statute] though content-based, is constitutional because it is a reasonable, viewpoint-neutral regulation of a non-public forum."

STEVENS, J., joined by O'Connor and Souter, JJ., did not address the question of whether the area around a polling place was a public forum, but agreed with Blackmun, J., that the regulation could not be upheld without showing that it was necessary to serve a compelling state interest by means narrowly tailored to that end. He contended that the existence of the secret ballot was a sufficient safeguard against intimidation and that the fear of fraud from last minute campaigning could not be reconciled with *Mills v. Alabama*, 384 U.S. 214 (1966)(prohibition on election day editorials unconstitutional). In addition, Stevens, J., argued that the prohibition disproportionately affects candidates with "fewer resources, candidates from lesser visibility offices, and 'grassroots' candidates" who specially profit from "last-minute campaigning near the polling place. [The] hubbub of campaign workers outside a polling place may be a nuisance, but it is also the sound of a vibrant democracy."

Questions about polling place electioneering persist, and in MINNESOTA VOTERS ALLIANCE v. MANSKY, 138 S.Ct. 1876 (2018), the Court addressed a Minnesota ban wearing political apparel inside a polling place on the day of an election. Specifically, the statute, which dated to the late nineteenth century, provided that a "political badge, political button, or other political insignia may not be worn at or about the polling place." The statute was challenged by a coalition of individuals and political groups. One of the individuals wished to wear a shirt on which was written "Please I.D. Me," accompanied by the telephone number and address of a group called the Election Integrity Watch. Other challengers included individuals who attempted to vote while wearing shirts with the words, "Don't Tread on Me," or with various Tea Party symbols and slogans.

Writing for the majority, ROBERTS, C.J., recapitulated his understanding of existing public forum doctrine: "[O]ur cases recognize three types of government-controlled spaces: traditional public forums, designated public forums, and nonpublic forums. In a traditional public forum—parks, streets, sidewalks, and the like—the government may impose reasonable time, place, and manner restrictions on private speech, but restrictions based on content must satisfy strict scrutiny, and those based on viewpoint are prohibited. The same standards apply in designated public forums—spaces that have 'not traditionally been regarded as a public forum' but which the government has 'intentionally opened up for that purpose.' In a nonpublic forum, on the other hand—a space that 'is not by tradition or designation a forum for public communication'—the government has much more flexibility to craft rules limiting speech," [as long as] there is "not an effort to suppress expression merely because public officials oppose the speaker's view. [Accordingly,] our decisions have long recognized that the government may impose some content-based restrictions on speech in nonpublic forums, including restrictions that exclude political advocates and forms of political advocacy."

Concluding that a polling place "qualifies as a nonpublic forum," the majority agreed that some forms of political advocacy could be entirely "excluded from the polling place," and that "Minnesota may choose to prohibit certain apparel there because of the message it conveys, so that voters may focus on the important decisions immediately at hand." But the Court then balked at Minnesota's broad and amorphous definition of the "political," and at the vague and confusing regulations and examples that the state and county election officials had adopted and applied. "[If] a State wishes to set its polling places apart as areas free of partisan discord, it must employ a more discernible approach than the one Minnesota has offered here."

In a dissenting opinion, SOTOMAYOR, J., joined by Breyer, J., agreed with the majority's broad analysis, but thought the majority too quick to invalidate the law, as opposed to obtaining "guidance from the State's highest court on the proper interpretation of that state law. [Especially] where there are undisputedly many constitutional applications of a state law that further weighty state interests, the Court should be wary of invalidating a law without giving the State's highest court an opportunity to pass upon it[, and without taking] the obvious step of certification in this case."

II. PRIVACY AND THE PUBLIC FORUM

HILL v. COLORADO
530 U.S. 703, 120 S.Ct. 2480, 147 L.Ed.2d 597 (2000).

JUSTICE STEVENS delivered the opinion of the Court.

[A Colorado statute makes it unlawful, within 100 feet of the entrance to any health care facility, for any person to "knowingly approach" within eight feet of another person, without that person's consent, "for the purpose of passing a leaflet or handbill to, displaying a sign to, or engaging in oral protest, education, or counseling with such other person * * * ." The statute] does not require a standing speaker to move away from anyone passing by. Nor does it place any restriction on the content of any message that anyone may wish to communicate to anyone else, either inside or outside the regulated areas. It does, however, make it more difficult to give unwanted advice, particularly in the form of a handbill or leaflet, to persons entering or leaving medical facilities.

[P]etitioners emphasize three propositions. First, they accurately explain that the areas protected by the statute encompass all the public ways within 100 feet of every entrance to every health care facility everywhere in the State of Colorado [even] though the legislative history makes it clear that its enactment was primarily motivated by activities in the vicinity of abortion clinics. Second, they correctly state that their leafletting, sign displays, and oral communications are protected by the First Amendment. The fact that the messages conveyed by those communications may be offensive to their recipients does not deprive them of constitutional protection. Third, the public sidewalks, streets, and ways affected by the statute are 'quintessential' public forums for free speech.

On the other hand, it is a traditional exercise of the States' "police powers to protect the health and safety of their citizens." That interest may justify a special focus on unimpeded access to health care facilities and the avoidance of potential trauma to patients associated with confrontational protests.

It is also important when conducting this interest analysis to recognize the significant difference between state restrictions on a speaker's right to address a willing audience and those that protect listeners from unwanted communication. This statute deals only with the latter. [The] right to avoid unwelcome speech has special force in the privacy of the home, *Rowan v. Post Office Dept.*, 397 U.S. 728 (1970), and its immediate surroundings, *Frisby v. Schultz*, 487 U.S. 474 (1988)[13] but can also be protected in confrontational settings. * * *

The dissenters argue that we depart from precedent by recognizing a "right to avoid unpopular speech in a public forum," We, of course, are not addressing whether there is such a "right." Rather, we are merely noting that our cases have repeatedly recognized the interests of unwilling listeners in situations where "the degree of captivity makes it impractical for the unwilling viewer or auditor to avoid exposure." * * *

[The] Colorado statute's regulation [places] no restrictions on—and clearly does not prohibit—either a particular viewpoint or any subject matter that may be discussed by a speaker. Rather, it simply establishes a minor place restriction on an extremely broad category of communications with unwilling listeners. Instead of drawing distinctions based on the subject that the approaching speaker may

---

[13]   Anti-abortion demonstrators picketed on a number of occasions outside a doctor's home. In response, the Town Board passed an ordinance prohibiting picketing taking place solely in front of, and directed at, a residence. *Frisby*, per O'Connor, J., upheld the ordinance: "The state's interest in protecting the well-being, tranquility, and privacy of the home is certainly of the highest order in a free and civilized society." Brennan, J., joined by Marshall, J., dissenting, would have permitted the town to regulate the number of residential picketers, the hours, and the noise level of the pickets. Stevens, J., dissenting, would have limited the ban to conduct that "unreasonably interferes with the privacy of the home and does not serve a reasonable communicative purpose." He worried that a sign such as "GET WELL CHARLIE—OUR TEAM NEEDS YOU," would fall within the sweep of the ordinance.

wish to address, the statute applies equally to used car salesmen, animal rights activists, fundraisers, environmentalists, and missionaries.

Here, the statute's restriction seeks to protect those who enter a health care facility from the harassment, the nuisance, the persistent importuning, the following, the dogging, and the implied threat of physical touching that can accompany an unwelcome approach within eight feet of a patient by a person wishing to argue vociferously face-to-face and perhaps thrust an undesired handbill upon her. The statutory phrases, "oral protest, education, or counseling," distinguish speech activities likely to have those consequences from speech activities (such as Justice Scalia's "happy speech") that are most unlikely to have those consequences. The statute does not distinguish among speech instances that are similarly likely to raise the legitimate concerns to which it responds. Hence, the statute cannot be struck down for failure to maintain "content neutrality," or for "underbreadth."

[The] contention that a statute is 'viewpoint based' simply because its enactment was motivated by the conduct of the partisans on one side of a debate is without support. The antipicketing ordinance upheld in *Frisby*, a decision in which both of today's dissenters joined, was obviously enacted in response to the activities of antiabortion protesters * * * . We nonetheless summarily concluded that the statute was content neutral.

[The statute is a reasonable place regulation.] The 8-foot separation between the speaker and the audience should not have any adverse impact on the readers' ability to read signs displayed by demonstrators. In fact, the separation might actually aid the pedestrians' ability to see the signs by preventing others from surrounding them and impeding their view. Furthermore, the statute places no limitations on the number, size, text, or images of the placards. And, as with all of the restrictions, the 8-foot zone does not affect demonstrators with signs who remain in place.

With respect to oral statements, the distance certainly can make it more difficult for a speaker to be heard, particularly if the level of background noise is high and other speakers are competing for the pedestrian's attention. Notably, the statute places no limitation on the number of speakers or the noise level, including the use of amplification equipment, although we have upheld such restrictions in past [cases]. Finally, here there is a "knowing" requirement that protects speakers "who thought they were keeping pace with the targeted individual" at the proscribed distance from inadvertently violating the statute.

[The] burden on the ability to distribute handbills is more serious because it seems possible that an 8-foot interval could hinder the ability of a leafletter to deliver handbills to some unwilling recipients. The statute does not, however, prevent a leafletter from simply standing near the path of oncoming pedestrians and proffering his or her material, which the pedestrians can easily accept.

[The statute] will sometimes inhibit a demonstrator whose approach in fact would have proved harmless. But the statute's prophylactic aspect is justified by the great difficulty of protecting, say, a pregnant woman from physical harassment with legal rules that focus exclusively on the individual impact of each instance of behavior. [Such] individualized characterization of each individual movement is often difficult to make accurately. [A] bright-line prophylactic rule may be the best way to provide protection, and, at the same time, by offering clear guidance and avoiding subjectivity, to protect speech itself. * * *

[There] are two parts to petitioners' "overbreadth" argument. On the one hand, they argue that the statute is too broad because it protects too many people in too many places, rather than just the patients at the facilities where confrontational speech had occurred. Similarly, it burdens all speakers, rather than just persons with a history of bad conduct. On the other hand, petitioners also contend that the statute is overbroad because it "bans virtually the universe of protected expression, including displays of signs, distribution of literature, and mere verbal statements."

[T]hat the coverage of a statute is broader than the specific concern that led to its enactment is of no constitutional significance. What is important is that all persons entering or leaving health care facilities share the interests served by the statute. It is precisely because the Colorado Legislature made a general policy choice that the statute is assessed under the constitutional standard set forth in *Ward*, rather than a more strict standard. In this case, it is not disputed that the regulation affects protected speech activity, the question is thus whether it is a "reasonable restrictio[n] on the time, place, or manner of protected speech." * * *

The second part of the argument is based on a misreading of the statute [, which] does not "ban" any messages, [nor] any signs, literature, or oral statements. It merely regulates the places where communications may occur. [Petitioners] have not persuaded us that the impact of the statute on the conduct of other speakers will differ from its impact on their own sidewalk counseling. Like petitioners' own activities, the conduct of other protesters and counselors at all health care facilities are encompassed within the statute's "legitimate sweep." Therefore, the statute is not overly broad. * * *

JUSTICE SOUTER, with whom JUSTICE O'CONNOR, JUSTICE GINSBURG, and JUSTICE BREYER, join concurring. * * *

It is important to recognize that the validity of punishing some expressive conduct, and the permissibility of a time, place, or manner restriction, does not depend on showing that the particular behavior or mode of delivery has no association with a particular subject or opinion. Draft card burners disapprove of the draft, see *O'Brien*, and abortion protesters believe abortion is morally wrong. There is always a correlation with subject and viewpoint when the law regulates conduct that has become the signature of one side of a controversy. But that does not mean that every regulation of such distinctive behavior is content based as First Amendment doctrine employs that term. The correct rule, rather, is captured in the formulation that a restriction is content based only if it is imposed because of the content of the speech. * * *

No one disputes the substantiality of the government's interest in protecting people already tense or distressed in anticipation of medical attention (whether an abortion or some other procedure) from the unwanted intrusion of close personal importunity by strangers. The issues dividing the Court, then, go to the content neutrality of the regulation, its fit with the interest to be served by it, and the availability of other means of expressing the desired message (however offensive it may be even without physically close communication).

Each of these issues is addressed principally by the fact that [the statute does] not declare any view as unfit for expression within the 100-foot zone or beyond it. [A]ll it forbids is approaching another person closer than eight feet (absent permission) to deliver the message. * * *

JUSTICE SCALIA, with whom JUSTICE THOMAS joins, dissenting.

[What] is before us [is] a speech regulation directed against the opponents of abortion, and it therefore enjoys the benefit of the "ad hoc nullification machine" that the Court has set in motion to push aside whatever doctrines of constitutional law stand in the way of that highly favored practice. [T]he regulation as it applies to oral communications is obviously and undeniably content-based. A speaker wishing to approach another for the purpose of communicating any message except one of protest, education, or counseling may do so without first securing the other's consent. Whether a speaker must obtain permission before approaching within eight [feet] depends entirely on *what he intends to say* when he gets there. I have no doubt that this regulation would be deemed content-based *in an instant* if the case before us involved antiwar protesters, or union members seeking to 'educate' the public about the reasons for their strike. * * *

The Court asserts that this statute is not content-based for purposes of our First Amendment analysis because it neither (1) discriminates among viewpoints nor (2) places restrictions on "any subject matter that may be discussed by a speaker." But we have never held that the universe of content-based regulations is limited to those two categories, and such a holding would be absurd. Imagine, for instance, special place-and-manner restrictions on all speech except that which "conveys a sense of contentment or happiness." This "happy speech" limitation would not be "viewpoint-based"—citizens would be able to express their joy in equal measure at either the rise or fall of the NASDAQ, at either the success or the failure of the Republican Party—and would not discriminate on the basis of subject matter, since gratification could be expressed about anything at all. Or consider a law restricting the writing or recitation of poetry—neither viewpoint-based nor limited to any particular subject matter. Surely this Court would consider such regulations to be "content-based" and deserving of the most exacting scrutiny.

[The] Court's confident assurance that the statute poses no special threat to First Amendment freedoms because it applies alike to "used car salesmen, animal rights activists, fundraisers, environmentalists, and missionaries," is a wonderful replication (except for its lack of sarcasm) of Anatole France's observation that "[t]he law, in its majestic equality, forbids the rich as well as the poor to sleep under bridges." [We] know what the Colorado legislators, by their careful selection of content ('protest, education, and counseling'), were taking aim at, for they set it forth in the statute itself: the 'right to protest or counsel against certain medical procedures' on the sidewalks and streets surrounding health care facilities.

The Court is unpersuasive in its attempt to equate the present restriction with content-neutral regulation of demonstrations and picketing—as one may immediately suspect from the opinion's wildly expansive definitions of demonstrations as "public display[s] of sentiment for or against a person or cause," and of picketing as an effort "to persuade or otherwise influence." (On these terms, Nathan Hale was a demonstrator and Patrick Henry a picket.) When the government regulates "picketing," or "demonstrating," it restricts a particular manner of expression that is, as the author of today's opinion has several times explained, "a mixture of conduct and communication." [Today], Justice Stevens gives us an opinion restricting not only handbilling but even one-on-one conversation of a particular content. * * *

[T]he "right to be let alone" [is] not an interest that may be legitimately weighed against the speakers' First Amendment rights (which the Court demotes to the status of First Amendment 'interests'). We have consistently held that "the Constitution does not permit the government to decide which types of otherwise protected speech are sufficiently offensive to require protection *for the unwilling listener or viewer.*" * * *

[T]he public forum involved here—the public spaces outside of health care facilities—has become, by necessity and by virtue of this Court's decisions, a forum of last resort for those who oppose abortion. [Those] whose concern is for the physical safety and security of clinic patients, workers, and doctors should take no comfort from today's decision. Individuals or groups intent on bullying or frightening women out of an abortion, or doctors out of performing that procedure, will not be deterred by Colorado's statute; bullhorns and screaming from eight feet away will serve their purposes well. But those who would accomplish their moral and religious objectives by peaceful and civil means, by trying to persuade individual women of the rightness of their cause, will be deterred; and that is not a good thing in a democracy. * * *

JUSTICE KENNEDY, dissenting.

[For] the first time, the Court approves a law which bars a private citizen from passing a message, in a peaceful manner and on a profound moral issue, to a fellow citizen on a public sidewalk. [We] would close our eyes to reality were we to deny that 'oral protest, education, or counseling' outside the entrances to medical facilities concern a narrow range of topics—indeed, one topic in particular. [If], just a few decades ago, a State with a history of enforcing racial discrimination had enacted a statute like this one, regulating "oral protest, education, or counseling" within 100 feet of the entrance to any lunch counter, our predecessors would not have hesitated to hold it was content based or viewpoint based. [To] say that one citizen can approach another to ask the time or the weather forecast or the directions to Main Street but not to initiate discussion on one of the most basic moral and political issues in all of contemporary discourse, a question touching profound ideas in philosophy and theology, is an astonishing view of the First Amendment. * * *

————

Compare McCULLEN v. COAKLEY, 573 U.S. 464 (2014): With the exception of patients, employees, police and the like, Massachusetts prohibits anyone from standing on a public highway or street within 35 feet of a hospital where abortions are performed. McCullen and others challenged the law because they wished to counsel patients about abortion especially about access to alternatives. Without calling [*Hill*] into question, the Court, per ROBERTS, C.J., held that strict scrutiny did not apply, but that the 35 feet buffer zone was not sufficiently tailored to meet the demands of a place restriction. The fact that the restriction applied only to abortion facilities did not make the restriction content based. Harms like obstruction and threats to public safety were not caused by the content of the communication. Although exceptions for employees were not designed to promote pro-abortion speech, such speech by employees in the zones would be impermissible. Roberts, C.J. suggested alternatives in meeting the state objectives such as statutes designed to prevent obstruction and harassment as well as other statutes designed to protect public safety. He also suggested that injunctions could be employed against those who had engaged in prior bad conduct.

SCALIA, J., joined by Kennedy and Thomas, JJ., concurring, argued that strict scrutiny should apply because the statute was plainly directed at anti-abortion protesters and also because employees of abortion facilities would clearly speak in favor of abortion. He did not reach the narrow tailoring issue because he did not want to create a false image of unanimity. ALITO, J., concurring, essentially agreed with Scalia, J., on the content discrimination issue, but explicitly agreed with the majority on the narrow tailoring issue.

————

Social media as public forum? Is all or part of social media a public forum for First Amendment purposes? In PACKINGHAM v. NORTH CAROLINA, 137 S.Ct. 1730 (2017), the Court addressed the question in the context of a North Carolina law making it a felony for a registered sex offender "to access a commercial social networking Web site where the sex offender knows that the site permits minor children to become members or to create or maintain personal Web pages." Lester Packingham was one of about 20,000 people in North Carolina to whom the statute applied, and one of over 1000 people prosecuted for violating it. He challenged the restriction on First Amendment grounds, and the Supreme Court, KENNEDY, J., writing for the majority, held the law, as written, to violate the First Amendment.

"A fundamental principle of the First Amendment is that all persons have access to places where they can speak and listen, and then, after reflection, speak and listen once more. The Court has sought to protect the right to speak in this spatial context. [While] in the past there may have been difficulty in identifying the most important places (in a spatial sense) for the exchange of views, today the answer is clear. It is cyberspace [in] general [and] social media in particular. [Social] media users employ [various] websites to engage in a wide array of protected First Amendment activity. [This] case is one of the first this Court has taken to address the relationship between the First Amendment and the modern Internet. As a result, the Court must exercise extreme caution before suggesting that the First Amendment provides scant protection for access to vast networks in that medium."

Against this background, the Court assumed that the statute was content neutral and thus to be evaluated according to "intermediate scrutiny." But even under this standard, the Court found the restriction excessively broad. "[To] foreclose access altogether is to prevent the user from engaging in the legitimate exercise of First Amendment rights. [Even] convicted criminals—and in some instances especially convicted criminals—might receive legitimate benefits from these means for access to the world of ideas . . . [The] analogy to this case is [*Board of Airport Comm'rs of Los Angeles v. Jews for Jesus* (supra, Sec. 1, IV, C)]. [If] a law prohibiting 'all protected expression' at a single airport is not constitutional, it follows with even greater force that the State may not enact this complete bar to the exercise of First Amendment rights on websites integral to the fabric of our modern society and culture."

Concurring in the judgment, ALITO, J., joined by Roberts, C.J., and Thomas, J, objected to what he called the Court's "undisciplined dicta." "The Court is unable to resist musings that seem to equate the entirety of the internet with public streets and parks." Finding it unnecessary to address the question of the nature of the internet as a public forum, or not, Alito still believed the North Carolina law unduly restrictive. "Because protecting children from abuse is a compelling state interest and sex offenders can (and do) use the internet to engage in such abuse, it is legitimate and entirely reasonable for states to try to stop abuse from occurring before it happens. [But the] fatal problem for [North Carolina's law] is that its wide sweep precludes access to a large number of websites that are most unlikely to facilitate the commission of a sex crime against a child." Using Amazon.com, washingtonpost.com, and WebMD as examples, Alito found invalid a law that prohibits registered sex offenders "from receiving or engaging in speech that the First Amendment protects and does not appreciably advance the State's goal of protecting children from recidivist sex offenders. [But] if the entirety of the internet or just 'social media' sites are the 21st century equivalent of public streets and parks, then [the Court's loose rhetoric . . . gives the States] little ability to restrict the sites that may be visited by even the most dangerous sex offenders. May a State preclude an adult previously convicted of molesting children from visiting a dating site for teenagers? Or a site where minors communicate with each other about personal problems? The Court should be more attentive to the implications of its rhetoric [because] there are important differences between cyberspace and the physical world."

4. NEW CATEGORIES?

The categories of fighting words, obscenity, copyright, and (formerly) libel and commercial advertising are often described as "exceptions" to the First Amendment. But once we realize just how much human communication remains untouched by the First Amendment—contract law, the law of wills, prosecution for perjury and blackmail, and much else—the language of "exceptions" seems misleading. Indeed, it may not be misleading to describe the speech that is covered by the First Amendment as itself an exception to the general regulability of verbal conduct. Nevertheless, there is considerable pressure on the existing boundaries of First Amendment coverage. Should previously uncovered communication be subject to First Amendment scrutiny of some sort, as with libel and fighting words? Should forms of communication—violent videogames, for example—that are now inside the First Amendment be treated as lying outside? Such issues have been subject to a considerable amount of recent litigation, as the following materials indicate

I. HARM TO CHILDREN AND THE OVERBREADTH DOCTRINE

NEW YORK v. FERBER, 458 U.S. 747 (1982), per WHITE, J., upheld conviction of a seller of films depicting young boys masturbating, under N.Y.Penal Law § 263.15, for "promoting a sexual performance," defined as "any performance [which] includes sexual conduct[14] by a child" under 16. The Court addressed the "single question": " 'To prevent the abuse of children who are made to engage in sexual conduct for commercial purposes, could the New York State Legislature, consistent with the First Amendment, prohibit the dissemination of material which shows children engaged in sexual conduct, regardless of whether such material is obscene?'* * *

"The *Miller* standard, like its predecessors, was an accommodation between the state's interests in protecting the 'sensibilities of unwilling recipients' from exposure to pornographic material and the dangers of censorship inherent in unabashedly content-based laws. Like obscenity statutes, laws directed at the dissemination of child pornography run the risk of suppressing protected expression by allowing the hand of the censor to become unduly heavy. For the following reasons, however, we are persuaded that the States are entitled to greater leeway in the regulation of pornographic depictions of children.

---

[14] Sec. 263.3 defined "sexual conduct" as "actual or simulated sexual intercourse, deviate sexual intercourse, sexual bestiality, masturbation, sado-masochistic abuse, or lewd exhibition of the genitals."

"First. [The] prevention of sexual exploitation and abuse of children constitutes a government objective of surpassing importance. The legislative findings accompanying passage of the New York laws reflect this concern. * * *

"We shall not second-guess this legislative judgment. Respondent has not intimated that we do so. Suffice it to say that virtually all of the States and the United States have passed legislation proscribing the production of or otherwise combating 'child pornography.' The legislative judgment, as well as the judgment found in the relevant literature, is that the use of children as subjects of pornographic materials is harmful to the physiological, emotional, and mental health of the child. That judgment, we think, easily passes muster under the First Amendment.

"Second. The distribution of photographs and films depicting sexual activity by juveniles is intrinsically related to the sexual abuse of children in at least two ways. First, the materials produced are a permanent record of the children's participation and the harm to the child is exacerbated by their circulation. Second, the distribution network for child pornography must be closed if the production of material which requires the sexual exploitation of children is to be effectively controlled. Indeed, there is no serious contention that the legislature was unjustified in believing that it is difficult, if not impossible, to halt the exploitation of children by pursuing only those who produce the photographs and movies. While the production of pornographic materials is a low-profile, clandestine industry, the need to market the resulting products requires a visible apparatus of distribution. The most expeditious if not the only practical method of law enforcement may be to dry up the market for this material by imposing severe criminal penalties on persons selling, advertising, or otherwise promoting the product. Thirty-five States and Congress have concluded that restraints on the distribution of pornographic materials are required in order to effectively combat the problem, and there is a body of literature and testimony to support these legislative conclusions.

"[The] *Miller* standard, like all general definitions of what may be banned as obscene, does not reflect the State's particular and more compelling interest in prosecuting those who promote the sexual exploitation of children. Thus, the question under the *Miller* test of whether a work, taken as a whole, appeals to the prurient interest of the average person bears no connection to the issue of whether a child has been physically or psychologically harmed in the production of the work. Similarly, a sexual explicit depiction need not be 'patently offensive' in order to have required the sexual exploitation of a child for its production. In addition, a work which, taken on the whole, contains serious literary, artistic, political, or scientific value may nevertheless embody the hardest core of child pornography. 'It is irrelevant to the child [who has been abused] whether or not the material [has] a literary, artistic, political, or social value.' We therefore cannot conclude that the *Miller* standard is a satisfactory solution to the child pornography problem.

"Third. The advertising and selling of child pornography provides an economic motive for and is thus an integral part of the production of such materials, an activity illegal throughout the nation. 'It rarely has been suggested that the constitutional freedom for speech and press extends its immunity to speech or writing used as an integral part of conduct in violation of a valid criminal statute.' * * *

"Fourth. The value of permitting live performances and photographic reproductions of children engaged in lewd sexual conduct is exceedingly modest, if not de minimis. We consider it unlikely that visual depictions of children performing sexual acts or lewdly exhibiting their genitals would often constitute an important and necessary part of a literary performance or scientific or educational work. As the trial court in this case observed, if it were necessary for literary or artistic value, a person over the statutory age who perhaps looked younger could be utilized. * * *

"Fifth. Recognizing and classifying child pornography as a category of material outside the protection of the First Amendment is not incompatible with our earlier decisions. 'The question whether speech is or is not protected by the First Amendment often depends on the content of the speech.' *Young v. American Mini Theatres, Inc.*, 427 U.S. 50 (1976). [When] a definable class of material, such as that covered by § 263.15, bears so heavily and pervasively on the welfare of children engaged in its production, we think the balance of competing interests is clearly struck and that it is permissible to consider these materials as without the protection of the First Amendment.

"There are, of course, limits on the category of child pornography which, like obscenity, is unprotected by the First Amendment. As with all legislation in this sensitive area, the conduct to be prohibited must be adequately defined by the applicable state law, as written or authoritatively construed. Here the nature of the harm to be combated requires that the state offense be limited to works that *visually* depict sexual conduct by children below a specified age. The category of 'sexual conduct' proscribed must also be suitably limited and described.

"The test for child pornography is separate from the obscenity standard enunciated in *Miller,* but may be compared to it for purpose of clarity. The *Miller* formulation is adjusted in the following respects: A trier of fact need not find that the material appeals to the prurient interest of the average person; it is not required that sexual conduct portrayed be done so in a patently offensive manner; and the material at issue need not be considered as a whole. We note that the distribution of descriptions or other depictions of sexual conduct, not otherwise obscene, which do not involve live performance or photographic or other visual reproduction of live performances, retains First Amendment protection. As with obscenity laws, criminal responsibility may not be imposed without some element of scienter on the part of the defendant. * * *

"It remains to address the claim that the New York statute is unconstitutionally overbroad because it would forbid the distribution of material with serious literary, scientific, or educational value or material which does not threaten the harms sought to be combated by the State. * * *

"The traditional rule is that a person to whom a statute may constitutionally be applied may not challenge that statute on the ground that it may conceivably be applied unconstitutionally to others in situations not before the Court. *Broadrick v. Oklahoma,* 413 U.S. 601 (1973). In *Broadrick,* we recognized that this rule reflects two cardinal principles of our constitutional order: the personal nature of constitutional rights and prudential limitations on constitutional adjudication. [By] focusing on the factual situation before us, and similar cases necessary for development of a constitutional rule, we face 'flesh-and-blood' legal problems with data 'relevant and adequate to an informed judgment.' This practice also fulfills a valuable institutional purpose: it allows state courts the opportunity to construe a law to avoid constitutional infirmities.

"What has come to be known as the First Amendment overbreadth doctrine is one of the few exceptions to this principle and must be justified by weighty countervailing policies. The doctrine is predicated on the sensitive nature of protected expression: persons whose expression is constitutionally protected may well refrain from exercising their rights for fear of criminal sanctions by a statute susceptible of application to protected expression. * * *

"In *Broadrick,* we explained [that]: '[T]he plain import of our cases is, at the very least, that facial overbreadth adjudication is an exception to our traditional rules of practice and that its function, a limited one at the outset, attenuates as the otherwise unprotected behavior that it forbids the State to sanction moves from "pure speech" toward conduct and that conduct—even if expressive—falls within the scope of otherwise valid criminal laws that reflect legitimate state interests in maintaining comprehensive controls over harmful, constitutionally unprotected conduct. * * *'

"[*Broadrick*] examined a regulation involving restrictions on political campaign activity, an area not considered 'pure speech,' and thus it was unnecessary to consider the proper overbreadth test when a law arguably reaches traditional forms of expression such as books and films. As we intimated in *Broadrick,* the requirement of substantial overbreadth extended 'at the very least' to cases involving conduct plus speech. This case, which poses the question squarely, convinces us that the rationale of *Broadrick* is sound and should be applied in the present context involving the harmful employment of children to make sexually explicit materials for distribution.

"[Applying] these principles, we hold that § 263.15 is not substantially overbroad. We consider this the paradigmatic case of a state statute whose legitimate reach dwarfs its arguably impermissible applications. [While] the reach of the statute is directed at the hard core of child pornography, the Court of Appeals was understandably concerned that some protected expression, ranging from medical textbooks to pictorials in the National Geographic would fall prey to the statute. How often, if ever, it may be necessary to employ children to engage in conduct clearly within the reach of § 263.15 in order to produce educational, medical, or artistic works cannot be known with certainty. Yet we seriously doubt

[that] these arguably impermissible applications of the statute amount to more than a tiny fraction of the materials within the statute's reach."

———

Digital child pornography. The Child Pornography Act of 1996 (the "CPPA") in addition to outlawing child pornography involving minors, extends its coverage to prohibit images that "appear to be, of a minor engaging in sexually explicit conduct" or marketed in a way that "conveys the impression" that it depicts a "minor engaging in sexually explicit conduct."

ASHCROFT v. FREE SPEECH COALITION, 535 U.S. 234 (2002), per KENNEDY, J., declared these provisions to be unconstitutional: "The CPPA [extends] to images that appear to depict a minor engaging in sexually explicit activity without regard to the *Miller* requirements. The materials need not appeal to the prurient interest. Any depiction of sexually explicit activity, no matter how it is presented, is proscribed. The CPPA applies to a picture in a psychology manual, as well as a movie depicting the horrors of sexual abuse. It is not necessary, moreover, that the image be patently offensive. Pictures of what appear to be 17-year-olds engaging in sexually explicit activity do not in every case contravene community standards.

"The CPPA prohibits speech despite its serious literary, artistic, political, or scientific value. The statute proscribes the visual depiction of [the idea] of teenagers engaging in sexual activity that is a fact of modern society and has been a theme in art and literature throughout the ages." Kennedy, J., argued that the Act could potentially apply to versions of Romeo and Juliet and films like Traffic and American Beauty.

"[The government] argues that the CPPA is necessary because pedophiles may use virtual child pornography to seduce children. There are many things innocent in themselves, however, such as cartoons, video games, and candy, that might be used for immoral purposes, yet we would not expect those to be prohibited because they can be misused. The Government, of course, may punish adults who provide unsuitable materials to children, and it may enforce criminal penalties for unlawful solicitation. The precedents establish, however, that speech within the rights of adults to hear may not be silenced completely in an attempt to shield children from it. [The Government] submits further that virtual child pornography whets the appetites of pedophiles and encourages them to engage in illegal conduct. This rationale cannot sustain the provision in question. The mere tendency of speech to encourage unlawful acts is not a sufficient reason for banning it. * * *

THOMAS, J., concurred: "In my view, the Government's most persuasive asserted interest [is] the prosecution rationale that persons who possess and disseminate pornographic images of real children may escape conviction by claiming that the images are computer-generated, thereby raising a reasonable doubt as to their guilt. At this time, however, the Government asserts only that defendants raise such defenses, not that they have done so successfully. In fact, the

Government points to no case in which a defendant has been acquitted based on a computer-generated images defense. While this speculative interest cannot support the broad reach of the CPPA, technology may evolve to the point where it becomes impossible to enforce actual child pornography laws because the Government cannot prove that certain pornographic images are of real children. * * *

O'CONNOR, J., concurring in part and dissenting in part, agreed that the act's attempt to ban sexually explicit images of adults that appear to be children was overbroad, but, in a portion of her opinion joined by Rehnquist, C.J., and Scalia, J., she argued that the prohibitions of computer generated sexually explicit images appearing to be children or conveying that impression were constitutional: "[D]efendants indicted for the production, distribution, or possession of actual-child pornography may evade liability by claiming that the images attributed to them are in fact computer-generated. Respondents may be correct that no defendant has successfully employed this tactic. But, given the rapid pace of advances in computer-graphics technology, the Governments concern is reasonable. Computer-generated images lodged with the Court bear a remarkable likeness to actual human beings. [T]his Court's cases do not require Congress to wait for harm to occur before it can legislate against it."

REHNQUIST, C.J., joined in part by Scalia, J., dissenting, would have construed the statute to apply to "visual depictions of youthful looking adult actors engaged in actual sexual activity; mere suggestions of sexual activity, such as youthful looking adult actors squirming under a blanket, are more akin to written descriptions than visual depictions, and thus fall outside the purview of the statute. The reference to simulated has been part of the definition of sexually explicit conduct since the statute was first passed. But the inclusion of simulated conduct, alongside actual conduct, does not change the hard core nature of the image banned. The reference to simulated conduct simply brings within the statute's reach depictions of hard core pornography that are made to look genuine including the main target of the CPPA, computer generated images virtually indistinguishable from real children engaged in sexually explicit conduct. Neither actual conduct nor simulated conduct, however, is properly construed to reach depictions such as those in a film portrayal of Romeo and Juliet which are far removed from the hard core pornographic depictions that Congress intended to reach."

After *Free Speech Coalition,* UNITED STATES v. WILLIAMS, 553 U.S. 285 (2008), per SCALIA, J., held that "offers to provide or requests to obtain child pornography are categorically excluded from the First Amendment" even if the material offered is not actually child pornography. *Free Speech Coalition* was distinguished on the ground that it "went beyond pandering to prohibit possession of material that could not otherwise be proscribed."

II. HARM TO WOMEN: FEMINISM AND PORNOGRAPHY

Catharine MacKinnon and Andrea Dworkin drafted an anti-pornography ordinance that was considered in a number of jurisdictions. The Indianapolis version of the anti-pornography civil rights ordinance was struck down in AMERICAN BOOKSELLERS ASS'N v. HUDNUT, 771 F.2d 323 (7th Cir.1985), affirmed, 475 U.S. 1001 (1986). The Seventh Circuit, per EASTERBROOK, J., ruled that the definition of pornography infected the entire ordinance (including provisions against trafficking, coercion into pornography, forcing pornography on a person, and assault or physical attack due to pornography) because it impermissibly discriminated on the basis of point of view: "Indianapolis enacted an ordinance defining 'pornography' as a practice that discriminates against women. * * *

"The Indianapolis ordinance does not refer to the prurient interest, to offensiveness, or to the standards of the community. It demands attention to particular depictions, not to the work judged as a whole. It is irrelevant under the ordinance whether the work has literary, artistic, political, or scientific value. The City and many amici point to these omissions as virtues. They maintain that pornography influences attitudes, and the statute is a way to alter the socialization of men and women rather than to vindicate community standards of offensiveness. And as one of the principal drafters of the ordinance has asserted, 'if a woman is subjected, why should it matter that the work has other value?' Catharine MacKinnon, *Pornography, Civil Rights, and Speech*, 20 Harv.C.R.-C.L.L.Rev. 1 (1985).

"Civil rights groups and feminists have entered this case as amici on both sides. Those supporting the ordinance say that it will play an important role in reducing the tendency of men to view women as sexual objects, a tendency that leads to both unacceptable attitudes and discrimination in the workplace and violence away from it. Those opposing the ordinance point out that much radical feminist literature is explicit and depicts women in ways forbidden by the ordinance and that the ordinance would reopen old battles. It is unclear how Indianapolis would treat works from James Joyce's *Ulysses* to Homer's *Iliad;* both depict women as submissive objects for conquest and domination.

"We do not try to balance the arguments for and against an ordinance such as this. The ordinance discriminates on the ground of the content of the speech. Speech treating women in the approved way—in sexual encounters 'premised on equality'—is lawful no matter how sexually explicit. Speech treating women in the disapproved way—as submissive in matters sexual or as enjoying humiliation—is unlawful no matter how significant the literary, artistic, or political qualities of the work taken as a whole. The state may not ordain preferred viewpoints in this way. The Constitution forbids the state to declare one perspective right and silence opponents. [Under] the First Amendment the government must leave to the people the evaluation of ideas. Bald or subtle, an idea is as powerful as the audience allows it to be. A belief may be pernicious—the beliefs of Nazis led to the death of millions, those of the Klan to the repression of millions. A pernicious belief may prevail. Totalitarian governments today rule much of the planet, practicing suppression of billions and spreading dogma that may enslave others. One of the things that separates our society from theirs is our absolute right to propagate opinions that the government finds wrong or even hateful. * * *

"Under the ordinance graphic sexually explicit speech is 'pornography' or not depending on the perspective the author adopts. Speech that 'subordinates' women and also, for example, presents women as enjoying pain, humiliation, or rape, or even simply presents women in 'positions of servility or submission or display' is forbidden, no matter how great the literary or political value of the work taken as a whole. Speech that portrays women in positions of equality is lawful, no matter how graphic the sexual content. This is thought control. It establishes an 'approved' view of women, of how they may react to sexual encounters, of how the sexes may relate to each other. Those who espouse the approved view may use sexual images; those who do not, may not.

"Indianapolis justifies the ordinance on the ground that pornography affects thoughts. Men who see women depicted as subordinate are more likely to treat them so. Pornography is an aspect of dominance.[1] It does not persuade people so much as change them. It works by socializing, by establishing the expected and the permissible. In this view pornography is not an idea; pornography is the injury.

"There is much to this perspective. Beliefs are also facts. People often act in accordance with the images and patterns they find around them. People raised in a religion tend to accept the tenets of that religion, often without independent examination. People taught from birth that black people are fit only for slavery rarely rebelled against that creed; beliefs coupled with the self-interest of the masters established a social structure that inflicted great harm while enduring for centuries. Words and images act at the level of the subconscious before they persuade at the level of the conscious. Even the truth has little chance unless a statement fits within the framework of beliefs that may never have been subjected to rational study.

"Therefore we accept the premises of this legislation. Depictions of subordination tend to perpetuate subordination. The subordinate status of women

---

[1]   **[Ct's Note]** "Pornography constructs what a woman is in terms of its view of what men want sexually. * * * Pornography's world of equality is a harmonious and balanced place. Men and women are perfectly complementary and perfectly bipolar. [All] the ways men love to take and violate women, women love to be taken and violated. [What] pornography *does* goes beyond its content: It eroticizes hierarchy, it sexualizes inequality. It makes dominance and submission sex. Inequality is its central dynamic; the illusion of freedom coming together with the reality of force is central to its working. [P]ornography is neither harmless fantasy nor a corrupt and confused misrepresentation of an otherwise neutral and healthy sexual situation. It institutionalizes the sexuality of male supremacy, fusing the erotization of dominance and submission with the social construction of male and female. * * * Men treat women as who they see women as being. Pornography constructs who that is. Men's power over women means that the way men see women defines who women can be. Pornography [is] a sexual reality." MacKinnon, supra, at 17–18 (emphasis in original).

in turn leads to affront and lower pay at work, insult and injury at home, battery and rape on the streets. * * *

"Yet this simply demonstrates the power of pornography as speech. All of these unhappy effects depend on mental intermediation. Pornography affects how people see the world, their fellows, and social relations. If pornography is what pornography does, so is other speech. Hitler's orations affected how some Germans saw Jews. Communism is a world view, not simply a *Manifesto* by Marx and Engels or a set of speeches. Efforts to suppress communist speech in the United States were based on the belief that the public acceptability of such ideas would increase the likelihood of totalitarian government. [Many] people believe that the existence of television, apart from the content of specific programs, leads to intellectual laziness, to a penchant for violence, to many other ills. The Alien and Sedition Acts passed during the administration of John Adams rested on a sincerely held belief that disrespect for the government leads to social collapse and revolution—a belief with support in the history of many nations. Most governments of the world act on this empirical regularity, suppressing critical speech. In the United States, however, the strength of the support for this belief is irrelevant. Seditious libel is protected speech unless the danger is not only grave but also imminent.

"Racial bigotry, anti-semitism, violence on television, reporters' biases—these and many more influence the culture and shape our socialization. None is directly answerable by more speech, unless that speech too finds its place in the popular culture. Yet all is protected as speech, however insidious. Any other answer leaves the government in control of all of the institutions of culture, the great censor and director of which thoughts are good for us.

"Sexual responses often are unthinking responses, and the association of sexual arousal with the subordination of women therefore may have a substantial effect. But almost all cultural stimuli provoke unconscious responses. Religious ceremonies condition their participants. Teachers convey messages by selecting what not to cover; the implicit message about what is off limits or unthinkable may be more powerful than the messages for which they present rational argument. Television scripts contain unarticulated assumptions. People may be conditioned in subtle ways. If the fact that speech plays a role in a process of conditioning were enough to permit governmental regulation, that would be the end of freedom of speech. * * *

"Much of Indianapolis's argument rests on the belief that when speech is 'unanswerable,' and the metaphor that there is a 'marketplace of ideas' does not apply, the First Amendment does not apply either. The metaphor is honored; Milton's *Aeropagitica* and John Stuart Mill's *On Liberty* defend freedom of speech on the ground that the truth will prevail, and many of the most important cases under the First Amendment recite this position. The Framers undoubtedly believed it. As a general matter it is true. But the Constitution does not make the dominance of truth a necessary condition of freedom of speech. To say that it does would be to confuse an outcome of free speech with a necessary condition for the application of the amendment.

"A power to limit speech on the ground that truth has not yet prevailed and is not likely to prevail implies the power to declare truth. At some point the government must be able to say (as Indianapolis has said): 'We know what the truth is, yet a free exchange of speech has not driven out falsity, so that we must now prohibit falsity.' If the government may declare the truth, why wait for the failure of speech? Under the First Amendment, however, there is no such thing as a false idea, *Gertz,* so the government may not restrict speech on the ground that in a free exchange truth is not yet dominant. * * *

"We come, finally, to the argument that pornography is 'low value' speech, that it is enough like obscenity that Indianapolis may prohibit it. [But] pornography is not low value speech within the meaning of the [relevant] cases. Indianapolis seeks to prohibit certain speech because it believes this speech influences social relations and politics on a grand scale, that it controls attitudes at home and in the legislature. This precludes a characterization of the speech as low value. True, pornography and obscenity have sex in common. But Indianapolis left out of its definition any reference to literary, artistic, political, or scientific value. The ordinance applies to graphic sexually explicit subordination in works great and small. The Court sometimes balances the value of speech against the costs of its restriction, but it does this by category of speech and not by the content of particular works. Indianapolis has created an approved point of view and so loses the support of these cases.

III. ANIMAL CRUELTY AND THE FLIGHT FROM NEW CATEGORIES

18 U.S.C. § 48 criminalizes the knowing creation, sale, or possession of a depiction of animal cruelty, if done for commercial gain in interstate or foreign commerce. A depiction of animal cruelty is defined as one "in which a living animal is intentionally maimed, mutilated, tortured, wounded, or killed," if that conduct violates federal or state law where "the creation, sale, or possession takes place." The law exempts any depiction "that has serious religious, political, scientific, educational, journalistic, historical, or artistic value." Respondent was convicted under the statute for selling videos of dog fighting, but argued that the statute violated the First Amendment on its face.

UNITED STATES v. STEVENS, 559 U.S. 460 (2010) per ROBERTS, C.J., rejected this contention and held that the statute was substantially overbroad, but it left room for Congress to pass a more narrowly drawn statute: "The Government's primary submission is that [the] banned depictions of animal cruelty, as a class, are categorically unprotected by the First Amendment. We disagree.

"[From] 1791 to the present,' [the] First Amendment has 'permitted restrictions upon the content of speech in a few limited areas,' and has never 'include[d] a freedom to disregard these traditional limitations.' These 'historic and traditional categories [ ]'—including obscenity, *Roth*, defamation, *Beauharnais*, fraud, *Virginia Bd.*, incitement, *Brandenburg*, and speech integral to criminal conduct, *Giboney v. Empire Storage & Ice Co.*, 336 U.S. 490 (1949)—are 'well-defined and narrowly limited classes of speech, the prevention and punishment of which have never been thought to raise any Constitutional problem.' *Chaplinsky*.

"The Government argues that 'depictions of animal cruelty' should be added to the list. It contends that depictions of 'illegal acts of animal cruelty' that are 'made, sold, or possessed for commercial gain' necessarily 'lack expressive value,' and may accordingly 'be regulated as *unprotected* speech.' * * *

"The Government contends that 'historical evidence' about the reach of the First Amendment is not 'a necessary prerequisite for regulation today,' and that categories of speech may be exempted from the First Amendment's protection without any long-settled tradition of subjecting that speech to regulation. Instead, the Government points to Congress's 'legislative judgment that . . . depictions of animals being intentionally tortured and killed [are] of such minimal redeeming value as to render [them] unworthy of First Amendment protection,' and asks the Court to uphold the ban on the same basis. The Government thus proposes that a claim of categorical exclusion should be considered under a simple balancing test: 'Whether a given category of speech enjoys First Amendment protection depends upon a categorical balancing of the value of the speech against its societal costs.'

"As a free-floating test for First Amendment coverage, that sentence is startling and dangerous. The First Amendment's guarantee of free speech does not extend only to categories of speech that survive an ad hoc balancing of relative social costs and benefits. The First Amendment itself reflects a judgment by the American people that the benefits of its restrictions on the Government outweigh the costs. * * *

"To be fair to the Government, its view did not emerge from a vacuum. As the Government correctly notes, this Court has often *described* historically unprotected categories of speech as being 'of such slight social value as a step to truth that any benefit that may be derived from them is clearly outweighed by the social interest in order and morality.' In *Ferber*, we noted that within these categories of unprotected speech, 'the evil to be restricted so overwhelmingly outweighs the expressive interests, if any, at stake, that no process of case-by-case adjudication is required,' because 'the balance of competing interests is clearly struck,' The Government derives its proposed test from these descriptions in our precedents.

"But such descriptions are just that-descriptive. They do not set forth a test that may be applied as a general matter to permit the Government to imprison any speaker so long as his speech is deemed valueless or unnecessary, or so long as an ad hoc calculus of costs and benefits tilts in a statute's favor. When we have identified categories of speech as fully outside the protection of the First Amendment, it has not been on the basis of a simple cost-benefit analysis. In *Ferber*, for example, we classified child pornography as such a category. We noted that the State of New York had a compelling interest in protecting children from abuse, and that the value of using children in these works (as opposed to simulated conduct or adult actors) was de minimis. But our decision did not rest on this 'balance of competing interests' alone. We made clear that *Ferber* presented a special case: The market for child pornography was 'intrinsically related' to the underlying abuse, and was therefore 'an integral part of the production of such materials, an activity illegal throughout the Nation.' * * *

"Our decisions in *Ferber* and other cases cannot be taken as establishing a freewheeling authority to declare new categories of speech outside the scope of the First Amendment. Maybe there are some categories of speech that have been historically unprotected, but have not yet been specifically identified or discussed as such in our case law. But if so, there is no evidence that 'depictions of animal cruelty' is among them. We need not foreclose the future recognition of such additional categories to reject the Government's highly manipulable balancing test as a means of identifying them." * * *

ALITO, J., dissented: "The Court strikes down in its entirety a valuable statute that was enacted not to suppress speech, but to prevent horrific acts of animal cruelty-in particular, the creation and commercial exploitation of 'crush videos,' a form of depraved entertainment that has no social value. [A] sample crush video, which has been lodged with the Clerk, records the following event: '[A] kitten, secured to the ground, watches and shrieks in pain as a woman thrusts her high-heeled shoe into its body, slams her heel into the kitten's eye socket and mouth loudly fracturing its skull, and stomps repeatedly on the animal's head. The kitten hemorrhages blood, screams blindly in pain, and is ultimately left dead in a moist pile of blood-soaked hair and bone.'

"It is undisputed that the *conduct* depicted in crush videos may constitutionally be prohibited. All 50 States and the District of Columbia have enacted statutes prohibiting animal cruelty. But before the enactment of § 48 the underlying conduct depicted in crush videos was nearly impossible to prosecute. These videos, which 'often appeal to persons with a very specific sexual fetish,' were made in secret, generally without a live audience, and 'the faces of the women inflicting the torture in the material often were not shown, nor could the location of the place where the cruelty was being inflicted or the date of the activity be ascertained from the depiction.' Thus, law enforcement authorities often were not able to identify the parties responsible for the torture. * * *"

"I do not have the slightest doubt that Congress, in enacting § 48, had no intention of restricting the creation, sale, or possession of depictions of hunting. Proponents of the law made this point clearly. [But] even if § 48 did impermissibly reach the sale or possession of depictions of hunting in a few unusual situations (for example, the sale in Oregon of a depiction of hunting with a crossbow in Virginia or the sale in Washington State of the hunting of a sharp-tailed grouse in Idaho, those isolated applications would hardly show that § 48 bans a substantial amount of protected speech."

IV. INTENTIONAL INFLICTION
OF EMOTIONAL DISTRESS

The father of a deceased Marine brought an action for intentional infliction of emotional distress, intrusion upon seclusion, and civil conspiracy against a fundamentalist church and its members for demonstrating near the Marine's funeral with signs whose content is detailed in the Court's opinion in SNYDER v. PHELPS, 562 U.S. 443 (2011), which is set out above.

V. VIOLENT VIDEO GAMES

California prohibits the sale or rental of "violent video games" to minors. The prohibition covers games "in which the range of options available to a player includes killing, maiming, dismembering, or sexually assaulting an image of a human being, if those acts are depicted" in a manner that "[a] reasonable person, considering the game as a whole, would find appeals to a deviant or morbid interest of minors," that is "patently offensive to prevailing standards in the community as to what is suitable for minors," and that "causes the game, as a whole, to lack serious literary, artistic, political, or scientific value for minors."

BROWN v. ENTERTAINMENT MERCHANTS ASS'N, 564 U.S. 786 (2011), per SCALIA, J., held that the law did not meet First Amendment standards for establishing a new category of unprotected speech: "Last Term, in *Stevens,* we held that new categories of unprotected speech may not be added to the list [of unprotected categories] by a legislature that concludes certain speech is too harmful to be tolerated. [The] Government argued in *Stevens* that it could create new categories of unprotected speech by applying a 'simple balancing test' that weighs the value of a particular category of speech against its social costs and then punishes that category of speech if it fails the test. We emphatically rejected that 'startling and dangerous' proposition. [W]ithout persuasive evidence that a novel restriction on content is part of a long (if heretofore unrecognized) tradition of proscription, a legislature may not revise the 'judgment [of] the American people,' embodied in the First Amendment, 'that the benefits of its restrictions on the Government outweigh the costs.'

"That holding controls this case. As in *Stevens,* California has tried to make violent speech regulation look like obscenity regulation by appending a saving clause required for the latter. That does not suffice. Our cases have been clear that the obscenity exception to the First Amendment does not cover whatever a legislature finds shocking, but only depictions of 'sexual conduct.' Because speech about violence is not obscene, it is of no consequence that California's statute mimics the New York statute regulating obscenity-for-minors that we upheld in *Ginsberg v. New York,* [fn. 70 in *Miller v. California,* Sec. 1, IV, B]. That case approved a prohibition on the sale to minors of sexual material that would be obscene from the perspective of a child. We held that the legislature could 'adjus[t] the definition of obscenity "to social realities by permitting the appeal of this type of material to be assessed in terms of the sexual interests" of . . . minors.' And because 'obscenity is not protected expression,' the New York statute could be sustained so long as the legislature's judgment that the proscribed materials were harmful to children 'was not irrational.' "

"California's argument would fare better if there were a longstanding tradition in this country of specially restricting children's access to depictions of violence, but there is [none.] California claims that video games present special problems because they are 'interactive,' in that the player participates in the violent action on screen and determines its outcome. The latter feature is nothing new: Since at least the publication of The Adventures of You: Sugarcane Island in 1969, young readers of choose-your-own-adventure stories have been able to make decisions that determine the plot by following instructions about which page to turn to. As for the argument that video games enable participation in the violent action, that seems to us more a matter of degree than of kind.

"Justice Alito has done considerable independent research to identify video games in which 'the violence is astounding,' 'Victims are dismembered, decapitated, disemboweled, set on fire, and chopped into little pieces. . . . Blood gushes, splatters, and pools.' Justice Alito recounts all these disgusting video games in order to disgust us—but disgust is not a valid basis for restricting expression. And the same is true of Justice Alito's description of those video games he has discovered that have a racial or ethnic motive for their violence "ethnic cleansing" [of] African Americans, Latinos, or Jews.' To what end does he relate this? Does it somehow increase the 'aggressiveness' that California wishes to suppress? Who knows? But it does arouse the reader's ire, and the reader's desire to put an end to this horrible message. Thus, ironically, Justice Alito's argument highlights the precise danger posed by the California Act: that the *ideas* expressed by speech—whether it be violence, or gore, or racism—and not its objective effects, may be the real reason for governmental proscription."

ALITO, J., joined by Roberts, C.J., concurring, argued that California's statute was unconstitutionally vague because the standards for what is inappropriate for children had been more clearly developed in the arena of sex than they have in the area of violence. He suggested that the statute would be on a stronger footing if it "targeted a narrower class of graphic depictions." At the same time, he argued that the majority was too casually dismissive of the "effect of exceptionally violent video games on impressionable minors, who often spend countless hours immersed in the alternative worlds that these games create. [When] all of the characteristics of video games are taken into account, there is certainly a reasonable basis for thinking that the experience of playing a video game may be quite different from the experience of reading a book, listening to a radio broadcast, or viewing a movie. And if this is so, then for at least some minors, the effects of playing violent video games may also be quite different. The Court acts prematurely in dismissing this possibility out of [hand.] I would hold only that the particular law at issue here fails to provide the clear notice that the Constitution requires. I would not squelch legislative efforts to deal with what is perceived by some to be a significant and developing social problem. If differently framed statutes are enacted by the States or by the Federal Government, we can consider the constitutionality of those laws when cases challenging them are presented to us."

THOMAS, J., dissenting, argued that the "Court's decision today does not comport with the original public understanding of the First Amendment. As originally understood, the First Amendment's protection against laws 'abridging the freedom of speech' did not extend to all speech. 'There are certain well-defined and narrowly limited classes of speech, the prevention and punishment of which have never been thought to raise any Constitutional problem. 'Laws regulating such speech do not 'abridg[e] the freedom of speech' because such speech is understood to fall outside 'the freedom of speech. * * *

"In my view, the 'practices and beliefs held by the Founders' reveal another category of excluded speech: speech to minor children bypassing their parents. The historical evidence shows that the founding generation believed parents had absolute authority over their minor children and expected parents to use that authority to direct the proper development of their children. It would be absurd to suggest that such a society understood 'the freedom of speech' to include a right to speak to minors (or a corresponding right of minors to access speech) without going through the minors' parents. The founding generation would not have considered it an abridgment of 'the freedom of speech' to support parental authority by restricting speech that bypasses minors' parents."

BREYER, J., dissented:

"[The] majority's claim that the California statute, if upheld, would create a 'new categor[y] of unprotected speech,' is overstated. No one here argues that depictions of violence, even extreme violence, *automatically* fall outside the First Amendment's protective scope as, for example, do obscenity and depictions of child pornography. We properly speak of *categories* of expression that lack protection when, like 'child pornography,' the category is broad, when it applies automatically, and when the State can prohibit everyone, including adults, from obtaining access to the material within it. But where, as here, careful analysis must precede a narrower judicial conclusion (say, denying protection to a shout of "fire" in a crowded theater, or to an effort to teach a terrorist group how to peacefully petition the United Nations), we do not normally describe the result as creating a 'new category of unprotected speech.'

"[Like] the majority, I believe that the California law must be 'narrowly tailored' to further a 'compelling interest,' without there being a 'less restrictive' alternative that would be 'at least as effective.' I would not apply this strict standard 'mechanically.' Rather, in applying it, I would evaluate the degree to which the statute injures speech-related interests, the nature of the potentially-justifying 'compelling interests,' the degree to which the statute furthers that interest, the nature and effectiveness of possible alternatives, and, in light of this evaluation, whether, overall, 'the statute works speech-related harm . . . out of proportion to the benefits that the statute seeks to provide.'

"[There] are many scientific studies that support California's views. Social scientists, for example, have found *causal* evidence that playing these games results in harm. Longitudinal studies, which measure changes over time, have found that increased exposure to violent video games causes an increase in aggression over the same period. Experimental studies in laboratories have found that subjects randomly assigned to play a violent video game subsequently displayed more characteristics of aggression than those who played nonviolent games. Surveys of 8th and 9th grade students have found a correlation between playing violent video games and aggression. Cutting-edge neuroscience has shown that 'virtual violence in video game playing results in those neural patterns that are considered characteristic for aggressive cognition and behavior.' And 'meta-analyses,' *i.e.*, studies of all the studies, have concluded that exposure to violent video games 'was positively associated with aggressive behavior, aggressive cognition, and aggressive affect,' and that 'playing violent video games is a *causal* risk factor for long-term harmful outcomes.'

"Some of these studies take care to explain in a commonsense way why video games are potentially more harmful than, say, films or books or television. In essence, they say that the closer a child's behavior comes, not to watching, but to *acting* out horrific violence, the greater the potential psychological harm. Experts debate the conclusions of all these studies. Like many, perhaps most, studies of human behavior, each study has its critics, and some of those critics have produced studies of their own in which they reach different conclusions. (I list both sets of research in the appendixes.) I, like most judges, lack the social science expertise to say definitively who is right. But associations of public health professionals who do possess that expertise have reviewed many of these studies and found a significant risk that violent video games, when compared with more passive media, are particularly likely to cause children harm. * * *

"Unlike the majority, I would find sufficient grounds in these studies and expert opinions for this Court to defer to an elected legislature's conclusion that the video games in question are particularly likely to harm children. * * * I add that the majority's different conclusion creates a serious anomaly in First Amendment law. *Ginsberg v. New York,* 390 U.S. 629 (1968), makes clear that a State can prohibit the sale to minors of depictions of nudity; today the Court makes clear that a State cannot prohibit the sale to minors of the most violent interactive video games. But what sense does it make to forbid selling to a 13-year-old boy a magazine with an image of a nude woman, while protecting a sale to that 13-year-old of an interactive video game in which he actively, but virtually, binds and gags the woman, then tortures and kills her? What kind of First Amendment would permit the government to protect children by restricting sales of that extremely violent video game only when the woman—bound, gagged, tortured, and killed—is also topless?

"This anomaly is not compelled by the First Amendment. It disappears once one recognizes that extreme violence, where interactive, and without literary, artistic, or similar justification, can prove at least as, if not more, harmful to children as photographs of nudity. And the record here is more than adequate to support such a view. That is why I believe that *Ginsberg* controls the outcome here a fortiori. And it is why I believe California's law is constitutional on its face."

VI. STOLEN VALOR AND THE PROBLEM OF NON-DEFAMATORY FALSITY

At his first public meeting of the Three Valley Water District Board, Board Member Xavier Alvarez introduced himself: "I'm a retired marine of 25 years. I retired in the year 2001. Back in 1987, I was awarded the Congressional Medal of Honor. I got wounded many times by the same guy." These statements were false, and Alvarez was indicted under the Stolen Valor Act, 18 U.S.C. § 704 which provides that "Whoever falsely represents himself or herself, verbally or in writing, to have been awarded any decoration or medal authorized by Congress for the Armed Forces of the United States . . . shall be fined under this title, imprisoned not more than six months, or both." The Act further provides that if the false representation relates to an award of the Congressional Medal of Honor, the possible imprisonment could rise to a year.

UNITED STATES v. ALVAREZ, 567 U.S. 709 (2012), held that the Stolen Valor Act violated the First Amendment. KENNEDY, J., joined by Roberts, C.J., and Ginsburg and Sotomayor, JJ., found the Act defective using the interpretive approach employed in *Stevens* and *Brown*: "In light of the substantial and expansive threats to free expression posed by content-based restrictions, this Court has rejected as 'startling and dangerous' a 'free-floating test for First Amendment coverage [based on] an ad hoc balancing of relative social costs and benefits.' *Stevens*. Instead, content-based restrictions on speech have been permitted, as a general matter, only when confined to the few 'historic and traditional categories [of expression] long familiar to the bar.' * * *

"Absent from those few categories [is] any general exception to the First Amendment for false statements. This comports with the common understanding that some false statements are inevitable if there is to be an open and vigorous expression of views in public and private conversation, expression the First Amendment guarantee. See *Sullivan* ('Th[e] erroneous statement is inevitable in free debate')."

Kennedy, J., argued that prior statements by the Court to the effect that false statements of fact have no constitutional value (see, e.g., *Gertz*), did not mean that false statements of fact were an unprotected category of speech. He maintained that the cases containing such language "all derive from cases discussing defamation, fraud, or some other legally cognizable harm associated with a false statement, such as an invasion of privacy or the costs of vexatious litigation. In those decisions the falsity of the speech at issue was not irrelevant to our analysis, but neither was it determinative. The Court has never endorsed the categorical rule the Government advances: that false statements receive no First Amendment protection. Our prior decisions have not confronted a measure, like the Stolen Valor Act, that targets falsity and nothing more. * * *

"The Government gives three examples of regulations on false speech that courts generally have found permissible: first, the criminal prohibition of a false statement made to a Government official, 18 U.S.C. § 1001; second, laws punishing perjury; and third, prohibitions on the false representation that one is speaking as a Government official or on behalf of the Government, see, e.g., § 912; § 709. These restrictions, however, do not establish a principle that all proscriptions of false statements are exempt from exacting First Amendment scrutiny. [§]1001's prohibition on false statements made to Government officials, in communications concerning official matters, does not lead to the broader proposition that false statements are unprotected when made to any person, at any time, in any context. The same point can be made about what the Court has confirmed is the 'unquestioned constitutionality of perjury statutes,' both the federal statute, § 1623, and its state-law equivalents. It is not simply because perjured statements are false that they lack First Amendment protection. Perjured testimony 'is at war with justice' because it can cause a court to render a 'judgment not resting on truth.' Perjury undermines the function and province of the law and threatens the integrity of judgments that are the basis of the legal system. Unlike speech in other contexts, testimony under oath has the formality and gravity necessary to remind the witness that his or her statements will be the basis for official governmental action, action that often affects the rights and liberties of others. Sworn testimony is quite distinct from lies not spoken under oath and simply intended to puff up oneself. Statutes that prohibit falsely representing that one is speaking on behalf of the Government, or that prohibit impersonating a Government officer, also protect the integrity of Government processes, quite apart from merely restricting false speech. [These] examples, to the extent that they implicate fraud or speech integral to criminal conduct, are inapplicable here. As our law and tradition show, then, there are instances in which the falsity of speech bears upon whether it is protected. Some false speech may be prohibited even if analogous true speech could not be. This opinion does not imply that any of these targeted prohibitions are somehow vulnerable. But it also rejects the notion that false speech should be in a general category that is presumptively unprotected.

"[T]he Stolen Valor Act, by its plain terms applies to a false statement made at any time, in any place, to any person. It can be assumed that it would not apply to, say, a theatrical performance. Still, the sweeping, quite unprecedented reach of the statute puts it in conflict with the First Amendment. Here the lie was made in a public meeting, but the statute would apply with equal force to personal, whispered conversations within a home. The statute seeks to control and suppress all false statements on this one subject in almost limitless times and settings. And it does so entirely without regard to whether the lie was made for the purpose of material gain. Permitting the government to decree this speech to be a criminal offense, whether shouted from the rooftops or made in a barely audible whisper, would endorse government authority to compile a list of subjects about which false statements are punishable. That governmental power has no clear limiting principle. Our constitutional tradition stands against the idea that we need Oceania's Ministry of Truth."

Kennedy, J., concluded that the Stolen Valor Act could not meet the exacting scrutiny required. He did not question that the statute attempted to further a compelling interest, but he denied that the statute was "actually necessary" to achieve it: "The Government points to no evidence to support its claim that the public's general perception of military awards is diluted by false claims such as those made by Alvarez. [Moreover,] the Government has not shown, and cannot show, why counterspeech would not suffice to achieve its interest. The facts of this case indicate that the dynamics of free speech, of counterspeech, of refutation, can overcome the lie. Respondent lied at a public meeting. Even before the FBI began investigating him for his false statements 'Alvarez was perceived as a phony,' [H]e was ridiculed online [and] his actions were reported in the press. [There] is good reason to believe that a similar fate would befall other false claimants. * * *

"The American people do not need the assistance of a government prosecution to express their high regard for the special place that military heroes hold in our tradition. Only a weak society needs government protection or intervention before it pursues its resolve to preserve the truth. Truth needs neither handcuffs nor a badge for its vindication."

BREYER, J., joined by Kagan, J., concurring in the judgment, departed from the approach taken in *Stevens*: "In determining whether a statute violates the First Amendment, this Court has often found it appropriate to examine the fit between statutory ends and means. In doing so, it has examined speech-related harms, justifications, and potential alternatives. In particular, it has taken account of the seriousness of the speech-related harm the provision will likely cause, the nature and importance of the provision's countervailing objectives, the extent to which the provision will tend to achieve those objectives, and whether there are other, less restrictive ways of doing so. Ultimately the Court has had to determine whether the statute works speech-related harm that is out of proportion to its justifications.

"Sometimes the Court has referred to this approach as 'intermediate scrutiny,' sometimes as 'proportionality' review, sometimes as an examination of 'fit,' and sometimes it has avoided the application of any label at all. Regardless of the label, some such approach is necessary if the First Amendment is to offer proper protection in the many instances in which a statute adversely affects constitutionally protected interests but warrants neither near-automatic condemnation (as 'strict scrutiny' implies) nor near-automatic approval (as is implicit in 'rational basis' review). But in this case, the Court's term 'intermediate scrutiny' describes what I think we should do.

"As the dissent points out, 'there are broad areas in which any attempt by the state to penalize purportedly false speech would present a grave and unacceptable danger of suppressing truthful speech.' Laws restricting false statements about philosophy, religion, history, the social sciences, the arts, and the like raise such

concerns, and in many contexts have called for strict scrutiny. But this case does not involve such a law. The dangers of suppressing valuable ideas are lower where, as here, the regulations concern false statements about easily verifiable facts that do not concern such subject matter. Such false factual statements are less likely than are true factual statements to make a valuable contribution to the marketplace of ideas. And the government often has good reasons to prohibit such false speech. But its regulation can nonetheless threaten speech-related harms.
* * *

"I must concede, as the Government points out, that this Court has frequently said or implied that false factual statements enjoy little First Amendment protection. But these judicial statements cannot be read to mean 'no protection at all.' False factual statements can serve useful human objectives, for example: in social contexts, where they may prevent embarrassment, protect privacy, shield a person from prejudice, provide the sick with comfort, or preserve a child's innocence; in public contexts, where they may stop a panic or otherwise preserve calm in the face of danger; and even in technical, philosophical, and scientific contexts, where (as Socrates' methods suggest) examination of a false statement (even if made deliberately to mislead) can promote a form of thought that ultimately helps realize the truth. Moreover, as the Court has often said, the threat of criminal prosecution for making a false statement can inhibit the speaker from making true statements, thereby 'chilling' a kind of speech that lies at the First Amendment's heart. * * *

"Further, the pervasiveness of false statements, made for better or for worse motives, made thoughtlessly or deliberately, made with or without accompanying harm, provides a weapon to a government broadly empowered to prosecute falsity without more. And those who are unpopular may fear that the government will use that weapon selectively, say by prosecuting a pacifist who supports his cause by (falsely) claiming to have been a war hero, while ignoring members of other political groups who might make similar false claims.

"I also must concede that many statutes and common law doctrines make the utterance of certain kinds of false statements unlawful. Those prohibitions, however, tend to be narrower than the statute before us, in that they limit the scope of their application, sometimes by requiring proof of specific harm to identifiable victims; sometimes by specifying that the lies be made in contexts in which a tangible harm to others is especially likely to occur; and sometimes by limiting the prohibited lies to those that are particularly likely to produce harm."

Breyer, J., proceeded to argue that this was true of fraud, defamation, the intentional infliction of emotional distress, perjury, materially false statements made to federal officials, false claims of terrorist attacks, impersonation of government officials, and trademark infringements: "While this list is not exhaustive, it is sufficient to show that few statutes, if any, simply prohibit without limitation the telling of a lie, even a lie about one particular matter. Instead, in virtually all these instances limitations of context, requirements of proof of injury, and the like, narrow the statute to a subset of lies where specific harm is more likely to occur. The limitations help to make certain that the statute does not allow its threat of liability or criminal punishment to roam at large, discouraging or forbidding the telling of the lie in contexts where harm is unlikely or the need for the prohibition is small.

"The statute before us lacks any such limiting features. It may be construed to prohibit only knowing and intentional acts of deception about readily verifiable facts within the personal knowledge of the speaker, thus reducing the risk that valuable speech is chilled. But it still ranges very broadly. And that breadth means that it creates a significant risk of First Amendment harm. As written, it applies in family, social, or other private contexts, where lies will often cause little harm. It also applies in political contexts, where although such lies are more likely to cause harm, the risk of censorious selectivity by prosecutors is also high. Further, given the potential haziness of individual memory along with the large number of military awards covered (ranging from medals for rifle marksmanship to the Congressional Medal of Honor), there remains a risk of chilling that is not completely eliminated by mens rea requirements; a speaker might still be worried about being prosecuted for a careless false statement, even if he does not have the intent required to render him liable. And so the prohibition may be applied where it should not be applied, for example, to bar stool braggadocio or, in the political arena, subtly but selectively to speakers that the Government does not like. * * *

"[I]t should be possible significantly to diminish or eliminate these remaining risks by enacting a similar but more finely tailored statute. For example, not all military awards are alike. Congress might determine that some warrant greater protection than others. And a more finely tailored statute might, as other kinds of statutes prohibiting false factual statements have done, insist upon a showing that the false statement caused specific harm or at least was material, or focus its coverage on lies most likely to be harmful or on contexts where such lies are most likely to cause harm. I recognize that in some contexts, particularly political contexts, such a narrowing will not always be easy to achieve. In the political arena a false statement is more likely to make a behavioral difference (say, by leading the listeners to vote for the speaker) but at the same time criminal prosecution is particularly dangerous (say, by radically changing a potential election result) and consequently can more easily result in censorship of speakers and their [ideas.] I would also note, like the plurality, that in this area more accurate information will normally counteract the lie. And an accurate, publicly available register of military awards, easily obtainable by political opponents, may well adequately protect the integrity of an award against those who would falsely claim to have earned it. And so it is likely that a more narrowly tailored statute combined with such information-disseminating devices will effectively serve Congress' end.

"The Government has provided no convincing explanation as to why a more finely tailored statute would not work. [That] being so, I find the statute as presently drafted works disproportionate constitutional harm. It consequently fails intermediate scrutiny, and so violates the First Amendment."

ALITO, J., joined by Scalia and Thomas, JJ., dissented: "Time and again, this Court has recognized that as a general matter false factual statements possess no intrinsic First Amendment value. Consistent with this recognition, many kinds of false factual statements have long been proscribed without 'rais[ing] any Constitutional problem.' Laws prohibiting fraud, perjury, and defamation, for example, were in existence when the First Amendment was adopted, and their constitutionality is now beyond question. We have also described as falling outside the First Amendment's protective shield certain false factual statements that were neither illegal nor tortious at the time of the Amendment's adoption. The right to freedom of speech has been held to permit recovery for the intentional infliction of emotional distress by means of a false statement. And in *Hill*, the Court concluded that the free speech right allows recovery for the even more modern tort of false-light invasion of privacy.

"In line with these holdings, it has long been assumed that the First Amendment is not offended by prominent criminal statutes with no close common-law analog. The most well known of these is probably 18 U.S.C. § 1001. [Unlike] perjury, § 1001 is not limited to statements made under oath or before an official government tribunal. Nor does it require any showing of 'pecuniary or property loss to the government.' Instead, the statute is based on the need to protect 'agencies from the perversion which *might* result from the deceptive practices described.'

"Still other statutes make it a crime to falsely represent that one is speaking on behalf of, or with the approval of, the Federal Government. We have recognized that § 912, like § 1001, does not require a showing of pecuniary or property loss and that its purpose is to 'maintain the general good repute and dignity' of Government service. All told, there are more than 100 federal criminal statutes that punish false statements made in connection with areas of federal agency concern. These examples amply demonstrate that false statements of fact merit no First Amendment protection in their own right. It is true, as Justice Breyer notes, that many in our society either approve or condone certain discrete categories of false statements, including false statements made to prevent harm to innocent victims and so-called 'white lies.' But respondent's false claim to have received the Medal of Honor did not fall into any of these categories. His lie did not 'prevent embarrassment, protect privacy, shield a person from prejudice, provide the sick with comfort, or preserve a child's innocence.' Nor did his lie 'stop a panic or otherwise preserve calm in the face of danger' or further philosophical or scientific debate. Respondent's claim, like all those covered by the Stolen Valor Act, served no valid purpose. [The] lies covered by the Stolen Valor Act have no intrinsic value and thus merit no First Amendment protection unless their prohibition would chill other expression that falls within the Amendment's scope. * * *

"[T]here are broad areas in which any attempt by the state to penalize purportedly false speech would present a grave and unacceptable danger of suppressing truthful speech. Laws restricting false statements about philosophy, religion, history, the social sciences, the arts, and other matters of public concern would present such a threat. The point is not that there is no such thing as truth or falsity in these areas or that the truth is always impossible to ascertain, but rather that it is perilous to permit the state to be the arbiter of truth. * * *

"In stark contrast to hypothetical laws prohibiting false statements about history, science, and similar matters, the Stolen Valor Act presents no risk at all that valuable speech will be suppressed. The speech punished by the Act is not only verifiably false and entirely lacking in intrinsic value, but it also fails to serve any instrumental purpose that the First Amendment might protect. Tellingly, when asked at oral argument what truthful speech the Stolen Valor Act might chill, even respondent's counsel conceded that the answer is none.

"Neither of the two opinions endorsed by Justices in the majority claims that the false statements covered by the Stolen Valor Act possess either intrinsic or instrumental value. Instead, those opinions appear to be based on the distinct concern that the Act suffers from overbreadth." Alito, J., referred to the plurality's concern about "personal, whispered conversations within a home") and Breyer, J.'s argument that the Act "applies in family, social, or other private contexts" and in "political contexts." But, Alito, J., argued that "to strike down a statute on the basis that it is overbroad, it is necessary to show that the statute's 'overbreadth [is] substantial, not only in an absolute sense, but also relative to [its] plainly legitimate sweep.' The plurality and the concurrence do not even attempt to make this showing. The plurality additionally worries that a decision sustaining the Stolen Valor Act might prompt Congress and the state legislatures to enact laws criminalizing lies about 'an endless list of subjects.' The plurality apparently fears that we will see laws making it a crime to lie about civilian awards such as college degrees or certificates of achievement in the arts and sports.

"This concern is likely unfounded. With very good reason, military honors have traditionally been regarded as quite different from civilian awards. Nearly a century ago, Congress made it a crime to wear a military medal without authorization; we have no comparable tradition regarding such things as Super Bowl rings, Oscars, or Phi Beta Kappa keys. In any event, if the plurality's concern is not entirely fanciful, it falls outside the purview of the First Amendment. The problem that the plurality foresees—that legislative bodies will enact unnecessary and overly intrusive criminal laws—applies regardless of whether the laws in question involve speech or nonexpressive conduct. If there is a problem with, let us say, a law making it a criminal offense to falsely claim to have been a high school valedictorian, the problem is not the suppression of speech but the misuse of the criminal law, which should be reserved for conduct that inflicts or threatens truly serious societal harm. The objection to this hypothetical law would be the same as the objection to a law making it a crime to eat potato chips during the graduation ceremony at which the high school valedictorian is recognized. The safeguard against such laws is democracy, not the First Amendment. Not every foolish law is unconstitutional.* * *

"The Stolen Valor Act is a narrow law enacted to address an important problem, and it presents no threat to freedom of expression. I would sustain the constitutionality of the Act, and I therefore respectfully dissent."

VII. "INDECENT" OR "NEAR OBSCENE" SPEECH

RENTON v. PLAYTIME THEATRES, INC., 475 U.S. 41 (1986), per REHNQUIST, J., upheld a zoning ordinance prohibiting adult motion theaters from within 1,000 feet of any residential zone, church, park, or school. The effect was to exclude such theaters from approximately 94% of the land in the city. Of the remaining 520 acres, a substantial part was occupied by a sewage disposal and treatment plant, a horse racing track and environs, a warehouse and manufacturing facilities, a Mobil Oil tank farm, and a shopping center: "[T]he resolution of this case is largely dictated by our decision in *Young v. American Mini Theatres, Inc.*, 427 U.S. 50 (1976). There, although five Members of the Court did not agree on a single rationale for the decision, we held that the city of Detroit's zoning ordinance, which prohibited locating an adult theater within 1,000 feet of any two other 'regulated uses' or within 500 feet of any residential zone, did not violate the First and Fourteenth amendments. The Renton ordinance, like the one in *Young,* does not ban adult theaters altogether, but merely provides that such theaters may not be located within 1,000 feet of any residential zone, single-or multiple-family dwelling, church, park, or school. The ordinance is therefore properly analyzed as a form of time, place, and manner regulation.

"This Court has long held that regulations enacted for the purpose of restraining speech on the basis of its content presumptively violate the First Amendment. See *Chicago Police Dept. v. Mosley,* supra. On the other hand, so-called 'content-neutral' time, place, and manner regulations are acceptable so long as they are designed to serve a substantial governmental interest and do not unreasonably limit alternative avenues of communication.

"At first glance, the Renton ordinance, like the ordinance in *Young,* does not appear to fit neatly into either the 'content-based' or the 'content-neutral' category. To be sure, the ordinance treats theaters that specialize in adult films differently from other kinds of theaters. Nevertheless, [the] City Council's '*predominate* concerns' were with the secondary effects of adult theaters, and not with the content of adult films themselves. * * *

"[This] finding as to 'predominate' intent is more than adequate to establish that the city's pursuit of its zoning interests here was unrelated to the suppression of free expression. The ordinance by its terms is designed to prevent crime, protect the city's retail trade, maintain property values, and generally 'protec[t] and preserv[e] the quality of [the city's] neighborhoods, commercial districts, and the quality of urban life,' not to suppress the expression of unpopular views. As Justice Powell observed in *Young,* '[i]f [the city] had been concerned with restricting the message purveyed by adult theaters, it would have tried to close them or restrict their number rather than circumscribe their choice as to location.'

"In short, the [ordinance] does not contravene the fundamental principle that underlies our concern about 'content-based' speech regulations: that 'government may not grant the use of a forum to people whose views it finds acceptable, but deny use to those wishing to express less favored or more controversial views.' *Mosley.*

"It was with this understanding in mind that, in *Young,* a majority of this Court decided that at least with respect to businesses that purvey sexually explicit materials, zoning ordinances designed to combat the undesirable secondary effects of such businesses are to be reviewed under the standards applicable to 'content-neutral' time, place, and manner regulations.[2]

"The appropriate inquiry in this case, then, is whether the Renton ordinance is designed to serve a substantial governmental interest and allows for reasonable alternative avenues of communication." After concluding that the ordinance [served] substantial government interests, the Court ruled that the Renton ordinance allowed "for reasonable alternative avenues of communication": "[W]e note that the ordinance leaves some 520 acres, or more than five percent of the entire land area of Renton, open to use as adult theater sites. [T]he First Amendment requires only that Renton refrain from effectively denying respondents a reasonable opportunity to open and operate an adult theater within the city, and the ordinance before us easily meets this requirement. * * * "

BRENNAN, J., joined by Marshall, J., dissented: "The fact that adult movie theaters may cause harmful 'secondary' land use effects may arguably give Renton a compelling reason to regulate such establishments; it does not mean, however, that such regulations are content-neutral. [The] ordinance discriminates on its face against certain forms of speech based on content. Movie theaters specializing in 'adult motion pictures' may not be located within 1,000 feet of any residential zone, single-or multiple-family dwelling, church, park, or school. Other motion picture theaters, and other forms of 'adult entertainment,' such as bars, massage parlors, and adult bookstores, are not subject to the same restrictions. This selective treatment strongly suggests that Renton was interested not in controlling the 'secondary effects' associated with adult businesses, but in discriminating against adult theaters based on the content of the films they exhibit."

Renton's "secondary effects" notion was revisited by several justices in BOOS v. BARRY, 485 U.S. 312 (1988): A District of Columbia ordinance banned the display of any sign within 500 feet of a foreign embassy that would tend to bring the embassy into "public odium" or "public disrepute." O'CONNOR, J., joined by Stevens and Scalia, JJ., distinguished *Renton:* "Respondents and the United States

---

[2] **[Ct's Note]** See *Young* (plurality opinion) ("[I]t is manifest that society's interest in protecting this type of expression is of a wholly different, and lesser, magnitude than the interest in untrammeled political debate * * * ."). [The plurality opinion in *Young* stated that "[f]ew of us would march our sons and daughters off to war to see 'Specified Sexual Activities' exhibited in the theaters of our choice."].

do not point to the 'secondary effects' of picket signs in front of embassies. They do not point to congestion, to interference with ingress or egress, to visual clutter, or to the need to protect the security of embassies. Rather, they rely on the need to protect the dignity of foreign diplomatic personnel by shielding them from speech that is critical of their governments. This justification focuses *only* on the content of the speech and the direct impact that speech has on its listeners. The emotive impact of speech on its audience is not a 'secondary effect.' Because the display clause regulates speech due to its potential primary impact, we conclude it must be considered content-based."

BRENNAN, J., joined by Marshall, J., agreed with the conclusion that the ordinance was content-based, but objected to O'Connor, J.'s "assumption that the *Renton* analysis applies not only outside the context of businesses purveying sexually explicit materials but even to political speech."

———

LOS ANGELES v. ALAMEDA BOOKS, 535 U.S. 425 (2002), per O'CONNOR, J., reaffirmed *Renton* and found a sufficient showing of secondary effects to permit Los Angeles not only to disperse adult businesses, but also to prohibit more than one adult entertainment business within the same building, i.e., a company could not have an adult bookstore and an adult video arcade in the same building.

SCALIA, J., concurring, would have gone further: "[I]n a case such as this our First Amendment traditions make secondary effects analysis quite unnecessary. The Constitution does not prevent those communities that wish to do so from regulating, or indeed entirely suppressing, the business of pandering sex."

Four Justices expressed doubts about the conception of "content" employed in *Renton*. KENNEDY, J., concurring, criticized *Renton's* conception of "content": "*Renton* described a similar ordinance as "content neutral," and I agree with the dissent that the designation is imprecise. [T]he ordinance in *Renton* 'treat[ed] theaters that specialize in adult films differently from other kinds of theaters.' The fiction that this sort of ordinance is content neutral—or 'content neutral'—is perhaps more confusing than helpful. [These] ordinances are content based, and we should call them so."

Nonetheless, Kennedy, J., adhered to the "intermediate scrutiny" of *Renton* and required a city to "advance some basis to show that its regulation has the purpose and effect of suppressing secondary effects, while leaving the quantity and accessibility of speech substantially intact." Kennedy, J., found that Los Angeles ordinance met this burden.

SOUTER, J., joined by Stevens and Ginsburg, and in part by Breyer, JJ., dissented: "[W]hile it may be true that an adult business is burdened only because of its secondary effects, it is clearly burdened only if its expressive products have adult content. Thus, the Court has recognized that this kind of regulation, though called content neutral, occupies a kind of limbo between full-blown, content-based restrictions and regulations that apply without any reference to the substance of what is said."

Five years after *Renton*, the Court held that an Indiana statute prohibiting the knowing or intentional appearing in a public place in a state of nudity could constitutionally be applied to require that any female dancer at a minimum wear "pasties" and a "G-string" when she dances.

BARNES v. GLEN THEATRE, INC., 501 U.S. 560 (1991). The Justices upholding the ordinance were divided upon the rationale for doing so. Rehnquist, C.J., joined by O'Connor and Kennedy, JJ., applied the *O'Brien* test, characterized the statute as a "public indecency" statute, and concluded that the interests in order and morality justified the statute. Souter, J., concurring, also applied the *O'Brien* test, but concluded that the statute was justified by the "secondary effects" of prostitution, sexual assaults, and other criminal activity even though this justification had not been articulated by the Indiana legislature or its courts. Scalia, J., argued that the case law did not support the plurality's contention that the interest in morality was substantial enough to pass muster under *O'Brien*; nonetheless, he voted to uphold the statute by repudiating the *O'Brien* test. White, J. joined by Marshall, Blackmun and Stevens, JJ., dissented.

The fragmented character of the *Barnes* majority created interpretive difficulties for the Pennsylvania Supreme Court in considering an Erie, Pennsylvania ordinance. Like Indiana, Erie's ordinance forbade knowingly or intentionally appearing in a public "state of nudity." Unlike Indiana, however, the preamble to the ordinance stated that the "Council specifically wishes to adopt the concept of Public Indecency prohibited by the laws of the State of Indiana, which was approved by the U.S. Supreme Court in *Barnes*, (for) the purpose of limiting a recent increase in nude live entertainment within the City," which led to prostitution and other crime.

Pap's A.M., operated "Kandyland," featuring nude erotic dancing by women. To comply with the ordinance, these dancers had to minimally wear "pasties" and a "G-string." Pap's sought an injunction against the ordinance's enforcement. The Pennsylvania Supreme Court, unable to find a lowest common denominator uniting the *Barnes* majority, felt free to reach an independent judgment, and found that the ordinance, although also directed at secondary effects, was primarily directed at expression and did not survive close scrutiny.

In ERIE v. PAP'S A.M., 529 U.S. 277 (2000), the plurality, per O'CONNOR, J., joined by Rehnquist, C.J., and Kennedy and Breyer, JJ., upheld application of the ordinance to prevent nude dancing: "Being 'in a state of nudity' is not an inherently expressive condition. [N]ude dancing of the type at issue here is expressive conduct, although we think that it falls only within the outer ambit of the First

Amendment's protection. [G]overnment restrictions on public nudity such as the ordinance at issue here should be evaluated under the framework set forth in *O'Brien* for content-neutral restrictions on symbolic speech. * * *

SCALIA, J., joined by Thomas., J., concurred: "In *Barnes*, I voted to uphold the challenged Indiana statute 'not because it survives some lower level of First Amendment scrutiny, but because, as a general law regulating conduct and not specifically directed at expression, it is not subject to First Amendment scrutiny at all.' Erie's ordinance, too, by its terms prohibits not merely nude dancing, but the act—irrespective of whether it is engaged in for expressive purposes—of going nude in public."

"Moreover, even were I to conclude that the city of Erie had specifically singled out the activity of nude dancing, I still would not find that this regulation violated the First Amendment unless I could be persuaded (as on this record I cannot) that it was the communicative character of nude dancing that prompted the ban. When conduct other than speech itself is regulated, it is my view that the First Amendment is violated only '[w]here the government prohibits conduct precisely because of its communicative attributes.' I do not feel the need, as the Court does, to identify some 'secondary effects.' [The] traditional power of government to foster good morals (bonos mores), and the acceptability of the traditional judgment (if Erie wishes to endorse it) that nude public dancing *itself* is immoral, have not been repealed by the First Amendment."

SOUTER, J., concurred in part and dissented in part: "I [agree] with the analytical approach that the plurality employs in deciding this case. [But] intermediate scrutiny requires a regulating government to make some demonstration of an evidentiary basis for the harm it claims to flow from the expressive activity, and for the alleviation expected from the restriction imposed. [What] is clear is that the evidence of reliance must be a matter of demonstrated fact, not speculative supposition.

"By these standards, the record before us today is deficient. [The] plurality does the best it can with the materials to hand, but the pickings are slim. [T]he ordinance's preamble assert[s] that over the course of more than a century the city council had expressed 'findings' of detrimental secondary effects flowing from lewd and immoral profitmaking activity in public places. But however accurate the recital may be and however honestly the councilors may have held those conclusions to be true over the years, the recitation does not get beyond conclusions on a subject usually fraught with some emotionalism. * * *

STEVENS, J., joined by Ginsburg, J., dissented: "Far more important than the question whether nude dancing is entitled to the protection of the First Amendment are the dramatic changes in legal doctrine that the Court endorses today. Until now, the 'secondary effects' of commercial enterprises featuring indecent entertainment have justified only the regulation of their location. For the first time, the Court has now held that such effects may justify the total suppression of protected speech. * * *

"[Never] before have we approved the use of ['the so-called "secondary effects" test'] to justify a total ban on protected First Amendment expression. On the contrary, we have been quite clear that the doctrine would not support that end."

VIII. PRIVATE SPEECH

Dun & Bradstreet, Inc., a credit reporting agency, falsely and negligently reported to five of its subscribers that Greenmoss Builders, Inc. had filed a petition for bankruptcy and also negligently misrepresented Greenmoss' assets and liabilities. In the ensuing defamation action, Greenmoss recovered $50,000 in compensatory damages and $300,000 in punitive damages. Dun & Bradstreet argued that, under *Gertz,* its First Amendment rights had been violated because presumed and punitive damages had been imposed without instructions requiring a showing of *New York Times* malice. Greenmoss argued that the *Gertz* protections did not extend to non-media defendants and, in any event, did not extend to commercial speech.

DUN & BRADSTREET, INC. v. GREENMOSS BUILDERS, INC., 472 U.S. 749 (1985), rejected Dun & Bradstreet's contention, but there was no opinion of the Court. The common theme of the five justices siding with Greenmoss was that the First Amendment places less value on "private" speech than upon "public" speech.

POWELL, J., joined by Rehnquist and O'Connor, JJ., noted that the Vermont Supreme Court below had held "as a matter of federal constitutional law" that "the media protections outlined in *Gertz* are inapplicable to nonmedia defamation actions." In affirming, Powell, J., stated that his reasons were "different from those relied upon by the Vermont Supreme Court": "Like every other case in which this Court has found constitutional limits to state defamation laws, *Gertz* involved expression on a matter of undoubted public concern. * * *

"We have never considered whether the *Gertz* balance obtains when the defamatory statements involve no issue of public concern. To make this determination, we must employ the approach approved in *Gertz* and balance the State's interest in compensating private individuals for injury to their reputation against the First Amendment interest in protecting this type of expression. This state interest is identical to the one weighed in *Gertz.* * * *

"The First Amendment interest, on the other hand, is less important than the one weighed in *Gertz.* We have long recognized that not all speech is of equal First Amendment importance. It is speech on 'matters of public concern' that is 'at the heart of the First Amendment's protection.' [In] contrast, speech on matters of purely private concern is of less First Amendment concern. As a number of state courts, including the court below, have recognized, the role of the Constitution in regulating state libel law is far more limited when the concerns that activated *New York Times* and *Gertz* are absent.

"While such speech is not totally unprotected by the First Amendment, its protections are less stringent. [In] light of the reduced constitutional value of speech involving no matters of public concern, we hold that the state interest adequately supports awards of presumed and punitive damages—even absent a showing of 'actual malice.'

"We conclude that permitting recovery of presumed and punitive damages in defamation cases absent a showing of 'actual malice' does not violate the First Amendment when the defamatory statements do not involve matters of public concern."

Although expressing the view that *Gertz* should be overruled and that the *New York Times* malice definition should be reconsidered, BURGER, C.J., concurring, stated that: "The single question before the Court today is whether *Gertz* applies to this case. The plurality opinion holds that *Gertz* does not apply because, unlike the challenged expression in *Gertz,* the alleged defamatory expression in this case does not relate to a matter of public concern. I agree that *Gertz* is limited to circumstances in which the alleged defamatory expression concerns a matter of general public importance, and that the expression in question here relates to a matter of essentially private concern. I therefore agree with the plurality opinion to the extent that it holds that *Gertz* is inapplicable in this case for the two reasons indicated. No more is needed to dispose of the present case."

WHITE, J., who had dissented in *Gertz,* was prepared to overrule that case or to limit it, but he disagreed with Powell, J.'s, suggestion that the plurality's resolution of the case was faithful to *Gertz:* "It is interesting that Justice Powell declines to follow the *Gertz* approach in this case. I had thought that the decision in *Gertz* was intended to reach cases that involve any false statements of fact injurious to reputation, whether the statement is made privately or publicly and whether or not it implicates a matter of public importance."

BRENNAN, J., joined by Marshall, Blackmun and Stevens, JJ., dissented: "This case involves a difficult question of the proper application of *Gertz* to credit reporting—a type of speech at some remove from that which first gave rise to explicit First Amendment restrictions on state defamation law—and has produced a diversity of considered opinions, none of which speaks for the Court. Justice Powell's plurality opinion affirming the judgment below would not apply the *Gertz* limitations on presumed and punitive damages [because] the speech involved a subject of purely private concern and was circulated to an extremely limited audience. * * * Justice White also would affirm; he would not apply *Gertz* to this case on the ground that the subject matter of the publication does not deal with a matter of general or public importance. The Chief Justice apparently agrees with Justice White. The four who join this opinion would reverse the judgment of the Vermont Supreme Court. We believe that, although protection of the type of expression at issue is admittedly not the 'central meaning of the First Amendment,' *Gertz* makes clear that the First Amendment nonetheless requires restraints on presumed and punitive damage awards for this expression. [Respondent] urged that *Gertz* be restricted] to cases in which the defendant is a 'media' entity. Such a distinction is irreconcilable with the fundamental First Amendment principle that '[t]he inherent worth [of] speech in terms of its capacity for informing the public does not depend upon the identity of its source, whether corporation, association, union, or individual.' *First National Bank v. Bellotti* [Sec. 10 infra]."

"Even if the subject matter of credit reporting were properly considered—in the terms of Justice White and Justice Powell—as purely a matter of private discourse, this speech would fall well within the range of valuable expression for which the First Amendment demands protection. Much expression that does not directly involve public issues receives significant protection. Our cases do permit some diminution in the degree of protection afforded one category of speech about economic or commercial matters. 'Commercial speech'—defined as advertisements that 'do no more than propose a commercial transaction'—may be more closely regulated than other types of speech. [Credit] reporting is not 'commercial speech' as this Court has defined the term."

5. PRIOR RESTRAINTS

Prior restraint is a technical term in First Amendment law, referring to requirements that speech be licensed in advance of its delivery, or to injunctions against speeches (or publications) yet to be delivered. Of course a criminal statute prohibiting all advocacy of violent action would *restrain* speech and would have been enacted *prior* to any restrained communication. The statute would be overbroad, but it would not in this technical sense be a prior restraint. A prior restraint refers only to closely related, distinctive methods of regulating expression that are said to have their own peculiar set of evils and problems, in addition to those that accompany most any governmental interference with free expression. "The issue is not whether the government may impose a particular restriction of substance in an area of public expression, such as forbidding obscenity in newspapers, but whether it may do so by a particular method, such as advance screening of newspaper copy. In other words, restrictions which could be validly imposed when enforced by subsequent punishment are, nevertheless, forbidden if attempted by prior restraint." Thomas Emerson, *The Doctrine of Prior Restraint*, 20 Law and Contemp.Prob. 648 (1955).

The classic prior restraints were the English licensing laws which required a license in advance to print any material or to import or to sell any book. One of the questions raised in this chapter concerns the types of government conduct beyond the classic licensing laws that should be characterized as prior restraints.

I. FOUNDATION CASES

A. Licensing

LOVELL v. GRIFFIN, 303 U.S. 444 (1938), per Hughes, C.J., invalidated an ordinance prohibiting the distribution of handbooks, advertising or literature within the city of Griffin, Georgia without obtaining written permission of the City Manager: "[T]he ordinance is invalid on its face. Whatever the motive which induced its adoption, its character is such that it strikes at the very foundation of the freedom of the press by subjecting it to license and censorship. The struggle for the freedom of the press was primarily directed against the power of the licensor. It was against that power that John Milton directed his assault by his 'Appeal for the Liberty of Unlicensed Printing.' And the liberty of the press became initially a right to publish *without* a license what formerly could be published only *with* one.' While this freedom from previous restraint upon publication cannot be regarded as exhausting the guaranty of liberty, the prevention of that restraint was a leading purpose in the adoption of the constitutional provision. Legislation of the type of the ordinance in question would restore the system of license and censorship in its baldest form.

"The liberty of the press is not confined to newspapers and periodicals. It necessarily embraces pamphlets and leaflets. These indeed have been historic weapons in the defense of liberty, as the pamphlets of Thomas Paine and others in our own history abundantly attest. The press in its historic connotation comprehends every sort of publication which affords a vehicle of information and opinion. * * *

"The ordinance cannot be saved because it relates to distribution and not to publication. 'Liberty of circulating is as essential to that freedom as liberty of publishing; indeed, without the circulation, the publication would be of little value.' *Ex parte Jackson*, 96 U.S. (6 Otto) 727, 733 (1877).

"[As] the ordinance is void on its face, it was not necessary for appellant to seek a permit under it. She was entitled to contest its validity in answer to the charge against her."

———

WATCHTOWER BIBLE & TRACT SOCIETY v. STRATTON, 536 U.S. 150 (2002), per STEVENS, J., struck down a village ordinance requiring door to door advocates or distributors of literature to register with the mayor: "It is offensive—not only to the values protected by the First Amendment, but to the very notion of a free society—that in the context of everyday public discourse a citizen must first inform the government of her desire to speak to her neighbors and then obtain a permit to do so. Even if the issuance of permits by the mayor's office is a ministerial task that is performed promptly and at no cost to the applicant, a law requiring a permit to engage in such speech constitutes a dramatic departure from our national heritage and constitutional tradition."

B. Injunctions

NEAR v. MINNESOTA

283 U.S. 697, 51 S.Ct. 625, 75 L.Ed. 1357 (1931).

CHIEF JUSTICE HUGHES delivered the opinion of the Court.

[The *Saturday Press* published articles charging that through graft and incompetence named public officials failed to expose and punish gangsters responsible for gambling, bootlegging, and racketeering in Minneapolis. It demanded a special grand jury and special prosecutor to deal with the situation and to investigate an alleged attempt to assassinate one of its publishers. Under a statute that authorized abatement of a "malicious, scandalous and defamatory newspaper" the state secured, and its supreme court affirmed, a court order that "abated" the Press and perpetually enjoined the defendants from publishing or circulating "any publication whatsoever which is a malicious, scandalous or defamatory newspaper." The order did not restrain the defendants from operating a newspaper "in harmony with the general welfare."]

The object of the statute is not punishment, in the ordinary sense, but suppression of the offending newspaper. [In] the case of public officers, it is the reiteration of charges of official misconduct, and the fact that the newspaper [is] principally devoted to that purpose, that exposes it to suppression. [T]he operation and effect of the statute [is] that public authorities may bring the owner or publisher of a newspaper or periodical before a judge upon a charge of conducting a business of publishing scandalous and defamatory matter—in particular that the matter consists of charges against public officers of official dereliction—and, unless the owner or publisher is able and disposed to bring competent evidence to satisfy the judge that the charges are true and are published with good motives and for justifiable ends, his newspaper or periodical is suppressed and further publication is made punishable as a contempt. This is of the essence of censorship.

The question is whether a statute authorizing such proceedings [is] consistent with the conception of the liberty of the press as historically conceived and guaranteed. [I]t has been generally, if not universally, considered that it is the chief purpose of the guaranty to prevent previous restraints upon publication. The struggle in England, directed against the legislative power of the licenser, resulted in renunciation of the censorship of the press. The liberty deemed to be established was thus described by Blackstone: "The liberty of the press is indeed essential to the nature of a free state; but this consists in laying no *previous* restraints upon publications, and not in freedom from censure for criminal matter when published. Every freeman has an undoubted right to lay what sentiments he pleases before the public; to forbid this, is to destroy the freedom of the press; but if he publishes what is improper, mischievous or illegal, he must take the consequence of his own temerity." [The] criticism upon Blackstone's statement has not been because immunity from previous restraint upon publication has not been regarded as deserving of special emphasis, but chiefly because that immunity cannot be deemed to exhaust the conception of the liberty guaranteed by State and Federal Constitutions.

[T]he protection even as to previous restraint is not absolutely unlimited. But the limitation has been recognized only in exceptional cases. [N]o one would question but that a government might prevent actual obstruction to its recruiting service or the publication of the sailing dates of transports or the number and location of troops. On similar grounds, the primary requirements of decency may be enforced against obscene publications. The security of the community life may be protected against incitements to acts of violence and the overthrow by force of orderly [government]. * * *

The fact that for approximately one hundred and fifty years there has been almost an entire absence of attempts to impose previous restraints upon publications relating to the malfeasance of public officers is significant of the deep-seated conviction that such restraints would violate constitutional right. Public officers, whose character and conduct remain open to debate and free discussion in the press, find their remedies for false accusations in actions under libel laws providing for redress and punishment, and not in proceedings to restrain the publication of newspapers and periodicals. [The] fact that the liberty of the press may be abused by miscreant purveyors of scandal does not make any the less necessary the immunity of the press from previous restraint in dealing with official misconduct. Subsequent punishment for such abuses as may exist is the appropriate remedy, consistent with constitutional [privilege].

The statute in question cannot be justified by reason of the fact that the publisher is permitted to show, before injunction issues, that the matter published is true and is published with good motives and for justifiable ends. If such a statute, authorizing suppression and injunction on such a basis, is constitutionally valid, it would be equally permissible for the Legislature to provide that at any time the publisher of any newspaper could be brought before a court, or even an administrative officer (as the constitutional protection may not be regarded as resting on mere procedural details), and required to produce proof of the truth of his publication, or of what he intended to publish and of his motives, or stand enjoined. If this can be done, the Legislature may provide machinery for determining in the complete exercise of its discretion what are justifiable ends and restrain publication accordingly. And it would be but a step to a complete system of censorship.

[For] these reasons we hold the statute, so far as it authorized the proceedings in this action, [to] be an infringement of the liberty of the press guaranteed by the Fourteenth Amendment. * * *

JUSTICE BUTLER (dissenting).

[T]he *previous restraints* referred to by [Blackstone] subjected the press to the arbitrary will of an administrative officer. [The] Minnesota statute does not operate as a *previous* restraint on publication within the proper meaning of that phrase. It does not authorize administrative control in advance such as was formerly exercised by the licensers and censors, but prescribes a remedy to be enforced by a suit in equity. In this case [t]he business and publications unquestionably constitute an abuse of the right of free press. [A]s stated by the state Supreme Court [they] threaten morals, peace, and good order. [The] restraint authorized is only in respect of continuing to do what has been duly adjudged to constitute a nuisance. [It] is fanciful to suggest similarity between the granting or enforcement of the decree authorized by this statute to prevent *further* publication of malicious, scandalous, and defamatory articles and the *previous restraint* upon the press by licensers as referred to by Blackstone and described in the history of the times to which he alludes. * * *

It is well known, as found by the state supreme court, that existing libel laws are inadequate effectively to suppress evils resulting from the kind of business and publications that are shown in this case. The doctrine [of this decision] exposes the peace and good order of every community and the business and private affairs of every individual to the constant and protracted false and malicious assaults of any insolvent publisher who may have purpose and sufficient capacity to contrive and put into effect a scheme or program for oppression, blackmail or extortion. * * *

The collateral bar rule. Consider the collateral bar rule, which sheds light on the relationship between prior restraints and injunctions. That rule insists "that a court order must be obeyed until it is set aside, and that persons subject to the order who disobey it may not defend against the ensuing charge of criminal contempt on the ground that the order was erroneous or even unconstitutional." Stephen Barnett, *The Puzzle of Prior Restraint*, 29 Stan.L.Rev. 539 (1977).

WALKER v. BIRMINGHAM, 388 U.S. 307 (1967) upheld the rule against a First Amendment challenge in affirming the contempt conviction of defendants for violating an ex parte injunction issued by an Alabama court enjoining them from engaging in street parades without a municipal permit issued pursuant to the city's parade ordinance. The Court, per STEWART, J., (Warren, C.J., Brennan, Douglas, and Fortas, JJ., dissenting) held that because the petitioners neither moved to dissolve the injunction nor sought to comply with the city's parade ordinance, their claim that the injunction and ordinance were unconstitutional[15] did not need to be considered: "This Court cannot hold that the petitioners were constitutionally free to ignore all the procedures of the law and carry their battle to the streets. [R]espect for judicial process is a small price to pay for the civilizing hand of law, which alone can give abiding meaning to constitutional freedom." Although *Walker* suggested that its holding might be different if the court issuing the injunction lacked jurisdiction or if the injunction were "transparently invalid or had only a frivolous pretense to validity," it held that Alabama's invocation of the collateral bar rule was not itself unconstitutional.

---

[15]   Indeed, the ordinance in question was declared unconstitutional two years later. *Shuttlesworth v. Birmingham*, 394 U.S. 147 (1969) (ordinance conferring unbridled discretion to prohibit any parade or demonstration is unconstitutional prior restraint).

II. PRIOR RESTRAINTS AND
NATIONAL SECURITY

NEW YORK TIMES CO. V. UNITED STATES
[THE PENTAGON PAPERS CASE]
403 U.S. 713, 91 S.Ct. 2140, 29 L.Ed.2d 822 (1971).

PER CURIAM.

We granted certiorari in these cases in which the United States seeks to enjoin the *New York Times* and the *Washington Post* from publishing the contents of a classified study entitled "History of U.S. Decision-Making Process on Viet Nam Policy."[16]

"Any system of prior restraints of expression comes to this Court bearing a heavy presumption against its constitutional validity." *Bantam Books;* see also *Near.* The Government "thus carries a heavy burden of showing justification for the enforcement of such a restraint." [The district court in the *Times* case and both lower federal courts] in the *Post* case held that the Government had not met that burden. We agree. [T]he stays entered [by this Court five days previously] are vacated. * * *

JUSTICE BLACK, with whom JUSTICE DOUGLAS joins, concurring.

I adhere to the view that the Government's case against the *Post* should have been dismissed and that the injunction against the *Times* should have been vacated without oral argument when the cases were first presented to this Court. I believe that every moment's continuance of the injunctions against these newspapers amounts to a flagrant, indefensible, and continuing violation of the First Amendment. Furthermore, after oral arguments, I agree [with] the reasons stated by my Brothers Douglas and Brennan. In my view it is unfortunate that some of my Brethren are apparently willing to hold that the publication of news may sometimes be enjoined. Such a holding would make a shambles of the First Amendment.

[F]or the first time in the 182 years since the founding of the Republic, the federal courts are asked to hold that the First Amendment does not mean what it says, but rather means that the Government can halt the publication of current news of vital importance to the people of this country. * * *

The Government does not even attempt to rely on any act of Congress. Instead it makes the bold and dangerously far-reaching contention that the courts should take it upon themselves to "make" a law abridging freedom of the press in the name of equity, presidential power and national security, even when the representatives of the people in Congress have adhered to the command of the First Amendment

---

[16]   On June 12–14, 1971 the *New York Times* and on June 18 the *Washington Post* published portions of this "top secret" Pentagon study. Government actions seeking temporary restraining orders and injunctions progressed through two district courts and two courts of appeals between June 15–23. After a June 26 argument, ten Supreme Court opinions were issued on June 30, 1971.

and refused to make such a law. To find that the President has "inherent power" to halt the publication of news by resort to the courts would wipe out the First Amendment and destroy the fundamental liberty and security of the very people the Government hopes to make "secure." [The] word "security" is a broad, vague generality whose contours should not be invoked to abrogate the fundamental law embodied in the First Amendment. * * *

JUSTICE DOUGLAS, with whom JUSTICE BLACK joins, concurring.

While I join the opinion of the Court I believe it necessary to express my views more fully.

[The First Amendment leaves] no room for governmental restraint on the press. There is, moreover, no statute barring the publication by the press of the material which the *Times* and *Post* seek to use. [These] disclosures may have a serious impact. But that is no basis for sanctioning a previous restraint on the press * * * .

The dominant purpose of the First Amendment was to prohibit the widespread practice of governmental suppression of embarrassing information. [A] debate of large proportions goes on in the Nation over our posture in Vietnam. That debate antedated the disclosure of the contents of the present documents. The latter are highly relevant to the debate in progress.

Secrecy in government is fundamentally anti-democratic, perpetuating bureaucratic errors. Open debate and discussion of public issues are vital to our national health. [The] stays in these cases that have been in effect for more than a week constitute a flouting of the principles of the First Amendment as interpreted in *Near*.

JUSTICE BRENNAN, concurring.

I write separately [to] emphasize what should be apparent: that our judgment in the present cases may not be taken to indicate the propriety, in the future, of issuing temporary stays and restraining orders to block the publication of material sought to be suppressed by the Government. So far as I can determine, never before has the United States sought to enjoin a newspaper from publishing information in its possession. * * *

The entire thrust of the Government's claim throughout these cases has been that publication of the material sought to be enjoined "could," or "might," or "may" prejudice the national interest in various ways. But the First Amendment tolerates absolutely no prior judicial restraints of the press predicated upon surmise or conjecture that untoward consequences may result. Our cases, it is true, have indicated that there is a single, extremely narrow class of cases in which the First Amendment's ban on prior judicial restraint may be overridden. Our cases have thus far indicated that such cases may arise only when the Nation "is at war," [*Schenck*]. Even if the present world situation were assumed to be tantamount to a time of war, or if the power of presently available armaments would justify even in peacetime the suppression of information that would set in motion a nuclear holocaust, in neither of these actions has the Government presented or even alleged that publication of items from or based upon the material at issue would cause the happening of an event of that nature. [Thus,] only governmental allegation and proof that publication must inevitably, directly and immediately cause the occurrence of an event kindred to imperiling the safety of a transport already at sea can support even the issuance of an interim restraining order. In no event may mere conclusions be sufficient: for if the Executive Branch seeks judicial aid in preventing publication, it must inevitably submit the basis upon which that aid is sought to scrutiny by the judiciary. And therefore, every restraint issued in this case, whatever its form, has violated the First Amendment—and not less so because that restraint was justified as necessary to afford the courts an opportunity to examine the claim more thoroughly. Unless and until the Government has clearly made out its case, the First Amendment commands that no injunction may issue.

JUSTICE STEWART, with whom JUSTICE WHITE joins, concurring.

[I]n the cases before us we are asked neither to construe specific regulations nor to apply specific laws. [We] are asked, quite simply, to prevent the publication by two newspapers of material that the Executive Branch insists should not, in the national interest, be published. I am convinced that the Executive is correct with respect to some of the documents involved. But I cannot say that disclosure of any of them will surely result in direct, immediate, and irreparable damage to our Nation or its people. That being so, there can under the First Amendment be but one judicial resolution of the issues before us. I join the judgments * * * .

JUSTICE WHITE, with whom JUSTICE STEWART joins, concurring.

I concur in today's judgments, but only because of the concededly extraordinary protection against prior restraints enjoyed by the press under our constitutional system. I do not say that in no circumstances would the First Amendment permit an injunction against publishing information about government plans or operations. Nor, after examining the materials the Government characterizes as the most sensitive and destructive, can I deny that revelation of these documents will do substantial damage to public interests. Indeed, I am confident that their disclosure will have that result. But I nevertheless agree that the United States has not satisfied the very heavy burden which it must meet to warrant an injunction against publication in these cases, at least in the absence of express and appropriately limited congressional authorization for prior restraints in circumstances such as these.

The Government's position is simply stated: The responsibility of the Executive for the conduct of the foreign affairs and for the security of the Nation is so basic that the President is entitled to an injunction against publication of a newspaper story whenever he can convince a court that the information to be revealed threatens "grave and irreparable" injury to the public interest; and the injunction should issue whether or not the material to be published is classified, whether or not publication would be lawful under relevant criminal statutes enacted by Congress and regardless of the circumstances by which the newspaper came into possession of the information.

At least in the absence of legislation by Congress, based on its own investigations and findings, I am quite unable to agree that the inherent powers of the Executive and the courts reach so far as to authorize remedies having such sweeping potential for inhibiting publications by the press. [To] sustain the Government in these cases would start the courts down a long and hazardous road that I am not willing to travel at least without congressional guidance and direction.

* * * Prior restraints require an unusually heavy justification under the First Amendment; but failure by the Government to justify prior restraints does not measure its constitutional entitlement to a conviction for criminal publication. That the Government mistakenly chose to proceed by injunction does not mean that it could not successfully proceed in another way.

* * * Congress has addressed itself to the problems of protecting the security of the country and the national defense from unauthorized disclosure of potentially damaging information. It has not, however, authorized the injunctive remedy against threatened publication. It has apparently been satisfied to rely on criminal sanctions and their deterrent effect on the responsible as well as the irresponsible press. * * *

JUSTICE HARLAN, with whom THE CHIEF JUSTICE and JUSTICE BLACKMUN join, dissenting. * * *

With all respect, I consider that the Court has been almost irresponsibly feverish in dealing with these cases. Both [the] Second Circuit and [the] District of Columbia Circuit rendered judgment on June 23. [This] Court's order setting a hearing before us on June 26 at 11 a.m., a course which I joined only to avoid the possibility of even more peremptory action by the Court, was issued less than 24 hours before. The record in the *Post* case was filed with the Clerk shortly before 1 p.m. on June 25; the record in the *Times* case did not arrive until 7 or 8 o'clock that same night. The briefs of the parties were received less than two hours before argument on June 26.

This frenzied train of events took place in the name of the presumption against prior restraints created by the First Amendment. Due regard for the extraordinarily important and difficult questions involved in these litigations should have led the Court to shun such a precipitate timetable. In order to decide the merits of these cases properly, some or all of the following questions should have been faced: * * *

2. Whether the First Amendment permits the federal courts to enjoin publication of stories which would present a serious threat to national security. See *Near* (dictum). * * *

4. Whether the unauthorized disclosure of any of these particular documents would seriously impair the national security.

5. What weight should be given to the opinion of high officers in the Executive Branch of the Government with respect to [question 4]. * * *

7. Whether the threatened harm to the national security or the Government's possessory interest in the documents justifies the issuance of an injunction against publication in light of—

a. The strong First Amendment policy against prior restraints on publication; b. The doctrine against enjoining conduct in violation of criminal statutes; and c. The extent to which the materials at issue have apparently already been otherwise disseminated.

These are difficult questions of fact, of law, and of judgment; the potential consequences of erroneous decision are enormous. The time which has been available to us, to the lower courts, and to the parties has been wholly inadequate for giving these cases the kind of consideration they deserve. It is a reflection on the stability of the judicial process that these great issues—as important as any that have arisen during my time on the Court—should have been decided under the pressures engendered by the torrent of publicity that has attended these litigations from their inception.

Forced as I am to reach the merits of these cases, I dissent from the opinion and judgments of the Court. Within the severe limitations imposed by the time constraints under which I have been required to operate, I can only state my reasons in telescoped form, even though in different circumstances I would have felt constrained to deal with the cases in the fuller sweep indicated above.

[It] is plain to me that the scope of the judicial function in passing upon the activities of the Executive Branch of the Government in the field of foreign affairs is very narrowly restricted. This view is, I think, dictated by the concept of separation of powers upon which our constitutional system [rests.] I agree that, in performance of its duty to protect the values of the First Amendment against political pressures, the judiciary must review the initial Executive determination to the point of satisfying itself that the subject matter of the dispute does lie within the proper compass of the President's foreign relations power. Constitutional considerations forbid "a complete abandonment of judicial control." Moreover, the judiciary may properly insist that the determination that disclosure of the subject matter would irreparably impair the national security be made by the head of the Executive Department concerned—here the Secretary of State or the Secretary of Defense—after actual personal consideration by that officer. This safeguard is required in the analogous area of executive claims of privilege for secrets of state.

But in my judgment the judiciary may not properly go beyond these two inquiries and redetermine for itself the probable impact of disclosure on the national security. "[T]he very nature of executive decisions as to foreign policy is political, not judicial. Such decisions are wholly confided by our Constitution to the political departments of the government, Executive and Legislative. They are delicate, complex, and involve large elements of prophecy. They are and should be undertaken only by those directly responsible to the people whose welfare they advance or imperil. They are decisions of a kind for which the judiciary has neither aptitude, facilities nor responsibility and which has long been held to belong in the domain of political power not subject to judicial intrusion or inquiry." *Chicago & S. Air Lines v. Waterman S.S. Corp.* (Jackson, J.), 333 U.S. 103 (1948).

Even if there is some room for the judiciary to override the executive determination, it is plain that the scope of review must be exceedingly narrow. I can see no indication in the opinions of either the District Court or the Court of Appeals in the *Post* litigation that the conclusions of the Executive were given even the deference owing to an administrative agency, much less that owing to a co-equal branch of the Government operating within the field of its constitutional prerogative. * * *

Pending further hearings in each case conducted under the appropriate ground rules, I would continue the restraints on publication. I cannot believe that the doctrine prohibiting prior restraints reaches to the point of preventing courts from maintaining the status quo long enough to act responsibly in matters of such national importance as those involved here.

JUSTICE BLACKMUN, dissenting.

[The First Amendment] is only one part of an entire Constitution. Article II of the great document vests in the Executive Branch primary power over the conduct of foreign affairs and places in that branch the responsibility for the Nation's safety. Each provision of the Constitution is important, and I cannot subscribe to a doctrine of unlimited absolutism for the First Amendment at the cost of downgrading other provisions. First Amendment absolutism has never commanded a majority of this Court. What is needed here is a weighing, upon properly developed standards, of the broad right of the press to print and of the very narrow right of the Government to prevent. Such standards are not yet developed. The parties here are in disagreement as to what those standards should be. But even the newspapers concede that there are situations where restraint is in order and is constitutional. Mr. Justice Holmes gave us a suggestion when he said in *Schenck,* "It is a question of proximity and degree. When a nation is at war many things that might be said in time of peace are such a hindrance to its effort that their utterance will not be endured so long as men fight and that no Court could regard them as protected by any constitutional right."

I therefore would remand these cases to be developed expeditiously, of course, but on a schedule permitting the orderly presentation of evidence from both sides [and] with the preparation of briefs, oral argument and court opinions of a quality better than has been seen to this point. [T]hese cases and the issues involved and the courts, including this one, deserve better than has been produced thus far. * * *

———

Consider UNITED STATES v. PROGRESSIVE, INC., 467 F.Supp. 990 (W.D.Wis.) (preliminary injunction issued Mar. 28, 1979), request for writ of mandamus den. sub nom. *Morland v. Sprecher,* 443 U.S. 709 (1979), case dismissed, 610 F.2d 819 (7th Cir.1979).[17] *The Progressive* planned to publish an article. "The H-Bomb Secret—How We Got It, Why We're Telling It," maintaining that the article would contribute to informed opinion about nuclear weapons and demonstrate the inadequacies of a system of secrecy and classification. Although the government conceded that at least some of the information contained in the article was "in the public domain" or had been "declassified," it argued that "national security" permitted it to censor information originating in the public domain "if when drawn together, synthesized and collated, such information acquires the character of presenting immediate, direct and irreparable harm to the interests of the United States." The Secretary of State stated that publication would increase thermonuclear proliferation and that this would "irreparably impair the national security of the United States." The Secretary of Defense maintained that dissemination of the Morland article would lead to a substantial increase in the risk of thermonuclear proliferation and to use or threats that would "adversely affect the national security of the United States."

Although recognizing that this constituted "the first instance of prior restraint against a publication in this fashion in the [nation's history]," the district court enjoined defendants, pending final resolution of the litigation, from publishing or otherwise disclosing any information designated by the government as "restricted data" within the meaning of The Atomic Energy Act of 1954: "What is involved here is information dealing with the most destructive weapon in the history of mankind, information of sufficient destructive potential to nullify the right to free speech and to endanger the right to life itself. [Faced] with a stark choice between upholding the right to continued life and the right to freedom of the press, most jurists would have no difficulty in opting for the chance to continue to breathe and function as they work to achieve perfect freedom of expression.

"[A] mistake in ruling against *The Progressive* will seriously infringe cherished First Amendment rights. [A] mistake in ruling against the United States could pave the way for thermonuclear annihilation for us all. In that event, our right to life is extinguished and the right to publish becomes moot.

"[W]ar by foot soldiers has been replaced in large part by machines and bombs. No longer need there be any advance warning or any preparation time before a nuclear war could be commenced. [In light of these factors] publication of the technical information on the hydrogen bomb contained in the article is analogous to publication of troop movements or locations in time of war and falls within the extremely narrow exception to the rule against prior restraint [recognized in *Near*].

"The government has met its burden under § 2274 of The Atomic Energy Act[, which authorizes injunctive relief against one who would communicate or disclose restricted data 'with reason to believe such data will be utilized to. injure the United States or to secure an advantage to any foreign nation.']. [I]t has also met

---

[17]   The government's action against *The Progressive* was abandoned after information similar to that it sought to enjoin was published elsewhere.

the test enunciated by two Justices in *Pentagon Papers,* namely grave, direct, immediate and irreparable harm to the United States."

6. JUSTICE AND NEWSGATHERING

I. PUBLICITY ABOUT TRIALS

In a number of cases, defendants have asserted that their rights to a fair trial have been abridged by newspaper publicity.

SHEPPARD v. MAXWELL, 384 U.S. 333 (1966), is probably the most notorious "trial by newspaper" case. The Court, per CLARK, J., (Black, J. dissenting) agreed with the "finding" of the Ohio Supreme Court that the atmosphere of defendant's murder trial was that of a " 'Roman holiday' for the news media." The courtroom was jammed with reporters. And in the corridors outside the courtroom, "a host of photographers and television personnel" photographed witnesses, counsel and jurors as they entered and left the courtroom. Throughout the trial, there was a deluge of publicity, much of which contained information never presented at trial, yet the jurors were not sequestered until the trial was over and they had begun their deliberations.

The Court placed the primary blame on the trial judge. He could "easily" have prevented "the carnival atmosphere of the trial" since "the courtroom and courthouse premises" were subject to his control. For example, he should have provided privacy for the jury, insulated witnesses from the media, instead of allowing them to be interviewed at will, and "made some effort to control the release of leads, information, and gossip to the press by police officers, witnesses, and the counsel for both sides." No one "coming under the jurisdiction of the court should be permitted to frustrate its function."

The Court recognized that "there is nothing that proscribes the press from reporting events that transpire in the courtroom. But where there is a reasonable likelihood that prejudicial news prior to trial will prevent a fair trial, the judge should continue the case until the threat abates, or transfer it to another county not so permeated with publicity. In addition, sequestration of the jury was something the judge should have raised sua sponte with counsel. If publicity during the proceedings threatens the fairness of the trial, a new trial should be ordered. But we must remember that reversals are but palliatives; the cure lies in those remedial measures that will prevent the prejudice at its inception."

The Court, however, reiterated its extreme reluctance "to place any direct limitations on the freedom traditionally exercised by the news media for '[w]hat transpires in the courtroom is public property.' " The press "does not simply publish information about trials but guards against the miscarriage of justice by subjecting the police, prosecutors, and judicial processes to extensive public scrutiny and criticism."

In anticipation of the trial of Simants for a mass murder which had attracted widespread news coverage, the county court prohibited everyone in attendance from, inter alia, releasing or authorizing for publication "any testimony given or evidence adduced." Simants' preliminary hearing (open to the public) was held the same day, subject to the restrictive order. Simants was bound over for trial. Respondent Nebraska state trial judge then entered an order which, as modified by the state supreme court, restrained the press and broadcasting media from reporting any confessions or incriminating statements made by Simants to law enforcement officers or third parties, except members of the press, and from reporting other facts "strongly implicative" of the defendant. The order expired when the jury was impaneled.

In NEBRASKA PRESS ASS'N v. STUART, 427 U.S. 539 (1976), the Court granted review while Simants' conviction was pending on appeal in the state supreme court. The Court, per BURGER, C.J., struck down the state court order: "To the extent that the order prohibited the reporting of evidence adduced at the open preliminary hearing, it plainly violated settled principles: 'There is nothing that proscribes the press from reporting events that transpire in the courtroom.' *Sheppard.*" To the extent that the order prohibited publication "based on information gained from other sources, [the] heavy burden imposed as a condition to securing a prior restraint was not met." The portion of the order regarding "implicative" information was also "too vague and too broad" to survive scrutiny of restraints on First Amendment rights.

"[P]retrial publicity—even pervasive, adverse publicity—does not inevitably lead to an unfair trial. The capacity of the jury eventually impaneled to decide the case fairly is influenced by the tone and extent of the publicity, which is in part, and often in large part, shaped by what attorneys, police and other officials do to precipitate news coverage. [T]he measures a judge takes or fails to take to mitigate the effects of pretrial publicity—the measures described in *Sheppard*—may well determine whether the defendant receives a trial consistent [with] due process.

"[The] Court has interpreted [First Amendment] guarantees to afford special protection against orders that prohibit the publication or broadcast of particular information or commentary—orders that impose [a] 'prior' restraint on speech. None of our decided cases on prior restraint involved restrictive orders entered to protect a defendant's right to a fair and impartial jury, but [they] have a common thread relevant to this case. * * *

"The thread running through [*Near* and *Pentagon Papers*], is that prior restraints on speech and publication are the most serious and the least tolerable infringement on First Amendment rights. A criminal penalty or a judgment in a defamation case is subject to the whole panoply of protections afforded by deferring the impact of the judgment until all avenues of appellate review have been exhausted. [But] a prior restraint [has] an immediate and irreversible sanction." [We] reaffirm that the guarantees of freedom of expression are not an absolute prohibition under all circumstances, but the barriers to prior restraint remain high and the presumption against its use continues intact. We hold that, with respect to the order entered in this case [the] heavy burden imposed as a condition to securing a prior restraint was not [met]."

BRENNAN, J., joined by Stewart and Marshall, JJ., concurring, would hold that "resort to prior restraints on the freedom of the press is a constitutionally impermissible method for enforcing [the right to a fair trial by a jury]; judges have at their disposal a broad spectrum of devices for ensuring that fundamental fairness is accorded the accused without necessitating so drastic an incursion on the equally fundamental and salutary constitutional mandate that discussion of public affairs in a free society cannot depend on the preliminary grace of judicial censors": " * * * Settled case law concerning the impropriety and constitutional invalidity of prior restraints on the press compels the conclusion that there can be no prohibition on the publication by the press of any information pertaining to pending judicial proceedings or the operation of the criminal justice system, no matter how shabby the means by which the information is obtained. This does not imply, however, any subordination of Sixth Amendment rights, for an accused's right to a fair trial may be adequately assured through methods that do not infringe First Amendment values."

II. NEWSGATHERING

A. Protection of Confidential Sources

BRANZBURG V. HAYES

408 U.S. 665, 92 S.Ct. 2646, 33 L.Ed.2d 626 (1972).

JUSTICE WHITE delivered the opinion of the Court.

[Branzburg, a Kentucky reporter, wrote articles describing his observations of local hashish-making and other drug violations. He refused to testify before a grand jury regarding his information. The state courts rejected his claim of a First Amendment privilege.

[Pappas, a Massachusetts TV newsman-photographer, was allowed to enter and remain inside a Black Panther headquarters on condition he disclose nothing. When an anticipated police raid did not occur, he wrote no story. Summoned before a local grand jury, he refused to answer any questions about what had occurred inside the Panther headquarters or to identify those he had observed. The state courts denied his claim of a First Amendment privilege.

[Caldwell, a N.Y. Times reporter covering the Black Panthers, was summoned to appear before a federal grand jury investigating Panther activities. A federal court issued a protective order providing that although he had to divulge information given him "for publication," he could withhold "confidential" information "developed or maintained by him as a professional journalist." Maintaining that absent a specific need for his testimony he should be excused from attending the grand jury altogether, Caldwell disregarded the order and was held in contempt. The Ninth Circuit reversed, holding that absent "compelling reasons" Caldwell could refuse even to attend the grand jury, because of the potential impact of such an appearance on the flow of news to the public.]

[Petitioners' First Amendment claims] may be simply put: that to gather news it is often necessary to agree either not to identify [sources] or to publish only part of the facts revealed, or both; that if the reporter is nevertheless forced to reveal these confidences to a grand jury, the source so identified and other confidential sources of other reporters will be measurably deterred from furnishing publishable information, all to the detriment of the free flow of information protected by the First Amendment. Although petitioners do not claim an absolute privilege [they] assert that the reporter should not be forced either to appear or to testify before a grand jury or at trial until and unless sufficient grounds are shown for believing that the reporter possesses information relevant to a crime the grand jury is investigating, that the information the reporter has is unavailable from other sources, and that the need for the information is sufficiently compelling to override the claimed invasion of First Amendment interests occasioned by the disclosure. [The] heart of the claim is that the burden on news gathering resulting from compelling reporters to disclose confidential information outweighs any public interest in obtaining the information.

[We agree] that news gathering [qualifies] for First Amendment protection; without some protection for seeking out the news, freedom of the press could be eviscerated. But this case involves no intrusions upon speech [and no] command that the press publish what it prefers to withhold. [N]o penalty, civil or criminal, related to the content of published material is at issue here. The use of confidential sources by the press is not forbidden or restricted; reporters remain free to seek news from any source by means within the law. No attempt is made to require the press to publish its sources of information or [disclose] them on request. The sole issue before us is the obligation of reporters to respond to grand jury subpoenas as other citizens do and to answer questions relevant to an investigation into the commission of crime.

[T]he First Amendment does not guarantee the press a constitutional right of special access to information not available to the public generally. [Although] news gathering may be hampered, the press is regularly excluded from grand jury proceedings, our own conferences, the meetings of other official bodies gathered in executive session, and the meetings of private organizations. Newsmen have no constitutional right of access to the scenes of crime or disaster when the general public is excluded, and they may be prohibited from attending or publishing information about trials if such restrictions are necessary to assure a defendant a fair trial before an impartial tribunal. [It] is thus not surprising that the great weight of authority is that newsmen are not exempt from the normal duty of appearing before a grand jury and answering questions relevant to a criminal investigation.

[A number] of States have provided newsmen a statutory privilege of varying breadth, [but] none has been provided by federal statute. [We decline to create one] by interpreting the First Amendment to grant newsmen a testimonial privilege that other citizens do not enjoy. [On] the records now before us, we perceive no basis for holding that the public interest in law enforcement and in ensuring effective grand jury proceedings is insufficient to override the consequential, but uncertain, burden on news gathering which is said to result from insisting that reporters, like other citizens, respond to relevant questions put to them in the course of a valid grand jury investigation or criminal trial.

This conclusion [does not] threaten the vast bulk of confidential relationships between reporters and their sources. Grand juries address themselves to the issues of whether crimes have been committed and who committed them. Only where news sources themselves are implicated in crime or possess information relevant to the grand jury's task need they or the reporter be concerned about grand jury subpoenas. Nothing before us indicates that a large number or percentage of *all* confidential news sources fall into either category and would in any way be deterred by [our holding]. * * *

Accepting the fact, however, that an undetermined number of informants not themselves implicated in crime will nevertheless, for whatever reason, refuse to talk to newsmen if they fear identification by a reporter in an official investigation, we cannot accept the argument that the public interest in possible future news about crime from undisclosed, unverified sources must take precedence over the public interest in pursuing and prosecuting those crimes reported to the press by informants and in thus deterring the commission of such crimes in the future. * * *

[The] privilege claimed here is conditional, not absolute; given the suggested preliminary showings and compelling need, the reporter would be required to testify. [If] newsmen's confidential sources are as sensitive as they are claimed to be, the prospect of being unmasked whenever a judge determines the situation justifies it is hardly a satisfactory solution to the problem. For them, it would appear that only an absolute privilege would suffice.

We are unwilling to embark the judiciary on a long and difficult journey to such an uncertain destination. The administration of a constitutional newsman's privilege would present practical and conceptual difficulties of a high order. Sooner or later, it would be necessary to define those categories of newsmen who qualified for the privilege, a questionable procedure in light of the traditional doctrine that liberty of the press is the right of the lonely pamphleteer who uses carbon paper or a mimeograph just as much as of the large metropolitan publisher who utilizes the latest photocomposition methods. [The] informative function asserted by representatives of the organized press in the present cases is also performed by lecturers, political pollsters, novelists, academic researchers, and dramatists. Almost any author may quite accurately assert that he is contributing to the flow of information to the public, that he relies on confidential sources of information, and that these sources will be silenced if he is forced to make disclosures before a grand jury.

[At] the federal level, Congress has freedom to determine whether a statutory newsman's privilege is necessary and desirable and to fashion standards and rules as narrow or broad as deemed necessary [and], equally important, to re-fashion those rules as experience from time to time may dictate. There is also merit in leaving state legislatures free, within First Amendment limits, to fashion their own standards in light of the conditions and problems with respect to the relations between law enforcement officials and press in their own [areas]. * * *

JUSTICE POWELL, concurring in the opinion of the Court.

I add this brief statement to emphasize what seems to me to be the limited nature of the Court's holding. The Court does not hold that newsmen, subpoenaed to testify before a grand jury, are without constitutional rights with respect to the gathering of news or in safeguarding their sources. [As] indicated in the concluding portion of the opinion, the Court states that no harassment of newsmen will be tolerated. If a newsman believes that the grand jury investigation is not being conducted in good faith he is not without remedy. Indeed, if the newsman is called upon to give information bearing only a remote and tenuous relationship to the subject of the investigation, or if he has some other reason to believe that his testimony implicates confidential source relationships without a legitimate need of law enforcement, he will have access to the Court on a motion to quash and an appropriate protective order may be entered. The asserted claim to privilege should be judged on its facts by the striking of a proper balance between freedom of the press and the obligation of all citizens to give relevant testimony with respect to criminal conduct. The balance of these vital constitutional and societal interests on a case-by-case basis accords with the tried and traditional way of adjudicating such questions.

In short, the courts will be available to newsmen under circumstances where legitimate First Amendment interests require protection.

JUSTICE DOUGLAS, dissenting.

[T]here is no "compelling need" that can be shown [by the Government] which qualifies the reporter's immunity from appearing or testifying before a grand jury, unless the reporter himself is implicated in a crime. His immunity in my view is therefore quite complete, for absent his involvement in a crime, the First Amendment protects him against an appearance before a grand jury and if he is involved in a crime, the Fifth Amendment stands as a barrier. Since in my view there is no area of inquiry not protected by a privilege, the reporter need not appear for the futile purpose of invoking one to each [question.]

Two principles which follow from [Alexander Meiklejohn's] understanding of the First Amendment are at stake here. One is that the people, the ultimate governors, must have absolute freedom of and therefore privacy of their individual opinions and beliefs regardless of how suspect or strange they may appear to others. Ancillary to that principle is the conclusion that an individual must also have absolute privacy over whatever information he may generate in the course of testing his opinions and beliefs. In this regard, Caldwell's status as a reporter is less relevant than is his status as a student who affirmatively pursued empirical research to enlarge his own intellectual viewpoint. The second principle is that effective self-government cannot succeed unless the people are immersed in a steady, robust, unimpeded, and uncensored flow of opinion and reporting which are continuously subjected to critique, rebuttal, and re-examination. In this respect, Caldwell's status as a newsgatherer and an integral part of that process becomes critical. * * *

JUSTICE STEWART, with whom JUSTICE BRENNAN and JUSTICE MARSHALL join, dissenting.

The Court's crabbed view of the First Amendment reflects a disturbing insensitivity to the critical role of an independent press in our society. [While] Mr. Justice Powell's enigmatic concurring opinion gives some hope of a more flexible view in the future, the Court in these cases holds that a newsman has no First Amendment right to protect his sources when called before a grand jury. The Court thus invites state and federal authorities to undermine the historic independence of the press by attempting to annex the journalistic profession as an investigative arm of government. Not only will this decision impair performance of the press' constitutionally protected functions, but it will, I am convinced, in the long run, harm rather than help the administration of justice.

[As] private and public aggregations of power burgeon in size and the pressures for conformity necessarily mount, there is obviously a continuing need for an independent press to disseminate a robust variety of information and opinion through reportage, investigation and criticism, if we are to preserve our constitutional tradition of maximizing freedom of choice by encouraging diversity of expression. * * *

A corollary of the right to publish must be the right to gather news. [This right] implies, in turn, a right to a confidential relationship between a reporter and his source. This proposition follows as a matter of simple logic once three factual predicates are recognized: (1) newsmen require informants to gather news; (2) confidentiality—the promise or understanding that names or certain aspects of communications will be kept off-the-record—is essential to the creation and maintenance of a news-gathering relationship with informants; and (3) the existence of an unbridled subpoena power—the absence of a constitutional right protecting, in *any* way, a confidential relationship from compulsory process—will either deter sources from divulging information or deter reporters from gathering and publishing information. * * *

After today's decision, the potential informant can never be sure that his identity or off-the-record communications will not subsequently be revealed through the compelled testimony of a newsman. A public spirited person inside government, who is not implicated in any crime, will now be fearful of revealing corruption or other governmental wrong-doing, because he will now know he can subsequently be identified by use of compulsory process. The potential source must, therefore, choose between risking exposure by giving information or avoiding the risk by remaining silent.

The reporter must speculate about whether contact with a controversial source or publication of controversial material will lead to a subpoena. In the event of a subpoena, under today's decision, the newsman will know that he must choose between being punished for contempt if he refuses to testify, or violating his profession's ethics and impairing his resourcefulness as a reporter if he discloses confidential information. * * *

The impairment of the flow of news cannot, of course, be proven with scientific precision, as the Court seems to demand. [But] we have never before demanded that First Amendment rights rest on elaborate empirical studies demonstrating beyond any conceivable doubt that deterrent effects exist; we have never before required proof of the exact number of people potentially affected by governmental action, who would actually be dissuaded from engaging in First Amendment activity. * * *

———

Evaluating Powell, J.'s concurrence. Does Powell, J.'s suggested test—the privilege claim "should be judged on its facts by [balancing the] vital constitutional and societal interests on a case-by-case basis"—resemble Stewart, J.'s dissenting approach more than White, J.'s? Extrajudicially, Stewart, J., referred to *Branzburg* as a case which rejected claims for a journalist's privilege "by a vote of 5–4, or, considering Mr. Justice Powell's concurring opinion, perhaps by a vote of 4½–4½." Potter Stewart, *"Or of the Press,"* 26 Hast.L.J. 631 (1975). Indeed, some courts earlier concluded that Powell, J.'s opinion read together with the dissents supported a qualified privilege. But the prevailing view is that because Powell, J. joined the majority opinion (unlike in *Bakke*, Ch. 9, Sec. 2, IV), the *Branzburg* majority opinion rejecting the privilege is controlling and the concurrence has no operative effect. See *In re Grand Jury Subpoena, Judith Miller*, 438 F.3d 1141 (D.C. Cir. 2005); *McKevitt v. Pallasch*, 339 F.3d 530 (7th Cir. 2003).

B. Access to Trials and Other Governmentally Controlled Information and Institutions

By 1978, no Supreme Court holding contradicted Burger, C.J.'s contention for the plurality in *Houchins v. KQED*, 438 U.S. 1 (1978) that, "neither the First Amendment nor the Fourteenth Amendment mandates a right of access to government information or sources of information within the government's control." Or as Stewart, J., put it in an often-quoted statement, "The Constitution itself is neither a Freedom of Information Act nor an Official Secrets Act." *"Or of the Press,"* 26 Hast.L.J. 631, 636 (1975). *Richmond Newspapers,* infra, constitutes the Court's first break with its past denials of First Amendment rights to information within governmental control.

RICHMOND NEWSPAPERS, INC. V. VIRGINIA

448 U.S. 555, 100 S.Ct. 2814, 65 L.Ed.2d 973 (1980).

[At the commencement of his fourth trial on a murder charge (his first conviction having been reversed and two subsequent retrials having ended in mistrials), defendant moved, without objection by the prosecutor or two reporters present, that the trial be closed to the public—defense counsel stating that he did not "want any information being shuffled back and forth when we have a recess as [to] who testified to what." The trial judge granted the motion, stating that "the statute gives me that power specifically." He presumably referred to Virginia Code § 19.2–266, providing that in all criminal trials "the court may, in its discretion, exclude [any] persons whose presence would impair the conduct of a fair trial, provided that the [defendant's right] to a public trial shall not be violated." Later the same day the trial court granted appellants' request for a hearing on a motion to vacate the closure order. At the closed hearing, appellants observed that prior to the entry of its closure order the court had failed to make any evidentiary findings or to consider any other, less drastic measures to ensure a fair trial. Defendant stated that he "didn't want information to leak out," be published by the media, perhaps inaccurately, and then be seen by the jurors. Noting inter alia that "having people in the Courtroom is distracting to the jury" and that if "the rights of the defendant are infringed in any way [and if his closure motion] doesn't completely override all rights of everyone else, then I'm inclined to go along with" the defendant, the court denied the motion to vacate the closure order. Defendant was subsequently found not guilty.]

CHIEF JUSTICE BURGER announced the judgment of the Court and delivered an opinion in which JUSTICE WHITE and JUSTICE STEVENS joined.

[T]he precise issue presented here has not previously been before this Court for decision. [*Gannett Co. v. DePasquale*, 443 U.S. 368 (1979)] was not required to decide whether a right of access to *trials,* as distinguished from hearings on *pre*trial motions, was constitutionally guaranteed. The Court held that the Sixth Amendment's guarantee to the accused of a public trial gave neither the public nor the press an enforceable right of access to a *pre*trial suppression hearing. One concurring opinion specifically emphasized that "a hearing on a motion before trial to suppress evidence is not a *trial.*" (Burger, C.J., concurring). Moreover, the Court did not decide whether the First and Fourteenth Amendments guarantee a right of the public to attend trials; nor did the dissenting opinion reach this issue. [H]ere for the first time the Court is asked to decide whether a criminal trial itself may be closed to the public upon the unopposed request of a defendant, without any demonstration that closure is required to protect the defendant's superior right to a fair trial, or that some other overriding consideration requires closure.

[T]he historical evidence demonstrates conclusively that at the time when our organic laws were adopted, criminal trials both here and in England had long been presumptively open[, thus giving] assurance that the proceedings were conducted fairly to all concerned, [and] discourag[ing] perjury, the misconduct of participants, and decisions based on secret bias or partiality. [Moreover, the] early history of open trials in part reflects the widespread acknowledgment [that] public trials had significant therapeutic value. [When] a shocking crime occurs, a community reaction of outrage and public protest often follows. Thereafter the open processes of justice serve an important prophylactic purpose, providing an outlet for community concern, hostility, and emotion.

[From] this unbroken, uncontradicted history, supported by reasons as valid today as in centuries past, we are bound to conclude that a presumption of openness inheres in the very nature of a criminal trial under our system of criminal justice. [Nevertheless,] the State presses its contention that neither the Constitution nor the Bill of Rights contains any provision which by its terms guarantees to the public the right to attend criminal trials. Standing alone, this is correct, but there remains the question whether, absent an explicit provision, the Constitution affords protection against exclusion of the public from criminal trials.

[The] expressly guaranteed [First Amendment] freedoms share a common core purpose of assuring freedom of communication on matters relating to the functioning of government. Plainly it would be difficult to single out any aspect of government of higher concern and importance to the people than the manner in which criminal trials are conducted. [In] the context of trials is that the First Amendment guarantees of speech and press, standing alone, prohibit government from summarily closing courtroom doors which had long been open to the public at the time that amendment was adopted.

[The] right of access to places traditionally open to the public, as criminal trials have long been, may be seen as assured by the amalgam of the First Amendment guarantees of speech and press; and their affinity to the right of assembly is not without relevance. From the outset, the right of assembly was regarded not only as an independent right but also as a catalyst to augment the free exercise of the other First Amendment rights with which it was deliberately linked by the draftsmen. [Subject] to the traditional time, place, and manner restrictions, streets, sidewalks, and parks are places traditionally open, where First Amendment rights may be exercised; a trial courtroom also is a public place where the people generally—and representatives of the media—have a right to be present, and where their presence historically has been thought to enhance the integrity and quality of what takes place. * * *

Reversed.

JUSTICE BRENNAN, with whom JUSTICE MARSHALL joins, concurring in the judgment.

[*Gannett*] held that the Sixth Amendment right to a public trial was personal to the accused, conferring no right of access to pretrial proceedings that is separately enforceable by the public or the press. [This case] raises the question whether the First Amendment, of its own force and as applied to the States through the Fourteenth Amendment, secures the public an independent right of access to trial proceedings. Because I believe that [it does secure] such a public right of access, I agree [that], without more, agreement of the trial judge and the parties cannot constitutionally close a trial to the public.

While freedom of expression is made inviolate by the First Amendment, and with only rare and stringent exceptions, may not be suppressed, the First Amendment has not been viewed by the Court in all settings as providing an equally categorical assurance of the correlative freedom of access to information. Yet the Court has not ruled out a public access component to the First Amendment in every circumstance. Read with care and in context, our decisions must therefore be understood as holding only that any privilege of access to governmental information is subject to a degree of restraint dictated by the nature of the information and countervailing interests in security or confidentiality. [Cases such as *Houchins*, *Saxbe* and *Pell*] neither comprehensively nor absolutely deny that public access to information may at times be implied by the First Amendment and the principles which animate it. [The] First Amendment embodies more than a commitment to free expression and communicative interchange for their own sakes; it has a *structural* role to play in securing and fostering our republican system of self-government. Implicit in this structural role is not only "the principle that debate on public issues should be uninhibited, robust, and wide-open," but the antecedent assumption that valuable public debate—as well as other civic behavior—must be informed. The structural model links the First Amendment to that process of communication necessary for a democracy to survive, and thus entails solicitude not only for communication itself, but for the indispensable conditions of meaningful communication. * * *

JUSTICE STEWART, concurring in the judgment.

Whatever the ultimate answer [may] be with respect to pretrial suppression hearings in criminal cases, the First and Fourteenth Amendments clearly give the press and the public a right of access to trials themselves, civil as well as criminal. * * *

But this does not mean that the First Amendment right of members of the public and representatives of the press to attend civil and criminal trials is absolute. Just as a legislature may impose reasonable time, place and manner restrictions upon the exercise of First Amendment freedoms, so may a trial judge impose reasonable limitations upon the unrestricted occupation of a courtroom by representatives of the press and members of the public. * * *

JUSTICE WHITE, concurring.

This case would have been unnecessary had *Gannett* construed the Sixth Amendment to forbid excluding the public from criminal proceedings except in narrowly defined circumstances. But the Court there rejected the submission of four of us to this effect, thus requiring that the First Amendment issue involved here be addressed. * * *

JUSTICE BLACKMUN, concurring in the judgment.

My opinion and vote in partial dissent [in] *Gannett* compels my vote to reverse the judgment. [It] is gratifying [to] see the Court now looking to and relying upon legal history in determining the fundamental public character of the criminal trial. * * *

The Court's ultimate ruling in *Gannett,* with such clarification as is provided by the opinions in this case today, apparently is now to the effect that there is no *Sixth* Amendment right on the part of the public—or the press—to an open hearing on a motion to suppress. I, of course, continue to believe that *Gannett* was in error, both in its interpretation of the Sixth Amendment generally, and in its application to the suppression hearing, for I remain convinced that the right to a public trial is to be found where the Constitution explicitly placed it—in the Sixth Amendment.

[But] with the Sixth Amendment set to one side, I am driven to conclude, as a secondary position, that the First Amendment must provide some measure of protection for public access to the trial. * * *

JUSTICE STEVENS, concurring.

This is a watershed case. Until today the Court has accorded virtually absolute protection to the dissemination of information or ideas, but never before has it squarely held that the acquisition of newsworthy matter is entitled to any constitutional protection whatsoever. An additional word of emphasis is therefore appropriate.

Twice before, the Court has implied that any governmental restriction on access to information [would] be constitutionally acceptable so long as it did not single out the press for special disabilities not applicable to the public at large. [Today, for] the first time, the Court [holds] that an arbitrary interference with access to important information [abridges the] First Amendment.* * * .

JUSTICE REHNQUIST, dissenting.

[I] do not believe that [anything in the Constitution] require[s] that a State's reasons for denying public access to a trial, where both [the prosecution and defense] have consented to [a court-approved closure order], are subject to any additional constitutional review at our hands.

7.   GOVERNMENT SPEECH

I.   SUBSIDIES OF SPEECH

Pleasant Grove, Utah permitted private groups to place a number of permanent monuments in its Pioneer Park including a Ten Commandments monument provided by the Fraternal Order of Eagles. Summum, a religious organization, requested permission to erect a monument containing Seven Aphorisms which it believes were presented by God to Moses. The city refused and Summum challenged the refusal on the ground that the city was engaging in unacceptable content discrimination in a public forum.

PLEASANT GROVE CITY v. SUMMUM, 555 U.S. 460 (2009), per ALITO, J., upheld the city's action: "[A]lthough a park is a traditional public forum for speeches and other transitory expressive acts, the display of a permanent monument in a public park is not a form of expression to which forum analysis applies. Instead, the placement of a permanent monument in a public park is best viewed as a form of government speech and is therefore not subject to scrutiny under the Free Speech Clause. [If] government entities must maintain viewpoint neutrality in their selection of donated monuments, they must either 'brace themselves for an influx of clutter' or face the pressure to remove longstanding and cherished monuments. Every jurisdiction that has accepted a donated war memorial may be asked to provide equal treatment for a donated monument questioning the cause for which the veterans fought. New York City, having accepted a donated statue of one heroic dog (Balto, the sled dog who brought medicine to Nome, Alaska, during a diphtheria epidemic) may be pressed to accept monuments for other dogs who are claimed to be equally worthy of commemoration. The obvious truth of the matter is that if public parks were considered to be traditional public forums for the purpose of erecting privately donated monuments, most parks would have little choice but to refuse all such donations." Earlier in the opinion, the Court recited limits on government speech: "This does not mean that there are no restraints on government speech. For example, government speech must comport with the Establishment Clause. The involvement of public officials in advocacy may be limited by law, regulation, or practice. And of course, a government entity is ultimately 'accountable to the electorate and the political process for its advocacy.' 'If the citizenry objects, newly elected officials later could espouse some different or contrary position.' "

WALKER V. TEXAS DIVISION, SONS OF CONFEDERATE VETERANS, INC.
576 U.S. 200, 135 S.Ct. 2239, 192 L.Ed.2d 274 (2015).

JUSTICE BREYER delivered the opinion of the Court.

Texas offers automobile owners a choice between ordinary and specialty license plates. Those who want the State to issue a particular specialty plate may propose a plate design, comprising a slogan, a graphic, or (most commonly) both. If the Department of Motor Vehicles Board approves the design, the State will make it available for display on vehicles registered in Texas.

In this case, the Texas Division of the Sons of Confederate Veterans proposed a specialty license plate design featuring a Confederate battle flag. The Board rejected the proposal. We must decide whether that rejection violated the Constitution's free speech guarantees. We conclude that it did not.

I.　　A. Texas law requires all motor vehicles operating on the State's roads to display valid license plates. And Texas makes available several kinds of plates. Drivers may choose to display the State's general-issue license plates. Each of these plates contains the word "Texas," a license plate number, a silhouette of the State, a graphic of the Lone Star, and the slogan "The Lone Star State." In the alternative, drivers may choose from an assortment of specialty license plates. Each of these plates contains the word "Texas," a license plate number, and one of a selection of designs prepared by the State. Finally, Texas law provides for personalized plates (also known as "vanity plates"). Pursuant to the personalization program, a vehicle owner may request a particular alphanumeric pattern for use as a plate number, such as "BOB" or "TEXPL8." Here we are concerned only with the second category of plates, namely specialty license plates, not with the personalization program. Texas offers vehicle owners a variety of specialty plates, generally for an annual fee. And Texas selects the designs for specialty plates through three distinct processes.

First, the state legislature may specifically call for the development of a specialty license plate. The legislature has enacted statutes authorizing, for example, plates that say "Keep Texas Beautiful" and "Mothers Against Drunk Driving," plates that "honor" the Texas citrus industry, and plates that feature an image of the World Trade Center towers and the words "Fight Terrorism." Second, the Board may approve a specialty plate design proposal that a state-designated private vendor has created at the request of an individual or organization. Among the plates created through the private-vendor process are plates promoting the "Keller Indians" and plates with the slogan "Get it Sold with RE/MAX." Third, the Board "may create new specialty license plates on its own initiative or on receipt of an application from a" nonprofit entity seeking to sponsor a specialty plate. A nonprofit must include in its application "a draft design of the specialty license plate." And Texas law vests in the Board authority to approve or to disapprove an application. The relevant statute says that the Board "may refuse "[for] a number of reasons, for example "if the design might be offensive to any member of the public . . . or for any other reason established by rule." Specialty plates that the Board has sanctioned through this process include plates featuring the words "The Gator Nation," together with the Florida Gators logo, and plates featuring the logo of Rotary International and the words "SERVICE ABOVE SELF."

B.   In 2009, the Sons of Confederate Veterans, Texas Division (a nonprofit entity), applied to sponsor a specialty license plate through this last-mentioned process. [At] the bottom of the proposed plate were the words "SONS OF CONFEDERATE VETERANS." At the side was the organization's logo, a square Confederate battle flag framed by the words "Sons of Confederate Veterans 1896." A faint Confederate battle flag appeared in the background on the lower portion of the plate. [In] the middle of the plate was the license plate number, and at the top was the State's name and silhouette. In 2010, SCV renewed [a previously denied] application before the Board. The Board invited public comment on its website and at an open meeting. After considering the responses, including a number of letters sent by elected officials who opposed the proposal, the Board voted unanimously against issuing the plate. The Board explained that it had found "it necessary to deny th[e] plate design application, specifically the confederate flag portion of the design, because public comments ha[d] shown that many members of the general public find the design offensive, and because such comments are reasonable." The Board added "that a significant portion of the public associate the confederate flag with organizations advocating expressions of hate directed toward people or groups that is demeaning to those people or groups." * * *

II. When government speaks, it is not barred by the Free Speech Clause from determining the content of what it says. [*Summum*]. [Were] the Free Speech Clause interpreted otherwise, government would not work. How could a city government create a successful recycling program if officials, when writing householders asking them to recycle cans and bottles, had to include in the letter a long plea from the local trash disposal enterprise demanding the contrary? How could a state government effectively develop programs designed to encourage and provide vaccinations, if officials also had to voice the perspective of those who oppose this type of immunization? * * *

We have therefore refused "[t]o hold that the Government unconstitutionally discriminates on the basis of viewpoint when it chooses to fund a program dedicated to advance certain permissible goals, because the program in advancing those goals necessarily discourages alternative goals." [*Rust v. Sullivan*, infra]. * * *

III. In our view, specialty license plates issued pursuant to Texas's statutory scheme convey government speech. Our reasoning rests primarily on our analysis in *Summum*. [First,] the history of license plates shows that, insofar as license plates have conveyed more than state names and vehicle identification numbers, they long have communicated messages from the States. In 1917, Arizona became the first State to display a graphic on its plates. The State presented a depiction of the head of a Hereford steer. In the years since, New Hampshire plates have featured the profile of the "Old Man of the Mountain," Massachusetts plates have included a representation of the Commonwealth's famous codfish, and Wyoming plates have displayed a rider atop a bucking bronco.

In 1928, Idaho became the first State to include a slogan on its plates. The Idaho plate proclaimed "Idaho Potatoes" and featured an illustration of a brown potato, onto which the license plate number was superimposed in green. The brown potato did not catch on, but slogans on license plates did. Over the years, state plates have included the phrases "North to the Future" (Alaska), "Keep Florida Green" (Florida), "Hoosier Hospitality" (Indiana), "The Iodine Products State" (South Carolina), "Green Mountains" (Vermont), and "America's Dairyland" (Wisconsin). * * *

Texas, too, has selected various messages to communicate through its license plate designs. By 1919, Texas had begun to display the Lone Star emblem on its plates. In 1936, the State's general-issue plates featured the first slogan on Texas license plates: the word "Centennial." In 1968, Texas plates promoted a San Antonio event by including the phrase "Hemisfair 68." [And] in 1995, Texas plates celebrated "150 Years of Statehood." Additionally, the Texas Legislature has specifically authorized specialty plate designs stating, among other things, "Read to Succeed" [and] "Houston Livestock Show and Rodeo."

[Texas] license plate designs "are often closely identified in the public mind with the [State]." Each Texas license plate is a government article serving the governmental purposes of vehicle registration and identification. The governmental nature of the plates is clear from their faces: The State places the name "TEXAS" in large letters at the top of every plate. Moreover, the State requires Texas vehicle owners to display license plates, and every Texas license plate is issued by the State. * * *

Texas license plates are, essentially, government IDs. And issuers of ID "typically do not permit" the placement on their IDs of "message[s] with which they do not wish to be associated Consequently, "persons who observe" designs on IDs "routinely—and reasonably—interpret them as conveying some message on the [issuer's] behalf." Indeed, a person who displays a message on a Texas license plate likely intends to convey to the public that the State has endorsed that message. If not, the individual could simply display the message in question in larger letters on a bumper sticker right next to the plate. But the individual prefers a license plate design to the purely private speech expressed through bumper stickers. That may well be because Texas's license plate designs convey government agreement with the message displayed.

[Texas] maintains direct control over the messages conveyed on its specialty plates. Texas law provides that the State "has sole control over the design, typeface, color, and alphanumeric pattern for all license plates." The Board must approve every specialty plate design proposal before the design can appear on a Texas plate. And the Board and its predecessor have actively exercised this authority. Texas asserts, and SCV concedes, that the State has rejected at least a dozen proposed designs. * * *

This final approval authority allows Texas to choose how to present itself and its constituency. Thus, Texas offers plates celebrating the many educational institutions attended by its citizens. But it need not issue plates deriding schooling. Texas offers plates that pay tribute to the Texas citrus industry. But it need not issue plates praising Florida's oranges as far better. And Texas offers plates that say "Fight Terrorism." But it need not issue plates promoting al Qaeda. * * *

SCV believes that Texas's specialty license plate designs are not government speech, at least with respect to the designs [proposed] by private parties. According to SCV, the State does not engage in expressive activity through such slogans and graphics, but rather provides a forum for private speech by making license plates available to display the private parties' designs. We cannot agree.

We have previously used what we have called "forum analysis" to evaluate government restrictions on purely private speech that occurs on government property. But [because] the State is speaking on its own behalf, the First Amendment strictures that attend the various types of government-established forums do not apply.

The parties agree that Texas's specialty license plates are not a "traditional public forum," such as a street or a park. ["The] Court has rejected the view that traditional public forum status extends beyond its historic confines." And state-issued specialty license plates lie far beyond those confines.

It is equally clear that Texas's specialty plates are neither a " 'designated public forum,' " which exists where "government property that has not traditionally been regarded as a public forum is intentionally opened up for that purpose," nor a "limited public forum," which exists where a government has "reserv[ed a forum] for certain groups or for the discussion of certain topics." * * *

Texas's policies and the nature of its license plates indicate that the State did not intend its specialty license plates to serve as either a designated public forum or a limited public forum. First, the State exercises final authority over each specialty license plate design. [Second,] Texas takes ownership of each specialty plate design, making it particularly untenable that the State intended specialty plates to serve as a forum for public discourse. Finally, Texas license plates have traditionally been used for government speech, are primarily used as a form of government ID, and bear the State's name. These features of Texas license plates indicate that Texas explicitly associates itself with the speech on its plates. * * *

The fact that private parties take part in the design and propagation of a message does not extinguish the governmental nature of the message or transform the government's role into that of a mere forum-provider. [In] this case, as in *Summum,* the "government entity may exercise [its] freedom to express its views" even "when it receives assistance from private sources for the purpose of delivering a government-controlled message." * * *

[Reversed].

JUSTICE ALITO, with whom THE CHIEF JUSTICE, JUSTICE SCALIA, and JUSTICE KENNEDY join, dissenting.

The Court's decision passes off private speech as government speech and, in doing so, establishes a precedent that threatens private speech that government finds displeasing. Under our First Amendment cases, the distinction between government speech and private speech is critical. The First Amendment "does not regulate government speech," and therefore when government speaks, it is free "to select the views that it wants to express." By contrast, "[i]n the realm of private speech or expression, government regulation may not favor one speaker over another."

Unfortunately, the Court's decision categorizes private speech as government speech and thus strips it of all First Amendment protection. The Court holds that all the privately created messages on the many specialty plates issued by the State of Texas convey a government message rather than the message of the motorist displaying the plate. Can this possibly be correct?

Here is a test. Suppose you sat by the side of a Texas highway and studied the license plates on the vehicles passing by. You would see, in addition to the standard

Texas plates, an impressive array of [more than 350] specialty plates. You would likely observe plates that honor numerous colleges and universities. You might see plates bearing the name of a high school, a fraternity or sorority, the Masons, the Knights of Columbus, the Daughters of the American Revolution, a realty company, a favorite soft drink, a favorite burger restaurant, and a favorite NASCAR driver.

As you sat there watching these plates speed by, would you really think that the sentiments reflected in these specialty plates are the views of the State of Texas and not those of the owners of the cars? If a car with a plate that says "Rather Be Golfing" passed by at 8:30 am on a Monday morning, would you think: "This is the official policy of the State—better to golf than to work?" If you did your viewing at the start of the college football season and you saw Texas plates with the names of the University of Texas's out-of-state competitors in upcoming games—Notre Dame, Oklahoma State, the University of Oklahoma, Kansas State, Iowa State— would you assume that the State of Texas was officially (and perhaps treasonously) rooting for the Longhorns' opponents? And when a car zipped by with a plate that reads "NASCAR—24 Jeff Gordon," would you think that Gordon (born in California, raised in Indiana, resides in North Carolina) is the official favorite of the State government?

The Court says that [these] messages are government speech [because] it is essential that government be able to express its own viewpoint. [and] otherwise, how would it promote its programs, like recycling and vaccinations? So when Texas issues a "Rather Be Golfing" plate, but not a "Rather Be Playing Tennis" or "Rather Be Bowling" plate, it is furthering a state policy to promote golf but not tennis or bowling. And when Texas allows motorists to obtain a Notre Dame license plate but not a University of Southern California plate, it is taking sides in that long-time rivalry.

[Specialty] plates may seem innocuous. [But] the precedent this case sets is dangerous. While all license plates unquestionably contain *some* government speech (e.g., the name of the State and the numbers and/or letters identifying the vehicle), the State of Texas has converted the remaining space on its specialty plates into little mobile billboards on which motorists can display their own messages. And what Texas did here was to reject one of the messages that members of a private group wanted to post on some of these little billboards because the State thought that many of its citizens would find the message offensive. That is blatant viewpoint discrimination. If the State can do this with its little mobile billboards, could it do the same with big, stationary billboards? * * *

What if a state college or university did the same thing with a similar billboard or a campus bulletin board or dorm list serve? What if it allowed private messages that are consistent with prevailing views on campus but banned those that disturbed some students or faculty? * * *

[II.A.] In relying almost entirely on one precedent—*Summum*—the Court holds that messages that private groups succeed in placing on Texas license plates are government messages. The Court badly misunderstands *Summum*. [First,] governments have long used monuments as a means of expressing a government message. As we put it, "[s]ince ancient times, kings, emperors, and other rulers have erected statues of themselves to remind their subjects of their authority and power." [Thus,] long experience has led the public to associate public monuments with government speech.

Second, there is no history of landowners allowing their property to be used by third parties as the site of large permanent monuments that do not express messages that the landowners wish to convey. While "[a] great many of the monuments that adorn the Nation's public parks were financed with private funds or donated by private parties," "cities and other jurisdictions take some care in accepting donated monuments" and select those that "conve[y] a government message." We were not presented in *Summum* with examples of public parks that had been thrown open for private groups or individuals to put up whatever monuments they desired.

Third, spatial limitations played a prominent part in our analysis. "[P]ublic parks can accommodate only a limited number of permanent monuments," and consequently permanent monuments "monopolize the use of the land on which they stand and interfere permanently with other uses of public space." * * *

B.1. [As] we said in *Summum,* governments have used monuments since time immemorial to express important government messages, and there is no history of governments giving equal space to those wishing to express dissenting views. In 1775, when a large gilded equestrian statue of King George III dominated Bowling Green, a small park in lower Manhattan, the colonial governor surely would not have permitted the construction on that land of a monument to the fallen at Lexington and Concord. When the United States accepted the Third French Republic's gift of the Statue of Liberty in 1877, Congress, it seems safe to say, would not have welcomed a gift of a Statue of Authoritarianism if one had been offered by another country. Nor is it likely that the National Park Service today would be receptive if private groups, pointing to the Lincoln Memorial, the Martin Luther King, Jr., Memorial, and the Vietnam Veterans Memorial on the National Mall, sought permission to put up monuments to Jefferson Davis, Orval Faubus, or the North Vietnamese Army. Governments have always used public monuments to express a government message, and members of the public understand this.

The history of messages on license plates is quite different. After the beginning of motor vehicle registration in 1917, more than 70 years passed before the proliferation of specialty plates in Texas. It was not until the 1990s that motorists were allowed to choose from among 10 messages, such as "Read to Succeed" and "Keep Texas Beautiful." Up to this point, the words on the Texas plates can be considered government speech. The messages were created by the State, and they plausibly promoted state programs. But when, at some point within the last 20 years or so, the State began to allow private entities to secure plates conveying their own messages, Texas crossed the line. * * *

2.   The Texas specialty plate program also does not exhibit the "selective receptivity" present in *Summum*. To the contrary, Texas's program is *not* selective by design. The Board's chairman, who is charged with approving designs, explained that the program's purpose is "to encourage private plates" in order to "generate additional revenue for the state." And most of the time, the Board "base[s] [its] decisions on rules that primarily deal with reflectivity and readability." A Department brochure explains: "Q. Who provides the plate design? A. You do, though your design is subject to reflectivity, legibility, and design standards."* * *

The Court believes that messages on privately created plates are government speech because motorists want a seal of state approval for their messages and therefore prefer plates over bumper stickers. This is dangerous reasoning. There is a big difference between government speech (that is, speech by the government in furtherance of its programs) and governmental blessing (or condemnation) of private speech. * * *

3.   A final factor that was important in *Summum* was space. A park can accommodate only so many permanent monuments. Often large and made of stone, monuments can last for centuries and are difficult to move. License plates, on the other hand, are small, light, mobile, and designed to last for only a relatively brief time. The only absolute limit on the number of specialty plates that a State could issue is the number of registered vehicles. The variety of available plates is limitless, too. Today Texas offers more than 350 varieties. In 10 years, might it be 3,500? * * *

III.   What Texas has done by selling space on its license plates is to create what we have called a limited public forum. It has allowed state property [to] be used by private speakers according to rules that the State prescribes. Under the First Amendment, however, those rules cannot discriminate on the basis of viewpoint. * * *

The Confederate battle flag is a controversial symbol. To the Texas Sons of Confederate Veterans, it is said to evoke the memory of their ancestors and other soldiers who fought for the South in the Civil War. To others, it symbolizes slavery, segregation, and hatred. Whatever it means to motorists who display that symbol and to those who see it, the flag expresses a viewpoint. The Board rejected the plate design because it concluded that many Texans would find the flag symbol offensive. That was pure viewpoint discrimination.

If the Board's candid explanation of its reason for rejecting the SCV plate were not alone sufficient to establish this point, the Board's approval of the Buffalo Soldiers plate at the same meeting dispels any doubt. The proponents of both the SCV and Buffalo Soldiers plates saw them as honoring soldiers who served with bravery and honor in the past. To the opponents of both plates, the images on the plates evoked painful memories. The Board rejected one plate and approved the other. * * *

[* * * I] respectfully dissent.

RUST V. SULLIVAN

500 U.S. 173, 111 S.Ct. 1759, 114 L.Ed.2d 233 (1991).

CHIEF JUSTICE REHNQUIST delivered the opinion of the Court.

These cases concern a facial challenge to Department of Health and Human Services (HHS) regulations which limit the ability of Title X fund recipients to engage in abortion-related activities. * * *

A.   In 1970, Congress enacted Title X of the Public Health Service Act, which provides federal funding for family-planning services. The Act authorizes the Secretary to "make grants to and enter into contracts with public or nonprofit private entities to assist in the establishment and operation of voluntary family planning projects which shall offer a broad range of acceptable and effective family planning methods and services." Grants and contracts under Title X must "be made in accordance with such regulations as the Secretary may promulgate." Section 1008 of the Act, however, provides that "[n]one of the funds appropriated under this subchapter shall be used in programs where abortion is a method of family planning." * * *

The [HHS] regulations attach three principal conditions on the grant of federal funds for Title X projects. First, the regulations specify that a "Title X project may not provide counseling concerning the use of abortion as a method of family planning or provide referral for abortion as a method of family planning." Second, the regulations broadly prohibit a Title X project from engaging in activities that "encourage, promote or advocate abortion as a method of family planning." Third, the regulations require that Title X projects be organized so that they are "physically and financially separate" from prohibited abortion activities.

[T]here is no question but that the statutory prohibition contained in § 1008 is constitutional. [The] Government can, without violating the Constitution, selectively fund a program to encourage certain activities it believes to be in the public interest, without at the same time funding an alternate program which seeks to deal with the problem in another way. In so doing, the Government has not discriminated on the basis of viewpoint; it has merely chosen to fund one activity to the exclusion of the other. * * *

The challenged regulations implement the statutory prohibition by prohibiting counseling, referral, and the provision of information regarding abortion as a method of family planning. They are designed to ensure that the limits of the federal program are observed. The Title X program is designed not for prenatal care, but to encourage family planning. A doctor who wished to offer prenatal care to a project patient who became pregnant could properly be prohibited from doing so because such service is outside the scope of the federally funded program. The regulations prohibiting abortion counseling and referral are of the same ilk; "no funds appropriated for the project may be used in programs where abortion is a method of family planning," and a doctor employed by the project may be prohibited in the course of his project duties from counseling abortion or referring for abortion. This is not a case of the Government "suppressing a dangerous idea," but of a prohibition on a project grantee or its employees from engaging in activities outside of its scope.

To hold that the Government unconstitutionally discriminates on the basis of viewpoint when it chooses to fund a program dedicated to advance certain permissible goals, because the program in advancing those goals necessarily discourages alternate goals, would render numerous government programs constitutionally suspect. When Congress established a National Endowment for Democracy to encourage other countries to adopt democratic principles, 22 U.S.C. § 4411(b), it was not constitutionally required to fund a program to encourage competing lines of political philosophy such as Communism and Fascism. Petitioners' assertions ultimately boil down to the position that if the government chooses to subsidize one protected right, it must subsidize analogous counterpart rights. But the Court has soundly rejected that proposition. Within far broader limits than petitioners are willing to concede, when the government appropriates public funds to establish a program it is entitled to define the limits of that program.* * *

JUSTICE BLACKMUN, with whom JUSTICE MARSHALL joins, with whom JUSTICE STEVENS joins as to Parts II and III, and with whom JUSTICE O'CONNOR joins as to Part I, dissenting. * * *

II.   A. Until today, the Court never has upheld viewpoint-based suppression of speech simply because that suppression was a condition upon the acceptance of public funds. Whatever may be the Government's power to condition the receipt of its largess upon the relinquishment of constitutional rights, it surely does not extend to a condition that suppresses the recipient's cherished freedom of speech based solely upon the content or viewpoint of that speech. * * *

It cannot seriously be disputed that the counseling and referral provisions at issue in the present cases constitute content-based regulation of speech. Title X grantees may provide counseling and referral regarding any of a wide range of family planning and other topics, save abortion.

The Regulations are also clearly viewpoint-based. While suppressing speech favorable to abortion with one hand, the Secretary compels anti-abortion speech with the other. [Moreover,] the Regulations command that a project refer for prenatal care each woman diagnosed as pregnant, irrespective of the woman's expressed desire to continue or terminate her pregnancy. If a client asks directly about abortion, a Title X physician or counselor is required to say, in essence, that the project does not consider abortion to be an appropriate method of family planning. Both requirements are antithetical to the First Amendment. * * *

––––––

Rust distinguished. The University of Virginia subsidized the printing costs of a wide variety of student organizations, but refused to fund religious activities (those that "primarily promote or manifest a particular belief in or about a deity or an ultimate reality").

ROSENBERGER v. UNIVERSITY OF VIRGINIA, 515 U.S. 819 (1995), per KENNEDY, J., also set forth Ch. 8, Sec. I infra held that the refusal to fund religious speech violated the free speech clause: "[In *Rust*] the government did not create a program to encourage private speech but instead used private speakers to transmit specific information pertaining to its own program. We recognized that when the government appropriates public funds to promote a particular policy of its own it is entitled to say what it wishes.

"It does not follow [that] viewpoint-based restrictions are proper when the University does not itself speak or subsidize transmittal of a message it favors but instead expends funds to encourage a diversity of views from private speakers."

SOUTER, J., joined by Stevens, Ginsburg and Breyer, JJ., dissented: "If the Guidelines were written or applied so as to limit only such Christian advocacy and no other evangelical efforts that might compete with it, the discrimination would be based on viewpoint. But that is not what the regulation authorizes; it applies to Muslim and Jewish and Buddhist advocacy as well as to Christian. And since it limits funding to activities promoting or manifesting a particular belief not only 'in' but 'about' a deity or ultimate reality, it applies to agnostics and atheists as well as it does to deists and theists. The Guidelines [thus] do not skew debate by funding one position but not its competitors. [T]hey simply deny funding for hortatory speech that 'primarily promotes or manifests' any view on the merits of religion; they deny funding for the entire subject matter of religious apologetics."

Rust v. Sullivan relied almost exclusively on framing the case as one in which the government could decide, even on viewpoint-based grounds, to decide what to fund and what not to fund, and thus what to say and what not to say. In NATIONAL INSTITUTE OF FAMILY AND LIFE ADVOCATES v. BECERRA, 138 S.Ct. 2361 (2018), a related issue arose in a context not involving government funding or government programs. California had passed a law—The California Reproductive Freedom, Accountability, Comprehensive Care, and Transparency Act—that required state-licensed and unlicensed clinics offering pregnancy-related services to notify women of the availability of state provided pregnancy services, including abortions, and that required unlicensed clinics to notify women, by use of a state-drafted notice, that the clinics were not licensed to provide medical services.

A coalition of pro-life pregnancy counseling clinics challenged the law, arguing that its "compelled speech" requirements violated the First Amendment. Writing for a 5–4 majority, THOMAS, J. agreed, and ruled the statute unconstitutional. California had argued that the professional speech offered in pregnancy counseling clinics was subject to greater regulation because of its professional nature, and because of the state's interest in regulating various professional practices. But the

Court resisted that characterization, and resisted as well the idea that there was a broad category of professional speech deserving of less First Amendment scrutiny, saying that neither the precedents requiring the disclosure of factual information in a commercial speech context nor the precedents allowing regulation of professional conduct were applicable here. Rather, the Court saw this as a content-based regulation of noncommercial speech, and one in which the under-inclusiveness of the statute, when combined with the availability of other alternatives for providing the relevant information, made the law inconsistent with the First Amendment. "[N]either California nor the Ninth Circuit has identified a persuasive reason for treating [licensed] professional speech as a unique category that is exempt from ordinary First Amendment principles. [California] asserts a single interest[:] providing low-income women with information about state-sponsored services. Assuming that this is a substantial state interest, the [required notice] is not sufficiently [narrowly] drawn to achieve it." For similar reasons, the Court held the requirement as to unlicensed facilities was also "unduly burdensome," and could not withstand First Amendment scrutiny.

KENNEDY, J., joined by Roberts, C.J., Alito, J., and Gorsuch, J., concurred, emphasizing that for them the fundamental flaw in the California statute was its viewpoint-based discrimination between pro-life and pro-choice messages and clinics. "Governments must not be allowed to force persons to express a message contrary to their deepest convictions."

BREYER, J., dissented, joined by Ginsburg, J., Sotomayor, J., and Kagan, J. For Justice Breyer, the statute was not relevantly different from a wide range of health-related and public-interest-related required warnings and notifications, including those applicable to the securities laws, to trash disposal procedures, to petting zoos, to elevators, and to countless health care facilities and services. Moreover, he argued, the Court's prior abortion cases had upheld various forms of required notification. [If] a state can lawfully require a doctor to tell a woman seeking an abortion about adoption services (see *Akron v. Akron Center for Reproductive Health*, discussed in *Planned Parenthood of Southeastern Pennsylvania v. Casey*, Ch. 6, Sec. 2), why should it not be able, as here, to require a medical counselor to tell a woman seeking prenatal care or other reproductive healthcare about childbirth and abortion services? As the question suggests, there is no convincing reason to distinguish between information about adoption and information about abortion in this context."

———

Funding arts and science. The government funds scientific projects on the basis of their perceived merit. Can Congress constitutionally prohibit the funding of "indecent" art? Would this be content discrimination or viewpoint discrimination? Does it matter? The extent to which the government may make such judgments and the role that political actors may play in the process was debated in *National Endowment for the Arts v. Finley*, 524 U.S. 569 (1998) but not resolved.

II. GOVERNMENT AS EDUCATOR AND EDITOR

TINKER V. DES MOINES SCHOOL DISTRICT
393 U.S. 503, 89 S.Ct. 733, 21 L.Ed.2d 731 (1969).

JUSTICE FORTAS delivered the opinion of the Court.

[Petitioners, two high school students and one junior high student, wore black armbands to school to publicize their objections to the Vietnam conflict and their advocacy of a truce. They refused to remove the armbands when asked to do so. In accordance with a ban on armbands which the city's school principals had adopted two days before in anticipation of such a protest, petitioners were sent home and suspended from school until they would return without the armbands. They sought a federal injunction restraining school officials from disciplining them, but the lower federal courts upheld the constitutionality of the school authorities' action on the ground that it was reasonable in order to prevent a disturbance which might result from the wearing of the armbands.]

[T]he wearing of armbands in the circumstances of this case was entirely divorced from actually or potentially disruptive conduct by those participating in it. It was closely akin to "pure speech" which, we have repeatedly held, is entitled to comprehensive protection under the First Amendment. * * *

First Amendment rights, applied in light of the special characteristics of the school environment, are available to teachers and students. It can hardly be argued that either students or teachers shed their constitutional rights to freedom of speech or expression at the schoolhouse gate. This has been the unmistakable holding of this Court for almost 50 years. In *Meyer*, this Court [held that fourteenth amendment due process] prevents States from forbidding the teaching of a foreign language to young students. Statutes to this effect, the Court held, unconstitutionally interfere with the liberty of teacher, student, and parent. * * *

The problem presented by the present case does not relate to regulation of the length of skirts or the type of clothing, to hair style or deportment. [It] does not concern aggressive, disruptive action or even group demonstrations. Our problem involves direct, primary First Amendment rights akin to "pure speech."

The school officials banned and sought to punish petitioners for a silent, passive, expression of opinion, unaccompanied by any disorder or disturbance on the part of petitioners. There is here no evidence whatever of petitioners' interference, actual or nascent, with the school's work or of collision with the rights of other students to be secure and to be let alone. Accordingly, this case does not concern speech or action that intrudes upon the work of the school or the rights of other students.

Only a few of the 18,000 students in the school system wore the black armbands. Only five students were suspended for wearing them. There is no indication that the work of the school or any class was disrupted. Outside the classrooms, a few students made hostile remarks to the children wearing armbands, but there were no threats or acts of violence on school premises.

[I]n our system, undifferentiated fear or apprehension of disturbance [the District Court's basis for sustaining the school authorities' action] is not enough to overcome the right to freedom of expression. Any departure from absolute regimentation may cause trouble. Any variation from the majority's opinion may inspire fear. Any words spoken, in class, in the lunchroom or on the campus, that deviates from the views of another person, may start an argument or cause a disturbance. But our Constitution says we must take this risk [and] our history says that it is this sort of hazardous freedom—this kind of openness—that is the basis of our national strength and of the independence and vigor of Americans who grow up and live in this relatively permissive, often disputatious society.

In order for the State in the person of school officials to justify prohibition of a particular expression of opinion, it must be able to show that its action was caused by something more than a mere desire to avoid the discomfort and unpleasantness that always accompany an unpopular viewpoint. Certainly where there is no finding and no showing that the exercise of the forbidden right would "materially and substantially interfere with the requirements of appropriate discipline in the operation of the school," the prohibition cannot be sustained.

In the present case, the District Court made no such finding, and our independent examination of the record fails to yield evidence that the school authorities had reason to anticipate that the wearing of the armbands would substantially interfere with the work of the school or impinge upon the rights of other students. Even an official memorandum prepared after the suspension that listed the reasons for the ban on wearing the armbands made no reference to the anticipation of such disruption.

On the contrary, the action of the school authorities appears to have been based upon an urgent wish to avoid the controversy which might result from the expression, even by the silent symbol of armbands, of opposition to this Nation's part in the conflagration in Vietnam. * * *

It is also relevant that the school authorities did not purport to prohibit the wearing of all symbols of political or controversial significance. The record shows that students in some of the schools wore buttons relating to national political campaigns, and some even wore the Iron Cross, traditionally a symbol of Nazism. The order prohibiting the wearing of armbands did not extend to these. Instead, a particular symbol—black armbands worn to exhibit opposition to this Nation's involvement in Vietnam—was singled out for prohibition. Clearly, the prohibition of expression of one particular opinion, at least without evidence that it is necessary to avoid material and substantial interference with school work or discipline, is not constitutionally permissible.

In our system, state-operated schools may not be enclaves of totalitarianism. School officials do not possess absolute authority over their students. Students in school as well as out of school are "persons" under our Constitution. They are possessed of fundamental rights which the State must respect, just as they themselves must respect their obligations to the State. In our system, students may not be regarded as closed-circuit recipients of only that which the State chooses to communicate. They may not be confined to the expression of those sentiments that are officially approved. In the absence of a specific showing of constitutionally valid reasons to regulate their speech, students are entitled to freedom of expression of their views.

[The principle of prior cases underscoring the importance of diversity and exchange of ideas in the schools,] is not confined to the supervised and ordained discussion which takes place in the classroom. The principal use to which the schools are dedicated is to accommodate students during prescribed hours for the purpose of certain types of activities. Among those activities is personal intercommunication among the students. This is not only an inevitable part of the process of attending school. It is also an important part of the educational process.

A student's rights therefore, do not embrace merely the classroom hours. When he is in the cafeteria, or on the playing field, or on the campus during the authorized hours, he may express his opinions, even on controversial subjects like the conflict in Vietnam, if he does so "[without] materially and substantially interfering [with] appropriate discipline in the operation of the school" and without colliding with the rights of others. *Burnside.* But conduct by the student, in class or out of it, which for any reason—whether it stems from time, place, or type of behavior—materially disrupts classwork or involves substantial disorder or invasion of the rights of others is, of course, not immunized by the [First Amendment].

We properly read [the First Amendment] to permit reasonable regulation of speech-connected activities in carefully restricted circumstances. But we do not confine the permissible exercise of First Amendment rights to a telephone booth or the four corners of a pamphlet, or to supervised and ordained discussion in a school classroom. * * *

Reversed and remanded.

JUSTICE STEWART, concurring.

Although I agree with much of what is said in the Court's opinion, and with its judgment in this case, I cannot share the Court's uncritical assumption that, school discipline aside, the First Amendment rights of children are co-extensive with those of adults. * * *

JUSTICE BLACK, dissenting. * * *

Assuming that the Court is correct in holding that the conduct of wearing armbands for the purpose of conveying political ideas is protected by the First Amendment [, the] crucial remaining questions are whether students and teachers may use the schools at their whim as a platform for the exercise of free speech— "symbolic" or "pure"—and whether the Courts will allocate to themselves the function of deciding how the pupils' school day will be spent. * * *

While the record does not show that any of these armband students shouted, used profane language, or were violent in any manner, detailed testimony by some of them shows their armbands caused comments, warnings by other students, the poking of fun at them, and a warning by an older football player that other, nonprotesting students had better let them alone. [While] the absence of obscene or boisterous and loud disorder perhaps justifies the Court's statement that the few armband students did not actually "disrupt" the classwork, I think the record overwhelmingly shows that the armbands did exactly what the elected school officials and principals foresaw it would, that is, took the students' minds off their classwork and diverted them to thoughts about the highly emotional subject of the Vietnam war. * * *

JUSTICE HARLAN, dissenting.

I certainly agree that state public school authorities in the discharge of their responsibilities are not wholly exempt from the requirements of the Fourteenth Amendment respecting the freedoms of expression and association. At the same time I am reluctant to believe that there is any disagreement between the majority and myself on the proposition that school officials should be accorded the widest authority in maintaining discipline and good order in their institutions. To translate that proposition into a workable constitutional rule, I would, in cases like this, cast upon those complaining the burden of showing that a particular school measure was motivated by other than legitimate school concerns—for example, a desire to prohibit the expression of an unpopular point of view, while permitting expression of the dominant opinion.

MORSE v. FREDERICK, 551 U.S. 393 (2007), per ROBERTS, C.J., upheld the suspension of a high school student for refusing to take down a banner at a school sponsored event that read "BONG HiTS 4 JESUS": "The concern is not that Frederick's speech is offensive, but that it was reasonably viewed as promoting illegal drug use."

ALITO, J., joined by Kennedy, J., concurring, joined the Court's opinion on the understanding that it "goes no further than to hold that a public school may restrict speech that a reasonable observer would interpret as advocating illegal drug use" and provides no support for restricting comments on political or social issues including "the wisdom of the war on drugs or legalizing marijuana for medicinal use."

THOMAS, J., concurring, would overrule *Tinker*: "In light of the history of American public education, it cannot be seriously suggested that the First Amendment 'freedom of speech' encompasses a student's right to speak in public schools. Early public schools gave total control to teachers, who expected obedience and respect from students."

STEVENS, J., joined by Souter and Ginsburg, JJ., dissenting, thought it was not reasonable to conclude that the message on the banner advocated drug use or that it would persuade students to use drugs.

HAZELWOOD SCHOOL DISTRICT V. KUHLMEIER
484 U.S. 260, 108 S.Ct. 562, 98 L.Ed.2d 592 (1988).

JUSTICE WHITE delivered the opinion of the Court. * * *

Petitioners are the Hazelwood School District in St. Louis County, Missouri; various school officials; Robert Eugene Reynolds, the principal of Hazelwood East High School, and Howard Emerson, a teacher in the school district. Respondents are three former Hazelwood East students who were staff members of Spectrum, the school newspaper. * * *

The practice at Hazelwood East during the spring 1983 semester was for the journalism teacher to submit page proofs of each Spectrum issue to Principal Reynolds for his review prior to publication. On May 10, Emerson delivered the proofs of the May 13 edition to Reynolds, who objected to two of the articles scheduled to appear in that edition. One of the stories described three Hazelwood East students' experiences with pregnancy; the other discussed the impact of divorce on students at the school.

Reynolds was concerned that, although the pregnancy story used false names "to keep the identity of these girls a secret," the pregnant students still might be identifiable from the text. He also believed that the article's references to sexual activity and birth control were inappropriate for some of the younger students at the school. In addition, Reynolds was concerned that a student identified by name in the divorce story had complained [about] her father * * * . Reynolds believed that the student's parents should have been given an opportunity to respond to these remarks or to consent to their publication. He was unaware that Emerson had deleted the student's name from the final version of the article.

Reynolds believed that there was no time to make the necessary changes in the stories before the scheduled press run and that the newspaper would not appear before the end of the school year if printing were delayed to any significant extent. He concluded that his only options under the circumstances were to publish a four-page newspaper instead of the planned six-page newspaper, eliminating the two pages on which the offending stories appeared, or to publish no newspaper at all. Accordingly, he directed Emerson to withhold from publication the two pages containing the stories on pregnancy and divorce. He informed his superiors of the decision, and they concurred. * * *

[T]he First Amendment rights of students in the public schools "are not automatically coextensive with the rights of adults in other settings," *Bethel School District No. 403 v. Fraser*, 478 U.S. 675 (1986), and must be "applied in light of the special characteristics of the school environment." *Tinker*. A school need not tolerate student speech that is inconsistent with its "basic educational mission,"

Fraser, even though the government could not censor similar speech outside the school. Accordingly, we held in *Fraser* that a student could be disciplined for having delivered a speech that was "sexually explicit" but not legally obscene at an official school [assembly]. We thus recognized that "[t]he determination of what manner of speech in the classroom or in school assembly is inappropriate properly rests with the school board," rather than with the federal courts. * * *

We deal first with the question whether Spectrum may appropriately be characterized as a forum for public expression. [T]he evidence relied upon by the Court of Appeals fails to demonstrate the "clear intent to create a public forum," that existed in cases in which we found public forums to have been created. School [officials] "reserve[d] the forum for its intended purpos[e]," as a supervised learning experience for journalism students. Accordingly, school officials were entitled to regulate the contents of Spectrum in any reasonable manner. * * *

The question whether the First Amendment requires a school to tolerate particular student speech—the question that we addressed in *Tinker*—is different from the question whether the First Amendment requires a school affirmatively to promote particular student speech. The former question addresses educators' ability to silence a student's personal expression that happens to occur on the school premises. The latter question concerns educators' authority over school-sponsored publications, theatrical productions, and other expressive activities that students, parents, and members of the public might reasonably perceive to bear the imprimatur of the school. These activities may fairly be characterized as part of the school curriculum, whether or not they occur in a traditional classroom setting, so long as they are supervised by faculty members and designed to impart particular knowledge or skills to student participants and audiences.

[Accordingly,] we conclude that the standard articulated in *Tinker* for determining when a school may punish student expression need not also be the standard for determining when a school may refuse to lend its name and resources to the dissemination of student expression. Instead, we hold that educators do not offend the First Amendment by exercising editorial control over the style and content of student speech in school-sponsored expressive activities so long as their actions are reasonably related to legitimate pedagogical concerns. * * *

JUSTICE BRENNAN, with whom JUSTICE MARSHALL and JUSTICE BLACKMUN join, dissenting.

[I] fully agree with the Court that the First Amendment should afford an educator the prerogative not to sponsor the publication of a newspaper article that is "ungrammatical, poorly written, inadequately researched, biased or prejudiced," or that falls short of the "high standards [for] student speech that is disseminated under [the school's] auspices." But we need not abandon *Tinker* to reach that conclusion; we need only apply it. The enumerated criteria reflect the skills that the curricular newspaper "is designed to teach." The educator may, under *Tinker,* constitutionally "censor" poor grammar, writing, or research because to reward such expression would "materially disrup[t]" the newspaper's curricular purpose. * * *

The Court relies on bits of testimony to portray the principal's conduct as a pedagogical lesson to Journalism II students who "had not sufficiently mastered those portions of [the] curriculum that pertained to the treatment of controversial issues and personal attacks, the need to protect the privacy of individuals [and] 'the legal, moral, and ethical restrictions imposed upon journalists * * * .'"

But the principal never consulted the students before censoring their work. [T]hey learned of the deletions when the paper was released. [Further,] he explained the deletions only in the broadest of generalities. In one meeting called at the behest of seven protesting Spectrum staff members (presumably a fraction of the full class), he characterized the articles as " 'too sensitive' for 'our immature audience of readers,' " and in a later meeting he deemed them simply "inappropriate, personal, sensitive and unsuitable for the newspaper." The Court's supposition that the principal intended (or the protesters understood) those generalities as a lesson on the nuances of journalistic responsibility is utterly incredible. If he did, a fact that neither the District Court nor the Court of Appeals found, the lesson was lost on all but the psychic Spectrum staffer.

[Official] censorship of student speech on the ground that it addresses "potentially sensitive topics" is, for related reasons, equally impermissible. I would not begrudge an educator the authority to limit the substantive scope of a school-sponsored publication to a certain, objectively definable topic, such as literary criticism, school sports, or an overview of the school year. Unlike those determinate limitations, "potential topic sensitivity" is a vaporous nonstandard [that] invites manipulation to achieve ends that cannot permissibly be achieved through blatant viewpoint discrimination and chills student speech to which school officials might not object. * * *

MAHANOY AREA SCHOOL DISTRICT V. B. L.
594 U.S. ___, 141 S.Ct. 2038, 206 L.Ed.2d ___ (2021).

JUSTICE BREYER delivered the opinion of the Court.

A public high school student used, and transmitted to her Snapchat friends, vulgar language and gestures criticizing both the school and the school's cheerleading team. The student's speech took place outside of school hours and away from the school's campus. In response, the school suspended the student for a year from the cheerleading team. We must decide whether [the] school's decision violated the First Amendment. Although we do not agree with the reasoning of the Third Circuit panel's majority, we do agree with its conclusion that the school's disciplinary action violated the First Amendment.

B. L. was a student at Mahanoy Area High School in Mahanoy City, Pennsylvania. At the end of her freshman year, B. L. tried out for a position on the school's varsity cheerleading squad. [She] did not make the varsity cheerleading team [but] was offered a spot on the cheerleading squad's junior varsity team. B. L. did not accept the coach's decision with good grace, particularly because the squad coaches had placed an entering freshman on the varsity team.

That weekend, B. L. and a friend visited [a] local convenience store. There, B. L. used her smartphone to post two photos on Snapchat, a social media application that allows users to post photos and videos that disappear after a set period of time. B. L. posted the images to her Snapchat "story," a feature of the application that allows any person in the user's "friend" group (B. L. had about 250 "friends") to view the images for a 24 hour period. The first image B. L. posted showed B. L. and a friend with middle fingers raised; it bore the caption: "Fuck school fuck softball fuck cheer fuck everything." The second image was blank but for a caption, which read: "Love how me and [another student] get told we need a year of jv before we make varsity but tha[t] doesn't matter to anyone else?" The caption also contained an upside-down smiley- face emoji.

B. L.'s Snapchat "friends" included other Mahanoy Area High School students, some of whom also belonged to the cheerleading squad. At least one of them, using a separate cellphone, took pictures of B. L.'s posts and shared them with other members of the cheerleading squad. One of the students who received these photos showed them to her mother (who was a cheerleading squad coach), and the images spread. That week, several cheerleaders and other students approached the cheerleading coaches "visibly upset" about B. L.'s posts. Questions about the posts persisted during an Algebra class taught by one of the two coaches. After discussing the matter with the school principal, the coaches decided that because the posts used profanity in connection with a school extracurricular activity, they violated team and school rules. As a result, the coaches suspended B. L. from the junior varsity cheerleading squad for the upcoming year. B. L.'s subsequent apologies did not move school officials. The school's athletic director, principal, superintendent, and school board all affirmed B. L.'s suspension from the team. In response, B. L., with her parents, filed this lawsuit in Federal District Court.

The District Court found in B. L.'s favor, [finding] that B. L.'s Snapchats had not caused substantial disruption at the school. [The] District Court declared that B. L.'s punishment violated the First Amendment, awarded B. L. nominal damages and attorneys' fees, and ordered the school to expunge her disciplinary record. On appeal, a panel of the Third Circuit affirmed. [The] majority noted that *Tinker* [held] that a public high school could not constitutionally prohibit a peaceful student political demonstration consisting of "'pure speech'" on school property during the school day. In *Tinker*, this Court emphasized that there was no evidence the student protest would "substantially interfere with the work of the school or impinge upon the rights of other students." . . .

Many courts have taken this statement as setting a standard [that] allows schools considerable freedom on campus to discipline students for conduct that the First Amendment might otherwise protect. But here, the panel majority held that this additional freedom did "not apply to off-campus speech," which it defined as "speech that is outside school-owned, -operated, or -supervised channels and that is not reasonably interpreted as bearing the school's imprimatur." Because B. L.'s speech took place off campus, the panel concluded that [*Tinker*] did not apply and the school consequently could not discipline B. L. for engaging in a form of pure speech.

[We] have made clear that students do not "shed their constitutional rights to freedom of speech or expression," even "at the school house gate." But we have also made clear that courts must apply the First Amendment "in light of the special characteristics of the school environment." One such characteristic [is] that schools at times stand *in loco parentis*, *i.e.*, in the place of parents. This Court has [outlined] three specific categories of student speech that schools may regulate in certain circumstances: (1) "indecent," "lewd," or "vulgar" speech uttered during a school assembly on school grounds. *Bethel.* (2) speech, uttered during a class trip, that promotes "illegal drug use," *Morse* v. *Frederick*; and (3) speech that others may reasonably perceive as "bear[ing] the imprimatur of the school," [as] in a school-sponsored newspaper, *Kuhlmeier*. Finally, in *Tinker*, we said schools have a special interest in regulating speech that "materially disrupts classwork or involves substantial disorder or invasion of the rights of others."

Unlike the Third Circuit, we do not believe the special characteristics that give schools additional license to regulate student speech always disappear when a school regulates speech that takes place off campus. The school's regulatory interests remain significant in some off-campus circumstances. [These] include serious or severe bullying or harassment targeting particular individuals; threats aimed at teachers or other students; the failure to follow rules concerning lessons, the writing of papers, the use of computers, or participation in other online school activities; and breaches of school security devices, including material maintained within school computers.

Even B. L. herself and the *amici* supporting her would redefine the Third Circuit's off-campus/on-campus distinction, treating as on campus: all times when the school is responsible for the student; the school's immediate surroundings; travel en route to and from the school; all speech taking place over school laptops or on a school's website; speech taking place during remote learning; activities taken for school credit; and communications to school e- mail accounts or phones. And it may be that speech related to extracurricular activities, such as team sports, would also receive special treatment under B. L.'s proposed rule.

We are uncertain as to the length or content of any such list of appropriate exceptions or carveouts to the Third Circuit majority's rule. [Particularly] given the advent of computer-based learning, we hesitate to determine precisely which of many school-related off-campus activities belong on such a list. Neither do we now know how such a list might vary, depending upon a student's age, the nature of the school's off-campus activity, or the impact upon the school itself. Thus, we do not now set forth a broad, highly general First Amendment rule stating just what counts as "off campus" speech and whether or how ordinary First Amendment standards must give way off campus to a school's special need to prevent, *e.g.*, substantial disruption of learning-related activities or the protection of those who make up a school community.

We can, however, mention three features of off-campus speech that [distinguish] schools' efforts to regulate that speech from their efforts to regulate on-campus speech. [*First*,] a school, in relation to off-campus speech, will rarely stand *in loco parentis*. The doctrine of *in loco parentis* treats school administrators as standing in the place of students' parents under circumstances where the children's actual parents cannot protect, guide, and discipline them. Geographically speaking, off-campus speech will normally fall within the zone of parental, rather than school-related, responsibility. *Second*, from the student speaker's perspective, regulations of off-campus speech, when coupled with regulations of on-campus speech, include all the speech a student utters during the full 24-hour day. That means courts must be more skeptical of a school's efforts to regulate off-campus speech, for doing so may mean the student cannot engage in that kind of speech at all. When it comes to political or religious speech that occurs outside school or a school program or activity, the school will have a heavy burden to justify intervention. *Third*, the school itself has an interest in protecting a student's unpopular expression, especially when the expression takes place off campus. America's public schools are the nurseries of democracy. . . .

Given the many different kinds of off-campus speech, [we] can [say] little more than this: Taken together, these three features of much off-campus speech mean that the leeway the First Amendment grants to schools [is] diminished. We leave for future cases to decide where, when, and how these features mean the speaker's off-campus location will make the critical difference. This case can, however, provide one example. [Putting] aside the vulgar language, the listener would hear criticism of the team, the team's coaches, and the school—[i.e., criticism] of the rules of a community of which B. L. forms a part. This criticism did not involve features that place it outside the First Amendment's ordinary protection. B. L.'s posts, while crude, did not amount to fighting words. And while B. L. used vulgarity, her speech was not obscene as this Court has understood that term. To the contrary, B. L. uttered the kind of pure speech to which, were she an adult, the First Amendment would provide strong protection.

Consider too when, where, and how B. L. spoke. Her posts appeared outside of school hours from a location outside the school. She did not identify the school in her posts or target any member of the school community with vulgar or abusive language. B. L. also transmitted her speech through a personal cellphone, to an audience consisting of her private circle of Snapchat friends. These features of her speech, while risking transmission to the school itself, nonetheless diminish the school's interest in punishing B. L.'s utterance.

But what about the school's interest [in] prohibiting students from using vulgar language to criticize a school team or its coaches—at least when that criticism might well be transmitted to other students, team members, coaches, and faculty? We can break that general interest into three parts.

First, we consider the school's interest in teaching good manners and consequently in punishing the use of vulgar language aimed at part of the school community. The strength of this anti-vulgarity interest is weakened considerably by the fact that B. L. spoke outside the school on her own time. B. L. spoke under circumstances where the school did not stand *in loco parentis*. And there is no reason to believe B. L.'s parents had delegated to school officials their own control of B. L.'s behavior at the [convenience store]. Moreover, the vulgarity in B. L.'s posts encompassed a message, an expression of B. L.'s irritation with, and criticism of, the school and cheerleading communities. . . . .

Second, the school argues that it was trying to prevent disruption [within] the bounds of a school-sponsored extracurricular activity. But we can find no evidence [of] the sort of "substantial disruption" of a school activity or a threatened harm to the rights of others that might justify the school's action. Rather, the record shows that discussion of the matter took, at most, 5 to 10 minutes of an Algebra class "for just a couple of days" and that some members of the cheerleading team were "upset" about the content of B. L.'s Snapchats. [As] we said in *Tinker*, "for the State in the person of school officials to justify prohibition of a particular expression of opinion, it must be able to show that its action was caused by something more than a mere desire to avoid the discomfort and unpleasantness that always accompany an unpopular viewpoint."

Third, the school presented some evidence that expresses [a] concern for team morale. There is [little,] however, that suggests any serious decline in team morale—to the point where it could create a substantial interference in, or disruption of, the school's efforts to maintain team cohesion. As we have said [in *Tinker*,] simple "undifferentiated fear or apprehension . . . is not enough to overcome the right to freedom of expression."

[Although] we do not agree with the reasoning of the Third Circuit majority, [we] agree that the school violated B. L.'s First Amendment rights. [Affirmed.]

JUSTICE ALITO, with whom JUSTICE GORSUCH joins, concurring.

I join the opinion of the Court but write separately to explain [the] framework within which I think cases like this should be analyzed. This is the first case in which we have considered [a] public school's attempt to regulate true off-premises student speech, and it is important that our opinion not be misunderstood.[2]

The Court holds—and I agree—that: the First Amendment permits public schools to regulate *some* student speech that does not occur on school premises during the regular school day. [I] also agree that it is not prudent for us to attempt

---

[2] This case does not involve speech by a student at a public college or university. For several reasons, including the age, independence, and living arrangements of such students, regulation of their speech may raise very different questions from those presented here. I do not understand the decision in this case to apply to such students.

at this time to "set forth a broad, highly general First Amendment rule" governing all off-premises speech. But [it] is helpful to consider the framework within which efforts to regulate off-premises speech should be analyzed.

[I] start with this threshold question: Why does the First Amendment ever allow the free-speech rights of public school students to be restricted to a greater extent than the rights of other juveniles who do not attend a public school? As the Court recognized in *Tinker*, when a public school regulates student speech, it acts as an arm of the State in which it is located. Suppose that B. L. had been enrolled in a private school and did exactly what she did in this case. [Pennsylvania] would have had no legal basis to punish her and almost certainly would not have even tried. So why should her status as a public school student give the Commonwealth any greater authority to punish her speech?

Our cases involving the regulation of student speech have not directly addressed this question. All those cases involved either in-school speech or speech that was tantamount to in-school speech. And in those cases, the Court appeared to take it for granted that "the special characteristics of the school environment" justified special rules. Why the Court took this for granted is not hard to imagine. As a practical matter, it is impossible to see how a school could function if administrators and teachers could not regulate on-premises student speech, including by imposing content-based restrictions in the classroom. In a math class, for example, the teacher can insist that students talk about math, not some other subject. In addition, when a teacher asks a question, the teacher must have the authority to insist that the student respond to that question and not some other question, and a teacher must also have the authority to speak without interruption and to demand that students refrain from interrupting one another. Practical necessity likewise dictates that teachers and school administrators have related authority with respect to other in-school activities like auditorium programs attended by a large audience. [But] when a public school regulates what students say or write when they are not on school grounds and are not participating in a school program, the school has the obligation to answer the question with which I began: Why should enrollment in a public school result in the diminution of a student's free-speech rights? The only plausible answer [is that] by enrolling a child in a public school, parents consent on behalf of the child to the relinquishment of some of the child's free-speech rights.

[When] it comes to children, courts [have] analyzed the issue of consent by adapting the common-law doctrine of *in loco parentis*. Under the common law, as Blackstone explained, "[a father could] delegate part of his parental authority . . . to the tutor or schoolmaster of his child; who is then *in loco parentis*, and has *such a portion of the power of the parent* committed to his charge, [namely,] that of restraint and correction, *as may be necessary to answer the purposes for which he is employed*." [Today,] of course, the educational picture is quite different. [If] *in loco parentis* is transplanted [to] the 21st century United States, what it amounts to is simply a doctrine of inferred parental consent to a public school's exercise of a degree of authority that is commensurate with the task that the parents ask the school to perform. [So] how much authority to regulate speech do parents implicitly delegate when they enroll a child at a public school? The answer must be that parents are treated as having relinquished the measure of authority that the schools must be able to exercise in order to carry out their state-mandated educational mission, as well as the authority to perform any other functions to which parents expressly or implicitly agree—for example, by giving permission for a child to participate in an extracurricular activity or to go on a school trip.

I have already explained what this delegated authority means with respect to student speech during standard classroom instruction. And [this] authority extends to periods when students are in school but are not in class, for example, when they are walking in a hall, eating lunch, congregating outside before the school day starts, or waiting for a bus after school. [A] public school's regulation of off-premises student speech is a different matter. While the decision to enroll a student in a public school may be regarded as conferring the authority to regulate *some* off-premises speech, [enrollment] cannot be treated as a complete transfer of parental authority over a student's speech. [It] would be far-fetched to suggest that enrollment implicitly confers the right to regulate what a child says or writes at all times of day and throughout the calendar year.

[The] degree to which enrollment in a public school can be regarded as a delegation of authority over off-campus speech depends on the nature of the speech and the circumstances under which it occurs. [One] category of off-premises student speech falls easily within the scope of the authority that parents implicitly or explicitly provide. This category includes speech that takes place during or as part of what amounts to a temporal or spatial extension of the regular school program, *e.g.,* online instruction at home, assigned essays or other homework, and transportation to and from school. Also included are statements made during other school activities in which students participate with their parents' consent, such as school trips, school sports and other extracurricular activities that may take place after regular school hours or off school premises, and after-school programs for students who would otherwise be without adult supervision during that time. Abusive speech that occurs while students are walking to and from school may also fall into this category on the theory that it is school attendance that puts students on that route and in the company of the fellow students who engage in the abuse. The imperatives that justify the regulation of student speech while in school [apply] more or less equally to these off-premises activities.

[At] the other end of the spectrum, there is a category of speech that is almost always beyond the regulatory authority of a public school. This is student speech that is not expressly and specifically directed at the school, school administrators, teachers, or fellow students and that addresses matters of public concern, including sensitive subjects like politics, religion, and social relations. Speech on such matters lies at the heart of the First Amendment's protection, and the connection between student speech in this category and the ability of a public school to carry out its instructional program is tenuous. If a school tried to regulate such speech, the most that it could claim is that offensive off-premises speech on important matters may cause controversy and recriminations among students and may thus disrupt instruction and good order on school premises. But it is a "bedrock principle" that speech may not be suppressed simply because it expresses ideas that are "offensive or disagreeable." . . .

[Between] these two extremes (*i.e.*, off-premises speech that is tantamount to on-campus speech and general statements made off premises on matters of public concern) lie the categories of off-premises student speech that appear to have given rise to the most litigation. A survey of lower court cases reveals several prominent categories. [One] group of cases involves perceived threats to school administrators, teachers, other staff members, or students. Laws that apply to everyone prohibit defined categories of threats. [Another] common category involves speech that criticizes or derides school administrators, teachers, or other staff members. Schools may assert that parents who send their children to a public school implicitly authorize the school to demand that the child exhibit the respect that is required for orderly and effective instruction, but parents surely do not relinquish their children's ability to complain in an appropriate manner about wrongdoing, dereliction, or even plain incompetence. Perhaps the most difficult category involves criticism or hurtful remarks about other students. Bullying and severe harassment are serious (and age-old) problems, but these concepts are not easy to define with the precision required for a regulation of speech.

The present case does not fall into any of these categories. Instead, it simply involves criticism (albeit in a crude manner) of the school and an extracurricular activity. Unflattering speech about a school or one of its programs is different from speech that criticizes or derides particular individuals, and [the] school's justifications for punishing B. L.'s speech were weak. [The] school did not claim that the messages caused any significant disruption of classes. [As] for the messages' effect on the morale of the cheerleading squad, the coach of a team sport may wish to take group cohesion and harmony into account in selecting members of the team, in assigning roles, and in allocating playing time, but it is self-evident that this authority has limits. [There] is, finally, the matter of B. L.'s language. There are parents who would not have been pleased with B. L.'s language and gesture, but whatever B. L.'s parents thought about what she did, it is not reasonable to infer that they gave the school the authority to regulate her choice of language when she was off school premises and not engaged in any school activity.

[The] overwhelming majority of school administrators, teachers, and coaches are men and women who are deeply dedicated to the best interests of their students, but it is predictable that there will be occasions when some will get carried away, as did the school officials in the case at hand. If today's decision teaches any lesson, it must be that the regulation of many types of off-premises student speech raises serious First Amendment concerns, and school officials should proceed cautiously before venturing into this territory.

JUSTICE THOMAS, dissenting.

B. L., a high school student, sent a profanity-laced message to hundreds of people, including classmates and team- mates. The message included a picture of B. L. raising her middle finger and captioned "F*** school" and "f*** cheer." This message was juxtaposed with another, which explained that B. L. was frustrated that she failed to make the varsity cheerleading squad. The cheerleading coach responded by disciplining B. L.

The Court overrides that decision—without even mentioning the 150 years of history supporting the coach. [When] students are on campus, the majority says, schools have authority *in loco parentis* [to] discipline speech and conduct. Off campus, the authority of schools is somewhat less. At that level of generality, I agree. But the majority omits important detail. What authority does a school have when it operates *in loco parentis*? How much less authority do schools have over off-campus speech and conduct? And how does a court decide if speech is on or off campus?

Disregarding these important issues, the majority simply posits three vague considerations and reaches an outcome. A more searching review reveals that schools historically could discipline students in circumstances like those presented here. Because the majority does not attempt to explain why we should not apply this historical rule and does not attempt to tether its approach to anything stable, I respectfully dissent.

[While] the majority entirely ignores the relevant history, I would begin the assessment of the scope of free-speech rights incorporated against the States by looking to "what 'ordinary citizens' at the time of [the Fourteenth Amendment's] ratification would have understood" the right to encompass. Cases and treatises from that era reveal that public schools retained substantial authority to discipline students: [A school could] regulate speech when it occurs off campus, so long as it has a proximate tendency to harm the school, its faculty or students, or its programs. [If] there is a good constitutional reason to depart from this historical rule, the majority and the parties fail to identify it.

[Our] modern doctrine is not to the contrary. "[T]he penalties imposed in this case were unrelated to any political viewpoint" or religious viewpoint. And although the majority sugar coats this speech as "criticism," it is well settled that schools can punish "vulgar" speech—at least when it occurs on campus. The discipline here—a 1-year suspension from the team—may strike some as disproportionate. But [there is] no textual or historical evidence to suggest that federal courts generally can police the proportionality of school disciplinary decisions in the name of the First Amendment.

The majority declines to consider [this] history, instead favoring a few pragmatic guideposts. [Consider] the Court's longtime failure to grapple with the historical doctrine of *in loco parentis*. [The] Fourteenth Amendment was ratified against the background legal principle that publicly funded schools [as] delegated substitutes of parents. This principle freed schools from the constraints the Fourteenth Amendment placed on other government actors. [Plausible] arguments can be raised in favor of departing from that historical doctrine. When the Fourteenth Amendment was ratified, just three jurisdictions had compulsory-education laws. One might argue that [*in*] *loco parentis* applies only when delegation is voluntary. The Court, however, did not make that (or any other) argument against this historical doctrine. [It] acknowledges that schools act *in loco parentis* when students speak on campus [but] fails to address the historical contours of that doctrine, whether the doctrine applies to off-campus speech, or why the Court has abandoned it. [Moreover,] the majority uncritically adopts the assumption that B. L.'s speech, in fact, was off campus. But the location of her speech is a much trickier question than the majority acknowledges. Because speech travels, schools sometimes may be able to treat speech as on campus even though it originates off campus. Nobody doubts, for example, that can discipline [a student] when he passes out vulgar flyers on campus—even if he creates those flyers off campus. The same may be true in many contexts when social media speech is generated off campus but received on campus. [Here,] it makes sense to treat B. L.'s speech as off-campus speech. There is little evidence that B. L.'s speech was received on campus. [But] the majority mentions none of this. It simply, and uncritically, assumes that B. L.'s speech was off campus. . . .

[The] Court transparently takes a common-law approach to today's decision. It states just one rule: Schools can regulate speech less often when that speech occurs off campus. It then identifies this case as an "example" and "leav[es] for future cases" the job of developing this new common-law doctrine. But the Court's foundation is untethered from anything stable, and courts (and schools) will almost certainly be at a loss as to what exactly the Court's opinion today means. [Because] it reaches the wrong result under the appropriate historical test, I respectfully dissent.

III. GOVERNMENT AS EMPLOYER

Ceballos, a supervising district attorney, wrote a disposition memorandum in which he recommended dismissal of a case on the ground that the affidavit in support of a search warrant contained false representations. As a result of the memorandum, which he characterized as protected speech, Ceballos maintained he was unconstitutionally transferred to a less desirable work location and denied a promotion in retaliation.

GARCETTI v. CEBALLOS, 547 U.S. 410 (2006), per KENNEDY, J., held that the memorandum was pursuant to his official duties as a supervising district attorney and, therefore, not protected by the First Amendment: "*Pickering v. Bd. of Educ.*, 391 U.S. 563 (1968)[18] and the cases decided in its wake identify two inquiries to guide interpretation of the constitutional protections accorded to public employee speech. The first requires determining whether the employee spoke as a citizen on a matter of public concern. If the answer is no, the employee has no First Amendment cause of action based on his or her employer's reaction to the speech.

---

[18]   *Pickering* held that the First Amendment protected a teacher who published a letter in a newspaper criticizing the Board of Education.

If the answer is yes, then the possibility of a First Amendment claim arises. The question becomes whether the relevant government entity had an adequate justification for treating the employee differently from any other member of the general public. This consideration reflects the importance of the relationship between the speaker's expressions and employment. A government entity has broader discretion to restrict speech when it acts in its role as employer, but the restrictions it imposes must be directed at speech that has some potential to affect the entity's operations. * * *

"When a citizen enters government service, the citizen by necessity must accept certain limitations on his or her freedom. Government employers, like private employers, need a significant degree of control over their employees 'words and actions; without it, there would be little chance for the efficient provision of public services. Public employees, moreover, often occupy trusted positions in society. When they speak out, they can express views that contravene governmental policies or impair the proper performance of governmental functions.

"At the same time, the Court has recognized that a citizen who works for the government is nonetheless a citizen. The First Amendment limits the ability of a public employer to leverage the employment relationship to restrict, incidentally or intentionally, the liberties employees enjoy in their capacities as private citizens. So long as employees are speaking as citizens about matters of public concern, they must face only those speech restrictions that are necessary for their employers to operate efficiently and effectively. * * *

"The controlling factor in Ceballos' case is that his expressions were made pursuant to his duties as a calendar deputy. That consideration—the fact that Ceballos spoke as a prosecutor fulfilling a responsibility to advise his supervisor about how best to proceed with a pending case—distinguishes Ceballos' case from those in which the First Amendment provides protection against discipline. We hold that when public employees make statements pursuant to their official duties, the employees are not speaking as citizens for First Amendment purposes, and the Constitution does not insulate their communications from employer discipline. * * *

"This result is consistent with our precedents' attention to the potential societal value of employee speech. Refusing to recognize First Amendment claims based on government employees' work product does not prevent them from participating in public debate. The employees retain the prospect of constitutional protection for their contributions to the civic discourse. This prospect of protection, however, does not invest them with a right to perform their jobs however they see fit. [Displacement] of managerial discretion by judicial supervision finds no support in our precedents. When an employee speaks as a citizen addressing a matter of public concern, the First Amendment requires a delicate balancing of the competing interests surrounding the speech and its consequences. When, however, the employee is simply performing his or her job duties, there is no warrant for a similar degree of scrutiny. To hold otherwise would be to demand permanent judicial intervention in the conduct of governmental operations to a degree inconsistent with sound principles of federalism and the separation of powers.

[Justice] Souter suggests today's decision may have important ramifications for academic freedom, at least as a constitutional value. There is some argument that expression related to academic scholarship or classroom instruction implicates additional constitutional interests that are not fully accounted for by this Court's customary employee-speech jurisprudence. We need not, and for that reason do not, decide whether the analysis we conduct today would apply in the same manner to a case involving speech related to scholarship or teaching."

SOUTER, J., joined by Stevens and Ginsburg, JJ., dissented: "In *Givhan v. Western Line School Dist.*, 439 U.S. 410 (1979), we followed *Pickering* when a teacher was fired for complaining to a superior about the racial composition of the school's administrative, cafeteria, and library [staffs]. The difference between a case like *Givhan* and this one is that the subject of Cembalos' speech fell within the scope of his job responsibilities, whereas choosing personnel was not what the teacher was hired to do. The effect of the majority's constitutional line between these two cases, then, is that a *Givhan* schoolteacher is protected when complaining to the principal about hiring policy, but a school personnel officer would not be if he protested that the principal disapproved of hiring minority job applicants. This is an odd place to draw a distinction, and while necessary judicial line-drawing sometimes looks arbitrary, any distinction obliges a court to justify its choice. Here, there is no adequate justification for the majority's line categorically denying *Pickering* protection to any speech uttered 'pursuant [to] official duties.'

"Nothing [accountable] on the individual and public side of the *Pickering* balance changes when an employee speaks 'pursuant' to public duties.[19] On the side of the government employer, however, something is different, and to this extent, I agree with the majority of the Court. The majority is rightly concerned that the employee who speaks out on matters subject to comment in doing his own work has the greater leverage to create office uproars and fracture the government's authority to set policy to be carried out coherently through the ranks. [Up] to a point, then, the majority makes good points: government needs civility in the workplace, consistency in policy, and honesty and competence in public service. * * *

"[T]he basic *Pickering* balancing scheme is perfectly feasible here. First, the extent of the government's legitimate authority over subjects of speech required by a public job can be recognized in advance by setting in effect a minimum heft for comments with any claim to outweigh it. Thus, the risks to the government are great enough for us to hold from the outset that an employee commenting on

---

[19] Later in his opinion, Souter, J., observed: "This ostensible domain beyond the pale of the First Amendment is spacious enough to include even the teaching of a public university professor, and I have to hope that today's majority does not mean to imperil First Amendment protection of academic freedom in public colleges and universities, whose teachers necessarily speak and write 'pursuant to official duties.' "

subjects in the course of duties should not prevail on balance u
a matter of unusual importance and satisfies high standards (
the way he does it. The examples I have already given indicate ;
matter, and it is fair to say that only comment on official disho1
unconstitutional action, other serious wrongdoing, or threats to
can weigh out in an employee's favor. If promulgation of this sta
to discourage meritless actions [before] they get filed, the standar
them out at the summary-judgment stage."

BREYER, J., dissented: "The majority [holds] that 'when public employees
make statements pursuant to their official duties, the employees are not speaking
as citizens for First Amendment purposes, and the Constitution does not insulate
their communications from employer discipline.' In a word, the majority says,
'never.' That word, in my view, is too absolute.

"[The] First Amendment sometimes does authorize judicial actions based
upon a government employee's speech that both (1) involves a matter of public
concern and also (2) takes place in the course of ordinary job-related duties. But it
does so only in the presence of augmented need for constitutional protection and
diminished risk of undue judicial interference with governmental management of
the public's affairs."

8. THE ELECTRONIC MEDIA

I. ACCESS TO THE MASS MEDIA

MIAMI HERALD PUB. CO. v. TORNILLO, 418 U.S. 241 (1974), per BURGER,
C.J., unanimously struck down a Florida "right of reply" statute, which required
any newspaper that "assails" the personal character or official record of a candidate
in any election to print, on demand, free of cost, any reply the candidate may make
to the charges, in as conspicuous a place and the same kind of type, provided the
reply takes up no more space than the charges. The opinion carefully explained the
aim of the statute to "ensure that a wide variety of views reach the public" even
though "chains of newspapers, national newspapers, national wire and news
services, and one-newspaper towns, are the dominant features of a press that has
become noncompetitive and enormously powerful and influential in its capacity to
manipulate popular opinion and change the course of events," placing "in a few
hands the power to inform the American people and shape public opinion."
Nonetheless, the Court concluded that to require the printing of a reply violated
the First Amendment: "Compelling editors or publishers to publish that which
' "reason" tells them should not be published' is what is at issue in this case. The
Florida statute operates as a command in the same sense as a statute or regulation
forbidding appellant from publishing specified matter. [The] Florida statute exacts
a penalty on the basis of the content of a newspaper. The first phase of the penalty
resulting from the compelled printing of a reply is exacted in terms of the cost in
printing and composing time and materials and in taking up space that could be
devoted to other material the newspaper may have preferred to print. It is correct,

as appellee contends, that a newspaper is not subject to the finite technological limitations of time that confront a broadcaster but it is not correct to say that, as an economic reality, a newspaper can proceed to infinite expansion of its column space to accommodate the replies that a government agency determines or a statute commands the readers should have available.

"Faced with the penalties that would accrue to any newspaper that published news or commentary arguably within the reach of the right of access statute, editors might well conclude that the safe course is to avoid controversy and that, under the operation of the Florida statute, political and electoral coverage would be blunted or reduced. Government enforced right of access inescapably 'dampens the vigor and limits the variety of public debate,' *New York Times*.

"Even if a newspaper would face no additional costs to comply with a compulsory access law and would not be forced to forego publication of news or opinion by the inclusion of a reply, the Florida statute fails to clear the barriers of the First Amendment because of its intrusion into the function of editors. A newspaper is more than a passive receptacle or conduit for news, comment, and advertising. The choice of material to go into a newspaper, and the decisions made as to limitations on the size of the paper, and content, and treatment of public issues and public officials—whether fair or unfair—constitutes the exercise of editorial control and judgment. It has yet to be demonstrated how governmental regulation of this crucial process can be exercised consistent with First Amendment guarantees of a free press as they have evolved to this time."

––––––––

The Federal Communications Commission for many years imposed on radio and television broadcasters the "fairness doctrine"—requiring that stations (1) devote a reasonable percentage of broadcast time to discussion of public issues and (2) assure fair coverage for each side. At issue in RED LION BROADCASTING CO. v. FCC, 395 U.S. 367 (1969), were the application of the fairness doctrine to a particular broadcast and two related specific access regulations: (1) the "political editorial" rule, requiring that when a broadcaster, in an editorial, "endorses or opposes" a political candidate, it must notify the candidate opposed, or the rivals of the candidate supported, and afford them a "reasonable opportunity" to respond; (2) the "personal attack" rule, requiring that "when, during the presentation of views on a controversial issue of public importance, an attack is made on the honesty, character [or] integrity [of] an identified person or group," the person or group attacked must be given notice, a transcript of the attack, and an opportunity to respond. "[I]n view of [the] scarcity of broadcast frequencies, the Government's role in allocating those frequencies, and the legitimate claims of those unable without government assistance to gain access to those frequencies for expression of their views," a 7–0 majority, per WHITE, J., upheld both access regulations:

"[The broadcasters] contention is that the First Amendment protects their desire to use their allotted frequencies continuously to broadcast whatever they choose, and to exclude whomever they choose from ever using that frequency. No man may be prevented from saying or publishing what he thinks, or from refusing in his speech or other utterances to give equal weight to the views of his opponents. This right, they say, applies equally to broadcasters.

"Although broadcasting is clearly a medium affected by a First Amendment interest, differences in the characteristics of new media justify differences in the First Amendment standards applied to [them]. Just as the Government may limit the use of sound-amplifying equipment potentially so noisy that it drowns out civilized private speech, so may the Government limit the use of broadcast equipment. The right of free speech of a broadcaster, the user of a sound truck, or any other individual does not embrace a right to snuff out the free speech of [others].

"Where there are substantially more individuals who want to broadcast than there are frequencies to allocate, it is idle to posit an unabridgeable First Amendment right to broadcast comparable to the right of every individual to speak, write, or publish. [It] would be strange if the First Amendment, aimed at protecting and furthering communications, prevented the Government from making radio communication possible by requiring licenses to broadcast and by limiting the number of licenses so as not to overcrowd the spectrum. * * *

"By the same token, as far as the First Amendment is concerned those who are licensed stand no better than those to whom licenses are refused. A license permits broadcasting, but the licensee has no constitutional right [to] monopolize a radio frequency to the exclusion of his fellow citizens. There is nothing in the First Amendment which prevents the Government from requiring a licensee to share his frequency with others and to conduct himself as a proxy or fiduciary with obligations to present those views and voices which are representative of his community and which would otherwise, by necessity, be barred from the airwaves.

"[The] people as a whole retain their interest in free speech by radio and their collective right to have the medium function consistently with the ends and purposes of the First Amendment. It is the right of the viewers and listeners, not the right of the broadcasters, which is paramount. [It] is the purpose of the First Amendment to preserve an uninhibited marketplace of ideas in which truth will ultimately prevail, rather than to countenance monopolization of that market, whether it be by the Government itself or a private licensee. [It] is the right of the public to receive suitable access to social, political, esthetic, moral, and other ideas and experiences which is crucial [here.]

"In terms of constitutional principle, and as enforced sharing of a scarce resource, the personal attack and political editorial rules are indistinguishable from the equal-time provision of § 315 [of the Communications Act], a specific enactment of Congress requiring [that stations allot equal time to qualified candidates for public office] and to which the fairness doctrine and these constituent regulations are important complements. [Nor] can we say that it is inconsistent with the First Amendment goal of producing an informed public capable of conducting its own affairs to require a broadcaster to permit answers to personal attacks occurring in the course of discussing controversial issues, or to require that the political opponents of those endorsed by the station be given a chance to communicate with the public. Otherwise, station owners and a few networks would have unfettered power to make time available only to the highest bidders, to communicate only their own views on public issues, people and candidates, and to permit on the air only those with whom they agreed. There is no sanctuary in the First Amendment for unlimited private censorship operating in a medium not open to all.

"[It is contended] that if political editorials or personal attacks will trigger an obligation in broadcasters to afford the opportunity for expression to speakers who need not pay for time and whose views are unpalatable to the licensees, then broadcasters will be irresistibly forced to self-censorship and their coverage of controversial public issues will be eliminated or at least rendered wholly ineffective. Such a result would indeed be a serious matter, [but] that possibility is at best speculative. [If these doctrines turn out to have this effect], there will be time enough to reconsider the constitutional implications. The fairness doctrine in the past has had no such overall effect. That this will occur now seems unlikely, however, since if present licensees should suddenly prove timorous, the Commission is not powerless to insist that they give adequate and fair attention to public issues. It does not violate the First Amendment to treat licensees given the privilege of using scarce radio frequencies as proxies for the entire community, obligated to give suitable time and attention to matters of great public concern. To condition the granting or renewal of licenses on a willingness to present representative community views on controversial issues is consistent with the ends and purposes of those constitutional provisions forbidding the abridgment of freedom of speech and freedom of the press."

***

The fairness doctrine repealed. The FCC concluded a 15 month administrative proceeding with an official denunciation of the fairness doctrine, pointing in particular to the marked increase in the information services marketplace since *Red Lion* and the effects of the doctrine in application. FCC, [*General*] *Fairness Doctrine Obligations of Broadcast Licensees*, 102 F.C.C.2d 143 (1985). *Syracuse Peace Council*, 2 FCC Rcd 5043 (1987) held that "under the constitutional standard established by *Red Lion* and its progeny, the fairness doctrine contravenes the First Amendment and its enforcement is no longer in the public interest."

Candidate debates on public television. A third party candidate was excluded from a debate sponsored by a public television station on the ground that he had little popular support. He claimed a right of access.

ARKANSAS EDUCATIONAL TELEVISION COMM'N v. FORBES, 523 U.S. 666 (1998), concluded that a candidate debate sponsored by a state-owned public television broadcaster was a nonpublic forum subject to constitutional restraints (because the views expressed were those of the candidates, not the broadcaster and because of the importance of such debates to the political process), but that the broadcaster's decision to exclude a candidate was reasonable: "We conclude that, unlike most other public television programs, the candidate debate was subject to constitutional constraints applicable to nonpublic fora under our forum precedents. Even so, the broadcaster's decision to exclude the candidate was a reasonable, viewpoint-neutral exercise of journalistic discretion."

II. THE ELECTRONIC MEDIA AND CONTENT REGULATION

FCC v. PACIFICA FOUNDATION

438 U.S. 726, 98 S.Ct. 3026, 57 L.Ed.2d 1073 (1978).

JUSTICE STEVENS delivered the opinion of the Court (Parts I, II, III, and IV-C) and an opinion in which CHIEF JUSTICE BURGER and JUSTICE REHNQUIST joined (Parts IV-A and IV-B).

[In an early afternoon weekday broadcast which was devoted that day to contemporary attitudes toward the use of language, respondent's New York radio station aired a 12-minute selection called "Filthy Words," from a comedy album by a satiric humorist, George Carlin. The monologue, which had evoked frequent laughter from a live theater audience, began by referring to Carlin's thought about the seven words you can't say on the public airwaves, "the ones you definitely wouldn't say ever." He then listed the words ("shit," "piss," "fuck," "motherfucker," "cocksucker," "cunt," and "tits"), "the ones that will curve your spine, grow hair on your hands and (laughter) maybe, even bring us, God help us, peace without honor (laughter) um, and a bourbon (laughter)," and repeated them over and over in a variety of colloquialisms. Immediately prior to the monologue, listeners were advised that it included sensitive language which some might regard as offensive. Those who might be offended were advised to change the station and return in fifteen minutes.

[The FCC received a complaint from a man stating that while driving in his car with his young son he had heard the broadcast of the Carlin monologue. The FCC issued an order to be "associated with the station's license file, and in the event that subsequent complaints are received, the Commission will then decide whether it should utilize any of the available sanctions it has been granted by Congress."]

The Commission characterized the language used in the Carlin monologue as "patently offensive," though not necessarily obscene, and expressed the opinion that it should be regulated by principles analogous to those found in the law of nuisance where the "law generally speaks to *channeling* behavior more than actually prohibiting [it]."

Applying these considerations to the language used in the monologue as broadcast by respondent, the Commission concluded that certain words depicted sexual and excretory activities in a patently offensive manner, noted that they "were broadcast at a time when children were undoubtedly in the audience (i.e., in the early afternoon)," and that the prerecorded language, with these offensive words "repeated over and over," was "deliberately broadcast." In summary, the Commission stated: "We therefore hold that the language as broadcast was indecent [under 18 U.S.C. 1464]."

IV. Pacifica [argues] that the Commission's construction of the statutory language broadly encompasses so much constitutionally protected speech that reversal is required even if Pacifica's broadcast of the "Filthy Words" monologue is not itself protected by the First Amendment. * * *

A.   The first argument fails because our review is limited to the question whether the Commission has the authority to proscribe this particular broadcast. As the Commission itself emphasized, its order was "issued in a specific factual context." That approach is appropriate for courts as well as the Commission when regulation of indecency is at stake, for indecency is largely a function of context—it cannot be adequately judged in the abstract. * * *

It is true that the Commission's order may lead some broadcasters to censor themselves. At most, however, the Commission's definition of indecency will deter only the broadcasting of patently offensive references to excretory and sexual organs and activities. * * *

B.   [The] words of the Carlin monologue are unquestionably "speech" within the meaning of the First Amendment. [The] question in this case is whether a broadcast of patently offensive words dealing with sex and excretion may be regulated because of its content. Obscene materials have been denied the protection of the First Amendment because their content is so offensive to contemporary moral standards. But the fact that society may find speech offensive is not a sufficient reason for suppressing it. Indeed, if it is the speaker's opinion that gives offense, that consequence is a reason for according it constitutional protection. For it is a central tenet of the First Amendment that the government must remain neutral in the marketplace of ideas. If there were any reason to believe that the Commission's characterization of the Carlin monologue as offensive could be traced to its political content—or even to the fact that it satirized contemporary attitudes about four letter words—First Amendment protection might be required. But that is simply not this case. These words offend for the same reasons that obscenity offends. Their place in the hierarchy of First Amendment values was aptly sketched by Justice Murphy when he said, "such utterances are no essential part of any exposition of ideas, and are of such slight social value as a step to truth that any benefit that may be derived from them is clearly outweighed by the social interest in order and morality." *Chaplinsky.*

Although these words ordinarily lack literary, political, or scientific value, they are not entirely outside the protection of the First Amendment. Some uses of even the most offensive words are unquestionably protected. Indeed, we may assume, arguendo, that this monologue would be protected in other contexts. [It] is a characteristic of speech such as this that both its capacity to offend and its "social value," to use Justice Murphy's term, vary with the circumstances. Words that are commonplace in one setting are shocking in another. To paraphrase Justice Harlan, one occasion's lyric is another's vulgarity. Cf. *Cohen v. California.*

In this case it is undisputed that the content of Pacifica's broadcast was "vulgar," "offensive," and "shocking." Because content of that character is not entitled to absolute constitutional protection under all circumstances, we must consider its context in order to determine whether the Commission's action was constitutionally permissible.

C.   We have long recognized that each medium of expression presents special First Amendment problems. And of all forms of communication, it is broadcasting that has received the most limited First Amendment [protection.]

The reasons for these distinctions are complex, but two have relevance to the present case. First, the broadcast media have established a uniquely pervasive presence in the lives of all Americans. Patently offensive, indecent material presented over the airwaves confronts the citizen, not only in public, but also in the privacy of the home, where the individual's right to be let alone plainly outweighs the First Amendment rights of an intruder. Because the broadcast audience is constantly tuning in and out, prior warnings cannot completely protect the listener or viewer from unexpected program content. To say that one may avoid further offense by turning off the radio when he hears indecent language is like saying that the remedy for an assault is to run away after the first blow.[27] * * *

Second, broadcasting is uniquely accessible to children, even those too young to read. Although Cohen's written message might have been incomprehensible to a first grader, Pacifica's broadcast could have enlarged a child's vocabulary in an instant. Other forms of offensive expression may be withheld from the young without restricting the expression at its source. Bookstores and motion picture theaters, for example, may be prohibited from making indecent material available to children. * * *

It is appropriate, in conclusion, to emphasize the narrowness of our holding. This case does not involve a two-way radio conversation between a cab driver and a dispatcher, or a telecast of an Elizabethan comedy. We have not decided that an occasional expletive in either setting would justify any sanction or, indeed, that this broadcast would justify a criminal prosecution. The Commission's decision rested entirely on a nuisance rationale under which context is all-important.

[R]eversed.

JUSTICE POWELL, with whom JUSTICE BLACKMUN joins, concurring.

[T]he language employed is, to most people, vulgar and offensive. It was chosen specifically for this quality, and it was repeated over and over as a sort of

---

[27]   **[Ct's Note]** Outside the home, the balance between the offensive speaker and the unwilling audience may sometimes tip in favor of the speaker, requiring the offended listener to turn away.

verbal shock treatment. [In] essence, the Commission sought to "channel" the monologue to hours when the fewest unsupervised children would be exposed to it. In my view, this consideration provides strong support for the Commission's holding.

[M]y views are generally in accord with what is said in Part IV(C) of Justice Stevens's opinion. I therefore join that portion of his opinion. I do not join Part IV(B), however, because I do not subscribe to the theory that the Justices of this Court are free generally to decide on the basis of its content which speech protected by the First Amendment is most "valuable" and hence deserving of the most protection, and which is less "valuable" and hence deserving of less protection. In my view, the result in this case does not turn on whether Carlin's monologue, viewed as a whole, or the words that comprise it, have more or less "value" than a candidate's campaign speech. This is a judgment for each person to make, not one for the judges to impose upon him. * * *

JUSTICE BRENNAN, with whom JUSTICE MARSHALL joins, dissenting.

[T]he Court refuses to embrace the notion, completely antithetical to basic First Amendment values, that the degree of protection the First Amendment affords protected speech varies with the social value ascribed to that speech by five Members of this Court. See opinion of Justice Powell. Moreover, [all] Members of the Court agree that [the monologue] does not fall within one of the categories of speech, such as "fighting words," or obscenity, that is totally without First Amendment protection. [Yet] a majority of the Court nevertheless finds that, on the facts of this case, the FCC is not constitutionally barred from imposing sanctions on Pacifica for its airing of the Carlin monologue. * * *

[A]n individual's actions in switching on and listening to communications transmitted over the public airways and directed to the public at-large do not implicate fundamental privacy interests, even when engaged in within the home. Instead, because the radio is undeniably a public medium, these actions are more properly viewed as a decision to take part, if only as a listener, in an ongoing public discourse. Although an individual's decision to allow public radio communications into his home undoubtedly does not abrogate all of his privacy interests, the residual privacy interests he retains vis-à-vis the communication he voluntarily admits into his home are surely no greater than those of the people present in the corridor of the Los Angeles courthouse in [*Cohen*].* * *

Because the Carlin monologue is obviously not an erotic appeal to the prurient interests of children, the Court, for the first time, allows the government to prevent minors from gaining access to materials that are not obscene, and are therefore protected, as to them. [As] surprising as it may be to individual Members of this Court, some parents may actually find Mr. Carlin's unabashed attitude towards the seven "dirty words" healthy, and deem it desirable to expose their children to the manner in which Mr. Carlin defuses the taboo surrounding the words. Such parents may constitute a minority of the American public, but the absence of great numbers willing to exercise the right to raise their children in this fashion does not alter the right's [existence]. * * *

[My] Brother Stevens [finds] solace in his conviction that "[t]here are few, if any, thoughts that cannot be expressed by the use of less offensive language." The idea that the content of a message and its potential impact on any who might receive it can be divorced from the words that are the vehicle for its expression is transparently fallacious. A given word may have a unique capacity to capsule an idea, evoke an emotion, or conjure up an image. Indeed, for those of us who place an appropriately high value on our cherished First Amendment rights, the word "censor" is such a word. Justice Harlan, speaking for the Court, recognized the truism that a speaker's choice of words cannot surgically be separated from the ideas he desires to express when he warned that "we cannot indulge the facile assumption that one can forbid particular words without also running a substantial risk of suppressing ideas in the process." * * *

Other media. (a) *Telephonic "indecency" compared.* SABLE COMMUNICATIONS v. FCC, 492 U.S. 115 (1989), per WHITE, J., unanimously invalidated a congressional ban on "indecent" interstate commercial telephone messages, i.e., "dial-a-porn." The Court thought *Pacifica* was "readily distinguishable from this case, most obviously because it did not involve a total ban on broadcasting indecent material. [Second,] there is no 'captive audience' problem here; callers will generally not be unwilling listeners. [Third,] the congressional record contains no legislative findings that would justify us in concluding that there is no constitutionally acceptable less restrictive means, short of a total ban, to achieve the Government's interest in protecting minors."

(b) *Internet "indecency" compared.* Two provisions of the Communications Decency Act ("CDA") sought to protect minors from indecent or patently offensive material on the Internet. 47 U.S.C. § 223(a) prohibited the knowing transmission of indecent messages to any recipient under 18 years of age. 47 U.S.C. § 223(d) prohibited the knowing sending or displaying of patently offensive messages in a manner that is available to a person under 18 years of age. Patently offensive was defined as any "image or other communication that in context, depicts or describes, in terms patently offensive as measured by contemporary community standards, sexual or excretory activities or organs."

RENO v. AMERICAN CIVIL LIBERTIES UNION, 521 U.S. 844 (1997), per STEVENS, J., invalidated both provisions: "The breadth of the CDA's coverage is wholly unprecedented. Unlike the regulations upheld in *Ginsberg* and *Pacifica,* the scope of the CDA is not limited to commercial speech or commercial entities. [The] general, undefined terms 'indecent' and 'patently offensive' cover large amounts of nonpornographic material with serious educational or other value. Moreover, the 'community standards' criterion as applied to the Internet means that any communication available to a nation-wide audience will be judged by the standards of the community most likely to be offended by the message. [This could] also extend to discussions about prison rape or safe sexual practices, artistic images that include nude subjects, and arguably the card catalogue of the Carnegie Library. Compare *Ashcroft v. American Civil Liberties Union* (II), 542 U.S. 656 (2004), per Kennedy, J., invalidating the Child Online Protection Act prohibiting placing material obscene for children on the web unless proof of age for access was required. The Court concluded that Congress could encourage the use of software to block pornography as a less restrictive alternative. Scalia, J., dissenting, argued that strict scrutiny was inappropriate and Breyer, J., argued that encouraging filtering software had been tried and found wanting.

9. THE RIGHT NOT TO SPEAK, THE RIGHT TO ASSOCIATE, AND THE RIGHT NOT TO ASSOCIATE

NAACP v. Alabama ex rel. Patterson, 357 U.S. 449 (1958), per Harlan, J., held that the Constitution barred Alabama from compelling production of NAACP membership lists. The opinion used the phrase freedom of association repeatedly, "elevat[ing] freedom of association to an independent right, possessing an equal status with the other rights specifically enumerated in the First Amendment." Thomas Emerson, *Freedom of Association and Freedom of Expression*, 74 Yale L.J. 1 (1964).

I. THE RIGHT NOT TO BE ASSOCIATED WITH PARTICULAR IDEAS

WEST VIRGINIA STATE BD. OF EDUC. v. BARNETTE, 319 U.S. 624 (1943), per JACKSON, J., upheld the right of public school students to refuse to salute the flag. "To sustain the compulsory flag salute we are required to say that a Bill of Rights which guards the individual's right to speak his own mind, left it open to public authorities to compel him to utter what is not in his mind. * * * Struggles to coerce uniformity of sentiment in support of some end thought essential to their time and country have been waged by many good as well as by evil men. [Ultimate] futility of such attempts to compel coherence is the lesson of every such effort from the Roman drive to stamp out Christianity as a disturber of its pagan unity, the Inquisition, as a means to religious and dynastic unity, the Siberian exiles as a means to Russian unity, down to the fast failing efforts of our present totalitarian enemies. Those who begin coercive elimination of dissent soon find themselves exterminating dissenters. Compulsory unification of opinion achieves only the unanimity of the graveyard. * * *

"If there is any fixed star in our constitutional constellation, it is that no official, high or petty, can prescribe what shall be orthodox in politics, nationalism, religion, or other matters of opinion or force citizens to confess by word or act their faith therein. If there are any circumstances which permit an exception, they do not now occur to us. We think the action of the local authorities in compelling the flag salute and pledge transcends constitutional limitations on their power and invades the sphere of intellect and spirit which it is the purpose of the First Amendment to our Constitution to reserve from all official control."

———

New Hampshire required that noncommercial vehicles bear license plates embossed with the state motto, "Live Free or Die." "Refus[ing] to be coerced by the State into advertising a slogan which I find morally, ethically, religiously and politically abhorrent," appellee, a Jehovah's Witness, covered up the motto on his license plate, a misdemeanor under state law. After being convicted several times of violating the misdemeanor statute, appellee sought federal injunctive and declaratory relief.

WOOLEY v. MAYNARD, 430 U.S. 705 (1977), per BURGER, C.J., held that requiring appellee to display the motto on his license plates violated his First Amendment right to "refrain from speaking": "[T]he freedom of thought protected by the First Amendment [includes] both the right to speak freely and the right to refrain from speaking at all. See *Barnette*. The right to speak and the right to refrain from speaking are complementary components of the broader concept of 'individual freedom of mind.' This is illustrated [by] *Miami Herald* [infra], where we held unconstitutional a Florida statute placing an affirmative duty upon newspapers to publish the replies of political candidates whom they had criticized.

" * * * Compelling the affirmative act of a flag salute [the situation in *Barnette*] involved a more serious infringement upon personal liberties than the passive act of carrying the state motto on a license plate, but the difference is essentially one of degree. Here, as in *Barnette,* we are faced with a state measure which forces an individual as part of his daily life—indeed constantly while his automobile is in public view—to be an instrument for fostering public adherence to an ideological point of view he finds unacceptable. In doing so, the State 'invades the sphere of intellect and spirit which it is the purpose of the First Amendment [to] reserve from all official control.' *Barnette*.

"New Hampshire's statute in effect requires that appellees use their private property as a 'mobile billboard' for the State's ideological message—or suffer a penalty, as Maynard already has. [The] fact that most individuals agree with the thrust of [the] motto is not the test; most Americans also find the flag salute acceptable. The First Amendment protects the right of individuals to hold a point of view different from the majority and to refuse to foster, in the way New Hampshire commands, an idea they find morally objectionable." * * *

REHNQUIST, J., joined by Blackmun, J., dissented, not only agreeing with what he called "the Court's implicit recognition that there is no protected 'symbolic speech' in this case," but maintaining that "that conclusion goes far to undermine the Court's ultimate holding that there is an element of protected expression here. The State has not forced appellees to 'say' anything; and it has not forced them to communicate ideas with nonverbal actions reasonably likened to 'speech,' such as wearing a lapel button promoting a political candidate or waving a flag as a symbolic gesture. The State has simply required that *all* noncommercial automobiles bear license tags with the state motto. [Appellees] have not been forced to affirm or reject that motto; they are simply required by the State [to] carry a state auto license tag for identification and registration purposes. [The] issue, unconfronted by the Court, is whether appellees, in displaying, as they are required to do, state license tags, the format of which is known to all as having been prescribed by the State, would be considered to be advocating political or ideological views. * * *

———

Use of private property as a forum for the speech of others. Appellees sought to enjoin a shopping center from denying them access to the center's central courtyard in order to solicit signatures from passersby for petitions opposing a U.N. resolution. The California Supreme Court held they were entitled to conduct their activity at the center, construing the state constitution to protect "speech and petitioning, reasonably exercised, in shopping centers, even [when] privately owned." The shopping center appealed, arguing that its First Amendment rights had been violated.

PRUNEYARD SHOPPING CENTER v. ROBINS, 447 U.S. 74 (1980), per REHNQUIST, J., disagreed with the shopping center: "[In *Wooley,*] the government itself prescribed the message, required it to be displayed openly on appellee's personal property that was used 'as part of his daily life,' and refused to permit him [to] cover up the motto even though the Court found that the display of the motto served no important state interest. Here, by contrast, [the center] is not limited to the personal use of appellants, [but is] a business establishment that is open to the public to come and go as they please. The views expressed by members of the public in passing out pamphlets or seeking signatures for a petition thus will not likely be identified with those of the owner. Second, no specific message is dictated by the State to be displayed on appellants' property. There consequently is no danger of government discrimination for or against a particular message. Finally, [it appears] appellants can expressly disavow any connection with the message by simply posting signs in the area where the speakers or handbillers stand." * * *

POWELL, J., joined by White, J., concurring in the judgment, maintained that "state action that transforms privately owned property into a forum for the expression of the public's views could raise serious First Amendment questions": "I do not believe that the result in *Wooley* would have changed had [the state] directed its citizens to place the slogan 'Live Free or Die' in their shop windows rather than on their automobiles. [*Wooley*] protects a person who refuses to allow use of his property as a market place for the ideas of others. [One] who has merely invited the public onto his property for commercial purposes cannot fairly be said to have relinquished his right 'to decline to be an instrument for fostering public adherence to an ideological point of view he finds unacceptable.' *Wooley.*

"[E]ven when [as here] no particular message is mandated by the State, First Amendment interests are affected by state action that forces a property owner to admit third-party speakers. [A] right of access [may be] no less intrusive than speech compelled by the State itself. [A] law requiring that a newspaper permit others to use its columns imposes an unacceptable burden upon the newspaper's First Amendment right to select material for publication. *Miami Herald.*

"[On this record] I cannot say that customers of this vast center [occupying several city blocks and containing more than 65 shops] would be likely to assume that appellees' limited speech activity expressed the views of [the center]. [Moreover, appellants] have not alleged that they object to [appellees' views, nor asserted] that some groups who reasonably might be expected to speak at [the center] will express views that are so objectionable as to require a response even when listeners will not mistake their source. [Thus,] I join the judgment of the Court, [but] I do not interpret our decision today as a blanket approval for state efforts to transform privately owned commercial property into public forums."

––––––––

Paraders' rights. Boston authorized the South Boston Allied War Veterans Council to conduct the St. Patrick's Day-Evacuation parade (commemorating the evacuation of British troops from the city in 1776). The Veterans Council refused to let the Irish-American Gay, Lesbian and Bisexual Group of Boston march in the parade, but the Massachusetts courts ruled that the Council's refusal violated a public accommodations law in that the parade was an "open recreational event."

HURLEY v. IRISH-AMERICAN GAY, LESBIAN AND BISEXUAL GROUP OF BOSTON, 515 U.S. 557 (1995), per SOUTER, J., held that "[t]his use of the State's power violates the fundamental rule of protection under the First Amendment, that a speaker has the autonomy to choose the content of his own message. * * *

"[The Council's] claim to the benefit of this principle of autonomy to control one's own speech is as sound as the South Boston parade is expressive. Rather like a composer, the Council selects the expressive units of the parade from potential participants, and though the score may not produce a particularized message, each contingent's expression in the Council's eyes comports with what merits celebration on that day. Even if this view gives the Council credit for a more considered judgment than it actively made, the Council clearly decided to exclude a message it did not like from the communication it chose to make, and that is enough to invoke its right as a private speaker to shape its expression by speaking on one subject while remaining silent on another. * * *

"Unlike the programming offered on various channels by a cable network, the parade does not consist of individual, unrelated segments that happen to be transmitted together for individual selection by members of the audience. Although each parade unit generally identifies itself, each is understood to contribute something to a common theme, and accordingly there is no customary practice whereby private sponsors disavow any 'identity of viewpoint' between themselves and the selected participants. Practice follows practicability here, for such disclaimers would be quite curious in a moving parade. [*PruneYard* found] that the proprietors were running 'a business establishment that is open to the public to come and go as they please,' that the solicitations would 'not likely be identified with those of the owner,' and that the proprietors could 'expressly disavow any connection with the message by simply posting signs in the area where the speakers or handbillers stand.' "

———

Economic pressure to engage in political activity. NAACP v. CLAIBORNE HARDWARE CO., 458 U.S. 886 (1982): The NAACP organized a consumer boycott whose principal objective was, according to the lower court, "to force the white merchants [to] bring pressure upon [the government] to grant defendants' demands or, in the alternative, to suffer economic ruin." Mississippi characterized the boycott as a tortious and malicious interference with the plaintiffs' businesses. The Court, per STEVENS, J., held for the NAACP: Although labor boycotts for economic ends have long been subject to prohibition, "speech to protest racial discrimination" was "essential political speech lying at the core of the First Amendment" and was distinguishable. Is the boycott protected association? Are there association rights on the other side? Does the state have a legitimate interest in protecting merchants from being forced to support political change they oppose? Cf. *NLRB v. Retail Store Employees Union*, 447 U.S. 607 (1980) (ban on labor picketing encouraging consumer boycott of neutral employer upheld).

———

Compelled monetary subsidies. A series of cases have invalidated government forced monetary contributions for support of speech opposed by the contributors. *Abood v. Detroit Bd. of Educ.*, 431 U.S. 209 (1977), held that members of a public employee bargaining unit who are not members of the union can be compelled to pay a service fee to the union for its collective bargaining expenses (because they would otherwise be free riders and that would endanger labor peace and because of the importance of stable unions), but they may not be charged for political expenses if they object to the use of union funds supporting political candidates or political views. Similarly, *Keller v. State Bar of California*, 496 U.S. 1 (1990), held that the use of compulsory dues to finance political and ideological activities with which members disagreed violated their First Amendment right of free speech when such expenditures were not necessarily or reasonably incurred for purpose of regulating the legal profession or the improving quality of legal services. *International Ass'n of Machinists v. Street*, 367 U.S. 740 (1961), held that "dissent is not to be presumed" and that only employees who have affirmatively made known to the union their opposition to political uses of their funds are entitled to relief for political expenditures. *Chicago Teachers v. Hudson*, 475 U.S. 292 (1986), spoke to the process for determining which part of the fees was germane to collective bargaining and which was political, holding that "constitutional requirements for the Union's collection of agency fees include an adequate explanation of the basis for the fee, a reasonably prompt opportunity to challenge the amount of the fee before an impartial decisionmaker, and an escrow for the amounts reasonably in dispute while such challenges are pending."

KNOX v. SERVICE EMPLOYEES INT'L UNION, 567 U.S. 298 (2012), per ALITO, J., held that unions that have a special assessment for political purposes must issue a *Hudson* notice and may not exact funds from non-union members of a bargaining unit without their affirmative consent. In lengthy dicta, Alito, J., suggested that the practice of requiring non-members to opt out of supporting political expenditures authorized by *Hudson*, may not only be statutorily changed to an opt in requirement as was held in *Davenport v. Washington Educ. Ass'n*, 551 U.S. 177 (2007), but may be required under the First Amendment even when the dues assessment is not special.

HARRIS v. QUINN, 573 U.S. 616 (2014), per ALITO, J, ruled that an Illinois rule, requiring some home health workers who objected to their union to pay for bargaining expenses, violated the First Amendment right to freedom of association. These "personal assistants" were hired and fired by home-care recipients and subject to their control, but the working relationship albeit broad in scope was controlled by some government regulations and the assistants were paid by government. Alito, J., declined to extend *Abood* to this situation because of its "questionable" foundations and because the personal assistants were not like the "full-fledged" public employees present in *Abood*.

After Knox and Harris, many observers suspected that the Court was heading in the direction of explicitly overruling of Abood and the various cases that had relied on it. The Court appeared to be taking this route when it granted certiorari in *Friedrichs v. California Teachers Ass'n*, 136 S.Ct. 1083 (2016), but the death of Justice Scalia after argument but prior to decision in that case produced an affirmance of the decision below, without opinion, by a 4–4 equally divided Court. In JANUS v. AMERICAN FEDERATION OF STATE, COUNTY, AND MUNICIPAL EMPLOYEES, COUNCIL 31, 138 S.Ct. 2448 (2018), however, the Court took the widely-expected course and explicitly overruled Abood on First Amendment grounds.

Writing for a 5–4 majority, ALITO, J., characterized the case as one in which, "[u]nder Illinois law, public employees are forced to subsidize a union, even if they choose not to join and strongly object to the positions the union takes in collective bargaining and related activities." At issue was an Illinois statute allowing the creation of public employee unions, and providing, as in *Abood*, that a majority of employees in a bargaining unit could designate a union as their sole bargaining representative. After such a designation, the union was permitted to charge those employees who chose not to join the union an "agency fee" designed to compensate the union for the costs of bargaining and related activities. In *Janus*, the agency fee charged to non-members amounted $535 per year, which was slightly more than 78% of the full union dues for union members.

Justice Alito and the majority relied initially on *Pickering v. Board of Education* (1968, Ch. 7, Sec. 7, C, above) for the basic proposition that public employees do not relinquish their free speech rights by virtue of taking public employment, and went on to describe the compelled payment of the agency fee as a restriction on the free speech rights of public employees, in particular the employees who not only did not wish to join the union, but who also objected to the positions that the union took or might take as part of the collective bargaining process. For the majority, "[c]ompelling individuals to [support views] they find objectionable violates [a] cardinal constitutional command. [When] speech is compelled, [individuals] are coerced into betraying their convictions." Justice Alito commenced with the premise that for a state to force individuals, even public employees, to "voice ideas with which they disagree," especially on matters of public concern, would be a plain violation of the First Amendment, and "[c]ompelling a person to subsidize the speech of other private speakers raises similar First Amendment concerns."

Because the First Amendment was implicated in this way, the majority concluded, the restriction would be tested against something more stringent than "minimal scrutiny," although the majority declined to decide whether the Illinois scheme would be tested against "strict scrutiny," finding that the scheme could not survive the somewhat less stringent standard noted in *Knox* and *Harris*. Applying that standard, the Court concluded that neither the interest in labor peace, at least on the facts presented here, nor the interest in deterring free riding by non-member employees who nevertheless benefited from the collective bargaining agreement, was sufficient to justify the imposition of the agency fee. And although the Court used *Pickering* as the touchstone for the basic proposition that public employees retain extensive First Amendment rights, and for the additional proposition that *Pickering* protected public employee speech on matters of public concern, the Court rejected the full analytic framework of *Pickering*, a framework that, in its most relevant dimension, required weighing the employee's interests against those of the public employer. But the Court found that such a weighing process to be inapplicable to the compelled speech situation, and inapplicable to pervasive regulatory programs, as opposed to individual supervisory decisions. Instead the Court treated the compelled speech of a public employee on a matter of public concern as something close to presumptively unconstitutional.

In explicitly overruling *Abood*, the Court acknowledged the constraints of stare decisis, but held those constraints insufficient in this case to allow *Abood* to stand. For the Court, the constraints of *stare decisis* were weaker in constitutional interpretation because the only alternative to overruling is constitutional amendment. "And *stare decisis* applies with perhaps least force of all to decisions that wrongly denied First Amendment rights." In addition, five factors—the quality of the reasoning in the earlier decision, the workability of the previous rule, the consistency between the earlier decision and the larger body of law of which it was a part, the degree of reliance on the earlier decision, and legal and other developments since the earlier decision—all inclined against following a prior decision just because of its status as prior. Concluding that "*Abood* is an 'anomaly' in our First Amendment jurisprudence," and especially "when viewed against our cases holding that public employees generally may not be required to support a political party" (e.g., *Elrod v. Burns* (1976) above, Sec. 7, III), the majority held that "States and public-sector unions may no longer extract agency fees from nonconsenting employees," and thus that "*Abood* was wrongly decided and is now overruled."

KAGAN, J. writing for herself and Ginsburg, Breyer, and Sotomayor, JJ. dissented. Accusing the majority and the challengers of "weaponizing" the First Amendment by using it to attack the kinds of traditionally acceptable economic arrangements that receive great deference in the post-*Lochner* era, she rejected the majority's conclusion that *Abood* was an anomaly, arguing that '[t]he Court's decisions have long made plain that government entities have substantial latitude to regulate their employees' speech—especially about terms of employment—in the interest of operating their workplaces effectively." Moreover, the Court's decision "will have large scale consequences. Public employee unions will lose a secure source of financial support. State and local governments that thought fair-share provisions furthered their interests will need to find new ways of managing their workforces. [And thus] the relationships of public employees and employers will alter in both predictable and unexpected ways."

Justice Kagan relied heavily on *Pickering*'s deference to a public employer's "managerial interests" and "respect—even solicitude—for the government's prerogatives as an employer." In rejecting this approach, the majority, she argued, "subverts all known principles of *stare decisis*." Even accepting for the sake of argument that *Abood* was wrongly decided, "respecting *stare decisis* means sticking to some wrong decisions. Any departure from settled precedent [demands] a 'special justification'—over and above the belief that the precedent was wrongly decided. And the majority does not have anything close. To the contrary: all that is 'special' in this case—especially the massive reliance interests at stake—demands retaining *Abood*, beyond even the normal precedent."

––––––––––

Anonymous political speech. McINTYRE v. OHIO ELECTIONS COMM'N, 514 U.S. 334 (1995), per STEVENS, J., held that Ohio's prohibition against the distribution of anonymous campaign literature was unconstitutional: "Under our Constitution, anonymous pamphleteering is not a pernicious, fraudulent practice, but an honorable tradition of advocacy and of dissent. [The] State may and does punish fraud directly. But it cannot seek to punish fraud indirectly by indiscriminately outlawing a category of speech, based on its content, with no necessary relationship to the danger sought to be prevented."

THOMAS, J., concurred, but argued that instead of asking whether " 'an honorable tradition' of free speech has existed throughout American history, [we] should seek the original understanding when we interpret the Speech and Press clauses, just as we do when we read the Religion Clauses of the First Amendment."

According to Thomas, J., the original understanding approach also protected anonymous speech.

SCALIA, joined by Rehnquist, C.J., dissenting, asserted that it was the "Court's (and society's) traditional view that the Constitution bears its original meaning and is unchanging." Applying that approach, he concluded that anonymous political speech is not protected under the First Amendment.

II. INTIMATE ASSOCIATION AND EXPRESSIVE ASSOCIATION

ROBERTS v. UNITED STATES JAYCEES, 468 U.S. 609 (1984): Appellee U.S. Jaycees, a nonprofit national membership corporation whose objective is to pursue educational and charitable purposes that promote the growth and development of young men's civic organizations, limits regular membership to young men between the ages of 18 and 35. Associate membership is available to women and older men. An associate member may not vote or hold local or national office. Two local chapters in Minnesota violated appellee's bylaws by admitting women as regular members. When they learned that revocation of their charters was to be considered, members of both chapters filed discrimination charges with the Minnesota Department of Human Rights, alleging that the exclusion of women from full membership violated the Minnesota Human Rights Act (Act), which makes it an "unfair discriminatory practice" to deny anyone "the full and equal enjoyment of goods, services, facilities, privileges, advantages, and accommodations of a place of public accommodation" because, inter alia, of sex. Before a hearing on the state charge took place, appellee brought federal suit, alleging that requiring it to accept women as regular members would violate the male members' constitutional "freedom of association."

In rejecting appellee's claims, the Court, per BRENNAN, J., pointed out that the Constitution protects " 'freedom of association' in two distinct senses," what might be called "freedom of intimate association" and "freedom of expressive association": "In one line of decisions, the Court has concluded that choices to enter into and maintain certain intimate human relationships must be secured against undue intrusion by the State because of the role of such relationships in safeguarding the individual freedom that is central to our constitutional scheme. In this respect, freedom of association receives protection as a fundamental element of personal liberty. In another set of decisions, the Court has recognized a right to associate for the purpose of engaging in those activities protected by the First Amendment—speech, assembly, petition for the redress of grievances, [and] religion. The Constitution guarantees freedom of association of this kind as an indispensable means of preserving other individual liberties."

The freedom of intimate association was deemed important because, "certain kinds of personal bonds have played a critical role in the culture and traditions of the Nation by cultivating and transmitting shared ideals and beliefs; they thereby foster diversity and act as critical buffers between the individual and the power of the State. Moreover, the constitutional shelter afforded such relationships reflects the realization that individuals draw much of their emotional enrichment from close ties with others. Protecting these relationships from unwarranted state interference therefore safeguards the ability independently to define one's identity that is central to any concept of liberty. [In] this case, however, several features of the Jaycees clearly place the organization outside of the category of relationships worthy of this kind of constitutional protection.

"[T]he local chapters of the Jaycees are large and basically unselective groups. [Apart] from age and sex, neither the national organization nor the local chapters employs any criteria for judging applicants for membership, and new members are routinely recruited and admitted with no inquiry into their backgrounds. In fact, a local officer testified that he could recall no instance in which an applicant had been denied membership on any basis other than age or sex. [Furthermore], numerous non-members of both genders regularly participate in a substantial portion of activities central to the decision of many members to associate with one another, including many of the organization's various community programs, awards ceremonies, and recruitment meetings.

"[We] turn therefore to consider the extent to which application of the Minnesota statute to compel the Jaycees to accept women infringes the group's freedom of expressive association. * * *

"Government actions that may unconstitutionally infringe upon [freedom of expressive association] can take a number of forms. Among other things, government may seek to impose penalties or withhold benefits from individuals because of their membership in a disfavored group; it may attempt to require disclosure of the fact of membership in a group seeking anonymity; and it may try to interfere with the internal organization or affairs of the group. [There] can be no clearer example of an intrusion into the internal structure or affairs of an association than a regulation that forces the group to accept members it does not desire. Such a regulation may impair the ability of the original members to express only those views that brought them together. Freedom of association therefore plainly presupposes a freedom not to associate.

"The right to associate for expressive purposes is not, however, absolute. Infringements on that right may be justified by regulations adopted to serve compelling state interests, unrelated to the suppression of ideas, that cannot be achieved through means significantly less restrictive of associational freedoms.

"In applying the Act to the Jaycees, the State has advanced [compelling] interests through the least restrictive means of achieving its ends. Indeed, the Jaycees have failed to demonstrate that the Act imposes any serious burdens on the male members' freedom of expressive association. [There] is, however, no basis in the record for concluding that admission of women as full voting members will impede the organization's ability to engage in these protected activities or to disseminate its preferred views. * * *

O'CONNOR, J., concurring, joined the Court's opinion except for its analysis of freedom of expressive association: "[T]he Court has adopted a test that unadvisedly casts doubt on the power of States to pursue the profoundly important goal of ensuring nondiscriminatory access to commercial opportunities" yet "accords insufficient protection to expressive associations and places inappropriate burdens on groups claiming the protection of the First Amendment":

"[The] Court declares that the Jaycees' right of association depends on the organization's making a 'substantial' showing that the admission of unwelcome members 'will change the message communicated by the group's speech.' [The] Court's readiness to inquire into the connection between membership and message reveals a more fundamental flaw in its analysis. The Court pursues this inquiry as part of its mechanical application of a 'compelling interest' test, [and] entirely neglects to establish at the threshold that the Jaycees is an association whose activities or purposes should engage the strong protections that the First Amendment extends to expressive associations.

"On the one hand, an association engaged exclusively in protected expression enjoys First Amendment protection of both the content of its message and the choice of its members. * * * Protection of the association's right to define its membership derives from the recognition that the formation of an expressive association is the creation of a voice, and the selection of members is the definition of that voice. [A] ban on specific group voices on public affairs violates the most basic guarantee of the First Amendment—that citizens, not the government, control the content of public discussion.

"On the other hand, there is only minimal constitutional protection of the freedom of *commercial* association. There are, of course, some constitutional protections of commercial speech—speech intended and used to promote a commercial transaction with the speaker. But the State is free to impose any rational regulation on the commercial transaction itself. The Constitution does not guarantee a right to choose employees, customers, suppliers, or those with whom one engages in simple commercial transactions, without restraint from the State." * * *

––––––––

James Dale's position as an assistant scoutmaster of a New Jersey troop of the Boy Scouts of America was revoked. The Scouts learned that he was gay and the co-President of the Rutgers University Lesbian/Gay Alliance. Dale had been publicly quoted on the importance in his own life on the need for gay role models. Dale sued, and the New Jersey Supreme Court ultimately held that New Jersey's anti-discrimination public accommodation law required that the Scouts readmit him.

BOY SCOUTS OF AMERICA v. DALE, 530 U.S. 640 (2000), per REHNQUIST, C.J., held that the New Jersey law violated the expressive association rights of the Boy Scouts: "The First Amendment's protection of expressive association is not reserved for advocacy groups. But to come within its ambit, a group must engage in some form of expression, whether it be public or private."

Rehnquist, C.J., cited portions of the Scout Oath requiring Scouts to be "morally straight" and to be "Clean": "The Boy Scouts [says] that it 'teach[es] that homosexual conduct is not morally straight' * * * . We need not inquire further to determine the nature of the Boy Scouts' expression with respect to homosexuality. But because the record before us contains written evidence of the Boy Scouts' viewpoint, we look to it as instructive, if only on the question of the sincerity of the professed beliefs. * * *

"We must [also] give deference to an association's view of what would impair its expression. [That] is not to say that an expressive association can erect a shield against antidiscrimination laws simply by asserting that mere acceptance of a member from a particular group would impair its message. But here Dale, by his own admission, is one of a group of gay Scouts who have 'become leaders in their community and are open and honest about their sexual orientation.' [His] presence in the Boy Scouts would, at the very least, force the organization to send a message, both to the youth members and the world, that the Boy Scouts accepts homosexual conduct as a legitimate form of behavior. * * *

STEVENS, J., joined by Souter, Ginsburg, and Breyer, JJ., dissenting, contended that: "at a minimum, a group seeking to prevail over an antidiscrimination law must adhere to a clear and unequivocal view" and that the Scouts had not done so. Nor did precedent favor the Scouts claim: "Several principles are made perfectly clear by *Jaycees* and *Rotary Club*. First, to prevail on a claim of expressive association in the face of a State's antidiscrimination law, it is not enough simply to engage in *some kind* of expressive activity. Both the Jaycees and the Rotary Club engaged in expressive activity protected by the First Amendment, yet that fact was not dispositive. Second, it is not enough to adopt an openly avowed exclusionary membership policy. Both the Jaycees and the Rotary Club did that as well. Third, it is not sufficient merely to articulate *some* connection between the group's expressive activities and its exclusionary policy." Stevens, J., argued that it was necessary to show a serious burden on the association's expression: "The evidence before this Court makes it exceptionally clear that BSA has, at most, simply adopted an exclusionary membership policy and has no shared goal of disapproving of homosexuality [or] collective effort to foster a belief about homosexuality at all—let alone one that is significantly burdened by admitting homosexuals." Stevens argued that the majority's deferential posture toward the allegations of the Scouts reflected "an astounding view of the law. I am unaware of any previous instance in which our analysis of the scope of a constitutional right was determined by looking at what a litigant asserts in his or her brief and inquiring no further."

10. WEALTH, EQUALITY, AND THE POLITICAL PROCESS

BUCKLEY V. VALEO
424 U.S. 1, 96 S.Ct. 612, 46 L.Ed.2d 659 (1976).

PER CURIAM.

[In this portion of a lengthy opinion dealing with the validity of the Federal Election Campaign Act of 1971, as amended in 1974, the Court considers those parts of the Act limiting *contributions* to a candidate for federal office (all sustained), and those parts limiting *expenditures* in support of such candidacy (all held invalid).]

A. *General Principles.* The Act's contribution and expenditure limitations operate in an area of the most fundamental First Amendment activities. Discussion of public issues and debate on the qualifications of candidates are integral to the operation of the system of government established by our Constitution.

[Appellees] contend that what the Act regulates is conduct, and that its effect on speech and association is incidental at most. Appellants respond that contributions and expenditures are at the very core of political speech, and that the Act's limitations thus constitute restraints on First Amendment liberty that are both gross and [direct.]

We cannot share the view [that] the present Act's contribution and expenditure limitations are comparable to the restrictions on conduct upheld in *O'Brien* [Sec. 2 supra]. The expenditure of money simply cannot be equated with such conduct as destruction of a draft card. Some forms of communication made possible by the giving and spending of money involve speech alone, some involve conduct primarily, and some involve a combination of the two. Yet this Court has never suggested that the dependence of a communication on the expenditure of money operates itself to introduce a non-speech element or to reduce the exacting scrutiny required by the First Amendment. * * *

Even if the categorization of the expenditure of money as conduct were accepted, the limitations challenged here would not meet the *O'Brien* test because the governmental interests advanced in support of the Act involve "suppressing communication." The interests served by the Act include restricting the voices of people and interest groups who have money to spend and reducing the overall scope of federal election campaigns. [Unlike] *O'Brien,* where [the] interest in the preservation of draft cards was wholly unrelated to their use as a means of communication, it is beyond dispute that the interest in regulating the alleged "conduct" of giving or spending money "arises in some measure because the communication allegedly integral to the conduct is itself thought to be harmful." * * *

A restriction on the amount of money a person or group can spend on political communication during a campaign necessarily reduces the quantity of expression by restricting the number of issues discussed, the depth of their exploration, and the size of the audience reached. This is because virtually every means of communicating ideas in today's mass society requires the expenditure of [money].

The expenditure limitations contained in the Act represent substantial rather than merely theoretical restraints on the quantity and diversity of political speech. The $1,000 ceiling on spending "relative to a clearly identified candidate," 18 U.S.C. § 608(e)(1), would appear to exclude all citizens and groups except candidates, political parties and the institutional press from any significant use of the most effective modes of communication.* * *

By contrast with a limitation upon expenditures for political expression, a limitation [on] the amount of money a person may give to a candidate or campaign organization [involves] little direct restraint on his political communication, for it permits the symbolic expression of support evidenced by a contribution but does not in any way infringe the contributor's freedom to discuss candidates and issues. While contributions may result in political expression if spent by a candidate or an association to present views to the voters, the transformation of contributions into political debate involves speech by someone other than the contributor.

[There] is no indication [that] the contribution limitations imposed by the Act would have any dramatic adverse effect on the funding of campaigns and political associations. The overall effect of the Act's contribution ceilings is merely to require candidates and political committees to raise funds from a greater number of persons and to compel people who would otherwise contribute amounts greater than the statutory limits to expend such funds on direct political expression, rather than to reduce the total amount of money potentially available to promote political expression. * * *

In sum, although the Act's contribution and expenditure limitations both implicate fundamental First Amendment interests, its expenditure ceilings impose significantly more severe restrictions on protected freedoms of political expression and association than do its limitations on financial contributions.

B.   *Contribution Limitations.* [Section] 608(b) provides, with certain limited exceptions, that "no person shall make contributions to any candidate with respect to any election for Federal office which, in the aggregate, exceeds $1,000." * * *

Appellants contend that the $1,000 contribution ceiling unjustifiably burdens First Amendment freedoms, employs overbroad dollar limits, and discriminates against candidates opposing incumbent officeholders and against minor-party candidates in violation of the Fifth Amendment.

[It] is unnecessary to look beyond the Act's primary purpose—to limit the actuality and appearance of corruption resulting from large individual financial contributions—in order to find a constitutionally sufficient justification for the $1,000 contribution limitation. [The] increasing importance of the communications media and sophisticated mass mailing and polling operations to effective campaigning make the raising of large sums of money an ever more essential ingredient of an effective candidacy. To the extent that large contributions are given to secure political quid pro quos from current and potential office holders, the integrity of our system of representative democracy is undermined. Although the scope of such pernicious practices can never be reliably ascertained, the deeply disturbing examples surfacing after the 1972 election demonstrate that the problem is not an illusory one.

Of almost equal concern as the danger of actual quid pro quo arrangements is the impact of the appearance of corruption stemming from public awareness of the opportunities for abuse inherent in a regime of large individual financial contributions. [Here,] Congress could legitimately conclude that the avoidance of the appearance of improper influence "is also critical [if] confidence in the system of representative Government is not to be eroded to a disastrous extent."

Appellants contend that the contribution limitations must be invalidated because bribery laws and narrowly-drawn disclosure requirements constitute a less restrictive means of dealing with "proven and suspected quid pro quo arrangements." But laws [against] bribes deal with only the most blatant and specific attempts of those with money to influence governmental action. [And] Congress was surely entitled to conclude that disclosure was only a partial measure, and that contribution ceilings were a necessary legislative concomitant to deal with the reality or appearance of corruption inherent in a system permitting unlimited financial contributions, even when the identities of the contributors and the amounts of their contributions are fully disclosed.

The Act's $1,000 contribution limitation focuses precisely on the problem of large campaign contributions—the narrow aspect of political association where the actuality and potential for corruption have been identified—while leaving persons free to engage in independent political expression, to associate actively through volunteering their services. [The] Act's contribution limitations [do] not undermine to any material degree the potential for robust and effective discussion of candidates and campaign [issues]. * * *

C. *Expenditure Limitations.* [1.] Section 608(e)(1) provides that "[n]o person may make any expenditure [relative] to a clearly identified candidate during a calendar year which, when added to all other expenditures made by such person during the year advocating the election or defeat of such candidate, exceeds $1,000." [Its] plain effect [is] to prohibit all individuals, who are neither candidates nor owners of institutional press facilities, and all groups, except political parties and campaign organizations, from voicing their views "relative to a clearly identified candidate" through means that entail aggregate expenditures of more than $1,000 during a calendar year. The provision, for example, would make it a federal criminal offense for a person or association to place a single one-quarter page advertisement "relative to a clearly identified candidate" in a major metropolitan newspaper.

[Although] "expenditure," "clearly identified," and "candidate" are defined in the Act, there is no definition clarifying what expenditures are "relative to" a candidate. [But the "when" clause in § 608(e)(1)] clearly permits, if indeed it does not require, the phrase "relative to" a candidate to be read to mean "advocating the election or defeat of" a candidate.

But while such a construction of refocuses the vagueness question, [it hardly] eliminates the problem of unconstitutional vagueness altogether. For the distinction between discussion of issues and candidates and advocacy of election or defeat of candidates may often dissolve in practical application. Candidates, especially incumbents, are intimately tied to public issues involving legislative proposals and governmental actions. Not only do candidates campaign on the basis of their positions on various public issues, but campaigns themselves generate issues of public interest.

[Constitutionally deficient uncertainty which "compels the speaker to hedge and trim"] can be avoided only by reading § 608(e)(1) as limited to communications that include explicit words of advocacy of election or defeat of a candidate, much as the definition of "clearly identified" in § 608(e)(2) requires that an explicit and unambiguous reference to the candidate appear as part of the communication. This is the reading of the provision suggested by the non-governmental appellees in arguing that "[f]unds spent to propagate one's views on issues without expressly calling for a candidate's election or defeat are thus not covered." We agree that in order to preserve the provision against invalidation on vagueness grounds, § 608(e)(1) must be construed to apply only to expenditures for communications that in express terms advocate the election or defeat of a clearly identified candidate for federal office.

We turn then to the basic First Amendment question—whether § 608(e)(1), even as thus narrowly and explicitly construed, impermissibly burdens the constitutional right of free expression. * * *

We find that the governmental interest in preventing corruption and the appearance of corruption is inadequate to justify § 608(e)(1)'s ceiling on independent expenditures. First, assuming arguendo that large independent expenditures pose the same dangers of actual or apparent quid pro quo arrangements as do large contributions, § 608(e)(1) does not provide an answer that sufficiently relates to the elimination of those dangers. Unlike the contribution limitations' total ban on the giving of large amounts of money to candidates, § 608(e)(1) prevents only some large expenditures. So long as persons and groups eschew expenditures that in express terms advocate the election or defeat of a clearly identified candidate, they are free to spend as much as they want to promote the candidate and his views. The exacting interpretation of the statutory language necessary to avoid unconstitutional vagueness thus undermines the limitation's effectiveness as a loophole-closing provision by facilitating circumvention by those seeking to exert improper influence upon a candidate or office-holder. It would naively underestimate the ingenuity and resourcefulness of persons and groups desiring to buy influence to believe that they would have much difficulty devising expenditures that skirted the restriction on express advocacy of election or defeat but nevertheless benefitted the candidate's campaign. * * *

Second, [the] independent advocacy restricted by the provision does not presently appear to pose dangers of real or apparent corruption comparable to those identified with large campaign contributions. The parties defending § 608(e)(1) contend that it is necessary to prevent would-be contributors from avoiding the contribution limitations by the simple expedient of paying directly for media advertisements or for other portions of the candidate's campaign activities. [Section] 608(b)'s contribution ceilings rather than § 608(e)(1)'s independent expenditure limitation prevent attempts to circumvent the Act through prearranged or coordinated expenditures amounting to disguised contributions. By contrast, § 608(e)(1) limits expenditures for express advocacy of candidates made totally independently of the candidate and his campaign. [The] absence of prearrangement and coordination of an expenditure with the candidate or his agent not only undermines the value of the expenditure to the candidate, but also alleviates the danger that expenditures will be given as a quid pro quo for improper commitments from the candidate. Rather than preventing circumvention of the contribution limitations, § 608(e)(1) severely restricts all independent advocacy despite its substantially diminished potential for abuse.

While the independent expenditure ceiling thus fails to serve any substantial governmental interest in stemming the reality or appearance of corruption in the electoral process, it heavily burdens core First Amendment expression. [Advocacy] of the election or defeat of candidates for federal office is no less entitled to protection under the First Amendment than the discussion of political policy generally or advocacy of the passage or defeat of legislation.

It is argued, however, that the ancillary governmental interest in equalizing the relative ability of individuals and groups to influence the outcome of elections serves to justify the limitation on express advocacy of the election or defeat of candidates imposed by § 608(e)(1)'s expenditure ceiling. But the concept that government may restrict the speech of some elements of our society in order to enhance the relative voice of others is wholly foreign to the First Amendment, which was designed "to secure 'the widest possible dissemination of information from diverse and antagonistic sources,' " and " 'to assure unfettered interchange of ideas for the bringing about of political and social changes desired by the people.' " *New York Times Co. v. Sullivan.* The First Amendment's protection against governmental abridgement of free expression cannot properly be made to depend on a person's financial ability to engage in public discussion.

[For] the reasons stated, we conclude that § 608(e)(1)'s independent expenditure limitation is unconstitutional under the First Amendment. * * *

2.   [The] Act also sets limits on expenditures by a candidate "from his personal funds, or the personal funds of his immediate family, in connection with his campaigns during any calendar year." § 608(a)(1).

The ceiling on personal expenditures by candidates on their own behalf [imposes] a substantial restraint on the ability of persons to engage in protected First Amendment expression. The candidate, no less than any other person, has a First Amendment right to engage in the discussion of public issues and vigorously and tirelessly to advocate his own election and the election of other candidates. Indeed, it is of particular importance that candidates have the unfettered opportunity to make their views known so that the electorate may intelligently evaluate the candidates' personal qualities and their positions on vital public issues before choosing among them on election day. [Section] 608(a)'s ceiling on personal expenditures by a candidate in furtherance of his own candidacy thus clearly and directly interferes with constitutionally protected freedoms.

The primary governmental interest served by the Act—the prevention of actual and apparent corruption of the political process—does not support the limitation on the candidate's expenditure of his own personal funds. [Indeed], the use of personal funds reduces the candidate's dependence on outside contributions and thereby counteracts the coercive pressures and attendant risks of abuse to which the Act's contribution limitations are directed.

The ancillary interest in equalizing the relative financial resources of candidates competing for elective office, therefore, provides the sole relevant rationale for Section 608(a)'s expenditure ceiling. That interest is clearly not sufficient to justify the provision's infringement of fundamental First Amendment rights. First, the limitation may fail to promote financial equality among candidates. [Indeed], a candidate's personal wealth may impede his [fundraising efforts]. Second, and more fundamentally, the First Amendment simply cannot tolerate § 608(a)'s restriction upon the freedom of a candidate to speak without legislative limit on behalf of his own candidacy. We therefore hold that § 608(a)'s restrictions on a candidate's personal expenditures is unconstitutional.

3.   [Section] 608(c) of the Act places limitations on overall campaign expenditures by candidates [seeking] election to federal office. [For Presidential candidates the ceiling is $10,000,000 in seeking nomination and $20,000,000 in the general election campaign; for House of Representatives candidates it is $70,000 for each campaign—primary and general; for candidates for Senator the ceiling depends on the size of the voting age population.]

No governmental interest that has been suggested is sufficient to justify [these restrictions] on the quantity of political expression. [The] interest in alleviating the corrupting influence of large contributions is served by the Act's contribution limitations and disclosure provisions rather than by § 608(c)'s campaign expenditure ceilings. [There] is no indication that the substantial criminal penalties for violating the contribution ceilings combined with the political repercussion of such violations will be insufficient to police the contribution provisions. Extensive reporting, auditing, and disclosure requirements applicable to both contributions and expenditures by political campaigns are designed to facilitate the detection of illegal contributions. * * *

The interest in equalizing the financial resources of candidates competing for federal office is no more convincing a justification for restricting the scope of federal election campaigns. Given the limitation on the size of outside contributions, the financial resources available to a candidate's campaign, like the number of volunteers recruited, will normally vary with the size and intensity of the candidate's support. There is nothing invidious, improper, or unhealthy in permitting such funds to be spent to carry the candidate's message to the electorate. Moreover, the equalization of permissible campaign expenditures might serve not to equalize the opportunities of all candidates but to handicap a candidate who lacked substantial name recognition or exposure of his views before the start of the campaign.

The campaign expenditure ceilings appear to be designed primarily to serve the governmental interests in reducing the allegedly skyrocketing costs of political campaigns. [But the] First Amendment denies government the power to determine that spending to promote one's political views is wasteful, excessive, or unwise. In the free society ordained by our Constitution it is not the government but the people individually as citizens and candidates and collectively as associations and political committees who must retain control over the quantity and range of debate on public issues in a political campaign.[65]

For these reasons we hold that § 608(c) is constitutionally invalid. * * *

CHIEF JUSTICE BURGER, concurring in part and dissenting in part.

[I] agree fully with that part of the Court's opinion that holds unconstitutional the limitations the Act puts on campaign expenditures. [Yet] when it approves similarly stringent limitations on contributions, the Court ignores the reasons it finds so persuasive in the context of expenditures. For me contributions and expenditures are two sides of the same First Amendment coin.

[Limiting] contributions, as a practical matter, will limit expenditures and will put an effective ceiling on the amount of political activity and debate that the Government will permit to take place.

The Court attempts to separate the two communicative aspects of political contributions—the "moral" support that the gift itself conveys, which the Court suggests is the same whether the gift is of $10 or $10,000, and the fact that money translates into communication. The Court dismisses the effect of the limitations on the second aspect of contributions: "[T]he transformation of contributions into political debate involves speech by someone other than the contributor." On this premise—that contribution limitations restrict only the speech of "someone other than the contributor"—rests the Court's justification for treating contributions differently from expenditures. The premise is demonstrably flawed; the contribution limitations will, in specific instances, limit exactly the same political

---

[65]   **[Ct's Note]** [Congress] may engage in public financing of election campaigns and may condition acceptance of public funds on an agreement by the candidate to abide by specified expenditure limitations. Just as a candidate may voluntarily limit the size of the contributions he chooses to accept he may decide to forgo private fundraising and accept public funding.

activity that the expenditure ceilings limit, and at least one of the "expenditure" limitations the Court finds objectionable operates precisely like the "contribution" limitations.[8]

The Court's attempt to distinguish the communication inherent in political *contributions* from the speech aspects of political *expenditures* simply will not wash. We do little but engage in word games unless we recognize that people— candidates and contributors—spend money on political activity because they wish to communicate ideas, and their constitutional interest in doing so is precisely the same whether they or someone else utter the words.

[T]he restrictions are hardly incidental in their effect upon particular campaigns. Judges are ill-equipped to gauge the precise impact of legislation, but a law that impinges upon First Amendment rights requires us to make the attempt. It is not simply speculation to think that the limitations on contributions will foreclose some candidacies. The limitations will also alter the nature of some electoral contests drastically.[10]

[In] striking down the limitations on campaign expenditures, the Court relies in part on its conclusion that other means—namely, disclosure and contribution ceilings—will adequately serve the statute's aim. It is not clear why the same analysis is not also appropriate in weighing the need for contribution ceilings in addition to disclosure requirements. Congress may well be entitled to conclude that disclosure was a "partial measure," but I had not thought until today that Congress could enact its conclusions in the First Amendment area into laws immune from the most searching review by this Court. * * *

JUSTICE WHITE, concurring in part and dissenting in part. * * *

I [agree] with the Court's judgment upholding the limitations on contributions. I dissent [from] the Court's view that the expenditure limitations [violate] the First Amendment. [This] case depends on whether the nonspeech interests of the Federal Government in regulating the use of money in political campaigns are sufficiently urgent to justify the incidental effects that the limitations visit upon the First Amendment interests of candidates and their supporters.

[The Court] accepts the congressional judgment that the evils of unlimited contributions are sufficiently threatening to warrant restriction regardless of the impact of the limits on the contributor's opportunity for effective speech and in turn

---

[8]   **[Ct's Note]** The Court treats the Act's provisions limiting a candidate's spending from his *personal resources* as *expenditure* limits, as indeed the Act characterizes them, and holds them unconstitutional. As Mr. Justice Marshall points out, infra, by the Court's logic these provisions could as easily be treated as limits on *contributions,* since they limit what the candidate can give to his own campaign.

[10]   **[Ct's Note]** Under the Court's holding, candidates with personal fortunes will be free to contribute to their own campaigns as much as they like, since the Court chooses to view the Act's provisions in this regard as unconstitutional "expenditure" limitations rather than "contribution" limitations.

on the total volume of the candidate's political communications by reason of his inability to accept large sums from those willing to give.

The congressional judgment, which I would also accept, was that other steps must be taken to counter the corrosive effects of money in federal election campaigns. One of these steps is § 608(e), which [limits] what a contributor may independently spend in support or denigration of one running for federal office. Congress was plainly of the view that these expenditures also have corruptive potential; but the Court strikes down the provision, strangely enough claiming more insight as to what may improperly influence candidates than is possessed by the majority of Congress that passed this Bill and the President who signed it. Those supporting the Bill undeniably included many seasoned professionals who have been deeply involved in elective processes and who have viewed them at close range over many years.

It would make little sense to me, and apparently made none to Congress, to limit the amounts an individual may give to a candidate or spend with his approval but fail to limit the amounts that could be spent on his behalf. Yet the Court permits the former while striking down the latter limitation. [I] would take the word of those who know—that limiting independent expenditures is essential to prevent transparent and widespread evasion of the contribution limits. * * *

The Court also rejects Congress' judgment manifested in § 608(c) that the federal interest in limiting total campaign expenditures by individual candidates justifies the incidental effect on their opportunity for effective political speech. I disagree both with the Court's assessment of the impact on speech and with its narrow view of the values the limitations will serve.

[M]oney is not always equivalent to or used for speech, even in the context of political campaigns. [There are] many expensive campaign activities that are not themselves communicative or remotely related to speech. Furthermore, campaigns differ among themselves. Some seem to spend much less money than others and yet communicate as much or more than those supported by enormous bureaucracies with unlimited financing. The record before us no more supports the conclusion that the communicative efforts of congressional and Presidential candidates will be crippled by the expenditure limitations than it supports the contrary. The judgment of Congress was that reasonably effective campaigns could be conducted within the limits established by the Act and that the communicative efforts of these campaigns would not seriously suffer. In this posture of the case, there is no sound basis for invalidating the expenditure limitations, so long as the purposes they serve are legitimate and sufficiently substantial, which in my view they are.

[E]xpenditure ceilings reinforce the contribution limits and help eradicate the hazard of corruption. [Without] limits on total expenditures, campaign costs will inevitably and endlessly escalate. Pressure to raise funds will constantly build and with it the temptation to resort in "emergencies" to those sources of large sums, who, history shows, are sufficiently confident of not being caught to risk flouting contribution [limits.]

The ceiling on candidate expenditures represents the considered judgment of Congress that elections are to be decided among candidates none of whom has overpowering advantage by reason of a huge campaign war chest. At least so long as the ceiling placed upon the candidates is not plainly too low, elections are not to turn on the difference in the amounts of money that candidates have to spend. This seems an acceptable purpose and the means chosen a common sense way to achieve [it.]

I also disagree with the Court's judgment that § 608(a), which limits the amount of money that a candidate or his family may spend on his campaign, violates the Constitution. Although it is true that this provision does not promote any interest in preventing the corruption of candidates, the provision does, nevertheless, serve salutary purposes related to the integrity of federal campaigns. By limiting the importance of personal wealth, § 608(a) helps to assure that only individuals with a modicum of support from others will be viable candidates. This in turn would tend to discourage any notion that the outcome of elections is primarily a function of money. Similarly, § 608(a) tends to equalize access to the political arena, encouraging the less wealthy, unable to bankroll their own campaigns, to run for political office.

––––––––

Vermont's 1997 campaign finance statute limited the amount that state candidates could spend on their campaigns and that individuals, organizations, and parties could contribute to those campaigns.

RANDALL v. SORRELL, 548 U.S. 230 (2006), struck down both the expenditure limitations and the contribution limitations with a diversity of views concerning the authority of *Buckley*. BREYER, J., announced the judgment of the Court in an opinion joined by Roberts, C.J., and, in part, by Alito, J. He determined that the expenditure provision was unconstitutional on the strength of *Buckley*. On the basis of stare decisis, he declined what he perceived to be an invitation to overrule *Buckley's* ruling on candidate expenditure limits, and he rejected the view that *Buckley* could be distinguished on the ground that it failed to consider the argument that such limitations are justified because they help to prevent candidates from spending too much time raising money. With respect to the contribution limits, Breyer, J., maintained that they were too restrictive, noting, for example, that the limit on contributions for governor (adjusted for inflation) was slightly more than one-twentieth of the limit on contributions to federal office before the Court in *Buckley*. He also determined that Vermont's per election contribution limit was the lowest in the nation. Breyer, J., concluded that such limits would impair the ability of some candidates running against incumbent officeholder to mount an effective challenge.

THOMAS, J., joined by Scalia, J., concurred in the judgment, demanding strict scrutiny in examining both expenditure and contributions limitations, and arguing that the plurality's attempt to distinguish permissible from impermissible contribution limits could not be administered in a principled way: "[T]he plurality's determination that this statute clearly lies on the *impermissible* side of the constitutional line gives no assistance in drawing this line, and it is clear that no such line can be drawn rationally. There is simply no way to calculate just how much money a person would need to receive before he would be corrupt or perceived to be corrupt (and such a calculation would undoubtedly vary by person). Likewise, there is no meaningful way of discerning just how many resources must be lost before speech is 'disproportionately burden[ed].' "

STEVENS, J., dissenting, would depart from *Buckley's* strict scrutiny of candidate expenditure limits. He would uphold such limits "so long as the purposes they serve are legitimate and sufficiently substantial:" "The interest in freeing candidates from the fundraising straitjacket [is] compelling. Without expenditure limits, fundraising devours the time and attention of political leaders, leaving them too busy to handle their public responsibilities effectively. That fact was well recognized by backers of the legislation reviewed in *Buckley,* by the Court of Appeals judges who voted to uphold the expenditure limitations in that statute, and by Justice White—who not incidentally had personal experience as an active participant in a Presidential campaign. The validity of their judgment has surely been confirmed by the mountains of evidence that has been accumulated in recent years concerning the time that elected officials spend raising money for future campaigns and the adverse effect of fundraising on the performance of their official duties."

SOUTER, J., joined by Ginsburg, J., and, on the contributions issue, by Stevens, J., dissented, arguing that the question whether to relax *Buckley's* standard on expenditure requirements was not properly before the Court. He voted to affirm the Court of Appeals decision to remand on the expenditures issue to determine if the record met the requirements of *Buckley,* and to uphold the contribution limits: "I believe the Court of Appeals correctly rejected the challenge to the contribution limits. Low though they are, one cannot say that 'the contribution limitation[s are] so radical in effect as to render political association ineffective, drive the sound of a candidate's voice below the level of notice, and render contributions pointless.' *Nixon* v. *Shrink Missouri Government PAC,* 528 U.S. 377 (2000). The limits set by Vermont are not remarkable departures either from those previously upheld by this Court or from those lately adopted by other States. The plurality concedes that on a per-citizen measurement Vermont's limit for statewide elections 'is slightly more generous,' than the one set by the Missouri statute approved by this Court in *Shrink.*"

———

Aggregate contribution limits. Federal election law set limits to the amount contributors could give to candidates, to national party committees, to state or local party committees, and to political action committees. In addition to these "base" limits, the law sets aggregate limits. A contributor can give $5,200 to a particular federal election candidate ($2,600 in the primary and $2,600 in the general election), but can fully support no more than nine candidates because the aggregate limit for candidates is $48,600. The maximum amount that could be given in the aggregate to all of a contributor's potential beneficiaries is $123,200.

McCUTCHEON v. FEC, 572 U.S. 185 (2014), per ROBERTS, C.J., joined by SCALIA, KENNEDY, and ALITO, JJ., announced the judgment that the aggregate contribution limits as applied to candidates and committees violated the First Amendment and argued that the limits did little to combat corruption because the base limits would still apply to any additional candidates or committees supported, and the interest in stopping circumvention of the base limits was based on speculation and was already served by other loophole closing devices. On the other hand, the aggregate limits seriously restricted participation in the democratic process.

BREYER, J., joined by Ginsburg, Sotomayor, and Kagan, JJ., dissenting, primarily argued that the plurality's conception of corruption was too narrow in that it excluded influence over or access to elected officials and political parties, and that the loophole closing devices mentioned by the plurality are more complicated and ineffective than it understands.

CITIZENS UNITED V. FEC
588 U.S. 310, 130 S.Ct. 876, 175 L.Ed.2d 753 (2010).

JUSTICE KENNEDY delivered the opinion of the Court.

[In January 2008, Citizens United, a nonprofit corporation that accepts a small portion of its funds from for-profit companies, released a film entitled *Hillary: The Movie.* The film was a documentary arguing that Senator Hilary Clinton was an unsuitable candidate for President. Citizens United had released its film in theaters and on DVD, but it also wished to make the film available through video-on-demand on cable and to promote the film with ads on broadcast and cable television.]

Federal law prohibits corporations and unions from using their general treasury funds to make independent expenditures for speech defined as an "electioneering communication" or for speech expressly advocating the election or defeat of a candidate. Federal Election Campaign Act of 1971, 2 U.S.C. § 441b. Limits on electioneering communications were upheld in *McConnell v. Federal Election Comm'n,* (2003). The holding of *McConnell* rested to a large extent on an earlier case, *Austin v. Michigan Chamber of Commerce,* 494 U.S. 652 (1990). *Austin* had held that political speech may be banned based on the speaker's corporate identity.

In this case we are asked to reconsider *Austin* and, in effect, *McConnell.* * * * We [hold] that stare decisis does not compel the continued acceptance of *Austin.*

The Government may regulate corporate political speech through disclaimer and disclosure requirements, but it may not suppress that speech altogether.

Before the Bipartisan Campaign Reform Act of 2002 (BCRA), federal law prohibited-and still does prohibit—corporations and unions from using general treasury funds to make direct contributions to candidates or independent expenditures that expressly advocate the election or defeat of a candidate, through any form of media, in connection with certain qualified federal elections. BCRA § 203 amended § 441b to prohibit any "electioneering communication" as [well,] defined as "any broadcast, cable, or satellite communication" that "refers to a clearly identified candidate for a Federal office" and is made [well] within 30 days of a primary or 60 days of a general [election.][20] Corporations and unions [may] establish, however, a "separate segregated fund" (known as a political action committee, or PAC) for these purposes. The moneys received by the segregated fund are limited to donations from stockholders and employees of the corporation or, in the case of unions, members of the union. * * *

[T]he following acts would all be felonies under § 441b: The Sierra Club runs an ad, within the crucial phase of 60 days before the general election, that exhorts the public to disapprove of a Congressman who favors logging in national forests; the National Rifle Association publishes a book urging the public to vote for the challenger because the incumbent U.S. Senator supports a handgun ban; and the American Civil Liberties Union creates a Web site telling the public to vote for a Presidential candidate in light of that candidate's defense of free speech. These prohibitions are classic examples of censorship.

[A] PAC is a separate association from the corporation. So the PAC exemption from § 441b's expenditure ban does not allow corporations to speak. Even if a PAC could somehow allow a corporation to speak—and it does not—the option to form PACs does not alleviate the First Amendment problems with § 441b. PACs are burdensome alternatives; they are expensive to administer and subject to extensive regulations. For example, every PAC must appoint a treasurer, forward donations to the treasurer promptly, keep detailed records of the identities of the persons making donations, preserve receipts for three years, and file an organization statement and report changes to this information within 10 days. * * *

By taking the right to speak from some and giving it to others, the Government deprives the disadvantaged person or class of the right to use speech to strive to establish worth, standing, and respect for the speaker's voice. The Government may not by these means deprive the public of the right and privilege to determine for itself what speech and speakers are worthy of consideration. The First Amendment protects speech and speaker, and the ideas that flow from each.

The Court has upheld a narrow class of speech restrictions that operate to the disadvantage of certain persons, but these rulings were based on an interest in

---

[20]   The law exempted any news story, commentary, or editorial distributed through the facilities of any broadcasting station, newspaper, magazine, or other periodical publication, unless such facilities are owned or controlled by any political party, political committee, or candidate.

allowing governmental entities to perform their functions. See, e.g., *Bethel School Dist. No. v. Fraser*, 478 U.S. 675 (1986) (protecting the "function of public school education"); *Jones v. North Carolina Prisoners' Labor Union, Inc.*, 433 U.S. 119 (furthering "the legitimate penological objectives of the corrections system"); *Parker v. Levy*, 417 U.S. 733 (1974) (ensuring "the capacity of the Government to discharge its [military] responsibilities"); *Civil Service Comm'n v. Letter Carriers*, 413 U.S. 548 (1973) ("[F]ederal service should depend upon meritorious performance rather than political service"). The corporate independent expenditures at issue in this case, however, would not interfere with governmental functions, so these cases are inapposite. These precedents stand only for the proposition that there are certain governmental functions that cannot operate without some restrictions on particular kinds of speech. By contrast, it is inherent in the nature of the political process that voters must be free to obtain information from diverse sources in order to determine how to cast their votes. At least before *Austin,* the Court had not allowed the exclusion of a class of speakers from the general public dialogue.

[Laws] that burden political speech are "subject to strict scrutiny," which requires the Government to prove that the restriction "furthers a compelling interest and is narrowly tailored to achieve that interest." *Austin* identified a new governmental interest in limiting political speech: an antidistortion interest. *Austin* found a compelling governmental interest in preventing "the corrosive and distorting effects of immense aggregations of wealth that are accumulated with the help of the corporate form and that have little or no correlation to the public's support for the corporation's political ideas." [As] for *Austin's* antidistortion rationale, the Government does little to defend it. * * *

If the First Amendment has any force, it prohibits Congress from fining or jailing citizens, or associations of citizens, for simply engaging in political speech. If the antidistortion rationale were to be accepted, however, it would permit Government to ban political speech simply because the speaker is an association that has taken on the corporate form. The Government contends that *Austin* permits it to ban corporate expenditures for almost all forms of communication stemming from a corporation. If *Austin* were correct, the Government could prohibit a corporation from expressing political views in media beyond those presented here, such as by printing books. The Government responds "that the FEC has never applied this statute to a book," and if it did, "there would be quite [a] good as-applied challenge." This troubling assertion of brooding governmental power cannot be reconciled with the confidence and stability in civic discourse that the First Amendment must secure. * * *

Austin sought to defend the antidistortion rationale as a means to prevent corporations from obtaining "an unfair advantage in the political marketplace" by using "resources amassed in the economic marketplace." But *Buckley* rejected the premise that the Government has an interest "in equalizing the relative ability of individuals and groups to influence the outcome of elections." *Buckley* was specific in stating that "the skyrocketing cost of political campaigns" could not sustain the governmental prohibition. The First Amendment's protections do not depend on the speaker's "financial ability to engage in public discussion."

[*Austin*] undertook to distinguish wealthy individuals from corporations on the ground that "[s]tate law grants corporations special advantages—such as limited liability, perpetual life, and favorable treatment of the accumulation and distribution of assets." This does not suffice, however, to allow laws prohibiting speech. "It is rudimentary that the State cannot exact as the price of those special advantages the forfeiture of First Amendment rights."

It is irrelevant for purposes of the First Amendment that corporate funds may "have little or no correlation to the public's support for the corporation's political ideas." All speakers, including individuals and the media, use money amassed from the economic marketplace to fund their speech. The First Amendment protects the resulting speech, even if it was enabled by economic transactions with persons or entities who disagree with the speaker's ideas.

Austin's antidistortion rationale would produce the dangerous, and unacceptable, consequence that Congress could ban political speech of media corporations [now] exempt from § 441b's ban on corporate expenditures. Yet media corporations accumulate wealth with the help of the corporate form, the largest media corporations have "immense aggregations of wealth," and the views expressed by media corporations often "have little or no correlation to the public's support" for those views. Thus, under the Government's reasoning, wealthy media corporations could have their voices diminished to put them on par with other media entities. There is no precedent for permitting this [nor any] precedent supporting laws that attempt to distinguish between corporations which are deemed to be exempt as media corporations and those which are not. "We have consistently rejected the proposition that the institutional press has any constitutional privilege beyond that of other speakers." * * *

[T]he Government falls back on the argument that corporate political speech can be banned in order to prevent corruption or its appearance. In *Buckley,* the Court found this interest "sufficiently important" to allow limits on contributions but did not extend that reasoning to expenditure limits. * * *

With regard to large direct contributions, *Buckley* reasoned that they could be given "to secure a political quid pro quo," and that "the scope of such pernicious practices can never be reliably ascertained." The practices *Buckley* noted would be covered by bribery laws if a quid pro quo arrangement were proved. The Court, in consequence, has noted that restrictions on direct contributions are preventative, because few if any contributions to candidates will involve quid pro quo arrangements. The *Buckley* Court, nevertheless, sustained limits on direct contributions in order to ensure against the reality or appearance of corruption. That case did not extend this rationale to independent expenditures, and the Court does not do so here. * * *

When *Buckley* identified a sufficiently important governmental interest in preventing corruption or the appearance of corruption, that interest was limited to quid pro quo corruption. The fact that speakers may have influence over or access to elected officials does not mean that these officials are corrupt: "[It] is in the nature of an elected representative to favor certain policies, and, by necessary corollary, to favor the voters and contributors who support those policies. It is well understood that a substantial and legitimate reason, if not the only reason, to cast a vote for, or to make a contribution to, one candidate over another is that the candidate will respond by producing those political outcomes the supporter favors. Democracy is premised on responsiveness." Reliance on a "generic favoritism or influence theory . . . is at odds with standard First Amendment analyses because it is unbounded and susceptible to no limiting principle."

The appearance of influence or access, furthermore, will not cause the electorate to lose faith in our democracy. By definition, an independent expenditure is political speech presented to the electorate that is not coordinated with a candidate. The fact that a corporation, or any other speaker, is willing to spend money to try to persuade voters presupposes that the people have the ultimate influence over elected officials. This is inconsistent with any suggestion that the electorate will refuse "to take part in democratic governance" because of additional political speech made by a corporation or any other speaker.

The *McConnell* record was "over 100,000 pages" long, yet it "does not have any direct examples of votes being exchanged for . . . expenditures," This confirms *Buckley*'s reasoning that independent expenditures do not lead to, or create the appearance of, quid pro quo corruption. In fact, there is only scant evidence that independent expenditures even ingratiate. Ingratiation and access, in any event, are not corruption. The BCRA record establishes that certain donations to political parties, called "soft money," were made to gain access to elected officials. This case, however, is about independent expenditures, not soft money. [If] elected officials succumb to improper influences from independent expenditures; if they surrender their best judgment; and if they put expediency before principle, then surely there is cause for concern. We must give weight to attempts by Congress to seek to dispel either the appearance or the reality of these influences. The remedies enacted by law, however, must comply with the First Amendment; and, it is our law and our tradition that more speech, not less, is the governing rule.

The Government contends further that corporate independent expenditures can be limited because of its interest in protecting dissenting shareholders from being compelled to fund corporate political speech. This asserted interest, like *Austin*'s antidistortion rationale, would allow the Government to ban the political speech even of media corporations. Assume, for example, that a shareholder of a corporation that owns a newspaper disagrees with the political views the newspaper expresses. Under the Government's view, that potential disagreement could give the Government the authority to restrict the media corporation's political speech. The First Amendment does not allow that power. There is, furthermore, little evidence of abuse that cannot be corrected by shareholders "through the procedures of corporate democracy."

Those reasons are sufficient to reject this shareholder-protection interest; and, moreover, the statute is both underinclusive and overinclusive. As to the first, if Congress had been seeking to protect dissenting shareholders, it would not have banned corporate speech in only certain media within 30 or 60 days before an election. A dissenting shareholder's interests would be implicated by speech in any media at any time. As to the second, the statute is overinclusive because it covers all corporations, including nonprofit corporations and for-profit corporations with only single shareholders. As to other corporations, the remedy is not to restrict speech but to consider and explore other regulatory mechanisms. The regulatory mechanism here, based on speech, contravenes the First Amendment.

[441b] is not limited to corporations or associations that were created in foreign countries or funded predominately by foreign shareholders. Section 441b therefore would be overbroad even if we assumed, arguendo, that the Government has a compelling interest in limiting foreign influence over our political process.

Austin is overruled, [thus] "effectively invalidat[ing] not only BCRA Section 203, but also 441b's prohibition on the use of corporate treasury funds for express advocacy." Section 441b's restrictions on corporate independent expenditures are therefore invalid and cannot be applied to *Hillary*.

Given our conclusion we are further required to overrule the part of *McConnell* that upheld BCRA § 203's extension of § 441b's restrictions on corporate independent expenditures. * * *

JUSTICE STEVENS, with whom JUSTICE GINSBURG, JUSTICE BREYER, and JUSTICE SOTOMAYOR join, concurring in part and dissenting in part.

Pervading the Court's analysis is the ominous image of a "categorical ba[n]" on corporate speech. [But our] cases have repeatedly pointed out that, "[c]ontrary to the [majority's] critical assumptions," the statutes upheld in *Austin* and *McConnell* do "not impose an *absolute* ban on all forms of corporate political spending." For starters, both statutes provide exemptions for PACs, separate segregated funds established by a corporation for political purposes. "The ability to form and administer separate segregated funds," we observed in *McConnell,* "has provided corporations and unions with a constitutionally sufficient opportunity to engage in express advocacy. That has been this Court's unanimous view."

A significant and growing number of corporations avail themselves of this option; during the most recent election cycle, corporate and union PACs raised nearly a billion dollars. Administering a PAC entails some administrative burden, but so does complying with the disclaimer, disclosure, and reporting requirements that the Court today upholds, and no one has suggested that the burden is severe for a sophisticated for-profit corporation. To the extent the majority is worried about this issue, it is important to keep in mind that we have no record to show how substantial the burden really is, just the majority's own unsupported factfinding.

The laws upheld in *Austin* and *McConnell* leave open many additional avenues for corporations' political speech. Consider the statutory provision we are ostensibly evaluating in this case, BCRA § 203. It has no application to genuine issue advertising—a category of corporate speech Congress found to be far more substantial than election-related advertising or to Internet, telephone, and print advocacy. [It] also allows corporations to spend unlimited sums on political communications with their executives and shareholders, to fund additional PAC activity through trade associations, to distribute voting guides and voting records, to underwrite voter registration and voter turnout activities, to host fundraising events for candidates within certain limits, and to publicly endorse candidates through a press release and press conference. * * *

In many ways, then, § 203 functions as a source restriction or a time, place, and manner restriction. It applies in a viewpoint-neutral fashion to a narrow subset of advocacy messages about clearly identified candidates for federal office, made during discrete time periods through discrete channels. In the case at hand, all Citizens United needed to do to broadcast *Hillary* right before the primary was to abjure business contributions or use the funds in its PAC, which by its own account is "one of the most active conservative PACs in America."

[Laws] such as § 203 target a class of communications that is especially likely to corrupt the political process, that is at least one degree removed from the views of individual citizens, and that may not even reflect the views of those who pay for it. Such laws burden political speech, and that is always a serious matter, demanding careful scrutiny. But the majority's incessant talk of a "ban" aims at a straw man. * * *

The second pillar of the Court's opinion is its assertion that "the Government cannot restrict political speech based on the speaker's . . . identity." [Yet] in a variety of contexts, we have held that speech can be regulated differentially on account of the speaker's identity, when identity is understood in categorical or institutional terms. The Government routinely places special restrictions on the speech rights of students, prisoners, members of the Armed Forces, foreigners, and its own employees. When such restrictions are justified by a legitimate governmental interest, they do not necessarily raise constitutional problems. [T]he Court, of course, is right that the First Amendment closely guards political speech. But in [the election] context, too, the authority of legislatures to enact viewpoint-neutral regulations based on content and identity is well settled. We have, for example, allowed state-run broadcasters to exclude independent candidates from televised debates. We have upheld statutes that prohibit the distribution or display of campaign materials near a polling place. Although we have not reviewed them directly, we have never cast doubt on laws that place special restrictions on campaign spending by foreign nationals. And we have consistently approved laws that bar Government employees, but not others, from contributing to or participating in political [activities].

* * * Undergirding the majority's approach to the merits is the claim that the only "sufficiently important governmental interest in preventing corruption or the appearance of corruption" is one that is "limited to quid pro quo corruption." [On] numerous occasions we have recognized Congress' legitimate interest in preventing the money that is spent on elections from exerting an "undue influence on an officeholder's judgment" and from creating "the appearance of such influence," beyond the sphere of quid pro quo relationships. Corruption can take many forms. Bribery may be the paradigm case. But the difference between selling a vote and selling access is a matter of degree, not kind. And selling access is not qualitatively different from giving special preference to those who spent money on one's behalf. Corruption operates along a spectrum, and the majority's apparent belief that quid pro quo arrangements can be neatly demarcated from other improper influences does not accord with the theory or reality of politics. It certainly does not accord with the record Congress developed in passing BCRA, a record that stands as a remarkable testament to the energy and ingenuity with which corporations, unions, lobbyists, and politicians may go about scratching each other's backs-and which amply supported Congress' determination to target a limited set of especially destructive practices.

Stevens, J., then quoted the district court: "The factual findings of the Court illustrate that corporations and labor unions routinely notify Members of Congress as soon as they air electioneering communications relevant to the Members' elections. The record also indicates that Members express appreciation to organizations for the airing of these election-related advertisements. Indeed, Members of Congress are particularly grateful when negative issue advertisements are run by these organizations, leaving the candidates free to run positive advertisements and be seen as 'above the fray.' Political consultants testify that campaigns are quite aware of who is running advertisements on the candidate's behalf, when they are being run, and where they are being run. Likewise, a prominent lobbyist testifies that these organizations use issue advocacy as a means to influence various Members of Congress. [Finally], a large majority of Americans (80%) are of the view that corporations and other organizations that engage in electioneering communications, which benefit specific elected officials, receive special consideration from those officials when matters arise that affect these corporations and organizations."

[When] private interests are seen to exert outsized control over officeholders solely on account of the money spent on (or withheld from) their campaigns, the result can depart so thoroughly "from what is pure or correct" in the conduct of Government that it amounts to a "subversion [of] the electoral process." [Starting] today, corporations with large war chests to deploy on electioneering may find democratically elected bodies becoming much more attuned to their interests. * * *

The fact that corporations are different from human beings might seem to need no elaboration, except that the majority opinion almost completely elides it. *Austin* set forth some of the basic differences. Unlike natural persons, corporations have "limited liability" for their owners and managers, "perpetual life," separation of ownership and control, "and favorable treatment of the accumulation and distribution of assets [that] enhance their ability to attract capital and to deploy their resources in ways that maximize the return on their shareholders' investments." [It] might also be added that corporations have no consciences, no beliefs, no feelings, no thoughts, no desires. Corporations help structure and facilitate the activities of human beings, to be sure, and their "personhood" often serves as a useful legal fiction. But they are not themselves members of "We the People" by whom and for whom our Constitution was established. * * *

It is an interesting question "who" is even speaking when a business corporation places an advertisement that endorses or attacks a particular candidate. Presumably it is not the customers or employees, who typically have no say in such matters. It cannot realistically be said to be the shareholders, who tend to be far removed from the day-to-day decisions of the firm and whose political preferences may be opaque to management. Perhaps the officers or directors of the corporation have the best claim to be the ones speaking, except their fiduciary duties generally prohibit them from using corporate funds for personal ends. * * *

In critiquing *Austin's* antidistortion rationale and campaign finance regulation more generally, our colleagues place tremendous weight on the example of media corporations. Yet it is not at all clear that *Austin* would permit § 203 to be applied to them. The press plays a unique role not only in the text, history, and structure of the First Amendment but also in facilitating public discourse * * *. Our colleagues have raised some interesting and difficult questions about Congress' authority to regulate electioneering by the press, and about how to define what constitutes the press. *But that is not the case before us.* Section 203 does not apply to media corporations, and even if it did, Citizens United is not a media corporation. * * *

Interwoven with *Austin's* concern to protect the integrity of the electoral process is a concern to protect the rights of shareholders from a kind of coerced speech: electioneering expenditures that do not "reflec[t] [their] support." When corporations use general treasury funds to praise or attack a particular candidate for office, it is the shareholders, as the residual claimants, who are effectively footing the bill. Those shareholders who disagree with the corporation's electoral message may find their financial investments being used to undermine their political convictions.

The PAC mechanism, by contrast, helps assure that those who pay for an electioneering communication actually support its content and that managers do not use general treasuries to advance personal agendas. [The] shareholder protection rationale has been criticized as underinclusive, in that corporations also spend money on lobbying and charitable contributions in ways that any particular shareholder might disapprove. But those expenditures do not implicate the selection of public officials, an area in which "the interests of unwilling ... corporate shareholders [in not being] forced to subsidize that speech" "are at their zenith." And in any event, the question is whether shareholder protection provides a basis for regulating expenditures in the weeks before an election, not whether additional types of corporate communications might similarly be conditioned on voluntariness.

Recognizing the limits of the shareholder protection rationale, the *Austin* Court did not hold it out as an adequate and independent ground for sustaining the statute in question. Rather, the Court applied it to reinforce the antidistortion rationale, in two main ways. First, the problem of dissenting shareholders shows that even if electioneering expenditures can advance the political views of some members of a corporation, they will often compromise the views of others. Second, it provides an additional reason, beyond the distinctive legal attributes of the corporate form, for doubting that these "expenditures reflect actual public support for the political ideas espoused." * * *

While American democracy is imperfect, few outside the majority of this Court would have thought its flaws included a dearth of corporate money in politics.

Soft money. *Citizens United* reopens a loophole that the Bipartisan Campaign Reform Act [BCRA] sought to close. But the same Act sought to close another loophole as well. As interpreted, the Federal Election Campaign Act of 1971 ("FECA") distinguishes between hard and soft money. Hard money is contributed money that falls under the specified contribution limits and complies with certain source limitations. Soft money encompasses contributions not subject to those restrictions which are for the most part ostensibly designed to encourage party-building activities benefitting the political parties in general, but not specific candidates. Under FECA, as interpreted, however, wealthy donors were able to use soft money directly or indirectly in ways that benefited federal candidates.

BRCA sought to close the soft money loophole. It forbids national party committees from soliciting, receiving, or directing the use of soft-money; prohibits state and local party committees from using soft money (although it permits their use of hard money and some additional funding) for activities affecting federal elections, including voter registration activity during the 120 days before a federal election, and get-out-the-vote drives conducted in connection with an election in which a federal candidate appears on the ballot; forbids the use of soft money by state and local party committees or state and local candidates and officeholders for any public communication that supports or attacks a federal candidate, whether or not the communication specifically asks for a vote for or against a particular candidate.

McCONNELL v. FEC, 540 U.S. 93 (2003), per STEVENS and O'CONNOR, JJ., joined by Souter, Ginsburg and Breyer, JJ. (the "Joint Opinion"), upheld the soft money provisions of the Act against a facial constitutional challenge: "Of the two major parties' total spending, soft money accounted for 5% ($21.6 million) in 1984, 11% ($45 million) in 1988, 16% ($80 million) in 1992, 30% ($272 million) in 1996, and 42% ($498 million) in 2000. The national parties transferred large amounts of their soft money to the state parties, which were allowed to use a larger percentage of soft money to finance mixed-purpose activities under FEC rules. In the year 2000, for example, the national parties diverted $280 million—more than half of their soft money—to state parties.

"Many contributions of soft money were dramatically larger than the contributions of hard money permitted by FECA. For example, in 1996 the top five corporate soft-money donors gave, in total, more than $9 million in nonfederal funds to the two national party committees. In the most recent election cycle the political parties raised almost $300 million—60% of their total soft-money fundraising—from just 800 donors, each of which contributed a minimum of $120,000. Moreover, the largest corporate donors often made substantial contributions to both parties. Such practices corroborate evidence indicating that many corporate contributions were motivated by a desire for access to candidates and a fear of being placed at a disadvantage in the legislative process relative to other contributors, rather than by ideological support for the candidates and parties."

Despite the fact that many of the soft money restrictions regulated spending, the Joint Opinion concluded that the less than strict scrutiny applied to the contribution limits in *Buckley* and *Nixon v. Shrink Missouri Government PAC*, 528 U.S. 377 (2000), was appropriately applied to the soft money restrictions: "The relevant inquiry is whether the mechanism adopted to implement the contribution limit, or to prevent circumvention of that limit, burdens speech in a way that a direct restriction on the contribution itself would not. That is not the case here." Applying the *Buckley* contribution limits standard, it concluded that the soft money restrictions were "closely drawn to match the important governmental interests of preventing corruption and the appearance of corruption."

––––––––––

Wisconsin Right to Life, Inc., a non profit advocacy corporation, ran three broadcast ads from its treasury funds, which included contributions of $50,000 from business corporations, for the ads. Wisconsin Right to Life had previously campaigned against Senator Feingold, and one of its concerns was his support of filibustering of judicial nominees. The ads spoke out against filibustering and asked citizens to contact Senators Feingold and McCain without referring to Feingold's position on the issue (though his position was well known in Wisconsin). The ads appeared to violate BCRA § 203.

FEC v. WISCONSIN RIGHT TO LIFE, INC., 551 U.S. 449 (2007), per ROBERTS, C.J., joined only by Alito, J., concluded that § 203 was constitutional only as applied to ads that are "susceptible of no reasonable interpretation other than as an appeal to vote for or against a specific candidate." Because of the importance of political speech, any doubt on the matter was to be resolved in favor of the ads. Neither the intent nor the effect of the ads counted in the determination. Roberts, C.J., found Wisconsin Right to Life's ads to be protected under the First Amendment.

SOUTER, J., joined by Stevens, Ginsburg, and Breyer, JJ., dissenting, found it hard to imagine that the majority would ever find an ad unprotected unless it contained words of express advocacy.

Judicial elections. In most but not all American states, judges are elected. When judges are running for election or re-election, do the principles of *Buckley v. Valeo, Citizens United*, and most of the other campaign finance cases discussed above apply in the same way that they apply to legislative and executive elections? In WILLIAMS-YULEE v. FLORIDA BAR, 575 U.S. 433 (2015), a sharply and intricately divided 5–4 Court, per ROBERTS, C.J., on most of the issues, said "no," concluding that concerns with judicial integrity upheld restrictions on solicitation of campaign funds by judges, restrictions that would have been invalidated on First Amendment grounds with respect to candidates for non-judicial offices.

CHAPTER 8

FREEDOM OF RELIGION

■ ■ ■

This chapter concerns the "Religion Clauses" of the First Amendment, respectively the "Establishment Clause" (forbidding laws "respecting an establishment of religion") and the "Free Exercise Clause" (forbidding laws "prohibiting the free exercise thereof"). It is difficult to explore either clause in isolation from the other. The extent to which the clauses interact may be illustrated by the matter of public financial aid to parochial schools, Sec. 1, II. On one hand, does public financial support for religious education violate the Establishment Clause? On the other, does a state's failure to provide such aid when it provides aid for other forms of education violate the Free Exercise Clause? Another example of the potential conflict between the clauses—also considered in the materials below—is whether, on one hand, a state's exemption of church buildings from property taxes contravenes the Establishment Clause or whether, on the other, a state's taxing these buildings contravenes the Free Exercise Clause.

1. THE ESTABLISHMENT CLAUSE

I. INTRODUCTION

Many authorities view the Establishment Clause as seeking to assure some form of separation of church and state in a nation that has become characterized by religious pluralism. Prior to 1947, only two decisions concerning the Establishment Clause produced any significant consideration by the Court. *Bradfield v. Roberts*, 175 U.S. 291 (1899), upheld federal appropriations to a hospital in the District of Columbia, operated by the Catholic Church, for ward construction and care of indigent patients. *Quick Bear v. Leupp*, 210 U.S. 50 (1908), upheld federal disbursement of funds, held in trust for the Sioux Indians, to Catholic schools designated by the Sioux for payment of tuition costs.

In the Court's first modern decision, *Everson v. Board of Educ.* (1947), Part II infra, Rutledge, J., observed that "no provision of the Constitution is more closely tied to or given content by its generating history than the religious clause of the First Amendment." Black, J., writing for the majority, recounted that the Religion Clauses "reflected in the minds of early Americans a vivid mental picture of conditions and practices which they fervently wished to stamp out in order to preserve liberty for themselves and for their posterity." Black, J., detailed the history of religious persecution in Europe "before and contemporaneous with the colonization of America" and the "repetition of many of the old world practices" in the colonies. For example, in Massachusetts, Quakers, Baptists, and other religious minorities suffered harshly and were taxed for the state's established Congregational Church. In 1776, the Maryland Declaration of Rights stated that "only persons professing the Christian religion" were entitled to religious freedom, and not until 1826 were Jews permitted to hold public office. The South Carolina Constitution of 1778 stated that "the Christian Protestant religion shall be [the] established religion of this state." Black, J., explained that "abhorrence" of these practices "reached its dramatic climax in Virginia in 1785–86" when "Madison wrote his great Memorial and Remonstrance" against renewal of "Virginia's tax levy for support of the established church and the Virginia Assembly "enacted the famous 'Virginia Bill for Religious Liberty,'" originally written by Thomas Jefferson. [T]he provisions of the First Amendment, in the drafting and adoption of which Madison and Jefferson played such leading roles, had the same objective and were intended to provide the same protection against governmental intrusion on religious liberty as the Virginia statute."

Still, the specific historical record suggests that rather than disclosing any coherent intent of the Framers, those who influenced the framing of the First Amendment were animated by several distinct and sometimes conflicting goals. Thus, Jefferson once wrote that the integrity of government could be preserved only by erecting "a wall of separation" between church and state. A sharp division of authority was essential, in his view, to insulate the democratic process from ecclesiastical depredations and excursions. Madison shared this view, but also perceived church-state separation as benefiting religious institutions. Even more strongly, Roger Williams, one of the earliest colonial proponents of religious freedom, posited an evangelical theory of separation, believing it vital to protect the sanctity of the church's "garden" from the "wilderness" of the state. Finally, there is evidence that one purpose of the Establishment Clause was to protect the existing state-established churches from the newly ordained national government. (Indeed, although disestablishment was then well under way, it did not end until 1833, when Massachusetts finally relinquished official state support of Congregationalism).

The varied ideologies that prompted the founders do, however, disclose a dominant theme: constitutional status for the integrity of individual religious conscience. Moreover, in Virginia's Bill for Religious Liberty, a practice seen by many as anathema to religious freedom was forcing the people to support religion through compulsory taxation, although there was a division of opinion as to whether non-preferential aid to religion violated liberty of conscience.

A final matter involving the history of the Establishment Clause concerns *Everson*'s unanimous ruling that it was "made applicable to the states" by the Fourteenth Amendment.

II. AID TO RELIGION

EVERSON v. BOARD OF EDUC., 330 U.S. 1 (1947), involved one of the major areas of controversy under the Establishment Clause: public financial assistance to church-related institutions (mainly parochial schools). A New Jersey township reimbursed parents for the cost of sending their children "on regular buses operated by the public transportation system," to and from schools, including nonprofit private and parochial schools. The Court, per BLACK, J., rejected a municipal taxpayer's contention that payment for Catholic parochial school students violated the Establishment Clause:

"The 'establishment of religion' clause of the First Amendment means at least this: Neither a state nor the Federal Government can set up a church. Neither can pass laws which aid one religion, aid all religions, or prefer one religion over another. Neither can force nor influence a person to go to or to remain away from church against his will or force him to profess a belief or disbelief in any religion. No person can be punished for entertaining or professing religious beliefs or disbeliefs, for church attendance or non-attendance. No tax in any amount, large or small can be levied to support any religious activities or institutions, whatever they may be called, or whatever form they may adopt to teach or practice religion. Neither a state nor the Federal Government can, openly or secretly, participate in the affairs of any religious organizations or groups and vice versa. In the words of Jefferson, the clause against establishment of religion by law was intended to erect 'a wall of separation between Church and State.'

"We must [not invalidate the New Jersey statute] if it is within the state's constitutional power even though it approaches the verge of that power. New Jersey [cannot] contribute tax-raised funds to the support of an institution which teaches the tenets and faith of any church. On the other hand, other language of the amendment commands that New Jersey cannot hamper its citizens in the free exercise of their own religion. Consequently, it cannot exclude individual Catholics, Lutherans, Mohammedans, Baptists, Jews, Methodists, Non-believers, Presbyterians, or the members of any other faith, *because of their faith, or lack of it*, from receiving the benefits of public welfare legislation. While we do not mean to intimate that a state could not provide transportation only to children attending public schools, we must be careful, in protecting the citizens of New Jersey against state-established churches, to be sure that we do not inadvertently prohibit New Jersey from extending its general State law benefits to all its citizens without regard to their religious belief."

Noting that "the New Jersey legislature has decided that a public purpose will be served" by having children "ride in public buses to and from schools rather than run the risk of traffic and other hazards incident to walking or 'hitchhiking,' " the Court conceded "that children are helped to get to church schools. There is even a possibility that some of the children might not be sent to the church schools if the parents were compelled to pay their children's bus fares out of their own pockets when transportation to a public school would have been paid for by the State. [But] state-paid policemen, detailed to protect children going to and from church schools from the very real hazards of traffic, would serve much the same [purpose]. Similarly, parents might be reluctant to permit their children to attend schools which the state had cut off from such general government services as ordinary police and fire protection, connections for sewage disposal, public highways and sidewalks. Of course, cutting off church schools from these services, so separate and so indisputably marked off from the religious function, would make it far more difficult for the schools to operate. But such is obviously not the purpose of the First Amendment. That Amendment requires the state to be a neutral in its relations with groups of religious believers and non-believers; it does not require the state to be their adversary. * * *

"This Court has said that parents may, in the discharge of their duty under state compulsory education laws, send their children to a religious rather than a public school if the school meets the secular educational requirements which the state has power to impose. See *Pierce v. Society of Sisters*, [Ch. 7, Sec. 7, II]. It appears that these parochial schools meet New Jersey's requirements. The State contributes no money to the schools. [Its] legislation, as applied, does no more than provide a general program to help parents get their children, regardless of their religion, safely and expeditiously to and from accredited schools.

"The First Amendment has erected a wall between church and state. That wall must be kept high and impregnable. We could not approve the slightest breach. New Jersey has not breached it here."

RUTLEDGE, J., joined by Frankfurter, Jackson and Burton, JJ., filed the principal dissent, arguing that the statute aided children "in a substantial way to get the very thing which they are sent to the particular school to secure, namely, religious training and [teaching.] Commingling the religious with the secular teaching does not divest the whole of its religious permeation and emphasis or make them of minor part, if proportion were material. Indeed, on any other view, the constitutional prohibition always could be brought to naught by adding a modicum of the secular. [T]ransportation is [no] less essential to education, whether religious or secular, than payment for tuitions, for teachers' salaries, for buildings, equipment and necessary materials. [Now], as in Madison's time, not the amount but the principle of assessment is wrong.

" * * * Public money devoted to payment of religious costs, educational or other, brings the quest for more. It brings too the struggle of sect against sect for the larger share or for any. Here one by numbers alone will benefit most, there another. That is precisely the history of societies which have had an established religion and dissident groups. It is the very thing Jefferson and Madison experienced and sought to guard [against]. The dominating group will achieve the dominant benefit; or all will embroil the state in their dissensions. [Nor] is the case comparable to one of furnishing fire or police protection, or access to public highways. These things are matters of common right, part of the general need for safety. Certainly the fire department must not stand idly by while the church burns." [Jackson, J., joined by Frankfurter, J., also filed a dissent.]

––––––––––

The Court did not again confront the subject of aid to parochial schools for more than two decades. During the intervening years, however, the Court continued to develop its Establishment Clause rationale in cases involving other issues, emphasizing the "purpose and primary effect" of the challenged government action (see Part III infra).

WALZ v. TAX COMM'N, 397 U.S. 664 (1970), per BURGER, C.J., upheld state tax exemption for "property used exclusively for religious, educational or charitable purposes": The purpose "is neither the advancement nor the inhibition of religion; it is neither sponsorship nor hostility. [We] must also be sure that the end result— the effect—is not an excessive government entanglement with religion. The test is inescapably one of degree. * * * Elimination of exemption would tend to expand the involvement of government by giving rise to tax valuation of church property, tax liens, tax foreclosures, and the direct confrontations and conflicts that follow in the train of those legal processes.

"Granting tax exemptions to churches necessarily operates to afford an indirect economic benefit and also gives rise to some, but yet a lesser, involvement than taxing them. [Finally,] no one acquires a vested or protected right in violation of the Constitution by long use * * * . Yet an unbroken practice of according the exemption to churches [is] not something to be lightly cast aside."

Only DOUGLAS, J., dissented: "The financial support rendered here is to the church, the place of worship. A tax exemption is a subsidy."

––––––––––

"Neutrality" and "endorsement." TEXAS MONTHLY, INC. v. BULLOCK, 489 U.S. 1 (1989), held violative of the Establishment Clause a Texas sales tax exemption for books and "periodicals that are published or distributed by a religious faith and that consist wholly of writings promulgating the teaching of the faith." BRENNAN, J., joined by Marshall and Stevens, JJ., referred to several important themes in the Court's developing Establishment Clause doctrine: "[*Walz*] emphasized that the benefits derived by religious organizations flowed to a large number of nonreligious groups as [well]. However, when government directs a subsidy exclusively to religious organizations [that] either burdens nonbeneficiaries markedly or cannot reasonably be seen as removing a significant state-imposed deterrent to the free exercise of religion, as Texas has done, it 'provide[s] unjustifiable awards of assistance to religious organizations' and cannot but 'conve[y] a message of endorsement' to slighted members of the community. This is particularly true where, as here, the subsidy is targeted at writings that *promulgate* the teachings of religious faiths. [This] lacks a secular objective."

White, J., concurred on freedom of press grounds. Scalia, J., joined by Rehnquist, C.J., and Kennedy, J., dissented from Brennan, J.'s distinction of *Walz*.

LEMON v. KURTZMAN, 403 U.S. 602 (1971), per BURGER C.J., which invalidated state salary supplements to teachers of secular subjects in nonpublic schools, articulated a three-part test for judging Establishment Clause issues. This test remains frequently invoked by the lower courts and—as the materials that follow indicate—has never been overruled:

"First, the statute must have a secular legislative purpose; second, its principal or primary effect must be one that neither advances nor inhibits religion;" third, the statute must not foster "an excessive government entanglement with religion."

MITCHELL v. HELMS, 530 U.S. 793 (2000), involved a federal program that lends "secular, neutral and nonideological" educational materials (mainly for libraries and computers)—which may not "supplant funds from non-Federal sources"—to elementary and secondary schools, both public and private. THOMAS, J., joined by Rehnquist, C.J., and Scalia and Kennedy, JJ., upheld the program. [I]f the government, seeking to further some legitimate secular purpose, offers aid on the same terms, without regard to religion, to all who adequately further that purpose, then it is fair to say that any aid going to a religious recipient only has the effect of furthering that secular purpose. [The] religious nature of a recipient should not matter to the constitutional analysis, so long as the recipient adequately furthers the government's secular purpose. [T]he inquiry into the recipient's religious views required by a focus on whether a school is pervasively sectarian is not only unnecessary but also offensive. It is well established [that] courts should refrain from trolling through a person's or institution's religious beliefs * * * .

ZELMAN V. SIMMONS-HARRIS

536 U.S. 639, 122 S.Ct. 2460, 153 L.Ed.2d 604 (2002).

CHIEF JUSTICE REHNQUIST delivered the opinion of the Court.

* * * In 1995, a Federal District Court declared a "crisis of magnitude" and placed the entire Cleveland school district under state control. Shortly thereafter, the state auditor found that Cleveland's public schools [had] failed to meet any of the 18 state standards for minimal acceptable performance. [More] than two-thirds of high school students either dropped or failed out before graduation. [Of] those students who did graduate, few could read, write, or compute at levels comparable to their counterparts in other cities.

It is against this backdrop that Ohio enacted, among other initiatives, its Pilot Project Scholarship Program [which] provides financial assistance to families in any Ohio school district that is or has been "under federal court order requiring supervision" [and] Cleveland is the only Ohio school district to fall within that category.

[First,] the program provides tuition aid for students [to] attend a participating public or private school of their parent's choosing. Second, the program provides tutorial aid for students who choose to remain enrolled in public school. [Any] private school, whether religious or nonreligious, may participate in the tuition aid portion [so] long as the school is located within the boundaries of a covered district and meets statewide educational standards. Participating private schools must agree not to discriminate on the basis of race, religion, or ethnic background, or to "advocate or foster unlawful behavior or teach hatred of any person or group on the basis of race, ethnicity, national origin, or religion." Any public school located in a school district adjacent to the covered district may also participate [and is] eligible to receive a $2,250 tuition grant for each program student accepted in addition to the full amount of per-pupil state funding attributable to each additional student.

Tuition aid is distributed to parents according to financial need. Families with incomes below 200% of the poverty line are given priority [and] receive 90% of private school tuition up to $2,250. For these lowest-income families, participating private schools may not charge a parental co-payment greater than $250. For all other families, the program pays 75% of tuition costs, up to $1,875, with no co-payment cap. [If] parents choose a private school, checks are made payable to the parents who then endorse the checks over to the chosen school.

[In] the 1999–2000 school year, 56 private schools participated in the program, 46 (or 82%) of which had a religious affiliation. None of the public schools in districts adjacent to Cleveland have elected to participate. More than 3,700 students participated [most] of whom (96%) enrolled in religiously affiliated schools. Sixty percent of these students were from families at or below the poverty line. * * *

The program is part of a broader undertaking by the State to enhance the educational options of Cleveland's schoolchildren in response to the 1995 takeover. That undertaking includes programs governing community and magnet schools. Community schools are funded under state law but are run by their own school boards, not by local school districts. These schools enjoy academic independence to hire their own teachers and to determine their own curriculum. They can have no religious affiliation and are required to accept students by lottery. During the 1999–2000 school year, there were 10 start-up community schools in the Cleveland City School District with more than 1,900 students enrolled. For each child enrolled in a community school, the school receives state funding of $4,518, twice the funding a participating program school may receive.

Magnet schools are public schools operated by a local school board that emphasize a particular subject area, teaching method, or service to students. For each student enrolled in a magnet school, the school district receives $7,746, including state funding of $4,167, the same amount received per student enrolled at a traditional public school. As of 1999, parents in Cleveland were able to choose from among 23 magnet schools, which together enrolled more than 13,000 students in kindergarten through eighth grade. These schools provide specialized teaching methods, such as Montessori, or a particularized curriculum focus, such as foreign language, computers, or the arts.

[There] is no dispute that the program challenged here was enacted for the valid secular purpose of providing educational assistance to poor children in a demonstrably failing public school system. Thus, the question presented is whether the Ohio program nonetheless has the forbidden "effect" of advancing or inhibiting religion.

To answer that question, our decisions have drawn a consistent distinction between government programs that provide aid directly to religious schools, *Mitchell*; *Rosenberger v. University of Virginia*, 515 U.S. 819 (1995), and programs of true private choice, in which government aid reaches religious schools only as a result of the genuine and independent choices of private individuals. While our jurisprudence with respect to the constitutionality of direct aid programs has "changed significantly" over the past two decades, our jurisprudence with respect to true private choice programs has remained consistent and unbroken. Three times we have confronted Establishment Clause challenges to neutral government programs that provide aid directly to a broad class of individuals, who, in turn, direct the aid to religious schools or institutions of their own choosing. Three times we have rejected such challenges.

In *Mueller v. Allen* [supra], we rejected an Establishment Clause challenge to a Minnesota program authorizing tax deductions for various educational expenses, including private school tuition costs, even though the great majority of the program's beneficiaries (96%) were parents of children in religious schools. [In] *Witters v. Washington Dept. of Servs. for Blind*, 474 U.S. 481 (1986), we used identical reasoning to reject an Establishment Clause challenge to a vocational scholarship program that provided tuition aid to a student studying at a religious institution to become a pastor. [Finally,] in *Zobrest v. Catalina Foothills School Dist.*, 509 U.S. 1 (1993), we applied *Mueller* and *Witters* to reject an Establishment Clause challenge to a federal program that permitted sign-language interpreters to assist deaf children enrolled in religious schools. * * *

Mueller, *Witters*, and *Zobrest* thus make clear that where a government aid program is neutral with respect to religion, and provides assistance directly to a broad class of citizens who, in turn, direct government aid to religious schools wholly as a result of their own genuine and independent private choice, the program is not readily subject to challenge under the Establishment Clause. [The] incidental advancement of a religious mission, or the perceived endorsement of a religious message, is reasonably attributable to the individual recipient, not to the government, whose role ends with the disbursement of benefits [citing the opinions of the plurality and O'Connor, J., in *Mitchell*]. [It] is precisely for these reasons that we have never found a program of true private choice to offend the Establishment Clause.

We believe that the program challenged here is a program of true private choice. [It] is neutral in all respects toward religion. It is part of a general and multifaceted undertaking by the State of Ohio to provide educational opportunities to the children of a failed school district. It confers educational assistance directly to a broad class of individuals defined without reference to religion. [The] program permits the participation of *all* schools within the district, religious or nonreligious. Adjacent public schools also may participate and have a financial incentive to do so. [The] only preference stated anywhere in the program is a preference for low-income families* * * .

There are no "financial incentive[s]" that "ske[w]" the program toward religious schools. *Witters.* [The] program here in fact creates financial *dis*incentives for religious schools, with private schools receiving only half the government assistance given to community schools and one-third the assistance given to magnet schools. Adjacent public schools, should any choose to accept program students, are also eligible to receive two to three times the state funding of a private religious [school]. Parents that choose to participate in the scholarship program [in] a private school (religious or nonreligious) must copay a portion of the school's tuition. Families that choose a community school, magnet school, or traditional public school pay [nothing.] [Any] objective observer familiar with the full history and context of the Ohio program would reasonably view it as one aspect of a broader undertaking to assist poor children in failed schools, not as an endorsement of religious schooling in general.

There also is no evidence that the program fails to provide genuine opportunities for Cleveland parents to select secular educational options for their school-age children. Cleveland schoolchildren [may] remain in public school as before, remain in public school with publicly funded tutoring aid, obtain a scholarship and choose a religious school, obtain a scholarship and choose a nonreligious private school, enroll in a community school, or enroll in a magnet school. That 46 of the 56 private schools now participating in the program are religious schools does not condemn it as [t]he Establishment Clause question is whether Ohio is coercing parents into sending their children to religious schools, and that question must be answered by evaluating *all* options * * * .

Justice Souter speculates that because more private religious schools currently participate in the program, the program itself must somehow discourage the participation of private nonreligious schools. But Cleveland's preponderance of religiously affiliated private schools [is] a phenomenon common to many American cities. Indeed, by all accounts the program has captured a remarkable cross-section of private schools, religious and nonreligious. It is true that 82% of Cleveland's participating private schools are religious schools, but it is also true that 81% of private schools in Ohio are religious schools. To attribute constitutional significance to this figure, moreover, would lead to the absurd result that a neutral school-choice program might [be] constitutional in some States, such as Maine or Utah, where less than 45% of private schools are religious schools, but not in other States, such as Nebraska or Kansas, where over 90% of private schools are religious schools.

Respondents and Justice Souter claim [that] the fact that 96% of scholarship recipients have enrolled in religious schools [alone] proves parents lack genuine choice, even if no parent has ever said so. [This] was flatly rejected in *Mueller*. [The] constitutionality of a neutral educational aid program simply does not turn on whether and why, in a particular area, at a particular time, most private schools are run by religious organizations, or most recipients choose to use the aid at a religious school. As we said in *Mueller*, "[s]uch an approach would scarcely provide the certainty that this field stands in need of, nor can we perceive principled standards by which such statistical evidence might be evaluated." This point is aptly illustrated here. The 96% figure upon which respondents and Justice Souter rely discounts entirely (1) the more than 1,900 Cleveland children enrolled in alternative community schools, (2) the more than 13,000 children enrolled in alternative magnet schools, and (3) the more than 1,400 children enrolled in traditional public schools with tutorial assistance. Including some or all of these children in the denominator of children enrolled in nontraditional schools during the 1999–2000 school year drops the percentage enrolled in religious schools from 96% to under 20%. The 96% figure also represents but a snapshot of one particular school year. In the 1997–1998 school year, by contrast, only 78% of scholarship recipients attended religious schools. The difference was attributable to two private nonreligious schools that had accepted 15% of all scholarship students electing instead to register as community schools, in light of larger per-pupil funding for community schools and the uncertain future of the scholarship program generated by this litigation.* * *

Respondents finally claim that we should look to *Committee for Public Ed. & Religious Liberty v. Nyquist*, 413 U.S. 756 (1973) [involving a state partial tuition tax credit to parents who sent their children to nonpublic schools; for parents too poor to be liable for income taxes and therefore unable to benefit from a tax credit, the state gave an outright grant of up to fifty percent of tuition] to decide these cases. We disagree for two reasons. First, the program in *Nyquist* [was] "unmistakably to provide desired financial support for nonpublic, sectarian institutions." Its genesis, we said, was that private religious schools faced "increasingly grave fiscal problems." [It] provided tuition reimbursements designed explicitly to "offe[r] an incentive to parents to send their children to sectarian schools." Indeed, the program flatly prohibited the participation of any public school, or parent of any public school enrollee. Ohio's program shares none of these features. Second, [we] expressly reserved judgment with respect to "a case involving some form of public assistance (e.g., scholarships) made available generally without regard to the sectarian-nonsectarian, or public-nonpublic nature of the institution benefited." That, of course, is the very question now before us, and it has since been answered [in *Mueller*, *Witters*, and *Zobrest*].

The judgment of the Court of Appeals is reversed.

JUSTICE O'CONNOR, concurring. * * *

These cases are different from prior indirect aid cases in part because a significant portion of the funds appropriated for the voucher program reach religious schools without restrictions on the use of these funds. The share of public resources that reach religious schools is not, however, as significant as respondents suggest. [Even if] all voucher students came from low-income families and that each voucher student used up the entire $2,250 voucher, at most $8.2 million of public funds flowed to religious schools under the voucher program in 1999–2000. [This] is minor compared to the $114.8 million the State spent on students in the Cleveland magnet schools [alone, and] pales in comparison to the amount of funds that federal, state, and local governments already provide religious institutions. Religious organizations may qualify for exemptions from the federal corporate income tax, the corporate income tax in many States, and property taxes in all 50 States, and clergy qualify for a federal tax break on income used for housing expenses. In addition, the Federal Government provides [a] tax deduction for charitable contributions to qualified religious groups. Finally, the Federal Government and certain state governments provide tax credits for educational expenses, many of which are spent on education at religious schools [reducing] federal tax revenues by nearly $25 billion annually * * * .

JUSTICE SOUTER, with whom JUSTICE STEVENS, JUSTICE GINSBURG, and JUSTICE BREYER join, dissenting.

[In] Cleveland the overwhelming proportion of large appropriations for voucher money must be spent on religious schools if it is to be spent at all, and will be spent in amounts that cover almost all of tuition. The money will thus pay for eligible students' instruction not only in secular subjects but in religion as well, in schools that can fairly be characterized as founded to teach religious doctrine and to imbue teaching in all subjects with a religious dimension.* * *

The majority's statements of Establishment Clause doctrine cannot be appreciated without some historical perspective on the Court's announced limitations on government aid to religious education. [My] object here [is] to set out the broad doctrinal stages covered in the modern era, and to show that doctrinal bankruptcy has been reached today. [F]rom 1947 to 1968, the basic principle of no aid to religion through school benefits was unquestioned. Thereafter for some 15 years, the Court termed its efforts as attempts to draw a line against aid that would be divertible to support the religious, as distinct from the secular, activity of an institutional beneficiary. Then, starting in 1983, concern with divertibility was gradually lost in favor of approving aid in amounts unlikely to afford substantial benefits to religious schools, when offered evenhandedly without regard to a recipient's religious character, and when channeled to a religious institution only by the genuinely free choice of some private individual. Now, the three stages are succeeded by a fourth, in which the substantial character of government aid is held to have no constitutional significance, and the espoused criteria of neutrality in offering aid, and private choice in directing it, are shown to be nothing but examples of verbal formalism.

[Souter, J., began with *Everson* and continued with *Board of Educ. v. Allen*, 392 U.S. 236 (1968), upholding a program for lending state approved secular textbooks to all schoolchildren, including those attending church-related schools.] The Court relied [on] the theory that the in-kind aid could only be used for secular educational purposes, and found it relevant that "no funds or books are furnished [directly] to parochial schools, and the financial benefit is to parents and children, not to schools." * * *

Allen recognized the reality that "religious schools pursue two goals, religious instruction and secular education;" if state aid could be restricted to serve the second, it might be permissible under the Establishment Clause. But in the retrenchment that followed, the Court saw that the two educational functions were so intertwined in religious primary and secondary schools that aid to secular education could not readily be segregated, and the intrusive monitoring required to enforce the line itself raised Establishment Clause concerns about the entanglement of church and state. See *Lemon*. To avoid the entanglement, the Court's focus in the post-*Allen* cases was on the principle of divertibility. [The] greater the risk of diversion to religion (and the monitoring necessary to avoid it), the less legitimate the aid scheme was under the no-aid principle. On the one hand, the Court tried to be practical, and when the aid recipients were not so "pervasively sectarian" that their secular and religious functions were inextricably intertwined, the Court generally upheld aid earmarked for secular use. See, e.g., *Roemer v. Board of Public Works*, 426 U.S. 736 (1976); *Hunt v. McNair*, 413 U.S. 734 (1973); *Tilton v. Richardson*, 403 U.S. 672 (1971). But otherwise the principle of nondivertibility was enforced strictly, with its violation being presumed in most cases, even when state aid seemed secular on its face. Compare, e.g., *Levitt v. Committee for Public Ed. & Religious Liberty*, 413 U.S. 472 (1973) (striking down state program reimbursing private schools' administrative costs for teacher-prepared tests in compulsory secular subjects), with *Wolman* (upholding similar program using standardized tests [and] permitting state aid for diagnostic speech, hearing, and psychological testing).

The fact that the Court's suspicion of divertibility reflected a concern with the substance of the no-aid principle is apparent in its rejection of stratagems invented to dodge it. [The] *Nyquist* Court dismissed warranties of a "statistical guarantee," that the scheme provided at most 15% of the total cost of an education at a religious school which could presumably be matched to a secular 15% of a child's education at the school. And it rejected the idea that the path of state aid to religious schools might be dispositive: "[that] aid is disbursed to parents rather than to the schools is only one among many factors to be considered." The point was that "the effect of the aid is unmistakably to provide desired financial support for nonpublic, sectarian institutions." [The Court's object] had always been a realistic assessment of facts aimed at respecting the principle of no aid. [But] *Mueller* started down the road from realism to formalism. [If] public expenditure is still predominantly on public schools, then the majority's reasoning would find neutrality in a scheme of vouchers available for private tuition in districts with no secular private schools at all. "Neutrality" as the majority employs the term is, literally, verbal and nothing more. * * *

The majority addresses the issue of choice the same way [which] ignores the whole point of the choice test: it is a criterion for deciding whether indirect aid to a religious school is legitimate because it passes through private hands that can spend or use the aid in a secular school. [The] majority now has transformed this question about private choice in channeling aid into a question about selecting from examples of state spending (on education) including direct spending on magnet and community public schools that goes through no private hands and could never reach a religious school under any circumstance. [And] because it is unlikely that any participating private religious school will enroll more pupils than the generally available public system, it will be easy to generate numbers suggesting that aid to religion is not the significant intent or effect of the voucher scheme.* * *

If, contrary to the majority, we ask the right question about genuine choice to use the vouchers, the answer shows that something is influencing choices in a way that aims the money in a religious direction: * * * 96.6% of all voucher recipients go to religious schools, only 3.4% to nonreligious [ones.] One answer to these statistics, for example, which would be consistent with the genuine choice claimed to be operating, might be that 96.6% of families [choose] to educate their children in schools of their own religion. This would not, in my view, render the scheme constitutional, but it would speak to the majority's choice criterion. Evidence shows, however, that almost two out of three families [made] it clear they had not chosen the schools because they wished their children to be proselytized in a religion not their own, or in any religion, but because of educational opportunity.

Even so, [that] some 2,270 students chose to apply their vouchers to schools of other religions might be consistent with true choice if the students "chose" their religious schools over a wide array of private nonreligious options, or if it could be shown [that] Ohio's program had no effect on educational choices and thus no impermissible effect of advancing religious education. But both possibilities are contrary to fact. First, even if all existing nonreligious private schools in Cleveland were willing to accept large numbers of voucher students, [the] total enrollment at all nonreligious private schools in Cleveland for kindergarten through eighth grade is only 510 children, and there is no indication that these schools have many open seats. Second, the $2,500 cap that the program places on tuition for participating low-income pupils has the effect of curtailing the participation of nonreligious schools: "nonreligious schools with higher tuition (about $4,000) stated that they could afford to accommodate just a few voucher students." By comparison, the average tuition at participating Catholic schools in Cleveland in 1999–2000 was $1,592, almost $1,000 below the cap.

Of course, the obvious fix would be to increase the value of vouchers so that existing nonreligious private and non-Catholic religious schools would be able to enroll more voucher students, and to provide incentives for educators to create new such schools given that few presently exist. [But] it is simply unrealistic to [even approach] the statewide program for vocational and higher education in *Witters*. And to get to that hypothetical point would require that such massive financial support be made available to religion as to disserve every objective of the Establishment Clause even more than the present scheme does.

[P]ublic schools in adjacent districts hardly have a financial incentive to participate in the Ohio voucher program, and none has. [It] is entirely irrelevant that the State did not deliberately design the network of private schools for the sake of channeling money into religious institutions. The criterion is one of genuinely free choice on the part of the private individuals who choose, and a Hobson's choice is not a choice, whatever the reason for being Hobsonian. * * *

The scale of the aid to religious schools approved today is unprecedented. [In] paying for practically the full amount of tuition for thousands of qualifying students, the scholarships purchase everything that tuition purchases, be it instruction in math or indoctrination in faith. [T]he majority makes no pretense that substantial amounts of tax money are not systematically underwriting religious practice and indoctrination. [E]very objective underlying the prohibition of religious establishment is betrayed by this scheme. [The first objective is] respect for freedom of conscience. Jefferson described it as the idea that no one "shall be compelled [to] support any religious worship, place, or ministry whatsoever."

As for the second objective, to save religion from its own corruption, [a] condition of receiving government money under the program is that [the] school may not give admission preferences to children who are members of the patron faith. [In addition], a participating religious school may well be forbidden to choose a member of its own clergy to serve as teacher or principal over a layperson of a different religion claiming equal qualification for the job. Indeed, a separate condition that "[t]he school [not] teach hatred of any person or group on the basis [of] religion," could be understood (or subsequently broadened) to prohibit religions from teaching traditionally legitimate articles of faith as to the error, sinfulness, or ignorance of [others].

[T]here is no question that religious schools in Ohio are on the way to becoming bigger businesses with budgets enhanced to fit their new stream of tax-raised income. See, e.g., People for the American Way Foundation, A Painful Price 5, 9, 11 (Feb. 14, 2002) (of 91 schools participating in the Milwaukee program, 75 received voucher payments in excess of tuition, 61 of those were religious and averaged $185,000 worth of overpayment per school, justified in part to "raise low salaries"). [A] move in the Ohio State Senate [would] raise the current maximum value of a school voucher from $2,250 to the base amount of current state spending on each public school student ($4,814 for the 2001 fiscal year). Ohio, in fact, is merely replicating the experience in Wisconsin. [T]he odds are that increases in government aid will bring the threshold voucher amount closer to the tuition at even more expensive religious schools. * * *

JUSTICE BREYER, with whom JUSTICE STEVENS and JUSTICE SOUTER join, dissenting.

[T]he Court's 20th century Establishment Clause cases—both those limiting the practice of religion in public schools and those limiting the public funding of private religious education—focused directly upon social conflict, potentially created when government becomes involved in religious education. [The] Court appreciated the religious diversity of contemporary American society. [It] understood the Establishment Clause to prohibit (among other things) [favoring some religions at the expense of others]. Yet *how* did the Clause achieve that objective? Did it simply require the government to give each religion an equal chance to introduce religion into the primary schools? [T]he Court concluded that the Establishment Clause required "separation," in part because an "equal opportunity" approach was not workable. [D]id not history show that efforts to obtain equivalent funding for the private education of children whose parents did not hold popular religious beliefs only exacerbated religious strife? * * * America boasts more than 55 different religious groups and subgroups with a significant number of members. [I]f widely adopted, ["voucher programs"] may well provide billions of dollars. [Why] will different religions not become concerned about, and seek to influence, the criteria used to channel this money to religious schools? Why will they not want to examine the implementation of the programs that provide this money—to determine, for example, whether implementation has biased a program toward or against particular sects, or whether recipient religious schools are adequately fulfilling a program's criteria? If so, just how is the State to resolve the resulting controversies without provoking legitimate fears of the kinds of religious favoritism that, in so religiously diverse a Nation, threaten social dissension? * * *

I concede that the Establishment Clause currently permits States to channel various forms of assistance to religious schools, for example, transportation costs for students, computers, and secular texts. [V]oucher programs differ, however, in both *kind* and *degree* [because] they direct financing to a core function of the church: the teaching of religious truths to young [children]. History suggests, not that such private school teaching of religion is undesirable, but that *government funding* of this kind of religious endeavor is far more contentious than providing funding for secular textbooks, computers, vocational training, or even funding for adults who wish to obtain a college education at a religious university. [H]istory also shows that government involvement in religious primary education is far more divisive than state property tax exemptions for religious institutions or tax deductions for charitable contributions, both of which come far closer to exemplifying the neutrality that distinguishes, for example, fire protection on the one hand from direct monetary assistance on the other. [T]he "parental choice" aspect of the voucher [program] cannot help the taxpayer who does not want to finance the religious education of children. It will not always help the parent who may see little real choice between inadequate nonsectarian public education and adequate education at a school whose religious teachings are contrary to his own.

It will not satisfy religious minorities unable to participate because they are too few in number to support the creation of their own private schools. It will not satisfy groups whose religious beliefs preclude them from participating in a government-sponsored program, and who may well feel ignored as government funds primarily support the education of children in the doctrines of the dominant religions. And it does little to ameliorate the entanglement problems or the related problems of social division * * * .

III. RELIGION AND PUBLIC SCHOOLS

WALLACE V. JAFFREE
472 U.S. 38, 105 S.Ct. 2479, 86 L.Ed.2d 29 (1985).

JUSTICE STEVENS delivered the opinion of the Court.

[In 1978, Alabama enacted § 16–1–20 authorizing a one-minute period of silence in all public schools "for meditation"; in 1981, it enacted § 16–1–20.1 authorizing a period of silence "for meditation or voluntary prayer." Appellees] have not questioned the holding that § 16–1–20 is valid. Thus, the narrow question for decision [concerns § 16–1–20.1].

[T]he Court has [recognized] that the political interest in forestalling intolerance extends beyond intolerance among Christian sects—or even intolerance among "religions"—to encompass intolerance of the disbeliever and the uncertain. [Under *Lemon*,] even though a statute that is motivated in part by a religious purpose may satisfy the first criterion, [a] statute must be invalidated if it is entirely motivated by a purpose to advance religion. In applying the purpose test, it is appropriate to ask "whether government's actual purpose is to endorse or disapprove of religion." In this case, the answer to that question is dispositive. * * *

The sponsor of the bill that became § 16–1–20.1, Senator Donald Holmes, inserted into the legislative record—apparently without dissent—a statement indicating that the legislation was an "effort to return voluntary prayer" to the public schools. Later [in] District Court[,] he stated: "No, I did not have no other purpose in mind."[44] The State did not present evidence of *any* secular purpose. * * *

The legislative intent to return prayer to the public schools is, of course, quite different from merely protecting every student's right to engage in voluntary prayer during an appropriate moment of silence during the school day. The 1978 statute already protected that right, containing nothing that prevented any student from engaging in voluntary prayer during a silent minute of meditation. [The] legislature enacted § 16–1–20.1, despite the existence of § 16–1–20 for the sole purpose of expressing the State's endorsement of prayer activities for one

---

[44]   **[Ct's Note]** [The] evidence presented to the District Court elaborated on the express admission of the Governor of Alabama (then Fob James) that the enactment of § 16–1–20.1 was intended to "clarify [the State's] intent to have prayer as part of the daily classroom activity," and that the "expressed legislative purpose in enacting Section 16–1–20.1 (1981) was to 'return voluntary prayer to public schools.'"

minute at the beginning of each schoolday [as] a favored practice. Such an endorsement is not consistent with the established principle that the government must pursue a course of complete neutrality toward religion.

The importance of that principle does not permit us to treat this as an inconsequential case involving nothing more than a few words of symbolic speech on behalf of the political majority.[51] For whenever the State itself speaks on a religious subject, one of the questions [is] "whether the government intends to convey a message of endorsement or disapproval of religion." * * *

JUSTICE O'CONNOR concurring in the judgment.

* * * Although a distinct jurisprudence has enveloped each of [the Religion] Clauses, their common purpose is to secure religious liberty. [O]ur goal should be "to frame a principle for constitutional adjudication that is not only grounded in the history and language of the first amendment, but one that is also capable of consistent application to the relevant problems." Jesse H. Choper, *Religion in the Public Schools: A Proposed Constitutional Standard*, 47 Minn.L.Rev. 329 (1962). Last Term, I proposed a refinement of the *Lemon* test with this goal in mind. *Lynch v. Donnelly* (concurring opinion).

The *Lynch* concurrence suggested that the religious liberty protected by the Establishment Clause is infringed when the government makes adherence to religion relevant to a person's standing in the political community. Direct government action endorsing religion or a particular religious practice is invalid under this approach because it "sends a message to nonadherents that they are outsiders, not full members of the political community, and an accompanying message to adherents that they are insiders, favored members of the political community." [In] this country, church and state must necessarily operate within the same community. [Thus], it is inevitable that the secular interests of government and the religious interests of various sects and their adherents will frequently intersect, conflict, and combine. A statute that ostensibly promotes a secular interest often has an incidental or even a primary effect of helping or hindering a sectarian belief. Chaos would ensue if every such statute were invalid under the Establishment Clause. For example, the State could not criminalize murder for fear that it would thereby promote the Biblical command against killing.[1] The task for the Court is to sort out those statutes and government

---

51   **[Ct's Note]** As this Court stated in *Engel v. Vitale*, [infra]: "The Establishment Clause, unlike the Free Exercise Clause, does not depend upon any showing of direct governmental compulsion and is violated by the enactment of laws which establish an official religion whether those laws operate directly to coerce nonobserving individuals or not." Moreover, this Court has noted that "[w]hen the power, prestige and financial support of government is placed behind a particular religious belief, the indirect coercive pressure upon religious minorities to conform to the prevailing officially approved religion is plain." * * *

1   On this analysis, *McGowan v. Maryland*, 366 U.S. 420 (1961), per Warren, C.J., upheld Maryland's Sunday Closing Laws. Although "the original laws which dealt with Sunday labor were motivated by religious forces," the Court showed that secular emphases in language and interpretation had come about, that recent "legislation was supported by labor groups and trade associations," and that "secular justifications have been advanced for making Sunday a day of rest, a day when people may recover from the labors of the week just passed and may physically and

practices whose purpose and effect go against the grain of religious liberty protected by the First Amendment.

The endorsement test [precludes] government from conveying or attempting to convey a message that religion or a particular religious belief is favored or preferred. Such an endorsement infringes the religious liberty of the nonadherent * * * .

Twenty-five states permit or require public school teachers to have students observe [a] moment of silence at the beginning of the schoolday during which students may meditate, pray, or reflect on the activities of the day. * * * Relying on this Court's decisions disapproving vocal prayer and Bible reading in the public schools, see *School Dist. v. Schempp*, 374 U.S. 203 (1963); *Engel v. Vitale*, 370 U.S. 421 (1962), the courts that have struck down the moment of silence statutes generally conclude that their purpose and effect are to encourage prayer in public schools.

The *Engel* and *Schempp* decisions are not dispositive. [In] *Engel*, a New York statute required teachers to lead their classes in a vocal prayer.[2] The Court concluded that "it is no part of the business of government to compose official prayers for any group of the American people to recite as part of a religious program carried on by the government." In *Schempp*, the Court addressed Pennsylvania and Maryland statutes that authorized morning Bible readings in public schools.[3] The Court reviewed the purpose and effect of the statutes, concluded that they required religious exercises, and therefore found them to violate the Establishment Clause. Under all of these statutes, a student who did not share the religious beliefs expressed in the course of the exercise was left with the choice of participating, thereby compromising the nonadherent's beliefs, or withdrawing, thereby calling attention to his or her nonconformity. The decisions acknowledged the coercion implicit under the statutory schemes, see *Engel*, but they expressly turned only on the fact that the government was sponsoring a manifestly religious exercise.

A state-sponsored moment of silence in the public schools is different from state-sponsored vocal prayer or Bible reading. First, a moment of silence, [unlike] prayer or Bible reading, need not be associated with a religious exercise. Second, [d]uring a moment of silence, a student who objects to prayer is left to his or her own thoughts, and is not compelled to listen to the prayers or thoughts of others.

---

mentally prepare for the week's work to come. [It] would seem unrealistic for enforcement purposes and perhaps detrimental to the general welfare to require a State to choose a common day of rest other than that which most persons would select of their own accord."

[2] The prayer, composed by the N.Y. Board of Regents, provided: "Almighty God, we acknowledge our dependence upon Thee, and we beg Thy blessings upon us, our parents, our teachers and our country."

[3] Reading the Bible, without comment, was followed by recitation of the Lord's Prayer. In Pennsylvania, various students read passages they selected from any version of the Bible. Plaintiff father testified that "specific religious doctrines purveyed by a literal reading of the Bible" were contrary to the family's Unitarian religious beliefs; one expert testified that "portions of the New Testament were offensive to Jewish tradition" and, if "read without explanation, they could [be] psychologically harmful to the child and had caused a divisive force within the social media of the school"; a defense expert testified "that the Bible [was] non-sectarian within the Christian faiths."

[It] is difficult to discern a serious threat to religious liberty from a room of silent, thoughtful school children.

[E]ven if a statute specifies that a student may choose to pray silently during a quiet moment, [it] is also possible that a moment of silence statute, either as drafted or as actually implemented, could effectively favor the child who prays over the child who does not. For example, the message of endorsement would seem inescapable if the teacher exhorts children to use the designated time to pray. Similarly, the fact of the statute or its legislative history may clearly establish that it seeks to encourage or promote voluntary prayer over other alternatives. [The] crucial question is whether the State has conveyed or attempted to convey the message that children should use the moment of silence for prayer. This question [requires] courts to examine the history, language, and administration of a particular statute to determine whether it operates as an endorsement of religion.

[T]he inquiry into the purpose of the legislature in enacting a moment of silence law should be deferential and limited. [If] a legislature expresses a plausible secular purpose for a moment of silence statute in either the text or the legislative history, or if the statute disclaims an intent to encourage prayer over alternatives during a moment of silence, then courts should generally defer to that stated intent. It is particularly troublesome to denigrate an expressed secular purpose due to postenactment testimony by particular legislators or by interested persons who witnessed the drafting of the statute. Even if the text and official history of a statute express no secular purpose, the statute should be held to have an improper purpose only if it is beyond purview that endorsement of religion or a religious belief "was and is the law's reason for existence." *Epperson v. Arkansas*, [note 3(b) infra. * * *

[It is] possible that a legislature will enunciate a sham secular purpose for a statute. I have little doubt that our courts are capable of distinguishing a sham secular purpose from a sincere one, or that the *Lemon* inquiry into the effect of an enactment would help decide those close cases where the validity of an expressed secular purpose is in doubt. [The] issue is whether an objective observer, acquainted with the text, legislative history, and implementation of the statute, would perceive it as a state endorsement of prayer in public schools. [However] deferentially one examines its text and legislative history, [the] conclusion is unavoidable that the purpose of [§ 16–1–20.1] is to endorse prayer in public schools.* * *

CHIEF JUSTICE BURGER dissenting.

* * * Today's decision recalls the observations of Justice Goldberg: "[U]ntutored devotion to the concept of neutrality can lead [to] results which partake not simply of that noninterference and noninvolvement with the religious which the Constitution commands, but of a brooding and pervasive dedication to the secular and a passive, or even active, hostility to the religious. Such results are not only not compelled by the Constitution, but, it seems to me, are prohibited by it." *Schempp* (concurring opinion). * * *

Curiously, the opinions do not mention that *all* of the sponsor's statements relied upon—including the statement "inserted" into the Senate Journal—were made *after* the legislature had passed the statute; [there] is not a shred of evidence that the legislature as a whole shared the sponsor's motive or that a majority in either house was even aware of the sponsor's view of the bill when it was passed. [T]he sponsor also testified that one of his purposes in drafting [the] moment-of-silence bill was to clear up a widespread misunderstanding that a schoolchild is legally *prohibited* from engaging in silent, individual prayer once he steps inside a public school building. That testimony is at least as important as the statements the Court relies upon, and surely that testimony manifests a permissible purpose. * * *

The several preceding opinions conclude that [the] sole purpose behind the inclusion of the phrase "or voluntary prayer" in § 16–1–20.1 was to endorse and promote prayer. This reasoning is simply a subtle way of focusing exclusively on the religious component of the statute rather than examining the statute as a whole. [It] would lead the Court to hold, for example, that a state may enact a statute that provides reimbursement for bus transportation to the parents of all schoolchildren, but may not *add* parents of parochial school students to an existing program providing reimbursement for parents of public school students.

* * * Without pressuring those who do not wish to pray, the statute simply creates an opportunity to think, to plan, or to pray if one wishes—as Congress does by providing chaplains and chapels. [If] the government may not accommodate religious needs when it does so in a wholly neutral and noncoercive manner, the "benevolent neutrality" that we have long considered the correct constitutional standard will quickly translate into the "callous indifference" that the Court has consistently held the Establishment Clause does not require. * * *

JUSTICE REHNQUIST, dissenting.

[There] is simply no historical foundation for the proposition that the Framers intended to build the "wall of separation" that was constitutionalized in *Everson*. [And the "purpose and effect" tests] are in no way based on either the language or intent of the drafters. [If] the purpose prong is intended to void those aids to sectarian institutions accompanied by a stated legislative purpose to aid religion, the prong will condemn nothing so long as the legislature utters a secular purpose and says nothing about aiding religion. [I]f the purpose prong is aimed to void all statutes enacted with the intent to aid sectarian institutions, whether stated or not, then most statutes providing any aid, such as textbooks or bus rides for sectarian school children, will fail because one of the purposes behind every statute, whether stated or not, is to aid the target of its largesse. * * *

If a constitutional theory has no basis in the history of the amendment it seeks to interpret, is difficult to apply and yields unprincipled results, I see little use in it. [It] would come as much of a shock to those who drafted the Bill of Rights as it will to a large number of thoughtful Americans today to learn that the Constitution [prohibits] the Alabama Legislature from "endorsing" prayer. George Washington himself, at the request of the very Congress which passed the Bill of Rights, proclaimed a day of "public thanksgiving and prayer, to be observed by acknowledging with grateful hearts the many and signal favors of Almighty God." History must judge whether it was the Father of his Country in 1789, [or] the Court today, which has strayed from the meaning of the Establishment Clause. * * *

NOTES AND QUESTIONS

1. **Released time.** (a) McCOLLUM v. BOARD OF EDUC., 333 U.S. 203 (1948), per BLACK, J., held that a public school released time program violated the Establishment Clause. Privately employed religious teachers held weekly classes, on public school premises, in their respective religions, for students whose parents signed request cards, while non-attending students pursued secular studies in other parts of the building: "[N]ot only are the state's tax-supported public school buildings used for the dissemination of religious doctrines. The State also affords sectarian groups an invaluable aid in that it helps to provide pupils for their religious classes through use of the state's compulsory public school machinery."

(b) ZORACH v. CLAUSON, 343 U.S. 306 (1952), per DOUGLAS, J., upheld a released time program when the religious classes were held in church buildings: Unlike *McCollum*, "[t]his involves neither religious instruction in public school classrooms nor the expenditure of public funds. All costs, including the application blanks, are paid by the religious organizations. [N]ullification of this law would have wide and profound effects. A Catholic student applies to his teacher for permission to leave the school during hours on a Holy Day of Obligation to attend a mass. A Jewish student asks his teacher for permission to be excused for Yom Kippur. A Protestant wants the afternoon off for a family baptismal ceremony. In each case the teacher requires parental consent in writing [and] to make sure the student is not a truant, goes further and requires a report from the priest, the rabbi, or the minister. The teacher in other words cooperates in a religious program to the extent of making it possible for her students to participate in it. Whether she does it occasionally for a few students, regularly for one, or pursuant to a systematized program designed to further the religious needs of all the students does not alter the character of the act.

"We are a religious people whose institutions presuppose a Supreme Being. [When] the state encourages religious instruction or cooperates [by] adjusting the schedule of public events to sectarian needs, [it] respects the religious nature of our people and accommodates the public service to their spiritual needs. To hold that it may not would [be] preferring those who believe in no religion over those who do believe. [The] problem, like many problems in constitutional law, is one of degree."

2. **Secular purpose.** Several decisions, in addition to *Jaffree*, have invalidated public school practices because their "purpose" has been found to be "religious":

(a) STONE v. GRAHAM, 449 U.S. 39 (1980), per curiam, held that a Kentucky statute—requiring "the posting of a copy of the Ten Commandments, purchased with private contributions, on the wall of each public classroom in the State," with the notation at the bottom that "The secular application of the Ten Commandments is clearly seen in its adoption as the fundamental legal code of Western Civilization and the Common Law of the United States"—had "no secular legislative purpose": "The Ten Commandments is undeniably a sacred text in the Jewish and Christian faiths, and no legislative recitation of a supposed secular purpose can blind us to that [fact]. Posting of religious texts on the wall serves [no] educational function. If [they] are to have any effect at all, it will be to induce the school children to read, meditate upon, perhaps to venerate and obey, the Commandments. However desirable this might be as a matter of private devotion, it is not a permissible state objective under the Establishment Clause."[4]

(b)   EPPERSON v. ARKANSAS, 393 U.S. 97 (1968), per FORTAS, J., held that an "anti-evolution" statute, forbidding public school teachers "to teach the theory or doctrine that mankind ascended or descended from a lower order of animals," violated both religion clauses: "Arkansas' law selects from the body of knowledge a particular segment which it proscribes for the sole reason that it is deemed to conflict with a particular religious doctrine." Citing newspaper advertisements and letters supporting adoption of the statute in 1928, the Court found it "clear that fundamentalist sectarian conviction was and is the law's reason for existence.* * * Arkansas did not seek to excise from the curricula [all] discussion of the origin of man."

(c)   EDWARDS v. AGUILLARD, 482 U.S. 578 (1987), per BRENNAN, J., held that a Louisiana statute, barring "teaching of the theory of evolution in public schools unless accompanied by instruction in 'creation science,'" had "no clear secular purpose": "True, the Act's stated purpose is to protect academic freedom. [While] the Court is normally deferential to a State's articulation of a secular purpose, it is required that the statement of such purpose be sincere and not a sham. [It] is clear from the legislative history [that] requiring schools to teach creation science with evolution does not advance academic freedom. The Act does not grant teachers a flexibility that they did not already possess to supplement the present science curriculum with the presentation of theories, besides evolution, about the origin of life. [If] the Louisiana legislature's purpose was solely to maximize the comprehensiveness and effectiveness of science instruction, it would have encouraged the teaching of all scientific theories about the origins of humankind. But [the] legislative history documents that the Act's primary purpose was to change the science curriculum of public schools in order to provide persuasive advantage to a particular religious doctrine that rejects the factual basis of evolution in its entirety [and that] embodies the religious belief that a supernatural creator was responsible for the creation of humankind."

---

[4]   Rehnquist, J., dissented from "the Court's summary rejection of a secular purpose articulated by the legislature and confirmed by the state court." Stewart, J., also dissented. Burger, C.J., and Blackmun, J., dissented from not giving the case plenary consideration. For recent decisions on the Ten Commandments in public places, see Part IV infra.

SCALIA, J., joined by Rehnquist, C.J., dissented: "Even if I agreed with the questionable premise that legislation can be invalidated under the Establishment Clause on the basis of its motivation alone, without regard to its effects, I would still find no justification for today's decision. [The] Legislature explicitly set forth its secular purpose ('protecting academic freedom') [which] meant: *students'* freedom from *indoctrination*. The legislature wanted to ensure that students would be free to decide for themselves how life began, based upon a fair and balanced presentation of the scientific evidence. [It] is undoubtedly true that what prompted the Legislature [was] its awareness of the tension between evolution and the religious beliefs of many children. But [a] valid secular purpose is not rendered impermissible simply because its pursuit is prompted by concern for religious sensitivities."

3. ***Purpose, primary effect, and "neutrality."*** (a) BOARD OF EDUC. v. MERGENS, 496 U.S. 226 (1990), interpreted the federal Equal Access Act to apply to public secondary schools that (a) receive federal financial aid and (b) give official recognition to noncurriculum related student groups (e.g., chess club and scuba diving club in contrast to Latin club and math club) in such ways as allowing them to meet on school premises during noninstructional time. The Act prohibited these schools from discriminating against student groups "on the basis of the religious, political, philosophical, or other content of the speech at [their] meetings." O'CONNOR, J., joined by Rehnquist, C.J., and White and Blackmun, JJ., held that the Establishment Clause did not forbid Westside High School from including within its thirty recognized student groups a Christian club "to read and discuss the Bible, to have fellowship and to pray together."

(b)   GOOD NEWS CLUB v. MILFORD CENTRAL SCHOOL, 533 U.S. 98 (2001), per THOMAS, J., used similar analysis to find no Establishment Clause violation for a public school's permitting a Christian organization to use schoolrooms for weekly after school meetings, which involved religious instruction and worship, when the school allowed such use by other groups for "the moral and character development of children."

IV. OFFICIAL ACKNOWLEDGMENT OF RELIGION

ALLEGHENY COUNTY V. ACLU
492 U.S. 573, 109 S.Ct. 3086, 106 L.Ed.2d 472 (1989).

JUSTICE BLACKMUN announced the judgment of the Court and delivered the opinion of the Court with respect to Parts III-A, IV, and V, an opinion with respect to Parts I and II, in which JUSTICE O'CONNOR and JUSTICE STEVENS join, an opinion with respect to Part III-B, in which JUSTICE STEVENS joins, and an opinion with respect to Part VI.

This litigation concerns the constitutionality of two recurring holiday displays located on public property in downtown Pittsburgh. The first is a crèche placed on the Grand Staircase of the Allegheny County Courthouse. The second is a

Chanukah menorah placed just outside the City-County Building, next to a Christmas tree and a sign saluting liberty. * * *

I.A. [The] crèche [is] a visual representation of the scene in the manger in Bethlehem shortly after the birth of Jesus. [The] crèche includes [an] angel bearing a banner that proclaims "Gloria in Excelsis Deo!" A plaque stated it had been donated by the Holy Name Society.

[III.A.] Although "the myriad, subtle ways in which Establishment Clause values can be eroded," are not susceptible to a single verbal formulation, this Court has attempted to encapsulate the essential precepts. [Thus,] in *Everson*, the Court gave this often-repeated summary [stating the second ¶ on p. 1210 supra]. In *Lemon*, the Court sought to refine these principles by focusing on three "tests." [In] recent years, we have paid particularly close attention to whether the challenged governmental practice either has the purpose or effect of "endorsing" religion. [See] *Lynch* (O'Connor, J., concurring).

B. [In *Lynch*,] we considered whether the city of Pawtucket, R.I., had violated the Establishment Clause by including a crèche in its annual Christmas display, located in a private [park]. By a 5–4 decision[,] the Court [held] that the inclusion of the crèche did [not]. Justice O'Connor['s] concurrence [provides] a sound analytical framework for evaluating governmental use of religious symbols. First and foremost, [it recognizes] any endorsement of religion as "invalid," because it "sends a message to nonadherents that they are outsiders, not full members of the political community, and an accompanying message to adherents that they are insiders, favored members of the political community." Second, [it] articulates a method for determining whether the government's use of an object with religious meaning has the effect of endorsing religion[:] the question is "what viewers may fairly understand to be the purpose of the display." That inquiry, of necessity, turns upon the context in which the contested object appears: "a typical museum setting, though not neutralizing the religious content of a religious painting, negates any message of endorsement of that content." * * *

The concurrence applied this mode of analysis to the Pawtucket crèche, seen in the context of that city's holiday celebration as a whole. In addition to the crèche the city's display contained: a Santa Claus House with a live Santa distributing candy, reindeer pulling Santa's sleigh; a live 40-foot Christmas tree strung with lights; statues of carolers in old-fashioned dress; candy-striped poles; a "talking" wishing well; a large banner proclaiming "SEASONS GREETINGS"; a miniature "village" with several houses and a church, and various "cut-out" figures, including those of a clown, a dancing elephant, a robot, and a teddy bear. The concurrence concluded that both because the crèche is "a traditional symbol" of Christmas, a holiday with strong secular elements, and because the crèche was "displayed along with purely secular symbols," the crèche's setting "changes what viewers may fairly understand to be the purpose of the display" and "negates any message of endorsement" of "the Christian beliefs represented by the crèche."

[D]espite divergence at the bottom line, the five Justices in concurrence and dissent in *Lynch* agreed upon the relevant constitutional principles [which] have been adopted by the Court in subsequent cases. [*Grand Rapids.*]

IV.   We turn first to the county's crèche display. [U]nlike *Lynch*, nothing in the context of the display detracts from the crèche's religious message. [T]he crèche sits on the Grand Staircase, the "main" and "most beautiful part" of the building that is the seat of county government. No viewer could reasonably think that it occupies this location without the support and approval of the government [which] has chosen to celebrate Christmas in a way that has the effect of endorsing a patently Christian message: Glory to God for the birth of Jesus Christ. * * *

V.   Justice Kennedy and the three Justices who join [him] require a response in some depth:

A.   In *Marsh v. Chambers*, 463 U.S. 783 (1983) [upholding the practice of legislative prayer], the Court relied specifically on the fact that Congress authorized legislative prayer at the same time that it produced the Bill of Rights. Justice Kennedy, however, argues that *Marsh* legitimates all "practices with no greater potential for an establishment of religion" than those "accepted traditions dating back to the Founding." Otherwise, the Justice asserts, such practices as our national motto ("In God We Trust") and our Pledge of Allegiance (with the phrase "under God," added in 1954) are in danger of invalidity.

Our previous opinions have considered in dicta the motto and the pledge, characterizing them as consistent with the proposition that government may not communicate an endorsement of religious belief. We need not return to the subject of "ceremonial deism,"[5] because there is an obvious distinction between crèche displays and references to God in the motto and the pledge. However history may affect the constitutionality of nonsectarian references to religion by the government, history cannot legitimate practices that demonstrate the government's allegiance to a particular sect or creed. [The] history of this Nation, it is perhaps sad to say, contains numerous examples of official acts that endorsed Christianity specifically [but] this heritage of official discrimination against non-Christians has no place in the jurisprudence of the Establishment Clause. * * *

C.   Although Justice Kennedy repeatedly accuses the Court of harboring a "latent hostility" or "callous indifference" toward religion, nothing could be further from the truth. [The] government does not discriminate against any citizen on the basis of the citizen's religious faith if the government is secular in its functions and operations. On the contrary, the Constitution mandates that the government remain secular [in] order to avoid discriminating among citizens on the basis of

---

[5]   Brennan, J., joined by Marshall, Blackmun and Stevens, JJ., dissenting in *Lynch* "suggest[ed] that such practices as the designation of 'In God We Trust' as our national motto, or the references to God contained in the Pledge of Allegiance can best be understood [as] a form of 'ceremonial deism,' protected from Establishment Clause scrutiny chiefly because they have lost through rote repetition any significant religious content."

their religious faiths. [A] secular state establishes neither atheism nor religion as its official creed. * * *

VI. The display of the Chanukah menorah. [The] question for Establishment Clause purposes is whether the combined display of the tree, the sign, and the menorah has the effect of endorsing both Christian and Jewish faiths, or rather simply recognizes that both Christmas and Chanukah are part of the same winter-holiday season, which has attained a secular status in our society. Of the two interpretations of this particular display, the latter seems far more plausible * * * .

The Christmas tree, unlike the menorah, is not itself a religious symbol. [The] widely accepted view of the Christmas tree as the preeminent secular symbol of the Christmas holiday season serves to emphasize the secular component of the message communicated by other elements of an accompanying holiday display, including the Chanukah menorah. The tree, moreover, is clearly the predominant element in the city's display. The 45-foot tree occupies the central position [in] the City-County Building; the 18-foot menorah is positioned to one side. Given this configuration, it is much more sensible to interpret the meaning of the menorah in light of the tree, rather than vice versa. * * *

Although the city has used a symbol with religious meaning as its representation of Chanukah, this is not a case in which the city has reasonable alternatives that are less religious in nature. [Where] the government's secular message can be conveyed by two symbols, only one of which carries religious meaning, an observer reasonably might infer from the fact that the government has chosen to use the religious symbol that the government means to promote religious faith. See *Schempp* (Brennan, J., concurring) (Establishment Clause forbids use of religious means to serve secular ends when secular means suffice). But where, as here, no such choice has been made, this inference of endorsement is not present.

The Mayor's sign further diminishes the possibility that the tree and the menorah will be interpreted as a dual endorsement of Christianity and Judaism. The sign states that during the holiday season the city salutes liberty. Moreover, the sign draws upon the theme of light, common to both Chanukah and Christmas as winter festivals, and links that theme with this Nation's legacy of freedom, which allows an American to celebrate the holiday season in whatever way he wishes, religiously or otherwise. [While] an adjudication of the display's effect must take into account the perspective of one who is neither Christian nor Jewish, as well as of those who adhere to either of these religions, the constitutionality of its effect must also be judged according to the standard of a "reasonable observer." When measured against this standard, the menorah need not be excluded from this particular display.

The conclusion [here] does not foreclose the possibility that the display of the menorah might violate either the "purpose" or "entanglement" prong of the *Lemon* analysis. These issues [may] be considered [on] remand. * * *

JUSTICE KENNEDY, with whom THE CHIEF JUSTICE, JUSTICE WHITE, and JUSTICE SCALIA join, concurring in the judgment in part and dissenting in part. * * *

I.   In keeping with the usual fashion of recent years, the majority applies the *Lemon* [test]. Persuasive criticism of *Lemon* has emerged. Our cases often question its utility in providing concrete answers to Establishment Clause questions, calling it but a "helpful signpos[t]" or "guidelin[e]," to assist our deliberations rather than a comprehensive test. *Mueller;* see *Lynch* ("we have repeatedly emphasized our unwillingness to be confined to any single test or criterion in this sensitive area"). Substantial revision of our Establishment Clause doctrine may be in order; but it is unnecessary [for] even the *Lemon* test, when applied with proper sensitivity to our traditions and our caselaw, supports the conclusion that both the crèche and the menorah are permissible displays in the context of the holiday season.

[T]he Establishment Clause permits government some latitude in recognizing and accommodating the central role religion plays in our society. *Lynch; Walz.* Any approach less sensitive to our heritage would border on latent hostility toward religion, as it would require government in all its multifaceted roles to acknowledge only the secular. [A]s the modern administrative state expands to touch the lives of its citizens in such diverse ways and redirects their financial choices through programs of its own, it is difficult to maintain the fiction that requiring government to avoid all assistance to religion can in fairness be viewed as serving the goal of neutrality. [Our] cases disclose two limiting principles: government may not coerce anyone to support or participate in any religion or its exercise; and it may not [give] direct benefits to religion in such a degree that it in fact "establishes a [state] religion or religious faith, or tends to do so." *Lynch.* These two principles, while distinct, are not unrelated, for it would be difficult indeed to establish a religion without some measure of more or less subtle coercion, be it in the form of taxation to supply the substantial benefits that would sustain a state-established faith, direct compulsion to observance, or governmental exhortation to religiosity that amounts in fact to proselytizing.

[S]ome of our recent cases reject the view that coercion is the sole touchstone of an Establishment Clause violation. See *Engel* (dictum) [see fn. 53 in *Jaffree*]; *Schempp; Nyquist.* That may be true if by "coercion" is meant *direct* coercion in the classic sense of an establishment of religion that the Framers knew. But coercion need not be a direct tax in aid of religion or a test oath. Symbolic recognition or accommodation of religious faith may violate the Clause in an extreme case. I doubt not, for example, that the Clause forbids a city to permit the permanent erection of a large Latin cross on the roof of city hall. This is not because government speech about religion is per se suspect, as the majority would have it, but because such an obtrusive year-round religious display would place the government's weight behind an obvious effort to proselytize on behalf of a particular religion. Speech may coerce in some circumstances, but this does not justify a ban on all government recognition of religion. [Absent] coercion, the risk of infringement of religious liberty by passive or symbolic accommodation is minimal. [In] determining whether there exists an establishment, or a tendency toward one, we refer to the other types of church-state contacts that have existed unchallenged throughout our history, or that have been found permissible in our caselaw [discussing *Lynch* and *Marsh*].

II.   These principles are not difficult to apply to the facts of the case before us. [If] government is to participate in its citizens' celebration of a holiday that contains both a secular and a religious component, enforced recognition of only the secular aspect would signify the callous indifference toward religious faith[; the] government would be refusing to acknowledge [the] historical reality, that many of its citizens celebrate its religious aspects as well. * * *

There is no suggestion here that the government's power to coerce has been used to further the interests of Christianity or Judaism in any way. No one was compelled to observe or participate in any religious ceremony or activity. Neither the city nor the county contributed significant amounts of tax money to serve the cause of one religious faith. The crèche and the menorah are purely passive symbols of religious holidays. Passersby who disagree with the message conveyed by these displays are free to ignore them, or even to turn their [backs]. Whether the crèche be surrounded by poinsettias, talking wishing wells, or carolers, the conclusion remains the same, for the relevant context is not the items in the display itself but the season as a whole. * * *

[III.] [The endorsement test is a] most unwelcome, addition to our tangled Establishment Clause jurisprudence. [*Marsh*] stands for the proposition, not that specific practices common in 1791 are an exception to the otherwise broad sweep of the Establishment Clause, but rather that the meaning of the Clause is to be determined by reference to historical practices and understandings. Whatever test we choose to apply must permit not only legitimate practices two centuries old but also any other practices with no greater potential for an establishment of religion. [Few] can withstand scrutiny under a faithful application [the endorsement test].

Some examples suffice. [Since] the Founding of our Republic, American Presidents have issued Thanksgiving Proclamations establishing a national day of celebration and prayer [and] the forthrightly religious nature of these proclamations has not waned with the years. [It] requires little imagination to conclude that these proclamations would cause non-adherents to feel excluded.* * * .

The Executive has not been the only Branch of our Government to recognize the central role of religion in our society. [T]his Court opens its sessions with the request that "God save the United States and this honorable Court." [The] Legislature has gone much further, not only employing legislative chaplains, but also setting aside a special prayer room in the Capitol for use by Members of the House and Senate. The [room] depicts President Washington kneeling in prayer; around him is etched the first verse of the 16th Psalm: "Preserve me, O God, for in Thee do I put my trust." * * * Congress has directed the President to "set aside and proclaim a suitable day each year [as] a National Day of Prayer, on which the people of the United States may turn to God in prayer and meditation at churches, in groups, and as individuals." [Also] by statute, the Pledge of Allegiance to the Flag describes the United States as "one Nation under God." To be sure, no one is obligated to recite this phrase, see *West Virginia State Bd. of Educ. v. Barnette*, [Sec. 2, I infra] but it borders on sophistry to suggest that the " 'reasonable' " atheist would not feel less than a " 'full membe[r] of the political community' " every time his fellow Americans recited, as part of their expression of patriotism and love for country, a phrase he believed to be false. Likewise, our national motto, "In God we trust," which is prominently engraved in the wall above the Speaker's dias in the Chamber of the House of Representatives and is reproduced on every coin minted and every dollar printed by the Federal Government, must have the same effect.

If the intent of the Establishment Clause is to protect individuals from mere feelings of exclusion, then legislative prayer cannot escape invalidation. It has been argued that "[it serves] the legitimate secular purposes of solemnizing public occasions [in] society." *Lynch* (O'Connor, J., concurring). I fail to see why prayer is the only way to convey these messages; appeals to patriotism. [No] doubt prayer is "worthy of appreciation," but that is most assuredly not because it is secular. Even accepting the secular-solemnization explanation at face value, moreover, it seems incredible to suggest that the average observer of legislative prayer who either believes in no religion or whose faith rejects the concept of God would not receive the clear message that his faith is out of step with the political norm. * * *

[IV.] The case before us is admittedly a troubling one. It must be conceded that, however neutral the purpose of the city and county, the eager proselytizer may seek to use these symbols for his own ends [and] that some devout adherents of Judaism or Christianity may be as offended by the holiday display as are nonbelievers, if not more so. [For] these reasons, I might have voted against installation [were] I a local legislative official. But [the] principles of the Establishment Clause and our Nation's historic traditions of diversity and pluralism allow communities to make reasonable judgments respecting the accommodation or acknowledgment of holidays with both cultural and religious aspects. * * *

JUSTICE O'CONNOR with whom JUSTICE BRENNAN and JUSTICE STEVENS join as to Part II, concurring in part and concurring in the judgment. * * *

II.   * * * Justice Kennedy asserts that the endorsement test "is flawed in its fundamentals and unworkable in practice." * * *

An Establishment Clause standard that prohibits only "coercive" practices or overt efforts at government proselytization, but fails to take account of the numerous more subtle ways that government can show favoritism to particular beliefs or convey a message of disapproval to others, would [not] adequately protect the religious liberty or respect the religious diversity of the members of our pluralistic political community. Thus, this Court has never relied on coercion alone as the touchstone of Establishment Clause analysis. To require a showing of coercion, even indirect coercion, as an essential element of an Establishment Clause violation would make the Free Exercise Clause a redundancy. [Moreover,] as even Justice Kennedy recognizes, any Establishment Clause test limited to "*direct* coercion" clearly would fail to account for forms of "[s]ymbolic recognition or accommodation of religious faith" that may violate the Establishment Clause.

[To] be sure, the endorsement test depends on a sensitivity to the unique circumstances and context of a particular challenged practice and, like any test that is sensitive to context, it may not always yield results with unanimous agreement at the margins. But that is true of many standards in constitutional law, and even the modified coercion test offered by Justice Kennedy involves judgment and hard choices at the margin. He admits as much by acknowledging that the permanent display of a Latin cross at city hall would violate the Establishment Clause, as would the display of symbols of Christian holidays alone. Would the display of a Latin cross for six months have such an unconstitutional effect, or the display of the symbols of most Christian holidays and one Jewish holiday? Would the Christmas-time display of a crèche inside a courtroom be "coercive" if subpoenaed witnesses had no opportunity to "turn their backs" and walk away? Would displaying a crèche in front of a public school violate the Establishment Clause under Justice Kennedy's test? * * *

Justice Kennedy submits that the endorsement test [would] invalidate many traditional practices. [But] historical acceptance of a practice does not in itself validate that practice under the Establishment Clause if the practice violates the values protected by that Clause, just as historical acceptance of racial or gender based discrimination does not immunize such practices from scrutiny under the 14th Amendment. [The "history and ubiquity" of a practice is relevant because it provides part of the context in which a reasonable observer evaluates whether a challenged governmental practice conveys a message of endorsement of religion. [Thus,] the celebration of Thanksgiving as a public holiday, despite its religious origins, is now generally understood as a celebration of patriotic values rather than particular religious beliefs. * * *

III. [I]n Part VI * * * Justice Blackmun's new rule that an inference of endorsement arises every time government uses a symbol with religious meaning if a "more secular alternative" is available, is too blunt an instrument for Establishment Clause analysis, which depends on sensitivity to the context and circumstances presented by each [case.]

JUSTICE BRENNAN, with whom JUSTICE MARSHALL and JUSTICE STEVENS join, concurring in part and dissenting in part.

* * * I continue to believe that the display of an object that "retains a specifically Christian [or other] religious meaning," is incompatible with the separation of church and state demanded by our Constitution. I therefore agree with the Court that Allegheny County's display of a crèche at the county courthouse signals an endorsement of the Christian faith in violation of the Establishment Clause, and join Parts III-A, IV, and V of the Court's opinion. I cannot agree,

however, [with] the decision as to the menorah [which] rests on three premises: the Christmas tree is a secular symbol; Chanukah is a holiday with secular dimensions, symbolized by the menorah; and the government may promote pluralism by sponsoring or condoning displays having strong religious associations on its property.

[I.]   Even though the tree alone may be deemed predominantly secular, it can hardly be so characterized when placed next to such a forthrightly religious symbol. Consider a poster featuring a star of David, a statue of Buddha, a Christmas tree, a mosque, and a drawing of Krishna. [W]hen found in such company, the tree serves as an unabashedly religious symbol. * * *

[II.] The menorah is indisputably a religious symbol, used ritually in a celebration that has deep religious significance. * * * Pittsburgh's secularization of an inherently religious symbol [recalls] the effort in *Lynch* to render the crèche a secular symbol. As I said then: "To suggest [that] such a symbol is merely 'traditional' and therefore no different from Santa's house or reindeer is not only offensive to those for whom the crèche has profound significance, but insulting to those who insist for religious or personal reasons that the story of Christ is in no sense a part of 'history' nor an unavoidable element of our national 'heritage.' " * * *

III.   * * * I know of no principle under the Establishment Clause [that] governmental promotion of religion is acceptable so long as one religion is not favored. We have, on the contrary, interpreted that Clause to require neutrality, not just among religions, but between religion and nonreligion. [The] uncritical acceptance of a message of religious pluralism also ignores [that many] religious faiths are hostile to each other, and indeed, refuse even to participate in ecumenical services designed to demonstrate the very pluralism Justices Blackmun and O'Connor extol. * * *

JUSTICE STEVENS, with whom JUSTICE BRENNAN and JUSTICE MARSHALL join, concurring in part and dissenting in part. * * *

In my opinion the Establishment Clause should be construed to create a strong presumption against the display of religious symbols on public property. [Even] though "[p]assersby who disagree with the message conveyed by these displays are free to ignore them, or even turn their backs," displays of this kind inevitably have a greater tendency to emphasize sincere and deeply felt differences among individuals than to achieve an ecumenical goal. The Establishment Clause does not allow public bodies to foment such disagreement.

Application of a strong presumption [will not] "require a relentless extirpation of all contact between government and religion," (Kennedy, J., concurring and dissenting), for it will prohibit a display only when its message, evaluated in the context in which it is presented, is nonsecular. For example, a carving of Moses holding the Ten Commandments, if that is the only adornment on a courtroom wall, conveys an equivocal message, perhaps of respect for Judaism, for religion in general, or for law. The addition of carvings depicting Confucius and Mohammed may honor religion, or particular religions, to an extent that the First Amendment does not tolerate any more than it does "the permanent erection of a large Latin cross on the roof of city hall." Placement of secular figures such as Caesar Augustus, William Blackstone, Napoleon Bonaparte, and John Marshall alongside these three religious leaders, however, signals respect not for great proselytizers but for great lawgivers. It would be absurd to exclude such a fitting message from a courtroom, as it would to exclude religious paintings by Italian Renaissance masters from a public museum. Far from "border[ing] on latent hostility toward religion," this careful consideration of context gives due regard to religious and nonreligious members of our society. * * *

    McCREARY COUNTY v. ACLU, 545 U.S. 844 (2005), per SOUTER, J. held that posting copies of the Ten Commandments in two Kentucky county courthouses violated the Establishment Clause because of a "predominantly religious purpose": "When government acts with the ostensible and predominant purpose of advancing religion, it violates that central Establishment Clause value of official religious neutrality * * *.

    "Examination of purpose is a staple of statutory interpretation [and] is a key element of a good deal of constitutional doctrine, e.g., *Washington v. Davis*, [Ch. 9, Sec. 2, III] (discriminatory purpose required for Equal Protection violation); *Hunt v. Washington State Apple Advertising Comm'n*, [Ch. 4, Sec. 2, I] (discriminatory purpose relevant to dormant Commerce Clause claim); *Church of Lukumi Babalu Aye, Inc. v. Hialeah*, [Sec. 2, I infra] (discriminatory purpose raises level of scrutiny required by free exercise claim). [S]crutinizing purpose make[s] practical sense, [where] an understanding of official objective emerges from readily discoverable fact, without any judicial psychoanalysis of a drafter's heart of hearts[, and when "openly available data supported a commonsense conclusion that a religious objective permeated the government's action."] The eyes that look to purpose belong to an 'objective observer,' one who takes account of the traditional external signs that show up in the 'text, legislative history, and implementation of the statute,' or comparable official act. *Santa Fe Ind. School Dist.* [note 3 infra]. [A]lthough a legislature's stated reasons will generally get deference, the secular purpose required has to be genuine, not a sham, and not merely secondary to a religious objective."

    The Court's detailed examination of the record showed that the counties first posted only the Ten Commandments. When suit was filed, the counties adopted "resolutions reciting that the Ten Commandments are 'the precedent legal code upon which the civil and criminal codes [of] Kentucky are founded,' and stating several grounds for taking that position," most of which were related to religion. The displays were expanded to include "eight other documents in smaller frames, each either having a religious theme or excerpted to highlight a religious element," including the Preamble to the Constitution, the Mayflower Compact, and Presidential Proclamations. After a preliminary injunction was issued, the counties installed another display, "the third within a year," entitled "The Foundations of American Law and Government Display," made up "of nine framed documents of equal size" including the Bill of Rights and a picture of Lady Justice, all with statements about their historical and legal significance.

"[T]he Commandments 'are undeniably a sacred text in the Jewish and Christian faiths' [*Stone v. Graham*]. This is not to deny that the Commandments have had influence on civil or secular law; [but where] the text is set out, the insistence of the religious message is hard to avoid in the absence of a context plausibly suggesting a message going beyond an excuse to promote the religious point of view. * * *

SCALIA, joined by Rehnquist, C.J., and Thomas, J., dissented: "[B]oth historical fact [pointing to actions beginning with President Washington and the First Congress to Congress's unanimous action in 2002 approving "under God" in the Pledge of Allegiance] and current practice ["federal, state and local governments across the Nation" have displayed the Ten Commandments] [contradict] the demonstrably false principle that the government cannot favor religion over irreligion. [T]he principle that the government cannot favor one religion over another [is valid] where public aid or assistance to religion [or] where the free exercise of religion is at issue, but it necessarily applies in a more limited sense to public acknowledgment of the Creator.

VAN ORDEN v. PERRY, 545 U.S. 677 (2005), upheld the display of a monument, donated by the Eagles, inscribed with the Ten Commandments on the Texas State Capitol grounds "between the Capitol and the Supreme Court building. [The] 22 acres contain 17 monuments and 21 historical markers commemorating the 'people, ideals, and events that compose Texan identity.'[1] [A]n eagle grasping the American flag, an eye inside of a pyramid, and two small tablets with what appears to be an ancient script are carved above the text of the Ten Commandments. Below the text are two Stars of David and the superimposed Greek letters Chi and Rho, which represent Christ. The bottom of the monument bears the inscription 'PRESENTED TO THE PEOPLE AND YOUTH OF TEXAS BY THE FRATERNAL ORDER OF EAGLES OF TEXAS 1961.' " REHNQUIST, C.J., joined by Scalia, Kennedy, and Thomas, JJ. wrote the plurality opinion: "Our institutions presuppose a Supreme Being, yet these institutions must not press religious observances upon their citizens. Reconciling [these] requires that we neither abdicate our responsibility to maintain a division between church and state nor evince a hostility to religion by disabling the government from in some ways recognizing our religious heritage. * * *

---

[1]   **[Ct's Note]** The monuments are: Heroes of the Alamo, Hood's Brigade, Confederate Soldiers, Volunteer Fireman, Terry's Texas Rangers, Texas Cowboy, Spanish-American War, Texas National Guard, Ten Commandments, Tribute to Texas School Children, Texas Pioneer Woman, The Boy Scouts' Statue of Liberty Replica, Pearl Harbor Veterans, Korean War Veterans, Soldiers of World War I, Disabled Veterans, and Texas Peace Officers.

"Whatever may be the fate of the *Lemon* test in the larger scheme of Establishment Clause jurisprudence, we think it not useful in dealing with the sort of passive monument that Texas has erected on its Capitol grounds. Instead, our analysis is driven both by the nature of the monument and by our Nation's history. As we explained in *Lynch*, 'There is an unbroken history of official acknowledgment by all three branches of government of the role of religion in American life from at least 1789.' [Recognition] of the role of God in our Nation's heritage has also been reflected in our decisions. We have acknowledged, for example, that 'religion has been closely identified with our history and government,' *Schempp*, and that '[t]he history of man is inseparable from the history of religion,' *Engel*. This recognition has led us to hold that the Establishment Clause permits a state legislature to open its daily sessions with a prayer by a chaplain paid by the State. Such a practice, we thought, was 'deeply embedded in the history and tradition of this country.' [In] this case we are faced with a display of the Ten Commandments on government property outside the Texas State Capitol. [Such] acknowledgments [are] common throughout America [and] can be seen throughout a visitor's tour of our Nation's Capital. * * *

BREYER, J. concurred only in the judgment: "[T]he Establishment Clause does not compel the government to purge from the public sphere all that in any way partakes of the religious. Such absolutism is not only inconsistent with our national traditions, but would also tend to promote the kind of social conflict the Establishment Clause seeks to avoid. Thus, [the] Court has found no single mechanical formula that can accurately draw the constitutional line in every case."

"Here [the] Fraternal Order of Eagles, a private civic (and primarily secular) organization, while interested in the religious aspect of the Ten Commandments, sought to highlight the Commandments' role in shaping civic morality as part of that organization's efforts to combat juvenile delinquency. [The] monument sits in a large park containing 17 monuments and 21 historical markers, all designed to illustrate the 'ideals' of those who settled in Texas and of those who have lived there since that time. The setting does not readily lend itself to meditation or any other religious activity. [T]he context suggests that the State intended the display's moral message—an illustrative message reflecting the historical 'ideals' of Texans—to predominate. [The] 40 years [that] passed in which the presence of this monument, legally speaking, went unchallenged suggest [that] the public visiting the capitol grounds has considered the religious aspect of the tablets' message as part of what is a broader moral and historical message reflective of a cultural heritage. [This] case also differs from *McCreary County*, where the short (and stormy) history of the courthouse Commandments' displays demonstrates the substantially religious objectives of those who mounted them, and the effect of this readily apparent objective upon those who view them. [This] display has stood apparently uncontested for nearly two generations. That experience helps us understand that as a practical matter of *degree* this display is unlikely to prove divisive. And this matter of degree is, I believe, critical in a borderline case such as this one. At the same time, to reach a contrary conclusion [would], I fear, lead the law to exhibit a hostility toward religion [that] might well encourage disputes concerning the removal of longstanding depictions of the Ten Commandments from public buildings across the Nation. And it could thereby create the very kind of religiously based divisiveness that the Establishment Clause seeks to avoid."

STEVENS, J., joined by Ginsburg, J., dissented: "Viewed on its face, Texas' display has no purported connection to God's role in the formation of Texas or the founding of our Nation; nor does it provide the reasonable observer with any basis to guess that it was erected to honor any individual or organization. The message [is:] This State endorses the divine code of the 'Judeo-Christian' God. [In] my judgment [the] Establishment Clause has created a strong presumption against the display of religious symbols on public property. [This] Court has often recognized 'an unbroken history of official acknowledgment [of] the role of religion in American life.' [This] case, however, is not about historic preservation or the mere recognition of religion. [This] Nation's resolute commitment to neutrality with respect to religion is flatly inconsistent with the plurality's wholehearted validation of an official state endorsement of the message that there is one, and only one, God.

SOUTER, J., joined by Stevens and Ginsburg, JJ., also dissented: "A governmental display of an obviously religious text cannot be squared with neutrality, except in a setting that plausibly indicates that the statement is not placed in view with a predominant purpose on the part of government either to adopt the religious message or to urge its acceptance by others. "[A] pedestrian happening upon the monument at issue here needs no training in religious doctrine to realize that the statement of the Commandments, quoting God himself, proclaims that the will of the divine being is the source of obligation to obey the rules, including the facially secular ones. [The] word 'Lord' appears in all capital letters (as does the word 'am'), so that the most eye-catching segment of the quotation is the declaration 'I AM the LORD thy God.' [T]he government of Texas is telling everyone who sees the monument to live up to a moral code because God requires it, [as] the inheritances specifically of Jews and Christians. [It] stands in contrast to any number of perfectly constitutional depictions of [the Commandments], the frieze of our own Courtroom providing a good example, where the figure of Moses stands among history's great lawgivers. [N]o one looking at the lines of figures in marble relief is likely to see a religious purpose. [T]he viewers may just as naturally see the tablets of the Commandments (showing the later ones, forbidding things like killing and theft, but without the divine preface) as background from which the concept of law emerged. [But] 17 monuments with no common appearance, history, or esthetic role scattered over 22 acres is not a museum, and anyone strolling around the lawn would surely take each memorial on its own terms.

———

Whatever life may have been left in the *Lemon* test appears to have expired after AMERICAN LEGION v. AMERICAN HUMANIST ASSOCIATION, 139 S.Ct.

2067 (2019), whose multiple and complex opinions both followed *Van Orden* in important respects and made clear that *Lemon* no longer commands the support of a majority of the Court. At issue was a large Latin cross in Bladensburg, Maryland, originally planned in 1918 to honor the 49 American soldiers from Prince George's County who had been killed in the World War I. Finally completed in 1925, the publicly-owned cross stood on public land adjacent to and highly visible from a well-traveled highway. On a challenge that the cross violated the Establishment Clause as a public symbol of Christianity, the Court, per ALITO, J., with only Justices Ginsburg and Sotomayor dissenting, rejected the challenge and tracked *Van Orden* in concluding that the use of the cross in this way neither had the original purpose nor the current effect of endorsing Christianity.

Unlike the Ten Commandments in *Van Orden*, the so-called Peace Cross was not part of a larger collection of other symbols and monuments. Nevertheless, Justice Alito found neither state endorsement of Christianity nor anything that could properly be characterized as coercion. Most significantly, Justice Alito's opinion, along with the separate opinions of Justices Breyer and Kagan, explicitly rejected the *Lemon* analysis, leaving *Lemon* as historical artifact and no longer, even implicitly, the Court's test for the Establishment Clause.

————

Differing interpretations of the "coercion" test. LEE v. WEISMAN, 505 U.S. 577 (1992), per KENNEDY, J., held violative of the Establishment Clause the practice of public school officials inviting members of the clergy to offer invocation and benediction prayers at graduation ceremonies: "[The] school district's supervision and control of a high school graduation ceremony places public pressure, as well as peer pressure, on attending students to stand as a group or, at least, maintain respectful silence during the Invocation and Benediction. [Finding] no violation [would] place objectors in the dilemma of participating, with all that implies, or protesting. * * * Research in psychology supports the common assumption that adolescents are often susceptible to pressure from their peers towards conformity, and that the influence is strongest in matters of social convention. [That] the intrusion was in the course of promulgating religion that sought to be civic or nonsectarian rather than pertaining to one sect does not lessen the offense or isolation to the objectors. At best it narrows their number, at worst increases their sense of isolation and affront."

BLACKMUN, J., joined by Stevens and O'Connor, JJ., who joined the Court's opinion, concurred: "[I]t is not enough that the government restrain from compelling religious practices: it must not engage in them either. [To] that end, our cases have prohibited government endorsement of religion, its sponsorship, and active involvement in religion, whether or not citizens were coerced to conform."

SCALIA, J., joined by Rehnquist, C.J., and White and Thomas, JJ., dissented: "Three terms ago, I joined an opinion recognizing that 'the meaning of the [Establishment] Clause is to be determined by reference to historical practices and understandings.' * * * *Allegheny County* (Kennedy, J., concurring in judgment in part and dissenting in part). These views of course prevent me from joining today's opinion, [which] lays waste a tradition that is as old as public-school graduation ceremonies themselves. [Since] the Court does not dispute that students exposed to prayer at graduation ceremonies retain (despite 'subtle coercive pressures,') the free will to sit, there is absolutely no basis for the Court's decision. It is fanciful enough to say that 'a reasonable dissenter,' standing head erect in a class of bowed heads, 'could believe that the group exercise signified her own participation or approval of it.' It is beyond the absurd to say that she could entertain such a belief while pointedly declining to rise. But let us assume the very worst, that the nonparticipating graduate is 'subtly coerced' [to] stand! Even that half of the disjunctive does not remotely establish a 'participation' (or an 'appearance of participation') in a religious exercise. * * *

"The deeper flaw in the Court's opinion does not lie in its wrong answer to the question whether there was state-induced 'peer-pressure' coercion; it lies, rather, in the Court's making violation of the Establishment Clause hinge on such a precious question. The coercion that was a hallmark of historical establishments of religion was coercion of religious orthodoxy and of financial support by force of *law and threat of penalty.* [I] concede that our constitutional tradition [has] ruled out of order government-sponsored endorsement of religion—even when no legal coercion is present, and indeed even when no ersatz, 'peer-pressure' psycho-coercion is present—where the endorsement is sectarian, in the sense of specifying details upon which men and women who believe in a benevolent, omnipotent Creator and Ruler of the world, are known to differ (for example, the divinity of Christ). But there is simply no support for the proposition that the officially sponsored nondenominational invocation and benediction read by Rabbi Gutterman—with no one legally coerced to recite them—violated the Constitution of the United States. To the contrary, they are so characteristically American they could have come from the pen of George Washington or Abraham Lincoln himself.

"The Court relies on our 'school prayer' cases, *Engel* and *Schempp.* But whatever the merit of those cases, they [do] not constitute an exception to the rule, distilled from historical practice, that public ceremonies may include prayer; rather, they simply do not fall within the scope of the rule (for the obvious reason that school instruction is not a public ceremony). Second, we have made clear our understanding that school prayer occurs within a framework [of] legal coercion to attend [school]. Voluntary prayer at graduation—a one-time ceremony at which parents, friends and relatives are present—can hardly be thought to raise the same concerns."

GREECE v. GALLOWAY, 572 U.S. 565 (2014): A town invited or permitted "ministers or laypersons ["within its borders"] of any persuasion, including [in 2008] an atheist, [a] Jewish layman and the chairman of the local Baha'i temple [and] a Wiccan priestess" to give an opening prayer at monthly town board meetings. The invocations, however, reflecting "the predominantly Christian identity of the town's congregations," often invoked Jesus Christ and similar

"Christian themes" and said "let us pray" and asked the "audience members to stand and bow their heads."

The Court, per KENNEDY, J., held "that the Establishment Clause must be interpreted 'by reference to historical practices and understandings,'" and noted that "since the framing of the Constitution," Congress "and the majority of the other States had the same, consistent practice": [An] insistence on nonsectarian or ecumenical prayer as a single, fixed standard is not consistent with our tradition," and that "Congress continues to permit [its] chaplains to express themselves in a religious idiom." The "contention that legislative prayer must be generic or nonsectarian derives from dictum in *County of Allegheny* that was disputed when written and has been repudiated in later cases. [To] hold that invocations must be nonsectarian would force the legislatures that sponsor prayers and the courts that are asked to decide these cases to act as supervisors and censors of religious speech, a rule that would involve government in religious matters" and produce "the difficulty, indeed the futility, of sifting sectarian from nonsectarian speech, [a] form of government entanglement with religion that is far more troublesome than the current approach.

"[T]he Court does not imply that no constraints remain. [If the] practice over time shows that the invocations denigrate nonbelievers or religious minorities, threaten damnation, or preach conversion, many present may consider the prayer to fall short of the desire to elevate the purpose of the occasion and to unite lawmakers in their common effort. [But] our tradition assumes that adult citizens, firm in their own beliefs, can tolerate and perhaps appreciate a ceremonial prayer delivered by a person of a different faith. [That] a prayer is given in the name of Jesus, Allah, or Jehovah, or that it makes passing reference to religious doctrines, does not remove it from that tradition."

KENNEDY, J., joined by Roberts, C.J., and Alito, J., distinguished *Lee*: "The inquiry [regarding coercion] remains a fact-sensitive one that considers both the setting in which the prayer arises and the audience to whom it is directed. [T]he reasonable observer is acquainted with [and] understands that its purposes are to lend gravity to public proceedings and to acknowledge the place religion holds in the lives of many private citizens, not to afford government an opportunity to proselytize. [Although] board members themselves stood, bowed their heads, or made the sign of the cross during the prayer, they at no point solicited similar gestures by the public. [T]he circumstances [in *Lee*] are not present in this case, [which involves] mature adults, who 'presumably' are 'not readily susceptible to religious indoctrination or peer pressure.'"

KAGAN, J., joined by Ginsburg, Breyer, and Sotomayor, JJ., dissented: "[U]nder *Marsh*, legislative prayer has a distinctive constitutional warrant by virtue of tradition," but the Greece "Board's meetings are also occasions for ordinary citizens to engage with and petition their government." The prayers were "addressed directly to the Town's citizenry [with "10 or so citizens in attendance"], and the speaker [might ask the audience] to recite a common prayer with him.

[Thus, they] were *more* sectarian, and *less* inclusive, than [in] *Marsh*. [I]n this citizen-centered venue, government officials must take steps to ensure—as none of Greece's Board members ever did—that opening prayers are inclusive of different faiths, rather than always identified with a single religion." In *Marsh* some of the Presbyterian minister's "earlier prayers explicitly invoked Christian beliefs, but he 'removed all references to Christ' after a single legislator complained," whereas in Greece, "[a]bout two-thirds of the prayers given over this decade or so invoked 'Jesus,' 'Christ,' 'Your Son,' or 'the Holy Spirit.' "* * *

"Let's say that a Muslim citizen of Greece goes before the Board to share her views on policy or request some permit. [She] must think—it is hardly paranoia, but only the truth—that Christian worship has become entwined with local governance," and she is put "to the unenviable choice of either pretending to pray like the majority or declining to join its communal activity, at the very moment of petitioning their elected leaders. [When] a person goes to court, a polling place, or an immigration proceeding, [etc.], government officials do not engage in sectarian worship, nor do they ask her to do likewise. [Why] not, then, at a town meeting?

" * * * Greece had multiple ways of incorporating prayer into its town meetings [so as to] forge common bonds, rather than divide. [It] might have invited clergy of many faiths to serve as chaplains [as] Congress does. [T]he Board 'maintains [that] it would welcome a prayer by any minister or layman who wishe[s] to give one,' [but that] representation has never been publicized; nor has the Board (except for a few months surrounding this suit's filing) offered the chaplain's role to any non-Christian clergy or layman."

ELK GROVE UNIFIED SCHOOL DIST. v. NEWDOW, 542 U.S. 1 (2004), reversed the Ninth Circuit's decision that daily classroom recitation by the teacher of the Pledge of Allegiance, with the words "Under God" added in 1954 by Congress, violates the Establishment Clause. The Court held that the father of the schoolgirl had no standing, see Ch. 12, Sec. 2, I. Three Justices reached the merits and would reverse. REHNQUIST, C.J., joined by O'Connor, J., noted that the sponsor of the 1954 amendment "said its purpose was to contrast this country's belief in God with the Soviet Union's embrace of atheism. We do not know what other Members of Congress [thought]. Following the decision of the Court of Appeals in this case, Congress [made] extensive findings about the historic role of religion in the political development of the Nation and reaffirmed the text of the Pledge. To the millions of people who regularly recite the Pledge, and who have no access to, or concern with, such legislation or legislative history, 'under God' might mean several different [things]. Examples of patriotic invocations of God and official acknowledgments of religion's role in our Nation's history abound. * * *

"I do not believe that the phrase 'under God' in the Pledge converts its recital into a 'religious exercise' of the sort described in *Lee*. [It is] in no sense a prayer, nor an endorsement of any religion. [It] is a patriotic exercise, not a religious one; participants promise fidelity to our flag and our Nation, not to any particular God, faith, or church."

O'CONNOR, J., added: "For centuries, we have marked important occasions or pronouncements with references to God and invocations of divine assistance. [These] can serve to solemnize an occasion instead of to invoke divine provenance. The reasonable observer[,] fully aware of our national history and the origins of such practices, would not perceive these [as] signifying a government endorsement of any specific religion, or even of religion over non-religion.

"There are no de minimis violations of the Constitution. [But] government can, in a discrete category of cases, acknowledge or refer to the divine without offending the Constitution. This category of 'ceremonial deism' most clearly encompasses such things as the national motto ("In God We Trust"), religious references in traditional patriotic songs such as the Star-Spangled Banner, and the words with which the Marshal of this Court opens each of its sessions. See *Allegheny County* (opinion of O'Connor, J.). [Although] it is a close question, I conclude that [the Pledge is "an instance of ceremonial deism." It] complies with [the] requirement [that "no religious acknowledgment could claim to be an instance of ceremonial deism if it explicitly favored one particular religious belief system over another"]. It does not refer to a nation 'under Jesus' or 'under Vishnu,' but instead acknowledges religion in [a] simple reference to a generic 'God.' Of course, some religions—Buddhism, for instance—are not based upon a belief in a separate Supreme Being. But one would be hard pressed to imagine a brief solemnizing reference to religion that would adequately encompass every religious belief expressed by any citizen of this Nation."

THOMAS, J., also concurred: "Adherence to *Lee* would require us to strike down the Pledge [but] *Lee* was wrongly decided. [The] kind of coercion implicated by the Religion Clauses is that accomplished *by force of law and threat of penalty. Lee* (Scalia, J., dissenting). Peer pressure, unpleasant as it may be, is not coercion."

Differing interpretations of the "endorsement" test. CAPITOL SQUARE REVIEW & ADVISORY BOARD v. PINETTE, 515 U.S. 753 (1995), per SCALIA, J., relying on *Widmar* and *Lamb's Chapel*, held that petitioner's permitting the Ku Klux Klan to place a Latin cross in Capitol Square—"A 10-acre, state-owned plaza surrounding the Statehouse in Columbus, Ohio"—when it had also permitted such other unattended displays as "a State-sponsored lighted tree during the Christmas season, a privately-sponsored menorah during Chanukah, a display showing the progress of a United Way fundraising campaign, and booths and exhibits during an arts festival," did not violate the Establishment Clause: "The State did not sponsor respondents' expression, the expression was made on government property that had been opened to the public for speech, and permission was requested through the same application process [for] other private groups."

The seven-justice majority divided, however, on the scope of the "endorsement" test. SCALIA, J., joined by Rehnquist, C.J., and Kennedy and Thomas, JJ., rejected petitioners' claim based on "the forum's proximity to the seat of government, which, they contend, may produce the perception that the cross bears the State's approval": "[W]e have consistently held that it is no violation for government to enact neutral policies that happen to benefit religion. Where we have tested for endorsement of religion, the subject [was] either expression by the government itself, *Lynch*, or else government action alleged to discriminate in favor of private religious expression or activity, *Allegheny County*. [O]ne can conceive of a case in which a governmental entity manipulates its administration of a public forum close to the seat of government (or within a government building) in such a manner that only certain religious groups take advantage of it, creating an impression of endorsement that is in fact accurate. But those situations, which involve governmental favoritism, do not exist here. * * *

"The contrary view [by] Justice Stevens [infra], but endorsed by Justice Souter and Justice O'Connor [and Breyer, J.] as well, [infra], exiles private religious speech to a realm of less-protected expression. [It] is no answer to say that the Establishment Clause tempers religious speech. [T]hat Clause applies only to the words and acts of government. It [has] never been read by this Court to serve as an impediment to purely private religious speech connected to the State only through its occurrence in a public forum."

O'CONNOR, J., joined by Souter and Breyer, JJ., concurred in part: "Where the government's operation of a public forum has the effect of endorsing religion, even if the governmental actor neither intends nor actively encourages that result, [the] State's own actions (operating the forum in a particular manner and permitting the religious expression to take place therein), and their relationship to the private speech at issue, actually convey a message of endorsement."

STEVENS, J., dissented: "[A] paramount purpose of the Establishment Clause is to protect "[a reasonable observer"] from being made to feel like an outsider in matters of faith. [If] a reasonable person [does so], then the State may not allow its property to be used as a forum for that [display.]

"[The] very fact that a sign is installed on public property implies official recognition and reinforcement of its message. That implication is especially strong when the sign stands in front of the seat of the government itself. [Even] if the disclaimer at the foot of the cross (which stated that the cross was placed there by a private organization) were legible, that inference would remain, because a property owner's decision to allow a third party to place a sign on her property conveys the same message of endorsement as if she had erected it herself. * * *

"The battle over the Klan cross underscores the power of such symbolism. The menorah prompted the Klan to seek permission to erect an anti-semitic symbol, [which] not only prompted vandalism but also motivated other sects to seek permission to place their own symbols in the Square. These facts illustrate the potential for insidious entanglement that flows from state-endorsed proselytizing."

GINSBURG, J., also dissented, reserving the question of whether an unequivocal disclaimer, "legible from a distance," "that Ohio did not endorse the display's message" would suffice: "Near the stationary cross were the government's flags and the government's statues. [No] other private display was in sight. No plainly visible sign informed the public that the cross belonged to the Klan and that Ohio's government did not endorse the display's message."

SALAZAR v. BUONO, 559 U.S. 700 (2010): In 1934, members of the Veterans of Foreign Wars placed a Latin cross on federal land to honor American soldiers who died in World War I. Easter services have been regularly held there over the years. After a federal court held this violative of the Establishment Clause, Congress directed the Secretary of the Interior to transfer the cross and land to VFW in exchange for privately owned land elsewhere in the Preserve. The statute provided that the property would revert to the Government if not maintained "as a memorial commemorating United States participation in World War I and honoring the American veterans of that war." A splintered 5–4 majority reversed on grounds of (1) rules pertaining to the law of injunctions or (2) standing. Four Justices reached the constitutional issue but their discussion was somewhat influenced by their view of injunction doctrine.

ALITO, J., who was part of the majority, would uphold the statute: "Assuming that it is appropriate to apply the so-called 'endorsement test,' [the "reasonable observer"] would be familiar with the origin and history of the monument and would also know both that the land on which the monument is located is privately owned. [A] well-informed observer would appreciate that the transfer represents an effort by Congress to address a unique situation and to find a solution that best accommodates conflicting concerns [to] commemorate our Nation's war dead and to avoid the disturbing symbolism that would have been created by the destruction of the monument."

STEVENS, J., joined by Ginsburg and Sotomayor, JJ., dissented: "[I]t is undisputed that the Latin cross is the preeminent symbol of Christianity. It is exclusively a Christian symbol, [I] certainly agree that the Nation should memorialize the service of those who fought and died in World War I, but it cannot lawfully do so by continued endorsement of a starkly sectarian message.

"[T]he transfer [statute] would not end government endorsement. [First,] after the transfer it would continue to appear to any reasonable observer that the Government has endorsed the cross, notwithstanding that the name has changed on the title to a small patch of underlying land. [T]he Government has designated the cross as a national memorial, [and] endorsement continues regardless of whether the cross sits on public or private land. [Second,] Congress' intent to preserve the display of the cross maintains the Government's endorsement of the cross."

2. THE FREE EXERCISE CLAUSE AND RELATED STATUTORY ISSUES

I. CONFLICT WITH STATE REGULATION

On its face, the Free Exercise clause of the First Amendment bars the banning of entire religions, and prevents Congress and (after incorporation through the

Fourteenth Amendment) the states from prohibiting religious practices just because of their religious origins. But however real such worries were in 1791, and however real they are in parts of the world now, such governmental are now so rare in the United States as never to have generated a Supreme Court decision. In reality, the most common problem respecting Free Exercise of religion now has involved a generally applicable government regulation, whose purpose is nonreligious, that either makes illegal (or otherwise burdens) conduct that is dictated by some religious belief, or requires (or otherwise encourages) conduct that is forbidden by some religious belief.

REYNOLDS v. UNITED STATES, 98 U.S. 145 (1878), the first major Free Exercise Clause decision, upheld a federal law making polygamy illegal as applied to a Mormon whose religious duty was to practice polygamy: "Congress was deprived of all legislative power over mere opinion, but was left free to reach actions which were in violation of social duties or subversive of good order."

Beginning with *Cantwell v. Connecticut*, 310 U.S. 296 (1940)—which first held that the Fourteenth Amendment made the free exercise guarantee applicable to the states—a number of cases invalidated application of state laws to conduct undertaken pursuant to religious beliefs. Like *Cantwell*, these decisions, a number of which are set forth in Ch. 7, rested in whole or in part on the freedom of expression protections of the First and Fourteenth Amendments. Similarly, WEST VIRGINIA STATE BD. OF EDUC. v. BARNETTE, 319 U.S. 624 (1943), held that compelling a flag salute by public school children whose religious scruples forbade it violated the First Amendment: "[The] freedoms of speech and of press, of assembly, and of worship [are] susceptible of restriction only to prevent grave and immediate danger to interests which the state may lawfully protect. [The] freedom asserted by these appellees does not bring them into collision with rights asserted by any other individual. It is such conflicts which most frequently require intervention of the State to determine where the rights of one end and those of another begin. [T]he compulsory flag salute and pledge requires *affirmation of a belief* and an *attitude of mind*. [If] there is any fixed star in our constitutional constellation, it is that no official, high or petty, can prescribe what shall be orthodox in politics, nationalism or other matters of opinion or force citizens to confess by word or act their faith therein."

Not until 1963, in *Sherbert v. Verner* (discussed in *Hobbie* below), did the Court held conduct protected by the Free Exercise Clause alone.

HOBBIE v. UNEMPLOYMENT APPEALS COMM'N
480 U.S. 136, 107 S.Ct. 1046, 94 L.Ed.2d 190 (1987).

JUSTICE BRENNAN delivered the opinion of the Court.

Appellant's employer discharged her when she refused to work certain scheduled hours because of sincerely-held religious convictions adopted after beginning employment. [Under] our precedents, the [Florida] Appeals Commission's disqualification of appellant from receipt of [unemployment compensation] benefits violates the Free Exercise [Clause]. *Sherbert v. Verner*, 374 U.S. 398 (1963); *Thomas v. Review Board*, 450 U.S. 707 (1981). In *Sherbert* we considered South Carolina's denial of unemployment compensation benefits to a Sabbatarian who, like Hobbie, refused to work on Saturdays. The Court held that the State's disqualification of Sherbert "force[d] her to choose between following the precepts of her religion and forfeiting benefits, on the one hand, and abandoning one of the precepts of her religion in order to accept work, on the other hand. Governmental imposition of such a choice puts the same kind of burden upon the free exercise of religion as would a fine imposed against [her] for her Saturday worship." * * *

In *Thomas*, [a] Jehovah's Witness, held religious beliefs that forbade his participation in the production of armaments. He was forced to leave his job when the employer closed his department and transferred him to a division that fabricated turrets for tanks. Indiana then denied Thomas unemployment compensation benefits. [We] see no meaningful distinction among the situations [and] again affirm, as stated in *Thomas:* "Where the state conditions receipt of an important benefit upon conduct proscribed by a religious faith, *or where it denies such a benefit because of conduct mandated by religious belief, thereby putting substantial pressure on an adherent to modify his behavior and to violate his beliefs,* a burden upon religion exists. While the compulsion may be indirect, the infringement upon free exercise is nonetheless substantial" (emphasis added).

Both *Sherbert* and *Thomas* held that such infringements must be subjected to strict scrutiny and could be justified only by proof by the State of a compelling interest. The Appeals Commission does not seriously contend that its denial of benefits can withstand strict scrutiny; rather it urges that we hold that its justification should be determined under the less rigorous standard articulated in Chief Justice Burger's opinion in *Bowen v. Roy:* "the Government meets its burden when it demonstrates that a challenged requirement for governmental benefits, neutral and uniform in its application, is a reasonable means of promoting a legitimate public interest." 476 U.S. 693 (1986). Five Justices expressly rejected this argument in *Roy*. [See] also *Wisconsin v. Yoder*, 406 U.S. 205 (1972)[6] ("[O]nly those interests of the highest order and those not otherwise served can overbalance legitimate claims to the free exercise of religion"). * * *

The Appeals Commission also attempts to distinguish this case by arguing that [in] *Sherbert* and *Thomas*, the employees held their respective religious beliefs at the time of hire; subsequent changes in the conditions of employment made *by the employer* caused the conflict between work and belief. In this case, Hobbie's

---

[6]   *Yoder* invalidated a law compelling school attendance to age 16 as applied to Amish parents who refused on religious grounds to send their children to high school, noting no "showing that upon leaving the Amish community Amish children, with their practical agricultural training and habits of industry and self-reliance, would become burdens on society because of educational shortcomings. [The] independence and successful social functioning of the Amish community for a period approaching almost three centuries [is] strong evidence that there is at best a speculative gain, [in] meeting the duties of citizenship from an additional one or two years of compulsory formal education."

beliefs changed during the course of her employment. [We] decline [to] single out the religious convert for different, less favorable treatment. * * *

Finally, we reject the Appeals Commission's argument that the awarding of benefits to Hobbie would violate the Establishment Clause. This Court has long recognized that the government may (and sometimes must) accommodate religious practices and that it may do so without violating the Establishment Clause.

Reversed.

CHIEF JUSTICE REHNQUIST, dissenting.

I adhere to the views I stated in dissent in *Thomas* [where Rehnquist, J., stated: "As to the proper interpretation of the Free Exercise Clause, I would accept the decision of *Braunfeld v. Brown*, 366 U.S. 599 (1961), and the dissent in *Sherbert*. In *Braunfeld*, we held that Sunday closing laws do not violate the First Amendment rights of Sabbatarians. Chief Justice Warren explained that the statute did not make unlawful any religious practices of appellants; it simply made the practice of their religious beliefs more expensive. We concluded that '[t]o strike down, without the most critical scrutiny, legislation which imposes only an indirect burden on the exercise of religion, i.e., legislation which does not make unlawful the religious practice itself, would radically restrict the operating latitude of the legislature.' Likewise in this case, it cannot be said that the State discriminated against Thomas on the basis of his religious beliefs or that he was denied benefits *because* he was a Jehovah's Witness. Where, as here, a State has enacted a general statute, the purpose and effect of which is to advance the State's secular goals, the Free Exercise Clause does not in my view require the State to conform that statute to the dictates of religious conscience of any group."]

Rejections of Free Exercise claims. (a) *Taxation.* (i) JIMMY SWAGGART MINISTRIES v. BOARD OF EQUAL., 493 U.S. 378 (1990), per O'CONNOR, J., unanimously held that the Free Exercise Clause does not prohibit imposing a sales and use tax on sale of religious materials by a religious organization: "[T]o the extent that imposition of a generally applicable tax merely decreases the amount of money appellant has to spend on its religious activities, any such burden is not constitutionally significant. [B]ecause appellant's religious beliefs do not forbid payment of the sales and use tax, appellant's reliance on *Sherbert* and its progeny is misplaced. [Although] it is of course possible to imagine that a more onerous tax, even if generally applicable, might effectively choke off an adherent's religious practices, we face no such situation in this case." UNITED STATES v. LEE, 455 U.S. 252 (1982), per BURGER, C.J., held that the Free Exercise Clause does not require an exemption for members of the Old Order Amish from payment of social security taxes even though "both payment and receipt of social security benefits is forbidden by the Amish faith": "The state may justify a limitation on religious liberty by showing that it is essential to accomplish an overriding governmental interest [and] mandatory participation is indispensable to the fiscal vitality of the social security system. [To] maintain an organized society that guarantees religious freedom to a great variety of faiths requires that some religious practices yield to the common good. [The] tax system could not function if denominations were allowed to challenge the tax system because tax payments were spent in a manner that violates their religious belief."

(b) *Conscription.* (i) GILLETTE v. UNITED STATES, 401 U.S. 437 (1971), per MARSHALL, J., held that the Free Exercise Clause does not forbid Congress from "conscripting persons who oppose a particular war on grounds of conscience and religion. * * *": "The conscription laws [are] not designed to interfere with any religious ritual or practice, and do not work a penalty against any theological position. The incidental burdens felt by [petitioners] are strictly justified by substantial governmental interests [in] procuring the manpower necessary for military purposes."

DOUGLAS, J., dissented: "[M]y choice is the dicta of Chief Justice Hughes who, dissenting in *Macintosh*, spoke for Holmes, Brandeis, and Stone: '[Among] the most eminent statesmen here and abroad have been those who condemned the action of their country in entering into wars they thought to be unjustified."

(ii) In JOHNSON v. ROBISON, 415 U.S. 361 (1974), a federal statute granted educational benefits for veterans who served on active duty but disqualified conscientious objectors who performed alternate civilian service. The Court, per BRENNAN, J., found a "rational basis" for the classification and thus no violation of equal protection, because the "disruption caused by military service is quantitatively greater [and] qualitatively different." Further, the statute "involves only an incidental burden upon appellee's free exercise of religion—if, indeed, any burden exists at [all.]" Douglas, J., dissented.

(c) *Tax exemption.* BOB JONES UNIV. v. UNITED STATES, 461 U.S. 574 (1983), per BURGER, C.J., held that IRS denial of tax exempt status to private schools that practice racial discrimination on the basis of sincerely held religious beliefs does not violate the Free Exercise Clause: "[T]he Government has a fundamental, overriding interest in eradicating racial discrimination in education [which] substantially outweighs [petitioners'] exercise of their religious beliefs. The interests asserted by petitioners cannot be accommodated with that compelling governmental interest, see *Lee;* and no 'less restrictive means' are available to achieve the governmental interest."

(d) *Internal government affairs.* LYNG v. NORTHWEST INDIAN CEMETERY PROTECTIVE ASS'N, 485 U.S. 439 (1988), per O'CONNOR, J., held the federal government's building a road in a national forest did not violate the Free Exercise rights of American Indian tribes even though this would "virtually destroy the Indians' ability to practice their religion" because it would irreparably damage "sacred areas which are an integral and necessary part of [their] belief systems": "In *Bowen v. Roy*, we considered a challenge to a federal statute that required the States to use Social Security numbers in administering certain welfare programs. Two applicants [contended] that their religious beliefs prevented them from acceding to the use of a Social Security number [that had been assigned to] their two-year-old daughter because the use of a numerical identifier would ' "rob the spirit" of [their] daughter and prevent her from attaining greater spiritual power.' [The] Court rejected [this]: 'The Free Exercise Clause simply cannot be understood to require the Government to conduct its own internal affairs in ways that comport with the religious beliefs of particular citizens."

"[The] dissent now offers to distinguish [*Roy*] by saying that the Government was acting there 'in a purely internal manner,' whereas land-use decisions 'are likely to have substantial external effects.' [But robbing] the spirit of a child, and preventing her from attaining greater spiritual power, is both a 'substantial external effect' and one that is remarkably similar to the injury claimed [today]."

BRENNAN, J., joined by Marshall and Blackmun, JJ., dissented: "[T]oday's ruling sacrifices a religion at least as old as the Nation itself, along with the spiritual well-being of its approximately 5,000 adherents, so that the Forest Service can build a six-mile segment of road that two lower courts found had only the most marginal and speculative utility, both to the Government itself and to the private lumber interests that might conceivably use it." Kennedy, J., did not participate.

EMPLOYMENT DIVISION v. SMITH
494 U.S. 872, 110 S.Ct. 1595, 108 L.Ed.2d 876 (1990).

JUSTICE SCALIA delivered the opinion of the Court. * * *

Respondents [were] fired from their jobs with a private drug rehabilitation organization because they ingested peyote for sacramental purposes at a ceremony of the Native American Church, of which both are members. When respondents applied to petitioner [for] unemployment compensation, they were determined to be ineligible for benefits because they had been discharged for work-related "misconduct." [We believe] that "if a State has prohibited through its criminal laws certain kinds of religiously motivated conduct without violating the First Amendment, it certainly follows that it may impose the lesser burden of denying unemployment compensation benefits to persons who engage in that conduct."

[The] free exercise of religion means [the] right to believe and profess whatever religious doctrine one desires. [But] the "exercise of religion" often involves not only belief and profession but the performance of (or abstention from) physical acts: assembling with others for a worship service, participating in sacramental use of bread and wine, proselytizing, abstaining from certain foods or certain modes of transportation. It would be true, we think (though no case of ours has involved the point), that a state would be "prohibiting the free exercise [of religion]" if it sought to ban such acts or abstentions only when they are engaged in for religious reasons. [But respondents] contend that their religious motivation for using peyote places them beyond the reach of a criminal law that is not specifically directed at their religious practice, and that is concededly constitutional as applied to those who use the drug for other reasons. [As] a textual matter, we do not think the words must be given that meaning. It is no more necessary to regard the collection of a general tax, for example, as "prohibiting the free exercise [of religion]" by those citizens who believe support of organized government to be sinful, than it is to regard the same tax as "abridging the freedom [of] the press" of those publishing companies that must pay the tax as a condition of staying in business. It is a permissible reading of the text [to] say that if prohibiting the exercise of religion (or burdening the activity of printing) is not the object of the tax but merely the incidental effect of a generally applicable and otherwise valid provision, the First Amendment has not been offended.

Our decisions reveal that the latter reading is the correct one. We have never held that an individual's religious beliefs excuse him from compliance with an otherwise valid law prohibiting conduct that the State is free to regulate. [In] *Prince v. Massachusetts*, 321 U.S. 158 (1944), we held that a mother could be prosecuted under the child labor laws for using her children to dispense literature in the streets, her religious motivation notwithstanding. [The opinion also discusses *Braunfeld, Gillette,* and *Lee.*]

The only decisions in which we have held that the First Amendment bars application of a neutral, generally applicable law to religiously motivated action have involved [the] Free Exercise Clause in conjunction with other constitutional protections, such as freedom of speech and of the press, see *Cantwell* (invalidating a licensing system for religious and charitable solicitations under which the administrator had discretion to deny a license to any cause he deemed nonreligious); *Murdock*; *Follett*, or the right of parents, acknowledged in *Pierce v. Society of Sisters* [Sec. 2 supra] to direct the education of their children, see *Yoder*. Some of our cases prohibiting compelled expression, decided exclusively upon free speech grounds, have also involved freedom of religion, cf. *Wooley v. Maynard* [Ch. 7, Sec. 9, I] (invalidating compelled display of a license plate slogan that offended individual religious beliefs); *Barnette*. And it is easy to envision a case in which a challenge on freedom of association grounds would likewise be reinforced by Free Exercise Clause concerns. Cf. *Roberts v. United States Jaycees* [Ch. 7, Sec. 9, III] ("An individual's freedom to speak, to worship [could] not be vigorously protected from interference by the State [if] a correlative freedom to engage in group effort toward those ends were not also guaranteed."). * * *

Respondents argue that [the] claim for a religious exemption must be evaluated under the balancing test set forth in *Sherbert*[:] governmental actions that substantially burden a religious practice must be justified by a compelling governmental interest. [We] have never invalidated any governmental action on the basis of the *Sherbert* test except the denial of unemployment compensation. Although we have sometimes purported to apply the *Sherbert* test in contexts other than that, we have always found the test satisfied, see *Lee, Gillette*. In recent years we have abstained from applying the *Sherbert* test (outside the unemployment compensation field) at all [discussing *Roy* and *Lyng*]. In *Goldman v. Weinberger*, 475 U.S. 503 (1986), we rejected application of the *Sherbert* test to military dress regulations that forbade the wearing of yarmulkes. In *O'Lone v. Shabazz*, 482 U.S.

342 (1987), we sustained, without mentioning the *Sherbert* test, a prison's refusal to excuse inmates from work requirements to attend worship services.

[The] *Sherbert* test [was] developed in a context that lent itself to individualized governmental assessment of the reasons for the relevant conduct. [O]ur decisions in the unemployment cases stand for the proposition that where the State has in place a system of individual exemptions, it may not refuse to extend that system to cases of "religious hardship" without compelling reason.

Whether or not the decisions are that limited, they at least have nothing to do with an across-the-board criminal prohibition on a particular form of conduct. [T]he sounder approach [is] to hold the test inapplicable to such challenges. [To] make an individual's obligation to obey such a law contingent upon the law's coincidence with his religious beliefs, except where the State's interest is "compelling"— permitting him, by virtue of his beliefs, "to become a law unto himself," *Reynolds*— contradicts both constitutional tradition and common sense.

The "compelling government interest" requirement [as] the standard that must be met before the government may accord different treatment on the basis of race, see [Ch. 9, Sec. 2, I], or before the government may regulate the content of speech, is not remotely comparable to using it for the purpose asserted here. What it produces in those other fields—equality of treatment, and an unrestricted flow of contending speech—are constitutional norms; what it would produce here—a private right to ignore generally applicable laws—is a constitutional anomaly.

Nor is it possible to [require] a "compelling state interest" only when the conduct prohibited is "central" to the individual's religion. It is no more appropriate for judges to determine the "centrality" of religious beliefs [than] it would be for them to determine the "importance" of ideas before applying the "compelling interest" test in the free speech field. [I]n many different contexts, we have warned that courts must not presume to determine the place of a particular belief in a religion or the plausibility of a religious claim.

[I]f "compelling interest" really means what it says (and watering it down here would subvert its rigor in the other fields where it is applied), many laws will not meet the test. Any society adopting such a system would be courting anarchy, but that danger increases in direct proportion to the society's diversity of religious [beliefs]. Precisely because "we are a cosmopolitan nation made up of people of almost every conceivable religious preference," and precisely because we value and protect that religious divergence, we cannot afford the luxury of deeming *presumptively invalid*, as applied to the religious objector, every regulation of conduct that does not protect an interest of the highest order. [It] would open the prospect of constitutionally required religious exemptions from civic obligations of almost every conceivable kind—ranging from compulsory military service, see, e.g., *Gillette*, to the payment of taxes, see, e.g., *Lee*, to health and safety regulation such as manslaughter and child neglect laws, compulsory vaccination laws, drug laws, and traffic laws, to social welfare legislation such as minimum wage laws, see *Tony and Susan Alamo Foundation v. Secretary of Labor*, 471 U.S. 290 (1985), child labor laws, see *Prince;* animal cruelty laws, environmental protection laws, and laws providing for equality of opportunity for the races, see e.g., *Bob Jones University.* The First Amendment's protection of religious liberty does not require this.

[A] number of States have made an exception to their drug laws for sacramental peyote use. But to say that a nondiscriminatory religious-practice exemption is permitted, or even that it is desirable, is not to say that it is constitutionally required, and that the appropriate occasions for its creation can be discerned by the courts. It may fairly be said that leaving accommodation to the political process will place at a relative disadvantage those religious practices that are not widely engaged in; but that unavoidable consequence of democratic government must be preferred to a system in which each conscience is a law unto itself or in which judges weigh the social importance of all laws against the centrality of all religious beliefs. * * *

JUSTICE O'CONNOR, with whom JUSTICE BRENNAN, JUSTICE MARSHALL, and JUSTICE BLACKMUN join as to [Part II], concurring in the judgment. * * *

II.   "[T]o agree that religiously grounded conduct must often be subject to the broad police power of the State is not to deny that [a] regulation neutral on its face may, in its application, nonetheless offend the constitutional requirement for government neutrality if it unduly burdens the free exercise of religion," [*Yoder*, and in] each of the other cases cited by the Court to support its categorical rule, we rejected the particular constitutional claims before us only after carefully weighing the competing interests. [A] neutral criminal law prohibiting conduct that a State may legitimately regulate is, if anything, *more* burdensome than a neutral civil statute placing legitimate conditions on the award of a state benefit.

[Even] if, as an empirical matter, a government's criminal laws might usually serve a compelling interest in health, safety, or public order, the First Amendment at least requires a case-by-case determination of the question, sensitive to the facts of each particular claim. Given the range of conduct that a State might legitimately make criminal, we cannot assume, merely because a law carries criminal sanctions and is generally applicable, that the First Amendment *never* requires the State to grant a limited exemption for religiously motivated conduct.

Moreover, we have not "rejected" or "declined to apply" the compelling interest test in our recent cases. [In] both *Roy* and *Lyng*, for example, we expressly distinguished *Sherbert* on the ground that the First Amendment does not "require the Government *itself* to behave in ways that the individual believes will further his or her spiritual development. * * * " This distinction makes sense because "the Free Exercise Clause is written in terms of what the government cannot do to the individual, not in terms of what the individual can exact from the government." *Sherbert* (Douglas, J., concerning). Because [this case] plainly falls into the former category, I would apply those established precedents to the facts of this case.

Similarly, the other cases cited by the Court for the proposition that we have rejected application of the *Sherbert* test outside the unemployment compensation field are distinguishable because they arose in the narrow, specialized contexts in which we have not traditionally required the government to justify a burden on religious conduct by articulating a compelling interest. *Goldman v. Weinberger* and *O'Lone v. Shabazz* [military and prison regulations] say nothing about whether the test should continue to apply in paradigm free exercise cases such as the one presented here. [Our] free speech cases similarly recognize that neutral regulations that affect free speech values are subject to a balancing, rather than categorical, approach. See, e.g., *United States v. O'Brien*, [Ch. 7, Sec. 2].

Finally, the Court today suggests that [accommodating] minority religions [must] be left to the political process. In my view, however, the First Amendment was enacted precisely to protect the rights of those whose religious practices are not shared by the majority and may be viewed with hostility. The history of our free exercise doctrine amply demonstrates the harsh impact majoritarian rule has had on unpopular or emerging religious groups such as the Jehovah's Witnesses and the Amish. * * *

III. The Court's holding today [is] unnecessary to this [case.] Oregon has a significant interest in enforcing laws that control the possession and use of controlled substances by its citizens [and] a compelling interest in prohibiting the possession of peyote. [Although] the question is close, I would conclude that uniform application of Oregon's criminal prohibition is "essential to accomplish," *Lee*, its overriding interest in preventing the physical harm caused by the use of a [federal] Schedule I controlled substance. [R]egardless of the motivation of the user, [use] for religious purposes, violates the very purpose of the laws that prohibit them. [T]hat the Federal Government and several States provide exemptions for the religious use of peyote [does not result in] Oregon, with its specific asserted interest in uniform application of its drug laws, being *required* to do so by the First Amendment * * *

JUSTICE BLACKMUN, with whom JUSTICE BRENNAN and JUSTICE MARSHALL join, dissenting.

This Court over the years painstakingly has [held that] a state statute that burdens the free exercise of religion [and] may stand only if the law in general, and the State's refusal to allow a religious exemption in particular, are justified by a compelling interest that cannot be served by less restrictive means.

[T]he state interest involved [here is the] State's narrow interest in refusing to make an exception for the religious, ceremonial use of peyote. [The] State cannot plausibly assert that [is] essential to fulfill any compelling interest [as it] has never sought to prosecute respondents, and does not claim that it has made significant enforcement efforts against other religious users of peyote. The State's asserted interest thus amounts only to the symbolic preservation of an unenforced prohibition. * * *

Similarly, this Court's prior decisions [have] demanded evidentiary support for a refusal to allow a religious exception. [In] this case, the State [offers] no evidence that the religious use of peyote has ever harmed anyone. The factual findings of other courts cast doubt on the State's assumption that religious use of peyote is harmful. See *State v. Whittingham*, 504 P.2d 950 (Ariz.App. 1973) ("the State failed to prove that the quantities of peyote used in the sacraments of the Native American Church are sufficiently harmful to the health and welfare of the participants * * * "); *People v. Woody*, 40 Cal.Rptr. 69, 394 P.2d 813 (1964) ("as the Attorney General [admits,] the opinion of scientists and other experts is 'that peyote [works] no permanent deleterious injury to the Indian' "). [The] Federal Government [does] not find peyote so dangerous as to preclude an exemption for religious use.

The carefully circumscribed ritual context in which respondents used peyote is far removed from the irresponsible and unrestricted recreational use of unlawful drugs. * * * [J]ust as in *Yoder*, the values and interests of those seeking a religious exemption in this case are congruent, to a great degree, with those the State seeks to promote through its drug laws. See *Yoder* (since the Amish accept formal schooling up to 8th grade, and then provide "ideal" vocational education, State's interest in enforcing its law against the Amish is "less substantial than [for] children generally"). Not only does the Church's doctrine forbid nonreligious use of peyote; it also generally advocates self-reliance, familial responsibility, and abstinence from alcohol. There is considerable evidence that the spiritual and social support provided by the Church has been effective in combatting the tragic effects of alcoholism on the Native American population. * * *

The State also seeks to support its refusal to make an exception [by] invoking its interest in abolishing drug trafficking. There is, however, practically no illegal traffic in peyote. Also, the availability of peyote for religious use [would] still be strictly controlled by federal regulations, see 21 U.S.C. §§ 821–823 (registration requirements for distribution of controlled substances); and by the State of Texas, the only State in which peyote grows in significant quantities. * * *

Finally, the State argues that, [if] it grants an exemption for religious peyote use, a flood of other claims to religious exemptions will follow. [But almost] half the States, and the Federal Government, have maintained an exemption for religious peyote use for many years, and apparently have not found themselves overwhelmed by claims to other religious exemptions. [The] unusual circumstances that make the religious use of peyote compatible with the State's interests in health and safety and in preventing drug trafficking would not apply to other religious claims. Some religions, for example, might not restrict drug use to a limited ceremonial context, as does the Native American Church. See, e.g., *Olsen* ("the Ethiopian Zion Coptic Church [teaches] that marijuana is properly smoked 'continually all day' "). Some religious claims involve drugs such as marijuana and heroin, in which there is significant illegal traffic, [so] that it would be difficult to grant a religious exemption without seriously compromising law enforcement efforts. [Though] the State must treat all religions equally, and not favor one over another, this obligation is fulfilled by the uniform application of the "compelling interest" *test* to all free exercise claims, not by reaching uniform *results* as to all claims. * * *

Respondents believe, and their sincerity has *never* been at issue, that the peyote plant embodies their deity, and eating it is an act of worship and communion[,] the essential ritual of their religion. * * *[7]

NOTES

1. *Discrimination.* (a) CHURCH OF THE LUKUMI BABALU AYE, INC. v. HIALEAH, 508 U.S. 520 (1993), per KENNEDY, J., held that city ordinances barring ritual animal sacrifice violated the Free Exercise Clause: "[I]f the object of a law is to infringe upon or restrict practices because of their religious motivation, the law is not neutral, see *Smith;* and it is invalid unless it is justified by a compelling interest and is narrowly tailored to advance that interest. [The] ordinances had as their object the suppression of [the Santeria] religion. The [record] discloses animosity to Santeria adherents and their religious practices; the ordinances by their own terms target this religious exercise; the texts of the

---

[7] In 1993, Congress passed the Religious Freedom Restoration Act, which effectively reinstated the *Sherbert-Yoder* test for generally applicable laws that burden religious practices. RFRA was held unconstitutional in *Boerne v. Flores,* Ch. 11, Sec. 3, but only as applied to state (and not to federal) legislation, and the *Sherbert-Yoder* test thus continues to apply to the national government as a result of RFRA's mandate. *Burwell v. Hobby Lobby Stores, Inc.,* 573 U.S. 682 (2014), per Alito, J., held that RFRA exempted two closely held for-profit corporations from the obligation to provide employees with contraception coverage under the Affordable Care Act (see Ch. 2, Sec. 2, IV) because their owners' religious beliefs were opposed to after-conception contraceptives. The Court assumed that a guarantee of cost-free contraceptives is a "compelling government interest," but found that there are "less restrictive alternatives" available to the government to satisfy it, e.g., the government might pay for the insurance itself or require insurers to pay. Ginsburg, J., joined by Breyer, Sotomayor and Kagan, JJ., dissented in a lengthy opinion, contending that complying with the statute did not "substantially" burden the corporations, and that "none of the preferred alternatives would serve the compelling interests to which Congress responded." In a part of her opinion joined only by Sotomayor, J., Ginsburg, J., also concluded that for-profit corporations were not "persons" entitled to religious exemptions under RFRA.

The *Hobby Lobby* litigation spawned an extensive literature on the extent to which, if at all, corporations and other non-natural entities can have or exercise Free Exercise rights. A good collection of perspectives is *The Rise of Corporate Religious Liberty* (Micah Schwartzman, Zoe Robinson & Chad Flanders, eds., 2016). For the view that the *Hobby Lobby* exception violates the Establishment Clause "by shifting the material costs of accommodating contraception beliefs from employers to their employees," see Frederick M. Gedicks & Rebecca G. Van Tassell, *Exceptions from the Contraception Mandate: An Unconstitutional Accommodation of Religion,* 49 Harv.C.R.-C.L.L.Rev. 343 (2014).

Litigation regarding the contraceptive mandate of the Affordable Care Act has continued, with the issue of religious exemptions to the mandate raising numerous statutory issues. In *Little Sisters of the Poor Saints Peter and Paul Home v. Pennsylvania,* 140 S.Ct. 2367 (2020), a Supreme Court majority reversed a Third Circuit ruling and upheld the statutory authority of the Departments of Health and Human Services, Labor, and Treasury to create exemptions from the contraceptive mandate for employers with religious or moral objections to the mandate's requirements. Writing for the majority, Thomas, J., noted that no constitutional question had been raised in the litigation, and concluded that the plain language of the Affordable Care Act authorized all three departments to create the religious and moral exemptions. In a concurring opinion, Alito, J., joined by Gorsuch, J., argued that the religious exemption was required by the Religious Freedom Restoration Act, and thus would be necessary even apart from the language of the Affordable Care Act. Kagan, J., joined by Breyer, J., concurred only in the judgment, and emphasized that on remand the exemption would have to be measured against the administrative law requirement of "reasoned decisionmaking," and hinted that the exemption in its existing form might not satisfy this requirement. Ginsburg, J., joined by Sotomayor, J., dissented, arguing that the Women's Health Amendment to the Affordable Care Act required that contraceptive services be made available even in the face of a claimed exemption by employers.

ordinances were gerrymandered with care to proscribe religious killings of animals but to exclude almost all secular killings; and the ordinances suppress much more religious conduct than is necessary in order to achieve the legitimate ends asserted in their defense. [A] law that targets religious conduct for distinctive treatment or advances legitimate governmental interests only against conduct with a religious motivation will survive strict scrutiny only in rare cases."

SOUTER, J., concurred specially, noting that "the Court should re-examine the rule *Smith* declared." BLACKMUN, J., joined by O'Connor, J., concurred only in the judgment, contending that "when a law discriminates against religion as such, as do the ordinances in this case, it automatically will fail strict scrutiny [because] a law that targets religious practice for disfavored treatment both burdens the free exercise of religion and, by definition, is not precisely tailored to a compelling governmental interest." Finally, "this case does not [decide] whether the Free Exercise Clause would require a religious exemption from a law that sincerely pursued the goal of protecting animals from cruel treatment. [That] is not a concern to be treated lightly."

(b)　LOCKE v. DAVEY, 540 U.S. 712 (2004), per REHNQUIST, C.J., held that the exclusion (as required by the state constitution) from Washington's Promise Scholarship Program to assist academically gifted postsecondary students, of pursuit of a devotional theology degree (i.e., one "designed to induce religious faith"), did not violate the Free Exercise Clause: "[W]e have long said that 'there is room for play in the joints' between [the religion clauses]. *Walz* [i.e.,] there are some state actions permitted by the Establishment Clause but not required by the Free Exercise Clause. [And] there is no doubt that the State could, consistent with the Federal Constitution, permit Promise Scholars to pursue a degree in devotional theology, see *Witters* * * * .

"[Respondent] contends that [under] *Lukumi*, the program is presumptively unconstitutional because it is not facially neutral with respect to religion. [But here], the State's disfavor of religion (if it can be called that) is of a far milder kind [than in *Lukumi*]. It imposes neither criminal nor civil sanctions on any type of religious service or rite. It does not deny to ministers the right to participate in the political affairs of the community. See *McDaniel*. And it does not require students to choose between their religious beliefs and receiving a government benefit. *Sherbert*. The State has merely chosen not to fund a distinct category of instruction.

"[M]ajoring in devotional theology is akin to a religious calling as well as an academic pursuit. [T]he interest that [the Washington constitution] seeks to further is scarcely novel. [Since] the founding of our country, there have been popular uprisings against procuring taxpayer funds to support church leaders, which was one of the hallmarks of an 'established' religion. [Most] States that sought to avoid such an establishment around the time of the founding placed in their constitutions formal prohibitions against using tax funds to support the ministry. [T]hat early state constitutions saw no problem in explicitly excluding *only* the ministry from receiving state dollars reinforces the conclusion that religious instruction is of a different ilk. Far from evincing the hostility toward religion which was manifest in *Lukumi*, we believe that the entirety of the Promise Scholarship Program goes a long way toward including religion in its benefits. The program permits students to attend pervasively religious schools, so long as they are accredited [and] students are still eligible to take devotional theology courses."

SCALIA, J., joined by Thomas, J., dissented, finding *Lukumi* "irreconcilable with today's decision": "When the State makes a public benefit generally available, that benefit becomes part of the baseline against which burdens on religion are measured; and when the State withholds that benefit from some individuals solely on the basis of religion, it violates the Free Exercise Clause no less than if it had imposed a special tax.

"[The history relied on by the Court] involved not the inclusion of religious ministers in public benefits programs like the one at issue here, but laws that singled them out for financial aid. [No] one would seriously contend, for example, that the Framers would have barred ministers from using public roads on their way to church.

"[T]he State already has all the play in the joints it needs. [It] could make the scholarships redeemable only at public universities (where it sets the curriculum), or only for select courses of study. Either option would replace a program that facially discriminates against religion with one that just happens not to subsidize it.

"[T]he interest to which the Court defers is not fear of a conceivable Establishment Clause violation, budget constraints, avoidance of endorsement, or substantive neutrality[, but] a pure philosophical preference: the State's opinion that it would violate taxpayers' freedom of conscience *not* to discriminate against candidates for the ministry. This sort of protection of 'freedom of conscience' has no logical limit and can justify the singling out of religion for exclusion from public programs in virtually any context. The Court never says whether it deems this interest compelling (the opinion is devoid of any mention of standard of review) but, self-evidently, it is not.

"The Court [identifies] two features thought to render its discrimination less offensive. The first is the lightness of Davey's burden. The Court offers no authority for approving facial discrimination against religion simply because its material consequences are not severe. I might understand such a test if we were still in the business of reviewing facially neutral laws that merely happen to burden some individual's religious exercise, but we are not. See *Smith*. Discrimination *on the face of a statute* is something else. The indignity of being singled out for special burdens on the basis of one's religious calling is so profound that the concrete harm produced can never be dismissed as insubstantial[,] see e.g., *Brown v. Board of Education*, and it should not do so here. * * *

"The other reason the Court thinks this particular facial discrimination less offensive is that the scholarship program was not motivated by animus toward religion. [We] do sometimes look to legislative intent to smoke out more subtle instances of discrimination, but we do so as a *supplement* to the core guarantee of facially equal treatment, not as a replacement for it.

"[Most] citizens of this country identify themselves as professing some religious belief, but [t]hose the statutory exclusion actually affects—those whose belief in their religion is so strong that they dedicate their study and their lives to its ministry—are a far narrower set. One need not delve too far into modern popular culture to perceive a trendy disdain for deep religious conviction."

(c)   In TRINITY LUTHERAN CHURCH OF COLUMBUS, INC. v. COMER, 137 S.Ct. 2012 (2017), Missouri refused to reimburse a church for the cost of gravel produced by the state pursuant to its program to dispose of scrapped tires. The church wished to use the gravel to resurface its school's playground. The state relied on a provision of the state constitution forbidding aid to churches. The Court, per ROBERTS, C.J., held that this violated the Free Exercise Clause: The state's "policy expressly discriminates against otherwise eligible recipients." Consequently, it "imposes a penalty on the free exercise of religion that triggers the most exacting scrutiny, *Lukumi*." *Locke* is distinguishable because its use of tax funds to pay for training of clergy involved an "essentially religious endeavor," totally unlike Missouri's program to use recycled tires to resurface playgrounds.

Thomas, J., joined by Gorsuch J., concurred in part. Gorsuch, J., joined by Thomas, J. also concurred in part. Breyer, J., concurred in the result and would limit it to the fact that the program here was "designed to secure or to improve the health and safety of children."

SOTOMAYOR, J., joined by Ginsburg, J. dissented: The Court holds "for the first time, that the Constitution requires the government to provide public funds directly to a church. [The] Establishment Clause does not allow Missouri to grant the Church's funding requests because the Church uses the Learning Center, including its playground, in conjunction with its religious mission. The Court's silence on this front signals its misunderstanding of the facts of this case or a departure from our precedents."

2.   *Choosing a "minister."* In HOSANNA-TABOR EVANGELICAL LUTHERAN CHURCH AND SCHOOL v. EQUAL EMPLOYMENT OPPORTUNITY COMM'N, 565 U.S. 171 (2012), after the church school terminated Perich, a teacher who had completed the church's academic requirements to become a "minister," she filed a claim with the EEOC that her termination violated the Americans with Disabilities Act. Although "the Courts of Appeals have uniformly recognized [a] ministerial exception barring certain employment discrimination claims against religious institutions—an exception 'rooted in the First Amendment's guarantees of religious freedom,'" the Sixth Circuit concluded that Perich "did not qualify as a 'minister' under the exception." A unanimous Court, per ROBERTS, C.J., reversed: "The Establishment Clause prevents the Government from appointing ministers, and the Free Exercise Clause prevents it from interfering with the freedom of religious groups to select [those] who will personify its beliefs."

The Court was "reluctant [to] adopt a rigid formula for deciding when an employee qualifies as a minister," but noted that the church "held Perich out as a minister," and that she "held herself out as a minister of the church" in various ways. "Perich's title as a minister reflected a significant degree of religious training followed by a formal process of commissioning. [S]he had to pass an oral examination by a faculty committee at a Lutheran college. It took Perich six years to fulfill these requirements. [She] taught her students religion four days a week, and led them in prayer three times a day. Once a week, she took her students to a school-wide chapel service, and—about twice a year—she took her turn leading [it.]" Finally, in regarding "the relative amount of time Perich spent performing religious functions as largely determinative" (this "consumed only 45 minutes of each workday") rather than just "relevant," the Sixth Circuit "gave too much weight to the fact that lay teachers at the school performed the same religious duties. [The] heads of congregations themselves often have a mix of duties, including secular ones such as helping to manage the congregations' finances, supervising purely secular personnel, and overseeing the upkeep of facilities."

Alito, J., joined by Kagan, J., concurred, urging that "courts should focus on the function performed by persons who work for religious bodies. [The] 'ministerial' exception [should] apply to any 'employee' who leads a religious organization, conducts worship services or important religious ceremonies or rituals, or serves as a messenger or teacher of its faith."

The scope of the so-called ministerial exemption from much of state and federal employment law was expanded at the end of the 2019 Term in OUR LADY OF GUADALUPE SCHOOL v. MORRISSEY-BERRU, 140 S.Ct. 2049 (2020). Although the teacher in *Hosanna-Tabor* had been formally designated by her religious school employer as a "minister," and although she had received considerable religious training, the Court in *Our Lady of Guadalupe* held that neither of these attributes were necessary for the application of the ministerial exemption. Writing for a 7–2 majority, ALITO, J., emphasized that the criteria set forth in *Hosanna-Tabor* were not to be understood as a rigid formula, and that the teachers whose employment was at issue in the two consolidated cases had substantial responsibilities for religious education in their respective religious schools. Even though neither was designated as a minister, even though both had been trained in the liberal arts and not in religion, and even though both were involved in teaching non-religious subjects, their actual job duties included a sufficient amount of religious instruction and inculcation to qualify them for the ministerial exemption. THOMAS, J., joined by Gorsuch, J., concurred in the Court's judgment and opinion, but wrote separately to emphasize that the religion clauses did not permit the courts to second-guess the good-faith determination by a religious institution of who did or did not qualify as a minister. SOTOMAYOR, J., joined by Ginsburg, J., dissented, charging the majority with having distorted the facts, with granting undue deference to a religious institution's determination of the nature of the employee's responsibilities, and of being insufficiently attentive to the basic principle of *Employment Division v. Smith, supra,* that "religious entities" must "abide by generally applicable laws," especially laws dealing with discrimination in employment.

3. ***Purpose—again.*** In MASTERPIECE CAKESHOP, LTD. v. COLORADO CIVIL RIGHTS COMM'N, 138 S.Ct. 1719 (2018), the Court, per KENNEDY, J., relied on *Church of the Lukumi Babalu Aye* in using evidence of anti-religious statements from several members of the Colorado Civil Rights Commission's hearings to invalidate that Commission's conclusion, upheld in the Colorado courts, that a baker who refused to bake a wedding cake for a same-sex couple's wedding because of the baker's religious convictions was not entitled to an exemption from the requirements of Colorado law prohibiting discrimination on grounds of sexual orientation. In rejecting the Commission's rejection of the baker's claim, the Court said that "[t]he neutral and respectful consideration to which Phillips (the baker) was entitled was compromised." The Court noted some number of statements by commissioners that supported this conclusion, but emphasized one in which a commissioner had said that "[f]reedom of religion and religion has been used to justify all kinds of discrimination throughout history, whether it be slavery, whether it be the holocaust, whether it be—I mean, we—we can list hundreds of situations where freedom of religion has been used to justify discrimination. And to me it is one of the most despicable pieces of rhetoric that people can use to—to use their religion to hurt others." Because of its reliance on what it took to be explicit hostility both to the baker's sincerity and to religion in general, especially the statement just quoted, one unchallenged by any other commissioner, the majority did not address the continuing question of the extent to which religious convictions would entitle someone to a constitutionally mandated exemption from a religiously neutral law of general application that was neutrally applied without hostility. Justice Kagan's concurring opinion, joined by Justice Breyer, agreed with most of the majority's reasoning, especially on the issue of overt hostility, but questioned whether differential treatment by the commission of this and cases in which religious-conscience-based claims by bakers who had refused to bake cakes opposed to same-sex marriage was itself evidence of hostility, as the majority had, in part, argued. Justice Thomas's concurring opinion, focused substantially on free speech issues, but Justice Ginsburg's dissenting opinion, joined by Justice Sotomayor, concentrated on the free exercise issue, questioning both whether statements largely challenging the baker's sincerity amounted to the kind of hostility present in *Church of the Lukumi Babalu Aye* and also whether the statements of "one or two" commissioners were sufficient to invalidate an action taken by the entire commission.

TRUMP v. HAWAII
585 U.S. ___, 138 S.Ct. 2392, 201 L.Ed.2d 775 (2018).

CHIEF JUSTICE ROBERTS delivered the opinion of the Court.

[T]he Immigration and Nationality Act [vests] the President with authority to restrict the entry of aliens whenever he finds that their entry "would be detrimental to the interests of the United States." [T]he President concluded that it was necessary to impose entry restrictions on nationals of countries that present national security risks. * * *

I. A.   Shortly after taking office, President Trump signed Executive Order No. 13769, Protecting the Nation From Foreign Terrorist Entry Into the United States. (EO-1). EO-1 directed the Secretary of Homeland Security to conduct a [worldwide] review to examine the adequacy of information provided by foreign governments about their nationals seeking to enter the United States. Pending that review, the order suspended for 90 days the entry of foreign nationals from seven countries—Iran, Iraq, Libya, Somalia, Sudan, Syria, and Yemen—that had been previously identified by Congress or prior administrations as posing heightened terrorism risks. The District Court for the Western District of Washington entered a temporary restraining order blocking the entry restrictions, and the Court of Appeals for the Ninth Circuit denied the Government's request to stay that order.

In response, the President revoked EO-1, replacing it with [EO-2, which] temporarily restricted the entry (with case-by-case waivers) of foreign nationals from six of the countries covered by EO-1: Iran, Libya, Somalia, Sudan, Syria, and Yemen. [T]hose countries had been selected because each "is a state sponsor of terrorism, has been significantly compromised by terrorist organizations, or contains active conflict zones." The entry restriction was to stay in effect for 90 days, pending completion of the worldwide review.

[The] interim measures were immediately challenged in court. The District Courts for the Districts of Maryland and Hawaii entered nationwide preliminary injunctions [and] the respective Courts of Appeals upheld those injunctions, albeit on different grounds. This Court granted certiorari and stayed the injunctions—allowing the entry suspension to go into effect—with respect to foreign nationals who lacked a "credible claim of a bona fide relationship" with a person or entity in the United States. The temporary restrictions in EO-2 expired before this Court took any action, and we vacated the lower court decisions as moot.

September 24, 2017, after completion of the worldwide review, the President issued the Proclamation before us. [It] sought to improve vetting procedures by identifying ongoing deficiencies in the information needed to assess whether nationals of particular countries present "public safety threats." To further that purpose, the Proclamation placed entry restrictions on the nationals of eight foreign states whose systems for managing and sharing information about their nationals the President deemed inadequate.

The Proclamation described how foreign states were selected for inclusion based on the review undertaken pursuant to EO-2. As part of that review, the Department of Homeland Security (DHS), in consultation with the State Department and several intelligence agencies, developed a "baseline" for the information required from foreign governments to confirm the identity of individuals seeking entry into the United States, and to determine whether those individuals pose a security threat. The baseline included three components. The first, "identity-management information," focused on whether a foreign government ensures the integrity of travel documents by issuing electronic passports, reporting lost or stolen passports, and making available additional identity-related information. Second, the agencies considered the extent to which the country discloses information on criminal history and suspected terrorist links, provides travel document exemplars, and facilitates the U.S. Government's receipt of information about airline passengers and crews traveling to the United States. Finally, the agencies weighed various indicators of national security risk, including whether the foreign state is a known or potential terrorist safe haven and whether it regularly declines to receive returning nationals following final orders of removal from the United States.

DHS collected and evaluated data regarding all foreign governments. It identified 16 countries [as] presenting national security concerns, and another 31 countries as "at risk" of similarly failing to meet the baseline. The State Department then undertook diplomatic efforts over a 50-day period to encourage all foreign governments to improve their practices. As a result of that effort, numerous countries provided DHS with travel document exemplars and agreed to share information on known or suspected terrorists.

Following the 50-day period, the Acting Secretary of Homeland Security concluded that eight countries—Chad, Iran, Iraq, Libya, North Korea, Syria, Venezuela, and Yemen—remained deficient in terms of their risk profile and willingness to provide requested information. The Acting Secretary recommended that the President impose entry restrictions on certain nationals from all of those countries except Iraq. She also concluded that although Somalia generally satisfied the information-sharing component of the baseline standards, its "identity-management deficiencies" and "significant terrorist presence" presented special circumstances justifying additional limitations. She therefore recommended entry limitations for certain nationals of that country. As for Iraq, the Acting Secretary found that entry limitations on its nationals were not warranted [given] Iraq's commitment to combating ISIS.

After consulting with multiple Cabinet members and other officials, [the] President determined that certain entry restrictions were necessary to "prevent the entry of those foreign nationals about whom the United States Government lacks sufficient information"; "elicit improved identity-management and information-sharing protocols and practices from foreign governments"; and otherwise "advance [the] foreign policy, national security, and counterterrorism objectives" of the United States.

[The] Proclamation imposed a range of restrictions that vary based on the "distinct circumstances" in each of the eight countries. [It] further directs DHS to assess on a continuing basis whether entry restrictions should be modified or continued, and to report to the President every 180 days. Upon completion of the first such review period, the President, on the recommendation of the Secretary of

Homeland Security, determined that Chad had sufficiently improved its practices, and he accordingly lifted restrictions on its nationals.

B.   Plaintiffs in this case are the State of Hawaii, three individuals, [and] the Muslim Association of Hawaii. The State operates the University of Hawaii system, which recruits students and faculty from the designated countries. [Plaintiffs] argued that the Proclamation contravenes provisions in the Immigration and Nationality Act (INA) [and] the Establishment Clause of the First Amendment, because it was motivated not by concerns pertaining to national security but by animus toward Islam.

The District Court granted a nationwide preliminary injunction barring enforcement of the entry restrictions. [The] Government requested expedited briefing and sought a stay pending appeal. The Court of Appeals for the Ninth Circuit granted a partial stay, permitting enforcement of the Proclamation with respect to foreign nationals who lack a bona fide relationship with the United States. This Court then stayed the injunction in full pending disposition of the Government's appeal.

III.   The INA establishes numerous grounds on which an alien abroad may be inadmissible to the United States and ineligible for a visa. Congress has also delegated to the President authority [to] "suspend the entry of all aliens or any class of aliens" whenever he "finds" that their entry "would be detrimental to the interests of the United States." * * *

The text of § 1182(f) states: "Whenever the President finds that the entry of any aliens or of any class of aliens into the United States would be detrimental to the interests of the United States, he may by proclamation, and for such period as he shall deem necessary, suspend the entry of all aliens or any class of aliens as immigrants or nonimmigrants, or impose on the entry of aliens any restrictions he may deem to be appropriate."

By its terms, § 1182(f) exudes deference to the President in every clause. [The] sole prerequisite set forth in § 1182(f) is that the President "find[ ]" that the entry of the covered aliens "would be detrimental to the interests of the United States." The President has undoubtedly fulfilled that requirement here. He first ordered DHS and other agencies to conduct a comprehensive evaluation of every single country's compliance with the information and risk assessment baseline. The President then issued a Proclamation setting forth extensive findings describing how deficiencies in the practices of select foreign governments—several of which are state sponsors of terrorism—deprive the Government of "sufficient information to assess the risks [those countries' nationals] pose to the United States." * * *

Plaintiffs believe that these findings are insufficient. [But] even assuming that some form of review is appropriate, plaintiffs' attacks on the sufficiency of the President's findings cannot be sustained. The 12-page Proclamation [is] more detailed than any prior order a President has issued under § 1182(f). Contrast Presidential Proclamation No. 6958 (President Clinton, explaining in one sentence why suspending entry of members of the Sudanese government and armed forces "is in the foreign policy interests of the United States"); Presidential Proclamation No. 4865, 3 CFR 50–51 (1981) (President Reagan explaining in five sentences why measures to curtail "the continuing illegal migration by sea of large numbers of undocumented aliens into the southeastern United States" are "necessary").

Moreover, plaintiffs' request for a searching inquiry into the persuasiveness of the President's justifications is inconsistent with the broad statutory text and the deference traditionally accorded the President in this sphere. * * *

The Proclamation also comports with the remaining textual limits in § 1182(f). We agree with plaintiffs that the word "suspend" often connotes a "defer[ral] till later." [But] 1182(f) authorizes the President to suspend entry "for such period as he shall deem necessary." [To] that end, the Proclamation establishes an ongoing process to engage covered nations and assess every 180 days whether the entry restrictions should be modified or terminated. [Finally,] the Proclamation properly identifies a "class of aliens"—nationals of select countries— whose entry is suspended. [In] short, the language of § 1182(f) is clear, and the Proclamation does not exceed any textual limit on the President's authority.

B.   Confronted with this "facially broad grant of power," plaintiffs focus their attention on statutory structure and legislative [purpose.] Plaintiffs' structural argument starts with the premise that § 1182(f) does not give the President authority to countermand Congress's considered policy judgments. The President, they say, may supplement the INA, but he cannot supplant it. [But] the Proclamation supports Congress's individualized approach for determining admissibility. The INA sets forth various inadmissibility grounds based on connections to terrorism and criminal history, but those provisions can only work when the consular officer has sufficient (and sufficiently reliable) information to make that determination. The Proclamation promotes the effectiveness of the vetting process by helping to ensure the availability of such information. [Nor] is there a conflict between the Proclamation and the Visa Waiver Program. The Program allows travel without a visa for short-term visitors from 38 countries that have entered into a "rigorous security partnership" with the United States. Eligibility for that partnership involves "broad and consequential assessments of [the country's] foreign security standards and operations." * * *

Congress's decision to authorize a benefit for "many of America's closest allies," did not implicitly foreclose the Executive from imposing tighter restrictions on nationals of certain high-risk countries. [Fairly] read, the provision vests authority in the President to impose additional limitations on entry beyond the grounds for exclusion set forth in the INA—including in response to circumstances that might affect the vetting system or other "interests of the United States." * * *

C.   Plaintiffs' final statutory argument is that the President's entry suspension violates § 1152(a)(1)(A), which provides that "no person shall . . . be discriminated against in the issuance of an immigrant visa because of the person's race, sex, nationality, place of birth, or place of residence." They contend that we should interpret the provision as prohibiting nationality-based discrimination throughout the *entire* immigration process, despite the reference in § 1152(a)(1)(A) to the act of visa issuance alone. [W]e reject plaintiffs' interpretation because it ignores the basic distinction between admissibility determinations and visa issuance that runs throughout the INA. [Once] § 1182 sets the boundaries of admissibility into the United States, § 1152(a)(1)(A) prohibits discrimination in the allocation of immigrant visas based on nationality and other traits. * * *

IV. A.   We now turn to plaintiffs' claim that the Proclamation was issued for the unconstitutional purpose of excluding Muslims.

[B.] Plaintiffs believe that the Proclamation [operates] as a "religious gerrymander," in part because most of the countries covered by the Proclamation have Muslim-majority populations [and] that the primary purpose of the Proclamation was religious animus and that the President's stated concerns about vetting protocols and national security were but pretexts for discriminating against Muslims.

At the heart of plaintiffs' case is a series of statements by the President and his advisers casting doubt on the official objective of the Proclamation. For example, while a candidate on the campaign trail, the President published a "Statement on Preventing Muslim Immigration" that called for a "total and complete shutdown of Muslims entering the United States until our country's representatives can figure out what is going [on."] Then-candidate Trump also stated that "Islam hates us" and asserted that the United States was "having problems with Muslims coming into the country." Shortly after being elected, when asked whether violence in Europe had affected his plans to "ban Muslim immigration," the President replied, "You know my plans. All along, I've been proven to be right."

One week after his inauguration, the President issued EO-1. In a television interview, one of the President's campaign advisers explained that when the President "first announced it, he said, 'Muslim ban.' He called me up. He said, 'Put a commission together. Show me the right way to do it legally.' " The adviser said he assembled a group of Members of Congress and lawyers that "focused on, instead of religion, danger. . . . [The order] is based on places where there [is] substantial evidence that people are sending terrorists into our country."

Plaintiffs also note that after issuing EO-2 to replace EO-1, the President expressed regret that his prior order had been "watered down" and called for a "much tougher version" of his "Travel Ban." Shortly before the release of the Proclamation, he stated that the "travel ban . . . should be far larger, tougher, and more specific," but "stupidly that would not be politically correct." More recently, on November 29, 2017, the President retweeted links to three anti-Muslim propaganda videos. In response to questions about those videos, the President's deputy press secretary denied that the President thinks Muslims are a threat to the United States, explaining that "the President has been talking about these security issues for years now, from the campaign trail to the White House" and "has addressed these issues with the travel order that he issued earlier this year and the companion proclamation."

The President of the United States possesses an extraordinary power to speak to his fellow citizens and on their behalf. Our Presidents have frequently used that power to espouse the principles of religious freedom and tolerance on which this Nation was founded. * * *

Plaintiffs argue that this President's words strike at fundamental standards of respect and tolerance, in violation of our constitutional tradition. But the issue before us is not whether to denounce the statements. It is instead the significance of those statements in reviewing a Presidential directive, neutral on its face, addressing a matter within the core of executive responsibility. In doing so, we must consider not only the statements of a particular President, but also the authority of the Presidency itself.

The case before us differs in numerous respects from the conventional Establishment Clause claim. Unlike the typical suit involving religious displays or school prayer, plaintiffs seek to invalidate a national security directive regulating the entry of aliens abroad. [The] Proclamation, moreover, is facially neutral toward religion. Plaintiffs therefore ask the Court to probe the sincerity of the stated justifications for the policy by reference to extrinsic statements—many of which were made before the President took the oath of office. These various aspects of plaintiffs' challenge inform our standard of review.

C.   For more than a century, this Court has recognized that the admission and exclusion of foreign nationals is a "fundamental sovereign attribute exercised by the Government's political departments largely immune from judicial control." [Because] decisions in these matters may implicate "relations with foreign powers," or involve "classifications defined in the light of changing political and economic circumstances," such judgments "are frequently of a character more appropriate to either the Legislature or the Executive." *Mathews v. Diaz*, 426 U.S. 67 (1976).

Nonetheless, although foreign nationals seeking admission have no constitutional right to entry, this Court has engaged in a circumscribed judicial inquiry when the denial of a visa allegedly burdens the constitutional rights of a U.S. citizen. [But] we limited our review to whether the Executive gave a "facially legitimate and bona fide" reason for its action. [This] narrow standard of review "has particular force" in admission and immigration cases that overlap with "the area of national security." * * *

The upshot of our cases in this context is clear: "Any rule of constitutional law that would inhibit the flexibility" of the President "to respond to changing world conditions should be adopted only with the greatest caution," and our inquiry into matters of entry and national security is highly constrained. We need not define the precise contours of that inquiry in this case. A conventional application of [the precedents], asking only whether the policy is facially legitimate and bona fide, would put an end to our review. [For] our purposes today, we assume that we may look behind the face of the Proclamation to the extent of applying rational basis review. [As] a result, we may consider plaintiffs' extrinsic evidence, but will uphold the policy so long as it can reasonably be understood to result from a justification independent of unconstitutional grounds.

D.   Given the standard of review, it should come as no surprise that [it] cannot be said that it is impossible to "discern a relationship to legitimate state interests" or that the policy is "inexplicable by anything but animus." * * *

The Proclamation is expressly premised on legitimate purposes: preventing entry of nationals who cannot be adequately vetted and inducing other nations to improve their practices. The text says nothing about religion. [T]he policy covers just 8% of the world's Muslim population and is limited to countries that were previously designated by Congress or prior administrations as posing national security risks. * * *

The Proclamation, moreover, reflects the results of a worldwide review process undertaken by multiple Cabinet officials and their agencies. [As] for Iraq, the Secretary of Homeland Security determined that entry restrictions were not warranted in light of the close cooperative relationship between the U.S. and Iraqi Governments and the country's key role in combating terrorism in the region. It [is] difficult to see how exempting one of the largest predominantly Muslim countries in the region from coverage under the Proclamation can be cited as evidence of animus toward Muslims.

[While] we of course "do not defer to the Government's reading of the First Amendment," the Executive's evaluation of the underlying facts is entitled to appropriate weight, particularly in the context of litigation involving "sensitive and weighty interests of national security and foreign affairs."

Three additional features of the entry policy support the Government's claim of a legitimate national security interest. First, since the President introduced entry restrictions in January 2017, three Muslim-majority countries—Iraq, Sudan, and Chad—have been removed from the list of covered countries. * * *

Second, for those countries that remain subject to entry restrictions, the Proclamation includes significant exceptions for various categories of foreign nationals. [The] Proclamation also exempts permanent residents and individuals who have been granted asylum.

Third, the Proclamation creates a waiver program open to all covered foreign nationals seeking entry as immigrants or nonimmigrants. According to the Proclamation, consular officers are to consider in each admissibility determination whether the alien demonstrates that (1) denying entry would cause undue hardship; (2) entry would not pose a threat to public safety; and (3) entry would be in the interest of the United States. [The] Proclamation also directs DHS and the State Department to issue guidance elaborating upon the circumstances that would justify a waiver.

Finally, the dissent invokes *Korematsu* (1944, Ch. 9, Sec. 2). Whatever rhetorical advantage the dissent may see in doing so, *Korematsu* has nothing to do with this case. [The] dissent's reference to *Korematsu*, however, affords this Court the opportunity to make express what is already obvious: *Korematsu* was gravely wrong the day it was decided, has been overruled in the court of history, and—to be clear—"has no place in law under the Constitution." 323 U.S., at 248 (Jackson, J., dissenting). * * *

JUSTICE KENNEDY, concurring.

I join the Court's opinion in full.

There may be some common ground between the opinions in this case, in that the Court does acknowledge that in some instances, governmental action may be subject to judicial review to determine whether or not it is "inexplicable by anything but animus," *Romer* v. *Evans* (1996, Ch. 9, Sec. 4), which in this case would be animosity to a religion. Whether judicial proceedings may properly continue in this case, in light of the substantial deference that is and must be accorded to the Executive in the conduct of foreign affairs, and in light of today's decision, is a matter to be addressed in the first instance on remand. And even if further proceedings are permitted, it would be necessary to determine that any discovery and other preliminary matters would not themselves intrude on the foreign affairs power of the Executive. * * *

THOMAS, J., concurring.

I join the Court's opinion, which highlights just a few of the many problems with the plaintiffs' claims. There are several more. Section 1182(f) does not set forth any judicially enforceable limits that constrain the President. Nor could it, since the President has *inherent* authority to exclude aliens from the country. See *United States ex rel. Knauff v. Shaughnessy*, 338 U.S. 537 (1950). The plaintiffs cannot raise any other First Amendment claim, since the alleged religious discrimination in this case was directed at aliens abroad. See *United States v. Verdugo-Urquidez*, 494 U.S. 259, 265 (1990). And, even on its own terms, the plaintiffs' proffered evidence of anti-Muslim discrimination is unpersuasive. * * *

JUSTICE SOTOMAYOR, with whom JUSTICE GINSBURG joins, dissenting.

[The] Court's decision [leaves] undisturbed a policy first advertised openly and unequivocally as a "total and complete shutdown of Muslims entering the United States" because the policy now masquerades behind a façade of national-security concerns. But [b]ased on the evidence in the record, a reasonable observer would conclude that the Proclamation was motivated by anti-Muslim animus. That alone suffices to show that plaintiffs are likely to succeed on the merits of their Establishment Clause claim.

[A.] [T]his Court has long acknowledged that governmental actions that favor one religion "inevitabl[y]" foster "the hatred, disrespect and even contempt of those who [hold] contrary beliefs." *Engel v. Vitale* (1962, Ch. 8, Sec. 1).

"When the government acts with the ostensible and predominant purpose" of disfavoring a particular religion, "it violates that central Establishment Clause value of official religious neutrality, there being no neutrality when the government's ostensible object is to take sides." *McCreary County v. ACLU* (2005, Ch. 8, Sec. 1). To determine whether plaintiffs have proved an Establishment Clause violation, the Court asks whether a reasonable observer would view the government action as enacted for the purpose of disfavoring a religion.

In answering that question, this Court has generally considered the text of the government policy, its operation, and any available evidence regarding "the historical background of the decision under challenge, the specific series of events leading to the enactment or official policy in question, and the legislative or administrative history, including contemporaneous statements made by" the decisionmaker. *Church of the Lukumi Babalu Aye v. Hialeah* (1993, Ch. 8, Sec. 2).

B. 1. [T]he full record paints [a] picture, from which a reasonable observer would readily conclude that the Proclamation was motivated by hostility and animus toward the Muslim faith. During his Presidential campaign, then-candidate Donald Trump issued a formal statement "calling for a total and complete shutdown of Muslims entering the United States." * * *

On December 8, 2015, Trump justified his proposal during a television interview by noting that President Franklin D. Roosevelt "did the same thing" with respect to the internment of Japanese Americans during World War II. In January 2016, during a Republican primary debate, Trump was asked whether he wanted to "rethink [his] position" on "banning Muslims from entering the country." He answered, "No." [In] March 2016, he expressed his belief that "Islam hates us. . . . [W]e can't allow people coming into this country who have this hatred of the United States . . . [a]nd of people that are not Muslim." * * *

As Trump's presidential campaign progressed, he began to describe his policy proposal in slightly different terms. In June 2016, for instance, he characterized the policy proposal as a suspension of immigration from countries "where there's a proven history of terrorism." [Asked] in July 2016 whether he was "pull[ing] back from" his pledged Muslim ban, Trump responded, "I actually don't think it's a rollback. In fact, you could say it's an expansion."

On January 27, 2017, one week after taking office, President Trump signed Executive Order No. 13769 (EO-1), entitled "Protecting the Nation From Foreign Terrorist Entry Into the United States." [That] same day, President Trump explained to the media that, under EO-1, Christians would be given priority for entry as refugees into the United States. In particular, he bemoaned the fact that in the past, "[i]f you were a Muslim [refugee from Syria] you could come in, but if you were a Christian, it was almost impossible." [The] following day, one of President Trump's key advisers candidly drew the connection between EO-1 and the "Muslim ban" that the President had pledged to implement if elected. * * *

On March 6, 2017, President Trump issued [a] new executive order, which, like its predecessor, imposed temporary entry and refugee bans (EO-2). [T]he

White House Press Secretary told reporters that, by issuing EO-2, President Trump "continue[d] to deliver on . . . his most significant campaign promises." [While] litigation over EO-2 was ongoing, President Trump repeatedly made statements alluding to a desire to keep Muslims out of the country. For instance, he said at a rally of his supporters that EO-2 was just a "watered down version of the first one" and had been "tailor[ed]" at the behest of "the lawyers." [And] in June 2017, the President stated on Twitter that the Justice Department had submitted a "watered down, politically correct version" of the "original Travel Ban" "to S[upreme] C[ourt]." The President went on to tweet: "[W]e need a TRAVEL BAN for certain DANGEROUS countries, not some politically correct term that won't help us protect our people!" [In] September 2017, President Trump tweeted that "[t]he travel ban into the United States should be far larger, tougher and more specific—but stupidly, that would not be politically correct!"

[2.] Taking all the relevant evidence together, a reasonable observer would conclude that the Proclamation was driven primarily by anti-Muslim animus, rather than by the Government's asserted national-security justifications. Even before being sworn into office, then-candidate Trump [promised] to enact a "total and complete shutdown of Muslims entering the United States." The President continued to make similar statements well after his inauguration, as detailed above.

Moreover, despite several opportunities to do so, President Trump has never disavowed any of his prior statements about Islam. Instead, he has continued to make remarks that a reasonable observer would view as an unrelenting attack on the Muslim religion and its followers. [I]t is unsurprising that the President's lawyers have, at every step in the lower courts, failed in their attempts to launder the Proclamation of its discriminatory taint. [Ultimately,] what began as a policy explicitly "calling for a total and complete shutdown of Muslims entering the United States" has since morphed into a "Proclamation" putatively based on national-security concerns. But this new window dressing cannot conceal an unassailable fact: the words of the President and his advisers create the strong perception that the Proclamation is contaminated by impermissible discriminatory animus against Islam and its followers.

II. [The majority] incorrectly applies a watered-down legal standard in an effort to short circuit plaintiffs' Establishment Clause claim.

The majority begins its constitutional analysis by noting that this Court, at times, "has engaged in a circumscribed judicial inquiry when the denial of a visa allegedly burdens the constitutional rights of a U.S. citizen." As the majority notes, *Kleindienst v. Mandel*, 408 U.S. 753 (1972), held that when the Executive Branch provides "a facially legitimate and bona fide reason" for denying a visa, "courts will neither look behind the exercise of that discretion, nor test it by balancing its justification." [T]he majority rightly declines to apply *Mandel*'s "narrow standard of review" and "assume[s] that we may look behind the face of the Proclamation." In doing so, however, the Court, without explanation or precedential support, limits its review of the Proclamation to rational-basis scrutiny. That approach is perplexing, given that in other Establishment Clause cases, including those involving claims of religious animus or discrimination, this Court has applied a more stringent standard of review.

But even under rational-basis review, the Proclamation must fall. [The] President's statements, which the majority utterly fails to address in its legal analysis, strongly support the conclusion that the Proclamation was issued to express hostility toward Muslims and exclude them from the country. Given the overwhelming record evidence of anti-Muslim animus, it simply cannot be said that the Proclamation has a legitimate basis. * * *

The majority insists that the Proclamation furthers two interrelated national-security interests: "preventing entry of nationals who cannot be adequately vetted and inducing other nations to improve their practices." [E]ven a cursory review of the Government's asserted national-security rationale reveals that the Proclamation is nothing more than a " 'religious gerrymander.' " *Lukumi.*

The majority first emphasizes that the Proclamation "says nothing about religion." Even so, the Proclamation, just like its predecessors, overwhelmingly targets Muslim-majority nations. Given the record here, including all the President's statements linking the Proclamation to his apparent hostility toward Muslims, it is of no moment that the Proclamation also includes minor restrictions on two non-Muslim majority countries, North Korea and Venezuela, or that the Government has removed a few Muslim-majority countries from the list of covered countries since EO-1 was issued. * * *

The majority next contends that the Proclamation "reflects the results of a worldwide review process under-taken by multiple Cabinet officials." [But] the worldwide review does little to break the clear connection between the Proclamation and the President's anti-Muslim statements. The President campaigned on a promise to implement a "total and complete shutdown of Muslims" entering the country, translated that campaign promise into a concrete policy, and made several statements linking that policy [to] anti-Muslim animus.

Ignoring all this, the majority empowers the President to hide behind an administrative review process that the Government refuses to disclose to the public. [But] judicial notice indicates that the multiagency review process could not have been very thorough. Ongoing litigation under the Freedom of Information Act shows that the September 2017 report the Government produced after its review process was a mere 17 pages. That the Government's analysis of the vetting practices of hundreds of countries boiled down to such a short document raises serious questions about the legitimacy of the [national-security] rationale.

Beyond that, Congress has already addressed the national-security concerns supposedly undergirding the Proclamation through an "extensive and complex" framework governing "immigration and alien status." *Arizona* v. *United States*, 567 U.S. 387 (2012). The Immigration and Nationality Act sets forth, in painstaking detail, a reticulated scheme regulating the admission of individuals to the United

States. Generally, admission to the United States requires a valid visa or other travel document. To obtain a visa, an applicant must produce "certified cop[ies]" of documents proving her identity, background, and criminal history. [T]he Government also rigorously vets the information-sharing and identity-management systems of other countries, as evidenced by the Visa Waiver Program, which permits certain nationals from a select group of countries to skip the ordinary visa-application process. To determine which countries are eligible for the Visa Waiver Program, the Government considers whether they can satisfy numerous criteria—*e.g.*, using electronic, fraud-resistant passports, 24-hour reporting of lost or stolen passports, and not providing a safe haven for terrorists. The Secretary of Homeland Security, in consultation with the Secretary of State, also must determine that a country's inclusion in the program will not compromise "the law enforcement and security interests of the United States." [T]ellingly, the Government remains wholly unable to articulate any credible national-security interest that would go unaddressed by the current statutory scheme absent the Proclamation. * * *

For many of these reasons, several former national-security officials from both political parties—including former Secretary of State Madeleine Albright, former State Department Legal Adviser John Bellinger III, former Central Intelligence Agency Director John Brennan, and former Director of National Intelligence James Clapper—have advised that the Proclamation and its predecessor orders "do not advance the national-security or foreign policy interests of the United States, and in fact do serious harm to those interests."

Moreover, the Proclamation purports to mitigate national-security risks by excluding nationals of countries that provide insufficient information to vet their nationals. Yet, [the] Proclamation broadly denies immigrant visas to all nationals of those countries, including those whose admission would likely not implicate these information deficiencies (*e.g.*, infants, or nationals of countries included in the Proclamation who are long-term residents of and traveling from a country not covered by the Proclamation). In addition, the Proclamation permits certain nationals from the countries named in the Proclamation to obtain nonimmigrant visas, which undermines the Government's assertion that it does not already have the capacity and sufficient information to vet these individuals adequately.

Equally unavailing is the majority's reliance on the Proclamation's waiver program. [T]here is reason to suspect that the Proclamation's waiver program is nothing more than a sham. The remote possibility of obtaining a waiver pursuant to an ad hoc, discretionary, and seemingly arbitrary process scarcely demonstrates that the Proclamation is rooted in a genuine concern for national security. * * *

In sum, [w]hat the unrebutted evidence actually shows is that a reasonable observer would conclude, quite easily, that the primary purpose and function of the Proclamation is to disfavor Islam by banning Muslims from entering our country. * * *

IV.   [In] holding that the First Amendment gives way to an executive policy that a reasonable observer would view as motivated by animus against Muslims, the majority opinion upends this Court's precedent, repeats tragic mistakes of the past, and denies countless individuals the fundamental right of religious liberty. * * *

Our Constitution demands, and our country deserves, a Judiciary willing to hold the coordinate branches to account when they defy our most sacred legal commitments. Because the Court's decision today has failed in that respect, with profound regret, I dissent.

JUSTICE BREYER, with whom JUSTICE KAGAN joins, dissenting.

[I]f the government is applying the exemption and waiver provisions as written, then its argument for the Proclamation's lawfulness is strengthened. For one thing, the Proclamation then resembles more closely the two important Presidential precedents on point, President Carter's Iran order and President Reagan's Cuba proclamation, both of which contained similar categories of persons authorized to obtain case-by-case exemptions. For another thing, the Proclamation then follows more closely the basic statutory scheme, which provides for strict case-by-case scrutiny of applications. It would deviate from that system, not across the board, but where circumstances may require that deviation.

Further, since the case-by-case exemptions and waivers apply without regard to the individual's religion, application of that system would help make clear that the Proclamation does not deny visas to numerous Muslim individuals (from those countries) who do not pose a security threat. And that fact would help to rebut the First Amendment claim that the Proclamation rests upon anti-Muslim bias rather than security need. Finally, of course, the very fact that Muslims from those countries would enter the United States (under Proclamation-provided exemptions and waivers) would help to show the same thing.

[I]f the Government is not applying the Proclamation's exemption and waiver system, the claim that the Proclamation is a "Muslim ban," rather than a "security-based" ban, becomes much stronger. [Unfortunately] there is evidence that supports the [possibility] that the Government is not applying the Proclamation as written. The Proclamation provides that the Secretary of State and the Secretary of Homeland Security "shall coordinate to adopt guidance" for consular officers to follow when deciding whether to grant a waiver. Yet, to my knowledge, no guidance has issued. * * *

An examination of publicly available statistics also provides cause for concern. The State Department reported that during the Proclamation's first month, two waivers were approved out of 6,555 eligible applicants. [T]he Government claims that number increased from 2 to 430 during the first four months of implementation. That number, 430, however, when compared with the number of pre-Proclamation visitors, accounts for a miniscule percentage of those likely eligible for visas, in such categories as persons requiring medical treatment, academic visitors, students, family members, and others belonging to groups that, when considered as a group (rather than case by case), would not seem to pose security threats.

Amici have suggested that there are numerous applicants who could meet the waiver criteria. For instance, the Proclamation anticipates waivers for those with "significant business or professional obligations" in the United States, and amici identify many scholars who would seem to qualify. The Proclamation also anticipates waivers for those with a "close family member (*e.g.*, a spouse, child, or parent)" in the United States, and amici identify many such individuals affected by the Proclamation. * * *

Other data suggest the same. The Proclamation does not apply to asylum seekers or refugees. While more than 15,000 Syrian refugees arrived in the United States in 2016, only 13 have arrived since January 2018. Similarly few refugees have been admitted since January from Iran (3), Libya (1), Yemen (0), and Somalia (122).

The Proclamation also exempts individuals applying for several types of nonimmigrant visas: lawful permanent residents, parolees, those with certain travel documents, dual nationals of noncovered countries, and representatives of governments or international organizations. It places no restrictions on the vast majority of student and exchange visitors, covering only those from Syria, which provided 8 percent of student and exchange visitors from the five countries in 2016. Visitors from Somalia are eligible for any type of nonimmigrant visa, subject to "additional scrutiny." If nonimmigrant visa applications under the Proclamation resemble those in 2016, 16 percent of visa applicants would be eligible for exemptions.

In practice, however, only 258 student visas were issued to applicants from Iran (189), Libya (29), Yemen (40), and Somalia (0) in the first three months of 2018. This is less than a quarter of the volume needed to be on track for 2016 student visa levels. And only 40 nonimmigrant visas have been issued to Somali nationals, a decrease of 65 percent from 2016. While this is but a piece of the picture, it does not provide grounds for confidence. * * *

Finally, in a pending case in the Eastern District of New York, a consular official has filed a sworn affidavit asserting that he and other officials do not, in fact, have discretion to grant waivers. [Another] report similarly indicates that the U.S. Embassy in Djibouti, which processes visa applications for citizens of Yemen, received instructions to grant waivers "only in rare cases of imminent danger," with one consular officer reportedly telling an applicant that " '[e]ven for infants, we would need to see some evidence of a congenital heart defect or another medical issue of that degree of difficulty that ... would likely lead to the child's developmental harm or death.' "

[The] Government has not had an opportunity to respond, and a court has not had an opportunity to decide. But, given the importance of the decision in this case, the need for assurance that the Proclamation does not rest upon a "Muslim ban," and the assistance in deciding the issue that answers to the "exemption and waiver" questions may provide, I would send this case back to the District Court for further proceedings. And, I would leave the injunction in effect while the matter is litigated. Regardless, the Court's decision today leaves the District Court free to explore these issues on remand.

If this Court must decide the question without this further litigation, I would, on balance, find the evidence of antireligious bias, including statements on a website taken down only after the President issued the two executive orders preceding the Proclamation, along with the other statements also set forth in Justice Sotomayor's opinion, a sufficient basis to set the Proclamation aside.

II. NON-MAINSTREAM RELIGIOUS BELIEFS AND PRACTICES

1. *Validity and sincerity.* In UNITED STATES v. BALLARD, 322 U.S. 78 (1944), defendant was indicted for mail fraud. He had solicited funds for the "I Am" movement, asserting, inter alia, that he had been selected as a divine messenger, had divine power of healing incurable diseases, and had talked with Jesus and would transmit these conversations to mankind. The Court, per DOUGLAS, J., held that the First Amendment barred submitting to the jury the question whether these religious beliefs were true: "Men may believe what they cannot [prove.] Religious experiences real as life to some may be incomprehensible to others. [The] miracles of the New Testament, the Divinity of Christ, life after death, the power of prayer are deep in the religious convictions of many. If one could be sent to jail because a jury in a hostile environment found those teachings false, little indeed would be left of religious freedom."

2. *What is "religion"?* May the Court determine that asserted religious beliefs and practices do not constitute a valid religion? Consider Jonathan Weiss, *Privilege, Posture and Protection—"Religion" in the Law*, 73 Yale L.J. 593 (1964): "[A]ny definition of religion would seem to violate religious freedom in that it would dictate to religions, present and future, what they must [be]. Furthermore, an attempt to define religion, even for purposes of increasing freedom for religions, would run afoul of the Establishment Clause as excluding some religions, or even as establishing a notion respecting religion."

TORCASO v. WATKINS, per BLACK, J., 367 U.S. 488 (1961), invalidated a Maryland provision requiring a declaration of belief in God as a test for public office: "[Government cannot] impose requirements which aid all religions as against nonbelievers, and neither can aid those religions based on a belief in the existence of God as against those religions founded on different beliefs." The Court noted that "among religions [that] do not teach what would generally be considered a belief in the existence of God are Buddhism, Taoism, Ethical Culture, Secular Humanism and others."

UNITED STATES v. SEEGER, 380 U.S. 163 (1965): § 6(j) of the Universal Military Training and Service Act exempted from combat any person "who, by reason of religious training and belief, is conscientiously opposed to participation in war in any form. Religious training and belief in this [means] an individual's belief in a relation to a Supreme Being involving duties superior to those arising from any human relation, but does not include essentially political, sociological or philosophical views or a merely personal moral code." The Court, per CLARK, J., avoided constitutional questions and upheld claims for exemption of three conscientious objectors. One declared "that he preferred to leave the question as to his belief in a Supreme Being open, [and] that his was a 'belief in and devotion to goodness and virtue for their own sakes, and a religious faith in a purely ethical creed.'" Another said "that he felt it a violation of his moral code to take human life and that he considered this belief superior to his obligation to the state. [He quoted] Reverend John Haynes Holmes' definition of religion as 'the consciousness of some power manifest in nature which helps man in the ordering of his life in harmony with its demands * * *; it is man thinking his highest, feeling his deepest, and living his best.' The source of his conviction he attributed to reading and meditation 'in our democratic American culture, with its values derived from the western religious and philosophical tradition.' As to his belief in a Supreme Being, Peter stated that he supposed 'you could call that a belief in the Supreme Being or God. These just do not happen to be the words I use.'"

The Court "concluded that Congress, in using the expression 'Supreme Being' [was] merely clarifying the meaning of religious training and belief so as to embrace all religions and to exclude essentially political, sociological, or philosophical views [and that] the test [is] whether a given belief that is sincere and meaningful occupies a place in the life of its possessor parallel to that filled by the orthodox belief in God of one who clearly qualifies for the exemption. [No] party claims to be an atheist. [We] do not deal with [that. The] use by Congress of the words 'merely personal' seems to us to restrict the exception to a moral code which [is] in no way related to a Supreme Being. [Congress did] not distinguish between externally and internally derived beliefs. Such a determination [would] prove impossible as a practical matter.

3. PREFERENCE AMONG RELIGIONS

In BOARD OF EDUC. OF KIRYAS JOEL v. GRUMET, 512 U.S. 687 (1994), a New York statute constituted the Village of Kiryas Joel—"a religious enclave of Satmar Hasidim, practitioners of a strict form of Judaism"—as a separate school district. Most of the children attend pervasively religious private schools. The newly created district "currently runs only a special education program for handicapped [Satmar] children" who reside both inside and outside the village. The statute was passed "to enable the village's handicapped children to receive a secular, public-school education" because when they previously attended public schools in the larger school district outside the village, they suffered "panic, fear and trauma [in] leaving their own community and being with people whose ways were so different." The Court, per SOUTER, J., invoked "a principle at the heart of the Establishment Clause, that government should not prefer one religion to another. [As] Kiryas Joel did not receive [its] new authority simply as one of many communities eligible for equal treatment under a general law, we have no assurance that the next similarly situated group seeking a school district of its own will receive one; [and] a legislature's failure to enact a special law is itself unreviewable. [Here] the benefit flows only to a single sect, [and] therefore crosses the line from permissible accommodation to impermissible establishment."

KENNEDY, J., concurred in the judgment: "Whether or not the purpose is accommodation and whether or not the government provides similar gerrymanders to people of all religious faiths, the Establishment Clause forbids the government to use religion [as] a criterion to draw political or electoral lines."

SCALIA, J., joined by Rehnquist, C.J., and Thomas, J., dissented: "[A]ll the residents of the Kiryas Joel Village School District are Satmars. But all its residents also wear unusual dress, have unusual civic customs, and have not much to do with people who are culturally different from them. [I]t was not theology but dress, language, and cultural alienation that posed the educational problem for the children [and caused the Legislature to] provide a public education for these students, in the same way it addressed, by a similar law, the unique needs of children institutionalized in a hospital. [T]he creation of a special, one-culture school district for the benefit of [children whose] parents were nonreligious commune dwellers, or American Indians, or gypsies [would] pose no problem. The neutrality demanded by the Religion Clauses requires the same indulgence towards cultural characteristics that are accompanied by religious belief."[8]

NOTES

1. ***Delegation of government power.*** In *Kiryas Joel*, SOUTER, J., joined by Blackmun, Stevens and Ginsburg, JJ., found an additional ground for invalidating the statute: "delegating the State's discretionary authority over public schools to a group defined by its character as a religious community, in a legal and historical context that gives no assurance that governmental power has been or will be exercised neutrally." They relied on LARKIN v. GRENDEL'S DEN, INC., 459 U.S. 116 (1982), per BURGER, C.J., which held that a Massachusetts law (§ 16C), giving churches and schools the power "to veto applications for liquor licenses within a five hundred foot radius of the church or school, violates the Establishment Clause": "§ 16C [delegates] discretionary governmental powers [to] religious bodies.

"[The] valid secular objectives [of protecting] from the 'hurly-burly' associated with liquor outlets [can] be readily accomplished by [an] absolute legislative ban on liquor outlets within reasonable prescribed distances from churches, schools, hospitals and like institutions, or by ensuring a hearing for the views of affected institutions at licensing proceedings. [But the] churches' power under the statute is standardless [and] may therefore be used [for] example, favoring liquor licenses for members of that congregation. [And] the mere appearance of a joint exercise of

---

[8] Is this persuasive when there is total congruence between a religion and distinctive cultural needs *and* the cultural distinctiveness is defined by the religion?

legislative authority by Church and State provides a significant symbolic benefit to religion in the minds of some. [T]he statute can be seen as having a 'primary' and 'principal' effect of advancing religion. [Finally, § 16C] enmeshes churches in the processes of government and creates the danger of 'political fragmentation and divisiveness along religious lines.' "

REHNQUIST, J., dissented: A "flat ban [on] the grant of an alcoholic beverages license to any establishment located within 500 feet of a church or a [school], which the majority concedes is valid, is more protective of churches and more restrictive of liquor sales than the present § 16C [which] does not sponsor or subsidize any religious group or activity. It does not encourage, much less compel, anyone to participate in religious activities or to support religious institutions. [If] a church were to [favor] its members [for licenses], there would be an occasion to determine whether it had violated any right of an unsuccessful applicant for a liquor license."

SCALIA, J., joined by Rehnquist, C.J., and Thomas, J., dissenting in *Kiryas Joel*, argued that *Grendel's Den* had ruled that "a state may not delegate its civil authority *to a church*," not to "groups of people sharing a common religious and cultural heritage": "If the conferral of governmental power upon a religious institution *as such* (rather than upon American citizens who belong to the religious institution) is not the test of *Grendel's Den* invalidity, [it] might have made the entire States of Utah and New Mexico unconstitutional at the time of their admission to the Union."

2. ***"Excessive government entanglement" in ecclesiastical disputes.*** In JONES v. WOLF, 443 U.S. 595 (1979), a majority of the Vineville Presbyterian Church voted to separate from the Presbyterian Church in the United States (PCUS). A commission of PCUS, acting pursuant to the PCUS constitution (called the Book of Church Order), declared the Vineville minority to be "the true congregation." The minority sued for the local church property. The state court applied "the 'neutral principles of law' method for resolving church property disputes. The court examined the deeds to the properties, the state statutes dealing with implied trusts, and the Book of Church Order, to determine whether there was any basis for a trust in favor of the general church. Finding [none], the court awarded the property on the basis of legal title, which was in the local church."

The Court, per BLACKMUN, J., stated the established principle that "the First Amendment prohibits civil courts from resolving church property disputes on the basis of religious doctrine and practice. *Presbyterian Church v. Hull Church*, 393 U.S. 440 (1969). [The] Amendment requires that civil courts defer to the resolution of issues of religious doctrine [by] the highest court of a hierarchical church organization. *Serbian Eastern Orthodox Diocese v. Milivojevich*, 426 U.S. 696 (1976). Subject to these limitations, [however,] 'a State may adopt *any* of various approaches for settling church property [disputes].'

"[W]e think the 'neutral principles of law' approach is consistent with the foregoing constitutional principles. [It] relies extensively on objective, well-established concepts of trust and property law [to] free civil courts completely from entanglement in questions of religious doctrine, polity, and practice. Furthermore, [it affords] flexibility [to] reflect the intentions of the parties. [R]eligious societies can specify what is to happen to church property in the event of a particular contingency. [The] neutral principles method [does require] a civil court to examine certain religious documents, such as a church constitution, for language of trust in favor of the general church. [A] civil court must take special care to scrutinize the document in purely secular terms [in] determining whether the document indicates that the parties have intended to create a trust. [If] the interpretation of the instruments of ownership would require the civil court to resolve a religious controversy, then the court must defer to [the] authoritative ecclesiastical body. *Serbian.*"

POWELL, J., joined by Burger, C.J., and Stewart and White, JJ., dissented, finding that the neutral principles "approach inevitably will increase the involvement of civil courts in church controversies [rather than relying on whether] the rules of polity, accepted by its members[, had] placed ultimate authority over the use of the church property. The courts, in answering this question have recognized two broad categories of church government. One is congregational, in which authority over questions of church doctrine, practice, and administration rests entirely in the local congregation or some body within [it]. The second is hierarchical [and] this Court has held that the civil courts must give effect to the duly made decisions of the highest body within the hierarchy that has considered the dispute." See generally 1 Greenawalt ch. 16.

––––––––

LARSON v. VALENTE, 456 U.S. 228 (1982): The Unification Church ("Moonies") challenged "a Minnesota statute, imposing certain registration and reporting requirements upon only those religious organizations that solicit more than fifty per cent of their funds from nonmembers." The Court, per BRENNAN, J., noting that "the clearest command of the Establishment Clause is that one religious denomination cannot be officially preferred over another, [*Everson*]," and that this "is inextricably connected with the continuing vitality of the Free Exercise Clause," held that the statute violated the Establishment Clause because it did not survive "strict scrutiny." Assuming that the state's "valid secular purpose [in] protecting its citizens from abusive practices in the solicitation of funds for charity" is "compelling," the state "failed to demonstrate that the fifty per cent rule [is] 'closely fitted' " to furthering that interest. Moreover, the statute failed the third *Lemon* "test": "The [rule] effects the *selective* legislative imposition of burdens and advantages upon particular denominations. The 'risk of politicizing religion' that inheres in such legislation [is] confirmed by the provision's legislative history [which] demonstrates that the provision was drafted with the explicit intention of including particular religious denominations and excluding others."

WHITE, J., joined by Rehnquist, J., dissented: "The rule [names] no churches or denominations. [Some] religions will qualify and some will not, but this depends on the source of their contributions, not on their brand of religion."

4. CONFLICT BETWEEN THE CLAUSES

CORPORATION OF THE PRESIDING BISHOP OF THE CHURCH OF JESUS CHRIST OF LATTER-DAY SAINTS v. AMOS

483 U.S. 327, 107 S.Ct. 2862, 97 L.Ed.2d 273 (1987).

JUSTICE WHITE delivered the opinion of the Court.

Section 702 of the Civil Rights Act of 1964 exempts religious organizations from Title VII's prohibition against discrimination in employment on the basis of religion. [The] Deseret Gymnasium (Gymnasium) in Salt Lake City, Utah, is a nonprofit facility, open to the public, run by [the] Mormon or LDS Church. Appellee Mayson worked at the Gymnasium [as a] building engineer. He was discharged because he failed to qualify for [a] certificate that he is a member of the Church and eligible to attend its temples. Mayson [contended that] § 702 violates the Establishment Clause. * * *

"This Court has long recognized that the government may (and sometimes must) accommodate religious practices [without] violating the Establishment Clause." It is well established, too, that "[t]he limits of permissible state accommodation to religion are by no means co-extensive with the noninterference mandated by the Free Exercise Clause." *Walz.* [At] some point, accommodation may devolve into "an unlawful fostering of religion," but [this is not such a case].

Lemon [does] not mean that the law's purpose must be unrelated to religion [but] aims at preventing the relevant governmental decisionmaker—in this case, Congress—from abandoning neutrality and acting with the intent of promoting a particular point of view in religious matters.

Under the *Lemon* analysis, it is a permissible legislative purpose to alleviate significant governmental interference with the ability of religious organizations to define and carry out their religious missions. [§ 702 originally] exempted only the religious activities of such employers from the statutory ban on religious discrimination. [Nonetheless,] it is a significant burden on a religious organization to require it [to] predict which of its activities a secular court will consider religious. The line is hardly a bright one, and an organization might understandably be concerned that a judge would not understand its religious tenets [and] affect the way an organization carried out what it understood to be its religious mission. * * *

The second requirement under *Lemon* is that the law in question have "a principal or primary effect [that] neither advances nor inhibits religion." Undoubtedly, religious organizations are better able now to advance their purposes than they were prior to [the] amendment to § 702. But religious groups have been better able to advance their purposes on account of many laws that have passed constitutional muster: for example, the property tax exemption at issue in *Walz*, or the loans of school books to school children, including parochial school students, upheld in *Allen*. A law is not unconstitutional simply because it *allows* churches to advance religion, which is their very purpose. For a law to have forbidden "effects" under *Lemon*, it must be fair to say that the *government itself* has advanced religion through its own activities and influence. [Moreover,] we find no persuasive evidence in the record before us that the Church's ability to propagate its religious doctrine through the Gymnasium is any greater now than it was prior to the passage of the Civil Rights Act in 1964. In such circumstances, we do not see how any advancement of religion achieved by the Gymnasium can be fairly attributed to the Government, as opposed to the Church.

We find unpersuasive [that] § 702 singles out religious entities for a benefit. [The Court] has never indicated that statutes that give special consideration to religious groups are per se invalid. [Our cases provide] ample room for accommodation of religion under the Establishment Clause. Where, as here, government acts with the proper purpose of lifting a regulation that burdens the exercise of religion, we see no reason to require that the exemption come packaged with benefits to secular [entities.] *Larson* indicates that laws discriminating *among* religions are subject to strict scrutiny, and that laws "affording a uniform benefit to *all* religions" should be analyzed under *Lemon*. In a case such as this, where a statute is neutral on its face and motivated by a permissible purpose of limiting governmental interference with the exercise of religion, [it] passes the *Lemon* [test.] § 702 is rationally related to the legitimate purpose of alleviating significant governmental interference with the ability of religious organizations to define and carry out their religious missions. * * *

JUSTICE BRENNAN, with whom JUSTICE MARSHALL joins, concurring in the judgment.

[E]xemption from Title VII's proscription on religious discrimination [says] that a person may be put to the choice of either conforming to certain religious tenets or losing a job opportunity. [The] potential for coercion created by such a provision [is] in serious tension with our commitment to individual freedom of conscience in matters of religious belief. [But] religious organizations have an interest in [d]etermining that certain activities are in furtherance of an organization's religious mission, and that only those committed to that mission should conduct [them]. Solicitude for a church's ability to do so reflects the idea that furtherance of the autonomy of religious organizations often furthers individual religious freedom as well.

[I]deally, religious organizations should be able to discriminate on the basis of religion *only* with respect to religious activities [because] the infringement on religious liberty that results from conditioning performance of *secular* activity upon religious belief cannot be defended as necessary for the community's self-definition. Furthermore, the authorization of discrimination in such circumstances is not an accommodation that simply enables a church to gain members by the normal means of prescribing the terms of membership. [Rather,] it puts at the disposal of religion the added advantages of economic leverage in the secular realm.

[A] religious-secular distinction [as] the character of an activity is not self-evident [and] requires a searching case-by-case analysis. This results in considerable ongoing government entanglement in religious affairs [and] raises concern that a religious organization may be chilled in its Free Exercise activity. [The] risk [is] most likely to arise with respect to *nonprofit* activities. The fact that an operation is not organized as a profit-making commercial enterprise makes colorable a claim that it is not purely secular in orientation. * * *

Sensitivity to individual religious freedom dictates that religious discrimination be permitted only with respect to employment in religious activities. Concern for the autonomy of religious organizations demands that we avoid the entanglement and the chill on religious expression that a case-by-case determination would produce. We cannot escape the fact that these aims are in tension. Because of the nature of nonprofit activities, I believe that a categorical exemption for such enterprises appropriately balances these competing concerns. * * *

JUSTICE O'CONNOR, concurring in the judgment * * *

In *Jaffree*, I noted [that, "on] the one hand, a rigid application of the *Lemon* test would invalidate legislation exempting religious observers from generally applicable government obligations. By definition, such legislation has a religious purpose and effect in promoting the free exercise of religion. On the other hand, [a]lmost any government benefit to religion could be recharacterized as simply "allowing" a religion to better advance itself," unless perhaps it involved actual proselytization by government agents. In nearly every case of a government benefit to religion, the religious mission would not be advanced if the religion did not take advantage of the benefit * * * .

The necessary first step in evaluating an Establishment Clause challenge to a government action lifting from religious organizations a generally applicable regulatory burden is to recognize that such government action *does* have the effect of advancing religion. The necessary second step is to separate those benefits to religion that constitutionally accommodate the free exercise of religion from those that provide unjustifiable awards of assistance to religious organizations. [T]he inquiry framed by the *Lemon* test should be "whether government's purpose is to endorse religion and whether the statute actually conveys a message of endorsement" [and] how it would be perceived by an objective observer, acquainted with the text, legislative history, and implementation of the statute. [Because] there is a probability that a nonprofit activity of a religious organization will itself be involved in the organization's religious mission, in [this case] the objective observer should perceive the government action as an accommodation of the exercise of religion rather than as a government endorsement of religion. * * *

NOTES AND QUESTIONS

1. ***Draft exemption.*** Did the statute in *Gillette*, exempting only "religious" conscientious objectors, impermissibly prefer religion over nonreligion? In WELSH v. UNITED STATES, Sec. 2, II supra, WHITE, J., joined by Burger, C.J., and Stewart, J., found it valid: "First, § 6(j) may represent a purely practical judgment

that religious objectors, however admirable, would be of no more use in combat than many others unqualified for military service. [T]he exemption has neither the primary purpose nor the effect of furthering religion. [Second], Congress may have [believed that] to deny the exemption would violate the Free Exercise Clause or at least raise grave problems in this respect. [It] cannot be ignored that the First Amendment itself contains a religious classification [and the Free Exercise Clause] protects conduct as well as religious belief and speech. [It] was not suggested [in *Braunfeld*] that the Sunday closing laws in 21 States exempting Sabbatarians and others violated the Establishment Clause because no provision was made for others who claimed nonreligious reasons for not working on some particular day of the week. Nor was it intimated in *Zorach* that the no-establishment holding might be infirm because only those pursuing religious studies for designated periods were released from the public school routine; neither was it hinted that a public school's refusal to institute a released time program would violate the Free Exercise Clause. The Court in *Sherbert* construed the Free Exercise Clause to require special treatment for Sabbatarians under the State's unemployment compensation law. But the State could deal specially with Sabbatarians whether the Free Exercise Clause required it or [not]."

HARLAN, J., disagreed, believing that "having chosen to exempt, [Congress] cannot draw the line between theistic or nontheistic religious beliefs on the one hand and secular beliefs on the other. [I]t must encompass the class of individuals it purports to exclude, those whose beliefs emanate from a purely moral, ethical, or philosophical source. The common denominator must be the intensity of moral [conviction]. *Everson*, *McGowan* and *Allen*, all sustained legislation on the premise that it was neutral [notwithstanding] that it may have assisted religious groups by giving them the same benefits accorded to nonreligious groups. To the extent that *Zorach* and *Sherbert* stand for the proposition that the Government may (*Zorach*), or must (*Sherbert*), shape its secular programs to accommodate the beliefs and tenets of religious groups, I think these cases unsound."

2. ***Unemployment compensation.*** Did the Court's decisions in *Sherbert*, *Thomas* and *Hobbie* impermissibly prefer religion? In THOMAS v. REVIEW BD., Sec. 2 supra, REHNQUIST, J., dissented, finding the result "inconsistent with many of our prior Establishment Clause cases": "If Indiana were to legislate [an] unemployment compensation law which permitted benefits to be granted to those persons who quit their jobs for religious reasons—the statute would 'plainly' violate the Establishment Clause as interpreted in such cases as [*Lemon*]. First, [the] proviso would clearly serve only a religious purpose. It would grant financial benefits for the sole purpose of accommodating religious beliefs. Second, [the] primary effect of the proviso would be to 'advance' religion by facilitating the exercise of religious belief. Third, [it] would surely 'entangle' the State in religion. [By] granting financial benefits to persons solely on the basis of their religious beliefs, the State must necessarily inquire whether the claimant's belief is 'religious' and whether it is sincerely [held.] Conversely, governmental assistance which does not have the effect of 'inducing' religious belief, but instead merely

'accommodates' or implements an independent religious choice does not impermissibly involve the government in religious choices and therefore does not violate the Establishment Clause. * * * "

3.   ***Breadth of exemption.*** In TEXAS MONTHLY, INC. v. BULLOCK, Sec. 1, II supra, SCALIA, J., joined by Rehnquist, C.J., and Kennedy, J., charged that according to Brennan, J.'s plurality opinion, "no law is constitutional whose 'benefits [are] confined to religious organizations,' except [those] that are unconstitutional *unless* they contain benefits confined to religious organizations. [But] 'the limits of permissible state accommodation to religion are by no means co-extensive with the noninterference mandated by the Free Exercise Clause.' Breadth of coverage is essential to constitutionality whenever a law's benefiting of religious activity [is] defended [as] merely the incidental consequence of seeking to benefit *all* activity that achieves a particular secular goal. But [w]here accommodation of religion is the justification, by definition religion is being singled out. [And] if the exemption comes so close to being a constitutionally required accommodation, there is no doubt that it is at least a permissible one."

BRENNAN, J., joined by Marshall and Stevens, JJ., responded: "[W]e in no way suggest that *all* benefits conferred exclusively upon religious groups or upon individuals on account of their religious beliefs are forbidden by the Establishment Clause unless they are mandated by the Free Exercise Clause. [Permissible benefits] however, involve legislative exemptions that did not or would not impose substantial burdens on nonbeneficiaries while allowing others to act according to their religious beliefs. [Thus,] the application of Title VII's exemption for religious organizations that we approved in *Amos* though it had some adverse effect on those holding or seeking employment with those organizations (if not on taxpayers generally), prevented potentially serious encroachments on protected religious freedoms. Texas' tax exemption, by contrast, does not remove a demonstrated and possible grave imposition on religious activity sheltered by the Free Exercise Clause. Moreover, it burdens nonbeneficiaries by increasing their tax bills by whatever amount is needed to offset the benefit bestowed on subscribers to religious publications."

4.   ***Sabbath observance.*** THORNTON v. CALDOR, INC., 472 U.S. 703 (1985), per BURGER, C.J., held that a Connecticut law—"that those who observe a Sabbath any day of the week as a matter of religious conviction must be relieved of the duty to work on that day, no matter what burden or inconvenience this imposes on the employer or fellow workers"—"has a primary effect that impermissibly advances a particular religious practice" and thus violates the Establishment Clause: "The statute arms Sabbath observers with an absolute and unqualified right not to work on whatever day they designate as their Sabbath [and thus] goes beyond having an incidental or remote effect of advancing religion."

O'CONNOR, J., joined by Marshall, J., concurred, distinguishing "the religious accommodation provisions of Title VII of the Civil Rights Act [which] require private employers to reasonably accommodate the religious practices of employees unless to do so would cause undue hardship to the employer's business": "Since Title VII calls for reasonable rather than absolute accommodation and extends [to] all religious beliefs and practices rather than protecting only the Sabbath observance, I believe an objective observer would perceive it as an anti-discrimination law rather than an endorsement of religion or a particular religious practice."

In *Kiryas Joel*, Sec. 3 supra, SCALIA, J., joined by Rehnquist, C.J., and Thomas, J., disagreed with the Court's conclusion that New York had impermissibly preferred one religion: "[M]ost efforts at accommodation seek to solve a problem that applies [to] only one or a few religions. Not every religion uses wine in its sacraments, but that does not make an exemption from Prohibition for sacramental wine-use impermissible, nor does it require the State granting such an exemption to explain [how] it will treat every other claim for dispensation from its controlled-substances laws." Kennedy, J., expressed a similar view.

5. ***Unanimous approval.*** CUTTER v. WILKINSON, 544 U.S. 709 (2005), per GINSBURG, J., relying on *Amos* held that the Religious Land Use and Institutionalized Persons Act of 2000—"No government shall impose a substantial burden on the religious exercise of a person residing [in] an institution," unless it survives strict scrutiny—does not violate the Establishment Clause: RLUIPA "does not, on its face, exceed the limits of permissible government accommodation [because] it alleviates exceptional government-created burdens on private religious exercise [and] does not founder on shoals the Court's prior decisions. [C]ourts must take adequate account of the burdens a requested accommodation may impose on nonbeneficiaries, see *Caldor*, and they must be satisfied that the Act's prescriptions [are] administered neutrally among different faiths, see *Kiryas Joel*. [It] covers state-run institutions—mental hospitals, prisons, and the like—in which the government exerts a degree of control unparalleled in civilian society and severely disabling to private religious exercise. * * * [RLUIPA's sponsors] anticipated that courts would apply the Act's standard with 'due deference to the experience and expertise of prison and jail [administrators']."

6. ***School prayer.*** In *Jaffree*, O'CONNOR, J., applied her "solution" to Alabama's moment of silence law: "No law prevents a student who is so inclined from praying silently in public schools. [Of] course, the State might argue that § 16–1–20.1 protects not silent prayer, but rather group silent prayer under State sponsorship. Phrased in these terms, the burden lifted by the statute is not one imposed by the State of Alabama, but by the Establishment Clause."

CHAPTER 9

EQUAL PROTECTION

■ ■ ■

Laws frequently classify (or "discriminate") by imposing special burdens (or granting exemptions from such burdens) or by conferring benefits on some people and not others. To take uncontroversial examples, only those who can pass an examination and possess good eyesight qualify for driver's licenses. Those with expensive homes frequently must pay higher taxes than those with less expensive homes. People who are not high school graduates typically are denied admission to state universities. Against this background of accepted practice, under what circumstances do legislative classifications violate the Fourteenth Amendment's command that no state shall "deny to any person within its jurisdiction the equal protection of the laws"?

Although the language of the Equal Protection Clause is not confined to racial discrimination, the *Slaughter-House Cases,* Ch. 5, Sec. 1, II supra (one of the first decisions interpreting the Civil War amendments), "doubt[ed] very much whether any action of a State not directed by way of discrimination against the negroes as a class, or on account of their race, will ever be held to come within the purview of this provision." At least as early as 1897, however, the Court invoked the Equal Protection Clause to invalidate a commonplace economic regulation that obligated railroad defendants (but not others) to pay the attorneys' fees of successful plaintiffs. The Court acknowledged that "as a general proposition, [it] is undeniably true" that "it is not within the scope of the Fourteenth Amendment to withhold from States the power of classification." But, the Court continued, "it must appear" that a classification is "based upon some reasonable ground—some difference which bears a just and proper relation to the attempted classification—and is not a mere arbitrary selection." *Gulf, Colo. & Santa Fé Ry. Co. v. Ellis,* 165 U.S. 150 (1897).[1]

Sec. 1 of this Chapter considers this "traditional approach" under the Equal Protection Clause to general economic and social welfare regulations. Sec. 2 then deals with the "strict scrutiny" given to explicit racial and ethnic classifications, which the Court has deemed "suspect," as well as with related issues involving race. Sec. 3 reviews the Court's treatment of gender-based classifications. Sec. 4 addresses the use of a nondeferential standard of review for governmental action that disadvantages several other groups. Finally, Sec. 5 examines standards for

---

[1]   For an even earlier invocation of the Equal Protection Clause to invalidate a classification of transportation rates, see *Reagan v. Farmers' Loan & Trust Co.,* 154 U.S. 362 (1894).

equal protection review of classifications affecting what the Court classifies as "fundamental" rights.

One potential source of confusion should be kept in mind throughout. By its terms, the Equal Protection Clause—the relevant language of which provides that "[n]o *State* shall . . ."—does not apply to the federal government. Nonetheless, at least since its 1954 decision in *Bolling v. Sharpe*, Sec. 2, II infra, the Court has held that the Due Process Clause of the Fifth Amendment incorporates equal protection norms binding on the federal government. The *Bolling* Court explained: "The Fifth Amendment, which is applicable in the District of Columbia, does not contain an equal protection clause as does the Fourteenth Amendment which applies only to the states. But the concepts of equal protection and due process, both stemming from our American ideal of fairness, are not mutually exclusive. [D]iscrimination may be so unjustifiable as to be violative of due process."

In applying equal protection norms to the federal government, the Court's pattern of decisions has not been perfectly consistent, as will be explained in the materials that follow. For the most part, however, the Court has insisted that the "approach to Fifth Amendment equal protection claims [is] precisely the same as to equal protection claims under the Fourteenth Amendment." *Weinberger v. Wiesenfeld,* Sec. 3, III infra; see also *Adarand Constructors, Inc. v. Pena,* Sec. 2, V infra.[2] Accordingly, in many parts of this Chapter, challenges to federal legislation under the Due Process Clause will be treated as offering de facto interpretations of the Equal Protection Clause.

1. TRADITIONAL APPROACH

As seen in Ch. 5, the Due Process Clause was the usual provision invoked by the Court in the first third of the twentieth century to overturn a great many economic and social welfare regulations. But despite Justice Holmes's dismissive reference to the Equal Protection Clause as "the usual last resort of constitutional arguments,"[3] the Court held during this period that approximately twenty state and local laws violated equal protection. For the most part, the Court at least purported to take a deferential approach that granted the states "a broad discretion in classification in the exercise of [their] power of regulation" and interposed the "constitutional guaranty of equal protection" only "against discriminations that are entirely arbitrary."[4] But compare the formulation used in *F.S. Royster Guano Co. v. Virginia,* 253 U.S. 412 (1920): "[T]he classification must be reasonable, not arbitrary, and must rest upon some ground of difference having a fair and substantial relation to the object of the legislation, so that all persons similarly circumstanced shall be treated alike."

---

[2]   The principal exception to this general rule of "congruence" involves the treatment of aliens. Current doctrine subjects state discriminations against aliens to more searching judicial scrutiny than federal discriminations against aliens—a disparity considered in Sec. 4, II infra.

[3]   *Buck v. Bell,* 274 U.S. 200 (1927).

[4]   *Smith v. Cahoon,* 283 U.S. 553 (1931).

The materials that follow concern the Court's equal protection scrutiny of economic and social welfare regulations since the late 1930s, when it abandoned searching substantive due process review of such legislation.

RAILWAY EXPRESS AGENCY V. NEW YORK
336 U.S. 106, 69 S.Ct. 463, 93 L.Ed. 533 (1949).

JUSTICE DOUGLAS delivered the opinion of the Court.

[T]he Traffic Regulations of the City of New York [provide]: "No person shall operate [on] any street an advertising vehicle; [except for] business notices upon business delivery vehicles, so long as such vehicles are engaged in the usual business [of] the owner and not used merely or mainly for advertising."

Appellant [operates] about 1,900 trucks in New York City and sells the space on the exterior sides of these trucks for advertising [for] the most part unconnected with its own business. It was convicted * * * .

The court [below] concluded that advertising on [vehicles] constitutes a distraction to vehicle drivers and to pedestrians alike and therefore affects the safety of the public in the use of the streets. We do not sit to weigh evidence on the due process issue in order to determine whether the regulation is sound or appropriate; nor is it our function to pass judgment on its wisdom. See *Olsen v. Nebraska* [Ch. 5, Sec. 3 supra]. We would be trespassing on one of the most intensely local and specialized of all municipal problems if we held that this regulation had no relation to the traffic problem of New York City. It is the judgment of the local authorities that it does have such a relation.

[The] question of equal protection of the laws is pressed more strenuously on us. [It] is said, for example, that one of appellant's trucks carrying the advertisement of a commercial house would not cause any greater distraction of pedestrians and vehicle drivers than if the commercial house carried the same advertisement on its own truck. Yet the regulation allows the latter to do what the former is forbidden from doing. It is therefore contended that the classification which the regulation makes has no relation to the traffic problem since a violation turns not on what kind of advertisements are carried on trucks but on whose trucks they are carried.

That, however, is a superficial way of analyzing the [problem]. The local authorities may well have concluded that those who advertised their own wares on their trucks do not present the same traffic problem in view of the nature or extent of the advertising which they use. * * *

We cannot say that that judgment is not an allowable one. Yet if it is, the classification has relation to the purpose for which it is made and does not contain the kind of discrimination against which the Equal Protection Clause affords protection. It is by such practical considerations based on experience rather than by theoretical inconsistencies that the question of equal protection is to be answered. And the fact that New York City sees fit to eliminate from traffic this kind of distraction but does not touch what may be even greater ones in a different category, such as the vivid displays on Times Square, is immaterial. It is no requirement of equal protection that all evils of the same genus be eradicated or none at all. * * *

Affirmed.

JUSTICE RUTLEDGE acquiesces in the Court's opinion and judgment, dubitante on the question of equal protection of the laws.

JUSTICE JACKSON, concurring. * * *

The burden should rest heavily upon one who would persuade us to use the Due Process Clause to strike down a substantive [law]. Even its provident use against municipal regulations frequently disables all government—state, municipal and federal—from dealing with the conduct in question because the requirement of due process is also applicable to State and Federal Governments. * * *

Invocation of the Equal Protection Clause, on the other hand, does not disable any governmental body from dealing with the subject at hand. It merely means that the prohibition or regulation must have a broader impact. I regard it as a salutary doctrine that cities, states and the Federal Government must exercise their powers so as not to discriminate between their inhabitants except upon some reasonable differentiation fairly related to the object of regulation. [T]here is no more effective practical guaranty against arbitrary and unreasonable government than to require that the principles of law which officials would impose upon a minority must be imposed generally. Conversely, nothing opens the door to arbitrary action so effectively as to allow those officials to pick and choose only a few to whom they will apply legislation and thus to escape the political retribution that might be visited upon them if larger numbers were affected. Courts can take no better measure to assure that laws will be just than to require that laws be equal in operation. * * *

In this case, if the City of New York should assume that display of any advertising on vehicles tends and intends to distract the attention of persons using the highways and to increase the dangers of its traffic, I should think it fully within its constitutional powers to forbid it all. [Instead], however, the City seeks to reduce the hazard only by saying that while some may, others may not exhibit such appeals. The same display, for example, advertising cigarettes, which this appellant is forbidden to carry on its trucks, may be carried on the trucks of a cigarette dealer. [The] courts of New York have declared that the sole nature and purpose of the regulation before us is to reduce traffic hazards. There is not even a pretense here that the traffic hazard created by the advertising which is forbidden is in any manner or degree more hazardous than that which is permitted. * * *

* * * I do not think differences of treatment under law should be approved on classification because of differences unrelated to the legislative purpose. The Equal Protection Clause ceases to assure either equality or protection if it is avoided by

any conceivable difference that can be pointed out between those bound and those left free. This Court has often announced the principle that the differentiation must have an appropriate relation to the object of the [legislation].

The question in my mind comes to this. Where individuals contribute to an evil or danger in the same way and to the same degree, may those who do so for hire be prohibited, while those who do so for their own commercial ends but not for hire be allowed to continue? I think the answer has to be that the hireling may be put in a class by himself and may be dealt with differently than those who act on their own. But this is not merely because such a discrimination will enable the lawmaker to diminish the evil. That might be done by many classifications, which I should think wholly unsustainable. It is rather because there is a real difference between doing in self-interest and doing for hire, so that it is one thing to tolerate action from those who act on their own and it is another thing to permit the same action to be promoted for a price. * * *

NEW ORLEANS V. DUKES
427 U.S. 297, 96 S.Ct. 2513, 49 L.Ed.2d 511 (1976).

PER CURIAM.

[A 1972 New Orleans ordinance banned all pushcart food vendors in the French Quarter ("Vieux Carre") except those who had continuously operated there for eight or more years. Two vendors had done so for twenty or more years and qualified under the "grandfather clause." Appellee, who had operated a pushcart for only two years, attacked the ordinance.]

When local economic regulation is challenged solely as violating the Equal Protection Clause, this Court consistently defers to legislative determinations as to the desirability of particular statutory discriminations. Unless a classification trammels fundamental personal rights or is drawn upon inherently suspect distinctions such as race, religion, or alienage, our decisions presume the constitutionality of the statutory discriminations and require only that the classification challenged be rationally related to a legitimate state interest. States are accorded wide latitude in the regulation of their local economies under their police powers, and rational distinctions may be made with substantially less than mathematical exactitude. Legislatures may implement their program step by step in such economic areas, adopting regulations that only partially ameliorate a perceived evil and deferring complete elimination of the evil to future regulations. See, e.g., *Williamson v. Lee Optical Co.*[5] In short, the judiciary may not sit as a

---

[5] In *Lee Optical*, Ch. 5, Sec. 3 supra, a statute that otherwise prohibited the fitting of eyeglasses without a prescription exempted businesses that sold ready-to-wear glasses. The Court found no violation of equal protection: "Evils in the same field may be of different dimensions and proportions, requiring different remedies. Or so the legislature may think. Or the reform may take one step at a time, addressing itself to the phase of the problem which seems most acute to the legislative mind. The legislature may select one phase of one field and apply a remedy there, neglecting the others. [For] all this record shows, the ready-to-wear branch of this business may not loom large in Oklahoma or may present problems of regulation distinct from the other branch."

superlegislature to judge the wisdom or desirability of legislative policy determinations made in areas that neither affect fundamental rights nor proceed along suspect lines; in the local economic sphere, it is only the invidious discrimination, the wholly arbitrary act, which cannot stand consistently with the Fourteenth Amendment. See, e.g., *Ferguson v. Skrupa.*

[New Orleans'] classification rationally furthers the purpose which [the] city had identified as its objective in enacting the provision, that is, as a means "to preserve the appearance and custom valued by the Quarter's residents and attractive to tourists." The legitimacy of that objective is obvious. The City Council plainly could further that objective by making the reasoned judgment that street peddlers and hawkers tend to interfere with the charm and beauty of an historic area [and] that to ensure the economic vitality of that area, such businesses should be substantially curtailed in the Vieux Carre, if not totally banned.

It is suggested that the "grandfather provision" [was] a totally arbitrary and irrational method of achieving the city's purpose. But rather than proceeding by the immediate and absolute abolition of all pushcart food vendors, the city could rationally [decide] that newer businesses were less likely to have built up substantial reliance interests in continued operation in the Vieux Carre and that the two vendors who qualified under the "grandfather clause" [had] themselves become part of the distinctive character and charm that distinguishes the Vieux Carre. We cannot say that these judgments so lack rationality that they constitute a constitutionally impermissible denial of equal protection. * * *

Reversed.

JUSTICE MARSHALL concurs in the judgment.

JUSTICE STEVENS took no part in [the] case.

––––––––––

NEW YORK CITY TRANSIT AUTH. v. BEAZER, 440 U.S. 568 (1979), upheld the exclusion of all methadone users from any Transit Authority (TA) employment. An estimated 75% of "patients who have been on methadone maintenance for at least a year [were] free from illicit drug use" and, if they could be properly identified, would pose no special safety risk. In addition, the exclusion applied to non-safety-sensitive as well as to safety-sensitive jobs. Nevertheless, the Court, per STEVENS, J., rejected the finding of the lower court that the methadone exclusion had "no rational relation to the demands of the job to be performed": "[T]he District Court [concluded] that employment in nonsensitive jobs could not be denied to methadone users who had progressed satisfactorily with their treatment for one year, and who, when examined individually, satisfied the TA's employment criteria. [But] any special rule short of total exclusion that TA might adopt is likely to be less precise—and will assuredly be more costly—than the one that it currently enforces. If eligibility is marked at any intermediate point—whether after one year of treatment or later—the classification will inevitably discriminate between employees or applicants equally or almost equally apt to achieve full recovery. [By] contrast, the 'no drugs' policy now enforced by TA is supported by the legitimate inference that as long as a treatment program (or other drug use) continues, a degree of uncertainty persists.* * *

"[T]he District Court's conclusion was that TA's rule is broader than necessary to exclude those methadone users who are not actually qualified to work for TA. We may assume [that] it is probably unwise for a large employer like TA to rely on a general rule instead of individualized consideration of every job applicant. But these assumptions concern matters of personnel policy that do not implicate the principle safeguarded by the Equal Protection Clause. As the District Court recognized, the special classification created by TA's rule serves the general objectives of safety and efficiency. Moreover, the exclusionary line challenged by respondents [does] not circumscribe a class of persons characterized by some unpopular trait or affiliation, it does not create or reflect any special likelihood of bias on the part of the ruling majority. Under these circumstances, it is of no constitutional significance that the degree of rationality is not as great with respect to certain ill-defined subparts of the classification as it is with respect to the classification as a whole."

WHITE, J., joined by Marshall, J., dissented: Both courts below "found that those who have been maintained on methadone for at least a year and who are free from the use of illicit drugs and alcohol can easily be identified through normal personnel procedures and, for a great many jobs, are as employable as and present no more risk than applicants from the general population. [On] the facts as found [one] can reach the Court's result only if [equal protection] imposes no real constraint at all in this situation. * * *

"Of course, the District Court's order permitting total exclusion of all methadone users maintained for less than one year, whether successfully or not, would still exclude some employables and would to this extent be overinclusive. [But although] many of those who have not been successfully maintained for a year are employable, as a class they, unlike the protected group, are not as employable as the general population. Thus, even assuming the bad risks could be identified, serving the end of employability would require unusual efforts to determine those more likely to revert. But that legitimate secondary goal is not fulfilled by excluding the protected [class]. Accordingly, the rule's classification of successfully maintained persons as dispositively different from the general population is left without any justification and, with its irrationality and invidiousness thus uncovered, must fall before the Equal Protection Clause."

Justice White added in a footnote: "I have difficulty also with the Court's easy conclusion that the challenged rule was '[q]uite plainly' not motivated 'by any special animus against a specific group of persons.' Heroin addiction is a special problem of the poor, and the addict population is composed largely of racial minorities that the Court has previously recognized as politically powerless and historical subjects of majoritarian neglect. Persons on methadone maintenance have few interests in common with members of the majority, and thus are unlikely to have their interests protected, or even considered, in governmental decisionmaking. Indeed, petitioners stipulated that '[o]ne of the reasons for [the] drug policy is the fact that [petitioners] feel[ ] an adverse public reaction would result if it were generally known that [petitioners] employed persons with a prior history of drug abuse, including persons participating in methadone maintenance programs.' It is hard for me to reconcile that stipulation of animus against former addicts with our past holdings that 'a bare [desire] to harm a politically unpopular group cannot constitute a *legitimate* governmental interest.' *U.S. Dept. of Agriculture v. Moreno*, [infra]. On the other hand, the afflictions to which petitioners are more sympathetic, such as alcoholism and mental illness, are shared by both white and black, rich and poor.

"Some weight should also be given to the history of the rule. Petitioners admit that it was not the result of a reasoned policy decision and stipulated that they had never studied the ability of those on methadone maintenance to perform petitioners' jobs. Petitioners are not directly accountable to the public, are not the type of official body that normally makes legislative judgments of fact such as those relied upon by the majority today, and are by nature more concerned with business efficiency than with other public policies for which they have no direct responsibility. Both the State and City of New York, which do exhibit those democratic characteristics, hire persons in methadone programs for similar jobs.

"These factors together strongly point to a conclusion of invidious discrimination. * * * "

———

Although the Supreme Court almost invariably upholds statutes pursuant to rational basis review, there are exceptions. UNITED STATES DEPT. OF AGRICULTURE v. MORENO, 413 U.S. 528 (1973), per BRENNAN, J., applying " 'traditional' equal protection analysis," held that a provision of the Food Stamp Act—excluding "any household containing an individual who is unrelated to any other member of the household"—was "wholly without any rational basis": The exclusion "is clearly irrelevant to the stated purposes of the Act [to] raise levels of nutrition among low-income households. [Thus], the challenged classification must rationally further some legitimate governmental interest other than those specifically stated in the Congressional 'Declaration of Policy.'

"[The] little legislative history [that] does exist" indicates that the provision "was intended to [prevent] 'hippie communes' from participating in the food stamp program. [But equal protection] at the very least mean[s] that a bare congressional desire to harm a politically unpopular group cannot constitute a *legitimate* governmental interest." Nor does the classification "operate so as rationally to further the prevention of fraud" because, under the Act, "two *unrelated* persons living together" may "avoid the 'unrelated person' exclusion simply by altering their living arrangements so as [to] create two separate 'households,' both of which are eligible for assistance. [Thus], in practical operation, the [provision] excludes from participation [not] those persons who are 'likely to abuse the program' but, rather, only those persons who are so desperately in need of aid that they cannot even afford to alter their living arrangements so as to retain their eligibility."

Douglas, J., concurred: "I could not say that [this] provision has no 'rational' relation to control of fraud. We deal here, however, with the right of association, protected by the First Amendment." Thus, the classification "can be sustained only on a showing of a 'compelling' governmental interest."

Rehnquist, J., joined by Burger, C.J., dissented: "Congress attacked the problem with a rather blunt instrument, [b]ut I do not think it is unreasonable for Congress to conclude that the basic unit which it was willing to support [with] food stamps is some variation on the family as we know it—a household consisting of related individuals. This unit provides a guarantee which is not provided by households containing unrelated individuals that the household exists for some purpose other than to collect federal food stamps.

"Admittedly, [the] limitation will make ineligible many households which have not been formed for the purpose of collecting federal food stamps, and will [not] wholly deny food stamps to those households which may have been formed in large part to take advantage of the program. But, as the Court concedes, 'traditional' equal protection analysis does not require that every classification be drawn with precise mathematical nicety."

Since *Moreno*, the Court has occasionally found impermissible purposes in other cases, mostly ones involving classifications—such as those based on sexual orientation or intellectual disability—that some commentators think the Court regards as quasi-suspect, and that therefore trigger an elevated form of "rational basis plus." See *Romer v. Evans*, Sec. 4, I infra (involving "animus" against gays); *United States v. Windsor*, Sec. 4, I infra (finding "purpose" of harming parties to same-sex marriages); *Cleburne v. Cleburne Living Center, Inc.*, 473 U.S. 432 (1985) (invalidating action predicated on "irrational prejudice against the mentally retarded"). But even apart from cases involving impermissible purposes, there are at least a few modern cases in which the Court, although employing the traditional "rational basis" standard, has held laws violative of equal protection. See, e.g., Katie R. Eyer, *The Canon of Rational Basis Review*, 93 Notre Dame L.Rev. 1317 (2018).

2. RACE AND ETHNIC ANCESTRY

I. HISTORICAL BACKGROUND

Racism and practices of race discrimination are deeply embedded in American constitutional history. According to David O. Stewart, *The Summer of 1787*, at 70–71 (2007), in 1787, Massachusetts was the only state that wholly "banned slavery, and that state's prohibition came from a court ruling, not from a legislative act."[6]

---

[6]   "Four other states (New Hampshire, Connecticut, Rhode Island, and Pennsylvania) had 'gradual emancipation' laws that freed children of slave parents. New York adopted gradual emancipation in 1799, and New Jersey followed in 1804. [In] 1802, Virginia enacted a

At least six of the thirteen original colonies—Maryland, Delaware, Virginia, the Carolinas, and Georgia—gave express legal support to slavery. At the Constitutional Convention, the existence of slavery was accepted as a political fact. There was no serious discussion of the Constitution forbidding slavery altogether. On the contrary, at least three provisions of the original Constitution recognized and arguably promoted slavery: Art. I, § 2, which based a state's representation in the House of Representatives on its free population and three-fifths of "all other Persons" within its territory; Art. I, § 9, which barred Congress from abolishing the slave trade before 1808; and Art. IV, § 2, which provided that "no Person held to Service or Labor" under the laws of one state could escape that status upon flight to another state but, on the contrary, "shall be delivered up on the Claim of the Party to whom such Service or Labour may be due." Even in many "free" states, at the time of the Constitutional Convention and thereafter African Americans were denied the vote, excluded from jury service, and separated from whites in public conveyances.

In the antebellum years, the Supreme Court decided major cases involving the African slave trade,[7] the return of fugitive slaves,[8] slavery in the federal territories, and the rights of slaves in transit through free states—virtually all in a manner accepting slavery's basic lawfulness. The most notorious of the antebellum decisions involving slavery came in the *Dred Scott* case.

———

The plaintiff-appellant in DRED SCOTT v. SANDFORD, 60 U.S. (19 How.) 393 (1857), was born in slavery in Virginia but, in the company of his master, later traveled in the free state of Illinois and the territory of Wisconsin, where slavery was prohibited by federal statute under the Missouri Compromise. Following his return to Missouri, a slave state, Dred Scott brought suit against his owner, John Sandford, in federal court, arguing that he had attained his freedom under Illinois and federal law. Scott predicated his claim of federal jurisdiction on diversity of citizenship, alleging that he was a citizen of Missouri and Sandford a citizen of New York. The Court, per TANEY, C.J., dismissed the suit by a vote of 7–2. It held (1) that Scott was incapable of becoming a "citizen" of Missouri eligible to invoke federal diversity jurisdiction; (2) that Congress's effort in the Missouri Compromise to abolish slavery in federal territories was unconstitutional; and (3) that whatever Scott's status in Illinois, after he had returned to Missouri his status was governed by the law of Missouri, which treated him as a slave:

---

manumission law allowing masters to set slaves free, but not many took the opportunity to do so." Id.

[7]   See, e.g., *The Antelope*, 23 U.S. (10 Wheat.) 66 (1825) (recognizing the right of foreigners to engage in the slave trade, if the laws of their nation permitted them to do so, but upholding prosecutions against American slave traders).

[8]   See *Prigg v. Pennsylvania*, 41 U.S. (16 Pet.) 539 (1842) (upholding the federal Fugitive Slave Act of 1793, which established federal procedures for the capture and return of runaway slaves, and invalidating a Pennsylvania law creating impediments to the recapture of slaves).

"The question before us is, whether the class of persons described in the plea in abatement [are 'citizens' capable of invoking federal jurisdiction based on diversity of citizenship]. We think they are not, and that they are not included, and were not intended to be included, under the word 'citizens' in the Constitution, and can therefore claim none of the rights and privileges which that instrument provides for and secures to citizens of the United States. On the contrary, they were at that time considered as a subordinate and inferior class of beings, who had been subjugated by the dominant race, and, whether emancipated or not, yet remained subject to their authority, and had no rights or privileges but such as those who held the power and the Government might choose to grant them. [It] is difficult at this day to realize the state of public opinion in relation to that unfortunate race, which prevailed in the civilized and enlightened portions of the world at the time of the Declaration of Independence, and when the Constitution of the United States was framed and adopted. But the public history of every European nation displays it in a manner too plain to be mistaken. [Negroes] had for more than a century before been regarded as beings of inferior order, and altogether unfit to associate with the white race, either in social or political relations; and so far inferior, that they had no rights which the white man was bound to respect; and that the negro might justly and lawfully be reduced to slavery for his benefit. He was bought and sold, and treated as an ordinary article of merchandise and traffic, whenever a profit could be made by it. This opinion was at that time fixed and universal in the civilized portion of the white race. It was regarded as an axiom in morals as well as in politics, which no one thought of disputing, or supposed to be open to dispute; and men in every grade and position in society daily and habitually acted upon it in their private pursuits, as well as in matters of public concern, without doubting for a moment the correctness of this opinion.

"But it is too clear for dispute, that the enslaved African race were not intended to be included, and formed no part of the people who framed and adopted this declaration; for if the language, as understood in that day, would embrace them, the conduct of the distinguished men who framed the Declaration of Independence would have been utterly and flagrantly inconsistent with the principles they asserted; and instead of the sympathy of mankind, to which they so confidently appealed, they would have deserved and received universal rebuke and reprobation.

"Yet the men who framed this declaration were great men—high in literary acquirements—high in their sense of honor, and incapable of asserting principles inconsistent with those on which they were acting. They perfectly understood the meaning of the language they used, and how it would be understood by others; and they knew that it would not in any part of the civilized world be supposed to embrace the negro race, which, by common consent, had been excluded from civilized Governments and the family of nations, and doomed to slavery. They spoke and acted according to the then established doctrines and principles, and in the ordinary language of the day, no one misunderstood them. The unhappy black race were separated from the white by indelible marks, and laws long before established, and were never thought of or spoken of except as property, and when the claims of the owner or the profit of the trader were supposed to need protection. * * *

"No one, we presume, supposes that any change in public opinion or feeling, in relation to this unfortunate race, in the civilized nations of Europe or in this country, should induce the court to give to the words of the Constitution a more liberal construction in their favor than they were intended to bear when the instrument was framed and adopted. Such an argument would be altogether inadmissible in any tribunal called on to interpret it. If any of its provisions are deemed unjust, there is a mode prescribed in the instrument itself by which it may be amended; but while it remains unaltered, it must be construed now as it was understood at the time of its adoption. [Any] other rule of construction would abrogate the judicial character of this court, and make it the mere reflex of the popular opinion or passion of the day. This court was not created by the Constitution for such purposes. Higher and graver trusts have been confided to it, and it must not falter in the path of duty. * * *

"[Nor does Article IV, § 3, cl. 2, which empowers Congress to 'make all needful Rules and Regulations respecting the Territory and other Property of the United States,' authorize Congress to prohibit slavery in the territories. As the language indicates, this grant of power applies only to those territories that were already a part of one of the States in 1789, the cession of which to the United States was therefore contemplated. Moreover, general regulatory powers] in relation to rights of person, which it is not necessary here to enumerate, are, in express and positive terms, denied to the General Government; and the rights of private property have been guarded with equal care. Thus the rights of property are united with the rights of persons, and placed on the same ground by the fifth amendment to the Constitution, which provides that no person shall be deprived of life, liberty, and property, without due process of law. And an act of Congress which deprives a citizen of the United States of his liberty or property merely because he came himself or brought his property into a particular Territory of the United States, and who had committed no offence against the laws, could hardly be dignified with the name of due process of law.

"[The] powers of the Government, and the rights of the citizen under it, are positive and practical regulations plainly written down. [It] has no power over the person or property of a citizen but what the citizens of the United States have granted. And no laws or usages of other nations, or reasoning of statesmen or jurists upon the relations of master and slave, can enlarge the powers of the Government, or take from the citizens the rights they have reserved. And if the Constitution recognizes the right of property of the master in a slave, and makes no distinction between that description of property and other property owned by a citizen, no tribunal, acting under the authority of the United States, whether it be legislative, executive, or judicial, has a right to draw such a distinction, or deny to it the benefit of the provisions and guarantees which have been provided for the protection of private property against the encroachments of the Government.

"Now, as we have already said in an earlier part of this opinion, upon a different point, the right of property in a slave is distinctly and expressly affirmed in the Constitution. The right to traffic in it, like an ordinary article of merchandise and property, was guarantied to the citizens of the United States, in every State that might desire it, for twenty years. And the Government in express terms is pledged to protect it in all future time, if the slave escapes from his owner. This is done in plain words—too plain to be misunderstood. And no word can be found in the Constitution which gives Congress a greater power over slave property, or which entitles property of that kind to less protection than property of any other description. The only power conferred is the power coupled with the duty of guarding and protecting the owner in his rights.

"Upon these considerations, it is the opinion of the court that the act of Congress which prohibited a citizen from holding and owning property of this kind in the territory of the United States north of the line therein mentioned, is not warranted by the Constitution, and is therefore void; and that neither Dred Scott himself, nor any of his family, were made free by being carried into this territory; even if they had been carried there by the owner, with the intention of becoming a permanent resident."

CURTIS, J., dissented: "The first section of the second article of the Constitution uses the language, 'a citizen of the United States at the time of the adoption of the Constitution.' One mode of approaching this question is, to inquire who were citizens of the United States at the time of the adoption of the Constitution. * * * At the time of the ratification of the Articles of Confederation, all free native-born inhabitants of the States of New Hampshire, Massachusetts, New York, New Jersey, and North Carolina, though descended from African slaves, were not only citizens of those States, but such of them as had the other necessary qualifications possessed the franchise of electors, on equal terms with other citizens. * * * I can find nothing in the Constitution which, proprio vigore, deprives of their citizenship any class of persons who were citizens of the United States at the time of its adoption, or who should be native-born citizens of any State after its adoption; nor any power enabling Congress to disfranchise persons born on the soil of any State, and entitled to citizenship of such State by its Constitution and laws. And my opinion is, that, under the Constitution of the United States, every free person born on the soil of a State, who is a citizen of that State by force of its Constitution or laws, is also a citizen of the United States. * * *

"[A]s, in my opinion, the Circuit Court had jurisdiction, I am obliged to consider the question [whether] the plaintiff's status, as a slave, was so changed by his residence within [free territory] that he was not a slave in the State of Missouri, at the time this action was brought. * * *

"First. The rules of international law respecting the emancipation of slaves, by the rightful operation of the laws of another State or country upon the status of the slave, while resident in such foreign State or country, are part of the common law of Missouri, and have not been abrogated by any statute law of that State.

Second. The laws of the United States, constitutionally enacted, which operated directly on and changed the status of a slave coming into the Territory of Wisconsin with his master, who went thither to reside for an indefinite length of time, in the performance of his duties as an officer of the United States, had a rightful operation on the status of the slave, and it is in conformity with the rules of international law that this change of status should be recognised everywhere. * * *

"I have thus far assumed, merely for the purpose of the argument, that the laws of the United States, respecting slavery in this Territory, were constitutionally enacted by Congress. It remains to inquire whether they are constitutional and binding laws. [When] the Federal Constitution was framed, and presented to the people of the several States for their consideration, the unsettled territory was viewed as justly applicable to the common benefit, so far as it then had or might attain thereafter a pecuniary value; and so far as it might become the seat of new States, to be admitted into the Union upon an equal footing with the original States. * * * The importance of conferring on the new Government regular powers commensurate with the objects to be attained, and thus avoiding the alternative of a failure to execute the trust assumed by the acceptance of the cessions made and expected, or its execution by usurpation, could scarcely fail to be perceived. That it was in fact perceived, is clearly shown by the Federalist, (No. 38,) where this very argument is made use of in commendation of the Constitution. * * * Keeping these facts in view, it may confidently be asserted that there is very strong reason to believe, before we examine the Constitution itself, that the necessity for a competent grant of power to hold, dispose of, and govern territory, ceded and expected to be ceded, could not have escaped the attention of those who framed or adopted the Constitution; and that if it did not escape their attention, it could not fail to be adequately provided for.

"[Article IV thus provides:] 'The Congress shall have power to dispose of and make all needful rules and regulations respecting the territory or other property belonging to the United States; and nothing in this Constitution shall be so construed as to prejudice any claims of the United States or any particular State.' * * * No reason has been suggested why any reluctance should have been felt, by the framers of the Constitution, to apply this provision to all the territory which might belong to the United States, or why any distinction should have been made, founded on the accidental circumstance of the dates of the cessions; a circumstance in no way material as respects the necessity for rules and regulations, or the propriety of conferring on the Congress power to make them. And if we look at the course of the debates in the Convention on this article, we shall find that the then unceded lands, so far from having been left out of view in adopting this article, constituted, in the minds of members, a subject of even paramount importance.

"[With Congress's power to prohibit slavery in the territories otherwise being clear, the] the position, that a prohibition to bring slaves into a Territory deprives any one of his property without due process of law, [will not] bear examination. It must be remembered that this restriction on the legislative power is not peculiar to the Constitution of the United States; it was borrowed from Magna Charta; was brought to America by our ancestors, as part of their inherited liberties, and has existed in all the States, usually in the very words of the great charter. It existed in every political community in America in 1787, when the [Northwest] ordinance prohibiting slavery north and west of the Ohio was passed. * * *

"It was certainly understood by the Convention which framed the Constitution, and has been so understood ever since, that, under the power to regulate commerce, Congress could prohibit the importation of slaves; and the exercise of the power was restrained till 1808. A citizen of the United States owns slaves in Cuba, and brings them to the United States, where they are set free by the legislation of Congress. Does this legislation deprive him of his property without due process of law? If so, what becomes of the laws prohibiting the slave trade? If not, how can a similar regulation respecting a Territory violate the fifth amendment of the Constitution? * * *

"In my opinion, the judgment of the Circuit Court should be reversed."[9]

II. DISCRIMINATION AGAINST RACIAL AND ETHNIC MINORITIES

The "evil to be remedied" by the Equal Protection Clause, declared the *Slaughter-House Cases*, was "the existence of laws in the States where the newly emancipated negroes resided, which discriminated with gross injustice and hardship against them as a class."

STRAUDER v. WEST VIRGINIA, 100 U.S. 303 (1880)—the first post-Civil War race discrimination case to reach the Court—per STRONG, J., invalidated the state murder conviction of an African American on the ground that state law forbade blacks from serving on grand or petit juries. In the course of its opinion, the Court observed that "the true spirit and meaning" of the Civil War amendments was "securing to a race recently emancipated [the] enjoyment of all the civil rights that under the law are enjoyed by [whites]. What is [equal protection but] that all persons, whether colored or white, shall stand equal before the laws of the States, and, in regard to the colored race, for whose protection the amendment was primarily designed, that no discrimination shall be made against them by law because of their color? The words of the amendment [contain] a positive immunity or right, most valuable to the colored race,—the right to exemption from unfriendly legislation against them distinctively as colored,—exemption from legal discriminations, implying inferiority in civil society, lessening the security of their enjoyment of the rights which others enjoy, and discriminations which are steps towards reducing them to the condition of a subject race.

"That the West Virginia statute respecting juries [is] such a discrimination ought not to be doubted. [And if] in those States where the colored people constitute a majority of the entire population a law should be enacted excluding all white men from jury service, [we] apprehend no one would be heard to claim that it would not

---

    [9]   Other concurring and dissenting opinions in the case are omitted.

be a denial to white men of the equal protection of the laws. Nor if a law should be passed excluding all naturalized Celtic Irishmen, would there be any doubt of its inconsistency with the spirit of the amendment. * * *

"We do not say that within the limits from which it is not excluded by the amendment a State may not prescribe the qualifications of its jurors, and in so doing make discriminations. It may confine the selection to males, to freeholders, to citizens, to persons within certain ages, or to persons having educational qualifications. We do not believe the Fourteenth Amendment was ever intended to prohibit this. Looking at its history, it is clear it had no such purpose. Its aim was against discrimination because of race or color."

PLESSY v. FERGUSON
163 U.S. 537, 16 S.Ct. 1138, 41 L.Ed. 256 (1896).

JUSTICE BROWN delivered the opinion of the Court.

[An 1890 Louisiana law required that railway passenger cars have "equal but separate accommodations for the white, and colored races." Plessy, alleging that he "was seven-eighths Caucasian and one-eighth African blood; that the mixture of colored blood was not discernible in him; and that he was entitled to every right [of] the white race," was arrested for refusing to vacate a seat in a coach for whites.]

That [the challenged statute] does not conflict with the Thirteenth Amendment [is] too clear for argument. Slavery implies involuntary servitude,—a state of bondage * * * . This amendment [was] regarded by the statesmen of that day as insufficient to protect the colored race from certain laws [imposing] onerous disabilities and burdens, and curtailing their rights in the pursuit of life, liberty, and property to such an extent that their freedom was of little value; [and] the Fourteenth Amendment was devised to meet this exigency. * * *

The object of the amendment was undoubtedly to enforce the absolute equality of the two races before the law, but, in the nature of things, it could not have been intended to abolish distinctions based upon color, or to enforce social, as distinguished from political equality, or a commingling of the two races upon terms unsatisfactory to either. Laws permitting, and even requiring, their separation, in places where they are liable to be brought into contact do not necessarily imply the inferiority of either race to the other, and have been generally, if not universally, recognized as within the competency of the state legislatures in the exercise of their police power. The most common instance of this is connected with the establishment of separate schools for white and colored children, which have been [upheld] even by courts of states where the political rights of the colored race have been longest and most earnestly enforced [citing cases from Mass., Ohio, Mo., Cal., La., N.Y., Ind., and Ky.].

Laws forbidding the intermarriage of the two races may be said in a technical sense to interfere with the freedom of contract, and yet have been universally recognized as within the police power of the state. The distinction between laws interfering with the political equality of the negro and those requiring the separation of the two races in schools, theatres and railway carriages have been frequently drawn by this court. Thus in *Strauder v. West Virginia* it was held that a law of West Virginia [forbidding blacks to serve on juries] was a discrimination which implied a legal inferiority in civil society, which lessened the security of the colored race, and was a step toward reducing them to a condition of servility.

[S]tatutes for the separation of the two races upon public conveyances were held to be constitutional in [federal decisions and cases from Pa., Mich., Ill., Tenn. and N.Y. Almost] directly on point is [a Mississippi case] wherein the railway company was indicted for a violation of a statute of Mississippi, enacting that all railroads carrying passengers should provide equal, but separate, accommodations for the white and colored races. [It is suggested] that the same argument that will justify the state legislature in requiring railways to provide separate accommodations for the two races will also authorize them to require separate cars to be provided for people whose hair is of a certain color, or who are aliens, or who belong to certain nationalities, or to enact laws requiring colored people to walk upon one side of the street, and white people upon the other, or requiring white men's houses to be painted white, and colored men's black, or their vehicles or business signs to be of different colors, upon the theory that one side of the street is as good as the other, or that a house or vehicle of one color is as good as one of another color. The reply to all this is that every exercise of the police power must be reasonable, and extend only to such laws as are enacted in good faith for the promotion of the public good, and not for the annoyance or oppression of a particular class. [In] determining the question of reasonableness, [the state] is at liberty to act with reference to the established usages, customs, and traditions of the people, and with a view to the promotion of their comfort, and the preservation of the public peace and good order. Gauged by this standard, we cannot say [this law] is unreasonable, or more obnoxious to the Fourteenth Amendment than the [acts] requiring separate schools for colored children in the District of Columbia, the constitutionality of which does not seem to have been questioned, or the corresponding acts of state legislatures.

We consider the underlying fallacy of the plaintiff's argument to consist in the assumption that the enforced separation of the two races stamps the colored race with a badge of inferiority. If this be so, it is not by reason of anything found in the act, but solely because the colored race chooses to put that construction upon it. [The] argument also assumes that social prejudices may be overcome by legislation, and that equal rights cannot be secured to the negro except by an enforced commingling of the two races. We cannot accept this proposition. If the two races are to meet upon terms of social equality, it must be the result [of] voluntary consent of individuals. * * * Legislation is powerless to eradicate racial instincts, or to abolish distinctions based upon physical differences, and the attempt to do so can only result in accentuating the difficulties of the present situation. If the civil and political rights of both races be equal, one cannot be inferior to the other civilly or politically. If one race be inferior to the other socially, the Constitution of the United States cannot put them on the same plane. * * *

JUSTICE BREWER did [not] participate in the decision of this case.

JUSTICE HARLAN, dissenting.

[No] legislative body or judicial tribunal may have regard to the race of citizens when the civil rights of those citizens are involved. * * *

It was said in argument that the statute of Louisiana does not discriminate against either race, but prescribes a rule applicable alike to white and colored citizens. But [e]very one knows that [it] had its origin in the purpose, not so much to exclude white persons from railroad cars occupied by blacks, as to exclude colored people from coaches occupied by or assigned to white persons. [The] fundamental objection, therefore, to the statute is that it interferes with the personal freedom of citizens. * * *

The white race deems itself to be the dominant race in this country. And so it is, in prestige, in achievements, in education, in wealth, and in power. So, I doubt not, it will continue to be for all time, if it remains true to its great heritage, and holds fast to the principles of constitutional liberty. But in view of the constitution, in the eye of the law, there is in this country no superior, dominant, ruling class of citizens. There is no caste here. Our constitution is color-blind * * * .

In my opinion, the judgment this day rendered will, in time, prove to be quite as pernicious as the decision made by this tribunal in the *Dred Scott Case.* [What] can more certainly arouse race hate, what more certainly create and perpetuate a feeling of distrust between these races, than state enactments which, in fact, proceed on the ground that colored citizens are so inferior and degraded that they cannot be allowed to sit in public coaches occupied by white citizens? [The] thin disguise of "equal" accommodations for passengers in railroad coaches will not mislead any one, nor atone for the wrong this day done. * * *

I do not deem it necessary to review the decisions of state courts to which reference was made in argument. Some [are] inapplicable, because rendered prior to the adoption of the last amendments of the [Constitution]. Others were made at a time [when] race prejudice was, practically, the supreme law of the land. Those decisions cannot be guides in the era introduced by the recent amendments of the supreme law, which established universal civil freedom * * * .

KOREMATSU V. UNITED STATES
323 U.S. 214, 65 S.Ct. 193, 89 L.Ed. 194 (1944).

JUSTICE BLACK delivered the opinion of the Court.

[Following the Japanese attack on Pearl Harbor, President Franklin Roosevelt signed Executive Order 9066, which gave military officials the legal authority to exclude any or all persons from designated areas on the west coast in order to insure against sabotage and espionage. Congress implicitly ratified the

Executive Order by providing that the violation of an implementing order by a military commander constituted a misdemeanor punishable by fine or imprisonment. Under the authority of the Executive Order, the War Relocation Authority subjected all persons of Japanese ancestry on the west coast to a curfew, excluded them from their homes, detained them in assembly centers, and then evacuated them to "relocation centers" in California, Idaho, Utah, Arizona, Wyoming, Colorado, and Arkansas. By the end of 1942, roughly 112,000 persons—over 65,000 of whom were U.S. citizens—had been involuntarily removed to relocation centers.]

The petitioner, an American citizen of Japanese descent, was convicted in a federal district court for remaining in San Leandro, California, a "Military Area," contrary to Civilian Exclusion Order No. 34 of the Commanding General of the Western Command, U.S. Army, which directed that after May 9, 1942, all persons of Japanese ancestry should be excluded from that area. No question was raised as to petitioner's loyalty to the United States. * * *

[A]ll legal restrictions which curtail the civil rights of a single racial group are immediately suspect. That is not to say that all such restrictions are unconstitutional. It is to say that courts must subject them to the most rigid scrutiny. Pressing public necessity may sometimes justify the existence of such restrictions; racial antagonism never can. * * *

Exclusion Order No. 34 [was] one of a number of military orders. [In] *Hirabayashi v. United States*, 320 U.S. 81 (1943), we sustained a conviction [for] violation of [a] curfew order [applicable only to persons of Japanese ancestry as] an exercise of the power [to] take steps necessary to prevent espionage and sabotage in an area threatened by Japanese attack.

In the light of the principles we announced in the *Hirabayashi* case, we are unable to conclude that it was beyond the war power of Congress and the Executive to exclude those of Japanese ancestry from the West Coast war area at the time they did. [Nothing] short of apprehension by the proper military authorities of the gravest imminent danger to the public safety can constitutionally justify either [the *Hirabayashi* curfew order or Exclusion Order No. 34]. But exclusion from a threatened area, no less than curfew, has a definite and close relationship to the prevention of espionage and sabotage. * * *

Here, as in *Hirabayashi,* "we cannot reject as unfounded the judgment of the military authorities and of Congress that there were disloyal members of that population, whose number and strength could not be precisely and quickly ascertained. We cannot say that the war-making branches of the Government did not have ground for believing that in a critical hour such persons could not readily be isolated and separately dealt with, and constituted a menace to the national defense and safety, which demanded that prompt and adequate measures be taken to guard against it."

[This] answers the contention that the exclusion was in the nature of group punishment based on antagonism to those of Japanese origin. That there were members of the group who retained loyalties to Japan has been confirmed by investigations made subsequent to the exclusion. Approximately five thousand American citizens of Japanese ancestry refused to swear unqualified allegiance to the United States [and] several thousand evacuees requested repatriation to Japan.

[H]ardships are part of war, and war is an aggregation of hardships. [E]xclusion of large groups of citizens from their homes, except under circumstances of direst emergency and peril, is inconsistent with our basic governmental institutions. But when under conditions of modern warfare our shores are threatened by hostile forces, the power to protect must be commensurate with the threatened danger. * * *

It is said that we are dealing here with the case of imprisonment of a citizen in a concentration camp solely because of his ancestry, without evidence or inquiry concerning his loyalty and good disposition towards the United States. [But] we are dealing specifically with nothing but an exclusion order. To cast this case into outlines of racial prejudice, without reference to the real military dangers which were presented, merely confuses the issue. Korematsu was not excluded from the Military Area because of hostility to him or his race. He was excluded because we are at war with the Japanese Empire, because the properly constituted military authorities feared an invasion of our West Coast and felt constrained to take proper security measures, because they decided that the military urgency of the situation demanded that all citizens of Japanese ancestry be segregated from the West Coast temporarily, and finally, because Congress, reposing its confidence in this time of war in our military leaders—as inevitably it must—determined that they should have the power to do just this. There was evidence of disloyalty on the part of some, the military authorities considered the need for action was great, and time was short. We cannot—by availing ourselves of the calm perspective of hindsight—now say that at that time these actions were unjustified.

Affirmed.

JUSTICE FRANKFURTER, concurring.

[To] find that the Constitution does not forbid the military measures now complained of does not carry with it approval of that which Congress and the Executive did. That is their business, not ours.

JUSTICE MURPHY, dissenting.

[T]he exclusion, either temporarily or permanently, of all persons with Japanese blood in their veins [must] rely for its reasonableness upon the assumption that *all* persons of Japanese ancestry may have a dangerous tendency to commit sabotage and espionage and [it] is difficult to believe that reason, logic or experience could be marshalled in support of such an assumption. [The] reasons appear, instead, to be largely an accumulation of much of the misinformation, half-truths and insinuations that for years have been directed against Japanese Americans by people with racial and economic prejudices—the same people who have been among the foremost advocates of the evacuation. A military judgment based upon such racial and sociological considerations is not entitled to the great weight ordinarily given the judgments based upon strictly military considerations. Especially is this so when every charge relative to race, religion, culture, geographical location, and legal and economic status has been substantially discredited by independent studies made by experts in these matters. * * *

Moreover, there was no adequate proof that the FBI and the military and naval intelligence services did not have the espionage and sabotage situation well in hand during this long period. Nor is there any denial of the fact that not one person of Japanese ancestry was accused or convicted of espionage or sabotage after Pearl Harbor while they were still free, a fact which is some evidence of the loyalty of the vast majority of these individuals and of the effectiveness of the established methods of combatting these evils. It seems incredible that under these circumstances it would have been impossible to hold loyalty hearings for the mere 112,000 persons involved—or at least for the 70,000 American citizens—especially when a large part of this number represented children and elderly men and women. Any inconvenience that may have accompanied an attempt to conform to procedural due process cannot be said to justify violations of constitutional [rights].

JUSTICE JACKSON, dissenting.

Korematsu was born on our soil, of parents born in Japan. [Had] Korematsu been one of four—the others being, say, a German alien enemy, an Italian alien enemy, and a citizen of American-born ancestors, convicted of treason but out on parole—only Korematsu's presence would have violated the order. The difference between their innocence and his crime would result, not from anything he did, said, or thought, different than they, but only in that he was born of different racial stock.

Now, if any fundamental assumption underlies our system, it is that guilt is personal and not inheritable. [If] Congress in peace-time legislation should enact such a criminal law, I should suppose this Court would refuse to enforce it.

But [it] would be impracticable and dangerous idealism to expect or insist that each specific military command in an area of probable operations will conform to conventional tests of constitutionality. When an area is so beset that it must be put under military control at all, the paramount consideration is that its measures be successful, rather than legal. * * * I cannot say, from any evidence before me, that the orders of General DeWitt were not reasonably expedient military precautions, nor could I say that they were. But even if they were permissible military procedures, I deny that it follows that they are constitutional. If, as the Court holds, it does follow, then we may as well say that any military order will be constitutional and have done with it.

The limitation under which courts always will labor in examining the necessity for a military order are illustrated by this case. How does the Court know that these orders have a reasonable basis in necessity? No evidence whatever on that subject has been taken by this or any other court. There is sharp controversy as to the credibility of the DeWitt report. So the Court, having no real evidence before it, has no choice but to accept General DeWitt's own unsworn, self-serving statement, untested by any cross-examination, that what he did was reasonable. And thus it will always be when courts try to look into the reasonableness of a military order. * * *

[A] judicial construction of the Due Process Clause that will sustain this order is a far more subtle blow to liberty than the promulgation of the order itself. A military order, however unconstitutional, is not apt to last longer than the military emergency. [But] once a judicial opinion rationalizes [the] Constitution to show that the Constitution sanctions such an order, the Court for all time has validated the principle of racial discrimination in criminal procedure and of transplanting American citizens. The principle then lies about like a loaded weapon ready for the hand of any authority that can bring forward a plausible claim of an urgent need. * * *

My duties as a justice as I see them do not require me to make a military judgment as to whether General DeWitt's evacuation and detention program was a reasonable military necessity. I do not suggest that the courts should have attempted to interfere with the Army in carrying out its task. But I do not think they may be asked to execute a military expedient that has no place in law under the Constitution. I would reverse the judgment and discharge the prisoner.[10]

———————

In TRUMP v. HAWAII, 138 S.Ct. 2392 (2018), Ch. 8, Sec. 2, I supra, which upheld a presidential proclamation that restricted entry into the United States by nationals of six predominantly Muslim countries and also of North Korea and Venezuela, a dissenting opinion by SOTOMAYOR, J., joined by Ginsburg, J., invoked *Korematsu* as an analogy (based on alleged "dangerous stereotypes," "animus," and the government's "unwilling[ness] to reveal its own intelligence agencies' views of the alleged security concerns"). The Court, per ROBERTS, C.J., responded: "*Korematsu* has nothing to do with this case. The forcible relocation of U.S. citizens to concentration camps, solely and explicitly on the basis of race, is objectively unlawful and outside the scope of Presidential authority. But it is wholly inapt to liken that morally repugnant order to a facially neutral policy denying certain foreign nationals the privilege of admission. * * * The dissent's reference to *Korematsu*, however, affords this Court the opportunity to make express what is already obvious: *Korematsu* was gravely wrong the day it was decided, has been overruled in the court of history, and—to be clear—'has no place in law under the Constitution.' [*Korematsu*] (Jackson, J., dissenting)."

———

10   The dissenting opinion of Roberts, J., is omitted.

BROWN V. BOARD OF EDUCATION
347 U.S. 483, 74 S.Ct. 686, 98 L.Ed. 873 (1954).

CHIEF JUSTICE WARREN delivered the opinion of the Court.

These cases come to us from the States of Kansas, South Carolina, Virginia, and Delaware. * * *

In each of the cases, minors of the Negro race [seek] the aid of the courts in obtaining admission to the public schools of their community on a nonsegregated basis. [In] each of the cases other than the Delaware case, a three-judge federal district court denied relief to the plaintiffs on the so-called "separate but equal" doctrine announced by this Court in [*Plessy*]. In the Delaware case, the Supreme Court of Delaware adhered to that doctrine, but ordered that the plaintiffs be admitted to the white schools because of their superiority to the Negro schools.

* * * Argument was heard in the 1952 Term, and reargument was heard this Term on certain questions propounded by the Court.

Reargument was largely devoted to the circumstances surrounding the adoption of the Fourteenth Amendment in 1868. It covered exhaustively consideration of the Amendment in Congress, ratification by the states, then existing practices in racial segregation, and the views of proponents and opponents of the Amendment. This discussion and our own investigation convince us that, although these sources cast some light, it is not enough to resolve the problem with which we are faced. At best, they are inconclusive. The most avid proponents of the post-War Amendments undoubtedly intended them to remove all legal distinctions among "all persons born or naturalized in the United States." Their opponents, just as certainly, were antagonistic to both the letter and the spirit of the Amendments and wished them to have the most limited effect. What others in Congress and the state legislatures had in mind cannot be determined with any degree of certainty.

An additional reason for the inconclusive nature of the Amendment's history, with respect to segregated schools, is the status of public education at that time. In the South, the movement toward free common schools, supported by general taxation, had not yet taken hold. Education of white children was largely in the hands of private groups. Education of Negroes was almost nonexistent, and practically all of the race were illiterate. In fact, any education of Negroes was forbidden by law in some states. Today, in contrast, many Negroes have achieved outstanding success in the arts and sciences as well as in the business and professional world. It is true that public school education at the time of the Amendment had advanced further in the North, but the effect of the Amendment on Northern States was generally ignored in the congressional debates. Even in the North, the conditions of public education did not approximate those existing today. The curriculum was usually rudimentary; ungraded schools were common in rural areas; the school term was but three months a year in many states; and compulsory school attendance was virtually unknown. As a consequence, it is not surprising that there should be so little in the history of the Fourteenth Amendment relating to its intended effect on public education.

In the first cases in this Court construing the Fourteenth Amendment, decided shortly after its adoption, the Court interpreted it as proscribing all state-imposed discriminations against the Negro race.[5] The doctrine of "separate but equal" did not make its appearance in this Court until 1896 in *Plessy,* involving not education but transportation. [In] this Court, there have been six cases involving the "separate but equal" doctrine in the field of public education. In *Cumming v. Board of Education,* 175 U.S. 528, and *Gong Lum v. Rice,* 275 U.S. 78, the validity of the doctrine itself was not challenged.[8] In more recent cases, all on the graduate school level, inequality was found in that specific benefits enjoyed by white students were denied to Negro students of the same educational qualifications. *Missouri ex rel. Gaines v. Canada,* 305 U.S. 337;[11] *Sipuel v. Oklahoma,* 332 U.S. 631; *Sweatt v. Painter,* 339 U.S. 629;[12] *McLaurin v. Oklahoma State Regents,* 339 U.S. 637.[13] In none of these cases was it necessary to re-examine the doctrine to grant relief to the Negro plaintiff. And in *Sweatt,* the Court expressly reserved decision on the question whether *Plessy* should be held inapplicable to public education.

In the instant cases, that question is directly presented. [T]here are findings below that the Negro and white schools involved have been equalized, or are being equalized, with respect to buildings, curricula, qualifications and salaries of teachers, and other "tangible" factors. Our decision, therefore, cannot turn on merely a comparison of these tangible factors in the Negro and white schools involved in each of the cases. We must look instead to the effect of segregation itself on public education.

---

[5]   [Ct's Note] *Slaughter-House Cases*; *Strauder* * * * . See also *Virginia v. Rives,* 1879, 100 U.S. 313, 318; *Ex parte Virginia,* 1879, 100 U.S. 339, 344–345. [See generally Brief for the Committee of Law Teachers Against Segregation in Legal Education, *Segregation and the Equal Protection Clause,* 34 Minn.L.Rev. 289 (1950).]

[8]   [Ct's Note] In the *Cumming* case, Negro taxpayers sought an injunction requiring the defendant school board to discontinue the operation of a high school for white children until the board resumed operation of a high school for Negro children. Similarly, in the *Gong Lum* case, the plaintiff, a child of Chinese descent, contended only that state authorities had misapplied the doctrine by classifying him with Negro children and requiring him to attend a Negro school.

[11]   *Gaines,* in 1938, invalidated the refusal to admit blacks to the University of Missouri School of Law, despite the state's offer to pay petitioner's tuition at an out-of-state law school pending establishment of a state law school for African-Americans.

[12]   *Sweatt,* in 1950, required admission of African Americans to the University of Texas Law School, despite the recent establishment of a state law school for blacks: "In terms of number of the faculty, variety of courses and opportunity for specialization, size of the student body, scope of the library, availability of law review and similar activities, the University of Texas Law School is superior. [Equally troubling is that the] law school to which Texas is willing to admit petitioner excludes from its student body members of the racial groups which number 85% of the population of the State and include most of the lawyers, witnesses, jurors, judges and other officials with whom petitioner will inevitably be dealing when he becomes a member of the Texas Bar."

[13]   *McLaurin,* in 1950, held violative of equal protection requirements that African-American graduate students at the University of Oklahoma sit at separate desks adjoining the classrooms and separate tables outside the library reading room, and eat at separate times in the school cafeteria.

In approaching this problem, we cannot turn the clock back to 1868 when the Amendment was adopted, or even to 1896 when *Plessy* was written. We must consider public education in the light of its full development and its present place in American life throughout the Nation. Only in this way can it be determined if segregation in public schools deprives these plaintiffs of the equal protection of the laws.

Today, education is perhaps the most important function of state and local governments. Compulsory school attendance laws and the great expenditures for education both demonstrate our recognition of the importance of education to our democratic society. It is required in the performance of our most basic public responsibilities, even service in the armed forces. It is the very foundation of good citizenship. Today it is a principal instrument in awakening the child to cultural values, in preparing him for later professional training, and in helping him to adjust normally to his environment. In these days, it is doubtful that any child may reasonably be expected to succeed in life if he is denied the opportunity of an education. Such an opportunity, where the state has undertaken to provide it, is a right which must be made available to all on equal terms.

We come then to the question presented: Does segregation of children in public schools solely on the basis of race, even though the physical facilities and other "tangible" factors may be equal, deprive the children of the minority group of equal educational opportunities? We believe that it does.

In *Sweatt,* in finding that a segregated law school for Negroes could not provide them equal educational opportunities, this Court relied in large part on "those qualities which are incapable of objective measurement but which make for greatness in a law school." In *McLaurin,* the Court, in requiring that a Negro admitted to a white graduate school be treated like all other students, again resorted to intangible considerations: "[his] ability to study, to engage in discussions and exchange views with other students, and in general, to learn his profession." Such considerations apply with added force to children in grade and high schools. To separate them from others of similar age and qualifications solely because of their race generates a feeling of inferiority as to their status in the community that may affect their hearts and minds in a way unlikely ever to be undone. The effect of this separation on their educational opportunities was well stated by a finding in the Kansas case by a court which nevertheless felt compelled to rule against the Negro plaintiffs: "Segregation of white and colored children in public schools has a detrimental effect upon the colored children. The impact is greater when it has the sanction of the law; for the policy of separating the races is usually interpreted as denoting the inferiority of the Negro group. A sense of inferiority affects the motivation of a child to learn. Segregation with the sanction of law, therefore, has a tendency to [retard] the educational and mental development of Negro children and to deprive them of some of the benefits they would receive in a racial[ly] integrated school system."[10] Whatever may have been

---

[10]   [Ct's Note] A similar finding was made in the Delaware case: "I conclude from the testimony that in our Delaware society, State-imposed segregation in education itself results in

the extent of psychological knowledge at the time of *Plessy,* this finding is amply supported by modern authority.[11] Any language in *Plessy* contrary to this finding is rejected.

We conclude that in the field of public education the doctrine of "separate but equal" has no place. Separate educational facilities are inherently unequal. Therefore, we hold that the plaintiffs and others similarly situated for whom the actions have been brought are, by reason of the segregation complained of, deprived of [equal protection].

Because these are class actions, because of the wide applicability of this decision, and because of the great variety of local conditions, the formulation of decrees in these cases presents problems of considerable complexity. On reargument, the consideration of appropriate relief was necessarily subordinated to the primary question—the constitutionality of segregation in public education. We have now announced that such segregation is a denial of the equal protection of the laws. In order that we may have the full assistance of the parties in formulating decrees, the cases will be restored to the docket, and the parties are requested to present further argument on Questions 4 and 5 previously propounded by the Court for the reargument this Term.[13] * * *

---

the Negro children, as a class, receiving educational opportunities which are substantially inferior to those available to white children otherwise similarly situated."

[11]   **[Ct's Note]** K. B. Clark, *Effect of Prejudice and Discrimination on Personality Development* (Midcentury White House Conference on Children and Youth, 1950); Witmer and Kotinsky, *Personality in the Making* (1952), c. VI; Deutscher and Chein, *The Psychological Effects of Enforced Segregation: A Survey of Social Science Opinion,* 26 J.Psychol. 259 (1948); Chein, *What are the Psychological Effects of Segregation Under Conditions of Equal Facilities?,* 3 Int.J. Opinion and Attitude Res. 229 (1949); Brameld, *Educational Costs in Discrimination and National Welfare* (MacIver, ed., 1949), 44–48; Frazier, *The Negro in the United States* (1949), 674–681. And, see generally Gunnar Myrdal, *An American Dilemma* (1944).

[13]   **[Ct's Note]** "4. Assuming it is decided that segregation in public schools violates the Fourteenth Amendment

      "(a) would a decree necessarily follow providing that, within the limits set by normal geographic school districting, Negro children should forthwith be admitted to schools of their choice, or

      "(b) may this Court, in the exercise of its equity powers, permit an effective gradual adjustment to be brought about from existing segregated systems to a system not based on color distinctions?

      "5. On the assumption on which questions 4(a) and (b) are based, and assuming further that this Court will exercise its equity powers to the end described in question 4(b),

      "(a) should this Court formulate detailed decrees in these cases;

      "(b) if so, what specific issues should the decrees reach;

      "(c) should this Court appoint a special master to hear evidence with a view to recommending specific terms for such decrees;

      "(d) should this Court remand to the courts of first instance with directions to frame decrees in these cases, and if so what general directions should the decrees of this Court include and what procedures should the courts of first instance follow in arriving at the specific terms of more detailed decrees?"

BOLLING v. SHARPE, 347 U.S. 497 (1954), per WARREN, C.J., held—on the same day as *Brown*—that public school segregation in the District of Columbia "constitutes an arbitrary deprivation [of] liberty in violation of the Due Process Clause" of the Fifth Amendment: "The Fifth Amendment [does] not contain an Equal Protection Clause as does the Fourteenth Amendment which applies only to the states. But the concepts of equal protection and due process, both stemming from our American ideal of fairness, are not mutually exclusive. The 'equal protection of the laws' is a more explicit safeguard of prohibited unfairness than 'due process of law,' and, therefore, we do not imply that the two are always interchangeable phrases. But, as this Court has recognized, discrimination may be so unjustifiable as to be violative of due process.

"Classifications based solely upon race must be scrutinized with particular care, since they are contrary to our traditions and hence constitutionally suspect. *Korematsu*. ['Liberty'] extends to the full range of conduct which the individual is free to pursue, and it cannot be restricted except for a proper governmental objective. Segregation in public education is not reasonably related to any proper governmental objective * * * .

"In view of our decision that the Constitution prohibits the states from maintaining racially segregated public schools, it would be unthinkable that the same Constitution would impose a lesser duty on the Federal Government."

BROWN V. BOARD OF EDUCATION (II)
349 U.S. 294, 75 S.Ct. 753, 99 L.Ed. 1083 (1955).

CHIEF JUSTICE WARREN delivered the opinion of the Court.

These cases were decided on May 17, 1954. [There] remains for consideration the manner in which relief is to be accorded. * * *

Full implementation of these constitutional principles may require solution of varied local school problems. School authorities have the primary responsibility for elucidating, assessing, and solving [them]; courts will have to consider whether the action of school authorities constitutes good faith implementation of the governing constitutional principles. Because of their proximity to local conditions and the possible need for further hearings, the courts which originally heard these cases can best perform this judicial appraisal. Accordingly, we believe it appropriate to remand the cases to those courts.

In fashioning and effectuating the decrees, the courts will be guided by equitable principles. Traditionally, equity has been characterized by a practical flexibility in shaping its remedies and by a facility for adjusting and reconciling public and private needs. [A]t stake is the personal interest of the plaintiffs in admission to public schools as soon as practicable on a nondiscriminatory basis. To effectuate this interest may call for elimination of a variety of obstacles in making the transition to school systems operated in accordance with the constitutional principles set forth in our May 17, 1954, decision. Courts of equity may properly take into account the public interest in the elimination of such obstacles in a systematic and effective manner. But it should go without saying that the vitality of these constitutional principles cannot be allowed to yield simply because of disagreement with them.

While giving weight to these public and private considerations, the courts will require that the defendants make a prompt and reasonable start toward full compliance with our May 17, 1954, ruling. Once such a start has been made, the courts may find that additional time is necessary to carry out the ruling in an effective manner. The burden rests upon the defendants to establish that such time is necessary in the public interest and is consistent with good faith compliance at the earliest practicable date. To that end, the courts may consider problems related to administration, arising from the physical condition of the school plant, the school transportation system, personnel, revision of school districts and attendance areas into compact units to achieve a system of determining admission to the public schools on a nonracial basis, and revision of local laws and regulations which may be necessary in solving the foregoing problems. They will also consider the adequacy of any plans the defendants may propose to meet these problems and to effectuate a transition to a racially nondiscriminatory school system. During this period of transition, the courts will retain jurisdiction of these cases.

The [cases are remanded] to take such proceedings and enter such orders and decrees consistent with this opinion as are necessary and proper to admit to public schools on a racially nondiscriminatory basis with all deliberate speed the parties to these cases. * * *

LOVING V. VIRGINIA
388 U.S. 1, 87 S.Ct. 1817, 18 L.Ed.2d 1010 (1967).

CHIEF JUSTICE WARREN delivered the opinion of the Court.

This case presents a constitutional question never addressed by this Court: whether a statutory scheme adopted by Virginia to prevent marriages between persons solely on the basis of racial classifications violates [the] Fourteenth Amendment. [Appellants, a black woman and white man, were married in the District of Columbia, returned to reside in Virginia, and were convicted under the state antimiscegenation statute.]

Virginia is now one of 16 States which prohibit and punish marriages on the basis of racial classifications.[5] [The] state court concluded that the State's legitimate purposes were "to preserve the racial integrity of its citizens," and to prevent "the corruption of blood," "a mongrel breed of citizens," and "the obliteration of racial pride," obviously an endorsement of the doctrine of White Supremacy. [T]he State [argues] that the meaning of the Equal Protection Clause, as illuminated by the statements of the Framers, is only that state penal laws

---

    [5]   **[Ct's Note]** [Over] the past 15 years, 14 States have repealed laws outlawing interracial marriages * * * .

containing an interracial element as part of the definition of the offense must apply equally to whites and Negroes in the sense that members of each race are punished to the same degree. * * *

Because we reject the notion that the mere "equal application" of a statute containing racial classifications is enough to remove the classifications from the Fourteenth Amendment's proscription of all invidious racial discriminations, we do not accept the State's contention that these statutes should be upheld if there is any possible basis for concluding that they serve a rational purpose. [Here], we deal with statutes containing racial classifications, and the fact of equal application does not immunize the statute from the very heavy burden of justification which the Fourteenth Amendment has traditionally required of state statutes drawn according to race.

The State argues that statements in the Thirty-ninth Congress about the time of the passage of the Fourteenth Amendment indicate that the Framers did not intend the Amendment to make unconstitutional state miscegenation laws. Many of the statements [have] some relevance to the intention of Congress in submitting the Fourteenth Amendment, [but] it must be understood that they pertained to the passage of specific statutes and not to the broader, organic purpose of a constitutional amendment. As for the various statements directly concerning the Fourteenth Amendment, we have said in connection with a related problem, that although these historical sources "cast some light" they are not sufficient to resolve the problem; "[a]t best, they are inconclusive." *Brown.* We have rejected the proposition that the debates in the Thirty-ninth Congress or in the state legislatures which ratified the Fourteenth Amendment supported the theory [that equal protection] is satisfied by penal laws defining offenses based on racial classifications so long as white and Negro participants in the offense were similarly punished. *McLaughlin v. Florida*, 379 U.S. 184 (1964).[14]

The State finds support for its "equal application" theory [in] *Pace v. Alabama*, 106 U.S. 583 (1883). In that case, the Court upheld a conviction under an Alabama statute forbidding adultery or fornication between a white person and a Negro which imposed a greater penalty than that of a statute proscribing similar conduct by members of the same race. The Court reasoned that the statute could not be said to discriminate against Negroes because the punishment for each participant in the offense was the same. However, as recently as the 1964 Term, in rejecting the reasoning of that case, we stated "*Pace* represents a limited view of the Equal Protection Clause which has not withstood analysis in the subsequent decisions of this Court." *McLaughlin.* [The] clear and central purpose of the Fourteenth Amendment was to eliminate all official state sources of invidious racial discrimination in the States. [At] the very least, the Equal Protection Clause demands that racial classifications, especially suspect in criminal statutes, be subjected to the "most rigid scrutiny," and, if they are ever to be upheld, they must be shown to be necessary to the accomplishment of some permissible state

---

14   *McLaughlin* invalidated a statute making interracial cohabitation a crime.

objective, independent of the racial discrimination which it was the object of the Fourteenth Amendment to eliminate.[15] Indeed, two [justices] have already stated that they "cannot conceive of a valid legislative purpose [which] makes the color of a person's skin the test of whether his conduct is a criminal offense." *McLaughlin* (Stewart, J., joined by Douglas, J., concurring).

There is patently no legitimate overriding purpose independent of invidious racial discrimination which justifies this classification. The fact that Virginia only prohibits interracial marriages involving white persons demonstrates that the racial classifications must stand on their own justification, as measures designed to maintain White Supremacy.[11] We have consistently denied the constitutionality of measures which restrict the rights of citizens on account of race. There can be no doubt that restricting the freedom to marry solely because of racial classifications violates the central meaning of the Equal Protection Clause.

These statutes also deprive the Lovings of liberty without [due process].

Marriage is one of the "basic civil rights of man," fundamental to our very existence and survival. *Skinner v. Oklahoma* [Ch. 6, Sec. 2 supra]. To deny this fundamental freedom on so unsupportable a basis as the racial classifications embodied in these statutes [surely denies due process].

Reversed.

JUSTICE STEWART, concurring.

I have previously expressed the belief that "it is simply not possible for a state law to be valid under our Constitution which makes the criminality of an act depend upon the race of the actor." *McLaughlin* (concurring opinion). Because I adhere to that belief, I concur in the judgment of the Court.

————

PALMORE v. SIDOTI, 466 U.S. 429 (1984), per BURGER, C.J., held that Florida's denial of child custody to a white mother because her new husband was black violated equal protection: "There is a risk that a child living with a step-parent of a different race may be subject to a variety of pressures and stresses not present if the child were living with parents of the same racial or ethnic origin. [But the] effects of racial prejudice, however real, cannot justify a racial

---

[15] *McLaughlin* also stated that racial classifications were " 'in most circumstances irrelevant' to any constitutionally acceptable legislative purpose." Harlan, J., concurring, added that "necessity, not mere reasonable relationship, is the proper test"; this "test which developed to protect free speech against state infringement should be equally applicable in a case involving state racial discrimination—prohibition of which lies at the very heart of the Fourteenth Amendment."

[11] **[Ct's Note]** [While] Virginia prohibits whites from marrying any nonwhite (subject to the exception for the descendants of Pocahontas), Negroes, Orientals and any other racial class may intermarry without statutory interference. Appellants contend that this distinction renders Virginia's miscegenation statutes arbitrary and unreasonable even assuming the constitutional validity of an official purpose to preserve "racial integrity." We need not reach this contention because we find the racial classifications in these statutes repugnant to the Fourteenth Amendment, even assuming an evenhanded state purpose to protect the "integrity" of all races.

classification removing an infant child from the custody of its natural mother found to be an appropriate person to have such custody."

———

JOHNSON v. CALIFORNIA, 543 U.S. 499 (2005), held that the "strict scrutiny" test developed in prior race discrimination cases (under which racial classifications will be upheld only if proven to be "narrowly tailored" to further "compelling governmental interests") applied to a policy of the California Department of Corrections (CDC) to assign newly arrived prisoners to temporary cells "based on a number of factors, [but] predominantly race." The Court, per O'CONNOR, J., rejected arguments for applying "the deferential standard of review articulated in *Turner v. Safley*, 482 U.S. 78 (1987)," under which courts will ordinarily uphold any prison regulation that is "reasonably related" to "legitimate penological interests." Unlike burdens on prisoners' rights to privacy, speech, and religion, "[t]he right not to be discriminated against based on one's race is not susceptible to the logic of *Turner*. It is not a right that need necessarily be compromised for the sake of proper prison administration."

Although Stevens, J., agreed with the majority about the applicable standard of review, he dissented from the Court's decision to remand the case to the district court to apply the compelling interest test and would have held squarely that the challenged policy violated the Equal Protection Clause. Thomas, J., joined by Scalia, J., dissented. In light of the threats of race-based prison violence and the general needs of prison administration, he would have upheld the CDC's policy on the basis of *Turner*.

III. HISTORY OF SCHOOL DESEGREGATION

1. ***Massive resistance.*** (a) Although there was prompt compliance with *Brown* in the District of Columbia and some border states, the initial response in the Deep South was "massive resistance." Reports Michael J. Klarman, *From Jim Crow to Civil Rights: The Supreme Court and the Struggle for Racial Equality* 350–51 (2004): "For personal and political reasons, school board members resisted prompt and effective action toward desegregation. [Board] members were elected officials, who could ill afford to ignore public opinion. [Such] officials also had personal incentives to delay and evade compliance with *Brown*, as they had to live in communities that were staunchly opposed to desegregation. [School] board members had [particularly] strong reasons not to be the first in a state or region to desegregate, which would make them the focal point of segregationist pressure."

(b)　In the late 1950s, some states sought to comply with *Brown* by simply permitting students to apply for transfer from one previously all-black or all-white school to another school. Procedures were complex and time-consuming; standards were vague, making it difficult to show that denials were due to race. But the Court generally took a hands-off stance, leaving the burden of grappling with the "massive resistance" campaign largely to the lower federal courts. The justices' most notable intervention in the immediate post-*Brown* decade came in COOPER

v. AARON, 358 U.S. 1 (1958), also discussed in Ch. 1, Sec. 1 supra. At issue in *Cooper* was a request by the Little Rock, Arkansas, School Board to stay an integration plan that had been in operation at Central High School during the 1957–58 school year. During that year, implementation of the plan became possible only after President Eisenhower sent federal troops to protect black students from "extreme public hostility" fueled by inflammatory opposition by the governor and state legislature. The opinion, unprecedented in that it was signed by all nine Justices (including those appointed since *Brown*), "unanimously reaffirmed" *Brown* and further asserted that the decision "can neither be nullified openly and directly by state legislators or state executive or judicial officers, nor nullified indirectly by them through evasive schemes."

(c)   Despite these firm-sounding words, little school desegregation ensued in *Cooper*'s immediate aftermath. Relevant developments occurred on other fronts, however. A growing civil rights movement galvanized attention, much of it sympathetic. Largely in response, and with firm leadership by President Lyndon Johnson, Congress in 1964 enacted a sweeping civil rights act, two titles of which specifically dealt with schools. Title IV authorized the attorney general to assist in the development and implementation of school desegregation plans and, where such plans were not adopted voluntarily, empowered the attorney general to initiate lawsuits to remedy racial discrimination. Title VI barred federal financial assistance for any program, including school programs, administered in a racially discriminatory manner.

2.   *Court demands for desegregation.* Whatever the cause, 1964 marked a turning point in the Court's demands for actual desegregation.

(a)   GRIFFIN v. COUNTY SCHOOL BD., 377 U.S. 218 (1964), addressed the situation in Prince Edward County, Virginia, which in 1959 closed its public schools rather than comply with a desegregation order. Private schools, supported by state and local tuition grants and tax credits, were operated for whites. The Court, per BLACK, J., held that the closing denied African Americans equal protection: "[Whatever] nonracial grounds might support a state's allowing a county to abandon public schools, the object must be a constitutional one, and grounds of race and opposition to desegregation do not qualify."

(b)   In GREEN v. COUNTY SCHOOL BD., 391 U.S. 430 (1968), the Court, per BRENNAN, J., invalidated a "freedom-of-choice" plan that Virginia's rural, sparsely populated New Kent County had grudgingly adopted to remain eligible for federal financial aid: "There is no residential segregation in the county; persons of both races reside throughout. The school system has only two schools[. When the litigation began in 1965, the] 'School Board [still] operate[d] one white combined elementary and high school (New Kent), and one Negro combined elementary and high school (George W. Watkins). There are no attendance zones. Each school serves the entire county.' "

Following adoption of the freedom-of-choice plan (implemented after litigation had commenced), enrolled students could annually choose between the county's previously all-white and all-black high schools, with pupils who did not register an alternative preference being automatically reassigned to the school they had attended the year before. After three years, however, no white child had chosen to go to the black school that 85% of the black children continued to attend. For the system to operate as it did, "21 school buses—11 serving the Watkins school and 10 serving the New Kent school—travel[ed] overlapping routes throughout the county to transport pupils to and from the two schools.

"[It] is of course true that for the time immediately after *Brown II* the concern was with making an initial break in a long-established pattern of excluding Negro children from schools attended by white children. The principal focus was on obtaining for those Negro children courageous enough to break with tradition a place in the 'white' schools. Under *Brown II* that immediate goal was only the first step, however. The transition to a unitary, nonracial system of public education was and is the ultimate end to be brought about; it was because of the 'complexities arising from the transition to a system of public education freed of racial discrimination' that we provided for 'all deliberate speed' in the implementation of the principles of *Brown I*.

"[Thirteen] years after *Brown II* commanded the abolition of dual systems we must measure the effectiveness of respondent School Board's 'freedom-of-choice' plan to achieve that end. [The] New Kent School Board's 'freedom-of-choice' plan," which was not adopted "until some 11 years after *Brown I* was decided and 10 years after *Brown II* directed the making of a 'prompt and reasonable start,'" cannot "be accepted as a sufficient step to 'effectuate a transition' to a unitary system. [It] is incumbent upon the School Board to establish that its proposed plan promises meaningful and immediate progress toward disestablishing state-imposed segregation. [The School] Board must be required [to] fashion steps which promise realistically to convert promptly to a system without a 'white' school and a 'Negro' school, but just schools."

(c) SWANN v. CHARLOTTE-MECKLENBURG BD. OF EDUC., 402 U.S. 1 (1971), per BURGER, C.J., affirmed a lower court order establishing flexible mathematical targets for permissible racial balance in individual schools and requiring school busing as a tool for achieving those goals in an urban district that had previously practiced de jure segregation. The Court opinion invited voluntary efforts to achieve broad racial integration: "School authorities are traditionally charged with broad power to formulate and implement educational policy and might well conclude, for example, that in order to prepare students to live in a pluralistic society each school should have a prescribed ratio of Negro to white students reflecting the proportion for the district as a whole."

At a minimum, however, previously segregated districts were obliged to "to eliminate from the public schools all vestiges of state-imposed segregation." If they failed to do so, "judicial authority may be invoked. [When] school authorities present a district court with a 'loaded game board,' affirmative action in the form of remedial altering of attendance zones is proper to achieve truly nondiscriminatory assignments. [The] importance of bus transportation as a normal and accepted tool of educational policy is readily discernible. [The lower court's] decree provided that [trips] for elementary school pupils average about seven miles and the District Court found that they would take 'not over 35 minutes at the most.' This system compares favorably with the transportation plan previously operated in Charlotte under which each day 23,600 students on all grade levels were transported an average of 15 miles one way for an average trip requiring over an hour. In these circumstances, we find no basis for holding that the local school authorities may not be required to employ bus transportation as one tool of school desegregation. Desegregation plans cannot be limited to the walk-in school."

3. ***Limits of the remedial obligation.*** The Court's demand that previously unconstitutionally segregated school districts root out the vestiges of past segregation raised the question of how long remedial policies—including court-ordered busing—must continue. In OKLAHOMA CITY BD. OF EDUC. v. DOWELL, 498 U.S. 237 (1991), a school district that previously had been under a desegregation order that included forced busing satisfied the district court that "unitariness had been achieved." Eight years later, the school board adopted a new neighborhood assignment plan that resulted in about half the schools becoming primarily uniracial. Successors to the parties in the initial action then challenged the school board's actions as incompatible with prior judicial orders, which they maintained continued in effect. The Court, per REHNQUIST, C.J., held that the previously entered desegregation decree should be dissolved, even if a substantial reduction in actual integration would occur, if the board has "complied in good faith [since the injunction] was entered" and "the vestiges of past discrimination have been eliminated to the extent practicable. [The] District Court should then evaluate the Board's decision to implement the [new assignment plan] under appropriate equal protection principles [that tolerate government decisions that are not explicitly race-based unless they are made with a racially discriminatory intent]. See *Washington v. Davis,* [Sec. 2, IV, infra]."

MARSHALL, J., joined by Blackmun and Stevens, JJ., dissented: "I believe a desegregation decree cannot be lifted so long as conditions likely to inflict the stigmatic injury condemned in *Brown I* persist and there remain feasible methods of eliminating such conditions." Souter, J., did not participate.

PARENTS INVOLVED IN COMMUNITY SCHOOLS v. SEATTLE SCHOOL DIST.

551 U.S. 701, 127 S.Ct. 2738, 168 L.Ed.2d 508 (2007).

ROBERTS, C.J., announced the judgment of the Court, and delivered the opinion of the Court with respect to Parts I, II, III-A, and III-C, and an opinion with respect to Parts III-B and IV, in which JUSTICES SCALIA, THOMAS, and ALITO join.

The school districts in these cases [in Seattle, Washington, and Jefferson County, Kentucky] voluntarily adopted student assignment plans that rely upon race to determine which public schools certain children may attend. * * *

I.　　Both cases present the same underlying legal question—whether a public school that had not operated legally segregated schools or has been found to be unitary may choose to classify students by race and rely upon that classification in making school assignments.

[The Seattle School District was never officially segregated by law, but racial imbalances led to threatened and actual lawsuits in the 1960s and 1970s and to a series of steps to settle those lawsuits that once included mandatory busing, despite the fact that official discrimination was never proved nor admitted. In 1998, the district] adopted the plan at issue in this case for assigning students to [its ten high] schools. The plan allows incoming ninth graders to choose from among any of the district's high schools, ranking however many schools they wish in order of preference. [If] too many students list the same school as their first choice, the district employs a series of "tiebreakers" to determine who will fill the open slots at the oversubscribed school. The first tiebreaker selects for admission students who have a sibling currently enrolled in the chosen school. The next tiebreaker depends upon the racial composition of the particular school and the race of the individual student. [This second tiebreaker comes into play if a school's enrollment deviates by more than 10% from the district's overall balance of approximately 41% white and 59% nonwhite students.]

Jefferson County Public Schools operates the public school system in metropolitan Louisville, Kentucky. [In] 2001, after [a judicially mandated school desegregation] decree had been dissolved, Jefferson County adopted the voluntary student assignment plan at issue in this case. [That plan, which covers 97,000 students—roughly 34% of whom are black and the remaining 66% of whom are mostly white—] requires all nonmagnet schools to maintain a minimum black enrollment of 15 percent, and a maximum black enrollment of 50 percent. [The requirements can sometimes block initial assignments and transfers, including assignments and transfers to neighborhood schools, that would otherwise occur.]

III.　A. It is well established that when the government distributes burdens or benefits on the basis of individual racial classifications, that action is reviewed under strict scrutiny. *Johnson* v. *California*; *Grutter* v. *Bollinger,* [Sec. 2, V infra].

As the Court recently reaffirmed, " 'racial classifications are simply too pernicious to permit any but the most exact connection between justification and classification.' " *Gratz v. Bollinger*, [Sec. 2, V]. In order to satisfy this searching standard of review, the school districts must demonstrate that the use of individual racial classifications in the assignment plans here under review is "narrowly tailored" to achieve a "compelling" government interest.

[O]ur prior cases, in evaluating the use of racial classifications in the school context have recognized two interests that qualify as compelling. The first is [remedying] the effects of past intentional discrimination. See *Freeman* v. *Pitts*.

Yet the Seattle public schools have not shown that they were ever segregated by law, and were not subject to court-ordered desegregation decrees. The Jefferson County public schools [have been found to have] "eliminated the vestiges associated with [their] former policy of segregation and its pernicious effects" and thus [to have] achieved "unitary" status. Jefferson County accordingly does not rely upon an interest in remedying the effects of past intentional discrimination in defending its present use of race in assigning students. Nor could it. We have emphasized [that] "the Constitution is not violated by racial imbalance in the schools, without more." *Milliken v. Bradley.*

[The] second government interest we have recognized as compelling for purposes of strict scrutiny is the interest in diversity in higher education upheld in *Grutter* [which sustained an affirmative plan that took race into account in law school admissions]. [The] diversity interest was not focused on race alone but encompassed "all factors that may contribute to student body diversity." [The] entire gist of the analysis in *Grutter* was that the admissions program at issue there focused on each applicant as an individual, and not simply as a member of a particular racial group.

[In] the present cases, by contrast, race is not considered as part of a broader effort to achieve "exposure to widely diverse people, cultures, ideas, and viewpoints"; race, for some students, is determinative standing alone. [Even] when it comes to race, the plans here employ only a limited notion of diversity, viewing race exclusively in white/nonwhite terms in Seattle and black/"other" terms in Jefferson County. [Under] the Seattle plan, a school with 50 percent Asian-American students and 50 percent white students but no African-American, Native-American, or Latino students would qualify as balanced, while a school with 30 percent Asian-American, 25 percent African-American, 25 percent Latino, and 20 percent white students would not. [The] present cases are not governed by *Grutter*.

B.   Each school district argues that educational and broader socialization benefits flow from a racially diverse learning environment, and each contends that because the diversity they seek is racial diversity—not the broader diversity at issue in *Grutter*—it makes sense to promote that interest directly by relying on race alone. The parties and their amici dispute whether racial diversity in schools in fact has a marked impact on test scores and other objective yardsticks or achieves intangible socialization benefits. The debate is not one we need to resolve, however, because it is clear that the racial classifications employed by the districts are not narrowly tailored to the goal of achieving the educational and social benefits asserted to flow from racial diversity. In design and operation, the plans are directed only to racial balance, pure and simple, an objective this Court has repeatedly condemned as illegitimate. [The] districts offer no evidence that the level of racial diversity necessary to achieve the asserted educational benefits happens to coincide with the racial demographics of the respective school districts—or rather the white/nonwhite or black/"other" balance of the districts, since that is the only diversity addressed by the plans. * * *

C. The districts assert, as they must, that the way in which they have employed individual racial classifications is necessary to achieve their stated ends. The minimal effect these classifications have on student assignments, however, suggests that other means would be effective. Seattle's racial tiebreaker results, in the end, only in shifting a small number of students between schools. [T]he district could identify only 52 students who were ultimately affected adversely by the racial tiebreaker in that it resulted in assignment to a school they had not listed as a preference and to which they would not otherwise have been assigned.

[Similarly,] Jefferson County's use of racial classifications has only a minimal effect on the assignment of [students.] Jefferson County estimates that the racial guidelines account for only 3 percent of assignments. While we do not suggest that *greater* use of race would be preferable, the minimal impact of the districts' racial classifications on school enrollment casts doubt on the necessity of using racial classifications. In *Grutter*, the consideration of race was viewed as indispensable in more than tripling minority representation at the law school-from 4 to 14.5 percent.

[The] districts have also failed to show that they considered methods other than explicit racial classifications to achieve their stated goals. Narrow tailoring requires "serious, good faith consideration of workable race-neutral alternatives." *Grutter*.

IV. Justice Breyer's dissent [fails] to ground the result it would reach in law. [It] seeks to justify the plans at issue under our precedents recognizing the compelling interest in remedying past intentional discrimination. [But the] distinction between segregation by state action and racial imbalance caused by other factors has been central to our jurisprudence in this area for generations. [*Swann* and the other cases relied on by the dissent to establish once-prevailing legal assumptions were decided "before this Court definitively determined that 'all racial classifications [must] be analyzed by a reviewing court under strict scrutiny.'" *Adarand Constructors, Inc. v. Pena*, [Sec. 2, V infra].

In *Brown* v. *Board of Education*, we held that segregation deprived black children of equal educational opportunities regardless of whether school facilities and other tangible factors were equal, because government classification and separation on grounds of race themselves denoted inferiority. [The] parties and their amici debate which side is more faithful to the heritage of *Brown*, but the position of the plaintiffs in *Brown* was spelled out in their brief and could not have been clearer: "[T]he Fourteenth Amendment prevents states from according differential treatment to American children on the basis of their color or race." Before *Brown*, schoolchildren were told where they could and could not go to school based on the color of their skin. The school districts in these cases have not carried the heavy burden of demonstrating that we should allow this once again—even for very different reasons. For schools that never segregated on the basis of race, such as Seattle, or that have removed the vestiges of past segregation, such as Jefferson County, the way "to achieve a system of determining admission to the public schools on a nonracial basis," is to stop assigning students on a racial basis. The way to stop discrimination on the basis of race is to stop discriminating on the basis of race.

JUSTICE THOMAS, concurring.

* * * Most of the dissent's criticisms of today's result can be traced to its rejection of the color-blind Constitution. [The] dissent appears to pin its interpretation of the Equal Protection Clause to current societal practice and expectations, deference to local officials, likely practical consequences, and reliance on previous statements from this and other courts. Such a view was ascendant [in] *Plessy,* where the Court asked whether a state law providing for segregated railway cars was "a reasonable regulation." [In] place of the color-blind Constitution, the dissent would permit measures to keep the races together and proscribe measures to keep the races apart. Although no such distinction is apparent in the Fourteenth Amendment, the dissent would constitutionalize today's faddish social theories that embrace that distinction. The Constitution is not that malleable. [Can] we really be sure that the racial theories that motivated *Dred Scott* and *Plessy* are a relic of the past or that future theories will be nothing but beneficent and progressive? That is a gamble I am unwilling to take, and it is one the Constitution does not allow.

JUSTICE KENNEDY, concurring in part and concurring in the judgment.

I.   * * * Diversity, depending on its meaning and definition, is a compelling educational goal a school district may pursue. [But the] government bears the burden of justifying its use of individual racial classifications. * * *

II.   [Parts] of the opinion by The Chief Justice imply an all-too-unyielding insistence that race cannot be a factor in instances when, in my view, it may be taken into account. The plurality opinion is too dismissive of the legitimate interest government has in ensuring all people have equal opportunity regardless of their race. [To] the extent the plurality opinion suggests the Constitution mandates that state and local school authorities must accept the status quo of racial isolation in schools, it is, in my view, profoundly mistaken.

[In] the administration of public schools by the state and local authorities it is permissible to consider the racial makeup of schools and to adopt general policies to encourage a diverse student body, one aspect of which is its racial composition. Cf. *Grutter* (Kennedy, J., dissenting). If school authorities are concerned that the student-body compositions of certain schools interfere with the objective of offering an equal educational opportunity to all of their students, they are free to devise race-conscious measures to address the problem in a general way and without treating each student in different fashion solely on the basis of a systematic, individual typing by race.

School boards may pursue the goal of bringing together students of diverse backgrounds and races through other means, including strategic site selection of new schools; drawing attendance zones with general recognition of the demographics of neighborhoods; allocating resources for special programs; recruiting students and faculty in a targeted fashion; and tracking enrollments, performance, and other statistics by race. These mechanisms are race conscious but do not lead to different treatment based on a classification that tells each student he or she is to be defined by race, so it is unlikely any of them would demand strict scrutiny to be found permissible. Executive and legislative branches, which for generations now have considered these types of policies and procedures, should be permitted to employ them with candor and with confidence that a constitutional violation does not occur whenever a decisionmaker considers the impact a given approach might have on students of different races. Assigning to each student a personal designation according to a crude system of individual racial classifications is quite a different matter; and the legal analysis changes accordingly. * * *

III. [In relying on lower court opinions that have upheld explicitly race-conscious student-assignment plans, the dissent] ignores the dangers presented by individual classifications, dangers that are not as pressing when the same ends are achieved by more indirect means. When the government classifies an individual by race, it must first define what it means to be of a race. Who exactly is white and who is nonwhite? To be forced to live under a state-mandated racial label is inconsistent with the dignity of individuals in our society. And it is a label that an individual is powerless to change. Governmental classifications that command people to march in different directions based on racial typologies can cause a new divisiveness. The practice can lead to corrosive discourse, where race serves not as an element of our diverse heritage but instead as a bargaining chip in the political process. On the other hand, race-conscious measures that do not rely on differential treatment based on individual classifications present these problems to a lesser degree. * * *

JUSTICE STEVENS, dissenting.

While I join Justice Breyer's eloquent and unanswerable dissent in its entirety, it is appropriate to add these words. [If] we look at cases decided during the interim between *Brown* and *Adarand,* we can see how [the Court's] rigid adherence to tiers of scrutiny obscures *Brown*'s clear message. Perhaps the best example is provided by our approval of the decision of the Supreme Judicial Court of Massachusetts in 1967 upholding a state statute mandating racial integration in that State's school system. See *School Comm. of Boston* v. *Board of Education*, 352 Mass. 693, 227 N. E. 2d 729. [Our] ruling on the merits simply stated that the appeal was "dismissed for want of a substantial federal question." *School Comm. of Boston* v. *Board of Education*, 389 U.S. 572 (1968) (per curiam). The Court has changed significantly since it decided *School Comm. of Boston* in 1968. It was then more faithful to *Brown* and more respectful of our precedent than it is today. It is my firm conviction that no Member of the Court that I joined in 1975 would have agreed with today's decision.

JUSTICE BREYER, with whom JUSTICE STEVENS, JUSTICE SOUTER, and JUSTICE GINSBURG, join, dissenting. * * *

I.   The historical and factual context in which these cases arise is critical. In *Brown*, this Court held that the government's segregation of schoolchildren by race violates the Constitution's promise of equal protection. [In] dozens of subsequent cases, this Court told school districts previously segregated by law what they must do at a minimum to comply with *Brown*'s constitutional holding. The measures required by those cases often included race-conscious practices, such as mandatory busing and race-based restrictions on voluntary transfers. Beyond those minimum requirements, the Court left much of the determination of how to achieve integration to the judgment of local communities. Thus, in respect to race-conscious desegregation measures that the Constitution *permitted,* but did not *require* (measures similar to those at issue here), this Court unanimously stated: "School authorities are traditionally charged with broad power to formulate and implement educational policy and might well conclude, for example, that in order to prepare students to live in a pluralistic society each school should have a prescribed ratio of Negro to white students reflecting the proportion for the district as a whole. *To do this as an educational policy is within the broad discretionary powers of school authorities.*" *Swann* (emphasis added).

As a result [of this and similar signals from the Court], different districts—some acting under court decree, some acting in order to avoid threatened lawsuits, some seeking to comply with federal administrative orders, some acting purely voluntarily—adopted, modified, and experimented with hosts of different kinds of plans, including race-conscious plans, all with a similar objective: greater racial integration of public schools. [Overall] these efforts brought about considerable racial integration. More recently, however, progress has stalled [and then reversed direction]. [In] light of the evident risk of a return to school systems that are in fact (though not in law) resegregated, many school districts have felt a need to maintain or to extend their integration efforts.

[Breyer, J., here offered a lengthy recitation of the historical context in Seattle and Louisville as "typical" of "school integration stories" throughout the country. His account of events in Seattle emphasized that although there was never a formal finding of school segregation, a 1956 school board memo spoke of discriminatory policies making it difficult for blacks to transfer from one city school to another, and many of the school district's desegregation efforts in the 1960s and 1970s occurred in response to threatened and actual litigation. More generally, his account emphasized ongoing, adaptive efforts by the Seattle and Louisville school districts to achieve meaningful integration through politically acceptable mechanisms.]

Is Seattle free on remand to say that its schools were de jure segregated, just as in 1956 a memo for the School Board admitted? The plurality does not seem confident as to the answer. * * *

Moreover, Louisville's history makes clear that a community under a court order to desegregate might submit a race-conscious remedial plan *before* the court dissolved the order, but with every intention of following that plan even *after* dissolution. How could such a plan be lawful the day before dissolution but then become unlawful the very next day? On what legal ground can the majority rest its contrary view? * * *

II.   A longstanding and unbroken line of legal authority tells us that the Equal Protection Clause permits local school boards to use race-conscious criteria to achieve positive race-related goals, even when the Constitution does not compel it. [The plain dicta of *Swann*, supra, established] a basic principle of constitutional law—a principle of law that has found "wide acceptance in the legal culture." [In] fact, without being exhaustive, I have counted 51 federal statutes that use racial classifications. I have counted well over 100 state statutes that similarly employ racial classifications. Presidential administrations for the past half-century have used and supported various race-conscious measures. And during the same time, hundreds of local school districts have adopted student assignment plans that use race-conscious criteria.

That *Swann*'s legal statement should find such broad acceptance is not surprising. [There] is reason to believe that those who drafted [the Fourteenth Amendment] would have understood the legal and practical difference between the use of race-conscious criteria [to] keep the races apart, and the use of race-conscious criteria to [bring] the races together.

[No] case—not *Adarand, Gratz, Grutter*, or any other—has ever held that the test of "strict scrutiny" means that all racial classifications—no matter whether they seek to include or exclude—must in practice be treated the same. [Nonetheless,] in light of *Grutter* and other precedents, I shall [apply] the version of strict scrutiny that those cases embody. * * *

III.   The principal interest advanced in these cases to justify the use of race-based criteria goes by various names. Sometimes a court refers to it as an interest in achieving racial "diversity." Other times a court, like the plurality here, refers to it as an interest in racial "balancing." [Regardless] of its name, however, the interest at stake possesses three essential elements. First, there is a historical and remedial element: an interest in setting right the consequences of prior conditions of segregation. This refers back to a time when public schools were highly segregated, often as a result of legal or administrative policies that facilitated racial segregation in public schools. It is an interest in continuing to combat the remnants of segregation caused in whole or in part by these school-related policies, which have often affected not only schools, but also housing patterns, employment practices, economic conditions, and social attitudes. * * *

Second, there is an educational element: an interest in overcoming the adverse educational effects produced by and associated with highly segregated schools. * * * Third, there is a democratic element: an interest in producing an educational environment that reflects the "pluralistic society" in which our children will live. It is an interest in helping our children learn to work and play together with children of different racial backgrounds. It is an interest in teaching children to engage in the kind of cooperation among Americans of all races that is necessary to make a land of three hundred million people one Nation. [This] Court from *Swann* to *Grutter* has treated these civic effects as an important virtue of racially diverse education.

[In] light of this Court's conclusions in *Grutter,* the "compelling" nature of these interests in the context of primary and secondary public education follows here a fortiori. [If] an educational interest that combines these three elements is not "compelling," what is? * * *

Justice Kennedy suggests that school boards "may pursue the goal of bringing together students of diverse backgrounds and races through other means * * * ." But, as to "strategic site selection," Seattle has built one new high school in the last 44 years (and that specialized school serves only 300 students). [As] to "drawing" neighborhood "attendance zones" on a racial basis, Louisville tried it, and it worked only when forced busing was also part of the plan. As to "allocating resources for special programs," Seattle and Louisville have both experimented with this; indeed, these programs are often referred to as "magnet schools," but the limited desegregation effect of these efforts extends at most to those few schools to which additional resources are granted. In addition, there is no evidence from the experience of these school districts that it will make any meaningful impact. * * *

V.   * * * The plurality, or at least those who follow Justice Thomas' "color-blind" approach, may feel confident that, to end invidious discrimination, one must end *all* governmental use of race-conscious criteria including those with inclusive objectives. By way of contrast, I do not claim to know how best to stop harmful discrimination; how best to create a society that includes all Americans; how best to overcome our serious problems of increasing de facto segregation, troubled inner city schooling, and poverty correlated with race. [But] I do know that the Constitution does not authorize judges to dictate solutions to these problems.

VI.   [To] invalidate the plans under review is to threaten the promise of *Brown.* The plurality's position, I fear, would break that promise. This is a decision that the Court and the Nation will come to regret.

IV.   DE JURE VS. DE FACTO DISCRIMINATION

Part II of this Section involved laws that explicitly discriminate against racial and ethnic minorities by drawing facially race-based lines. But intentional (or "de jure") discrimination may exist even though the law in question is racially "neutral" on its face: the law may be deliberately administered in a discriminatory way; or the law, although neutral in its language and applied in accordance with its terms, may have been enacted with a purpose (or motive) of disadvantaging a "suspect" class. This section begins by considering the Court's response to cases involving actual or alleged discrimination in the administration of laws that would be unobjectionable if applied fairly. It then examines the Court's response to laws that are racially neutral in on their faces but have a discriminatory effect or impact that the legislature (or comparable body) either may or may not have intended to produce.

Yick Wo v. Hopkins
118 U.S. 356, 6 S.Ct. 1064, 30 L.Ed. 220 (1886).

Justice Matthews delivered the opinion of the Court.

[A San Francisco ordinance made it unlawful to operate a laundry in a wood building without the consent of the board of supervisors. Yick Wo, a Chinese alien who had operated a laundry for 22 years, had certificates from the health and fire authorities, but was refused consent by the board. It was admitted that "there were about 320 laundries in the city [and] about 240 were owned [by] subjects of China, and of the whole number, viz., 320, about 310 were constructed of wood"; that "petitioner, and more than 150 of his countrymen, have been arrested" for violating the ordinance "while those who are not subjects of China, and who are conducting 80 odd laundries under similar conditions, are left unmolested."]

[T]he facts shown establish an administration directed so exclusively against a particular class of persons as to warrant and require the conclusion that, whatever may have been the intent of the ordinances as adopted, they are applied [with] a mind so unequal and oppressive as to amount to a practical denial by the State of [equal protection]. Though the law itself be fair on its face and impartial in appearance, yet, if it is applied and administered by public authority with an evil eye and an unequal hand, so as practically to make unjust and illegal discriminations between persons in similar circumstances, material to their rights, the denial of equal justice is still within the prohibition of the Constitution. [The] fact of this discrimination is admitted. No reason for it is shown, and the conclusion cannot be resisted that no reason for it exists except hostility to [Yick Wo's] race and nationality * * * .

———

UNITED STATES v. ARMSTRONG, 517 U.S. 456 (1996), per Rehnquist, C.J., held that the defendants had failed to make out a prima facie case of racially selective prosecution in cases involving the sale and possession of cocaine and thus were not entitled to discovery on the issue of prosecutorial intent to discriminate. The evidence showed that all 24 defendants in "crack" cocaine cases closed by a Public Defender's office in the Central District of California during the previous year were black. In addition, the defendants submitted "an affidavit alleging that an intake coordinator at a drug treatment center had told her that there are 'an equal number of caucasian users and dealers to minority users and dealers,' [an] affidavit from a criminal defense attorney alleging that in his experience many nonblacks are prosecuted in state court for crack offenses, and a newspaper article reporting that Federal 'crack criminals [are] being punished far more severely than if they had been caught with powder cocaine, and almost every single one of them is black.'" But this was not enough: "the claimant must show that similarly situated individuals of a different race were not prosecuted." STEVENS, J., dissented: "I am persuaded that the District Judge did not abuse her discretion when she concluded that the factual showing was sufficiently disturbing to require some response from the United States Attorney's Office."

WASHINGTON V. DAVIS

426 U.S. 229, 96 S.Ct. 2040, 48 L.Ed.2d 597 (1976).

JUSTICE WHITE delivered the opinion of the Court.

This case involves the validity of a qualifying test administered to applicants for positions as police officers in the District of Columbia. [T]he police recruit was required to satisfy certain physical and character standards, to be a high school graduate or its equivalent and to receive a grade of at least 40 out of 80 on "Test 21," which is "an examination that is used generally throughout the federal service," which "was developed by the Civil Service Commission, not the Police Department," and which was "designed to test verbal ability, vocabulary, reading and comprehension."

[The evidence showed that roughly four times as many blacks as whites failed Test 21. Apart from the test, however, the Police Department had systematically and affirmatively sought to enroll black officers. As a result, 44% of new police force recruits had been black in the years immediately preceding the litigation. There was, accordingly, no allegation that the Department had acted with discriminatory intent—only that a test with a substantially discriminatory impact could not be used, at least in the absence of a showing that performance on Test 21 bore a substantial and demonstrated relationship to performance on the job.]

[The] District Court rejected the assertion that Test 21 was culturally slanted to favor whites and was "satisfied that the undisputable facts prove the test to be reasonably and directly related to the requirements of the police recruit training program and that it is neither so designed nor operates to discriminate against otherwise qualified blacks." [The Court of Appeals held] that lack of discriminatory intent in designing and administering Test 21 was irrelevant; the critical fact was rather [that] four times as many [blacks] failed the test than did whites. This disproportionate impact [was] held sufficient to establish a constitutional violation, absent proof by petitioners that the test was an adequate measure of job performance in addition to being an indicator of probable success in the training program, a burden which the court ruled petitioners had failed to discharge. * * *

The central purpose of the Equal Protection Clause [is] the prevention of official conduct discriminating on the basis of race. It is also true that the Due Process Clause of the Fifth Amendment contains an equal protection component prohibiting the United States from invidiously discriminating between individuals or groups. But our cases have not embraced the proposition that a law or other official act, without regard to whether it reflects a racially discriminatory purpose, is unconstitutional *solely* because it has a racially disproportionate impact.

Almost 100 years ago, *Strauder* established that the exclusion of Negroes from grand and petit juries in criminal proceedings violated the Equal Protection Clause, but the fact that a particular jury or a series of juries does not statistically reflect the racial composition of the community does not in itself make out an invidious discrimination forbidden by the Clause. "A purpose to discriminate must be present which may be proven by systematic exclusion of eligible jurymen of the prescribed race or by an unequal application of the law to such an extent as to show intentional discrimination." * * *

The school desegregation cases have also adhered to the basic equal protection principle that the invidious quality of a law claimed to be racially discriminatory must ultimately be traced to a racially discriminatory purpose. That there are both predominantly black and predominantly white schools in a community is not alone violative of the Equal Protection Clause. The essential element ["differentiating] between de jure segregation and so-called de facto segregation [is] *purpose* or *intent* to segregate." *Keyes v. School Dist.*, [Sec. 2, III supra].

This is not to say that the necessary discriminatory racial purpose must be express or appear on the face of the statute, or that a law's disproportionate impact is irrelevant. [A] statute, otherwise neutral on its face, must not be applied so as invidiously to discriminate on the basis of race. *Yick Wo.* It is also clear from the cases dealing with racial discrimination in the selection of juries that [a] prima facie case of discriminatory purpose may be proved [by] the absence of Negroes on a particular jury combined with the failure of the jury commissioners to be informed of eligible Negro jurors in a community, or with racially non-neutral selection procedures. With a prima facie case made out, "the burden of proof shifts to the State to rebut the presumption of unconstitutional action by showing that permissible racially neutral selection criteria and procedures have produced the monochromatic result."

Necessarily, an invidious discriminatory purpose may often be inferred from the totality of the relevant facts, including [that] the law bears more heavily on one race than another. It is also not infrequently true that the discriminatory impact— in the jury cases for example, the total or seriously disproportionate exclusion of Negroes from jury venires—may for all practical purposes demonstrate unconstitutionality because in various circumstances the discrimination is very difficult to explain on nonracial grounds. Nevertheless, we have not held that a law, neutral on its face and serving ends otherwise within the power of government to pursue, is invalid under the Equal Protection Clause simply because it may affect a greater proportion of one race than of another. Disproportionate impact is not irrelevant, but it is not the sole touchstone of an invidious racial discrimination forbidden by the Constitution. Standing alone, it does not trigger the rule that racial classifications are to be subjected to the strictest scrutiny and are justifiable only by the weightiest of considerations.

[Test 21] seeks to ascertain whether those who take it have acquired a particular level of verbal skill; and it is untenable that the Constitution prevents the government from seeking modestly to upgrade the communicative abilities of its employees rather than to be satisfied with some lower level of competence, particularly where the job requires special ability to communicate orally and in writing. * * *Nor on the facts of the case before us would the disproportionate impact of Test 21 warrant the conclusion that it is a purposeful device to discriminate against Negroes. [T]he test is neutral on its face and rationally may be said to serve a purpose the government is constitutionally empowered to pursue. Even agreeing with the District Court that the differential racial effect of Test 21 called for further inquiry, we think the District Court correctly held that the affirmative efforts of the Metropolitan Police Department to recruit black officers, the changing racial composition of the recruit classes and of the force in general, and the relationship of the test to the training program negated any inference that the Department discriminated on the basis of race * * * .

Under Title VII [of the Civil Rights Act of 1964], Congress provided that when hiring and promotion practices disqualifying substantially disproportionate numbers of blacks are challenged, discriminatory purpose need not be proved, and that it is an insufficient response to demonstrate some rational basis for the challenged practices. It is necessary, in addition, that they be "validated" in terms of job performance * * * . However this process proceeds, it involves a more probing judicial review of, and less deference to, the seemingly reasonable acts of administrators and executives than is appropriate under the Constitution where special racial impact, without discriminatory purpose, is claimed. We are not disposed to adopt this more rigorous standard for the purposes of applying the Fifth and the Fourteenth Amendments in cases such as this.

A rule that a statute designed to serve neutral ends is nevertheless invalid, absent compelling justification, if in practice it benefits or burdens one race more than another would be far-reaching and would raise serious questions about, and perhaps invalidate, a whole range of tax, welfare, public service, regulatory, and licensing statutes that may be more burdensome to the poor and to the average black than to the more affluent white.[14]

Given that rule, such consequences would perhaps be likely to follow. However, in our view, extension of the rule beyond those areas where it is already applicable by reason of statute, such as in the field of public employment, should await legislative prescription. * * *[16]

---

[14]   **[Ct's Note]** Goodman, *De Facto School Segregation: A Constitutional and Empirical Analysis*, 60 Calif.L.Rev. 275, 300 (1972), suggests that disproportionate-impact analysis might invalidate "tests and qualifications for voting, draft deferment, public employment, jury service, and other government-conferred [benefits]; [s]ales taxes, bail schedules, utility rates, bridge tolls, license fees, and other state-imposed charges." It has also been argued that minimum wage and usury laws as well as professional licensing requirements would require major modifications in light of the unequal-impact rule. William Silverman, *Equal Protection, Economic Legislation, and Racial Discrimination*, 25 Vand.L.Rev. 1183 (1972). * * *

[16]   The Court also found no violation of the relevant statutory provisions. Stewart, J., joined only the constitutional aspects of the Court's opinion. Brennan, J., joined by Marshall, J., did not address the constitutional questions but dissented on statutory grounds.

JUSTICE STEVENS, concurring. * * *

The requirement of purposeful discrimination is a common thread running through the cases summarized [by the Court. But] in each of these contexts, the burden of proving a prima facie case may well involve differing evidentiary considerations. The extent of deference that one pays to the trial court's determination of the factual issue, and indeed, the extent to which one characterizes the intent issue as a question of fact or a question of law, will vary in different contexts.

Frequently the most probative evidence of intent will be objective evidence of what actually happened rather than evidence describing the subjective state of mind of the actor. For normally the actor is presumed to have intended the natural consequences of his deeds. This is particularly true in the case of governmental action which is frequently the product of compromise, of collective decisionmaking, and of mixed motivation. It is unrealistic, on the one hand, to require the victim of alleged discrimination to uncover the actual subjective intent of the decisionmaker or conversely, to invalidate otherwise legitimate action simply because an improper motive affected the deliberation of a participant in the decisional process. A law conscripting clerics should not be invalidated because an atheist voted for it.

My point [is] to suggest that the line between discriminatory purpose and discriminatory impact is not nearly as bright, and perhaps not quite as critical, as the reader of the Court's opinion might assume. I agree [that] a constitutional issue does not arise every time some disproportionate impact is shown. On the other hand, when the disproportion is as dramatic as in *Gomillion v. Lightfoot*, 364 U.S. 339 (1960),[17] or *Yick Wo*, it really does not matter whether the standard is phrased in terms of purpose or effect. * * *

————

Although *Washington v. Davis* rejected the "disparate impact" theory and held that a facially neutral statute violates the Equal Protection Clause only if motivated by a discriminatory purpose, the Court did not address in detail what counts as a discriminatory purpose. The leading case addressing that issue involved gender, not race, but the Court's approach to identifying forbidden intent or purposes appears to be the same in both contexts.

PERSONNEL ADMINISTRATOR v. FEENEY, 442 U.S. 256 (1979), per STEWART, J., upheld Massachusetts' "absolute lifetime preference to veterans" for state civil service positions, even though "the preference operates overwhelmingly to the advantage of males": "When a statute gender-neutral on its face is challenged

---

17   In *Gomillion,* an Alabama statute changed the Tuskegee city boundaries from a square to a 28-sided figure, allegedly removing "all save only four or five of its 400 Negro voters while not removing a single white voter or resident." The Court held that the complaint "amply alleges a claim of racial discrimination" in violation of the Fifteenth Amendment: "If these allegations upon a trial remained uncontradicted or unqualified, the conclusion would be irresistible, tantamount for all practical purposes to a mathematical demonstration, that the legislation is solely concerned with segregating white and colored voters by fencing Negro citizens out of town so as to deprive them of their pre-existing municipal vote."

on the ground that its effects upon women are disproportionately adverse, a two-fold inquiry [is] appropriate. The first question is whether the statutory classification is indeed neutral * * * . If the classification itself, covert or overt, is not based upon gender, the second question is whether the adverse effect reflects invidious gender-based discrimination. In this second inquiry, impact provides an 'important starting point,' but purposeful discrimination is 'the condition that offends the Constitution.' "

As to the first question, "The District Court [found] first, that ch. 31 serves legitimate and worthy purposes; second, that the absolute preference was not established for the purpose of discriminating against women. [Thus,] the distinction between veterans and nonveterans drawn by ch. 31 is not a pretext for gender discrimination. * * *

"If the impact of this statute could not be plausibly explained on a neutral ground, impact itself would signal that the real classification made by the law was in fact not neutral. But there can be but one answer to the question whether this veteran preference excludes significant numbers of women from preferred state jobs because they are women or because they are nonveterans. [Although] few women benefit from the preference, * * * significant numbers of nonveterans are men, and all nonveterans—male as well as female—are placed at a disadvantage. Too many men are affected by ch. 31 to permit the inference that the statute is but a pretext for preferring men over women. * * *

"The dispositive question, then, is whether the appellee has shown that a gender-based discriminatory purpose has, at least in some measure, shaped [ch. 31. Her] contention that this veterans' preference is 'inherently non-neutral' or 'gender-biased' presumes that the State, by favoring veterans, intentionally incorporated into its public employment policies the panoply of sex-based and assertedly discriminatory federal laws that have prevented all but a handful of women from becoming veterans. There are two serious difficulties with this argument. First, it is wholly at odds with the District Court's central finding that Massachusetts has not offered a preference to veterans for the purpose of discriminating against women. Second, [t]o the extent that the status of veteran is one that few women have been enabled to achieve, every hiring preference for veterans, however modest or extreme, is inherently gender-biased. If Massachusetts by offering such a preference can be said intentionally to have incorporated into its state employment policies the historical gender-based federal military personnel practices, the degree of the preference would or should make no constitutional difference. Invidious discrimination does not become less so because the discrimination accomplished is of a lesser magnitude.[23] Discriminatory intent is simply not amenable to calibration. It either is a factor that has influenced the legislative choice or it is not. The District Court's conclusion that the absolute

---

[23]   **[Ct's Note]** This is not to say that the degree of impact is irrelevant to the question of intent. But it is to say that a more modest preference, while it might well lessen impact and, as the State argues, might lessen the effectiveness of the statute in helping veterans, would not be any more or less "neutral" in the constitutional sense.

veterans' preference was not originally enacted or subsequently reaffirmed for the purpose of giving an advantage to males as such necessarily compels the conclusion that the State intended nothing more than to prefer 'veterans.' * * *

"To be sure, this case is unusual in that it involves a law that by design is not neutral. [As] opposed to the written test at issue in *Davis,* it does not purport to define a job related characteristic. To the contrary, it confers upon a specifically described group—perceived to be particularly deserving—a competitive head start. But the District Court found, and the appellee has not disputed, that this legislative choice was legitimate. [Thus, it] must be analyzed as is any other neutral law that casts a greater burden upon women as a group than upon men as a group. The enlistment policies of the armed services may well have discriminated on the basis of sex. But the history of discrimination against women in the military is not on trial in this case.

"The appellee's ultimate argument rests upon the presumption, common to the criminal and civil law, that a person intends the natural and foreseeable consequences of his voluntary actions. * * *

" 'Discriminatory purpose,' however, implies more than intent as volition or intent as awareness of consequences. It implies that the decisionmaker, in this case a state legislature, selected or reaffirmed a particular course of action at least in part 'because of,' not merely 'in spite of,' its adverse effects upon an identifiable group.[25] Yet nothing in the record demonstrates that this preference for veterans was originally devised or subsequently re-enacted because it would accomplish the collateral goal of keeping women in a stereotypic and predefined place in the Massachusetts Civil Service."

STEVENS, J., joined by White, J., concurred in the Court's opinion, adding: "[F]or me the answer is largely provided by the fact that the number of males disadvantaged by Massachusetts' Veterans Preference (1,867,000) is sufficiently large—and sufficiently close to the number of disadvantaged females (2,954,000)— to refute the claim that the rule was intended to benefit males as a class over females as a class."

MARSHALL, J., joined by Brennan, J., dissented: "In my judgment, [ch. 31] evinces purposeful gender-based discrimination. [That] a legislature seeks to advantage one group does not, as a matter of logic or of common sense, exclude the possibility that it also intends to disadvantage another. Individuals in general and lawmakers in particular frequently act for a variety of reasons. [S]ince reliable evidence of subjective intentions is seldom obtainable, resort to inference based on

---

[25]   **[Ct's Note]** This is not to say that the inevitability or foreseeability of consequences of a neutral rule has no bearing upon the existence of discriminatory intent. Certainly, when the adverse consequences of a law upon an identifiable group are as inevitable as the gender-based consequences of ch. 31, a strong inference that the adverse effects were desired can reasonably be drawn. But in this inquiry—made as it is under the Constitution—an inference is a working tool, not a synonym for proof. When as here, the impact is essentially an unavoidable consequence of a legislative policy that has in itself always been deemed to be legitimate, and when, as here, the statutory history and all of the available evidence affirmatively demonstrate the opposite, the inference simply fails to ripen into proof.

objective factors is generally unavoidable. To discern the purposes underlying facially neutral policies, this Court has therefore considered the degree, inevitability, and foreseeability of any disproportionate impact as well as the alternatives reasonably available.

"[T]he impact of the Massachusetts statute on women is undisputed. Any veteran with a passing grade on the civil service exam must be placed ahead of a nonveteran, regardless of their respective scores. [Because] less than 2% of the women in Massachusetts are veterans, the absolute preference formula has rendered desirable state civil service employment an almost exclusively male prerogative. [Where] the foreseeable impact of a facially neutral policy is so disproportionate, the burden should rest on the State to establish that sex-based considerations played no part in the choice of the particular legislative scheme.

"Clearly, that burden was not sustained here. The legislative history of the statute reflects the Commonwealth's patent appreciation of the impact the preference system would have on women, and an equally evident desire to mitigate that impact only with respect to certain traditionally female occupations. Until 1971, the statute [and] regulations exempted from operation of the preference any job requisitions 'especially calling for women.' In practice, this exemption, coupled with the absolute preference for veterans, has created a gender-based civil service hierarchy, with women occupying low grade clerical and secretarial jobs and men holding more responsible and remunerative positions. [Particularly] when viewed against the range of less discriminatory alternatives available to assist veterans,[2] Massachusetts's choice of a formula that so severely restricts public employment opportunities for women cannot reasonably be thought gender-neutral. The Court's conclusion to the contrary—that 'nothing in the record' evinces a 'collateral goal of keeping women in a stereotypic and predefined place in the Massachusetts Civil Service'—displays a singularly myopic view of the facts established below.[3]"

V. AFFIRMATIVE ACTION

Prior to *Brown v. Board of Education*, public policies that drew race-based distinctions almost invariably did so for the purpose of advantaging whites by disadvantaging racial minorities. In the decades that followed, however, some state universities and other public institutions began to implement "affirmative action" programs that expressly took race into account not to exclude racial minorities but to increase their representation in higher education, employment, and government contracts. Affirmative action programs raise a variety of issues under the Equal Protection Clause. One involves the appropriate standard of judicial review:

---

[2]   [Ct's Note] Only four States afford a preference comparable in scope. . . . Other States and the Federal Government grant point or tie-breaking preferences that do not foreclose opportunities for women.

[3]   [Ct's Note] Although it is relevant that the preference statute also disadvantages a substantial group of men, it is equally pertinent that 47% of Massachusetts men over 18 are veterans, as compared to 0.8% of Massachusetts women. Given this disparity, and the indicia of intent noted supra, the absolute number of men denied preference cannot be dispositive, especially since they have not faced the barriers to achieving veteran status confronted by women.

Should strict judicial scrutiny be triggered whenever the government classifies on the basis of race, or only when racial classifications disadvantage "discrete and insular minorities," see *United States v. Carolene Products*, as opposed to the white majority? Are all race-based classifications inherently objectionable, or only those that subordinate or stigmatize on the basis of race? A second issue involves government purposes in implementing affirmative action programs. Are some, such as remedying past discrimination or promoting diversity, more weighty or acceptable than others (such as achieving racial proportionality, for example)?

The first major affirmative action case to be decided by the Supreme Court on the merits, REGENTS OF UNIV. OF CALIFORNIA v. BAKKE, 438 U.S. 265 (1978), presented a challenge to the affirmative action program of the Medical School of the University of California at Davis, which reserved 16 out of 100 places in its entering class for members of minority groups, which the University defined as "Blacks," "Chicanos," "Asians," and "American Indians." The constitutionality of the program was challenged by Allan Bakke, a white male applicant who was rejected, even though some applicants were admitted under the affirmative action program who had "significantly lower" grade point averages and test scores. The issues presented by the case divided the Court almost literally down the middle. Four Justices—Burger, C.J., and Stewart, Rehnquist, and Stevens, JJ.—believed that a federal statute, Title VI of the 1964 Civil Rights Act, forbade schools receiving federal funds from taking any account of race in their admissions processes. Four other Justices—Brennan, White, Marshall, and Blackmun— concluded that all aspects of the Medical School's policy passed muster under a level of judicial scrutiny less searching than "strict scrutiny." With the Court thus divided, the determining vote lay with Justice Lewis Powell, who sought to stake out an intermediate position in an opinion that was not joined in some critical sections by even a single other Justice.

In a part of his opinion joined by Brennan, White, Marshall, and Blackmun, JJ., POWELL, J., first found that Title VI of the Civil Rights Act of 1964—which provides that "No person in the United States shall, on the ground of race, color, or national origin, be excluded from participation in, be denied the benefits of, or be subjected to discrimination under any program or activity receiving Federal financial assistance"—proscribes "only those racial classifications that would violate the Equal Protection Clause or the Fifth Amendment." Then, writing mostly only for himself, he turned to the equal protection arguments: "[P]etitioner argues that the court below erred in applying strict scrutiny to the special admissions program because white males, such as respondent, are not a 'discrete and insular minority' requiring extraordinary protection from the majoritarian political process. *Carolene Products Co.*, n. 4 [Ch. 5, Sec. 3 supra. These] characteristics may be relevant in deciding whether or not to add new types of classifications to the list of 'suspect' categories or whether a particular classification survives close examination. Racial and ethnic classifications, however, are subject to stringent examination without regard to these additional characteristics.

"[This] perception of racial and ethnic distinctions is rooted in our Nation's constitutional and demographic history. [T]he white 'majority' itself is composed of various minority groups, most of which can lay claim to a history of prior discrimination at the hands of the State and private individuals. [It] is the individual who is entitled to judicial protection against classifications based upon his racial or ethnic background. [When legal classifications] touch upon an individual's race or ethnic background, he is entitled to a judicial determination that the burden he is asked to bear on that basis is precisely tailored to serve a compelling governmental interest.

"[The] special admissions program purports to serve the purposes of: (i) 'reducing the historic deficit of traditionally disfavored minorities in medical schools and the medical profession,' (ii) countering the effects of societal discrimination; (iii) increasing the number of physicians who will practice in communities currently underserved; and (iv) obtaining the educational benefits that flow from an ethnically diverse student body.

"[If] petitioner's purpose is to assure within its student body some specified percentage of a particular group merely because of its race or ethnic origin, such a preferential purpose must be rejected not as insubstantial but as facially invalid. Preferring members of any one group for no reason other than race or ethnic origin is discrimination for its own sake. This the Constitution forbids. E.g., *Loving; Brown.*

"The State certainly has a legitimate and substantial interest in ameliorating, or eliminating where feasible, the disabling effects of identified discrimination. [That] goal [is] far more focused than the remedying of the effects of 'societal discrimination,' an amorphous concept of injury that [would *not* provide a compelling justification for affirmative action]. We have never approved a classification that aids persons perceived as members of relatively victimized groups at the expense of other innocent individuals in the absence of judicial, legislative, or administrative findings of constitutional or statutory violations. [Without] such findings of constitutional or statutory violations, [which have not been made in this case,] it cannot be said that the government has any greater interest in helping one individual than in refraining from harming another. [To] hold otherwise would be to convert a remedy heretofore reserved for violations of legal rights into a privilege that all institutions throughout the Nation could grant at their pleasure to whatever groups are perceived as victims of societal discrimination.

"Petitioner identifies, as another purpose of its program, improving the delivery of health-care services to communities currently underserved. It may be assumed that in some situations a State's interest in facilitating the health care of its citizens is sufficiently compelling to support the use of a suspect classification. But there is virtually no evidence in the record indicating that petitioner's special admissions program is either needed or geared to promote that goal. The court below addressed this failure of proof: 'The University concedes it cannot assure that minority doctors who entered under the program, all of whom express an 'interest' in participating in a disadvantaged community, will actually do so.'

"[The] fourth goal asserted by petitioner is the attainment of a diverse student body. This is clearly a permissible goal for an institution of higher education. * * * Ethnic diversity, however, is only one element in a range of factors a university properly may consider in attaining the goal of a heterogeneous student body. Although a university must have wide discretion in making the sensitive judgments as to who should be admitted, constitutional limitations protecting individual rights may not be disregarded. [As] the interest of diversity is compelling in the context of a university's admissions program, the question remains whether the program's racial classification is necessary to promote this interest.

"[P]etitioner's argument that this is the only effective means of serving the interest of diversity is seriously flawed. [The] diversity that furthers a compelling state interest encompasses a far broader array of qualifications and characteristics of which racial or ethnic origin is but a single though important element. Petitioner's special admissions program, focused *solely* on ethnic diversity, would hinder rather than further attainment of genuine diversity. * * * "

Powell, J., then referred favorably to the Harvard College admissions program, under which, "when the Committee on Admissions reviews the large middle group of applicants who are 'admissible' and deemed capable of doing good work in their courses, the race of an applicant may tip the balance in his favor just as geographic origin or a life spent on a farm may tip the balance in other candidates' cases. [This] kind of program treats each applicant as an individual in the admissions process. The applicant who loses out [to] another candidate receiving a 'plus' on the basis of ethnic background will not have been foreclosed from all consideration simply because he was not the right color or had the wrong surname. It would mean only that his combined qualifications, which may have included similar nonobjective factors, did not outweigh those of the other applicant. His qualifications would have been weighed fairly and competitively and he would have no basis to complain of unequal treatment under the Fourteenth Amendment."

Because the Medical School had applied a quota system, Powell, J., found it invalid, despite his recognition that a properly tailored affirmative action program designed to promote diversity could survive strict judicial scrutiny.

In a joint opinion, BRENNAN, WHITE, MARSHALL, and BLACKMUN, JJ., concurred in part and dissented in part: "[W]hites as a class [do not] have any of the traditional indicia of suspectness: the class is not saddled with such disabilities, or subjected to such a history of purposeful unequal treatment, or relegated to such a position of political powerlessness as to command extraordinary protection from the majoritarian political process. [On] the other hand, the fact that this case does not fit neatly into our prior analytic framework for race cases does not mean that it should be analyzed by applying the very loose rational-basis [standard]. Instead, a number of considerations—developed in gender discrimination cases but which carry even more force when applied to racial classifications—lead us to conclude that racial classifications designed to further remedial purposes 'must serve important governmental objectives and must be substantially related to achievement of those objectives.' *Craig v. Boren*, [Sec. 3, I infra].

"[Davis'] articulated purpose of remedying the effects of past societal discrimination is, under our cases, sufficiently important to justify the use of race-conscious admissions programs where there is a sound basis for concluding that minority underrepresentation is substantial and chronic, and that the handicap of past discrimination is impeding access of minorities to the medical school. * * *

"[Davis'] special admissions program cannot be said to violate the Constitution simply because it has set aside a predetermined number of places for qualified minority applicants rather than using minority status as a positive factor to be considered in evaluating the applications of disadvantaged minority applicants. For purposes of constitutional adjudication, there is no difference between the two approaches. In any admissions program which accords special consideration to disadvantaged racial minorities, a determination of the degree of preference to be given is unavoidable, and any given preference that results in the exclusion of a white candidate is no more or less constitutionally acceptable than a program such as that at Davis."

MARSHALL, J., also wrote a separate opinion: "[I]t must be remembered that, during most of the past 200 years, the Constitution as interpreted by this Court did not prohibit the most ingenious and pervasive forms of discrimination against the Negro. Now, when a State acts to remedy the effects of that legacy of discrimination, I cannot believe that this same Constitution stands as a barrier. [In] light of the sorry history of discrimination and its devastating impact on the lives of Negroes, bringing the Negro into the mainstream of American life should be a state interest of the highest order. To fail to do so is to ensure that America will forever remain a divided society. * * *

"Since the Congress that considered and rejected the objections to the 1866 Freedmen's Bureau Act concerning special relief to Negroes also proposed the Fourteenth Amendment, it is inconceivable that the Fourteenth Amendment was intended to prohibit all race-conscious relief measures. [T]o hold that it barred state action to remedy the effects [of] discrimination [would] pervert the intent of the framers by substituting abstract equality for the genuine equality the amendment was intended to achieve."

STEVENS, J, with whom Burger, C.J. and Stewart and Rehnquist, JJ., joined, did not reach any constitutional issue. He thought that the specific admissions program challenged in the case was illegal under Title VI and that "the question whether race can ever be used as a factor in an admissions decision" was "not an issue in this case" nor one appropriate for the Court to consider under the circumstances.

After *Bakke*, the Supreme Court did not revisit the issues raised by affirmative action in the context of admissions to educational institutions for another twenty-five years. In the meantime, however, it invalidated affirmative action programs involving teacher lay-offs in 1986, see *Wygant v. Jackson Bd. of Educ.*, 476 U.S. 267, and municipal preferences for minority-owned businesses in 1989, see *Richmond v. J.A. Croson Co.*, 488 U.S. 469, and made clear more generally that all affirmative action programs would trigger strict judicial scrutiny. By 2003, many regarded the continuing constitutionality of educational affirmative action as very much in doubt, even though a number of state schools continued to practice affirmative action in reliance on Powell, J.'s, *Bakke* opinion.

GRUTTER V. BOLLINGER
539 U.S. 306, 123 S.Ct. 2325, 156 L.Ed.2d 304 (2003).

JUSTICE O'CONNOR delivered the opinion of the Court.

This case requires us to decide whether the use of race as a factor in student admissions by the University of Michigan Law School (Law School) is unlawful.

I A. The Law School ranks among the Nation's top law schools. It receives more than 3,500 applications each year for a class of around 350 students. [The] hallmark of [the Law School's admission] policy is its focus on academic ability coupled with a flexible assessment of applicants' talents, experiences, and potential "to contribute to the learning of those around them." By] enrolling a " 'critical mass' of [underrepresented] minority students," the Law School seeks to "ensur[e] their ability to make unique contributions to the character of the Law School."

II.　We last addressed the use of race in public higher education over 25 years ago [in] the landmark *Bakke* case[. Justice] Powell approved the university's use of race to further only one interest: "the attainment of a diverse student body." * * * [We] apply strict scrutiny to all racial classifications to " 'smoke out' illegitimate uses of race by assuring that [government] is pursuing a goal important enough to warrant use of a highly suspect tool." *Richmond v. J.A. Croson Co.* Strict scrutiny is not "strict in theory, but fatal in fact." *Adarand Constructors, Inc. v. Pena*, 515 U.S. 200 (1995). [When] race-based action is necessary to further a compelling governmental interest, such action does not violate the constitutional guarantee of equal protection so long as the narrow-tailoring requirement is also satisfied.

III A.　[Although] some language in [past] opinions might be read to suggest that remedying past discrimination is the only permissible justification for race-based governmental action[, we] have never held that the only governmental use of race that can survive strict scrutiny is remedying past discrimination. [The] Law School has a compelling interest in attaining a diverse student body. The Law School's educational judgment that such diversity is essential to its educational mission is one to which we defer. * * *

As part of its goal of "assembling a class that is both exceptionally academically qualified and broadly diverse," the Law School seeks to "enroll a 'critical mass' of minority students." The Law School's interest is not simply "to assure within its student body some specified percentage of a particular group merely because of its race or ethnic origin." That would amount to outright racial balancing, which is patently unconstitutional. Rather, the Law School's concept of critical mass is defined by reference to the educational benefits that diversity is designed to produce.

These benefits are substantial. As the District Court emphasized, the Law School's admissions policy promotes "cross-racial understanding," helps to break down racial stereotypes, and "enables [students] to better understand persons of different races." [Major] American businesses have made clear that the skills needed in today's increasingly global marketplace can only be developed through exposure to widely diverse people, cultures, ideas, and viewpoints. What is more, high-ranking retired officers and civilian leaders of the United States military assert that, "[b]ased on [their] decades of experience," a "highly qualified, racially diverse officer corps . . . is essential to the military's ability to fulfill its principle mission to provide national security." The primary sources for the Nation's officer corps are the service academies and the Reserve Officers Training Corps (ROTC), the latter comprising students already admitted to participating colleges and universities. At present, "the military cannot achieve an officer corps that is *both* highly qualified *and* racially diverse unless the service academies and the ROTC used limited race-conscious recruiting and admissions policies." To fulfill its mission, the military "must be selective in admissions for training and education for the officer corps, and it must train and educate a highly qualified, racially diverse officer corps in a racially diverse setting." We agree that "[i]t requires only a small step from this analysis to conclude that our country's other most selective institutions must remain both diverse and selective."

[U]niversities, and in particular, law schools, represent the training ground for a large number of our Nation's leaders. *Sweatt v. Painter*. [In] order to cultivate a set of leaders with legitimacy in the eyes of the citizenry, it is necessary that the path to leadership be visibly open to talented and qualified individuals of every race and ethnicity. All members of our heterogeneous society must have confidence in the openness and integrity of the educational institutions that provide this training. * * *

B.   Even in the limited circumstance when drawing racial distinctions is permissible to further a compelling state interest, government is still "constrained in how it may pursue that [end.]" [A] university may consider race or ethnicity only as a " 'plus' in a particular applicant's file," without "insulat[ing] the individual from comparison with all other candidates for the available seats." [We] find that the Law School's admissions program bears the hallmarks of a narrowly tailored plan. [The] Law School's goal of attaining a critical mass of underrepresented minority students does not transform its program into a quota. [Nor] does the Law School's consultation of the "daily reports," which keep track of the racial and ethnic composition of the class (as well as of residency and gender), "sugges[t] there was no further attempt at individual review save for race itself" during the final stages of the admissions process. To the contrary, the Law School's admissions officers testified without contradiction that they never gave race any more or less weight based on the information contained in these reports. Moreover, [between] 1993 and 1998, the number of African-American, Latino, and Native-American students in each class at the Law School varied from 13.5 to 20.1 percent, a range inconsistent with a quota.

[Petitioner] and the United States argue that the Law School's plan is not narrowly tailored because race-neutral means exist to obtain the educational benefits of student body diversity that the Law School seeks. We disagree. Narrow tailoring does not require exhaustion of every conceivable race-neutral alternative. Nor does it require a university to choose between maintaining a reputation for excellence or fulfilling a commitment to provide educational opportunities to members of all racial groups. [The] District Court took the Law School to task for failing to consider race-neutral alternatives such as "using a lottery system" or "decreasing the emphasis for all applicants on undergraduate GPA and LSAT scores." But these alternatives would require a dramatic sacrifice of diversity, the academic quality of all admitted students, or both. [The] United States advocates "percentage plans," recently adopted by public undergraduate institutions in Texas, Florida, and California to guarantee admission to all students above a certain class-rank threshold in every high school in the State. [In part because some high schools have disproportionately large minority enrollments, these programs help to increase minority admissions, though often less so than explicitly race-based affirmative action programs.] The United States does not, however, explain how such plans could work for graduate and professional schools.

[We] acknowledge that "there are serious problems of justice connected with the idea of preference itself." [It] has been 25 years since Justice Powell first approved the use of race to further an interest in student body diversity in the context of public higher education. Since that time, the number of minority applicants with high grades and test scores has indeed increased. We expect that 25 years from now, the use of racial preferences will no longer be necessary to further the interest approved today.

JUSTICE GINSBURG, with whom JUSTICE BREYER joins, concurring.

[From] today's vantage point, one may hope, but not firmly forecast, that over the next generation's span, progress toward nondiscrimination and genuinely equal opportunity will make it safe to sunset affirmative action.

CHIEF JUSTICE REHNQUIST, with whom JUSTICE SCALIA, JUSTICE KENNEDY, and JUSTICE THOMAS join, dissenting.

I agree with the Court that, "in the limited circumstance when drawing racial distinctions is permissible," the government must ensure that its means are narrowly tailored to achieve a compelling state interest. I do not believe, however, that the University of Michigan Law School's (Law School) means are narrowly tailored to the interest it asserts. [Stripped] of its "critical mass" veil, the Law School's program is revealed as a naked effort to achieve racial balancing.

[From] 1995 through 2000, the Law School admitted between 1,130 and 1,310 students. Of those, between 13 and 19 were Native American, between 91 and 108 were African-Americans, and between 47 and 56 were Hispanic. If the Law School is admitting between 91 and 108 African-Americans in order to achieve "critical mass," thereby preventing African-American students from feeling "isolated or like spokespersons for their race," one would think that a number of the same order of magnitude would be necessary to accomplish the same purpose for Hispanics and Native Americans. Similarly, even if all of the Native American applicants admitted in a given year matriculate, which the record demonstrates is not at all the case,* how can this possibly constitute a "critical mass" of Native Americans in a class of over 350 students? * * *

[Only] when the "critical mass" label is discarded does a likely explanation for these numbers emerge. [The] correlation between the percentage of the Law School's pool of applicants who are members of the three minority groups and the percentage of the admitted applicants who are members of these same groups is far too precise to be dismissed as merely the result of the school paying "some attention to [the] numbers." As the tables below show, from 1995 through 2000 the percentage of admitted applicants who were members of these minority groups closely tracked the percentage of individuals in the school's applicant pool who were from the same groups. [This] is precisely the type of racial balancing that the Court itself calls "patently unconstitutional."

JUSTICE KENNEDY, dissenting. * * *

JUSTICE SCALIA, with whom JUSTICE THOMAS joins, concurring in part and dissenting in part.

The "educational benefit" that the University of Michigan seeks to achieve by racial discrimination consists, according to the Court, of "cross-racial understanding," and "better prepar[ation of] students for an increasingly diverse workforce and society," all of which is necessary not only for work, but also for good "citizenship." This is not, of course, an "educational benefit" on which students will be graded on their Law School transcript (Works and Plays Well with Others: B+) or tested by the bar examiners (Q: Describe in 500 words or less your cross-racial understanding). For it is a lesson of life rather than law—essentially the same lesson taught to (or rather learned by, for it cannot be "taught" in the usual sense) people three feet shorter and twenty years younger than the full-grown adults at the University of Michigan Law School, in institutions ranging from Boy Scout troops to public-school kindergartens. If properly considered an "educational benefit" at all, it is surely not one that is either uniquely relevant to law school or uniquely "teachable" in a formal educational setting. *And therefore*: If it is

---

*   [Ct's Note] Indeed, during this 5-year time period, enrollment of Native American students dropped to as low as three such students. Any assertion that such a small group constituted a "critical mass" of Native Americans is simply absurd.

appropriate for the University of Michigan Law School to use racial discrimination for the purpose of putting together a "critical mass" that will convey generic lessons in socialization and good citizenship, surely it is no less appropriate—indeed, *particularly* appropriate—for the civil service system of the State of Michigan to do so. There, also, those exposed to "critical masses" of certain races will presumably become better Americans, better Michiganders, better civil servants. And surely private employers cannot be criticized—indeed, should be praised—if they also "teach" good citizenship to their adult employees through a patriotic, all-American system of racial discrimination in hiring. The nonminority individuals who are deprived of a legal education, a civil service job, or any job at all by reason of their skin color will surely understand. * * *

JUSTICE THOMAS, with whom JUSTICE SCALIA joins as to Parts I-VII, concurring in part and dissenting in part.

Frederick Douglass, speaking to a group of abolitionists almost 140 years ago, delivered a message lost on today's majority: "[I]n regard to the colored people, there is always more that is benevolent, I perceive, than just, manifested towards us. What I ask for the negro is not benevolence, not pity, not sympathy, but simply *justice*. . . . And if the negro cannot stand on his own legs, let him fall. . . . All I ask is, give him a chance to stand on his own legs! Let him alone! [Y]our interference is doing him positive injury." [Like] Douglass, I believe blacks can achieve in every avenue of American life without the meddling of university administrators. Because I wish to see all students succeed whatever their color, I share, in some respect, the sympathies of those who sponsor the type of discrimination advanced by the University of Michigan Law School (Law School). The Constitution does not, however, tolerate institutional devotion to the status quo in admissions policies when such devotion ripens into racial discrimination. Nor does the Constitution countenance the unprecedented deference the Court gives to the Law School, an approach inconsistent with the very concept of "strict scrutiny."

III. [Justice] Powell's opinion in *Bakke* and the Court's decision today rest on the fundamentally flawed proposition that racial discrimination can be contextualized so that a goal, such as classroom aesthetics, can be compelling in one context but not in another. [Under] the proper standard, there is no pressing public necessity in maintaining a public law school at all and, it follows, certainly not an elite law school. Likewise, marginal improvements in legal education do not qualify as a compelling state interest. * * *

VI. [I] believe what lies beneath the Court's decision today are the benighted notions that one can tell when racial discrimination benefits (rather than hurts) minority groups, and that racial discrimination is necessary to remedy general societal ills. [I] must contest the notion that the Law School's discrimination benefits those admitted as a result of it. The Court spends considerable time discussing the impressive display of amicus support for the Law School in this case from all corners of society. But nowhere in any of the filings in this Court is any evidence that the purported "beneficiaries" of this racial discrimination prove themselves by performing at (or even near) the same level as those students who receive no preferences.

[The] Law School tantalizes unprepared students with the promise of a University of Michigan degree and all of the opportunities that it offers. These overmatched students take the bait, only to find that they cannot succeed in the cauldron of competition. And this mismatch crisis is not restricted to elite institutions. [While] these students may graduate with law degrees, there is no evidence that they have received a qualitatively better legal education (or become better lawyers) than if they had gone to a less "elite" law school for which they were better prepared.

[It] is uncontested that each year, the Law School admits a handful of blacks who would be admitted in the absence of racial discrimination. Who can differentiate between those who belong and those who do not? The majority of blacks are admitted to the Law School because of discrimination, and because of this policy all are tarred as undeserving. This problem of stigma does not depend on determinacy as to whether those stigmatized are actually the "beneficiaries" of racial discrimination. When blacks take positions in the highest places of government, industry, or academia, it is an open question today whether their skin color played a part in their advancement. The question itself is the stigma— because either racial discrimination did play a role, in which case the person may be deemed "otherwise unqualified," or it did not, in which case asking the question itself unfairly marks those blacks who would succeed without discrimination.

———

In GRATZ v. BOLLINGER, 539 U.S. 244 (2003), the Court, per REHNQUIST, C.J., invalidated a rigid program for undergraduate admissions to the University of Michigan under which applicants from underrepresented minorities received a fixed total of 20 points out of a possible 150 on the school's admission index. The index assigned 110 points for high school grades, standardized test scores, and rigor of academic program. "Legacy" applicants whose parents had attended the school received four points. Apart from race, the index awarded 20 points to students from socioeconomically disadvantaged backgrounds, recruited athletes, and those specially designated by the provost. Focusing solely on the race-based preference, the Court assumed that the university had a compelling interest in achieving a diverse student body, but it ruled that the uniform, 20-point, race-based bonus was too large and mechanical to be narrowly tailored the kind of diversity in student background and outlook that Powell, J., had approved in *Bakke*. Breyer, J., concurred in the judgment only.

GINSBURG, J., joined by Souter, J., dissented: "The stain of generations of racial oppression is still visible in our society, and the determination to hasten its removal remains vital. One can reasonably anticipate, therefore, that colleges and universities will seek to maintain their minority enrollment—and the networks and opportunities thereby opened to minority graduates—whether or not they can do so in full candor through adoption of affirmative action plans of the kind here at issue. Without recourse to such plans, institutions of higher education may resort to camouflage. For example, schools may encourage applicants to write of their cultural traditions in the essays they submit, or to indicate whether English is their second language. Seeking to improve their chances for admission, applicants may highlight the minority group associations to which they belong, or the Hispanic surnames of their mothers or grandparents. In turn, teachers' recommendations may emphasize who a student is as much as what he or she has accomplished. If honesty is the best policy, surely Michigan's accurately described, fully disclosed College affirmative action program is preferable to achieving similar numbers through winks, nods, and disguises."

STEVENS, J., also dissented.

———

Roughly following the approach adopted in Grutter, FISHER v. UNIVERSITY OF TEXAS, 136 S.Ct. 2198 (2016), per KENNEDY, J., upheld an affirmative action program at the University of Texas at Austin. (The Court had previously ruled in *Fisher v. University of Texas (I)*, 570 U.S. 297 (2013), that the court of appeals had given undue deference to the University's arguments concerning the narrow tailoring of its program to the compelling interest in educational diversity.) The University had an unusual two-tiered admissions process. Roughly 75% of students are admitted based on their high school class rank—pursuant to a Top Ten Percent Plan—if they attended high school in Texas. The remaining 25% were admitted pursuant to a holistic assessment that took race into account.

"Petitioner's [failure to challenge] the Top Ten Percent Plan complicates [judicial] review [because] it has led to a record that is almost devoid of information about the students who secured admission [through] the Plan. The Court thus cannot know how students admitted solely based on their class rank differ in their contribution to diversity from students admitted through holistic review. [The] fact that this case has been litigated on a somewhat artificial basis, furthermore, may limit its value for prospective guidance.

"[In] seeking to reverse the judgment of the Court of Appeals, petitioner [argues first] that the University has not articulated its compelling interest with sufficient clarity. According to petitioner, the University must set forth more precisely the level of minority enrollment that would constitute a "critical mass." [As] this Court's cases have made clear, however, the compelling interest that justifies consideration of race in college admissions is not an interest in enrolling a certain number of minority students. Rather, a university may institute a race-conscious admissions program as a means of obtaining "the educational benefits that flow from student body diversity." * * *

"The record reveals that in first setting forth its current admissions policy, the University articulated concrete and precise goals. On the first page of its 2004 'Proposal to Consider Race and Ethnicity in Admissions,' the University identifies the educational values it seeks to realize through its admissions process: the destruction of stereotypes, the 'promot[ion of] cross-racial understanding,' the preparation of a student body 'for an increasingly diverse workforce and society,' and the 'cultivat[ion of] a set of leaders with legitimacy in the eyes of the citizenry.'

"[Second,] petitioner argues that the University has no need to consider race because it had already "achieved critical mass" by 2003 using the Top Ten Percent Plan and race-neutral holistic review. Petitioner is correct that a university bears a heavy burden in showing that it had not obtained the educational benefits of diversity before it turned to a race-conscious plan. The record reveals, however, that, at the time of petitioner's application, the University could not be faulted on this score. Before changing its policy the University conducted "months of study and deliberation, including retreats, interviews, [and] review of data," and concluded that "[t]he use of race-neutral policies and programs ha[d] not been successful in achieving" sufficient racial diversity at the University. At no stage in this litigation has petitioner challenged the University's good faith in conducting its studies, and the Court properly declines to consider the extrarecord materials the dissent relies [upon.]

"The record itself contains significant evidence, both statistical and anecdotal, in support of the University's position. To start, the demographic data the University has submitted show consistent stagnation in terms of the percentage of minority students enrolling at the University from 1996 to 2002. In 1996, for example, 266 African-American freshmen enrolled, a total that constituted 4.1 percent of the incoming class. In 2003, the year *Grutter* was decided, 267 African-American students enrolled—again, 4.1 percent of the incoming class. The numbers for Hispanic and Asian-American students tell a similar story. Although demographics alone are by no means dispositive, they do have some value as a gauge of the University's ability to enroll students who can offer underrepresented perspectives.

"In addition to this broad demographic data, the University put forward evidence that minority students admitted under the [previous] regime experienced feelings of loneliness and isolation. * * *

"[Third,] petitioner argues that considering race was not necessary because such consideration has had only a " 'minimal impact' in advancing the [University's] compelling interest." Again, the record does not support this assertion. In 2003, 11 percent of the Texas residents enrolled through holistic review were Hispanic and 3.5 percent were African-American. In 2007, by contrast, 16.9 percent of the Texas holistic-review freshmen were Hispanic and 6.8 percent were African-American. Those increases—of 54 percent and 94 percent, respectively—show that consideration of race has had a meaningful, if still limited, effect on the diversity of the University's freshman class. In any event, it is not a failure of narrow tailoring for the impact of racial consideration to be minor. The fact that race consciousness played a role in only a small portion of admissions decisions should be a hallmark of narrow tailoring, not evidence of unconstitutionality. * * *

"Petitioner's final suggestion is to uncap the Top Ten Percent Plan, and admit more—if not all—the University's students through a percentage plan. As an initial matter, petitioner overlooks the fact that the Top Ten Percent Plan, though facially neutral, cannot be understood apart from its basic purpose, which is to boost minority enrollment. Percentage plans are "adopted with racially segregated neighborhoods and schools front and center stage." *Fisher I* (Ginsburg, J., dissenting). "It is race consciousness, not blindness to race, that drives such plans." Id. Consequently, petitioner cannot assert simply that increasing the University's reliance on a percentage plan would make its admissions policy more race neutral. * * *"

JUSTICE THOMAS, dissenting.

"I join Justice Alito's dissent. [I] write separately to reaffirm that 'a State's use of race in higher education admissions is categorically prohibited by the Equal Protection Clause.' *Fisher I* (Thomas, J., dissenting)."

[In his concurring opinion in *Fisher I*, Thomas, J. wrote: "My view of the Constitution is the one advanced by the plaintiffs in *Brown*: '[N]o State has any authority under the equal-protection clause of the Fourteenth Amendment to use race as a factor in affording educational opportunities among its citizens.' [This] principle is neither new nor difficult to understand. In 1868, decades before *Plessy*, the Iowa Supreme Court held that schools may not discriminate against applicants based on their skin color. In *Clark v. Board of Directors*, 24 Iowa 266 (1868), a school denied admission to a student because she was black, and 'public sentiment [was] opposed to the intermingling of white and colored children in the same schools.' The Iowa Supreme Court rejected that flimsy justification, holding that 'all the youths are equal before the law, and there is no discretion vested in the board [or] elsewhere, to interfere with or disturb that equality.'[18]

["The] worst forms of racial discrimination in this Nation have always been accompanied by straight-faced representations that discrimination helped minorities. Slaveholders argued that slavery was a 'positive good' that civilized blacks and elevated them in every dimension of life. [A] century later, segregationists similarly asserted [that] separate schools protected black children from racist white students and teachers.

["The] University's discrimination 'stamp[s] [blacks and Hispanics] with a badge of inferiority.' [Although] most blacks and Hispanics attending the University were admitted without discrimination under the Top Ten Percent plan, [no] one can distinguish those students from the ones whose race played a role in their admission."]

JUSTICE ALITO, with whom ROBERTS, C.J., and THOMAS, J., join, dissenting.

"[Because] UT has failed to define its interest in using racial preferences with clarity, [the] narrow tailoring inquiry is impossible, and UT cannot satisfy strict scrutiny. When UT adopted its challenged policy, it characterized its compelling

---

[18]   The decision was based on Iowa law, not the Fourteenth Amendment.

interest as obtaining a 'critical mass' of underrepresented minorities. [But] to this day, UT has not explained in anything other than the vaguest terms what it means by 'critical mass.' In fact, UT argues that it need not identify any interest more specific than 'securing the educational benefits of diversity.' [This] intentionally imprecise interest is designed to insulate UT's program from meaningful judicial review. [Without] knowing in reasonably specific terms what critical mass is or how it can be measured, a reviewing court cannot conduct the requisite "careful judicial inquiry" into whether the use of race was 'necessary.' *Fisher I.* [The aims that the University has advanced] are laudable goals, but they are not concrete or precise, and they offer no limiting principle for the use of racial preferences. For instance, how will a court ever be able to determine whether stereotypes have been adequately destroyed? Or whether cross-racial understanding has been adequately achieved? [By] accepting these amorphous goals as sufficient for UT to carry its burden, the majority violates decades of precedent rejecting blind deference to government officials defending 'inherently suspect' classifications. *Miller v. Johnson*, 515 U.S. 900 (1995).

"[Although] UT's primary argument is that it need not point to any interest more specific than 'the educational benefits of diversity,' it has—at various points in this litigation—identified four more specific goals. [First], both UT and the majority cite demographic data as evidence that African-American and Hispanic students are 'underrepresented' at UT and that racial preferences are necessary to compensate for this underrepresentation. [To] the extent that UT is pursuing parity with Texas demographics, that is nothing more than 'outright racial balancing,' which this Court has time and again held 'patently unconstitutional.' *Fisher I.*

"[The] other major explanation UT offered in the Proposal [to resume taking race into account in admissions] was its desire to promote classroom diversity. [UT] now equivocates, disclaiming any discrete interest in classroom diversity. [Nor] is there any indication that UT instructed admissions officers to search for African-American and Hispanic applicants who would fill particular gaps at the classroom level.

"[While] both the majority and the Fifth Circuit rely on UT's classroom study, they completely ignore its finding that Hispanics are better represented than Asian-Americans in UT classrooms. In fact, they act almost as if Asian-American students do not exist. [The] District Court acknowledged the impact of UT's policy on Asian-American students[, those of whom who are admitted through holistic review tend to have higher scores that whites, African-Americans, or Hispanics, but] it brushed aside this impact, concluding—astoundingly—that UT can pick and choose which racial and ethnic groups it would like to favor. [This] reasoning, which the majority implicitly accepts by blessing UT's reliance on the classroom study, places the Court on the "tortuous" path of 'decid[ing] which races to favor.' [By] accepting the classroom study as proof that UT satisfied strict scrutiny, the majority "move[s] us from 'separate but equal' to 'unequal but benign.' "

"[UT] also alleges—and the majority embraces—an interest in avoiding 'feelings of loneliness and isolation' among minority students. In support of this argument, they cite only demographic data and anecdotal statements by UT officials that some students (we are not told how many) feel 'isolated.' This vague interest cannot possibly satisfy strict scrutiny.

"[Even] assuming UT is correct that, under *Grutter*, it need only cite a generic interest in the educational benefits of diversity, its plan still fails strict scrutiny because it is not narrowly tailored. [If] "a ' "nonracial approach [could] promote the substantial interest about as well and at tolerable administrative expense," ' then the university may not consider race." *Fisher I*. Here, there is no evidence that race-blind, holistic review would not achieve UT's goals at least "about as well" as UT's race-based policy. In addition, UT could have adopted other approaches to further its goals, such as intensifying its outreach efforts, uncapping the Top Ten Percent Law, or placing greater weight on socioeconomic factors.

"[The] fact that UT's racial preferences are unnecessary to achieve its stated goals is further demonstrated by their minimal effect on UT's diversity. In 2004, when race was not a factor, 3.6% of non-Top Ten Percent Texas enrollees were African-American and 11.6% were Hispanic. It would stand to reason that at least the same percentages of African-American and Hispanic students would have been admitted through holistic review in 2008 even if race were not a factor. If that assumption is correct, then race was determinative for only 15 African-American students and 18 Hispanic students in 2008 (representing 0.2% and 0.3%, respectively, of the total enrolled first-time freshmen from Texas high schools).

"[UT] has long been aware that it bears the burden of justifying its racial discrimination under strict scrutiny. [The] majority's willingness to cite UT's "good faith" as the basis for excusing its failure to adduce evidence is particularly inappropriate in light of UT's well-documented absence of good faith. [The] majority concludes that UT has met its heavy burden [of satisfying strict scrutiny]. This conclusion is remarkable—and remarkably wrong."

KAGAN, J., did not participate.

———

In ADARAND CONSTRUCTORS, INC. v. PENA, 515 U.S. 200 (1995), the Court, per O'CONNOR, J., overruled its earlier decision in *Metro Broadcasting, Inc. v. FCC*, 497 U.S. 547 (1990),[19] which had held that affirmative action programs implemented by the federal government, need only satisfy intermediate scrutiny. But the Court also said that "we wish to dispel the notion that strict scrutiny is

---

[19]   *Metro Broadcasting*, per Brennan, J., upheld FCC policies granting preferences to minority ownerships in the acquisition and transfer of broadcast licenses on the basis of the governmental interest "in enhancing broadcast diversity." The opinion was joined by Justice White, who had joined the plurality opinion in *Croson*; it distinguished *Croson* as having established the level of scrutiny applicable to affirmative action programs initiated by state and local governments, not to federal affirmative action. O'Connor, J., joined by Rehnquist, C.J., and Scalia and Kennedy, JJ., dissented.

'strict in theory, but fatal in fact.' The unhappy persistence of both the practice and the lingering effects of racial discrimination against minority groups in this country is an unfortunate reality, and government is not disqualified from acting in response to it. As recently as 1987, for example, every Justice of this Court agreed that the Alabama Department of Public Safety's 'pervasive, systematic, and obstinate discriminatory conduct' justified a narrowly tailored race-based remedy. See *United States v. Paradise*, 480 U.S. 149 (1987).[20] When race-based action is necessary to further a compelling interest, such action is within constitutional constraints if it satisfies the 'narrow tailoring' test this Court has set out in previous cases."

STEVENS, J., joined by Ginsburg, J., dissented: "The majority in *Metro Broadcasting* [was] not alone in relying upon a critical distinction between federal and state programs. In his separate opinion in [*Croson*], Justice Scalia discussed the basis for this distinction. He observed that 'it is one thing to permit racially based conduct by the Federal Government—whose legislative powers concerning matters of race were explicitly enhanced by the Fourteenth Amendment—and quite another to permit it by the precise entities against whose conduct in matters of race that Amendment was specifically directed.' [In] her plurality opinion in *Croson,* Justice O'Connor also emphasized the importance of this distinction when she responded to the City's argument that *Fullilove* was controlling. [It] is one thing to say (as no one seems to dispute) that the Fifth Amendment encompasses a general guarantee of equal protection as broad as that contained within the Fourteenth Amendment. It is another thing entirely to say that Congress' institutional competence and constitutional authority entitles it to no greater deference when it enacts a program designed to foster equality than the deference due a State legislature."[21]

3. DISCRIMINATIONS BASED ON GENDER

I. DEFINING THE LEVEL OF SCRUTINY

Prior to 1971, the Court used the deferential "traditional approach" (see Sec. 1 supra) to test the constitutionality of classifications based on gender. *Muller v. Oregon*, 208 U.S. 412 (1908), per Brewer, J., upheld a law barring factory work by women for more than ten hours a day, reasoning that "as healthy mothers are essential to vigorous offspring, the physical well-being of a woman becomes an object of public interest and care."[22] *Goesaert v. Cleary*, 335 U.S. 464 (1948), per Frankfurter, J., upheld a law denying bartender's licenses to most women,

---

[20] *Paradise* upheld a *judicially* ordered race-conscious remedy. The Court was unanimous that the federal government has a compelling interest in remedying proven race discrimination. Per Brennan, J., it found the particular order at issue to be "narrowly tailored," and thus upheld it, by a closely divided vote of 5–4.

[21] The dissenting opinions of Souter, J., joined by Ginsburg and Breyer, JJ., and of Ginsburg, J., joined by Breyer, J., are omitted.

[22] But see *Adkins v. Children's Hospital*, 261 U.S. 525 (1923) (minimum wage for women violates due process), overruled, *West Coast Hotel Co. v. Parrish*, Ch. 5, Sec. 3 supra.

reasoning that "the fact that women may now have achieved the virtues that men have long claimed as their prerogatives and now indulge in vices that men have long practiced, does not preclude the States from drawing a sharp line between the sexes, certainly in such matters as the regulation of the liquor traffic."[23] As recently as 1961, *Hoyt v. Florida*, 368 U.S. 57, per Harlan, J., sustained a law placing women on the jury list only if they made special request, stating that a "woman is still regarded as the center of home and family life."[24] The first decision holding sex discrimination violative of equal protection, REED v. REED, 404 U.S. 71 (1971), per BURGER, C.J., involved a law preferring males to females when two persons were otherwise equally entitled to be the administrator of an estate: "A classification 'must be reasonable, not arbitrary, and must rest upon some ground of difference having a fair and substantial relation to the object of the [law].' The question" is whether the classification "bears a rational relationship to a state objective that is sought to be advanced by the [law]." It was contended that the law had the reasonable "objective of reducing the workload on probate courts by eliminating one class of contests" and that the legislature might reasonably have "concluded that in general men are better qualified to act as an administrator than are women." But "to give a mandatory preference to members of either sex over members of the other, merely to accomplish the elimination of hearings on the merits, is to make the very kind of arbitrary legislative choice forbidden by [equal protection]."

———

Reed was followed by FRONTIERO v. RICHARDSON, 411 U.S. 677 (1973), which invalidated a federal statute permitting males in the armed services an automatic dependency allowance for their wives but requiring servicewomen to prove that their husbands were dependent. BRENNAN, J., joined by Douglas, White, and Marshall, JJ., argued that "classifications based upon sex [are] inherently suspect and must therefore be subjected to close judicial scrutiny." The plurality found "at least implicit support for such an approach in [*Reed's*] departure from 'traditional' rational basis analysis": "[O]ur Nation has had a long and unfortunate history of sex discrimination. Traditionally, such discrimination was rationalized by an attitude of 'romantic paternalism' which, in practical effect, put women not on a pedestal, but in a cage. * * *

"As a result of notions such as these, [statutes] became laden with gross, stereotypical distinctions between the sexes and, indeed, throughout much of the

---

[23]   See also the concurring opinion of Bradley, J., joined by Swayne and Field, JJ., in *Bradwell v. Illinois*, 83 U.S. (16 Wall.) 130 (1873), which upheld a statute denying women the right to practice law against challenge based on the Privileges or Immunities Clause: "[T]he natural and proper timidity and delicacy which belongs to the female sex evidently unfits it for many of the occupations of civil life. [The] paramount destiny and mission of woman are to fulfill the noble and benign offices of wife and mother. This is the law of the Creator."

[24]   *Hoyt* was effectively overruled in *Taylor v. Louisiana*, 419 U.S. 522 (1975), holding that a similar statute, operating largely to exclude women from jury service, deprived a criminal defendant of the Sixth and Fourteenth Amendment right to an impartial jury drawn from a fair cross section of the community.

19th century the position of women in our society was, in many respects, comparable to that of blacks under the pre-Civil War slave codes. Neither slaves nor women could hold office, serve on juries, or bring suit in their own names, and married women traditionally were denied the legal capacity to hold or convey property or to serve as legal guardians of their own children. And although blacks were guaranteed the right to vote in 1870, women were denied even [that] until adoption of the Nineteenth Amendment half a century later.

"It is true, of course, that the position of women in America has improved markedly in recent decades. [But] in part because of the high visibility of the sex characteristic, women still face pervasive, although at times more subtle, discrimination in our educational institutions, on the job market and, perhaps most conspicuously, in the political arena.[17]

"Moreover, since sex, like race and national origin, is an immutable characteristic [the] imposition of special disabilities [would] seem to violate 'the basic concept of our system that legal burdens should bear some relationship to individual responsibility.' And what differentiates sex from such non-suspect statuses as intelligence or physical disability [is] that the sex characteristic frequently bears no relation to ability to perform or contribute to society.

"[The] Government [maintains] that, as an empirical matter, wives in our society frequently are dependent upon their husbands, while husbands rarely are dependent upon their wives. Thus, the Government argues that Congress might reasonably have concluded that it would be both cheaper and easier simply conclusively to presume that wives of male members are financially dependent upon their husbands, while burdening female members with the task of establishing dependency in fact.

"The Government offers no concrete evidence, however, tending to support its view that such differential treatment in fact saves the Government any money. [And any] statutory scheme which draws a sharp line between the sexes, *solely* [for] administrative convenience [violates equal protection]."

POWELL, J., joined by Burger, C.J., and Blackmun, J., concurring, would rely "on the authority of *Reed* and reserve for the future any expansion of its rationale." Stewart, J., concurred, "agreeing that the [statutes] work an invidious discrimination." Rehnquist, J., dissented.

———————

In CRAIG v. BOREN, 429 U.S. 190 (1976), the Court, in an opinion by BRENNAN, J., for the first time subjected a statute that discriminated on the basis of sex to a standard of scrutiny intermediate between rational basis review and strict judicial scrutiny: "[To] withstand constitutional challenge, [classifications] by gender must serve important governmental objectives and must be

---

[17]   **[Ct's Note]** It is true ... that when viewed in the abstract, women do not constitute a small and powerless minority. Nevertheless, in part because of past discrimination, women are vastly underrepresented in this Nation's decisionmaking councils. * * *

substantially related to achievement of those objectives." Pursuant to that standard, the Court invalidated an Oklahoma statute that prohibited the sale of "nonintoxicating" 3.2% beer to males under the age of 21 but allowed females to purchase the beverage beginning at 18.

"[We] accept for purposes of discussion the District Court's identification of the objective underlying [the challenged statute] as the enhancement of traffic safety. Clearly, the protection of public health and safety represents an important function of state and local governments. However, appellees' statistics in our view cannot support the conclusion that the gender-based distinction closely serves to achieve that objective and therefore the distinction cannot under *Reed* withstand equal protection challenge. The appellees introduced a variety of statistical surveys [to support the statute, but the] most focused and relevant of the statistical surveys, arrests of 18–20-year-olds for alcohol-related driving offenses, exemplifies the ultimate unpersuasiveness of this evidentiary record. Viewed in terms of the correlation between sex and the actual activity that Oklahoma seeks to regulate— driving while under the influence of alcohol—the statistics broadly establish that .18% of females and 2% of males in that age group were arrested for that offense. While such a disparity is not trivial in a statistical sense, it hardly can form the basis for employment of a gender line as a classifying device. Certainly if maleness is to serve as a proxy for drinking and driving, a correlation of 2% must be considered an unduly tenuous 'fit.' [Indeed,] prior cases have consistently rejected the use of sex as a decisionmaking factor even though the statutes in question certainly rested on far more predictive empirical relationships than this.

"[W]hen it is further recognized that Oklahoma's statute prohibits only the selling of 3.2% beer to young males and not their drinking the beverage once acquired (even after purchase by their 18–20-year-old female companions), the relationship between gender and traffic safety becomes far too tenuous to satisfy *Reed*'s requirement that the gender-based difference be substantially related to achievement of the statutory objective. We hold, therefore, that [Oklahoma's] 3.2% beer statute invidiously discriminates against males 18–20 years of age."

REHNQUIST, J., with whom CHIEF JUSTICE BURGER was "in general agreement," dissented: "The Court's disposition of this case is objectionable on two grounds. First is its conclusion that *men* challenging a gender-based statute which treats them less favorably than women may invoke a more stringent standard of judicial review than pertains to most other types of classifications. Second is the Court's enunciation of this standard, without citation to any source, as being that 'classifications by gender must serve *important* governmental objectives and must be *substantially* related to achievement of those objectives.' [I] think the Oklahoma statute challenged here need pass only the "rational basis" equal protection analysis expounded in [prior cases].

"[Under the] applicable rational-basis test [the] evidence suggests clear differences between the drinking and driving habits of young men and women. Those differences are grounds enough for the State reasonably to conclude that young males pose by far the greater drunk-driving hazard, both in terms of sheer numbers and in terms of hazard on a per-driver basis. The gender-based difference in treatment in this case is therefore not irrational."

UNITED STATES V. VIRGINIA
518 U.S. 515, 116 S.Ct. 2264, 135 L.Ed.2d 735 (1996).

JUSTICE GINSBURG delivered the opinion of the Court.

Virginia's public institutions of higher learning include an incomparable military college, Virginia Military Institute (VMI). The United States maintains that the Constitution's equal protection guarantee precludes Virginia from reserving exclusively to men the unique educational opportunities VMI affords. We agree.

Founded in 1839, VMI is today the sole single-sex school among Virginia's 15 public institutions of higher learning. VMI's distinctive mission is to produce "citizen-soldiers." [Assigning] prime place to character development, VMI uses an "adversative method" modeled on English public schools and once characteristic of military instruction. [This model] features "physical rigor, mental stress, absolute equality of treatment, absence of privacy, minute regulation of behavior, and indoctrination in desirable values." [VMI] cadets live in spartan barracks where surveillance is constant and privacy nonexistent. [Entering] students are incessantly exposed to the rat line, "an extreme form of the adversative model," [which] bonds new cadets to their fellow sufferers and, when they have completed the 7-month experience, to their former tormentors.

In 1990, prompted by a complaint filed with the Attorney General by a female high-school student seeking admission to VMI, the United States sued the Commonwealth of Virginia and VMI, alleging that VMI's exclusively male admission policy violated the Equal Protection Clause of the Fourteenth Amendment. [The district court upheld the policy, but the court of appeals reversed, finding an equal protection violation. Following the remand, the state of Virginia proposed a remedial plan, under which the state would adopt] a parallel program for women: Virginia Women's Institute for Leadership (VWIL). The 4-year, state-sponsored undergraduate program would be located at Mary Baldwin College, a private liberal arts school for women, and would be open, initially, to about 25 to 30 students. Although VWIL would share VMI's mission—to produce "citizen-soldiers"—the VWIL program would differ, as does Mary Baldwin College, from VMI in academic offerings, methods of education, and financial resources.

The average combined SAT score of entrants at Mary Baldwin is about 100 points lower than the score for VMI freshmen. [While] VMI offers degrees in liberal arts, the sciences, and engineering, Mary Baldwin, at the time of trial, offered only bachelor of arts degrees. [Under the proposed remedial plan,] VWIL students would participate in ROTC programs [but in] lieu of VMI's adversative method, [VWIL would offer] "a cooperative method which reinforces self-esteem."

Virginia represented that it will provide equal financial support for in-state VWIL students and VMI cadets, and the VMI Foundation agreed to supply a $5.4625 million endowment for the VWIL program. Mary Baldwin's own endowment is about $19 million; VMI's is $131 million. Mary Baldwin will add $35 million to its endowment based on future commitments; VMI will add $220 million. [Both the district court and the court of appeals held that the proposed remedial plan satisfied the Equal Protection Clause.]

The cross-petitions in this case present two ultimate issues. First, does Virginia's exclusion of women from the educational opportunities provided by VMI—extraordinary opportunities for military training and civilian leadership development—deny to women "capable of all of the individual activities required of VMI cadets," the equal protection of the laws guaranteed by the Fourteenth Amendment? Second, if VMI's "unique" situation—as Virginia's sole single-sex public institution of higher education—offends the Constitution's equal protection principle, what is the remedial requirement?

We note, once again, the core instruction of this Court's pathmarking decisions in *J.E.B. v. Alabama ex rel. T.B.*, [511 U.S. 127 (1994) (finding gender-based peremptory challenges in a criminal case to be based on stereotypes and not substantially related to an important state interest)], and *Mississippi Univ. for Women*, [Part III infra]: Parties who seek to defend gender-based government action must demonstrate an "exceedingly persuasive justification" for that action. [The] burden of justification is demanding and it rests entirely on the State. The State must show "at least that the [challenged] classification serves 'important governmental objectives and that the discriminatory means employed' are 'substantially related to the achievement of those objectives.' " The justification must be genuine, not hypothesized or invented post hoc in response to litigation. And it must not rely on overbroad generalizations about the different talents, capacities, or preferences of males and females.

The heightened review standard our precedent establishes does not make sex a proscribed classification. Supposed "inherent differences" are no longer accepted as a ground for race or national origin classifications. See *Loving v. Virginia*. Physical differences between men and women, however, are enduring. Inherent differences between men and women, we have come to appreciate, remain cause for celebration, but not for denigration of the members of either sex or for artificial constraints on an individual's opportunity. Sex classifications may be used to compensate women "for particular economic disabilities [they have] suffered," *Califano v. Webster*, [Part III infra], to "promote equal employment opportunity," see *California Federal Sav. & Loan Assn. v. Guerra*, [Part III infra], [and] to advance full development of the talent and capacities of our Nation's people.[7] But

---

[7]   [Ct's Note] Several amici have urged that diversity in educational opportunities is an altogether appropriate governmental pursuit and that single-sex schools can contribute importantly to such diversity. Indeed, it is the mission of some single-sex schools "to dissipate, rather than perpetuate, traditional gender classifications." We do not question the State's prerogative evenhandedly to support diverse educational opportunities. We address specifically and only an educational opportunity recognized by the District Court and the Court of Appeals as

such classifications may not be used, as they once were, to create or perpetuate the legal, social, and economic inferiority of women. [Measuring] the record in this case against the review standard just described, we conclude that Virginia has shown no "exceedingly persuasive justification" for excluding all women from the citizen-soldier training afforded by VMI.

[Single-sex] education affords pedagogical benefits to at least some students, Virginia emphasizes, and that reality is uncontested in this litigation. Similarly, it is not disputed that diversity among public educational institutions can serve the public good. But Virginia has not shown that VMI was established, or has been maintained, with a view to diversifying, by its categorical exclusion of women, educational opportunities within the State. In cases of this genre, our precedent instructs that "benign" justifications proffered in defense of categorical exclusions will not be accepted automatically; a tenable justification must describe actual state purposes, not rationalizations for actions in fact differently grounded.

[Neither] recent nor distant history bears out Virginia's alleged pursuit of diversity through single-sex educational options. In 1839, when the State established VMI, a range of educational opportunities for men and women was scarcely contemplated. [In] admitting no women, VMI followed the lead of [the] University of Virginia, founded in 1819. [Beginning in 1884,] Virginia eventually provided for several women's seminaries and colleges. [By] the mid-1970s, [however,] all [had] become coeducational. [The] University of Virginia introduced coeducation [in 1970] and, in 1972, began to admit women on an equal basis with men.

[Virginia] describes the current absence of public single-sex higher education for women as "an historical anomaly." But the historical record indicates action more deliberate than anomalous: First, protection of women against higher education; next, schools for women far from equal in resources and stature to schools for men; finally, conversion of the separate schools to coeducation. [In] sum, we find no persuasive evidence in this record that VMI's male-only admission policy "is in furtherance of a state policy of 'diversity.'"

[Virginia] next argues that VMI's adversative method of training provides educational benefits that cannot be made available, unmodified, to women. Alterations to accommodate women would necessarily be "radical," so "drastic," Virginia asserts, as to transform, indeed "destroy," VMI's program. [The] District Court [found] that coeducation would materially affect "at least these three aspects of VMI's program—physical training, the absence of privacy, and the adversative approach." And it is uncontested that women's admission would require accommodations, primarily in arranging housing assignments and physical training programs for female cadets. It is also undisputed, however, that "the VMI methodology could be used to educate women."

"unique," an opportunity available only at Virginia's premier military institute, the State's sole single-sex public university or college.

[The] notion that admission of women would downgrade VMI's stature, destroy the adversative system and, with it, even the school, is a judgment hardly proved, a prediction hardly different from other "self-fulfilling prophecies" once routinely used to deny rights or opportunities. [Women's] successful entry into the federal military academies, and their participation in the Nation's military forces, indicate that Virginia's fears for the future of VMI may not be solidly grounded. [Virginia], in sum, "has fallen far short of establishing the 'exceedingly persuasive justification'" that must be the solid base for any gender-defined classification.

In the second phase of the litigation, Virginia presented its remedial plan— maintain VMI as a male-only college and create VWIL as a separate program for women. [Having] violated the Constitution's equal protection requirement, Virginia was obliged to show that its remedial proposal "directly addressed and related to" the violation, i.e., the equal protection denied to women ready, willing, and able to benefit from educational opportunities of the kind VMI offers. Virginia described VWIL as a "parallel program," and asserted that VWIL shares VMI's mission of producing "citizen-soldiers" and VMI's goals of providing "education, military training, mental and physical discipline, character [and] leadership development." [But] VWIL affords women no opportunity to experience the rigorous military training for which VMI is famed. Instead, the VWIL program "deemphasizes" military education, and uses a "cooperative method" of education "which reinforces self-esteem."

[Virginia] maintains that these methodological differences are "justified pedagogically," based on "important differences between men and women in learning and developmental needs," "psychological and sociological differences" Virginia describes as "real" and "not stereotypes." [As] earlier stated, [however], generalizations about "the way women are," estimates of what is appropriate for most women, no longer justify denying opportunity to women whose talent and capacity place them outside the average description. "[S]ome women, at least, would want to attend [VMI] if they had the opportunity"; "some women are capable of all of the individual activities required of VMI cadets" and "can meet the physical standards [VMI] now imposes on men". It is on behalf of these women that the United States has instituted this suit, and it is for them that a remedy must be crafted.[19]

[In] myriad respects other than military training, VWIL does not qualify as VMI's equal. VWIL's student body, faculty, course offerings, and facilities hardly match VMI's. Nor can the VWIL graduate anticipate the benefits associated with VMI's 157-year history, the school's prestige, and its influential alumni network.

[Virginia's] VWIL solution is reminiscent of the remedy Texas proposed 50 years ago, in response to a state trial court's 1946 ruling that, given the equal protection guarantee, African-Americans could not be denied a legal education at

---

[19]   **[Ct's Note]** Admitting women to VMI would undoubtedly require alterations necessary to afford members of each sex privacy from the other sex in living arrangements, and to adjust aspects of the physical training programs. Experience [at the United States military academies] shows such adjustments are manageable.

a state facility. See *Sweatt v. Painter*, [Sec. 2, II supra]. Reluctant to admit African-Americans to its flagship University of Texas Law School, the State set up a separate school for Heman Sweatt and other black law students. [This] Court contrasted resources at the new school with those at the school from which Sweatt had been excluded. Accordingly, the Court held, the Equal Protection Clause required Texas to admit African-Americans to the University of Texas Law School. In line with *Sweatt,* we rule here that Virginia has not shown substantial equality in the separate educational opportunities the State supports at VWIL and VMI. * * *

JUSTICE THOMAS took no part in the consideration or decision of this case.

CHIEF JUSTICE REHNQUIST, concurring in the judgement.

Two decades ago in *Craig v. Boren,* we announced that "to withstand constitutional challenge, * * * classifications by gender must serve important governmental objectives and must be substantially related to achievement of those objectives." [While] the majority adheres to this test today, it also says that the State must demonstrate an " 'exceedingly persuasive justification' " to support a gender-based classification. [To] avoid introducing potential confusion, I would have adhered more closely to our traditional [standard].

[I] agree with the Court that there is scant evidence in the record that [diversity] was the real reason that Virginia decided to maintain VMI as men only. [Even] if diversity in educational opportunity were the Commonwealth's actual objective, the Commonwealth's position would still be problematic. The difficulty is that the diversity benefited only one sex.

[Virginia] offers a second justification for the single-sex admissions policy: maintenance of the adversative method. [But a] State does not have substantial interest in the adversative methodology unless it is pedagogically beneficial. While considerable evidence shows that a single-sex education is pedagogically beneficial for some students, and hence a State may have a valid interest in promoting that methodology, there is no similar evidence in the record that an adversative method is pedagogically beneficial or is any more likely to produce character traits than other methodologies.

The Court defines the constitutional violation in this case as "the categorical exclusion of women from an extraordinary educational opportunity afforded to men." By defining the violation in this way, [the] Court necessarily implies that the only adequate remedy would be the admission of women to the all-male institution. [I] would not define the violation in this way; it is not the "exclusion of women" that violates the Equal Protection Clause, but the maintenance of an all-men school without providing any—much less a comparable—institution for women. * * *

JUSTICE SCALIA, dissenting.

* * * Much of the Court's opinion is devoted to deprecating the closed-mindedness of our forebears with regard to women's education, and even with

regard to the treatment of women in areas that have nothing to do with education. Closed-minded they were—as every age is, including our own, with regard to matters it cannot guess, because it simply does not consider them debatable. The virtue of a democratic system with a First Amendment is that it readily enables the people, over time, to be persuaded that what they took for granted is not so, and to change their laws accordingly. That system is destroyed if the smug assurances of each age are removed from the democratic process and written into the Constitution. So to counterbalance the Court's criticism of our ancestors, let me say a word in their praise: they left us free to change. The same cannot be said of this most illiberal Court, which has embarked on a course of inscribing one after another of the current preferences of the society (and in some cases only the counter-majoritarian preferences of the society's law-trained elite) into our Basic Law. Today it enshrines the notion that no substantial educational value is to be served by an all-men's military academy—so that the decision by the people of Virginia to maintain such an institution denies equal protection to women who cannot attend that institution but can attend others.

[In] my view the function of this Court is to preserve our society's values regarding (among other things) equal protection, not to revise them. [Whatever] abstract tests we may choose to devise, they cannot supersede—and indeed ought to be crafted so as to reflect—those constant and unbroken national traditions that embody the people's understanding of ambiguous constitutional texts. More specifically, it is my view that "when a practice not expressly prohibited by the text of the Bill of Rights bears the endorsement of a long tradition of open, widespread, and unchallenged use that dates back to the beginning of the Republic, we have no proper basis for striking it down."

The all-male constitution of VMI comes squarely within such a governing tradition. For almost all of VMI's more than a century and a half of existence, its single-sex status reflected the uniform practice for government-supported military colleges.

[To] reject the Court's disposition today, however, it is [only] necessary to apply honestly the test the Court has been applying to sex-based classifications for the past two decades. [Only] the amorphous "exceedingly persuasive justification" phrase, and not the standard elaboration of intermediate scrutiny, can be made to yield [the] conclusion that VMI's single-sex composition is unconstitutional because there exist several women (or, one would have to conclude under the Court's reasoning, a single woman) willing and able to undertake VMI's program. Intermediate scrutiny has never required a least-restrictive-means analysis, but only a "substantial relation" between the classification and the state interests that it serves.

[It] is beyond question that Virginia has an important state interest in providing effective college education for its citizens. That single-sex instruction is an approach substantially related to that interest should be evident enough from the long and continuing history in this country of men's and women's colleges. But beyond that, [there was] "virtually uncontradicted" [expert evidence introduced in this case tending to show the benefits of single-sex education].

[Besides] its single-sex constitution, VMI [employs] a "distinctive educational method," sometimes referred to as the "adversative, or doubting, model of education." [It] was uncontested that "if the state were to establish a women's VMI-type [i.e., adversative] program, the program would attract an insufficient number of participants to make the program work"; and it was found by the District Court that if Virginia were to include women in VMI, the school "would eventually find it necessary to drop the adversative system altogether." Thus, Virginia's options were an adversative method that excludes women or no adversative method at all.

There can be no serious dispute that single-sex education and a distinctive educational method "represent legitimate contributions to diversity in the Virginia higher education system." As a theoretical matter, Virginia's educational interest would have been best served (insofar as the two factors we have mentioned are concerned) by six different types of public colleges—an all-men's, an all-women's, and a coeducational college run in the "adversative method," and an all-men's, an all-women's, and a coeducational college run in the "traditional method." But as a practical matter, of course, Virginia's financial resources, like any State's, are not limitless, and the Commonwealth must select among the available options. [In] these circumstances, Virginia's election to fund one public all-male institution and one on the adversative model—and to concentrate its resources in a single entity that serves both these interests in diversity—is substantially related to the State's important educational interests.

[The] Court argues that VMI would not have to change very much if it were to admit women. The principal response to that argument is that it is irrelevant: If VMI's single-sex status is substantially related to the government's important educational objectives, as I have demonstrated above and as the Court refuses to discuss, that concludes the inquiry. [But] if such a debate were relevant, the Court would certainly be on the losing side.

[Finally], the absence of a precise "all-women's analogue" to VMI is irrelevant. [VWIL] was carefully designed by professional educators who have long experience in educating young women. [None] of the United States' own experts in the remedial phase of this case was willing to testify that VMI's adversative method was an appropriate methodology for educating women.

[The] Court's decision today will have consequences that extend far beyond the parties to the case. [Under] the constitutional principles announced and applied today, single-sex public education is unconstitutional. [Although] the Court [purports] to have said nothing of relevance to other public schools [and to have considered] only an educational opportunity recognized [as] "unique," [footnote 7, supra], I suggest that the single-sex program that will not be capable of being characterized as "unique" is not only unique but nonexistent.

[A broader] potential of today's decision for widespread disruption of existing institutions lies in its application to private single-sex education. Government support is immensely important to private educational institutions. [When government funding is challenged, the] issue will be not whether government assistance turns private colleges into state actors, but whether the government itself would be violating the Constitution by providing state support to single-sex colleges. For example, in *Norwood v. Harrison*, [Ch. 10, Sec. 3 infra], we saw no room to distinguish between state operation of racially segregated schools and state support of privately run segregated schools. [The] only hope for state-assisted single-sex private schools is that the Court will not apply in the future the principles of law it has applied today. * * *

II.　DIFFERENCES—REAL AND IMAGINED

Whatever standard of scrutiny applies, the Court has consistently assumed that differences between men and women sometimes justify different treatment. But a recurrent problem has been to distinguish "real" differences and permissible distinctions based upon them from impermissible reliance on and reinforcement of gender-based stereotypes. As you read the cases in this section, consider how consistent and successful the Court's efforts have been, and how much the Court has been aided—if at all—by the doctrinal tests that it has purported to apply.

———

GEDULDIG v. AIELLO, 417 U.S. 484 (1974), per STEWART, J., held that exclusion of "disability that accompanies normal pregnancy and childbirth" from California's disability insurance system "does not exclude [anyone] because of gender * * * . While it is true that only women can become pregnant, it does not follow that every legislative classification concerning pregnancy is [sex-based]. Absent a showing that distinctions involving pregnancy are mere pretexts designed to effect an invidious discrimination against the members of one sex or the other, lawmakers are constitutionally free to include or exclude pregnancy from the coverage of legislation such as this on any reasonable basis, just as with respect to any other physical condition. [The] program divides potential recipients into two groups—pregnant women and nonpregnant persons. While the first group is exclusively female, the second includes members of both sexes. The fiscal and actuarial benefits of the program thus accrue to members of both sexes. [There] is no risk from which men are protected and women are not. Likewise, there is no risk from which women are protected and men are not.[21]"

BRENNAN, J., joined by Douglas and Marshall, JJ., dissented, finding "sex discrimination" in the state's "singling out for less favorable treatment a gender-linked disability peculiar to women [while] men receive full compensation for all

———

[21]　[Ct's Note] Indeed, the [data indicated] that both the annual claim rate and the annual claim cost are greater for women than for [men.]

disabilities suffered, including those that affect only or primarily their sex, such as prostatectomies, circumcision, hemophilia and gout."[25]

———

NGUYEN v. INS, 533 U.S. 53 (2001), upheld a provision of the Immigration and Naturalization Act that distinguishes between American citizen mothers and American citizen fathers who are the parents of out-of-wedlock children born abroad: Whereas the mothers pass their American citizenship automatically to their out-of-wedlock offspring, the statute establishes various procedural barriers before the nonmarital child of a citizen father can become a citizen. Writing for the Court, KENNEDY, J., recognized that heightened scrutiny applied, but he found the different treatment of mothers and fathers of out-of-wedlock children to be substantially related to two important governmental interests: "assuring that a biological parent-child relationship exists" and "ensur[ing] that the child and the citizen parent have some demonstrated opportunity or potential to develop [a] relationship [that] consists of the real, everyday ties that provide a connection between child and citizen parent and, in turn, the United States. In the case of a citizen mother and a child born overseas, the opportunity for a meaningful relationship between citizen parent and child inheres in the very event of birth, an event so critical to our constitutional and statutory understandings of citizenship. The mother knows that the child is in being and is hers and has an initial point of contact with him. * * *

"To fail to acknowledge even our most basic biological differences—such as the fact that a mother must be present at birth but the father need not be—risks making the guarantee of equal protection superficial, and so disserving it."

O'CONNOR, J., joined by Souter, Ginsburg, and Breyer, JJ., dissented: "While the Court invokes heightened scrutiny, the manner in which it [applies] this standard is a stranger to our precedents." According to O'Connor, J., no real differences justified the differential treatment. As a result of "[m]odern DNA testing," it was not substantially more difficult to determine biological fatherhood than motherhood in most cases. And if Congress cared about parent-child relationships, it "could require some degree of regular contact between the child and the citizen parent over a period of time" in order for either a mother or a father to be able to pass on American citizenship to an illegitimate child born abroad: "[The statute] finds support not in biological differences but instead in a stereotype—i.e., 'the generalization that mothers are significantly more likely than fathers [to] develop caring relationships with their children.' [No] one should mistake the majority's analysis for a careful application of this Court's equal protection jurisprudence concerning sex-based classifications. Today's decision instead represents a deviation from a line of cases in which we have vigilantly applied heightened scrutiny."

---

[25]   Cf. *Cleveland Bd. of Educ. v. LaFleur*, 414 U.S. 632 (1974) (invalidating a requirement that pregnant teachers go on leave on the ground that an "irrebuttable presumption" of inability to teach during pregnancy violated due process).

Do you agree? Does the Court's decision at least indicate—contrary to the conclusion that some had drawn from *United States v. Virginia*, supra—that the Justices remain far more tolerant of gender-based than of race-based discriminations? Consider William N. Eskridge, Jr., *Some Effects of Identity-Based Social Movements on Constitutional Law in the Twentieth Century*, 100 Mich.L.Rev. 2062 (2002): "The Court's disposition[ ] reflects the continued difference between race and sex distinctions in equality jurisprudence. Is there much doubt that the Court would have overturned a law making one's citizenship turn in any way on the race of one's American (or non-American) parent?"

———

SESSIONS v. MORALES-SANTANA, 137 S.Ct. 1678 (2017), invalidated a provision of the Immigration and Nationality Act that gave unmarried mothers who are U.S. citizens a preference over unmarried citizen fathers and even married citizen couples in passing on U.S. citizenship to children born outside the U.S. The provision conditioned the capacity to pass on citizenship to offspring born abroad on a citizen's having resided in the U.S. for a number of years, but required fewer years for unwed citizen mothers than for other citizen parents. GINSBURG, J., reasoned: "Prescribing one rule for mothers, another for fathers, [requires] an 'exceedingly persuasive justification.' [Moreover], the classification must substantially serve an important governmental interest *today*, for 'in interpreting the [e]qual [p]rotection [guarantee], [we have] recognized that new insights and societal understandings can reveal unjustified inequality . . . that once passed unnoticed and unchallenged.' [No] 'important [governmental] interest' is served by laws grounded [in] the obsolescing view that 'unwed fathers [are] invariably less qualified and entitled than mothers' to take responsibility for nonmarital children. Overbroad generalizations of that order [have] a constraining impact, descriptive though they may be of the way many people still order their lives.[13] Laws according or denying benefits in reliance on '[s]tereotypes about women's domestic roles' [may] 'creat[e] a self-fulfilling cycle of discrimination that force[s] women to continue to assume the role of primary family caregiver.'

"[A] man needs no more time in the United States than a woman 'in order to have assimilated citizenship-related values to transmit to [his] child.' " The Court rejected the argument that because an "unwed mother [is] the child's only 'legally recognized' parent at the time of childbirth[, a] longer physical connection to the United States is warranted for the unwed father [to counteract] the 'competing national influence' of the alien mother. [One] cannot see in this driven-by-gender scheme the close means-end fit required to survive heightened scrutiny." The Government also argued that "[Congress] established the gender-based residency differential [in order to] reduce the risk that a foreign-born child of a U.S. citizen would be born stateless. [But] there is little reason to believe that a statelessness

---

[13] **[Ct's Note]** "Even if stereotypes frozen into legislation have 'statistical support,' our decisions reject measures that classify unnecessarily and overbroadly by gender when more accurate and impartial lines can be drawn."

concern prompted the diverse physical-presence requirements. Nor has the Government shown that the risk of statelessness disproportionately endangered the children of unwed mothers."

Ginsburg, J., distinguished *Nguyen* on the ground that it involved the legitimacy of a "paternal-acknowledgment requirement on fathers" as a means of establishing "a biological parent-child relationship" that the Government did not dispute.

III. "BENIGN" OR "REMEDIAL" DISCRIMINATION

CALIFANO V. WEBSTER
430 U.S. 313, 97 S.Ct. 1192, 51 L.Ed.2d 360 (1977).

PER CURIAM.

[Social Security Act § 215(b)(3)'s formula—which has since been amended—afforded the chance of higher old-age benefits to female wage earners than to similarly situated males.]

To withstand scrutiny under [equal protection], "classifications by gender must serve important governmental objectives and must be substantially related to achievement of those objectives." *Craig*. Reduction of the disparity in economic condition between men and women caused by the long history of discrimination against women has been recognized as such an important governmental objective. *Schlesinger v. Ballard*, 419 U.S. 498 (1975);[26] *Kahn v. Shevin*, 416 U.S. 351 (1974).[27] But "the mere recitation of a benign, compensatory purpose is not an automatic shield which protects against any inquiry into the actual purposes underlying a statutory scheme." *Weinberger v. Wiesenfeld*, 420 U.S. 636 (1975).[28] Accordingly, we have rejected attempts to justify gender classifications as compensation for past discrimination against women when the classifications in

---

[26]   *Schlesinger*, per Stewart, J., upheld a federal statute providing for the discharge of naval "line" officers who had not been promoted for nine years (males) or thirteen years (females): Because of Navy restrictions on combat and sea duty for women, "Congress [may] quite rationally have believed that women line officers had less opportunity for promotion than did their male counterparts, and that a longer period of tenure for women officers would, therefore, be consistent with the goal to provide women officers with 'fair and equitable career advancement programs.' "

[27]   *Kahn*, per Douglas, J., upheld a property tax exemption for widows (but not widowers) on the ground that the law was "reasonably designed to further the state policy of cushioning the financial impact of spousal loss upon the sex for whom that loss imposes a disproportionately heavy burden."

[28]   *Weinberger*, per Brennan, J., held that Social Security Act § 402(g)'s payment of benefits to the wife—but not to the husband—of a deceased wage earner with minor children violated equal protection because it "unjustifiably discriminated against women wage-earners": as in *Frontiero*, an " 'archaic and overbroad' generalization [underlies] the distinction drawn by § 402(g), namely, that male [but not female] workers' earnings are vital to the support of their families." Unlike in *Kahn*, "[i]t is apparent both from the statutory scheme itself and from the legislative history of § 402(g) that Congress' purpose [was] not to provide an income to women who were, because of economic discrimination, unable to provide for themselves."

fact penalized women wage earners, *Califano v. Goldfarb,* 430 U.S. 199 (1977);[29] *Wiesenfeld,* or when the statutory structure and its legislative history revealed that the classification was not enacted as compensation for past discrimination. *Goldfarb; Wiesenfeld.*

[The] more favorable treatment of the female wage earner enacted here was not a result of "archaic and overbroad generalizations" about women, or of "the role-typing society has long imposed" upon women such as casual assumptions that women are "the weaker sex" or are more likely to be child-rearers or dependents. Rather, "the only discernible purpose of [§ 215's more favorable treatment is] the permissible one of redressing our society's longstanding disparate treatment of women." *Goldfarb.*

The challenged statute operated directly to compensate women for past economic discrimination. Retirement benefits [are] based on past earnings. But as we have recognized: "Whether from overt discrimination or from the socialization process of a male-dominated culture, the job market is inhospitable to the woman seeking any but the lowest paid jobs." *Kahn.* Thus, allowing women, who as such have been unfairly hindered from earning as much as men, to eliminate additional low-earning years from the calculation of their retirement benefits works directly to remedy some part of the effect of past discrimination.[5]

[T]he legislative history is clear that the differing treatment of men and women in former § 215(b)(3) was not "the accidental byproduct of a traditional way of thinking about females," *Goldfarb* (Stevens, J., concurring in the result), but rather was deliberately enacted to compensate for particular economic disabilities suffered by women. * * *

Reversed.

CHIEF JUSTICE BURGER, with whom JUSTICE STEWART, JUSTICE BLACKMUN, and JUSTICE REHNQUIST join, concurring in the judgment.

* * * I question whether certainty in the law is promoted by hinging the validity of important statutory schemes on whether five Justices view them to be more akin to the "offensive" provisions struck down in *Wiesenfeld* and *Frontiero,* or more like the "benign" provisions upheld in *Ballard* and *Kahn.* I therefore concur in the judgment [for] reasons stated by Mr. Justice Rehnquist in his dissenting opinion in *Goldfarb*: ["Favoring aged widows is scarcely an invidious discrimination. [It] in no way perpetuates the economic discrimination which has been the basis for heightened scrutiny of gender-based classifications, and is, in fact, explainable as a measure to ameliorate the characteristically depressed condition of aged widows."]

---

[29]   *Goldfarb* held that Social Security Act § 402(f)'s payment of benefits to a widow of a covered employee, but not to a widower unless he proves dependency on his deceased wife-employee, violated equal protection.

[5]   **[Ct's Note]** Even with the advantage[,] women on the average received lower retirement benefits than men. "As of December 1972, the average monthly retirement insurance benefit for males was $179.60 and for females, $140.50."

MISSISSIPPI UNIV. FOR WOMEN V. HOGAN

458 U.S. 718, 102 S.Ct. 3331, 73 L.Ed.2d 1090 (1982).

JUSTICE O'CONNOR delivered the opinion of the Court.

[Mississippi University for Women ("MUW"), "the oldest state-supported all-female college in the United States," denied Hogan admission to its School of Nursing solely because of his sex.[30]] Our decisions [establish] that the party seeking to uphold a statute that classifies individuals on the basis of their gender must carry the burden of showing an "exceedingly persuasive justification" for the classification. The burden is met only by showing at least that the classification serves "important governmental objectives and that the discriminatory means employed" are "substantially related to the achievement of those objectives."[9] * * *

The State's primary justification for maintaining the single-sex admissions policy of MUW's School of Nursing is that it compensates for discrimination against women and, therefore, constitutes educational affirmative action. [A] state can evoke a compensatory purpose to justify an otherwise discriminatory classification only if members of the gender benefited by the classification actually suffer a disadvantage related to the classification. We considered such a situation in *Webster* [and *Ballard*].

In sharp contrast, Mississippi has made no showing that women lacked opportunities to obtain training in the field of nursing or to attain positions of leadership in that field when the MUW School of Nursing opened its door or that women currently are deprived of such opportunities. In fact, in 1970, the year before the School of Nursing's first class enrolled, women earned 94 percent of the nursing baccalaureate degrees conferred in Mississippi and 98.6 percent of the degrees earned nationwide.

Rather than compensate for discriminatory barriers faced by women, MUW's [policy] tends to perpetuate the stereotyped view of nursing as an exclusively woman's job.[15] By assuring that Mississippi allots more openings in its state-supported nursing schools to women than it does to men, MUW's admissions policy lends credibility to the old view that women, not men, should become nurses, and makes the assumption that nursing is a field for women a self-fulfilling prophecy. Thus, we conclude that, although the State recited a "benign, compensatory purpose," it failed to establish that the alleged objective is the actual purpose underlying the discriminatory classification.

---

[30]   The Court declined "to address the question of whether MUW's admissions policy, as applied to males seeking admission to schools other than the School of Nursing, violates the Fourteenth Amendment."

[9]   [Ct's Note] [Because] we conclude that the challenged statutory classification is not substantially related to an important objective, we need not decide whether classifications based upon gender are inherently suspect.

[15]   [Ct's Note] Officials of the American Nurses Association have suggested that excluding men from the field has depressed nurses' wages. To the extent the exclusion of men has that effect, MUW's admissions policy actually penalizes the very class the State purports to benefit. Cf. *Wiesenfeld*.

The policy is invalid also because [the] State has made no showing that the gender-based classification is substantially and directly related to its proposed compensatory objective. To the contrary, MUW's policy of permitting men to attend classes as auditors fatally undermines its claim that women, at least those in the School of Nursing, are adversely affected by the presence of men.

Affirmed.

CHIEF JUSTICE BURGER, dissenting.

I agree generally with Justice Powell's dissenting opinion. I write separately, however, to emphasize that [s]ince the Court's opinion relies heavily on its finding that women have traditionally dominated the nursing profession, it suggests that a State might well be justified in maintaining, for example, the option of an all-women's business school or liberal arts program.

JUSTICE POWELL, with whom JUSTICE REHNQUIST joins, dissenting.[31]

[T]he Court errs seriously by assuming [that] the equal protection standard generally applicable to sex discrimination is appropriate here. That standard was designed to free women from "archaic and overbroad generalizations." *Ballard.* In no previous case have we applied it to invalidate state efforts to *expand* women's choices. * * *

By applying heightened equal protection analysis to this case, the Court frustrates the liberating spirit of the Equal Protection Clause. It forbids the States from providing women with an opportunity to choose the type of university they prefer. And yet it is these women whom the Court regards as the *victims* of an illegal, stereotyped perception of the role of women in our society. The Court reasons this way in a case in which no woman has complained, and the only complainant is a man who advances no claims on behalf of anyone else. His claim [is] not that he is being denied a substantive educational opportunity, or even the right to attend an all-male or a coeducational college. It is *only* that the colleges open to him are located at inconvenient distances.

* * * I would sustain Mississippi's right to continue MUW on a rational basis analysis. But I need not apply this "lowest tier" of scrutiny. [More] than 2,000 women presently evidence their preference for MUW by having enrolled [there.] Generations of our finest minds, both among educators and students, have believed that single-sex, college-level institutions afford distinctive benefits. There are many persons, of course, who have different views. But simply because there are these differences is no reason—certainly none of constitutional dimension—to conclude that no substantial state interest is served when such a choice is made available.

---

[31]   Blackmun, J.'s brief dissent—agreeing essentially with Powell, J.—is omitted.

NOTE

"Affirmative action" preferences for women. Does *Webster* suggest that classifications enacted to remedy past discrimination against women will be tested under "intermediate" scrutiny, rather than the strict scrutiny applicable to race-based affirmative action? Does *Hogan* alter or supplement the framework for analysis? Consider, too, the possible relevance of *United States v. Virginia,* in which the Court said: "Sex classifications may be used to compensate women 'for particular economic disabilities [they have] suffered,' *Califano v. Webster,* to 'promote equal employment opportunity, see *California Federal Sav. & Loan Assn. v. Guerra,* [and] to advance full development of the talent and capacities of our Nation's people. But such classifications may not be used, as they once were, to create or perpetuate the legal, social, and economic inferiority of women."

4. SPECIAL SCRUTINY FOR OTHER CLASSIFICATIONS: DOCTRINE AND DEBATES

Are there other classifications besides race and gender that should be subject to special scrutiny? If so, by what criteria should they be identified?

I. SEXUAL ORIENTATION

ROMER V. EVANS
517 U.S. 620, 116 S.Ct. 1620, 134 L.Ed.2d 855 (1996).

JUSTICE KENNEDY delivered the opinion of the Court.

One century ago, the first Justice Harlan admonished this Court that the Constitution "neither knows nor tolerates classes among citizens." *Plessy v. Ferguson* (dissenting opinion). [T]his principle [requires] us to hold invalid a provision of Colorado's Constitution.

[The] enactment challenged in this case is an amendment to the Constitution of the State of Colorado, adopted in a 1992 statewide referendum [and referred to] as "Amendment 2." [It] reads: "No Protected Status Based on Homosexual, Lesbian, or Bisexual Orientation. Neither the State of Colorado, through any of its branches or departments, nor any of its agencies, political subdivisions, municipalities or school districts, shall enact, adopt or enforce any statute, regulation, ordinance or policy whereby homosexual, lesbian or bisexual orientation, conduct, practices or relationships shall constitute or otherwise be the basis of or entitle any person or class of persons to have or claim any minority status, quota preferences, protected status or claim of discrimination. This Section of the Constitution shall be in all respects self-executing."

[The] State's principal argument in defense of Amendment 2 is that it puts gays and lesbians in the same position as all other persons. So, the State says, the measure does no more than deny homosexuals special rights. This reading of the amendment's language is implausible. We rely not upon our own interpretation of the amendment but upon the authoritative construction of Colorado's Supreme Court, [which held that] "The immediate objective of Amendment 2 is, at a minimum, to repeal existing statutes, regulations, ordinances, and policies of state and local entities that barred discrimination based on sexual orientation." [Under Amendment 2 as thus construed, homosexuals], by state decree, are put in a solitary class with respect to transactions and relations in both the private and governmental spheres. The amendment withdraws from homosexuals, but no others, specific legal protection from the injuries caused by discrimination, and it forbids reinstatement of these laws and policies.

The change that Amendment 2 works in the legal status of gays and lesbians in the private sphere is far-reaching, both on its own terms and when considered in light of the structure and operation of modern antidiscrimination laws. "[At] common law, innkeepers, smiths, and others who 'made profession of a public employment,' were prohibited from refusing, without good reason, to serve a customer." The duty was a general one and did not specify protection for particular groups. The common law rules, however, proved insufficient in many instances, and [most] States have chosen to counter discrimination by enacting detailed statutory schemes.

Colorado's state and municipal laws typify this emerging tradition of statutory protection and follow a consistent pattern. The laws first enumerate the persons or entities subject to a duty not to discriminate. [The] Boulder ordinance, for example, include[s] "any place of business engaged in any sales to the general public and any place that offers services, facilities, privileges, or advantages to the general public or that receives financial support through solicitation of the general public or through governmental subsidy of any kind."

[These] statutes and ordinances also depart from the common law by enumerating the groups or persons within their ambit of protection. [In] following this approach, Colorado's state and local governments have not limited anti-discrimination laws to groups that have so far been given the protection of heightened equal protection scrutiny under our cases. [They] [include] age, military status, marital status, pregnancy, parenthood, custody of a minor child, political affiliation, physical or mental disability of an individual or of his or her associates—and, in recent times, sexual orientation.

Amendment 2 bars homosexuals from securing protection against the injuries that these public-accommodations laws address. That in itself is a severe consequence, but there is more. Amendment 2, in addition, nullifies specific legal protections for this targeted class in all transactions in housing, sale of real estate, insurance, health and welfare services, private education, and employment.

[Not] confined to the private sphere, Amendment 2 also operates to repeal and forbid all laws or policies providing specific protection for gays or lesbians from discrimination by every level of Colorado government. The State Supreme Court cited two examples of protections in the governmental sphere that are now rescinded and may not be reintroduced. The first is [an] Executive Order which forbids employment discrimination against " 'all state employees, classified and exempt' on the basis of sexual orientation." Also repealed, and now forbidden, are "various provisions prohibiting discrimination based on sexual orientation at state colleges."

Amendment 2's reach may not be limited to specific laws passed for the benefit of gays and lesbians. It is a fair, if not necessary, inference from the broad language of the amendment that it deprives gays and lesbians even of the protection of general laws and policies that prohibit arbitrary discrimination [such as statutes subjecting agency action to judicial review under the arbitrary and capricious standard and making it a criminal offense for a public servant knowingly, arbitrarily, or capriciously to refrain from performing a duty imposed by law]. At some point in the systematic administration of these laws, an official must determine whether homosexuality is an arbitrary and thus forbidden basis for decision. Yet a decision to that effect would itself amount to a policy prohibiting discrimination on the basis of homosexuality, and so would appear to be no more valid under Amendment 2 than the specific prohibitions against discrimination the state court held invalid.

[The] state court did not decide whether the amendment has this effect, however, and neither need we. [Even] if, as we doubt, homosexuals could find some safe harbor in laws of general application, we cannot accept the view that Amendment 2's prohibition on specific legal protections does no more than deprive homosexuals of special rights. To the contrary, the amendment imposes a special disability upon those persons alone. Homosexuals are forbidden the safeguards that others enjoy or may seek without constraint. They can obtain specific protection against discrimination only by enlisting the citizenry of Colorado to amend the state constitution or perhaps, on the State's view, by trying to pass helpful laws of general applicability. This is so no matter how local or discrete the harm, no matter how public and widespread the injury. We find nothing special in the protections Amendment 2 withholds. These are protections taken for granted by most people either because they already have them or do not need them; these are protections against exclusion from an almost limitless number of transactions and endeavors that constitute ordinary civic life in a free society.

[If] a law neither burdens a fundamental right nor targets a suspect class, we will uphold the legislative classification so long as it bears a rational relation to some legitimate end. Amendment 2 fails, indeed defies, even this conventional inquiry.

[It] is at once too narrow and too broad. It identifies persons by a single trait and then denies them protection across the board. [It] is not within our constitutional tradition to enact laws of this sort. Central both to the idea of the rule of law and to our own Constitution's guarantee of equal protection is the principle that government and each of its parts remain open on impartial terms to all who seek its assistance. [Respect] for this principle explains why laws singling out a certain class of citizens for disfavored legal status or general hardships are rare. A law declaring that in general it shall be more difficult for one group of citizens than for all others to seek aid from the government is itself a denial of equal protection of the laws in the most literal sense. * * *

[A] second and related point is that laws of the kind now before us raise the inevitable inference that the disadvantage imposed is born of animosity toward the class of persons affected. "[I]f the constitutional conception of 'equal protection of the laws' means anything, it must at the very least mean that a bare * * * desire to harm a politically unpopular group cannot constitute a *legitimate* governmental interest." *Moreno*, [Sec. 1 supra]. Even laws enacted for broad and ambitious purposes often can be explained by reference to legitimate public policies which justify the incidental disadvantages they impose on certain persons. Amendment 2, however, in making a general announcement that gays and lesbians shall not have any particular protections from the law, inflicts on them immediate, continuing, and real injuries that outrun and belie any legitimate justifications that may be claimed for it.

[The] primary rationale the State offers for Amendment 2 is respect for other citizens' freedom of association, and in particular the liberties of landlords or employers who have personal or religious objections to homosexuality. Colorado also cites its interest in conserving resources to fight discrimination against other groups. The breadth of the Amendment is so far removed from these particular justifications that we find it impossible to credit them. [It] is a status-based enactment divorced from any factual context from which we could discern a relationship to legitimate state interests; it is a classification of persons undertaken for its own sake, something the Equal Protection Clause does not permit. * * *

JUSTICE SCALIA, with whom THE CHIEF JUSTICE and JUSTICE THOMAS join, dissenting.

[In] rejecting the State's arguments that Amendment 2 "puts gays and lesbians in the same position as all other persons," and "does no more than deny homosexuals special rights," [the] Court considers it unnecessary to decide the validity of the State's argument that Amendment 2 does not deprive homosexuals of the "protection [afforded by] general laws and policies that prohibit arbitrary discrimination in governmental and private settings." I agree that we need not resolve that dispute, because the Supreme Court of Colorado has resolved it for us. [The] Colorado court stated: "[I]t is significant to note that Colorado law currently proscribes discrimination against persons who are not suspect classes, including discrimination based on age, marital or family status, veterans' status, and for any legal, off-duty conduct such as smoking tobacco. *Of course Amendment 2 is not intended to have any effect on this legislation, but seeks only to prevent the adoption of antidiscrimination laws intended to protect gays, lesbians, and bisexuals.*" (emphasis added). [This] analysis, which is fully in accord with (indeed, follows inescapably from) the text of the constitutional provision, lays to rest such horribles [as] the prospect that assaults upon homosexuals could not be prosecuted. The amendment prohibits *special treatment* of homosexuals, and nothing more. It would not affect, for example, a requirement of state law that pensions be paid to all retiring state employees with a certain length of service; homosexual employees, as well as others, would be entitled to that benefit. But it would prevent the State or any municipality from making death-benefit payments to the "life partner" of a homosexual when it does not make such payments to the long-time roommate of a nonhomosexual employee.

[Despite] all of its hand-wringing about the potential effect of Amendment 2 on general antidiscrimination laws, the Court's opinion ultimately does not dispute all this, but assumes it to be true. The only denial of equal treatment it contends homosexuals have suffered is this: They may not obtain *preferential* treatment without amending the state constitution. That is to say, the principle underlying the Court's opinion is that one who is accorded equal treatment under the laws, but cannot as readily as others obtain *preferential* treatment under the laws, has been denied equal protection of the laws. If merely stating this alleged "equal protection" violation does not suffice to refute it, our constitutional jurisprudence has achieved terminal silliness.

The central thesis of the Court's reasoning is that any group is denied equal protection when, to obtain advantage (or, presumably, to avoid disadvantage), it must have recourse to a more general and hence more difficult level of political decisionmaking than others. The world has never heard of such a principle, which is why the Court's opinion is so long on emotive utterance and so short on relevant legal citation. And it seems to me most unlikely that any multilevel democracy can function under such a principle. For *whenever* a disadvantage is imposed, or conferral of a benefit is prohibited, at one of the higher levels of democratic decisionmaking (i.e., by the state legislature rather than local government, or by the people at large in the state constitution rather than the legislature), the affected group has (under this theory) been denied equal protection. To take the simplest of examples, consider a state law prohibiting the award of municipal contracts to relatives of mayors or city councilmen. Once such a law is passed, the group composed of such relatives must, in order to get the benefit of city contracts, persuade the state legislature—unlike all other citizens, who need only persuade the municipality. It is ridiculous to consider this a denial of equal protection, which is why the Court's theory is unheard of. * * *

I turn next to whether there was a legitimate rational basis for the substance of the constitutional amendment—for the prohibition of special protection for homosexuals.[1] It is unsurprising that the Court avoids discussion of this question, since the answer is so obviously yes. The case most relevant to the issue before us

---

[1]   **[Ct's Note]** The Court evidently agrees that "rational basis"—the normal test for compliance with the Equal Protection Clause—is the governing standard. The trial court rejected respondents' argument that homosexuals constitute a "suspect" or "quasi-suspect" class, and respondents elected not to appeal that ruling to the Supreme Court of Colorado. And the Court implicitly rejects the Supreme Court of Colorado's holding that Amendment 2 infringes upon a "fundamental right" of "independently identifiable class[es]" to "participate equally in the political process."

today is not even mentioned in the Court's opinion: In *Bowers v. Hardwick*, [Ch. 6, Sec. 4 supra], we held that the Constitution does not prohibit what virtually all States had done from the founding of the Republic until very recent years—making homosexual conduct a crime. [If] it is constitutionally permissible for a State to make homosexual conduct criminal, surely it is constitutionally permissible for a State to enact other laws merely *disfavoring* homosexual conduct. [And] a fortiori it is constitutionally permissible for a State to adopt a provision *not even* disfavoring homosexual conduct, but merely prohibiting all levels of state government from bestowing *special protections* upon homosexual conduct. Respondents (who, unlike the Court, cannot afford the luxury of ignoring inconvenient precedent) counter *Bowers* with the argument that a greater-includes-the-lesser rationale cannot justify Amendment 2's application to individuals who do not engage in homosexual acts, but are merely of homosexual "orientation."

[Assuming] that, in Amendment 2, a person of homosexual "orientation" is someone who does not engage in homosexual conduct but merely has a tendency or desire to do so, *Bowers* still suffices to establish a rational basis for the provision. If it is rational to criminalize the conduct, surely it is rational to deny special favor and protection to those with a self-avowed tendency or desire to engage in the conduct.

[The] Court's opinion contains grim, disapproving hints that Coloradans have been guilty of "animus" or "animosity" toward homosexuality, as though that has been established as Unamerican. Of course it is our moral heritage that one should not hate any human being or class of human beings. But I had thought that one could consider certain conduct reprehensible—murder, for example, or polygamy, or cruelty to animals—and could exhibit even "animus" toward such conduct. Surely that is the only sort of "animus" at issue here: moral disapproval of homosexual conduct, the same sort of moral disapproval that produced the centuries-old criminal laws that we held constitutional in *Bowers*.

[But] though Coloradans are, as I say, *entitled* to be hostile toward homosexual conduct, the fact is that the degree of hostility reflected by Amendment 2 is the smallest conceivable.

[The] constitutions of the States of Arizona, Idaho, New Mexico, Oklahoma, and Utah *to this day* contain provisions stating that polygamy is "forever prohibited." Polygamists, and those who have a polygamous "orientation," have been "singled out" by these provisions for much more severe treatment than merely denial of favored status; and that treatment can only be changed by achieving amendment of the state constitutions. The Court's disposition today suggests that these provisions are unconstitutional, and that polygamy must be permitted in these States on a state-legislated, or perhaps even local-option, basis—unless, of course, polygamists for some reason have fewer constitutional rights than homosexuals.

[To] suggest [that] this constitutional amendment springs from nothing more than " 'a bare * * * desire to harm a politically unpopular group,' " is nothing short of insulting. (It is also nothing short of preposterous to call "politically unpopular" a group which enjoys enormous influence in American media and politics, and which, as the trial court here noted, though composing no more than 4% of the population had the support of 46% of the voters on Amendment 2.) [When] the Court takes sides in the culture wars, it tends to be with the knights rather than the villeins—and more specifically with the Templars, reflecting the views and values of the lawyer class from which the Court's Members are drawn. How that class feels about homosexuality will be evident to anyone who wishes to interview job applicants at virtually any of the Nation's law schools. The interviewer may refuse to offer a job because the applicant is a Republican; because he is an adulterer; [or] because he went to the wrong prep school or belongs to the wrong country club. But if the interviewer should wish not to be an associate or partner of an applicant because he disapproves of the applicant's homosexuality, *then* he will have violated the pledge which the Association of American Law Schools requires all its member-schools to exact from job interviewers: "assurance of the employer's willingness" to hire homosexuals. This law-school view of what "prejudices" must be stamped out may be contrasted with the more plebeian attitudes that apparently still prevail in the United States Congress, which has been unresponsive to repeated attempts to extend to homosexuals the protections of federal civil rights laws. * * *

———

LAWRENCE v. TEXAS, Ch. 6, Sec. 4 supra, per KENNEDY, J., overruled *Bowers* and held that a Texas statute prohibiting homosexual but not heterosexual sodomy lacked a legitimate purpose and violated a liberty right protected under the Due Process Clause. The Court passed quickly by an equal protection argument: "[P]etitioners [contend] that *Romer* provides the basis for declaring the Texas statute invalid under the Equal Protection Clause. That is a tenable argument, but we conclude the instant case requires us to address whether *Bowers* [has] continuing validity." In characterizing the equal protection argument as "tenable," did the majority endorse it?

O'CONNOR, J., concurring, would have put the decision wholly on equal protection grounds: "When a law exhibits [a bare] desire to harm a politically unpopular group, we have applied a more searching form of rational basis review to strike down such laws under the Equal Protection Clause. [And we] have been most likely to apply rational basis review to hold a law unconstitutional under the Equal Protection Clause where, as here, the challenged legislation inhibits personal relationships. [O'Connor, J., here cited, inter alia, *Moreno*, *Eisenstadt v. Baird*, and *Romer*.] The statute at issue here [treats] the same conduct differently based solely on the participants. Those harmed by this law are people who have a same-sex sexual orientation. [The] Texas statute makes homosexuals unequal in the eyes of the law by making particular conduct—and only that conduct—subject to criminal sanction. [Texas] attempts to justify its law [by] arguing that the statute satisfies rational basis review because it furthers the legitimate governmental interest of the promotion of morality. In *Bowers*, we [rejected] the argument that no rational basis existed to justify [a prohibition against sodomy], pointing to the government's interest in promoting morality. [But] *Bowers* did not hold that moral disapproval of a group is a rational basis under the Equal Protection Clause to criminalize homosexual sodomy when heterosexual sodomy is not punished. [Moral] disapproval of a group cannot be a legitimate governmental interest under the Equal Protection Clause because legal classifications must not be 'drawn for the purpose of disadvantaging the group burdened by the law.' Texas' invocation of moral disapproval as a legitimate state interest proves nothing more than Texas' desire to criminalize homosexual sodomy. But the Equal Protection Clause prevents a State from creating 'a classification of persons undertaken for its own sake.'

"Texas argues [that] the law discriminates only against homosexual conduct. While it is true that the law applies only to conduct, the conduct targeted by this law is conduct that is closely correlated with being homosexual. Under such circumstances, Texas' sodomy law is targeted at more than conduct. It is instead directed toward gay persons as a class."

SCALIA, J., joined by Rehnquist, C.J., and Thomas, J., dissenting, rejected the equal protection as well as the due process argument: "On its face [the challenged statute] applies equally to all persons. [To] be sure, § 21.06 does distinguish between the sexes insofar as concerns the partner with whom the sexual acts are performed: men can violate the law only with other men, and women only with other women. But this cannot itself be a denial of equal protection, since it is precisely the same distinction regarding partner that is drawn in state laws prohibiting marriage with someone of the same sex while permitting marriage with someone of the opposite sex.

"Justice O'Connor argues that [this law discriminates] with regard to the sexual proclivity of the principal actor. [But a similar claim could be made about] any law. A law against public nudity targets 'the conduct that is closely correlated with being a nudist,' and hence 'is targeted at more than conduct'; it is 'directed toward nudists as a class.' But be that as it may. Even if the Texas law does deny equal protection to 'homosexuals as a class,' that denial still does not need to be justified by anything more than a rational basis, which our cases show is satisfied by the enforcement of traditional notions of sexual morality."

In OBERGEFELL v. HODGES, 576 U.S. 644 (2015), Ch. 6, Sec. 2 supra, the Court, again per KENNEDY, J., held that the Fourteenth Amendment creates a fundamental liberty right encompassing same-sex marriage. After finding a right of same-sex couples to marry under the Due Process Clause, the Court adverted briefly to equal protection: "The right of same-sex couples to marry that is part of the liberty promised by the Fourteenth Amendment is derived, too, from that Amendment's guarantee of the equal protection of the laws. The Due Process

Clause and the Equal Protection Clause are connected in a profound way, though they set forth independent principles. [In] any particular case one Clause may be thought to capture the essence of the right in a more accurate and comprehensive way, even as the two Clauses may converge in the identification and definition of the right. [The] Court's cases touching upon the right to marry reflect this dynamic. In *Loving* the Court invalidated a prohibition on interracial marriage under both the Equal Protection Clause and the Due Process Clause. The Court first declared the prohibition invalid because of its unequal treatment of interracial couples. It stated: 'There can be no doubt that restricting the freedom to marry solely because of racial classifications violates the central meaning of the Equal Protection Clause.' With this link to equal protection the Court proceeded to hold the prohibition offended central precepts of liberty: 'To deny this fundamental freedom on so unsupportable a basis as the racial classifications embodied in these statutes, classifications so directly subversive of the principle of equality at the heart of the Fourteenth Amendment, is surely to deprive all the State's citizens of liberty without due process of law.' The reasons why marriage is a fundamental right became more clear and compelling from a full awareness and understanding of the hurt that resulted from laws barring interracial unions.

"[It] is now clear that the challenged laws burden the liberty of same-sex couples, and it must be further acknowledged that they abridge central precepts of equality. Here the marriage laws enforced by the respondents are in essence unequal: same-sex couples are denied all the benefits afforded to opposite-sex couples and are barred from exercising a fundamental right. Especially against a long history of disapproval of their relationships, this denial to same-sex couples of the right to marry works a grave and continuing harm. The imposition of this disability on gays and lesbians serves to disrespect and subordinate them. And the Equal Protection Clause, like the Due Process Clause, prohibits this unjustified infringement of the fundamental right to marry."

ROBERTS, C.J., joined by Scalia and Thomas, JJ., dissented: "[The] marriage laws at issue here do not violate the Equal Protection Clause, because distinguishing between opposite-sex and same-sex couples is rationally related to the States' 'legitimate state interest' in 'preserving the traditional institution of marriage' [as a union of one man and one woman that 'arose in the nature of things to meet a vital need: ensuring that children are conceived by a mother and father committed to raising them in the stable conditions of a lifelong relationship.'] It is important to note with precision which laws petitioners have challenged. Although they discuss some of the ancillary legal benefits that accompany marriage, such as hospital visitation rights and recognition of spousal status on official documents, petitioners' lawsuits target the laws defining marriage generally rather than those allocating benefits specifically. The equal protection analysis might be different, in my view, if we were confronted with a more focused challenge to the denial of certain tangible benefits."

SCALIA, J., THOMAS, J., and ALITO, J., also filed dissenting opinions.

II. ALIENAGE

The doctrine governing the equal protection rights of lawful aliens is complex. (The Court has never held that *undocumented* immigrants are a suspect class or, with one important exception, that discrimination against undocumented immigrants triggers elevated scrutiny.) Discrimination by the federal government is subject only to rational basis review. By contrast, state discrimination against lawfully admitted aliens sometimes triggers elevated scrutiny and sometimes does not. As you read this section, try to keep in mind distinctions between (1) state and federal statutes that classify on the basis of status as a lawfully admitted alien and (2) documented (or lawfully admitted) and undocumented aliens.

A. State Discriminations Against Lawfully Admitted Aliens

Up to the late 1940s, the Supreme Court found a "special public interest"[32] that justified rejecting almost all challenges to *state* as well as federal discriminations against aliens, including those lawfully admitted into the United States. But *Takahashi v. Fish & Game Comm'n*, 334 U.S. 410 (1948), relying on both Congress' "broad constitutional powers in determining what aliens shall be admitted to the United States" and the Fourteenth Amendment's "general policy" of "equality," invalidated California's denial of licenses for commercial fishing in coastal waters to aliens lawfully residing in the state.

GRAHAM v. RICHARDSON, 403 U.S. 365 (1971), Part I supra, took a much further step. Reasoning that "aliens as a class are a prime example of a 'discrete and insular minority,' " the Court ruled that "classifications based on alienage [are] inherently suspect" and held that state laws denying welfare benefits to legal aliens violate equal protection.

SUGARMAN v. DOUGALL, 413 U.S. 634 (1973), applied the close scrutiny prescribed by *Graham* to Section 53 of New York's Civil Service Law, which required citizenship as a condition of public employment in positions subject to competitive examination. The Court, per BLACKMUN, J., held that Section 53 unconstitutionally discriminated against aliens:

"[We] recognize a State's interest in establishing its own form of government, and in limiting participation in that government to those who are within 'the basic conception of a political community.' We recognize, too, the State's broad power to define its political community. But in seeking to achieve this substantial purpose, with discrimination against aliens, the means the State employs must be precisely drawn in light of the acknowledged purpose. Section 53 is neither narrowly confined nor precise in its application. Its imposed ineligibility may apply to the 'sanitation man, class B,' to the typist, and to the office worker, as well as to the person who directly participates in the formulation and execution of important state policy. [In] view of the breadth and imprecision of § 53 in the context of the

---

[32] *Truax v. Raich*, 239 U.S. 33 (1915). *Truax*, however, invalidated Arizona's forbidding employers of five or more persons from hiring over 20% aliens.

State's interest, we conclude that the statute does not withstand close judicial scrutiny."

AMBACH V. NORWICK

441 U.S. 68, 99 S.Ct. 1589, 60 L.Ed.2d 49 (1979).

JUSTICE POWELL delivered the opinion of the Court.

This case presents the question whether a State, consistently with the Equal Protection Clause, may refuse to employ as elementary and secondary school teachers aliens who are eligible for United States citizenship but who refuse to seek naturalization. * * *

[*Graham* for] the first time treated classifications based on alienage as "inherently suspect and subject to close judicial scrutiny." [In] *Sugarman,* [however,] we recognized that a State could, "in an appropriately defined class of positions, require citizenship as a qualification for office." [*Sugarman* thus contemplated that the] exclusion of aliens from [influential] governmental positions would not invite as demanding scrutiny from this Court.

The rule for governmental functions, which is an exception to the general standard applicable to classifications based on alienage, rests on important principles inherent in the Constitution. The distinction between citizens and aliens, though ordinarily irrelevant to private activity, is fundamental to the definition and government of a State. [Citizenship] denotes an association with the polity which, in a democratic republic, exercises the powers of governance. The form of this association is important; an oath of allegiance or similar ceremony cannot substitute for the unequivocal legal bond citizenship represents. It is because of this special significance of citizenship that governmental entities, when exercising the functions of government, have wider latitude in limiting the participation of noncitizens. * * *

[Applying the rational basis standard, we held last Term that New York could exclude aliens from the ranks of its police force. *Foley v. Connelie*, 435 U.S. 291 (1978). Because the police function fulfilled "a most fundamental obligation of government to its constituency" and by necessity cloaked policemen with substantial discretionary powers, we viewed the police force as being one of those appropriately defined classes of positions for which a citizenship requirement could be imposed.[33]]

Public education, like the police function, "fulfills a most fundamental obligation of government to its constituency." *Foley.* The importance of public schools in the preparation of individuals for participation as citizens, and in the preservation of the values on which our society rests, long has been recognized by our decisions [*Brown I*]. Within the public school system, teachers play a critical

---

[33]   *Cabell v. Chavez-Salido*, 454 U.S. 432 (1982), extended *Foley* to probation officers. Marshall, J., joined by Brennan, Blackmun, and Stevens, JJ., dissented in *Foley*. Blackmun, J., joined by Brennan, Marshall, and Stevens, JJ., dissented in *Cabell*.

part in developing students' attitude toward government and understanding of the role of citizens in our society. [In] shaping the students' experience to achieve educational goals, teachers by necessity have wide discretion over the way the course material is communicated to students. [Further], a teacher serves as a role model for his students, exerting a subtle but important influence over their perceptions and values. Thus, [a] teacher has an opportunity to influence the attitudes of students toward government, the political process, and a citizen's social responsibilities. This influence is crucial to the continued good health of a democracy. * * *

As the legitimacy of the State's interest in furthering the educational goals outlined above is undoubted, it remains only to consider whether [the statute] bears a rational relationship to this interest. The restriction is carefully framed to serve its purpose, as it bars from teaching only those aliens who have demonstrated their unwillingness to obtain United States citizenship. * * *

Reversed.

JUSTICE BLACKMUN, with whom JUSTICE BRENNAN, JUSTICE MARSHALL, and JUSTICE STEVENS, join, dissenting.

[T]he New York classification is irrational. Is it better to employ a poor citizen-teacher than an excellent resident alien teacher? Is it preferable to have a citizen who has never seen Spain or a Latin American country teach Spanish to eighth graders and to deny that opportunity to a resident alien who may have lived for 20 years in the culture of Spain or Latin America? The State will know how to select its teachers responsibly, wholly apart from citizenship, and can do so selectively and intelligently. * * *

———

PLYLER v. DOE, 457 U.S. 202 (1982), Sec. 5, IV, infra, "reject[ed] the claim that 'illegal aliens' are a 'suspect class.' [U]ndocumented status is not irrelevant to any proper legislative goal. Nor is [it] an absolutely immutable characteristic since it is the product of conscious, indeed unlawful, action." But the Court, per BRENNAN, J, invalidated a Texas statute denying free public education to undocumented alien children, stressing both the special status of the children—who can "affect neither their parents' conduct nor their own status"—and the importance of education, both to the children themselves and to the nation more generally, since so many were almost certain to remain in the United States.[34]

B. Federal Discriminations Against Aliens

The Court has never, under any circumstances, subjected *federal* statutes that discriminate against aliens to elevated scrutiny under equal protection norms, largely due to the long-recognized power of the national government "to exclude aliens altogether from the United States, or to prescribe the terms and conditions

---

[34]   Burger, C.J., joined by White, Rehnquist, and O'Connor, JJ., dissented.

upon which they may come to this country." *Lem Moon Sing v. United States*, 158 U.S. 538 (1895). Relying on the traditional federal authority to regulate immigration, MATHEWS v. DIAZ, 426 U.S. 67 (1976), per STEVENS, J., upheld a federal statute denying Medicare benefits to aliens unless they have (i) been admitted for permanent residence and (ii) resided for at least five years in the United States. Although "aliens and citizens alike, are protected by the Due Process Clause, [i]n the exercise of its broad power over naturalization and immigration, Congress regularly makes rules that would be unacceptable if applied to citizens.

"[T]he responsibility for regulating the relationship between the United States and [aliens] has been committed to the political branches of the Federal Government. Since decisions in these matters may implicate our relations with foreign powers, and since a wide variety of classifications must be defined in the light of changing political and economic circumstances, such decisions are frequently of a character more appropriate to either the Legislature or the Executive than to the Judiciary. [The] reasons that preclude judicial review of political questions also dictate a narrow standard of review of decisions made by the Congress or the President in the area of immigration and naturalization.

"Since it is obvious that Congress has no constitutional duty to provide *all aliens* with the welfare benefits provided to citizens, the party challenging the constitutionality of the particular line Congress has drawn" [—allowing benefits to some aliens but not to others—] "has the burden of advancing principled reasoning that will at once invalidate that line and yet tolerate a different line separating some aliens from others. [Since neither of the two requirements] is wholly irrational, this case essentially involves nothing more than a claim that it would have been more reasonable for Congress to select somewhat different requirements of the same kind. [But] it remains true that some line is essential, that any line must produce some harsh and apparently arbitrary consequences, and, of greatest importance, that those who qualify under the test Congress has chosen may reasonably be presumed to have a greater affinity with the United States than those who do not."

C. A Note on Aliens' Constitutional Rights Other than Equal Protection

Although equal protection doctrine leaves the federal government free to distinguish between citizens and non-citizens for many purposes, Congress' power to exclude aliens or impose conditions on their admission to the United States does not imply a power to deny them *all* constitutional rights while they are here, even if Congress arguably might have a rational basis for doing so. Important cases upholding aliens' rights under a variety of constitutional provisions include, e.g., *Boumediene v. Bush*, 553 U.S. 723 (2008) (habeas corpus); *Almeida-Sanchez v. United States*, 413 U.S. 266, 273 (1973) (Fourth Amendment); *Wong Wing v. United States*, 163 U.S. 228, 237 (1896) (Fifth and Sixth Amendments).

Questions involving aliens' rights under constitutional guarantees other than that of equal protection are often complex and fraught. See, e.g., Gerald L. Neuman, *Strangers to the Constitution: Immigrants, Borders, and Fundamental Law* (1996). Such rights are a central focus of courses on Immigration Law. For current purposes, two main points should be emphasized. First, equal protection norms are not the only, or even necessarily the most important, source of constitutional rights for aliens, especially insofar as they are threatened with or might be singled out for *criminal* punishment. Second, aliens are most threatened with distinctively adverse treatment (in comparison with citizens) in connection with violations or suspected violations of the immigration laws. Unlike citizens, aliens are not only vulnerable to being excluded from the United States, but also to being removed from the country once they have arrived here, and the Court has given immigration officials broad (but not unlimited) license in investigating suspected violations of the immigration laws. For example, in the aftermath of the September 11, 2001 terrorist attacks, the government relied on its immigration powers to detain more than a thousand aliens while it conducted investigations, purportedly for immigration violations.

III. OTHER CHALLENGED BASES FOR DISCRIMINATION

1.   *Out-of-wedlock children.* The Court long subjected statutes that discriminated against children born out of wedlock—especially for purposes of inheritance and other survivorship benefits—only to rational basis review. MATHEWS v. LUCAS, 427 U.S. 495 (1976), involved a challenge to a provision of the Social Security Act that required most minor children born out of wedlock, but not others, to prove dependency in order to be eligible for survivorship benefits upon the death of a wage-earning parent. The Court, per BLACKMUN, J., rejected an equal protection challenge: "[It] is true, of course, that the legal status of illegitimacy, however defined, is, like race or national origin, a characteristic determined by causes not within the control of the illegitimate individual, and it bears no relation to the individual's ability to participate in and contribute to society. The Court recognized in *Weber v. Aetna Casualty & Surety Co.*, 406 U.S. 164 (1972), that visiting condemnation upon that child in order to express society's disapproval of the parents' liaisons "is illogical and unjust. [But] where the law is arbitrary in such a way, we have had no difficulty in finding the discrimination impermissible on less demanding standards than those advocated here. *Levy v. Louisiana*, 391 U.S. 68 (1968).[35] And such irrationality in some classifications does not in itself demonstrate that other, possibly rational, distinctions made in part on the basis of legitimacy are inherently untenable. Moreover, [discrimination]

---

[35]   *Levy,* per Douglas, J., invalidated a statute denying illegitimate children the right to recover for the wrongful death of their mother: "[The test] is whether the line drawn is a rational one [but] we have been extremely sensitive when it comes to basic civil rights and have not hesitated to strike down an invidious classification even though it had history and tradition on its side."

against illegitimates has never approached the severity or pervasiveness of the historic legal and political discrimination against women and Negroes. * * *

"Applying [rational basis review], we think that the statutory classifications challenged here are justified as reasonable empirical judgments that are consistent with a design to qualify entitlement to benefits upon a child's dependency at the time of the parent's death. [Under] all but one of the statutes [struck down in prior cases], not only was the legitimate child automatically entitled to benefits, but an illegitimate child was denied benefits solely and finally on the basis of illegitimacy, and regardless of any demonstration of dependency or other legitimate factor. [Here], the statute does not broadly discriminate between legitimates and illegitimates without more, but is carefully tuned to alternative considerations.

STEVENS, J., joined by Brennan and Marshall, JJ., dissented: "[In] the name of 'administrative convenience' the Court allows these survivors' benefits to be allocated on grounds which have only the most tenuous connection to the supposedly controlling factor—the child's dependency on his father. I am persuaded that the classification [is] more probably the product of a tradition of thinking of illegitimates as less deserving persons than legitimates. The sovereign should firmly reject that tradition."

Compare CLARK v. JETER, 486 U.S. 456 (1988), which unanimously concluded that between the "extremes of rational basis review and strict scrutiny lies a level of intermediate scrutiny, which generally has been applied to discriminatory classifications based on sex or illegitimacy. To withstand intermediate scrutiny, a statutory classification must be substantially related to an important governmental objective." Applying that standard, *Clark* invalidated a statute providing that child-support actions for out-of-wedlock children must be brought before the child turns six. Although acknowledging an important state interest in avoiding litigation of stale or fraudulent claims, the Court found the six-year statute of limitations not substantially related to that interest. The six-year period was not necessarily a reasonable one, given the social pressures that might stop an unmarried mother from filing a claim, and "increasingly sophisticated tests for genetic markers permit the exclusion of over 99% of those who might be accused of paternity" regardless of when a claim is filed.

2.   *Age.* MASSACHUSETTS BD. OF RETIREMENT v. MURGIA, 427 U.S. 307 (1976), per curiam, upheld—"under the rational basis standard"—a law requiring uniformed state police officers to retire at age 50. After first rejecting the contention "that a right of governmental employment per se is fundamental" and thus makes the legislative classification subject to "strict scrutiny" (see Sec. 5 infra), the Court continued: "While the treatment of the aged in this Nation has not been wholly free of discrimination, such persons, unlike, say, those who have been discriminated against on the basis of race or national origin, have not experienced a 'history of purposeful unequal treatment' or been subjected to unique disabilities on the basis of stereotyped characteristics not truly indicative of their abilities. The [Massachusetts statute] cannot be said to discriminate only against

the elderly. Rather, it draws the line at a certain age in middle life. But even old age does not define a 'discrete and insular' group, *Carolene Products,* n.4, in need of 'extraordinary protection from the majoritarian political process.' Instead, it marks a stage that each of us will reach if we live out our normal span. Even if the statute could be said to impose a penalty upon a class defined as the aged, it would not impose a distinction sufficiently akin to those classifications that we have found suspect to call for strict judicial scrutiny."

MARSHALL, J., dissented from "the rigid two-tier model [that] still holds sway as the Court's articulated description of the equal protection test," urging a "flexible equal protection standard" of the kind discussed in his concurring opinion in *Cleburne,* supra: "[T]he Court is quite right in suggesting that distinctions exist between the elderly and traditional suspect classes such as [blacks]. The elderly are protected not only by certain antidiscrimination legislation, but by legislation that provides them with positive benefits not enjoyed by the public at large. Moreover, the elderly are not isolated in society, and discrimination against them is not pervasive but is centered primarily in employment. The advantage of a flexible equal protection standard, however, is that it can readily accommodate such variables. The elderly are undoubtedly discriminated against, and when legislation denies them an important benefit—employment—I conclude that to sustain the legislation the Commonwealth must show a reasonably substantial interest and a scheme reasonably closely tailored to achieving that interest."

3. ***Poverty.*** Laws that explicitly distinguish on the basis of wealth or poverty, and work directly to the disadvantage of the poor, are rare. But cf. *Edwards v. California,* 314 U.S. 160 (1941) (invalidating, under the Commerce Clause, a California statute making it a misdemeanor knowingly to transport a non-resident indigent into the state). Today, laws seldom if ever prescribe that the poor cannot vote, attend public universities, utilize legal processes, or receive medical care in public hospitals. The disadvantage experienced by the poor more typically arises from the discriminatory impact of statutes that condition opportunities on the payment of money, or that draw lines—such as those separating relatively poor from relatively wealthy school districts—that strongly correlate with wealth. Equal protection issues involving discriminatory impact on the poor are discussed in Sec. 5, II–IV, infra.

Rare though they may be, should explicit discriminations against poor people be held "suspect"? Although the Warren Court *stated* on several occasions that "lines drawn on the basis of wealth or property" "render a classification highly suspect,"[36] the Burger Court observed in 1973 that the Court had "never held that wealth discrimination alone provides an adequate basis for invoking strict scrutiny,"[37] and, in 1980, *Harris v. McRae,* Ch. 6, Sec. 2 supra, said that "this Court

---

[36]   *Harper v. Virginia Bd. of Elections,* Sec. 5, I infra, and *McDonald v. Board of Elec. Comm'rs,* 394 U.S. 802 (1969).

[37]   *San Antonio Ind. School Dist. v. Rodriguez,* Sec. 5, IV infra.

has held repeatedly that poverty, standing alone, is not a suspect classification. See, e.g. *James v. Valtierra*."

JAMES v. VALTIERRA, 402 U.S. 137 (1971), per BLACK, J., upheld Art. 34 of the California Constitution, which provided that no "low-rent housing project"—defined as any development "for persons of low income"—could be constructed unless approved by local referendum: "Provisions for referendums demonstrate devotion to democracy, not to bias, discrimination, or prejudice." A "law making procedure that 'disadvantages' a particular group does not always deny equal protection." Nor were "persons advocating low-income [housing] singled out": Mandatory referendums were "required for approval of state constitutional amendments, for the issuance of general obligation long-term bonds by local governments, and for certain municipal territorial annexations."

MARSHALL, J., joined by Brennan and Blackmun, JJ., dissented. Under California law, "publicly assisted housing developments designed to accommodate the aged, veterans, state employees, persons of moderate income, or any class of citizens other than the poor, need not be approved by prior referenda. [Art. 34 is] an explicit classification on the basis of poverty—a suspect classification which demands exacting judicial scrutiny."[38]

5. FUNDAMENTAL RIGHTS

In the equal protection cases studied thus far, the crucial variable has been the basis on which the government draws classificatory lines. Suspect bases for classification trigger strict judicial scrutiny, whereas statutory lines that disadvantage most other groups attract only rational basis review. For the most part, the nature of the benefit or burden being distributed, and its relative importance or unimportance, have not mattered. Beginning in the late 1950s, however, and especially in the 1960s and 1970s, the Court began to develop the notion that discriminatory classifications burdening "fundamental" rights will trigger strict judicial scrutiny even if they do not employ an otherwise suspect classification. In other words, the Court adopted a methodology pursuant to which there are two distinct ways to trigger strict scrutiny under the Equal Protection Clause (and the equal protection component of the Fifth Amendment), one involving suspect classifications and the other involving fundamental rights.

As with the Due Process Clause, fundamental rights cases under the Equal Protection Clause have often proved controversial, partly because of the difficulty of identifying fundamental rights to which the Constitution makes no explicit reference (even if they can fairly be regarded as implicit in the Constitution). Indeed, the Court's methodology in identifying fundamental rights under the Equal Protection Clause does not seem clearly different from its methodology in identifying fundamental rights under the Due Process Clause—whatever that methodology either is or ought to be. Many of the methodological controversies studied in Chapter Six thus recur in equal protection fundamental rights cases. If

---

[38]   Douglas, J., did not participate.

there is any difference, it may be this: If a right counts as fundamental under the Due Process Clause, then the government has an obligation to recognize that right and extend it to everyone. By contrast, if a right is a fundamental right under the Equal Protection Clause, then strict scrutiny may become applicable only when the government denies the right to some, while allowing it to others (absent a compelling countervailing interest). Voting rights, the first example of an equal protection fundamental right to be studied in this section, provide an illustration. A city may not need to allow anyone to vote for candidates for mayor. If the mayor were chosen by an elected city council, no constitutional issue would arise.[39] But if a city has mayoral elections at all, then rules allowing some residents to vote, while denying the vote to others, would trigger strict judicial scrutiny.

This Section begins by examining two rights that the Court has recognized as fundamental under the Equal Protection Clause: the right to vote and the right to travel. It then examines cases in which the Court has refused to classify the rights to welfare and to education as fundamental for purposes of equal protection analysis.

I. VOTING

A. Denial or Qualification of the Right

HARPER v. VIRGINIA STATE BD. OF ELECS., 383 U.S. 663 (1966), built upon earlier cases—a number of which are discussed below—to overrule *Breedlove v. Suttles*, 302 U.S. 277 (1937), and hold that Virginia's $1.50 poll tax as "a prerequisite of voting" violated the Equal Protection Clause because the right to vote was a fundamental right. Writing for the Court, DOUGLAS, J., held that "the right to vote in state elections is nowhere expressly mentioned" in the Constitution, but "once the franchise is [granted] lines may not be drawn which [violate equal protection]."[3]

"Long ago in *Yick Wo*, [Sec. 2, IV supra], the Court referred to 'the political franchise of voting' as a 'fundamental political right, because preservative of all rights.' * * * Wealth, like race, creed, or color, is not germane to one's ability to participate intelligently in the electoral process. Lines drawn on the basis of wealth or property, like those of race, are traditionally disfavored. See *Edwards v. California*, [Sec. 4, IV supra] (Jackson, J., concurring); *Griffin v. Illinois; Douglas v. California*, [Part III infra]. To introduce wealth or payment of a fee as a measure of a voter's qualifications is to introduce a capricious or irrelevant factor. * * *

---

[39]   Cf. *Fortson v. Morris*, 385 U.S. 231 (1966), upholding a Georgia election procedure under which, if no gubernatorial candidate received a majority of the popular vote, the state legislature elected the governor from the two candidates receiving the most votes: There is no federal constitutional provision "which either expressly or impliedly dictates the method a state must use to select its governor. A method which would be valid if initially employed is equally valid when employed as an alternative."

[3]   **[Ct's Note]** [While] the "Virginia poll tax was born of a desire to disenfranchise the Negro," we do not stop to determine whether [the] Virginia tax in its modern setting serves the same end.

"In determining what lines are unconstitutionally discriminatory, we have never been confined to historic notions of equality" and "notions of what constitutes equal treatment for purposes of the Equal Protection Clause *do* change [citing *Plessy* and *Brown*, Sec. 2, II supra]. * * * Our conclusion, like that in *Reynolds v. Sims*,[40] is founded not on what we think governmental policy should be, but on what the Equal Protection Clause requires.

"We have long been mindful that where fundamental rights and liberties are asserted under the Equal Protection Clause, classifications which might invade or restrain them must be closely scrutinized and carefully confined. See, e.g., *Reynolds; Carrington v. Rash*."[41]

BLACK, J., dissented: "[P]oll tax legislation can 'reasonably,' 'rationally' and without an 'invidious' or evil purpose to injure anyone be found to rest on a number of state policies including (1) the State's desire to collect its revenue, and (2) its belief that voters who pay a poll tax will be interested in furthering the State's welfare when they vote. [H]istory is on the side of 'rationality' of the State's poll tax policy. Property qualifications existed in the Colonies and were continued by many States after the Constitution was adopted. [The Court] seems to be using the old 'natural-law-due-process formula' to justify striking down state laws as violations of [equal protection]."

HARLAN, J., joined by Stewart, J., dissented: "The [equal protection] test evolved by this Court [is whether] a classification can be deemed to be founded on some rational and otherwise constitutionally permissible state [policy].[3] *Reynolds* marked a departure from these traditional and wise principles. [I]t was probably accepted as sound political theory by a large percentage of Americans through most of our history, that people with some property have a deeper stake in community affairs, and are consequently more responsible, more educated, more knowledgeable, more worthy of [confidence. It] is all wrong, in my view, for the Court to adopt the political doctrines popularly accepted at a particular moment of our history and to declare all others to be irrational and invidious."

---

[40]   *Reynolds*, Part B infra, was among the first of the Court's so-called "one-person, one-vote" decisions requiring that voting districts have roughly equal populations.

[41]   *Carrington*, 380 U.S. 89 (1965), invalidated as an "invidious discrimination" a Texas provision barring members of the military who moved to Texas from voting in state elections, so long as they remained in the military: "We deal here with matters close to the core of our constitutional system." Only "where military personnel are involved has Texas been unwilling to develop more precise tests to determine the bona fides on an individual claiming to have actually made his home in the state long enough to vote. * * * 'Fencing out' from the franchise a sector of the population because of the way they may vote is constitutionally impermissible."

[3]   [Ct's Note] I think the somewhat different application of the Equal Protection Clause to racial discrimination cases finds justification in the fact that insofar as that clause may embody a particular value in addition to rationality, the historical origins of the Civil War Amendments might attribute to racial equality this special status. * * *

KRAMER V. UNION FREE SCHOOL DISTRICT
395 U.S. 621, 89 S.Ct. 1886, 23 L.Ed.2d 583 (1969).

CHIEF JUSTICE WARREN delivered the opinion of the Court.

[§ 2012 of the New York Education Law] provides that in certain New York school districts residents [may] vote in the school district election only if they [or their spouse] (1) own (or lease) taxable real property within the district, or (2) are parents (or have custody of) children enrolled in the local public schools. Appellant, a bachelor who neither owns nor leases taxable real property, [claimed] § 2012 denied him equal protection * * * .

[I]t is important to note what is *not* at issue in this case. The requirements of § 2012 that school district voters must (1) be citizens of the United States, (2) be bona fide residents of the school district, and (3) be at least 21 years of age are not challenged. * * *

In determining whether or not [this statute] violates the Equal Protection Clause, [we] must give the statute a close and exacting examination. [This] careful examination is necessary because statutes distributing the franchise constitute the foundation of our representative society. Any unjustified discrimination in determining who may participate in political affairs or in the selection of public officials undermines the legitimacy of representative government. [Therefore,] if a [statute] grants the right to vote to some bona fide residents of requisite age and citizenship and denies the franchise to others, the Court must determine whether the exclusions are necessary to promote a compelling state interest. See *Carrington*.

[The] presumption of constitutionality and the approval given "rational" classifications in other types of enactments are based on an assumption that the institutions of state government are structured so as to represent fairly all the people. However, when the challenge to the statute is in effect a challenge of this basic assumption, the assumption can no longer serve as the basis for presuming constitutionality. And, the assumption is no less under attack because the legislature which decides who may participate at the various levels of political choice is fairly elected. * * *

The need for exacting judicial scrutiny of statutes distributing the franchise is undiminished simply because, under a different statutory scheme, the offices subject to election might have been filled through appointment[11] [since] "once the franchise is granted to the electorate, lines may not be drawn which are inconsistent with [equal protection]." *Harper*. Nor is the need for close judicial examination affected because the district [and] the school board do not have "general" legislative powers. Our exacting examination is not necessitated by the

---

[11]   **[Ct's Note]** Similarly, no less a showing of a compelling justification for disenfranchising residents is required merely because the questions scheduled for the election need not have been submitted to the voters.

subject of the election [but] because some resident citizens are permitted to participate and some are not. * * *

Besides appellant and others who similarly live in their parents' homes, the statute also disenfranchises the following persons (unless they are parents or guardians of children enrolled in the district public school): senior citizens and others living with children or relatives; clergy, military personnel and others who live on tax-exempt property; boarders and lodgers; parents who neither own nor lease qualifying property and whose children are too young to attend school [or] attend private schools.

[A]ppellees argue that the State has a legitimate interest in limiting the franchise in school district elections [to] those "primarily interested in such elections" [and] that the State may reasonably and permissibly conclude that "property taxpayers" (including lessees of taxable property who share the tax burden through rent payments) and parents of the children enrolled in the district's schools are those "primarily interested" in school affairs. * * *

[A]ssuming, arguendo, that New York legitimately might limit the franchise in these school district elections to those "primarily interested in school affairs," close scrutiny of the § 2012 classifications demonstrates that they do not accomplish this purpose with sufficient precision to justify denying appellant the franchise.

[T]he classifications must be tailored so that the exclusion of appellant and members of his class is necessary to achieve the articulated state goal.[14] Section 2012 does not meet the exacting standard of precision [because it permits] inclusion of many persons who have, at best, a remote and indirect interest in school affairs and on the other hand, exclude[s] others who have a distinct and direct interest in the school meeting decisions.[15] * * *

JUSTICE STEWART, with whom JUSTICE BLACK and JUSTICE HARLAN join, dissenting. * * *

Clearly a State may reasonably assume that its residents have a greater stake in the outcome of elections held within its boundaries than do other persons [and] that residents, being generally better informed regarding state affairs than are nonresidents, will be more likely [to] vote responsibly. And the same may be said of legislative assumptions regarding the electoral competence of adults and literate persons on the one hand, and of minors and illiterates on the other. It is clear, of course, that lines thus drawn cannot infallibly perform their intended legislative function. Just as "[i]lliterate people may be intelligent voters," nonresidents or minors might also in some instances be interested, informed, and intelligent

---

14   [Ct's Note] Of course, if the exclusions are necessary to promote the articulated state interest, we must then determine whether the interest promoted by limiting the franchise constitutes a compelling state interest. We do not reach that issue in this case.

15   [Ct's Note] For example, appellant resides with his parents in the school district, pays state and federal taxes and is interested in and affected by school board decisions [but cannot vote, whereas] an uninterested unemployed young man who pays no state or federal taxes, but who rents an apartment in the district, can [vote].

participants in the electoral process. Persons who commute across a state line to work may well have a great stake in the affairs of the State in which they are employed; some college students under 21 may be both better informed and more passionately interested in political affairs than many adults. But such discrepancies are the inevitable concomitant of the line-drawing that is essential to lawmaking. So long as the classification is rationally related to a permissible legislative end, therefore—as are residence, literacy, and age requirements imposed with respect to voting—there is no denial of equal protection.

Thus judged, the statutory classification involved here seems to me clearly to be valid [and] the Court does not really argue the contrary. Instead, it [asserts] that the traditional equal protection standard is [inapt]. But the asserted justification for applying [a stricter] standard cannot withstand analysis. [The] voting qualifications at issue have been promulgated not by Union Free School District, but by the New York State Legislature, and the appellant is of course fully able to participate in the election of representatives in that body. There is simply no claim whatever here that the state government is not "structured so as to represent fairly all the people," including the appellant.

[§ 2012] does not involve racial classifications [and] is not one that impinges upon a constitutionally protected right, and that consequently can be justified only by a "compelling" state interest. For "the Constitution of the United States does not confer the right of suffrage upon any one."

In any event, it seems to me that under *any* equal protection standard, short of a doctrinaire insistence that universal suffrage is somehow mandated by the Constitution, the appellant's claim must be rejected. * * *

———

In CRAWFORD v. MARION COUNTY ELEC. BD., 553 U.S. 181 (2008), the Court rejected a facial challenge to an Indiana law requiring each voter to present government-issued photo identification as a condition of voting. STEVENS, J., announced the judgment in a plurality opinion joined by Roberts, C.J., and Kennedy, J.: "Under the standard applied in *Harper* [*v. Virginia Bd. of Elections,*] even rational restrictions on the right to vote are invidious [and unconstitutional] if they are unrelated to voter qualifications [but] 'evenhanded restrictions that protect the integrity and reliability of the electoral process itself' are not invidious" and may be upheld based on "relevant and legitimate state interests 'sufficiently weighty to justify the limitation.' [T]he state interests [asserted by Indiana, including deterring voter fraud and safeguarding voter confidence,] are both neutral and sufficiently strong to require us to reject petitioners' facial attack." Stevens, J., left open the possibility, however, that some otherwise qualified voters might be able to establish on an individual basis that they faced such severe difficulties in obtaining government-issued photo identification that the statute would be unconstitutional as applied to them.

SCALIA, J., joined by Thomas and Alito, J., concurred in the judgment: "*Burdick v. Takushi*, 504 U.S. 428 (1992),[42] [calls] for application of a deferential [standard] for nonsevere, nondiscriminatory restrictions, reserving strict scrutiny for laws that severely restrict the right to vote. [T]he Indiana photo-identification law is a generally applicable, nondiscriminatory voting regulation" that easily survives deferential review, and does not trigger the "balancing" approach apparently contemplated by Stevens, J. The law's effects on individual voters should not matter: "A voter complaining about [the] law's effect on him has no valid equal protection claim because, without proof of discriminatory intent, a generally applicable law with disparate impact is not unconstitutional."

SOUTER, J., joined by Ginsburg, J., dissented: "Indiana's 'Voter ID Law' threatens to impose nontrivial burdens on the voting rights of [an estimated 43,000 citizens, or roughly 1% of all eligible voters,] and a significant number of those individuals are likely to be deterred from voting [by the costs of time and money involved in traveling to the offices of the Bureau of Motor Vehicles where photo identification must be obtained.] Poor, old, and disabled voters who do not drive a car [may] find the trip prohibitive. [A] state may not burden the right to vote merely by invoking abstract interests, [but] must make a particular, factual showing. [T]he State has made no such justification here. [Without] a shred of evidence that in-person voter impersonation is a problem in the State, [Indiana] has adopted one of the most restrictive photo identification requirements in the country."

B. "Dilution" of the Right: Apportionment

Distinct from the question of who gets to cast a vote in elections are questions involving how the lines dividing electoral districts are drawn and, relatedly, whether it is constitutionally permissible for voters in some districts to have proportionally more voting power than voters in others.

REYNOLDS V. SIMS

377 U.S. 533, 84 S.Ct. 1362, 12 L.Ed.2d 506 (1964).

CHIEF JUSTICE WARREN delivered the opinion of the Court.

[Although the Alabama constitution required the legislature to reapportion decennially on the basis of population, no such reapportionment had taken place since 1901. The federal district court held the existing malapportionment violative of equal protection. Under] 1960 census figures, only 25.1% of the State's total population resided in districts represented by a majority of the members of the Senate, and only 25.7% lived in counties which could elect a majority of the members of the House of Representatives. Population-variance ratios of up to about 41-to-1 existed in the Senate, and up to about 16-to-1 in the House. * * *

---

[42] *Burdick* held that a state prohibition against write-in ballots did not impermissibly burden the right to vote.

We indicated in *Baker,* Ch1, supra, that the Equal Protection Clause provides discoverable and manageable standards for [determining] the constitutionality of a state legislative apportionment scheme. [In this case] we are faced with the problem [of] determining the basic standards and stating the applicable guidelines for implementing our decision in *Baker.*

Gray v. Sanders, 372 U.S. 368 (1963),[43] and *Wesberry v. Sanders,* 376 U.S. 1 (1964),[44] are of course [relevant to but] not dispositive [of] these cases involving state legislative [apportionment]. But neither are they wholly inapposite. [*Gray*] established the basic principle of equality among voters within a State, [and] *Wesberry* clearly established that the fundamental principle of representative government in this country is one of equal representation for equal numbers of people, without regard to race, sex, economic status, or place of residence within a State. Our problem, then, is to ascertain [whether] there are any constitutionally cognizable principles which would justify departures from the basic standard of equality among voters in the apportionment of seats in state legislatures.

A predominant consideration in determining whether a State's legislative apportionment scheme constitutes an invidious discrimination [is] that the rights allegedly impaired are individual and personal in nature. [Since] the right of suffrage is a fundamental matter in a free and democratic society [and] is preservative of other basic civil and political rights, any alleged infringement [must] be carefully and meticulously scrutinized. * * *

Legislators represent people, not trees or acres. Legislators are elected by voters, not farms or cities or economic interests. [It] is inconceivable that a state law to the effect that, in counting votes for legislators, the votes of citizens in one part of the State would be multiplied by two, five, or 10, while the votes of persons in another area would be counted only at face value, could be [constitutional]. Of course, the effect of state legislative districting schemes which give the same number of representatives to unequal numbers of constituents is identical. * * *

Logically, in a society ostensibly grounded on representative government, it would seem reasonable that a majority of the people of a State could elect a majority of that State's legislators. [T]o sanction minority control of state legislative bodies would appear to deny majority rights in a way that far surpasses any possible denial of minority rights that might otherwise be thought to result. [[Any] suggested criteria for the differentiation of citizens are insufficient to justify

---

[43]   *Gray* invalidated the "county unit system" employed in Georgia primaries for statewide offices, under which the candidate receiving the highest number of votes in each county obtained "two votes for each representative to which the county is entitled in the lower House of the General Assembly," and the winner was determined on the basis of the county unit vote. Because counties were not represented in the state legislature in accordance with their population, counties comprising only a third of the state's population had "a clear majority of county units." *Gray* was not dispositive in *Reynolds* since it involved "the weighing of votes in statewide elections."

[44]   *Wesberry* struck down Georgia's congressional districting statute, under which some districts had more than twice the population of others: "[T]he command of Art. I, § 2, that representatives be chosen 'by the people of the several states' means that as nearly as is practicable one man's vote in a congressional election is to be worth as much as another's."

any discrimination, as to the weight of their votes, unless relevant to the permissible purposes of legislative apportionment. Since the achieving of fair and effective representation for all citizens is concededly the basic aim of legislative apportionment, we conclude that the Equal Protection Clause guarantees the opportunity for equal participation by all voters in the election of state legislators. [Diluting] the weight of votes because of place of residence impairs basic constitutional rights under the Fourteenth Amendment just as much as invidious discriminations based upon factors such as race, or economic status. Our constitutional system amply provides for the protection of minorities by means other than giving them majority control of state legislatures. * * *

We are told that the matter of apportioning representation in a state legislature is a complex and many-faceted one. We are advised that States can rationally consider factors other than [population]. We are admonished not to restrict the power of the States to impose differing views as to political philosophy on their citizens. We are cautioned about the dangers of entering into political thickets and mathematical quagmires. Our answer is this: a denial of constitutionally protected rights demands judicial protection; our oath and our office require no less of us. [To] the extent that a citizen's right to vote is debased, he is that much less a citizen. * * *

We hold that, as a basic constitutional standard, the Equal Protection Clause requires that the seats in both houses of a bicameral state legislature must be apportioned on a population basis. [We] find the federal analogy inapposite and irrelevant to state legislative districting schemes. [T]he Founding Fathers clearly had no intention of establishing a pattern or model for the apportionment of seats in state legislatures when the system of representation in the Federal Congress was adopted. Demonstrative of this is the fact that the Northwest Ordinance, adopted in the same year, 1787, as the Federal Constitution, provided for the apportionment of seats in territorial legislatures solely on the basis of population.

The system of representation in the two Houses of the Federal Congress [is] based on the consideration that in establishing our type of federalism a group of formerly independent States bound themselves together under one national government. [A] compromise between the larger and smaller States on this matter averted a deadlock in the Constitutional Convention * * * .

Political subdivisions of States [never] have been considered as sovereign entities. Rather, they have been traditionally regarded as subordinate governmental instrumentalities created by the State. * * *

We do not believe that the concept of bicameralism is rendered anachronistic and meaningless when the predominant basis of representation in the two state legislative bodies is required to be the same—population. A prime reason for bicameralism, modernly considered, is to insure mature and deliberate consideration of, and to prevent precipitate action on, proposed legislative measures. [T]he Equal Protection Clause requires that a State make an honest and good faith effort to construct districts, in both houses of its legislature, as nearly of equal population as is practicable. We realize that it is a practical impossibility to arrange legislative districts so that each one has an identical number of residents, or citizens, or voters.

[So] long as the divergences from a strict population standard are based on legitimate considerations incident to the effectuation of a rational state policy, some deviations from the equal-population principle are constitutionally permissible, [b]ut neither history alone, nor economic or other sorts of group interests, are permissible factors in attempting to justify disparities from population-based representation. Citizens, not history or economic interests, cast votes.

* * * Decennial reapportionment appears to be a rational approach to readjustment of legislative representation in order to take into account population shifts and growth [and] if reapportionment were accomplished with less frequency, it would assuredly be constitutionally suspect. * * *[45]

[Clark and Stewart, JJ., concurred in the result in *Reynolds,* but STEWART, J., joined by Clark, J., dissented in two of the companion cases in an opinion sharply at odds with the *Reynolds* rationale:]

[My] own understanding of the various theories of representative government is that no one theory has ever commanded unanimous [assent]. But even if it were thought that the rule announced today by the Court is, as a matter of political theory, the most desirable, [I] could not join in the fabrication of a constitutional mandate which imports and forever freezes one theory of political thought into our Constitution, and forever denies to every State any opportunity for enlightened and progressive innovation * * * .

[The] fact of geographic districting, the constitutional validity of which the Court does not question, carries with it an acceptance of the idea of legislative representation of regional needs and interests. Yet if geographical residence is irrelevant, as the Court suggests, and the goal is solely that of equally "weighted" votes, I do not understand why the Court's constitutional rule does not require the abolition of districts and the holding of all elections at large. * * *

JUSTICE HARLAN, dissenting [in all the cases decided that day.]

The Court's constitutional discussion [is] remarkable [for] its failure to address itself at all to the Fourteenth Amendment as a whole or to the legislative history of the Amendment pertinent to the matter at hand. [I] am unable to understand the Court's utter disregard of [§ 2 of the Fourteenth Amendment], which expressly recognizes the States' power to deny "or in any way" abridge the right of their inhabitants to vote for "the members of the [State] Legislature," and

---

[45]   In addition to striking down Alabama's apportionment scheme in *Reynolds,* the Court invalidated apportionments in Colorado, *Lucas v. Forty-Fourth Gen. Assembly,* 377 U.S. 713; Delaware, *Roman v. Sincock,* 377 U.S. 695; Maryland, *Maryland Comm. for Fair Rep. v. Tawes,* 377 U.S. 656; New York, *WMCA, Inc. v. Lomenzo,* 377 U.S. 633; and Virginia, *Davis v. Mann,* 377 U.S. 678.

its express provision of a remedy for such denial or abridgement.[46] The comprehensive scope of the second section and its particular reference to the state legislatures precludes the suggestion that the first section was intended to have the result reached by the [Court].

The history of the adoption of the Fourteenth Amendment provides conclusive evidence that neither those who proposed nor those who ratified the Amendment believed that the Equal Protection Clause limited the power of the States to apportion their legislatures as they saw fit. Moreover, the history demonstrates that the intention to leave this power undisturbed was deliberate and was widely believed to be essential to the adoption of the Amendment. [N]ote should [also] be taken of the Fifteenth and Nineteenth Amendments. [If] constitutional amendment was the only means by which all men and, later, women, could be guaranteed the right to vote at all, even for *federal* officers, how can it be that the far less obvious right to a particular kind of apportionment of *state* legislatures—a right to which is opposed a far more plausible conflicting interest of the State than the interest which opposes the general right to vote—can be conferred by judicial construction of the Fourteenth Amendment?

[The] consequence of today's decision is that in all but the handful of States which may already satisfy the new requirements the [courts] are given blanket authority and the constitutional duty to supervise apportionment of the State Legislatures. It is difficult to imagine a more intolerable and inappropriate interference by the judiciary with the independent legislatures of the States. * * *

C. "Dilution" of the Right: Issues Involving Race

Voters in equally populous districts do not necessarily have equal political influence in electing representatives of their choice. Among the groups that may be advantaged or disadvantaged by the drawing of district lines are groups defined by race. What guarantees, if any, does the Equal Protection Clause give to minority groups that they will be able to cast *effective* votes (as opposed to votes that satisfy the one-person, one-vote principle but are otherwise ineffectual)? A voting scheme that was deliberately structured to disadvantage racial minorities would of course violate the Equal Protection Clause because of its discriminatory intent under the rule of *Washington v. Davis*. But does or should the *fundamental* status of the right to vote trigger heightened judicial scrutiny of voting schemes that make it hard for racial minorities to elect a representative of their choice even if those schemes do not reflect a demonstrably discriminatory purpose?

---

[46]   Section 2 of the Fourteenth Amendment provides, in relevant part: "[W]hen the right to vote at any election for . . . the members of the Legislature [of a State], is denied to any of the male inhabitants of such State, being twenty-one years of age, and citizens of the United States, or in any way abridged, except for participation in rebellion, or other crime, the basis of representation therein shall be reduced in the proportion which the number of such male citizens shall bear to the whole number of male citizens twenty-one years of age in such State."

MOBILE V. BOLDEN

446 U.S. 55, 100 S.Ct. 1490, 64 L.Ed.2d 47 (1980).

JUSTICE STEWART announced the judgment of the Court and delivered an opinion in which THE CHIEF JUSTICE, JUSTICE POWELL, and JUSTICE REHNQUIST join.

The City of Mobile, Ala., has since 1911 been governed by a City Commission consisting of three members elected by the voters of the city at-large. [This] is the same basic electoral system that is followed by literally thousands of municipalities and other local governmental units throughout the Nation.

[The] constitutional objection to multimember districts is not and cannot be that, as such, they depart from apportionment on a population basis in violation of *Reynolds* and its progeny. Rather the focus in such cases has been on the lack of representation multimember districts afford various elements of the voting population in a system of representative legislative democracy. "Criticism [of multimember districts] is rooted in their winner-take-all aspects, their tendency to submerge minorities, [a] general preference for legislatures reflecting community interests as closely as possible and disenchantment with political parties and elections as devices to settle policy differences between contending interests." *Whitcomb v. Chavis*, 403 U.S. 124 (1971).

Despite repeated constitutional attacks upon multimember legislative districts, the Court has consistently held that they are not unconstitutional per se, e.g., *White v. Regester*, 412 U.S. 755 (1973); *Burns v. Richardson*, supra. We have recognized, however, that such legislative apportionments could violate the Fourteenth Amendment if their purpose were invidiously to minimize or cancel out the voting potential of racial or ethnic minorities. To prove such a purpose it is not enough to show that the group allegedly discriminated against has not elected representatives in proportion to its numbers. A plaintiff must prove that the disputed plan was "conceived or operated as [a] purposeful devic[e] to further racial discrimination."

This burden of proof is simply one aspect of the basic principle that only if there is purposeful discrimination can there be a violation of [equal protection]. See *Washington v. Davis; Arlington Heights; Personnel Adm'r v. Feeney*, [Sec. 2, IV supra]. Although dicta may be drawn from a few of the Court's earlier opinions suggesting that disproportionate effects alone may establish a claim of unconstitutional racial vote dilution, the fact is that such a view is not supported by any decision of this Court. More importantly, such a view is not consistent with the meaning of the Equal Protection Clause as it has been understood in a variety of other contexts involving alleged racial discrimination. *Davis* (employment); *Arlington Heights* (zoning); *Keyes* (public schools); *Akins v. Texas*, 325 U.S. 398 (1945) (jury selection).

[It] is clear that the evidence in the present case fell far short of showing [purposeful] discrimination. [T]he District Court [affirmed by the Court of Appeals] based its conclusion of unconstitutionality primarily on the fact that no Negro had ever been elected to the City Commission, apparently because of the pervasiveness of racially polarized voting in Mobile. The trial court also found that city officials had not been as responsive to the interests of Negroes as to those of white persons. On the basis of these findings, the court concluded that the political processes in Mobile were not equally open to Negroes, despite its seemingly inconsistent findings that there were no inhibitions against Negroes becoming candidates, and that in fact Negroes had registered and voted without hindrance. [But] past discrimination cannot, in the manner of original sin, condemn governmental action that is not itself unlawful. The ultimate question remains whether a discriminatory intent has been proved in a given [case].

[We] turn finally [to] Justice Marshall's dissenting opinion. The theory [appears] to be that every "political group," or at least every such group that is in the minority, has a federal constitutional right to elect candidates in proportion to its numbers. Moreover, a political group's "right" to have its candidates elected is said to be a "fundamental interest," the infringement of which may be established without proof that a State has acted with the purpose of impairing anybody's access to the political process. This dissenting opinion finds the "right" infringed [because] no Negro has been elected to the Mobile City Commission.

Whatever appeal the dissenting opinion's view may have as a matter of political theory, it is not the law. The Equal Protection Clause [does] not require proportional representation as an imperative of political organization. * * *

It is of course true that a law that impinges upon a fundamental right explicitly or implicitly secured by the Constitution is presumptively unconstitutional. See *Shapiro v. Thompson,* [Part II infra]. See also *San Antonio Ind. School Dist. v. Rodriguez,* [Part IV infra]. But plainly "[i]t is not the province of this Court to create substantive constitutional rights in the name of guaranteeing equal protection of the laws," id. [In] *Whitcomb,* the trial court had found that a multimember state legislative district had invidiously deprived Negroes and poor persons of rights guaranteed them by the Constitution, notwithstanding the absence of any evidence whatever of discrimination against them. Reversing the trial court, this Court said: "The District Court's holding, although on the facts of this case limited to guaranteeing one racial group representation, is not easily contained. It is expressive of the more general proposition that any group with distinctive interests must be represented in legislative halls if it is numerous enough to command at least one seat and represents a majority living in an area sufficiently compact to constitute a single-member district. This approach would make it difficult to reject claims of Democrats, Republicans, or members of any political [organization]. There are also union oriented workers, the university community, religious or ethnic groups occupying identifiable areas of our heterogeneous cities and urban areas. Indeed, it would be difficult for a great many, if not most, multi-member districts to survive analysis under the District Court's view unless combined with some voting arrangement such as proportional representation or cumulative voting aimed at providing representation for minority parties or interests. At the very least, affirmance [would] spawn endless litigation concerning the multi-member district systems now widely employed in this country." * * *

JUSTICE BLACKMUN, concurring in the result.

Assuming that proof of intent is a prerequisite to appellees' prevailing on their constitutional claim of vote dilution, I am inclined to agree with Justice White that, in this case, "the findings of the District Court amply support an inference of purposeful discrimination." I concur in the Court's judgment of reversal, however, because I believe that the relief afforded appellees by the District Court [ordering a new form of government "of a Mayor and a City Council with members elected from single-member districts"] was not commensurate with the sound exercise of judicial discretion. * * *

JUSTICE STEVENS, concurring in the judgment.

[The antidiscrimination command] is applicable, not merely to gerrymanders directed against racial minorities, but to those aimed at religious, ethnic, economic and political groups as well. My conclusion that the same standard should be applied to racial groups as is applied to other groups leads me also to conclude that the standard cannot condemn every adverse impact on one or more political groups without spawning more dilution litigation than the judiciary can manage. [N]othing comparable to the mathematical yardstick used in apportionment cases is available to identify the difference between permissible and impermissible adverse impacts on the voting strength of political groups. * * *

In my view, the proper standard is suggested by three characteristics of the gerrymander condemned in *Gomillion:* (1) the 28-sided configuration [was] manifestly not the product of a routine or a traditional political decision; (2) it had a significant adverse impact on a minority group; and (3) it was unsupported by any neutral justification and thus was either totally irrational or entirely motivated by a desire to curtail the political strength of the minority. These characteristics suggest that a proper test should focus on the objective effects of the political decision rather than the subjective motivation of the decisionmaker. [A] political decision that is supported by valid and articulable justifications cannot be invalid simply because some participants in the decisionmaking process were motivated by a purpose to disadvantage a minority group. [A] contrary view "would spawn endless litigation concerning the multimember districts now widely employed in this Country," and would entangle the judiciary in a voracious political thicket.

JUSTICE MARSHALL, dissenting. * * *

The Court does not dispute the proposition that multimember districting can have the effect of submerging electoral minorities. [Further], we decided a series of vote-dilution cases under the Fourteenth Amendment that were designed to protect electoral minorities from precisely the combination of electoral laws and historical and social factors found in the present cases.[4] [Although] we have held that multimember districts are not unconstitutional per se, there is simply no basis for the plurality's conclusion that under our prior cases proof of discriminatory intent is a necessary condition for the invalidation of multimember districting.

[Under] this line of cases, an electoral districting plan is invalid if it has the effect of affording an electoral minority "less opportunity [than] other residents in the district to participate in the political processes and to elect legislators of their choice," *Regester*. It is also apparent that the Court in *Regester* considered equal access to the political process as meaning more than merely allowing the minority the opportunity to vote. *Regester* stands for the proposition that an electoral system may not relegate an electoral minority to political impotence by diminishing the importance of its [vote].

The plurality fails to apply the discriminatory effect standard of *Regester* because that approach conflicts with what the plurality takes to be an elementary principle of law. "[O]nly if there is purposeful discrimination," announces the plurality, "can there be a violation of [equal protection]." That proposition [fails] to distinguish between two distinct lines of equal protection decisions: those involving suspect classifications, and those involving fundamental rights. * * *

Under the Equal Protection Clause, if a classification "impinges upon a fundamental right explicitly or implicitly protected by the [Constitution], strict judicial scrutiny" is required, *Rodriguez,* regardless of whether the infringement was intentional. As I will explain, our cases recognize a fundamental right to equal electoral participation that encompasses protection against vote dilution. Proof of discriminatory purpose is, therefore, not required to support a claim of vote dilution.[10] The plurality's erroneous conclusion to the contrary is the result of a failure to recognize the central distinction between *Regester* and *Davis*: the former involved an infringement of a constitutionally protected right, while the latter dealt with a claim of racially discriminatory distribution of an interest to which no citizen has a constitutional entitlement. * * *

---

[4]   **[Ct's Note]** [T]hough municipalities must be accorded some discretion in arranging their affairs, see *Abate*, there is all the more reason to scrutinize assertions that municipal, rather than State, multi-member districting dilutes the vote of an electoral minority: "In statewide elections, it is possible that a large minority group in one multi-member district will be unable to elect any legislators, while in another multi-member district where the same group is a slight majority, they will elect the entire slate of legislators. [In] at-large elections, [t]here is no way to balance out the discrimination against a particular minority group because the entire city is one huge election district. The minority's loss is absolute." Barbara Berry & Thomas Dye, *The Discriminatory Effects of At-Large Elections*, 7 Fla.St.U.L.Rev. 85, 87 (1979). * * *

[10]   **[Ct's Note]** [Although] the right to vote is indistinguishable for present purposes from the other fundamental rights our cases have recognized, surely the plurality would not require proof of discriminatory purpose in those cases. The plurality fails to articulate why the right to vote should receive such singular treatment. Furthermore, the plurality refuses to recognize the disutility of requiring proof of discriminatory purpose in fundamental rights cases. For example, it would make no sense to require such a showing when the question is whether a state statute regulating abortion violates the right of personal choice recognized in *Roe v. Wade*. The only logical inquiry is whether, regardless of the legislature's motive, the statute has the effect of infringing that right. See, e.g., *Planned Parenthood v. Danforth*, [428 U.S. 52 (1976)].

Reynolds and its progeny focused solely on the discriminatory *effects* of malapportionment. [In] the present cases, the alleged vote dilution, though caused by the combined effects of the electoral structure and social and historical factors rather than by unequal population distribution, is analytically the same concept: the unjustified abridgement of a fundamental right. It follows, then, that a showing of discriminatory intent is just as unnecessary under the vote-dilution approach adopted in *Dorsey* and applied in *Regester,* as it is under our reapportionment cases. * * *

The plurality's response is that my approach amounts to nothing less than a constitutional requirement of proportional representation for groups. That assertion amounts to nothing more than a red herring. [Appellees] proved that no Negro had ever been elected to the Mobile City Commission, despite the fact that Negroes constitute about one-third of the electorate, and that the persistence of severe racial bloc voting made it highly unlikely that any Negro could be elected at-large in the foreseeable future. Contrary to the plurality's contention, however, I do not find unconstitutional vote dilution in this case simply because of that showing. The plaintiffs convinced the District Court that Mobile Negroes were unable to use alternative avenues of political influence. They showed that Mobile Negroes still suffered pervasive present effects of massive historical official and private discrimination, and that the city commission had been quite unresponsive to the needs of the minority community. Mobile has been guilty of such pervasive racial discrimination in hiring employees that extensive intervention by the Federal District Court has been required. Negroes are grossly underrepresented on city boards and committees. The city's distribution of public services is racially discriminatory. City officials and police were largely unmoved by Negro complaints about police brutality and "mock lynchings." The District Court concluded that "[t]his sluggish and timid response is another manifestation of the low priority given to the needs of the black citizens and of the [commissioners'] political fear of a white backlash vote when black citizens' needs are at stake."

[The] plurality's requirement of proof of *intentional discrimination* [may] represent an attempt to bury the legitimate concerns of the minority beneath the soil of a doctrine almost as impermeable as it is specious. If so, the superficial tranquility created by such measures can be but short-lived. If this Court refuses to honor our long-recognized principle that the Constitution "nullifies sophisticated as well as simple-minded modes of discrimination," it cannot expect the victims of discrimination to respect political channels of seeking redress. I dissent.[47]

ROGERS v. LODGE, 458 U.S. 613 (1982), per WHITE, J., affirmed a decision that the at-large election system for a Georgia County Board of Commissioners violated equal protection: "The district court [demonstrated] its understanding of the controlling standard by observing that a determination of discriminatory intent

---

[47]   The dissenting opinions of Brennan, J., and White, J., are omitted.

is 'a requisite to a finding of unconstitutional vote dilution' [and] concluded that the [system] 'although racially neutral when adopted, is being *maintained* for invidious purposes.' [For] the most part, the district court dealt with the evidence in terms of the factors [that had been used by the district court in *Mobile*], but as the court of appeals stated: 'Judge Alaimo [did] not treat [those factors] as absolute, but rather considered them only to the extent that they were relevant to the question of discriminatory intent.' Although a tenable argument can be made to the contrary, we are not inclined to disagree with the court of appeals' conclusion that the district court applied the proper legal standard. * * *

"The Court of Appeals [stated that the] District Court correctly anticipated *Mobile* and required appellees to prove that the at-large voting system was maintained for a discriminatory purpose. The Court of Appeals also held that the District Court's findings not only were not clearly erroneous, but its conclusion that the at-large system was maintained for invidious purposes was 'virtually mandated by the overwhelming proof.' [This Court has] noted that issues of intent are commonly treated as factual matters [and] has frequently noted its reluctance to disturb findings of fact concurred in by two lower courts."

POWELL, J., joined by Rehnquist, J., dissented: "[T]he Court's opinion cannot be reconciled persuasively with [*Mobile*]. There are some variances in the largely sociological evidence presented in the two cases. But *Mobile* held that this *kind* of evidence was not enough. * * * I would hold that the factors cited by the Court of Appeals are too attenuated as a matter of law to support an inference of discriminatory intent."

———

Whereas *Mobile v. Bolden* involved issues of minority vote dilution, partly symmetrical issues may arise in cases in which legislatures act with the goal of *increasing* the voting power of racial minorities through the deliberate design of so-called majority-minority districts. There are a variety of reasons that legislatures might seek to create majority-minority districts, including the need to comply with the Voting Rights Act of 1965, supra. As noted immediately above, § 2 of the VRA prohibits minority vote dilution as defined by effects, without need for proof of discriminatory intent. In addition, during the period when the Court decided the cases that follow immediately, § 5 mandated that any proposed districting changes in covered jurisdictions (identified on the basis of prior histories of exclusion of minority voters prior to 1965) should not be "retrogressive" with respect to the representation of racial minorities. To enforce this requirement, § 5 provided that covered jurisdictions must "pre-clear" proposed districting changes with either a federal court or the Department of Justice. As a result of these provisions, the VRA not only permits, but sometimes actually requires, policy-makers to be race-conscious in drawing electoral districts. See Daniel Hays Lowenstein, *You Don't Have to Be Liberal to Hate the Racial Gerrymandering Cases*, 50 Stan.L.Rev. 779 (1998).

The Court's 2013 decision in *Shelby County v. Holder*, Ch. 11, Sec. 3 infra, effectively rendered § 5 of the Voting Rights Act inoperative by invalidating the "coverage" provision that made it applicable to some jurisdictions but not to others. Nevertheless, in part because of the continued operation of § 2, the issues raised by the cases that follow—involving the deliberate creation of majority-minority voting districts—have not been mooted.

SHAW V. RENO

509 U.S. 630, 113 S.Ct. 2816, 125 L.Ed.2d 511 (1993).

JUSTICE O'CONNOR delivered the opinion of the Court.

[As] a result of the 1990 census, North Carolina became entitled to a twelfth seat in the United States House of Representatives. The General Assembly enacted a reapportionment plan that included one majority-black congressional district. After the Attorney General of the United States objected to the plan pursuant to § 5 of the Voting Rights Act of 1965, the General Assembly passed new legislation creating a second majority-black district. Appellants allege that the revised plan, which contains district boundary lines of dramatically irregular shape, constitutes an unconstitutional racial gerrymander. * * *

The voting age population of North Carolina is approximately 78% white, 20% black, and 1% Native American; the remaining 1% is predominantly Asian. The black population is relatively dispersed; blacks constitute a majority of the general population in only 5 of the State's 100 counties. [The] largest concentrations of black citizens live in the Coastal Plain, primarily in the northern part. The General Assembly's first redistricting plan contained one majority-black district centered in that area of the State. [I]t moves southward until it tapers to a narrow band; then, with finger-like extensions, it reaches far into the southern-most part of the State near the South Carolina border. District 1 has been compared to a "Rorschach ink-blot test," and a "bug splattered on a windshield."

The second majority-black district, District 12, is even more unusually shaped. It is approximately 160 miles long and, for much of its length, no wider than the I-85 corridor. It winds in snake-like fashion through tobacco country, financial centers, and manufacturing areas "until it gobbles in enough enclaves of black neighborhoods." Northbound and southbound drivers on I-85 sometimes find themselves in separate districts in one county, only to "trade" districts when they enter the next county. Of the 10 counties through which District 12 passes, five are cut into three different districts; even towns are divided. At one point the district remains contiguous only because it intersects at a single point with two other districts before crossing over them. One state legislator has remarked that "[i]f you drove down the interstate with both car doors open, you'd kill most of the people in the district." * * *

An understanding of the nature of appellants' claim is critical to our resolution of the case. In their complaint, appellants did not claim that the General Assembly's reapportionment plan unconstitutionally "diluted" white voting strength. They did not even claim to be white. Rather, appellants' complaint alleged that the deliberate segregation of voters into separate districts on the basis of race violated their constitutional right to participate in a "color-blind" electoral process. [This] Court never has held that race-conscious state decisionmaking is impermissible in all circumstances. What appellants object to is redistricting legislation that is so extremely irregular on its face that it rationally can be viewed only as an effort to segregate the races for purposes of voting, without regard for traditional districting principles and without sufficiently compelling justification. For the reasons that follow, we conclude that appellants have stated a claim upon which relief can be granted under the Equal Protection Clause.

[R]edistricting differs from other kinds of state decisionmaking in that the legislature always is aware of race when it draws district lines, just as it is aware of age, economic status, religious and political persuasion, and a variety of other demographic factors. That sort of race consciousness does not lead inevitably to impermissible race discrimination. [W]hen members of a racial group live together in one community, a reapportionment plan that concentrates members of the group in one district and excludes them from others may reflect wholly legitimate purposes. The district lines may be drawn, for example, to provide for compact districts of contiguous territory, or to maintain the integrity of political subdivisions.

The difficulty of proof, of course, does not mean that a racial gerrymander, once established, should receive less scrutiny under the Equal Protection Clause than other state legislation classifying citizens by race. Moreover, it seems clear to us that proof sometimes will not be difficult at all. In some exceptional cases, a reapportionment plan may be so highly irregular that, on its face, it rationally cannot be understood as anything other than an effort to "segregat[e] voters" on the basis of race. *Gomillion*, in which a tortured municipal boundary line was drawn to exclude black voters, was such a case. So, too, would be a case in which a State concentrated a dispersed minority population in a single district by disregarding traditional districting principles such as compactness, contiguity, and respect for political subdivisions. We emphasize that these criteria are important not because they are constitutionally required—they are not—but because they are objective factors that may serve to defeat a claim that a district has been gerrymandered on racial lines.

[A] reapportionment plan that includes in one district individuals who belong to the same race, but who are otherwise widely separated by geographical and political boundaries, and who may have little in common with one another but the color of their skin, bears an uncomfortable resemblance to political apartheid. It reinforces the perception that members of the same racial group—regardless of their age, education, economic status, or the community in which they live—think alike, share the same political interests, and will prefer the same candidates at the polls. We have rejected such perceptions elsewhere as impermissible racial stereotypes. By perpetuating such notions, a racial gerrymander may exacerbate the very patterns of racial bloc voting that majority-minority districting is sometimes said to counteract.

The message that such districting sends to elected representatives is equally pernicious. When a district obviously is created solely to effectuate the perceived common interests of one racial group, elected officials are more likely to believe that their primary obligation is to represent only the members of that group, rather than their constituency as a whole. This is altogether antithetical to our system of representative democracy. * * *

For these reasons, we conclude that a plaintiff challenging a reapportionment statute under the Equal Protection Clause may state a claim by alleging that the legislation, though race-neutral on its face, rationally cannot be understood as anything other than an effort to separate voters into different districts on the basis of race, and that the separation lacks sufficient justification. * * *

Racial gerrymandering, even for remedial purposes, may balkanize us into competing racial factions; it threatens to carry us further from the goal of a political system in which race no longer matters—a goal that the Fourteenth and Fifteenth Amendments embody, and to which the Nation continues to aspire. It is for these reasons that race-based districting by our state legislatures demands close judicial scrutiny. * * *

JUSTICE WHITE, with whom JUSTICE BLACKMUN and JUSTICE STEVENS join, dissenting.

[The] question in gerrymandering cases is "whether a particular group has been unconstitutionally denied its chance to effectively influence the political process."

[It] strains credulity to suggest that North Carolina's purpose in creating a second majority-minority district was to discriminate against members of the majority group by "impair[ing] or burden[ing their] opportunity [to] participate in the political process." The State has made no mystery of its intent, which was to respond to the Attorney General's objections by improving the minority group's prospects of electing a candidate of its choice. I doubt that this constitutes a discriminatory purpose as defined in the Court's equal protection cases—i.e., an intent to aggravate "the unequal distribution of electoral power." But even assuming that it does, there is no question that appellants have not alleged the requisite discriminatory effects. Whites constitute roughly 76 percent of the total population and 79 percent of the voting age population in North Carolina. Yet, under the State's plan, they still constitute a voting majority in 10 (or 83 percent) of the 12 congressional districts. * * *

[In other cases] we have put the plaintiff challenging district lines to the burden of demonstrating that the plan was meant to, and did in fact, exclude an identifiable racial group from participation in the political process. Not so, apparently, when the districting "segregates" by drawing odd-shaped lines. In that case, [it] is the State that must rebut the allegation that race was taken into account, a fact that, together with the legislators' consideration of ethnic, religious, and other group characteristics, I had thought we practically took for granted.

[Although] I disagree with the holding that appellants' claim is cognizable, the Court's discussion of the level of scrutiny it requires warrants a few comments. I have no doubt that a State's compliance with the Voting Rights Act clearly constitutes a compelling interest. [The] Court, while seemingly agreeing with this position, warns that the State's redistricting effort must be "narrowly tailored" to further its interest in complying with the law. It is evident to me, however, that what North Carolina did was precisely tailored to meet the objection of the Attorney General to its prior plan. * * *

State efforts to remedy minority vote dilution are wholly unlike what typically has been labeled "affirmative action." To the extent that no other racial group is injured, remedying a Voting Rights Act violation does not involve preferential treatment. It involves, instead, an attempt to equalize treatment, and to provide minority voters with an effective voice in the political process. The Equal Protection Clause of the Constitution, surely, does not stand in the way. * * *

JUSTICE STEVENS, dissenting.

[If] it is permissible to draw boundaries to provide adequate representation for rural voters, for union members, for Hasidic Jews, for Polish Americans, or for Republicans, it necessarily follows that it is permissible to do the same thing for members of the very minority group whose history in the United States gave birth to the Equal Protection Clause. A contrary conclusion could only be described as perverse.

JUSTICE SOUTER, dissenting.

[Unlike] other contexts in which we have addressed the State's conscious use of race, see, e.g., *Croson*; *Wygant*, electoral districting calls for decisions that nearly always require some consideration of race for legitimate reasons where there is a racially mixed population. As long as members of racial groups have the commonality of interest implicit in our ability to talk about concepts like "minority voting strength," and "dilution of minority votes," and as long as racial bloc voting takes place, legislators will have to take race into account in order to avoid dilution of minority voting strength in the districting plans they adopt. [In] addition, the mere placement of an individual in one district instead of another denies no one a right or benefit provided to others. [Under] our cases there is in general a requirement that in order to obtain relief under the Fourteenth Amendment, the purpose and effect of the districting must be to devalue the effectiveness of a voter compared to what, as a group member, he would otherwise be able to enjoy. * * *

There is thus no theoretical inconsistency in having two distinct approaches to equal protection analysis, one for cases of electoral districting and one for most other types of state governmental decisions. Nor, because of the distinctions between the two categories, is there any risk that Fourteenth Amendment districting law as such will be taken to imply anything for purposes of general

Fourteenth Amendment scrutiny about "benign" racial discrimination, or about group entitlement as distinct from individual protection, or about the appropriateness of strict or other heightened scrutiny. * * *

COOPER V. HARRIS
___ U.S. ___, 137 S.Ct. 1455, 197 L.Ed.2d 837 (2017).

JUSTICE KAGAN delivered the opinion of the Court.

The Equal Protection Clause of the Fourteenth Amendment [prevents] a State, in the absence of "sufficient justification," from "separating its citizens into different voting districts on the basis of race." When a voter sues state officials for drawing such race-based lines, our decisions call for a two-step analysis. First, the plaintiff must prove that "race was the predominant factor motivating the legislature's decision to place a significant number of voters within or without a particular district." *Miller v. Johnson*, 515 U.S. 900 (1995).[1] [Second,] if racial considerations predominated over others, [the] burden thus shifts to the State to prove that its race-based sorting of voters serves a "compelling interest" and is "narrowly tailored" to that end.

This Court has long assumed that one compelling interest is complying with operative provisions of the Voting Rights Act of 1965 (VRA or Act). Two provisions of the VRA—§ 2 and § 5—are involved in this case. Section 2 prohibits "vote dilution"—brought about, most relevantly here, by the "dispersal of [a group's members] into districts in which they constitute an ineffective minority of voters." *Thornburg v. Gingles*. Section 5, [before] *Shelby County v. Holder*, [required various] North Carolina counties to pre-clear voting changes with the Department of Justice, so as to forestall "retrogression" in the ability of racial minorities to elect their preferred candidates.

This case concerns North Carolina's most recent redrawing of two congressional districts, both of which have long included substantial populations of black voters. Both have quite the history before this Court[, beginning] in *Shaw v. Reno*, [which] held [that the predecessors of the same districts challenged in this case, Districts 1 and 12] were unwarranted racial gerrymanders. [After *Shaw*,] the State responded with a new districting plan[, and the Court upheld] a new District 12. See *Hunt v. Cromartie*, 526 U.S. 541 (1999) (*Cromartie I*); *Easley v. Cromartie*, 532 U.S. 234 (2001) (*Cromartie II*). Racial considerations, we held, did not predominate in designing the revised District 12. Rather, that district was the result of a political gerrymander—[a constitutionally permissible] effort to engineer, mostly "without regard to race," a safe Democratic seat.

Another census, in 2010, necessitated [the] congressional map [at] issue in this case. State Senator Robert Rucho and State Representative David Lewis, both

---

    [1]   **[Ct's Note]** A plaintiff succeeds at this stage even if the evidence reveals that a legislature elevated race to the predominant criterion in order to advance other goals, including political ones.

Republicans, chaired the two committees jointly responsible for preparing the revamped plan. They hired Dr. Thomas Hofeller, a veteran political mapmaker, to assist them in redrawing district lines. [After the] 2010 census had revealed District 1 to be substantially underpopulated, [the] State needed to place almost 100,000 new people within the district's boundaries. Rucho, Lewis, and Hofeller chose to take most of those people from heavily black areas of Durham, requiring a finger-like extension of the district's western line. With that addition, District 1's [black voting-age population or] BVAP rose from 48.6% to 52.7%. [Although] District 12 [had] no need for significant total-population changes, Rucho, Lewis, and Hofeller decided to reconfigure the district, further narrowing its already snakelike body while adding areas at either end. [As] the district gained some 35,000 African-Americans of voting age and lost some 50,000 whites of that age, its BVAP increased from 43.8% to 50.7%. After a bench trial, a three-judge District Court [ruled] that racial considerations predominated in the design of [both Districts 1 and 12 and that both were constitutionally invalid].

[With regard to District 1, uncontested] evidence [shows] that the State's mapmakers [purposefully] established a racial target [as the predominant factor in their revisions[3]]: African-Americans should make up no less than a majority of the voting-age population[.] [The] more substantial question is whether District 1 can survive the strict scrutiny applied to racial gerrymanders. [The State argues that it] had "good reasons to believe it needed to draw [District 1] as a majority-minority district to avoid Section 2 liability" for vote dilution. [But] electoral history provided no evidence that a § 2 plaintiff could demonstrate the third *Gingles* prerequisite [in addition to the requirements that a minority community be large and compact enough to constitute a district-wide majority and that it be politically cohesive]—effective white bloc-voting. For most of the twenty years prior to the new plan's adoption, African-Americans had made up less than a majority of District 1's voters; the district's BVAP usually hovered between 46% and 48%. Yet throughout those two decades, as the District Court noted, District 1 was "an extraordinarily safe district for African-American preferred candidates." [In] the lingo of voting law, District 1 functioned [as] a "crossover" district, in which members of the majority help a "large enough" minority to elect its candidate of choice. [Because] this Court has made clear that unless each of the three *Gingles* prerequisites is established, "there neither has been a wrong nor can be a remedy," [the challenge to District 1 must be upheld].

[The legality of District 12] turns solely on which of two possible reasons predominantly explains its most recent reconfiguration[—race or Republican political advantage]. [Because] "racial identification is highly correlated with

---

3   [Ct's Note] The State's argument to the contrary rests on a legal proposition that [racial] considerations cannot predominate in drawing district lines unless there is an "actual conflict" between those lines and "traditional districting principles." But we rejected that view earlier this Term, holding that when (as here) race furnished "the overriding reason for choosing one map over others," a further showing of "inconsistency between the enacted plan and traditional redistricting criteria" is unnecessary to a finding of racial predominance. *Bethune-Hill v. Virginia State Bd. of Elections*, 137 S.Ct. 788 (2017).

political affiliation," [and because Republicans can gain an overall electoral advantage in other districts by "packing" as many additional Democrats as possible into a district that Democrats would easily carry anyway, the trial court] must make "a sensitive inquiry" into all "circumstantial and direct evidence of intent" to assess whether the plaintiffs have managed to disentangle race from politics and prove that the former drove a district's lines.[7] Our job is different—and generally easier. [W]e review a district court's finding as to racial predominance only for clear error, except when the court made a legal mistake.

[By further slimming a district in which no substantial population changes were necessary] (and adding a couple of knobs to its snakelike body), [the] General Assembly incorporated tens of thousands of new voters and pushed out tens of thousands of old ones. And those changes followed racial lines. [The] Assembly thus turned District 12 [into] a majority-minority district. Rucho and Lewis had publicly stated that racial considerations lay behind District 12's augmented BVAP. In a release issued along with their draft districting plan, the two legislators ascribed that change to the need to achieve preclearance of the plan under § 5 of the VRA.

[The] State's contrary story—that politics alone drove decisionmaking—came into the trial mostly through Hofeller's testimony. Hofeller explained that Rucho and Lewis instructed him, first and foremost, to make the map as a whole "more favorable to Republican candidates." [The] District Court, however, disbelieved Hofeller's asserted indifference to the new district's racial composition.

[The] State mounts a final, legal rather than factual, attack on the District Court's finding of racial predominance. When race and politics are competing explanations of a district's lines, argues North Carolina, [quoting *Cromartie II*,] the party challenging the district must [introduce] "an alternative [map] that achieves the legislature's political objectives while improving racial balance." [We] have no doubt that an alternative districting plan, of the kind North Carolina describes, can serve as key evidence in a race-versus-politics dispute. But in no area of our equal protection law have we forced plaintiffs to submit one particular form of proof to prevail.

THOMAS, J., concurring.

I join the opinion of the Court because it correctly applies our precedents [and] represents a welcome course correction to this Court's [previously insufficiently deferential] application of the clear-error standard.

ALITO, J., joined by ROBERTS, C.J., and KENNEDY, J., concurring in the judgment in part and dissenting in part.

---

7   [Ct's Note] As earlier noted, that inquiry is satisfied when legislators have "place[d] a significant number of voters within or without" a district predominantly because of their race, regardless of [whether they] use race as their predominant districting criterion with the end goal of advancing their partisan interests. [In] other words, the sorting of voters on the grounds of their race remains suspect even if race is meant to function as a proxy for other (including political) characteristics.

[I concur in the judgment of the Court regarding Congressional District 1. The State concedes that the district was intentionally created as a majority-minority districts. And appellants have not satisfied strict scrutiny.]

[District 12 is governed by the rule of *Cromartie II*, under which] "the party attacking the legislatively drawn boundaries must show at the least that the legislature could have achieved its legitimate political objectives in alternative ways that are comparably consistent with traditional districting principles [and] that those districting alternatives would have brought about significantly greater racial balance."

[C]ourts are obligated to "exercise extraordinary caution in adjudicating claims that a State has drawn district lines on the basis of race." [As] we have acknowledged, "[p]olitics and political considerations are inseparable from districting and apportionment," and it is well known that state legislative majorities very often attempt to gain an electoral advantage through that process. See *Davis v. Bandemer*, [Part D infra]. [W]hile some might find [that practice] distasteful, "[o]ur prior decisions have made clear that a jurisdiction may engage in constitutional political gerrymandering, even if it so happens that the most loyal Democrats happen to be black Democrats and even if the State were conscious of that fact." *Cromartie I*. [And if] around 90% of African-American voters cast their ballots for the Democratic candidate, as they have in recent elections, a plan that packs Democratic voters will look very much like a plan[ ] that packs African-American voters.

[*Cromartie II*'s rule that challengers] must submit an alternative map demonstrating that the legislature could have achieved its political goals without the racial effects giving rise to the racial gerrymandering allegation [should be applied in this case]. [When] a federal court says that race was a legislature's predominant purpose in drawing a district, it accuses the legislature of "offensive and demeaning" conduct. [That] is a grave accusation. [In] addition, "[f]ederal-court review of districting legislation represents a serious intrusion on the most vital of local functions" because "[i]t is well settled that reapportionment is primarily the duty and responsibility of the State." [Finally, unless] courts "exercise extraordinary caution" in distinguishing race-based redistricting from politics-based redistricting, they will invite the losers in the redistricting process to seek to obtain in court what they could not achieve in the political arena.

Even if we set aside the challengers' failure to submit an alternative map, the District Court's finding that race predominated in the drawing of District 12 is clearly erroneous. The State offered strong and coherent evidence that politics, not race, was the legislature's predominant aim, and the evidence supporting the District Court's contrary finding is weak.[48]

---

[48]   In response to this line of argument, the majority countered: "[The] dissent repeatedly flips the appropriate standard of review. [It] mistakes the rule that a legislature's good faith should be presumed 'until a claimant makes a showing sufficient to support th[e] allegation' of 'race-based decisionmaking' for a kind of super-charged, pro-State presumption on appeal, trumping clear-error review." The dissent in turn replied: "Because the evidence [the plaintiffs] put forward is so

The basic shape of District 12 was legitimately taken as a given. Dr. Hofeller began with the prior version of District 12 [and, he testified,] moved more Democratic voters into District 12 in order to "increase Republican opportunities in the surrounding districts." [The] results of subsequent congressional elections show that Dr. Hofeller's plan achieved its goal.

D. "Dilution" of the Right: Partisan Gerrymanders

According to Pamela S. Karlan, *The Rights to Vote: Some Pessimism about Formalism*, 71 Tex.L.Rev. 1705 (1993), "Chief Justice Warren called *Reynolds v. Sims* his most important opinion 'because it insured that henceforth elections would reflect the collective public interest—embodied in the "one-man, one-vote" standard—rather than the machinations of special interests.' " "Measured against that ambition," Karlan writes, "*Reynolds* has been a spectacular failure. Advances in the technology of districting [which allow partisan legislatures to engage in partisan gerrymanders even while maintaining equal-sized districts] have stripped the substantive principles of one-person, one-vote of any real constraining force."

The question whether the Equal Protection Clause creates rights to be free from partisan gerrymanders has sharply divided the Supreme Court. In *Davis v. Bandemer*, 478 U.S. 109 (1986), the Court divided over the test to apply to identify constitutionally forbidden partisan gerrymanders under the Equal Protection Clause. White, J., joined by Brennan, Marshall, and Blackmun, JJ., would have required proof of "intentional discrimination against an identifiable political group and an actual discriminatory effect on that group." Powell, J., joined by Stevens, J., would have focused on "whether the boundaries of the voting districts have been distorted deliberately and arbitrarily to achieve illegitimate ends." A dissenting opinion, by O'Connor, J., joined by Burger, C.J., and Rehnquist, J., would have held that challenges to partisan gerrymanders pose nonjusticiable political questions because the Equal Protection Clause simply "does not supply judicially manageable standards for resolving" them.

The view that challenges to partisan gerrymanders present political questions, which gained the support of a plurality of the Justices in *Vieth v. Jubelirer*, 541 U.S. 267 (2004), prevailed, by a vote of 5 to 4, in *Rucho v. Common Cause*, Ch. 1, Sec. 2. *Rucho*, which you should re-read at this time, states the governing law on the constitutional permissibility of partisan gerrymanders. As you re-read Roberts, C.J.'s, majority opinion, consider what practical difference there is, if any, between its ruling that challengers to political gerrymanders pose nonjusticiable political questions and an "on the merits" conclusion that partisan gerrymanders do not violate the Equal Protection Clause or any other provision of the Constitution.

---

weak, they have failed to carry [their] burden, and it was clear error for the District Court to hold otherwise."

E. Equality in the Counting and Recounting of Votes

BUSH V. GORE
531 U.S. 98, 121 S.Ct. 525, 148 L.Ed.2d 388 (2000).

PER CURIAM.

[After a machine count and recount of ballots in the 2000 Florida presidential election, Democrat Albert Gore trailed Republican George W. Bush by fewer than 1,000 votes. Returns from other states made it clear that the winner of Florida's electoral votes would have an electoral college majority. With the election thus in the balance, Gore sought further manual recounts in selected, heavily Democratic Florida counties, and a complex series of legal battles unfolded. Among the signal events was a United States Supreme Court decision, entered on December 4, vacating a decision of the Florida Supreme Court that effectively extended the deadline established by Florida's Secretary of State for the completion of recounts. When the deadline for "recounts" passed with a full manual recount having been completed in only one county, the legal battles entered a second phase in which Florida law permits legal "contests" of disputed elections. In an appeal from a lower court ruling, the Florida Supreme Court, by 4–3, ordered a manual recount of all so-called "undervotes"—ballots on which the earlier machine counts had failed to record any presidential choice—in one of the counties in which Gore had sought a recount and further directed a manual recount of "undervotes" in all counties. Many of the "undervote" ballots were punchcards on which voters using a stylus had apparently left hanging "chads" or produced "dimples" but made no full perforation. In determining when votes should be recorded, the Florida Supreme Court said only that election officials and lower court judges should follow the legislatively prescribed standard of attempting to discern "the will of the voter."]

[Bush immediately sought a Supreme Court stay of the Florida Supreme Court's ruling, alleging that the state court's decision lacked any foundation in pre-existing Florida law and thus violated both a federal statute and the command of Art. II of the federal constitution that the choice of presidential electors should occur "in such Manner as the [state] Legislature"—as distinguished, Bush argued, from the state constitution or state courts—"may direct." Bush also contended that the unelaborated "will of the voter" standard for counting or not counting ballots with hanging chads and dimples would produce unjustified disparities and violate the Due Process and Equal Protection Clauses. The Supreme Court stayed the Florida Supreme Court's order on Saturday, December 9—just three days before what a majority of the Justices understood to be a Florida statutory deadline of December 12 for the completion of proceedings bearing on the final certification of the state's electors. The Court held oral argument in the case on Monday December 11 and handed down its decision shortly after 10 p.m. on December 12.]

[When] the state legislature vests the right to vote for President in its people, the right to vote as the legislature has prescribed is fundamental; and one source of its fundamental nature lies in the equal weight accorded to each vote and the equal dignity owed to each voter. See [*McPherson v. Blacker*, 146 U.S. 1, 35 (1892)].

The right to vote is protected in more than the initial allocation of the franchise. Equal protection applies as well to the manner of its exercise. Having once granted the right to vote on equal terms, the State may not, by later arbitrary and disparate treatment, value one person's vote over that of another. See, e.g., *Harper v. Virginia Bd. of Elections*, [supra]. * * *

The question before us [is] whether the recount procedures the Florida Supreme Court has adopted are consistent with its obligation to avoid arbitrary and disparate treatment of the members of its electorate. * * *

For purposes of resolving the equal protection challenge, it is not necessary to decide whether the Florida Supreme Court had the authority under the legislative scheme for resolving election disputes to define what a legal vote is and to mandate a manual recount implementing that definition. The recount mechanisms implemented in response to the decisions of the Florida Supreme Court do not satisfy the minimum requirement for non-arbitrary treatment of voters necessary to secure the fundamental right. Florida's basic command for the count of legally cast votes is to consider the "intent of the voter." This is unobjectionable as an abstract proposition and a starting principle. The problem inheres in the absence of specific standards to ensure its equal application.

[T]he standards for accepting or rejecting contested ballots might vary not only from county to county but indeed within a single county from one recount team to another. The record provides some examples. A monitor in Miami-Dade County testified at trial that he observed that three members of the county canvassing board applied different standards in defining a legal vote. * * *

[The Court also expressed concern about the disparate treatment of so-called "overvotes," involving ballots on which a voter made a mark next to the name of more than one candidate. Under the recount scheme mandated by the Florida Supreme Court,] the citizen whose ballot was not read by a machine because he failed to vote for a candidate in a way readable by machine may still have his vote counted in a manual recount; on the other hand, the citizen who marks two candidates in a way discernable by the machine will not have the same opportunity to have his vote count, even if a manual examination of the ballot would reveal the requisite indicia of intent. * * *

In addition [the] Florida Supreme Court's [order] did not specify who would recount the ballots. The county canvassing boards were forced to pull together ad hoc teams comprised of judges from various Circuits who had no previous training in handling and interpreting ballots. Furthermore, while others were permitted to observe, they were prohibited from objecting during the recount.

The recount process, in its features here described, is inconsistent with the minimum procedures necessary to protect the fundamental right of each voter in the special instance of a statewide recount under the authority of a single state judicial officer. Our consideration is limited to the present circumstances, for the problem of equal protection in election processes generally presents many complexities.

The question before the Court is not whether local entities, in the exercise of their expertise, may develop different systems for implementing elections. Instead, we are presented with a situation where a state court with the power to assure uniformity has ordered a statewide recount with minimal procedural safeguards. When a court orders a statewide remedy, there must be at least some assurance that the rudimentary requirements of equal treatment and fundamental fairness are satisfied. * * *

Upon due consideration of the difficulties identified to this point, it is obvious that the recount cannot be conducted in compliance with the requirements of equal protection and due process without substantial additional work. * * *

The Supreme Court of Florida has said that the legislature intended the State's electors to [be chosen] by December 12. That date is upon us, and there is no recount procedure in place under the State Supreme Court's order that comports with minimal constitutional standards. Because it is evident that any recount seeking to meet the December 12 date will be unconstitutional for the reasons we have discussed, we reverse the judgment of the Supreme Court of Florida ordering a recount to proceed. * * *

[Rehnquist, C.J., joined by Scalia and Thomas, JJ., joined the per curiam opinion, but wrote separately, concluding that the Florida Supreme Court violated Art. II by applying rules of decision at odds with those mandated by the Florida legislature.]

JUSTICE STEVENS, with whom JUSTICES GINSBURG and BREYER, join, dissenting.

* * * [Although we have previously found equal protection violations] when individual votes within the same State were weighted unequally, [we] have never before called into question the substantive standard by which a State determines that a vote has been legally cast. And there is no reason to think that the guidance provided to the factfinders, specifically the various canvassing boards, by the "intent of the voter" standard is any less sufficient—or will lead to results any less uniform—than, for example, the "beyond a reasonable doubt" standard employed everyday by ordinary citizens in courtrooms across this country.

Admittedly, the use of differing substandards for determining voter intent in different counties employing similar voting systems may raise serious concerns. Those concerns are alleviated—if not eliminated—by the fact that a single impartial magistrate will ultimately adjudicate all objections arising from the recount process. Of course, as a general matter, "[t]he interpretation of constitutional principles must not be too literal. We must remember that the machinery of government would not work if it were not allowed a little play in its joints." *Bain Peanut Co. of Tex. v. Pinson*, 282 U.S. 499, 501 (1931) (Holmes, J.). If it were otherwise, Florida's decision to leave to each county the determination of what balloting system to employ—despite enormous differences in accuracy—might run afoul of equal protection. So, too, might the similar decisions of the vast majority of state legislatures to delegate to local authorities certain decisions with respect to voting systems and ballot design. * * *

If we assume—as I do—that the [Florida Supreme Court] and the judges who would have carried out its mandate are impartial, its decision does not even raise a colorable federal question. What must underlie petitioners' entire [case] is an unstated lack of confidence in the impartiality and capacity of the state judges who would make the critical decisions if the vote count were to proceed. [The] endorsement of that position by a majority of this Court can only lend credence to the most cynical appraisal of the work of judges throughout the land. [Although] we may never know with complete certainty the winner of this year's Presidential election, the identity of the loser is perfectly clear. It is the Nation's confidence in the judge as an impartial guardian of the rule of law.

JUSTICE SOUTER, with whom JUSTICE BREYER, joins, dissenting.

* * * I would [remand] the case to the courts of Florida with instructions to establish uniform standards for evaluating the several types of ballots that have prompted differing treatments, to be applied within and among counties when passing on such identical ballots in any further recounting (or successive recounting) that the courts might order. * * *

JUSTICE GINSBURG, with whom JUSTICE STEVENS, joins, dissenting:

* * * Ideally, perfection would be the appropriate standard for judging the recount. But we live in an imperfect world, one in which thousands of votes have not been counted. I cannot agree that the recount adopted by the Florida court, flawed as it may be, would yield a result any less fair or precise than the certification that preceded that recount. See, e.g., *McDonald v. Board of Election Comm'rs of Chicago*, 394 U.S. 802, 807 (1969) (even in the context of the right to vote, the state is permitted to reform " 'one step at a time' "). * * *

JUSTICE BREYER, with whom JUSTICE STEVENS, JUSTICE SOUTER, and JUSTICE GINSBURG, join, dissenting.

* * * By halting the manual recount, and thus ensuring that the uncounted legal votes will not be counted under any standard, this Court crafts a remedy out of proportion to the asserted harm. [I]n a system that allows counties to use different types of voting systems, voters already arrive at the polls with an unequal chance that their votes will be counted. I do not see how the fact that this results from counties' selection of different voting machines rather than a court order makes the outcome any more fair. Nor do I understand why the Florida Supreme Court's recount order, which helps to redress this inequity, must be entirely prohibited based on a deficiency that could easily be remedied. * * *

II. TRAVEL

The Court has long held that there is a constitutionally protected right to travel. An early case is *Crandall v. Nevada*, 73 U.S. (6 Wall.) 35 (1867), which struck down a state tax of $1 on rail and stage tickets for out-of-state destinations. In ruling as it did, however, the Court pointedly declined to identify any particular provision of the Constitution as the source of the right. "The people of these United States constitute one nation," the Court emphasized, and it further suggested that implicit in the idea of nationhood was a prohibition against state interferences with the right to travel from one state to another. Since *Crandall*, the Court has consistently recognized a right to travel, but it has had far more difficulty identifying the specific bounds of that right.

SAENZ V. ROE
526 U.S. 489, 119 S.Ct. 1518, 143 L.Ed.2d 689 (1999).

JUSTICE STEVENS delivered the opinion of the Court.

In 1992, California enacted a statute limiting the maximum welfare benefits available to newly arrived residents. The scheme limits the amount payable to a family that has resided in the State for less than 12 months to the amount payable by the State of the family's prior residence. The questions presented by this case are whether the 1992 statute was constitutional when it was enacted and, if not, whether an amendment to the Social Security Act enacted by Congress in 1996 affects that determination. * * *

The word "travel" is not found in the text of the Constitution. Yet the "constitutional right to travel from one State to another" is firmly embedded in our jurisprudence. [In] *Shapiro v. Thompson*, 394 U.S. 618 (1969)]), we reviewed the constitutionality of three statutory provisions that denied welfare to residents of [states] who had resided within those respective jurisdictions less than one year immediately preceding their applications for assistance. Without pausing to identify the specific source of the right, [we] squarely held that it was "constitutionally impermissible" for a State to enact durational residency requirements for the purpose of inhibiting the migration by needy persons into the State. We further held that a classification that had the effect of imposing a penalty on the exercise of the right to travel violated the Equal Protection Clause "unless shown to be necessary to promote a *compelling* governmental interest" and that no such showing had been made. In this case, California argues that [its statute], unlike the legislation reviewed in *Shapiro*, [does] not penalize the right to travel because new arrivals are not ineligible for benefits during their first year of residence. California submits that, instead of being subjected to the strictest scrutiny, the statute should be upheld if it is supported by a rational basis and that the State's legitimate interest in saving over $10 million a year satisfies that test.

[The] "right to travel" discussed in our cases embraces at least three different components. It protects the right of a citizen of one State to enter and to leave another State, the right to be treated as a welcome visitor rather than an unfriendly alien when temporarily present in the second State, and, for those travelers who elect to become permanent residents, the right to be treated like other citizens of that State.* * *

What is at issue in this case [is the] third aspect of the right to travel—the right of the newly arrived citizen to the same privileges and immunities enjoyed by other citizens of the same State. That right is protected not only by the new arrival's status as a state citizen, but also by her status as a citizen of the United States. That additional source of protection is plainly identified in the opening words of the Fourteenth Amendment: "All persons born or naturalized in the United States, and subject to the jurisdiction thereof, are citizens of the United States and of the State wherein they reside. No state shall make or enforce any law which shall abridge the privileges or immunities of citizens of the United States."

Despite fundamentally differing views concerning the coverage of the Privileges or Immunities Clause of the Fourteenth Amendment, most notably expressed in the majority and dissenting opinions in the *Slaughter-House Cases*, [Ch. 5. Sec. 1, II supra] it has always been common ground that this Clause protects the third component of the right to travel. Writing for the majority in the *Slaughter-House Cases*, Justice Miller explained that one of the privileges conferred by this Clause "is that a citizen of the United States can, of his own volition, become a citizen of any State of the Union by a *bona fide* residence therein, with the same rights as other citizens of that State." * * *

Neither mere rationality nor some intermediate standard of review should be used to judge the constitutionality of a state rule that discriminates against some of its citizens because they have been domiciled in the State for less than a year. The appropriate standard may be more categorical than that articulated in *Shapiro*, but it is surely no less strict. * * *

Because this case involves discrimination against citizens who have completed their interstate travel, the State's argument that its welfare scheme affects the right to travel only "incidentally" is beside the point. Were we concerned solely with actual deterrence of migration, we might be persuaded that a partial withholding of benefits constitutes a lesser incursion on the right to travel than an outright denial of all benefits. But since the right to travel embraces the citizen's right to be treated equally in her new State of residence, the discriminatory classification is itself a penalty.

It is undisputed that respondents and the members of the class that they represent are citizens of California and that their need for welfare benefits is unrelated to the length of time that they have resided in California. We thus have no occasion to consider what weight might be given to a citizen's length of residence if the bona fides of her claim to state citizenship were questioned. Moreover, because whatever benefits they receive will be consumed while they remain in California, there is no danger that recognition of their claim will encourage citizens of other States to establish residency for just long enough to acquire some readily portable benefit, such as a divorce or a college education, that will be enjoyed after they return to their original domicile.[49] * * *

Disavowing any desire to fence out the indigent, California has instead advanced an entirely fiscal justification for its [scheme]. The enforcement of [the statute] will save the State approximately $10.9 million a year. The question is not whether such saving is a legitimate purpose but whether the State may accomplish that end by the discriminatory means it has chosen. An evenhanded, across-the-board reduction of about 72 cents per month for every beneficiary would produce the same result. But our negative answer to the question does not rest on the weakness of the State's purported fiscal justification. It rests on the fact that the Citizenship Clause of the Fourteenth Amendment expressly equates citizenship with residence: "That Clause does not provide for, and does not allow for, degrees of citizenship based on length of residence." *Zobel.* [Neither] the duration of respondents' California residence, nor the identity of their prior States of residence, has any relevance to their need for benefits. Nor do those factors bear any relationship to the State's interest in making an equitable allocation of the funds to be distributed among its needy citizens. As in *Shapiro*, we reject any contributory rationale for the denial of benefits to new residents. [S]ee also *Zobel.* In short, the State's legitimate interest in saving money provides no justification for its decision to discriminate among equally eligible citizens.

The question that remains is whether congressional approval of durational residency requirements in the 1996 amendment to the Social Security Act somehow resuscitates the constitutionality of [the statute]. That question is readily answered, for we have consistently held that Congress may not authorize the States to violate the Fourteenth Amendment.

CHIEF JUSTICE REHNQUIST, with whom JUSTICE THOMAS joins, dissenting:

The Court today breathes new life into the previously dormant Privileges or Immunities Clause of the Fourteenth Amendment—a Clause relied upon by this Court in only one other decision, *Colgate v. Harvey*, 296 U.S. 404 (1935), overruled five years later by *Madden v. Kentucky*, 309 U.S. 83 (1940). It uses this Clause to strike down what I believe is a reasonable measure falling under the head of a "good-faith residency requirement." Because I do not think any provision of the Constitution—and surely not a provision relied upon for only the second time since its enactment 130 years ago—requires this result, I dissent. * * *

I agree with the proposition that a "citizen of the United States can, of his own volition, become a citizen of any State of the Union by a *bona fide* residence therein, with the same rights as other citizens of that State." *Slaughter-House Cases.* But I cannot see how the right to become a citizen of another State is a necessary "component" of the right to travel, or why the Court tries to marry these separate and distinct rights. A person is no longer "traveling" in any sense of the word when

---

[49]   The Court had approved statutes imposing durational residency requirements for divorce and in-state tuition in Sosna v. Iowa, 419 U.S. 393 (1975), and Vlandis v. Kline, 412 U.S. 411 (1973).

he finishes his journey to a State which he plans to make his home. Indeed, under the Court's logic, the protections of the Privileges or Immunities Clause recognized in this case come into play only when an individual *stops* traveling with the intent to remain and become a citizen of a new State.

[No] doubt the Court has, in the past 30 years, essentially conflated the right to travel with the right to equal state citizenship in striking down durational residence requirements similar to the one challenged here. [The] Court today tries to clear much of the underbrush created by these prior right-to-travel cases, abandoning its effort to define what residence requirements deprive individuals of "important rights and benefits" or "penalize" the right to travel. Under its new analytical framework, a State, outside certain ill-defined circumstances, cannot classify its citizens by the length of their residence in the State without offending the Privileges or Immunities Clause of the Fourteenth Amendment.

[In] unearthing from its tomb the right to become a state citizen and to be treated equally in the new State of residence, however, the Court ignores a State's need to assure that only persons who establish a bona fide residence receive the benefits provided to current residents of the State. [T]he Court has consistently recognized that while new citizens must have the same opportunity to enjoy the privileges of being a citizen of a State, the States retain the ability to use bona fide residence requirements to ferret out those who intend to take the privileges and run.* * *

If States can require individuals to reside in-state for a year before exercising the right to educational benefits, the right to terminate a marriage, or the right to vote in primary elections that all other state citizens enjoy, then States may surely do the same for welfare benefits. Indeed, there is no material difference between a 1-year residence requirement applied to the level of welfare benefits given out by a State, and the same requirement applied to the level of tuition subsidies at a state university.

[The] Court today recognizes that States retain the ability to determine the bona fides of an individual's claim to residence, but then tries to avoid the issue. It asserts that because respondents' need for welfare benefits is unrelated to the length of time they have resided in California, it has "no occasion to consider what weight might be given to a citizen's length of residence if the bona fides of her claim to state citizenship were questioned." * * *

The Court tries to distinguish education and divorce benefits by contending that the welfare payment here will be consumed in California, while a college education or a divorce produces benefits that are "portable" and can be enjoyed after individuals return to their original domicile. But this "you can't take it with you" distinction is more apparent than real, and offers little guidance to lower courts who must apply this rationale in the future. Welfare payments are a form of insurance, giving impoverished individuals and their families the means to meet the demands of daily life while they receive the necessary training, education, and time to look for a job. The cash itself will no doubt be spent in California, but the benefits from receiving this income and having the opportunity to become employed or employable will stick with the welfare recipient if they stay in California or go back to their true domicile. Similarly, tuition subsidies are "consumed" in-state but the recipient takes the benefits of a college education with him wherever he goes. A welfare subsidy is thus as much an investment in human capital as is a tuition subsidy, and their attendant benefits are just as "portable." More importantly, this foray into social economics demonstrates that the line drawn by the Court borders on the metaphysical, and requires lower courts to plumb the policies animating certain benefits like welfare to define their "essence" and hence their "portability." * * *

I therefore believe that the durational residence requirement challenged here is a permissible exercise of the State's power to "assur[e] that services provided for its residents are enjoyed only by residents."

JUSTICE THOMAS, with whom THE CHIEF JUSTICE joins, dissenting.

[Because] I believe that the demise of the Privileges or Immunities Clause has contributed in no small part to the current disarray of our Fourteenth Amendment jurisprudence, I would be open to reevaluating its meaning in an appropriate case. Before invoking the Clause, however, we should endeavor to understand what the framers of the Fourteenth Amendment thought that it meant. We should also consider whether the Clause should displace, rather than augment, portions of our equal protection and substantive due process jurisprudence. The majority's failure to consider these important questions raises the specter that the Privileges or Immunities Clause will become yet another convenient tool for inventing new rights, limited solely by the "predilections of those who happen at the time to be Members of this Court." * * *

III. WELFARE AND EDUCATION

Based on a number of Warren Court decisions that seemed to have as their practical aim ensuring that the poor would have access to opportunities that are routinely enjoyed by the economically better off, by the late 1960s a number of commentators thought that the Justices might be poised either to recognize fundamental rights to education and possibly welfare or to identify the poor as a suspect class. The Court, however, never formally confronted whether to do so during the Warren years. Subsequent decisions have rejected claims that welfare and education are fundamental rights for purposes of equal protection analysis.

———

DANDRIDGE v. WILLIAMS, 397 U.S. 471 (1970): Maryland's Aid to Families With Dependent Children Program gave most eligible families their computed "standard of need," but imposed a "maximum limitation" on the total amount any family could receive. The Court, per STEWART, J., held that the statutory ceiling did not violate equal protection: "[H]ere we deal with state regulation in the social and economic field, not affecting freedoms guaranteed by the Bill of Rights, and claimed to violate the Fourteenth Amendment only because the regulation results in some disparity in grants of welfare payments to the largest AFDC families.[16] In [this area] a state does not violate [equal protection] merely because the classifications made by its laws are imperfect." "It is enough that the state's action be rationally based and free from invidious discrimination."

"To be sure, [many cases] enunciating this [standard] have in the main involved state regulation of business or industry. The administration of public welfare assistance, by contrast, involves the most basic economic needs of impoverished human beings, [but] we can find no basis for applying a different constitutional standard. [By] combining a limit on the recipient's grant with permission to retain money earned, without reduction in the amount of the grant, Maryland provides an incentive to seek gainful employment. And by keeping the maximum family AFDC grants to the minimum wage a steadily employed head of a household receives, the State maintains some semblance of an equitable balance between families on welfare and those supported by an employed breadwinner.

"It is true that in some AFDC families there may be no person who is employable. It is also true that with respect to AFDC families whose determined standard of need is below the regulatory maximum, [the] employment incentive is absent. But the Equal Protection Clause does not require that a State must choose between attacking every aspect of a problem or not attacking the problem at all. [T]he intractable economic, social, and even philosophical problems presented by public welfare assistance programs are not the business of this Court."[50]

MARSHALL, J., joined by Brennan, J., dissented:[51] "[T]he only distinction between those children with respect to whom assistance is granted and those [denied] is the size of the family into which the child permits himself to be born. [This] is grossly underinclusive in terms of the class which the AFDC program was designed to assist, namely *all* needy dependent children, [and requires] a persuasive justification * * * .

"The Court never undertakes to inquire for such a justification; rather it avoids the task by focusing upon the abstract dichotomy between two different approaches to equal protection problems which have been utilized by this Court.

"[The] cases relied on by the Court, in which a 'mere rationality' test was actually used, [involve] regulation of business interests. The extremes to which the Court has gone in dreaming up rational bases for state regulation in that area may in many instances be ascribed to a healthy revulsion from the Court's earlier excesses in using the Constitution to protect interests which have more than enough power to protect themselves in the legislative halls. This case, involving the literally vital interests of a powerless minority—poor families without

---

16   **[Ct's Note]** Cf. *Shapiro*, [Part II supra,] where, by contrast, the Court found state interference with the constitutionally protected freedom of interstate travel.

50   See also *Lindsey v. Normet*, 405 U.S. 56 (1972) (the assurance of adequate housing is not a fundamental right).

51   Douglas, J., dissented on the ground (agreed to also by Marshall and Brennan, JJ.) that the Maryland law was inconsistent with the Social Security Act.

breadwinners—is far removed from the area of business regulation, as the Court concedes. * * *

"In my view, equal protection analysis of this case is not appreciably advanced by the a priori definition of a 'right,' fundamental [and thus invoking the 'compelling' interest test] or otherwise.[14] Rather, concentration must be placed upon the character of the classification in question, the relative importance to individuals in the class discriminated against of the governmental benefits which they do not receive, and the asserted state interests in support of the classification. * * *

"It is the individual interests here [that] most clearly distinguish this case from the 'business regulation' [cases]. AFDC support to needy dependent children provides the stuff which sustains those children's lives: food, clothing, shelter. And this Court has already recognized [that] when a benefit, even a 'gratuitous' benefit, is necessary to sustain life, stricter constitutional standards, both procedural[17] and substantive,[18] are applied to the deprivation of that benefit.

"Nor is the distinction upon which the deprivation is here based—the distinction between large and small families—one which readily commends [itself]. Indeed, governmental discrimination between children on the basis of a factor over which they have no control [bears] some resemblance to the classification between legitimate and illegitimate children which we condemned [in cases discussed in Sec. 4, IV supra]."

On examination, the asserted state interests were either "arbitrary," impermissible, of "minimum rationality," "drastically overinclusive," or "grossly underinclusive." "The existence of [other] alternatives [to satisfy asserted state interests] does not, of course, conclusively establish the invalidity of the maximum grant regulation. It is certainly relevant, however, in appraising the overall interest of the State in the maintenance of the regulation [against] a fundamental constitutional challenge."

SAN ANTONIO IND. SCHOOL DIST. V. RODRIGUEZ
411 U.S. 1, 93 S.Ct. 1278, 36 L.Ed.2d 16 (1973).

JUSTICE POWELL delivered the opinion of the Court.

This suit attacking the Texas system of financing public education was initiated by Mexican-American parents [as] a class action on behalf of

---

[14]   **[Ct's Note]** [T]he Court's insistence that equal protection analysis turns on the basis of a closed category of "fundamental rights" involves a curious value judgment. It is certainly difficult to believe that a person whose very survival is at stake would be comforted by the knowledge that his "fundamental" rights are preserved intact. * * *

[17]   **[Ct's Note]** See *Goldberg v. Kelly*, [397 U.S. 254 (1970)].

[18]   **[Ct's Note]** [See] *Kirk v. Board of Regents*, 273 Cal.App.2d 430, 440–441 (1969), appeal dismissed, 396 U.S. 554 (1970), upholding a one-year residency requirement for tuition-free graduate education at state university, and distinguishing *Shapiro* on the ground that it "involved the immediate and pressing need for preservation of life and health of persons unable to live without public assistance, and their dependent children."

schoolchildren throughout the State who are members of minority groups or who are poor and reside in school districts having a low property tax base. * * *

Recognizing the need for increased state funding to help offset disparities in local spending [because of sizable differences in the value of assessable property between local school districts,] the state legislature [established the] Minimum Foundation School Program [which] accounts for approximately half of the total educational expenditures in Texas. [It] calls for state and local contributions to a fund earmarked specifically for teacher salaries, operating expenses, and transportation costs. The State [finances] approximately [80%]. The districts' share, known as the Local Fund Assignment, is apportioned among the school districts under a formula designed to reflect each district's relative taxpaying ability. * * *

The school district in which appellees reside, [Edgewood,] has been compared throughout this litigation with the Alamo Heights [District. Edgewood] is situated in the core-city sector of San Antonio in a residential neighborhood that has little commercial or industrial property. [A]pproximately 90% of the student population is Mexican-American and over 6% is Negro. The average assessed property value per pupil is $5,960—the lowest in the metropolitan area—and the median family income ($4,686) is also the lowest. At an equalized tax rate of $1.05 per $100 of assessed property—the highest in the metropolitan area—the district contributed $26 to the education of each child for the 1967–1968 school year above its Local Fund Assignment for the Minimum Foundation Program. The Foundation Program contributed $222 per pupil for a state-local total of $248. Federal funds added another $108 for a total of $356 per pupil.

Alamo Heights is the most affluent school district in San Antonio. [Its] school population [has] only 18% Mexican-Americans and less than 1% Negroes. The assessed property value per pupil exceeds $49,000 and the median family income is $8,001. In 1967–1968 the local tax rate of $.85 per $100 of valuation yielded $333 per pupil over and above its contribution to the Foundation Program. Coupled with the $225 provided from that Program, the district was able to supply $558 per student. Supplemented by a $36 per pupil grant from federal sources, Alamo Heights spent $594 per pupil.

[M]ore recent partial statistics indicate that [the] trend of increasing state aid has been significant. For the 1970–1971 school year, the Foundation School Program allotment for Edgewood was $356 per [pupil and] Alamo Heights [received] $491 per [pupil].[35] These recent figures also reveal the extent to which

---

35   [Ct's Note] [I]t is apparent that Alamo Heights has enjoyed a larger gain [due] to the emphasis in the State's allocation formula on the guaranteed minimum salaries for teachers. Higher salaries are guaranteed to teachers having more years of experience and possessing more advanced degrees. Therefore, Alamo Heights, which has a greater percentage of experienced personnel with advanced degrees, receives more State support. [Because] more dollars have been given to districts that already spend more per pupil, such Foundation formulas have been described as "anti-equalizing." The formula, however, is anti-equalizing only if viewed in absolute terms. The percentage disparity between the two Texas districts is diminished substantially by State aid. Alamo Heights derived in 1967–1968 almost 13 times as much money from local taxes

these two districts' allotments were funded from their own required contributions to the Local Fund Assignment. Alamo Heights, because of its relative wealth, was required to contribute out of its local property tax collections approximately $100 per pupil, or about 20% of its Foundation grant. Edgewood, on the other hand, paid only $8.46 per pupil, which is about 2.4% of its grant. [Finding] that wealth is a "suspect" classification and that education is a "fundamental" interest, the District Court held that the Texas system could be sustained only if the State could show that it was premised upon some compelling state interest. * * *

II.   [The] wealth discrimination discovered [is] quite unlike any of the forms of wealth discrimination heretofore reviewed by this Court. [The] individuals [who] constituted the class discriminated against in our prior cases shared two distinguishing characteristics: because of their impecunity they were completely unable to pay for some desired benefit, and as a consequence, they sustained an absolute deprivation of a meaningful opportunity to enjoy that benefit. [For example,] *Douglas v. California* [provides] no relief for those on whom the burdens of paying for a criminal defense are, relatively speaking, great but not insurmountable. Nor does it deal with relative differences in the quality of counsel acquired by the less wealthy.

[Neither] of the two distinguishing characteristics of wealth classifications can be found here. First, [there] is reason to believe that the poorest families are not necessarily clustered in the poorest property districts. A [recent] Connecticut study found, not surprisingly, that the poor were clustered around commercial and industrial areas—those same areas that provide the most attractive sources of property tax income for school districts. * * *

Second, [lack] of personal resources has not occasioned an absolute deprivation of the desired benefit. The argument here is not that the children [are] receiving no public education; rather, it is that they are receiving a poorer quality education [than] children in districts having more assessable wealth. [A] sufficient answer to appellees' argument is that at least where wealth is involved the Equal Protection Clause does not require absolute equality or precisely equal advantages. [Texas] asserts that the Minimum Foundation Program provides an "adequate" education for all children in the State. [No] proof was offered at trial persuasively discrediting or refuting the State's assertion. * * * 60

This brings us [to] the third way in which the classification scheme might be defined—*district* wealth discrimination. Since the only correlation indicated by the evidence is between district property wealth and expenditures, it may be argued

---

as Edgewood did. The State aid grants to each district in 1970–1971 lowered the ratio to approximately two to [one].

60   **[Ct's Note]** [If] elementary and secondary education were made available by the State only to those able to pay a tuition assessed against each pupil, there would be a clearly defined class of "poor" people—definable in terms of their inability to pay the prescribed sum—who would be absolutely precluded from receiving an education. That case would present a far more compelling set of circumstances for judicial assistance than [this one].

that discrimination might be found without regard to the individual income characteristics of district residents. * * *

However described, it is clear that appellees' suit asks this Court to extend its most exacting scrutiny to review a system that allegedly discriminates against a large, diverse, and amorphous class, unified only by the common factor of residence in districts that happen to have less taxable wealth than other districts. The system of alleged discrimination and the class it defines have none of the traditional indicia of suspectness: the class is not saddled with such disabilities, or subjected to such a history of purposeful unequal treatment, or relegated to such a position of political powerlessness as to command extraordinary protection from the majoritarian political process.

We thus conclude that the Texas system does not operate to the peculiar disadvantage of any suspect class.

[Recognizing] that this Court has never heretofore held that wealth discrimination alone provides an adequate basis for invoking strict scrutiny, appellees [also] assert that the State's system impermissibly interferes with the exercise of a "fundamental" right [requiring] the strict standard of judicial review. * * *

Nothing this Court holds today in any way detracts from our historic dedication to public education. [But] the importance of a service performed by the State does not determine whether it must be regarded as fundamental for purposes of examination under the Equal Protection Clause. [In *Shapiro,* the] right to interstate travel had long been recognized as a right of constitutional significance, and the Court's decision, therefore, did not require an ad hoc determination as to the social or economic importance of that right. [In *Dandridge*], the central importance of welfare benefits to the poor was not an adequate foundation for requiring the State to justify its law by showing some compelling state interest. * * *

The lesson of these cases [is that it] is not the province of this Court to create substantive constitutional rights in the name of guaranteeing equal protection of the laws. Thus the key to discovering whether education is "fundamental" is not to be found in comparisons of the relative societal significance of education as opposed to subsistence or housing [or] by weighing whether education is as important as the right to travel. Rather, the answer lies in assessing whether there is a right to education explicitly or implicitly guaranteed by the Constitution. *Dunn;*[74] *Skinner.*[76]

---

[74]   [Ct's Note] *Dunn* fully canvasses this Court's voting rights cases and explains that "this Court has made clear that a citizen has a *constitutionally protected right* to participate in elections on an equal basis with other citizens in the jurisdiction." (emphasis supplied). The constitutional underpinnings of [this right] can no longer be doubted even though, as the Court noted in *Harper,* "the right to vote in state elections is nowhere explicitly mentioned."

[76]   [Ct's Note] *Skinner* applied the standard of close scrutiny to a state law permitting forced sterilization of "habitual criminals." Implicit in the Court's opinion is the recognition that

Education, of course, is not among the rights afforded explicit protection under [the] Constitution. Nor do we find any basis for saying it is implicitly so protected. [But] appellees [contend] that education is distinguishable from other services and benefits provided by the State because it bears a peculiarly close relationship to other rights and liberties accorded protection under the Constitution [in that] it is essential to the effective exercise of First Amendment freedoms and to intelligent utilization of the right to vote. In asserting a nexus between speech and education, appellees urge that the right to speak is meaningless unless the speaker is capable of articulating his thoughts intelligently and persuasively. [A] similar line of reasoning is pursued with respect to the right to [vote]: a voter cannot cast his ballot intelligently unless his reading skills and thought processes have been adequately developed.

We need not dispute any of these propositions. [Yet] we have never presumed to possess either the ability or the authority to guarantee to the citizenry the most *effective* speech or the most *informed* electoral choice. That these may be desirable goals [is] not to be doubted. [But] they are not values to be implemented by judicial intrusion into otherwise legitimate state activities.

[The] logical limitations on appellees' nexus theory are difficult to perceive. [Empirical] examination might well buttress an assumption that the ill-fed, ill-clothed, and ill-housed are among the most ineffective participants in the political process and that they derive the least enjoyment from the benefits of the First Amendment. * * *

[The] present case, in another basic sense, is significantly different from any of the cases in which the Court has applied strict scrutiny [to] legislation touching upon constitutionally protected rights. [These] involved legislation which "deprived," "infringed," or "interfered" with the free exercise of some such fundamental personal right or liberty. [We] think it plain that, in substance, the thrust of the Texas system is affirmative and reformatory and, therefore, should be scrutinized under judicial principles sensitive to the nature of the State's efforts and to the rights reserved to the States under the Constitution.

[A] century of Supreme Court adjudication under the Equal Protection Clause affirmatively supports the application of the traditional standard of review, which requires only that the State's system be shown to bear some rational relationship to legitimate state purposes. This case represents [a] direct attack on the way in which Texas has chosen to raise and disburse state and local tax revenues. [This] Court has often admonished against such interferences with the State's fiscal policies under the Equal Protection Clause [and] we continue to acknowledge that the Justices of this Court lack both the expertise and the familiarity with local problems so necessary to the making of wise decisions with respect to the raising and disposition of public revenues. Yet, we are urged to direct the States either to alter drastically the present system or to throw out the property tax altogether in

---

the right of procreation is among the rights of personal privacy protected under the Constitution. See *Roe v. Wade*.

favor of some other form of taxation. No scheme of taxation [has] yet been devised which is free of all discriminatory impact. In such a complex arena in which no perfect alternatives exist, the Court does well not to impose too rigorous a standard of scrutiny lest all local fiscal schemes become subjects of criticism under the Equal Protection Clause.

[T]his case also involves the most persistent and difficult questions of educational policy, another area in which this Court's lack of specialized knowledge and experience counsels against premature interference with the informed judgments made at the state and local levels. [I]t would be difficult to imagine a case having a greater potential impact on our federal system than the one now before us, in which we are urged to abrogate systems of financing public education presently in existence in virtually every State. * * *

Reversed.

JUSTICE BRENNAN, dissenting.

Although I agree with my Brother White that the Texas statutory scheme is devoid of any rational basis, [I] also record my disagreement with the Court's rather distressing assertion that a right may be deemed "fundamental" for the purposes of equal protection analysis only if it is "explicitly or implicitly guaranteed by the Constitution." As my Brother Marshall convincingly demonstrates our prior cases stand for the proposition that "fundamentality" is, in large measure, a function of the right's importance in terms of the effectuation of those rights which are in fact constitutionally guaranteed. * * *

JUSTICE WHITE, with whom JUSTICE DOUGLAS and JUSTICE BRENNAN join, dissenting.

[T]his case would be quite different if it were true that the Texas system, while insuring minimum educational expenditures in every district through state funding, extended a meaningful option to all local districts to increase their per-pupil [expenditures. But for] districts with a low per-pupil real estate tax base [the] Texas system utterly fails to extend a realistic choice to parents because the property tax, which is the only revenue-raising mechanism extended to school districts, is practically and legally unavailable. * * *

In order to equal the highest yield in any other Bexar County district, Alamo Heights would be required to tax at the rate of 68 cents per $100 of assessed valuation. Edgewood would be required to tax at the prohibitive rate of $5.76 per $100. But state law places a $1.50 per $100 ceiling on the maintenance tax [rate]. Requiring the State to establish only that unequal treatment is in furtherance of a permissible goal, without also requiring the State to show that the means chosen to effectuate that goal are rationally related to its achievement, makes equal protection analysis no more than an empty gesture. * * *

JUSTICE MARSHALL, with whom JUSTICE DOUGLAS, concurs, dissenting.

[T]he majority's holding can only be seen as a retreat from our historic commitment to equality of educational opportunity. [At] the very least, in view of the substantial interdistrict disparities in funding, [the] burden of proving that these disparities do not in fact affect the quality of children's education must fall upon the appellants. Yet [they] have argued no more than that the relationship is ambiguous. * * *

Nor can I accept the appellants' apparent suggestion [that equal protection] cannot be offended by substantially unequal state treatment of persons who are similarly situated so long as the State provides everyone with some unspecified amount of education which evidently is "enough." [The] Equal Protection Clause is not addressed to the minimal sufficiency but rather to the unjustifiable inequalities of state action. [In] light of the data introduced before the District Court, the conclusion that the school children of property poor districts constitute a sufficient class for our purposes seems indisputable to me. [Whether] this discrimination against [them] is violative of the Equal Protection Clause is the question to which we must now turn.

[The] Court apparently seeks to establish [that] equal protection cases fall into one of two neat categories which dictate the appropriate standard of review—strict scrutiny or mere rationality. But [a] principled reading of what this Court has done reveals that it has applied a spectrum of standards [which] clearly comprehends variations in the degree of care with which the Court will scrutinize particular classifications, depending [on] the constitutional and societal importance of the interest adversely affected and the recognized invidiousness of the basis upon which the particular classification is drawn. * * *

I therefore cannot accept the majority's labored efforts to demonstrate that fundamental interests, which call for strict scrutiny of the challenged classification, encompass only established rights which we are somehow bound to recognize from the text of the Constitution itself. * * *

I would like to know where the Constitution guarantees the right to procreate, *Skinner,* or the right to vote in state elections, e.g., *Reynolds v. Sims,* or the right to an appeal from a criminal conviction, e.g., *Griffin.* These are instances in which, due to the importance of the interests at stake, the Court has displayed a strong concern with the existence of discriminatory state treatment. But the Court has [never] indicated that these are interests which independently enjoy full-blown constitutional protection. * * *

The majority is, of course, correct when it suggests that the process of determining which interests are fundamental is a difficult one. But I do not think the problem is insurmountable. [The task] should be to determine the extent to which constitutionally guaranteed rights are dependent on interests not mentioned in the Constitution. As the nexus between the specific constitutional guarantee and the nonconstitutional interest draws closer, the nonconstitutional interest becomes more fundamental and the degree of judicial scrutiny applied when the interest is infringed on a discriminatory basis must be adjusted accordingly. * * * Procreation is now understood to be important because of its interaction with the established constitutional right of privacy. The exercise of the state franchise is closely tied to basic civil and political rights inherent in the First Amendment. And access to criminal appellate processes enhances the integrity of the range of rights implicit in the Fourteenth Amendment guarantee of due process of law. Only if we closely protect the related interests from state discrimination do we ultimately ensure the integrity of the constitutional guarantee itself. This is the real lesson that must be taken from our previous decisions involving interests deemed to be fundamental.

[It] is true that this Court has never deemed the provision of free public education to be required by the Constitution. [But] the fundamental importance of education is amply indicated by the prior decisions of this Court, by the unique status accorded public education by our society, and by the close relationship between education and some of our most basic constitutional [values].

[I] do not question that local control of public education, as an abstract matter, constitutes a very substantial state interest. [But] on this record, it is apparent that the State's purported concern with local control is offered primarily as an excuse rather than as a justification for interdistrict inequality.

In Texas statewide laws regulate [the] most minute details of local public education. For example, the State prescribes required courses. All textbooks must be submitted for state [approval]. The State has established the qualifications necessary for teaching in Texas public schools and the procedures for obtaining certification. The State has even legislated on the length of the school [day.]

Moreover, even if we accept Texas' general dedication to local control in educational matters, [i]f Texas had a system truly dedicated to local fiscal control one would expect the quality of the educational opportunity provided in each district to vary with the decision of the voters in that district as to the level of sacrifice they wish to make for public education. [But local] districts cannot choose to have the best education [by] imposing the highest tax rate. Instead, the quality of the educational opportunity offered by any particular district is largely determined by the amount of taxable property located in the district—a factor over which local voters can exercise no control.

[In] my judgment, any substantial degree of scrutiny of the operation of the Texas financing scheme reveals that the State has selected means wholly inappropriate to secure its purported interest in assuring its school districts local fiscal control.[96] At the same time, appellees have pointed out a variety of alternative financing schemes which may serve the State's purported interest in local control as well as, if not better than, the present scheme without the current

---

[96] **[Ct's Note]** [Although] my Brother White purports to reach this result by application of that lenient standard of mere rationality, [it] seems to be that the care with which he scrutinizes the practical effectiveness of the present local property tax as a device for affording local fiscal control reflects the application of a more stringent standard of [review].

impairment of the educational opportunity of vast numbers of Texas schoolchildren.[98] * * *

The Court distinguished *Rodriguez*, per BRENNAN, J., in PLYLER v. DOE (1982), Sec. 4, IV supra, which invalidated a Texas statute that denied free public education to undocumented alien children. In an opinion that was joined by Powell, J., the author of the Court opinion in *Rodriguez*, Brennan, J., stressed "the importance of education": "Persuasive arguments support the view that a State may withhold its beneficence from those whose very presence within the United States is the product of their own unlawful conduct. [But] § 21.031 [imposes] its discriminatory burden on the basis of a legal characteristic over which children can have little control. It is thus difficult to conceive of a rational justification for penalizing these children for their presence within the United States. * * *

"Public education is not a 'right' granted to individuals by the Constitution. *Rodriguez*. But neither is it merely some governmental 'benefit' indistinguishable from other forms of social welfare legislation. Both the importance of education in maintaining our basic institutions, and the lasting impact of its deprivation on the life of the child, mark the distinction. [We] cannot ignore the significant social costs borne by our Nation when select groups are denied the means to absorb the values and skills upon which our social order rests.[20] [Thus], the discrimination contained in § 21.031 can hardly be considered rational unless it furthers some substantial goal of the State.

"[First,] appellants appear to suggest that the State may seek to protect the State from an influx of illegal immigrants. While a State might have an interest in mitigating the potentially harsh economic effects of sudden shifts in population, [t]here is no evidence in the record suggesting that illegal entrants impose any significant burden on the State's economy. To the contrary, the available evidence suggests that illegal aliens underutilize public services, while contributing their labor to the local economy and tax money to the State fisc. The dominant incentive for illegal entry [into] Texas is the availability of employment; few if any illegal immigrants come to this country [to] avail themselves of a free education. * * *

"Second, [appellants] suggest that undocumented children are appropriately singled out for exclusion because of the special burdens they impose on the State's ability to provide high quality public education. [In] terms of educational cost and

------

[98]   **[Ct's Note]** [Central] financing would leave in local hands the entire gamut of local educational policy-making—teachers, curriculum, school sites, the whole process of allocating resources among alternative educational objectives. [A] second possibility is the much discussed theory of district power equalization [under which] each school district would receive a fixed amount of revenue per pupil for any particular level of tax effort regardless of the level of local property tax base. * * *

[20]   **[Ct's Note]** * * * Whatever the current status of these children, the courts below concluded that many will remain here permanently and that some indeterminate number will eventually become citizens. * * *

need, however, undocumented children are 'basically indistinguishable' from legally resident alien children.

"Finally, appellants suggest that undocumented children are appropriately singled out because their unlawful presence within the United States renders them less likely than other children to remain within the boundaries of the State, and to put their education to productive social or political use within the State. Even assuming that such an interest is legitimate, it is an interest that is most difficult to quantify. The State has no assurance that any child, citizen or not, will employ the education provided by the State within the confines of the State's borders. In any event, the record is clear that many of the undocumented children disabled by this classification will remain in this country indefinitely, and that some will become lawful residents or citizens of the United States. It is difficult to understand precisely what the State hopes to achieve by promoting the creation and perpetuation of a subclass of illiterates within our boundaries, surely adding to the problems and costs of unemployment, welfare, and crime. It is thus clear that whatever savings might be achieved [are] wholly insubstantial in light of the costs involved to these children, the State, and the Nation."

POWELL, J., who joined the Court's opinion, concurred "to emphasize the unique character of the case": "[These children] have been singled out for a lifelong penalty and stigma. A legislative classification that threatens the creation of an underclass of future citizens and residents cannot be reconciled with one of the fundamental purposes of the Fourteenth Amendment. In these unique circumstances, the Court properly may require that the State's interests be substantial and that the means bear a 'fair and substantial relation' to these interests.[3]"

BURGER, C.J., joined by White, Rehnquist, and O'Connor, JJ., dissented: "[B]y patching together bits and pieces of what might be termed quasi-suspect-class and quasi-fundamental-rights analysis, the Court spins out a theory custom-tailored to the facts[, and its] opinion rests on such a unique confluence of theories and rationales that it will likely stand for little beyond the results in these particular [cases].

"[Once] it is conceded—as the Court does—that illegal aliens are not a suspect class, and that education is not a fundamental right, our inquiry should focus on and be limited to whether the legislative classification at issue bears a rational relationship to a legitimate state purpose. [I]t simply is not 'irrational' for a State to conclude that it does not have the same responsibility to provide benefits for persons whose very presence in the State and this country is illegal as it does to provide for persons lawfully present."

---

[3]   [Ct's Note] [I]n *Rodriguez* no group of children was singled out by the State and then penalized because of their parents' status. [Nor] was any group of children totally deprived of all education as in this case. If the resident children of illegal aliens were denied welfare assistance, made available by government to all other children who qualify, this also—in my opinion—would be an impermissible penalizing of children because of their parents' status.

CHAPTER 10

THE CONCEPT OF STATE ACTION

■ ■ ■

1. INTRODUCTION

The Supreme Court has long held that most provisions of the Constitution that protect individual rights—including Art. 1, §§ 9 and 10, the Bill of Rights, and the Fourteenth and Fifteenth Amendments—impose restrictions or obligations only on the government and its officials. The "state action doctrine" grows out of this restriction. On the one hand, public officials who act under color of governmental authority are "state actors" who are subject to constitutional norms and who can almost invariably be sued for violating the Constitution. These include legislators, the president, executive officials, public prosecutors, and state and local police, to name just a few.[1] On the other hand, private citizens who are not governmental officials will rarely be deemed to be state actors. Outside of certain exceptional circumstances, they are not bound by the Constitution and cannot be sued for violating it. Most of this chapter concerns the relatively anomalous situations in which entities and people who are neither governmental bodies nor public officials will be deemed to be "state actors" and therefore to be subject to judicially enforceable constitutional constraints. As you read the following materials, however, you should not forget the general rule: governmental officials are nearly invariably state actors and those who are not public officials are almost never directly subject to constitutional restrictions.

The state action doctrine received its first extensive treatment in the *Civil Rights Cases* (which follow immediately). The issue directly before the Court involved Congress' authority under the final sections of the Thirteenth and Fourteenth Amendments to "enforce" those amendments' substantive provisions "by appropriate legislation" (a topic to be considered in detail in Ch. 11). The Court held that neither the Thirteenth nor the Fourteenth Amendment empowered Congress to pass the Civil Rights Act of 1875, making racial discrimination unlawful in public accommodations (inns, public conveyances, places of public amusement, etc.). Thus, "no other ground of authority for its passage being suggested, [the Act] must necessarily be declared void." The Court's holding about Congress' power to "enforce" the Fourteenth Amendment depended on its logically

---

[1]   In rare cases, the conduct of some public employees may not constitute state action. For example, in *Polk County v. Dodson*, 454 U.S. 312 (1981), the Supreme Court explained that a public defender does "not ac[t] on behalf of the State; he is the State's adversary." Public defenders are "not amenable to administrative direction in the same sense as other employees of the State," are "professional[ly] independent" of the state, and have ethical obligations to their client that supersede their employment by the state.

antecedent determination that § 1 of the Fourteenth Amendment applied only to "state action" and imposed no antidiscrimination obligations on private citizens. Because the Fourteenth Amendment did not bar private discrimination, the Court reasoned, congressional legislation purporting to ban private discrimination did not lie within Congress' authority to "enforce" the Fourteenth Amendment. Although the *Civil Rights Cases* focused more on Congress' enforcement power than on judicially enforceable constitutional obligations in the absence of congressional legislation, the Court's discussion of "state action" remains the classic exposition.

CIVIL RIGHTS CASES
109 U.S. 3, 3 S.Ct. 18, 27 L.Ed. 835 (1883).

JUSTICE BRADLEY delivered the opinion of the Court.

These cases are all founded on the first and second sections of the act of Congress known as the "Civil Rights Act," passed March 1, 1875, entitled "An Act to protect all citizens in their civil and legal rights." Two of the cases [are] indictments for denying to persons of color the accommodations and privileges of an inn or hotel; two of them [are] for denying to individuals the privileges and accommodations of a theater, the information against Ryan being for refusing a colored person a seat.

[Under the Fourteenth Amendment,] individual invasion of individual rights is not [prohibited. The Fourteenth Amendment] nullifies and makes void all state legislation, and state action of every kind, which impairs the privileges and immunities of citizens of the United States, or which injures them in life, liberty, or property without due process of law, or which denies to any of them the equal protection of the laws. [T]he last section of the amendment [does] not authorize Congress to create a code of municipal law for the regulation of private rights; but to provide modes of redress against the operation of state laws, and the action of state officers, executive or judicial, when these are subversive of the fundamental rights specified in the amendment. * * *

An inspection of the [Civil Rights Act of 1875] shows that [it] proceeds ex directo to declare that certain acts committed by individuals shall be deemed offenses. [It] does not profess to be corrective of any constitutional wrong committed by the states; [it] applies equally to cases arising in states which have the justest laws respecting the personal rights of citizens, and whose authorities are ever ready to enforce such laws as to those which arise in states that may have violated the prohibition of the amendment. In other words, it steps into the domain of local jurisprudence, and lays down rules for the conduct of individuals in society towards each other. [C]ivil rights, such as are guaranteed by the Constitution against state aggression, cannot be impaired by the wrongful acts of individuals, unsupported by state authority in the shape of laws, customs, or judicial or executive proceedings. [An] individual cannot deprive a man of his right to vote, to hold property, to buy and to sell, to sue in the courts, or to be a witness or a juror;

he may, by force or fraud, interfere with the enjoyment of the right in a particular case; [but] unless protected in these wrongful acts by some shield of state law or state authority, he cannot destroy or injure the right; he will only render himself amenable [to] the laws of the state where the wrongful acts are committed. [The] abrogation and denial of rights, for which the states alone were or could be responsible, was the great seminal and fundamental wrong which was intended to be remedied. * * *

[The Thirteenth Amendment] is not a mere prohibition of state laws establishing or upholding slavery, but an absolute declaration that slavery or involuntary servitude shall not exist in any part of the United States [and] that the power vested in Congress to enforce the article by appropriate legislation, clothes Congress with power to pass all laws necessary and proper for abolishing all badges and incidents of slavery, in the United States. [T]he civil rights bill of 1866, passed in view of the Thirteenth Amendment, before the fourteenth was adopted, undertook to wipe out these burdens and disabilities, [and to confer] the same right to make and enforce contracts, to sue, be parties, give evidence, and to inherit, purchase, lease, sell, and convey property, as is enjoyed by white citizens. [At] that time (in 1866) Congress did not assume, under the authority given by the Thirteenth Amendment, to adjust what may be called the social rights of men and races in the community; but only to declare and vindicate those fundamental rights which appertain to the essence of citizenship, and the enjoyment or deprivation of which constitutes the essential distinction between freedom and slavery. * * *

[It] would be running the slavery argument into the ground to make it apply to every act of discrimination which a person may see fit to make as to the guests he will entertain, or as to the people he will take into his coach or cab or car, or admit to his concert or theater, or deal with in other matters of intercourse or business.

HARLAN, J., dissented.

Although the basic principles underlying the state action doctrine are well settled, and although the presence or absence of state action is nearly self-evident in most instances, issues involving the presence or absence of state action have generated significant controversy in some categories of cases. The remainder of this chapter traces the Court's response. Although the doctrine is highly complex, the Court has most frequently insisted that a private citizen or entity should be deemed to be a "state actor" only insofar as it (a) is performing a "government function" or (b) is sufficiently "involved" or "entwined" with or "encouraged by" the state to be held to the state's constitutional obligations. Controversy has also attended the question whether state failures to act—for example, by failing to come to the aid of their citizens—constitute judicially reviewable state action. State failure to act will be discussed at the end of this chapter.

2. "GOVERNMENT FUNCTION"

The Court has defined the category of "public function" as involving activities that are "traditionally and exclusively reserved to the State." But many of the leading cases finding state action date from the 1940s, 1950s, and 1960s and involved racial discrimination. As you read this Section, you should consider whether subsequent decisions declining to find state action are persuasively distinguishable from the older cases or whether they have deprived the race-based cases of generative significance for other modern issues.

I. ELECTORAL FUNCTIONS: THE "WHITE PRIMARY" CASES

SMITH v. ALLWRIGHT, 321 U.S. 649 (1944), held that the Fifteenth Amendment forebade exclusion of African-Americans from primary elections conducted by the Democratic Party of Texas, pursuant to party resolution. The Court, per REED, J., reasoned that state delegation to a party of the power to fix the qualifications of primary elections is delegation of a state function that may make the party's action the action of the state. "[The] right to participate in the choice of elected officials without restriction by any state because of race [is] not to be nullified by a state through casting its electoral process in a form which permits a private organization to practice racial discrimination in the election." Frankfurter, J., concurred in the result. Roberts, J., dissented.

TERRY v. ADAMS, 345 U.S. 461 (1953), involved the exclusion of African-Americans from the "pre-primary" elections of the Jaybird Democratic Association, an organization of all the white voters in a Texas county. The Jaybird Democratic Association was run like a regular political party, and its preferred candidates nearly always ran unopposed in the regular Democratic primary and won the general election. The record showed "complete absence of any [Jaybird coordination or] cooperation [with] the State." The Court held the Jaybird primary subject to the Fifteenth Amendment but reached no majority opinion.

BLACK, J., joined by Douglas and Burton, JJ., found that "the admitted party purpose" was "to escape the Fifteenth Amendment's command." The "Amendment excludes social or business clubs" but "no election machinery could be sustained if its purpose or effect was to deny Negroes on account of their race an effective voice in the governmental affairs. [The] only election that has counted in this Texas county for more than fifty years has been that held by the Jaybirds. [For] a state to permit such a duplication of its election processes is to permit a flagrant abuse [of] the Fifteenth Amendment."

CLARK, J., joined by Vinson, C.J., and Reed and Jackson, JJ., described the Jaybirds as not merely a "private club" "organized to influence public candidacies or political action," but rather a "part and parcel of the Democratic Party, an organization existing under the auspices of Texas law. [W]hen a state structures its electoral apparatus in a form which devolves upon a political organization the uncontested choice of public officials, that organization itself, in whatever disguise, takes on those attributes of government which draw the Constitution's safeguards into play."[2]

MINTON, J., dissented: The Jaybird's activity "seems to differ very little from situations common in many other places [where] a candidate must obtain the approval of a religious group. [E]lections and other public business are influenced by all sorts of pressures from carefully organized groups. [Far] from the activities of these groups being properly labeled as state action, [they] are to be considered as attempts to influence or obtain state action."

II. MUNICIPAL FUNCTIONS: PRIVATELY OWNED SPACES OPEN TO THE PUBLIC

MARSH v. ALABAMA, 326 U.S. 501 (1946): A Jehovah's Witness sought "to distribute religious literature on the premises of a company-owned town contrary to the wishes of the town's management." The town, owned by a shipbuilding company, had "all the characteristics of any other American town." Appellant was warned that she could not distribute the literature. When she refused to leave the sidewalk of the town's "business block," a deputy sheriff, who was paid by the company to serve as the town's policeman, arrested her, and she was convicted of trespass.

The Court, per BLACK, J., reversed: Under *Lovell v. Griffin,* Ch. 7, Sec. 5, I, an ordinary municipality could not have barred appellant's activities, and the fact that "a single company had legal title to all the town" should not result in the impairment of "channels of communication" that would otherwise be available to its inhabitants or those persons passing through. "Ownership does not always mean absolute dominion. The more an owner, for his advantage, opens up his property for use by the public in general, the more do his rights become circumscribed by the statutory and constitutional rights of those who use it. Thus, the owners of privately held bridges, ferries, turnpikes and railroads may not operate them as freely as a farmer does his farm. Since these facilities are built and operated primarily to benefit the public and since their operation is essentially a public function, it is subject to state regulation." In balancing property rights against freedom of press and religion, "the latter occupy a preferred position," and the former do not "justify the State's permitting a corporation to govern a community of citizens so as to restrict their fundamental liberties and the

---

[2]   Frankfurter, J., stated that the "vital requirement is State responsibility" and found it as "a matter of practical politics": "[W]e may assume [those] charged by State law with the duty of assuring all eligible voters an opportunity to participate in the selection of candidates at the primary—the county election officials who are normally leaders in their communities—participate by voting in the Jaybird primary [and] condone [a] wholly successful effort to withdraw significance from the State-prescribed primary, to subvert the operation of what is formally the law of the State for primaries in this county."

enforcement of such restraint by the application of a State statute." Frankfurter, J., concurred. Jackson, J., did not participate.

III. REFUSALS TO FIND "GOVERNMENTAL FUNCTION"

JACKSON V. METROPOLITAN EDISON CO.
419 U.S. 345, 95 S.Ct. 449, 42 L.Ed.2d 477 (1974).

JUSTICE REHNQUIST delivered the opinion of the Court.

Respondent, "a heavily regulated private utility" with a state certificate of public convenience to sell electricity, terminated service to petitioner for nonpayment pursuant to a provision of its general tariff that had been filed with the Pennsylvania Public Utilities Commission. Petitioner claimed that termination "without adequate notice and a hearing before an impartial body" deprived her of property without due process of law.

[The] mere fact that a business is subject to state regulation does not by itself convert its action into that of the State for purposes of the Fourteenth Amendment. [It] may well be that acts of a heavily regulated utility with at least something of a governmentally protected monopoly will more readily be found to be "state" acts than will the acts of an entity lacking these characteristics. But the inquiry must be whether there is a sufficiently close nexus between the State and the challenged action of the regulated entity so that the action of the latter may be fairly treated as that of the State itself. * * *

Petitioner first argues that "state action" is present because of the monopoly status allegedly conferred upon Metropolitan by the State of Pennsylvania. As a factual matter, it may well be doubted that the State ever granted or guaranteed Metropolitan a monopoly.[8] But assuming that it had, this fact is not determinative. * * *

Petitioner next urges that state action is present because respondent provides an essential public service [and] hence performs a "public function." We have, of course, found state action present in the exercise by a private entity of powers traditionally exclusively reserved to the State. See, e.g., *Terry* (election); *Marsh* (company town). If we were dealing with the exercise by Metropolitan of some power delegated to it by the State which is traditionally associated with sovereignty, such as eminent domain, our case would be quite a different one. But while the Pennsylvania statute imposes an obligation to furnish service on regulated utilities, it imposes no such obligation on the State. * * *

---

[8]   **[Ct's Note]** [In] fact Metropolitan does face competition within portions of its service area from another private utility company and from municipal utility companies. [As] petitioner admits, such public utility companies are natural monopolies created by the economic forces of high threshold capital requirements and virtually unlimited economy of scale. Regulation was superimposed on such natural monopolies as a substitute for competition and not to eliminate it. * * *

Perhaps in recognition of the fact that the supplying of utility service is not traditionally the exclusive prerogative of the State, petitioner urges a broad principle that all businesses "affected with the public interest" are state actors in all their actions.

We decline the invitation for reasons stated long ago in *Nebbia v. New York*, [Ch. 5, Sec. 3]: "It is clear that there is no closed class or category of businesses affected with a public interest. Doctors, optometrists, lawyers, Metropolitan, and Nebbia's upstate New York grocery selling a quart of milk are all in regulated businesses, providing arguably essential goods and services, 'affected with a public interest.' " We do not believe that such a status converts their every action, absent more, into that of the State.

We also reject the notion that Metropolitan's termination is state action because the State "has specifically authorized and approved" the termination [practice].[11] Although the Commission did hold hearings on portions of Metropolitan's general tariff relating to a general rate increase, it never even considered the reinsertion of this provision in the newly filed general tariff. * * *

Affirmed.

JUSTICE MARSHALL, dissenting. * * *

Our state-action cases have repeatedly relied on several factors clearly presented by this case: a state-sanctioned monopoly; an extensive pattern of cooperation between the "private" entity and the State; and a service uniquely public in nature. * * * The majority distinguishes this line of cases with a cryptic assertion that public utility companies are "natural monopolies." [I]t is far from obvious that an electric company would not be subject to competition if the market were unimpeded by governmental restrictions. [The] State has chosen to forbid the high profit margins that might invite private competition or increase pressure for state ownership and operation of electric power facilities[, thus] to ensure that the company's service will be the functional equivalent of service provided by the State. * * *

I agree with the majority that it requires more than a finding that a particular business is "affected with the public interest" before constitutional burdens can be imposed on that business. But when the activity in question is of such public importance that the State invariably either provides the service itself or permits private companies to act as state surrogates in providing it, much more is involved than just a matter of public interest. In those cases, the State has determined that if private companies wish to enter the field, they will have to surrender many of the prerogatives normally associated with private enterprise and behave in many ways like a governmental body. [The] majority's analysis would seemingly apply as well to a company that refused to extend service to Negroes, welfare recipients, or any other group that the company preferred, for its own reasons, not to serve. I

---

11   **[Ct's Note]** Petitioner does not contest the fact that Metropolitan had this right at common law before the advent of regulation.

cannot believe that this Court would hold that the State's involvement with the utility company was not sufficient to impose upon the company an obligation to meet the constitutional mandate of nondiscrimination.[3] * * *

––––––––

MANHATTAN COMMUNITY ACCESS CORP. v. HALLECK, 139 S.Ct. 1921 (2019), held that a private entity administering the public access channels on a New York cable system was not a state actor despite having been designated to perform that function by the City of New York. New York state law "requires cable operators in the State to set aside channels on their cable systems for public access" and further "requires that use of the public access channels be free of charge and first-come, first-served. Under state law, the cable operator operates the public access channels unless the local government in the area chooses to itself operate the channels or designates a private entity to operate the channels." For the Time-Warner cable system in Manhattan, New York City designated a private nonprofit corporation, Manhattan Neighborhood Network (MNN), to operate the legally mandated public access. After the respondents produced a film critical of MNN and MNN televised it, MNN suspended the respondents from further access to MNN facilities. Respondents then sued, alleging that the public access channels were a public forum and that MNN's actions violated their First Amendment rights.

Per KAVANAUGH, J., the Court, by 5–4, ordered dismissal on the ground that MNN is not a state actor. Although "a private entity may qualify as a state actor when it exercises 'powers traditionally exclusively reserved to the State,' " *Jackson v. Metropolitan Edison Co.*, the function of operating "public access channels on a cable system [h]as not traditionally and exclusively been performed by government. Since the 1970s, when public access channels became a regular feature on cable systems, a variety of private and public actors have operated public access channels, including: private cable operators; private nonprofit organizations; municipalities; and other public and private community organizations such as churches, schools, and libraries." As the Court ruled in *Hudgens* v. *NLRB*, "a private entity who provides a forum for speech is not transformed by that fact alone into a state actor. [G]rocery stores put up community bulletin boards. Comedy clubs host open mic nights."

Nor did it matter that New York City had "designated MNN to operate the public access channels" or that "New York State heavily regulates MNN with respect to the public access channels. [That] the government licenses, contracts with, or grants a monopoly to a private entity does not convert the private entity into a state actor—unless the private entity is performing a traditional, exclusive public function."

KAVANAUGH, J., dismissed an alternative contention that MNN was a state actor because it acted in the stead of New York City, which should be regarded as the owner or lessor of the public access channels under applicable New York law.

––––––––––––––––

[3]   Brennan, J., dissented on procedural grounds. Douglas, J.'s dissent is omitted.

"It does not matter that a provision in the franchise agreements between the City and Time Warner allowed the City to designate a private entity to operate the public access channels on Time Warner's cable system. [N]othing in the franchise agreements suggests that the City possesses any property interest in Time Warner's cable system, or in the public access channels on that system."

SOTOMAYOR, J., dissented: "New York City secured a property interest in public-access television channels when it granted a cable franchise to a cable company. State regulations require those public-access channels to be made open to the public on terms that render them a public forum. The City contracted out the administration of that forum to a private organization. [By] accepting that agency relationship, MNN stepped into the City's shoes and thus qualifies as a state actor. * * *

"[The majority] is wrong in two ways. First, the majority erroneously decides the property question against the plaintiffs as a matter of law. [S]econd, and more fundamentally, the majority mistakes a case about the government choosing to hand off responsibility to an agent for a case about a private entity that simply enters a marketplace. [The] majority's opinion erroneously fixates on a type of case that is not before us: one [such as *Jackson*] in which a private entity simply enters the marketplace and is then subject to government regulation. [But] MNN is not a private entity that simply ventured into the marketplace. It occupies its role because it was asked to do so by the City, which secured the public-access channels in exchange for giving up public rights of way, opened those channels up (as required by the State) as a public forum, and then deputized MNN to administer them." The Court's reliance on prior public function cases was therefore misguided. "[When] the government hires an agent, [that agent is a state actor, regardless of whether the government] hired the agent to do something that can be done in the private marketplace too."

FLAGG BROS., INC. V. BROOKS

436 U.S. 149, 98 S.Ct. 1729, 56 L.Ed.2d 185 (1978).

JUSTICE REHNQUIST delivered the opinion of the Court.

The question presented [is] whether a warehouseman's proposed sale of goods entrusted to him for storage, as permitted by New York Uniform Commercial Code § 7–210, is an action properly attributable to the State * * * .

[R]espondent Shirley Brooks and her family were evicted from their apartment in Mount Vernon, N.Y., on June 13, 1973. The city marshal arranged for Brooks' possessions to be stored by petitioner Flagg Brothers, Inc., in its warehouse. [A]fter a series of disputes over the validity of the charges being claimed by petitioner Flagg Brothers, Brooks received a letter demanding that her account be brought up to date within 10 days "or your furniture will be sold." Brooks thereupon initiated this class action [and] the declaration that such a sale pursuant to § 7–210 would violate [due process].

It must be noted that respondents have named no public officials as defendants in this action. The city marshal, who supervised their evictions, was dismissed from the case by the consent of all the parties. This total absence of overt official involvement plainly distinguishes this case from earlier decisions imposing procedural restrictions on creditors' remedies such as *North Georgia Finishing, Inc. v. Di-Chem, Inc.*, 419 U.S. 601 (1975); *Fuentes v. Shevin*, 407 U.S. 67 (1972); *Sniadach v. Family Finance Corp.*, 395 U.S. 337 (1969). * * *

Respondents' primary contention is that New York has delegated to Flagg Brothers a power "traditionally exclusively reserved to the State." *Jackson.* They argue that the resolution of private disputes is a traditional function of civil government, and that the State [has] delegated this function to Flagg Brothers. Respondents, however, have read too much into the language of our previous cases. While many functions have been traditionally performed by governments, very few have been "exclusively reserved to the State." * * *

[The] proposed sale by Flagg Brothers under § 7–210 is not the only means of resolving this purely private dispute. Respondent Brooks has never alleged that state law barred her from seeking a waiver of Flagg Brothers' right to sell her goods at the time she authorized their storage. Presumably, [a person] who alleges that she never authorized the storage of her goods, could have sought to replevy her goods at any time under state law. The challenged statute itself provides a damages remedy against the warehouseman for violations of its provisions. This system of rights and remedies, recognizing the traditional place of private arrangements in ordering relationships in the commercial world,[9] can hardly be said to have delegated to Flagg Brothers an exclusive prerogative of the sovereign.[10]

Whatever the particular remedies available under New York law, we do not consider a more detailed description of them necessary to our conclusion that the settlement of disputes between debtors and creditors is not traditionally an exclusive public function.[11] [T]here are a number of state and municipal functions

---

[9] **[Ct's Note]** Unlike the parade of horribles suggested by our Brother Stevens in dissent, this case does not involve state authorization of private breach of the peace.

[10] **[Ct's Note]** [It] would intolerably broaden [the] notion of state action [to] hold that the mere existence of a body of property law in a State, whether decisional or statutory, itself amounted to "state action" even though no state process or state officials were ever involved in enforcing that body of law.

This situation is clearly distinguishable from cases such as *North Georgia Finishing; Fuentes;* and *Sniadach.* In each of those cases a government official participated in the physical deprivation of what had concededly been the constitutional plaintiff's property under state law before the deprivation occurred. The constitutional protection attaches not because, as in *North Georgia Finishing,* a clerk issued a ministerial writ out of the court, but because as a result of that writ the property of the debtor was seized and impounded by the affirmative command of the law of Georgia. The creditor in *North Georgia Finishing* had not simply sought to pursue the collection of his debt by private means permissible under Georgia law; he had invoked the authority of the Georgia court, which in turn had ordered the garnishee not to pay over money which previously had been the property of the debtor. * * *

[11] **[Ct's Note]** It may well be, as my Brother Stevens' dissent contends, that "[t]he power to order legally binding surrenders of property and the constitutional restrictions on that power are necessary correlatives in our system." But here New York, unlike Florida in *Fuentes,* Georgia in *North Georgia Finishing,* and Wisconsin in *Sniadach,* has not ordered respondents to surrender any property whatever. It has merely enacted a statute which provides that a warehouseman

not covered by our election cases or governed by the reasoning of *Marsh* which have been administered with a greater degree of exclusivity by States and municipalities than has the function of so-called "dispute resolution." Among these are such functions as education, fire and police protection, and tax collection. We express no view as to the extent, if any, to which a city or State might be free to delegate to private parties the performance of such functions and thereby avoid the strictures of the Fourteenth Amendment. [This] Court, however, has never held that a State's mere acquiescence in a private action converts that action into that of the State. * * *

Here, the State of New York has not compelled the sale of a bailor's goods, but has merely announced the circumstances under which its courts will not interfere with a private sale. Indeed, the crux of respondents' complaint is not that the State *has* acted, but that it has *refused* to act. This statutory refusal to act is no different in principle from an ordinary statute of limitations whereby the State declines to provide a remedy for private deprivations of property after the passage of a given period of time. * * *

Reversed.

JUSTICE STEVENS, with whom JUSTICE WHITE and JUSTICE MARSHALL join, dissenting.

[Under the Court's] approach a State could enact laws authorizing private citizens to use self-help in countless situations without any possibility of federal challenge. [It] could authorize the warehouseman to retain all proceeds of the lien sale, even if they far exceeded the amount of the alleged debt; it could authorize finance companies to enter private homes to repossess merchandise; or indeed, it could authorize "any person with sufficient physical power" to acquire and sell the property of his weaker neighbor.

[In] this case, the State of New York, by enacting § 7–210 of the Uniform Commercial Code, has acted in the most effective and unambiguous way a State can act. This section specifically authorizes petitioner Flagg Brothers to sell respondents' possessions; it details the procedures that petitioner must follow; and it grants petitioner the power to convey good title to goods that are now owned by respondents to a third party.

---

conforming to the provisions of the statute may convert his traditional lien into good title. There is no reason whatever to believe that either Flagg Brothers or respondents could not, if they wished, seek resort to the New York courts in order to either compel or prevent the "surrenders of property" to which that dissent refers, and that the compliance of Flagg Brothers with applicable New York property law would be reviewed after customary notice and hearing in such a proceeding.

The fact that such a judicial review of a self-help remedy is seldom encountered bears witness to the important part that such remedies have played in our system of property rights. This is particularly true of the warehouseman's lien, which [is] burdened by procedural constraints and provides for a compensatory remedy and judicial relief against abuse, [and] is not atypical of creditors' liens historically, whether created by statute or legislatively enacted. The conduct of private actors in relying on the rights established under these liens to resort to self-help remedies does not permit their conduct to be ascribed to the State.

[Petitioners] argue that the nonconsensual transfer of property rights is not a traditional function of the sovereign. [T]he Court reasons that state action cannot be found because the State has not delegated to the warehouseman an *exclusive* sovereign function.[8] This distinction [is] inconsistent with the line of cases beginning with *Sniadach* [which have] scrutinized various state statutes regulating the debtor-creditor relationship for compliance with the Due Process Clause. [The] Court today seeks to explain these [on] the ground that in each case there was some element of "overt official involvement." [But] until today, this Court had never held that purely ministerial acts of "minor governmental functionaries" were sufficient to establish state action. [The] number of private actions in which a governmental functionary plays some ministerial role is legion;[12] to base due process review on the fortuity of such governmental intervention would demean the majestic purposes of the Due Process Clause.

[Here] the very defect that made the statutes in *Fuentes* and *North Georgia Finishing* unconstitutional—lack of state control—is, under today's decision, the factor that precludes constitutional review of the state statute. The Due Process Clause cannot command such incongruous results. If it is unconstitutional for a State to allow a private party to exercise a traditional state power because the state supervision of that power is purely mechanical, the State surely cannot immunize its actions from constitutional *scrutiny* by removing even the mechanical supervision. * * *

Finally, it is obviously true that the overwhelming majority of disputes in our society are resolved in the private sphere. But it is no longer possible, if it ever was, to believe that a sharp line can be drawn between private and public actions. [In] the broadest sense, we expect government "to provide a reasonable and fair framework of rules which facilitate commercial transactions." This "framework of rules" is premised on the assumption that the State will control nonconsensual deprivations of property and that the State's control will, in turn, be subject to the restrictions of the Due Process Clause. * * *[4]

---

[8]   **[Ct's Note]** [Even] if I were to accept the notion that sovereign functions must be "exclusive," the Court's description of exclusivity is incomprehensible. The question is whether a particular action is a uniquely sovereign function, not whether state law forecloses any possibility of recovering for damages for such activity. For instance, it is clear that the maintenance of a police force is a unique sovereign function, and the delegation of police power to a private party will entail state action. Under the Court's analysis, however, there would be no state action if the State provided a remedy, such as an action for wrongful imprisonment, for the individual injured by the "private" policeman. [Of] course, the availability of other state remedies may be relevant in determining whether the statute provides sufficient procedural protections under the Due Process Clause, but it is not relevant to the state-action issue.

[12]   **[Ct's Note]** For instance, state officials often perform ministerial acts in the transferring of ownership in motor vehicles or real estate. It is difficult to believe that the Court would hold that all car sales are invested with state action.

[4]   The separate dissent of Marshall, J., is omitted. Brennan, J., did not participate.

3. STATE "INVOLVEMENT"

The Court has also found that the conduct of private individuals or groups constitutes state action when a private entity is sufficiently "involved" or "entwined" with or "encouraged by" the state. Under this strand of state action analysis, the Court has *sometimes* found state action when a state court enforces private agreements, when the state legally or financially entwines itself with private actors, when the state licenses or authorizes private conduct, and when the state subsidizes or regulates private conduct. But the cases are not easy to reconcile with one another.

I. STATE ENFORCEMENT

SHELLEY V. KRAEMER
334 U.S. 1, 68 S.Ct. 836, 92 L.Ed. 1161 (1948).

CHIEF JUSTICE VINSON delivered the opinion of the Court.

[In two cases from Missouri and Michigan, petitioners were African-Americans who had purchased houses from whites despite the fact that the properties were subject to restrictive covenants, signed by most property owners in the block, providing that for a specified time (in one case fifty years from 1911) the property would be sold only to Caucasians. Respondents, owners of other property subject to the covenants, sued to enjoin the buyers from taking possession and to divest them of title. The state courts granted the relief.]

Equality in the enjoyment of property rights was regarded by the framers of [the Fourteenth] Amendment as an essential pre-condition to the realization of other basic civil rights and liberties which the Amendment was intended to guarantee.[7] Thus, [42 U.S.C. § 1982] derived from § 1 of the Civil Rights Act of 1866 which was enacted by Congress while the Fourteenth Amendment was also under consideration, provides: "All citizens of the United States shall have the same right, in every State and Territory, as is enjoyed by white citizens thereof to inherit, purchase, lease, sell, hold, and convey real and personal property." * * *

It is likewise clear that restrictions on the right of occupancy of the sort sought to be created by the private agreements in these cases could not be squared with the requirements of the Fourteenth Amendment if imposed by state statute or local ordinance. [But here] the particular patterns of discrimination and the areas in which the restrictions are to operate, are determined, in the first instance, by the terms of agreements among private individuals. Participation of the State consists in the enforcement of the restrictions so defined. * * *

Since [the] *Civil Rights Cases,* the principle has become firmly embedded in our constitutional law that the action inhibited by the first section of the Fourteenth Amendment is only such action as may fairly be said to be that of the

---

7   [Ct's Note] *Slaughter-House Cases* [Ch. 5, Sec. 1, II]. See Horace E. Flack, *The Adoption of the Fourteenth Amendment.*

States. That Amendment erects no shield against merely private conduct, however discriminatory or wrongful. We conclude, therefore, that the restrictive agreements standing alone cannot be regarded as a violation of any rights guaranteed to petitioners by the Fourteenth Amendment. So long as the purposes of those agreements are effectuated by voluntary adherence to their terms, it would appear clear that there has been no action by the State and the provisions of the Amendment have not been violated.

But here [the] purposes of the agreements were secured only by judicial enforcement by state courts of the restrictive terms of the agreements. [That] the action of state courts and of judicial officers in their official capacities is to be regarded as action of the State within the meaning of the Fourteenth Amendment, is a proposition which has long been established. * * *

One of the earliest applications of the prohibitions contained in the Fourteenth Amendment to action of state judicial officials occurred in cases in which Negroes had been excluded from jury service. [These] cases demonstrate, also, the early recognition by this Court that state action in violation of the Amendment's provisions is equally repugnant to the constitutional commands whether directed by state statute or taken by a judicial official in the absence of statute. * * *

But the examples of state judicial action which have been held by this Court to violate the Amendment's commands are not restricted to situations in which the judicial proceedings were found in some manner to be procedurally unfair. It has been recognized that the action of state courts in enforcing a substantive common-law rule formulated by those courts, may result in the denial of rights guaranteed by the Fourteenth Amendment. [Thus,] in *AFL v. Swing*, 312 U.S. 321 (1941), enforcement by state courts of the common-law policy of the State, which resulted in the restraining of peaceful picketing, was held to be state action of the sort prohibited by the Amendment's guaranties of freedom of discussion. In *Cantwell v. Connecticut*, 1940, [Ch. 8, Sec. 2, I], a conviction in a state court of the common-law crime of breach of the peace was, under the circumstances of the case, found to be a violation of the Amendment's commands relating to freedom of religion. * * *

We have no doubt that there has been state action in these cases in the full and complete sense of the phrase. The undisputed facts disclose that petitioners were willing purchasers of properties upon which they desired to establish homes. The owners of the properties were willing sellers; and contracts of sale were accordingly consummated. It is clear that but for the active intervention of the state courts, supported by the full panoply of state power, petitioners would have been free to occupy the properties in question without restraint.

These are not cases, as has been suggested, in which the States have merely abstained from action, leaving private individuals free to impose such discriminations as they see fit. Rather, these are cases in which the States have made available to such individuals the full coercive power of government to deny to petitioners, on the grounds of race or color, the enjoyment of property rights in premises which petitioners are willing and financially able to acquire and which the grantors are willing to sell. * * *

Respondents urge, however, that since the state courts stand ready to enforce restrictive covenants excluding white persons[,] enforcement of covenants excluding colored persons may not be deemed a denial of equal protection of the laws to the colored persons who are thereby affected. [But e]qual protection of the laws is not achieved through indiscriminate imposition of inequalities. * * *

Reversed.

JUSTICE REED, JUSTICE JACKSON, and JUSTICE RUTLEDGE took no part in the consideration or decision of these cases.

––––––––––

With *Shelley*, compare N.Y. TIMES CO. v. SULLIVAN, 376 U.S. 254 (1964), Ch. 7, Sec. 2, II, supra, which held that the common-law "rule of law applied by the Alabama courts is constitutionally deficient for failure to provide the safeguards for freedom of speech and of the press that are required by the First and Fourteenth Amendments in a libel action brought by a public official against critics of his official conduct." The Court explained that, even though the case concerned "a civil lawsuit between private parties," the federal Constitution applied because "[i]t matters not that the law has been applied in a civil action and that it is common law only, though supplemented by statute. The test is not the form in which state power has been applied but, whatever the form, whether such power has in fact been exercised."

The state action principle of *New York Times v. Sullivan* seems largely unquestioned: parties are always entitled to test the constitutional validity of a state law that is being applied against them at the time of its judicial application. Note that *Shelley* depends on a different principle (involving the judicial enforceability of a private agreement under the circumstances of the case).

II. SYMBIOTIC RELATIONSHIPS BETWEEN THE STATE AND PRIVATE ENTITIES

BURTON V. WILMINGTON PARKING AUTH.
365 U.S. 715, 81 S.Ct. 856, 6 L.Ed.2d 45 (1961).

JUSTICE CLARK delivered the opinion of the Court.

In this action for declaratory and injunctive relief it is admitted that the Eagle Coffee Shoppe, Inc., a restaurant located within an off-street automobile parking building in Wilmington, Delaware, has refused to serve appellant food or drink solely because he is a Negro.

The parking building is owned and operated by the Wilmington Parking Authority, an agency of the State of Delaware, and the restaurant is the Authority's lessee. Appellant claims that such refusal abridges his rights under the Equal Protection Clause of the Fourteenth Amendment to the United States Constitution. * * * In August 1958 appellant parked his car in the building and walked around to enter the restaurant by its front door on Ninth Street. Having entered and sought service, he was refused it. * * *

It is clear, as it always has been since the *Civil Rights Cases*, supra, that 'Individual invasion of individual rights is not the subject-matter of the amendment,' and that private conduct abridging individual rights does no violence to the Equal Protection Clause unless to some significant extent the State in any of its manifestations has been found to have become involved in it.* * *

The land and building were publicly owned. As an entity, the building was dedicated to 'public uses' in performance of the Authority's 'essential governmental functions.' The costs of land acquisition, construction, and maintenance are defrayed entirely from donations by the City of Wilmington, from loans and revenue bonds and from the proceeds of rentals and parking services out of which the loans and bonds were payable. * * * Upkeep and maintenance of the building, including necessary repairs, were responsibilities of the Authority and were payable out of public funds. It cannot be doubted that the peculiar relationship of the restaurant to the parking facility in which it is located confers on each an incidental variety of mutual benefits. Guests of the restaurant are afforded a convenient place to park their automobiles, even if they cannot enter the restaurant directly from the parking area. Similarly, its convenience for diners may well provide additional demand for the Authority's parking facilities. Should any improvements effected in the leasehold by Eagle become part of the realty, there is no possibility of increased taxes being passed on to it since the fee is held by a tax-exempt government agency. Neither can it be ignored, especially in view of Eagle's affirmative allegation that for it to serve Negroes would injure its business, that profits earned by discrimination not only contribute to, but also are indispensable elements in, the financial success of a governmental agency.

Addition of all these activities, obligations and responsibilities of the Authority, the benefits mutually conferred, together with the obvious fact that the restaurant is operated as an integral part of a public building devoted to a public parking service, indicates that degree of state participation and involvement in discriminatory action which it was the design of the Fourteenth Amendment to condemn. It is irony amounting to grave injustice that in one part of a single building, erected and maintained with public funds by an agency of the State to serve a public purpose, all persons have equal rights, while in another portion, also serving the public, a Negro is a second-class citizen, offensive because of his race, without rights and unentitled to service, but at the same time fully enjoys equal access to nearby restaurants in wholly privately owned buildings. * * * The State has so far insinuated itself into a position of interdependence with Eagle that it must be recognized as a joint participant in the challenged activity, which, on that account, cannot be considered to have been so 'purely private' as to fall without the scope of the Fourteenth Amendment.* * *

Specifically defining the limits of our inquiry, what we hold today is that when a State leases public property in the manner and for the purpose shown to have been the case here, the proscriptions of the Fourteenth Amendment must be complied with by the lessee as certainly as though they were binding covenants written into the agreement itself.[5] * * *

NOTES

1. ***State-private joint seizure of property.*** LUGAR v. EDMONDSON OIL CO., 457 U.S. 922 (1982), involved a statute that authorized a creditor to file a petition with a court clerk and thus obtain a prejudgment attachment of a debtor's property without any substantial judicial inquiry. The sheriff then executed the attachment. The Court, per WHITE, J., relied on debtor-creditor decisions such as *North Georgia Finishing, Inc. v. Di-Chem, Inc.*, supra; *Fuentes v. Shevin*, supra; and *Sniadach v. Family Finance Corp.*, supra, as establishing the doctrine "that a private party's joint participation with state officials in the seizure of disputed property is sufficient to characterize that party as a 'state actor' for purposes of the Fourteenth Amendment." POWELL, J., joined by Rehnquist and O'Connor, JJ., dissented: "It is unclear why a private party engages in state action when filing papers seeking an attachment of property, but not [when] summoning police to investigate a suspected crime." Burger, C.J., also dissented.

2. ***Jury selection.*** EDMONSON v. LEESVILLE CONCRETE CO., 500 U.S. 614 (1991), per KENNEDY, J., held that use by a private litigant in a civil trial of a peremptory challenge to exclude jurors on the basis of race violated "the excluded jurors' equal protection rights": "[I]n determining whether a particular action or course of conduct is governmental in character, it is relevant to examine the following: the extent to which the actor relies on governmental assistance and benefits, see *Burton;* whether the actor is performing a traditional governmental function, see *Terry*; *Marsh*; and whether the injury caused is aggravated in a unique way by the incidents of governmental authority, see *Shelley* * * * .

"Although private use of state-sanctioned private remedies or procedures does not rise, by itself, to the level of state action, our cases have found state action when private parties make extensive use of state procedures with 'the overt, significant assistance of state officials.' See *Lugar*. [The] government summons jurors, constrains their freedom of movement, and subjects them to public scrutiny and examination. The party who exercises a challenge invokes the formal authority of the court, which must discharge the prospective juror, thus effecting the 'final and practical denial' of the excluded individual's opportunity to serve on the petit jury. [By] enforcing a discriminatory peremptory challenge, the court 'has not only made itself a party to the [biased act], but has elected to place its power, property and prestige behind the [alleged] discrimination.' *Burton*.

---

[5] Stewart, J. concurred on other grounds. Harlan, J., joined by Whittaker, J., dissented, arguing that the Court should have remanded the case to the Delaware Supreme Court or held the case pending application to the state court for clarification of the issues in the case. The dissent of Frankfurter, J. is omitted.

"[Further, a] traditional function of government is evident here. The peremptory challenge is used in selecting an entity that is a quintessential governmental body, having no attributes of a private actor. [If] a government confers on a private body the power to choose the government's employees or officials, the private body will be bound by the constitutional mandate of race neutrality [*Terry*]. If peremptory challenges based on race were permitted, persons could be required by summons to be put at risk of open and public discrimination as a condition of their participation in the justice system. The injury to excluded jurors would be the direct result of governmental delegation and participation."

O'CONNOR, J., joined by Rehnquist, C.J., and Scalia, J., dissented: "It is the nature of a peremptory that its exercise is left wholly within the discretion of the litigant. [The] peremptory is, by design, an enclave of private action in a government-managed proceeding. [That] these actions may be necessary to a peremptory challenge [no] more makes the challenge state action than the building of roads and provision of public transportation makes state action of riding on a bus.

"[The] government 'normally can be held responsible for a private decision only when it has exercised coercive power or has provided such significant encouragement, either overt or covert, that the choice must in law be deemed to be that of the State.' *Blum.* [A] judge does not 'significantly encourage' discrimination by the mere act of excusing a juror in response to an unexplained request."

III.   STATE LICENSING AND AUTHORIZATION

MOOSE LODGE V. IRVIS
407 U.S. 163, 92 S.Ct. 1965, 32 L.Ed.2d 627 (1972).

JUSTICE REHNQUIST delivered the opinion of the Court.

Appellee Irvis, a Negro, [who] was refused service [as the guest of a member] by appellant Moose Lodge, [claimed] that because the Pennsylvania liquor board had issued appellant Moose Lodge a private club license that authorized the sale of alcoholic beverages on its premises, the refusal of service to him was "state action." * * *

While the principle is easily stated, the question of whether particular discriminatory conduct is private, on the one hand, or amounts to "state action," on the other hand, frequently admits of no easy answer. "Only by sifting facts and weighing circumstances can the non-obvious involvement of the State in private conduct be attributed its true significance." *Burton.* * * *

Here there is nothing approaching the symbiotic relationship between lessor and lessee that was present in [*Burton*]. Moose Lodge quite ostentatiously proclaims the fact that it is not open to the public at large. Nor is it located and operated in such surroundings that although private in name, it discharges a function or performs a service that would otherwise in all likelihood be performed by the State. In short, while Eagle was a public restaurant in a public building, Moose Lodge is a private social club in a private building.

With the exception hereafter noted, the Pennsylvania Liquor Control Board plays absolutely no part in establishing or enforcing the membership or guest policies of the club which it licenses to serve liquor.[3] [The] only effect that the state licensing of Moose Lodge to serve liquor can be said to have [is] that for some purposes club licenses are counted in the maximum number of licenses which may be issued in a given municipality. * * *

The District Court was at pains to [note that] an applicant for a club license must make such physical alterations in its premises as the board may require, must file a list of the names and addresses of its members and employees, and must keep extensive financial records. The board is granted the right to inspect the licensed premises at any time * * * .

However detailed this type of regulation may be in some particulars, it cannot be said to in any way foster or encourage racial discrimination. Nor can it be said to make the State in any realistic sense a partner or even a joint venturer in the club's enterprise. The limited effect of the prohibition against obtaining additional club licenses when the maximum number of retail licenses allotted to a municipality has been issued, when considered together with the availability of liquor from hotel, restaurant, and retail licensees falls far short of conferring upon club licensees a monopoly in the dispensing of liquor * * * . We therefore hold that, with the exception hereafter noted, the operation of the regulatory scheme enforced by the Pennsylvania Liquor Control Board does not sufficiently implicate the State in the discriminatory guest policies of Moose Lodge * * * .

The District Court found that [Liquor] Control Board [regulations] adopted pursuant to statute affirmatively require that "every club licensee shall adhere to all the provisions of its constitution and by-laws." Appellant argues that the purpose of this provision "is purely and simply and plainly the prevention of subterfuge." [There] can be no doubt that the label "private club" can and has been used to evade both regulations of State and local liquor authorities, and statutes requiring places of public accommodation to serve all persons without regard to race, color, religion, or national origin. * * *

Even though the Liquor Control Board regulation in question is neutral in its terms, the result of its application in a case where the constitution and by-laws of a club required racial discrimination [as Moose Lodge did in respect to membership and guest privileges] would be to invoke the sanctions of the State to enforce a concededly discriminatory private rule. * * * *Shelley v. Kraemer* makes it clear that the application of state sanctions to enforce such a rule would violate the Fourteenth Amendment. * * *

---

[3]   **[Ct's Note]** Unlike the situation in *Pollak,* where the regulatory agency had affirmatively approved the practice of the regulated entity after full investigation * * * .

Appellee was entitled to a decree enjoining the enforcement of § 113.09 [but] no more. The judgment of the District Court is reversed * * * .

JUSTICE DOUGLAS, with whom JUSTICE MARSHALL joins, dissenting.

Liquor licenses in Pennsylvania [are] not freely available to those who meet racially neutral qualifications. [There] is a complex quota system [and] the Harrisburg quota, where Moose Lodge No. 107 is located, has been full for many years. No more club licenses may be issued in that city.

This state-enforced scarcity of licenses restricts the ability of blacks to obtain liquor, for liquor is commercially available *only* at private clubs for a significant portion of each week.[3] [A] group desiring to form a nondiscriminatory club which would serve blacks must purchase a license held by an existing club, which can exact a monopoly price for the transfer [and] without a liquor license a fraternal organization would be hard-pressed to survive.

Thus, the State of Pennsylvania is putting the weight of its liquor license, concededly a valued and important adjunct to a private club, behind racial discrimination. * * *

JUSTICE BRENNAN, with whom JUSTICE MARSHALL joins, dissenting.

When Moose Lodge obtained its liquor license, the State of Pennsylvania became an active participant in the operation of the Lodge bar. Liquor licensing laws [are] primarily pervasive regulatory schemes under which the State dictates and continually supervises virtually every detail of the operation of the licensee's business. Very few, if any, other licensed businesses experience such complete state involvement. * * * Liquor licenses have been employed in Pennsylvania to regulate a wide variety of moral conduct, such as the presence and activities of homosexuals, performance by a topless dancer, lewd dancing, swearing, being noisy or disorderly. So broad is the state's power that the courts of Pennsylvania have upheld its restriction of freedom of expression of a licensee on the ground that in doing so it merely exercises its plenary power to attach conditions to the privilege of dispensing liquor which a licensee holds at the sufferance of the state. * * *

IV. STATE SUBSIDIZATION AND REGULATION

RENDELL-BAKER v. KOHN
457 U.S. 830, 102 S.Ct. 2764, 73 L.Ed.2d 418 (1982).

CHIEF JUSTICE BURGER delivered the opinion of the Court.

[New Perspectives is a private school that] specializes in dealing with students who have experienced difficulty completing public high [schools]. In

---

[3]   **[Ct's Note]** Hotels and restaurants may serve liquor between 7:00 a.m. and 2:00 a.m. the next day, Monday through Saturday. On Sunday, such licensees are restricted to sales between 12:00 a.m. and 2:00 a.m., and between 1:00 p.m. and 10:00 p.m. * * * Club licensees, however, are permitted to sell liquor to members and guests from 7:00 a.m. to 3:00 a.m. the next day, seven-days-a-week. * * *

recent years, nearly all of the students at the school have been referred to it by the Brookline or Boston school committees, or by the Drug Rehabilitation Division of the Massachusetts Department of Mental Health. [In] recent years, public funds have accounted for at least 90%, and in one year 99%, of respondent's operating budget. [T]he school must comply with a variety [of] detailed regulations concerning matters ranging from recordkeeping to student-teacher ratios. [T]he regulations require the school to [maintain] personnel standards and procedures, but they impose few specific requirements.

[Petitioners were teachers and a vocational counselor discharged by the school for, inter alia, supporting student criticisms against various school policies. The] core issue presented [is] not whether petitioners were discharged because of their speech or without adequate procedural protections, but whether the school's action in discharging them can fairly be seen as state action. * * *

In *Blum v. Yaretsky*, 457 U.S. 991 (1982), [the] Court considered whether certain nursing homes were state actors for the purpose of determining whether decisions regarding transfers of patients could [be] subjected to Fourteenth Amendment due process requirements. [Like] the New Perspectives School, the nursing homes were privately owned and operated. [T]he Court held that, "[A] State normally can be held responsible for a private decision only when it has exercised coercive power or has provided such significant encouragement, either overt or covert, that the choice must in law be deemed to be that of the State." In determining that the transfer decisions were not actions of the state, the Court considered each of the factors alleged by petitioners [here].

First, [the] State subsidized the operating and capital costs of the nursing homes, and paid the medical expenses of more than 90% of the patients. * * *

The school, like the nursing homes, is not fundamentally different from many private corporations whose business depends primarily on contracts to build roads, bridges, dams, ships, or submarines for the government. Acts of such private contractors do not become acts of the government by reason of their significant or even total engagement in performing public contracts. * * *

A second factor considered in *Blum* was the extensive regulation of the nursing homes by the State. There the State was indirectly involved in the transfer decisions challenged in that case because a primary goal of the State in regulating nursing homes was to keep costs down by transferring patients from intensive treatment centers to less expensive facilities when possible.[6] [The] nursing homes were extensively regulated in many other ways as well. The Court relied on *Jackson,* where we held that state regulation, even if "extensive and detailed," did not make a utility's actions state action.

---

[6]   Brennan, J., joined by Marshall, J., dissented in *Blum:* "[Not] only has the State established the system of treatment levels and utilization review in order to further its own fiscal goals, [but] the State prescribes with as much precision as is possible the standards by which individual determinations are to be made. [The] Court thus fails to perceive the decisive involvement of the State in the private conduct challenged by the respondents."

Here the decisions to discharge the petitioners were not compelled or even influenced by any state regulation. [The] most intrusive personnel regulation promulgated by the various government agencies was the requirement that the Committee on Criminal Justice had the power to approve persons hired as vocational counselors.[6] Such a regulation is not sufficient to make a decision to discharge, made by private management, state action.

The third factor asserted to show that the school is a state actor is that it performs a "public function." However, our holdings have made clear that the relevant question [is] whether the function performed has been "traditionally the *exclusive* prerogative of the State." [U]ntil recently the State had not undertaken to provide education for students who could not be served by traditional public schools. That a private entity performs a function which serves the public does not make its acts state action.[7]

Fourth, petitioners argue that there is a "symbiotic relationship" [as] in *Burton.* Such a claim was rejected in *Blum,* and we reject it here. In *Burton,* [i]n response to the argument that the restaurant's profits, and hence the State's financial position, would suffer if it did not discriminate, the Court concluded that this showed that the State profited from the restaurant's discriminatory conduct. [Here] the school's fiscal relationship with the State is not different from that of many contractors performing services for the government. * * *

Affirmed.

JUSTICE MARSHALL, with whom JUSTICE BRENNAN joins, dissenting.

[I]t is difficult to imagine a closer relationship between a government and a private enterprise. [The] school's very survival depends on the State. If the State chooses, it may exercise complete control over the school's operations simply by threatening to withdraw financial support if the school takes action that it considers objectionable. [Almost] every decision the school makes is substantially affected in some way by the State's regulations.[1]

[Under state law], the State is *required* to provide a free education to all children, including those with special needs. Clearly, if the State had decided to provide the service itself, its conduct would be measured against constitutional standards. The State should not be permitted to avoid constitutional requirements simply by delegating its statutory duty to a private entity. * * *

The majority repeatedly compares the school to a private contractor * * * . Although shipbuilders and dambuilders, like the school, may be dependent on

---

[6]   **[Ct's Note]** [The] Committee did not take any part in discharging Rendell-Baker; on the contrary, it attempted to use leverage to aid her. [T]here is no evidence that the Committee had any authority to take even those steps.

[7]   **[Ct's Note]** There is no evidence that the State has attempted to avoid its constitutional duties by a sham arrangement which attempts to disguise provision of public services as acts of private parties.]

[1]   **[Ct's Note]** [By] analyzing the various indicia of state action separately, without considering their cumulative impact, the majority commits a fundamental error.

government funds, they are not so closely supervised by the government. And unlike most private contractors, the school is performing a statutory duty of the State. * * *

4. STATE FAILURE TO ACT

DeShaney v. Winnebago County Dep't of Social Serv.

489 U.S. 189, 109 S.Ct. 998, 103 L.Ed.2d 249 (1989).

Chief Justice Rehnquist delivered the opinion of the Court.

[I]n January 1982, [the] Department of Social Services (DSS) interviewed [Joshua DeShaney's father about alleged child abuse], but he denied the accusations, and DSS did not pursue them. [In] January 1983, Joshua was admitted to a local hospital with multiple bruises and abrasions. The examining physician suspected child abuse and notified DSS. [T]he county convened an ad hoc "Child Protection Team" [which] decided that there was insufficient evidence of child abuse to retain Joshua in the custody of the court. The Team did, however, decide to recommend several measures to protect Joshua, including enrolling him in a preschool program, providing his father with certain counselling services, and encouraging his father's girlfriend to move out of the home. [A month later] emergency room personnel called the DSS caseworker handling Joshua's case to report that he had once again been treated for suspicious injuries. The caseworker concluded that there was no basis for action. [For] six months, the caseworker made monthly visits to the DeShaney home, during which she observed a number of suspicious injuries on Joshua's head; [and] that he had not been enrolled in school and that the girlfriend had not moved out. The caseworker dutifully recorded these incidents in her files, along with her continuing suspicions that someone in the DeShaney household was physically abusing Joshua, but she did nothing more. In November 1983, the emergency room notified DSS that Joshua had been treated once again for injuries that they believed to be caused by child abuse. On the caseworker's next two visits to the DeShaney home, she was told that Joshua was too ill to see her. Still DSS took no action.

In March 1984, Randy DeShaney beat 4-year-old Joshua so severely that he fell into a life-threatening coma [and] is expected to spend the rest of his life confined to an institution for the profoundly retarded. Randy DeShaney was subsequently tried and convicted of child abuse.

Joshua and his mother brought this action under 42 U.S.C. § 1983. [But] nothing in the language of the Due Process Clause itself requires the State to protect the life, liberty, and property of its citizens against invasion by private actors. [Nor] does history support such an expansive reading of the constitutional text. [The Clause's] purpose was to protect the people from the State, not to ensure that the State protected them from each other. The Framers were content to leave the extent of governmental obligation in the latter area to the democratic political processes. * * *

Petitioners contend, however, that even if the Due Process Clause imposes no affirmative obligation on the State to provide the general public with adequate protective services, such a duty may arise out of certain "special relationships" created or assumed by the State with respect to particular individuals [and] that such a "special relationship" existed here because the State knew that Joshua faced a special danger of abuse at his father's hands, and specifically proclaimed, by word and by deed, its intention to protect him against that danger. * * *

We reject this argument. It is true that in certain limited circumstances the Constitution imposes upon the State affirmative duties of care and protection with respect to particular individuals [discussing *Youngberg v. Romeo*, 457 U.S. 307 (1982); *Estelle v. Gamble*, 429 U.S. 97 (1976) (involving involuntary incarceration); and other cases]. But these [cases] stand only for the proposition that when the State takes a person into its custody and holds him there against his will, the Constitution imposes upon it a corresponding duty to assume some responsibility for his safety and general well-being. [I]ncarceration, institutionalization, or other similar restraint of personal liberty [is] the "deprivation of liberty" triggering the protections of the Due Process Clause. [While] the State may have been aware of the dangers that Joshua faced in the free world, it played no part in their creation, nor did it do anything to render him any more vulnerable to them. That the State once took temporary custody of Joshua does not alter the analysis, for when it returned him to his father's custody, it placed him in no worse position than that in which he would have been had it not acted at all. [The] most that can be said of the state functionaries in this case is that they stood by and did nothing when suspicious circumstances dictated a more active role for them. In defense of them it must also be said that had they moved too soon to take custody of the son away from the father, they would likely have been met with charges of improperly intruding into the parent-child relationship, charges based on the same Due Process Clause * * * .

JUSTICE BRENNAN, with whom JUSTICE MARSHALL and JUSTICE BLACKMUN join, dissenting.

* * * I [would] recognize, as the Court apparently cannot, that "the State's knowledge of [an] individual's predicament [and] its expressions of intent to help him" can amount to a "limitation of his freedom to act on his own behalf" or to obtain help from others. Thus, I would read *Youngberg* and *Estelle* to stand for the much more generous proposition that, if a State cuts off private sources of aid and then refuses aid itself, it cannot wash its hands of the harm that results from its inaction. * * *

The specific facts before us bear out this view of Wisconsin's system of protecting children. Each time someone voiced a suspicion that Joshua was being abused, that information was relayed to the Department for investigation and possible action. [If] DSS ignores or dismisses these suspicions, no one will step in to fill the gap. [Through] its child-protection program, the State actively intervened in Joshua's life and, by virtue of this intervention, acquired ever more certain knowledge that Joshua was in grave danger. * * * My disagreement with the Court arises from its failure to see that inaction can be every bit as abusive of power as action, that oppression can result when a State undertakes a vital duty and then ignores it. * * *7

JUSTICE BLACKMUN, dissenting. * * *

Like the antebellum judges who denied relief to fugitive slaves, the Court today claims that its decision, however harsh, is compelled by existing legal doctrine. [O]ur Fourteenth Amendment precedents may be read more broadly or narrowly depending upon how one [chooses]. I would adopt a "sympathetic" reading, one which comports with dictates of fundamental justice and recognizes that compassion need not be exiled from the province of judging. * * *

Poor Joshua! Victim of repeated attacks by an irresponsible, bullying, cowardly, and intemperate father, and abandoned by respondents who placed him in a dangerous predicament and who knew or learned what was going on, and yet did essentially nothing except, as the Court revealing observes * * * "dutifully recorded these incidents in [their] files." * * *

---

7   See also *Castle Rock v. Gonzales*, 545 U.S. 748 (2005).

CHAPTER 11

CONGRESSIONAL ENFORCEMENT
OF CIVIL RIGHTS

■ ■ ■

The exercise of congressional authority under the Commerce Clause to protect civil rights was examined in detail in Ch. 2, Sec. 2, III. But it is striking that the Supreme Court, in upholding the central provisions of the 1964 Civil Rights Act, relied on the Commerce Clause at all. Equally striking is that the Court did not invoke the federal legislative powers to enforce civil rights that are found in the final sections of the Thirteenth and Fourteenth Amendments, both of which authorize Congress to enforce the Amendment's substantive provisions "by appropriate legislation." Although the enforcement provisions of those Amendments possess modern significance, as does a parallel section of the Fifteenth Amendment, the Court's interpretations have been limited and controversial.

1. HISTORICAL FRAMEWORK

Reconstruction Congresses enacted a series of civil rights acts, beginning with the Civil Rights Act of 1866 and culminating in the Civil Rights Act of 1875, the latter of which the Court invalidated in the *Civil Rights Cases*, Ch. 10, Sec. 1. The Court's central analytical move in the *Civil Rights Cases* was to interpret the Fourteenth Amendment as barring only "state action" and, accordingly, as providing no authorization for legislation regulating "private individuals" as a means of enforcing Fourteenth Amendment rights.[1] As you read this chapter, pay careful attention to the dates of the cases adjudicating the constitutionality of the Reconstruction civil rights laws. After Reconstruction ended and the political tide shifted away from protecting African-Americans from systematic oppression, the civil rights laws played little meaningful role until the mid-twentieth century, when they reemerged during the Civil Rights Era.

---

[1]   See *United States v. Cruikshank*, 92 U.S. 542, 23 L.Ed. 588 (1876); *Virginia v. Rives*, 100 U.S. 313, 25 L.Ed. 667 (1879).

CIVIL RIGHTS CASES

109 U.S. 3, 3 S.Ct. 18, 27 L.Ed. 835 (1883).

JUSTICE BRADLEY delivered the opinion of the Court.

[The first and second sections of the 1875 Civil Rights Act—providing, inter alia, that "all persons within the jurisdiction of the United States shall be entitled to the full and equal enjoyment of the accommodations, advantages, facilities, and privileges of inns, public conveyances on land or water, theaters, and other places of public amusement; subject only to the conditions and limitations established by law, and applicable alike to citizens of every race and color, regardless of any previous condition of servitude"—are invalid. Individual] invasion of individual rights is not the subject-matter of the [Fourteenth] amendment [nor does the amendment] authorize Congress to create a code of municipal law for the regulation of private rights; but [only] to provide modes of redress against the operation of state laws, and the action of state officers, executive or judicial, when these are subversive of the fundamental rights specified in the amendment. * * *

[The Thirteenth Amendment] is not a mere prohibition of state laws establishing or upholding slavery, but an absolute declaration that slavery or involuntary servitude shall not exist in any part of the United States [and] that the power vested in Congress to enforce the article by appropriate legislation, clothes Congress with power to pass all laws necessary and proper for abolishing all badges and incidents of slavery, in the United States. [T]he civil rights bill of 1866, passed in view of the Thirteenth Amendment, before the fourteenth was adopted, undertook to wipe out these burdens and disabilities, the necessary incidents of slavery, constituting its substance and visible from; and to secure to all citizens of every race and color, and without regard to previous servitude, those fundamental rights which are the essence of civil freedom, namely, the same right to make and enforce contracts, to sue, be parties, give evidence, and to inherit, purchase, lease, sell, and convey property, as is enjoyed by white citizens. [At] that time (in 1866) Congress did not assume, under the authority given by the Thirteenth Amendment, to adjust what may be called the social rights of men and races in the community; but only to declare and vindicate those fundamental rights which appertain to the essence of citizenship, and the enjoyment or deprivation of which constitutes the essential distinction between freedom and slavery. * * *

[It] would be running the slavery argument into the ground to make it apply to every act of discrimination which a person may see fit to make as to the guests he will entertain, or as to the people he will take into his coach or cab or car, or admit to his concert or theater, or deal with in other matters of intercourse or business. * * * If the laws themselves make any unjust discrimination, amenable to the prohibitions of the Fourteenth Amendment, Congress has full power to afford a remedy under that amendment and in accordance with it.

JUSTICE HARLAN, dissenting. * * *

Was it the purpose of the nation [by the Thirteenth Amendment] simply to destroy the institution [of slavery], and remit the race, theretofore held in bondage, to the several states for such protection, in their civil rights, necessarily growing out of freedom, as those states [choose] to provide? [S]ince slavery [rested] wholly upon the inferiority, as a race, of those held in bondage, their freedom necessarily involved immunity from, and protection against, all discrimination against them, because of their race, in respect of such civil rights as belong to freemen of other races. Congress, therefore, [may] enact laws of a direct and primary character, operating upon states, their officers and agents, and also upon, at least, such individuals and corporations as exercise public functions and wield power and authority under the state. * * *

It remains now to inquire what are the legal rights of colored persons in respect of the accommodations * * * .

1.   As to public conveyances on land and water. [R]ailroads [are] none the less public highways because controlled and owned by private corporations; that it is a part of the function of government to make and maintain highways for the conveyance of the public; that no matter who is the agent, and what is the agency, the function performed is *that of the state* * * * .

Such being the relations these corporations hold to the public, it would seem that the right of a colored person to use an improved public highway, upon the terms accorded to freemen of other races, is as fundamental in the state of freedom, established in this country, as are any of the rights which my brethren concede to be so far fundamental as to be deemed the essence of civil freedom.

2.   As to inns. [A] keeper of an inn is in the exercise of a quasi public employment. The law gives him special privileges, and he is charged with certain duties and responsibilities to the public [which] forbids him from discriminating against any person asking admission as a guest on account of [race].

3.   As to places of public amusement. [W]ithin the meaning of the act of 1875, [they] are such as are established and maintained under direct license of the law. [The] local government granting the license represents [the colored race] as well as all other races within its jurisdiction. A license from the public to establish a place of public amusement, imports, in law, equality of right, at such [places].

[With regard to the Fourteenth Amendment,] the first clause of the first section—"all persons born or naturalized in the United States, and subject to the jurisdiction thereof, are citizens of the United States, and of the state wherein they reside"—is of a distinctly affirmative character. In its application to the colored race, previously liberated, it [granted] citizenship of the state in which they respectively resided. [Further], they were brought, by this supreme act of the nation, within the direct operation of that provision of the Constitution which declares that "the citizens of each state shall be entitled to all privileges and immunities of citizens in the several states." Article IV, § 2.

The citizenship thus acquired [may be protected] by congressional legislation of a primary direct character; this, because the power of Congress is not restricted to the enforcement of prohibitions upon state laws or state action. It is, in terms distinct and positive, to enforce "the *provisions of this article*" of amendment * * * *all* of the provisions,—affirmative and prohibitive * * * .

But what was secured to colored citizens of the United States—as between them and their respective states—by the grant to them of state citizenship? With what rights, privileges, or immunities did this grant from the nation invest them? There is one, if there be no others—exemption from race discrimination in respect of any civil right belonging to citizens of the white race in the same state [by] the state, or its officers, or by individuals, or corporations exercising public functions or authority. [It] was perfectly well known that the great danger to the equal enjoyment by citizens of their rights, as citizens, was to be apprehended, not altogether from unfriendly state legislation, but from the hostile action of corporations and individuals in the states. * * *

But if it were conceded that the power of Congress could not be brought into activity until the rights specified in the act of 1875 had been abridged or denied by some state law or state action, I maintain that the decision of the court is erroneous. [In] every material sense applicable to the practical enforcement of the Fourteenth Amendment, railroad corporations, keepers of inns, and managers of places of public amusement are agents of the state, because amenable, in respect of their public duties and functions, to public regulation. * * * I agree that if one citizen chooses not to hold social intercourse with another, he is not and cannot be made amenable to the law for his conduct in that regard. [The] rights which Congress, by the act of 1875, endeavored to secure and protect are legal, not social, rights. The right, for instance, of a colored citizen to use the accommodations of a public highway upon the same terms as are permitted to white citizens is no more a social right than his right, under the law, to use the public streets of a city, or a town, or a turnpike road, or a public market, or a post-office, or his right to sit in a public building with others, of whatever race, for the purpose of hearing the political questions of the day discussed.

2. REGULATION OF PRIVATE PERSONS

Congress repeatedly invoked the enforcement provisions of the Reconstruction Amendments to enact ambitious civil rights legislation in the early years after the Civil War. After the end of Reconstruction, however, the statutes went mostly unenforced for decades. They returned to relevance only in the mid-twentieth century—when the Court once again had occasion to construe them and to consider their constitutionality.

I. THIRTEENTH AMENDMENT

The Civil Rights Act of 1866, enacted pursuant to the Thirteenth Amendment, was the first Reconstruction Act that sought "to protect all persons in the United States in their civil rights." Its current provisions are:

42 U.S.C. § 1981. *"Equal rights under the law.* All persons within the jurisdiction of the United States shall have the same right in every State and Territory to make and enforce contracts, to sue, be parties, give evidence, and to the full and equal benefit of all laws and proceedings for the security of persons and property as is enjoyed by white citizens, and shall be subject to like punishment, pains, penalties, taxes, licenses, and exactions of every kind, and to no other."

42 U.S.C. § 1982. *"Property rights of citizens.* All citizens of the United States shall have the same right, in every State and Territory, as is enjoyed by white citizens thereof to inherit, purchase, lease, sell, hold, and convey real and personal property."

JONES V. ALFRED H. MAYER CO.
392 U.S. 409, 88 S.Ct. 2186, 20 L.Ed.2d 1189 (1968).

JUSTICE STEWART delivered the opinion of the Court.

[P]etitioners filed a complaint [that] respondents had refused to sell them a home [for] the sole reason that petitioner [is] a Negro. Relying in part upon 42 U.S.C. § 1982, the petitioners sought injunctive and other relief.[1] The [courts below] sustained the respondents' motion to dismiss [concluding] that § 1982 applies only to state action * * * .

[I]t is important to make clear precisely what this case does *not* involve. Whatever else it may be, § 1982 is not a comprehensive open housing law, [but] deals only with racial discrimination [and] does not deal specifically with discrimination in the provision of services or facilities in connection with the sale or rental of a dwelling. * * *

On its [face] § 1982 appears to prohibit *all* discrimination against Negroes in the sale or rental of property—discrimination by private owners as well as discrimination by public [authorities]. Stressing what they consider to be the revolutionary implications of so literal a reading of § 1982, the respondents argue that Congress cannot possibly have intended any such result. Our examination of the relevant history, however, persuades us that Congress meant exactly what it said.

In its original form, § 1982 was part [of] the Civil Rights Act of 1866. [The Court then extensively examined antecedent statutes and studies and debate in

---

[1]   **[Ct's Note]** To vindicate their rights under § 1982, the petitioners invoked the jurisdiction of the District Court to award "damages [or] equitable or other relief under any Act of Congress providing for the protection of civil rights * * * ." 28 U.S.C. § 1343(4). * * *

the Congress, contemporaneous with the proposal and ratification of the Thirteenth Amendment, in support of its conclusion respecting § 1982.] It is quite true that some members of Congress supported the Fourteenth Amendment "in order to eliminate doubt as to the constitutional validity of the Civil Rights Act as applied to the States." [*Hurd v. Hodge*, 334 U.S. 24 (1948)]. But it certainly does not follow that the adoption of the Fourteenth Amendment or the subsequent readoption of the Civil Rights Act were meant somehow to *limit* its application to state action. The legislative history furnishes not the slightest factual basis for any such speculation, and the conditions prevailing in 1870 make it highly implausible. * * *

The remaining question is whether Congress has power under the Constitution to do what § 1982 purports to [do]. Our starting point is the Thirteenth Amendment, for it was pursuant to that constitutional provision that Congress originally enacted what is now § 1982. [It] has never been [doubted] "that the power vested in Congress to enforce the article by appropriate legislation," [*Civil Rights Cases,*] includes the power to enact laws "direct and primary, operating upon the acts of individuals, whether sanctioned by State legislation or not." [Id.]

"By its own unaided force and effect," the Thirteenth Amendment "abolished slavery, and established universal freedom." *Civil Rights Cases.* Whether or not the Amendment *itself* did any more than that—a question not involved in this case—it is at least clear that the Enabling Clause of that Amendment empowered Congress to do much more.[2] For that clause clothed "Congress with power to pass *all laws necessary and proper for abolishing all badges and incidents of slavery in the United States."* Ibid. (Emphasis added.)

[The] majority leaders in Congress—who were, after all, the authors of the Thirteenth Amendment—had no doubt that its Enabling Clause contemplated the sort of positive legislation that was embodied in the 1866 Civil Rights Act. [Surely] Congress has the power under the Thirteenth Amendment rationally to determine what are the badges and the incidents of slavery, and the authority to translate that determination into effective legislation. Nor can we say that the determination Congress has made is an irrational one. For this Court recognized long ago that, whatever else they may have encompassed, the badges and incidents of slavery— its "burdens and disabilities"—included restraints upon "those fundamental rights which are the essence of civil freedom, namely the same right [to] inherit, purchase, lease, sell and convey property, as is enjoyed by white citizens." *Civil Rights Cases.* Just as the Black Codes, enacted after the Civil War to restrict the free exercise of those rights, were substitutes for the slave system, so the exclusion of Negroes from white communities became a substitute for the Black Codes. And when racial discrimination herds men into ghettos and makes their ability to buy property turn on the color of their skin, then it too is a relic of slavery.

---

[2]   For discussion of the use of judicial power under § 1, see Ch. 10, Sec. 1.

[At] the very least, the freedom that Congress is empowered to secure under the Thirteenth Amendment includes the freedom to buy whatever a white man can buy, the right to live wherever a white man can live. If Congress cannot say that being a free man means at least this much, then the Thirteenth Amendment made a promise the Nation cannot keep. * * *

Reversed.

JUSTICE HARLAN, whom JUSTICE WHITE joins, dissenting.

[In a lengthy opinion, Harlan, J., relied on statements in prior Court opinions, the use of the word "right" in § 1982, the legislative history and debates of the Civil Rights Act of 1866 and of companion legislation, and on the ethics of the times to insist that the Court's construction of § 1982 was "open to the most serious doubt" if not "wholly untenable."][3]

———

RUNYON v. McCRARY, 427 U.S. 160 (1976), per STEWART, J., relying on *Mayer's* interpretation of § 1982, held that § 1981 prohibits private schools from refusing to accept black students. POWELL, J., joined the opinion, but added that "choices, including those involved in entering into a contract, that are 'private' in the sense that they are not part of a commercial relationship offered generally or widely, and that reflect the selectivity exercised by an individual entering into a personal relationship, certainly were never intended to be restricted by" § 1981. Stevens, J., joined the Court's opinion, feeling bound by, but disagreeing with, the statutory interpretation in *Mayer*. White, J., joined by Rehnquist, J., dissented on grounds of statutory interpretation.

II. FOURTEENTH AMENDMENT

UNITED STATES v. MORRISON, Ch. 2, Sec. 2, IV, per REHNQUIST, C.J., held that Congress had no power under § 5 of the Fourteenth Amendment to grant a civil remedy to victims of gender-motivated violence: "[T]he language and purpose of the Fourteenth Amendment place certain limitations on the manner in which Congress may attack [gender discrimination. Foremost] is that the Fourteenth Amendment, by its very terms, prohibits only state action. * * *

"Shortly after the Fourteenth Amendment was adopted, we [decided] *United States v. Harris*, 106 U.S. 629 (1883), [which] considered a challenge to § 2 of the Civil Rights Act of 1871. That section sought to punish 'private persons' for 'conspiring to deprive any one of the equal protection of the laws enacted by the State.' We concluded that this law exceeded Congress' § 5 power because the law was 'directed exclusively against the action of private persons, without reference to the laws of the State, or their administration by her officers.' [We] reached a similar conclusion in the *Civil Rights Cases*. * * *

---

[3]   The concurring opinion of Douglas, J., is omitted.

Sec. 13981 "is directed not at any State or state actor, but at individuals who have committed criminal acts motivated by gender bias. [It] visits no consequence whatever on any Virginia public official involved in investigating or prosecuting [the rape involved in this case]. The section is, therefore, unlike any of the § 5 remedies that we have previously upheld."

BREYER, J., joined by Stevens, J., dissented[4]: "The Federal Government's argument [is] that Congress used § 5 to remedy the actions of *state actors*, namely, those States which, through discriminatory design or the discriminatory conduct of their officials, failed to provide adequate (or any) state remedies for women injured by gender-motivated violence—a failure that the States, and Congress, documented in depth." The *Civil Rights Cases* did not consider "this kind of claim," because the statute "did 'not profess to be corrective of any constitutional wrong committed by the States' [but] established 'rules for the conduct of individuals in society towards each other, [without] referring in any manner to any supposed action of the State or its authorities.'

"[W]hy can Congress not provide a remedy against private actors? Those private actors, of course, did not themselves violate the Constitution. But this Court has held that Congress at least sometimes can enact remedial 'legislation [that] prohibits conduct which is not itself unconstitutional.' The statutory remedy [may] lead state actors to improve their own remedial systems, primarily through example. It restricts private actors only by imposing liability for private conduct that is, in the main, already forbidden by state law. [To be permissible under *City of Boerne v. Flores*, Sec. 3, infra, legislation enacted pursuant to § 5 must be "congruent" and "proportional" to an identified pattern of constitutional violations. But why] is the remedy 'disproportionate'? And given the relation between remedy and violation—the creation of a federal remedy to substitute for constitutionally inadequate state remedies—where is the lack of 'congruence'?

" * * * Congress had before it the task force reports of at least 21 States documenting constitutional violations [involving officials' discrimination against the victims of gender-based violence]. And it made its own findings about pervasive gender-based stereotypes hampering many state legal systems, sometimes unconstitutionally so. [This] Court has not previously held that Congress must document the existence of a problem in every State prior to proposing a national solution."

3. REGULATION OF STATE ACTORS

After the *Civil Rights Cases*, no significant congressional action to enforce civil rights took place until the mid-twentieth century. Some of the most important civil rights legislation passed by Congress in the 1960s and after, including the Civil Rights Act of 1964, relied upon the Commerce Clause to circumvent the Fourteenth Amendment's state action requirement and forbid discrimination by private

---

[4]   Souter and Ginsburg, JJ., having found the law valid under the Commerce Clause, felt no occasion to reach the § 5 issue.

entities. But Congress also enacted important civil rights legislation that regulated the behavior of state actors under the enforcement provisions of the Fourteenth and Fifteenth Amendments. The scope of Congress' powers under those two amendments has been a continuing source of controversy, with more recent decisions taking a narrow view.

I.   FOURTEENTH AMENDMENT

BOERNE V. FLORES
521 U.S. 507, 117 S.Ct. 2157, 138 L.Ed.2d 624 (1997).

JUSTICE KENNEDY delivered the opinion of the Court.

A decision by local zoning authorities to deny a church a building permit was challenged under the Religious Freedom Restoration Act of 1993 (RFRA). * * *

Congress enacted RFRA in direct response to the Court's decision in *Employment Div. v. Smith*, [Ch. 8, Sec. 2, I]. *Smith* held that neutral, generally applicable laws may be applied to religious practices even when not supported by a compelling governmental interest. [Many] criticized the Court's reasoning, and this disagreement resulted in the passage of RFRA. * * *

RFRA prohibits "[g]overnment" from "substantially burden[ing]" a person's exercise of religion even if the burden results from a rule of general applicability unless the government can demonstrate the burden "(1) is in furtherance of a compelling governmental interest; and (2) is the least restrictive means of furthering that compelling governmental interest." * * * Legislation which deters or remedies constitutional violations can fall within the sweep of Congress' [Fourteenth Amendment] enforcement power even if in the process it prohibits conduct which is not itself unconstitutional and intrudes into "legislative spheres of autonomy previously reserved to the States." *Fitzpatrick v. Bitzer*, 427 U.S. 445 (1976). [As examples, the Court discussed the practices that Congress had made unlawful in *South Carolina v. Katzenbach*, 383 U.S. 301 (1966) (upholding a provision of the 1965 Voting Rights Act that required covered jurisdictions to obtain federal pre-clearance of changes in their voting laws); *Katzenbach v. Morgan*, 384 U.S. 641 (1966) (upholding provision of the 1965 Voting Rights Act providing that that no one who had completed the sixth grade in a non-English-speaking school in Puerto Rico could be denied the right to vote in covered U.S. jurisdictions on grounds of illiteracy); and *Rome v. United States*, 446 U.S. 156 (1980) (upholding a congressional prohibition against changes in voting rules by covered jurisdictions that would have a racially discriminatory effect, even in the absence of a discriminatory intent).] We agree with respondent, of course, that Congress can enact legislation under § 5 enforcing the constitutional right to the free exercise of religion. * * *

Congress' power under § 5, however, extends only to "enforc[ing]" the provisions of the Fourteenth Amendment. The Court has described this power as "remedial." The design of the Amendment and the text of § 5 are inconsistent with the suggestion that Congress has the power to decree the substance of the Fourteenth Amendment's restrictions on the States. Legislation which alters the meaning of the Free Exercise Clause cannot be said to be enforcing the Clause. [Were] it not so, what Congress would be enforcing would no longer be, in any meaningful sense, the "provisions of [the Fourteenth Amendment]."

While the line between measures that remedy or prevent unconstitutional actions and measures that make a substantive change in the governing law is not easy to discern, and Congress must have wide latitude in determining where it lies, the distinction exists and must be observed. There must be a congruence and proportionality between the injury to be prevented or remedied and the means adopted to that end. Lacking such a connection, legislation may become substantive in operation and effect. * * *

The Fourteenth Amendment's history confirms the remedial, rather than substantive, nature of the Enforcement Clause.[5] [The] objections to the [Joint] Committee's first draft of the Amendment ["The Congress shall have power to make all laws which shall be necessary and proper to secure to the citizens of each State all privileges and immunities of citizens in the several States, and to all persons in the several States equal protection in the rights of life, liberty, and property."] have a direct bearing on the central issue of defining Congress' enforcement power. * * * Members of Congress from across the political spectrum criticized the Amendment, and the criticisms had a common theme: The proposed Amendment gave Congress [a] power to intrude into traditional areas of state responsibility, a power inconsistent with the federal design central to the Constitution. [Under] the revised Amendment, Congress' power was no longer plenary but remedial [and] did not raise the concerns expressed earlier regarding broad congressional power to prescribe uniform national laws with respect to life, liberty, and property. * * *

The design of the Fourteenth Amendment has proved significant also in maintaining the traditional separation of powers between Congress and the Judiciary. The first eight Amendments to the Constitution set forth self-executing prohibitions on governmental action, and this Court has had primary authority to interpret those prohibitions. The [Joint Committee's first] draft, some thought, departed from that tradition by vesting in Congress primary power to interpret and elaborate on the meaning of the new Amendment through legislation. Under it, "Congress, and not the courts, was to judge whether or not any of the privileges

---

[5]   Contra, Douglas Laycock, *Conceptual Gulfs in Boerne v. Flores*, 39 Wm. & Mary L. Rev. 743, 766 (1998): "Senators and representatives argued [that] the enforcement power would add nothing if it were confined to the judicially enforceable meaning of the Amendment"; Evan Caminker, *"Appropriate" Means-End Constraints on Section 5 Powers*, 53 Stan. L. Rev. 1127, 1159 (2001): "[A]n originalist inquiry—whether focused on the Framers' actual subjective intentions, as the Court did with respect to the interpretation of Section 5 ends, or whether focused on the most likely public understanding of the amendment's plain language, as many contemporary originalists would do—firmly supports the conclusion that Section 5 was designed [and] understood as codifying Chief Justice Marshall's especially deferential ['necessary and proper' formulation] in *McCulloch*"; Ruth Colker, *The Supreme Court's Historical Errors in City of Boerne v. Flores*, 43 B.C. L. Rev. 783 (2002).

or immunities were not secured to citizens in the several States." [But the] power to interpret the Constitution in a case or controversy remains in the Judiciary. * * *

Any suggestion that Congress has a substantive, non-remedial power under the Fourteenth Amendment is not supported by our case law. In *Oregon v. Mitchell*, [400 U.S. 112 (1970)], a majority of the Court concluded Congress had exceeded its enforcement powers by enacting legislation lowering the minimum age of voters from 21 to 18 in state and local elections.[6] The five Members of the Court who reached this conclusion explained that [the] legislation was unconstitutional because the Constitution "reserves to the States the power to set voter qualifications in state and local elections." Four of these five were explicit in rejecting the position that § 5 endowed Congress with the power to establish the meaning of constitutional provisions. See (opinion of Harlan, J.); (opinion of Stewart, J., joined by Burger, C. J., and Blackmun, J.). * * *

There is language in our opinion in *Morgan* which could be interpreted as acknowledging a power in Congress to enact legislation that expands the rights contained in § 1 of the Fourteenth Amendment. This is not a necessary interpretation, however, or even the best one. [As] Justice Stewart explained in *Mitchell,* interpreting *Morgan* to give Congress the power to interpret the Constitution "would require an enormous extension of that decision's rationale."

If Congress could define its own powers by altering the Fourteenth Amendment's meaning, no longer would the Constitution be "superior paramount law, unchangeable by ordinary means." It would be "on a level with ordinary legislative acts, and, like other [acts,] alterable when the legislature shall please to alter it." *Marbury v. Madison.* Under this approach, it is difficult to conceive of a principle that would limit congressional power. Shifting legislative majorities could change the Constitution and effectively circumvent the difficult and detailed amendment process contained in Article V. * * *

Respondent contends that RFRA is a proper exercise of Congress' remedial or preventive power. The Act, it is [said,] prevents and remedies laws which are enacted with the unconstitutional object of targeting religious beliefs and practices. See *Church of the Lukumi Babalu Aye, Inc. v. Hialeah*, [Ch. 8, Sec. 2, I]. To avoid the difficulty of proving such violations, it is said, Congress can simply invalidate any law which imposes a substantial burden on a religious practice unless it is justified by a compelling interest and is the least restrictive means of accomplishing that interest. If Congress can prohibit laws with discriminatory effects in order to prevent racial discrimination in violation of the Equal Protection Clause, then it can do the same, respondent argues, to promote religious liberty.

While preventive rules are sometimes appropriate remedial measures, there must be a congruence between the means used and the ends to be achieved. * * *

---

[6]   A different majority—Black, Douglas, Brennan, White and Marshall, JJ.—voted to uphold this provision as to federal elections. Black, J., who was in both majorities, distinguished the situations on the ground (which no other justice joined) that Congress had power under Art. I, § 4 to set qualifications for voters in federal elections.

Strong measures appropriate to address one harm may be an unwarranted response to another, lesser one.

A comparison between RFRA and the Voting Rights Act is instructive. In contrast to the record which confronted Congress and the judiciary in the voting rights cases, RFRA's legislative record lacks examples of modern instances of generally applicable laws passed because of religious bigotry. [Rather,] the emphasis of the hearings was on laws of general applicability which place incidental burdens on religion. * * *

Regardless of the state of the legislative record, RFRA [is] so out of proportion to a supposed remedial or preventive object that it cannot be understood as responsive to, or designed to prevent, unconstitutional behavior. It appears, instead, to attempt a substantive change in constitutional protections. Preventive measures prohibiting certain types of laws may be appropriate when there is reason to believe that many of the laws affected by the congressional enactment have a significant likelihood of being unconstitutional.* * *

The reach and scope of RFRA distinguish it from other measures passed under Congress' enforcement power, even in the area of voting rights. * * * The provisions restricting and banning literacy tests, upheld in *Morgan,* attacked a particular type of voting qualification, one with a long history as a "notorious means to deny and abridge voting rights on racial grounds." [This] is not to say, of course, that § 5 legislation requires termination dates, geographic restrictions or egregious predicates. Where, however, a congressional enactment pervasively prohibits constitutional state action in an effort to remedy or to prevent unconstitutional state action, limitations of this kind tend to ensure Congress' means are proportionate to ends legitimate under § 5. * * *

The substantial costs RFRA exacts, both in practical terms of imposing a heavy litigation burden on the States and in terms of curtailing their traditional general regulatory power, far exceed any pattern or practice of unconstitutional conduct under the Free Exercise Clause as interpreted in *Smith.* [In] addition, the Act imposes in every case a least restrictive means requirement—a requirement that was not used in the pre-*Smith* jurisprudence RFRA purported to codify— which also indicates that the legislation is broader than is appropriate if the goal is to prevent and remedy constitutional violations.

When [the] political branches of the Government act against the background of a judicial interpretation of the Constitution already issued, it must be understood that in later cases and controversies the Court will treat its precedents with the respect due them under settled principles, including stare decisis, and contrary expectations must be disappointed. RFRA was designed to control cases and controversies, such as the one before us; but as the provisions of the federal statute here invoked are beyond congressional authority, it is this Court's precedent, not RFRA, which must control. * * *

JUSTICE STEVENS, concurring.

In my opinion, RFRA is a "law respecting an establishment of religion" that violates the First Amendment * * * .[7]

JUSTICE O'CONNOR, with whom JUSTICE BREYER joins except as to [the first sentence below].

* * * I agree with much of the reasoning set forth in [the] Court's opinion. [But] I remain of the view that *Smith* was wrongly decided, and I would use this case to reexamine the Court's holding there. Therefore, I would direct the parties to brief the question whether *Smith* represents the correct understanding of the Free Exercise Clause and set the case for reargument. If the Court were to correct the misinterpretation of the Free Exercise Clause set forth in *Smith,* it would simultaneously put our First Amendment jurisprudence back on course and allay the legitimate concerns of a majority in Congress who believed that *Smith* improperly restricted religious liberty. We would then be in a position to review RFRA in light of a proper interpretation of the Free Exercise Clause. * * *

FLORIDA PREPAID POSTSECONDARY EDUCATION EXPENSE BOARD v. COLLEGE SAVINGS BANK, 527 U.S. 627 (1999), per REHNQUIST, C.J., concerned Congress' § 5 power to make states subject to federal court actions for patent infringement: Although patents "have long been considered a species [of] 'property' of which no person may be deprived by a State without due process[,] Congress identified no pattern of patent infringement by the States, let alone a pattern of constitutional violations.* * *

"The legislative record thus suggests that the Patent Remedy Act does not respond to a history of 'widespread and persisting deprivation of constitutional rights' of the sort Congress has faced in enacting proper prophylactic § 5 legislation. [Because] of this lack, the provisions of the Patent Remedy Act are 'so out of proportion to a supposed remedial or preventive object that [they] cannot be understood as responsive to, or designed to prevent, unconstitutional behavior.' Boerne."

STEVENS, J., joined by Souter, Ginsburg and Breyer, JJ., dissented: "[Here, the Act] has no impact whatsoever on any substantive rule of state law, but merely effectuates settled federal policy to confine patent infringement litigation to federal judges. There is precise congruence between 'the means used' (abrogation of sovereign immunity in this narrow category of cases) and 'the ends to be achieved' (elimination of the risk that the defense of sovereign immunity will deprive some patentees of property without due process of law)."

----

[7]   The concurring opinion of Scalia, J., joined by Stevens, J., both of whom joined the Court's opinion, is omitted. Souter, J. would dismiss the writ of certiorari as improvidently granted.

KIMEL v. FLORIDA BD. OF REGENTS, 528 U.S. 62 (2000), per O'CONNOR, J., explored *Boerne's* scope in the context of Congress' exercising its § 5 power to make states subject to federal court actions for violating the Age Discrimination in Employment Act:[8] "We have [held that] age is not a suspect classification [Ch. 9, Sec. 4, IV]. Our Constitution permits States to draw lines on the basis of age when they have a rational basis for doing so at a class-based level, even if it 'is probably not true' that those reasons are valid in the majority of cases.

"Judged against the backdrop of our equal protection jurisprudence, it is clear that the ADEA is 'so out of proportion to a supposed remedial or preventive object that it cannot be understood as responsive to, or designed to prevent, unconstitutional behavior.' *Boerne.* The Act, through its broad restriction on the use of age as a discriminating factor, prohibits substantially more state employment decisions and practices than would likely be held unconstitutional under the applicable equal protection, rational basis standard.* * *

"Our examination of the ADEA's legislative record confirms [that] Congress never identified any pattern of age discrimination by the States, much less any discrimination whatsoever that rose to the level of constitutional violation. The evidence compiled by petitioners [consists] almost entirely of isolated sentences clipped from floor debates and legislative reports. * * *

"Our decision today does not signal the end of the line for [state employees who] are protected by state age discrimination statutes, and may recover money damages from their state employers, in almost every [State]."

STEVENS, J., joined by Souter, Ginsburg and Breyer, JJ., dissented: "Congress' power to authorize federal remedies against state agencies that violate federal statutory obligations is coextensive with its power [under the Commerce Clause] to impose those obligations on the States in the first place. Neither the Eleventh Amendment nor the doctrine of sovereign immunity places any limit on that power. "Federalism concerns do make it appropriate for Congress to speak clearly when it regulates state action. But when it does so, as it has in these cases, we can safely presume that the burdens the statute imposes on the sovereignty of the several States were taken into account during the deliberative process leading to the enactment of the measure."

———

NEVADA DEP'T OF HUMAN RESOURCES v. HIBBS, 538 U.S. 721 (2003), per REHNQUIST, C.J., upheld Congress' § 5 power to abrogate state sovereign immunity and provide state employees damages under the Family and Medical Leave Act which entitles eligible employees up to 12 work weeks of unpaid leave annually for several reasons, including onset of a "serious health condition" in an employee's spouse, child, or parent: "The FMLA aims to protect the right to be free from gender-based discrimination in the workplace. [According] to evidence that

---

8   Thomas, J., joined by Kennedy, J., concurred because the ADEA did not "reveal Congress' intention" to abrogate state immunity from private suits for damages.

was before Congress when it enacted the FMLA, States continue to rely on invalid gender stereotypes in the employment context, specifically in the administration of leave benefits.* * *

"As the FMLA's legislative record reflects, a 1990 Bureau of Labor Statistics (BLS) survey stated that 37 percent of surveyed private-sector employees were covered by maternity leave policies, while only 18 percent were covered by paternity leave policies. [The] data show an increase in the percentage of employees eligible for such leave, [but] they also show a widening of the gender gap [from 1989]. Thus, stereotype-based beliefs about the allocation of family duties remained firmly rooted, and employers' reliance on them in establishing discriminatory leave policies remained widespread.[3]

"Congress also heard testimony that '[p]arental leave for fathers [is] rare. Even [w]here child-care leave policies do exist, men, *both in the public and private sectors,* receive notoriously discriminatory treatment in their requests for such leave." [This] and other differential leave policies [e.g., state employers' collective bargaining agreements] were not attributable to any differential physical needs of men and women, but rather to the pervasive sex-role stereotype that caring for family members is women's work.[5]

"Finally, Congress [was also] aware of the 'serious problems with the discretionary nature of family leave,' because when 'the authority to grant leave and to arrange the length of that leave rests with individual supervisors,' it leaves 'employees open to discretionary and possibly unequal treatment.' * * *

"[Here, unlike *Kimel,*] Congress directed its attention to state gender discrimination, which triggers a heightened level of scrutiny [that makes it] easier for Congress to show a pattern of state constitutional violations.* * *

"We believe that Congress' chosen remedy [is] 'congruent and proportional to the targeted violation.' [By] setting a minimum standard of family leave for *all* eligible employees, irrespective of gender, the FMLA attacks the formerly state-sanctioned stereotype that only women are responsible for family caregiving, thereby reducing employers' incentives to engage in discrimination by basing hiring and promotion decisions on stereotypes.

KENNEDY, J., joined by Scalia and Thomas, JJ., dissented on the ground that Congress had failed "to make the requisite showing. [The] Act's findings of purpose are devoid of any discussion of the relevant evidence. * * *

---

[3]   **[Ct's Note]** While this and other material described leave policies in the private sector, a 50-state survey also before Congress demonstrated that "[t]he proportion and construction of leave policies available to public sector employees differs little from those offered private sector employees."

[5]   **[Ct's Note]** * * *Justice Kennedy's dissent ignores this common foundation that, as Congress found, has historically produced discrimination in the hiring and promotion of women. Consideration of such evidence does not, as the dissent contends, expand our § 5 inquiry to include "*general* gender-based stereotypes in employment." To the contrary, because parenting and family leave address very similar situations in which work and family responsibilities conflict, they implicate the same stereotypes.

"[If] Congress had been concerned about different treatment of men and women with respect to family leave, a congruent remedy would have sought to ensure the benefits of any leave program enacted by a State are available to men and women on an equal basis. Instead, the Act imposes, across the board, a requirement that States grant a minimum of 12 weeks of leave per year. This requirement may represent Congress' considered judgment as to the optimal balance. [It] does not follow, however, that if the States choose to enact a different benefit scheme, they should be deemed to engage in unconstitutional conduct and forced to open their treasuries to private suits for damages."

SCALIA, J., dissenting, added: "The constitutional violation that is a prerequisite to 'prophylactic' congressional action to 'enforce' the Fourteenth Amendment is a violation *by the State against which the enforcement action is taken.* There is no guilt by association, enabling the sovereignty of one State to be abridged under § 5 of the Fourteenth Amendment because of violations by another State, or by most other States, or even by 49 other States. [T]he Court does not even attempt to demonstrate that each one of the 50 States covered by [the Act] was in violation of the Fourteenth Amendment. [This] will not do. Prophylaxis in the sense of extending the remedy beyond the violation is one thing; prophylaxis in the sense of extending the remedy beyond the violator is something else."

II. FIFTEENTH AMENDMENT

SHELBY COUNTY V. HOLDER
570 U.S. 529, 133 S.Ct. 2612, 186 L.Ed.2d 651 (2013).

CHIEF JUSTICE ROBERTS delivered the opinion of the Court.

The Voting Rights Act of 1965 employed extraordinary measures to address an extraordinary problem. [Against the background of historic race-based discrimination with regard to voting rights,] Section 5 of the Act required States to obtain federal permission before enacting any law related to voting—a drastic departure from basic principles of federalism. And § 4 of the Act[, its "coverage" section,] applied that requirement only to some States—an equally dramatic departure from the principle that all States enjoy equal sovereignty. This was strong medicine, but [as] we explained in upholding the law [in *South Carolina*, supra], "exceptional conditions can justify legislative measures not otherwise appropriate." Reflecting the unprecedented nature of these measures, they were scheduled to expire after five years.

[As originally written, Section 4 "covered" those States that had maintained a test or device as a prerequisite to voting as of November 1, 1964 and that had less than 50 percent voter registration or turnout in the 1964 Presidential election. A covered jurisdiction could "bail out" of coverage if it had not used a test or device in the preceding five years, "for the purpose or with the effect of denying or abridging the right to vote on account of race or color." § 4(a). But for so long as a state remained covered, Section 5 provided that no change in voting procedures

could take effect until it was approved by federal authorities in Washington, D.C.—
either the Attorney General or a court of three judges. A jurisdiction could obtain
such "preclearance" only by proving that the change had neither "the purpose [nor]
the effect of denying or abridging the right to vote on account of race or color."]

[In] 1970, Congress reauthorized the Act for another five years, and extended
the coverage formula in § 4(b) to jurisdictions that had a voting test and less than
50 percent voter registration or turnout as of 1968. That swept in several counties
in California, New Hampshire, and New York. Congress also extended the ban in
§ 4(a) on tests and devices nationwide.

In 1975, Congress reauthorized the Act for seven more years, and extended
its coverage to jurisdictions that had a voting test and less than 50 percent voter
registration or turnout as of 1972. Congress also amended the definition of "test or
device" to include the practice of providing English-only voting materials in places
where over five percent of voting-age citizens spoke a single language other than
English. As a [result,] Alaska, Arizona, and Texas, as well as several counties in
California, Florida, Michigan, New York, North Carolina, and South Dakota,
became covered jurisdictions.

[In] 1982, Congress reauthorized the Act for 25 years, but did not alter its
coverage formula. [In] 2006, Congress again reauthorized the Voting Rights Act for
25 years, again without change to its coverage formula. [In *Northwest Austin
Municipal Utility Dist. v. Holder*, 557 U.S. 193 (2009), which "expressed serious
doubts about the Act's continued constitutionality," but construed the Act to avoid
that issue,] we stated that "the Act imposes current burdens and must be justified
by current needs." And we concluded that "a departure from the fundamental
principle of equal [state] sovereignty requires a showing that a statute's disparate
geographic coverage is sufficiently related to the problem that it targets." [D]espite
the tradition of equal sovereignty, the Act applies to only nine States (and several
additional counties).

[In 1966], the coverage formula [made] sense. We found that "Congress chose
to limit its attention to the geographic areas where immediate action seemed
necessary," "[where] voting discrimination ha[d] been most flagrant." Nearly 50
years later, things have changed dramatically. [In] the covered jurisdictions,
[v]oter turnout and registration rates now approach parity. Blatantly
discriminatory evasions of federal decrees are rare. * * * Census Bureau data from
the most recent election indicate that African-American voter turnout exceeded
white voter turnout in five of the six States originally covered by § 5, with a gap in
the sixth State of less than one half of one percent. [In] the first decade after
enactment of § 5, the Attorney General objected to 14.2 percent of proposed voting
changes. In the last decade before reenactment, the Attorney General objected to a
mere 0.16 percent. There is no doubt that these improvements are in large part
because of the Voting Rights Act. [Yet] the Act has not eased the restrictions in § 5
or narrowed the scope of the coverage formula in § 4(b) along the [way]—as if
nothing had changed.

[Respondents] do not deny that there have been improvements on the ground, but argue that much of this can be attributed to the deterrent effect of § 5, which dissuades covered jurisdictions from engaging in discrimination that they would resume should § 5 be struck down. Under this theory, however, § 5 would be effectively immune from scrutiny; no matter how 'clean' the record of covered jurisdictions, the argument could always be made that it was deterrence that accounted for the good behavior.

[The] Fifteenth Amendment [is] not designed to punish for the past; its purpose is to ensure a better future. To serve that purpose, Congress—if it is to divide the States—must identify those jurisdictions to be singled out on a basis that makes sense in light of current conditions. [If] Congress had started from scratch in 2006, it plainly could not have enacted the present coverage formula. It would have been irrational for Congress to distinguish between States in such a fundamental way based on 40-year-old data, when today's statistics tell an entirely different story [and] when such [voting] tests have been illegal since that time. But that is exactly what Congress has done. * * *

We issue no holding on § 5 itself, only on the coverage formula. Congress may draft another formula based on current conditions. Such a formula is an initial prerequisite to a determination that exceptional conditions still exist justifying such an "extraordinary departure from the traditional course of relations between the States and the Federal Government."[9]

JUSTICE GINSBURG, whom JUSTICES BREYER, SOTOMAYOR, and KAGAN join, dissenting.

[The] question this case presents is who decides whether, as currently operative, § 5 remains justifiable, this Court, or a Congress charged with the obligation to enforce the post-Civil War Amendments. [With] overwhelming support in both Houses, Congress concluded that, for two prime reasons, § 5 should continue in force, unabated. First, continuance would facilitate completion of the impressive gains thus far made; and second, continuance would guard against backsliding.

[Between] 1982 and 2006, DOJ objections blocked over 700 voting changes based on a determination that the changes were discriminatory. Congress found that the majority of DOJ objections included findings of discriminatory intent, and that the changes blocked by preclearance were ' "calculated decisions to keep minority voters from fully participating in the political process." ' * * * Congress received evidence that more than 800 proposed changes were altered or withdrawn since the last reauthorization in 1982. Congress also received empirical studies finding that DOJ's requests for more information had a significant effect on the degree to which covered jurisdictions "compl[ied] with their obligatio[n]" to protect minority voting rights. Congress also received evidence that litigation under § 2 of the VRA [which was discussed in Ch. 9, Sec. 5, I, supra] was an inadequate

---

[9]   Thomas, J., concurred on the ground that the Court's opinion "compellingly demonstrates" that § 5 is also unconstitutional.

substitute for preclearance in the covered jurisdictions. [This evidence] of preclearance's continuing efficacy in blocking constitutional violations in the covered jurisdictions[ ] itself grounded Congress' conclusion that the remedy should be retained for those jurisdictions.

[A study] of § 2 lawsuits in covered and noncovered jurisdictions [indicated] that racial discrimination in voting remains "concentrated in the jurisdictions singled out for preclearance."

[The] evidence before Congress, furthermore, indicated that voting in the covered jurisdictions was more racially polarized than elsewhere in the country. [T]he Court does not even deign to grapple with the legislative record. [In] 2008, for example, the city of Calera, located in Shelby County, requested preclearance of a redistricting plan that "would have eliminated the city's sole majority-black district, which had been created pursuant to the consent decree." [Although] DOJ objected to the plan, Calera forged ahead with elections based on the unprecleared voting changes, resulting in the defeat of the incumbent African-American councilman who represented the former majority-black district. The city's defiance required DOJ to bring a § 5 enforcement action that ultimately yielded appropriate redress, including restoration of the majority-black district. [These] recent episodes forcefully demonstrate that § 5's preclearance requirement is constitutional as applied to Alabama and its political subdivisions. And under our case law, that conclusion should suffice to resolve this case.

[Under the] VRA's exceptionally broad severability provision, [even] if the VRA could not constitutionally be applied to certain States—e.g., Arizona and Alaska—it calls for those unconstitutional applications to be severed, leaving the Act in place for jurisdictions as to which its application does not transgress constitutional limits. [W]ithout considering whether application of the VRA to Shelby County is constitutional, or even addressing the VRA's severability provision, the Court's opinion can hardly be described as an exemplar of restrained and moderate decisionmaking.

[Today's] unprecedented extension of the equal sovereignty principle outside its proper domain—the admission of new States—is capable of much mischief. Federal statutes that treat States disparately are hardly novelties. See, e.g., * * * 26 U.S.C. § 142(*l*) (EPA required to locate green building project in a State meeting specified population criteria); 42 U.S.C. § 3796bb (at least 50 percent of rural drug enforcement assistance funding must be allocated to States with "a population density of fifty-two or fewer persons per 589 square mile or a State in which the largest county has fewer than one hundred and fifty thousand people, based on the decennial census of 1990 through fiscal year 1997"); §§ 13925, 13971 (similar population criteria for funding to combat rural domestic violence); § 10136 (specifying rules applicable to Nevada's Yucca Mountain nuclear waste site, and providing that "[n]o State, other than the State of Nevada, may receive financial assistance under this subsection after December 22, 1987").

[The] situation Congress faced in 2006, when it took up reauthorization of the coverage formula, was not the same [as in 1965]. By [then,] *all* of the jurisdictions covered by it were "familiar to Congress by name." [There] was at that point no chance that the formula might inadvertently sweep in new areas that were not the subject of congressional findings. And Congress could determine from the record whether the jurisdictions captured by the coverage formula still belonged under the preclearance regime. If they did, there was no need to alter the formula. That is why the Court, in addressing prior reauthorizations of the VRA, did not question the continuing 'relevance' of the formula. [In] light of this record, Congress had more than a reasonable basis to conclude that the existing coverage formula was not out of sync with conditions on the ground in covered areas.

[The] record supporting the 2006 reauthorization of the VRA [was] described by the Chairman of the House Judiciary Committee as "one of the most extensive considerations of any piece of legislation that the United States Congress has dealt with in the 27½ years" he had served in the House. [That] determination of the body empowered to enforce the Civil War Amendments "by appropriate legislation" merits this Court's utmost respect.

CHAPTER 12

LIMITATIONS ON JUDICIAL POWER AND REVIEW

■ ■ ■

1. STANDING

I. THE STRUCTURE OF STANDING DOCTRINE

ALLEN V. WRIGHT

468 U.S. 737, 104 S.Ct. 3315, 82 L.Ed.2d 556 (1984).

JUSTICE O'CONNOR delivered the opinion of the Court.

Parents of black public school children allege in this nation-wide class action that the Internal Revenue Service (IRS) has not adopted sufficient standards and procedures to fulfill its obligation to deny tax-exempt status to racially discriminatory private schools. They assert that the IRS thereby harms them directly and interferes with the ability of their children to receive an education in desegregated public schools. The issue before us is whether plaintiffs have standing to bring this suit. We hold that they do not.

[Respondents] allege in their complaint that many racially segregated private schools were created or expanded in their communities at the time the public schools were undergoing desegregation. According to the complaint, many such private schools, including 17 schools or school systems identified by name in the complaint (perhaps some 30 schools in all), receive tax exemptions either directly or through the tax-exempt status of "umbrella" organizations that operate or support the [schools].[11] Respondents allege that the IRS grant of tax exemptions to such racially discriminatory schools is unlawful [under federal statutes and the Constitution, and they seek declaratory and injunctive relief].

[R]espondents do not allege that their children have been the victims of discriminatory exclusion from the schools whose tax exemptions they challenge as unlawful. [Rather,] respondents claim a direct injury from the mere fact of the challenged Government conduct and, as indicated by the restriction of the plaintiff class to parents of children in desegregating school districts, injury to their children's opportunity to receive a desegregated education. * * *

---

[11]   **[Ct's Note]** * * * Contrary to Justice Brennan's statement, the complaint does not allege that each desegregating district in which they reside contains one or more racially discriminatory private schools unlawfully receiving a tax exemption.

II. Article III of the Constitution confines the federal courts to adjudicating actual "cases" and "controversies." As the Court explained in *Valley Forge Christian College v. Americans United for Separation of Church and State, Inc.*, [Part III infra,] the "case or controversy" requirement defines with respect to the Judicial Branch the idea of separation of powers on which the Federal Government is founded. The several doctrines that have grown up to elaborate that requirement are "founded in concern about the proper—and properly limited—role of the courts in a democratic society." * * *

The Art. III doctrine that requires a litigant to have "standing" to invoke the power of a federal court is perhaps the most important of these doctrines. In essence the question of standing is whether the litigant is entitled to have the court decide the merits of the dispute or of particular issues. Standing doctrine embraces several judicially self-imposed limits on the exercise of federal jurisdiction, such as the general prohibition on a litigant's raising another person's legal rights, the rule barring adjudication of generalized grievances more appropriately addressed in the representative branches, and the requirement that a plaintiff's complaint fall within the zone of interests protected by the law invoked. The requirement of standing, however, has a core component derived directly from the Constitution. A plaintiff must allege personal injury fairly traceable to the defendant's allegedly unlawful conduct and likely to be redressed by the requested relief.

Like the prudential component, the constitutional component of standing doctrine incorporates concepts concededly not susceptible of precise definition. The injury alleged must be, for example, "distinct and palpable," and not "abstract" or "conjectural" or "hypothetical," *Los Angeles v. Lyons*, [infra]. The injury must be "fairly" traceable to the challenged action, and relief from the injury must be "likely" to follow from a favorable decision. See *Simon v. Eastern Kentucky Welfare Rights Org.*, [infra]. These terms cannot be defined so as to make application of the constitutional standing requirement a mechanical exercise.

The absence of precise definitions, however, [hardly] leaves courts at sea in applying the law of standing. Like most legal notions, the standing concepts have gained considerable definition from developing case law. [More] important, the law of Art. III standing is built on a single basic idea—the idea of separation of powers. It is this fact which makes possible the gradual clarification of the law through judicial application. * * *

Respondents allege two injuries in their complaint to support their standing to bring this lawsuit. First, they say that they are harmed directly by the mere fact of Government financial aid to discriminatory private schools. Second, they say that the federal tax exemptions to racially discriminatory private schools in their communities impair their ability to have their public schools desegregated. [N]either suffices to support respondents' standing.

Respondents' first claim of injury [might] be a claim simply to have the Government avoid the violation of law alleged in respondents' complaint. Alternatively, it might be a claim of stigmatic injury, or denigration, suffered by all members of a racial group when the Government discriminates on the basis of race. Under neither interpretation is this claim of injury judicially cognizable.

This Court has repeatedly held that an asserted right to have the Government act in accordance with law is not sufficient, standing alone, to confer jurisdiction on a federal court. In *Schlesinger v. Reservists Committee to Stop the War*, 418 U.S. 208 (1974), for example, the Court rejected a claim of citizen standing to challenge Armed Forces Reserve commissions held by Members of Congress as violating the Incompatibility Clause of Art. I, § 6, of the Constitution. As citizens, the Court held, plaintiffs alleged nothing but "the abstract injury in nonobservance of the Constitution." More recently, in *Valley Forge*, we rejected a claim of standing to challenge a Government conveyance of property to a religious institution. Insofar as the plaintiffs relied simply on "their shared individuated right" to a Government that made no law respecting an establishment of religion, we held that plaintiffs had not alleged a judicially cognizable injury. * * *

Neither do they have standing to litigate their claims based on the stigmatizing injury often caused by racial discrimination. There can be no doubt that this sort of noneconomic injury is one of the most serious consequences of discriminatory government action and is sufficient in some circumstances to support standing. Our cases make clear, however, that such injury accords a basis for standing only to "those persons who are personally denied equal treatment" by the challenged discriminatory conduct. [If an] abstract stigmatic injury were cognizable, standing would extend nationwide to all members of the particular racial groups against which the Government was alleged to be discriminating by its grant of a tax exemption to a racially discriminatory school, regardless of the location of that school. [A] black person in Hawaii could challenge the grant of a tax exemption to a racially discriminatory school in Maine. Recognition of standing in such circumstances would transform the federal courts into "no more than a vehicle for the vindication of the value interests of concerned bystanders." *United States v. SCRAP*, [infra]. Constitutional limits on the role of the federal courts preclude such a transformation.

It is in their complaint's second claim of injury that respondents allege harm to a concrete, personal interest that can support standing in some circumstances. The injury they identify—their children's diminished ability to receive an education in a racially integrated school—is, beyond any doubt, not only judicially cognizable but, as shown by cases [since] *Brown v. Board of Education*, [Ch. 9, Sec. 2, II supra,] one of the most serious injuries recognized in our legal system. Despite the constitutional importance of curing the injury alleged by respondents, however, the federal judiciary may not redress it unless standing requirements are met. In this case, respondents' second claim of injury cannot support standing because the injury alleged is not fairly traceable to the Government conduct respondents challenge as unlawful.[22]

---

[22]   **[Ct's Note]** Respondents' stigmatic injury, though not sufficient for standing in the abstract form in which their complaint asserts it, is judicially cognizable to the extent that respondents are personally subject to discriminatory treatment. See *Heckler v. Mathews*, [infra]

The illegal conduct challenged by respondents is the IRS's grant of tax exemptions to some racially discriminatory schools. The line of causation between that conduct and desegregation of respondents' schools is attenuated at best. From the perspective of the IRS, the injury to respondents is highly indirect and "results from the independent action of some third party not before the court." *Simon.* * * *

The diminished ability of respondents' children to receive a desegregated education would be fairly traceable to unlawful IRS grants of tax exemptions only if there were enough racially discriminatory private schools receiving tax exemptions in respondents' communities for withdrawal of those exemptions to make an appreciable difference in public school integration. Respondents have made no such allegation. It [is] entirely speculative, as respondents themselves conceded in the Court of Appeals, whether withdrawal of a tax exemption from any particular school would lead the school to change its policies. It is just as speculative whether any given parent of a child attending such a private school would decide to transfer the child to public school as a result of any changes in educational or financial policy made by the private school once it was threatened with loss of tax-exempt status. It is also pure speculation whether, in a particular community, a large enough number of the numerous relevant school officials and parents would reach decisions that collectively would have a significant impact on the racial composition of the public schools. * * *

The Court of Appeals relied for its contrary conclusion on *Gilmore v. City of Montgomery*, [417 U.S. 556 (1974), and] *Norwood v. Harrison*, 413 U.S. 455 (1973). [Neither], however, requires that we find standing in this lawsuit.

In *Gilmore*, the plaintiffs [alleged] that the city was violating [their] equal protection right by permitting racially discriminatory private schools and other groups to use the public parks. The Court recognized plaintiffs' standing to challenge this city policy insofar as the policy permitted the exclusive use of the parks by racially discriminatory private [schools]. Standing in *Gilmore* thus rested on an allegation of direct deprivation of a right to equal use of the parks. * * *

In *Norwood v. Harrison*, parents of public school children in Tunica County, Miss., filed a statewide class action challenging the State's provision of textbooks to students attending racially discriminatory private schools in the State. The Court held the State's practice unconstitutional because it breached "the State's acknowledged duty to establish a unitary school system." The Court did not expressly address the basis for the plaintiffs' standing.

[involving the denial of monetary benefits on an allegedly discriminatory basis]. The stigmatic injury thus requires identification of some concrete interest with respect to which respondents are personally subject to discriminatory treatment. That interest must independently satisfy the causation requirement of standing doctrine.

[Here,] respondents identify only one interest that they allege is being discriminatorily impaired—their interest in desegregated public school education. Respondents' asserted stigmatic injury, therefore, is sufficient to support their standing in this litigation only if their school-desegregation injury independently meets the causation requirement of standing doctrine.

In *Gilmore*, however, the Court identified the basis for standing in *Norwood*: "The plaintiffs in Norwood were parties to a school desegregation order and the relief they sought was directly related to the concrete injury they suffered." Through the school-desegregation decree, the plaintiffs had acquired a right to have the State "steer clear" of any perpetuation of the racially dual school system that it had once sponsored. The interest acquired was judicially cognizable because it was a personal interest, created by law, in having the State refrain from taking specific actions. * * *

III. "The necessity that the plaintiff who seeks to invoke judicial power stand to profit in some personal interest remains an Art. III requirement." *Simon*. Respondents have not met this fundamental requirement. The judgment of the Court of Appeals is accordingly reversed, and the injunction issued by that court is vacated.

JUSTICE BRENNAN, dissenting.

[In] these cases, the respondents have alleged at least one type of injury that satisfies the constitutional requirement of "distinct and palpable injury."[3] In particular, they claim that the IRS's grant of tax-exempt status to racially discriminatory private schools directly injures their children's opportunity and ability to receive a desegregated education. * * *

The Court acknowledges that this alleged injury is sufficient to satisfy constitutional standards. [Moreover,] in light of the injuries they claim, the respondents have alleged a direct causal relationship between the Government action they challenge and the injury they suffer: [Common] sense alone would recognize that the elimination of tax-exempt status for racially discriminatory private schools would serve to lessen the impact that those institutions have in defeating efforts to desegregate the public schools.

The Court admits that "[t]he diminished ability of respondents' children to receive a desegregated education would be fairly traceable to unlawful IRS grants of tax exemptions [if] there were enough racially discriminatory private schools receiving tax exemptions in respondents' communities for withdrawal of those exemptions to make an appreciable difference in public school integration," but concludes that "[r]espondents have made no such allegation." With all due respect, the Court has either misread the complaint or is improperly requiring the respondents to prove their case on the merits in order to defeat a motion to dismiss. For example, the respondents specifically refer by name to at least 32 private schools that discriminate on the basis of race and yet continue to benefit illegally from tax-exempt status. Eighteen of those schools [are] located in the city of Memphis, Tenn., which has been the subject of several court orders to desegregate. * * *

---

[3]   **[Ct's Note]** Because I conclude that the second injury alleged by the respondents is sufficient to satisfy constitutional requirements, I do not need to reach what the Court labels the "stigmatic injury." * * *

More than one commentator has noted that the causation component of the Court's standing inquiry is no more than a poor disguise for the Court's view of the merits of the underlying claims. The Court today does nothing to avoid that criticism. * * *

JUSTICE STEVENS, with whom JUSTICE BLACKMUN joins, dissenting.

[In the] final analysis, the wrong respondents allege that the Government has committed is to subsidize the exodus of white children from schools that would otherwise be racially integrated. The critical question in these cases, therefore, is whether respondents have alleged that the Government has created that kind of subsidy.

[If] the granting of preferential tax treatment would "encourage" private segregated schools to conduct their "charitable" activities, it must follow that the withdrawal of the treatment would "discourage" them, and hence promote the process of desegregation. [This] causation analysis is nothing more than a restatement of elementary economics: when something becomes more expensive, less of it will be purchased. [W]ithout tax-exempt status, private schools will either not be competitive in terms of cost, or have to change their admissions policies, hence reducing their competitiveness for parents seeking "a racially segregated alternative" to public schools, which is what respondents have alleged many white parents in desegregating school districts seek.

[Because] [c]onsiderations of tax policy, economics, and pure logic all confirm the conclusion that respondents' injury in fact is fairly traceable to the Government's allegedly wrongful conduct[,] [t]he Court [is] forced to introduce the concept of "separation of powers" into its analysis. [In doing so,] the Court could be saying that it will require a more direct causal connection when it is troubled by the separation of powers implications of the case before it. That approach confuses the standing doctrine with the justiciability of the issues that respondents seek to raise. The purpose of the standing inquiry is to measure the plaintiff's stake in the outcome, not whether a court has the authority to provide it with the outcome it seeks.

[As the Court has previously recognized,] the " 'fundamental aspect of standing' is that it focuses primarily on the *party* seeking to get his complaint before the federal court rather than 'on the issues he wishes to have adjudicated,' " *United States v. Richardson*, 418 U.S. 166 (1974). [If] a plaintiff presents a nonjusticiable issue, or seeks relief that a court may not award, then its complaint should be dismissed for those reasons, and not because the plaintiff lacks a stake in obtaining that relief and hence has no standing. Imposing an undefined but clearly more rigorous standard for redressability for reasons unrelated to the causal nexus between the injury and the challenged conduct can only encourage undisciplined, ad hoc litigation.

[Alternatively], the Court could be saying that it will not treat as legally cognizable injuries that stem from an administrative decision concerning how enforcement resources will be allocated. This surely is an important point.

Respondents do seek to restructure the IRS's mechanisms for enforcing the legal requirement that discriminatory institutions not receive tax-exempt status. Such restructuring would dramatically affect the way in which the IRS exercises its prosecutorial discretion. The Executive requires latitude to decide how best to enforce the law, and in general the Court may well be correct that the exercise of that discretion, especially in the tax context, is unchallengeable.

However, as the Court also recognizes, this principle does not apply when suit is brought "to enforce specific legal obligations whose violation works a direct harm." [Here,] respondents contend that the IRS is violating a specific constitutional limitation on its enforcement discretion. There is a solid basis for that contention. In *Norwood*, we wrote: "A State's constitutional obligation requires it to steer clear, not only of operating the old dual system of racially segregated schools, but also of giving significant aid to institutions that practice racial or other invidious discrimination."

Deciding whether the Treasury has violated a specific legal limitation on its enforcement discretion does not intrude upon the prerogatives of the Executive, for in so deciding we are merely saying "what the law is." * * *

In short, I would deal with the question of the legal limitations on the IRS's enforcement discretion on its merits, rather than by making the untenable assumption that the granting of preferential tax treatment to segregated schools does not make those schools more attractive to white students and hence does not inhibit the process of desegregation.[1]

NOTES

1. ***The doctrinal requirement of injury-in-fact.*** The Court's insistence that standing minimally requires injury-in-fact has occasioned sharp disputes about what constitutes an "injury" in the constitutional sense. Although unwilling to find an actionable stigmatic injury in *Allen*, the Court has regularly accepted the proposition that non-economic injuries can satisfy the constitutional requirement, provided that they are pleaded with sufficient specificity. For example, FRIENDS OF THE EARTH, INC. v. LAIDLAW ENVIRONMENTAL SERVICES (TOC), INC., 528 U.S. 167 (2000), upheld standing under the citizen suit provisions of the Clean Water Act. The defendant argued that standing was defeated because the District Court, in imposing a penalty, ruled that the defendant's illegal actions had not been proved to "result in any health risk or environmental harm." But the Court, per GINSBURG, J., held that the relevant injury "is not injury to the environment but injury to the plaintiff" and that the plaintiffs suffered injury from their "reasonable concerns" that pollution had damaged land that they otherwise would have used. Scalia, J., joined by Thomas, J., dissented.

In HECKLER v. MATHEWS, 465 U.S. 728 (1984), a challenged statute gave larger Social Security benefits to women than to men and further provided that if

---

[1]   Marshall, J., did not participate in the decision.

a court should find the disparity unconstitutional, then women's benefits should be reduced to the men's level. Despite the fact that the male plaintiffs could achieve no material benefit from a decision in their favor, the Court, per BRENNAN, J., upheld standing: "[T]he right to equal treatment guaranteed by the Constitution is not co-extensive with any substantive rights to the benefits denied the party discriminated against. [Rather,] discrimination itself [can] cause serious non-economic injuries to those persons who are personally denied equal treatment solely because of their membership in a disfavored group. Accordingly, [the] appropriate remedy is a *mandate* of equal treatment, a result that can be accomplished by withdrawal of benefits from the favored class as well as by extension of benefits to the excluded class."

Threatened future injuries pose additional problems. In CLAPPER v. AMNESTY INTERNATIONAL, 568 U.S. 398 (2013), U.S. citizens residing in the United States challenged the constitutionality of an amendment to the Foreign Intelligence Surveillance Act under which, they alleged, their communications with non-Americans abroad were likely to be intercepted. Despite the plaintiffs' specific allegations that their professional activities (including as lawyers and journalists) required them to be in regular contact with organizations abroad that were likely targets of government surveillance, the Court, per ALITO, J., denied standing based on the plaintiffs' failure to establish that an injury-in-fact was "certainly impending" in light, inter alia, of the opacity of the Government's criteria for seeking foreign-security wiretaps. The Court also said: "[W]e have often found a lack of standing in cases in which the Judiciary has been requested to review actions of the political branches in the fields of intelligence gathering and foreign affairs. [The] assumption that if respondents have no standing to sue, no one would have standing, is not a reason to find standing."

BREYER, J., joined by Ginsburg, Sotomayor, and Kagan, JJ., dissenting, maintained that although some past Court decisions had referred to a need for "certainly impending" injury, future injury was seldom if ever "absolutely certain" and that "federal courts frequently [and appropriately] entertain actions for injunctions and for declaratory relief aimed at preventing future injures that are reasonably likely or highly likely [to] take place."

Compare *Susan B. Anthony List v. Driehaus*, 573 U.S. 149 (2014), upholding standing to seek an injunction against enforcement of a penal statute alleged to violate the First Amendment and affirming that "a plaintiff satisfies the injury-in-fact requirement where he alleges 'an intention to engage in [conduct] arguably affected with a constitutional interest, but proscribed by a statute, and there exists a credible threat of prosecution.'" Should a credible threat of prosecution, as in *Susan B. Anthony List,* be easier to establish than the threat of being subjected to allegedly unconstitutional surveillance involved in *Clapper*?

2.   ***Causation requirement.*** With the application of the causation requirement in *Allen,* compare REGENTS OF THE UNIVERSITY OF CALIFORNIA v. BAKKE, Ch. 9, Sec. 2, V supra, in which the Court upheld the

standing of a white plaintiff to challenge a special admissions program for minority applicants to medical school. A standing question arose because it was not clear that the existence of an affirmative action program caused Bakke's rejection (he might have been turned down anyway). Rebuffing a standing challenge, POWELL, J., wrote for a majority of five that Bakke suffered injury through his deprivation, on grounds of race, of the chance to compete for every place in the entering class regardless of whether the affirmative action program caused his being ultimately rejected.[2]

The Court denied standing based on a causation analysis in CALIFORNIA v. TEXAS, 141 S.Ct. 2104 (2021), in which the plaintiffs argued that a change in law since the Court's prior cases involving the Affordable Care Act (ACA) rendered the statute facially invalid and therefore unenforceable. In *National Federation of Independent Business v. Sebelius*, 567 U.S. 519 (2012), Ch. 2, Sections 2 and 3, a divided Court held that Congress had no authority under the Commerce Clause to require individuals to purchase health insurance, but it upheld the individual mandate, which was enforced via a penalty payable to the Internal Revenue Service, as a valid exercise of the taxing power. After Congress subsequently reduced the penalty for non-purchase of insurance to $0, two individuals and a number of states sought invalidation of the entire ACA. According to the plaintiffs, the individual mandate could no longer be characterized as a tax, and all of the ACA's other provisions were so interconnected with the mandate that if the mandate was unconstitutional, the other provisions were not "severable" or separately enforceable.

Per BREYER, J., the Court found, by 7–2, that because none of the plaintiffs had standing to bring the action against the Secretary of Health and Human Services and the other defendant executive officials, it need not determine either the continuing validity of the now-unenforceable individual mandate or the severability of the mandate from the remainder of the ACA. Although the individual plaintiffs had alleged injury in the form of costs for the purchase of health insurance, they failed to satisfy the causation prong of the standing test: "Our cases have consistently spoken of the need to assert an injury that is the result of a statute's actual or threatened enforcement." In the absence of any credible threat that the defendants would enforce the mandate to purchase insurance, any harm that the plaintiffs had suffered when they bought insurance was not "fairly traceable" to the defendants.

BREYER, J., then turned to the claims of the plaintiff states, who had alleged that they suffered financial injuries from provisions of the ACA other than the individual mandate. In concluding that they lacked standing to challenge the

---

[2]   *Northeastern Florida Chapter of the Associated General Contractors of America v. Jacksonville*, 508 U.S. 656 (1993), per Thomas, J., pursued a similar analysis, holding that the challenger to an affirmative action set-aside program need not show that, but for the program, the challenger would have received a concrete benefit: "The 'injury in fact' in an equal protection case of this variety is the denial of equal treatment resulting from the imposition of [a barrier that makes it more difficult for members of a group to obtain a benefit], not the ultimate inability to obtain the benefit."

mandate's validity, Breyer, J., again relied on causation principles. He dismissed the states' claim that the mandate led state residents to enroll in state-operated insurance programs that cost the states money by emphasizing the benefits that those programs provide. "[N]either logic nor intuition suggests that the presence of the minimal essential coverage requirement would lead an individual to enroll in one of those programs that its absence would lead them to ignore," he wrote, when the programs' benefits afforded another possible motive for their actions.

BREYER, J., acknowledged that provisions of the ACA other than the individual mandate imposed costs on the plaintiff states, including those incurred in providing information to residents and furnishing information to the Internal Revenue Service. But "no one" claimed that those other provisions, which "operate independently of" the individual mandate, violate the Constitution. The states' averments thus failed to establish standing to challenge the mandate, which they had not shown to be causally responsible for costs in complying with other provisions.

ALITO, J., joined by GORSUCH, J., dissented. "[T]he individual plaintiffs' claim to standing raise[d] a novel question," he thought, but it did not need to be addressed, since "the States have standing for reasons that are straightforward and meritorious." Alito, J., began his analysis of the states' standing with the premise that they had suffered financial injuries in complying with provisions of the ACA other than the individual mandate. Building on that premise, he further reasoned that if the states were correct (1) that the individual mandate was constitutionally invalid and (2) that other provisions of the ACA could not be severed from it, then the states' financial injuries were "indeed traceable to the mandate." According to Alito, J., the Court had granted standing to plaintiffs mounting facial challenges to statutes on grounds of statutory nonseverability in a number of prior cases and then treated the question of statutory severability as one to be resolved on the merits. That was the correct approach, he argued.

BREYER, J., did not respond the substance of Alito, J.'s, standing analysis, which he characterized as a "novel theory" that was neither argued by the plaintiffs in the lower courts nor presented in the plaintiffs' cert petitions and that "[w]e accordingly decline to consider." Thomas, J., filed a concurring opinion in which he agreed with and elaborated upon the "waiver" argument that Breyer, J., asserted more cryptically and that Alito, J., disputed.

Waiver arguments aside, Alito, J., appears correct in his contention that a number of the Court's prior decisions entertaining facial challenges to federal statutes have implicitly relied on a standing-though-nonserverability analysis under which plaintiffs who were directly harmed by one provision of a statute were permitted to argue for facial invalidation based on an alleged defect in another provision of an allegedly non-severable statute. (A recent example is *Seila Law LLC v. Consumer Financial Protection Bureau* (CFPB), 140 S.Ct. 2183 (2020), Ch. 3 of this Supplement, in which a law firm that suffered harm pursuant to a statute's enforcement provisions was permitted to challenge another provision involving the appointment and removal of the CFPB's Director. Although the Court ultimately rejected the plaintiff's argument that an invalid limitation on presidential removal was not severable from the rest of the statute, it did so only after recognizing the plaintiff's standing to mount the facial challenge.) As Thomas, J., noted in his concurring opinion, however, "this Court has not addressed standing-through-inseverability in any detail, largely relying on it through implications."

When the Court more straightforwardly considers the soundness of the theory of "standing-through-inseverability," it will need to wrestle with complex principles of severability and non-severability law that have often provoked sharp divisions. For an introduction to some of the central concepts and their relationship to one another, see Richard H. Fallon, Jr., *Facial Challenges, Saving Constructions, and Statutory Severability*, 99 Tex.L.Rev. 215 (2020).

3. ***Redressability.*** In perhaps the majority of cases, the requirement that an injury be redressable can be viewed as an aspect of the causation requirement: if a defendant has caused injury, relief against the defendant will ordinarily remedy the injury. Occasionally, however, the redressability requirement exercises independent bite.

In LOS ANGELES v. LYONS, 461 U.S. 95 (1983), for example, the plaintiff had been choked to unconsciousness by the Los Angeles police after being stopped for a traffic violation. Alleging that the department had a policy of applying life-threatening chokeholds unnecessarily, Lyons sued for injunctive relief. Standing could not be grounded on the threat of future injury, the Court held, because it was too speculative that Lyons himself would be subjected to a choke-hold again. And, although Lyons undoubtedly had suffered an injury in the past, that injury could not be redressed by an injunction against future police conduct.[3]

Although courts will not order injunctive relief to redress "past" injuries that are unlikely to be repeated, UZUEGBUNAM v. PRECZEWSKI, 141 S.Ct. 792 (2021), held that a claim for nominal damages can suffice to establish standing and thus permit an adjudication of the merits of a plaintiff's constitutional claim. *Uzuegbunam* arose from a complaint that a public college and its officials violated the plaintiff's free speech rights to engage in religious proselytization on the college campus. By the time the case reached the Supreme Court, the college had withdrawn the policies that it enforced against Uzuegbunam, and Uzuebbunam was no longer a student at the college. Nonetheless, the Court held, by 8–1, that the plaintiff had alleged injury in fact, caused by the defendants, and that nominal damages would redress his injury: "By permitting plaintiffs to pursue nominal damages whenever they suffered a personal legal injury, the common law"—which provided relevant backdrop for the Court's interpretation of Article III—"avoided the oddity of privileging small-dollar economic rights over important, but not easily quantifiable, nonpecuniary rights."

---

[3] Marshall, J., joined by Brennan, Blackmun, and Stevens, JJ., dissented.

ROBERTS, C.J., dissented, arguing that the common law cases clearly established only that plaintiffs could sue for nominal damages as a form of relief against ongoing or threatened future harms and that cases involving purely past injuries were different. He also thought that allowing nominal damages for past injuries conflicted with "modern justiciability principles" that authorize suit only when judicial relief will "compensate[e] the plaintiff for a past loss" or prevent "an ongoing or future harm."

II. CONGRESSIONAL POWER
TO CREATE STANDING

In nearly all of the cases considered so far, plaintiffs based their claim to standing directly on the Constitution. Does Congress have the power to confer standing where it would not otherwise exist? And if so, how far does Congress' power extend?

LUJAN V. DEFENDERS OF WILDLIFE
504 U.S. 555, 112 S.Ct. 2130, 119 L.Ed.2d 351 (1992).

JUSTICE SCALIA delivered the opinion of the Court with respect to Parts I, II, III-A, and IV, and an opinion with respect to Part III-B in which the CHIEF JUSTICE, JUSTICE WHITE, and JUSTICE THOMAS join.

[The Endangered Species Act of 1973 (ESA) § 7(a)(2) requires federal agencies to consult with the Secretary of the Interior to "insure" that projects that they fund do not threaten endangered species. Regulations promulgated in 1978 construed the consultation requirement as extending to actions taken in foreign nations. In 1986, however, the Department of the Interior reinterpreted the ESA to require consultation only for actions taken in the United States or on the high seas. Several organizations filed suits challenging the new regulation as contrary to law.]

III-A. [The Court first held that the groups and their members had failed to present sufficient evidence of injury-in-fact. Although affidavits testified that at least two members had previously traveled abroad to observe endangered species and intended to do so again,] [t]hat the women "had visited" the areas of [identified] projects before the projects commenced proves nothing. [And] the affiants' profession of an "inten[t]" to return to the places they had visited [before]—without any description of concrete plans, or indeed even any specification of *when* the some day will be—do not support a finding of the "actual or imminent" injury that our cases require.

[No more persuasive are] a series of novel standing theories, [including] the "animal nexus" approach, whereby anyone who has an interest in studying or seeing the endangered animals anywhere on the globe has standing; and the "vocational nexus" approach, under which anyone with a professional interest in such animals can sue. Under these theories, anyone who goes to see Asian elephants in the Bronx Zoo, and anyone who is a keeper of Asian elephants in the

Bronx Zoo, has standing to sue because the Director of AID did not consult with the Secretary regarding the AID-funded project in Sri Lanka. This is beyond all reason. [It is] pure speculation and fantasy, to say that anyone who observes or works with an endangered species, anywhere in the world, is appreciably harmed by a single project affecting some portion of that species with which he has no more specific connection.

B. Besides failing to show injury, respondents failed to demonstrate redressability. [Since] the agencies funding the projects were not parties to the case, the District Court could accord relief only against the Secretary. [There was no assurance that other agencies would feel bound by the Secretary's regulation, or that the withdrawal of American funding would cause projects to be terminated and the threat to endangered species thereby eliminated.]

IV. The Court of Appeals found that respondents had standing for an additional reason: because they had suffered a "procedural injury." The so-called "citizen-suit" provision of the ESA provides, in pertinent part, that "any person may commence a civil suit on his own behalf (A) to enjoin any person, including the United States and any other governmental instrumentality or agency [who] is alleged to be in violation of any provision of this chapter." The court held that, because § 7(a)(2) requires inter-agency consultation, the citizen-suit provision creates a "procedural righ[t]" to consultation in all "persons"—so that *anyone* can file suit in federal court to challenge the Secretary's (or presumably any other official's) failure to follow the assertedly correct consultative procedure, notwithstanding their inability to allege any discrete injury flowing from that failure. To understand the remarkable nature of this holding one must be clear about what it does *not* rest upon: This is not a case where plaintiffs are seeking to enforce a procedural requirement the disregard of which could impair a separate concrete interest of theirs (*e.g.*, the procedural requirement for a hearing prior to denial of their license application, or the procedural requirement for an environmental impact statement before a federal facility is constructed next door to them).[7] Nor is it simply a case where concrete injury has been suffered by many persons, as in mass fraud or mass tort situations. Nor, finally, is it the unusual case in which Congress has created a concrete private interest in the outcome of a suit against a private party for the government's benefit, by providing a cash bounty for the victorious plaintiff. Rather, the court held that the injury-in-fact requirement had been satisfied by congressional conferral upon *all* persons of an

---

[7] [Ct's Note] There is this much truth to the assertion that "procedural rights" are special: The person who has been accorded a procedural right to protect his concrete interests can assert that right without meeting all the normal standards for redressability and immediacy. Thus, under our case-law, one living adjacent to the site for proposed construction of a federally licensed dam has standing to challenge the licensing agency's failure to prepare an Environmental Impact Statement, even though he cannot establish with any certainty that the Statement will cause the license to be withheld or altered, and even though the dam will not be completed for many years. (That is why we do not rely, in the present case, upon the Government's argument that, *even if* the other agencies were obliged to consult with the Secretary, they might not have followed his advice.) What respondents' "procedural rights" argument seeks, however, is quite different from this: standing for persons who have no concrete interests affected—persons who live (and propose to live) at the other end of the country from the dam.

abstract, self-contained, non-instrumental "right" to have the Executive observe the procedures required by law.

[The] question presented here is whether the public interest in proper administration of the laws (specifically, in agencies' observance of a particular, statutorily prescribed procedure) can be converted into an individual right by a statute that denominates it as such, and that permits all citizens (or, for that matter, a subclass of citizens who suffer no distinctive concrete harm) to sue. If the concrete injury requirement has the separation-of-powers significance we have always said, the answer must be obvious: To permit Congress to convert the undifferentiated public interest in executive officers' compliance with the law into an "individual right" vindicable in the courts is to permit Congress to transfer from the President to the courts the Chief Executive's most important constitutional duty, to "take Care that the Laws be faithfully executed," Art. II, § 3. It would enable the courts, with the permission of Congress, "to assume a position of authority over the governmental acts of another and co-equal department," *Frothingham*, and to become "virtually continuing monitors of the wisdom and soundness of Executive action." *Allen*. We have always rejected that vision of our role * * * .

Nothing in this contradicts the principle that "[the] injury required by Art. III may exist solely by virtue of 'statutes creating legal rights, the invasion of which creates standing.' " *Warth v. Seldin*, 422 U.S. 490 (1975). [T]he cases [previously cited by the Court] as an illustration of that principle involved Congress's elevating to the status of legally cognizable injuries concrete, de facto injuries that were previously inadequate in law (namely, injury to an individual's personal interest in living in a racially integrated community, see *Trafficante v. Metropolitan Life Ins. Co.*, 409 U.S. 205 (1972), and injury to a company's interest in marketing its product free from competition, see *Hardin v. Kentucky Utilities Co.*, 390 U.S. 1 (1968)). As we said in *Sierra Club v. Morton*, 505 U.S. 727 (1972), "[Statutory] broadening [of] the categories of injury that may be alleged in support of standing is a different matter from abandoning the requirement that the party seeking review must himself have suffered an injury." Whether or not the principle set forth in *Warth* can be extended beyond that distinction, it is clear that in suits against the government, at least, the concrete injury requirement must remain.

JUSTICE KENNEDY, with whom JUSTICE SOUTER joins, concurring in part and concurring in the judgment.

[I] join Part IV of the Court's opinion with the following observations. As government programs and policies become more complex and far-reaching, we must be sensitive to the articulation of new rights of action that do not have clear analogs in our common-law tradition. Modern litigation has progressed far from the paradigm of Marbury suing Madison to get his commission. [In] my view, Congress has the power to define injuries and articulate chains of causation that will give rise to a case or controversy where none existed before, and I do not read the Court's opinion to suggest a contrary view. [In] exercising this power, however,

Congress must at the very least identify the injury it seeks to vindicate and relate the injury to the class of persons entitled to bring suit. The citizen-suit provision of the Endangered Species Act does not meet these minimal requirements, because [it] does not of its own force establish that there is an injury in "any person" by virtue of any "violation."

The Court's holding that there is an outer limit to the power of Congress to confer rights of action is a direct and necessary consequence of the case and controversy limitations found in Article III. I agree that it would exceed those limitations if, at the behest of Congress and in the absence of any showing of concrete injury, we were to entertain citizen-suits to vindicate the public's nonconcrete interest in the proper administration of the laws. While it does not matter how many persons have been injured by the challenged action, the party bringing suit must show that the action injures him in a concrete and personal way. This requirement is not just an empty formality. It preserves the vitality of the adversarial process by assuring both that the parties before the court have an actual, as opposed to professed, stake in the outcome, and that "the legal questions presented [will] be resolved, not in the rarefied atmosphere of a debating society, but in a concrete factual context conducive to a realistic appreciation of the consequences of judicial action." *Valley Forge.* In addition, the requirement of concrete injury confines the Judicial Branch to its proper, limited role in the constitutional framework of government. * * *

JUSTICE STEVENS, concurring in the judgment.

Because I am not persuaded that Congress intended the consultation requirement in § 7(a)(2) [to] apply to activities in foreign countries, I concur in the judgment of reversal. I do not, however, agree with the Court's conclusion that respondents lack standing because the threatened injury to their interest in protecting the environment and studying endangered species is not "imminent." Nor do I agree with the plurality's additional conclusion that respondents' injury is not "redressable" in this [litigation].

JUSTICE BLACKMUN, with whom JUSTICE O'CONNOR joins, dissenting.

I part company with the Court in this case in two respects. First, I believe that respondents have raised genuine issues of fact—sufficient to survive summary judgment—both as to injury and as to redressability. Second, I question the Court's breadth of language in rejecting standing for "procedural" injuries. * * *

The Court concludes that any "procedural injury" suffered by respondents is insufficient to confer standing. It rejects the view that the "injury-in-fact requirement [is] satisfied by congressional conferral upon *all* persons of an abstract, self-contained, noninstrumental 'right' to have the Executive observe the procedures required by law." Whatever the Court might mean with that very broad language, it cannot be saying that "procedural injuries" *as a class* are necessarily insufficient for purposes of Article III standing.

Most governmental conduct can be classified as "procedural." [When] the Government, for example, "procedurally" issues a pollution permit, those affected by the permittee's pollutants are not without standing to sue. Only later cases will tell just what the Court means by its intimation that "procedural" injuries are not constitutionally cognizable injuries. In the meantime, I have the greatest of sympathy for the courts across the country that will struggle to understand the Court's standardless exposition of this concept today.

The Court expresses concern that allowing judicial enforcement of "agencies' observance of a particular, statutorily prescribed procedure" would "transfer from the President to the courts the Chief Executive's most important constitutional duty, to 'take Care that the Laws be faithfully executed,' Art. II, sec. 3." In fact, the principal effect of foreclosing judicial enforcement of such procedures is to transfer power into the hands of the Executive at the expense—not of the courts—but of Congress, from which that power originates and emanates.

Under the Court's anachronistically formal view of the separation of powers, Congress legislates pure, substantive mandates and has no business structuring the procedural manner in which the Executive implements these mandates. To be sure, in the ordinary course, Congress does legislate in black-and-white terms of affirmative commands or negative prohibitions on the conduct of officers of the Executive Branch. In complex regulatory areas, however, Congress often legislates, as it were, in procedural shades of gray. That is, it sets forth substantive policy goals and provides for their attainment by requiring Executive Branch officials to follow certain procedures, for example, in the form of reporting, consultation, and certification requirements.

[There] may be factual circumstances in which a congressionally imposed procedural requirement is so insubstantially connected to the prevention of a substantive harm that it cannot be said to work any conceivable injury to an individual litigant. But, as a general matter, the courts owe substantial deference to Congress' substantive purpose in imposing a certain procedural requirement. In all events, [t]here is no room for a per se rule or presumption excluding injuries labeled "procedural" in [nature].

———

FEC v. AKINS, 524 U.S. 11 (1998), per BREYER, J., upheld the power of Congress to confer standing on any "aggrieved" person who suffers the harm of "inability to obtain information" as a result of a decision by the FEC that reporting and disclosure requirements are not applicable to a private party. Although the interest in acquiring information was not protected at common law, and although "prudential" considerations might have precluded recognition of standing to sue based on so widespread an injury in the absence of a statute, Congress had specifically authorized suit under the Federal Election Campaign Act. Judicially imposed "prudential" limitations on standing therefore had to give way; the "failure to obtain relevant information" is a "concrete" enough injury to satisfy the requirements of Art. III.

SCALIA, J., joined by O'Connor and Thomas, JJ., dissented on the ground that the asserted injury was too generalized and undifferentiated to support standing, and a statute could not cure the constitutional defect. "If today's decision is correct, it is within the power of Congress to authorize any interested person to manage (through the courts) the Executive's enforcement of any law that includes a requirement for the filing and public availability of a piece of paper. This is not the system we have had, and it is not the system we should desire."

———

In SPOKEO, INC. v. ROBINS, 136 S.Ct. 1540 (2016), the Court, per ALITO, J., reaffirmed that "Congress may 'elevat[e] to the status of legally cognizable injuries concrete, *de facto* injuries that were previously inadequate in law.' " But Alito, J., also emphasized once again that "Congress' role in identifying and elevating intangible harms does not mean that a plaintiff automatically satisfies the injury-in-fact requirement whenever a statute grants a person a statutory right and purports to authorize that person to sue to vindicate that right." To satisfy Article III, the plaintiff must allege an injury that is both "particularized" and "concrete," Alito, J., affirmed.

Spokeo involved a dispute under the Fair Credit Reporting Act, which requires consumer reporting agencies to "follow reasonable procedures to assure maximum possible accuracy of" consumer reports and provides that " '[a]ny person who willfully fails to comply with any requirement [of the Act] with respect to any [individual] is liable to that [individual].' " Robins brought suit against Spokeo, a "people search engine," which falsely reported, inter alia, that he was married, had a graduate degree, and was economically well off, when in fact he was out of work and seeking employment.

Alito, J.'s opinion recognized that Robins—who relied on the authorization to sue based on procedural deficiencies by consumer reporting agencies—had alleged an injury particularized to him, but noted that "not all inaccuracies [resulting from procedural violations] cause harm or present any material risk of harm," as illustrated by the example of the dissemination of an incorrect zip code. Having distinguished the particularity and concreteness inquiries, Alito, J., concluded that the lower court had failed to analyze "whether the particular procedural violations alleged in this case entail a degree of risk sufficient to meet the concreteness requirement." In light of this analytical defect, the Court remanded the case for further proceedings without deciding whether Robins "adequately alleged an injury in fact."

GINSBURG, J., joined by Sotomayor, J., dissented. Although Ginsburg, J., "agree[d] with much of the Court's opinion," she would have affirmed the lower court's decision to uphold standing without a remand, based on the allegation in Robins's complaint that "Spokeo's misinformation 'cause[s] actual harm to [his] employment prospects.' "

The Court clarified and arguably stiffened the "concrete" injury requirement in TRANSUNION LLC v. RAMIREZ, 141 S.Ct. 2190 (2021), another case under the Fair Credit Reporting Act (FCRA), which "requires consumer reporting agencies to 'follow reasonable procedures to assure maximum possible accuracy' in consumer reports and creates a cause of action for "any consumer" whose rights under the Act are violated. The TransUnion case grew out of a product marketed by a major credit reporting firm to alert its customers when consumers had names matching those on a U.S. government list of terrorists, drug traffickers, and other serious criminals. In determining which individuals to flag as "potential match[es]" with names on the government list, TransUnion initially conducted no investigation beyond a comparison of first and last names. Ramirez, who was misleadingly identified as a "potential match" and was rebuffed in his attempt to purchase a car as a result, sued TransUnion for failure to follow the "reasonable procedures" that FCRA requires. He also sought to certify a class of all 8,185 people to whom TransUnion sent a mailing during the period from January 1, 2011, to July 26, 2011, containing the information that their credit files contained alerts flagging them as possible terrorists or serious criminals. Within that seven-month period, however, TransUnion actually disseminated the potential-terrorist alerts with regard to only 1,853 consumers; although its files included alerts concerning 6,332 others, as well, it had not furnished those alerts to any customers within the seventh-month period subject to the parties' factual stipulations.

The Court, per KAVANAUGH, J., held by 5–4 that only the 1,853 individuals about whom false or misleading information was disseminated to TransUnion's customers suffered the "concrete" injury required for Article III standing. "The mere existence of a misleading [alert] in a consumer's internal credit file" did not constitute a concrete injury in the absence of publication or an analogue. Nor could standing be predicated on the risk that misleading information in the plaintiffs' credit files would be disseminated in the future. Although a risk of future injury will sometimes ground standing to seek injunctive relief, "in a suit for damages, the mere risk of future harm, standing alone, cannot qualify as a concrete harm— at least unless the exposure to the risk of future harm itself causes a separate concrete harm." The Court rejected the argument that credit reports on many of the 6,332 class members who claimed standing were likely sent to creditors outside of the seven-month period for which the parties had stipulated that only 1,853 of the plaintiffs' reports were actually distributed but within the nearly four-year period during which the plaintiffs claimed that TransUnion had violated their rights under FCRA. According to the Court, speculation about probabilities would not suffice; it was the plaintiffs' "burden to prove at trial that their reports were actually sent."

THOMAS, J., joined BREYER, SOTOMAYOR, and KAGAN, JJ., dissented. According to Thomas, J., Founding-era practice that informed the meaning of Article III drew a distinction between whether a plaintiff sued "based on the violation of a duty owed broadly to the whole community" or "asserts his or her own rights." Where a plaintiff sued to enforce a "public right" or a duty to the public as a whole, such as a general duty to obey or enforce the law, the existence of a justiciable case or controversy required a showing of concrete harm. But where a plaintiff sought to enforce a right or duty that was private or personal to her – such as a right to be free from trespass to her land – the plaintiff "needed only to allege the violation. * * * Courts typically did not require any showing of actual damage."

In the case before the Court, each of the plaintiffs had "established a violation of his or her private rights, because all of the FCRA provisions under which they sued created "duties [that] are owed to individuals, not to the community writ large." By extending the demand for concrete harm to cases involving congressionally created private rights, Thomas, J., maintained, the Court had adopted an approach "remarkable in both its novelty and effects. Never before has this Court declared that legal injury is inherently insufficient to support standing."

"Even assuming that this Court should be in the business of second-guessing private rights," Thomas, J., thought that the plaintiffs had all pleaded concrete injuries: "[O]one need only tap into common sense to know that receiving a letter identifying you as a potential drug trafficker or terrorist is harmful. All the more so when the information comes in the context of a credit report, the entire purpose of which is to demonstrate that a person can be trusted." According to Thomas, J., the errors in TransUnion's files created a real risk of disclosure at some time other than within the seven-month period in which TransUnion had disseminated erroneous credit reports involving roughly 25 percent of the plaintiff class. "Twenty-five percent over just a 7-month period seems, to me, 'a degree of risk sufficient to meet the concreteness requirement.'"

Kagan, J., also filed a separate dissent, joined by Breyer and Sotomayor, JJ., to explain that she "differ[ed] with Justice Thomas on just one matter. *** In his view, any 'violation of an individual right' created by Congress gives rise to Article III standing." By contrast, the Court had said in *Spokeo*, and she continued to believe, that "Article III requires a concrete injury even in the context of a statutory violation." Nevertheless, she thought that her view would lead to the same result as Thomas, J.'s "in all but highly unusual cases" due to the deference that the courts owed to Congress in determining "when something causes a harm or risk of harm in the real world."

III. TAXPAYER STANDING AND OTHER STATUS-BASED STANDING ISSUES

In FROTHINGHAM v. MELLON, 262 U.S. 447 (1923), a federal taxpayer contended that a federal statute providing funds to states undertaking programs to reduce maternal and infant mortality exceeded Congress' power, and "that the effect of the appropriations complained of will be to increase the burden of future taxation and thereby take her property without due process of law." The Court, per SUTHERLAND, J., dismissed "for want of jurisdiction." A federal taxpayer's "interest in the moneys of the treasury [is] shared with millions of others, is comparatively minute and indeterminable, and the effect upon future taxation, of any payment out of the funds, so remote, fluctuating and uncertain, that no basis is afforded for an appeal to the preventive powers of a court of equity." To permit such suits might result in attacks on "every other appropriation act and statute whose administration requires the outlay of public money * * * . The bare suggestion of such a result, with its attendant inconveniences, goes far to sustain the conclusion which we have reached, that a suit of this character cannot be maintained." A person asking the Court to hold a federal act unconstitutional "must be able to show, not only that the statute is invalid, but that he has sustained or is immediately in danger of sustaining some direct injury as the result of its enforcement, and not merely that he suffers in some indefinite way in common with people generally." Here, the complaint "is merely that [federal officials] will execute an act of Congress asserted to be unconstitutional; and this we are asked to prevent. To do so would be, not to decide a judicial controversy, but to assume a position of authority over the governmental acts of another and coequal department, an authority which plainly we do not possess."

———

FLAST v. COHEN, 392 U.S. 83 (1968), per WARREN, C.J., upheld the standing of federal taxpayers to challenge federal expenditures for parochial schools under the religion clauses of the First Amendment. The Court noted, at the outset, that standing doctrine blends "constitutional requirements and policy considerations" and implied that *Frothingham* rested largely on policy grounds. It framed the essence of the standing inquiry as distinct from the fitness of the issues presented for resolution on the merits: "[The] fundamental aspect of standing is that it focuses on the party seeking to get his complaint before a federal court and not on the issues he wishes to have adjudicated." But the Court then acknowledged that "in ruling on standing, it is both appropriate and necessary to look to the substantive issues [to] determine whether there is a logical nexus between the status asserted and the claim sought to be adjudicated [to] assure that [the litigant] is a proper and appropriate party to invoke federal judicial power [so as] to satisfy Article III requirements": "The nexus demanded of federal taxpayers has two aspects to it. First, the taxpayer must establish a logical link between that status and the type of legislative enactment attacked. [Secondly,] the taxpayer must establish a nexus between that status and the precise nature of the constitutional infringement alleged."

"The taxpayer-appellants in this case have satisfied both nexuses * * * ." With respect to the first, it sufficed that the "constitutional challenge is made to an exercise by Congress of its power under Art. I, § 8, to spend for the general welfare, and the challenged program involves a substantial expenditure of federal tax funds." With respect to the second, "appellants have alleged that the challenged expenditures violate the Establishment and Free Exercise Clauses of the First Amendment." In light of its historic purposes, the Establishment Clause "operates as a specific constitutional limitation upon the exercise by Congress of the taxing and spending power conferred by Art. I, § 8."

Frothingham was distinguishable. Although the "taxpayer in *Frothingham* attacked a federal spending program [and therefore] established the first nexus required," her general allegation that "Congress [had] exceeded the general powers delegated to it" failed to identify any specific limitation on spending that Congress had breached. The Court reserved the question whether "the Constitution contains other specific limitations" that would support standing by taxpayers to challenge federal expenditures.

HARLAN, J., dissenting, protested that the Court's dual nexus standard for taxpayer standing was "entirely unrelated" to the purportedly controlling standard of whether the plaintiff had the requisite personal stake to justify standing. "It is surely clear that a plaintiff's interest in the outcome of a suit in which he challenges the constitutionality of a federal expenditure is not made greater or smaller" by the nature of the program being attacked or the constitutional provision under which the attack is mounted. "[H]ow can it be said that Mrs. Frothingham's interests in her suit were, as a consequence of her choice of a constitutional claim, necessarily less intense than those, for example, of the present appellants?"

The plaintiffs' claim did not rest on any distinctive individual stake in the outcome, but involved an assertion of standing to represent the public interest— shared equally by all citizens—in the observance of the establishment clause. "[I]ndividual litigants have standing to represent the public interest, despite their lack of economic or other personal interests, if [but only if] Congress has appropriately authorized such suits. [Any] hazards to the proper allocation of authority among the three branches of the Government would be substantially diminished if public actions had been pertinently authorized by Congress and the President."

––––––––––

Although *Flast* has never been formally overruled, subsequent decisions have limited it nearly to its facts.

VALLEY FORGE CHRISTIAN COLLEGE v. AMERICANS UNITED FOR SEPARATION OF CHURCH AND STATE, INC., 454 U.S. 464 (1982), per REHNQUIST, J., held that respondents lacked standing as taxpayers or citizens to challenge, as violating the Establishment Clause, the giving of surplus federal property to a church college that trained students "for Christian services as either ministers or laymen": " '[R]espondents fail the first prong of the [*Flast*] test for taxpayer standing [in] two respects. First, the source of their complaint is not a congressional action, but a decision by HEW to transfer a parcel of federal property. *Flast* limited taxpayer standing to challenges directed 'only [at] exercises of congressional power.' * * * Second, [the] property transfer [was] not an exercise of authority conferred by the Taxing and Spending Clause of Art. I, § 8. The authorizing legislation [was] an evident exercise of Congress' power under the Property Clause, Art. IV, § 3, cl. 2. * * *

"The complaint in this case shares a common deficiency with those in *Schlesinger [v. Reservists Committee to Stop the War]* and *[United States v.] Richardson* [both cited in *Allen*]. Although [they] claim that the Constitution has been violated, [they] fail to identify any personal injury suffered by the plaintiffs *as a consequence* of the alleged constitutional error, other than the psychological consequence presumably produced by observation of conduct with which one disagrees. That is not an injury sufficient to confer standing under Art. III, even though the disagreement is phrased in constitutional terms. It is evident that respondents are firmly committed to the constitutional principle of separation of church and State, but standing is not measured by the intensity of the litigant's interest or the fervor of his advocacy."

BRENNAN, J., joined by Marshall and Blackmun, JJ.,[4] dissented: "The Court makes a fundamental mistake when it determines that a plaintiff has failed to satisfy [the] 'injury-in-fact' test, or indeed any other test of 'standing,' without first determining whether the Constitution [defines] injury, and creates a cause of action for redress of that injury, in precisely the circumstance presented to the Court. * * *[5] [One] of the primary purposes of the Establishment Clause was to prevent the use of tax moneys for religious purposes. *The taxpayer was the direct and intended beneficiary of the prohibition on financial aid to religion.* [Each], and indeed every, federal taxpayer suffers precisely the injury that the Establishment Clause guards against when the Federal Government directs that funds be taken from the pocketbooks of the citizenry and placed into the coffers of the ministry."

————

In HEIN v. FREEDOM FROM RELIGION FOUNDATION, INC., 549 U.S. 1109 (2007), the plurality opinion read *Flast v. Cohen* so narrowly that two concurring Justices and four dissenters believed that *Flast* was indistinguishable and should therefore be either overruled or applied. The case arose when the President, by executive orders, created a White House office and several "centers" within federal agencies to ensure that faith-based community groups would be eligible to apply for federal financial support for activities that were not inherently religious. Suing as taxpayers, respondents challenged a number of executive actions that, they said, violated the Establishment Clause by expending public funds to promote religious community groups over secular ones. The plurality opinion by ALITO, J., joined by Roberts, C.J., and Kennedy, J., held *Flast* distinguishable on the ground that the expenditures at issue were not made pursuant to any specific Act of Congress, as was the case in *Flast*, but rather occurred under general appropriations to the Executive Branch to fund day-to-day activities. *Flast*, the plurality said, "gave too little weight" to separation-of-powers concerns, and to extend it "would repeat and compound this mistake": "Because

---

4   Stevens, J., dissented separately.

5   **[Ct's Note]** When the Constitution makes it clear that a particular person is to be protected from a particular form of government action, then that person has a "right" to be free of that action; when that right is infringed, then there is injury, and a personal stake, within the meaning of Art. III.

almost all Executive Branch activity is ultimately funded by some congressional appropriation, extending the Flast exception to purely executive expenditures would effectively subject every federal action—be it a conference, proclamation, or speech—to Establishment Clause challenge by any taxpayer in federal court." Of the three Justices in the plurality, only KENNEDY, J., in a separate concurring opinion, affirmed expressly that "[i]n my view the result reached in *Flast* is correct and should not be called into question."

Concurring in the judgment, SCALIA, J., joined by Thomas, J., argued that *Flast* ultimately needed to rest on the indefensible principle that "Psychic Injury," rather than "Wallet Injury," sufficed to establish standing. Admission of that principle into the law rendered efforts to distinguish *Flast* arbitrary and unconvincing, he maintained, and it should be overruled so that its underlying rationale would be expunged: "*Flast*'s lack of a logical theoretical underpinning has rendered our taxpayer standing doctrine [a] jurisprudential disaster." SOUTER, J., joined by Stevens, Ginsburg, and Breyer, JJ., argued that "[w]hen executive agencies spend identifiable sums of tax money for religious purposes, no less than when Congress authorizes the same thing, taxpayers suffer injury."[5]

2. TIMING OF ADJUDICATION

I. MOOTNESS

DEFUNIS V. ODEGAARD
416 U.S. 312, 94 S.Ct. 1704, 40 L.Ed.2d 164 (1974).

PER CURIAM.

[Petitioner was admitted to the University of Washington Law School after a state trial court had sustained his claim that the school's special admissions policy violated equal protection. The Washington Supreme Court reversed, but its judgment was stayed. By the time the case was argued in the Supreme Court, petitioner had registered for the final term of his third year. Although the school stated that if its admissions policy were upheld, petitioner would be subject to it if he had to register for any additional terms, his present registration "would not be canceled [regardless] of the outcome of this litigation."]

---

[5]   See also *Arizona Christian School Tuition Org. v. Winn*, 563 U.S. 125 (2011), holding, per Kennedy, J., that taxpayers lack standing to challenge dollar-for-dollar tax credits for contributions to organizations that provide scholarships to children attending religious schools: "A dissenter whose tax dollars are 'extracted and spent' knows that he has in some small measure been made to contribute to an establishment of religion in violation of conscience. *Flast*. [By contrast, a] tax credit is not tantamount to a religious tax and does not visit the injury identified in *Flast*." Kagan, J., joined by Ginsburg, Breyer, and Sotomayor, JJ., dissented: In five previous cases challenging tax credits that subsidize religion, "we have [always] resolved the suit without questioning the plaintiffs' standing. [The] Court's opinion [offers] a roadmap—more truly, just a one-step instruction—to any government that wishes to insulate its financing of religious activity from legal challenge. Structure the funding as a tax expenditure, and *Flast* will not stand in the way."

The starting point for analysis is the familiar proposition that "federal courts are without power to decide questions that cannot affect the rights of litigants in the case before them." *North Carolina v. Rice*, 404 U.S. 244 (1971). The inability of the federal judiciary "to review moot cases derives from the requirement of Art. III of the Constitution under which the exercise of judicial power depends upon the existence of a case or controversy." *Liner v. Jafco, Inc.*, 375 U.S. 301 n.3 (1964).

[A]ll parties agree that DeFunis is now entitled to complete his legal studies at the University of Washington and to receive his degree from that institution. A determination by this Court of the legal issues tendered by the parties is no longer necessary to compel that result, and could not serve to prevent it. DeFunis did not cast his suit as a class action, and the only remedy he requested was an injunction commanding his admission to the Law School. He was not only accorded that remedy, but he now has also been irrevocably admitted to the final term of the final year of the Law School course. The controversy between the parties has thus clearly ceased to be "definite and concrete" and no longer "touch[es] the legal relations of parties having adverse legal interests." *Aetna Life Ins. Co. v. Haworth*, 300 U.S. 227 (1937).

[There] is a line of decisions in this Court standing for the proposition that the "voluntary cessation of allegedly illegal conduct does not deprive the tribunal of power to hear and determine the case, i.e., does not make the case moot." [E.g.,] *United States v. W.T. Grant Co.*, 345 U.S. 629 (1953). These decisions and the doctrine they reflect would be quite relevant if the question of mootness here had arisen by reason of a unilateral change in the *admissions procedures* of the Law School. For it was the admissions procedures that were the target of this litigation, and a voluntary cessation of the admissions practices complained of could make this case moot only if it could be said with assurance "that 'there is no reasonable expectation that the wrong will be repeated.'" *W.T. Grant Co.* Otherwise, "[t]he defendant is free to return to his old ways," id., and this fact would be enough to prevent mootness because of the "public interest in having the legality of the practices settled." Ibid. But mootness in the present case depends not at all upon a "voluntary cessation" of the admissions practices that were the subject of this litigation. It depends, instead, upon the simple fact that DeFunis is now in the final quarter of the final year of his course of study, and the settled and unchallenged policy of the Law School to permit him to complete the term for which he is now enrolled.

It might also be suggested that this case presents a question that is "capable of repetition, yet evading review," *Southern Pacific Terminal Co. v. ICC*, 219 U.S. 498, 515 (1911); *Roe v. Wade*, [Ch. 6, Sec. 2], and is thus amenable to federal adjudication even though it might otherwise be considered moot. But DeFunis will never again be required to run the gauntlet of the Law School's admission process, and so the question is certainly not "capable of repetition" so far as he is concerned. Moreover, just because this particular case did not reach the Court until the eve of the petitioner's graduation from law school, it hardly follows that the issue he raises will in the future evade review. If the admissions procedures of the Law

School remain unchanged, there is no reason to suppose that a subsequent case attacking those procedures will not come with relative speed to this Court, now that the Supreme Court of Washington has spoken. This case, therefore, in no way presents the exceptional situation in which the *Southern Pacific Terminal* doctrine might permit a departure from "[t]he usual rule in federal cases [that] an actual controversy must exist at stages of appellate or certiorari review, and not simply at the date the action is initiated." *Roe v. Wade.*

[W]e conclude that the Court cannot, consistently with the limitations of Art. III of the Constitution, consider the substantive constitutional issues tendered by the parties.[5]

JUSTICE BRENNAN, with whom JUSTICE DOUGLAS, JUSTICE WHITE, and JUSTICE MARSHALL concur, dissenting.[6]

[Many] weeks of the school term remain, and [a]ny number of unexpected events—illness, economic necessity, even academic failure—might prevent [petitioner's] graduation at the end of the term. Were that misfortune to befall, and were petitioner required to register for yet another term, the prospect that he would again face the hurdle of the admissions policy is real, not fanciful * * * .

In these circumstances, and because the University's position implies no concession that its admissions policy is unlawful, this controversy falls squarely within the Court's long line of decisions holding that the "[m]ere voluntary cessation of allegedly illegal conduct does not moot a case." *United States v. Concentrated Phosphate Export Ass'n*, 393 U.S. 199 (1968).

[T]he Court concedes that, if petitioner has lost his stake in this controversy, he did so only when he registered for the spring term. But petitioner took that action only after the case had been fully litigated in the state courts, briefs had been filed in this Court, and oral argument had been heard. The case is thus ripe for decision on a fully developed factual record with sharply defined and fully canvassed legal issues.

Moreover, in endeavoring to dispose of this case as moot, the Court clearly disserves the public interest. The constitutional issues which are avoided today concern vast numbers of people, organizations, and colleges and universities, as evidenced by the filing of twenty-six amicus curiae briefs. Few constitutional questions in recent history have stirred as much debate, and they will not disappear. [Because] avoidance of repetitious litigation serves the public interest, that inevitability counsels against mootness determinations, as here, not compelled by the record. * * *

---

   [5]   **[Ct's Note]** It is suggested in dissent that "[a]ny number of unexpected events—illness, economic necessity, even academic failure—might prevent his graduation at the end of the term." "But such speculative contingencies afford no basis for our passing on the substantive issues [the petitioner] would have us decide," *Hall v. Beals*, 396 U.S. 45 (1969), in the absence of "evidence that this is a prospect of 'immediacy and reality.'" *Golden v. Zwickler*, 394 U.S. 109 (1969).

   [6]   Douglas, J., also filed a separate dissent on the merits.

NOTES

1.   ***Mootness and standing.*** Although the Court on several occasions had characterized mootness as "the doctrine of standing set in a time frame,"[7] the Court reconsidered that description in FRIENDS OF THE EARTH v. LAIDLAW ENV. SERVS. (TOC), INC., 528 U.S. 167 (2000). After Friends of the Earth sued to enjoin a violation of the environmental laws, the defendants ceased their illegal conduct, and the court of appeals ordered the case dismissed as moot. Reasoning that all elements of Article III standing must persist throughout federal litigation, the lower court found it too unlikely that a judicial remedy would effectively redress any current injury to the plaintiffs.[8] The Court, per GINSBURG, J., reversed, holding that "the Court of Appeals confused mootness with standing": "[T]here are circumstances in which the prospect that a defendant will engage in (or resume) harmful conduct may be too speculative to support standing, but not too speculative to overcome mootness. [Standing] doctrine functions to ensure, among other things, that the scarce resources of the federal courts are devoted to those disputes in which the parties have a concrete stake. In contrast, by the time mootness is an issue, the case has been brought and litigated, often (as here) for years. To abandon the case at an advanced stage may prove more wasteful than frugal. This argument from sunk costs does not license courts to retain jurisdiction over cases in which one or both of the parties plainly lacks a continuing interest[, but it] surely highlights an important difference between the two doctrines." Scalia, J., joined by Thomas, J., dissented on the ground that the plaintiffs never possessed standing.

2.   ***Changes of law.*** In *New York State Rifle & Pistol Ass'n, Inc. v. City of New York*, 140 S.Ct. 1525 (2020), the Court ruled that a challenge to a New York City ordinance that barred licensed gun owners from transporting their weapons anywhere besides seven firing ranges within the City became moot after New York adopted an amended ordinance that allowed "direct[ ]" transport to and from other gun ranges and second homes. Dissenting, Alito, J., joined by Thomas and Gorsuch, JJ., maintained that because the amended ordinance continued to burden the petitioners' asserted right of "unrestricted access" to gun ranges, the dispute remained live.

3.   ***Mootness and class actions.*** The Supreme Court has asserted unequivocally that a plaintiff claiming standing to file a class action must have a personal stake at the time the lawsuit is filed; that other class members may have suffered injury will not suffice. See *Simon v. Eastern Kentucky Welfare Rights Org.*, 426 U.S. 26 n.20 (1976). But in cases such as *DeFunis,* in which the plaintiff has standing at the time suit is filed, the plaintiff's request for class certification may affect any subsequent mootness analysis. The leading case is UNITED STATES PAROLE COMM'N v. GERAGHTY, 445 U.S. 388 (1980), in which a federal

---

[7]   See *Arizonans for Official English v. Arizona*, 520 U.S. 43 n.22 (1997), quoting *United States Parole Comm'n v. Geraghty*, 445 U.S. 388 (1980), in turn quoting Henry P. Monaghan, *Constitutional Adjudication: The Who and When*, 82 Yale L.J. 1363 (1973).

[8]   The clearly available remedy under the Clean Water Act on which the "redressability" debate focused was a civil money penalty payable to the government, not to the plaintiffs.

prisoner filed a class action challenging the guidelines governing release on parole. The district court denied class certification and rejected the claim on the merits, and Geraghty himself had been released from prison before the case reached the Court. Nevertheless, the Court, per BLACKMUN, J., held the case not moot. "[A]n action brought on behalf of a class does not become moot upon expiration of the named plaintiff's substantive claim," and it made no difference that the plaintiff's substantive claim had been mooted before the class had been certified: "The proposed [class] representative retains a 'personal stake' in obtaining class certification sufficient to assure that Art. III values are not undermined. If the appeal results in a reversal of the class certification denial, and a class subsequently is properly certified, the merits of the class claim then may be adjudicated."

POWELL, J., joined by Burger, C.J., and Stewart and Rehnquist, JJ., dissented: "The Court makes no effort to identify any injury to respondent that may be redressed by, or any benefit to respondent that may accrue from, a favorable ruling on the certification question. Instead, respondent's 'personal stake' is said to derive from two factors having nothing to do with concrete injury or stake in the outcome. First, the Court finds that the Federal Rules of Civil Procedure create a 'right,' 'analogous to the private attorney general concept,' to have a class certified. Second, the Court thinks that the case retains the 'imperatives of a dispute capable of judicial resolution,' which are identified as (i) a sharply presented issue, (ii) a concrete factual setting, and (iii) a self-interested party actually contesting the case.

"The Court's reliance on some new 'right' inherent in Rule 23 is misplaced. We have held that even Congress may not confer federal court jurisdiction when Art. III does not. Far less so may a rule of procedure which 'shall not be construed to extend [the] jurisdiction of the United States district courts.' Fed. Rule Civ. Proc. 82. [Although] we have refused steadfastly to countenance the 'public action,' the Court's redefinition of the personal stake requirement leaves no principled basis for that practice."

But cf. *Genesis Healthcare Corp. v. Symczyk*, 569 U.S. 66 (2013) (holding, 5–4, that mootness doctrine required dismissal of a "collective action" under the Fair Labor Standards Act when a named plaintiff's personal claim had already become moot before she moved for "provisional certification" of a class).

II. RIPENESS

The ripeness doctrine seeks to identify and exclude from the federal courts cases that are somehow too abstract, premature, or ill-defined to be fit for adjudication. The ripeness doctrine is itself somewhat ill-defined, however, due to its uncertain relationship with standing. See, e.g., *Susan B. Anthony List v. Driehaus*, supra (treating standing and ripeness issues as overlapping and authorizing suit to enjoin enforcement of a penal statute alleged to violate the First Amendment where "there exists a credible threat of prosecution"). With the

Supreme Court sometimes treating ripeness as distinct, a persisting question is whether there might be cases in which a plaintiff has suffered sufficient injury to support standing but in which a court might think adjudication nevertheless premature, possibly due to uncertainty about the specific facts on which it should render judgment or to which it should shape a remedial decree.

Consider Erwin Chemerinsky, *Federal Jurisdiction* § 2.4.1 (6th ed. 2012): "Ripeness [is] a justiciability doctrine determining when review is appropriate. [I]n practice there is an obvious overlap between the doctrines of standing and ripeness. If no injury has occurred, the plaintiff might be denied standing or the case might be dismissed as not ripe. * * * However, for the sake of clarity, especially in those cases where the law of standing and ripeness is not identical, ripeness can be given a narrower definition that distinguishes it from standing and explains the existing case law. Ripeness properly should be understood as involving the question of *when may a party seek preenforcement review of a statute or regulation*. Customarily, a person can challenge the legality of a statute or regulation only when he or she is prosecuted for violating it. At that time, a defense can be that the law is invalid, for example, as being unconstitutional."

Insofar as ripeness is distinctively concerned with preenforcement review in suits for injunctions and declaratory judgments, ripeness inquiries blend with inquiries into the appropriateness of equitable relief in light of a balance of public and private interests. Leading cases largely accord with this conceptualization, but often without expressly characterizing ripeness as an equitable or otherwise discretionary doctrine. In a much quoted opinion in *Abbott Laboratories v. Gardner*, 387 U.S. 136 (1967), the Court characterized the ripeness inquiry as having two aspects: (i) "the hardship to the parties of withholding court consideration" and (ii) "the fitness of the issues for judicial decision."

APPENDIX A

THE JUSTICES OF THE SUPREME COURT

■ ■ ■

Originally prepared by JOHN J. COUND

Professor of Law, University of Minnesota

The following data summarize the prior public careers of the justices of the Supreme Court. The first dates in parentheses are those of birth and death; these are followed by the name of the appointing President and the dates of service on the Court. The states in which the justices were residing when appointed and their political affiliations at that time are then given. In detailing prior careers, I have followed chronological order, with two exceptions: I have listed first that a justice was a signer of the Declaration of Independence or the Federal Constitution, and I have indicated state legislative experience only once for each justice. I have not distinguished between different bodies in the state legislature, and I have omitted service in the Continental Congresses. Private practice, except where deemed especially significant, and law teaching have been omitted, except where a justice was primarily engaged therein upon or shortly before appointment. The activity in which a justice was engaged upon appointment has been italicized. Figures in parentheses indicate years of service in the position. In only a few cases, a justice's extra-Court or post-Court activity has been indicated or some other note made. An asterisk designates the Chief Justices.

The accompanying Table of Justices on pages [1754] and [56] has been planned so that the composition of the Court at any time can be readily ascertained.

(This material has been compiled from a great number of sources, but special acknowledgment must be made to the *Dictionary of American Biography* (Charles Scribner's Sons), the A.N. Marquis Company works, and Ewing, *The Judges of the Supreme Court, 1789–1937* (University of Minnesota Press, 1938).)

ALITO, JR., SAMUEL A. (1950–___; G.W. Bush, 2006–___). N.J.Rep.—U.S., Assistant U.S. Attorney (4); Assistant to Solicitor General (4); Deputy Assistant Attorney General (3); U.S. Attorney (4); Judge, Court of Appeals (16).

BALDWIN, HENRY (1780–1844; Jackson, 1830–1844). Pa.Dem.—U.S., House of Representatives (5). Private practice.

BARBOUR, PHILIP P. (1783–1841; Jackson, 1836–1841). Va.Dem.—Va., Legislature (2). U.S., House of Representatives (14). Va., Judge, General Court (2); President, State Constitutional Convention, 1829–30. U.S., Judge, District Court (5).

BARRETT, AMY CONEY (1972–___; Trump, 2020–___). Ind.Rep.—Professor (18). U.S., Judge, Court of Appeals (3).

BLACK, HUGO L. (1886–1971; F.D. Roosevelt, 1937–1971). Ala.Dem.—Captain, Field Artillery, World War I. Ala., Judge, Police Court (1); County Solicitor (2). U.S., Senate (10).

BLACKMUN, HARRY A. (1908–1999; Nixon, 1970–1994). Minn.Rep.—Resident Counsel, Mayo Clinic, (10). U.S., Judge, Court of Appeals (11).

BLAIR, JOHN (1732–1800; Washington, 1789–1796). Va.Fed.—Signer, U.S. Constitution, 1787. Va., Legislature (9); Judge and Chief Justice, General Court (2), Court of Appeals (9). His opinion in *Commonwealth v. Caton*, 4 Call 5, 20 (Va.1782), is one of the earliest expressions of the doctrine of judicial review.

BLATCHFORD, SAMUEL (1820–1893; Arthur, 1882–1893). N.Y.Rep.—U.S., Judge, District Court (5); Circuit Court (10).

BRADLEY, JOSEPH P. (1803–1892; Grant, 1870–1892). N.J.Rep.—Actuary. Private practice.

BRANDEIS, LOUIS D. (1856–1941; Wilson, 1916–1939). Mass.Dem.—Private practice. Counsel, variously for the government, for industry, and "for the people," in numerous administrative and judicial proceedings, both state and federal.

BRENNAN, WILLIAM J. (1906–1997; Eisenhower, 1956–1990). N.J.Dem.—U.S. Army, World War II. N.J., Judge, Superior Court (1); Appellate Division (2); Supreme Court (4).

BREWER, DAVID J. (1837–1910; B. Harrison, 1889–1910). Kans.Rep.—Kans., Judge, County Criminal and Probate Court (1), District Court (4); County Attorney (1); Judge, Supreme Court (14), U.S., Judge, Circuit Court (5).

BREYER, STEPHEN GERALD (1937–___; Clinton, 1994–___). Mass.Dem.—U.S., Special Assistant to Assistant Attorney General for Antitrust (2); Assistant Special Prosecutor (during Watergate) (1); Special Counsel of the Senate Judiciary Committee (1); Chief Counsel, same (2); Judge, Court of Appeals (10); Chief Judge, Court of Appeals (4).

BROWN, HENRY, B. (1836–1913; B. Harrison, 1890–1906). Mich.Rep.—U.S., Assistant U.S. Attorney (5). Mich., Judge, Circuit Court (1). U.S., Judge, District Court (15).

*BURGER, WARREN E. (1907–1995; Nixon, 1969–1986). Va.Rep.—U.S., Assistant Attorney General, Civil Division (3), Judge, Court of Appeals (13).

BURTON, HAROLD H. (1888–1964; Truman, 1945–1958). Ohio Rep.—Capt., U.S Army, World War I. Ohio, Legislature (2). Mayor, Cleveland, OH. (5). U.S., Senate (4).

BUTLER, PIERCE (1866–1939; Harding, 1922–1939). Minn.Dem.—Minn., County Attorney (4). Private practice.

BYRNES, JAMES F. (1879–1972; F.D. Roosevelt, 1941–1942). S.C.Dem.— S.C., Solicitor, Circuit Court (2). U.S., House of Representatives (14); Senate (12). Resigned from the Court to become U.S. Director of Economic Stabilization.

CAMPBELL, JOHN A. (1811–1889; Pierce, 1853–1861). Ala.Dem.—Private practice. After his resignation, he became Assistant Secretary of War, C.S.A.

CARDOZO, BENJAMIN N. (1870–1938; Hoover, 1932–1938). N.Y.Dem.— N.Y., Judge, Supreme Court (6 weeks); Associate Judge and Chief Judge, Court of Appeals (18).

CATRON, JOHN (1778–1865; Van Buren, 1837–1865). Tenn.Dem.—Tenn., Judge and Chief Justice, Supreme Court of Errors and Appeals (10). Private practice.

*CHASE, SALMON P. (1808–1873; Lincoln, 1864–1873). Ohio Rep.—U.S., Senate (6). Ohio, Governor (4). U.S., Secretary of the Treasury (3).

CHASE, SAMUEL (1741–1811; Washington, 1796–1811). Md.Fed.—Signer, U.S. Declaration of Independence, 1776. Md., Legislature (20); Chief Judge, Court of Oyer and Terminer (2), General Court (5). Impeached and acquitted, 1804–05.

CLARK, TOM C. (1899–1977; Truman, 1949–1967). Tex.Dem.—U.S. Army, World War I. Tex., Civil District Attorney (5). U.S., Assistant Attorney General (2), Attorney General (4).

CLARKE, JOHN H. (1857–1945; Wilson, 1916–1922). Ohio Dem.—U.S. Judge, District Court (2).

CLIFFORD, NATHAN (1803–1881; Buchanan, 1858–1881). Me.Dem.—Me., Legislature (4); Attorney General (4). U.S., House of Representatives (4); Attorney General (2); Minister Plenipotentiary to Mexico, 1848. Private practice.

CURTIS, BENJAMIN R. (1809–1874; Fillmore, 1851–1857). Mass.Whig.— Mass., Legislature (1). Private practice.

CUSHING, WILLIAM (1732–1810; Washington, 1789–1810). Mass.Fed.— Mass., Judge, Superior Court (3); Justice and Chief Justice, Supreme Judicial Court (14).

DANIEL, PETER V. (1784–1860; Van Buren, 1841–1860). Va.Dem.—Va., Legislature (3); Member, Privy Council (23). U.S., Judge, District Court (5).

DAVIS, DAVID (1815–1886; Lincoln, 1862–1877). Ill.Rep.—Ill., Legislature (2); Judge, Circuit Court (14). His resignation to become U.S. Senator upset the agreed-upon composition of the Hayes-Tilden Electoral Commission.

DAY, WILLIAM R. (1849–1923; T. Roosevelt, 1903–1922). Ohio Rep.—Ohio, Judge, Court of Common Pleas (4). U.S., Assistant Secretary of State (1), Secretary of State (½); Chairman, U.S. Peace Commissioners, 1898; Judge, Circuit Court of Appeals (4).

DOUGLAS, WILLIAM O. (1898–1980; F.D. Roosevelt, 1939–1975). Conn.Dem.—Pvt., U.S. Army, World War I. U.S., Chairman, Securities and Exchange Commission (3). His was the longest tenure in the history of the Court.

DUVAL(L), GABRIEL (1752–1844; Madison, 1811–1835). Md.Rep.—Declined to serve as delegate, U.S. Constitutional Convention, 1787. Md., State Council (3). U.S., House of Representatives (2). Md., Judge, General Court (6). U.S., Comptroller of the Treasury (9).

*ELLSWORTH, OLIVER (1745–1807; Washington, 1796–1800). Conn.Fed.—Delegate, U.S. Constitutional Convention, 1787. Conn., Legislature (2); Member, Governor's Council (4); Judge, Superior Court (5). U.S., Senate (7).

FIELD, STEPHEN J. (1816–1899; Lincoln, 1863–1897). Calif.Dem.—Calif., Justice, and Chief Justice, Supreme Court (6).

FORTAS, ABE (1910–1982; L.B. Johnson, 1965–1969). Tenn.Dem.—U.S. Government attorney and consultant (A.A.A., S.E.C., P.W.A., Dep't of Interior) (9); Undersecretary of Interior (4). Private practice in Washington, D.C. Nominated as Chief Justice; nomination withdrawn, 1968. Resigned.

FRANKFURTER, FELIX (1882–1965; F.D. Roosevelt, 1939–1962). Mass. Independent.—U.S., Assistant U.S. Attorney (4); Law Officer, War Department, Bureau of Insular Affairs (3); Assistant to Secretary of War (1). Professor (25).

*FULLER, MELVILLE W. (1833–1910; Cleveland, 1888–1910). Ill.Dem.—Ill., Legislature (2). Private practice.

GINSBURG, RUTH BADER (1933–2020; Clinton, 1993–2020); N.Y.Dem.—Professor (17). U.S., Judge, Court of Appeals (13).

GOLDBERG, ARTHUR J. (1908–1990; Kennedy, 1962–1965). Ill.Dem.—Major, U.S.A., World War II. General Counsel, USW-AFL-CIO (13). U.S., Secretary of Labor (1). Resigned to become Ambassador to U.N.

GORSUCH, NEIL M. (1967–____; Trump, 2017–____). Colo.Rep.—Private practice (1). U.S., Deputy Associate Attorney General (1). U.S., Judge, Court of Appeals (11).

GRAY, HORACE (1828–1902; Arthur, 1881–1902). Mass.Rep.—Mass., Associate Justice and Chief Justice, Supreme Judicial Court (18).

GRIER, ROBERT O. (1794–1870; Polk, 1846–1870). Pa.Dem.—Pa., Presiding Judge, District Court (13).

HARLAN, JOHN M. (1833–1911; Hayes, 1877–1911). Ky.Rep.—Ky., Judge, County Court (1). Col., Union Army, 1861–63. Ky., Attorney General (4). U.S., Member, President's Louisiana Commission, 1877. Private practice. Grandfather of:

HARLAN, JOHN M. (1899–1971; Eisenhower, 1955–1971). N.Y.Rep.—Col., U.S.A.A.F., World War II. N.Y. Chief Counsel, State Crime Commission (2). U.S., Judge, Court of Appeals (1).

HOLMES, OLIVER W., JR. (1841–1935; T. Roosevelt, 1902–1932). Mass.Rep.—Lt. Col., Mass. Volunteers, Civil War. Mass., Associate Justice, and Chief Justice, Supreme Judicial Court (20).

*HUGHES, CHARLES E. (1862–1948; Taft, 1910–1916, and Hoover, 1930–1941). N.Y.Rep.—N.Y., Counsel, legislative committees investigating gas and insurance industries (2); U.S., Special Assistant to Attorney General for Coal Investigation (1). N.Y., Governor (3). [Between appointments to the Supreme Court: Presidential Nominee, Republican Party, 1916. U.S., Secretary of State (4). Member, Permanent Court of Arbitration, The Hague (4). Judge, Permanent Court of International Justice (2).] Chief Justice on second appointment.

HUNT, WARD (1810–1886; Grant, 1872–1882). N.Y.Rep.—N.Y., Legislature (2). Mayor of Utica, N.Y. (1). N.Y., Associate Judge, and Chief Judge, Court of Appeals (4); Commissioner of Appeals (4). He did not sit from 1879 to his retirement in 1882.

IREDELL, JAMES (1750–1799; Washington, 1790–1799). N.C.Fed.—Comptroller of Customs (6), Collector of Port (2), Edenton, N.C. N.C., Judge, Superior Court (½); Attorney General (2); Member, Council of State, 1787; Reviser of Statutes (3).

JACKSON, HOWELL E. (1832–1895; B. Harrison, 1893–1895). Tenn.Dem.—Tenn., Judge, Court of Arbitration (4); Legislature (1). U.S., Senate (5); Judge, Circuit Court of Appeals (7).

JACKSON, ROBERT H. (1892–1954; F.D. Roosevelt, 1941–1954). N.Y.Dem.—U.S., General Counsel, Bureau of Internal Revenue (2); Assistant Attorney General (2); Solicitor General (2); Attorney General (1).

*JAY, JOHN (1745–1829; Washington, 1789–1795). N.Y.Fed.—N.Y., Chief Justice, Supreme Court (2). U.S., Envoy to Spain (2); Commissioner, Treaty of Paris, 1782–83; Secretary for Foreign Affairs (6). Co-author, The Federalist.

JOHNSON, THOMAS (1732–1819; Washington, 1791–1793). Md.Fed.—Md., Brigadier-General, Militia (1); Legislature (5); Governor (2); Chief Judge, General Court (1).

JOHNSON, WILLIAM (1771–1834; Jefferson, 1804–1834). S.C.Rep.—S.C., Legislature (4); Judge, Court of Common Pleas (6).

KAGAN, ELENA (1960–____; Obama, 2010–____). Mass.Dem.—U.S., Associate Counsel to the President (1); Deputy Assistant to the President for Domestic Policy (2). Professor and Dean (10). U.S., Solicitor General (1).

KAVANAUGH, BRETT M. (2018–___; Trump, 2018–___). D.C.Rep.—Associate Counsel to the Office of Independent Counsel (3); Private practice (3); Associate Counsel to the President (2); Staff Secretary to the President (3); U.S., Judge, Court of Appeals (12).

KENNEDY, ANTHONY M. (1936–____; Reagan, 1988–2018). Calif.Rep.—Calif. Army National Guard (1). U.S., Judge, Court of Appeals (11).

LAMAR, JOSEPH R. (1857–1916; Taft, 1910–1916). Ga.Dem.—Ga., Legislature (3); Commissioner to Codify Laws (3); Associate Justice, Supreme Court (4). Private practice.

LAMAR, LUCIUS Q.C. (1825–1893; Cleveland, 1888–1893). Miss.Dem.—Ga., Legislature (2). U.S., House of Representatives (4). Draftsman, Mississippi Ordinance of Secession, 1861. C.S.A., Lt. Col. (1); Commissioner to Russia (1); Judge-Advocate, III Corps. Army of No. Va. (1). U.S., House of Representatives (4); Senate (8); Secretary of the Interior (3).

LIVINGSTON, (HENRY) BROCKHOLST (1757–1823; Jefferson, 1806–1823). N.Y.Rep.—Lt. Col., Continental Army. N.Y., Judge, Supreme Court (4).

LURTON, HORACE H. (1844–1914; Taft, 1909–1914). Tenn.Dem.—Sgt. Major, C.S.A. Tenn., Chancellor (3); Associate Justice and Chief Justice, Supreme Court (7). U.S., Judge, Circuit Court of Appeals (16).

*MARSHALL, JOHN (1755–1835; J. Adams, 1801–1835). Va.Fed.—Va., Legislature (7); U.S., Envoy to France (1); House of Representatives (1); Secretary of State (1).

MARSHALL, THURGOOD (1908–1993; L.B. Johnson, 1967–1991). N.Y.Dem.—Counsel, Legal Defense and Educational Fund, NAACP (21). U.S., Judge, Court of Appeals (4); Solicitor General (2).

MATTHEWS, STANLEY (1824–1889; Garfield, 1881–1889). Ohio Rep.— Ohio, Judge, Court of Common Pleas (2); Legislature (3). U.S., District Attorney (3). Col., Ohio Volunteers. Ohio, Judge, Superior Court (2). Counsel before Hayes-Tilden Electoral Commission, 1877. U.S., Senate (2). Private practice. His first appointment to the Court by Hayes in 1881 was not acted upon by the Senate.

McKENNA, JOSEPH (1843–1926; McKinley, 1898–1925). Calif.Rep.—Calif., District Attorney (2); Legislature (2). U.S., House of Representatives (7); Judge, Circuit Court of Appeals (5); Attorney General (1).

McKINLEY, JOHN (1780–1852; Van Buren, 1837–1852). Ala.Dem.— Legislature (4). U.S., Senate (5); House of Representatives (2); re-elected to Senate, but appointed to Court before taking seat.

McLEAN, JOHN (1785–1861; Jackson, 1829–1861). Ohio Dem.—U.S., House of Representatives (4). Ohio, Judge, Supreme Court (6). U.S., Commissioner, General Land Office (1); Postmaster-General (6).

McREYNOLDS, JAMES C. (1862–1946; Wilson, 1914–1941). Tenn.Dem.— U.S., Assistant Attorney General (4); Attorney General (1).

MILLER, SAMUEL F. (1816–1890; Lincoln, 1862–1890). Iowa Rep.— Physician. Private practice.

MINTON, SHERMAN (1890–1965; Truman, 1949–1956). Ind.Dem.—Capt., Inf., World War I. U.S., Senate (6); Judge, Court of Appeals (8).

MOODY, WILLIAM H. (1853–1917; T. Roosevelt, 1906–1910). Mass.Rep.—U.S., District Attorney (5), House of Representatives (7); Secretary of the Navy (2); Attorney General (2).

MOORE, ALFRED (1755–1810; J. Adams, 1799–1804). N.C.Fed.—N.C., Col. of Militia; Legislature (2); Attorney General (9). U.S. Commissioner, Treaty with Cherokee Nation (1); N.C., Judge, Superior Court (1).

MURPHY, FRANK (1893–1949; F.D. Roosevelt, 1940–1949). Mich.Dem.—Capt., Inf., World War I. U.S., Assistant U.S. Attorney (1). Mich., Judge, Recorder's Court (7). Mayor, Detroit, Mich. (3). U.S., Governor-General, and High Commissioner, P.I. (3). Mich., Governor (2). U.S., Attorney General (1).

NELSON, SAMUEL (1792–1873; Tyler, 1845–1872). N.Y.Dem.—N.Y., Judge, Circuit Court (8); Associate Justice, and Chief Justice, Supreme Court (14).

O'CONNOR, SANDRA DAY (1930–____; Reagan, 1981–2006). Ariz.Rep.—Calif., Deputy County Attorney (2); Ariz., Assistant Attorney General (4); Legislature (6); Judge, Superior Court (4); Court of Appeals (2).

PATERSON, WILLIAM (1745–1806; Washington, 1793–1806). N.J.Fed.—Signer, U.S. Constitution, 1787. N.J., Legislature (2); Attorney General (7). U.S., Senate (1). N.J., Governor (3). Reviser of English Pre-Revolutionary Statutes in Force in N.J.

PECKHAM, RUFUS W. (1838–1909; Cleveland, 1895–1909). N.Y.Dem.—N.Y., District Attorney (1); Justice, Supreme Court (3); Associate Judge, Court of Appeals (9).

PITNEY, MAHLON (1858–1924; Taft, 1912–1922). N.J.Rep.—U.S., House of Representatives (4). N.J., Legislature (2); Associate Justice, Supreme Court (7); Chancellor (4).

POWELL, LEWIS F. (1907–1998; Nixon, 1972–1987). Va.Dem.—Col., U.S.A.A.F., World War II. U.S., Special Assistant to the Attorney General on Selective Service (4). Va., Member, State Board of Education (8). Private practice.

REED, STANLEY F. (1884–1980; F.D. Roosevelt, 1938–1957). Ky.Dem.—Ky., Legislature (4). 1st Lt., U.S.A., World War I. U.S., General Counsel, Federal Farm Board (3); General Counsel, Reconstruction Finance Corporation (3); Solicitor General (3).

*REHNQUIST, WILLIAM H. (1924–2005; Nixon, later Reagan, 1972–2005). Ariz.Rep.—U.S.A.F., World War II. U.S., Assistant Attorney General, Office of Legal Counsel (3).

*ROBERTS, JOHN G. (1955–____; G.W. Bush 2005–____). D.C. Rep.—U.S., Special Assistant to Attorney General (1); Associate Counsel to the President (4); Principal Deputy Solicitor General (4). Private practice (14). U.S., Judge, Court of Appeals (2).

ROBERTS, OWEN J. (1875–1955; Hoover, 1930–1945). Pa.Rep.—Pa., Assistant District Attorney (3). U.S., Special Deputy Attorney General in Espionage Act Cases, World War I; Special Prosecutor, Oil Cases, 1924. Private practice.

*RUTLEDGE, JOHN (1739–1800; Washington, 1789–1791, and Washington, 1795). S.C.Fed.—Signer, U.S. Constitution, 1787. S.C., Legislature (18); Attorney General (1); President and Governor (6); Chancellor (7). [Between appointments to the Supreme Court: S.C., Chief Justice, Court of Common Pleas and Sessions (4).] He did not sit under his first appointment; he sat with a recess appointment as Chief Justice, but his regular appointment was rejected by the Senate.

RUTLEDGE, WILEY B. (1894–1949; F.D. Roosevelt, 1943–1949). Iowa Dem.—Mo., then Iowa, Member, National Conference of Commissioners on Uniform State Laws (10). U.S., Judge, Court of Appeals (4).

SANFORD, EDWARD T. (1865–1930; Harding, 1923–1930). Tenn.Rep.— U.S., Assistant Attorney General (1); Judge, District Court (15).

SCALIA, ANTONIN (1936–2016; Reagan, 1986–2016). Va.Rep.—U.S., General Counsel, Office of Telecommunications Policy (1); Chairman, Administrative Conference of the United States (2); Assistant Attorney General, Office of Legal Counsel (3); Judge, Court of Appeals (4).

SHIRAS, GEORGE (1832–1924; B. Harrison, 1892–1903). Pa.Rep.—Private practice.

SOTOMAYOR, SONIA M. (1954–____; Obama, 2009–____). N.Y.Dem.—N.Y., Assistant District Attorney (4). U.S., Judge, District Court (6); Court of Appeals (11).

SOUTER, DAVID H. (1939–____; G.H.W. Bush, 1990–2009). N.H.Rep.—N.H., Assistant Attorney General (3); Deputy Attorney General (5); Attorney General (2); Associate Justice, Superior Court (5); Associate Justice, Supreme Court (7). U.S., Judge, Court of Appeals (½).

STEVENS, JOHN PAUL (1920–____; Ford, 1975–2010). Ill.Independent.— U.S.N.R., World War II. U.S., Associate Counsel, Subcommittee on the Study of Monopoly Power, Committee on the Judiciary, House of Representatives (1); Member, Attorney General's National Committee to Study the Antitrust Laws (2). Ill., Chief Counsel, Special Commission of the Supreme Court. U.S., Judge, Court of Appeals (5).

STEWART, POTTER (1915–1985; Eisenhower, 1958–1981). Ohio Rep.—Lt., U.S.N.R., World War II. U.S., Judge, Court of Appeals (4).

*STONE, HARLAN F. (1872–1946; Coolidge, later F.D. Roosevelt, 1925–1946). N.Y.Rep.—U.S., Attorney General (1). Chief Justice, 1941–1946.

STORY, JOSEPH (1779–1845; Madison, 1811–1845). Mass.Rep.—Mass., Legislature (5). U.S., House of Representatives (2). Private practice.

STRONG, WILLIAM (1808–1895; Grant, 1870–1880). Pa.Rep.—U.S., House of Representatives (4). Pa., Justice, Supreme Court (11). Private practice.

SUTHERLAND, GEORGE (1862–1942; Harding, 1922–1938). Utah Rep.—Utah, Legislature (4). U.S., House of Representatives (2); Senate (12). Private practice.

SWAYNE, NOAH H. (1804–1884; Lincoln, 1862–1881). Ohio Rep.—Ohio, County Attorney (4); Legislature (2). U.S., District Attorney (9). Private practice.

*TAFT, WILLIAM H. (1857–1930; Harding, 1921–1930). Conn.Rep.—U.S., Collector of Internal Revenue (1). Ohio, Judge, Superior Court (3). U.S., Solicitor General (2); Judge, Circuit Court of Appeals (8); Governor-General, P.I. (3); Secretary of War (4); President (4). Professor.

*TANEY, ROGER B. (1777–1864; Jackson, 1836–1864). Md.Dem.—Md., Legislature (7); Attorney General (2). U.S., Attorney General (2), Secretary of the Treasury (¾; rejected by the Senate). Private practice.

THOMAS, CLARENCE (1948–____; G.H.W. Bush, 1991–____). Ga.Rep.—Mo., Assistant Attorney General (3). U.S., Legislative Assistant (2); Assistant Secretary for Civil Rights, Department of Education (1); Chairman, Equal Employment Opportunity Commission (8); Judge, Court of Appeals (1).

THOMPSON, SMITH (1768–1843; Monroe, 1823–1843). N.Y.Rep.—N.Y., Legislature (2); Associate Justice, and Chief Justice, Supreme Court (16). U.S., Secretary of the Navy (4).

TODD, THOMAS (1765–1826; Jefferson, 1807–1826). Ky.Rep.—Ky., Judge, and Chief Justice, Court of Appeals (6).

TRIMBLE, ROBERT (1777–1828; J.Q. Adams, 1826–1828). Ky.Rep.—Ky., Legislature (2). Judge, Court of Appeals (2). U.S., District Attorney (4); Judge, District Court (9).

VAN DEVANTER, WILLIS (1859–1941; Taft, 1910–1937). Wyo.Rep.—Wyo., Legislature (2); Chief Justice, Supreme Court (1). U.S., Assistant Attorney General (Interior Department) (6); Judge, Circuit Court of Appeals (7).

*VINSON, FRED M. (1890–1953; Truman, 1946–1953). Ky.Dem.—Ky., Commonwealth Attorney (3). U.S., House of Representatives (14); Judge, Court of Appeals (5); Director, Office of Economic Stabilization (2); Federal Loan Administrator (1 mo.); Director, Office of War Mobilization and Reconversion (3 mo.); Secretary of the Treasury (1).

*WAITE, MORRISON R. (1816–1888; Grant, 1874–1888). Ohio Rep.—Ohio, Legislature (2). Counsel for United States, U.S.—Gr. Brit. Arbitration ("Alabama" Claims), 1871–72. Private practice.

*WARREN, EARL (1891–1974; Eisenhower, 1953–1969). Calif.Rep.—1st Lt., Inf., World War I. Deputy City Attorney (1); Deputy District Attorney (5); District Attorney (14); Attorney General (4); Governor (10).

WASHINGTON, BUSHROD (1762–1829; J. Adams, 1798–1829). Pa.Fed.—Va., Legislature (1). Private practice.

WAYNE, JAMES M. (1790–1867; Jackson, 1835–1867). Ga.Dem.—Ga., Officer, Hussars, War of 1812; Legislature (2). Mayor of Savannah, Ga. (2). Ga., Judge, Superior Court (5). U.S., House of Representatives (6).

WHITE, BYRON R. (1917–2002; Kennedy, 1962–1993). Colo.Dem.—U.S.N.R., World War II. U.S., Deputy Attorney General (1).

*WHITE, EDWARD D. (1845–1921; Cleveland, later Taft, 1894–1921). La.Dem.—La., Legislature (4); Justice, Supreme Court (2). U.S., Senate (3). Chief Justice, 1910–1921.

WHITTAKER, CHARLES E. (1901–1973; Eisenhower, 1957–1962). Mo.Rep.—U.S., Judge, District Court (2); Court of Appeals (1).

WILSON, JAMES (1724–1798; Washington, 1789–1798). Pa.Fed.—Signer, U.S. Declaration of Independence, 1776, and U.S. Constitution, 1787. Although he was strongly interested in western-land development companies for several years prior to his appointment, his primary activity in the period immediately preceding his appointment was in obtaining ratification of the Federal and Pennsylvania Constitutions.

WOODBURY, LEVI (1789–1851; Polk, 1845–1851). N.H. Dem.—N.H., Associate Justice, Superior Court (6); Governor (2); Legislature (1). U.S., Senate (6); Secretary of the Navy (3); Secretary of the Treasury (7); Senate (4).

WOODS, WILLIAM B. (1824–1887; Hayes, 1880–1887). Ga.Rep.—Mayor, Newark, Oh. (1). Ohio, Legislature (4). Brevet Major General, U.S. Vol., Civil War. Ala., Chancellor (1). U.S., Judge, Circuit Court (11).

Year	CJ	SEAT 1	SEAT 2	SEAT 3	SEAT 4	SEAT 5	SEAT 6	SEAT 7	SEAT 8	SEAT 9	SEAT 10
1789	Jay	Rutledge, J.	Cushing	Wilson	Blair						
1790						Iredell					
1791		Johnson, T.									
1793		Paterson									
1795	Rutledge, J.										
1796	Ellsworth				Chase, Samuel						
1798				Washington							
1799						Moore					
1801	Marshall, J.										
1804						Johnson, W.					
1806		Livingston									
Established February 24, 1807							**SEAT 6**				
1807							Todd				
1811			Story		Duval						
1823		Thompson									
1826							Trimble				
1829							McLean				
1830				Baldwin							
1835						Wayne					
1836	Taney				Barbour						
Established March 3, 1837								**SEAT 7**	**SEAT 8**	**SEAT 9**	
1837								Catron	McKinley		
1841					Daniel						
1845		Nelson	Woodbury								
1846				Grier							
1851			Curtis								
1853									Campbell		
1858			Clifford								
1862					Miller		Swayne		Davis		
1863										Field [1]	
1864	Chase, Salmon										
1865								1			
1866								Abolished			
1867						[1] Abolished					
Established April 10, 1869											**SEAT 10**
1870				Strong							Bradley
1872		Hunt									
1874	Waite										
1877									Harlan		
1880				Woods							

1 Catron (Seat 7) died in 1865, and Wayne (Seat 5) in 1867; their positions were abolished by Congress to prevent their being filled by President Johnson. Seat 10 was created in 1869, which traditionally has been regarded as a re-creation of Wayne's seat. Congress has left the Court's size at nine (Chief Justice and 8 Associate Justices) since then.

YEAR	CJ (1)	SEAT 1	SEAT 2	SEAT 3	SEAT 4	SEAT 5	SEAT 6	SEAT 7	SEAT 8	SEAT 9	SEAT 10
1881			Gray				Matthews				
1882		Blatchford									
1888	FULLER			Lamar, L.							
1889							Brewer				
1890					Brown						
1892											Shiras
1893				Jackson, H.							
1894		WHITE, E.									
1895				Peckham							
1898										McKenna	
1902			Holmes								
1903											Day
1906					Moody						
1909				Lurton							
1910	WHITE, E.[2]	Van Devanter			Lamar		Hughes				
1912									Pitney		
1914				McReynolds							
1916					Brandeis		Clarke				
1921	TAFT										
1922							Sutherland				Butler
1923									Sanford		
1925										STONE	
1930	HUGHES								Roberts, O.		
1932			Cardozo								
1937		Black									
1938							Reed				
1939			Frankfurter		Douglas						
1940											Murphy
1941	STONE[3]			Byrnes						Jackson, R.	
1943				Rutledge							
1945									Burton		
1946	VINSON										
1949				Minton							Clark
1953	WARREN										
1955										Harlan	
1956				Brennan							
1957							Whittaker				
1958									Stewart		
1962			Goldberg				White, B.				
1965			Fortas								
1967											Marshall, T.

2   Fuller died in 1910 and White was named Chief Justice.

3   Hughes resigned in 1941, and Stone was named Chief Justice.

YEAR	CJ (1)	SEAT 1	SEAT 2	SEAT 3	SEAT 4	SEAT 5	SEAT 6	SEAT 7	SEAT 8	SEAT 9	SEAT 10
1969	BURGER										
1970			Blackmun								
1972		Powell								REHNQUIST	
1975					Stevens						
1981									O'Connor		
1986	REHNQUIST [4]									Scalia	
1987											
1988		KENNEDY									
1989											
1990				Souter							
1991											THOMAS, C.
1993							GINSBURG				
1994			BREYER								
2005	ROBERTS, J.										
2006									ALITO		
2009				SOTOMAYOR							
2010					KAGAN						
2016										[5]	
2017										GORSUCH	
2018		KAVANAUGH									
2020							BARRETT [6]				

4 Burger resigned in 1986 and Rehnquist was named Chief Justice.

5 Scalia died in 2016. His seat was held open by Congress until after the 2016 election and then filled in 2017 by Gorsuch.

6 Ginsburg died in 2020 and Barrett was named as her replacement.

APPENDIX B

THE CONSTITUTION OF THE U.S.

■ ■ ■

We the People of the United States, in Order to form a more perfect Union, establish Justice, insure domestic Tranquility, provide for the common defence, promote the general Welfare, and secure the Blessings of Liberty to ourselves and our Posterity, do ordain and establish this Constitution for the United States of America.

ARTICLE I

Section 1. All legislative Powers herein granted shall be vested in a Congress of the United States, which shall consist of a Senate and House of Representatives.

Section 2. [1] The House of Representatives shall be composed of Members chosen every second Year by the People of the several States, and the Electors in each State shall have the Qualifications requisite for Electors of the most numerous Branch of the State Legislature.

[2] No Person shall be a Representative who shall not have attained to the Age of twenty five Years, and been seven Years a Citizen of the United States, and who shall not, when elected, be an Inhabitant of that State in which he shall be chosen.

[3] Representatives and direct Taxes shall be apportioned among the several States which may be included within this Union, according to their respective Numbers, which shall be determined by adding to the whole Number of free Persons, including those bound to Service for a Term of Years, and excluding Indians not taxed, three fifths of all other Persons. The actual Enumeration shall be made within three Years after the first Meeting of the Congress of the United States, and within every subsequent Term of ten Years, in such Manner as they shall by Law direct. The Number of Representatives shall not exceed one for every thirty Thousand, but each State shall have at Least one Representative; and until such enumeration shall be made, the State of New Hampshire shall be entitled to chuse three, Massachusetts eight, Rhode Island and Providence Plantations one, Connecticut five, New York six, New Jersey four, Pennsylvania eight, Delaware one, Maryland six, Virginia ten, North Carolina five, South Carolina five, and Georgia three.

[4] When vacancies happen in the Representation from any State, the Executive Authority thereof shall issue Writs of Election to fill such Vacancies.

[5]   The House of Representatives shall chuse their Speaker and other Officers; and shall have the sole Power of Impeachment.

Section 3. [1] The Senate of the United States shall be composed of two Senators from each State, chosen by the Legislature thereof, for six Years; and each Senator shall have one Vote.

[2]   Immediately after they shall be assembled in Consequence of the first Election, they shall be divided as equally as may be into three Classes. The Seats of the Senators of the first Class shall be vacated at the Expiration of the Second Year, of the second Class at the Expiration of the fourth Year, and of the third Class at the Expiration of the sixth Year, so that one third may be chosen every second Year; and if Vacancies happen by Resignation, or otherwise, during the Recess of the Legislature of any State, the Executive thereof may make temporary Appointments until the next Meeting of the Legislature, which shall then fill such Vacancies.

[3]   No Person shall be a Senator who shall not have attained to the Age of thirty Years, and been nine Years a Citizen of the United States, and who shall not, when elected, by an Inhabitant of that State for which he shall be chosen.

[4]   The Vice President of the United States shall be President of the Senate, but shall have no Vote, unless they be equally divided.

[5]   The Senate shall chuse their other Officers, and also a President pro tempore, in the Absence of the Vice President, or when he shall exercise the Office of President of the United States.

[6]   The Senate shall have the sole Power to try all Impeachments. When sitting for that Purpose, they shall be on Oath or Affirmation. When the President of the United States is tried, the Chief Justice shall preside: And no Person shall be convicted without the Concurrence of two thirds of the Members present.

[7]   Judgment in Cases of Impeachment shall not extend further than to removal from Office, and disqualification to hold and enjoy any Office of honor, Trust, or Profit under the United States: but the Party convicted shall nevertheless be liable and subject to Indictment, Trial, Judgment, and Punishment, according to Law.

Section 4. [1] The Times, Places and Manner of holding Elections for Senators and Representatives, shall be prescribed in each State by the Legislature thereof; but the Congress may at any time by Law make or alter such Regulations, except as to the Places of chusing Senators.

[2]   The Congress shall assemble at least once in every Year, and such Meeting shall be on the first Monday in December, unless they shall by Law appoint a different Day.

Section 5. [1] Each House shall be the Judge of the Elections, Returns, and Qualifications of its own Members, and a Majority of each shall constitute a Quorum to do Business; but a smaller Number may adjourn from day to day, and may be authorized to compel the Attendance of absent Members, in such Manner, and under such Penalties as each House may provide.

[2]   Each House may determine the Rules of its Proceedings, punish its Members for disorderly Behavior, and, with the Concurrence of two thirds, expel a Member.

[3]   Each House shall keep a Journal of its Proceedings, and from time to time publish the same, excepting such Parts as may in their Judgment require Secrecy; and the Yeas and Nays of the Members of either House on any question shall, at the Desire of one fifth of those Present, be entered on the Journal.

[4]   Neither House, during the Session of Congress, shall without the Consent of the other, adjourn for more than three days, nor to any other Place than that in which the two Houses shall be sitting.

Section 6. [1] The Senators and Representatives shall receive a Compensation for their Services, to be ascertained by Law, and paid out of the Treasury of the United States. They shall in all Cases, except Treason, Felony and Breach of the Peace, be privileged from Arrest during their Attendance at the Session of their respective Houses, and in going to and returning from the same; and for any Speech or Debate in either House, they shall not be questioned in any other Place.

[2]   No Senator or Representative shall, during the Time for which he was elected, be appointed to any civil Office under the Authority of the United States, which shall have been created, or the Emoluments whereof shall have been increased during such time; and no Person holding any Office under the United States, shall be a Member of either House during his Continuance in Office.

Section 7. [1] All Bills for raising Revenue shall originate in the House of Representatives; but the Senate may propose or concur with Amendments as on other Bills.

[2]   Every Bill which shall have passed the House of Representatives and the Senate, shall, before it become a Law, be presented to the President of the United States; If he approve he shall sign it, but if not he shall return it, with his Objections to the House in which it shall have originated, who shall enter the Objections at large on their Journal, and proceed to reconsider it. If after such Reconsideration two thirds of that House shall agree to pass the Bill, it shall be sent together with the Objections, to the other House, by which it shall likewise be reconsidered, and if approved by two thirds of that House, it shall become a Law. But in all such Cases the Votes of both Houses shall be determined by yeas and Nays, and the Names of the Persons voting for and against the Bill shall be entered on the Journal of each House respectively. If any Bill shall not be returned by the President within ten Days (Sundays excepted) after it shall have been presented to him, the Same shall be a Law, in like Manner as if he had signed it, unless the Congress by their Adjournment prevent its Return in which Case it shall not be a Law.

[3] Every Order, Resolution, or Vote, to Which the Concurrence of the Senate and House of Representatives may be necessary (except on a question of Adjournment) shall be presented to the President of the United States; and before the Same shall take Effect, shall be approved by him, or being disapproved by him, shall be repassed by two thirds of the Senate and House of Representatives, according to the Rules and Limitations prescribed in the Case of a Bill.

Section 8. [1] The Congress shall have Power To lay and collect Taxes, Duties, Imposts and Excises, to pay the Debts and provide for the common Defence and general Welfare of the United States; but all Duties, Imposts and Excises shall be uniform throughout the United States;

[2] To borrow money on the credit of the United States;

[3] To regulate Commerce with foreign Nations, and among the several States, and with the Indian Tribes;

[4] To establish an uniform Rule of Naturalization, and uniform Laws on the subject of Bankruptcies throughout the United States;

[5] To coin Money, regulate the Value thereof, and of foreign Coin, and fix the Standard of Weights and Measures;

[6] To provide for the Punishment of counterfeiting the Securities and current Coin of the United States;

[7] To Establish Post Offices and Post Roads;

[8] To promote the Progress of Science and useful Arts, by securing for limited Times to Authors and Inventors the exclusive Right to their respective Writings and Discoveries;

[9] To constitute Tribunals inferior to the supreme Court;

[10] To define and punish Piracies and Felonies committed on the high Seas, and Offenses against the Law of Nations;

[11] To declare War, grant Letters of Marque and Reprisal, and make Rules concerning Captures on Land and Water;

[12] To raise and support Armies, but no Appropriation of Money to that Use shall be for a longer Term than two Years;

[13] To provide and maintain a Navy;

[14] To make Rules for the Government and Regulation of the land and naval Forces;

[15] To provide for calling forth the Militia to execute the Laws of the Union, suppress Insurrections and repel Invasions;

[16] To provide for organizing, arming, and disciplining, the Militia, and for governing such Part of them as may be employed in the Service of the United States, reserving to the States respectively, the Appointment of the Officers, and

the Authority of training the Militia according to the discipline prescribed by Congress;

[17] To exercise exclusive Legislation in all Cases whatsoever, over such District (not exceeding ten Miles square) as may, by Cession of particular States, and the Acceptance of Congress, become the Seat of the Government of the United States, and to exercise like Authority over all Places purchased by the Consent of the Legislature of the State in which the Same shall be, for the Erection of Forts, Magazines, Arsenals, dock-Yards, and other needful Buildings;—And

[18] To make all Laws which shall be necessary and proper for carrying into Execution the foregoing Powers, and all other Powers vested by this Constitution in the Government of the United States, or in any Department or Officer thereof.

Section 9. [1] The Migration or Importation of Such Persons as any of the States now existing shall think proper to admit, shall not be prohibited by the Congress prior to the Year one thousand eight hundred and eight, but a Tax or duty may be imposed on such Importation, not exceeding ten dollars for each Person.

[2] The privilege of the Writ of Habeas Corpus shall not be suspended, unless when in Cases of Rebellion or Invasion the public Safety may require it.

[3] No Bill of Attainder or ex post facto Law shall be passed.

[4] No Capitation, or other direct, Tax shall be laid, unless in Proportion to the Census or Enumeration herein before directed to be taken.

[5] No Tax or Duty shall be laid on Articles exported from any State.

[6] No Preference shall be given by any Regulation of Commerce or Revenue to the Ports of one State over those of another: nor shall Vessels bound to, or from, one State be obliged to enter, clear, or pay Duties in another.

[7] No money shall be drawn from the Treasury, but in Consequence of Appropriations made by Law; and a regular Statement and Account of the Receipts and Expenditures of all public Money shall be published from time to time.

[8] No Title of Nobility shall be granted by the United States: And no Person holding any Office of Profit or Trust under them, shall, without the Consent of the Congress, accept of any present, Emolument, Office, or Title, of any kind whatever, from any King, Prince, or foreign State.

Section 10. [1] No State shall enter into any Treaty, Alliance, or Confederation; grant Letters of Marque and Reprisal; coin Money; emit Bills of Credit; make any Thing but gold and silver Coin a Tender in Payment of Debts; pass any Bill of Attainder, ex post facto Law, or Law impairing the Obligation of Contracts, or grant any Title of Nobility.

[2] No State shall, without the Consent of the Congress, lay any Imposts or Duties on Imports or Exports, except what may be absolutely necessary for executing it's inspection Laws: and the net Produce of all Duties and Imposts, laid

by any State on Imports or Exports, shall be for the Use of the Treasury of the United States; and all such Laws shall be subject to the Revision and Controul of the Congress.

[3] No State shall, without the Consent of Congress, lay any Duty of Tonnage, keep Troops, or Ships of War in time of Peace, enter into any Agreement or Compact with another State, or with a foreign Power, or engage in War, unless actually invaded, or in such imminent Danger as will not admit of delay.

ARTICLE II

Section 1. [1] The executive Power shall be vested in a President of the United States of America. He shall hold his Office during the Term of four Years, and, together with the Vice President, chosen for the same Term, be elected, as follows:

[2] Each State shall appoint, in such Manner as the Legislature thereof may direct, a Number of Electors, equal to the whole Number of Senators and Representatives to which the State may be entitled in the Congress; but no Senator or Representative, or Person holding an Office of Trust or Profit under the United States, shall be appointed an Elector.

[3] The Electors shall meet in their respective States, and vote by Ballot for two Persons, of whom one at least shall not be an Inhabitant of the same State with themselves. And they shall make a List of all the Persons voted for, and of the Number of Votes for each; which List they shall sign and certify, and transmit sealed to the Seat of the Government of the United States, directed to the President of the Senate. The President of the Senate shall, in the Presence of the Senate and House of Representatives, open all the Certificates, and the Votes shall then be counted. The Person having the greatest Number of Votes shall be the President, if such Number be a Majority of the whole Number of Electors appointed; and if there be more than one who have such Majority, and have an equal Number of Votes, then the House of Representatives shall immediately chuse by Ballot one of them for President; and if no Person have a Majority, then from the five highest on the List the said House shall in like Manner chuse the President. But in chusing the President, the Votes shall be taken by States the Representation from each State having one Vote; A quorum for this Purpose shall consist of a Member or Members from two thirds of the States, and a Majority of all the States shall be necessary to a Choice. In every Case, after the Choice of the President, the Person having the greater Number of Votes of the Electors shall be the Vice President. But if there should remain two or more who have equal Votes, the Senate shall chuse from them by Ballot the Vice President.

[4] The Congress may determine the Time of chusing the Electors, and the Day on which they shall give their Votes; which Day shall be the same throughout the United States.

[5] No person except a natural born Citizen, or a Citizen of the United States, at the time of the Adoption of this Constitution, shall be eligible to the Office of President; neither shall any Person be eligible to that Office who shall not have

attained to the Age of thirty five Years, and been fourteen Years a Resident within the United States.

[6]   In case of the removal of the President from Office, or of his Death, Resignation or Inability to discharge the Powers and Duties of the said Office, the Same shall devolve on the Vice President, and the Congress may by Law provide for the Case of Removal, Death, Resignation or Inability, both of the President and Vice President, declaring what Officer shall then act as President, and such Officer shall act accordingly, until the Disability be removed, or a President shall be elected.

[7]   The President shall, at stated Times, receive for his Services, a Compensation, which shall neither be increased nor diminished during the Period for which he shall have been elected, and he shall not receive within that Period any other Emolument from the United States, or any of them.

[8]   Before he enter on the Execution of his Office, he shall take the following Oath or Affirmation: "I do solemnly swear (or affirm) that I will faithfully execute the Office of President of the United States, and will to the best of my Ability, preserve, protect and defend the Constitution of the United States."

Section 2. [1] The President shall be Commander in Chief of the Army and Navy of the United States, and of the militia of the several States, when called into the actual Service of the United States; he may require the Opinion, in writing, of the principal Officer in each of the Executive Departments, upon any Subject relating to the Duties of their respective Offices, and he shall have Power to grant Reprieves and Pardons for Offenses against the United States, except in Cases of Impeachment.

[2]   He shall have Power, by and with the Advice and Consent of the Senate to make Treaties, provided two thirds of the Senators present concur; and he shall nominate, and by and with the Advice and Consent of the Senate, shall appoint Ambassadors, other public Ministers and Consuls, Judges of the supreme Court, and all other Officers of the United States, whose Appointments are not herein otherwise provided for, and which shall be established by Law; but the Congress may by Law vest the Appointment of such inferior Officers, as they think proper, in the President alone, in the Courts of Law, or in the Heads of Departments.

[3]   The President shall have Power to fill up all Vacancies that may happen during the Recess of the Senate, by granting Commissions which shall expire at the End of their next Session.

Section 3. He shall from time to time give to the Congress Information of the State of the Union, and recommend to their Consideration such Measures as he shall judge necessary and expedient; he may, on extraordinary Occasions, convene both Houses, or either of them, and in Case of Disagreement between them, with Respect to the Time of Adjournment, he may adjourn them to such Time as he shall think proper; he shall receive Ambassadors and other public Ministers; he shall take Care that the Laws be faithfully executed, and shall Commission all the Officers of the United States.

Section 4. The President, Vice President and all civil Officers of the United States, shall be removed from Office on Impeachment for, and Conviction of, Treason, Bribery, or other high Crimes and Misdemeanors.

ARTICLE III

Section 1. The judicial Power of the United States, shall be vested in one supreme Court, and in such inferior Courts as the Congress may from time to time ordain and establish. The Judges, both of the supreme and inferior Courts, shall hold their Offices during good Behaviour, and shall, at stated Times, receive for their Services a Compensation, which shall not be diminished during their Continuance in Office.

Section 2. [1] The judicial Power shall extend to all Cases, in Law and Equity, arising under this Constitution, the Laws of the United States, and Treaties made, or which shall be made, under their Authority;—to all Cases affecting Ambassadors, other public Ministers and Consuls;—to all Cases of admiralty and maritime Jurisdiction;—to Controversies to which the United States shall be a Party;—to Controversies between two or more States;—between a State and Citizens of another State;—between Citizens of different States;—between Citizens of the same State claiming Lands under the Grants of different States, and between a State, or the Citizens thereof, and foreign States, Citizens or Subjects.

[2] In all Cases affecting Ambassadors, other public Ministers and Consuls, and those in which a State shall be a Party, the supreme Court shall have original Jurisdiction. In all the other Cases before mentioned, the supreme Court shall have appellate Jurisdiction, both as to Law and Fact, with such Exceptions, and under such Regulations as the Congress shall make.

[3] The trial of all Crimes, except in Cases of Impeachment, shall be by Jury; and such Trial shall be held in the State where the said Crimes shall have been committed; but when not committed within any State, the Trial shall be at such Place or Places as the Congress may by Law have directed.

Section 3. [1] Treason against the United States, shall consist only in levying War against them, or, in adhering to their Enemies, giving them Aid and Comfort. No Person shall be convicted of Treason unless on the Testimony of two Witnesses to the same overt Act, or on Confession in open Court.

[2] The Congress shall have Power to declare the Punishment of Treason, but no Attainder of Treason shall work Corruption of Blood, or Forfeiture except during the Life of the Person attainted.

ARTICLE IV

Section 1. Full Faith and Credit shall be given in each State to the public Acts, Records, and judicial Proceedings of every other State. And the Congress may by general Laws prescribe the Manner in which such Acts, Records and Proceedings shall be proved, and the Effect thereof.

Section 2. [1] The Citizens of each State shall be entitled to all Privileges and Immunities of Citizens in the several States.

[2]   A Person charged in any State with Treason, Felony, or other Crime, who shall flee from Justice, and be found in another State, shall on demand of the executive Authority of the State from which he fled, be delivered up, to be removed to the State having Jurisdiction of the Crime.

[3]   No Person held to Service or Labour in one State, under the Laws thereof, escaping into another, shall, in Consequence of any Law or Regulation therein, be discharged from such Service or Labour, but shall be delivered up on Claim of the Party to whom such Service or Labour may be due.

Section 3. [1] New States may be admitted by the Congress into this Union; but no new State shall be formed or erected within the Jurisdiction of any other State; nor any State be formed by the Junction of two or more States, or Parts of States, without the Consent of the Legislatures of the States concerned as well as of the Congress.

[2]   The Congress shall have Power to dispose of and make all needful Rules and Regulations respecting the Territory or other Property belonging to the United States; and nothing in this Constitution shall be so construed as to Prejudice any Claims of the United States, or of any particular State.

Section 4. The United States shall guarantee to every State in this Union a Republican Form of Government, and shall protect each of them against Invasion; and on Application of the Legislature, or of the Executive (when the Legislature cannot be convened) against domestic Violence.

ARTICLE V

The Congress, whenever two thirds of both Houses shall deem it necessary, shall propose Amendments to this Constitution, or, on the Application of the Legislatures of two thirds of the several States, shall call a Convention for proposing Amendments, which, in either Case, shall be valid to all Intents and Purposes, as part of this Constitution, when ratified by the Legislatures of three fourths of the several States, or by Conventions in three fourths thereof, as the one or the other Mode of Ratification may be proposed by the Congress; Provided that no Amendment which may be made prior to the Year One thousand eight hundred and eight shall in any Manner affect the first and fourth Clauses in the Ninth Section of the first Article; and that no State, without its Consent, shall be deprived of its equal Suffrage in the Senate.

ARTICLE VI

[1]   All Debts contracted and Engagements entered into, before the Adoption of this Constitution shall be as valid against the United States under this Constitution, as under the Confederation.

[2] This Constitution, and the Laws of the United States which shall be made in Pursuance thereof; and all Treaties made, or which shall be made, under the Authority of the United States, shall be the supreme Law of the Land; and the Judges in every State shall be bound thereby, any Thing in the Constitution or Laws of any State to the Contrary notwithstanding.

[3] The Senators and Representatives before mentioned, and the Members of the several State Legislatures, and all executive and judicial Officers, both of the United States and of the several States, shall be bound by Oath or Affirmation, to support this Constitution; but no religious Test shall ever be required as a Qualification to any Office or public Trust under the United States.

ARTICLE VII

The Ratification of the Conventions of nine States shall be sufficient for the Establishment of this Constitution between the States so ratifying the Same.

AMENDMENTS OF THE CONSTITUTION OF THE UNITED STATES OF AMERICA, PROPOSED BY CONGRESS AND RATIFIED BY THE LEGISLATURES OF THE SEVERAL STATES PURSUANT TO THE FIFTH ARTICLE OF THE ORIGINAL CONSTITUTION.

AMENDMENT I [1791]

Congress shall make no law respecting an establishment of religion, or prohibiting the free exercise thereof; or abridging the freedom of speech, or of the press; or the right of the people peaceably to assemble, and to petition the Government for a redress of grievances.

AMENDMENT II [1791]

A well regulated Militia, being necessary to the security of a free State, the right of the people to keep and bear Arms, shall not be infringed.

AMENDMENT III [1791]

No Soldier shall, in time of peace be quartered in any house, without the consent of the Owner, nor in time of war, but in a manner to be prescribed by law.

AMENDMENT IV [1791]

The right of the people to be secure in their persons, houses, papers, and effects, against unreasonable searches and seizures, shall not be violated, and no Warrants shall issue, but upon probable cause, supported by Oath or affirmation and particularly describing the place to be searched, and the persons or things to be seized.

AMENDMENT V [1791]

No person shall be held to answer for a capital, or otherwise infamous crime, unless on a presentment or indictment of a Grand Jury, except in cases arising in the land or naval forces, or in the Militia, when in actual service in time of War or public danger; nor shall any person be subject for the same offence to be twice put in jeopardy of life or limb; nor shall be compelled in any criminal case to be a witness against himself, nor be deprived of life, liberty, or property, without due process of law; nor shall private property be taken for public use, without just compensation.

AMENDMENT VI [1791]

In all criminal prosecutions, the accused shall enjoy the right to a speedy and public trial, by an impartial jury of the State and district wherein the crime shall have been committed, which district shall have been previously ascertained by law, and to be informed of the nature and cause of the accusation; to be confronted with the witnesses against him; to have compulsory process for obtaining witnesses in his favor, and to have the Assistance of Counsel for his defence.

AMENDMENT VII [1791]

In Suits at common law, where the value in controversy shall exceed twenty dollars, the right of trial by jury shall be preserved, and no fact tried by jury, shall be otherwise re-examined in any Court of the United States, than according to the rules of the common law.

AMENDMENT VIII [1791]

Excessive bail shall not be required, nor excessive fines imposed, nor cruel and unusual punishments inflicted.

AMENDMENT IX [1791]

The enumeration in the Constitution, of certain rights, shall not be construed to deny or disparage others retained by the people.

AMENDMENT X [1791]

The powers not delegated to the United States by the Constitution, nor prohibited by it to the States, are reserved to the States respectively, or to the people.

AMENDMENT XI [1798]

The Judicial power of the United States shall not be construed to extend to any suit in law or equity, commenced or prosecuted against one of the United States by Citizens of another State, or by Citizens or Subjects of any Foreign State.

AMENDMENT XII [1804]

The Electors shall meet in their respective states and vote by ballot for President and Vice-President, one of whom, at least, shall not be an inhabitant of the same state with themselves; they shall name in their ballots the person voted for as President, and in distinct ballots the person voted for as Vice-President, and they shall make distinct lists of all persons voted for as President, and of all persons voted for as Vice-President, and of the number of votes for each, which lists they shall sign and certify, and transmit sealed to the seat of the government of the United States, directed to the President of the Senate;—The President of the Senate shall, in the presence of the Senate and House of Representatives, open all the certificates and the votes shall then be counted;—The person having the greatest number of votes for President, shall be the President, if such number be a majority of the whole number of Electors appointed; and if no person have such majority, then from the persons having the highest numbers not exceeding three on the list of those voted for as President, the House of Representatives shall choose immediately, by ballot, the President. But in choosing the President, the votes shall be taken by states, the representation from each state having one vote; a quorum for this purpose shall consist of a member or members from two-thirds of the states, and a majority of all the states shall be necessary to a choice. And if the House of Representatives shall not choose a President whenever the right of choice shall devolve upon them before the fourth day of March next following, then the Vice-President shall act as President, as in the case of the death or other constitutional disability of the President.—The person having the greatest number of votes as Vice-President, shall be the Vice-President, if such number be a majority of the whole number of Electors appointed, and if no person have a majority, then from the two highest numbers on the list, the Senate shall choose the Vice-President; a quorum for the purpose shall consist of two-thirds of the whole number of Senators, and a majority of the whole number shall be necessary to a choice. But no person constitutionally ineligible to the office of President shall be eligible to that of Vice-President of the United States.

AMENDMENT XIII [1865]

Section 1. Neither slavery nor involuntary servitude, except as a punishment for crime whereof the party shall have been duly convicted, shall exist within the United States, or any place subject to their jurisdiction.

Section 2. Congress shall have power to enforce this article by appropriate legislation.

AMENDMENT XIV [1868]

Section 1. All persons born or naturalized in the United States, and subject to the jurisdiction thereof, are citizens of the United States and of the State wherein they reside. No State shall make or enforce any law which shall abridge the privileges or immunities of citizens of the United States; nor shall any State deprive any person of life, liberty, or property, without due process of law; nor deny to any person within its jurisdiction the equal protection of the laws.

Section 2. Representatives shall be apportioned among the several States according to their respective numbers, counting the whole number of persons in each State, excluding Indians not taxed. But when the right to vote at any election for the choice of electors for President and Vice President of the United States, Representatives in Congress, the Executive and Judicial officers of a State, or the members of the Legislature thereof, is denied to any of the male inhabitants of such State, being twenty-one years of age, and citizens of the United States, or in any way abridged, except for participation in rebellion, or other crime, the basis of representation therein shall be reduced in the proportion which the number of such male citizens shall bear to the whole number of male citizens twenty-one years of age in such State.

Section 3. No person shall be a Senator or Representative in Congress, or elector of President and Vice President, or hold any office, civil or military, under the United States, or under any State, who having previously taken an oath, as a member of Congress, or as an officer of the United States, or as a member of any State legislature, or as an executive or judicial officer of any State, to support the Constitution of the United States, shall have engaged in insurrection or rebellion against the same, or given aid or comfort to the enemies thereof. But Congress may by a vote of two-thirds of each House, remove such disability.

Section 4. The validity of the public debt of the United States, authorized by law, including debts incurred for payment of pensions and bounties for services in suppressing insurrection or rebellion, shall not be questioned. But neither the United States nor any State shall assume or pay any debt or obligation incurred in aid of insurrection or rebellion against the United States, or any claim for the loss or emancipation of any slave; but all such debts, obligations and claims shall be held illegal and void.

Section 5. The Congress shall have power to enforce, by appropriate legislation, the provisions of this article.

AMENDMENT XV [1870]

Section 1. The right of citizens of the United States to vote shall not be denied or abridged by the United States or by any State on account of race, color, or previous condition of servitude.

Section 2. The Congress shall have power to enforce this article by appropriate legislation.

AMENDMENT XVI [1913]

The Congress shall have power to lay and collect taxes on incomes, from whatever source derived, without apportionment among the several States, and without regard to any census or enumeration.

AMENDMENT XVII [1913]

[1]   The Senate of the United States shall be composed of two Senators from each State, elected by the people thereof, for six years; and each Senator shall have one vote. The electors in each State shall have the qualifications requisite for electors of the most numerous branch of the State legislatures.

[2]   When vacancies happen in the representation of any State in the Senate, the executive authority of such State shall issue writs of election to fill such vacancies: *Provided,* That the legislature of any State may empower the executive thereof to make temporary appointments until the people fill the vacancies by election as the legislature may direct.

[3]   This amendment shall not be so construed as to affect the election or term of any Senator chosen before it becomes valid as part of the Constitution.

AMENDMENT XVIII [1919]

Section 1. After one year from the ratification of this article the manufacture, sale, or transportation of intoxicating liquors within, the importation thereof into, or the exportation thereof from the United States and all territory subject to the jurisdiction thereof for beverage purposes is hereby prohibited.

Section 2. The Congress and the several States shall have concurrent power to enforce this article by appropriate legislation.

Section 3. This article shall be inoperative unless it shall have been ratified as an amendment to the Constitution by the legislatures of the several States, as provided in the Constitution, within seven years from the date of the submission hereof to the States by the Congress.

AMENDMENT XIX [1920]

[1] The right of citizens of the United States to vote shall not be denied or abridged by the United States or by any State on account of sex.

[2] Congress shall have power to enforce this article by appropriate legislation.

AMENDMENT XX [1933]

Section 1. The terms of the President and Vice President shall end at noon on the 20th day of January, and the terms of Senators and Representatives at noon on the 3d day of January, of the years in which such terms would have ended if this article had not been ratified; and the terms of their successors shall then begin.

Section 2. The Congress shall assemble at least once in every year, and such meeting shall begin at noon on the 3d day of January, unless they shall by law appoint a different day.

Section 3. If, at the time fixed for the beginning of the term of the President, the President elect shall have died, the Vice President elect shall become President. If the President shall not have been chosen before the time fixed for the beginning of his term, or if the President elect shall have failed to qualify, then the Vice President elect shall act as President until a President shall have qualified; and the Congress may by law provide for the case wherein neither a President elect nor a Vice President elect shall have qualified, declaring who shall then act as President, or the manner in which one who is to act shall be selected, and such person shall act accordingly until a President or Vice President shall have qualified.

Section 4. The Congress may by law provide for the case of the death of any of the persons from whom the House of Representatives may choose a President whenever the right of choice shall have devolved upon them, and for the case of the death of any of the persons from whom the Senate may choose a Vice President whenever the right of choice shall have devolved upon them.

Section 5. Sections 1 and 2 shall take effect on the 15th day of October following the ratification of this article.

Section 6. This article shall be inoperative unless it shall have been ratified as an amendment to the Constitution by the legislatures of three-fourths of the several States within seven years from the date of its submission.

AMENDMENT XXI [1933]

Section 1. The eighteenth article of amendment to the Constitution of the United States is hereby repealed.

Section 2. The transportation or importation into any State, Territory, or possession of the United States for delivery or use therein of intoxicating liquors, in violation of the laws thereof, is hereby prohibited.

Section 3. This article shall be inoperative unless it shall have been ratified as an amendment to the Constitution by conventions in the several States, as provided in the Constitution, within seven years from the date of the submission hereof to the States by the Congress.

AMENDMENT XXII [1951]

Section 1. No person shall be elected to the office of the President more than twice, and no person who has held the office of President, or acted as President, for more than two years of a term to which some other person was elected President shall be elected to the office of President more than once. But this Article shall not apply to any person holding the office of President when this Article was proposed by the Congress, and shall not prevent any person who may be holding the office of President, or acting as President, during the term within which this Article becomes operative from holding the office of President or acting as President during the remainder of such term.

Section 2. This article shall be inoperative unless it shall have been ratified as an amendment to the Constitution by the legislatures of three-fourths of the several States within seven years from the date of its submission to the States by the Congress.

AMENDMENT XXIII [1961]

Section 1. The District constituting the seat of Government of the United States shall appoint in such manner as the Congress may direct:

A number of electors of President and Vice President equal to the whole number of Senators and Representatives in Congress to which the District would be entitled if it were a State, but in no event more than the least populous state; they shall be in addition to those appointed by the states, but they shall be considered, for the purposes of the election of President and Vice President, to be electors appointed by a state; and they shall meet in the District and perform such duties as provided by the twelfth article of amendment.

Section 2. The Congress shall have power to enforce this article by appropriate legislation.

AMENDMENT XXIV [1964]

Section 1. The right of citizens of the United States to vote in any primary or other election for President or Vice President, for electors for President or Vice President, or for Senator or Representative in Congress, shall not be denied or abridged by the United States or any State by reason of failure to pay any poll tax or other tax.

Section 2. The Congress shall have power to enforce this article by appropriate legislation.

AMENDMENT XXV [1967]

Section 1. In case of the removal of the President from office or of his death or resignation, the Vice President shall become President.

Section 2. Whenever there is a vacancy in the office of the Vice President, the President shall nominate a Vice President who shall take office upon confirmation by a majority vote of both Houses of Congress.

Section 3. Whenever the President transmits to the President pro tempore of the Senate and the Speaker of the House of Representatives his written declaration that he is unable to discharge the powers and duties of his office, and until he transmits to them a written declaration to the contrary, such powers and duties shall be discharged by the Vice President as Acting President.

Section 4. Whenever the Vice President and a majority of either the principal officers of the executive departments or of such other body as Congress may by law provide, transmit to the President pro tempore of the Senate and the Speaker of the House of Representatives their written declaration that the President is unable to discharge the powers and duties of his office, the Vice President shall immediately assume the powers and duties of the office as Acting President.

Thereafter, when the President transmits to the President pro tempore of the Senate and the Speaker of the House of Representatives his written declaration that no inability exists, he shall resume the powers and duties of his office unless the Vice President and a majority of either the principal officers of the executive department or of such other body as Congress may by law provide, transmit within four days to the President pro tempore of the Senate and the Speaker of the House of Representatives their written declaration that the President is unable to discharge the powers and duties of his office. Thereupon Congress shall decide the issue, assembling within forty-eight hours for that purpose if not in session. If the Congress, within twenty-one days after receipt of the latter written declaration, or, if Congress is not in session, within twenty-one days after Congress is required to assemble, determines by two-thirds vote of both Houses that the President is unable to discharge the powers and duties of his office, the Vice President shall continue to discharge the same as Acting President; otherwise, the President shall resume the powers and duties of his office.

AMENDMENT XXVI [1971]

Section 1. The right of citizens of the United States, who are eighteen years of age or older, to vote shall not be denied or abridged by the United States or by any State on account of age.

Section 2. The Congress shall have power to enforce this article by appropriate legislation.

AMENDMENT XXVII [1992]*

No law, varying compensation for the services of Senators and Representatives, shall take effect, until an election of Representatives shall have intervened.

---

* On May 7, 1992, more than 200 years after it was first proposed by James Madison, the Twenty-Seventh Amendment was ratified by a 38th State (Michigan). Although Congress set no time limit for ratification of this amendment, ten of the *other* amendments proposed at the same time (1789)—now known as the Bill of Rights—were ratified in a little more than two years. After all this time, is the ratification of the Twenty-Seventh Amendment valid? Does it matter that many of the states that ratified the amendment did not exist at the time it was first proposed? Very shortly after the Michigan ratification, the national archivist declared the Twenty-Seventh Amendment part of the Constitution, and a unanimous Senate and near-unanimous House quickly passed resolutions approving that declaration. Does that settle the question of the provision's validity?